D0202576

The Law of
PATENTS

EDITORIAL ADVISORS

Vicki Been
Boxer Family Professor of Law
New York University School of Law

Erwin Chemerinsky
Dean and Distinguished Professor of Law
University of California, Irvine, School of Law

Richard A. Epstein
Laurence A. Tisch Professor of Law
New York University School of Law
Peter and Kirsten Bedford Senior Fellow
The Hoover Institution
Senior Lecturer in Law
The University of Chicago

Ronald J. Gilson
Charles J. Meyers Professor of Law and Business
Stanford University
Marc and Eva Stern Professor of Law and Business
Columbia Law School

James E. Krier
Earl Warren DeLano Professor of Law
The University of Michigan Law School

Richard K. Neumann, Jr.
Professor of Law
Maurice A. Deane School of Law at Hofstra University

Robert H. Sitkoff
John L. Gray Professor of Law
Harvard Law School

David Alan Sklansky
Yosef Osheawich Professor of Law
University of California at Berkeley School of Law

Kent D. Syverud
Dean and Ethan A. H. Shepley University Professor
Washington University School of Law

ASPEN CASEBOOK SERIES

The Law of
PATENTS

Third Edition

Craig Allen Nard

Tom J.E. and Bette Lou Walker Professor of Law
Director, Center for Law, Technology & the Arts and the
FUSION Program in Design, Innovation & IP Management
Case Western Reserve University
School of Law

Wolters Kluwer
Law & Business

Copyright © 2014 CCH Incorporated.

Published by Wolters Kluwer Law & Business in New York.

Wolters Kluwer Law & Business serves customers worldwide with CCH, Aspen Publishers, and Kluwer Law International products. (www.wolterskluwerlb.com)

No part of this publication may be reproduced or transmitted in any form or by any means, electronic or mechanical, including photocopy, recording, or utilized by any information storage or retrieval system, without written permission from the publisher. For information about permissions or to request permissions online, visit us at www.wolterskluwerlb.com, or a written request may be faxed to our permissions department at 212-771-0803.

To contact Customer Service, e-mail customer.service@wolterskluwer.com, call 1-800-234-1660, fax 1-800-901-9075, or mail correspondence to:

Wolters Kluwer Law & Business
Attn: Order Department
PO Box 990
Frederick, MD 21705

Printed in the United States of America.

1 2 3 4 5 6 7 8 9 0

ISBN 978-1-4548-3150-1

Library of Congress Cataloging-in-Publication Data

Nard, Craig Allen, author.
    The law of patents / Craig Allen Nard, Tom J.E. and Bette Lou Walker Professor of Law, Director, Center for Law, Technology & the Arts and the FUSION Program in Design, Innovation & IP Management Case Western Reserve University School of Law.—Third Edition.
        pages. cm.
    Includes bibliographical references and index.
    ISBN 978-1-4548-3150-1 (alk. paper)
1. Patent laws and legislation—United States. I. Title.
    KF3095.N37 2013
    346.7304'86—dc23
                                    2013031241

SUSTAINABLE FORESTRY INITIATIVE

Certified Sourcing
www.sfiprogram.org
SFI-01234

SFI label applies to the text stock

About Wolters Kluwer Law & Business

Wolters Kluwer Law & Business is a leading global provider of intelligent information and digital solutions for legal and business professionals in key specialty areas, and respected educational resources for professors and law students. Wolters Kluwer Law & Business connects legal and business professionals as well as those in the education market with timely, specialized authoritative content and information-enabled solutions to support success through productivity, accuracy and mobility.

Serving customers worldwide, Wolters Kluwer Law & Business products include those under the Aspen Publishers, CCH, Kluwer Law International, Loislaw, ftwilliam.com and MediRegs family of products.

CCH products have been a trusted resource since 1913, and are highly regarded resources for legal, securities, antitrust and trade regulation, government contracting, banking, pension, payroll, employment and labor, and healthcare reimbursement and compliance professionals.

Aspen Publishers products provide essential information to attorneys, business professionals and law students. Written by preeminent authorities, the product line offers analytical and practical information in a range of specialty practice areas from securities law and intellectual property to mergers and acquisitions and pension/benefits. Aspen's trusted legal education resources provide professors and students with high-quality, up-to-date and effective resources for successful instruction and study in all areas of the law.

Kluwer Law International products provide the global business community with reliable international legal information in English. Legal practitioners, corporate counsel and business executives around the world rely on Kluwer Law journals, looseleafs, books, and electronic products for comprehensive information in many areas of international legal practice.

Loislaw is a comprehensive online legal research product providing legal content to law firm practitioners of various specializations. Loislaw provides attorneys with the ability to quickly and efficiently find the necessary legal information they need, when and where they need it, by facilitating access to primary law as well as state-specific law, records, forms and treatises.

ftwilliam.com offers employee benefits professionals the highest quality plan documents (retirement, welfare and non-qualified) and government forms (5500/PBGC, 1099 and IRS) software at highly competitive prices.

MediRegs products provide integrated health care compliance content and software solutions for professionals in healthcare, higher education and life sciences, including professionals in accounting, law and consulting.

Wolters Kluwer Law & Business, a division of Wolters Kluwer, is headquartered in New York. Wolters Kluwer is a market-leading global information services company focused on professionals.

For Patricia, Gabriel, Victor, and Elsa

SUMMARY OF CONTENTS

CONTENTS

CHAPTER **7**

Enforcing Patent Rights

CHAPTER **8**
Defenses to Patent Infringement   663

CHAPTER 9
Remedies 865

PREFACE TO THE THIRD EDITION

The last three years have witnessed an extraordinary amount of activity in the patent law space. First, Congress, after several years of deliberation, enacted the America Invents Act ("AIA"), which is the most far-reaching statutory reform since the 1952 Patent Act. The AIA eliminated the first-to-invent priority system and introduced a first-inventor-to-file mechanism; and the definition of novelty and statutory bars were modified in important ways. The Supreme Court decided the much anticipated case on the patentability of DNA sequences as well as cases at the intersection of contract, misuse, and antitrust law. And of course, the Federal Circuit has been quite busy. The court, now over three decades old, continues to manage and steer patent jurisprudence through its common law powers. Many of these changes required the USTPO to promulgate rules reflecting the altered landscape. With so much change brought about so quickly, a third edition of *The Law of Patents* was inescapable.

The third edition includes *Patent Reform Perspectives* that discuss the AIA in detail, particularly in Chapter Four. All of the Supreme Court patent law cases and noteworthy Federal Circuit caselaw are included as principal cases, followed by substantive Comments. And there are more subtle additions, including a discussion of some of the first-rate patent law scholarship that continues to be produced by my colleagues. Otherwise, *The Law of Patents* remains largely unchanged. There are still *Policy* and *Comparative Perspectives*, extensive Comments, relevant statutory sections reproduced in the back of the book, and a casebook website at law.case.edu/lawofpatents. This site provides PDFs of all of the patents-in-suit in the principal cases, relevant secondary material broken down by chapter, and links to important patent law/IP-related documents and websites. I have also created a stack of PowerPoint slides to accompany the book that I am happy to share upon request.

As with the prior editions, I welcome the comments of adopters and others steeped in patent law at craig.nard@case.edu.

Craig Allen Nard

Shaker Heights, Ohio
August 2013

PREFACE TO THE SECOND EDITION

Patent law jurisprudence has historically moved at a snail's pace, an accretion comparable to familiar first-year common law courses such as property and contracts. No longer. All of patent law's institutional players have become fully engaged over the past several years. The Supreme Court has renewed its interest in the useful arts, Congress has made it a yearly tradition to engage—unsuccessfully—in patent reform proposals, the USPTO has skillfully navigated the patent law landscape to effect change, and the Federal Circuit, which is patent law's principal policy driver, has asserted itself in a more pronounced way, fully cognizant that other actors are paying close attention. All of this means that a second edition of *The Law of Patents* is due. While there hasn't been much legislation to speak of, the courts and the USPTO have been busy. Since the first edition there have been significant developments relating to patent law's disclosure requirements, eligible subject matter, nonobviousness, enforcement, defenses, and remedies. All of these changes (or at least, what I think are the most important) are represented and discussed in the second edition. Moreover, I've made an attempt to provide a richer discussion of the prosecution process in Chapter 1, reflecting the divergence in practice among various industries as well as recent empirical findings.

In addition, there are two noteworthy structural changes to the second edition. First, a good portion of claim interpretation—which appeared entirely in Chapter 7 in the first edition—forms part of Chapter 2, thus emphasizing to a greater degree the importance of the claim in patent law. (The *Markman* case remains part of Chapter 7, however.) Second, the chapter on non-obviousness immediately follows the chapter on novelty, with statutory bars being covered after nonobviousness. Beyond the substantive and structural changes, *The Law of Patents* remains largely unchanged. There are still *Policy* and *Comparative Perspectives*, extensive Comments, relevant statutory sections reproduced in the back of the book, and a casebook website at http://law.case.edu/lawofpatents/. This site provides PDFs of all of the patents-in-suit in the principal cases, relevant secondary material broken down by chapter, and links to important patent law/IP-related documents and websites.

As with the first edition, I welcome the comments of adopters and others steeped in patent law at craig.nard@case.edu.

Craig Allen Nard

Shaker Heights, Ohio
October 2010

PREFACE TO THE FIRST EDITION

Patent law has rapidly assumed center stage in the global marketplace and information economy, presenting some of the most exciting, important, and complex issues facing not only our legal system, but also the business and technology communities. Indeed, patent law's presence in our legal, economic, and social fabric has increased dramatically in the past 25 years, and particularly, since the beginning of this century. The growing significance of patent law is understandable given the importance of intellectual capital to a firm's economic well being and the fact that for the past decade—and perhaps longer—a majority of firm value has been attributable to intangible assets. As such, legally protecting these assets—oftentimes with patents—is instrumental to a firm's business strategy. Constructing and judiciously managing a patent portfolio can lead to competitive advantages and lucrative revenue streams, through licensing, commercialization, or blocking competitor entry. Patent law's enhanced profile is manifested in the significant increase in patent applications filed in various countries throughout the world over the past several years. In the United States, for instance, 162,708 applications were filed in 1990; in 2006, there were 415,551.

In addition to raw numbers and corporate patent strategies, I am personally reminded of patent law's star power every academic year, not only because I teach and write about this particular area of the law, but also because of the number of law students who have an interest in pursuing careers in patent law. It was not uncommon for patent attorneys of my generation (I received my law degree in 1990) to "fall into" patent law after a few years working as an engineer or a chemist—law school just wasn't on the radar screen for many of us during college. While this remains an indirect route to the patent world, many more students today major in engineering or a physical or biological science fully expecting to go to law school with patent law in their sights. (Or, at least, students majoring in technical fields become aware of patent law soon after entering university.) This student demand prompted a number of law schools (including my own) to create centers and courses devoted to law and technology and intellectual property. Concomitantly, law schools hired people with an interest in teaching and writing in patent law, which has led to an extraordinary amount of patent law scholarship in recent years.

This book was designed with the aforementioned student and academic in mind. The book begins with a discussion of the history and economics of patent law, as well as an exploration of what a patent is and how one is obtained. With this foundation in place, chapter two introduces patent law's important disclosure and claiming requirements. These requirements are explored first because they introduce the student to the entire patent document and capture patent law's "big picture," namely the bargain between the inventor and society. Chapter three discusses eligible subject matter and the utility requirement. Chapters four through six explore, respectively, the patentability requirements of novelty (chapter four), statutory bars (chapter five), and non-obviousness (chapter six). Among these requirements, non-obviousness has the most practical significance and can be a particularly robust policy tool. This requirement demands that the inventor provide society with an invention that is more than simply new, what the Europeans call an "inventive step." Chapter seven is devoted to patent enforcement, and includes some of patent law's most controversial and important issues and doctrines such as claim interpretation and the doctrine of equivalents. Defenses to patent infringement are explored in chapter eight, including the role of antitrust and issues at the intersection of contract and patent law. And lastly, chapter nine is about remedies, namely money damages and equitable relief.

Four additional features of the book are worth mentioning. First, most of the chapters have *Comparative Perspectives* or *Policy Perspectives*. The former is designed to explore a particular issue through a comparative lens, with an emphasis on Europe and, less so, Japan. Patent law is a global affair, and having insight into how other jurisdictions approach a given issue can inform and enrich one's understanding of American patent law. The policy perspectives seek to provide a richer and more in depth discussion of a given issue, and introduce secondary, academic literature for further reading and exploration. Second, each case or set of cases is preceded by reference to applicable statutory section numbers, tailored to the specific issues raised in the cases. And the relevant *statutory provisions* are reproduced and integrated into the text (near the end of the book), thus eliminating the need for students to buy a separate statutory supplement. Third, each case or set of cases is preceded with a description of the issues to be discussed in the case and followed by *Comments* that explore the case and issues raised therein in greater detail. And fourth, I tried to include technologically accessible principal cases.It is a wonderfully propitious time to engage the rich world of patent law, and if you decide to continue reading *The Law of Patents*, I encourage you to contact me with your questions, comments, and suggestions at craig.nard@ case.edu.

Craig Allen Nard

Shaker Heights, Ohio
March 2008

ACKNOWLEDGMENTS

Composing an acknowledgements section for a patent law book is particularly appropriate because I am reminded of the inventive enterprise and the fact that we are all standing on the shoulders of those who came and created before us. For the past 30 years or so, scholars from the legal and economics communities provided us with a more sophisticated and deeper understanding of the inner workings of patent law and its relationship to innovation. I have benefitted a great deal from this rich literature.

I also have the good fortune of having generous friends and colleagues who read and commented on the *The Law of Patents* in its various stages. Indeed, the following people made *The Law of Patents* a better book: Andrew Beckerman-Rodau, Alan Bentley, Christopher Cotropia, Steve Errick, Troy Froebe, Giancarlo Frosio, Ed Hejlek, Timothy Holbrook, Dennis Karjala, Amy Landers, Jeff Lefstin, Mark Lemley, Clarisa Long, Joe Miller, Andy Morriss, Patricia Motta, Janice Mueller, Jason Rantanen, Josh Sarnoff, Sean Seymore, David Taylor, Mark Thurmon, and Polk Wagner.

And, of course, I must acknowledge my students at Case Western Reserve University, the University of Torino, and the WIPO Academy, whose comments and feedback made the book a more effective teaching tool.

The Law of
PATENTS

History and Architecture of the Patent System

INTRODUCTION

The term "patent" is short for "letters patent," derived from the Latin *litterae patentes*, meaning open letters.[1] Generally, letters patent were letters addressed by the sovereign "to all whom these presents shall come," reciting a grant of some dignity, office, franchise, or other privilege that had been given by the sovereign to the patentee.[2] The modern American patent is a government issued grant, which confers upon the patent owner the right to exclude others from "making, using, offering for sale, or selling the invention throughout the United States or importing the invention into the United States" for a period of 20 years ending from the filing date of the patent application.[3] A patent gives its owner the *right to exclude*; a patent does not provide a positive right to make, use, or sell the invention.[4] As Chief Justice Taney, in the mid-nineteenth century, stated, "[t]he franchise which the patent grants consists altogether in the right to

---

1. It should be noted that a patent for invention was just one form of "letters patent." In England, the Crown would conduct much of its state business by means of charters and letters patent, including the grant of privileges to inventors to practice their inventions. As William Blackstone writes in his COMMENTARIES:

> The King's grants are also matter[s] of public record. . . . These grants, whether of lands, honors, liberties, franchises, or aught besides, are contained in charters, or letters patent, that is, open letters, *litterae patentes*: so called, because they are not sealed up, but exposed to open view, with the great seal pendant at the bottom; and are usually directed or addressed by the King to all his subjects at large.

WILLIAM BLACKSTONE, 2 COMMENTARIES ON THE LAWS OF ENGLAND 316-317 (1768). The opposite of letters patent is letters close or *litterae clausae*, which are sealed so that only the addressee can read the contents of the letter.

2. ENCYCLOPEDIA BRITANNICA 969-970 (1942).

3. 35 U.S.C. § 154 (2006). Prior to June 8, 1995 (the effective date of the GATT-TRIPS legislation), the term for a United States patent was 17 years from the date the patent *issued*. In April 1994, the United States and several other countries participated in the Uruguay Round Agreements. The Uruguay Round included an "Agreement on Trade-Related Aspects of Intellectual Property" (TRIPS). The TRIPS patent section precipitated the change of the U.S. patent term from 17 years from date of issuance to 20 years from the filing date. As a result, the present patent term for applications filed before June 8, 1995, is (1) 17 years from date of issuance; or (2) 20 years measured from the filing date of the earliest referenced application, whichever is greater. For applications filed on or after June 8, 1995, the patent term is 20 years measured from the earliest claimed application filing date.

4. *See* FRANK Y. GLADNEY, RESTRAINTS OF TRADE IN PATENTED ARTICLES 1-17 (1910), for a good early twentieth-century discussion of the confusion that persisted in the lower courts as to what a patent granted to the inventor.

exclude everyone from making, using or vending the thing patented without the permission of the patentee. This is all that he obtains by the patent."[5]

In this regard, it is important to understand that while a patent provides its owner with a *legal* monopoly—a statutory right to exclude—it rarely allows for an *economic* monopoly. An economic monopoly refers to the presence of significant market power, which can be defined as the ability of a firm to price a product above marginal cost without losing substantial sales. The reason a patent typically does not confer market power is that there are usually viable substitutes for the patented good (e.g., if I charge too high a price for my patented mouse trap, the consumer will purchase a cat).[6] Thus, while a patentee with a marketable product has the opportunity to earn economic rents, he will typically—with rare exception[7]—have to contend with viable substitutes.

Moreover, the patent system neither guides inventors as to where they should channel their inventive energies, nor guarantees commercial success;[8] rather, it is the marketplace that signals to inventors where the financial rewards reside, and the costs and benefits of a given research project.[9] Thus, the patent system

5. *Bloomer v. McQuewan*, 14 How. 539, 549 (1852). The practical significance of this distinction is explored in section B of this chapter (Economics of Patent Law), in Chapter 2, section B, Comment 1 following the *Incandescent Lamp* case, and at the beginning of Chapter 7 on infringement. The right to exclude, without the right to use, is somewhat peculiar to patent law (as well as the law of copyright and negative easements). In contrast, the property right in real property (e.g., land) or personal property (e.g., a car or a computer) is a right to use that carries with it a logically subordinate right to exclude. That right to exclude exists to ensure the owner's full enjoyment of the right to use.

6. *See, e.g.*, WILLIAM M. LANDES & RICHARD A. POSNER, THE ECONOMIC STRUCTURE OF INTELLECTUAL PROPERTY LAW 374-375 (2003) (stating "[t]he *average* patent . . . confers too little market power on the patentee in a meaningful economic sense to interest a rational antitrust enforcer, and sometimes it confers no monopoly power at all") (emphasis in original); Michael A. Carrier, *Unraveling the Patent-Antitrust Paradox*, 150 U. PA. L. REV. 761, 791 (2002) (stating "patents typically do not demonstrate market power, and the set of technological substitutes that cannot be practiced because of the patent grant often has little overlap with the set of products that consumers view as economic substitutes").

7. *See* Thomas F. Cotter, *Refining the "Presumptive Illegality" Approach to Settlements of Patent Disputes Involving Reverse Payments: A Commentary on Hovenkamp, Janis and Lemley*, 87 MINN. L. REV. 1789, 1814 n.94 (2003) (stating "pharmaceutical patents . . . sometimes do confer market power").

8. *See* 1 HERBERT HOVENKAMP, MARK D. JANIS & MARK A. LEMLEY, IP AND ANTITRUST § 4.2a (2005) (noting a patent grant "is not even a guarantee of market success," let alone giving rise to an economic monopoly). But as Jacob Schmookler reminds us, "invention is largely an economic activity which, like other economic activities, is pursued for gain." JACOB SCHMOOKLER, INVENTION AND ECONOMIC GROWTH 206 (1966).

9. *See* B. ZORINA KHAN, THE DEMOCRATIZATION OF INVENTION: PATENTS AND COPYRIGHTS IN AMERICAN ECONOMIC DEVELOPMENT, 1790-1920 66 (2005) (stating that in the United States, patent "statutes from the earliest years ensured that the 'progress of science and useful arts' was to be achieved through a complementary relationship between law and the market in the form of a patent system"); STEVEN W. USSELMAN, REGULATING RAILROAD INNOVATION: BUSINESS, TECHNOLOGY, AND POLITICS IN AMERICA, 1840-1920 97-98 (2002) (stating "a patent in and of itself conveyed no rewards or special privileges. Inventors did not receive a bounty based on the perceived utility of their handiwork. Rather, a patent merely extended to creative individuals a legal claim upon those who wished to use their novelties. The market would determine the number of takers and the amount they were willing to pay"); NUNO PIRES DE CARVALHO, THE TRIPS REGIME OF PATENT RIGHTS 1-9 (2d ed. 2005) (discussing relationship between patent system and marketplace); BROOKE HINDLE, EMULATION AND INVENTION 18 (1981) (noting patent system "rested entirely upon the market economy"). Reflecting this sentiment, Henry Ellsworth, the superintendent of the patent office from 1835-1845, in his report to the Secretary of State about the need for patent reform, wrote "for no sooner are the wants of the public known than men of ingenuity attempt to supply them." REPORT FROM THE HON. HENRY L. ELLSWORTH TO THE SECRETARY OF STATE AND TRANSMITTED TO THE SELECT COMMITTEE ON THE PATENT LAWS 175, 177 (1836). *See also* JOEL MOKYR, THE GIFTS OF ATHENA:

embodies a self-selection process that works hand-in-hand with the marketplace to foster innovation in a decentralized setting.[10] In this setting, patent law can be viewed as an incentive-based system of laws that offers a potential financial reward as an inducement to invent, to disclose technical information, to invest capital in the innovation process, and to facilitate efficient use and manufacturing of invention through licensing.

Yet patent law's "reward structure cannot be modified according to the market structure in which the innovator operates,"[11] which means that some innovations will be over-rewarded while others are under-rewarded.[12] As two commentators have argued, a unitary patent system—one that generally does not discriminate among inventions—"simply cannot offer the range of proper incentives for the variety of technologies and industrial sectors it would need to serve."[13] In fact, some industries respond to patent law's incentives differently than others, and this holds true not only for established entities, but start-ups and entrepreneurs, as well.[14] For instance, the pharmaceutical and medical equipment industries rely heavily on patents, whereas the chemical process and communications equipment industries prefer trade secrecy and lead time into the market, respectively, relying less on patents.[15] And some industries seek patent

---

HISTORICAL ORIGINS OF THE KNOWLEDGE ECONOMY 76 (2002) (asking "which of all the problems that might be solved will an ingenious and creative individual apply his or her efforts to? The answer must be based in part on the signals that the market or another device sends to the potential inventor about the private and social benefits"). In the pharmaceutical space in particular, Daron Acemoglu and Joshua Linn have shown that "there is an economically and statistically significant response of the entry of new drugs to market size." Daron Acemoglu & Joshua Linn, *Market Size in Innovation: Theory and Evidence from the Pharmaceutical Industry*, QUARTERLY J. ECON. 1049-1090 (August 2004).

10. *See* Peter Menell & Suzanne Scotchmer, *Intellectual Property Law*, in HANDBOOK OF LAW & ECONOMICS 1477 (A. Mitchell Polinsky & Steven Shavell eds., 2007) (referring to decentralization in intellectual property systems as a "virtue" and stating "[p]robably the most important obstacle to effective public procurement is in finding ideas for invention that are widely distributed among firms and inventors. The lure of intellectual property protection does that automatically"). *See generally* MOKYR, GIFTS OF ATHENA, *supra* note 9, at 239 (noting overall welfare is enhanced in decentralized systems because they tend "to be more efficient than centralized ones in engendering technological progress because they do not depend on the personal judgment and survival of single-minded and strong-willed individuals"). Indeed, the decentralized nature of the American patent system is evident in the design of the patent and copyright clause of the Constitution. See notes 79-86, *infra*, for a discussion of this point.

11. SUZANNE SCOTCHMER, INNOVATION AND INCENTIVES 117 (2006).

12. *Id. See also* LANDES & POSNER, ECONOMIC STRUCTURE, *supra* note 6, at 300 (stating the "patent system makes no effort . . . to match the degree of patent protection" to variables relevant to determining whether a "given degree of patent protection is socially desirable").

13. DAN L. BURK & MARK A. LEMLEY, THE PATENT CRISIS AND HOW THE COURTS CAN SOLVE IT 101 (2009).

14. *See* Stuart J.H. Graham, Ted Sichelman, Robert P. Merges & Pamela Samuelson, *High Technology Entrepreneurs and the Patent System: Results of the 2008 Berkeley Patent Survey*, 24 BERKELEY TECH. L.J. 1255 (2010) (finding that "patents is more widespread among technology startups than has been previously reported, but that the patterns and drivers of holding patents are industry and context specific"); Ted Sichelman & Stuart J.H. Graham, *Patenting by Entrepreneurs*, 17 MICH. TELECOMM. & TECH. L. REV. 111 (2010) (exploring why start-ups and entrepreneurs choose to seek or not to seek patent protection); Stuart J.H. Graham & Ted Sichelman, *Why Do Start-Ups Patent?*, 23 BERKELEY TECH. L.J. 1063 (2008) (exploring reasons why start-ups decide to seek or not to seek patent protection).

15. *See* Wesley M. Cohen, Richard R. Nelson & John P. Walsh, *Protecting Their Intellectual Assets: Appropriability Conditions and Why U.S. Manufacturing Firms Patent (or Not)* (2004) (NBER Working Paper 7552) (finding different industries rely on different appropriability mechanisms to varying degrees. For instance, a majority of the industries surveyed noted that they rely on more than

protection with an eye towards commercialization and generating revenue, while others obtain patents to block competitors from developing competing products, to create freedom to operate (i.e., creating a space to pursue a line of research or practice a particular technology),[16] to enhance their bargaining position during cross-licensing negotiations, or, relatedly, to build a defensive posture,[17] particularly when a "complex" technology (i.e., a product or process that comprises several patented components) is involved.[18] Indeed, patent law is not a one-size-fits-all regime and demands a nuanced approach of its costs and benefits. As two commentators note:

one "appropriability mechanism" as part of their "appropriability strategy" (e.g., a combination of lead time and trade secrets or patents and lead time)); LANDES & POSNER, ECONOMIC STRUCTURE, *supra* note 6, at 312 ("Many highly progressive, research-intensive industries, notably including the computer software industry, do not rely heavily on patents as a method of preventing free riding on inventive activity"); Richard C. Levin, Alvin K. Klevorick, Richard R. Nelson & S.G. Winter, *Appropriating the Returns from Industrial Research and Development* (1987) (Brookings Papers on Economic Activity), 783-831. *Cf.* INTELLECTUAL PROPERTY IN THE U.S. ECONOMY: INDUSTRY IN FOCUS 7-8 (March 2012) (identifying several industries as "patent intensive" based on the ratio of number of patents to industry-specific jobs; industries included computer and communications equipment, semiconductor, navigational, measuring, and electromedical).

16. *See* Iain M. Cockburn & Rebecca Henderson, *Survey Results from the 2003 Intellectual Property Owners Association Survey on Strategic Management of Intellectual Property* 8 (Oct. 2003) (finding that 35% of corporate patent portfolios are used to establish freedom to operate). An example of building a blocking/licensing position is Toyota's strategy of filing over 2000 patent applications related to its gas-electric Prius. *See* John Murphy, *Toyota Builds Thicket of Patents Around Hybrid to Block Competitors*, WALL STREET JOURNAL (Asia Business, July 1, 2009) at http://online.wsj.com/article/SB124640553503576637.html.

17. *See* Graham & Sichelman, *Why Do Start-Ups Patent?*, *supra* note 14, at 1065 (stating "many companies acquire patents for what they claim are merely 'defensive' reasons. Far from using patents offensively to stop others from making or selling their products, these companies view patents as necessary evils that shield others from suing them for patent infringement. If a plaintiff sells products, an accused infringer can file a counterclaim accusing the plaintiff of infringing any of its patents that plausibly encompass those products. Any such game of "mutually assured destruction" raises the likelihood of a timely settlement or, if the defendant is known for countersuing, a settlement prior to the suit being filed"). In the IT industry, in particular, commentators such as Graham and Sichelman have employed the cold war term "mutually assured destruction" to describe the patenting strategies of firms in this space. The idea is that patents are filed to deter infringement suits. *See* Steven Vaughn-Nichols, *Software and Mutually Assured Destruction* at http://www.eweek.com/c/a/Linux-and-Open-Source/Software-Patents-and-Mutually-Assured-Destruction (March 23, 2005) (stating that in the IT industry, "if any one company tried to really strangle a large part of the market with an overly aggressive patent enforcement, they would be blasted by other companies with large patent portfolios. The end result would be that all of the companies involved would be locked into a software development doomsday, where nothing could be developed"); Ross Gittens, *Software's Game of Mutually Assured Damage* at http://www.smh.com.au/articles/2004/07/30/1091080437270.html (July 31, 2004) (noting "all the large software firms have big patent portfolios and they mainly go unused, in a sort of "mutually assured destruction" arrangement whereby each large firm is prevented from using their patent portfolio by fear of devastating reprisals"). *Cf.* James Bessen & Michael J. Meurer, *Lessons for Patent Policy from Empirical Research of Patent Litigation*, 9 LEWIS & CLARK L. REV. 1, 16 (2005) (asserting in the IT industry, "although it is individually rational for each firm to reduce its litigation risk by building a defensive portfolio, the collective equilibrium effect is to increase industry litigation hazards. This suggests that "defensive" patents are not used purely defensively").

18. *See* Cohen et al., *Protecting Their Intellectual Assets*, *supra* note 15; Petr Hanel, *Intellectual Property Rights Business Management Practices: A Survey of the Literature*, 26 TECHNOVATION 895, 896 (2007) (stating "[t]he rise of patenting and use of other IP instruments has often little to do with their effectiveness in protecting IP and much more with their usefulness in corporate strategies blocking competition and providing bargaining chips for cross-licensing"). *See also* Graham & Sichelman, *Why Do Start-Ups Patent?*, *supra* note 14, at 1071-1082 (identifying nine stated reasons and attendant empirical data relating to why firms patent).

In some areas, patent rights certainly are economically and socially productive in generating invention, spreading technological knowledge, inducing innovation and commercialization, and providing some degree of order in the development of broad technological prospects. However, in many areas of technology this is not the case. In a number of these, strong broad patent rights entail major economic costs while generating insufficient additional social benefits. And in some strong broad patents are simply counterproductive. One needs to be discriminating and cautious on this front.[19]

In the light of these divergent incentives among industries, patent law's non-discrimination principle is seemingly susceptible to criticism. Why paint with such a broad statutory brush? Why not create a patent system that reflects this diverse incentive dynamic?[20] One common response is grounded in public choice theory, which warns against the potential for rent-seeking that usually accompanies industry-specific legislation or at least legislation that reflects specific industry norms.[21] Indeed, the past several years of patent reform efforts in Congress witnessed an interest-group dynamic play out on Capitol Hill, the scope of which has heretofor been largely absent from legislative patent reform efforts.[22]

Accordingly, while the Congress and United States Patent and Trademark Office are important institutional players, it is the judiciary that has and continues to serve as patent law's principal policy driver. The patent code—much like the Sherman Act in antitrust law—can be viewed as a common law enabling statute, leaving ample room for courts to fill in the interstices of the patent code or to create doctrine emanating solely from Article III's domain. In fact,

---

19. Robert Mazzoleni & Richard R. Nelson, *The Benefits and Costs of Strong Patent Protection: A Contribution to the Current Debate*, 27 RESEARCH POLICY 273, 281 (1998). *See also* Keith E. Maskus & Jerome H. Reichman, *The Globalization of Private Knowledge Goods and the Privatization of Global Public Goods*, in INTERNATIONAL PUBLIC GOODS AND TRANSFER OF TECHNOLOGY UNDER A GLOBALIZED INTELLECTUAL PROPERTY REGIME 3-45 (Maskus & Reichman eds., 2005).

20. Two commentators have suggested this is already happening in Federal Circuit jurisprudence. *See* Dan L. Burk & Mark A. Lemley, *Is Patent Law Technology-Specific?*, 17 BERKELEY TECH. L.J. 1155, 1156 (2002) (noting "an increasing divergence between the rules themselves and the application of the rules to different industries," particularly in the biotechnology and computer software industries); *see also* Dan L. Burk & Mark A. Lemley, *Policy Levers in Patent Law*, 89 VA. L. REV. 1575, 1589-1595 (2003) (discussing the "industry-specific nature of the patent system").

21. *See* David E. Adelman, *A Fallacy of the Commons in Biotech Patent Policy*, 20 BERKELEY TECH. L.J. 985, 991 (2005) (stating that when it comes to patent reform proposals "[n]otably absent is a legislative approach, which commentators widely agree would fall prey to undue public choice pressures from specific industry interests"); Burk & Lemley, *Policy Levers, supra* note 20, at 1578 (arguing against elimination of uniform patent system because of "concerns about rent seeking and the inability of industry-specific statutes to respond to changing circumstances"). *See generally* Daniel A. Farber & Philip P. Frickey, *The Jurisprudence of Public Choice*, 65 TEX. L. REV. 873 (1987); Jonathan R. Macey, *Promoting Public-Regarding Legislation Through Statutory Interpretation: An Application to Constitutional Theory*, 86 COLUM. L. REV. 223 (1986).

22. Nonetheless, the resulting legislation, known as the America Invents Act of 2011, does not include industry-specific legislation, but not because of lack of effort. Rather, it is because legislators since at least 2005 ventured into territory that prompted competing reactions from interested parties where consensus was lacking. *See* DAN L. BURK & MARK A. LEMLEY, THE PATENT CRISIS AND HOW THE COURTS CAN SOLVE IT 101 (2009) (stating "[t]he pharmaceutical and biotechnology industries opposed virtually all elements of patent reform directed at abuse. . . . On the other side, the software, electronics, Internet, and telecommunications industries generally lined up behind reform, but expressed skepticism toward those few reforms the pharmaceutical industry supported"); Craig Allen Nard, *Legal Forms and the Common Law of Patents*, 90 B.U. L. REV. 51, 52 (2010) (referring to recent legislative efforts at patent reform as being "mired in a public choice brew"). Thus, while the America Invents Act made significant changes to the patent code that are discussed throughout the following chapters, the changes were largely procedural in nature or substantively neutral.

the common law has been the dominant legal force in the development of American patent law for over 200 years. As you will come to appreciate, a significant portion of American patent law, including some of the most important and controversial doctrines, is either built upon judicial interpretation of elliptical statutory phrases or is devoid of any statutory basis whatsoever. Thus, while Congress and the patent office each have a hand in constructing the latticework of patent law, judges are the principal architects.[23]

With this introduction in hand, this chapter is designed to introduce the history and economics of patent law, as well as the process by which patents are obtained. The goal is to provide you with a historical, doctrinal, and theoretical foundation to build upon as you proceed through the subsequent chapters.

A. A HISTORY OF PATENT LAW

1. The Classical Period

Dating back to ancient Greece, one can discern at least the idea of an incentive-based mechanism wherein a potential inventor is encouraged to disclose something new and useful to society. The incentive could take the form of a prize reward or exclusive right in the inventor's contribution. One of the earliest expressions of an incentive-based system can be found in Sybaris, a Greek colony in southern Italy that existed from 720 to 510 B.C. Known for their luxurious and decadent lifestyle, the Sybarites were said to have enacted a law that gave exclusive rights to those who created certain culinary delights. Quoting from the historian Phylarcus, the Greek writer Athenaeus states:

> The Sybarites, having given loose to their luxury, made a law that . . . if any confectioner or cook invented any peculiar and excellent dish, no other artist was allowed to make this for a year; but he alone who invented it was entitled to all the profits to be derived from the manufacture of it for that time; in order that others might be induced to labour at excelling in such pursuits. . . .[24]

Although the Sybaritic "law" is arguably "apocryphal,"[25] it should give us pause that the very idea of an incentive-based system expressed, remarkably, over 2,000

---

23. *See* Nard, *Legal Forms, supra* note 22 (discussing the dominance of the common law in the development of patent doctrine and policy). *See also* Peter S. Menell, *The Mixed Heritage of Federal Intellectual Property Law and Ramifications for Statutory Interpretation*, in INTELLECTUAL PROPERTY AND THE COMMON LAW (Shyam Balganesh ed., forthcoming 2013).

24. Giles S. Rich, *The "Exclusive Right" Since Aristotle* 2 (1990) (manuscript on file with the author). According to the intellectual property historian, F.D. Prager, it was said "that the more excellent cooks received golden crowns and other prizes usual in Greek cities." F.D. Prager, *The Early Growth and Influence of Intellectual Property*, 34 J. PAT. OFF. SOC'Y 106, 114 n.17 (1952). Even before the classical period, "primitive people assert[ed] personal ownership claims . . . to what we would consider intellectual property, namely songs, legends, designs, and magic incantations." RICHARD PIPES, PROPERTY AND FREEDOM 80 (2000). *See also* RICHARD H. LOWIE, PRIMITIVE SOCIETY 235-236 (1920) (characterizing some primitive society practices as corresponding to modern notions of patent and copyright laws).

25. In his history of American patent and copyright law, Bruce Bugbee writes that the Sybaritic law was "[w]ell-known—but apocryphal." *See* BRUCE BUGBEE, GENESIS OF AMERICAN PATENT AND

years ago, anticipates some of the very concepts that embody our modern patent code and demonstrates how closely tied patent law is to human nature.

A few centuries after the destruction of Sybaris, Aristotle addressed the notion of an exclusive right for those individuals who discovered something "good" for the state. Specifically, Aristotle addressed Hippodamus of Miletus, a noted city builder and contemporary of Pericles, who proposed that a law be enacted "to the effect that all who made discoveries advantageous to their country should receive honours."[26] Although prize rewards, primarily for aesthetic contributions, were common in classical Greece, Aristotle reacted negatively to Hippodamus's assertion, arguing that it would "lead to alterations to the constitution."[27] While Aristotle's concern was with new political and social ideas and not technological discoveries, he would probably have the same suspicion of the latter because technological change can no doubt alter the political landscape; but, perhaps more importantly, Aristotle viewed the "banausic" or useful arts with disdain,[28] writing that they "degrade the mind" and are unworthy of the free and thinking man.[29] Thus, although classical Greece is well known for its prominent scientists and mathematicians and certain inventions have their origins in Greece, the scientific culture placed emphasis on knowledge rather than the application or use of knowledge.

In Greece, exclusive rights were debated and rejected. In classical Rome, monopolies were outlawed. The Emperor Zeno (c. 480 A.D.) proclaimed that

> [n]o one shall exercise a monopoly over any . . . material, whether by his own authority or under that of an imperial rescript heretofore or hereafter promulgated.[30]

COPYRIGHT LAW 166, n.5 (1967). According to F.D. Prager, the Sybaritic law is a story that "was current in classic times but it was merely a joke. Even if the story was true, it was not taken seriously in the Greek cities or Hellenistic empires." Argues Prager, "[i]t seems that all this was merely in the spirit of revelry and carousing and that no 'law' was involved." Prager, *Early Growth, supra* note 24, at 114.

26. ARISTOTLE, POLITICS II (1268a6) (1981).

27. *Id.* at 1268b22. In short, Aristotle preferred political stability, and proposals of the sort made by Hippodamus were suspect.

28. Although it should be noted that Aristotle is credited for producing MECHANICS, the world's first engineering text. *See* FRANCIS & JOSEPH GIES, CATHEDRAL, FORGE, AND WATERWHEEL 21 (1994).

29. *Id.* Although for different reasons, Plato too considered the "banausic" as contemptible. F.D. Prager writes:

> [Plato] took no serious interest in any promotion of what is now called the useful arts. He was expressly opposed to most of the fine arts. In his ideal state there was no room for political or industrial development; only scientific research, and that only for few. He held that every craftsman should exercise only one craft, or even part of one craft only. . . . His reason for this strange view was metaphysical; he thought that in this manner the artisan might come closer to an eternal "idea" of the goods that he produced.

Prager, *Early Growth, supra* note 24, at 113. According to Bugbee, "Plato, who regarded the useful arts as 'base and mechanical' and the expression of 'base and mechanical handicraft' as one of reproach, assigned craftsmen and artisans to the lowest stratum of his ideal State." *See* BUGBEE, GENESIS, *supra* note 25, at 166 n.6.

30. *See* CORPUS JURIS CIVILIS v.XIII, Title LIX, p. 120 (S.P. Scott trans., 1932) ("We order that no one shall be so bold as to monopolize the sale of clothing of any kind, or of fish, combs, copper utensils, or anything else having reference to the nourishment or the common use of mankind, no matter of what material it may be composed, whether he does so by his own authority, or under that of a Rescript already promulgated, or which may hereafter be promulgated. . . ."). *See also* 4 WILLIAM BLACKSTONE, COMMENTARIES ON THE LAWS OF ENGLAND ch. 9 (1768) (expressly mentioning Zeno's law prohibiting monopolies).

Indeed, during the Roman period, with the exception of glassmaking, there was very little technological advancement.[31] This may be due in part to the lack of a government-sponsored, incentive-based system, which may have been derived from the anti-technological philosophy inherited from Aristotle and Plato.[32]

Although the ancient Greeks and Romans contributed a great deal to scientific knowledge and left a legacy of impressive structures and design,[33] they did not officially recognize a property interest in intangible goods.[34] There existed no incentive-based legal regime whereby novel and significant contributions to society were encouraged.

2. European Origins

a. The Italian Renaissance

The Middle Ages are widely considered to be a period of technological stagnation and intellectual darkness, or as Edward Gibbon wrote in his *Decline and Fall of the Roman Empire*, a society that witnessed "the triumph of barbarism and religion."[35] But scholars have since cast this characterization into doubt, arguing that, although the Aristotelian attitude toward the useful arts remained for the most part, technology was beginning to be viewed more favorably,[36] and

31. *See* GIES, CATHEDRAL, *supra* note 28, at 17 ("Nearly everything that sixth-century Europe knew about technology came to it from Rome. Rome, however, invented few of the tools and processes it bequeathed to the Middle Ages. Roman civilization achieved a high level of culture and sophistication and left many monuments, but most of its technology was inherited from the Stone, Bronze, and early Iron Ages."). *See also* BUGBEE, GENESIS, *supra* note 25, at 13.

32. *See* BUGBEE, GENESIS, *supra* note 25, at 13 (quoting a twentieth-century scholar's explanation of Rome's poor technological advancement: "'The central government did nothing to protect Italian industry. There was no legislation in the Imperial period comparable to modern legislation concerning patents. Everybody was free to imitate, and even to counterfeit, the products of a rival.'"). *See also* GIES, CATHEDRAL, *supra* note 28, at 36-37 ("[F]or the most part theoretical science was underemployed by the Romans in dealing with technical problems. One explanation that had been offered blames the rhetoric-based Roman education system, which in emphasizing composition, grammar, and logical expression rather than knowledge of nature, reflected what Lynn White called 'the anti-technological attitudes of the ruling class.' Yet another problem 'was in the realm of economics. . . . The economy, in short, was weak in the dynamics that make for the creation and diffusion of technological innovation.'").

33. For an account of technology and engineering during the classical period, *see* DONALD HILL, A HISTORY OF ENGINEERING IN CLASSICAL AND MEDIEVAL TIMES (1984).

34. *See* Edward C. Walterscheid, *The Early Evolution of the United States Patent Law: Antecedents (Part 1)*, 76 J. PAT. & TRAD. OFF. SOC'Y 697, 702 (1994) ("Despite occasional argument to the contrary, ancient law failed completely to recognize the concept of intellectual property. While accusations of theft and plagiarism were common in both the Greek and Roman worlds, they were almost always tied to concerns about honor, credit or fame."). *See also* P.O. Long, *Inventions, Authorship, "Intellectual Property," and the Origin of Patents: Notes Toward Conceptual History*, 32 TECHNOLOGY AND CULTURE 846, 854 (1991) (stating "[n]either Greek nor Roman laws included any notion of intellectual property").

35. EDWARD GIBBON, II DECLINE AND FALL OF THE ROMAN EMPIRE 1443 (Modern Library 2003).

36. *See* JOEL MOKYR, THE LEVER OF RICHES 30-56 (1990) (detailing technological advances during middle ages); NORMAN F. CANTOR, THE CIVILIZATION OF THE MIDDLE AGES 228-229 (1993) (noting technological innovations in horsepower, waterpower, and wind power); GIES, CATHEDRAL, *supra* note 28, at 13 (Middle Age thinkers were beginning to accept "technology as a part of human life, inferior to intellectual and spiritual elements but necessary and natural. Technology made life easier, freeing the mind from material concerns and supplementing man's innate powers").

indeed, several noteworthy technological advancements were made during the Middle Ages.[37] In an attempt to promote technological innovation within the confines of the state or to import such from abroad, several privileges, monopolies, and importation franchises were granted to local guilds or to artisans from afar in an attempt to lure them away from their home state.[38] Nevertheless, any notion of patent-like rights in inventive contributions was lacking.

It was not until the Renaissance, specifically Renaissance Italy, that the first true patent was issued, and the first true patent statute was enacted. The former occurred when the Republic of Florence, in 1421, issued a patent to the eminent architect and inventor, Filippo Brunelleschi, for his ship, which transported famed Carraran marble for his famous dome of the Duomo of Florence.[39] But Brunelleschi's ship sank in the Arno River and with it the Florentine patent system.[40] The Italian textile guilds, reflecting the growth of commercial activity, filled the void, enacting private rules granting exclusive rights to those members of the guild who invented "certain . . . designs and patterns" of silk or wool.[41] Indeed, in the Renaissance city-states of Italy and most of Europe at that time, commerce and the arts were "dominated by guilds,"[42] and these private guild rules led eventually to the first known patent statute, enacted on March 19, 1474, by the Venetian Republic, which had sought to "benefit" the "commonwealth" by encouraging technological innovation through the issuance of private grants and importation licenses. The statute read:

> WE HAVE among us men of great genius, apt to invent and discover ingenious devices; and in view of the grandeur and virtue of our city, more such men come to us every day from diverse parts. Now, if provision were made for the works and

37. GIES, CATHEDRAL, *supra* note 28, at 2 ("Today . . . the innovative technology of the Middle Ages appears as the silent contribution of many hands and minds working together. The most momentous changes are now understood not as single, explicit inventions but as gradual, imperceptible revolutions—in agriculture, in water and wind power, in building construction, in textile manufacture, in communications, in metallurgy, in weaponry—taking place through incremental improvements, large or small, in tools, techniques, and the organization of work. This new view is part of a broader change in historical theory that has come to perceive technological innovation in all ages as primarily a social process rather than a disconnected series of individual initiatives.").

38. *See* Walterscheid, *Early Evolution, supra* note 34, at 707; Prager, *Early Growth, supra* note 24, at 117-126; BUGBEE, GENESIS, *supra* note 25, at 12-17.

39. *See* F.D. PRAGER & GUSTINA SCAGLIA, BRUNELLESCHI: STUDIES OF HIS TECHNOLOGY AND INVENTIONS 111 (2004); BUGBEE, GENESIS, *supra* note 25, at 17-18; M. Frumkin, *The Origin of Patents*, 27 J. PAT. OFF. SOC'Y 143, 144 (1943). *See also* GIES, CATHEDRAL, *supra* note 28, at 254 (stating that Brunelleschi "pioneered patent protection for inventors"). *But see* Walterscheid, *Early Evolution, supra* note 34, at 707 ("While it is generally agreed that the custom of granting patents of monopoly, *i.e.*, exclusive right to practice a particular art, in return for its introduction into the state, originated in Italy, there is some question as to whether it began in Venice or in Florence."). For more on Brunelleschi's ship and his patent, *see* ROSS KING, BRUNELLESCHI'S DOME 112-113 (2000).

40. *See* Craig Allen Nard & Andrew P. Morriss, *Constitutionalizing Patents: From Venice to Philadelphia*, 2 REV. L. & ECON. 223, 250-256 (2006) (discussing reasons why patent system did not take hold in Florence). *Cf.* BUGBEE, GENESIS, *supra* note 25, at 19.

41. *See* Long, *Inventions, supra* note 34, at 870 ("In promoting attitudes of ownership toward intangible property—craft knowledge and processes as distinct from material products—the guilds developed the concept of 'intellectual property' without ever calling it that.").

42. *See* Walterscheid, *Early Evolution, supra* note 34, at 704 ("The example of glassmakers of Venice is particularly instructive. At the time of the Renaissance, Venetian glasswork was recognized as the finest in Europe. . . . There were detailed guild regulations covering a variety of matters, including legal workdays, election of guild officials, judicial procedures, apprenticeships, and relations between masters and patrons. Selling stolen, defective, or non-Venetian glass products was forbidden.").

devices discovered by such persons, so that others who may see them could not build them and take the inventor's honor away, more men would then apply their genius, would discover, and would build devices of great utility and benefit to our Commonwealth. Therefore:

Be it enacted that, by the authority of this Council, every person who shall build any *new and ingenious device* in this City, *not previously made in our Commonwealth,* shall give *notice* of it to the office of our General Welfare Board when it has been *reduced to perfection so that it can be used and operated.* It being forbidden to every other person in any of our territories and towns to make any further device conforming with and *similar* to said one, *without the consent and license of the author, for the term of 10 years.* And if anybody builds it in violation hereof, the aforesaid author and inventor shall be entitled to have him summoned before any magistrate of this City, by which magistrate the said infringer shall be constrained to *pay him hundred ducats*; *and the device shall be destroyed at once.* It being, however, within the power and discretion of the Government, in its activities, to take and use any such device and instrument, with this condition however that no one but the author shall operate it.[43]

The Venetian statute is notable for two reasons. First, it was written in Venetian—which was then a dialect of Italian—rather than Latin, suggesting the audience was the artisan and inventor, not the learned professional class. Second, and more importantly, every feature modern patent policymakers regard as fundamental can be found in the Venetian statute. For instance, the *quid pro quo*—the right to exclude is bestowed upon one who discloses a useful invention to society—is at the heart of the Venetian statute. Moreover, the invention

---

43. The statute is reproduced in Giulio Mandich, *Venetian Patents (1450-1550)*, 30 J. Pat. Off. Soc'y 166, 176-177 (1948) (emphasis added). For a detailed discussion of the development of patent rights in Renaissance Venice, *see* Nard & Morriss, *Constitutionalizing Patents, supra* note 40, at 233-258. For a discussion of Venetian guilds and patent law, *see* Ted M. Sichelman & Sean M. O'Connor, *Patents as Promoters of Competition: The Guild Origins of Patent Law in the Venetian Republic,* ___ San Diego L. Rev.___ (2013) at http://papers.ssrn.com/sol3/papers.cfm?abstract_id=2126944. Copyright law was also part of the Venetian landscape during this time. *See* J. Kostylo, *Commentary on the Venetian Statute on Industrial Brevets (1474),* in Primary Sources on Copyright (1450-1900) (L. Bently & M. Kretschmer eds., 2008) (http://www.copyrighthistory.org) (arguing "that in the realities of Renaissance Italy there was no strict separation between industrial brevets (protopatents) and book privileges and that there was much mutual influence between these two institutions"). In fact, prior to the enactment of the 1474 statute and germane to the development Venetian copyright law, the Venetian Council granted Johannes of Speyer a monopoly on printing or the first printing privilege:

> [w]hereas such an innovation, unique and particular to our age and entirely unknown to those ancients, must be supported and nourished with all our goodwill and resources and [whereas] the same Master Johannes, who suffers under the great expense of his household and the wages of his craftsmen, must be provided with the means so that he may continue in better spirits and consider his art of printing something to be expanded rather than something to be abandoned, in the same manner as usual in other arts, even much smaller ones, the undersigned lords of the present Council, in response to the humble and reverent entreaty of the said Master Johannes, have determined and by determining decreed that over the next five years no one at all should have the desire, possibility, strength or daring to practice the said art of printing books in this the renowned state of Venice and its dominion, apart from Master Johannes himself.

Johannes of Speyer's Printing Monopoly, Venice (1469), in Primary Sources on Copyright (1450-1900) (Joanna Kostylo trans., Lionel Bently & Martin Kretschmer eds.), available at http://www.copyrighthistory.org (describing the printing privilege as "unique in the history of Venetian copyright" and reflects "the early laissez-faire attitudes of the government towards the printing trade which combined with the natural play of economic forces to foster a thoroughly capitalistic structure of the book market in Venice").

must have possessed utility and novelty, implying an examination system.[44] The novelty requirement was also geographically limited to the Commonwealth. (The American novelty provision—section 102(a)—limits prior knowledge and use to the United States.) And it has been plausibly argued that the phrase "ingenious device" was the precursor to the nonobviousness requirement.[45] Third parties were prohibited from making the same or "similar" device, suggesting the grant of rights was not limited to the specific embodiment of the inventor. Furthermore, the statute required the invention be operable and to have been reduced to practice. There was also a temporal dimension to the exclusive right (i.e., 10 years), and a remedy was provided to the inventor for an infringing act, whereby the inventor could obtain damages from the infringer and have the latter's infringing device "destroyed at once." Indeed, the Venetian statute of 1474 established a foundation for the world's first patent system and prompted one historian to proclaim that "the international patent experience of nearly 500 years has merely brought amendments or improvements upon the solid core established in Renaissance Venice."[46] Or, to paraphrase the American philosopher, Alfred North Whitehead, all modern patent regimes consist of a series of footnotes to the Venetian patent statute of 1474.

Begun in Italy, the European patent custom spread rapidly throughout Europe, due largely to the migration of Venetian artisans and craftsman.[47] As a result, "a patent system almost identical with that of Venice grew up everywhere,

---

44. Mario Biagioli had this to say about the nature of the Venetian examination system:

The Venetian patent system involved some kind of examination, but not one that primarily centered on the performance of the invention or the soundness of its principles. . . . Technical examinations were common when inventors requested funds to develop inventions of particular public relevance, or pensions and rewards in exchange for communicating new military technologics to the state (Galileo's demonstration of his telescope to the Venetian Senate in 1609 is an example of this practice). Such tests, however, were rarely performed when inventors applied for privileges without the additional request of state funds. . . . Having effectively farmed out the technical tests to highly motivated patentees, the officials focused on the economic and bureaucratic aspects of the privilege. They assessed the local utility and novelty of the invention, its impact on local labor, commerce, and prices, and did preliminary checks to see whether someone else had already received a privilege for it.

Mario Biagioli, *Patent Republic: Representing Inventions, Constructing Rights and Authors*, SOCIAL RESEARCH, v. 73, pp. 1129, 1133 (Winter 2006).

45. Mandich, *Venetian Patents, supra* note 43, at 177 (arguing that "[t]here is reference to an 'inventive device' (*nuovo et ingegnoso artifico*); in outline, a requirement of inventive merit seems to emerge, according to which the invention must not be a trifling, all too obvious application of known technology").

46. BUGBEE, GENESIS, *supra* note 25, at 24. For a detailed discussion of the creation of the Venetian patent statute from a public choice perspective, *see* Nard & Morriss, *Constitutionalizing Patents, supra* note 40, at 233-258.

47. *See* Mandich, *Venetian Patents, supra* note 43, at 205 (noting Italian immigrants are among the first to seek monopoly patents); C.H. Greenstreet, *History of Patent Systems* 4 in MAINLY ON PATENTS (F. Liebesny ed., 1972) ("Familiar with the Venetian law and fearful of local competition, the glassmakers asked for and received patent protection wherever they settled abroad."); CHRISTINE MACLEOD, INVENTING THE INDUSTRIAL REVOLUTION: THE ENGLISH PATENT SYSTEM, 1660-1800 11 (1988) ("Emigrant Italian craftsmen, seeking protection against local competition and guild restrictions as a condition of imparting their skills disseminated knowledge of their patent systems around Europe.").

before 1600,"[48] including, France,[49] Germany,[50] the Netherlands,[51] and England, to which we now turn.

b. English Patent Policy and the Statute of Monopolies

England was not unlike its European neighbors in its attempt to attract foreign know-how to its shores and to cultivate domestic industry. During the fifteenth and sixteenth centuries, the English crown was fairly active in granting importation franchises and monopolistic privileges, particularly under Elizabeth I. With England still largely agricultural and lagging behind much of the rest of Europe in the industrial arts,[52] the Queen made aggressive use of patents of

48. Prager, *Early Growth*, *supra* note 24, at 139. *See also* MOKYR, LEVER OF RICHES, *supra* note 36, at 79 (noting the Venetian "example was followed widely and by the middle of the sixteenth century the idea had penetrated much of Europe"). It is not surprising that many of the initial patents issued by other European countries were to Italian artisans. *See* Walterscheid, *Early Evolution*, *supra* note 34, at 710.

49. *See* F.D. Prager, *A History of Intellectual Property from 1545 to 1787*, 26 J. PAT. OFF. SOC'Y 711, 723 (1944). It has been asserted that the first French patent was granted in 1551 to an Italian inventor for glassmaking, but Bugbee argues that the grant was more of an importation franchise than a patent, and the first French patent was "probably" given to Abel Foullon in 1551 for a "rangefinder." BUGBEE, GENESIS, *supra* note 25, at 25. Of some significance is the examination procedure adopted by France in 1699 to determine the novelty of an invention. This procedure was known by America's founding fathers and not surprisingly found its way into the 1790 Patent Act. France subjected inventions to the scrutinizing eye of trained examiners under the auspices of the Royal Academy of Sciences and required inventors who received a patent to deposit a model with the Academy. The 1699 French Act stated that:

> The Academy shall, on order of the King, examine all machines for which privileges are solicited from his majesty. It shall certify whether they are new and useful. The inventors of those which are approved shall leave a model thereof.

According to Prager, however, the "basic defect" of the examination procedure was "that it was not obligatory" and "[w]hile it was usual for the king's council and also for the Parliament to consult the academy, no such consultation was strictly necessary for either." Prager, *Intellectual Property from 1545 to 1787*, *supra* at 725. Furthermore, even though "the academy scrutinized novelty and 'utility' of the invention, the Parliament was most interested in the competitive chances and prospective tax value of the proposed enterprise" and the technical merits were not examined exclusively. *Id.* at 726.

50. *See* Walterscheid, *Early Evolution*, *supra* note 34, at 711; BUGBEE, GENESIS, *supra* note 25, at 26 (asserting that an "advanced patent institution flourished in the German states during most of the sixteenth century and the first three decades of the seventeenth before the destructive Thirty Years War brought its decline"). *See also* Hansjoerg Pohlmann, *The Inventor's Right in Early German Law*, 43 J. PAT. OFF. SOC'Y 121, 122-123 (1961).

51. It is arguable that the patent system of the Netherlands was the most advanced and sophisticated during the sixteenth and seventeenth centuries. *See generally* GERARD DOORMAN, PATENTS FOR INVENTIONS IN THE NETHERLANDS DURING THE 16TH, 17TH, AND 18TH CENTURIES (The Hague 1942). As one commentator writes:

> From the very beginning of the patent custom in the [Netherlands], the States General required the applicant to clearly delineate the subject matter to be covered by the patent grant. Typically, this was done before a committee appointed for the purpose. Initially, at least, a drawing or a specification had to be submitted. The purpose of the specification, drawing, or model was not to educate the public as to the nature of the invention, but rather solely to provide evidence as to the nature of the invention for purposes of granting the patent or to indicate the nature of the patented matter in the event of later litigation.

Walterscheid, *Early Evolution*, *supra* note 34, at 714.

52. *See* JOHN E. NEALE, THE ELIZABETHAN HOUSE OF COMMONS 19 (1949) ("Elizabethan England was primarily an agricultural community. Its chief wealth was in land and its ruling class was the landed gentry—the middling and big businessmen of a rural society."); MARK KISHLANSKY, A MONARCHY TRANSFORMED: BRITAIN 1603-1714, at 6 (1997) ("At the beginning of the seventeenth century most British people were farmers."); J.P. KENYON, STUART ENGLAND 15 (1978) (England

monopoly to encourage the growth of manufacturing and to lure skilled foreigners.[53] More than 50 patents of monopoly were granted from 1561 to 1590, for example.[54] In addition to expanding the number of patents, Elizabeth anglicized them as well. Over the course of her reign there was a gradual shift from the award of patents to foreigners to their award to locals.[55] There were thus more new ideas with potentially patentable consequences. Not only did scientific knowledge grow, but so did legal knowledge, caused by the "invasion of the universities and the Inns of Court by the gentry."[56]

After an initial tendency to reward innovation, "exhaustion of the Crown's reserves of patronage" forced her to increasingly bestow unwarranted and abusive privileges upon favorite courtiers such as Sir Walter Raleigh.[57] In fact, three of the most notorious patents (for vinegar, starch, and playing cards) were created late in Elizabeth's reign.[58] As Christine MacLeod has written, "without a committed, firm hand guiding the system to well-defined ends, malpractices began to creep in that were to bring it into disrepute and ultimately endanger its existence."[59] Some of the late-period patents granted rights to established techniques or items and so constituted attacks on established industries, spurring opposition to the most egregious.[60] Elizabeth's court had become "the Mecca of patronage, a place and incomparable profit to be had through the favour of the great ones of the land,"[61] making the abuse of patents no surprise.

Thus, it would not be long before a public outcry ensued leading to several celebrated cases by the Queen's Bench holding that monopolies were against the common law.[62] As a result, the abuses temporarily subsided, but it

---

"was a small, poor country with a single crop economy; her dependence on the exports of unfinished woolens put her on a par with the modern African cocoa state . . . her industries made a minuscule contribution toward the gross national product.").

53. *See* H.G. Fox, MONOPOLIES: A STUDY OF THE HISTORY AND FUTURE OF THE PATENT MONOPOLY 61 (Toronto 1947).

54. *See* Greenstreet, *History of Patent Systems, supra* note 47, at 6.

55. *See* Fox, MONOPOLIES, *supra* note 53, at 61.

56. NEALE, *supra* note 52, at 291. The education many received gave heavy emphasis to the classics and the Bible. "All this material trained members to see issues of high principle in the details of proposals which came before them, probably made their speeches longer, and made it far more improbable that they would meekly submit to proposals put before them." CONRAD RUSSELL, THE CRISIS OF PARLIAMENTS 181 (1971).

57. D.L. FARMER, BRITAIN AND THE STUARTS 3 (1967); ALAN G.R. SMITH, THE EMERGENCE OF A NATION STATE: THE COMMONWEALTH OF ENGLAND 1529-1660 240 (2d ed. 1984) ("One way she could reward [her courtiers and officials] without direct cost to the Crown was by granting them patents of monopoly" at a time when "the Queen was saving every penny she could for the war and had even less money than usual to bestow on her courtiers and officials.").

58. *See* E. Wyndham Hulme, *The History of the Patent System Under the Prerogative and at Common Law,* 16 L.Q. REV. 44, 53 (1896). *See also* WILLIAM HYDE PRICE, THE ENGLISH PATENTS OF MONOPOLY 8 (1906) ("In the course of the third decade (1581-1590), more obvious abuses crept in.").

59. MacLEOD, INDUSTRIAL REVOLUTION, *supra* note 47, at 14. *See also* Adam Mossoff, *Rethinking the Development of Patents: An Intellectual History, 1550-1800,* 52 HASTINGS L.J. 1255, 1266 (2001) ("During Queen Elizabeth's reign, the Privy Council's records are replete with patent monopolies issuing regardless of whether an industry was new to the realm or not, which was the original purpose and justification for the issuance of such letters patent); Michael Les Benedict, *Laissez-Faire and Liberty: A Re-Evaluation of the Meaning and Origins of Laissez-Faire Constitutionalism,* 3 LAW & HIST. REV. 293, 314 (1985) (noting that during the seventeenth century, the Crown "could bestow a monopoly in the privilege of selling salt as easily as he could bestow an escheated manor").

60. *See* PRICE, ENGLISH PATENTS, *supra* note 58, at 9.

61. NEALE, *supra* note 52, at 213.

62. *See Davenant v. Hurdis* (1599) and *Darcy v. Allin* (1602) (the latter case is also known as "The Case of Monopolies"). But while *Darcy* was the "first complete judicial pronouncement upon the common law principles concerning monopolies," FOX, MONOPOLIES, *supra* note 53, at 87, as

would not be long before the Crown, namely James I, who neither possessed the political savvy nor popularity of his predecessor, resumed granting "odious monopolies."[63] This led to yet another public outcry,[64] which ultimately culminated in parliamentary action. In 1624, Parliament enacted the Statute of Monopolies. Section I of the statute declared all monopolies and grants as void and contrary to law; however, Section VI provided a noteworthy exception:

> Provided also, and be it declared and enacted, that any declaration before mentioned shall not extend to any Letters Patents and grants of privilege for the term of 14 years or under hereafter to be made of the sole working or making of any manner of *new* manufacture within this Realm to the true and first inventor and inventors of such manufactures which others at the time of making such letters Patents and Grants shall not use so as also they be not contrary to law nor mischievous to the State.[65]

Most importantly, Section II "declared and enacted . . . that all monopolies . . . shall be forever hereafter examined, heard, tried, and determined by and according to the common laws." The statute decisively settled the question of the monarch's authority to issue patents of monopoly, sharply restricting the permissible grants.[66] The common law's limitation to grants that furthered the

---

Adam Mossoff suggests, the key to understanding *Darcy* was that "no one . . . was out to repudiate the Queen's royal prerogative *in toto,* but rather the judges simply enunciated the first common-law rule for adjudicating the *legitimacy* of a grant of monopoly privileges." Mossoff, *Rethinking the Development of Patents, supra* note 59, at 1269 (emphasis in original).

63. W.S. Holdsworth captures nicely the abusive mind-set of James I:

> James I was always hard up; and for a consideration he was prepared to grant many privileges both of the governmental and of the industrial varieties. . . . Of the second of these varieties of grants the following are a few examples: grant of an exclusive right to export calfskins; grant of an exclusive right to import cod and ling; grant of an exclusive right to make farthing tokens of copper.

W.S. Holdsworth, *The Common Debates 1621,* 52 L.Q. Rev. 481, 487 (1936). In the wake of *Davenant* and *Darcy* (*The Case of Monopolies*), James I, although eventually resuming his proclivity for granting undeserved monopolies, did make certain concessions. For example, he suspended all monopolies with the exception of "awards to corporations and companies of arts and for promoting commerce." Bugbee, Genesis, *supra* note 25, at 38. He also issued a declaration called the *Book of Bounty* (1610), which affirmed monopolies were against the common law, but reserved the right to grant monopolies for new contributions. The common law also made its mark in 1615 when the Queen's Bench, in *The Cloth Workers of Ipswich* case, held that royal grants of a limited duration for *new* manufactures were *not* against the common law.

64. *See* Fox, Monopolies, *supra* note 53, at 104.

65. Sir William Jarrett, *English Patent System,* 26 J. Pat. Off. Soc'y 761, 761 (1944) (emphasis added). According to Walterscheid, Lord Coke explained that a patent for invention is valid under Section 6 if seven conditions are met:

> the term of the patent may not exceed fourteen years, (2) the patent "must be granted to the first and true inventor," (3) "it must be of such manufactures, which any other at the making of such Letters Patents did not use," (4) it "must not be contrary to law," (5) it must not be "mischievous to the State by raising of prices of commodities at home," (6) it must not "hurt trade," and (7) it must not be "generally inconvenient."

Edward C. Walterscheid, *The Early Evolution of the United States Patent Law: Antecendents (Part II),* 76 J. Pat. & Trad. Off. Soc'y 849, 876-880 (1994).

66. *See* MacLeod, Industrial Revolution, *supra* note 47, at 17 (noting that in addition to invention patents, the Statute of Monopolies allowed "grants made or confirmed by Act of Parliament, warrants under the privy seal to justices of the courts of law and of the peace, patents for printing, making ordnance, gunpowder and alum, and the manufacturing patents granted to four named individuals; also exempted were charters to towns, corporations and companies"). Douglass North and Robert Thomas argue the statute of monopolies, particularly the shift of granting power to Parliament, played an important role in the development of Britain's Industrial Revolution. See Douglass C.

national interest would henceforth be enforced by the common law courts, not the Privy Council or the Star Chamber. By relocating the decision-making authority over the validity of particular patents, Parliament created a binding constraint on the issuance of monopoly patents, limiting them to cases of invention. But it is important to note that the common law did not enjoy prominence immediately after enactment.[67] Nor did the Statute of Monopolies end the abuses of the royal prerogative.[68] Patent law was only one of the many arenas in which the larger struggle for supremacy between Parliament and the monarchy was fought. Parliament's victory in the Statute of Monopolies, as important as it was,[69] was still only a single battle in a multi-century campaign. The point is that common law lawyers and members of Parliament shared a mutual interest in challenging the crown's abusive practices regarding monopolistic grants and acted pursuant to that interest to establish the principle of a neutral decision maker to evaluate the legitimacy of monopoly patents. Whether due to "pilot error" or "mechanical error," James's reign produced a fundamental shift in England's approach to patent law, introducing an institution capable of an independent evaluation of the legitimacy of particular patents.[70]

The Statute of Monopolies governed English patent law for more than 200 years, and it was not until the 1852 Patent Law Amendment Act that England witnessed significant patent law legislation.[71] But prior to the 1852 Act an important development occurred in English patent law: the *specification,* or "a full description of the invention and its operation which would show the scope of the patent."[72] Indeed, if we were inclined to isolate a noteworthy English contribution to patent law, it would have to be the development of the patent specification. Although the specification was part of the Continental patent systems, particularly in the Netherlands, it was England in the early eighteenth century

---

North and Robert P. Thomas, THE RISE OF THE WESTERN WORLD: A NEW ECONOMIC HISTORY (1973). But see Joel Mokyr, THE ENLIGHTENED ECONOMY: AN ECONOMIC HISTORY OF BRITAIN (2009).

67. *See* Mossoff, *Rethinking the Development of Patents, supra* note 59, at 1277 (noting the "Privy Council's obstinate refusal to concede jurisdiction" allowed it to continue to quash common law actions against patents in some cases); MACLEOD, INDUSTRIAL REVOLUTION, *supra* note 47, at 15 (stating "there were loopholes in the Act which the crown, desperate for new sources of patronage and revenue in the 1630s, was able to exploit").

68. *See* PRICE, ENGLISH PATENTS, *supra* note 58, at 35 (noting that crown used invention monopolies as a means to reduce existing industries to monopolies "under cover of technical improvements"). Fox notes that attacks on monopolies in Parliament continued into the "Long Parliament" that began in 1640. FOX, MONOPOLIES, *supra* note 53, at 7 ("The attacks upon it [patents of monopoly] were virulent and widespread. At the time of the Long Parliament it had few friends except those who personally profited by holding monopolies.").

69. *See, e.g.,* DOUGLASS NORTH, STRUCTURE AND CHANGE IN ECONOMIC HISTORY 164-165 (viewing the Statute of Monopolies as fundamental precondition for the Industrial Revolution).

70. *See* Nard & Morriss, *Constitutionalizing Patents, supra* note 40, for a discussion of the Statute of Monopolies from a public choice perspective. *See also* Thomas Nachbar, *Monopoly, Mercantilism, and Intellectual Property,* 91 VA. L. REV. 1313 (2005). Douglass North and Robert Thomas have argued that the Statute of Monopolies was instrumental in launching Great Britain's Industrial Revolution. *See* DOUGLASS C. NORTH & ROBERT P. THOMAS, THE RISE OF THE WESTERN WORLD: A NEW ECONOMIC HISTORY (1973).

71. For a discussion of the role of the patent system in the Industrial Revolution, *see* H. DUTTON, THE PATENT SYSTEM AND INVENTIVE ACTIVITY DURING THE INDUSTRIAL REVOLUTION, 1750-1852 (1984) (asserting the patent system had a powerful incentive effect in the rate of invention). *See also* R.J. Sullivan, *England's "Age of Invention": The Acceleration of Patents and Patentable Invention During the Industrial Revolution,* 26 EXPLORATIONS IN ECONOMIC HISTORY 424-452 (1989).

72. BUGBEE, GENESIS, *supra* note 25, at 41-42 (asserting that a specification "became a standard feature of [English] patents issued after 1734"); *see also* DOORMAN, PATENTS FOR INVENTIONS IN THE NETHERLANDS, *supra* note 51, at 22-23.

that adopted it as part of patent practice and required a much fuller disclosure.[73] This practice culminated in the well-known case of *Liardet v. Johnson,* decided in 1778, wherein Lord Mansfield held that the "consideration" for a patent grant was the specification rather than the introduction of a new industry.[74] No longer was the law only concerned with the introduction of an actual inventive device or product; rather, the inventor's contribution in the form of *information* was gradually assuming center stage.[75] The role of the specification was, and still is, the dissemination of knowledge. This focus on information and its dissemination continues to play an important role in modern patent systems.

3. The American Experience

The influence of the English patent custom on American patent practice is undeniable. There were several American colonies that granted patents;[76] and colonial patent practice, while limited, due largely to a predominantly agrarian society, influenced the subsequently developed patent custom of the states, as well as the federal patent system. The distractions of the American Revolution discouraged notions of "inventive property" at first, but as the Revolution continued, victory became less uncertain, and the Confederation witnessed a resumption of issued patents, especially during the 1780s.[77] Indeed, the demands of the Revolution coupled with colonial boycotts of British goods and notions of self-sufficiency stimulated industrial development, leading to the creation of various societies whose purpose was to encourage industry and manufacture.[78]

73. Prior to the creation of the specification as we appreciate it today, states required actual reduction to practice. According to Mario Biagioli, "privilege-granting authorities wanted to maximize local utility, not to disclose knowledge about the invention. What mattered was that inventions worked, not how they worked." Indeed, "the invention's local utility was vastly more important than its detailed description." *See* Mario Biagioli, *Patent Specification and Political Representations,* in MAKING AND UNMAKING INTELLECTUAL PROPERTY 27-28 (Woodmansee et al. eds., 2011).

74. *See* Jarrett, *English Patent System, supra* note 65, at 762. *See also* Edward C. Walterscheid, *The Early Evolution of the United States Patent Law: Antecedents (Part 3),* 77 J. PAT. & TRAD. OFF. SOC'Y 771 (1995).

75. Mario Biagioli argues that the transformation from requiring actual reduction to practice (showing the invention worked) to what we call today constructive reduction to practice (showing how the invention works through written disclosure) tracks the rise of political representation and the contract between inventors and citizens. *See* Biagioli, *Patent Specification, supra* note 73, at 25.

76. *See* BUGBEE, GENESIS, *supra* note 25, at 57-83; V. CLARK, I HISTORY OF MANUFACTURES IN THE UNITED STATES: 1607-1860 (1916). America's first colonial patent was issued in Massachusetts in 1641 to Samuel Winslow pertaining to the production of salt for the colony's fishing industry. The most active colonies in issuing patents were Massachusetts, Connecticut, and South Carolina. BUGBEE, GENESIS, *supra* note 25, at 75-83. It appears that Delaware, New Hampshire, New Jersey, and North Carolina did not issue patents. It is questionable whether Pennsylvania issued any patents during the Colonial period, whereas New York, Maryland, Rhode Island, and Virginia issued a combined total of ten. Edward C. Walterscheid, *The Early Evolution of United States Patent Law: Antecedents (5 Part I),* 78 J. PAT. & TRAD. OFF. SOC'Y 615, 630-631 (1996). Colonial patents were issued through private bills or special enactments, not general or public statutory schemes. *Id.* at 624-625.

77. In 1784, for example, South Carolina enacted the first American general patent provision, which essentially was a clause in the state's "Act for the Encouragement of Arts and Sciences." The clause read: "The Inventors of useful machines shall have a like exclusive privilege of making or vending their machines for the like term of 14 years, under the same privileges and restrictions hereby granted to, and imposed on, authors of books." BUGBEE, GENESIS, *supra* note 25, at 92-93.

78. *See* INLOW, THE PATENT GRANT 45 (1950); BUGBEE, GENESIS, *supra* note 25, at 85; Walterscheid, *Early Evolution, supra* note 74, at 632 n.80.

As domestic technology developed and national markets formed, the number of state-issued patents gradually increased, resulting in conflicting private legislative grants among states.[79] As the Constitutional Convention drew near, the problems with state patent custom became increasingly more apparent, thus giving rise to the desirability of a uniform system of patents.[80]

Therefore, in response to the driving forces of James Madison and Charles Pinckney, it was proposed, on Wednesday, September 5, 1787,[81] during the closing days of the Constitutional Convention, that Congress shall have the power

> [t]o promote the Progress of Science and useful Arts by securing for limited Times to Authors and Inventors the exclusive Right to their respective Writings and Discoveries.[82]

---

79. Take the famed Rumsey-Fitch steamboat dispute as an example. Both James Rumsey and John Fitch lobbied several state legislatures, each having distinct patent customs, for a monopoly for their respective steamboats. But interestingly, beyond the Fitch-Rumsey dispute, patents did not play a significant role in the development of the steamboat technology. As Louis Hunter wrote, "[t]hough the men who developed the machinery of the western steamboat possessed much ingenuity and inventive skill, the record shows that they had little awareness of or use for the patent system. . . . [N]o significant part of the engine, propelling mechanism, or boilers during the period of the steamboat's development to maturity was claimed and patented as a distinctive and original development." LOUIS HUNTER, STEAMBOATS ON THE WESTERN RIVERS 175-176 (1949).

80. *See* Nard & Morriss, *Constitutionalizing Patents, supra* note 40, at 290-304 (noting principal reason for federalizing patent system was desire for a nationally uniform patent policy). Prior to the ratification of the Constitution, there was no federal patent system. The states retained the power to issue patents because under Article II of the Articles of Confederation each state retained "every power, jurisdiction and right, which is not by the confederation expressly delegated to the United States, in Congress assembled." Edward C. Walterscheid, *To Promote the Progress of Useful Arts: American Patent Law and Administration, 1787-1836 (Part I)*, 79 J. PAT. & TRAD. OFF. SOC'Y 61, 65 (1997). Furthermore, as Bugbee noted:

> In 1777, when the Articles of Confederation were drafted, patent granting was temporarily in abeyance, and the framers of the Articles made no attempt to transfer the protection of inventive property to the national scene. Had this colonial prerogative been actively exercised at the time by the newly independent states, the Articles would probably have left it to them nevertheless. By 1787, however, the granting of state patents was at a peak, and the need for a centralized system was strongly indicated by the multiple applications of competing inventors. With the emergence of a small but significant class of manufacturers and promoters stimulated by the war, the economic stakes were now considerably greater than had been the case in colonial times. The merits and shortcomings of the state patent practice were therefore clearly visible to those state legislators who were about to transmit this experience to the national scene.

BUGBEE, GENESIS, *supra* note 25, at 103.

81. The delegates convened in Philadelphia on May 14, 1787. A draft Constitution was reported on August 6 without a patent and copyright clause. However, twelve days later, on August 18, Charles Pinckney of South Carolina, who was serving in the South Carolina legislature when it enacted America's first general patent and copyright provision in 1784, proposed that Congress have the power to enact patent legislation. Also, on August 18, James Madison submitted a similar proposal. David Brearley of New Jersey, a member of the Committee of Eleven, reported to the Convention what is essentially the patent and copyright clause embodied in Article I, Section 8, Clause 8 of the Constitution. *See* BUGBEE, GENESIS, *supra* note 25, at 125-131. *See also* Karl Fenning, *The Origin of the Patent and Copyright Clause of the Constitution*, 17 GEO. L.J. 114 (1929). Unfortunately, the historical record of the clause is sparse. Indeed, there is recorded debate on this provision. As one judge, writing in late nineteenth century, said when faced with interpreting the patent and copyright clause, "[w]hat immediate reasons operated upon the framers of the Constitution seem to be unknown." *McKeever v. United States*, 14 Ct. Cl. 396, 420 (1878).

82. Referring to the IP Clause, Michael Novak writes, "[t]he Constitution gives an incentive to discover new practical ideas and to bring them to the realistic service of one's neighbors. Perhaps no other practical device in history has so revolutionized the daily conditions of life. It has brought about a higher level of the common good than any people ever experienced before." MICHAEL NOVAK, BUSINESS AS A CALLING: WORK AND THE EXAMINED LIFE 144 (1996). The framers, employing

This provision, embodied in Article I, Section 8, Clause 8 of the Constitution, passed unanimously without debate and provides the foundation for American patent and copyright law. Indeed, Madison, in Federalist No. 43, wrote that

> [t]he utility of [Article I, Section 8, Clause 8] will scarcely be questioned. The copyright of authors has been solemnly adjudged, in Great Britain, to be a right of common law. The right to useful inventions seems with equal reason to belong to the inventors. The public good fully coincides in both cases with the claims of individuals.[83]

Of particular importance is the structure of the patent and copyright clause. The clause sets forth the specific means of exercising the enumerated power by permitting Congress to promote the progress of the useful arts (i.e., the enumerated power) only by granting *exclusive rights* for *limited times* to *inventors* for their *discoveries*. Ahkil Amar, citing the patent and copyright clause, asserts one method to deter "pretextual use of congressional power . . . was to specify the purpose of a particular power."[84] The decentralized nature of the clause reflects an aversion to special legislation and a desire to check Congressional

---

colonial syntax as one would expect, were respectively referring to works of authors and inventors when they used the terms "Science" and "useful Arts." In the eighteenth century, the term "Science," from the Latin, *scire*, "to know," meant learning or knowledge in general and had no particular connection to the physical or biological sciences like it does today. Thus, the operational relationships are between "authors," "science," and "writings" for copyright on the one hand and "inventors," "useful Arts," and "discoveries" for patents on the other. *See* Giles S. Rich, *Principles of Patentability*, in Nonobviousness, the Ultimate Condition of Patentability (John F. Witherspoon ed., 1980); Karl B. Lutz, *Patents and Science: A Clarification of the Patent Clause of the U.S. Constitution*, 18 Geo. Wash. L. Rev. 50 (1949); John F. Kasson, *Republican Values as a Dynamic Factor*, in The Industrial Revolution in America 6 (1998) (noting that the term *technology* "did not acquire its current meaning until the nineteenth century." In eighteenth century usage, "technology" denoted "a treatise on an art or the scientific study of the practical or industrial arts" or "useful knowledge"). *See generally* Kenneth J. Burchfield, *Revisiting the "Original" Patent Clause: Pseudohistory in Constitutional Construction*, 2 Harv. J.L. & Tech. 155 (1989).

83. The Federalist, A Commentary on the Constitution of the United States 278-279 (Modern Library 1937). The Supreme Court, in *Graham v. John Deere Co.*, 383 U.S. 1, 5-6 (1966), distinguished Article I, Section 8, Clause 8 from English patent custom by stressing that the constitutional clause was both a grant of and a limitation on Congress's power to make patent policy:

> The clause is both a grant of power and a limitation. This qualified authority, unlike the power often exercised in the sixteenth and seventeenth centuries by the English Crown, is limited to the promotion of advances in the "useful arts. It was written against this backdrop of the practices—eventually curtailed by the Statute of Monopolies—of the Crown in granting monopolies to court favorites in goods or businesses which had long before been enjoyed by the public. . . . The Congress in the exercise of the patent power may not overreach the restraints imposed by the stated constitutional purpose.

But see Adam Mossoff, *Who Cares What Thomas Jefferson Thought About Patents? Reevaluating the Patent "Privilege" in Historical Context*, 92 Cornell L. Rev. 953, 981-983 (2007) (asserting Madison was arguing in Federalist No. 43 that the policy justification for patents was grounded in natural rights theory). *See also* Novak, Business as a Calling, *supra* note 82, at 136-137 ("Only in one place in the body of the Constitution did the founders use the word *right*, to protect the 'right' of authors and inventors to the fruit of their original ideas. In mind, they saw, lies the primary cause of the wealth of nations. To genius of mind they added, as Lincoln admiringly noted, the 'fuel of interest.' To mind they gave incentives.").

84. Akhil Reed Amar, America's Constitution 112 (2005). *See also Graham v. John Deere Co.* 383 U.S. 1, 5-6 (1966) ("The [IP] clause is both a grant of power and a limitation. . . . It was written against this backdrop of the practices—eventually curtailed by the Statute of Monopolies—of the [English] Crown in granting monopolies to court favorites in goods or businesses which had long before been enjoyed by the public. . . ."); Robert Patrick Merges & Glenn Harlan Reynolds, *The Proper Scope of the Patent and Copyright Power*, 37 Harv. J. Leg. 45, 52-53 (2000) (asserting that "the constitutional footing for intellectual property protection was constructed with inherent limitations" that "originated in British analogues that were expressly designed to eliminate rent-seeking abuses").

overreaching. This desire is manifested by the proposals rejected by the delegates during the convention. In addition to the language that eventually found its way into Article I, Section 8, Madison and Pinckney proposed that Congress have the power to encourage the arts, sciences, and useful knowledge by offering rewards, chartering corporations, and establishing seminaries, public institutions, and universities.[85] These rejected proposals would have allowed for a great deal more Congressional intervention into market dynamics, rendering legislators more susceptible to interest-group pressures.[86] In fact, Alexander Hamilton recalled that a principal argument for limiting government involvement and its ability to direct the path of industry was that state intervention would "sacrifice the interest of the community to those of particular classes."[87] Moreover, the delegates were not operating in a vacuum; they most likely had knowledge of the Statute of Monopolies and, therefore, these structural limitations were arguably influenced by the antimonopoly tradition in England.[88]

Madison's fellow Virginian, Thomas Jefferson, while no stranger to the inventive process, was skeptical of monopolies and, initially, anything but a devotee of the patent system.[89] Nevertheless, he came to realize the importance of patents and played a prominent role in the early development of American patent law,[90] assuming primary administrative authority of the Patent Act of 1790,

---

85. *See* Dotan Oliar, *Making Sense of the Intellectual Property Clause: Promotion of Progress as a Limitation on Congress's Intellectual Property Power*, 94 GEO. L.J. 1771, 1791-1805 (2005).

86. *See* HINDLE, EMULATION, *supra* note 9, at 18 (stating the award of premiums by the government would invite "intrusive intervention into the economy," something that "flew in the face of the congenial laissez-faire atmosphere").

87. *Annals of Congress*, 2d Cong., 1st Sess., 972-973.

88. This is not to suggest that the Founders were aware of the common law cases interpreting the Statute of Monopolies, as those cases were largely decided in the second half of the eighteenth century. Nor is there direct evidence of the influence of the English experience on the structure of Article I, Section 8, Clause 8. *See* Thomas B. Nachbar, *Intellectual Property and Constitutional Norms*, 104 COLUM. L. REV. 272, 330-331 (2004). Nonetheless, a plausible inference can be made that the Founders were aware of the Statute of Monopolies and were at least sensitive to the English tradition. For instance, Blackstone, whose "Commentaries was the most widely read English law treatise in late-eighteenth-century America," John F. Manning, *Textualism and the Equity of the Statute*, 101 COLUM. L. REV. 1, 35 (2001), specifically mentioned the Statue of Monopolies in his Commentaries. *See* 4 WILLIAM BLACKSTONE, COMMENTARIES ON THE LAWS OF ENGLAND §9 (stating that royal abuse in granting monopolies was "in a great measure remedied by" the Statute of Monopolies, "which declares such monopolies to be contrary to law and void (except as to patents, not exceeding the grant of fourteen years, to the authors of new inventions)"). And there was arguably awareness of the English common law from the time of Justice Story's 1822 opinion in *Evans v. Eaton*, 20 U.S. (7 Wheat.) 356 (1822), but the extent of this awareness is difficult to discern.

89. *See* MERRILL D. PETERSON, THOMAS JEFFERSON AND THE NEW NATION 450 (1970) ("The first superintendent of patents did not fully subscribe to the principle of the system. He questioned that ingenuity is 'spurred on by the hopes of monopoly,' and thought 'the benefit even of limited monopolies . . . too doubtful to be opposed to that of their general suppression.'"). This sentiment was expressed by Jefferson in response to a draft of the Constitution sent to him by Madison. Jefferson wrote:

> I sincerely rejoice at the acceptance of our new constitution by nine states. It is a good canvas, on which some strokes only want retouching. What are these, I think are sufficiently manifested by the general voice from north to south, which calls for a bill of rights. It seems pretty generally understood that this should go to . . . Monopolies. . . . The saying there shall be no monopolies lessens the incitements to ingenuity, which spurred on by the hope of a monopoly for a limited time, as of 14 years; but the benefit even of limited monopolies is too doubtful to be opposed to that of their general suppression.

V WRITINGS OF THOMAS JEFFERSON 45, 47 (Ford ed., 1895).

90. In fact, shortly after the 1790 Act was passed, Jefferson, in a letter to British politician Benjamin Vaughan, wrote:

America's first patent statute signed into law on April 10, 1790 by President George Washington.[91] The 1790 Act authorized the issuance of patents for "any useful art, manufacture, engine, machine, or device, or any improvement therein not before known or used."[92] The Act did not create a patent office, but instead designated a patent board that would *examine* patent applications, comprising a specification and drawings, to determine if "the invention or discovery [was] sufficiently useful and important" so as to merit a patent. The board, self-dubbed the "Commissioners for the Promotion of the Useful Arts," comprised the Secretary of State (Thomas Jefferson), Secretary of War (Henry Knox), and the Attorney General (Edmund Randolph).[93] The first patent under the 1790

> An act of Congress authorizing the issue of patents for new discoveries has given a spring to invention beyond my conception. Being an instrument in granting the patents, I am acquainted with the discoveries. Many of them indeed are trifling, but there are some of great consequence, which have been proved of practice, and others which, if they stand the same proof, will produce greater effect.

ENCYCLOPEDIA VIRGINIA at www.encyclopediavirginia.org/Letter_from_Thomas_Jefferson_to_Benjamin_Vaughan_June_27_1790. A great deal has been written about Jefferson's role in the creation and support of the American patent system. *See, e.g.,* Kendall J. Dodd, *Patent Models and the Patent Law: 1790-1880 (Part I),* 65 J. PAT. & TRAD. OFF. SOC'Y 187, 196 (1983); Levi N. Fouts, *Jefferson the Inventor, and His Relation to the Patent System,* 4 J. PAT. OFF. SOC'Y 316, 322 (1922). *Cf.* Edward C. Walterscheid, *Patents and the Jeffersonian Mythology,* 29 JOHN MARSHALL L. REV. 269, 276-279 (1995) (questioning the historical scholarship on Jefferson); Mossoff, *Who Cares What Thomas Jefferson Thought About Patents?, supra* note 83, at 955 (noting that "Jefferson's hegemony over the history of American patent law is as indisputable as it is wrong").

91. Act of Apr. 10, 1790, ch. 7, 1 Stat. 109. A total of 55 patents were issued under the 1790 Act. The Patent Act of 1790 was passed on April 5, 1790, by the Congress of twelve states. Rhode Island did not join the Union as the thirteenth state until May 29, 1790, 49 days after President Washington signed the bill. *See* KENNETH W. DOBYNS, THE PATENT OFFICE PONY—A HISTORY OF THE EARLY PATENT OFFICE 22 (1994).

92. One issue that occupied the debate over the 1790 Act was whether to adopt a geographic specific novelty requirement. That is, should the statutory language read "not known or used in the United States" or simply "not known or used," as was ultimately adopted. (The current Patent Act, however, includes the words "not known or used . . . in this country," thus knowledge and use outside of the U.S. is not prior art.). The former would have allowed for patents of importation, which was for technology unknown in the United States, but already invented or in use outside of the U.S. American government officials and others in the United States knew that several European countries, most notably Great Britain, were successful in attracting foreign-developed technology through patents of importation. The most prominent government official favorably disposed to the introduction of technology from abroad was George Washington, who could not "forbear intimating to" Congress, in his State of the Union Address of January 8, 1790, of "the expediency of giving effectual encouragement . . . to the introduction of new and useful inventions from abroad." III Documentary History of the First Federal Congress of the United States of America, *House of Representatives Journal* (1977:253). Another significant proponent was Alexander Hamilton, who in his *Report on Manufactures,* strongly urged a government initiative aimed at encouraging the importation of technology and skilled artisans from abroad. *See* Alexander Hamilton, *Report on Manufactures,* in ALEXANDER HAMILTON: A PROFILE 308 (J.E. Cooke ed., 1964). There were voices who were adamantly opposed to patents of importation. The nascent American manufacturing class would be harmed if patents of importation were allowed since they would have to license foreign innovations, now available for free, from the first person to patent them domestically. Doron Ben-Atar speculates that the 1790 Act and its official rejection of patents of importation (or "technology piracy") was a façade for an unofficial policy designed to facilitate technology piracy. *See* DORON BEN-ATAR, TRADE SECRETS: INTELLECTUAL PROPERTY AND THE ORIGINS OF AMERICAN INDUSTRIAL POWER 168 (2004).

93. It was said of Jefferson that he "scrupulously guarded the privilege and investigated every claim to satisfy the statutory test of originality." PETERSON, THOMAS JEFFERSON, *supra* note 89, at 450. The United States was one of the first countries to enact a statute requiring patent applications to be subjected to an examination so as to ascertain the invention's usefulness and sufficiency. Other countries, most notably England, employed a registration system that was simply ministerial in nature. That is, no examination of the invention's validity or sufficiency is conducted.

Act issued to Samuel Hopkins for a method of "making Potash and Pearl ash by a new apparatus and Process."[94]

The examination system under the 1790 Act proved to be too burdensome for the three-member patent board, and in 1793 a new patent act was on the books. Although the 1793 Act contained several fundamental patent law concepts that are extant today,[95] the Act did away with the patent board and the examination proceedings and implemented a registration system, clerical in nature.[96] Needless to say, the lack of an examination requirement attracted several fraudulent or duplicative patents.[97] The 1793 Act lasted for 43 years, but during this time it came to be widely recognized that its provisions led to "unrestrained and promiscuous grants of patent privileges";[98] or, more generously, patents issued that "would not be capable of sustaining a just claim for the exclusive privileges acquired."[99] The result was a nineteenth-century version of a patent thicket, with conflicting and overlapping rights.

The shortcomings of the 1793 Act produced regular calls for reform and, eventually, the 1836 Act. In the interim, the patent bar had produced inno-

94. The original patent document is part of the collections of the Chicago Historical Society. There is presently some dispute as to the origins of Mr. Samuel Hopkins, the first patentee. For years it was thought that Hopkins was from Pittsford, Vermont, but a recent article convincingly argues that he was actually from Philadelphia. *See* David W. Maxey, *Samuel Hopkins, The Holder of the First U.S. Patent: A Study of Failure*, THE PENNSYLVANIA MAGAZINE OF HISTORY AND BIOGRAPHY 3-37 (Jan./April 1998). Eighteenth-century potash was a form of potassium carbonate that had several industrial applications. As David Maxey writes:

> Timber felled in the clearing of land that was not used for lumber or fuel was burned in huge bonfires; the ashes were segregated and saturated with water in a trough, and the resulting mixture was subjected to intense heat in containers that Hopkins and his contemporaries more often than not referred to as pots or kettles, but which actually amounted to cauldrons because of their size. The residue in the pot was potash, a black substance that with refluxing and the application of further heat to eliminate impurities evolved into pearlash.
>
> One authority would put potash in a class by itself as "America's first industrial chemical." From the vast forests that covered New England and portions of New York and Pennsylvania came the raw material which, through a primitive process accessible to the enterprising farmer or the frontier storekeeper, yielded an ingredient of value in the manufacture of soap, in glassmaking, in dying fabrics, and in the production of saltpeter for gunpowder. . . .

Id. at 10-11.
95. For example, Section 6 of the 1793 Act provided an accused patent infringer with certain defenses, namely that the invention was not novel, or was not sufficiently disclosed in the patent specification. Other examples are the all too important "public use" or "on-sale" defenses. Lastly, the 1793 Act gave us the four statutory subject matter categories that we use today (i.e., process, machine, manufacture, or composition of matter). The 1793 Act used the term "art," which meant process. The 1952 Act changed "art" to "process," and states that the term process "means process, art, or method." *See* 35 U.S.C. § 101.
96. *See* DOBYNS, THE PATENT OFFICE PONY, *supra* note 91, at 35 ("The Act of 1793 went from the extreme of rigid examination to the opposite extreme of no examination at all. The Patent Board was abolished. The State Department was to register patents, and the courts were to determine whether the patents were valid.").
97. *See* EDWARD WALTERSCHEID, TO PROMOTE THE PROGRESS OF THE USEFUL ARTS: AMERICAN PATENT LAW AND ADMINISTRATION 325 (stating "[t]hroughout the era of registration, a substantial number of useless or invalid patents would issue"). *See also* Senate Report accompanying Senate Bill 239, 14th Cong., 1st Sess. (April 1836), which led to the 1836 patent act (Senator Ruggles, the bill's sponsor, noted the 1793 Act was thought to lead to "the unrestrained and promiscuous grants of patent privileges").
98. Ruggles, Senate Report accompanying Senate Bill 239, *supra* note 97, at 4.
99. *See* JOHN REDMAN COXE, OF PATENTS, EMPORIUM ARTS & SCIENCES 76 (1812); T. COOPER, EMPORIUM ARTS & SCIENCES 435 (1812) (asserting that "patents, frivolous, absurd, and fraudulent, threaten to become taxes on the community"); WALTERSCHEID, AMERICAN PATENT LAW AND ADMINISTRATION, *supra* note 97, at 325 ("Throughout the era of registration, a substantial number of useless or invalid patents would issue").

vations such as the patent claim,[100] which was codified in the 1836 statute.[101] The 1836 Act introduced (and in some cases reintroduced) important features to patent law, including the creation of a Patent Office[102] as a distinct bureau of the Department of State, and vested it with greater responsibilities; created the position of Commissioner of Patents;[103] the present-day patent numbering system;[104] and an appellate structure for patent applicants seeking to appeal an examiner's refusal to issue a patent. Finally, and most importantly, the 1836 Act codified the claiming requirement[105] and re-instituted the patent examination proceeding that charged the Commissioner of the newly created Patent Office with performing "an examination of the alleged new invention or discovery."[106]

100. *See* John F. Duffy, *The* Festo *Decision and the Return of the Supreme Court to the Bar of Patents,* 2002 SUP. CT. REV. 273, 308 (noting the claim "arose not from any administrative, judicial, or legislative requirement. Instead, it was an innovation of patent attorneys, and it was formulated to protect and to expand the rights of patentees"); *Hilton Davis v. Warner-Jenkinson,* 62 F.3d 1512, 1530 (Fed. Cir. 1995) (*en banc*) (Newman, J., concurring) (noting the "development of claim style was guided by growing cadres of professional patent examiners and registered patent attorneys, along with the growth of prior art and competing technologies").

101. N.J. Brumbaugh, *History and Purpose of Claims in United States Patent Law,* 14 J. PAT. OFF. SOC'Y 273, 276 (1932) (referring to the patent claim, and stating the 1836 Act "merely endorsed and positively required what inventors had been doing voluntarily for years").

102. Mark Twain wrote, "the very first official thing I did, in my administration—and it was on the very first day of it too—was to start a patent office; for I knew that a country without a patent office and good patent laws was just a crab and couldn't travel any way but sideways or backways." A CONNECTICUT YANKEE IN KING ARTHUR'S COURT, Chapter 9 (Bantam Classics edition 1983). In 1810, Congress passed a law authorizing "a building suitable for the accommodation of the general post office, and of the office of the keeper of the patents, in such situation, and finished in such manner, as the interest of the United States and the safety and convenience of those offices respectively, and the arrangement of the models in the patent office shall, in his opinion, require." 11th Cong., Section 2, Chapter 34 (April 28, 1810). The Blodgett Hotel, home of the patent office from 1810-1836, was designed by James Hoban, the architect of the White House.

It is difficult to say when exactly the United States Patent Office was created. It was not a part of the Acts of 1790 and 1793. In 1802, Secretary of State James Madison, who was instrumental in the development of patent and copyright law during the early years of the Republic, made the Patent Office a distinct division of the Department of State by appointing the highly regarded Dr. William Thornton, the designer of the U.S. Capitol, at a salary of $1,400 a year to the full-time position of supervising the issuance of patents. Thus, one can argue that it was with this full-time appointment of Dr. Thornton in 1802 that the Patent Office was created. It was the 1836 Act, however, that gave the Patent Office legitimacy in the eyes of the law. Furthermore, the 1836 Act provided for the construction of a new building to house the Patent Office. That Patent Office was completely destroyed by fire on December 15, 1836.

103. Henry Leavitt Ellsworth (1791-1858), one of the twin sons of Justice Oliver Ellsworth, was appointed as the first Commissioner of Patents in 1836. In 1849, the Patent Office moved from the Department of State to the newly created Department of the Interior. It was not until 1925 that the Patent Office became part of the Department of Commerce, where it currently resides.

104. Patent Number 1 was issued to Senator John Ruggles of Maine, who was primarily responsible for the passage of the 1836 Act. Prior to 1836, patents were identified by the date they were issued. Unfortunately, the 10,000 pre-1836 patents were destroyed in a Patent Office fire in 1836. But through careful restoration of patent records and private files many of the pre-1836 patents have been reconstructed and models have been reproduced. (Those patents that could not be recovered were cancelled.) The restored pre-1836 patents were subsequently numbered chronologically and an "X" suffix was added to distinguish them from the new numbered patents. Thus, the first U.S. patent ever issued is number 1X issued to Samuel Hopkins. These older patents are now collectively referred to as the "X-patents."

105. See notes 100-101, *supra.*

106. Applicants, as under the 1790 and 1793 Acts, were required to submit a specification, drawings, and models with their application. For a discussion of the history and development of patent drawings, *see* William J. Rankin, *The "Person Skilled in the Art" Is Really Quite Conventional: U.S. Patent Drawings and the Persona of the Inventor, 1870-2005,* in MAKING AND UNMAKING INTELLECTUAL PROPERTY 55 (Woodmansee et al. eds., 2011). The 1836 Act required the Commissioner of Patents to publicly display the models. *See* F.D Prager, *Examination of Inventions from the Middle Ages to 1836,*

The 1836 Act, considered the first modern patent statute, laid the foundation for the modern patent system.[107] This Act reflected the changes in the American industrial landscape between 1793 and 1836. During this time, the new nation began to develop domestic manufacturing, national markets formed, and certainty in one's property rights became increasingly important.[108] As one commentator put it, the 1793 Act "may have been good enough for the agricultural country that founded it, but it was not sufficient for the manufacturing nation which had arisen through American ingenuity and intellect."[109]

The next noteworthy Congressional intervention came in 1870. Although the 1870 Patent Act was largely a re-codification of the 1836 Act, there was one significant exception: the 1870 Act placed more emphasis on the importance of the patent claim, and therefore the public notice function of patents. Whereas the 1836 Act required an inventor to "particularly specify or point out" what he regards as his invention, the 1870 Act required that inventors "particularly point out and *distinctly claim*" their inventions.[110] In the post-bellum era, the patent

---

46 J. Pat. Off. Soc'y 268, 289-291 (1964). For many years, patent models were a major tourist attraction in Washington until 1880 when models were no longer required to be submitted with a patent application. Several of these models are now housed in the Smithsonian Institution where they can presently be seen. Also, Judge Giles S. Rich of the United States Court of Appeals for the Federal Circuit has assembled a handsome collection of patent models, which are on display at the Federal Circuit court house.

107. *See* Bugbee, Genesis, *supra* note 25, at 152 ("With the act of 1836, the United States patent system came of age.").

108. For a discussion of the relationship among inventive activity, patenting, and market demand, *see* B. Zorina Khan & Kenneth L. Sokoloff, *"Schemes of Practical Utility": Entrepreneurship and Innovation Among "Great Inventors" in the United States, 1790-1865*, 53 J. Econ. History 289 (1993); Kenneth L. Sokoloff & B. Zorina Khan, *The Democratization of Invention During Early Industrialization: Evidence from the United States, 1790-1846*, 50 J. Econ. History 363 (1990).

109. Dobyns, The Patent Office Pony, *supra* note 91, at 100. During the post-bellum era, several patent wars were being waged. For example, Elias Howe, Jr. and Isaac Merrit Singer battled over the sewing machine; Alexander Graham Bell and his telephone went up against Elisha Gray; Thomas Edison and Emile Berliner clashed over the phonograph; and the reaper saw Cyrus McCormick involved in a patent dispute with Obed Hussey and John H. Manny. *See* Daniel J. Boorstin, The Americans: The Democratic Experience 57 (1973) ("There was hardly a major invention in the century after the Civil War which did not become a legal battlefield."). Of some interest is that Abraham Lincoln was "involved" in the McCormick case tried in Cincinnati, Ohio. But in his biography of Lincoln, David Herbert Donald explains that although Lincoln was retained by McCormick's eastern lawyers, they rebuffed him and treated him very rudely. According to Donald, McCormick's "lawyers made it clear to Lincoln that he could not participate in the trial. 'We were all at the same hotel,' [George] Harding recalled; but neither he nor [Edwin McMasters] Stanton 'ever conferred with him, ever had him at our table or sat with him, or asked him to our room, or walked to or from the court with him, or, in fact, had any intercourse with him.'" David Herbert Donald, Lincoln 186 (1995). Interestingly, Stanton would later become Lincoln's Secretary of War, a position he fulfilled admirably. Stanton grew fond of Lincoln and would later write, "No men were ever so deceived as we at Cincinnati." And upon Lincoln's death, Stanton was reported to say, "Now he belongs to the ages." *See* Doris Kearns Goodwin, Team of Rivals: The Political Genius of Abraham Lincoln (2005). One last notable point about Lincoln: he was the only American president to obtain a patent. *See* U.S. Patent No. 6,469, issued in 1849, entitled "Manner of Buoying Vessels."

110. Patent Act of 1870, ch. 230, §26, 116 Stat. 198, 201 (1871) (emphasis added). This new requirement, which came to be known as "peripheral claiming," highlighted the notice function of the claim and provided the applicant with more autonomy is setting forth the outer boundaries (periphery) of his invention. The public, it was thought, could now have more confidence on where the patentee's proprietary boundaries reside because peripheral claiming reduced the need for the DOE. Central claiming was officially dead, and the patent claim from 1870 to the present day has held center stage. *See, e.g., Merrill v. Yeomans*, 94 U.S. 568, 570 (1876) (asserting that the claim is of "primary importance" in ascertaining exactly what is patented).

claim would become increasingly more important.[111] As the author of the leading nineteenth-century patent law treatise wrote, the "claim is thus the life of the patent so far as the rights of the inventor are concerned, and by it the letters-patent, as a grant of an exclusive privilege, must stand or fall."[112]

After the 1870 Act, it would be 82 years before the patent code was meaningfully revised. But before discussing the important 1952 Patent Act, a brief discussion of the Supreme Court's attitude towards patents prior to the 1952 Act will shed light on the Act itself, as well as the driving forces behind the Act. From 1890 to 1930, patents were viewed favorably by the Court. But from about 1930 to 1950, the Court approached patents with a great deal of suspicion, emphasizing the monopolistic and social-cost aspects of patents.[113] For example, the Court expanded the patent misuse doctrine (*Mercoid*),[114] did away with the common practice of drafting claims in functional terms (*Halliburton*),[115] and, most significantly, enhanced the so-called requirement for invention by invoking the "flash of genius" test (*Cuno*),[116] and cast doubt on the patentability of "combination" patents (i.e., combination of old elements) by requiring a display of synergism (*Great Atlantic*);[117] that is, the combination, to be patentable, had to equal more than the sum of its parts. Indeed, this anti-patent fervor, led by Justices Douglas and Black, prompted Justice Jackson, in a dissenting opinion, to write that "the only patent that is valid is one which this Court has not been able to get its hands on."[118]

It was inevitable that members of the patent bar would take action. The 1952 Act, drafted primarily by Giles S. Rich, P.J. Federico, Paul Rose, and Henry Ashton, was largely a response to what was perceived to be the Supreme Court's anti-patent attitude. What did the 1952 Act, codified in Title 35 of the United States Code, accomplish? First, section 112 overturned *Halliburton*'s invalidation of functional claiming.[119] Second, sections 271(b), (c) and (d) overturned *Mercoid*'s broad reading of the misuse doctrine with respect to contributory

111. *See* RISDALE ELLIS, PATENT CLAIMS 3 (1949) (claims under the 1836 Act "served merely to call attention to what the inventor considered the salient features of his invention. The drawing and description were the main thing, the claims were a mere adjunct thereto. . . . The idea that the claim is just as important if not more important than the description and drawings did not develop until the Act of 1870 or thereabouts"). This is not to suggest the claim was an unimportant feature of the patent document. Recall, the claim was a pre-1836 creation of the patent bar, and as Woodward reminds us, applicants expended a "great deal of effort . . . in formulating claims, and the practice grew of presenting a profusion of claims of varying form and scope." William Redin Woodward, *Definiteness and Particularity in Patent Claims*, 46 MICH. L. REV. 755, 764 (1948). Our point is only that for much of the nineteenth century, the claim was not regarded as the central, institutionalized feature of the patent document.

112. WILLIAM C. ROBINSON, 2 THE LAW OF PATENTS § 505 (1890).

113. It is also interesting historically that the U.S government—during and shortly after World War II—filed numerous patent applications relating to the atomic bomb. *See* http://www.npr.org/templates/story/story.php?storyId=89127786&sc=emaf. The purpose behind the filing of some 2,100 applications (all held in secret under by law) was to protect the government from Manhattan Project scientists who maybe inclined to file their own applications or from foreign scientists wishing to do the same. *See also* Alex Wellerstein, *Patenting the Bomb: Nuclear Weapons, Intellectual Property, and Technological Control*, 99 THE HISTORICAL OF SCIENCE SOCIETY 57-87 (2008).

114. *Mercoid Corp. v. Mid-Continent Inv. Co.*, 320 U.S. 661 (1944). *See also Carbice Corp. v. American Patents Development Corp.*, 283 U.S. 27 (1931). See Chapter 8 for a discussion of patent misuse.

115. *Halliburton Oil Well Cementing Co. v. Walker*, 329 U.S. 1 (1946).

116. *Cuno Engineering Corp. v. Automatic Devices Corp.*, 314 U.S. 84 (1941).

117. *Great Atlantic & Pacific Tea Co. v. Supermarket Equipment Corp.*, 340 U.S. 147 (1950).

118. *Jungersen v. Ostby & Barton Co.*, 335 U.S. 560, 572 (1949).

119. See Chapter 7 for a discussion of means-plus-function claims.

Giles Sutherland Rich was born in Rochester, NY in 1904 and was a prominent patent attorney in New York City prior to being appointed to the Court of Customs and Patent Appeals in 1956 by President Eisenbhower. He served on the Federal Circuit from its creation in 1982 until his death in 1999. Judge Rich is widely regarded as one of the most influential figures in twentieth-century American patent jurisprudence.

Pasquale Joseph (P.J.) Federico was born in Monessen, PA in 1902, and graduated from the Case Institute of Technology. He was Chief Patent Examiner of the U.S. patent office for several years and along with his good friend, Giles Rich, was a principal draftsman of the 1952 Patent Act. His well-known Commentary on the 1952 Act is recommended reading. *See* 75 J. PAT. & TRADEMARK OFF. SOC'Y 161 (1993).

infringement.[120] Third, section 103 replaced the polysemous "invention" requirement with a less subjective standard of nonobviousness.[121] *Cuno*'s "flash of genius" test was no more. All of these issues are explored in the subsequent chapters.

The 1952 Act did a great deal to strengthen the patent system, but concerns, mainly procedural in nature, remained. The Evarts Act of 1891 created geographically situated regional circuit courts of appeal. Prior to 1982, regional circuits heard patent infringement appeals from their respective district courts, as they do presently, for example, with most criminal or civil (e.g., trademark and copyright infringement) cases. But there were disparities among the regional circuits in the treatment patents received with some circuits viewing patents very favorably, upholding their validity a vast majority of the time, and other circuits displaying a distinct anti-patent bias. This divergent treatment of patents,

---

120. See Chapters 7 and 8 for a discussion of contributory infringement and misuse, respectively.

121. See Chapter 5 for a discussion of the nonobviousness doctrine. For a history of section 103 of the 1952 Act, *see generally* NONOBVIOUSNESS, THE ULTIMATE CONDITION OF PATENTABILITY (John F. Witherspoon ed., 1980).

it was argued, led to forum shopping and a greatly weakened patent system. In response, Congress, in 1982, created the United States Court of Appeals for the Federal Circuit as a unified forum for patent appeals, with the intent of strengthening the American patent system.

While there were important revisions to the patent code in 1984, 1988, and 1999, the America Invents Act ("AIA") of 2011 is the most significant legislative reform since 1952. Among the many revisions embodied in the AIA, the most noteworthy is the shift from the first-to-invent system of priority to a first-inventor-to-file system. In so doing, the AIA redefined many aspects of prior art and the concept of novelty. In addition, several administrative mechanisms designed to challenge the issuance and validity of a patent were implemented, such as post-grant and *inter partes* review. These and other changes brought about by the AIA will be discussed throughout the book.

4. The U.S. Court of Appeals for the Federal Circuit

The United States Court of Appeals for the Federal Circuit (pictured) was created by Congress in 1982 as the nation's thirteenth federal court of appeals.[122] The creation of the Federal Circuit, which is located in Washington, D.C., has

been called "perhaps the single most significant institutional innovation in the field of intellectual property in the last quarter-century."[123] Indeed, the court represents the first significant consolidation of a particular area of law in American history.[124] The Federal Circuit has exclusive subject

122. Federal Courts Improvement Act of 1982, P.L. 97-164, 96 Stat. 25 (April 2, 1982). This Act merged the Court of Claims, which had seven judges, and the Court of Customs and Patent Appeals, which had five judges. The Federal Circuit came into existence on October 1, 1982. *See* THE UNITED STATES COURT OF APPEALS FOR THE FEDERAL CIRCUIT: A HISTORY (1991). For a discussion of some of the contested issues surrounding the creation of this new nationwide court, *see* Rochelle C. Dreyfuss, *The Federal Circuit: A Case Study in Specialized Courts*, 64 N.Y.U. L. REV. 1 (1989), and sources cited therein.

123. LANDES & POSNER, ECONOMIC STRUCTURE, *supra* note 6, at 7.

124. Efforts to create a national court for patent appeals began more than 100 years before the creation of the Federal Circuit. *See* Subcomm. on Patents, Trademarks & Copyrights, Senate Comm. on Judiciary, 85th Cong., 2d Sess., Study No. 20 (1959). For instance, in 1900, the American Bar Association's Section of Patent, Trademark and Copyright Law recommended the creation of a "Court of Patent Appeals" with national jurisdiction. *See* Report of the Committee of the Section of Patent, Trademark and Copyright Law, 23 ABA Rep. 543, 543 (1900). For an excellent discussion of the history of the Federal Circuit's creation and previous efforts to create a national court for patent appeals, *see* Paul M. Janicke, *To Be or Not to Be: The Long Gestation of the U.S. Court of Appeals for the Federal Circuit (1887-1992)*, 69 ANTITRUST L.J. 645 (2002).

matter jurisdiction over patent cases,[125] as well as numerous other areas of law.[126] (See the figure below.)

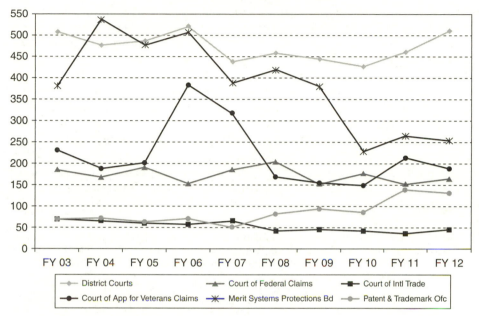

United States Court of Appeals for the Federal Circuit
Appeals Filed in Major Origins

Note: Includes reinstated, cross-, and consolidated appeals.

Some of the oft-cited reasons for the creation of the Federal Circuit are that—during the 1970s—there existed rampant forum shopping by patent litigants,[127] disparate circuit court treatment of patents, and accompanying

125. The court's patent-related cases are appealed from either a U.S. District Court (in a litigation context) or the USPTO (prosecution context). On occasion, other circuit courts will have jurisdiction to hear patent-related disputes. Jurisdictional issues are explored in Chapter 7.D. There were over 5,000 patent infringement cases filed in 2012, an increase over the previous two years. In 2012, the top five district courts in terms of patent filings were: (1) Eastern District, Texas; (2) Delaware; (3) Central District, California; (4) Northern District, Illinois; and (5) Northern District, California. Judicial Business of the United States Courts: 2012 Annual Report of the Director, Table C-7, available at http://www.uscourts.gov/uscourts/Statistics/JudicialBusiness/2012/appendices/ C07Sep12.pdf.

126. *See* 28 U.S.C. §1295. The court's docket includes appeals from, for example, the Court of International Trade, International Trade Commission, Merit Systems Protection Board, Court of Veterans Appeals, Court of Federal Claims, and United States Patent and Trademark Office. It was the intent of Congress to provide the court with a diverse jurisdiction. *See* H.R. Rep. No. 312, 97th Cong., 1st Sess. 20-22 (1981), at 19 ("The proposed new court is not a 'specialized court.' Its jurisdiction is not limited to one type of case, or even to two or three types of cases. Rather, it has a varied docket spanning a broad range of legal issues and types of cases."); S. Rep. No. 275, 97th Cong., 1st Sess. 5 (1981), at 6 ("[The Federal Circuit's] rich docket assures that the work of the . . . court will be a broad variety of legal problems. Moreover, the subject matter of the new court will be sufficiently mixed to prevent any special interest from dominating it."). For fiscal year 2012, 35 percent and 8 percent of merit-panel patent-related adjudications were from district court and patent office appeals, respectively. Approximately 50 percent of appeals were non-patent related, and pertained to either administrative law or money suits. *See* http://www.cafc.uscourts.gov/images/ stories/the-court/statistics/Caseload_by_Category_Appeals_Filed_2012.pdf.

127. *See* H.R. Rep. No. 312, *supra* note 126, at 20-22 ("Patent litigation long has been identified as a problem area, characterized by undue forum-shopping and unsettling inconsistency in

disuniformity in patent law.[128] In the first decade of its existence, the Federal Circuit earned praise for achieving a desirable degree of uniformity in place of regional circuit precedents perceived to be disjointed and conflicting.[129] And the court has had a significant impact on the patent landscape. Recent studies, for example, have shown the Federal Circuit has strengthened patent rights with respect to validity challenges, with the court affirming district court "decisions of invalidity significantly less often," resulting in patentees appealing "decisions of invalidity significantly more often, and district courts" holding "patents to be invalid significantly less often."[130]

But the Federal Circuit is not without critics.[131] For example, the court has been accused of producing precedents that "increase the cost of patent acquisition, augment the burdens of patent administration, and encourage free riders — trends that make both the patent system, and the process of innovation, less attractive alternatives."[132] And the court and its doctrine are said to "have brought less certainty and predictability to patent enforcement." Even commentators who are positive about the Federal Circuit experiment have acknowledged the "continuing problems perceived in the court's administration" of

---

adjudications."). But forum shopping has persisted at the district court level. *See* Kimberly A. Moore, *Forum Shopping in Patent Cases: Does Geographic Choice Affect Innovation?*, 79 N.C. L. Rev. 889 (2001). And some commentators have questioned whether forum shopping was as acute a problem as represented. *See* Scott Atkinson, Alan C. Marco & John L. Turner, *The Economics of a Centralized Judiciary: Uniformity, Forum Shopping, and the Federal Circuit*, http://ssrn.com/abstract=961035 (econometric study finding "strong evidence that forum shopping on the basis of validity rates ceased several years prior to the" Federal Circuit's creation); Testimony of James W. Geriak, Hearings Before the Committee on the Judiciary, Subcommittee on Courts, Civil Liberties and the Administration of Justice on H.R. 2405 (April 1981), 709 (stating that claims of forum shopping are "seriously exaggerated"); Cecil D. Quillen, *Innovation and the U.S. Patent System*, 1 Va. L. & Bus. Rev. 207, 228 (2006) (asserting forum shopping and outcome variability were not problematic during the 1970s).

128. *See* H.R. Rep. No. 312, *supra* note 126, at 20-22. ("[S]ome circuit courts are regarded as 'pro-patent' and others 'anti-patent,' and much time and money is expended in 'shopping' for a favorable venue." Furthermore, "the validity of a patent is too dependent upon geography (i.e., the accident of judicial venue) to make effective business planning possible. . . . A single court of appeals for patent cases will promote certainty where it is lacking to a significant degree and will reduce, if not eliminate, the forum-shopping that now occurs."). *See also* S. Rep. No. 275, *supra* note 126 ("The creation of the Court of Appeals for the Federal Circuit will produce desirable uniformity in this area of . . . [patent] law. Such uniformity will reduce the forum-shopping that is common to patent litigation.").

129. *See, e.g.*, Dreyfuss, *Federal Circuit*, *supra* note 122, at 74 (concluding that "[o]n the whole, the CAFC experiment has worked well for patent law, which is now more uniform, easier to apply, and more responsive to national interests"). Some have suggested the court "has had a significant positive effect on both the number of patent applications and the number of patent grants." Landes & Posner, Economic Structure, *supra* note 6, at 340.

130. *See* Matthew D. Henry & John L. Turner, *The Court of Appeals for the Federal Circuit's Impact on Patent Litigation*, 35 J. Leg. Stud. 85, 112 (2006); Joseph P. Cook, *On Understanding the Increase in U.S. Patent Litigation*, 9 Am. Law & Econ. Rev. 48-71 (2007). *See also* Glynn S. Lunney, *Patent Law, the Federal Circuit, and the Supreme Court: A Quiet Revolution*, 11 Sup. Ct. Econ. Rev. 1, 2 (2004) (finding since creation of Federal Circuit "patents have become routinely valid, but narrowly enforced").

131. Indeed, it is worth noting that there was not uniform support for the creation of the Federal Circuit. For instance, an ABA Report and Recommendation disapproving of the creation of the Federal Circuit was adopted by the ABA House of Delegates in 1980. *See* Testimony of Benjamin L. Zelenko, Hearings Before the Committee on the Judiciary, Subcommittee on Courts, Civil Liberties and the Administration of Justice on H.R. 2405 (April 1981), 423 (quoting the ABA recommendation). There was also Congressional testimony against the creation of the court. *See* Testimony of James W. Geriak, Hearings Before Committee, H.R. 2405, *supra* note 127, at 69 (stating "that would be a very, very substantial error for the subcommittee to conclude that all patent lawyers are agreed upon the desirability of the . . . Federal Circuit legislation").

132. John R. Thomas, *Formalism at the Federal Circuit*, 52 Am. U. L. Rev. 771, 773 (2003).

patent law.[133] These criticisms, some commentators argue, are largely due to the Federal Circuit's structural constraints in that the court does not enjoy the benefit of sister-circuit competition and a diversity of viewpoints.[134] Accordingly, it has been argued that "patent law's complex mixture of fact and law scenarios coupled with the fluid nature of innovation practices requires a competitive and diverse appellate enforcement model," one where diversity, competition, and incremental innovation are equally, if not more, important than uniformity.[135]

COMPARATIVE PERSPECTIVE
The European Patent Convention

The European Patent Convention ("EPC")—officially known as the "Convention on the Grant of European Patents"—took place on October 5, 1973, in Munich, Germany (sometimes the EPC is referred to as the "Munich Convention"). The EPC, which is not European Union legislation or an EU body, entered into force on October 7, 1977. The EPC created a centralized, unitary process for obtaining "European patents" through the newly created European Patent Office ("EPO") located in Munich, Germany with branches in Berlin and The Hague. The EPC is comprised of 178 Articles establishing various institutions, procedural rules, and substantive laws. *See* http://www.european-patent-office.org/legal/epc/e/ma1.html#CVN. For more on the European patent system and the EPC, *see* R. SINGER ET AL., THE EUROPEAN PATENT CONVENTION: A COMMENTARY. REVISED ENGLISH EDITION (R. LUNZER, SWEET & MAXWELL, LONDON, 1995).

Under the EPC, a member state defers to the EPO examination process; the member state's patent office does not need to conduct a separate or independent examination. But it is important to understand that the EPC only relates to obtaining patent rights; enforcement of patents remains with the EPC member states, of which there are currently 31. Thus, the term "European patent" is a misnomer because upon issuance, the patent loses its European character and becomes a national patent in those member countries that the applicant designates, and the patent is subsequently translated into the language of the designated state. In addition to the significant translation costs, there are high procedural costs associated with prosecuting a patent application through the EPO. It should come as no surprise then that obtaining a "European patent" has been estimated to be 11 and 13 times more expensive than a U.S. and Japanese patent, respectively. See Felix Addor and Claudia Mund, *A Patent Court for Europe: What's at Stake for Users?* 5, 4th Gallen Int'l Dispute Res. Conf. (2012). And in addition, the patentee must also pay renewal fees to each designated country after the patent issues.

Because of its distinct cost and efficiency advantages, a community patent has been part of the European patent agenda since the mid-1970s. *See*

---

133. Dreyfuss, *Federal Circuit, supra* note 122, at 773-786.
134. *See* Craig Allen Nard & John F. Duffy, *Rethinking Patent Law's Uniformity Principle*, 101 Nw. U. L. REV. 1619 (2007). *Cf.* S. Jay Plager & Lynne E. Pettigrew, *Rethinking Patent Law's Uniformity Principle: A Response to Nard and Duffy*, 101 Nw. U. L. REV. 1735 (2007); John M. Golden, *The Supreme Court as "Prime Percolator": A Prescription for Appellate Review of Questions of Law*, 56 UCLA L. Rev. 657 (2009).
135. Nard & Duffy, *Rethinking Uniformity, supra* note 134, at 1623.

Community Patent Convention (1975) and the Luxembourg Agreement (1989). *See also* V. Di Cataldo, *From the European Patent to a Community Patent*, in 8 COLUM. J. EUR. LAW, 2002, 19ff. But implementation has been blocked because of issues relating to translation of patents into the various national languages. As Laurent Manderieux explains, there has historically been no effective EU consensus on the community patent because:

> Several countries want their language to be an official one for patents, and at the same time, if too many translations are compulsory, operators would find no cost advantage over the present system, and thus they would show no interest in the new system. Also several states have reservations on how to establish an EU-wide jurisdiction which could decide on questions regarding an EU-wide patent right.

Laurent Manderieux, *Europe's IP Architecture*, in THE HANDBOOK OF EUROPEAN INTELLECTUAL PROPERTY MANAGEMENT 3-10 (Jolly & Philpott eds., 2007). Moreover, patent enforcement occurred in the respective member states, which meant that in the absence of a community patent, litigation over national patent rights could lead to disparate holdings and disuniformity.

To address these concerns, in December 2012, 25 member states of the EU—in a noteworthy development—adopted a unitary patent regime and unitary patent court. The unitary patent can be filed in any of the EU's 23 official languages, but thereafter *only* need be translated into English, French, or German for the patent to apply to the 25 participating states. (Spain and Italy did not participate because of objections to the final language regime.) According to the EPO, the "unitary patent will be a European patent granted by the EPO under the provisions of the [EPC] to which unitary effect for the territory of the 25 participating states is given after grant." The unified patent court will have a central division in Paris, with two sections, one in London for disputes involving chemistry and pharmaceuticals, and one in Munich for mechanical engineering disputes. The Paris, London, and Munich courts will have jurisdiction over revocation actions (invalidity) and declarations of noninfringement. In addition, there are local or regional divisions (also courts of first instance) that will hear infringement and counter-revocation claims. Revocation proceedings commenced in the central division or its two sections will be stayed if a subsequent infringement action has been filed with a local or regional court. The appellate court is located in Luxembourg. For more on both, *see* http://www.epo.org/law-practice/unitary.html.

Although it is common for a member state to enact domestic patent legislation that largely mirrors the EPC, some member states enjoy a greater percentage of designations from applicants. In 2012, the top designation countries for patent protection were Germany (99.1%), France (96%), and the U.K. (95.1%). Only these three countries had a designation rate of over 90%. Other countries with significant designations include Italy (86.1%), Spain (80.8%), the Netherlands (80.7%), and Sweden (79.3%). *See* EPO ANNUAL REPORT—STATISTICS AND TRENDS (2011) at http://www.epo.org/about-us/office/annual-report/2012.html.

B. ECONOMICS OF PATENT LAW

To fully appreciate the economic theories of patent law, it would first be helpful to have an understanding of the distinctive quality of information. The use, diffusion, and production of information are at the core of patent law. But information — unlike tangible property (e.g., a pen or olive oil) — is what economists call a public good, meaning that it is both non-rivalrous and non-excludable.[136] For example, many people can benefit from information without interfering in the pleasure others receive from the same information — it is non-rivalrous. One person's use of the creative ideas embodied in a word processing program, poem, or chemical formula does not interfere with another's use of those ideas. As Thomas Jefferson wrote, "He who receives an idea from me, receives instruction himself without lessening mine; as he who lights his taper at mine, receives light without darkening me."[137]

At the same time, once disclosed, it is extremely difficult to exclude others from using the information — it is non-excludable.[138] You cannot build a fence around your idea as you can your backyard or ranch. And therein lies the catch-22 for inventors. Inventors often need to disclose their ideas to facilitate licensing negotiations, secure venture capital, arrange for manufacturing capabilities, or otherwise efficiently utilize their invention. And even if the inventor obtains a contractual obligation from the person to whom the inventor's idea is disclosed, the inventor will likely remain fearful that his idea will be exploited by persons subject to the contractual arrangement or even persons not in a fiduciary relationship with the inventor. In other words, absent a property right transaction costs are prohibitively high, and the inventor will likely be reticent to disclose information for fear of inducing competition. Thus, there is an inherent conflict between the desire to disclose information and the need to limit access and use to those whom the inventor has authorized. This problem

---

136. *See* THE MIT DICTIONARY OF MODERN ECONOMICS 352 (David W. Pearce ed., 4th ed. 1992). *See also* ROBERT COOTER & THOMAS ULEN, LAW AND ECONOMICS 46 (4th ed. 2004) (noting that public goods have the characteristics of "nonrivalous consumption" and "nonexcludability"); F.M. Scherer, *Economics of Human Gene Patents*, ACADEMIC MEDICINE, Vol. 77, No. 2/Dec. 2002, 1348, 1354 (stating "[s]cientific knowledge is viewed by economists as the quintessential public good, that is, something whose use by one individual does not necessarily reduce the amount available for consumption by others, and whose use by anyone, once it is made known, is difficult to prevent except through special legal institutions such as patents"); Paul A. Samuelson, *The Pure Theory of Public Expenditure*, 36(4) REV. ECON. & STAT. 387-389 (Nov. 1954) (referring to "collective consumption goods" as that "which all enjoy in common in the sense that each individual's consumption of such a good leads to no subtractions from any other individual's consumption of that good").

137. Letter to Isaac McPherson (Aug. 13, 1813), reprinted in JEFFERSON WRITINGS 1291-1292 (M. Peterson ed., 1984). Elsewhere in Jefferson's letter, he wrote:

> If nature has made any one thing less susceptible than all others of exclusive property, it is the action of the thinking power called an idea, which an individual may exclusively possess as long as he keeps it to himself; but the moment it is divulged, it forces itself into the possession of every one, and the receiver cannot dispossess himself of it. Its peculiar character, too, is that no one possesses the less, because every other possesses the whole of it.

Id.

138. *See* FRANÇOIS LÉVÊQUE & YANN MÉNIÈRE, THE ECONOMICS OF PATENTS AND COPYRIGHT 17 (Berkeley Economic Press 2004) (stating "information is a non-excludable good: it is impossible to exclude an individual from information even if he does not contribute to the cost of its production").

is commonly referred to as "Arrow's Information Paradox," named after the economist, Kenneth Arrow.[139]

These two distinctive features of information goods (non-rivalrous and non-excludable) can lead to a free-rider problem—that is, consumers who exploit the information without sufficiently contributing to its creation.[140] As such, information will tend to be underproduced, or not produced at all, due to the riskiness associated with disclosing information or others discovering the information.[141] A common response to this problem is government intervention, which can—for example—take the form of research grants (subsidies), or using the taxing power to fund production or create incentives.[142] (National defense—a classic public good—is provided for through tax revenue.) Another form of government intervention is to create a private property right to induce the production of information goods,[143] which has been a government response in the form of patent legislation since 1790.

A patent system, however, is not a costless enterprise. With exclusivity comes the risk of reduced output, excessively high prices, and therefore less access to the patented product, because some consumers who value the good at a competitive price will not buy it at a supracompetitive price.[144] Economists refer to this as deadweight loss.[145] But to the extent these costs are cause for concern,

---

139. *See* Kenneth Arrow, *Economic Welfare and the Allocation of Resources for Invention*, in RATE AND DIRECTION OF INVENTIVE ACTIVITY 609 (NBER ed. 1962).

140. *See* U.S. CONGRESS, OFFICE OF TECHNOLOGY ASSESSMENT, FINDING A BALANCE: COMPUTER SOFTWARE, INTELLECTUAL PROPERTY AND THE CHALLENGE OF TECHNOLOGICAL CHANGE 185 (1992) (stating "individuals have an incentive not to pay for the good, or to undervalue it, in hopes of getting access as 'free riders'"); COOTER & ULEN, LAW AND ECONOMICS, *supra* note 136, at 46 (referring to public goods as a "source of market failure" and noting that "there is a strong inducement for consumers of the privately provided public good to try to be *free riders*: they hope to benefit at no cost to themselves from the payment of others") (emphasis in original).

141. *See* OFFICE OF TECHNOLOGY ASSESSMENT, *supra* note 140, at 185 ("The inability to exclude free riders distorts market signals and is thought to result in inefficient allocation of resources to nonexclusive goods and underproduction of them, relative to socially optimal quantities."). Adam Jaffe and Josh Lerner describe the difference between tangible and intangible assets as follows:

> Investment in new technology is . . . handicapped by riskiness, when compared to other forms of spending. . . . [W]hen a business builds a new factory or buys some equipment, it does not normally worry that its competitors will simply come and steal the equipment. When a business invests in R&D, it is "building" an asset that it hopes to profit from, just as it does when it builds a factory. But the asset you build with research is intangible. Being intangible, it is much easier for other firms to steal.

ADAM B. JAFFE & JOSH LERNER, INNOVATION AND ITS DISCONTENTS: HOW OUR BROKEN PATENT SYSTEM IS ENDANGERING INNOVATION AND PROGRESS, AND WHAT TO DO ABOUT IT? 43 (2004)

142. *See* MIT DICTIONARY OF MODERN ECONOMICS, *supra* note 136, at 163-164 (stating "[i]f the free rider phenomenon is a strong one, public goods will be systematically under-provided and there is a *prima facie* case for the good to be provided through government action").

143. For a discussion on patent rights as private property, *see* Adam Mossoff, *Patents as Constitutional Private Property: The Historical Protection of Patents Under the Takings Clause*, 87 B.U. L. REV. 689 (2007) (arguing nineteenth-century courts treated patents as constitutional private property under the takings clause).

144. *See* Joseph E. Stiglitz, *Knowledge as a Global Public Good*, in GLOBAL PUBLIC GOODS: INTERNATIONAL COOPERATION IN THE 21ST CENTURY 308, 311 (Inge Kaul, Isabelle Grunberg & Marc A. Stern eds., 1999) (stating with respect to patent rights "the gain in *dynamic* efficiency from the greater innovative activity is intended to balance out the lossess from *static* inefficiency from the underutilization of the knowledge or from the underproduction of the good protected by the patent").

145. *See* Mark A. Lemley, *Property, Intellectual Property and Free Riding*, 83 TEX. L. REV. 1031, 1059 (2005) (discussing "classic deadweight loss associated with deviations from competitive norm"); COOTER & ULEN, LAW AND ECONOMICS, *supra* note 136, at 122 (stating "monopolies impose social

they are thought to be offset by the benefits engendered by the availability of patent rights, which leads us to the economic theories underlying the patent system.

The historically predominant theory is the *incentive to invent,* which focuses on efficiency gains and the internalization of externalities.[146] (An externality is a cost or benefit that affects parties external to the given transaction.)[147] This theory seeks to address the effects of Arrow's Information Paradox, and holds that—due to the public goods nature of information—without the prospect of a property right, inventors would be unable to recoup (internalize) their research and development costs because third parties could simply copy the invention and compete with the inventor unencumbered by the need to recover fixed costs. In an increasingly competitive market, prices will be driven down, resulting in an under-investment in invention.[148]

---

costs in that too little of the monopolized good is produced and the price is too high"). While very few patents confer market power (an economic monopoly), patents do generally allow a patentee to price the patented product above marginal cost—otherwise, the incentive to invent would be greatly undercut.

Price discrimination—selling the patented product at different prices based on what various consumers are willing to pay—may reduce deadweight loss and allow the seller/producer to capture some of the market's consumer surplus. Thus, perfect price discrimination leads to market efficiency gains, but transfers wealth to the seller/producer. (In a competitive market, it is the consumer who captures most of this surplus.) But information deficiencies make perfect price discrimination highly unlikely because it is very difficult for sellers to know exactly each consumer's demand curve. And even if perfect price discrimination were possible, some economists remain doubtful of its effect on deadweight loss. *See, e.g.,* V. Bhaskar & Ted To, *Is Perfect Price Discrimination Really Efficient? An Analysis of Free Entry,* 35 RAND J. OF ECON. 762, 775 (2004).

146. *See* Harold Demsetz, *Toward a Theory of Property Rights,* 57 AM. ECON. REV. 347, 348, 359 (1967) (asserting the "primary function of property rights is that of guiding incentives to achieve a greater internalization of externalities," and further noting "if a new idea is freely appropriable by all, if there exist communal rights to new ideas, incentives for developing such ideas will be lacking. The benefits derivable from these ideas will not be concentrated on their originators. If we extend some degree of private rights to the originators, these ideas will come forth at a more rapid pace"); LANDES & POSNER, ECONOMICS STRUCTURE, *supra* note 6, at 294 (stating the "standard rationale of patent law is that it is an efficient method of enabling the benefits of research and development to be internalized, thus promoting innovation and technological progress"); DOUGLASS C. NORTH & ROBERT PAUL THOMAS, THE RISE OF THE WESTERN WORLD: A NEW ECONOMIC HISTORY 144-155 (1973) (discussing the significance of patents as a means of internalizing positive externalities). The same rationale exists for copyright law. *See* Neil Weinstock Netanel, *Copyright and a Democratic Civil Society,* 102 YALE L.J. 283, 312 n.117 (1996) (stating according to Demsetz, "[i]ntellectual property . . . exists in order to internalize the positive externalities of creating intellectual works. By according property rights in such works, copyright and patent concentrates the social benefits of original expression and invention in authors and inventors, giving them a greater incentive to engage in creative activity"). *Cf.* Brett M. Frischmann & Mark A. Lemley, *Spillovers,* 107 COLUM. L. REV. 257, 276 (2007) (stating "that there is no reason to think that complete internalization of externalities is necessary to optimize investment incentives; at some point, there are decreasing returns (in terms of improved incentives) to allowing property owners to capture more of the value from their inventions. Spillovers do not always interfere with incentives to invest; in some cases, spillovers actually drive further innovation").

147. *See* Demsetz, *Property Rights, supra* note 146, at 348 (stating "[w]hat converts a harmful or beneficial effect into an externality is that the cost of bringing the effect to bear on the decisions of one or more of the interacting persons is too high to make it worthwhile"); John F. Duffy, *Intellectual Property Isolationism and the Average Cost Thesis,* 83 TEX. L. REV. 1077, 1081 (2005) (stating externality "is defined as arising where 'some activity of party A imposes a cost or benefit on party B for which party A is not charged or compensated by the price system of a market economy'") (citing DAVID K. WHITCOMB, EXTERNALITIES AND WELFARE 6 (1972)).

148. *See* F.M. SCHERER, INDUSTRIAL MARKET STRUCTURE AND ECONOMIC PERFORMANCE 444 (2d ed. 1980) (stating "[i]f pure and perfect competition in the strictest sense prevailed continuously," then "incentives for invention and innovation would be fatally defective without a patent system or some equivalent substitute"); JAFFE & LERNER, INNOVATION AND ITS DISCONTENTS, *supra* note 141,

The second economic theory is the *incentive to disclose*. This theory, which is informed in part by the availability of trade secret protection, posits that the prospect of a property right will induce inventors to seek patent protection, and thereby disclose their inventions in accordance with patent law's disclosure requirements.[149] As explored in Chapter 2, the disclosure rules of section 112 require that the inventor—in return for a patent right—sufficiently disclose his invention to enable a person of ordinary skill in the art to make and use the invention. Without the availability of patent protection, this theory holds that inventors are more likely to opt for trade secret protection, thus depriving competitors (and the public generally) of a technical disclosure—that is, information that can be used by competitors to improve the patented technology or design around it,[150] activity that has potentially positive social value. Moreover, the importance of access to and dissemination of information to the pace of technological innovation and economic growth is well documented.[151]

The third economic theory is commonly referred to as the *incentive to innovate* (or incentive to commercialize).[152] An innovation is considered different from an invention,[153] and relates to a finished and commercialized product that actualizes an invention. As two commentators wrote, "invention is a subset

---

at 8 (stating "[p]otential inventors realize that without adequate protection rivals will rapidly copy their discoveries, and that therefore innovation is at best an uncertain route to future profit. As a result, companies would be unlikely to spend significant amounts of money on the Research and Development"); Kenneth Dam, *The Economic Underpinnings of Patent Law*, 23 J. LEGAL STUD. 247, 247 (1994) (stating it is "important to recognize the primary problem that the patent system solves. This problem—often called the 'appropriability problem'—is that, if a firm could not recover the costs of invention because the resulting information were available to all, then we could expect a much lower and indeed suboptimal level of innovation"). *Cf.* Frischmann & Lemley, *Spillovers*, *supra* note 146, at 276 (asserting that "inventors do not need to capture the full social value of their inventions in order to have sufficient incentive to create").

149. *See Universal Oil Products v. Globe Oil and Refining Co.*, 322 U.S. 471, 484 (1944) ("As a reward for inventions and to encourage their disclosure, the United States offers a seventeen-year monopoly to an inventor who refrains from keeping his invention a trade secret."); Rebecca Eisenberg, *Patents and the Progress of Science: Exclusive Rights and Experimental Use*, 56 U. CHI. L. REV. 1017, 1028 (1989) (stating "[t]he incentive to disclose argument . . . rests on the premise that in the absence of patent protection inventors would keep their inventions secret in order to prevent competitors from exploiting them. Secrecy prevents the public from gaining the full benefit of new knowledge and leads to wasteful duplicative research"); Margo A. Bagley, *Academic Discourse and Proprietary Rights: Putting Patents in Their Proper Place*, 47 B.C. L. REV. 217, 238 n.985 (2006) (stating "[p]roviding an incentive to disclose an invention is a well-established function of patent law").

150. *See* LANDES & POSNER, ECONOMIC STRUCTURE, *supra* note 6, at 328 (stating "[i]n the absence of a patent option, inventors would invest many more resources in maintaining trade secrets (and competitors in unmasking them) and inventive activity would be inefficiently biased toward inventions that can be kept secret").

151. *See* WILLIAM J. BAUMOL, THE FREE-MARKET INNOVATION MACHINE: ANALYZING THE GROWTH MIRACLE OF CAPITALISM 75 (2002) (stating "innovation and quick dissemination are two of the critical stimuli to economic growth"); MOKYR, GIFTS OF ATHENA, *supra* note 9, at 34 (asserting "[r]egardless of how one thinks of science, it seems incontrovertible that the rate of technological progress depends on the way human useful knowledge is generated, processed, and disseminated").

152. This theory is commonly associated with the work of Joseph Schumpeter. *See* JOSEPH SCHUMPETER, CAPITALISM, SOCIALISM, AND DEMOCRACY 81-110 (1950) and JOSEPH SCHUMPETER, 1 BUSINESS CYCLES 84-192 (1939).

153. Schumpeter is credited with making a distinction between invention and innovation. *See* RICHARD R. NELSON & SIDNEY G. WINTER, AN EVOLUTIONARY THEORY OF ECONOMIC CHANGE 263 (1982). *See also* Eisenberg, *Patents and the Progress of Science*, *supra* note 149, at 1038 (asserting Schumpeter "emphatically distinguishes innovation from invention, noting that invention itself produces 'no economically relevant effect at all'"); THE NATIONAL INTEREST 126 (Nov./Dec. 2007) ("Schumpeter's description of the entrepreneurial process found its first expression in *The Theory of Economic Development*. . . . Among its many conceptual contributions is the first clear expression of the vital distinction between invention and innovation—the latter being, to Schumpeter, far more

of innovation," which entails "[t]he entire process of research, development, and turning an idea into a finished product."[154] Thus, the incentive to innovate focuses on the role of patents in inducing the transformation of inventions into downstream, commercialized products by serving as a signal to relevant parties, namely investors (e.g., venture capitalists), potential licensees, and downstream players (e.g., entities with marketing, distribution, advertising, and manufacturing capabilities). In this sense, a patent is seen as a coordination tool that reduces transaction costs, resulting in the patent efficiently ending up in the hands of the party who is best suited to bring the technology to market.[155]

There are weaknesses to these incentive-based rationales, which predominate patent law's justificatory framework. For instance, the incentive to invent theory assumes the inventive act is driven by the prospect of a patent, rather than reputational gains, monetary prizes or rewards.[156] And to the extent a patent is the driving force behind creation, wasteful patent races (because the winner takes all), duplicative research,[157] and excessive rent-seeking[158] may ensue. With respect to the incentive to disclose theory, an "enabling" disclosure seldom

---

important than the former. Schumpeter stressed that an invention is of no economic significance until it is brought into use.").

154. Burk & Lemley, *Policy Levers, supra* note 20, at 1661.

155. *See* Edmund Kitch, *The Nature and Function of the Patent System*, 20 J.L. & ECON. 265, 276 (1977) (asserting a patentee with a broad property right will "coordinate the search for technological and market enhancement of the patent's value"). Kitch—who referred to this arrangement as the "prospect theory" because he analogized the United States patent system to a mineral claims system—viewed patent rights, as least in part, as solving Arrow's Information Paradox. *See* Dan L. Burk & Brent H. McDonnell, *The Goldilocks Hypothesis: Balancing Intellectual Property Rights at the Boundary of the Firm*, 2007 U. ILL. L. REV. 575, 585 (asserting "[b]y publicly disclosing technical information, while protecting it by exclusivity, patents circumvent the Arrow paradox. Patent licensing is no longer a bargain for disclosure, as that has already been accomplished by the publication of the patent. Licensees need only look at the patent to determine whether the information will be valuable to them. Neither need the patentee worry about unauthorized use of the disclosed invention, as it has been secured by a property right that covers the invention regardless of contractual protection"). Kitch's prospect theory is also relevant to the issue of claim scope and incentives to improve extant technology. This important issue is discussed in Chapter 2, following the *O'Reilly v. Morse* and *Incandescent Lamp* cases.

156. For a discussion of using non-IP related rewards as an incentive to create, *see* Brian Wright, *The Economics of Invention Incentives: Patents, Prizes and Research Contracts*, 73 AM. ECON. REV. 691 (1983); Michael Abramowicz, *Perfecting Patent Prizes*, 56 VAND. L. REV. 115 (2003); Steven Shavell & Tanguy van Ypersele, *Rewards Versus Intellectual Property Rights*, 44 J.L. & ECON. 525 (2001).

157. *But see* SCOTCHMER, INNOVATIONS AND INCENTIVES, *supra* note 11, at 100 (stating there is not necessarily duplication "if the successes and failures of different firms are independent," and thus "[i]f several researchers attempt a project, it may turn out ex post that all fail, or that several succeed." As such, one cannot infer "from an ex ante perspective the research plan was either deficient or duplicative"); LANDES & POSNER, ECONOMIC STRUCTURE, *supra* note 6, at 301 (stating "research expenditures of the losers of the race may not be wasted" because they "will generate information that the losers may be able to use in other projects"); John F. Duffy, *Rethinking the Prospect Theory of Patents*, 71 U. CHI. L. REV. 439 (2004) (asserting patent races bring about innovations quicker). On patent races, *see generally* G. Loury, *Market Structure and Innovation*, 93 QUARTERLY J. ECON. 395 (1979); P. Dasgupta & E. Maskin, *The Simple Economics of Research Portfolios*, 97 ECON. J. 581 (1987); P. Dasgupta & J. Stiglitz, *Uncertainty, Market Structure and the Speed of Research*, 11 BELL J. ECON. 1 (1980).

158. Rent-seeking has been defined as "behavior in institutional settings where individual efforts to maximize value generate social waste rather than social surplus." James M. Buchanan, *Rent Seeking and Profit Seeking*, in TOWARD A THEORY OF THE RENT-SEEKING SOCIETY (Buchanan et al. eds., 1980). Dennis Mueller elaborates, tying the term to the traditional evaluation of losses imposed by monopolies: "The government can, for example, help create, increase, or protect a group's monopoly position. In so doing, the government increases the monopoly rents of the favored groups, at the expense of the buyers of the group's products or services. The monopoly rents that

suffices for potential licensees to practice the claimed invention. This results in licensees asking the licensor/patentee to provide them with an "enabling package," which includes technical know-how and other forms of tacit knowledge not required to be disclosed under section 112.[159] Moreover, this theory does not fully take into account that trade secrecy is sometimes a viable, and indeed preferred, option even though patenting is available.[160] The incentive to innovate theory loses some of its force when one considers that oftentimes patentees neither commercialize, nor license their patented technology.[161] In other words, the development and realization of downstream products may not be consistent with the preferences of the patentee.

In addition, recent scholarship relating to patent law's relationship to innovation reveals that, "[t]aken as a whole, the empirical literature is inconclusive on the question of whether stronger patents increase *or* decrease innovation."[162] And while patents play an extremely important role in some industries (e.g., pharmaceutical), they are valued less in others, particularly compared to trade secret protection and lead-time into the market.[163] Moreover, patent law's relationship to R&D is uncertain,[164] and although there is good evidence that the

---

the government can help provide are a prize worth pursuing, and the pursuit of these rents has been given the name of rent seeking." DENNIS C. MUELLER, PUBLIC CHOICE II 229 (1989).

159. *See* Jeanne C. Fromer, *Patent Disclosure*, 94 IOWA L. REV. 539, 560 (2009) (stating "[n]otwithstanding the primacy of the patent document as a publicly available repository of information about a patented invention, a good deal of evidence suggests that technologists do not find that it contains pertinent information for their research"); Dan L. Burk, *The Role of Patent Law in Knowledge Codification*, 23 BERKELEY TECH. L.J. 1009, 1110 (2008) (asserting the disclosure rationale "has never been entirely satisfactory" because "[a]s a practical matter, patents are not production documents, and a good deal of the information that the technical community might like to divine from them is either accidentally or purposefully left out of the published patent"). *See also* MOKYR, GIFTS OF ATHENA, *supra* note 9, at 15 (stating "it would be too expensive to write a complete set of instructions for every technique. Judgment, dexterity, experience, and other forms of tacit knowledge inevitably come into play when a technique is executed").

160. *See* Cohen et al., *Protecting Their Intellectual Assets, supra* note 15 (finding trade secret protection a preferred form of appropriation for many industries).

161. *See* Mark A. Lemley, *Rational Ignorance at the Patent Office*, 95 Nw. U. L. REV. 1495, 1507 (2001) (approximating no more than 3.5% of patents are licensed without filing a lawsuit); John R. Allison, Mark A. Lemley, Kimberly A. Moore & R. Derek Trunkey, *Valuable Patents*, 92 GEO. L.J. 435 (2004) (asserting "[m]any patents are not worth enforcing—either because the inventions they cover turn out to be worthless, or because even if the invention has economic value the patent does not").

162. Robert W. Hahn, *The Economics of Patent Protection: Policy Implications from the Literature* 2 (AEI-Brookings Joint Center for Regulatory Studies 2003) (emphasis in original).

163. *See* Cohen et al., *Protecting Their Intellectual Assets, supra* note 15 (finding different industries rely on different appropriability mechanisms to varying degrees. For instance, a majority of the industries surveyed noted that they rely on more than one "appropriability mechanism" as part of their "appropriability strategy" (e.g., a combination of lead time and trade secrets or patents and lead time)); F.M. SCHERER & DAVID ROSS, INDUSTRIAL MARKET STRUCTURE AND ECONOMIC PERFORMANCE 628-630 (1980) (noting that for many industries, incentives to innovate other than patent rights are important, if not more important).

164. *See* Hahn, *Economics of Patent Protection, supra* note 162, at 2 (stating "[s]ome studies report that strengthening patents leads to more R&D, and thus more innovation. Others conclude patent protection and the pace of research are, at best, tenuously related"); Zvi Griliches, Ariel Pakes & Bronwyn H. Hall, *The Value of Patents as Indicators of Inventive Activity*, in ECONOMIC POLICY AND TECHNICAL PERFORMANCE 97, 120 (1987) (stating "while the aggregate value of patent rights appears to be quite high, it is estimated to be only on the order of 10 to 15 percent of total national expenditures on R&D"); SCOTCHMER, INNOVATIONS AND INCENTIVES, *supra* note 11, at 282 ("The evidence indicates that a remarkably small percentage of R&D expenditures are recovered as profit due to patent grants. . . . We should therefore make a clear distinction between the private value of an invention and the value of a patent. The value of an invention is usually greater than the incremental value of patenting it.") *Cf.* Ashish Arora, Marco Ceccagnoli & Wesley Cohen, *R&D*

private value of patents has increased,[165] and that technological innovation coupled with increases in human capital are agents of economic growth,[166] our understanding of patent law's effect on social welfare remains incomplete.[167] This latter point is important because American patent law is a utilitarian-based regime, designed to promote social welfare by encouraging technological innovation.[168] (Thus, patent law is not concerned with the manner—by accident or deliberately—in which an invention is brought into existence.)[169] In other words, the idea of a natural right in one's invention never firmly took hold in American patent law jurisprudence, despite early signs of a natural rights approach.[170] It is not surprising, therefore, that given some of the per-

---

and the Patent Premium (NBER Working Paper No. 9431) ("Although patent protection is found to provide a positive premium on average in only a few industries, our results also imply that it stimulates R&D across almost all manufactures industries, with the magnitude of that effect varying substantially.").

165. *See* Robert P. Merges, *As Many as Six Impossible Patents Before Breakfast: Property Rights for Business Concepts and Patent System Reform*, 14 BERKELEY TECH. L.J. 577, 603 (1999) (noting the "increase in the private value of patents since the early 1980s"). *See also* John R. Allison, Mark A. Lemley & Joshua Walker, *Extreme Value or Trolls on Top? The Characteristics of the Most-Litigated Patents*, 158 U. PA. L. REV. 1 (2009) (finding most-litigated patents to be most valuable and exploring the characteristics of these patents); Allison et al., *Valuable Patents, supra* note 161 (discussing what makes a patent have private value and how to identify those valuable patents).

166. *See* R.M. Solow, *Technical Change and the Aggregate Production Function*, 39 REV. ECON. STAT. 312 (1957); F.M. SCHERERT D. ROSS, INDUSTRIAL MARKET STRUCTURE AND ECONOMIC PERFORMANCE (1990).

167. *See* LANDES & POSNER, ECONOMIC STRUCTURE, *supra* note 6, at 310 ("Although there are powerful economic reasons in favor of creating property rights in inventions, there are also considerable social costs and whether the benefits exceed the costs is impossible to answer with confidence on the basis of present knowledge"); Richard Brunell, *Appropriability in Antitrust: How Much Is Enough*, 69 ANTITRUST L.J. 1, 4 (2001) ("[I]f the vast economics literature on intellectual property conveys one message, it is that the relationship between intellectual property protection and economic welfare is unclear"); Adam Jaffe, *The U.S. Patent System in Transition: Policy Innovation and the Innovation Process* (NBER Working Paper No. 7280) (stating "despite the significance of policy changes and the wide availability of detailed data relating to patenting, robust conclusions regarding the empirical consequences for technological innovation of changes in patent policy are few").

168. In support of this view, commentators point to the preamble of the Article I, §8, cl. 8 of the Constitution, which has come to be known as the IP clause. The preamble reads, Congress shall have the power "to promote the Progress of the useful Arts." In discussing the IP clause, the Supreme Court wrote in *Mazer v. Stein*, 347 U.S. 201 (1954), the "economic policy behind the clause empowering Congress to grant patents and copyrights is the conviction that it is the best way to advance public welfare." *See* section A.3 for a discussion of the IP clause.

169. For a list of nine well-known "things" invented by accident, *see* http://science.howstuffworks.com/9-things-invented-or-discovered-by-accident.htm (listing Play-Doh, fireworks, potato chips, Slinky, saccharin, Post-it® notes, Silly Putty, microwave ovens, and corn flakes). In Charles Slack's biography of Charles Goodyear, Slack describes how Goodyear discovered vulcanization:

> Sometime during the winter, probably in February or March, Goodyear accidentally dropped, placed, or spilled a quantity of rubber mixed with sulfur and white lead on a hot stove. When he retrieved the sample he discovered something remarkable: the sample had not melted, as he expected, but instead had hardened to the consistency of leather. Here, at last, was the final clue, the missing piece of the puzzle: heat.

CHARLES SLACK, NOBLE OBSESSION: CHARLES GOODYEAR, THOMAS HANCOCK, AND THE RACE TO UNLOCK THE GREATEST INDUSTRIAL SECRET OF THE NINETEENTH CENTURY 84 (2002).

170. For instance, Justice Story, the leading patent law jurist of the nineteenth century, wrote, "[t]he inventor has . . . a property in his inventions; a property which is often of very great value, and of which the law intended to give him the absolute enjoyment and possession." *Ex parte Wood*, 22 U.S. 603, 608 (1824). And in *Blanchard v. Sprague*, 3 F. Cas. 648, 650 (D. Mass. 1839), Justice Story wrote that "[p]atents . . . are clearly entitled to a liberal construction, since they are not granted as restrictions upon the rights of the community, but are granted "to promote science and useful arts." Circuit Justice Marshall was similarly disposed. In *Evans v. Jordan*, he stated that "the constitution and law, taken together, give to the inventor, from the moment of invention, an

ceived weaknesses of the incentive-based theories, some commentators have proposed non-incentive based theories to complement the traditional incentive rationale.[171]

The aforementioned discussion suggests that while scholars continue to unmask the benefits and shortcomings of the patent system, much remains to be discovered.[172] In 1958, economist Fritz Machlup conducted a study of the patent system and famously concluded that "[i]f we did not have a patent system, it would be irresponsible, on the basis of our present knowledge of its economic consequences, to recommend instituting one. But since we have had a patent system for a long time, it would be irresponsible on the basis of our present knowledge, to recommend abolishing it."[173] Our understanding of the patent system has increased tremendously since 1958, but Machlup's conclusion still resonates. And, to the extent answers remain unclear, Machlup encouraged us to continue "to muddle through."[174]

---

inchoate property therein, which is completed by suing out a patent." 8 F. Cas. 872, 873 (C.C. Va. 1813). In *Lowell v. Lewis*, the court wrote that "let the damages be estimated as high, as they can be, consistently with the rule of law on this subject, if the plaintiff's patent has been violated; wrongdoers may not reap the fruits of the labor and genius of other men." 15 F. Cas. 1018, 1019 (C.C. Mass. 1817). Favorable judicial disposition was matched by patent administrators such as William Thornton, the Superintendent of Patents from 1802 to 1828, who were of the view that the patent system was designed to serve and reward inventors. *See* WALTERSCHEID, To PROMOTE THE PROGRESS OF THE USEFUL ARTS, *supra* note 97, at 244 (noting that Thornton, "like many of his contemporaries, . . . viewed the patent system not so much as being embued [*sic*] with a public interest, but rather as a mechanism for rewarding legitimate inventors and protecting their rights"). For a discussion of William Thornton's tenure as Superintendent of Patents, *see* Daniel Preston, *The Administration and Reform of the U.S. Patent Office, 1790-1836*, 5 J. EARLY REPUBLIC 331 (1985); DOBYNS, PATENT OFFICE PONY, *supra* note 91, at 42-57. For a good discussion of the influence of natural rights theory in early American patent law, *see* Mossoff, *Rethinking the Development of Patents, supra* note 59, at 1266 (asserting natural rights theory played prominent role in IP development); Mossoff, *Who Cares What Thomas Jefferson Thought About Patents, supra* note 83.

171. *See, e.g.,* Burk, *Codification, supra* note 159, at 1034 (asserting patent system can serve "as a system of knowledge management and codification"); R. Polk Wagner & Gideon Parchomovsky, *Patent Portfolios*, 154 U. PA. L. REV. 1 (2005) (asserting firms recognize value of patents as part of a larger portfolio, not an individual benefit); Clarisa Long, *Patent Signals*, U. CHI. L. REV. 625 (2002) (arguing patents act as a signal for firms, thus reducing information costs regarding firm's financial and technologic strength); Paul J. Heald, A *Transactions Costs Theory of Patent Law*, 66 OHIO ST. L.J. 473 (2005) (asserting patent law serves to lower transaction costs).

172. *See* R. Polk Wagner, *The Supreme Court and the Future of Patent Reform*, 55-FEB FED. LAW. 35, 37 (Feb. 2008) (stating "[r]egardless of which theory one finds most attractive, the essential point is the same: the traditional appropriability theory of patents—that they generate social benefits by allowing a patentee to internalize otherwise nonexcludable benefits to an invention, thus solving a potential "public goods" problem with respect to the creation of new ideas—is no longer the sole, nor perhaps even the most important, way that patents are used in the marketplace").

173. ECONOMIC REVIEW OF THE PATENT SYSTEM: STUDY OF THE SUBCOMM. ON PATENTS, TRADEMARKS, & COPYRIGHTS OF THE COMM. ON THE JUDICIARY, 85th Cong. 80 (1958). For a copy of this study, see the casebook website at http://law.case.edu/lawofpatents. *See also* Edith Penrose, THE ECONOMICS OF THE INTERNATIONAL PATENT SYSTEM 40 (1951) (In the context of the nineteenth-century debate on whether to abolish patents, stating "[i]f national patent laws did not exist, it would be difficult to make a conclusive case for introducing them; but the fact that they do exist shifts the burden of proof and it is equally difficult to make a really conclusive case for abolishing them").

174. ECONOMIC REVIEW, *supra* note 173, at 80.

C. THE PATENT DOCUMENT AND PROCESS OF OBTAINING PATENT RIGHTS

There are three types of patents: utility, design, and plant. Approximately 90 percent of issued patents are utility, and therefore, the material in this and the remaining chapters pertains exclusively to utility patents.[175] Unlike trademark law, there is no such thing as common law patent rights. Nor do patent rights subsist upon fixation in a tangible medium of expression as provided for by copyright law. Rather, a United States patent can only be acquired by filing a patent application with the United States Patent and Trademark Office ("USPTO"). The USPTO is a federal agency that is under the Department of Commerce,[176] and is located in Alexandria, Virginia, just across the Potomac River from Washington, DC. The agency does not have jurisdiction over issues relating to infringement or enforcement. Rather, according to its 2012 Performance and Accountability Report, the agency's mission is:

> Fostering innovation, competitiveness and economic growth, domestically and abroad to deliver high quality and timely examination of patent and trademark applications, guiding domestic and international intellectual property policy, and delivering intellectual property information and education worldwide, with a highly skilled, diverse workforce.[177]

The agency is led by the Under Secretary of Commerce for Intellectual Property, who is also the Director of the USPTO.[178] The patent code states the "Director shall be responsible for providing policy direction and management supervision for the Office and for the issuance of patents and the registration of trademarks."[179] Several officials comprise the Director's staff, including the Deputy Under Secretary of Commerce and Deputy Director of the USPTO, the Commissioner for Patents, and the Commissioner for Trademarks.

The examination of patent applications is divided among eight technology centers, which are under the general supervision of the Deputy Commissioner for Patent Operations. Each center is led by a group director and subdivided into technological art units staffed by patent examiners.[180] In the fourth quarter of fiscal year 2012, the USPTO employed 7,935 patent examiners.[181]

---

175. Thus, unless expressly noted otherwise, utility patent is implied when the word "patent" is used in this book. The only exception is in Chapter 3, which devotes a small section to the discussion of design patents.

176. *See* 35 U.S.C. §1. For more on the history of USPTO, *see supra* note 102. *See also* DOBYNS, PATENT OFFICE PONY, *supra* note 91. *See also* the USPTO website at http://www.uspto.gov.

177. *See* USPTO PERFORMANCE AND ACCOUNTABILITY REPORT (2012) at page 8. *See* http://www.uspto.gov/about/stratplan/ar/index.jsp.

178. *See* 35 U.S.C. §3 (2006).

179. *See* 35 U.S.C. §3(a)(2) (2006).

180. For example, technology center 1600 is entitled "Biotechnology and Organic Chemistry." This center includes several art units such as Art Unit 1630, which handles patent applications related to "Molecular Biology, Bioinformatics, Nucleic Acids, Recombinant DNA and RNA, Gene Regulation, Nucleic Acid Amplification, Animals and Recombinant Plants, Combinatorial/Computational Chemistry." Technology Center 3700 is entitled "Mechanical Engineering, Manufacturing, and Products." One of its art units is 37E, "Medical Instruments, Diagnostic Equipment, Treatment Devices."

181. *See* PERFORMANCE AND ACCOUNTABILITY REPORT, *supra* note 177, at 10.

The process of applying for a patent is called *patent prosecution* (sometimes more generally referred to by patent professionals as "prep and pros" as in preparation and prosecution), and the record of the prosecution proceedings before the PTO is called the *prosecution history* (sometimes referred to as file history).[182] Prosecution is governed by three sets of rules and regulations: (1) the patent code set forth in Title 35; (2) Title 37 of the Code of Federal Regulations, which embodies the USPTO's rulemaking; and (3) the Manual of Patent Examining Procedure (commonly referred to as the "MPEP"), which provides important guidance to applicants and examiners, but does not have the force and effect of law.[183] The proceeding is *ex parte*, meaning that the prosecution is only between the applicant and the examiner.[184]

But the America Invents Act created several vehicles for third parties to challenge the issuance and validity of a patent. These vehicles include (1) pre-issuance submission of prior art; (2) post-grant review; and (3) *inter partes* review.

Pre-issuance submission of prior art permits third parties to submit "any patent, published patent application, or other printed publication of potential relevance to the examination of the application."[185] This new statutory provision overturns previous USPTO regulations by requiring that third-party submissions contain a "concise description" of the prior art's relevance. The submission period is also extended to the later of six months after publication of the application or the date of the first rejection under section 132.[186]

182. To prosecute a patent or otherwise represent clients before the PTO, one must be licensed to practice before the agency, which means one must have passed the patent bar exam. One does not have to be an attorney to sit for the patent bar and represent clients before the PTO. Non-attorneys who practice before the PTO are called patent agents. The exception to this licensure rule is pro se applicants; that is, an applicant representing himself before the USPTO. *See* http://www.uspto.gov/web/offices/dcom/gcounsel/oed.htm for more information about the patent bar and its eligibility requirements.While the idea to create a patent bar "to insure proper representation of the rights of applicants for patents" existed in the late nineteenth century, *see Patent Solicitors and the Proposed Patent Bar*, SCIENTIFIC AMERICAN (June 13, 1896), Vol. LXXIV (it was not until 1922 that the Commissioner of Patents was given the authority to require patent agents and attorneys to have certain qualifications before being permitted to practice before the office). For an historical discussion of the development of the patent practitioner in the late nineteenth century, *see* Kara W. Swanson, *The Emergence of the Professional Patent Practitioner*, 50 TECHNOLOGY & CULTURE 519-548 (July 2009).

183. All three sources can be found on the USPTO's website—http://www.uspto.gov as well as this casebook's website—http://law.case.edu/lawofpatents under "Laws, Regulations, and Treatises."

184. While the PTO has made significant strides in terms of efficiency, the process of obtaining a patent retains a level of complexity and nuance that would make Daedelus proud. Yet today's patent prosecution framework compares quite favorably to, for example, the nineteenth-century British patent system as uncharitably described by Dickens in *A Poor Man's Tale of a Patent*:

> Thereby I say nothing of my being tired of my life, while I was Patenting my invention. But I put this: Is it reasonable to make a man feel as if, in inventing an ingenious improvement meant to do good, he had done something wrong? How else can a man feel, when he is met by such difficulties at every turn? All inventors taking out a Patent MUST feel so. And look at the expense. How hard on me, and how hard on the country if there's any merit in me (and my invention is took up now, I am thankful to say, and doing well), to put me to all that expense before I can move a finger! Make the addition yourself, and it'll come to ninety-six pound, seven, and eightpence. No more, and no less.

At http://books.google.com/books?id=LfgbAQAAMAAJ&q=finger#search_anchor (page 20).

185. 35 U.S.C. §122(e).

186. *Id.*

Post-grant review allows anyone to challenge a patent's validity *within* nine months of issuance,[187] and is designed "to provide a meaningful opportunity to improve patent quality and restore confidence in the presumption of validity that comes with issued patents in court."[188] The challenge—which is heard by the Patent Trial and Appeal Board—can be based on "any ground that could be raised under paragraph (2) or (3) of section 282(b)," such as, for example, lack of novelty, on-sale and public use events of section 102, obviousness under section 103, and lack of enablement or other description deficiencies under section 112.[189] The USPTO "may not authorize post-grant review" unless it is deemed "more likely than not that at least 1 of the claims challenged in the petition is unpatentable."[190] Moreover, post-grant review can be based on "a novel or unsettled legal question that is important to other patents or patent applications," even if the aforementioned "more likely than not" standard is not met.[191] The USPTO has three months after the patent owner's response to decide whether to grant the petition.[192] The decision whether to invoke post-grant review is "final and not appealable";[193] once instituted, however, an adverse decision may be appealed to the Federal Circuit.[194] With rare exception, the post-grant review is available only for issued patents based on applications subject to the first-inventor-to-file provision, which applies to applications filed on or after March 16, 2013.

Importantly, invoking post-grant review is not without risk for the petitioner. A petitioner who receives a "final written decision" may not challenge the validity of the patent in district court or another USPTO proceeding "on any ground that the petitioner raised or reasonably could have raised during that post-grant review."[195]

Inter partes review permits the challenge of a patent's validity *after* either (1) nine months from issuance; or (2) if a post-grant review was invoked, the date of termination of the post-grant review.[196] Accordingly, the window for *inter partes* review opens after the post-grant review window closes. The USPTO "may not authorize *inter partes* review" unless the petitioner "shows that there is a reasonable likelihood that the petitioner would prevail with respect to at least

---

187. *Id.* at §321(c). Post-grant review—or opposition proceedings—have been part of the European patent law landscape for several years. For an empirical study of opposition proceedings, *see* Stuart J.H. Graham & Dietmar Harhoff, *Separating Patent Wheat from Chaff: Would the U.S. Benefit from Adopting a Patent Post-Grant Review* (2009), at http://papers.ssrn.com/sol3/papers.cfm?abstract_id=1489579 (stating that "the benefit of [post-grant] review in terms of social welfare per year—when put in dollar terms could be nearly $25 billion. The main parameter affecting this estimate is not savings on the cost of litigation, but the social costs of currently unlitigated patents that bestow excessive market power on some applications"). *See also* Stuart J.H. Graham & Dietmar Harhoff, *Can Post-Grant Reviews Improve Patent System Design? A Twin Study of U.S. and European Patents* (2006), at http://papers.ssrn.com/sol3/papers.cfm?abstract_id=921826. *See also* Bronwyn Hall, Stuart J.H. Graham, Dietmar Harhoff & David Mowery, *Prospects for Improving U.S. Patent Quality via Post-Grant Opposition*, at http://papers.ssrn.com/sol3/papers.cfm?abstract_id=410657.
188. Leahy-Smith America Invents Act, Committee of the Judiciary, H.R. Rep. No. 112-98, 112th Cong., 1st Sess., at 48 (June 1, 2011).
189. 35 U.S.C. §321(b).
190. *Id.* at §324(a).
191. *Id.* at §324(b).
192. *Id.* at §324(c).
193. *Id.* at §324(e).
194. *Id.* at §329.
195. *Id.* at §325(e)(1) and (2).
196. *Id.* at §311(c).

one of the claims challenged in the petition."[197] The decision whether to invoke *inter partes* review is "final and not appealable";[198] once instituted, however, an adverse decision may be appealed to the Federal Circuit.[199] Also, if a civil action is filed by the petitioner on or after the date he petitions for *inter partes* review, "that civil action shall be automatically stayed" until the patent owner either moves the court to lift the stay; alleging that the petitioner has infringed the patent; or the petitioner moves the court to dismiss the civil action.[200]

Unlike post-grant review, the grounds for invoking *inter partes* review are limited to patents and printed publications under sections 102 and 103.[201] But similar to post-grant review, *inter partes* review has a potential estoppel effect. Specifically, a petitioner who receives a "final written decision" may not challenge the validity of the patent in district court or another USPTO proceeding on grounds that "the petitioner raised or reasonably could have raised during that *inter partes* review."[202]

Prior to filing a patent application, an inventor or his attorney may conduct a prior art search. (Prior art is knowledge—for example, patents and publications—accessible to a person of ordinary skill in the art before the date of invention (pre-AIA timeframe) or before the effective filing date (post-AIA timeframe.) While there is no duty to conduct a search,[203] information gleaned from previous patents and publications may allow the inventor to get a better understanding of the patentability of the invention or potentially increase leverage during licensing negotiations or litigation.[204] But survey evidence suggests

197. *Id.* at §314(a).
198. *Id.* at §314(d).
199. *Id.* at §319.
200. *Id.* at §315(a)(2).
201. *Id.* at §311(b).
202. *Id.* at §315(e)(1) and (2).
203. But "[e]ach individual associated with the filing and prosecution of a patent application has a duty of candor and good faith in dealing with the Office," which means the individual has a duty to disclose to the USPTO "all information known to that individual to be material to patentability." 37 C.F.R. §1.56(a). Individuals include "(1) [e]ach inventor named in the application; (2) [e]ach attorney or agent who prepares or prosecutes the application; and (3) [e]very other person who is substantively involved in the preparation or prosecution of the application and who is associated with the inventor, with the assignee or with anyone to whom there is an obligation to assign the application." 37 C.F.R. §1.56(c). The definition of "material" information is explored in Section C of Chapter 8 under the heading "Inequitable Conduct and the Duty of Candor."
204. A court will likely be more deferential to the PTO if the challenger's invalidity defense is based solely on the same prior art the PTO considered during prosecution. *See PharmaStem Therapeutics, Inc. v. ViaCell, Inc.*, 491 F.3d 1342, 1366 (Fed. Cir. 2007) (stating "[w]hen a party asserting invalidity relies on references that were considered during examination or reexamination, that party 'bears the added burden of overcoming the deference that is due to a qualified government agency presumed to have done its job'"); *American Hoist & Derrick Co. v. Sowa & Sons, Inc.*, 725 F.2d 1350, 1359 (Fed. Cir. 1984) (stating "[w]hen no prior art other than that which was considered by the PTO examiner is relied on by the attacker, he has the added burden of overcoming the deference that is due to a qualified government agency"). *See also* John Allison & Mark Lemley, *The Growing Complexity of the United States Patent System*, 82 B.U. L. Rev. 77, 139 (2002) (stating "[c]iting more prior art will also make a patent more valuable in litigation, as it is much harder to prove a patent is invalid if the PTO has already considered and rejected the relevant prior art"); John R. Allison & Mark A. Lemley, *Empirical Evidence on the Validity of Litigated Patents*, 26 AIPLA Q.J. 185, 231-234 (1998) (providing empirical support for the proposition that citing more prior art makes proving invalidity more difficult).
A quick way to discern if a prior art reference was considered by the PTO is to look at the cover page of the patent under "References Cited." *See* bracket 56 ("[56]") on the cover page of the pizza box patent at the end of this chapter. There are several databases for searching patents. *See, e.g.*, http://www.uspto.gov/patents/ and http://www.google.com/patents.

prior art searches are not commonplace,[205] and the decision to perform a search varies from industry to industry.[206]

The patent application (and issued patent) is comprised of two parts: (1) the specification (oftentimes referred to more colloquially as the "spec"); and (2) the claims, both of which are written in highly stylized language. (The claims are technically part of the specification under 35 U.S.C. § 112, but it is common practice for patent professionals and courts to refer to and treat the "claims" and "specification" as distinct components of the patent, and this book will assume the same approach.) The claims are considered to be the most important part of the patent document because they delineate the patent owner's property right. To borrow real property terminology, the claims set forth the metes and bounds of the patentee's proprietary interest. The specification contains a disclosure of the claimed invention and can be viewed as a teaching device, informing its reader of the particulars of the claimed invention. As the Federal Circuit has noted, "Specifications teach. Claims claim."[207] (Claims and the specification are discussed in more detail in Chapter 2.)

An application is published 18 months after filing unless the applicant represents he will not seek foreign patent protection.[208] The application is examined by a patent examiner who is trained in the technology to which the claimed invention pertains. The examiner usually conducts a prior art search (both patent

---

205. *See* Cockburn & Henderson, *Survey Results, supra* note 16 at F.6 (finding that 65% percent of survey respondents—largely senior legal staff of corporations—"disagreed" or "strongly disagreed" with the following statement: "We always do a patent search before initiating any R&D or product development effort"). Some commentators have argued that applicants actually have a disincentive to conduct prior art searches. *See, e.g.,* R. Polk Wagner, *Reconsidering Estoppel: Patent Administration and the Failure of Festo,* 159 U. Pa. L. Rev. 159, 215 (2002) (asserting that a patentee has a motive "behave strategically" by, for example, "declining to conduct a thorough prior art search, thus transferring this cost to the public as well as increasing the possibility that the PTO will 'miss something' and allow the unwarranted scope").

206. In the information technology industry, for example, a prior art search is rare. *See* Mark A. Lemley, *Ignoring Patents,* 2008 Mich. St. L. Rev. 19, 21 (stating "both researchers and companies in component industries simply ignore patents. Virtually everyone does it. They do it at all stages of endeavor. Companies and lawyers tell engineers not to read patents in starting their research, lest their knowledge of the patent disadvantage the company by making it a willful infringer"). Bhaven Sampat has shown that applicants are more likely to perform prior art searches in "discrete product industries" (such as drugs and chemicals) that rely heavily upon patents for appropriating returns to R&D; but there is less of an incentive to conduct a search in "complex product industries" (such as electronics and telecommunications) where patents are viewed more as bargaining chips, rather than valuable tools for appropriating returns to R&D. *See* Bhaven Sampat, *When Do Applicants Search for Prior Art?,* 54 J.L. & Econ. (2010).

And in the context of academic research, it is not uncommon for investigators to express a willing ignorance or lack of concern with respect to patent rights. *See* Reaping the Benefits of Genomic and Proteomic Research: Intellectual Property Rights, Innovation, and Public Health 134 (National Research Council) (Steven A. Merrill & Anne-Marie Mazza eds., 2006) (stating "the lack of substantial evidence for a patent thicket or a patent blocking problem clearly is linked to a general lack of awareness or concern among academic investigators about existing intellectual property"); John P. Walsh, Charlene Cho & Wesley M. Cohen, *View from the Bench: Patents and Material Transfers,* 309 Science 2002, 2002 (2005) (stating "few academic bench scientists currently pay much attention to others' patents. Only 5 percent (18 out of 379) regularly check for patents on knowledge inputs related to their research").

207. *SRI Int'l v. Matsushita Elec. Corp. of America,* 775 F.2d 1107, 1121 n.14 (Fed. Cir. 1984).

208. *See* 35 U.S.C. § 122(a) and (b). Issued patents have a seven digit patent number in the upper right hand corner followed by either "B1"—indicating the application was not previously published—or "B2" indicating the application was published.

and non-patent references)[209] to determine if the claimed invention satisfies the novel and nonobvious requirements, explored in Chapters 4 and 5, respectively. The examiner will also determine whether the application satisfies the disclosure requirements, discussed in Chapter 2, and meets the utility and subject matter eligibility requirements, both of which are explored in Chapter 3.[210]

The examiner will then issue an initial *office action*, most likely rejecting some or all of the claims, and setting forth the reasons for the rejection. In fiscal year 2012, the average time for issuance of a first office action for all applications was 21.9 months, but there was variation depending on the technology at issue. For example, the average time for issuance of a first office action for communications-related inventions and software was 24.3 and 23.3 months, respectively; in contrast, for biotechnology-related inventions and semiconductors, the respective average time was 17.8 and 20.5 months. With respect to total pendency, the average across all technologies was 32.4 months, but with significant technology-specific variation.[211] Upon receipt of the office action, the inventor and his attorney can either abandon the application or, more commonly, reply to the office action by submitting an *amendment*. The amendment may cancel or modify claims, usually in a manner that narrows them, and put forward arguments aimed at persuading

209. *See* 37 C.F.R. §1.104(a)(1) ("On taking up an application for examination or a patent in a reexamination proceeding, the examiner shall make a thorough study thereof and shall make a thorough investigation of the available prior art relating to the subject matter of the claimed invention."). Prior art patents are considerably more accessible than non-patent related prior art (e.g., technical journals). *See* John R. Thomas, *Collusion and Collective Action in the Patent System: A Proposal for Patent Bounties*, 2001 ILL. L. REV. 305, 318 (stating "that the Patent Office has increasingly relied upon previously issued patents as prior art. Newly granted patents stress the citation of prior art patents, with diminished reference to such secondary literature as texts and journal articles. Tight examiner schedules appear to be the chief cause of this circumscribed searching strategy. In comparison to much of the secondary literature, patents are readily accessible, conveniently classified and printed in a common format. Identification of a promising secondary reference, and full comprehension of its contents, often prove to be more difficult tasks").

Prior art references that appear on the cover page of a patent (under the heading "References Cited") can be references disclosed by the applicant, discovered by the examiner, or a combination of both. (As of January 2001, examiner generated references are indicated with an asterisk.) One recent study, which looked at all U.S. patents issued between 2001-2003, found that for the "average patent . . . examiners introduced 63 percent of all patent citations" and "about 40 percent of patents granted over the period have *all* citations inserted by examiners, i.e., applicants did not add a single citations, whereas only 8 percent of patents had no examiner-inserted citations." *See* Juan Alcácer, Michelle Gittelman & Bhaven Sampat, *Applicant and Examiner Citations in U.S. Patents: An Overview and Analysis*, Working Paper 09-016 (Harvard Business School 2008), at 3-4 (emphasis in original). The authors looked at various "dimensions" to these data and found that "applicants with very high numbers of patents . . . receive higher shares of examiner citations than less-experienced applicants;" and that "non-U.S. applicants receive far higher shares than U.S. applicants." *Id.* And with respect to technology, "[e]xaminers account for *all* citations in 45 percent of patents in the computers/communications and electrical/electronic fields" and only 25 percent of citations for the drug and medical patents. *Id.* at 17 (emphasis in original). This discrepancy may be explained in part by the fact that in contrast to informational technology, a single (or relatively few) pharmaceutical patent can have tremendous commercial value, and therefore, applicants are more inclined to search for prior art as a means of strengthening the validity of the patent. *Id.* at 10-11. See also notes 181-182 (discussing prior art searching).

210. For a good discussion of the examination process, *see* Iain M. Cockburn, Samuel Kortum & Scott Stern, *Are All Patent Examiners Equal? Examiners, Patent Characteristics, and Litigation Outcomes*, in PATENTS IN THE KNOWLEDGE BASED ECONOMY (W. Cohen & W. Merrill eds., 2003). *See also* The Manual of Patent Examination Procedure ("MPEP") §2106 (July 2008), which provides a "Guidelines Flowchart" for examiners and inventors at http://www.uspto.gov/web/offices/pac/mpep/documents/2100_2106.htm#sect2106.

211. *See* USPatentStatistics.com at http://uspatentstatistics.com/averagependenciestechcenter .html. *See also* PERFORMANCE AND ACCOUNTABILITY REPORT, *supra* note 177, at 20.

the examiner to allow the application in its amended form. (The inventor and his attorney, as discussed in Chapter 7, have to be careful how they amend the application lest the amendment come back to haunt them during litigation, particularly with respect to claim scope.) At this stage in the prosecution, the examiner can either allow the application or reject it yet again. If the latter, the rejection is usually "final" as reflected in a *final office action*, which means that the inventor's options are more limited than they were after receipt of the initial office action. The inventor's choices are (1) appeal the decision to the Board of Patent Appeals and Interferences (the "BPAI"), an administrative body within the USPTO; (2) file a continuation application;[212] (3) file a continuation-in-part (C-I-P) application;[213] (4) request continued examination (RCE);[214] or (5) abandon the application.

Filing an application does not guarantee that a patent will issue; in fact, in 2012, 46.6 percent of originally filed applications resulted in issued patents.[215] But this figure is considerably higher once continuation applications[216] and pendency are taken into account. (Pendency refers to the amount of time between the original filing date and issuance or some form of final action.)[217] Taking these two factors into consideration, the percentage of issued patents has been

212. A continuation application enjoys the same filing date as the original application. The claims may be modified in the continuation, but the specification must remain the same. *See* 35 U.S.C. § 120; 37 C.F.R. § 1.53(b).

213. A continuation-in-part is an application filed during the lifetime of an earlier application, disclosing some or all of the earlier application and adding new matter not disclosed in the earlier application. A C-I-P has two filing dates, the filing date of the original application for the repeated information and the actual C-I-P filing date for the new matter. *See* 35 U.S.C. § 120; 37 C.F.R. § 1.53(b).

214. An RCE can be viewed as a request to keep the current application alive, without requiring the applicant to file a new application such as a continuation. According to § 706.07(h) the Manual of Patent Examination Procedure (MPEP):

> 35 U.S.C. 132(b) provides for continued examination of an application at the request of the applicant (request for continued examination or RCE) upon payment of a fee, without requiring the applicant to file a continuing application under 37 CFR 1.53(b). To implement the RCE practice, 37 CFR 1.114 provides a procedure under which an applicant may obtain continued examination of an application in which prosecution is closed (*e.g.*, the application is under final rejection or a notice of allowance) by filing a submission and paying a specified fee. Applicants cannot file an RCE to obtain continued examination on the basis of claims that are independent and distinct from the claims previously claimed and examined as a matter of right (*i.e.*, applicant cannot switch inventions). See 37 CFR 1.145. Any newly submitted claims that are directed to an invention that is independent and distinct from the invention previously claimed will be withdrawn from consideration and not entered. An RCE is not the filing of a new application. Thus, the Office will not convert an RCE to a new application such as an application filed under 37 CFR 1.53(b) or a continued prosecution application (CPA) under 37 CFR 1.53(d).

A significant advantage of filing a RCE is the relative quickness with which they are reviewed, but in an attempt to help examiners manage their workload, the PTO has moved to change the timing for consideration so that examiners are no longer required to act within two months of a RCE. *See* Notice of Change to Docketing Requests for Continued Examination (Oct. 19, 2009), at http://www.uspto.gov/patents/law/notices/rce_docket.pdf.

215. http://www.uspto.gov/web/offices/ac/ido/oeip/taf/us_stat.pdf.

216. For a discussion of the strategic use of continuation applications, *see* Mark A. Lemley & Kimberly A. Moore, 84 B.U. L. Rev. 63, 71-83 (2004) (detailing the abusive practices relating to the filing of continuation applications).

217. *Patent Pendency Statistics* at http://www.uspto.gov/patents/stats/patentpendency.jsp (FY 2009). The total average pendency for patent applications in fiscal year 2009 was 34.6 months; in 2003, it was 26.7 months. And the pendency rate, as with office actions, is technology-dependent. For instance, the total average pendency rate for communications-related inventions and software in FY 2009 was 42.7 and 40.7 months, respectively. The rate was 35.1 months for biotechnology-related inventions," and 29.7 months for semiconductor, electrical, optical systems and components. *Id.*

A Flow Chart of the Patent Prosecution Process

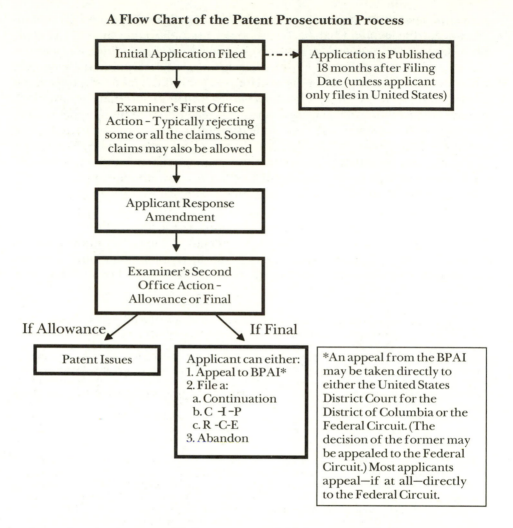

estimated to be between 71.8 percent and 75.9 percent.[218] And interestingly, one study has found that the most-litigated patents make "extraordinary use of patent continuations."[219]

---

218. *See* Mark A. Lemley & Bhavan Sampat, *Is the Patent Office a Rubber Stamp?*, 58 EMORY L.J. 181, 193 (2008) (updated as of April 2008). Another factor relating to issuance rates—a factor not entirely germane to the merits of the application—is the characteristics of the examiner. For instance, Lemley and Sampat studied nearly 10,000 patent applications that were filed in January 2001 and published before April 2006. Based on this study, they found "strong evidence that (a) more experienced examiners are more likely to grant patents; (b) this effect does not simply reflect differences in prior art search tendencies between experienced and unexperienced examiners, i.e., experience matters independently of these measures; and (c) even conditional on experience, the extent to which examiners search for prior art (as measured by the average share of citations they account for in their issued patents) is strongly related to the probability an application is granted." While the data do not lead to conclusions, they do suggest "that examiners are doing more work, and rejecting applications with more rigor, at early stages in their career, and both doing less work and allowing more patents as their tenure increases." Mark A. Lemley & Bhaven N. Sampat, *Examiner Characteristics and the Patent Grant Rate*, p. 12, at http://papers.ssrn.com/sol3/papers.cfm?abstract_id=1329091 (2009). See also, Mark A. Lemley and Bhaven Sampat, *Examiner Characteristics and Patent Office Outcomes*, 94 Rev. of Econ. and Stat. 817 (2012) (finding more experienced patent examiners cite less prior art and more likely to grant patents).

219. *See* Allison et al., *Extreme Value or Trolls on Top?*, *supra* note 165, at 12.

The issuance rate and long pendency periods must be viewed together. The longer the pendency periods, the greater the incentive to move applications through the system more quickly, which places greater time constraints on examiners to close out the prosecution (e.g., issue or deny the patent).[220] While internal PTO reforms have sought to ameliorate these issues, the time constraints placed on examiners, as well as limited resources and information flows,[221] high-volume patent strategies by firms,[222] and the general difficulties associated with applying the patentability standards, has led to concerns about patent quality and attendant calls for reform.[223]

The number of patent applications has increasingly grown over time and, naturally, a corresponding increase in issuances in terms of raw numbers. In 2001, there were 1,458,000 patent applications filed worldwide; in 2011, that

220. *See* Michael J. Meurer, *Patent Examination Priorities*, 51 WM. & MARY L. REV. 675, 679 (2009) (stating "examiners will make mistakes given the time constraints that they face"); Andrew Chin, *Search for Tomorrow: Some Side Effects of Patent Office Automation*, 87 N.C. L. REV. 1617, 1620 (2009) (noting that examiners "operate under time and other resource constraints that make it difficult to guarantee the adequacy of the cited prior art for analyzing patentability"); Mark A. Lemley, *Rational Ignorance at the Patent Office*, 95 NW. L. REV. 1496, 1497 n.3 (2001) (stating "[e]xaminers have astonishingly little time to spend on each application — on average, a total of eighteen hours, including the time spent reading the application, reading the submitted prior art, searching for and reading prior art in databases accessible to the PTO, comparing that prior art to the application, writing an office action, reading and responding to the response to office action, iterating the last two steps at least one and often more times, conducting an interview with the applicant, and ensuring that the diagrams and claims are in form for allowance. Because so many applications arrive at the PTO each year, examiners are rewarded for getting applications out the door"); Jay P. Kesan & Andres A. Gallo, *Why "Bad" Patents Survive in the Markets and How Should We Change?*, 55 EMORY L.J. 61, 66 (2006) (stating "the laws and regulations that dictate the behavior of the USPTO do not provide the correct incentives needed to grant valid patents. For example, the USPTO receives fees for each patent application and during prosecution of that application, but without any penalties for incorrectly issued patents").

221. A frequent complaint of USPTO officials and the inventive community has been Congressional diversion of patent office fees. As Clarisa Long states, historically "the PTO had been an unfashionable backwater, a bureau of the Department of Commerce that was perpetually underfunded, understaffed, and overlooked." Clarisa Long, *The PTO and the Market for Influence in Patent Law*, 157 U. PA. L. REV. 1965 (2009). But although the funding issue remains a "hot-button topic," Long points out the fee diversion situation has improved in recent years due in part to a combined lobbying effort of the PTO and inventive community. *Id.* at 1986-1987. With respect to information flows, *see, e.g.,* JAFFE & LERNER, INNOVATION AND ITS DISCONTENTS, *supra* note 141, at 21 (stating because relevant technical information resides in many different places, the "keys to a better [examination] system are therefore to create incentives to maximize the amount of information that different parties bring to the process while minimizing their incentive to use patent processes disruptively").

222. *See* R. Polk Wagner, *Understanding Patent-Quality Mechanisms*, 157 U. PA. L. REV. 2135, 2154-2155 (2009) (stating "having many patents, even if they are of low quality, can hedge against the difficulties in predicting the future noted above; by casting a broader net, with many patents in a particular field, less emphasis is placed on the need for any individual patent to endure into the future. Also, having many patents, even if they are of low quality, can hedge against changes in the law itself"); Gideon Parchomovsky & R. Polk Wagner, *Patent Portfolios*, 154 U. PA. L. REV. 1, 16-19 (2005) (discussing reasons for high-filing strategies).

223. *See, e.g.,* Beth Simone Noveck, *"Peer-to-Patent": Collective Intelligence, Open Review, and Patent Reform*, 20 HARV. J.L. & TECH. 123, 127 (2006) (discussing the difficulty examiners face in uncovering relevant prior art and proposing a "Peer-to-Patent" system whereby "the scientific community provides [to the examiner] what it knows best — scientific information relevant to determining the novelty and non-obviousness of a patent application"); Wagner, *Patent-Quality Mechanisms, supra* note 222 (discussing dynamics leading to poor patent quality and suggesting numerous reforms); JAFFE & LERNER, INNOVATION AND ITS DISCONTENTS, *supra* note 141, at 178 (proposing multiple levels of review of patent applications and greater information flows into the USPTO during examination).

number rose to 2,140,600.[224] In the United States, the USPTO received 543,815 applications in 2012 (334,445 applications were filed in 2002) and issued 253,155 patents.[225] In comparison, the European Patent Office (EPO) received 257,744 applications in 2012 (142,941 applications were filed in 2000) and issued 65,687 patents.[226] Not all patent offices are witnessing increases. The Japanese Patent Office (JPO), for instance, has seen fewer applications filed over the past 10 years. In 2001, 2006, and 2011, 439,175, 408,674, and 342,610 applications were filed, respectively.[227]

In addition to worldwide filing numbers, the origin of these filings is highly concentrated among five countries, with patent applicants from China, Germany, Japan, the Republic of South Korea, and the United States constituting the top five.[228] Of particular interest is the significant growth in filings from China, India, and South Korea. This may explain why a combination of non-U.S. applicants received a majority of U.S. patents issued every year beginning in 2008 (50.9%) to 2012 (52.2%). The number of "busy" patent offices is also highly concentrated. In addition to the USPTO, the largest recipient patent offices are Japan, China, the Republic of Korea, and Europe (i.e., the European Patent Office).[229] India has also witnessed a dramatic rise in patent filings over the past several years.[230]

What explains this steep increase in the number of patent filings? Commentators have offered a number of explanations. First, firms understand that intellectual property strategy is business strategy—a "boardroom issue"—and a policy of high-volume filing can be leveraged to create value and intellectual asset formation in the marketplace.[231] (This holds true even if a vast majority of patents have limited commercial value or are of low quality.) Indeed, a significant majority of market value for public corporations resides in intangible assets. And patents play an important role in this regard, particularly in certain industries. Second, it can be quite difficult to gauge commercial potential during the application phase;[232] in fact, commercial potential may not manifest itself—if at all—until several years after issuance, and therefore, applicants err

---

224. *See* 2012 WORLD INTELLECTUAL PROPERTY INDICATORS (2012 WIPO INDICATORS) at htpp://www.wipo.int/ipstats/en/wipi/figures.html#section_a.

225. *See* http://www.uspto.gov/web/offices/ac/ido/oeip/taf/us_stat.pdf.

226. *See* http://www.epo.org/about-us/annual-reports-statistics/statistics.html. According to the World Intellectual Property Organization there were nearly 1,979,133 patent applications filed worldwide in 2010, up 43.6 percent from 2000. *See* 2012 WIPO INDICATORS, *supra* note 224 at http://www.wipo.int/ipstats/en/wipi/figures.html (2011).

227. *See* htpp://www.jpo.go.jp/cgi/linke.cgi?url=/shiryou_e/toushin_e/kenkyukai_e/annual_report2012.htm.

228. *See* 2012 WIPO INDICATORS , *supra* note 224. In 2011, the most patent applications (in descending order) were filed by residents of Japan, China, United States, Republic of South Korea, and Germany.

229. *Id.* In 2011, the Chinese Patent Office had the most patent filings of any patent office in the world, including the United States. 2012 WIPO INDICATORS, *supra* note 224. As of this writing, the 2012 data for China is not available.

230. *Id.*

231. *See* Hanel, *Intellectual Property Rights*, *supra* note 18, at 895 (stating "[i]n the new economy, knowledge is the principal economic asset and its management and protection have become the cornerstones of corporate strategy"); Wagner, *Patent-Quality Mechanisms*, *supra* note 222, at 2154 (stating "[h]aving many patents, even if their quality is low, can provide much-needed marketplace power in a world where individual patents become increasingly less certain in scope and validity").

232. *See* F.M. Scherer, *The Innovation Lottery*, in EXPANDING THE BOUNDARIES OF INTELLECTUAL PROPERTY 3-21 (Dreyfuss et al. eds., 2001).

on the side of filing. Third, the creation of the United States Court of Appeals for the Federal Circuit, from its beginning in 1982, altered the legal landscape of patents, resulting in a significant strengthening of the patent grant.[233] Fourth, Congress has enacted patent and other forms of legislation that have incentivized certain technologic and industrial segments of society (e.g., research universities) to pursue patent protection on their innovations, particularly in the fields of biotechnology and genomics.[234] Fifth, a patent is an increasingly important tool to attract venture capital and financing.[235] Sixth, a patent can be used to reduce information costs by acting as a vehicle to publicize information, in addition to being used for privatizing information.[236] Seventh, there has been an increase in research productivity.[237] And lastly, patentees may simply want to block competitors from patenting similar technology,[238] or enhance their bargaining position during licensing negotiations.[239]

In addition to more filings, the cost of obtaining patent rights has increased. A recent survey of patent attorneys shows that the median costs (across geographic locations) for preparing and filing a patent application in 2012 for biotech/chemical applications was $10,000, for electrical/computer arts and for mechanical arts.[240] As these are median costs, some applications, depending on the complexity of the technology and geographic location of the law firm, can be considerably more. And there are, typically, after-filing costs that have a median range $1,800-3,000.[241]

As mentioned earlier, the patent claims are the most important part of the patent document. Although we will cover the claim's role in patent law in subsequent chapters, it is worth emphasizing here that claim drafting is a difficult endeavor that takes many years of practice to achieve a high level of competency.[242] Indeed, poorly drafted claims can be particularly costly if the patent is subject to licensing negotiations or eventually litigated. But a well-drafted claim can be worth millions of dollars.

---

233. *See* LANDES & POSNER, ECONOMIC STRUCTURE, *supra* note 6, at 337-344 (suggesting the Federal Circuit "has had a significant positive effect on both the number of patent applications and the number of patent grants"); John R. Allison & Mark A. Lemley, *Empirical Evidence on the Validity of Litigated Patents*, 26 AIPLA Q.J. 185, 241 (1998) (noting increase in patent validity rate after creation of Federal Circuit). *Cf.* Samuel Kortum & Josh Lerner, *Stronger Protection or Technological Revolution: What Is Behind the Recent Surge in Patenting?*, Carnegie-Rochester Series on Public Policy 48:247-304 (rejecting the "friendly court" hypothesis).

234. *See, e.g.,* 35 U.S.C. §§200-212 (2000) (the "Bayh-Dole Act").

235. *See* Bronwyn H. Hall, Adam B. Jaffe & Manuel Trajtenberg, *Market Value and Patent Citations*, 36 RAND J. ECON. 1 (2005); PAUL A. GOMPERS & JOSH LERNER, THE MONEY OF INVENTION: HOW VENTURE CAPITAL CREATES NEW WEALTH (2001); Mark A. Lemley, *Reconceiving Patents in the Age of Venture Capital*, 4 J. SMALL & EMERGING BUS. L. 137 (2000). *Cf.* Graham & Sichelman, *Why Do Start-Ups Patent?*, *supra* note 14 (discussing the challenges and decision-making calculus of start-up companies with respect to patenting).

236. *See* Clarisa Long, *Patent Signals*, 69 U. CHI. L. REV. 625 (2002).

237. *See* Kortum & Lerner, *Stronger Protection or Technological Revolution*, *supra* note 233 (finding the reason for the increase in patent filings resides outside the patent system such as increase in research productivity).

238. *See* Cohen et al., *Appropriability Conditions*, *supra* note 15, at 24.

239. *Id.*

240. *See* AMERICAN INTELLECTUAL PROPERTY LAW ASSOCIATION, REPORT OF THE ECONOMIC SURVEY 27 (2013). These numbers reflect attorneys' fees, not the PTO filing fees, which are relatively modest in comparison

241. *Id.* at I-132-133.

242. There are several excellent books on claim drafting; the most well known of these is ROBERT C. FABER, LANDIS ON THE MECHANICS OF PATENT CLAIM DRAFTING (2005).

Figure 1. Pizza Box
U.S. Patent 4,441,626

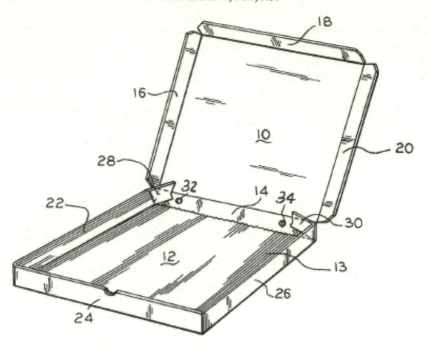

To illustrate the difficulty of claim drafting, consider the following familiar invention: a pizza box. How would you draft a claim to cover the fundamental features of this invention? Keep in mind you want to draft a claim with an eye toward litigation, meaning that you want a claim that provides the maximum amount of protection, but does not overlap with the prior art.

The following is an excerpt from the specification of the patent:

> As shown in FIG. 1, a pizza box constructed in accordance with the teachings of this invention comprises upper and lower members having a top panel **10**, a bottom panel **12** and a central panel **14**. The top panel **10** and the bottom panel **12** include side panels **16, 18, 20, 22, 24, 26** and various side flaps **28, 30**, to complete the folding and assembly of the box. . . .
>
> According to the invention, means are provided for venting the box . . . at holes **32** [and] **34**. . . . Research has found that proper ventilation should be attained inside the box to keep the pizza hot and still retain good crust quality, when approximately one square inch of ventilation is provided for each cubic foot of volume, to acquire a proper balance between heat and steam. . . .

There is a great deal of prior art showing many of the features of Figure 1 (e.g., upper and lower members with a central plane), but none of the prior art discloses flaps and ventilation holes together in a single pizza box. Think about the features of Figure 1 you want to protect, while also keeping in mind that you have to draft a claim that avoids the prior art. What features would you want to include and omit in a claim?

The point here is that no matter how basic or straightforward the invention, claim drafting is a difficult endeavor, yet one that is extremely important because of the legal weight claims assume within the patent system. As you read the actual claims in the 4,441,626 patent below, you will notice the highly structured nature of claim language, each word having significance, including words such as "said," "substantially," "intermediate," and "comprising."

Below is the cover page of issued U.S. Patent No. 4,441,626 entitled "Pizza Box." Notice that there are several important features on this page, including: [11] patent number and [22] filing date; [75] name of inventor and [73] assignee; [52] technical class that "pizza boxes" are a part of; for instance, U.S. Class 220/443 is for "receptacles coextensively bonded;" [56] references cited or prior art the PTO considered when examining the patent; and [57] abstract. Also, above the abstract are listed the names of the examiner and attorneys who prosecuted the patent application. A full copy of the pizza box patent is reproduced below, and the patent and its prosecution history can also be found on the casebook website at http://law.case.edu/lawofpatents. Please note that the patent claims only the box. As the prosecution history indicates, the process of making the box was originally claimed, but deleted during prosecution.

United States Patent [19]

Hall

[11]   **4,441,626**

[45]   **Apr. 10, 1984**

[54] **PIZZA BOX**

[75] Inventor: **Robert E. Hall**, Wheaton, Ill.

[73] Assignee: **Fidelity Grafcor, Inc.**, Elk Grove Village, Ill.

[21] Appl. No.: **330,674**

[22] Filed: **Dec. 14, 1981**

[51] Int. Cl.³ **B65D 81/24**; B65D 81/26
[52] U.S. Cl. .... **220/443**; 220/458; 229/2.5 R; 229/31; 229/33; 229/DIG. 14; 426/127
[58] Field of Search .... 220/441, 443, 418, 458; 229/2.5 R, 3.1, 33, 36, DIG. 14; 206/550, 545; 426/127, 124; 428/186

[56] **References Cited**

U.S. PATENT DOCUMENTS

1,184,749	5/1916	Hicks	428/186
1,449,409	3/1923	Hunt	220/443 X
1,865,742	7/1932	Chapman	229/2.5 R
1,945,397	1/1934	Gray	229/2.5 R
1,974,898	9/1934	Rutledge	229/2.5 R
2,164,025	6/1939	Schwertfeger	220/464 X
2,278,782	4/1942	Harvey et al.	220/411 X
2,434,466	1/1948	Marc	428/186 X
2,470,465	5/1949	Broeren et al.	426/127
2,497,203	2/1950	Bennett	426/127
2,782,977	2/1957	Thompson	220/441
3,067,921	12/1962	Reifers	229/2.5 R
3,145,904	8/1964	Bromley	220/76 X
3,291,367	12/1966	Carter	229/33
3,876,131	4/1975	Tolaas	206/491 X
4,058,214	11/1977	Mancuso	229/2.5 R X
4,237,171	12/1980	Laage et al.	229/33 X

Primary Examiner—Allan N. Shoap
Attorney, Agent, or Firm—Laff, Whitesel, Conte & Saret

[57]   **ABSTRACT**

A box is formed from a unitary, double-sided corrugated cardboard blank having a plurality of scored lines which enable a set up in box form. A bottom panel of the box has cemented thereto a single-sided, fluted corrugated cardboard medium with the fluted side facing upwardly. A moisture-resistant glue is used between the smooth faces of the fluted corrugated medium and the confronting liner of the blank to provide an impenetrable barrier which prevents grease from penetrating through the box. The boxes are manufactured on a conventional production line which is modified by, in effect, running one stage in a reverse direction in order to invert the single-sided medium and to apply the glue in a different manner to establish the moisture barrier.

9 Claims, 12 Drawing Figures

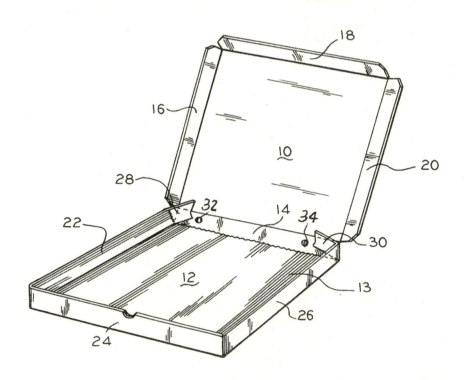

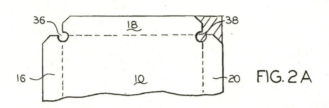

FIG. 2 A

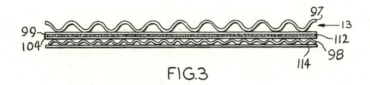

FIG.3

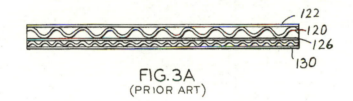

FIG.3A
(PRIOR ART)

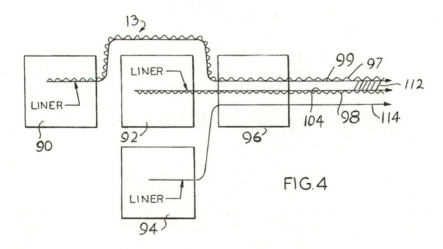

FIG.4

X

U.S. Patent   Apr. 10, 1984   Sheet 4 of 4   4,441,626

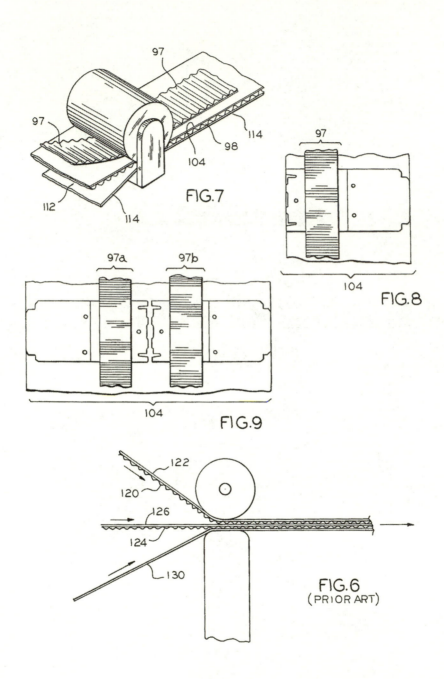

FIG.7

FIG.8

FIG.9

FIG.6
(PRIOR ART)

X

4,441,626

1

PIZZA BOX

This invention relates to boxes for packaging foods, and more particularly, to boxes for packaging and maintaining the temperature of foods such as pizza, in an optimal state, as during delivery, for example, and to methods for making the boxes.

Hereinafter, it will be convenient to refer to pizza boxes, by way of example. However, the invention is equally applicable to any of many similar foods, products, or the like, especially when it is desirable to keep the foods or products elevated above any liquid dripping off the foods or products. The box is designed to retain the temperature of either hot or cold food, or the like, over an extended period of time.

Conventional pizza boxes do not enable good air circulation or heat retention. They do not prevent a penetration of grease through the box. As a result, both the boxes and pizzas are often delivered in a soggy condition resulting in either damage to the pizzas or inconvenience to anyone or anything with which the boxes come in contact. Sometimes, the pizzas may be delivered inside large paper bags which can maintain the heat of the pizzas for only a few minutes. Usually, inserts in the form of corrugated cardboard discs must be added to the boxes or the bags. Thus, present day pizza boxes do not provide for delivery of pizzas in the same condition that they have when taken from the oven. These boxes require excessive set-up time for erecting boxes, installing inserts, etc.

Accordingly, an object of the invention is to provide new and improved packaging boxes, and particularly, food packaging boxes. More particularly, an object is to provide boxes which will enable grease or other liquids to drip or wick off pizzas, but not to penetrate through the boxes.

Here, an object is to provide boxes which help enable delivery of pizzas in a crisp, optimal state, without creating a greasy condition which may stain clothes, car seats, or the like.

Another object is to provide easy-to-assemble pizza boxes which set up with minimum effort, require no inserts, and enable a good air circulation and heat retention. Yet another object is to provide a method for assembling such pizza boxes.

In keeping with one aspect of this invention, a box is formed from a unitary, double-sided corrugated cardboard blank having a plurality of scored lines to enable a quick and easy folding of panels to set up the box form. The bottom panel of the box has a single-sided, fluted corrugated cardboard medium glued to the double-sided corrugated cardboard blank. The fluted side of the medium faces upwardly, out of the box. A moisture-resistant glue is used between the smooth faces of the fluted corrugated medium and the confronting liner of the blank to provide an impenetrable barrier which prevents grease from penetrating through the box. The boxes are manufactured on a conventional production line which is modified by, in effect, running one stage in a reverse direction in order to invert the single-sided medium and to apply the glue in a different manner to establish the moisture barrier.

The invention will be best understood by reference to the following description of an embodiment of the invention taken in conjunction with the accompanying drawings, in which:

2

FIG. 1 is a perspective view of the erected box, in an open position;

FIG. 2 is a plan view of a blank for the unerected box;

FIG. 2A is a view of the top panel of FIG. 2 which shows an alternative cutting of the box for ventilating the box without requiring holes made from loose parts;

FIG. 3 is a cross-section of the inventive box taken along line 3—3 of FIG. 2;

FIG. 3A is a cross-section of a conventional double-layer corrugated liner;

FIG. 4 is a block diagram of a production line for constructing the inventive box;

FIGS. 5 and 5A together show a diagrammatic view in side elevation of a corrugation cardboard production line for making the inventive box with a liner having upstanding flutes, such as that shown in FIG. 3;

FIG. 6 is a view of a work station in FIG. 5, showing a conventional method of making a double-layer corrugated liner, such as that shown in FIG. 3A;

FIG. 7 is a perspective view of the last work station in the production line of FIG. 5;

FIG. 8 is a plan view of the product of the production line, of FIG. 7, showing how the blank is cut for large boxes; and

FIG. 9 is a similar plan view showing how the blank is cut for smaller boxes.

As shown in FIG. 1, a pizza box constructed in accordance with the teachings of this invention comprises upper and lower members having a top panel 10, a bottom panel 12 and a central panel 14. The top panel 10 and the bottom panel 12 include side panels 16, 18, 20, 22, 24, 26 and various side flaps 28, 30, to complete the folding and assembly of the box.

If the pizza box described thus far is made of conventional corrugated cardboard, it is subject to two faults. First, bottom panel 12 does not prevent grease from penetrating through the box. Thus, a pizza which drips causes stains on clothes, auto seats, or anything else which may come into contact with the box. Second, the flat smooth surface of the bottom panel 12 does not provide for good air circulation and heat retention in the area under the pizza which leads to a soggy crust.

In keeping with one aspect of this invention, means are provided for preventing grease penetration and for enabling air circulation within the pizza box, and especially under the crust. In greater detail, a corrugated cardboard medium 13, with the upstanding flutes is glued to the bottom panel 12 with a moisture-resistant glue which forms an impenetrable layer or moisture barrier. The upstanding flutes are made of a material which wicks grease; thus grease not only drips, but also is positively wicked off the pizza and into the medium. However, that grease cannot penetrate through the layer of moisture resistant glue. The pizza and the box are kept in an optimal state. Air can also circulate around the pizza since it is held up and supported on the tops of the upstanding flutes of the corrugated medium, and out of any pool of grease or other liquid which may form in the bottom of the box.

According to the invention, means are also provided for venting the box either at holes 32, 34 in FIG. 2 or at several selvage enlargements which are cutout at 36, 38 when the blank is formed (FIG. 2A). Research has found that proper ventilation should be attained inside the box to keep the pizza hot and still retain good crust quality, when approximately one square inch of ventilation is provided for each cubic foot of volume, to acquire a proper balance between heat and steam. There-

4,441,626

3

fore, the size of the holes or cutouts is selected to enable just enough steam to escape to prevent the pizza from becoming soggy, but not so much that the pizza box will lose heat. Conveniently, the venting area may be controlled by selecting a correct number of holes so that one size punch will serve all box sizes.

FIG. 2 shows the basic, unitary blank for making the folded pizza box. The top panel **10** is defined by a plurality of scored lines **40, 42, 44, 46**. The bottom panel **12** is defined by scored lines **48, 50, 52, 54**. The bottom panel **12** has a medium **13** of single-faced corrugated cardboard glued to it with the exposed flutes facing upward as viewed in FIGS. 1, 2 and 3. In this embodiment, the top **10** and bottom **12** are joined by a central side panel **14** containing holes **32, 34** for venting steam without an undue loss of heat.

In FIG. 2, dashed lines are used to indicate where scoring forms fold lines and solid lines are used to indicate where blank cutting occurs. A semi-piercing rule die is used to form an alternating cut and score line at **46**, non-cutting rule dies form score lines elsewhere as indicated by dashed lines (e.g. line **42**), and cutting rule dies cut through the blank as indicated by solid lines, as at **56**, for example. The cutouts are formed at points **56–70** to make locking tabs and to reduce binding where the folding cardboard would otherwise form undue bulk, bind, or prevent smooth folds.

These score and cut lines divide the top panel **10** into matched side panels **16, 20** and an end panel **18**, and divide the bottom panel **12** into matched side panels **22, 26**, and a double end panel **24** divided by a scored line **72** into panels **74, 76**. Folding corner tabs or panels **78, 80** are formed on ends of the side panels **22, 26** at the front of the bottom panel **12** of the box. Corner tabs or panels **28, 30** are formed at the opposite ends of the side panels **22, 26** to hinge, fold inside, and support the sides and corners of the box. The corner tabs or panels **28, 30, 78, 80** enable and cause the side and end panels **14, 22, 26, 74, 76** to articulate and lock into a box configuration. A pair of locking tabs **82, 84** fit into cutouts at locations **56, 58** while tabs **78, 80** are captured between end panels **74, 76**, for locking the bottom panel **12** of the box into its fully-folded condition.

To fold and assemble the box, the side panels **22, 26** are first folded upwardly and out of the plane of the paper at lines **50, 54**, as viewed in FIG. 2. The corner panels **28, 30, 78, 80**, are folded inwardly toward the center of the box. Next, the double end panel **24** (divided into panels **74, 76**) is folded at line **52** upwardly out of the plane of the paper, and the panel **76** is then folded along two scored lines **72, 73** downwardly, over inturned corner panels **78, 80**, and into the box where locking tabs **82, 84** fit into the cutouts **56, 58**. Finally, side panels **16, 20** and end panel **18** are folded along lines **42, 44, 40** up out of the plane of the paper as shown in FIG. 2. The entire top panel **10** is then folded, at line **46**, upwardly, out of the plane of the paper as shown in FIG. 2. The side panels **16, 20** and end panel **18** tuck neatly into the bottom of the box. The circular hole punched at point **86** folds in half to provide a semi-circular cutout when panel **24** is folded along lines **72, 73** to provide a place where a person can place a thumb nail for an easy opening of the box.

FIG. 2A shows an alternative venting of the box wherein selvage cutouts **36, 38** replace holes **32, 34**. A possible problem with punched holes **32, 34** is that a cutout disc is formed which may not lift completely out of the remaining hole. If this should happen, someone

4

could eat the disc. Thus, the corner cutouts **36, 38** are desirable because each "disc" forming a hole is integral with a corner member (the selvage is cross-hatched in FIG. 2A) which may be removed as a unit so that there is no clean-out problem requiring a removal of the cut disc portions, such as might be required at **32, 34**. Thus, it is seen that, while present day machinery includes a certain amount of risk that the discs forming holes **32, 34** will not be cleaned out properly, the embodiment of FIG. 2A completely removes that risk. Therefore, none of the discs may fall into the box to be swallowed by a person who is eating the pizza.

The inventive production method of gluing the corrugated cardboard medium **13** is shown in the block diagram in FIG. 4. The back of corrugated cardboard medium **13** (with upstanding flutes) is cemented to and becomes integral with the bottom panel **12**, and with the fluted side of the cardboard medium **13** facing upwardly. More particularly, at a first work station **90**, an upper flute corrugated, single-face board is formed. At another work station **92**, a lower flute corrugated, double-face board is prepared. At work station **96** the smooth faces of the liners of the upper fluted single-face board and the lower fluted corrugated double-face boards are glued together with the use of a moisture resistant adhesive. The upper flutes are upstanding and a moisture resistant layer (shown by cross-hatching **112**) is formed inside the box. Work station **94** supplies a liner which is also added at work station **96** to complete the bottom of the double-faced corrugated board as shown in FIGS. 3 and 4.

The preferred embodiment (FIG. 3) uses "B" and "E" flutes for the upper and lower flutes **97, 98**, respectively. By industry standards, a "B" flute is relatively large, perhaps one-eighth inch in height, while an "E" flute is relatively small, about one-sixteenth inch in height. However, these particular dimensions are not critical and other flute sizes could be used.

A more detailed view of the production line of FIG. 4, for making the inventive box, is shown in FIG. 5 (with FIG. 5A placed to the right of and joining FIG. 5).

At work station **90**, a bleached white medium is corrugated into upper (preferably "B" size) flutes **97**. The bleached medium **97**, which comes into direct contact with the pizza is sanitary, and has a clean, fresh look (as compared to conventional brown Kraft paper). The medium **97** is then glued to a liner **99** pulled from a roll **100** of heavy Kraft paper. The bleached white flutes **97** are preferably adhered to liner **99** by a regular water resistant starch adhesive, altered by the addition of Ketones. The Ketones create an adequate moisture resistance to prevent delamination of the flute tips from the liner when the steam and grease from the pizza come into contact with them.

More particularly, the adhesive is added by glue applicator roll **102**. Since, the corn starch adhesive is not moisture-proof, pizza grease is able to both wick through the corrugated medium and drip into the bottom of the flutes. The flutes **97** should be large enough, for any food resting thereon, to be above any pool of grease or juices collected in the bottoms of the flutes.

At work station **92**, an unbleached Kraft paper medium is corrugated to form lower (preferably "E" size) flutes **98**. The "E"-fluted medium **98** is then glued to a heavy Kraft paper liner **104** from spool **106** with a conventional corn starch glue. The glue is added by glue applicator roll **108**. It should be noted that upper flutes

4,441,626

5

97 face upwardly while lower flutes **98** face downwardly so that the smooth liners **104, 99** form first and second substantially flat surfaces which come into face to face contact. The upper fluts **97** comprises a plurality of upwardly directed riges defining therebetween open 5 channels which are upwardly directed to convey heat and steam from under the pizza and toward vents **32, 34** or **36, 38**. The flat surface **104** is the upper surface of any suitable support layer, here elements **114, 98, 112**, by way of example. 10

The two, single-faced corrugated cardboards, thus formed at work stations **90, 92**, are transported in a more or less spaced parallel relationship to another work station **96** where the smooth faces **99, 104** of the liner are laminated together, with a moisture-resistant 15 glue **112** from gluer **110** which forms the moisuter barrier. The glue preferably used to bond the two liners **99, 104** to each other is a P.V.A. type adhesive **112** which creates a grease and moisture barrier. The P.V.A. adhesive conforms with the composition requirements of the 20 FDA Food Additives Regulation 175.105 for food packaging adhesives. A bottom liner **114** pulled from spool **94** is then glued to the lower fluted edge of medium **98** with a conventional corn starch glue, to complete the lower surface of the inventive material. 25

A station from a conventional production line for a double corrugation board is shown in FIG. 6, and the end product of this conventional production line is seen in FIG. 3A. A corrugated medium **120** is glued to a liner **122**, with the flutes facing downwardly. Another corru- 30 gated medium **124** is glued to the heavy Kraft center paper liner **126** with its flutes also facing downwardly. Then, the fluted medium **120**, with attached liner **122** is glued to the top of center paper liner **126** and a lower liner **130** is glued to the bottom of the double board. The 35 single sheet **126** is not covered with any moisture barrier and there is no space for an insertion of the barrier.

Compare FIGS. 3 and 3A, where the two liners **99, 104** are in a face to face relationship with the inventive moisture barrier **112** formed between them. There is no 40 way of placing the moisture barrier between two face-to-face liners in the layer **126**, by the conventional production methods since flutes **120** conventionally point downwardly and there is only one liner in the center. The inventive flutes **97** point upwardly and there are 45 two liners **99, 104** in the middle.

The inventive method achieves this result by, in effect, running work station **90** in a "backward" direction so that the medium **97** and liner **99** are manufactured in an upside down orientation. More particularly, there is 50 no need to physically turn the corrugating machine around in order to run it in a "backward" direction. These corrugation machines may conventionally be given either a "left-hand" or a "right-hand" drive, depending upon the layout of a production line. The "up- 55 side down" layer **97, 99** may be made by, in effect, using a "left-handed" drive on a "right-handed" production line, or vice versa. Hence, an advantage of the invention is that a conventional corrugation production line may be re-set in an unconventional manner to produce the 60 inventive box without requiring anything more than set-up time.

FIGS. 7-9 show how the insert layer of upwardly pointing flutes are formed in only the bottom of the box. In greater detail, (as best seen in FIGS. 7 and 8) the 65 E-fluted medium **98** which makes the double-faced corrugated cardboard **104, 114** has a full width, corresponding to the length of the blank of FIG. 2. The insert

6

of upwardly pointing flutes **97** has a restricted width, corresponding to the width of the bottom **12**.

Thus, the die for cutting the blank of FIG. 2 is positioned across the width of the product, as best seen in FIG. 8. Those portions of the blank which form the top **10** and the double end flap **24** are punched from the conventional double-sided corrugated cardboard **104**. The insert material having upwardly pointing flutes **97** are located in only the bottom area **12**. Thus, when the blank is cut, as shown in FIG. **8**, the insert automatically appears at the desired location, without requiring any extra labor.

The widths of the panel **104** and insert **97** may be made wider or more narrow to accommodate different box sizes. However, the boxes may become so small that it is no longer economically feasible to operate the production line. When this happens, two inserts **97a, 97b** are cemented onto the conventional cardboard **104**, as best seen in FIG. 9. Thus, two blanks are cut, end to end, or nested in a material saving manner. Likewise, any suitable number of insert stripes and of smaller boxes may be cut across the width of the cardboard, in a similar manner.

The many advantages of this pizza box should now be self-apparent. First, the exposed upstanding upper flutes enable grease to wick and flow off the pizza and into the lower areas of the box. The pizza is held at an elevation above the grease to keep it from becoming soggy. The upstanding corrugation also enables heat retention within the box while maintaining good air circulation around and under the pizza. Second, the moisture-resistant PVA adhesive, used to laminate the upper and lower single faced cardboards together, traps and prevents the pizza grease from penetrating through the box. Third, the size of the holes **32, 34** or cutouts **36, 38** enables controlled amounts of steam to escape, which might otherwise cause the pizza crust to lose crispness, and yet the holes or cutouts are small enough to retain the heat of the pizza. Of course, there are still other advantages which will be apparent to those skilled in the art.

While the principles of the invention have been described above in connection with specific apparatus and applications, it is to be understood that this description is made only by way of example and not as a limitation on the scope of the invention, and the claims are intended to cover all equivalents.

I claim:

1. A box comprising upper and lower members which close or open relative to each other to form a covered box, a bottom of said box being formed by said lower member and comprising three laminated layers, a first and outside one of said three laminated layers forming a supporting layer having a first and substantially flat surface on its interior side, a second and intermediate one of said three laminated layers extending over at least a substantial portion of said first flat interior surface, said second layer comprising barrier layer means resistant to at least moisture and being spread across said first flat interior surface, a third and inside one of said three layers having a second and substantially flat surface on its lower side with a plurality of spaced parallel flutes upstanding on its upper side, said first and second flat surfaces being bonded together in a face to face relationship with said barrier layer means interposed therebetween, said flutes comprising a plurality of upwardly directed ridges defining therebetween upwardly directed open channels, said ridges forming

4,441,626

7

means for supporting an article above the bottoms of said channels, and venting means formed in said box and located in a side wall of said box at the ends of said channels, the dimensions of said box being such that heat from an article resting on said flutes escapes through said ventilation means via said channels.

2. The box of claim 1 wherein said barrier layer means is an adhesive.

3. The box of either of the claims 1 or 2 wherein said flutes are made of a corrugated cardboard medium having a liner cemented to its lower tips and said barrier layer means is a water and grease resistant glue spread between the liner and the bottom of said lower member.

4. The box of claim 3 wherein said box is made from a unitary blank of double sided corrugated cardboard.

8

5. The box of either of the claims 1 or 2 wherein said flutes are bleached paper and said barrier layer means is a P.V.A. adhesive.

6. The box of any either the claims 1 or 2 wherein said flutes are made of paper which wicks moisture and grease and said barrier means is a P.V.A. adhesive.

7. The box of claim 1 wherein said venting means is in the order of substantially one square inch for each cubic foot enclosed within said box.

8. The box of claim 1 wherein said venting means is formed by holes in said box.

9. The box of claim 1 wherein said venting means is integrally formed by an enlargement in selvage which is cut from said box during the formation of a blank from which said box is erected.

* * * * *

X

CHAPTER

2

Claiming and Disclosing the Invention

INTRODUCTION

The disclosure requirements of section 112 are at the heart of patent law's goal of promoting the progress of the useful arts. Thus, it is here where we begin our substantive discussion of patent law. By requiring the patent applicant to claim the invention with clarity and to sufficiently disclose his invention to persons having ordinary skill in the art, patent law seeks to facilitate the dissemination of technical information and follow-on innovation.

This chapter is concerned with the patent claim and the patent specification as well as the relationship between these two parts of the patent document.[1] The claim and specification serve related, yet distinct functions. As the Federal Circuit noted, "while the role of the claims is to give public notice of the subject matter that is protected, the role of the specification is to teach, both what the invention is and how to make and use it."[2] Although this quote is informative, it understates the complexity of the relationship, and only hints at the profound centrality of the claim in American patent law.

Patent law is a property rights regime, and a patentee's property rights are set forth in the patent claims.[3] Claims are comprised of words, and these words must be given meaning (or interpreted). Accordingly, claim interpretation is relevant to both patent validity and infringement, and is thus a fundamental component of not only patent litigation, but also private transactions conducted either in the shadow of litigation such as licensing activity or outside the litigation context, namely due diligence investigations that typically accompany

---

1. You may find it helpful to revisit the claims and specification in the "Pizza Box" patent in Chapter 1. A PDF of the patent can also be found at the casebook website: http://law.case.edu/lawofpatents.

2. *University of Rochester v. G.D. Searle & Co., Inc.*, 358 F.3d 916, 922 n.5 (Fed. Cir. 2004). This function was quite different for most patent regimes prior to the nineteenth century. During this period, a description and actual model of the invention were viewed as evidence of "local utility," meaning that the invention actually worked and could be put into practice. As Mario Biagioli writes, patent granting authorities

> wanted to maximize local utility, not to disclose knowledge about the invention. (In the absence of international patent agreements, public disclosure of an invention could facilitate easy and undesirable transfer to nearby countries.) What mattered was that inventions worked, not how they worked.

Mario Biagioli, *Patent Specification and Political Representations*, in MAKING AND UNMAKING INTELLECTUAL PROPERTY 28 (Woodmansee et al. eds., 2011).

3. *See Phillips v. AWH Corp.*, 415 F.3d 1303, 1312 (Fed. Cir. 2005) (*en banc*) (stating "[i]t is a bedrock principle of patent law that the claims of a patent define the invention to which the patentee is entitled the right to exclude").

patent acquisitions. Relatedly, knowing the boundaries of the patentee's property rights helps competitors navigate follow-on improvement or design-around activity and decide with greater confidence whether a license is needed or whether they are free to operate.[4] As such, it is important that the rules of claim interpretation are clear and have a predictive quality.[5]

The most fundamental issue for *claim interpretation*, which is covered in section A, relates to what interpretive methodologies and evidentiary sources (and attendant weight of each source) are available to provide meaning to the claim language in question. (Another claim interpretation issue pertains to *who* interprets claim language—judge or jury—in the context of a patent infringement suit; we reserve this issue for Chapter 7.) Sections B and C of this chapter are devoted to the *enablement* and *written description* requirements, respectively. These requirements play an important role in fostering patent law's disseminative function and in determining *claim scope*, which is largely a policy decision that focuses on the extent of the patentee's property right. Thereafter, section D discusses the *definiteness* requirement, which demands the patentee draft clear and distinct claims to provide notice to competitors (and to the public generally) of the boundaries of the patentee's property rights and to distinguish the claimed invention from the prior art. And section E explores the *best mode* requirement. As the name suggests, this requirement obligates the patentee to disclose the best way of practicing the claimed invention during the examination of the patent application, but for actions commenced on or after September 16, 2011, failure to disclose the best mode cannot be used as a basis for challenging the validity of a patent.[6]

A. CLAIM INTERPRETATION

It would be difficult to overstate the importance of the patent claim. Patent claims are the touchstone of patent protection, what is often referred to as the

---

4. *See Festo Corp. v. Shoketsu Kinzoku Kogyo Kabushiki Co.*, 535 U.S. 722, 732 (2002) (stating "[i]f competitors cannot be certain about a patent's extent, they may be deterred from engaging in legitimate manufactures outside its limits, or they may invest by mistake in competing products that the patent secures").

5. *See* John M. Golden, *Construing Patent Claims According to Their "Interpretive Community": A Call for an Attorney-Plus-Artisan Perspective*, 21 HARV. J.L. & TECH. 321, 323 (2008) (asserting certainty in patent rights may "facilitate licensing that promotes efficient levels of inventive and productive activity"); Joseph Scott Miller, *Enhancing Patent Disclosure for Faithful Claim Construction*, 9 LEWIS & CLARK L. REV. 177, 196 (2005) (stating "it is well-accepted that clearer property boundaries promote efficiency by lowering transaction costs associated with bargaining over rights").

6. Removing the failure to comply with the best mode requirement as a basis for a validity challenge was part of the America Invents Act and went into effect for proceedings commenced on or after September 16, 2011. The requirement to disclose the best mode during examination was unchanged by the AIA. This compromise position sought to maintain, on the one hand, the quid pro quo between the inventor and society by still requiring the inventor to disclose the best mode and, on the other hand, the perceived need to curtail best mode civil challenges (and associated litigation costs) that require the very difficult task of discerning inventor intent. *For a discussion of these changes from someone who was closely involved with the America Invents Act, see A. Christal Shepard, Because Inquiring Minds Want to Know—Best Mode—Why Is It One-Sided?*, available at http://www.patentlyo.com/patent/2011/09/guest-post-because-inquiring-minds-want-to-know-best-mode-why-is-it-one-sided-.html.

"metes and bounds" of the patentee's protected interest. Indeed, in the context of litigation, once claims are interpreted, issues of validity and infringement are largely foregone conclusions,[7] or at least have crystallized to the point where the path toward resolution is more apparent.

What interpretive tools are or should be available when interpreting claim language is one of the more important and controversial questions in patent law. In developing this area of the law, the Federal Circuit has signaled a receptiveness to both "intrinsic evidence" (e.g., the claim, specification, and prosecution history) and certain forms of "extrinsic evidence" (e.g., dictionaries and technical treatises, and much less so, expert testimony). While there is an unmistakable preference for intrinsic evidence, questions remain regarding the relationship between intrinsic and extrinsic evidence, when it is proper to engage extrinsic evidence, and what distinctions, if any, exist among its various forms. The *en banc* case of *Phillips v. AWH* addresses the relationship between intrinsic and extrinsic evidence, and sets out an interpretive road map with an emphasis on context. Whether the court offered sufficient navigational guidance is an open question.

In addition to the intrinsic/extrinsic divide, there is a hierarchy within intrinsic evidence itself, with one school of interpretation placing a great deal of emphasis on the claim and the notice function of patent law. Another interpretive school, while not denying the importance of the claim, is more willing to consider all three forms of intrinsic evidence to discern claim meaning. The majority and dissent in the classic *Unique Concepts* case explore these two schools of thought.

PHILLIPS v. AWH CORP.

415 F.3d 1303 (Fed. Cir. 2005) (*en banc*)

BRYSON, Circuit Judge.

Edward H. Phillips invented modular, steel-shell panels that can be welded together to form vandalism-resistant walls. The panels are especially useful in building prisons because they are load-bearing and impact-resistant, while also insulating against fire and noise. Mr. Phillips obtained a patent on the invention, U.S. Patent No. 4,677,798 ("the '798 patent"), and he subsequently entered into an arrangement with AWH Corporation, Hopeman Brothers, Inc., and Lofton Corporation (collectively "AWH") to market and sell the panels. That arrangement ended in 1990. In 1991, however, Mr. Phillips received a sales brochure from AWH that suggested to him that AWH was continuing to use his trade secrets and patented technology without his consent. In a series of letters in 1991 and 1992, Mr. Phillips accused AWH of patent infringement. Correspondence between the parties regarding the matter ceased after that time.

In February 1997, Mr. Phillips brought suit in the United States District Court for the District of Colorado charging AWH with infringement of claims 1, 21, 22, 24, 25, and 26 of the '798 patent. The district court focused on the language of

---

7. *See, e.g., Markman v. Westview Instruments, Inc.*, 52 F.3d 967, 989 (Fed. Cir. 1995) (Mayer, J., concurring) (stating "to decide what the claims mean is nearly always to decide the case"). *See also* Mark A. Lemley, *The Changing Meaning of Patent Claim Terms*, 104 MICH. L. REV. 101, 102 (2005) (noting "once the court construes the claims, most patent cases settle, and those that do not are often decided on summary judgment").

claim 1, which recites "further means disposed inside the shell for increasing its load bearing capacity comprising internal steel baffles extending inwardly from the steel shell walls." The court interpreted that language as "a means . . . for performing a specified function," subject to 35 U.S.C. § 112, paragraph 6, which provides that such a claim "shall be construed to cover the corresponding structure, material, or acts described in the specification and equivalents thereof." Looking to the specification of the '798 patent, the court noted that "every textual reference in the Specification and its diagrams show baffle deployment at an angle other than 90 to the wall faces" and that "placement of the baffles at such angles creates an intermediate interlocking, but not solid, internal barrier." The district court therefore ruled that, for purposes of the '798 patent, a baffle must "extend inward from the steel shell walls at an oblique or acute angle to the wall face" and must form part of an interlocking barrier in the interior of the wall module. Because Mr. Phillips could not prove infringement under that claim construction, the district court granted summary judgment of noninfringement.

A panel of this court affirmed on both issues. As to the patent infringement claims, the panel was divided. The majority sustained the district court's summary judgment of noninfringement, although on different grounds. The dissenting judge would have reversed the summary judgment of noninfringement.

* * *

This court agreed to rehear the appeal *en banc* and vacated the judgment of the panel. [W]e reverse the portion of the court's judgment addressed to the issue of infringement.

I

Claim 1 of the '798 patent is representative of the asserted claims with respect to the use of the term "baffles." It recites:

> Building modules adapted to fit together for construction of fire, sound and impact resistant security barriers and rooms for use in securing records and persons, comprising in combination, an outer shell . . . , sealant means . . . and further means disposed inside the shell for increasing its load bearing capacity comprising internal steel baffles extending inwardly from the steel shell walls.

* * *

II

The first paragraph of section 112 of the Patent Act, 35 U.S.C. § 112, states that the specification

> shall contain a written description of the invention, and of the manner and process of making and using it, in such full, clear, concise, and exact terms as to enable any person skilled in the art to which it pertains . . . to make and use the same. . . .

The second paragraph of section 112 provides that the specification

> shall conclude with one or more claims particularly pointing out and distinctly claiming the subject matter which the applicant regards as his invention.

Those two paragraphs of section 112 frame the issue of claim interpretation for us. The second paragraph requires us to look to the language of the claims to determine what "the applicant regards as his invention." On the other hand, the first paragraph requires that the specification describe the invention set forth in the claims. The principal question that this case presents to us is the extent to which we should resort to and rely on a patent's specification in seeking to ascertain the proper scope of its claims.

This is hardly a new question. The role of the specification in claim construction has been an issue in patent law decisions in this country for nearly two centuries. We addressed the relationship between the specification and the claims at some length in our *en banc* opinion in *Markman v. Westview Instruments, Inc.* We again summarized the applicable principles in *Vitronics Corp. v. Conceptronic, Inc.*, and more recently in *Innova/Pure Water, Inc. v. Safari Water Filtration Systems, Inc.* What we said in those cases bears restating, for the basic principles of claim construction outlined there are still applicable, and we reaffirm them today. We have also previously considered the use of dictionaries in claim construction. What we have said in that regard requires clarification.

A

It is a "bedrock principle" of patent law that "the claims of a patent define the invention to which the patentee is entitled the right to exclude." *Innova*, 381 F.3d at 1115. That principle has been recognized since at least 1836, when Congress first required that the specification include a portion in which the inventor "shall particularly specify and point out the part, improvement, or combination, which he claims as his own invention or discovery." Act of July 4, 1836. In the following years, the Supreme Court made clear that the claims are "of primary importance, in the effort to ascertain precisely what it is that is patented." *Merrill v. Yeomans*, 94 U.S. 568, 570 (1876). Because the patentee is required to "define precisely what his invention is," the Court explained, it is "unjust to the public, as well as an evasion of the law, to construe it in a manner different from the plain import of its terms." *White v. Dunbar*, 119 U.S. 47, 52 (1886).

We have frequently stated that the words of a claim "are generally given their ordinary and customary meaning." *Vitronics*, 90 F.3d at 1582. We have made clear, moreover, that the ordinary and customary meaning of a claim term is the meaning that the term would have to a person of ordinary skill in the art in question at the time of the invention, *i.e.*, as of the effective filing date of the patent application. The inquiry into how a person of ordinary skill in the art understands a claim term provides an objective baseline from which to begin claim interpretation. That starting point is based on the well-settled understanding that inventors are typically persons skilled in the field of the invention and that patents are addressed to and intended to be read by others of skill in the pertinent art.

Importantly, the person of ordinary skill in the art is deemed to read the claim term not only in the context of the particular claim in which the disputed term appears, but in the context of the entire patent, including the specification. This court explained that point well in *Multiform Desiccants, Inc. v. Medzam, Ltd.*, 133 F.3d 1473, 1477 (Fed. Cir. 1998):

> It is the person of ordinary skill in the field of the invention through whose eyes the claims are construed. Such person is deemed to read the words used in the patent documents with an understanding of their meaning in the field, and to have knowledge of any special meaning and usage in the field. The inventor's words

that are used to describe the invention—the inventor's lexicography—must be understood and interpreted by the court as they would be understood and interpreted by a person in that field of technology. Thus the court starts the decision making process by reviewing the same resources as would that person, *viz.*, the patent specification and the prosecution history.

B

In some cases, the ordinary meaning of claim language as understood by a person of skill in the art may be readily apparent even to lay judges, and claim construction in such cases involves little more than the application of the widely accepted meaning of commonly understood words. In such circumstances, general purpose dictionaries may be helpful. In many cases that give rise to litigation, however, determining the ordinary and customary meaning of the claim requires examination of terms that have a particular meaning in a field of art. Because the meaning of a claim term as understood by persons of skill in the art is often not immediately apparent, and because patentees frequently use terms idiosyncratically, the court looks to "those sources available to the public that show what a person of skill in the art would have understood disputed claim language to mean." *Innova*, 381 F.3d at 1116. Those sources include "the words of the claims themselves, the remainder of the specification, the prosecution history, and extrinsic evidence concerning relevant scientific principles, the meaning of technical terms, and the state of the art." *Id.*

1

Quite apart from the written description and the prosecution history, the claims themselves provide substantial guidance as to the meaning of particular claim terms. To begin with, the context in which a term is used in the asserted claim can be highly instructive. To take a simple example, the claim in this case refers to "steel baffles," which strongly implies that the term "baffles" does not inherently mean objects made of steel.

Other claims of the patent in question, both asserted and unasserted, can also be valuable sources of enlightenment as to the meaning of a claim term. Because claim terms are normally used consistently throughout the patent, the usage of a term in one claim can often illuminate the meaning of the same term in other claims. Differences among claims can also be a useful guide in understanding the meaning of particular claim terms. For example, the presence of a dependent claim that adds a particular limitation gives rise to a presumption that the limitation in question is not present in the independent claim.

2

The claims, of course, do not stand alone. Rather, they are part of "a fully integrated written instrument," *Markman*, 52 F.3d at 978, consisting principally of a specification that concludes with the claims. For that reason, claims "must be read in view of the specification, of which they are a part." *Id.* at 979. As we stated in *Vitronics*, the specification "is always highly relevant to the claim construction analysis. Usually, it is dispositive; it is the single best guide to the meaning of a disputed term." 90 F.3d at 1582.

This court and its predecessors have long emphasized the importance of the specification in claim construction. In *Autogiro Co. of America v. United States*, 384 F.2d 391, 397-98 (Ct. Cl. 1967), the Court of Claims characterized the

specification as "a concordance for the claims," based on the statutory requirement that the specification "describe the manner and process of making and
using" the patented invention. The Court of Customs and Patent Appeals made
a similar point.

Shortly after the creation of this court, Judge Rich wrote that "[t]he descriptive part of the specification aids in ascertaining the scope and meaning of the
claims inasmuch as the words of the claims must be based on the description.
The specification is, thus, the primary basis for construing the claims." *Standard
Oil Co. v. Am. Cyanamid Co.*, 774 F.2d 448, 452 (Fed. Cir. 1985).

The importance of the specification in claim construction derives from its
statutory role. The close kinship between the written description and the claims
is enforced by the statutory requirement that the specification describe the
claimed invention in "full, clear, concise, and exact terms." 35 U.S.C. § 112, para.
1. In light of the statutory directive that the inventor provide a "full" and "exact"
description of the claimed invention, the specification necessarily informs the
proper construction of the claims. In *Renishaw*, this court summarized that point
succinctly:

> Ultimately, the interpretation to be given a term can only be determined and
> confirmed with a full understanding of what the inventors actually invented and
> intended to envelop with the claim. The construction that stays true to the claim
> language and most naturally aligns with the patent's description of the invention
> will be, in the end, the correct construction.

158 F.3d at 1250.

Consistent with that general principle, our cases recognize that the specification may reveal a special definition given to a claim term by the patentee that
differs from the meaning it would otherwise possess. In such cases, the inventor's lexicography governs. In other cases, the specification may reveal an intentional disclaimer, or disavowal, of claim scope by the inventor. In that instance
as well, the inventor has dictated the correct claim scope, and the inventor's
intention, as expressed in the specification, is regarded as dispositive.

The pertinence of the specification to claim construction is reinforced by the
manner in which a patent is issued. The Patent and Trademark Office ("PTO")
determines the scope of claims in patent applications not solely on the basis of
the claim language, but upon giving claims their broadest reasonable construction "in light of the specification as it would be interpreted by one of ordinary
skill in the art." *In re Am. Acad. of Sci. Tech. Ctr.*, 367 F.3d 1359, 1364 (Fed. Cir.
2004). Indeed, the rules of the PTO require that application claims must "conform to the invention as set forth in the remainder of the specification and the
terms and phrases used in the claims must find clear support or antecedent
basis in the description so that the meaning of the terms in the claims may be
ascertainable by reference to the description." 37 C.F.R. § 1.75(d)(1). It is therefore entirely appropriate for a court, when conducting claim construction, to
rely heavily on the written description for guidance as to the meaning of the
claims.

3

In addition to consulting the specification, we have held that a court "should
also consider the patent's prosecution history, if it is in evidence." *Markman*, 52
F.3d at 980. The prosecution history, which we have designated as part of the

"intrinsic evidence," consists of the complete record of the proceedings before the PTO and includes the prior art cited during the examination of the patent. Like the specification, the prosecution history provides evidence of how the PTO and the inventor understood the patent. Furthermore, like the specification, the prosecution history was created by the patentee in attempting to explain and obtain the patent. Yet because the prosecution history represents an ongoing negotiation between the PTO and the applicant, rather than the final product of that negotiation, it often lacks the clarity of the specification and thus is less useful for claim construction purposes. Nonetheless, the prosecution history can often inform the meaning of the claim language by demonstrating how the inventor understood the invention and whether the inventor limited the invention in the course of prosecution, making the claim scope narrower than it would otherwise be.

C

Although we have emphasized the importance of intrinsic evidence in claim construction, we have also authorized district courts to rely on extrinsic evidence, which "consists of all evidence external to the patent and prosecution history, including expert and inventor testimony, dictionaries, and learned treatises." *Markman,* 52 F.3d at 980, *citing Seymour v. Osborne,* 78 U.S. (11 Wall.) 516, 546 (1870). However, while extrinsic evidence "can shed useful light on the relevant art," we have explained that it is "less significant than the intrinsic record in determining 'the legally operative meaning of claim language.'" *C.R. Bard, Inc. v. U.S. Surgical Corp.,* 388 F.3d 858, 862 (Fed. Cir. 2004).

Within the class of extrinsic evidence, the court has observed that dictionaries and treatises can be useful in claim construction. We have especially noted the help that technical dictionaries may provide to a court "to better understand the underlying technology" and the way in which one of skill in the art might use the claim terms. Because dictionaries, and especially technical dictionaries, endeavor to collect the accepted meanings of terms used in various fields of science and technology, those resources have been properly recognized as among the many tools that can assist the court in determining the meaning of particular terminology to those of skill in the art of the invention. Such evidence, we have held, may be considered if the court deems it helpful in determining "the true meaning of language used in the patent claims." *Markman,* 52 F.3d at 980.

We have also held that extrinsic evidence in the form of expert testimony can be useful to a court for a variety of purposes, such as to provide background on the technology at issue, to explain how an invention works, to ensure that the court's understanding of the technical aspects of the patent is consistent with that of a person of skill in the art, or to establish that a particular term in the patent or the prior art has a particular meaning in the pertinent field. *See Key Pharms. v. Hercon Labs. Corp.,* 161 F.3d 709, 716 (Fed. Cir. 1998). However, conclusory, unsupported assertions by experts as to the definition of a claim term are not useful to a court. Similarly, a court should discount any expert testimony "that is clearly at odds with the claim construction mandated by the claims themselves, the written description, and the prosecution history, in other words, with the written record of the patent." *Key Pharms.,* 161 F.3d at 716.

We have viewed extrinsic evidence in general as less reliable than the patent and its prosecution history in determining how to read claim terms, for several reasons. First, extrinsic evidence by definition is not part of the patent and does not have the specification's virtue of being created at the time of patent pros-ecution for the purpose of explaining the patent's scope and meaning. Second, while claims are construed as they would be understood by a hypothetical per-son of skill in the art, extrinsic publications may not be written by or for skilled artisans and therefore may not reflect the understanding of a skilled artisan in the field of the patent. Third, extrinsic evidence consisting of expert reports and testimony is generated at the time of and for the purpose of litigation and thus can suffer from bias that is not present in intrinsic evidence. The effect of that bias can be exacerbated if the expert is not one of skill in the relevant art or if the expert's opinion is offered in a form that is not subject to cross-exam-ination. Fourth, there is a virtually unbounded universe of potential extrinsic evidence of some marginal relevance that could be brought to bear on any claim construction question. In the course of litigation, each party will naturally choose the pieces of extrinsic evidence most favorable to its cause, leaving the court with the considerable task of filtering the useful extrinsic evidence from the fluff. Finally, undue reliance on extrinsic evidence poses the risk that it will be used to change the meaning of claims in derogation of the "indisputable public records consisting of the claims, the specification and the prosecution history," thereby undermining the public notice function of patents. *Southwall Techs.*, 54 F.3d at 1578.

In sum, extrinsic evidence may be useful to the court, but it is unlikely to result in a reliable interpretation of patent claim scope unless considered in the context of the intrinsic evidence. Nonetheless, because extrinsic evidence can help educate the court regarding the field of the invention and can help the court determine what a person of ordinary skill in the art would under-stand claim terms to mean, it is permissible for the district court in its sound discretion to admit and use such evidence. In exercising that discretion, and in weighing all the evidence bearing on claim construction, the court should keep in mind the flaws inherent in each type of evidence and assess that evidence accordingly.

III

Although the principles outlined above have been articulated on numer-ous occasions, some of this court's cases have suggested a somewhat different approach to claim construction, in which the court has given greater emphasis to dictionary definitions of claim terms and has assigned a less prominent role to the specification and the prosecution history. The leading case in this line is *Texas Digital Systems, Inc. v. Telegenix, Inc.*, 308 F.3d 1193 (Fed. Cir. 2002). . . . [*Texas Digital*] placed too much reliance on extrinsic sources such as dictionar-ies, treatises, and encyclopedias and too little on intrinsic sources, in particular the specification and prosecution history. While the court noted that the speci-fication must be consulted in every case, it suggested a methodology for claim interpretation in which the specification should be consulted only after a deter-mination is made, whether based on a dictionary, treatise, or other source, as to the ordinary meaning or meanings of the claim term in dispute. Even then, recourse to the specification is limited to determining whether the specification excludes one of the meanings derived from the dictionary, whether the presump-tion in favor of the dictionary definition of the claim term has been overcome by "an explicit definition of the term different from its ordinary meaning," or whether the inventor "has disavowed or disclaimed scope of coverage, by using words or expressions of manifest exclusion or restriction, representing a clear disavowal of claim scope." 308 F.3d at 1204. In effect, the *Texas Digital* approach limits the role of the specification in claim construction to serving as a check on the dictionary meaning of a claim term if the specification requires the court to conclude that fewer than all the dictionary definitions apply, or if the specification contains a sufficiently specific alternative definition or disavowal. *See, e.g., Texas Digital,* 308 F.3d at 1202 ("unless compelled otherwise, a court will give a claim term the full range of its ordinary meaning"). That approach, in our view, improperly restricts the role of the specification in claim construction.

Assigning such a limited role to the specification, and in particular requiring that any definition of claim language in the specification be express, is inconsistent with our rulings that the specification is "the single best guide to the meaning of a disputed term," and that the specification "acts as a dictionary when it expressly defines terms used in the claims or when it defines terms by implication." *Vitronics,* 90 F.3d at 1582.

The main problem with elevating the dictionary to such prominence is that it focuses the inquiry on the abstract meaning of words rather than on the meaning of claim terms within the context of the patent. Properly viewed, the "ordinary meaning" of a claim term is its meaning to the ordinary artisan after reading the entire patent. Yet heavy reliance on the dictionary divorced from the intrinsic evidence risks transforming the meaning of the claim term to the artisan into the meaning of the term in the abstract, out of its particular context, which is the specification. The patent system is based on the proposition that claims cover only the invented subject matter. As the Supreme Court has stated, "[i]t seems to us that nothing can be more just and fair, both to the patentee and the public, than that the former should understand, and correctly describe, just what he has invented, and for what he claims a patent." *Merrill v. Yeomans,* 94 U.S. at 573-74. The use of a dictionary definition can conflict with that directive because the patent applicant did not create the dictionary to describe the invention. Thus, there may be a disconnect between the patentee's responsibility to describe and claim his invention, and the dictionary editors' objective of aggregating all possible definitions for particular words. . . .

[W]e do not intend to preclude the appropriate use of dictionaries. Dictionaries or comparable sources are often useful to assist in understanding the commonly understood meaning of words and have been used both by our court and the Supreme Court in claim interpretation. A dictionary definition has the value of being an unbiased source "accessible to the public in advance of litigation." *Vitronics,* 90 F.3d at 1585. As we said in *Vitronics,* judges are free to consult dictionaries and technical treatises

> at any time in order to better understand the underlying technology and may also rely on dictionary definitions when construing claim terms, so long as the dictionary definition does not contradict any definition found in or ascertained by a reading of the patent documents.

Id. at 1584 n.6.

We also acknowledge that the purpose underlying the *Texas Digital* line of cases — to avoid the danger of reading limitations from the specification into the claim — is sound. Moreover, we recognize that the distinction between using the specification to interpret the meaning of a claim and importing limitations from the specification into the claim can be a difficult one to apply in practice.

However, the line between construing terms and importing limitations can be discerned with reasonable certainty and predictability if the court's focus remains on understanding how a person of ordinary skill in the art would understand the claim terms. For instance, although the specification often describes very specific embodiments of the invention, we have repeatedly warned against confining the claims to those embodiments. In particular, we have expressly rejected the contention that if a patent describes only a single embodiment, the claims of the patent must be construed as being limited to that embodiment. That is not just because section 112 of the Patent Act requires that the claims themselves set forth the limits of the patent grant, but also because persons of ordinary skill in the art rarely would confine their definitions of terms to the exact representations depicted in the embodiments.

To avoid importing limitations from the specification into the claims, it is important to keep in mind that the purposes of the specification are to teach and enable those of skill in the art to make and use the invention and to provide a best mode for doing so. One of the best ways to teach a person of ordinary skill in the art how to make and use the invention is to provide an example of how to practice the invention in a particular case. Much of the time, upon reading the specification in that context, it will become clear whether the patentee is setting out specific examples of the invention to accomplish those goals, or whether the patentee instead intends for the claims and the embodiments in the specification to be strictly coextensive. The manner in which the patentee uses a term within the specification and claims usually will make the distinction apparent.

In the end, there will still remain some cases in which it will be hard to determine whether a person of skill in the art would understand the embodiments to define the outer limits of the claim term or merely to be exemplary in nature. While that task may present difficulties in some cases, we nonetheless believe that attempting to resolve that problem in the context of the particular patent is likely to capture the scope of the actual invention more accurately than either strictly limiting the scope of the claims to the embodiments disclosed in the specification or divorcing the claim language from the specification.

In *Vitronics*, this court grappled with the same problem and set forth guidelines for reaching the correct claim construction and not imposing improper limitations on claims. The underlying goal of our decision in *Vitronics* was to increase the likelihood that a court will comprehend how a person of ordinary skill in the art would understand the claim terms. In that process, we recognized that there is no magic formula or catechism for conducting claim construction. Nor is the court barred from considering any particular sources or required to analyze sources in any specific sequence, as long as those sources are not used to contradict claim meaning that is unambiguous in light of the intrinsic evidence. For example, a judge who encounters a claim term while reading a patent might consult a general purpose or specialized dictionary to begin to understand the meaning of the term, before reviewing the remainder of the patent to determine how the patentee has used the term. The sequence of steps used by the judge in consulting various sources is not important; what matters is for the court to attach the appropriate weight to be assigned to those sources in light of the statutes and policies that inform patent law. In *Vitronics*, we did not attempt to provide a rigid algorithm for claim construction, but simply attempted to explain why, in general, certain types of evidence are more valuable than others. Today, we adhere to that approach and reaffirm the approach to claim construction outlined in that case, in *Markman,* and in *Innova.* We now turn to the application of those principles to the case at bar.

IV

A

The critical language of claim 1 of the '798 patent—"further means disposed inside the shell for increasing its load bearing capacity comprising internal steel baffles extending inwardly from the steel shell walls"—imposes three clear requirements with respect to the baffles. First, the baffles must be made of steel. Second, they must be part of the load-bearing means for the wall section. Third, they must be pointed inward from the walls. Both parties, stipulating to a dictionary definition, also conceded that the term "baffles" refers to objects that check, impede, or obstruct the flow of something. The intrinsic evidence confirms that a person of skill in the art would understand that the term "baffles," as used in the '798 patent, would have that generic meaning.

The other claims of the '798 patent specify particular functions to be served by the baffles. For example, dependent claim 2 states that the baffles may be "oriented with the panel sections disposed at angles for deflecting projectiles such as bullets able to penetrate the steel plates." The inclusion of such a specific limitation on the term "baffles" in claim 2 makes it likely that the patentee did not contemplate that the term "baffles" already contained that limitation. Independent claim 17 further supports that proposition. It states that baffles are placed "projecting inwardly from the outer shell at angles tending to deflect projectiles that penetrate the outer shell." That limitation would be unnecessary if persons of skill in the art understood that the baffles inherently served such a function. *See TurboCare,* 264 F.3d at 1123 (claim terms should not be read to contain a limitation "where another claim restricts the invention in exactly the [same] manner"). Dependent claim 6 provides an additional requirement for the baffles, stating that "the internal baffles of both outer panel sections overlap and interlock at angles providing deflector panels extending from one end of the module to the other." If the baffles recited in claim 1 were inherently placed at specific angles, or interlocked to form an intermediate barrier, claim 6 would be redundant.

The specification further supports the conclusion that persons of ordinary skill in the art would understand the baffles recited in the '798 patent to be load-bearing objects that serve to check, impede, or obstruct flow. At several points, the specification discusses positioning the baffles so as to deflect projectiles. *See* '798 patent, col. 2, ll. 13-15; *id.,* col. 5, ll. 17-19. The patent states that one advantage of the invention over the prior art is that "[t]here have not been effective ways of dealing with these powerful impact weapons with inexpensive housing." *Id.,* col. 3, ll. 28-30. While that statement makes clear the invention envisions baffles that serve that function, it does not imply that in order to qualify as baffles within the meaning of the claims, the internal support structures must serve the projectile-deflecting function in all the embodiments of all the claims. The specification must teach and enable all the claims, and the section of the written description discussing the use of baffles to deflect projectiles serves that purpose for claims 2, 6, 17, and 23, which specifically claim baffles that deflect projectiles.

The specification discusses several other purposes served by the baffles. For example, the baffles are described as providing structural support. The patent states that one way to increase load-bearing capacity is to use "at least in part inwardly directed steel baffles 15, 16." '798 patent, col. 4, ll. 14-15. The baffle 16 is described as a "strengthening triangular baffle." *Id.*, col. 4, line 37. Importantly, Figures 4 and 6 do not show the baffles as part of an "intermediate interlocking, but not solid, internal barrier." In those figures, the baffle 16 simply provides structural support for one of the walls, as depicted below:

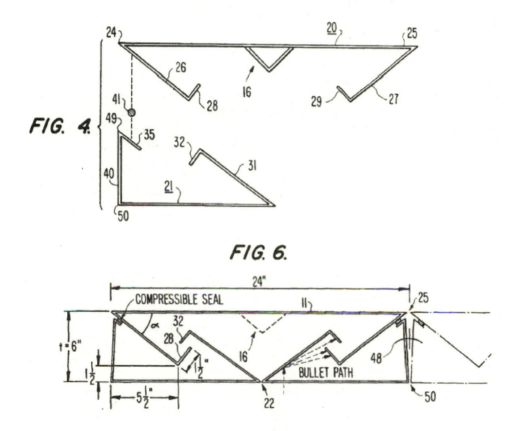

FIG. 4.

FIG. 6.

Other uses for the baffles are listed in the specification as well. In Figure 7, the overlapping flanges "provide for overlapping and interlocking the baffles to produce substantially an intermediate barrier wall between the opposite [wall] faces":

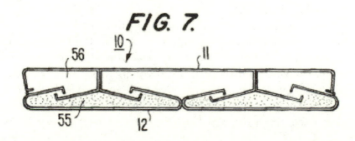

FIG. 7.

'798 patent, col. 5, ll. 26-29. Those baffles thus create small compartments that can be filled with either sound and thermal insulation or rock and gravel to stop projectiles. *Id.,* col. 5, ll. 29-34. By separating the interwall area into compartments (see, e.g., compartment 55 in Figure 7), the user of the modules can choose different types of material for each compartment, so that the module can be "easily custom tailored for the specific needs of each installation." *Id.,* col. 5, ll. 36-37. When material is placed into the wall during installation, the baffles obstruct the flow of material from one compartment to another so that this "custom tailoring" is possible.

The fact that the written description of the '798 patent sets forth multiple objectives to be served by the baffles recited in the claims confirms that the term "baffles" should not be read restrictively to require that the baffles in each case serve all of the recited functions. We have held that "[t]he fact that a patent asserts that an invention achieves several objectives does not require that each of the claims be construed as limited to structures that are capable of achieving all of the objectives." *Liebel-Flarsheim,* 358 F.3d at 908. Although deflecting projectiles is one of the advantages of the baffles of the '798 patent, the patent does not require that the inward extending structures always be capable of performing that function. Accordingly, we conclude that a person of skill in the art would not interpret the disclosure and claims of the '798 patent to mean that a structure extending inward from one of the wall faces is a "baffle" if it is at an acute or obtuse angle, but is not a "baffle" if it is disposed at a right angle.

* * *

VI

In our order granting rehearing *en banc,* we asked the parties to brief various questions, including the following: "Consistent with the Supreme Court's decision in *Markman v. Westview Instruments,* 517 U.S. 370 (1996), and our *en banc* decision in *Cybor Corp. v. FAS Technologies, Inc.,* 138 F.3d 1448 (Fed. Cir. 1998), is it appropriate for this court to accord any deference to any aspect of trial court claim construction rulings? If so, on what aspects, in what circumstances, and to what extent?" After consideration of the matter, we have decided not to address that issue at this time. We therefore leave undisturbed our prior *en banc* decision in *Cybor.*

* * *

MAYER, Circuit Judge, with whom NEWMAN, Circuit Judge, joins, dissenting.

Now more than ever I am convinced of the futility, indeed the absurdity, of this court's persistence in adhering to the falsehood that claim construction is a matter of law devoid of any factual component. Because any attempt to fashion a coherent standard under this regime is pointless, as illustrated by our many failed attempts to do so, I dissent.

This court was created for the purpose of bringing consistency to the patent field. *See* H.R. Rep. No. 312, 97th Cong., 1st Sess. 20-23 (1981). Instead, we have taken this noble mandate, to reinvigorate the patent and introduce predictability to the field, and focused inappropriate power in this court. In our quest to elevate our importance, we have, however, disregarded our role as an appellate court; the resulting mayhem has seriously undermined the legitimacy of the process, if not the integrity of the institution.

In the name of uniformity, *Cybor Corp. v. FAS Technologies, Inc.*, 138 F.3d 1448 (Fed. Cir. 1998) (*en banc*), held that claim construction does not involve subsidiary or underlying questions of fact and that we are, therefore, unbridled by either the expertise or efforts of the district court.[1] What we have wrought, instead, is the substitution of a black box, as it so pejoratively has been said of the jury, with the black hole of this court. Out of this void we emit "legal" pronouncements by way of "interpretive necromancy"; these rulings resemble reality, if at all, only by chance. Regardless, and with a blind eye to the consequences, we continue to struggle under this irrational and reckless regime, trying every alternative—dictionaries first, dictionaries second, never dictionaries, etc., etc., etc.

Again today we vainly attempt to establish standards by which this court will interpret claims. But after proposing no fewer than seven questions, receiving more than thirty *amici curiae* briefs, and whipping the bar into a frenzy of expectation, we say nothing new, but merely restate what has become the practice over the last ten years—that we will decide cases according to whatever mode or method results in the outcome we desire, or at least allows us a seemingly plausible way out of the case. I am not surprised by this. Indeed, there can be no workable standards by which this court will interpret claims so long as we are blind to the factual component of the task.

* * *

While this court may persist in the delusion that claim construction is a purely legal determination, unaffected by underlying facts, it is plainly not the case. Claim construction is, or should be, made in context: a claim should be interpreted both from the perspective of one of ordinary skill in the art and in view of the state of the art at the time of invention. These questions, which are critical to the correct interpretation of a claim, are inherently factual. They are hotly contested by the parties, not by resort to case law as one would expect for legal issues, but based on testimony and documentary evidence. During so called *Markman* "hearings," which are often longer than jury trials, parties battle over experts offering conflicting evidence regarding who qualifies as one of ordinary skill in the art; the meaning of patent terms to that person; the state of the art at the time of the invention; contradictory dictionary definitions and which would be consulted by the skilled artisan; the scope of specialized terms; the problem a patent was solving; what is related or pertinent art; whether a construction was disallowed during prosecution; how one of skill in the art would understand statements during prosecution; and on and on. In order to reconcile the parties' inconsistent submissions and arrive at a sound interpretation, the district court is required to sift through and weigh volumes of evidence. While this court treats the district court as an intake clerk, whose only role is to collect, shuffle and collate evidence, the reality, as revealed by conventional practice, is far different.

---

1. The Supreme Court did not suggest in affirming *Markman v. Westview Instruments, Inc.*, 52 F.3d 967 (1995) (*en banc*), that claim construction is a purely legal question. 517 U.S. 370 (1996). It held only that, as a policy matter, the judge, as opposed to the jury, should determine the meaning of a patent claim. *See Cybor*, 138 F.3d at 1464 (Mayer, C.J., dissenting) (explaining that "the [Supreme] Court chose not to accept our formulation of claim construction: as a pure question of law to be decided *de novo* in all cases on appeal").

* * *

While the court flails about in an attempt to solve the claim construction "conundrum," the solution to our plight is straightforward. We simply must follow the example of every other appellate court, which, regarding the vast majority of factual questions, reviews the trial court for clear error. Therefore, not only is it more efficient for the trial court to construct the record, the trial court is *better,* that is, more accurate, by way of both position and practice, at finding facts than appellate judges. Our rejection of this fundamental premise has resulted, not surprisingly, in several serious problems, including increased litigation costs, needless consumption of judicial resources, and uncertainty, as well as diminished respect for the court and less "decisional accuracy." We should abandon this unsound course.

If we persist in deciding the subsidiary factual components of claim construction without deference, there is no reason why litigants should be required to parade their evidence before the district courts or for district courts to waste time and resources evaluating such evidence. It is excessive to require parties, who "have already been forced to concentrate their energies and resources on persuading the trial judge that their account of the facts is the correct one," to "persuade three more judges at the appellate level." *Anderson,* 470 U.S. at 575. If the proceedings before the district court are merely a "tryout on the road," *id.,* as they are under our current regimen, it is wasteful to require such proceedings at all. Instead, all patent cases could be filed in this court; we would determine whether claim construction is necessary, and, if so, the meaning of the claims. Those few cases in which claim construction is not dispositive can be remanded to the district court for trial. In this way, we would at least eliminate the time and expense of the charade currently played out before the district court.

Eloquent words can mask much mischief. The court's opinion today is akin to rearranging the deck chairs on the Titanic — the orchestra is playing as if nothing is amiss, but the ship is still heading for Davey Jones' locker.

Comments

1. **The Phillips *Interpretive Road Map* and the Primacy of Context.** *Phillips* reaffirmed *Vitronics,* one of the first important claim interpretation cases following *Markman II.* In *Vitronics,* the court identified two different types of interpretive evidence: intrinsic and extrinsic. The former comprises the claims, specification, and prosecution history; the latter includes such things as expert testimony, dictionaries, and treatises, all of which are external to the patent document. The court expressed a preference for intrinsic evidence because it forms part of the public record and is consistent with the notice function of the patent claim. As the court stated in *Vitronics:*

   > The claims, specification, and file history, rather than extrinsic evidence, constitute the public record of the patentee's claim, a record on which the public is entitled to rely. In other words, competitors are entitled to review the public record, apply the established rules of claim construction, ascertain the scope of the patentee's claimed invention and, thus, design around the claimed invention.

90 F.3d 1576, 1584 (Fed. Cir. 1996). While the intrinsic/extrinsic distinction is helpful, *Vitronics* failed to provide a workable framework that would allow a judge to determine which types of interpretive sources are more relevant than others.

It was thought that *Phillips* would provide that framework, but the court arguably gave us little more than what was already established in patent doctrine and shied away from establishing specific interpretive rules. While *Phillips* reaffirmed the principle that claims are to be given their "ordinary and customary meaning" as interpreted by a person having ordinary skill in the art at the time of invention, the court also emphasized the importance of context. A contextual interpretation suggests that claim language is not determined in a vacuum, but should be harmonized with the intrinsic record, as understood within the technological field of the invention. In this regard, the *Phillips* court affirmed the specification's important role in claim interpretation. *See Sun Pharmaceutical Industries v. Eli Lilly & Co.*, 641 F.3d 1381, 1388 (Fed. Cir. 2010) ("*Phillips* as well as the rest of our claim construction precedent, expounds that a 'person of ordinary skill in the art is deemed to read the claim term not only in the context of the particular claim in which the disputed term appears, but in the context of the *entire patent, including the specification*.'") (emphasis in original); *Decision.com, Inc. v. Federated Dep't Stores, Inc.*, 527 F.3d 1300, 1308 (Fed. Cir. 2008) ("We must read the specification in light of its purposes in order to determine 'whether the patentee is setting out specific examples of the invention to accomplish those goals, or whether the patentee instead intends for the claims and the embodiments in the specification to be strictly coextensive. The manner in which the patentee uses a term within the specification and claims usually will make the distinction apparent.' Ultimately, our 'focus remains on understanding how a person of ordinary skill in the art would understand the claim terms.'").

Thus, while the claims are the starting point of any interpretive analysis, the specification is "always highly relevant to the claim construction analysis"; indeed, it is the single best guide to the meaning of a disputed term, and is "usually dispositive." As the Federal Circuit pithily noted in one of its earlier decisions: "Specifications teach. Claims claim." *SRI Int'l v. Matsushita Elec. Corp.*, 775 F.2d 1107, 1121 n.14 (Fed. Cir. 1985). One could argue that the emphasis on context is similar to the well-known school of statutory interpretation known as textualism. *See* John F. Manning, *Textualism and the Role of the Federalist in Constitutional Adjudication*, 66 GEO. WASH. L. REV. 1337, 1339 (1998) ("Textualists subscribe to an objective theory of interpretation, pursuant to which interpreters ask what a reasonable lawmaker, familiar with the relevant context, would have believed that he or she was voting for."); John F. Manning, *Textualism and Legislative Intent*, 91 VA. L. REV. 419, 420 (2005) (describing textualism as the "basic proposition that judges must seek and abide by the public meaning of the enacted text, understood in context (as all texts must be)").

Phillips was less enthusiastic about the value of prosecution history. While noting that "the prosecution history can often inform the meaning of the claim language by demonstrating how the inventor understood the invention and whether the inventor limited the invention in the course of prosecution," the court cautioned that because "the prosecution history represents an ongoing negotiation between the PTO and the applicant, rather than the final product of that negotiation, it often lacks the clarity of the specification and thus is less useful for claim construction purposes." 415 F.3d at 1317. But arguments made during prosecution remain important. *See MBO Laboratories v. Becton Dickinson & Co.*, 474 F.3d 1323, 1330 (Fed. Cir. 2007) (stating "[p]rosecution arguments . . . which draw distinctions between the patented invention and the prior art are useful for determining whether the patentee intended to surrender territory, since they indicate in the inventor's own words what the invention is not").

Extrinsic evidence is defined as "all evidence external to the patent and prosecution history, including expert and inventor testimony, dictionaries, and learned treatises." 415 F.3d at 1317. The *Phillips* court—echoing *Vitronics*—noted that extrinsic evidence is "less significant than the intrinsic record in determining the legally operative meaning of claim language." *Id.* The court provided several reasons for this preference, but they all can be explained by the fact that extrinsic evidence, to varying degrees, is not as publicly available as intrinsic evidence, is more of a moving target than the written intrinsic evidence, and therefore, does not serve the public notice function as well. Given the prominence of the specification and claims, even more acceptable forms of extrinsic evidence such as dictionaries, the Federal Circuit's *vade mecum* prior to *Phillips*, are viewed skeptically. The least acceptable form of extrinsic evidence is expert testimony, particularly "conclusory, unsupported assertions by experts as to the definition of a claim term," *id.*, and inventor testimony, which is "of little probative value for purposes of claim construction." *E-Pass Technologies, Inc. v. 3Com Corp.*, 343 F.3d 1364, 1370 n.5 (Fed. Cir. 2003). *See also Solomon v. Kimberly-Clark Corp.*, 216 F.3d 1372, 1379 (Fed. Cir. 2000) (stating "litigation-derived inventor testimony in the context of claim construction . . . is entitled to little, if any, probative value"). In short, "extrinsic evidence may be useful to the court, but it is unlikely to result in a reliable interpretation of patent claim scope unless considered in the context of the intrinsic evidence." *Phillips*, 415 F.3d at 1319.

In part, because *Phillips* emphasized context over rules, there continues to be an ongoing debate among Federal Circuit judges and commentators about the proper role of intrinsic and extrinsic evidence, which is comparable to the longstanding debate within contract law circles associated with the contrasting views of Samuel Williston and Arthur Corbin. Williston assumed a formalist approach to contract interpretation, what has been called the classical contract model. This model emphasized language of the contract and was reluctant to step outside the four corners of the express terms. In contrast, Corbin, in addition to the language of the contract, stressed the importance of custom and trade usage, items extrinsic to the contract and what Corbin referred to as "undisputed contexts." *Phillips* is more sympathetic to the Corbin approach. Indeed, several other notable thinkers such as Karl Llewellyn, in The Common Law Tradition: Deciding Appeals 268-285 (1960) (discussing what he referred to as "situation sense"), Pierre Bourdieu, in Outline of a Theory of Practice 72-95 (Richard Nice trans., 1977) (discussing the "habitus"), and John Searle, in The Construction of Social Realty 130 (1995) (referring to the "Background"), have expressed the importance of culture and extrinsic context in discerning meaning. Perhaps the most influential figure to do so was Ludwig Wittgenstein in his Philosophical

INVESTIGATIONS, wherein he famously wrote, "the meaning of a word is its use in the language." PHILOSOPHICAL INVESTIGATIONS § 43 (G.E.M. Anscombe trans., 2d ed. 1958).

Lord Hoffmann's remarks in *Kirin-Amgen v. Hoechst Marion Roussel* reveal the influence of the aforementioned works on his thinking and the importance of context for him in interpreting language:

> The attempt to treat the words of the claims as having meanings "in themselves" and without regard to the context in which or the purpose for which they were used was always a highly artificial exercise.

> The meaning of words is a matter of convention, governed by rules, which can be found in dictionaries. What the author would have been understood to mean by using those words is not simply a matter of rules. It is highly sensitive to context of and background to the particular utterance.

> It depends not only upon the words the author has chosen but also upon the identity of the audience he is taken to have been addressing and the knowledge and assumptions which one attributes to that audience.

[2004] UKHL 46, [2004] All ER (D) 286 (Oct. 1, 2004). For more on interpretive theory in the context of claim interpretation, *see* Craig Allen Nard, *A Theory of Claim Interpretation*, 14 HARV. J.L. & TECH. 1 (2000).

2. ***The Role of the Artisan in Claim Interpretation.*** As noted in Comment 1, it is a basic tenet of patent law—reaffirmed in *Phillips*—that claims are to be construed through the eyes of a person having ordinary skill in the art. But by circumscribing the role of expert testimony, one may ask whether *Phillips* and *Vitronics* pay too little attention to the central role of the artisan and technological context beyond the patent document. As Judge William Young stated in *Amgen, Inc. v. Hoechst Marion Roussel, Inc.*, 339 F. Supp. 2d 202, 227 n.23 (D. Mass. 2004) (emphasis in original):

> At first glance, the extrinsic evidence rule in *Vitronics* appears to create somewhat of a conundrum, in that it discourages resort to extrinsic evidence while at the same time urging courts to begin claim construction by considering the plain and customary meaning of a term *as understood by one skilled in the art*. How does a Court decipher the plain and customary meaning of a term as understood by one skilled in the art without resorting to extrinsic evidence about how one skilled in the art would construe the term?

The role of the artisan seems to be particularly important when words of degree (e.g., "substantial" or "about") are used in claims. *See BJ Services Co. v. Halliburton Energy Services, Inc.*, 338 F.3d 1368, 1372 (Fed. Cir. 2003) (noting that when words of degree are employed, the "question becomes whether one of ordinary skill in the art would understand what is claimed when the claim is read in light of the specification"). *Cf. Aventis Pharmaceuticals, Inc. v. Amino Chemicals Ltd.*, 715 F.3d 1363 (Fed. Cir. 2013) (relying on dictionary to define "substantially" to mean "largely but not wholly that which is specified"). But some commentators have asserted that claim interpretation is more akin to a legal determination. *See* John M. Golden, *Construing Patent Claims According to Their "Interpretive Community": A Call for an Attorney-Plus-Artisan Perspective*, 21 HARV. J.L. & TECH. 321, 328 (2008) (asserting that claim interpretation should be made from "the perspective of a patent attorney with access to the technological knowledge of an ordinary artisan").

3. *Canons of Claim Construction.* Over several decades of patent jurisprudence, the common law has developed various canons of claim construction. Two of the more interesting canons are: (1) "claims should be so construed, if possible, as to sustain their validity." *Rhine v. Casio, Inc.*, 183 F.3d 1342, 1345 (Fed. Cir. 1999). This canon is sometimes referred to as the "validity maxim." *See MBO Laboratories, Inc. v. Becton, Dickinson & Co.*, 474 F.3d 1323, 1332 (Fed. Cir. 2007). (2) "where there is an equal choice between a broader and a narrower meaning of a claim, and there is an enabling disclosure that indicates that the applicant is at least entitled to a claim having the narrower meaning," the notice function of the claim is best served by adopting the narrower meaning. *See Athletic Alternatives v. Prince Mfg.*, 73 F.3d 1573, 1581 (Fed. Cir. 1996). Other Federal Circuit panels have endorsed this canon. *See, e.g., Ethicon Endo-Surgery, Inc. v. United States Surgical Corp.*, 93 F.3d 1572, 1581-1582 (Fed. Cir. 1996); *Digital Biometrics, Inc. v. Identix, Inc.*, 149 F.3d 1335, 1344 (Fed. Cir. 1998).

The *Phillips* court cabined the validity maxim, stating "we have limited the maxim to cases in which 'the court concludes, after applying all the available tools of claim construction, that the claim is still ambiguous.'" 415 F.3d at 1327. According to *Phillips*, "we have looked to whether it is reasonable to infer that the PTO would not have issued an invalid patent, and that the ambiguity in the claim language should therefore be resolved in a manner that would preserve the patent's validity." *Id.* Is limiting the validity maxim to ambiguous claims consistent with the notice function of patent law, embodied in section 112, ¶2? Shouldn't a claim that is ambiguous be invalidated under section 112? Similarly, one could ask if the *Athletic Alternatives* principle is consistent with section 112, ¶2. As Judge Nies wrote in her concurrence:

> I do not agree that the adoption of the narrower of two equally plausible interpretations somehow flows from the requirement of section 112, ¶2 that the patentee must particularly point out and distinctly claim the subject matter which he regards as his invention. The majority analysis is illogical to me. Narrowness cannot be equated with definiteness. The majority, in effect, eviscerates the requirement of section 112, ¶2 for the patentee to particularly point out and distinctly claim his invention while purporting to rely on it.

Athletic Alternatives, 73 F.3d at 1583.

UNIQUE CONCEPTS, INC. v. BROWN
939 F.2d 1558 (Fed. Cir. 1991)

LOURIE, Circuit Judge.

BACKGROUND

A. The Patent in Suit

Unique is the exclusive licensee under U.S. Patent [4,018,260] ('260 patent), entitled "Fabric Wall Coverings," issued April 19, 1977, and owned by Floyd M. Baslow. Contrary to its title, the patent is not directed to wall coverings themselves, but to an "assembly of border pieces" used to attach a fabric wall covering to a wall. The assembly is made up of a number of "right angle corner border pieces" and "linear border pieces" which are arranged so as to form a frame around the area of a wall to be covered.

Below is Fig. 2 from the '260 patent, showing an exploded view of the assembly of border pieces forming the framework.

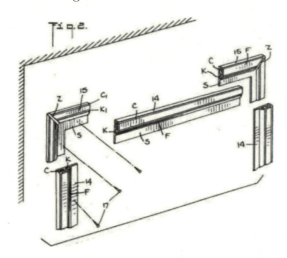

The '260 patent issued from application Serial No. 680,703, filed April 27, 1976 (Baslow application), which as originally filed contained 14 claims. Claim 1, the only independent claim, recited an assembly comprising "linear border pieces and right angle corner border pieces," each of the border pieces having a raised face, a storage channel, and a keyway. The original claims of the Baslow application were rejected by the Patent and Trademark Office (PTO) as being unpatentable in view of various references. The Examiner found that the references "show frames including corners in arrangements similar to that of applicant. . . ."

In response, the applicant amended his claims and argued against the references, stating that "[t]he main advantage of the present invention is that it greatly simplifies the mounting of a fabric covering. . . . Thus an amateur can practice the present invention. . . ."

The next item in the file history is a notice of allowability together with an examiner's amendment cancelling claims 1-3 and 5-14, and amending claim 4 to depend from claim 15. Application claims 15-17 and 4 issued as claims 1-4 of the '260 patent, respectively. Claim 1, the sole independent claim, reads:

> 1. An assembly of border pieces for creating a framework attachable to a wall or other flat surface for mounting a fabric sheet which is cut to dimensions at least sufficient to cover the surface, *said assembly comprising linear border pieces and right angle corner border pieces* which are arranged in end-to-end relation to define a framework that follows the perimeter of the area to be covered, *each piece* including a raised face, a storage channel running adjacent the outer edge of the piece and having a narrow inlet communicating with said face, the portion of the selvage of said sheet which includes fabric material in excess of that necessary to cover said surface being stuffed in said storage channel so that the exposed selvage of the sheet lies against said face to present a smooth appearance which extends to said inlet and is directly adjacent said perimeter, said linear pieces being formed of an integral one piece plastic material of sufficient elasticity to permit dilation of said inlet whereby said inlet may be temporarily expanded to admit said excess material and then contracted to retain said excess material in said storage channel.

(Emphasis added).

B. The Proceedings in the District Court

Unique brought the present suit in 1986, alleging that certain products made by Brown infringed claims 1-3 of the '260 patent. . . . Brown maintained that its accused products do not infringe [because] the accused products do not have corner pieces which were *preformed* at a right angle, but instead employ two linear pieces which are each mitered, *i.e.,* cut at a 45 degree angle, and then placed together to form a right angle. . . .

A trial was held, at which each party, by agreement, presented as its only witness a patent expert. After hearing the testimony, the judge entered judgment for Brown, finding that . . . the mitered linear pieces used by Brown do not meet the claim language "right angle corner border pieces," either literally or under the doctrine of equivalents. Unique appealed.

DISCUSSION

The '260 patent claims a framework for mounting a fabric sheet "comprising linear border pieces and right angle corner border pieces." The district court found the patent not infringed because, *inter alia,* the language "right angle corner pieces" is limited to preformed corner pieces, whereas the mitered linear pieces used by Brown do not meet this limitation either literally or under the doctrine of equivalents.

Unique argues that the district court erred in finding that the claims do not literally cover assemblies having mitered corners. To ascertain the meaning of claims, we consider three sources: the claims, the specification, and the prosecution history.

The language of claim 1 makes unambiguous reference to two distinct elements of the claimed structure: linear border pieces and right angle corner pieces. If, as Unique argues, linear border pieces of framing material, whose ends are mitered, are the same as linear border pieces *and* a right angle corner piece, the recitation of both types of pieces is redundant. Unique's argument for merging the two types of claim elements into one also violates the oft-quoted "all elements rule," the essence of which is that to prove infringement, every element in the claim must be found in the accused device either literally or equivalently. The district court thus correctly held that the plain language of the claim includes two distinct types of elements, including right angle corner border pieces, thereby precluding literal infringement.

The specification also shows that the claim language "right angle corner border piece" means a single preformed piece. The specification repeatedly refers to the preformed pieces 15 and 16, using only the words "right angle" border pieces or "corner pieces." In addition, the drawings show only preformed corner pieces and no mitered pieces.

The specification does refer once to "improvise[d] corner pieces" as an alternative to the preformed pieces:

> Instead of using preformed right-angle corner pieces of the type previously disclosed, one may improvise corner pieces by miter-cutting the ends of a pair of short linear border pieces at right angles to each other and providing a space between the cut ends to define the necessary storage slot. For this purpose, a temporary spacer may be used to provide exactly the right amount of storage space. The advantage of such corner pieces resides in the fact that linear pieces may be mass-produced at low cost by continuous extrusion, whereas preformed corner pieces must be molded or otherwise fabricated by more expensive techniques.

On the other hand, *a preformed corner piece is somewhat easier for a do-it-yourselfer to work with.*

Col. 8, lines 28-41 (emphasis added). However, this reference does not negate the claim language clearly reciting right angle corner pieces. This paragraph, rather than providing an illustration of a right angle corner border piece, as the dissent indicates, provides an alternative to it. The language right angle corner border piece is too clear to encompass linear pieces that are not right angle corner pieces. The fact that mitered linear border pieces meet to form a right angle corner does not make them right angle corner pieces, when the claim separately recites both linear border pieces and right angle corner border pieces. Such an interpretation would run counter to the clear meaning of the language. Linear border pieces are not right angle corner border pieces. Both types of pieces are required by the claim.

The statute requires that an inventor particularly point out and distinctly claim the subject matter of his invention. 35 U.S.C. §112 (1988). It would run counter to this statutory provision for an applicant for patent to expressly state throughout his specification and in his claims that his invention includes right angle corner border pieces and then be allowed to avoid that claim limitation in a later infringement suit by pointing to one paragraph in his specification stating an alternative that lacks that limitation, and thus interpret the claim contrary to its plain meaning. Such a result would encourage an applicant to escape examination of a more broadly-claimed invention by filing narrow claims and then, after grant, asserting a broader scope of the claims based on a statement in the specification of an alternative never presented in the claims for examination.

The claims as granted contain the right angle corner border piece limitation. All the limitations of a claim must be considered meaningful, and Brown's avoidance of that limitation avoids literal infringement.

It is also well-established that subject matter disclosed but not claimed in a patent application is dedicated to the public. *Edward Miller & Co. v. Bridgeport Brass Co.,* 104 U.S. 350, 352, 26 L. Ed. 783 (1881). That is what occurred here. If Unique intended to claim mitered linear border pieces as an alternative to its right angle corner border pieces, it had to persuade the examiner to issue such a claim. As will be shown below, Unique failed to do so.

The prosecution history also supports the district court's decision. During the prosecution of the '260 patent, the examiner understood the right angle corner pieces of Claim 1 to be distinct from mitered linear pieces, because he initially rejected the claims, citing and referring to other references as showing preformed, right angle corner pieces or braces. The applicant overcame the rejection by arguing the advantage of simplification for the do-it-yourselfer. As noted in the specification, a preformed corner piece is one of the advantages of the invention making it attractive to the do-it-yourselfer.

There then occurred a telephone interview between the attorney and the examiner, following which the Examiner cancelled certain claims. Among the cancelled claims was original Claim 9, which depended from original Claim 1 (also cancelled) and recited short linear mitered pieces as forming a right angle corner piece.

The dissent relies upon Claim 9 to construe what is now Claim 1 as including linear pieces which are mitered to form a corner piece. It interprets "linear pieces whose ends are mitered" to be a species of generic Claim 1's "right angle corner border pieces," and therefore within its scope. Such a construction is unjustified because the language of Claim 1 is clear and is inconsistent with Claim 9 being dependent thereon.

The record contains no indication of what transpired in the interview and why Claim 9 was cancelled. A plausible reason is that Claim 9 was cancelled because it was not properly dependent upon original Claim 1. The court referred to Brown's expert, who stated that the claim was cancelled because it did not encompass an invention suitable for a do-it-yourselfer. The dissent finds this expert testimony to be "wholly incredible." We do not know why Claim 9 was cancelled and cannot speculate on the reasons for the cancellation; we can only interpret the clear language of the claims as granted.

When the language of a claim is clear, as here, and a different interpretation would render meaningless express claim limitations, we do not resort to speculative interpretation based on claims not granted. *See White v. Dunbar,* 119 U.S. 47, 52 (1886) ("The claim is a statutory requirement, prescribed for the very purpose of making the patentee define precisely what his invention is; and it is unjust to the public, as well as an evasion of the law, to construe it in a manner different from the plain import of its terms."). Our interpretation gives full effect to the recitation of two distinct elements in the claimed structure: linear border pieces and right angle corner border pieces. It also gives full effect to the specification and the expert testimony, and a reasonable interpretation of the prosecution history.

* * *

CONCLUSION

The district court was correct in concluding that the claim language "right angle corner border pieces," properly construed with reference to the specification and prosecution history, requires a preformed corner piece.

RICH, Circuit Judge, dissenting.

* * *

In the present posture of this appeal, the sole question is whether the majority has correctly construed the meaning of a single limitation in claim 1, which claim is set forth in full in its opinion. That limitation is: "right-angle corner border pieces." I simply disagree with the majority's conclusions and with its attempted supporting reasoning. We arrive at different "plain meanings."

. . . We construe claims in the light of the *language of the claim* itself, the *specification* on which it is based, and the whole *prosecution history.* The majority has not properly done this and, in my judgment, has demonstrably come to a wrong conclusion. Significant statements in the specification and prosecution history are misapplied. I shall begin with the specification.

As the majority states, the specification first describes and illustrates the *one-piece* corner pieces 15 and 16, outside and inside corners respectively. True, these are the only corner pieces shown in drawings. Then the specification contains the significant statement quoted in the majority opinion from the patent at col. 8, lines 28-41. (*My* emphasis):

Instead of using *preformed* right-angle corner pieces of the type previously disclosed, one may improvise *corner pieces* by miter-cutting the ends of a pair of *short* linear border pieces placed *at right angles* to each other and providing a space between the cut ends to define the necessary storage slot. For this purpose, a temporary spacer may be used to provide exactly the right amount of storage space. The *advantage* of *such corner pieces* resides in the fact that linear pieces may be mass-produced at low cost by continuous extrusion, whereas *preformed* corner pieces must be molded or otherwise fabricated by more expensive techniques. On the other hand, a pre-formed corner piece is *somewhat* easier for a do-it-yourselfer to work with.

Perhaps this is a matter, on both sides, of seeing what you choose to see. Beyond question, however, the specification discloses *two species* of right-angle corner border pieces: (1) preformed one-piece and (2) mitered, *short,* linear pieces, arranged at right angles and properly spaced at their junction. The latter are to be joined to longer linear pieces. No drawing is needed to make (2) clear. In any case, there are always, in a single assembly, both *corner* pieces and *linear* pieces, even when the second species of corner is used.

Now I turn to the contents of the file-wrapper. From day one when the application was filed these two kinds of corners were not only described but claimed and we look to this, equally with the specification, to determine the correct construction of the claim 1 language. Original claim 1, as filed, used exactly the same terminology as patent claim 1, "right-angle corner border pieces." There were 14 original claims on day one. Among them was claim 9, depending from claim 1, reading:

> 9. An assembly as set forth in claim 1, wherein *said right-angle corner pieces are formed by a pair of short linear pieces whose ends are mitered and spaced from each other to define a slot therebetween* to receive the pucker of the selvage when the selvage is locked into the keyway. [My emphasis.]

Note that claim 9 is referring back to "right angle" corners *as described in claim 1* and is thus defining a species of that genus. Now, what does that tell one skilled in the art about the meaning of "right-angle corner border pieces"? It tells one that the claim 1 phrase is, and was clearly intended by the applicant to be, broad enough to cover the species recited in claim 9, which the majority says it does not cover. There is a genus-species relationship between the phrase in claim 1, which never changed throughout the prosecution, and the particular form of corner piece recited in claim 9.

I have to disagree with the majority's criticism or downplaying of my use of claim 9 as a construction aid in several particulars. The majority seems to start with an *a priori* assumption of what the "clear" language of claim 1 means. On the other hand, I am looking at the genealogical record of that claim to *find out* what it means.

The majority says, "we . . . cannot speculate on the reasons for the cancellation" of claim 9 because we have no idea of the content of the 'phone conversation between the examiner and the attorney which led to cancellation, along with many other claims. I agree. The majority then *speculates* that it may have been an improper dependent claim, though it is not apparent why and the majority gives no reason. I don't care why (or whether) claim 9 was cancelled—it was simply part of the original application and sheds a bright *light* on what claim 1 was intended to mean.

I see no significance to the fact that claim 9 was cancelled because it *is* part of the prosecution history, *all* of which is clearly before us. The majority correctly states that we must consider the prosecution history, of which claim 9 is a significant part.

The majority opines that the alternative corner piece described in claim 9 *has not been claimed* and is therefore dedicated to the public. This strange position begs the question. Of course it has not been claimed *specifically*. The question, however, is whether it is covered by or included in claim 1, which I say it is. Therefore, its subject matter is not "dedicated to the public."

35 U.S.C. § 112, which requires claims, is irrelevant to a consideration of what claims mean. Since Brown's so-called "expert"—expert only in the sense he was a patent lawyer—knew no more than the members of this panel, his speculations are of no value to us. The citation of cases is also of no help in finding out what claims mean.

To me, claim 9 is the only evidence of record, except for the specification itself, which is of any value in construing claim 1, and I think it is of great value.

The majority seems to say that my construction of claim 1 "would render meaningless express claim limitation." I await enlightenment on what those "express limitations" are. I have already said that I read both *corner* pieces and *linear* pieces in claim 1. The debate here is over the *kinds* of corner pieces claim 1 covers. It is clear that it is not limited to unitary or preformed or one-piece corner pieces as shown in the drawings at 15 and 16. That much is truly "clear."

Much has been made of the contention that using short mitered corner pieces is something that a "do-it-yourselfer"—an "amateur"—is unable to do. Defendants' expert speculated, with no support whatsoever, that, in his opinion, the examiner required claim 9 to be cancelled because "it was simply not something that a do-it-yourselfer could do." Both defendants and the district court relied heavily on this testimony. I find this opinion testimony to be wholly incredible. The sole basis given by the expert for his opinion was the fact that claim 9 was cancelled while claim 4 was not. However, there is absolutely nothing in the record showing *why* the examiner allowed certain claims and cancelled certain other claims.

The fact is that this whole "do-it-yourselfer" argument has been blown way out of proportion. The specification does not state that do-it-yourselfers are *incapable* of using mitered corner pieces; it merely states, as quoted above, that preformed corner pieces are "somewhat easier for a do-it-yourselfer to work with." Furthermore, the *only reference* to do-it-yourselfers during prosecution is a statement that certain known *prior art* arrangements are difficult for a do-it-yourselfer to use because the *fabric must be cut precisely to size* whereas according to the invention of the '260 patent, the fabric need merely be cut *roughly* to size, with the excess fabric being stuffed in the storage channel. This is equally true as to either kind of corner. To infer from this one statement that the claims must be limited to features not recited in the claims (i.e., "*preformed*" corner pieces) is contrary to established patent law practice.

Let us consider next another lesson about meaning to be learned from the specification. In the quotation above from column 8, in the opening sentence the drafter of the specification exhibits a clear consciousness of the distinction between "preformed right-angle corner pieces" and those made by mitering and placing at right angles two short pieces of linear border pieces. Claim 1 does not contain the limiting word "preformed" yet the majority, without justification, is reading it into the claim in holding that the claim does not cover corner pieces which are made up as clearly described in the specification.

I also point out that the term "right-angle" is not a limitation to *preformed* unitary pieces since the specification makes clear that the made-up variety of corners are also right-angle corner pieces when assembled.

The majority's argument based on alleged violation of the "all elements" rule is untenable. It overlooks the fact that the teaching in the specification is clear about making "corner pieces" by using two "*short* linear border pieces" (my emphasis) and then using such "improvised" *corner pieces in conjunction with linear pieces* to make the complete wall frame. Of course, it is the all-elements rule on which the defendants rely for non-infringement, arguing that they have no "corner pieces" when in fact they have a type of corner piece which is disclosed and claimed as an element of the combination of claim 1. I am not "merging the two types of claim elements into one"—whatever that may mean. I am simply saying that the element defined in claim 1 as "right-angle corner border pieces" is, as clearly shown by the patent and its prosecution history, a limitation generic to two types of corner pieces disclosed in the patent which is broad enough to read on defendants' structure because it is clearly *not* limited to "preformed" or "unitary" corner pieces, as held below and by the majority. That is the sum and substance of my position and it calls for reversal.

The prosecution history contains nothing contradictory to my position and much to support it, as shown above. I have not found any evidence to contradict it or to support the district court opinion which demonstrates a dismal failure to comprehend many patent law fundamentals and accepts, as established fact, opinion statements of defendants' expert witness unsupported by the record. The reader should also be aware that the district judge made no separate "findings of fact." He wrote a short, confused opinion which he concluded with the escape clause saying "The foregoing shall constitute the Findings of Fact and Conclusions of Law in accordance with Rule 54(b) [*sic*] of the Fed. R. Civ. P."

Comments

1. ***The Sometimes Uneasy Relationship Between the Claim and Specification.*** Even though *Unique Concepts* was decided several years before *Phillips*, the majority and dissent reveal what continues to be an ongoing debate among Federal Circuit judges as well as patent law scholars about the proper weight to be given the various forms of intrinsic evidence. Judge Lourie's emphasis on the claim in *Unique Concepts* is consistent with *Phillips*'s holding that a "bedrock principle" of claim interpretation is that claims define the invention and, therefore, the patentee's property right. This rule-oriented approach is also consistent with the distinctiveness requirement (see section D, below), which serves the notice function of patent law, and demands that an applicant "particularly point out and distinctly claim" his invention. 35 U.S.C. §112, ¶2.

   Of course, *Phillips* emphasized the interpretive importance of the specification, as well. Yet the question to what extent the specification can be used in this regard has proved to be particularly vexing. *See Retractable Technologies, Inc. v. Becton, Dickinson & Co.*, 659 F.3d 1369, 1370 (Fed. Cir. 2011) (Moore, J., dissenting from denial of petition for *en banc* review) (stating "[c]ommentators have observed that claim construction appeals are 'panel dependent' which leads to frustration and unpredictable results for both the litigants and the trial court. . . . Nowhere is the conflict more apparent than in our jurisprudence on the use of the specification in the interpretation of claim language"). This uneasy, yet mutually dependent, relationship between the claim and specification stems from two complementary principles of claim construction, both of which flow from the axiom that "it is the function and purpose of claims, not the written description part of the specification itself," to "delimit the right to exclude." *Markman I*, 52 F.3d at 980. The first holds that claims must be interpreted in the light of the specification. The second states that it is improper to import a limitation from the specification's general discussion, embodiments, and examples. *See Amgen, Inc. v. Hoechst Marion Roussel, Inc.*, 314 F.3d 1313, 1325 (Fed. Cir. 2003) ("Because the claims are best understood in light of the specification of which they are a part . . . courts must take extreme care when ascertaining the proper scope of the claims, lest they simultaneously import into the claims limitations that were unintended by the patentee"); *Innova/Pure Water, Inc. v. Safari Water Filtration Sys.*, 381 F.3d 1111, 1117 (Fed. Cir. 2004) ("[E]ven where a patent describes only a single embodiment, claims will not be read restrictively unless the patentee has demonstrated a clear intention to limit the claim scope using words or expressions of manifest exclusion or restriction."); *Silicon Graphics, Inc. v. ATI Techs., Inc.*, 607 F.3d 784, 792 (Fed. Cir. 2010) ("A construing court's reliance on the specification must not go so far as to import limitations into claims from examples or embodiments appearing only in a patent's written description unless the specification makes clear that the patentee intends for the claims and the embodiments in the specification to be strictly coextensive"). See Comment 3 for more on these principles.

With *Phillips* and the aforementioned caveats in mind, the court in *Retractable Technologies Inc. v. Becton, Dickinson & Co.*, 653 F.3d 1296, 1305 (Fed. Cir. 2011), viewed the specification primarily as a device to discern what was "actually invented," not as a dumping ground for information that could not be (or was not) claimed. The court turned to the "intrinsic record to construe the claims . . . to capture the scope of the actual invention, rather than strictly limit the scope of claims to disclosed embodiments or allow the claim language to become divorced from what the specification conveys is the invention." *Id.* In a concurring opinion, Judge Plager applauded the majority's approach, stating "I understand how a perfectly competent trial judge can be persuaded by the siren song of litigation counsel to give the jury wide scope regarding what is claimed. But it is a song to which courts should turn a deaf ear if patents are to serve the purposes for which they exist, including the obligation to make full disclosure of what is actually invented, and to claim that and nothing more." Accordingly, "[t]he bottom line of claim construction should be that the claims should not mean more than what the specification indicates, in one way or another, the inventors invented." *Arlington Industries, Inc. v. Bridgeport Fittings, Inc.*, 632 F.3d 1246, 1258 (Fed. Cir. 2011) (Lourie, J., concurring in part and dissenting in part).

The majority has been accused of using the specification not to interpret the claims, but to rewrite them—an approach arguably not supported by *Phillips. See Retractable Technologies*, 659 F.3d at 1372 (Moore, J., dissenting from the denial of the petition for rehearing *en banc*) (stating the majority erred in attempting to "rewrite the claims to better conform to what it discerns is the 'invention' of the patent instead of construing the language of claim. . . . Changing the plain meaning to tailor its scope to what the panel believes was the 'actual invention' is not supported by *Phillips*").

Phillips sets forth broad principles of claim construction, and both those who support the majority in *Retractable Techs.* and its detractors will be able to cite *Phillips* for support. In other words, the line between improper importation and appropriately reading claim language in the light of the specification will almost always be fuzzy enough to accommodate a given construction. As such, as a way to enhance early certainty, some judges on the Federal Circuit have urged greater deference to district court claim constructions as long as the lower court constructions are not "cryptic, unthinkable rulings." *Retractable Techs.*, 659 F.3d at 1375. As Judge O'Malley wrote:

> I do not criticize the panel majority for its legal analysis. The majority adhered to the broad principles of claim construction set forth in *Phillips* and reached a different conclusion than the trial judge. . . . The fact, however, that the panel members could not agree on the proper claim construction in this case, despite careful consideration of their respective obligations under *Phillips*, underscores the complicated and fact-intensive nature of claim construction and the need to rethink our approach to it.

Id. There is arguably much to be said for this approach, particularly when we consider "the inherent difficulties of using language to define the boundaries of abstract and intangible rights." Peter Menell, Matthew Powers & Steven Carlson, *Patent Claim Construction: A Modern Synthesis and Structured Framework*, 25 BERKELEY TECH. L.J. 711, 716 (2010). The dissent in *Unique Concepts* presumably understood these difficulties, as well. See Comment 2.

2. ***Can Claim Language Ever Be Clear on Its Face?*** The *Unique Concepts* dissent, like the majority, understood the importance of the claim, but is much more skeptical of finding clear meaning without visiting the specification and prosecution history. Recall Judge Rich's comment: "The majority seems to start with an *a priori* assumption of what the 'clear' language of claim 1 means. On the other hand, I am looking at the genealogical record of that claim to *find out* what it means." (Emphasis in original.) For Judge Rich, the claim cannot be read in isolation or in an overly literal fashion because to focus solely on the claim language is to adopt an acontextual approach to claim interpretation. As Richard Posner wrote, "meaning does not reside simply in the words of a text, for the words are always pointing to something outside." RICHARD A. POSNER, THE PROBLEMS OF JURISPRUDENCE 296 (1990); Stanley Fish, *Almost Pragmatism: Richard Posner's Jurisprudence*, 57 U. CHI. L. REV. 1447, 1456 (1990) ("No act of reading can stop at the plain meaning of a document, because that meaning itself will have emerged in the light of some stipulation of intentional circumstances, of purpose held by agents situated in real word situations."). For more on this issue, see Comment 1 after *Phillips* on the Corbin/Williston debate in contract law.

3. ***The Specification's Import-Export Rule.*** As noted in Comment 1, the Federal Circuit has recognized that "there is sometimes a fine line between reading a claim in light of the specification, and reading a limitation into the claim from the specification." *Comark Communications, Inc. v. Harris Corp.*, 156 F.3d 1182, 1186 (Fed. Cir. 1998). Indeed, Judge Dyk has written, "our decisions provide inadequate guidance as to when it is appropriate to look to the specification to narrow the claim by interpretation and when it is not

appropriate to do so. Until we provide better guidance, I fear that the lower courts and litigants will remain confused." *SciMed Life Systems, Inc. v. Advanced Cardiovascular Systems, Inc.*, 242 F.3d 1337, 1347 (Fed. Cir. 2001). This fine line was on display in *Unique Concepts*. Did the majority read in a limitation (i.e., "preformed") into the claim from the specification? Did the dissent ignore a claim limitation? This lack of clarity leads to predictable arguments during litigation, with the patentee citing improper importation; and the accused infringer asserting the court disregarded a claim limitation.

These seemingly contradictory canons of claim construction were at issue in *Alloc, Inc. v. International Trade Commission*, 342 F.3d 1361 (Fed. Cir. 2003). The claims of the patents at issue, which related to floor panels, did not explicitly require "play" (or spacing) between the panels. The court, however, interpreted the claim and specification as requiring this limitation:

> [T]his court recognizes that it must interpret the claims in light of the specification, yet avoid impermissibly importing limitations from the specification. That balance turns on how the specification characterizes the claimed invention. In this respect, this court looks to whether the specification refers to a limitation only as a part of less than all possible embodiments or whether the specification read as a whole suggests that the very character of the invention requires the limitation be a part of every embodiment. For example, it is impermissible to read the one and only disclosed embodiment into a claim without other indicia that the patentee so intended to limit the invention. On the other hand, where the specification makes clear at various points that the claimed invention is narrower than the claim language might imply, it is entirely permissible and proper to limit the claims. *SciMed Life Sys., Inc. v. Advance Cardiovascular Sys., Inc.*, 242 F.3d 1337, 1345 (Fed. Cir. 2001). . . . Here [as in *SciMed*], the [patent] specification read as a whole leads to the inescapable conclusion that the claimed invention must include play in every embodiment. . . . [T]he patent specification indicates that the invention is indeed exclusively directed toward flooring products including play. Moreover, unlike the patent-at-issue in *SunRace* [*Roots Enters. Co. v. SRAM Corp.*, 336 F.3d 1298 (Fed. Cir. 2003)], the [patent] specification also distinguished the prior art on the basis of play.

Id. at 1370-1371.

4. ***The Role of the Accused Device in Interpreting Claims.*** Another fundamental tenet of claim construction is that claims are not to be construed by reference to the accused device. *See SRI Int'l v. Matsushita Elec. Corp. of America*, 775 F.2d 1107, 1118 (Fed. Cir. 1985) (*en banc*); *NeoMagic Corp. v. Trident Microsystems, Inc.*, 287 F.3d 1062, 1074 (Fed. Cir. 2002). But recent decisions have suggested a greater role for the accused device. *See Wilson Sporting Goods Co. v. Hillerich & Bradsby Co.*, 442 F.3d 1322, 1326-1327 (Fed. Cir. 2006) ("While a trial court should certainly not prejudge the ultimate infringement analysis by construing claims with an aim to include or exclude an accused product or process, knowledge of that product or process provides meaningful context for the first step of the infringement analysis, claim construction."); *Lava Trading, Inc. v. Sonic Trading Management, Inc.*, 445 F.3d 1348 (Fed. Cir. 2006) ("Without knowledge of the accused products, this court cannot assess the accuracy of the infringement judgment under review and lacks a proper context for an accurate claim construction."); *Serio-US Industries, Inc. v. Plastic Recovery Technologies Corp.*, 459 F.3d 1311, 1319 (Fed. Cir. 2006) (stating "a trial court may consult the accused device for context that informs the claim construction process").

5. *The Doctrine of Claim Differentiation.* This doctrine presumes "each claim in a patent is presumptively different in scope." *Intermatic Inc. v. Lamson & Sessions Co.,* 273 F.3d 1355, 1364 (Fed. Cir. 2001). And this presumption is particularly applicable where "there is a dispute over whether a limitation found in a dependent claim should be read into an independent claim, and that limitation is the only meaningful difference between the two claims." *Id. See also Curtiss-Wright Flow Control Corp. v. Velan, Inc.,* 438 F.3d 1374, 1381 (Fed. Cir. 2006) (stating "claim differentiation takes on relevance in the context of a claim construction that would render additional, or different, language in another independent claim superfluous").

An example of the claim differentiation doctrine can be found in *Ecolab, Inc. v. Paraclipse, Inc.,* 285 F.3d 1362 (Fed. Cir. 2002). The patent-in-suit related to a flying insect trap. Independent claim 16 required "a flying insect trap using reflected and radiated light as an insect attractant." And dependent claim 17 stated: "The trap of claim 16 wherein the insect attractant light comprises a source of ultraviolet light." The alleged infringer argued "claim 16 requires reflected ultraviolet ("UV") light." The Federal Circuit rejected this proposed construction, noting that claim 16 does not require ultraviolet light "[b]ecause the only meaningful difference between claims 16 and 17 is the limitation of ultraviolet light." Accordingly, "under the doctrine of claim differentiation, claim 16 does not require ultraviolet light." *Id.* at 1376-1377. *See also Arlington Industries, Inc. v. Bridgeport Fittings, Inc.,* 632 F.3d 1246, 1253 (Fed. Cir. 2011) ("Claim 1 recites a 'spring metal adaptor being less than a complete circle,' while claim 8 omits the less than complete circle modifier. This difference indicates that, unlike the adaptor in claim 1, the spring metal adaptor of claim 8 can be either a complete circle or an incomplete circle. Similarly, independent claim 12 . . . recites 'a split circular spring metal adaptor,' while claim 8 of the patent omits the 'split' modifier. Thus, unlike the adaptor of claim 12, the spring metal adaptor of claim 8 can either be split or unsplit.").

Relatedly, a dependent claim can be a helpful interpretive tool when construing a term in an independent claim. Recall the *Phillips* court noted that "[d]ifferences among claims can also be a useful guide in understanding the meaning of particular claim terms," and that "the presence of a dependent claim that adds a particular limitation gives rise to a presumption that the limitation in question is not present in the independent claim." In *Intamin Ltd. v. Magetar Technologies,* 483 F.3d 1328 (Fed. Cir. 2007), claim 1 of the patent-in-suit claimed a rollercoaster "braking device" with "an intermediary disposed between adjacent pairs of . . . magnet elements." Dependent claim 2 stated, "[t]he braking device of claim 1 wherein said intermediary is non-magnetic." Based on its reading of the specification, which stated the "intermediary" related to non-magnetic substances only, the district court interpreted "intermediary" to mean a non-magnetic material between the adjacent magnetic elements. Relying on *Phillips,* the Federal Circuit reversed, stating the dependent claim implied a broader meaning for the term "intermediary" in claim 1. According to the court the "dependent claim shows both that the claim drafter perceived a distinction between magnetic and non-magnetic intermediaries and that independent claim 1 impliedly embraced magnetic intermediaries." *Id.* The court also cautioned that a narrow specification may not necessarily limit broader claim language; in this case, the "overall context of the patent . . . does not specifically disavow magnetic intermediaries," and "[t]he single reference does not expressly limit the entire invention but only describes a single embodiment." *Id.* For more on the doctrine of claim differentiation, *see* Mark A. Lemley, *The Limits of Claim Differentiation*, 22 BERKELEY TECH. L.J. 1389 (2007) (conducting an empirical review of Federal Circuit claim differentiation jurisprudence and suggesting "limiting principles that can be used to guide courts in their application of the doctrine").

POLICY PERSPECTIVE
Claim Construction Methodology

One of the most important questions in patent law is what interpretive methodology should a court adopt in construing claims. On the one hand, a methodology that is wedded to the intrinsic evidence has several virtues. For instance, it relies on publicly available information, which may lend itself to more predictability and is consistent with the important notice function of the claim. Moreover, a strict textual approach forces patent attorneys and agents to be more careful in drafting patent applications. And the concerns of the *Vitronics* court about expert testimony are certainly legitimate. The patentee's and defendant's well-trained, technical experts, who are not part of the public record, will almost invariably provide the court and jury with divergent testimony relating to identical claim language. On the other hand, an interpretive approach that is more receptive to context outside of the express text may more accurately reflect how a person having ordinary skill in the art would understand the claim language. Such an approach is also more sensitive to technologic custom and linguistic meaning—so-called facts on the ground. Everyone agrees that claims are to be construed through the eyes of the skilled artisan. This tenet makes sense because patents are technical documents written largely to a technical audience. District court judges rarely have the requisite technical training or background to fully comprehend, for example, biotechnological or computer-related principles. As such, there may be a concern about judicial presumptions regarding the meaning of technological descriptions without the aid of technical experts or, at least, technical dictionaries. This approach would also most likely lead to greater deference to district court judges, and therefore, instill greater certainty earlier in the litigation process.

For more on the interpretive methodology of claim construction, *see* Peter Menell, Matthew Powers & Steven Carlson, *Patent Claim Construction: A Modern Synthesis and Structured Framework*, 25 BERKELEY TECH. L.J. 711, 716 (2010); R. Polk Wagner & Lee Petherbridge, *Is the Federal Circuit Succeeding? An Empirical Assessment of Judicial Performance*, 152 U. PA. L. REV. 1105 (2004); Craig Allen Nard, *A Theory of Claim Interpretation*, 14 HARV. J.L. & TECH. 1 (2000); Christopher Cotropia, *Patent Claim Interpretation and Information Costs*, 9 LEWIS & CLARK L. REV. 57 (2005). *See also* Wagner's ongoing empirical assessment of the Federal Circuit's claim construction jurisprudence at http://www.claimconstruction.com.

B. ENABLEMENT

The enablement requirement can be viewed as serving two functions. The first
is facilitating information dissemination. Technical information disclosed in
the patent has potential immediate value to follow-on researchers interested in
improving the patented invention or to the public by contributing to the general storehouse of technical knowledge.[8]

The second function serves to keep claim scope on a leash by requiring
the specification to enable subject matter commensurate with the scope of the
claims. To satisfy the commensurability requirement, claim scope must be less
than or equal to the scope of the enablement, which means that the specification must enable a person having ordinary skill in the art to make and use
the claimed invention without "undue experimentation." In short, a patentee
cannot claim more than he discloses. What constitutes "undue experimentation" is discussed in *Cedarapids* and *Automotive Technologies*, the principal cases
in section B.2.

Subsumed within the information dissemination and commensurability functions of the enablement requirement is the very important question of optimal
claim scope; that is, the legal and policy determination relating to the breadth
of the patentee's property right that affects both ex ante and ex post incentives. Situating a patentee's claim scope on the narrow-broad continuum has
implications for not only the patentee, but also follow-on innovators who seek
to improve upon the patented technology and consumers who are the ultimate
beneficiaries of innovation. The *Morse* and *Incandescent Lamp* cases in section B.1
explore this dynamic. And we will revisit this issue in Chapter 7 in the context
of the Doctrine of Equivalents.

---

8. This view of the specification was embraced by the House of Lords in *Kirin-Amgen, Inc. v.
Hoechst Marion Roussel Ltd.*, wherein Lord Hoffmann wrote:

> [D]isclosure is not only to enable other people to perform the invention after the patent has
> expired. If that were all, the inventor might as well be allowed to keep it secret during the
> life of the patent. It is also to enable anyone to make immediate use of the information for
> any purpose which does not infringe the claims. The specifications of valid and subsisting
> patents are an important source of information for further research, as is abundantly shown
> by a reading of the sources cited in the specification for the patent in suit.

[2004] UKHL 46, [2004] All ER (D) 286 (Oct. 1, 2004). On the importance of access to and dissemination of information for technological innovation, *see* JOEL MOKYR, THE GIFTS OF ATHENA:
HISTORICAL ORIGINS OF THE KNOWLEDGE ECONOMY 28-77 (2002); WILLIAM J. BAUMOL, THE FREE-MARKET
INNOVATION MACHINE: ANALYZING THE GROWTH MIRACLE OF CAPITALISM 73-92 (2002). For a discussion
on the gradual nature of innovation, *see* GEORGE BASALLA, THE EVOLUTION OF TECHNOLOGY (1988).
Although some commentators have questioned the usefulness of the patent disclosure to subsequent researchers. *See, e.g.,* Jeanne C. Fromer, *Patent Disclosure*, 94 IOWA L. REV. 539, 560 (2009)
(stating "[n]otwithstanding the primacy of the patent document as a publicly available repository
of information about a patented invention, a good deal of evidence suggests that technologists do
not find that it contains pertinent information for their research"). In fact it is common in a patent
licensing transaction for the licensee to request an "enabling package," which includes access to
the inventor, know-how, and other forms of tacit knowledge not included in the specification.

STATUTE: Specification
35 U.S.C. § 112, ¶1

1. Enablement and Claim Scope

O'REILLY v. MORSE
56 U.S. 62 (1854)

Chief Justice TANEY delivered the opinion of the court.

* * *

[In a patent issued to Morse in 1840 and reissued in 1848, Morse described "a new and useful apparatus for, and a system of, transmitting intelligence between distant points by means of electro-magnetism, which puts in motion machinery for producing sounds or signs, and recording said signs upon paper or other suitable material, which invention I denominate the American Electro-Magnetic Telegraph. . . ." The patent described "the instruments and . . . mode of their operation," including the famed "Code." The patent continued and set forth the now famous claim eight:]

> Eighth. I do not propose to limit myself to the specific machinery, or parts of machinery, described in the foregoing specifications and claims; the essence of my invention being the use of the motive power of the electric or galvanic current, which I call electro-magnetism, however developed, for making or printing intelligible characters, letters, or signs, at any distances, being a new application of that power, of which I claim to be the first inventor or discovered.

* * *

We perceive no well-founded objection to the description which is given of the whole invention and its separate parts, nor to his right to a patent for the first seven inventions set forth in the specification of his claims. The difficulty arises on the eighth.

* * *

It is impossible to misunderstand the extent of this claim. He claims the exclusive right to every improvement where the motive power is the electric or galvanic current, and the result is the marking or printing intelligible characters, signs, or letters at a distance.

If this claim can be maintained, it matters not by what process or machinery the result is accomplished. For aught that we now know some future inventor, in the onward march of science, may discover a mode of writing or printing at a distance by means of the electric or galvanic current, without using any part of the process or combination set forth in the plaintiff's specification. His invention may be less complicated—less liable to get out of order—less expensive in construction, and in its operation. But yet if it is covered by this patent the inventor could not use it, nor the public have the benefit of it without the permission of this patentee.

Nor is this all, while he shuts the door against inventions of other persons, the patentee would be able to avail himself of new discoveries in the properties and powers of electro-magnetism which scientific men might bring to light. For he says he does not confine his claim to the machinery or parts of machinery, which he specifies; but claims for himself a monopoly in its use, however developed, for the purpose of printing at a distance. New discoveries in physical science may enable him to combine it with new agents and new elements, and by that means attain the object in a manner superior to the present process and altogether different from it. And if he can secure the exclusive use by his present patent he may vary it with every new discovery and development of the science, and need place no description of the new manner, process, or machinery, upon the records of the patent office. And when his patent expires, the public must apply to him to learn what it is. In fine he claims an exclusive right to use a manner and process which he has not described and

Chief Justice Roger Taney

indeed had not invented, and therefore could not describe when he obtained his patent. The court is of the opinion that the claim is too broad, and not warranted by law.

No one, we suppose will maintain that Fulton could have taken out a patent for his invention of propelling vessels by steam, describing the process and machinery he used, and claimed under it the exclusive right to use the motive power of steam, however developed, for the purpose of propelling vessels. It can hardly be supposed that under such a patent he could have prevented the use of the improved machinery which science has since introduced; although the motive power is steam, and the result is the propulsion of vessels. Neither could the man who first discovered that steam might, by a proper arrangement of machinery, be used as a motive power to grind corn or spin cotton, claim the right to the exclusive use of steam as a motive power for the purpose of producing such effects.

Again, the use of steam as a motive power in printing-presses is comparatively a modern discovery. Was the first inventor of a machine or process of this kind entitled to a patent, giving him the exclusive right to use steam as a motive power, however developed, for the purpose of marking or printing intelligible characters? Could he have prevented the use of any other press subsequently invented where steam was used? Yet so far as patentable rights are concerned both improvements must stand on the same principles. Both use a known motive power to print intelligible marks or letters; and it can make no difference in their legal rights under the patent laws, whether the printing is done near at hand or at a distance. Both depend for success not merely upon the motive power, but upon the machinery with which it is combined. And it has never, we believe, been supposed by any one, that the first inventor of a steam printing-press, was entitled to the exclusive use of steam, as a motive power, however developed, for marking or printing intelligible characters.

Indeed, the acts of the patentee himself are inconsistent with the claim made in his behalf. For in 1846 he took out a patent for his new improvement of local circuits, by means of which intelligence could be printed at intermediate places along the main line of the telegraph; and he obtained a reissued patent for this invention in 1848. Yet in this new invention the electric or galvanic current was the motive power, and writing at a distance the effect. The power was undoubtedly developed, by new machinery and new combinations. But if his eighth claim could be sustained, this improvement would be embraced by his first patent. And if it was so embraced, his patent for the local circuits would be illegal and void. For he could not take out a subsequent patent for a portion of his first invention, and thereby extend his monopoly beyond the period limited by law.

* * *

. . . Professor Morse has not discovered, that the electric or galvanic current will always print at a distance, no matter what may be the form of the machinery or mechanical contrivances through which it passes. You may use electro-magnetism as a motive power, and yet not produce the described effect, that is, print at a distance intelligible marks or signs. To produce that effect, it must be combined with, and passed through, and operate upon, certain complicated and delicate machinery, adjusted and arranged upon philosophical principles, and prepared by the highest mechanical skill. And it is the high praise of Professor Morse, that he has been able, by a new combination of known powers, of which electro-magnetism is one, to discover a method by which intelligible marks or signs may be printed at a distance. And for the method or process thus discovered, he is entitled to a patent. But he has not discovered that the electro-magnetic current, used as motive power, in any other method, and with any other combination, will do as well.

* * *

It is a well-settled principle of law, that the mere change in the form of the machinery (unless a particular form is specified as the means by which the effect described is produced) or an alteration in some of its unessential parts; or in the use of known equivalent powers, not varying essentially the machine, or its mode of operation or organization, will not make the new machine a new invention. It may be an improvement upon the former; but that will not justify its use without the consent of the first patentee.

* * *

Mr. Justice Grier.

. . . The . . . point, in which I cannot concur with the opinion of the majority, arises in the construction of the eighth claim of complainant's first patent, as finally amended.

* * *

The great art of printing, which has changed the face of human society and civilization, consisted in nothing but a new application of principles known to the world for thousands of years. No one could say it consisted in the type or the press, or in any other machine or device used in performing some particular function, more than in the hands which picked the types or worked the press. Yet if the inventor of printing had, under this narrow construction of our patent law, claimed his art as something distinct from his machinery, the doctrine now advanced, would have declared it unpatentable to its full extent as an art, and that the inventor could be protected in nothing but his first rough types and ill-contrived press.

Justice Grier

* * *

To say that a patentee, who claims the art of writing at a distance by means of electro-magnetism, necessarily claims all future improvements in the art, is to misconstrue it, or draws a consequence from it not fairly to be inferred from its language. An improvement in a known art is as much the subject of a patent as the art itself; so, also, is an improvement on a known machine. Yet, if the original machine be patented, the patentee of an improvement will not have a right to use the original. This doctrine has not been found to retard the progress of invention in the case of machines; and I can see no reason why a contrary one should be applied to an art.

* * *

The word telegraph is derived from the Greek, and signifies "to write afar off or at a distance." It has heretofore been applied to various contrivances or devices, to communicate intelligence by means of signals or semaphores, which speak to the eye for a moment. But in its primary and literal signification of writing, printing, or recording at a distance, it never was invented, perfected, or put into practical operation till it was done by Morse. He preceded Steinheil, Cook, Wheatstone, and Davy in the successful application of this mysterious power or element of electro-magnetism to this purpose; and his invention has entirely superseded their inefficient contrivances. It is not only "a new and useful art," if that term means any thing, but a most wonderful and astonishing invention, requiring tenfold more ingenuity and patient experiment to perfect it, than the art of printing with types and press, as originally invented.

* * *

Now the patent law requires an inventor, as a condition precedent to obtaining a patent, to deliver a written description of his invention or discovery, and to particularly specify what he claims to be his own invention or discovery. If he has truly stated the principle, nature and extent of his art or invention, how can the court say it is too broad, and impugn the validity of his patent for doing what the law requires as a condition for obtaining it? And if it is only in case of a machine that the law requires the inventor to specify what he claims as his own invention and discovery, and to distinguish what is new from what is old, then this eighth claim is superfluous and cannot affect the validity of his patent, provided his art is new and useful, and the machines and devices claimed separately, are of his own invention. If it be in the use of the words "however developed" that the claim is to be adjudged too broad, then it follows that a person using any other process for the purpose of developing the agent or element of electro-magnetism, than the common one now in use, and described in the patent, may pirate the whole art patented.

CONSOLIDATED ELECTRIC LIGHT CO. v. McKEESPORT LIGHT CO.
(*The Incandescent Lamp Case*)
159 U.S. 465 (1895)

This was a bill in equity, filed by the Consolidated Electric Light Company against the McKeesport Light Company, to recover damages for the infringement of letters patent No. 317,076, issued May 12, 1885, to the Electro-Dynamic Light Company, assignee of Sawyer and Man, for an electric light. The defendants justified under certain patents to Thomas A. Edison, particularly No. 223,898, issued January 27, 1880; denied the novelty and utility of the complainant's patent; and averred that the same had been fraudulently and illegally procured. The real defendant was the Edison Electric Light Company, and the case involved a contest between what are known as the Sawyer and Man and the Edison systems of electric lighting.

In their application, Sawyer and Man stated that their invention related to "that class of electric lamps employing an incandescent conductor enclosed in a transparent, hermetically sealed vessel or chamber, from which oxygen is excluded, and . . . more especially to the incandescing conductor, its substance, its form, and its combination with the other elements composing the lamp. Its object is to secure a cheap and effective apparatus; and our improvement consists, first, of the combination, in a lamp chamber, composed wholly of glass, as described in patent No. 205,144," upon which this patent was declared to be an improvement, "of an incandescing conductor of carbon made from a vegetable fibrous material, in contradistinction to a similar conductor made from mineral or gas carbon, and also in the form of such conductor so made from such vegetable carbon, and combined in the lighting circuit with the exhausted chamber of the lamp."

The following drawings exhibit the substance of the invention:

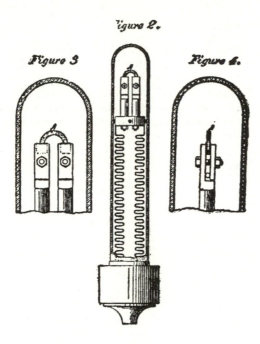

The specification further stated that:

In the practice of our invention, we have made use of carbonized paper, and also wood carbon. We have also used such conductors or burners of various shapes, such as pieces with their lower ends secured to their respective supports, and having their upper ends united so as to form an inverted V-shaped burner. We have also used conductors of varying contours, that is, with rectangular bends instead of curvilinear ones; but we prefer the arch shape.

No especial description of making the illuminating carbon conductors, described in this specification, and making the subject-matter of this improvement, is thought necessary, as any of the ordinary methods of forming the material to be carbonized to the desired shape and size, and carbonizing it while confined in retorts in powdered carbon, substantially according to the methods in practice before the date of this improvement, may be adopted in the practice thereof by any one skilled in the arts appertaining to the making of carbons for electric lighting or for other use in the arts.

An important practical advantage which is secured by the arch form of incandescing carbon is that it permits the carbon to expand and contract under the varying temperatures to which it is subjected when the electric current is turned on or off without altering the position of its fixed terminals. Thus, the necessity for a special mechanical device to compensate for the expansion and contraction which has heretofore been necessary is entirely dispensed with, and thus the lamp is materially simplified in its construction. . . .

The advantages resulting from the manufacture of the carbon from vegetable fibrous or textile material instead of mineral or gas carbon are many. Among them may be mentioned the convenience afforded for cutting and making the conductor in the desired form and size, the purity and equality of the carbon obtained, its susceptibility to tempering, both as to hardness and resistance, and its toughness and durability. . . .

The claims were as follows:

(1) An incandescing conductor for an electric lamp, of carbonized fibrous or textile material, and of an arch or horseshoe shape, substantially as hereinbefore set forth.

(2) The combination, substantially as hereinbefore set forth, of an electric circuit and an incandescing conductor of carbonized fibrous material, included in and forming part of said circuit, and a transparent, hermetically sealed chamber, in which the conductor is enclosed.

(3) The incandescing conductor for an electric lamp, formed of carbonized paper, substantially as described.

The commercial Edison lamp used by the appellee, and which is illustrated below, is composed of a burner, **A**, made of carbonized bamboo of a peculiar quality, discovered by Mr. Edison to be highly useful for the purpose, and having a length of about 6 inches, a diameter of about 5/1000 of an inch, and an electrical resistance of upward of 100 ohms. This filament of carbon is bent into the form of a loop, and its ends are secured by good electrical and mechanical connections to two fine platinum wires, **B, B**. These wires pass through a glass stem, **C**, the glass being melted and fused upon the platinum wires. A glass globe, **D**, is fused to the glass stem, **C**. This glass globe has originally attached to it, at the point **d**, a glass tube, by means of which a connection is made with highly organized and refined exhausting apparatus, which produces in the globe a high vacuum, whereupon the glass tube is melted off by a flame, and the globe is closed by the fusion of the glass at the point **d**.

Upon a hearing in the circuit court before Mr. Justice Bradley, upon pleadings and proofs, the court held the patent to be invalid, and dismissed the bill. Thereupon complainant appealed to this court.

Mr. Justice Brown, after stating the facts in the foregoing language, delivered the opinion of the court.

In order to obtain a complete understanding of the scope of the Sawyer and Man patent, it is desirable to consider briefly the state of the art at the time the application was originally made, which was in January, 1880.

Two general forms of electric illumination had for many years been the subject of experiments more or less successful, one of which was known as the "arc light," produced by the passage of a current of electricity between the points of two carbon pencils placed end to end, and slightly separated from each other. In its passage from one point to the other through the air, the electric current took the form of an arc, and gave the name to the light. This form of light had been produced by Sir Humphry Davy as early as 1810, and, by successive improvements in the carbon pencils and in their relative adjustment to each other, had come into general use as a means of lighting streets, halls, and other large spaces; but by reason of its intensity, the uncertain and flickering character of the light, and the rapid consumption of the carbon pencils, it was wholly unfitted for domestic use.

The second form of illumination is what is known as the "incandescent system," and consists generally in the passage of a current of electricity through a continuous strip or piece of refractory material, which is a conductor of electricity, but a poor conductor; in other words, a conductor offering a considerable resistance to the flow of the current through it. It was discovered early in this

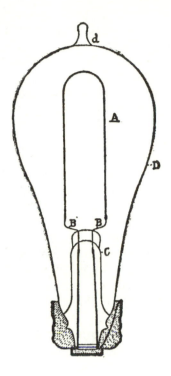

century that various substances might be heated to a white heat by passing a sufficiently strong current of electricity through them. . . .

For many years prior to 1880, experiments had been made by a large number of persons, in various countries, with a view to the production of an incandescent light which could be made available for domestic purposes, and could compete with gas in the matter of expense. Owing partly to a failure to find a proper material, which should burn but not consume, partly to the difficulty of obtaining a perfect vacuum in the globe in which the light was suspended, and partly to a misapprehension of the true principle of incandescent lighting, these experiments had not been attended with success; although it had been demonstrated as early as 1845 that, whatever material was used, the conductor must be enclosed in an arc-light bulb, to prevent it from being consumed by the oxygen in the atmosphere. The chief difficulty was that the carbon burners were subject to a rapid disintegration or evaporation, which electricians assumed was due to the disrupting action of the electric current, and hence the conclusion was reached that carbon contained in itself the elements of its own destruction, and was not a suitable material for the burner of an incandescent lamp.

It is admitted that the lamp described in the Sawyer and Man patent is no longer in use, and was never a commercial success; that it does not embody the principle of high resistance with a small illuminating surface; that it does not have the filament burner of the modern incandescent lamp; that the lamp chamber is defective; and that the lamp manufactured by the complainant, and put upon the market, is substantially the Edison lamp; but it is said that, in the conductor used by Edison (a particular part of the stem of the bamboo, lying directly beneath the siliceous cuticle, the peculiar fitness for which purpose was undoubtedly discovered by him), he made use of a fibrous or textile material covered by the patent to Sawyer and Man, and is therefore an infringer. It was admitted, however, that the third claim—for a conductor of carbonized paper—was not infringed.

The two main defenses to this patent are (1) that it is defective upon its face, in attempting to monopolize the use of all fibrous and textile materials for the purpose of electric illuminations; and (2) that Sawyer and Man were not in fact the first to discover that these were better adapted than mineral carbons to such purposes.

Is the complainant entitled to a monopoly of all fibrous and textile materials for incandescent conductors? If the patentees had discovered in fibrous and textile substances a quality common to them all, or to them generally, as distinguishing them from other materials, such as minerals, etc., and such quality or characteristic adapted them peculiarly to incandescent conductors, such claim might not be too broad. If, for instance, minerals or porcelains had always been used for a particular purpose, and a person should take out a patent for a similar article of wood, and woods generally were adapted to that purpose, the claim might not be too broad, though defendant used wood of a different kind from that of the patentee. But if woods generally were not adapted to the purpose, and yet the patentee had discovered a wood possessing certain qualities, which gave it a peculiar fitness for such purpose, it would not constitute an infringement for another to discover and use a different kind of wood, which was found to contain similar or superior qualities. The present case is an apt illustration of this principle. Sawyer and Man supposed they had discovered in carbonized paper the best material for an incandescent conductor. Instead of confining themselves to carbonized paper, as they might properly have done, and in fact did in their third claim, they made a broad claim for every fibrous or textile material, when in fact an examination of over 6,000 vegetable growths showed that none of them possessed the peculiar qualities that fitted them for that purpose. Was everybody, then, precluded by this broad claim from making further investigation? We think not.

The injustice of so holding is manifest in view of the experiments made, and continued for several months, by Mr. Edison and his assistants, among the different species of vegetable growth, for the purpose of ascertaining the one best adapted to an incandescent conductor. Of these he found suitable for his purpose only about three species of bamboo, one species of cane from the valley of the Amazon (impossible to be procured in quantities on account of the climate), and one or two species of fibers from the agave family. Of the special bamboo, the walls of which have a thickness of about 3/8 of an inch, he used only about 20/1000 of an inch in thickness. In this portion of the bamboo the fibers are more nearly parallel, the cell walls are apparently smallest, and the pithy matter between the fibers is at its minimum. It seems that carbon filaments cannot be made of wood, that is, exogenous vegetable growth, because the fibers are not parallel, and the longitudinal fibers are intercepted by radial fibers. The cells composing the fibers are all so large that the resulting carbon is very porous and friable. Lamps made of this material proved of no commercial value. After trying as many as 30 or 40 different woods of exogenous growth, he gave them up as hopeless. But finally, while experimenting with a bamboo strip which formed the edge of a palm-leaf fan, cut into filaments, he obtained surprising results. After microscopic examination of the material, he dispatched a man to Japan to make arrangements for securing the bamboo in quantities. It seems that the characteristic of the bamboo which makes it particularly suitable is that the fibers run more nearly parallel than in other species of wood. Owing to this, it can be cut up into filaments having parallel fibers, running throughout their length, and producing a homogeneous carbon. There is no generic quality, however, in vegetable fibers, because they are fibrous, which adapts them to the purpose. Indeed, the fibers are rather a disadvantage. If the bamboo grew solid, without fibers, but had its peculiar cellular formation, it would be a perfect material, and incandescent lamps would last at least six times as long as at present. All vegetable fibrous growths do not have a suitable cellular structure. In some the cells are so large that they are valueless for that purpose. No exogenous, and very few endogenous, growths are suitable. The messenger whom he dispatched to different parts of Japan and China sent him about 40 different kinds of bamboo, in such quantities as to enable him to make a number of lamps, and from a test of these different species he ascertained which was best for the purpose. From this it appears very clearly that there is no such quality common to fibrous and textile substances generally as makes them suitable for an incandescent conductor, and that the bamboo which was finally pitched upon, and is now generally used, was not selected because it was of vegetable growth, but because it contained certain peculiarities in its fibrous structure which distinguished it from every other fibrous substance. The question really is whether the imperfectly successful experiments of Sawyer and Man, with carbonized paper and wood carbon, conceding all that is claimed for them, authorize them to put under tribute the results of the brilliant discoveries made by others.

It is required by Rev. St. §4888, that the application shall contain "a written description of the device, and of the manner and process of making constructing, compounding, and using it in such full, clear, concise, and exact terms as to enable any person, skilled in the art or science to which it appertains or with which it is most nearly connected, to make, construct, compound, and use the same." The object of this is to apprise the public of what the patentee claims as his own, the courts of what they are called upon to construe, and competing manufacturers and dealers of exactly what they are bound to avoid. *Grant v. Raymond* [1832]. If the description be so vague and uncertain that no one can tell, except by independent experiments, how to construct the patented device, the patent is void.

It was said by Mr. Chief Justice Taney in *Wood v. Underhill* [1857], with respect to a patented compound for the purpose of making brick or tile, which did not give the relative proportions of the different ingredients:

> But when the specification of a new composition of matter gives only the names of the substances which are to be mixed together, without stating any relative proportion, undoubtedly it would be the duty of the court to declare the patent void. And the same rule would prevail where it was apparent that the proportions were stated ambiguously and vaguely; for in such cases it would be evident, on the face of the specification, that no one could use the invention without first ascertaining, by experiment, the exact proportion of the different ingredients required to produce the result intended to be obtained. . . . And if, from the nature and character of the ingredients to be used, they are not susceptible . . . of such exact description, the inventor is not entitled to a patent.

So in *Tyler v. Boston* [1868], wherein the plaintiff professed to have discovered a combination of fuel oil with the mineral and earthy oils, constituting a burning fluid, the patentee stated that the exact quantity of fuel oil which is necessary to produce the most desirable compound must be determined by experiment. And the court observed: "Where a patent is claimed for such a discovery, it should state the component parts of the new manufacture claimed with clearness and precision, and not leave a person attempting to use the discovery to find it out 'by experiment.'"

Applying this principle to the patent under consideration, how would it be possible for a person to know what fibrous or textile material was adapted to the purpose of an incandescent conductor, except by the most careful and painstaking experimentation? If, as before observed, there were some general quality, running through the whole fibrous and textile kingdom, which distinguished it from every other, and gave it a peculiar fitness for the particular purpose, the man who discovered such quality might justly be entitled to a patent; but that is not the case here. An examination of materials of this class carried on for months revealed nothing that seemed to be adapted to the purpose; and even the carbonized paper and wood carbons specified in the patent, experiments with which first suggested their incorporation therein, were found to be so inferior to the bamboo, afterwards discovered by Edison, that the complainant was forced to abandon its patent in that particular, and take up with the material discovered by its rival. Under these circumstances, to hold that one who had discovered that a certain fibrous or textile material answered the required purpose should obtain the right to exclude everybody from the whole domain of fibrous and textile materials, and thereby shut out any further efforts to discover a better specimen of that class than the patentee had employed, would be an unwarranted extension of his monopoly, and operate rather to discourage than to promote invention. If Sawyer and Man had discovered that a certain carbonized paper would answer the purpose, their claim to all carbonized paper would, perhaps, not be extravagant; but the fact that paper happens to belong to the fibrous kingdom did not invest them with sovereignty over this entire kingdom, and thereby practically limit other experimenters to the domain of minerals.

In fact, such a construction of this patent as would exclude competitors from making use of any fibrous or textile material would probably defeat itself, since, if the patent were infringed by the use of any such material, it would be anticipated by proof of the prior use of any such material. In this connection it would appear, not only that wood charcoal had been constantly used since the days of Sir Humphry Davy for arc lighting, but that in the English patent to Greener and Staite, of 1846, for an incandescent light, "charcoal, reduced to a state of powder," was one of the materials employed. So also, in the English patent of 1841 to De Moleyns, "a finely pulverized boxwood charcoal or plumbago" was used for an incandescent electric lamp. Indeed, in the experiments of Sir Humphry Davy, early in the century, pieces of well-burned charcoal were heated to a vivid whiteness by the electric current, and other experiments were made which evidently contemplated the use of charcoal heated to the point of incandescence. Mr. Broadnax, the attorney who prepared the application, it seems, was also of opinion that a broad claim for vegetable carbons could not be sustained, because charcoal had been used before in incandescent lighting. There is undoubtedly a good deal of testimony tending to show that, for the past 50 or 60 years, the word "charcoal" has been used in the art, not only to designate carbonized wood, but mineral or hard carbons, such as were commonly employed for the carbon pencils of arc lamps. But we think it quite evident that, in the patents and experiments above referred to, it was used in its ordinary sense of charcoal obtained from wood. The very fact of the use of such word to designate mineral carbons indicates that such carbons were believed to possess peculiar properties required for illumination, that before that had been supposed to belong to wood charcoal.

. . . [W]e are all agreed that the claims of this patent, with the exception of the third, are too indefinite to be the subject of a valid monopoly.

Comments

1. *Claim Scope and Commensurability.* The majority in *Morse* held claim eight invalid because the breadth of the claim was not commensurate with the specification. The commensurability requirement states that a patentee cannot claim more than he discloses; in other words, the claim scope must be commensurate with what is disclosed in the specification. (The *Cedarapids* and *Automotive Technologies* cases following these Comments discuss the test for commensurability.) The *Morse* case is perhaps the first time the Supreme Court invoked commensurability, because in a subsequent case, Justice Grier remarked: "Until the [*Morse*] decision was read in court, the patentee [Morse] had not the least reason to suspect his claim to be invalid. The decision was a surprise not only to him, but many others more learned in the law, who had carefully examined this claim, and advised the patentee that it was valid." *Silsby v. Foote*, 61 U.S. 378, 389 (1857) (Grier, J., dissenting).

Recall, the specification did not disclose all uses and improvements of the motive power of the electric or galvanic current. In claim 8, Morse sought patent protection on more than he actually invented. As such, the Court employed the enablement requirement to constrain claim scope, limiting Morse to his first seven claims. From a policy perspective, Justice Taney (pronounced "TAW-nee") was concerned that claim 8 would capture future improvements or alternatives that Morse did not invent or describe in his patent. (*See* Comment 5, below, for a discussion of Justice Taney that may partially explain why he was skeptical of Morse's claim 8.) As the majority stated: "For aught that we now know some future inventor" may improve upon Morse's invention yet "could not use it, not the public benefit of it without the permission of" Morse. Implicit in this statement is an awareness of inefficiencies associated with a "patent holdup" situation in the context of improvement activity. According to Tom Cotter, a patent holdup situation occurs when a:

> (1) patent owner (2) is able to exploit its bargaining power vis-à-vis downstream users (3) due to the possibility that the patent owner will be able to enjoin the manufacture, use, or sale of an end product that incorporates the patented invention, (4) in such a way as to threaten either (a) static deadweight loss far out of proportion to any likely increases in dynamic efficiency, or (b) dynamic efficiency losses due to downstream users' reduced incentives to invest in . . . follow-on innovation.

Thomas F. Cotter, *Patent Holdup, Patent Remedies, and Antitrust Responses*, 34 J. Corp. Law, 1151, 1154 (2009).

Justice Grier saw the case differently. By focusing on the significance of Morse's invention, Grier seemed to be making both a moral and instrumentalist argument based respectively on Morse's just deserts and contribution to society. (These two points are discussed in more detail later in this Comment.) But Justice Grier also advanced an economic argument by focusing on an improver's ability to obtain patent rights. Grier wrote, "An improvement in a known art is as much the subject of a patent as the art itself." To fully appreciate the significance of this statement, it is important to understand that one may obtain a patent on an invention and still infringe a preexisting patent. Consider the following example: Inventor 1 obtains a patent on a chair and claims a seat portion, a back portion, and four legs. Subsequently, Inventor 2 (the improver) invents a chair having a seat portion, a back portion *that reclines*, and four legs. Although Inventor 2 (as Justice Grier noted) may receive a patent (say because the reclining feature in combination with the other features were novel and not obvious), he cannot practice his claimed invention because it would infringe Inventor 1's patent. Infringement exists here because a commercial embodiment of Inventor 2's claimed invention has all of the limitations of Inventor 1's patent claim (i.e., a seat portion, a back portion, and four legs). While the reclining feature may have allowed Inventor 2 to patent his chair, this feature does not save Inventor 2 from infringement if he were to practice his invention. By the same token, Inventor 1 cannot practice Inventor 2's claimed invention. Thus, assuming Inventor 2's reclining feature is a marketable improvement, both inventors have an incentive to cross-license each other. This scenario is commonly referred to as "blocking patents," which is what Justice Grier may have had in mind when he wrote this "doctrine has not been found to retard the progress of invention." *Id.* But given the breadth of Morse's claim 8, how confident should we be that an improver would be able to obtain patent protection? That is, even if an improver develops a more efficient way of using electromagnetism for "making or printing intelligible chapters at any distances," claim 8's "however developed" language may nonetheless anticipate this improvement.

Interestingly, in some countries, such as Turkey, an improver who is unable to obtain permission from the original patentee may petition a court for a compulsory license to use the original patent. If granted, the original patentee may then seek a compulsory license to use the improvement patent. *See* Article 79, *Decree-Law No. 551 Pertaining to the Protection of Patent Rights* (stating "the right holder of the latter [improvement] patent may use . . . the prior patent where he has been authorized by the right holder of the prior patent to use same or has been granted compulsory license to use said prior patent"), and Article 101 ("Where patented inventions, dependent in the sense of Article 79, serve the same industrial purpose and where a compulsory license has been granted in favour of one of the dependent patents, the patentee of the dependent patent upon which compulsory license is granted may request from the court that a compulsory license be granted in his favour on the other dependent patent."). For a discussion of blocking patents, *see* Robert P. Merges, *Intellectual Property Rights and Bargaining Breakdown: The Case of Blocking Patents*, 62 TENN. L. REV. 75 (1994); Carl Shapiro, *Navigating the Patent Thickets: Cross Licenses, Patent Pools, and Standard Setting*, in 1 INNOVATION POLICY AND THE ECONOMY 119 (Adam B. Jaffe et al. eds., 2001). For more on the issue of patent holdups, *see* Mark A. Lemley & Carl Shapiro, *Patent Holdup and Royalty Stacking*, 85 TEX. L. REV. 1991 (2007); J. Gregory Sidak, *Holdup*,

Royalty Stacking, and the Presumption of Injunctive Relief for Patent Infringement: A Reply to Lemley and Shapiro, 92 MINN. L. REV. 714 (2008); Einer Elhauge, *Do Patent Holdup and Royalty Stacking Lead to Systematically Excessive Royalties?*, 4 J. COMPETITION L. & ECON. 535 (2008).

As noted above, Justice Grier also offered a moral and instrumentalist rationale. Contrary to the tenor of Justice Taney's opinion, Justice Grier referred to Morse's telegraph as "a most wonderful and astonishing invention, requiring tenfold more ingenuity and patient experiment to perfect it, than the art of printing with types and press, as originally invented." It was Morse, according to Justice Grier, who "invented, perfected, or put into practical operation" the telegraph. *Morse*, 56 U.S. at 134. Indeed, Morse's invention was significant as it divorced communication from transportation, and, along with the railroad, "facilitated nationwide commerce and diminished transaction costs." DAVID WALKER HOWE, WHAT HATH GOD WROUGHT: THE TRANSFORMATION OF AMERICA, 1815-1848 696 (2007). In fact, "[o]f all the celebrated inventions of an age that believed in progress, Morse's telegraph impressed observers the most." *Id.* at 696-697. As the New York Times observed in an 1852 editorial, this "slender wire has become the highway of thought." Grier somewhat overstated his case, however, when he wrote that Morse preceded Wheatstone in the telegraph's successful application, as the British had been operating a Wheatstone-designed electric telegraph since 1838; and there were others who preceded Morse and added important pieces to the telegraphy puzzle. But Morse's telegraph worked better, and the British would soon make the transition to Morse's system. As Kenneth Silverman wrote, Morse was not the first to employ the powers of electromagnetism, but compared to his competitors, his telegraph was "the cheapest, the most rugged, the most reliable, and the simplest to operate." KENNETH SILVERMAN, LIGHTING MAN: THE ACCURSED LIFE OF SAMUEL F.B. MORSE 322 (2003). Moreover, the famous Morse code greatly influenced the use of language. According to historian Maury Klein, the "leisurely, flowery flow of Victorian prose found itself challenged by the terse, snappy vignettes of the telegram, where more words meant higher costs." MAURY KLEIN, THE GENESIS OF INDUSTRIAL AMERICA, 1870-1920 77 (2007). What would Morse think of texting and tweeting?

2. ***Claim Scope and Ex Ante vs. Ex Post Incentives.*** The *Morse* case also highlights a broader policy issue in patent law, namely the determination of optimal claim scope—a very difficult endeavor. (See the Policy Perspective after these Comments.) An important part of this determination—namely, where the patentee's claim scope resides on the narrow-broad continuum—relates to how much improvement activity patentees such as Morse should be able to capture vis-à-vis follow-on improvers. Justices Taney and Grier provide competing perspectives on optimal claim scope. Whom do you agree with? Taney's approach provides follow-on improvers with more freedom to operate (emphasis on ex post incentives), whereas Grier places more emphasis on ex ante incentives and the role of blocking patents?

Before answering this question, consider the following discussion by economist Suzanne Scotchmer:

> When innovation is cumulative, the most important benefit of the innovation may be the boost it gives to later innovators. The boost can take at least three

forms. If the next innovation could not be invented without the first, then the social value of the first innovation includes at least part of the incremental social value provided by the second. If the first innovation merely reduces the cost of achieving the second, then the cost reduction is part of the social value provided by the first. And if the first innovation accelerates development of the second, then the social value includes the value of getting the second innovation sooner. *The problem introduced for incentive mechanisms is how to make sure that earlier innovators are compensated for their contributions, while ensuring that later innovators also have an incentive to invest.*

SUZANNE SCOTCHMER, INNOVATION AND INCENTIVES 127 (2006) (emphasis added). These considerations are not exclusive to patent law. As Judge Easterbrook wrote in a copyright case, during the creative enterprise every author is simultaneously both a "creator in part and a borrower in part." In this context, "[b]efore the first work is published, broad protection of intellectual property seems best; after it is published, narrow protection seems best." *Nash v. CBS, Inc.,* 899 F.2d 1537, 1540 (7th Cir. 1990). Nonetheless, "only one rule can be in force" and "[t]his single rule must achieve as much as possible of these inconsistent demands." *Id.* Easterbrook candidly acknowledged how difficult it is to address this challenge from an institutional perspective, as "[n]either Congress nor the courts has the information that would allow it to determine which is best. Both institutions must muddle through, using not a fixed rule but a sense of the consequences of moving dramatically in either direction." *Id.* at 1541. Consistent with this theme, William Robinson, the prominent nineteenth-century patent law treatise author, wrote in 1890 that "[w]ith very few exceptions, every invention is the result of the inventive genius of the age, working under the demand of its immediate wants, rather than the product of the individual mind." WILLIAM C. ROBINSON, THE LAW OF PATENTS §29 (1890). *See also* Mark A. Lemley, *The Economics of Improvement in Intellectual Property Law,* 75 TEX. L. REV. 989 (1997).

3. ***The Genus-Species Issue.*** In the *Incandescent Lamp* case, the Sawyer and Man specification disclosed a discovery that related to carbonized paper as a good incandescing conductor. But in claim 1, Sawyer and Man sought protection for "carbonized fibrous or textile material," language much broader than what was disclosed in the specification. In short, Sawyer and Man claimed a genus, but discovered a species. While they were entitled to protection of the species (as in claim 3), the enablement requirement prevented them from extending their patent protection to all "fibrous or textile material." As Justice Brown wrote, "the fact that paper belongs to the fibrous kingdom did not invest [Sawyer and Man] with sovereignty over this entire kingdom," particularly Edison's bamboo. Echoing Justice Taney's concern in *Morse,* Justice Brown continued:

> [T]o hold that one who had discovered that a certain fibrous or textile material answered the required purpose should obtain the right to exclude everybody from the whole domain of fibrous and textile materials, and thereby shut out any further efforts to discover a better specimen of that class than the patentee had employed, would be an unwarranted extension of his monopoly, and operate rather to discourage than to promote invention.

Patent law does permit applicants to claim generically without disclosing each and every species as long as the disclosure is sufficient. For example, as Justice Brown noted, "[i]f the patentees had discovered in fibrous and textile substances a quality common to them all, or to them generally, as distinguishing them from other materials, such as minerals." *See also Ariad Pharmaceuticals, Inc. v. Eli Lilly & Co.*, 598 F.3d 1336, 1350 (Fed. Cir. 2010) (*en banc*) ("We held that a sufficient description of a genus . . . requires the disclosure of either a representative number of species falling within the scope of the genus or structural features common to the members of the genus so that one of skill in the art can 'visualize or recognize' the members of the genus."). Not surprisingly, where the line is between a sufficient and insufficient description is sometimes difficult to discern, but the line must be drawn. In *In re Grimme*, 274 F.2d 949, 952 (CCPA 1960), for example, the applicant claimed generically and the court found the disclosure sufficient because the applicant provided several examples. According to the court, "[i]t is manifestly impracticable for an applicant who discloses a generic invention to give an example of every species falling within it, or even to name every such species." Just how many examples or species must be disclosed in a generic-claim context to satisfy the enablement requirement was addressed in *In re Shokal*, 242 F.2d 771, 773 (CCPA 1957):

> It appears to be well settled that a single species can rarely, if ever, afford sufficient support for a generic claim. The decisions do not however fix any definite number of species which will establish completion of a generic invention and it seems evident therefrom that such number will vary, depending on the circumstances of particular cases. Thus, in the case of a small genus such as the halogens, consisting of four species, a reduction to practice of three, or perhaps even two, might serve to complete the generic invention, while in the case of a genus comprising hundreds of species, a considerably larger number of reductions to practice would probably be necessary.

See also In re Angstadt, 537 F.2d 498, 502-503 (CCPA 1976) (deciding that applicants "are not required to disclose every species encompassed by their claims even in an unpredictable art" and that the disclosure of 40 working examples sufficiently described subject matter of claims directed to a generic process).

In a biological context, *see Capon v. Eshhar*, 418 F.3d 1349, 1359 (Fed. Cir. 2005) ("Precedent illustrates that the determination of what is needed to support generic claims to biological subject matter depends on a variety of factors, such as the existing knowledge in the particular field, the extent and content of the prior art, the maturity of the science or technology, the predictability of the aspect at issue, and other considerations appropriate to the subject matter. . . . It is not necessary that every permutation within a generally operable invention be effective in order for an inventor to obtain a generic claim, provided that the effect is sufficiently demonstrated to characterize a generic invention."). Technological unpredictability is indeed an important consideration. *See Bilstad v. Wakalopulos*, 386 F.3d 1116, 1125 (Fed. Cir. 2004) ("If the difference between members of the group is such that the person skilled in the art would not readily discern that other members of the genus would perform similarly to the disclosed members, i.e., if the art is unpredictable, then disclosure of more species is necessary to adequately show possession of the entire genus.").

As a prelude to the novelty section in Chapter 4, it is worth noting here that if the prior art discloses a species, an applicant cannot claim a genus because, by definition, part of the genus is not novel. *See In re Gosteli*, 872 F.2d 1008 (Fed. Cir. 1999). But the reverse is not always true. That is, an applicant may claim a species if the prior art discloses a genus. Courts have held that a prior art genus does not always anticipate a later claimed species, but *may* render the later claimed species obvious under section 103. Why? *See In re Baird*, 16 F.3d 380 (Fed. Cir. 1994), and *In re Jones*, 958 F.2d 347 (Fed. Cir. 1992).

4. ***Samuel Morse's Patent Troubles.*** Samuel Finley Breese Morse became wealthy and famous as an inventor, but before turning his attention to telegraphy, Morse was a professor of fine arts at New York University and a highly regarded portrait painter. Painting was undoubtedly less stressful, as Morse endured considerable frustrations resulting from his experience with patent litigation. Patent litigation, according to Morse, "is not the way to encourage the Arts, to drive the Artists into exile or to the insane hospital or to the grave." SILVERMAN, LIGHTING MAN, *supra* Comment 1, at 319. Morse was not alone in this sentiment. Charles Goodyear (who invented the rubber vulcanization process) wrote in his memoirs that patent litigation "is, to the inventor, a grievous hardship and wrong, and has no parallel in any other species of property." CHARLES SLACK, NOBEL OBSESSION: CHARLES GOODYEAR, THOMAS HANCOCK, AND THE RACE TO UNLOCK THE GREATEST INDUSTRIAL SECRET OF THE NINETEENTH CENTURY 165-166 (2002). In this vein, economic historian Joel Mokyr, referring to Goodyear and Eli Whitney (cotton gin inventor), writes that "[l]itigation over patent infringement could sap the creativity of great technical minds, and ruin inventors financially." JOEL MOKYR, LEVER OF RICHES 248-249 (1990).

5. ***Chief Justice Taney and Patent Law.*** Prior to the Civil War, for nearly 30 years, the Supreme Court was under the leadership of Chief Justice Roger B. Taney, appointed by President Andrew Jackson in 1836 after serving as Jackson's Attorney General and, during the "Bank War," as Secretary of Treasury. *See* HARRY L. WATSON, LIBERTY AND POWER: THE POLITICS OF JACKSONIAN AMERICA 164 (1990). Although Taney is largely remembered today for his opinion in the infamous *Dred Scott* case, he played a prominent role in the development of antebellum patent law. He was viewed as a "great technical lawyer with a better legal training than any of his predecessors" and his knowledge of the law and democratic philosophy "gave promise that his decisions would be made with a view to economic and social conditions, and not entirely from a coldly legalistic point of view." CHARLES W. SMITH, JR., ROGER B. TANEY: JACKSONIAN JURIST 16 (1936). Moreover, Taney held strong Jacksonian anti-monopoly views with respect to corporations, writing several opinions that "had undermined special corporate charters." JAMES MCPHERSON, BATTLE CRY OF FREEDOM: THE CIVIL WAR ERA 173 (1998). *See also* A. Samuel Oddi, *Regeneration in American Patent Law: Statutory Subject Matter*, 46 IDEA 491, 507 (2006) (asserting Taney "was ambivalent toward patents" and particularly skeptical of Justice Story's liberal construction of patent rights). In this light, one obtains a greater appreciation for why Taney may have been skeptical of Morse's claim 8.

6. *Thomas Edison's Quest for "Incandescent" Light.* By the 1870s, there were two known ways to derive light from electricity. The first was arc lighting (use of an electric arc), which formed light between two pieces of carbon. This type of lighting—associated with William Wallace and others—was used in public spaces and lighthouses, and was much brighter than an interior lamp. The other type of lighting employed a current to heat up a filament to such a degree that it became "incandescent." While incandescent lighting was conducive to indoor use, finding a filament that did not burn or melt was not immediately apparent. Enter Thomas Edison—backed by Wall Street financiers such as J.P. Morgan—and his quest to find the perfect filament. (The Edison Electric Light Company—formed in 1878—is the predecessor of today's General Electric Company.) Edison perused extant patents and literature on lighting systems and paid particular attention to the work of his "rivals," all in an attempt to create a practical and convenient lamp. He learned that delivering independent current to several individual lamps required a "parallel circuit," but such a circuit demanded the transfer of a great deal of energy. One way to deliver the requisite energy was to use either large currents or high voltage (Power = Voltage x Current), which required large conductors—a very expensive set up. Alternatively, high voltage could be delivered using small currents, but each lamp would require a high resistance (Voltage = Current x Resistance—Ohm's law). Indeed, "Edison's key insight was that any commercially viable lighting system must minimize electricity consumption and hence must use high-resistance filaments with lights connected in parallel across a constant-voltage system." VACLAV SMIL, CREATING THE TWENTIETH CENTURY: TECHNICAL INNOVATIONS OF 1867-1914 AND THEIR LASTING IMPACT 41 (2005). This insight required Edison and his team at Menlo Park, including Francis Upton, to search for a high-resistance filament. After a great deal of experimentation, a few inches of carbonized cotton thread proved feasible. Several months later, Edison and his Menlo Park researchers discovered Japanese bamboo, "whose core had perfect cellular structure and yielded a strong and highly resistant carbonized filament." *Id.* at 43.

Of course, Edison and Joseph Swan were not alone in their persistent inventive activities relating to incandescent light. Other researchers in the United States included Moses Farmer, William Sawyer, and Hiram Maxim. In the United Kingdom, in addition to Swan, St. George Lane-Fox was active in pursuing incandescent light. In fact, historians Robert Friedel and Paul Israel cite 22 prior "hopeful" inventors who tried "to make an incandescent electric light." *See* ROBERT FRIEDEL & PAUL ISRAEL, EDISON'S ELECTRIC LIGHT: BIOGRAPHY OF AN INVENTION 115 (1986). But it was Edison who succeeded in commercializing a practical lighting system, and thus, it is he who enjoys history's spotlight. In this regard, Edison is like Morse, each just one of many working in their respective technological spaces. And like Morse, Edison delivered a commercially viable system. According to Smil, the "fundamental importance of Edison's multifaceted and, even for him, frenzied activity that took place between 1879 and 1882 is that he put in place the world's first commercial system of electricity generation, transmission, and conversion." SMIL, CREATING THE TWENTIETH CENTURY, at 49.

7. *The Nineteenth-Century Technical Journal.* In the nineteenth century, several private technical journals, published by patent agencies, emerged to

further the goal of disseminating technical knowledge. For instance, *Scientific American* was published by Munn and Company, the largest nineteenth century patent agency; and *American Artisan* and the *American Inventor* were published by the patent agencies Brown, Coombs & Company and American Patent Agency, respectively. These publications and others were also used as a vehicle to bring inventors and capital together. *See* Naomi R. Lamoreaux & Kenneth L. Sokoloff, *Intermediaries in the U.S. Market for Technology, 1870-1920* in FINANCE, INTERMEDIARIES, AND ECONOMIC DEVELOPMENT 214-215 (Engerman et al. eds., 2003). On the historical and modern role of patent intermediaries, *see* Andrei Hagiu & David B. Yoffie, *The New Patent Intermediaries: Platforms, Defensive Aggregators, and Super-Aggregators,* in 27 J. ECON. PERSP. 45-66 (Winter 2013).

The excerpt below is relevant to the aforementioned discussion and the respective views of Justices Taney and Grier. We are reminded by Matt Richtel that the nature of innovation is typically comprised of many players contributing important pieces to any given technical puzzle. As A.P. Usher told his students, "[t]he inventor lives in the company of a great company of men, both dead and living.[9] History has forgotten or never discovered many of these individuals, yet their ideas and intellectual labor are very much a part of popularized innovation. The excerpt also reminds us that fame (and oftentimes fortune) is rewarded to those who understand market demands and deliver a product in a timely fashion.[10]

EDISON . . . WASN'T HE THE GUY WHO INVENTED EVERYTHING?[11]

Matt Richtel, N.Y. Times, Mar. 30, 2008, Ideas and Trends

Invention may be mothered by necessity. But determining the father can require a paternity test.

---

9. *See* Arthur Molella, *The Longue Duree of Abbott Payson Usher,* in 46 TECHNOLOGY AND CULTURE 789 n.21 (October 2005) (quoting from lecture notes taken by one of Usher's students in 1948). In the copyright context, Judge Easterbrook bluntly wrote, "No one invents even a tiny fraction of the ideas that make up our cultural heritage. . . . Every work uses scraps of thought from thousands of predecessors, far too many to compensate." *Nash v. CBS,* 899 F.2d 1537, 1540 (7th Cir. 1990). *See also* Malcolm Gladwell, *In the Air,* New Yorker (May 12, 2008) (www.newyorker.com/reporting/2008/05/12/080512fa_fact_gladwell) ("This phenomenon of simultaneous discovery—what science historians call 'multiples'—turns out to be extremely common"); Mark A. Lemley, *The Myth of the Sole Inventor,* 110 MICH. L. REV. 709, 712 (2012) (stating "[m]ultiple, independent studies show that what Merton calls 'singletons' are extraordinarily rare sorts of inventions") (citing Robert K. Merton, *Singletons and Multiples in Scientific Discovery: A Chapter in the Sociology of Science,* 105 PROC. AM. PHIL. SOC'Y 470, 470 (1961)).

10. *See* William Lyons, *Innovation, Innovation, Innovation,* WALL ST. J., May 27, 2010 (stating "Apple is one of a swathe of companies including Amazon.com Inc. and easyJet that in recent years have pioneered a growth strategy based on smart innovation. They have harnessed and ruthlessly exploited often intangible factors such as design, marketing, supply chain sales and organizational capital. In short they have redefined their respective marketplaces without actually inventing anything new"). *See also* John Kay, *Innovation Is Not About Wearing a White Coat,* Comment, FIN. TIMES (U.S.A.), Dec. 16, 2009, at 13 (asserting "innovation is about finding new ways of meeting consumers' needs. . . . Sometimes it comes from a laboratory scientist but, more often, the innovation that changes the business landscape comes from the imagination of Henry Ford or Walt Disney, Steve Jobs or Sir Stelios Haji-Ioannou," who is the founder of easyJet Airlines). Samuel Morse and Thomas Edison can be added to this list.

11. Copyright © 2008 by The New York Times Co. Reprinted with permission.

Take the sound recording. Researchers said last week that they had discovered a recording of a human voice, made by a little-known Frenchman two decades before Thomas Edison's invention of the phonograph.

An unusual case of innovation misconception? Hardly.

The reality is that the "Aha" moments of industrial creation are preceded by critical moments far less heralded. Behind and beside every big-name inventor are typically lots of others whom history forgot, or never knew. And it's unusual that an innovation is created in a vacuum (including the vacuum, which itself claims several progenitors).

"It's rare that you've got a major breakthrough that wasn't developed by multiple people at about the same time," said Mark Lemley, professor of intellectual property at Stanford Law School.

Or, for that matter, on the same day. Say, for instance, Feb. 14, 1876, when both Alexander Graham Bell and Elisha Gray filed papers with the United States Patent Office to register their competing telephone technologies. Years earlier, the Italian immigrant Antonio Meucci devised his own version of the telephone, but ultimately couldn't afford the patent application process to defend his innovation.

History remembers Bell, while his rivals are footnotes known mostly by aficionados of intellectual-property trivia.

"It's not that we wouldn't have had the telephone. Not only would we have had it, we would have had it the same day," Mr. Lemley said, adding: "The people who aren't the winners in the historical dispute sort of fade into obscurity."

Édouard-Léon Scott de Martinville has certainly been obscure, at least until now. Researchers say that in April 1860, the Parisian tinkerer used a device called a phonautograph to make visual recordings of a woman singing "Au Clair de la Lune." That was 17 years before Thomas Edison received a patent for the phonograph, and 28 years before his technology was used to capture and play back a piece of a section of a Handel oratorio.

Whom we credit with an invention often has less to do with who came up with an idea, and more to do with who translated it into something usable, accessible, commercial. Garages and laboratories, workbenches and scribbled napkins are filled with brilliant ideas unmatched with determination, resources and market sensibilities, said Jack Russo, a Silicon Valley intellectual-property lawyer.

"People run out of money, they can't find someone to manufacture for them. There are a gazillion reasons why it doesn't work out," Mr. Russo said.

A patent doesn't hurt, especially the right one. Edison also gets credit for the light bulb, though he got help from the Supreme Court, which in 1895 ruled that his technology did not infringe on a patent the court ruled was too broad, filed by competing (and now forgotten) innovators.

The Wright Brothers held a critical patent for an early airplane, and history rewards them for it. But lots of other innovators were making significant advances in the technology, Mr. Lemley noted.

Some part of the alchemy of anointing inventors has not to do with the innovator at all but with the rest of us—as audience and consumer. Sometimes we're finally receptive to an idea—whether it is a political meme like civil rights as proffered by the Rev. Dr. Martin Luther King Jr., or an online auction site, like eBay. Great ideas, while perhaps not novel, are delivered to us in palatable packaging just as we're hungry for them.

Oddly, by the time such a tipping point happens, the innovators of the original spark may find the ideas outdated.

"People come out of the woodwork and get a patent for something fundamental that the others in the field will think is trivial, understood and expected," said Dennis Allison, a lecturer in electrical engineering at Stanford University.

He has a bit of personal experience both with innovation and watching others get credit for it. In the early and mid-1970s, he was a co-founder of the PCC—People's Computer Company—which published papers and magazines describing essential early design and technology that begat the computer and then Internet revolution.

"Maybe I have a little bit of a claim—I and the people I was working with—to having invented the personal computer."

The names we remember are Gates and Jobs, and to a lesser extent Jobs's early partner, Steve Wozniak. They had an entrepreneurial zeal, marketing genius, a capacity and desire to translate the language of geeks into the products of the common people—just as our lifestyles and work styles and pocketbooks were ready to open up.

Mr. Allison, one among many of the early Silicon Valley innovators whose names seem not destined to be recorded by history, is peaceful with his relatively obscurity.

"I have my contribution," he said. "The people who I care about know what my role was."

POLICY PERSPECTIVE
Optimal Claim Scope and Patent Law's Delicate Balance

Determining the proper scope of Morse's patent (or any patent) is very difficult. A court must ascertain how much improvement activity patentees such as Morse should be able to capture vis-à-vis improver-competitors. A balance must be maintained, keeping in mind patent law's incentives to invent and commercialize, coordination of improvement activity, and reduce transaction costs (i.e., the costs associated with identifying owners of patents, negotiating licensing terms, etc.). On the one hand, a narrower claim scope may allow for more vigorous improvement activity by multiple players and is particularly useful when transaction costs are high (e.g., licensing terms) between the original and improver patentee relating to the improved technology. *See* Robert P. Merges & Richard Nelson, *On the Complex Economics of Claim Scope*, 90 COLUM. L. REV. 839, 873 (1990) (stating "with technological 'prospects' . . . no one knows for sure what possible inventions are in the technological pool. . . . Because of this uncertainty, development of technology is critically different from other common pool problems. The real problem is not controlling overfishing, but preventing underfishing after exclusive rights have been granted. The only way to find out what works and what does not is to let a variety of minds try").

But a narrow claim scope may dilute the initial incentive to invent, or to follow through in the commercialization process. In particular, improvers (follow-on innovators) will be the beneficiary of a narrow claim scope that is accompanied by an enabling disclosure, one that facilitates follow-on research and lowers costs. Yet a broader claim scope is conducive to efficient coordination efforts that focus on improvement activity and may incentivize the original patent owner himself to invest in sequential R&D. This perspective is known as the "Prospect Theory," which, as its name suggests, focuses more on encouraging post-patenting (ex post) investment in useful prospects and not on rewarding inventive activity before patenting. *See* Edmund W. Kitch, *The Nature and Function of the Patent System,* 20 J.L. & ECON. 265 (1977). But broad patent rights may also limit competition and the pace of technologic advancement due to high transaction costs. *See* Mark A. Lemley, *Ex Ante versus Ex Post Justifications for Intellectual Property,* 71 U. CHI. L. REV. 129, 139 (2004) (referring to the Prospect Theory as "fundamentally anti-market: it trusts the government's choice of whom to grant control over an area of research and development rather than trusting the market to pick the best researcher").

This incentive dynamic has been characterized by Clarisa Long as "trying to allocate fair compensation to the creators of valuable information assets . . . while assuring that other stakeholders have sufficient access to the same building blocks to provide the broader social benefits that the incentives also have been designed to provide." Clarisa Long, *The Dissonance of Scientific and Legal Norms,* SOC. EPISTEMOLOGY, 1999, Vol. 13, at 167. *See also* Suzanne Scotchmer, *Standing on the Shoulders of Giants: Cumulative Research and the Patent Law,* 5 J. ECON. PERSP. 29, 30 (Winter 1991) (stating "the challenge is to reward early innovators fully for the technological foundation they provide to later innovators, but to reward later innovators adequately for their improvements and new products as well"). And this issue is also present in copyright law. *See Nash v. CBS, Inc.,* 899 F.2d 1537, 1541 (7th Cir. 1990) (Easterbrook, J.) (stating "[b]efore the first work is published, broad protection of intellectual property seems best; after it is published, narrow protection seems best. At each instant some new works are in progress, and every author is simultaneously a creator in part and a borrower in part. In these roles, the same person has different objectives. Yet only one rule can be in force. This single rule must achieve as much as possible of these inconsistent demands").

2. Enablement and Undue Experimentation

Section 112 neither elaborates on how the enablement requirement is satisfied, nor does it set forth a framework for compliance. But through the common law process, the courts have developed a test, which states a disclosure is sufficient if it enables a person of ordinary skill in the art to make and use the claimed invention without "undue experimentation." Notably, this common law test uses the adjective "undue," thereby implying that some experimentation is allowed. Whether "undue experimentation" was required to make and use the claimed invention was at issue in *Cedarapids* and *Automotive Technologies.*

<u>CEDARAPIDS, INC. v. NORDBERG, INC.</u>

121 F.3d 727 (Fed. Cir. 1997)

ARCHER, Chief Judge.

Nordberg, Inc. (Nordberg) appeals the August 14, 1995 judgment of the United States District Court for the Northern District of Iowa granting summary judgment in favor of Cedarapids, Inc. (Cedarapids). The district court held that claim 1 of United States Patent No. 4,697,745 (the '745 patent) is invalid for failure to comply with the requirement[] for enablement under 35 U.S.C. § 112 (1994).

BACKGROUND

The '745 patent discloses a method for increasing efficiency and output of a rock crusher without increasing the size of the crusher chamber by simultaneously increasing speed and throw,[1] two aspects of crusher performance. . . . The district court held that claim 1 of the '745 patent does not enable one of ordinary skill in the art to practice the invention. The court found that the patent provides insufficient information about how much to increase the speed and throw.

DISCUSSION

I. Validity

A. *Enablement*

The district court concluded that claim 1 of the '745 patent is invalid for nonenablement. Claim 1 reads as follows:

1. A method for increasing the productivity of a conical crusher for comminuting a volume of material over unit time, said crusher having a fixed outer configuration, a fixed bowl liner having a maximum diameter, a specific volumetric capacity, a conical head with a specified diameter and gyrating within said bowl liner at a specified throw, said head also having a specified gyrational speed and power draw, and said crusher having a specified setting or gap between said bowl liner and said head, with the crushing action taking place when the gyrating head moves toward the bowl liner, said method comprising:

> increasing said throw of said head over the specified throw; and increasing said gyrational speed over the specified speed.

To be enabling, the specification must enable a person of ordinary skill in the art to make and use the invention. 35 U.S.C. § 112, ¶ 1 (1994). Enablement is a question of law that we review *de novo*.

The district court held that the '745 patent was not enabling because it did not provide the values for the increases to speed and throw for crushers of various sizes. The court also held that the specification was deficient in that it did not specify beginning points or the degree of adjustments to the two variables for the total range of crushers. The specification only provided values for the

---

1. "Speed" is the speed at which the head of the crusher gyrates. Throw, also known as stroke length, compares the smallest and largest distances between the head and the liner of the crusher as the head gyrates.

increases to a seven-foot crusher. The court found that "undue experimentation would be required to apply the process to other sizes of crushers."

All of the cases cited by the district court to support its conclusion that the specification of the '745 patent is not enabling are chemical cases. "In unpredictable art areas, this court has refused to find broad generic claims enabled by specifications that demonstrate the enablement of only one or a few embodiments and do not demonstrate with reasonable specificity how to make and use other potential embodiments across the full scope of the claim." *PPG Indus., Inc. v. Guardian Indus. Corp.,* 75 F.3d 1558, 1564 (Fed. Cir. 1996).

Rock crusher technology is not in the same category as the chemical arts where a slight variation in a method can yield an unpredictable result or may not work at all.

> In cases involving predictable factors, such as mechanical or electrical elements, a single embodiment provides broad enablement in the sense that, once imagined, other embodiments can be made without difficulty and their performance characteristics predicted by resort to known scientific laws. In cases involving unpredictable factors, such as most chemical and physiological activity, the scope of enablement obviously varies inversely with the degree of unpredictability of the factors involved.

In re Fisher, 427 F.2d 833, 839 (CCPA 1970). *See also Spectra-Physics, Inc. v. Coherent, Inc.,* 827 F.2d 1524, 1533 n.5 (Fed. Cir. 1987) ("If an invention pertains to an art where the results are predictable, e.g. mechanical as opposed to chemical arts, a broad claim can be enabled by disclosure of a single embodiment."). Our cases have, therefore, held that in the mechanical as opposed to chemical arts a broad claim can be enabled by disclosure of a single embodiment. It is not invalid for lack of enablement simply because it reads on another embodiment of the invention which is inadequately disclosed.

The fact that some experimentation is necessary does not preclude enablement; all that is required is that the amount of experimentation "must not be unduly extensive." *Atlas Powder Co. v. E.I. du Pont de Nemours & Co.,* 750 F.2d 1569, 1576 (Fed. Cir. 1984). While the district court acknowledged this it went on to find that undue experimentation would be necessary to practice the invention over the full range of crusher sizes. The district court, however, erred as a matter of law in holding the patent was not enabled for this reason.

All that is claimed is a method to increase productivity of rock crushers by simultaneously increasing speed and throw. While it may require experimentation to arrive at the optimum level of the simultaneous increases for various size crushers, we have never held that a patent must disclose information sufficient to manufacture a commercial product incorporating the invention. *See Christianson v. Colt Indus. Operating Corp.,* 822 F.2d 1544, 1562 (Fed. Cir. 1987) ("Patents are not production documents. . . . Thus the law has never required that a patentee who elects to manufacture its claimed invention must disclose in its patent the dimensions, tolerances, drawings, and other parameters of mass production not necessary to enable one skilled in the art to practice (as distinguished from mass-produce) the invention. Nor is it an objective of the patent system to supply, free of charge, production data and production drawings to competing manufacturers.").

The district court recognized that the specification enabled one skilled in the art to practice the invention on a seven-foot crusher in that it disclosed clearly that throw can be increased by as much as 40% and speed can be increased by as much as 100% over standard settings. The failure to recite the optimal amount of increase and relationship between speed and throw for crushers of various other sizes does not render the specification nonenabling. The district court found that the specified values for any conical crusher were readily ascertainable, that persons of skill in the art knew the characteristics of crusher performance, and that persons of skill in the art knew how to increase speed and/or throw. Accordingly, we reverse the district court's grant of summary judgment for nonenablement. . . .

AUTOMOTIVE TECHNOLOGIES INTERNATIONAL, INC. v. BMW OF NORTH AMERICA, INC.

501 F.3d 1274 (Fed. Cir. 2007)

LOURIE, Circuit Judge.

Automotive Technologies International, Inc. ("ATI") appeals from the decision of the United States District Court for the Eastern District of Michigan granting summary judgment of invalidity of claims 1-44 of U.S. Patent 5,231,253 (the "'253 patent") under 35 U.S.C. §112, ¶1. Because we conclude that the asserted claims of the '253 patent are invalid for lack of enablement, we affirm the decision of the district court granting summary judgment of invalidity.

BACKGROUND

The technology at issue involves crash sensing devices for deployment in an occupant protection apparatus, such as an airbag, during an impact or crash involving the side of a vehicle. ATI is the assignee of the '253 patent, entitled "Side Impact Sensors." The invention is directed to a velocity-type sensor placed in a position within a vehicle in order to sense a side impact. A velocity-type sensor is a sensor that triggers when a velocity change sensed in a crash exceeds a threshold value. Representative claim 1 reads as follows:

> A side impact crash sensor for a vehicle having front and rear wheels, said sensor comprising:
>   (a) a housing;
>   (b) a mass within said housing movable relative to said housing in response to accelerations of said housing;
>   (c) means responsive to the motion of said mass upon acceleration of said housing in excess of a predetermined threshold value, for initiating an occupant protection apparatus; and
>   (d) means for mounting said housing onto at least one of a side door of the vehicle and a side of the vehicle between the centers of the front and rear wheels, in such a position and a direction as to sense an impact into the side of said vehicle.

The prior art sensors used for sensing side impacts were crush sensors-devices configured to trigger only when crushed or deformed, thereby closing a circuit. Such sensors, however, are deficient in that they will not trigger during a crash in which a side door is not hit directly but the impact is severe enough such that the occupant would need the protection of an airbag. Velocity-type sensors, on the other hand, can be adjusted to a desired sensitivity to detect a side impact and deploy an airbag, even though the side door is not directly hit. According to ATI, conventional wisdom was that velocity-type sensors, which had been successfully used for sensing impacts to the front of a vehicle, would activate too slowly to deploy an airbag during a side impact crash. The inventors of the '253 patent discovered that velocity-type sensors when properly designed could successfully and timely operate to deploy an airbag in a side collision. An example of a velocity type sensor according to the invention is illustrated below:

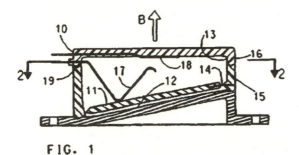

FIG. 1

When installed on a vehicle, the sensor faces the outside of the side door in the direction of the arrow **B**. When the sensor is subjected to a crash pulse of sufficient magnitude and duration, the flapper **11** moves toward the second contact **18**. The first contact **17** engages with the second contact **18** and closes an electrical circuit to initiate deployment of an airbag. Because side impact sensors require greater insensitivity for short, impulsive velocity changes, the specification discloses that an inertially damped sensor is the most suitable type of sensor for properly sensing side crashes. The specification states, however, that other sensors that are simpler and easier to manufacture, can be used to effectively sense a side impact. Such sensors include spring-mass sensors and viscously-damped sensors.

The specification also states that an electronic sensor assembly can be used to sense side impacts. The following figure, Figure **11**, depicts such an electronic sensor assembly:

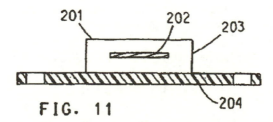

FIG. 11

The accompanying text states that Figure 11 is a "conceptional view of an electronic sensor assembly **201** built according to the teachings of this invention. This sensor contains a sensing mass **202** which moves relative to housing **203** in response to the acceleration of housing **203** which accompanies a side impact crash." The specification further states that the motion of the sensing mass "can be sensed by a variety of technologies using, for example, optics, resistance change, capacitance change or magnetic reluctance change." The enablement of this electronic side impact sensor is at issue in this appeal.

In May 2001, ATI filed a complaint against numerous defendants in the automotive industry, alleging infringement of the '253 patent. In September 2003, the district court issued an order construing the relevant claims. Relevant to this appeal, the court construed the phrase, "means responsive to the motion of said mass upon acceleration of said housing in excess of a predetermined threshold value, for initiating an occupant protection apparatus." The parties agreed, and the court found, that the limitation was in means-plus-function format and that the stated function is initiating an occupant protection apparatus. The parties disagreed as to the structure corresponding to the claimed function. ATI contended that the corresponding structure included not only mechanical switch assemblies, but also electronic switch assemblies, as identified in the specification. The defendants countered that the only clearly linked structure identified in the specification is a mechanical switch assembly. The district court agreed with ATI that the specification contains structure corresponding to the claimed function in the form of mechanical and electronic means.

* * *

Discussion

On appeal, ATI argues that because one embodiment of the invention is enabled, *viz.*, a mechanical side impact sensor, the enablement requirement is satisfied. According to ATI, there is a dichotomy in our case law—some of our cases hold that the enablement requirement is satisfied when one mode of practicing the invention is enabled, while others hold that every embodiment of the invention must be enabled in order for the enablement requirement to be met. According to ATI, the district court chose to follow the wrong line of cases. ATI further argues that, in any event, the specification does enable an electronic side impact sensor assembly. According to ATI, the specification discusses specific structure for an electronic side impact sensor and depicts such a structure in Figure 11. ATI contends that Delphi's expert never addressed whether making an electronic side impact sensor based on the disclosure would require undue experimentation. ATI also contends that electronic sensors, albeit for sensing frontal impacts, were widely known at the time of filing and therefore there was no need for the specification to describe them in detail.

Delphi responds that it is well established that the specification must enable the full scope of the claims as construed by the court, and the full scope of the claims includes mechanical side impact sensors and electronic side impact sensors. According to Delphi, providing an enabling disclosure of only mechanical side impact sensors is insufficient to satisfy the enablement requirement because the full scope of the claims is not enabled. Delphi further responds that the short recitation of an electronic sensor in the specification does not in fact enable an electronic side impact sensor because it does not teach one skilled in the art how to make and use such a sensor without undue experimentation. Delphi further responds that the specification expressly states that side impact sensing is a new field and hence ATI could not rely on the knowledge of one of ordinary skill in the art to supply the missing details. Moreover, Delphi asserts that the district court correctly found that the *Wands* factors, *viz.*, the quantity of experimentation, the lack of direction or guidance presented, and the nature of the prior art, favor a conclusion of invalidity for lack of enablement.

We agree with Delphi that the district court correctly granted summary judgment that the asserted claims are invalid for lack of enablement. The enablement requirement is set forth in 35 U.S.C. §112, ¶1 and provides in pertinent part that the specification shall describe "the manner and process of making and using [the invention], in such full, clear, concise, and exact terms as to enable any person skilled in the art to which it pertains, or with which it is most nearly connected, to make and use the [invention]." We have stated that the "enablement requirement is satisfied when one skilled in the art, after reading the specification, could practice the claimed invention without undue experimentation." *AK Steel*, 344 F.3d at 1244; *see also Wands*, 858 F.2d at 736-37.

The district court construed the relevant phrase "means responsive to the motion of said mass" to include both mechanical side impact sensors and electronic side impact sensors for performing the function of initiating an occupant protection apparatus. The parties do not dispute that construction; nor do they dispute that the specification enables mechanical side impact sensors. Under the district court's construction, however, that full scope must be enabled, and the district court was correct that the specification did not enable the full scope of the invention because it did not enable electronic side impact sensors.

Considering first the specification, although two full columns and five figures of the '253 patent detail mechanical side impact sensors, only one short paragraph and one figure relate to an electronic sensor. Importantly, that paragraph and figure do little more than provide an overview of an electronic sensor without providing any details of how the electronic sensor operates. Figure 11 shows a very general view of an electronic side impact sensor. That figure only shows a boxed housing and a sensing mass. In contrast, Figure 1 shows a mechanical sensor in much more detail, making it clear from the figure how the sensor operates. The specification even states that Figure 11 is a "conceptional view" of an electronic sensor. This is supported by the statement of one of the inventors that Figure 11 "is not meant to represent any specific design or sensor or anything, just a concept." Figure 11 represents a concept of an electronic sensor, not a figure providing details that would show one skilled in the art how to make or use an electronic side impact sensor.

Moreover, the textual description of Figure 11, which is the only description of an electronic sensor in the patent, provides little detail concerning how the electronic sensor is built or operated. The specification states the following:

> FIG. 11 is a conceptional view of an electronic sensor assembly 201 built according to the teachings of this invention. This sensor contains a sensing mass 202 which moves relative to housing 203 in response to the acceleration of housing 203 which accompanies a side impact crash. The motion of the sensing mass 202 can be sensed by a variety of technologies using, for example, optics, resistance change, capacitance change or magnetic reluctance change. Output from the sensing circuitry can be further processed to achieve a variety of sensor response characteristics as desired by the sensor designer.

'253 patent, col.10 ll.3-14. That general description, however, fails to provide a structure or description of how a person having ordinary skill in the art would make or use an electronic side impact sensor. Indeed, inventor Breed admitted that the specification fails to disclose structure for any of the technologies mentioned. Noticeably absent is any discussion of the circuitry involved in the electronic side impact sensor that would provide more detail on how the sensor operates. The mere boxed figure of the electronic sensor and the few lines of description fail to apprise one of ordinary skill how to make and use the electronic sensor.

ATI argues that despite this limited disclosure, the knowledge of one skilled in the art was sufficient to supply the missing information. We do not agree. In *Genentech, Inc. v. Novo Nordisk A/S,* 108 F.3d 1361, 1366 (Fed. Cir. 1997), we stated: "It is the specification, not the knowledge of one skilled in the art, that must supply the novel aspects of an invention in order to constitute adequate enablement." Although the knowledge of one skilled in the art is indeed relevant, the novel aspect of an invention must be enabled in the patent. The novel aspect of this invention is using a velocity-type sensor for side impact sensing. During prosecution, ATI stated that prior to its invention, "it was assumed that [conventional] inertial sensors would actuate too slowly to deploy an air bag in a side impact situation" and also that it "was unexpected that frontal impact sensors, properly designed, would work in sensing side impacts." ATI further stated that the "essential concept of the invention" is to use "an inertial or acceleration sensor on a motor vehicle for sensing side impacts." Thus, according to ATI, using inertial or acceleration sensors to sense side impacts represented a "breakthrough" in side impact crash sensing. Given that the novel aspect of the invention is side impact sensors, it is insufficient to merely state that known technologies can be used to create an electronic sensor. As we stated in *Genentech,* the rule that a specification need not disclose what is well known in the art is "merely a rule of supplementation, not a substitute for a basic enabling disclosure." 108 F.3d at 1366. We further stated that the "omission of minor details does not cause a specification to fail to meet the enablement requirement. However, when there is no disclosure of any specific starting material or of any of the conditions under which a process can be carried out, undue experimentation is required." *Id.*

Moreover, the specification states that: "Side impact sensing is a new field. The only prior art in the literature utilizes a crush sensing switch as a discriminating sensor to detect a side crash." '253 patent, col.8 ll. 45-47. In fact, ATI stated that at the time it filed the application for the '253 patent, it did not know of any electronic sensors used to sense side impact crashes. Given that side impact sensing was a new field and that there were no electronic sensors in existence that would detect side impact crashes, it was especially important for the specification to discuss how an electronic sensor would operate to detect side impacts and to provide details of its construction. As was the case in *Genentech,* the specification provides "only a starting point, a direction for further research" on using electronic sensors for sensing side impact crashes; it does not provide guidance to a person of ordinary skill in the art on how to make or use an electronic side impact sensor. 108 F.3d at 1366. The specification fails to provide "reasonable detail" sufficient to enable use of electronic side impact sensors. *Id.*

The inadequacy of the description of an electronic side impact sensor is highlighted by comparison with the extensive disclosure of how to make and use a mechanical side impact sensor, consisting of two full columns. If such a disclosure is needed to enable making and using a mechanical side impact sensor, why is not a similar disclosure needed to enable making and using an electronic side impact sensor, which is an essential aspect of the invention?

In determining that undue experimentation would have been required to make and use an electronic side impact sensor, the district court properly relied on testimony from Delphi's expert. Delphi's expert discussed at length how a "great deal of experimentation" would have been necessary to make an electronic side impact sensor after reading the specification of the '253 patent. He identified and discussed two distinct problems in developing an electronic side impact sensor: how to sense the motion of the mass in order to properly output a stream of data, and how to appropriately process the data. Moreover, Breed stated that based on his experience, electronic sensors for detecting side impact crashes could not be obtained commercially in 1990 and would have had to be developed. Inventor Breed admitted that he had never built an electronic sensor for side impact. The testimony from Delphi's expert and the inventor's own testimony provide additional support for the conclusion of a lack of enablement.

ATI argues that its expert, Dr. Dix, testified that one skilled in the art would know how to adapt then-existing technology to create an electronic side impact sensor and that his testimony creates a genuine issue of material fact. Dix's declaration states that electronic sensors were commercially available before the filing of the '253 patent and that, based on engineering texts in 1989, one would have known how to select a commercial accelerometer, how to use analog circuits, and how to program and interface a microprocessor to process the signal using the existing prior art. Dix's testimony, however, fails to discuss what types of tests would need to have been conducted to adapt existing electronic sensors for side impact sensing and does not provide any detail on how to adapt the existing technology. The testimony concludes that no undue experimentation was required to make an electronic side impact sensor, but, having failed to provide any detail regarding why no experimentation was necessary, the declaration does not create a genuine issue of material fact as to enablement.

We also reject ATI's argument that because the specification enables one mode of practicing the invention, *viz.*, mechanical side impact sensors, the enablement requirement is satisfied. We addressed and rejected a similar argument made in *Liebel-Flarsheim Co. v. Medrad, Inc.*, 481 F.3d 1371 (Fed. Cir. 2007). In that case, the invention was a front-loading fluid injector system with a replaceable syringe capable of withstanding high pressure for delivering a contrast agent to a patient. *Id.* at 1373. We construed the asserted claims, as urged by the patentee, to include an injector with and without a pressure jacket. Although the specification clearly enabled an injector with a pressure jacket, we concluded that it did not enable an injector without such a jacket and that the claims were invalid for lack of enablement. *Id.* at 1379. We stated that there "must be 'reasonable enablement of the scope of the range' which, in this case, includes both injector systems with and without a pressure jacket." *Id.* at 1380.

Similarly, in this case, the claim construction of the relevant claim limitation resulted in the scope of the claims including both mechanical and electronic side impact sensors. Disclosure of only mechanical side impact sensors does not permit one skilled in the art to make and use the invention as broadly as it was claimed, which includes electronic side impact sensors. Electronic side impact sensors are not just another known species of a genus consisting of sensors, but are a distinctly different sensor compared with the well-enabled mechanical side impact sensor that is fully discussed in the specification. Thus, in order to fulfill the enablement requirement, the specification must enable the full scope of the claims that includes both electronic and mechanical side impact sensors, which the specification fails to do.

We stated in *Liebel*: "The irony of this situation is that Liebel successfully pressed to have its claims include a jacketless system, but, having won that battle, it then had to show that such a claim was fully enabled, a challenge it could not meet." *Id.* at 1380. ATI sought to have the scope of the claims of the '253 patent include both mechanical and electronic side impact sensors. It succeeded, but then was unable to demonstrate that the claim was fully enabled. Claims must be enabled to correspond to their scope.

Comments

1. *Complying with the Enablement Requirement: Defining "Undue Experimentation."* The test for compliance with the enablement requirement is whether a person of ordinary skill in the art can make and use the claimed invention without "undue experimentation"; or as the *Cedarapids* court noted, the experimentation "must not be unduly extensive." Undue experimentation is a matter of degree, and as the adjective "undue" implies, some experimentation—trial and error—is permitted. In fact, "a considerable amount of experimentation is permissible," as long as it is "merely routine" or the specification "provides a reasonable amount of guidance" regarding the direction of experimentation. *Johns Hopkins Univ. v. CellPro, Inc.*, 152 F.3d 1342, 1360-1361 (Fed. Cir. 1998). But routine experimentation is "not without bounds." *Cephalon, Inc. v. Watson Pharm., Inc.*, 707 F.3d 1330, 1339 (Fed. Cir. 2013); *see Wyeth v. Abbott Labs*, 720 F.3d 1380 (Fed. Cir. 2013) (same).

The scope of enablement is comprised of what is disclosed in the claims, specification, and what is known to a person having ordinary skill in the art. *See AK Steel Corp. v. Sollac & Ugine*, 344 F.3d 1234, 1244 (Fed. Cir. 2003) (stating "artisan's knowledge of the prior art and routine experimentation can often fill gaps, interpolate between embodiments, and perhaps even extrapolate beyond the disclosed embodiments, depending upon the predictability of the art."); *Hybritech v. Monoclonal Antibodies, Inc.*, 802 F.2d 1367, 1384 (Fed. Cir. 1986) (stating "a patent need not teach, and preferably omits, what is well known in the art").

Several factors are considered in determining whether undue experimentation is needed, including: (1) the quantity of experimentation necessary, (2) the amount of direction or guidance presented, (3) presence or absence of working examples, (4) the nature of the invention, (5) the state of the prior art, (6) the relative skill of those in the art, (7) the predictability or unpredictability of the art, and (8) the breadth of the claims. *See In re Wands*, 858 F.2d 731, 737 (Fed. Cir. 1988). (Recall the *Automotive Technologies* court relied on *Wands*.) All of the *Wands* factors are illustrative, not mandatory. But two of them deserve further discussion, particularly "breadth of the claims"—which is explored in Comment 2, below—and "predictability or unpredictability of the art," which is discussed immediately below.

As reflected in *Cedarapids*, the courts have historically made a distinction between "predictable" (e.g., the mechanical and electrical arts) and "unpredictable" (e.g., chemical and biological arts) technologies in the context of what qualifies as undue experimentation. A PHOSITA (*p*erson *h*aving *o*rdinary *s*kill *i*n *t*he *a*rt) in electrical engineering, for instance, "can easily predict what will happen when circuits are combined," or in the context of the mechanical arts, "can use thermodynamics to predict how much power a new engine will produce." Sean B. Seymore, *Heightened Enablement in the*

Unpredictable Arts, 56 UCLA L. REV. 127, 136 (2008). In contrast, a PHOSITA in the unpredictable field of organic chemistry "cannot predict if a reaction protocol which works for one compound will work for others. Thus, there is a danger that embodiments not described either cannot be made or may require experimentation which is unduly extensive." *Id.* at 137-138. As the oft-quoted language in *In re Fisher* (quoted in *Cedarapids*) suggests, a single embodiment in the predictable arts can provide a broad enablement; but a more significant disclosure is required for unpredictable technologies.

Contrast *Edwards Lifesciences v. CoreValve, Inc.*, 699 F.3d 1305 (Fed. Cir. 2012), with *Amgen, Inc. v. Chugai Pharm. Co.*, 927 F.2d 1200 (Fed. Cir. 1991). In *Edwards*, the patentee, who owned the '552 patent, claimed a medical device — a "valve prosthesis for implantation in a body channel" — namely, a valve for insertion into the heart by a balloon catheter. The accused infringer argued that the patent was invalid because at the time the claimed invention was filed, the valve prosthesis had been implanted only in pigs, and that these experiments was not always successful, resulting in design changes. The patentee conceded that "more developmental work was required at the time of filing" relating to size, material, and design; and that "much more work had to be done before anybody ever even contemplated using this for a human." *Id.* at 1309. In short, at the time of filing, the claimed invention was a medical "device to perform testing" and "not a device to move in and treat patients." The court nonetheless held the '552 patent satisfied the enablement requirement, noting that "it has long been recognized that when experimentation on human subjects is inappropriate, as in the testing and development of drugs and medical devices, the enablement requirement may be met by animal tests or in vitro data." *Id.* Citing the *Wands* factors, the court continued that there was evidence the device was successfully implanted in pigs in accordance with the '552 specification, and further "[i]t was explained that pigs were a standard experimental animal for heart valve research"; and "[w]itnesses for both sides discussed the vascular anatomies of pigs and the established use of porcine valves in humans." *Id.* at 1310.

In *Amgen*, the patent generically claimed purified and isolated DNA sequences encoding erythropoietin ("EPO"), but "despite extensive statements in the specification concerning all the analogs of the EPO gene that can be made, there is little enabling disclosure of particular analogs and how to make them." *Id.* at 1213. The Federal Circuit—affirming the district court's lack of enablement finding—noted that the lower court correctly relied on *In re Fisher*:

> Considering the structural complexity of the EPO gene, the manifold possibilities for change in its structure, with attendant uncertainty as to what utility will be possessed by these analogs, we consider that more is needed concerning identifying the various analogs that are within the scope of the claim, methods for making them, and structural requirements for producing compounds with EPO-like activity. It is not sufficient, having made the gene and a handful of analogs whose activity has not been clearly ascertained, to claim all possible genetic sequences that have EPO-like activity.

Id. at 1214. *See also Pharmaceutical Resources, Inc. v. Roxane Laboratories, Inc.*, 253 Fed. Appx. 26, 28 (Fed. Cir. 2007) (noting because art was "highly unpredictable," patentee "set a high burden that its patent disclosure must meet to satisfy the requisite *quid pro quo* of patent enablement").

Relatedly, when nascent technology is involved, the breadth and depth of a skilled artisan's database of knowledge is not as great. Therefore, given the artisan's almost exclusive reliance on the patentee's specification, nascent technology "must be enabled with a specific and useful teaching." *Id.* In *Genentech, Inc. v. Novo Nordisk*, 108 F.3d 1361 (Fed. Cir. 1997), the invention related to a "cleavable fusion expression process for producing human growth hormone (HGH)." Although the disclosure was limited, the patentee argued that a person of ordinary skill in the art would be able to fill in the specification's gaps. The court was not persuaded, stating "[w]here, as here, the claimed invention is the application of an unpredictable technology in the early stages of development, an enabling description in the specification must provide those skilled in the art with a specific and useful teaching." *Id.* at 1367. Indeed, a patentee cannot "bootstrap a vague statement of a problem into an enabling disclosure sufficient to dominate someone else's solution of the problem." *Id.* at 1366. *See also Chiron Corp. v. Genentech, Inc.*, 363 F.3d 1247, 1254 (Fed. Cir. 2004) (stating that for nascent technology the specification must be "specific and useful . . . because a person of ordinary skill in the art has little or no knowledge independent from the patentee's instruction").

2. *Commensurability and the "Full Scope" of the Claimed Invention.* The Federal Circuit has held that the patentee's specification must enable a person having ordinary skill in the art to practice the *full scope* of the claimed invention. For example, in *Liebel-Flarsheim* (relied upon by *Automotive Technologies*), the patents related to a medical device, namely a "front-loading fluid injector with a replaceable syringe capable of withstanding high pressures for delivering a contrast agent to a patient." In a prior litigation, the patentee (Liebel) argued for a claim scope that would read on accused injectors that included a jacket or were jacketless. The Federal Circuit agreed with this interpretation. Accordingly, "[t]here must be 'reasonable enablement of the scope of the range' which, in this case, includes both injector systems with and without a pressure jacket." 481 F.3d at 1380. It was undisputed that an injector with a jacket was enabled; but there was an insufficient disclosure relating to a jacketless injector. In fact, the specification taught away from an injector without a jacket.

The Federal Circuit was mindful that a broad claim scope is a double-edged sword, noting "[t]he irony of this situation is that Liebel successfully pressed to have its claims include a jacketless system, but, having won that battle, it then had to show that such a claim was fully enabled, a challenge it could not meet. The motto, 'beware of what one asks for,' might be applicable here." 481 F.3d at 1380. The same was true in *Automotive Technologies*, where the patentee "sought to have the scope of the claims of the '253 patent include both mechanical and electronic side impact sensors," but, having succeeded, "was unable to demonstrate that the claim was fully enabled." *See also Sitrick v. Dreamworks*, 516 F.3d 993, 999 (Fed. Cir. 2008) (stating "[a] patentee who chooses broad claim language must make sure the broad claims are fully enabled"). Broad claim scope allows for greater protection, but also demands a more thorough disclosure.

Interestingly, both *Liebel-Flarsheim* and *Automotive Technologies* involved mechanical inventions, which, as noted in Comment 1, have historically been regarded as predictable technologies. What is the effect of these cases on enablement jurisprudence with respect to the predictable arts? Has the distinction between predictable and unpredictable arts narrowed (or vanished)? One can argue that *Liebel-Flarsheim* should be limited to cases where the specification expressly teaches away from the claimed invention. But teaching away was not present in *Automotive Technologies*; rather, the specification provided "'only a starting point, a direction for further research' on using electronic sensors for sensing side impact crashes; it does not provide guidance to a person of ordinary skill in the art on how to make or use an electronic side impact sensor." *Id.* at 1284.

In the United Kingdom, the House of Lords has taken a more generous view of sufficiency of disclosure with respect to product claims (which are typically the most commercially valuable). For instance, in *Lundbeck v. Generics (UK)*, [2008] EWCA Civ 311, Lord Hoffmann wrote "[i]n an ordinary product claim, the product is the invention. It is sufficiently enabled if the specification and common general knowledge enables the skilled person to make it. One method is enough."

3. ***Enablement Measured at Time of Filing.*** Congress was silent in defining the temporal dimension of the enablement requirement, namely *when* the requirement must be satisfied. The courts have filled this gap by holding that enablement is measured at the time of filing. Technical information or other informative material that arise post-filing cannot be used to satisfy the enablement requirement. *See Chiron Corp, supra*, 363 F.3d at 1255 (stating "the enablement requirement does not extend to technology that arises after the time of filing"). But while post-filing information cannot be used to supplement a deficient specification, it can be used as "evidence of the level of ordinary skill in the art *at the time* of the application and as evidence that the disclosed device would have been operative." *Gould v. Quigg*, 822 F.2d 1074, 1078 (Fed. Cir. 1987) (emphasis added).

The principal reason for this rule is that the filing date is proof of an inventor's latest date of invention, a date of crucial importance in American patent law because a patent is awarded to the party who can prove he was the first to invent the claimed invention. *See In re Glass*, 492 F.2d 1228 (CCPA 1974) (stating "the filing date becomes a date of constructive reduction to practice in determining priority of invention and this should not be the case unless at that time, without waiting for subsequent disclosures, any person skilled in the art could practice the invention from the disclosure of the application"). Chapter 4 explores proving date of invention.

C. WRITTEN DESCRIPTION

The first paragraph of section 112 provides that the "specification shall contain a *written description* of the invention." The written description requirement demands that the patent specification describe an invention understandable to a person of ordinary skill in the art and show the skilled artisan that the inventor actually invented what is claimed. The *Ariad* case explores the rationale for the written description requirement and how it differs from enablement. And *Gentry Gallery* provides an example of how the written description requirement can be used to rein in expansive claim scope, a function similar to the enablement requirement.

STATUTE: Specification

35 U.S.C. §112, ¶1

ARIAD PHARMACEUTICALS, INC. v. ELI LILLY AND COMPANY

598 F.3d 1336 (Fed. Cir. 2010) (*en banc*)

LOURIE, Circuit Judge.

Ariad Pharmaceuticals, Inc., Massachusetts Institute of Technology, the Whitehead Institute for Biomedical Research, and the President and Fellows of Harvard College (collectively, "Ariad") brought suit against Eli Lilly & Company ("Lilly") in the United States District Court for the District of Massachusetts, alleging infringement of U.S. Patent 6,410,516 ("the '516 patent"). After trial, at which a jury found infringement, but found none of the asserted claims invalid, a panel of this court reversed the district court's denial of Lilly's motion for judgment as a matter of law ("JMOL") and held the asserted claims invalid for lack of written description.

Ariad petitioned for rehearing *en banc,* challenging this court's interpretation of 35 U.S.C. §112, first paragraph, as containing a separate written description requirement. Because of the importance of the issue, we granted Ariad's petition and directed the parties to address whether §112, first paragraph, contains a written description requirement separate from the enablement requirement and, if so, the scope and purpose of that requirement. We now reaffirm that §112, first paragraph, contains a written description requirement separate from enablement, and we again reverse the district court's denial of JMOL and hold the asserted claims of the '516 patent invalid for failure to meet the statutory written description requirement.

BACKGROUND

The '516 patent relates to the regulation of gene expression by the transcription factor NF-κB. The inventors of the '516 patent were the first to identify NF-κB and to uncover the mechanism by which NF-κB activates gene expression underlying the body's immune responses to infection. The inventors discovered that NF-κB normally exists in cells as an inactive complex with a protein inhibitor, named "IκB" ("Inhibitor of kappa B"), and is activated by extracellular stimuli, such as bacterial-produced lipopolysaccharides, through a series of biochemical reactions that release it from IκB. Once free of its inhibitor, NF-κB travels into the cell nucleus where it binds to and activates the transcription of genes containing a NF-κB recognition site. The activated genes (e.g., certain cytokines), in turn help the body to counteract the extracellular assault. The production of cytokines can, however, be harmful in excess. Thus the inventors recognized that artificially interfering with NF-κB activity could reduce the harmful symptoms of certain diseases, and they filed a patent application on April 21, 1989, disclosing their discoveries and claiming methods for regulating cellular responses to external stimuli by reducing NF-κB activity in a cell.

The asserted claims, rewritten to include the claims from which they depend, are as follows:

80. [A method for modifying effects of external influences on a eukaryotic cell, which external influences induce NF-κB-mediated intracellular signaling, the method comprising altering NF-κB activity in the cells such that NF-κB-mediated effects of external influences are modified, wherein NF-κB activity in the cell is reduced] wherein reducing NF-κB activity comprises reducing binding of NF-κB to NF-κB recognition sites on genes which are transcriptionally regulated by NF-κB.

95. [A method for reducing, in eukaryotic cells, the level of expression of genes which are activated by extracellular influences which induce NF-κB mediated intracellular signaling, the method comprising reducing NF-κB activity in the cells such that expression of said genes is reduced,] carried out on human cells.

144. [A method for reducing bacterial lipopolysaccharide-induced expression of cytokines in mammalian cells, which method comprises reducing NF-κB activity in the cells so as to reduce bacterial lipopolysaccharide-induced expression of said cytokines in the cells] wherein reducing NF-κB activity comprises reducing binding of NF-κB to NF-κB recognition sites on genes which are transcriptionally regulated by NF-κB.

145. [A method for reducing bacterial lipopolysaccharide-induced expression of cytokines in mammalian cells, which method comprises reducing NF-κB activity in the cells so as to reduce bacterial lipopolysaccharide-induced expression of said cytokines in the cells,] carried out on human cells.

The claims are thus genus claims, encompassing the use of all substances that achieve the desired result of reducing the binding of NF-κB to NF-κB recognition sites. Furthermore, the claims, although amended during prosecution, use language that corresponds to language present in the priority application. Specifically, the asserted claims recite methods of reducing NF-κB activity, and more specifically reducing binding of NF-κB to NF-κB recognition sites, in cells in response to external influences like bacterial lipopolysaccha rides. The specification filed on April 21, 1989, similarly recites the desired goal of reducing NF-κB activity and binding to NF-κB recognition sites in cells in response to such external influences. The specification also hypothesizes three types of molecules with the potential to reduce NF-κB activity in cells: decoy, dominantly interfering, and specific inhibitor molecules.

* * *

DISCUSSION

I.

* * *

A.

As in any case involving statutory interpretation, we begin with the language of the statute itself. Section 112, first paragraph, reads as follows:

The specification shall contain a written description of the invention, and of the manner and process of making and using it, in such full, clear, concise, and exact terms as to enable any person skilled in the art to which it pertains, or with which it is most nearly connected, to make and use the same, and shall set forth the best mode contemplated by the inventor of carrying out his invention.

* * *

We . . . read the statute to give effect to its language that the specification "shall contain a written description of the invention" and hold that §112, first paragraph, contains two separate description requirements: a "written description [i] of the invention, *and* [ii] of the manner and process of making and using [the invention]. 35 U.S.C. §112, ¶1 (emphasis added). . . . If Congress had intended enablement to be the sole description requirement of §112, first paragraph, the statute would have been written differently. Specifically, Congress could have written the statute to read, "The specification shall contain a written description of the invention, in such full, clear, concise, and exact terms as to enable any person skilled in the art . . . to make and use the same," or "The specification shall contain a written description of the manner and process of making and using the invention, in such full, clear, concise, and exact terms as to enable any person skilled in the art . . . to make and use the same." Finally, a separate requirement to describe one's invention is basic to patent law. Every patent must describe an invention. It is part of the *quid pro quo* of a patent; one describes an invention, and, if the law's other requirements are met, one obtains a patent. The specification must then, of course, describe how to make and use the invention (i.e., enable it), but that is a different task. A description of the claimed invention allows the United States Patent and Trademark Office ("PTO") to examine applications effectively; courts to understand the invention, determine compliance with the statute, and to construe the claims; and the public to understand and improve upon the invention and to avoid the claimed boundaries of the patentee's exclusive rights. . . .

E.

* * *

[W]hile it is true that original claims are part of the original specification, *In re Gardner*, 480 F.2d 879, 879 (CCPA 1973), that truism fails to address the question whether original claim language necessarily discloses the subject matter that it claims. Ariad believes so, arguing that original claims identify whatever they state, e.g., a perpetual motion machine, leaving only the question whether the applicant has enabled anyone to make and use such an invention. We disagree that this is always the case. Although many original claims will satisfy the written description requirement, certain claims may not. For example, a generic claim may define the boundaries of a vast genus of chemical compounds, and yet the question may still remain whether the specification, including original claim language, demonstrates that the applicant has invented species sufficient to support a claim to a genus. The problem is especially acute with genus claims that use functional language to define the boundaries of a claimed genus. In such a case, the functional claim may simply claim a desired result, and may do so without describing species that achieve that result. But the specification must demonstrate that the applicant has made a generic invention that achieves the claimed result and do so by showing that the applicant has invented species sufficient to support a claim to the functionally-defined genus.

Recognizing this, we held in *Regents of the University of California v. Eli Lilly & Co.*, 119 F.3d 1559 (Fed. Cir. 1997), that an adequate written description of a claimed genus requires more than a generic statement of an invention's boundaries. The patent at issue in *Eli Lilly* claimed a broad genus of cDNAs purporting to encode many different insulin molecules, and we held that its generic claim language to "vertebrate insulin cDNA" or "mammalian insulin cDNA" failed to describe the claimed genus because it did not distinguish the genus from other materials in any way except by function, i.e., by what the genes do, and thus provided "only a definition of a useful result rather than a definition of what achieves that result." 119 F.3d at 1568.

We held that a sufficient description of a genus instead requires the disclosure of either a representative number of species falling within the scope of the genus or structural features common to the members of the genus so that one of skill in the art can "visualize or recognize" the members of the genus. *Id.* at 1568-69. We explained that an adequate written description requires a precise definition, such as by structure, formula, chemical name, physical properties, or other properties, of species falling within the genus sufficient to distinguish the genus from other materials. *Id.* at 1568 (quoting *Fiers v. Revel*, 984 F.2d 1164, 1171 (Fed. Cir. 1993)). We have also held that functional claim language can meet the written description requirement when the art has established a correlation between structure and function. But merely drawing a fence around the outer limits of a purported genus is not an adequate substitute for describing a variety of materials constituting the genus and showing that one has invented a genus and not just a species.

In fact, this case similarly illustrates the problem of generic claims. The claims here recite methods encompassing a genus of materials achieving a stated useful result, i.e., reducing NF-κB binding to NF-κB recognition sites in response to external influences. But the specification does not disclose a variety of species that accomplish the result. *See Eli Lilly*, 119 F.3d at 1568 ("The description requirement of the patent statute requires a description of an invention, not an indication of a result that one might achieve if one made that invention."). Thus, as indicated *infra*, that specification fails to meet the written description requirement by describing only a generic invention that it purports to claim.

F.

Since its inception, this court has consistently held that § 112, first paragraph, contains a written description requirement separate from enablement, and we have articulated a "fairly uniform standard," which we now affirm. *Vas-Cath Inc. v. Mahurkar*, 935 F.2d 1555, 1562-63 (Fed. Cir. 1991). Specifically, the description must "clearly allow persons of ordinary skill in the art to recognize that [the inventor] invented what is claimed." *Id.* at 1563. In other words, the test for sufficiency is whether the disclosure of the application relied upon reasonably conveys to those skilled in the art that the inventor had possession of the claimed subject matter as of the filing date. *Id.*

The term "possession," however, has never been very enlightening. It implies that as long as one can produce records documenting a written description of a claimed invention, one can show possession. But the hallmark of written description is disclosure. Thus, "possession as shown in the disclosure" is a more complete formulation. Yet whatever the specific articulation, the test requires an objective inquiry into the four corners of the specification from the perspective of a person of ordinary skill in the art. Based on that inquiry, the specification must describe an invention understandable to that skilled artisan and show that the inventor actually invented the invention claimed.

This inquiry, as we have long held, is a question of fact. Thus, we have recognized that determining whether a patent complies with the written description requirement will necessarily vary depending on the context. Specifically, the level of detail required to satisfy the written description requirement varies depending on the nature and scope of the claims and on the complexity and predictability of the relevant technology. For generic claims, we have set forth a number of factors for evaluating the adequacy of the disclosure, including "the existing knowledge in the particular field, the extent and content of the prior art, the maturity of the science or technology, [and] the predictability of the aspect at issue."

The law must be applied to each invention at the time it enters the patent process, for each patented advance has a novel relationship with the state of the art from which it emerges. Thus, we do not try here to predict and adjudicate all the factual scenarios to which the written description requirement could be applied. Nor do we set out any bright-line rules governing, for example, the number of species that must be disclosed to describe a genus claim, as this number necessarily changes with each invention, and it changes with progress in a field. Thus, whatever inconsistencies may appear to some to exist in the application of the law, those inconsistencies rest not with the legal standard but with the different facts and arguments presented to the courts.

There are, however, a few broad principles that hold true across all cases. We have made clear that the written description requirement does not demand either examples or an actual reduction to practice; a constructive reduction to practice that in a definite way identifies the claimed invention can satisfy the written description requirement. Conversely, we have repeatedly stated that actual "possession" or reduction to practice outside of the specification is not enough. Rather, as stated above, it is the specification itself that must demonstrate possession. And while the description requirement does not demand any particular form of disclosure, or that the specification recite the claimed invention *in haec verba*, a description that merely renders the invention obvious does not satisfy the requirement.

We also reject the characterization, cited by Ariad, of the court's written description doctrine as a "super enablement" standard for chemical and biotechnology inventions. The doctrine never created a heightened requirement to provide a nucleotide-by-nucleotide recitation of the entire genus of claimed genetic material; it has always expressly permitted the disclosure of structural features common to the members of the genus. It also has not just been applied to chemical and biological inventions.

Perhaps there is little difference in some fields between describing an invention and enabling one to make and use it, but that is not always true of certain inventions, including chemical and chemical-like inventions. Thus, although written description and enablement often rise and fall together, requiring a written description of the invention plays a vital role in curtailing claims that do not require undue experimentation to make and use, and thus satisfy enablement, but that have not been invented, and thus cannot be described. For example, a propyl or butyl compound may be made by a process analogous to a disclosed methyl compound, but, in the absence of a statement that the inventor invented propyl and butyl compounds, such compounds have not been described and are not entitled to a patent. *See In re DiLeone,* 58 C.C.P.A. 925, 436 F.2d 1404, 1405 n.1 (CCPA 1971) ("[C]onsider the case where the specification discusses only compound A and contains no broadening language of any kind. This might very well enable one skilled in the art to make and use compounds B and C; yet the class consisting of A, B and C has not been described.").

The written description requirement also ensures that when a patent claims a genus by its function or result, the specification recites sufficient materials to accomplish that function — a problem that is particularly acute in the biological arts. This situation arose not only in *Eli Lilly* but again in *University of Rochester v. G.D. Searle & Co., Inc.,* 358 F.3d 916 (Fed. Cir. 2004). In *Rochester,* we held invalid claims directed to a method of selectively inhibiting the COX-2 enzyme by administering a non-steroidal compound that selectively inhibits the COX-2 enzyme. *Id.* at 918. We reasoned that because the specification did not describe any specific compound capable of performing the claimed method and the skilled artisan would not be able to identify any such compound based on the specification's function description, the specification did not provide an adequate written description of the claimed invention. *Id.* at 927-28. Such claims merely recite a description of the problem to be solved while claiming all solutions to it and, as in Eli Lilly and Ariad's claims, cover any compound later actually invented and determined to fall within the claim's functional boundaries — leaving it to the pharmaceutical industry to complete an unfinished invention.

Ariad complains that the doctrine disadvantages universities to the extent that basic research cannot be patented. But the patent law has always been directed to the "useful Arts," U.S. Const. art. I, §8, cl. 8, meaning inventions with a practical use, *see Brenner v. Manson,* 383 U.S. 519, 532-36 (1966). Much university research relates to basic research, including research into scientific principles and mechanisms of action, and universities may not have the resources or inclination to work out the practical implications of all such research, i.e., finding and identifying compounds able to affect the mechanism discovered. That is no failure of the law's interpretation, but its intention. Patents are not awarded for academic theories, no matter how groundbreaking or necessary to the later patentable inventions of others. "[A] patent is not a hunting license. It is not a reward for the search, but compensation for its successful conclusion." *Rochester,* 358 F.3d at 930 n.10 (quoting *Brenner,* 383 U.S. at 536). Requiring a written description of the invention limits patent protection to those who actually perform the difficult work of "invention" — that is, conceive of the complete and final invention with all its claimed limitations — and disclose the fruits of that effort to the public.

That research hypotheses do not qualify for patent protection possibly results in some loss of incentive, although Ariad presents no evidence of any discernable impact on the pace of innovation or the number of patents obtained by universities. But claims to research plans also impose costs on downstream research, discouraging later invention. The goal is to get the right balance, and the written description doctrine does so by giving the incentive to actual invention and not "attempt[s] to preempt the future before it has arrived." *Fiers,*

984 F.2d at 1171. As this court has repeatedly stated, the purpose of the written description requirement is to "ensure that the scope of the right to exclude, as set forth in the claims, does not overreach the scope of the inventor's contribution to the field of art as described in the patent specification." *Rochester,* 358 F.3d at 920. It is part of the *quid pro quo* of the patent grant and ensures that the public receives a meaningful disclosure in exchange for being excluded from practicing an invention for a period of time.

II.

* * *

B.

Ariad claims methods comprising the single step of reducing NF-κB activity. Lilly argues that the asserted claims are not supported by a written description because the specification of the '516 patent fails to adequately disclose how the claimed reduction of NF-κB activity is achieved. The parties agree that the specification of the '516 patent hypothesizes three classes of molecules potentially capable of reducing NF-κB activity: specific inhibitors, dominantly interfering molecules, and decoy molecules. Lilly contends that this disclosure amounts to little more than a research plan, and does not satisfy the patentee's *quid pro quo* as described in *Rochester.* Ariad responds that Lilly's arguments fail as a matter of law because Ariad did not actually claim the molecules. According to Ariad, because there is no term in the asserted claims that corresponds to the molecules, it is entitled to claim the methods without describing the molecules. Ariad's legal assertion, however, is flawed.

In *Rochester,* as discussed above, we held very similar method claims invalid for lack of written description. 358 F.3d at 918-19 (holding the patent invalid because "Rochester did not present any evidence that the ordinarily skilled artisan would be able to identify any compound based on [the specification's] vague functional description"); *see also Fiers,* 984 F.2d at 1170-71 (holding a claim to a genus of DNA molecules not supported by written description of a method for obtaining the molecules); *cf. Eli Lilly,* 119 F.3d at 1567-68 (holding claims to a broad genus of genetic material invalid because the specification disclosed only one particular species). Ariad attempts to categorically distinguish *Rochester, Fiers,* and *Eli Lilly,* because in those cases, the claims explicitly included the non-described compositions. For example, in *Rochester,* the method claims recited a broad type of compound that we held was inadequately described in the specification of the patent:

> 1. A method for selectively inhibiting PGHS-2 activity in a human host, comprising administering a non-steroidal compound that selectively inhibits activity of the PGHS-2 gene product to a human host in need of such treatment.

Id. at 918. Ariad's attempt to distinguish these cases is unavailing. Regardless whether the asserted claims recite a compound, Ariad still must describe some way of performing the claimed methods, and Ariad admits that the specification suggests only the use of the three classes of molecules to achieve NF-κB reduction. Thus, to satisfy the written description requirement for the asserted claims, the specification must demonstrate that Ariad possessed the claimed methods by sufficiently disclosing molecules capable of reducing NF-κB activity so as to "satisfy the inventor's obligation to disclose the technologic knowledge upon which the patent is based, and to demonstrate that the patentee was in possession of the invention that is claimed." *Capon,* 418 F.3d at 1357.

Comments

1. **Ariad*'s Holding and Implications.* The *Ariad* court addressed whether there is a separate written description requirement—distinct from the enablement requirement—under 35 U.S.C. §112, ¶1, an issue that had been brewing for some time prior to *Ariad.* In recognizing a distinct written description requirement, the court, while not changing the law in a significant way, added clarity with respect to (1) its so-called possession test (see Comment 2 below); (2) the applicability of the written description requirement to originally filed claims (see Comment 3, below); and (3) the effect of the holding on research institutions and start-up companies, particularly in the context of life science research.

   Ariad makes the decision of *when* to file an application more important. Patent systems worldwide are designed to encourage early filing, but the written description requirement as interpreted by *Ariad* demands that the applicant provide enough information to demonstrate to a person of ordinary skill in the art "that the inventor actually invented the invention claimed." Here we get a generous peek behind the policy curtain, as reasonable minds can differ whether section 112 requires a separate written description requirement. (*See* Judge Rader's dissent in *Ariad.*) The court recognized that universities engage in a great deal of basic research (upstream) and that "universities may not have the resources or inclination to work out the practical implications of all such research." Yet, wrote the court, this is the law's intention. While it is true that research universities perform predominantly basic research, technology-transfer offices at many of these universities have contractual relationships with private firms to commercialize the research. Thus, it is unclear what the effect of *Ariad* will be on universities. Moreover, the court noted that Ariad presented no evidence to support its assertion that denying patent protection would result in a loss of incentives for universities. Yet the court—without any cited evidence—asserts that "claims to research plans also impose costs on down stream research, discouraging later invention." See Chapter 3, Comment 4 following *Myriad* for a discussion of the literature on the relationship between upstream patenting and downstream innovation.

2. *Complying with the Written Description Requirement: A Four Corners Approach.* To comply with the written description requirement the specification must clearly allow persons of ordinary skill in the art to recognize that the inventor actually invented what is claimed. This is sometimes known as the "possession" test. In *Vas-Cath v. Mahurkar,* 935 F.2d 1555 (Fed. Cir. 1991), the court wrote that the test for compliance with the written description requirement is "whether the disclosure of the application relied upon 'reasonably conveys to the artisan that the inventor had possession at that time of the later claimed subject matter.' " *Id.* at 1563. Yet, the *Ariad* court recognized that the term "possession" "has never been very enlightening" because "[i]t implies

that as long as one can produce records documenting a written description of a claimed invention, one can show possession." The court expressly anchored the written description requirement within the "four corners of the specification," and held that compliance is based on whether the specification conveys to a person of ordinary skill in the art "that the inventor actually invented the invention claimed." The court can look to "a number of factors" in making this determination, "including 'the existing knowledge in the particular field, the extent and content of the prior art, the maturity of the science or technology, [and] the predictability of the aspect at issue.'" 598 F.3d at 1351.

The written description requirement was not met in *Boston Scientific Corp. v. Johnson & Johnson*, 647 F.3d 1353 (Fed. Cir. 2011). The patents-in-suit related to the use of the stent drug rapamycin and its analogs to inhibit restenosis (the narrowing of a blood vessel). The patentees argued it "provided a template for those of ordinary skill to use for identifying analogs" of rapamycin, and therefore, did not have to disclose additional details. The court was not persuaded. First, the court noted the specification's lack of information on rapamycin's analogs, stating "[a]n *ipsis verbis* disclosure of a claimed genus (under the heading Experiments) is not per se sufficient to meet the written description requirement." *Id.* at 1364. Second, although examples can be used to satisfy section 112, "the universe of potential compounds that are structurally similar to rapamycin . . . is limitless." *Id.* The court noted the patents-in-suit were similar to those present in *Carnegie-Mellon Univ. v. Hoffman-LaRoche, Inc.*, 541 F.3d 1115 (Fed. Cir. 2008). Accordingly:

> In *Carnegie Mellon* the court noted that only three bacterial genes out of thousands of species had been cloned, and only one was disclosed in the specification. Here, no analogs are disclosed in the specification. While a small number of such analogs were known in the prior art, the claims cover tens of thousands of possible macrocyclic lactone analogs. With no guidance at all in the specification as to how to properly identify or choose the claimed analogs, and in light of the unpredictability and nascent state of using drug-eluting stents to treat restenosis, we agree with the district court that appellants have failed to create genuine issues of material fact.

647 F.3d at 1365.

But the specification does not have to disclose the invention "*in haec verba*" (verbatim) to satisfy the requirement. For instance, in *Application of Wertheim*, 541 F.2d 257, 265 (CCPA 1976), the patent claimed a particular range, "at least 35%," that was narrower than what was disclosed in the specification, which read "25% to 60%." The CCPA held that the specification supported the claim even though the precise range claimed was not exactly set forth in the specification.

3. ***Written Description and New Matter.*** Importantly, the applicant cannot add "new matter" to the specification and retain the original filing date. 35 U.S.C. §132(a) ("No amendment shall introduce new matter into the disclosure of the invention."). *See also TurboCare Div. of Demag Delaval Turbomachinery Corp. v. General Elec. Co.*, 264 F.3d 1111, 1118 (Fed. Cir. 2001) ("The written description requirement and its corollary, the new matter prohibition of 35 U.S.C. §132, both serve to ensure that the patent applicant was in full possession of the claimed subject matter on the application filing date. When the

applicant adds a claim or otherwise amends his specification after the original filing date, . . . the new claims or other added material must find support in the original specification."). If new matter is added to the specification, the applicant should file a continuation-in-part (C-I-P) application, wherein the new matter (and any claims that the new matter supports) would be entitled to the C-I-P filing date, and the information disclosed in the original application (and any claims that find support in the original disclosure) will retain the original filing date.

4. *Written Description Applied to Originally Filed Claims.* The *Ariad* court unequivocally held that the written description requirement applies to originally filed claims. The court was particularly concerned with the use of genus claims and whether, in this context, the applicant has invented a sufficient number of species to support the genus claim. (See Comment 3 after the *Incandescent Lamp* case.) The court provided the example of a genus claim that uses functional language to claim a desired result without an accompanying disclosure of species showing the result has been achieved.

Prior to *Ariad*, the Federal Circuit, in the context of biotechnology-related inventions, held that a specification describing a gene or DNA sequence only in terms of its biological function (e.g., to encode for a known protein) does not comply with the written description requirement, even as to an original claim directed to the functionally defined DNA sequence. *See Regents of the University of California v. Eli Lilly & Co.*, 119 F.3d 1559 (Fed. Cir. 1997). In *Fiers v. Revel*, 984 F.2d 1164 (Fed. Cir. 1993), the court explicitly linked conception with the issue of written description. The court noted that when DNA is at issue, the written description requirement demands "a description of the DNA itself" rather than a method of isolating the DNA. Consistent with *Fiers*, the *Eli Lilly* court wrote that a "written description of an invention involving a chemical genus, like a description of a chemical species, 'requires a precise definition, such as by structure, formula, [or] chemical name,' of the claimed subject matter sufficient to distinguish it from other materials." *Lilly*, 119 F.3d at 1566. Thus, "the description requirement . . . requires a description of an invention, not an indication of a result that one might achieve if one made that invention." *Id.* at 1568. Referring to the DNA simply by its biological function falls short of a sufficient written description, amounting to a mere "wish" or "plan." *Id.* at 1566.

It was long thought—as Ariad unsuccessfully asserted—that an original claim stands on its own. And some Federal Circuit judges have argued that applying the written description requirement to originally filed claims is improper because there is no after-filing amendment or continuation application at issue. *See, e.g., Enzo Biochem, Inc. v. Gen-Probe Inc.*, 323 F.3d 956, 979-980 (Fed. Cir. 2002) (rehearing *en banc* denied) (Rader, J., dissenting) (asserting that *Eli Lilly* is inconsistent with precedent because "for the first time, this court purported to apply [written description] as a general disclosure doctrine in place of enablement, rather than as a priority doctrine"); *Moba, B.V. v. Diamond Automation, Inc.*, 325 F.3d 1306, 1319 (Fed. Cir. 2003) ("The purpose of the written description requirement is to prevent an applicant from *later* asserting that he invented that which he did not; the applicant for a patent is therefore required 'to recount his invention in such detail that his *future* claims can be determined to be encompassed within his *original* creation.'") (emphasis in original). *See also In re Gardner*, 475

F.2d 1389, 1391 (CCPA 1973) (noting the original claim "itself constituted a description in the original disclosure. . . . Nothing more is necessary for compliance with the description requirement"). The *en banc Ariad* court laid this issue to rest.

5. ***Written Description Requirement and Functional Claim Language.*** Functional claim language "define[s] something by what it does, rather than by what it is (e.g., as evidenced by its specific structure or specific ingredients)." MANUAL PATENT EXAMINING PROCEDURE § 2173.05(g). While "[t]here is nothing inherently wrong with defining some part of an invention in functional terms," such language can render claim scope exceedingly broad. This is one of the reasons the Director of the USPTO — David Kappos — praised the *Ariad* decision:

> [T]he written description doctrine is particularly useful in examining claims that employ functional language, or that merely set forth a desired result without any indication of what achieves that result. I call these "result-orientated" or "results obtained" claims, and strongly support our examiners using the written description requirement to prevent issuance of such vastly overbroad recitations. Unless an applicant has devised every solution to a problem, the applicant is not entitled to patent every solution.

http://www.uspto.gov/blog/director. Director Kappos noted the functional language is particularly challenging when used in a genus claim. Mr. Kappos provided the following example: "[A] generic claim may define the boundaries of a vast genus of chemical compounds, and yet the question may still remain whether the specification, including original claim language, demonstrates that the applicant has invented species sufficient to support a claim to a genus." *Id.* Thus, functional claim language can be supported if the specification discloses an established correlation between structure and function. *See Boston Scientific,* 647 F.3d at 1366-1367 (holding the functional claim language was unsupported by the specification because it lacked any "information regarding structural characteristics" of rapamycin analogs and their function). For a case that does not involve genus claims or functional claim language and the written description requirement was satisfied, *see Crown Packaging Tech., Inc. v. Ball Metal Beverage Container Corp.,* 635 F.3d 1373, 1380 (Fed. Cir. 2011) (stating "'[i]nventors can frame their claims to address one problem or several, and the written description requirement will be satisfied as to each claim as long as the description conveys that the inventor was in possession of the invention recited in the claim'") (citing *Revolution Eyewear, Inc. v. Aspex Eyeware, Inc.,* 563 F.3d 1358 (Fed. Cir. 2009).

6. ***Written Description and Enablement.*** In prior cases, the Federal Circuit has distinguished the enablement and written description by stressing that the latter focuses on what the applicant actually invented, proof of which requires a level of specificity in the specification that may be unnecessary for enablement purposes. *See In re Ruschig,* 379 F.2d 990, 995 (CCPA 1967) ("[T]he question is not whether [one skilled in the art] would be so enabled but whether the specification discloses the compound to him, specifically, as something appellants actually invented."). Enablement, in contrast, focuses on whether the specification enables a person having ordinary skill in the art could make and use the claimed invention, an inquiry that is more objective that the inventor-centric written description requirement. Thus, it is possible

for a specification to satisfy enablement yet fall short of satisfying the written description requirement. As the Court of Customs and Patent Appeals noted in *In re DiLeone*, 436 F.2d 1404, 1405 (CCPA 1971), a specification that only discloses compound A with no broadening language "might very well enable one skilled in the art to make and use compounds B and C; yet the class consisting of A, B and C has not been described." Therefore, an applicant who later amends his claims to add B and C may comply with enablement, but not written description. In short, the "purpose of the 'written description' requirement is broader than to merely explain how to 'make and use'; the applicant must also convey with reasonable clarity to those skilled in the art that, as of the filing date sought, he or she was in possession of the invention. The invention is, for purposes of the 'written description' inquiry, whatever is now claimed." *Vas-Cath*, 935 F.2d at 1563-1564.

One way to think about the distinction between enablement and written description is the latter is primarily concerned with certainty (or notice) whereas enablement's is focus is on teaching a skilled artisan how to make and use the claimed invention. Both requirements use commensurability as a policy tool, but employ it from different angles. What do you think? Do you agree with the *Ariad* court's distinction between the written description requirement and the enablement requirement? Can you think of a situation where enablement is satisfied but not written description?

GENTRY GALLERY, INC. v. BERKLINE CORP.

134 F.3d 1473 (Fed. Cir. 1998)

LOURIE, Circuit Judge.

The Gentry Gallery appeals from the judgment of the United States District Court for the District of Massachusetts holding that the Berkline Corporation does not infringe U.S. Patent 5,064,244. Berkline cross-appeals from the decision that the patent was not shown to be invalid. [B]ecause the court clearly erred in finding that the written description portion of the specification supported certain of the broader claims asserted by Gentry, we reverse the decision that those claims are not invalid under 35 U.S.C. §112, ¶1 (1994).

BACKGROUND

Gentry owns the '244 patent, which is directed to a unit of a sectional sofa in which two independent reclining seats ("recliners") face in the same direction. Sectional sofas are typically organized in an L-shape with "arms" at the exposed ends of the linear sections. According to the patent specification, because recliners usually have had adjustment controls on their arms, sectional sofas were able to contain two recliners only if they were located at the exposed ends of the linear sections. Due to the typical L-shaped configuration of sectional sofas, the recliners therefore faced in different directions. *See* '244 patent; col. 1, ll. 15-19. Such an arrangement was "not usually comfortable when the occupants are watching television because one or both occupants must turn their heads to watch the same [television] set. Furthermore, the separation of the two reclining seats at opposite ends of a sectional sofa is not comfortable or conducive to intimate conversation." *Id.* at col. 1, ll. 19-25.

The invention of the patent solved this supposed dilemma by, *inter alia*, placing a "console" between two recliners which face in the same direction. This console "accommodates the controls for both reclining seats," thus eliminating the need to position each recliner at an exposed end of a linear section. *Id.* at col. 1, ll. 36-37. Accordingly, both recliners can then be located on the same linear section allowing two people to recline while watching television and facing in the same direction. Claim 1, which is the broadest claim of the patent, reads in relevant part:

> A sectional sofa comprising:
> a pair of reclining seats disposed in parallel relationship with one another in a double reclining seat sectional sofa section being without an arm at one end . . . , each of said reclining seats having a backrest and seat cushions and movable between upright and reclined positions . . . ,
> a *fixed console* disposed in the double reclining seat sofa section between the pair of reclining seats and with the console and reclining seats together comprising a unitary structure,
> said console including an armrest portion for each of the reclining seats; said arm rests remaining fixed when the reclining seats move from one to another of their positions, and
> a *pair of control means*, one for each reclining seat; *mounted on the double reclining seat sofa section.* . . .

Id. at col. 4, line 68 to col. 5, ll. 1-27 (emphasis added to most relevant claim language). Claims 9, 10, 12-15, and 19-21 are directed to a sectional sofa in which the control means are specifically located on the console.

In 1991, Gentry filed suit in the District of Massachusetts alleging that Berkline infringed the patent by manufacturing and selling sectional sofas having two recliners facing in the same direction. In the allegedly infringing sofas, the recliners were separated by a seat which has a back cushion that may be pivoted down onto the seat, so that the seat back may serve as a tabletop between the recliners. . . .

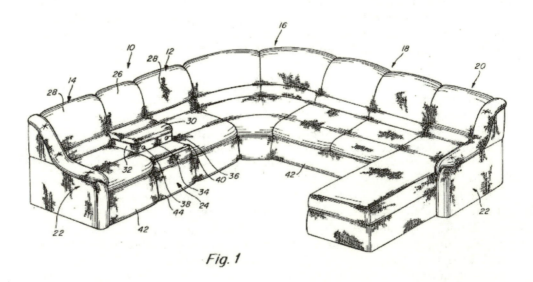

Fig. 1

* * *

B. Invalidity

. . . Berkline . . . argues that claims 1-8, 11, and 16-18 are invalid because they are directed to sectional sofas in which the location of the recliner controls is not limited to the console. According to Berkline, because the patent only describes sofas having controls on the console and an object of the invention is to provide a sectional sofa "with a console . . . that accommodates the controls for both the reclining seats," '244 patent, col. 1, ll. 35-37, the claimed sofas are not described within the meaning of §112, ¶1. Berkline also relies on Sproule's testimony that "locating the controls on the console is definitely the way we solved it [the problem of building sectional sofa with parallel recliners] on the original group [of sofas]." Gentry responds that the disclosure represents only Sproule's preferred embodiment, in which the controls are on the console, and therefore supports claims directed to a sofa in which the controls may be located elsewhere. Gentry relies on *Ethicon Endo-Surgery, Inc. v. United States Surgical Corp.*, 93 F.3d 1572, 1582 n.7 (Fed. Cir. 1996), and *In re Rasmussen*, 650 F.2d 1212, 1214 (CCPA 1981), for the proposition that an applicant need not describe more than one embodiment of a broad claim to adequately support that claim.

We agree with Berkline that the patent's disclosure does not support claims in which the location of the recliner controls is other than on the console. Whether a specification complies with the written description requirement of §112, ¶1, is a question of fact, which we review for clear error on appeal from a bench trial. To fulfill the written description requirement, the patent specification "must clearly allow persons of ordinary skill in the art to recognize that [the inventor] invented what is claimed." *In re Gosteli*, 872 F.2d 1008, 1012 (Fed. Cir. 1989). An applicant complies with the written description requirement "by describing *the invention,* with all its claimed limitations." *Lockwood v. American Airlines, Inc.*, 107 F.3d 1565, 1572 (1997).

It is a truism that a claim need not be limited to a preferred embodiment. However, in a given case, the scope of the right to exclude may be limited by a narrow disclosure. For example, as we have recently held, a disclosure of a television set with a keypad, connected to a central computer with a video disk player did not support claims directed to "an individual terminal containing a video disk player." *See id.* (stating that claims directed to a "distinct invention from that disclosed in the specification" do not satisfy the written description requirement); *see also Regents of the Univ. of Cal. v. Eli Lilly & Co.*, 119 F.3d 1559, 1568 (Fed. Cir. 1997) (stating that the case law does "not compel the conclusion that a description of a species always constitutes a description of a genus of which it is a part").

In this case, the original disclosure clearly identifies the console as the only possible location for the controls. It provides for only the most minor variation in the location of the controls, noting that the control "may be mounted on top or side surfaces of the console rather than on the front wall . . . without departing from this invention." '244 patent, col. 2, line 68 to col. 3, line 3.

No similar variation beyond the console is even suggested. Additionally, the only discernible purpose for the console is to house the controls. As the disclosure states, identifying the only purpose relevant to the console, "[a]nother object of the present invention is to provide . . . a console positioned between [the reclining seats] that accommodates the controls for both of the reclining seats." *Id.* at col. 1, ll. 33-37. Thus, locating the controls anywhere but on the console is outside the stated purpose of the invention. Moreover, consistent with this disclosure, Sproule's broadest original claim was directed to a sofa comprising, *inter alia,* "control means located upon the center console to enable each of the pair of reclining seats to move separately between the reclined and upright positions." Finally, although not dispositive, because one can add claims to a pending application directed to adequately described subject matter, Sproule admitted at trial that he did not consider placing the controls outside the console until he became aware that some of Gentry's competitors were so locating the recliner controls. Accordingly, when viewed in its entirety, the disclosure is limited to sofas in which the recliner control is located on the console.

Gentry's reliance on *Ethicon* is misplaced. It is true, as Gentry observes, that we noted that "an applicant . . . is generally allowed claims, when the art permits, which cover more than the specific embodiment shown." *Ethicon,* 93 F.3d at 1582 n.7. However, we were also careful to point out in that opinion that the applicant "was free to draft claim[s] broadly (within the limits imposed by the prior art) to exclude the lockout's exact location as a limitation of the claimed invention" only because he "did not consider the precise location of the lockout to be an element of his invention." *Id.* Here, as indicated above, it is clear that Sproule considered the location of the recliner controls on the console to be an essential element of his invention. Accordingly, his original disclosure serves to limit the permissible breadth of his later-drafted claims.

Similarly, *In re Rasmussen* does not support Gentry's position. In that case, our predecessor court restated the uncontroversial proposition that "a claim may be broader than the specific embodiment disclosed in a specification." 650 F.2d at 1215. However, the court also made clear that "[a]n applicant is entitled to claims as broad as the prior art *and his disclosure* will allow." *Id.* at 1214, 650 F.2d 1212 (emphasis added). The claims at issue in *Rasmussen,* which were limited to the generic step of "adheringly applying" one layer to an adjacent layer, satisfied the written description requirement only because "one skilled in the art who read [the] specification would understand that it is unimportant how the layers are adhered, so long as they are adhered." Here, on the contrary, one skilled in the art would clearly understand that it was not only important, but essential to Sproule's invention, for the controls to be on the console.

In sum, the cases on which Gentry relies do not stand for the proposition that an applicant can broaden his claims to the extent that they are effectively bounded only by the prior art. Rather, they make clear that claims may be no broader than the supporting disclosure, and therefore that a narrow disclosure will limit claim breadth. Here, Sproule's disclosure unambiguously limited the location of the controls to the console. Accordingly, the district court clearly erred in finding that he was entitled to claims in which the recliner controls are not located on the console. We therefore reverse the judgment that claims 1-8, 11, and 16-18, were not shown to be invalid.

Comments

1. **Gentry *and the So-Called Essential-Element Test.*** A key aspect of *Gentry* was that the patentee considered the location of the controls on the console to be an "essential element of his invention." The *Gentry* case generated a great deal of controversy because it was thought the court constructed a new test: the essential element test. In *Johnson Worldwide Assocs., Inc. v. Zebco Corp.*, 175 F.3d 985, 993 (Fed. Cir. 1999), for example, the Federal Circuit stated that "*Gentry Gallery* . . . considers the situation where the patent's disclosure makes crystal clear that a particular (i.e., narrow) understanding of a claim term is an 'essential element of [the inventor's] invention.' Here, however, the patent disclosure provides ample support for the breadth of the term 'heading'; it does not unambiguously limit[] the meaning of 'heading.'" But the court, in *Cooper Cameron Corp. v. Kvaerner Oilfield Products, Inc.*, 291 F.3d 1317 (Fed. Cir. 2002), stated that *Gentry* "did not announce a new 'essential element' test mandating an inquiry into what an inventor considers to be essential to his invention and requiring that the claims incorporate those elements." The court continued that *Gentry* "merely expounded upon the unremarkable proposition that a broad claim is invalid when the entirety of the specification clearly indicates that the invention is of a much narrower scope." *Id.* at 1323. *See also Amgen, Inc. v. Hoechst Marion Roussel, Inc.*, 314 F.3d 1313, 1333 (Fed. Cir. 2003) (stating *Gentry Gallery* does not mandate "an inquiry into what an inventor considers to be essential to his invention and requir[e] that the claims incorporate those elements").

2. ***Claim Scope Not Limited to Preferred Embodiment Unless.*** . . . The *Ethicon* case discussed in *Gentry* stands for the oft-noted principle that a patentee's claim scope is not limited to the preferred embodiment set forth in the specification. But this principle comes with an important caveat, namely, claim scope will be narrowed if the patentee "has demonstrated a clear intention to limit the claim's scope with words or expressions of manifest exclusion or restriction." *i4i Ltd. Partnership v. Microsoft*, 598 F.3d 831, 843 (Fed. Cir. 2010). In *Gentry*, Sproule's problem was not that he amended the claims post-filing to capture a competitive product, a maneuver that is legal and not uncommon; the problem was the amended claims did not have sufficient support in the specification. In fact, the specification suggested the claimed invention was of "much narrower scope." Sproule's intention was clear.

   In *ICU Medical v. Alaris Medical Systems*, 558 F.3d 1368 (Fed. Cir. 2009), the claims related to a valve mechanism for needleless IV drug delivery. The original claim language required the valves to have a "spike," but the claim was amended to remove the "spike" limitation, thus giving rise to so-called spikeless (or "spike-optional") claims. Thus, the court interpreted the amended claim as not having a "spike limitation." The specification, however, only spoke of a valve with a spike. The accused infringer, Alaris, asserted that the specification limited ICU's invention to valves with a spike and does not demonstrate that the inventor possessed a spikeless medical valve. In contrast, ICU argued that these claims are "spike-optional, i.e., because the claims contain no spike element, they cover valves with a spike and valves without a spike." Therefore, according to ICU, "the specification's disclosure of valves with a spike support claims that are neutral regarding whether the valve must include a spike." The

Federal Circuit agreed with Alaris and invalided the spikeless claims based on the written description requirement. According to the court:

> ICU's asserted spikeless claims are broader than its asserted spike claims because they do not include a spike limitation; these spikeless claims thus refer to medical valves generically—covering those valves that operate with a spike and those that operate without a spike. *But the specification describes only medical valves with spikes.*

Id. at 1378 (emphasis added).

And in *Revolution Eyewear v. Aspex Eyewear,* 563 F.3d 1368 (Fed. Cir. 2009), the Federal Circuit rejected the accused infringer's (Aspex) argument that the asserted claims are invalid under the written description requirement. The invention related to eyeglasses that can be fitted with sunglasses using magnets. The asserted advances over the prior art were a greater magnetic bond and greater stability support. Aspex argued that while the specification addresses both of these advances, the claims do not; and they therefore violate the written description requirement. The court was not convinced because "when the specification sets out two different problems present in the prior art, it is unnecessary for each and every claim in the patent to address both problems." *Id.* at 1367. The court noted that "[i]nventors can frame their claims to address one problem or several, and the written description requirement will be satisfied as to each claim as long as the description conveys that the inventor was in possession of the invention recited in the claim." *Id.* The court found the patentee did address the magnetic bond issue, thus satisfying the written description requirement. Should patent attorneys and agents be reluctant to discuss prior art deficiencies in the patent document? How do you distinguish your client's invention without discussing the prior art?

D. DEFINITENESS

The second paragraph of section 112 is commonly referred to as the "definiteness requirement." This section—which demands the patentee draft clear and distinct claims—has two purposes. First, a clearly drafted claim provides notice to competitors (and the public generally) of the boundaries of the patentee's property rights. The second purpose is to distinguish the claimed invention from the prior art. The *Datamize* and *Star Scientific* cases explore this requirement.

STATUTE: Specification
35 U.S.C. § 112, ¶2

DATAMIZE LLC v. PLUMTREE SOFTWARE, INC.
417 F.3d 1342 (Fed. Cir. 2005)

PROST, Circuit Judge.

Datamize, L.L.C. ("Datamize") appeals from a decision of the United States District Court for the Northern District of California holding each claim of

United States Patent No. 6,014,137 ("the '137 patent") invalid as indefinite under 35 U.S.C. § 112, ¶2. We affirm.

A. The '137 Patent and Related Prosecution History

The '137 patent, entitled "Electronic Kiosk Authoring System," discloses a software program that allows a person to author user interfaces for electronic kiosks. "The authoring system enables the user interface for each individual kiosk to be customized quickly and easily within wide limits of variation, yet subject to constraints adhering the resulting interface to good standards of aesthetics and user friendliness." '137 patent, Abstract; *see also id.* at col. 3, ll. 28-32.

The authoring system gives the system author a limited range of pre-defined design choices for stylistic and functional elements appearing on the screens. *Id.* at col. 3, ll. 52-57. "[M]ajor aesthetic or functional design choices . . . as well as hierarchical methods of retrieving information may be built into the system [while] taking into account the considered opinions of aesthetic design specialists, database specialists, and academic studies on public access kiosk systems and user preferences and problems." *Id.* at col. 3, ll. 57-64.

At issue in this appeal is the definiteness of "aesthetically pleasing" as it is used in the context of claim 1 of the '137 patent. The "aesthetically pleasing" claim language was not discussed by the inventor or the patent examiner during prosecution of the application that led to the '137 patent. The language was discussed, however, during prosecution of a continuation application to the '137 patent, which eventually issued as United States Patent No. 6,460,040 ("the '040 patent"). The patent examiner reviewing the application leading to the '040 patent rejected a claim as being indefinite for using the phrase "aesthetically pleasing." In response to this rejection, the inventor argued that the phrase is definite, but ultimately deleted it, stating in part that it is "not intended to identify qualities separate and apart from the remainder of this claim element" and is "superfluous and unnecessary."

* * *

Concluding that the phrase "aesthetically pleasing" in claim 1 is "hopelessly indefinite," the district court granted Plumtree's motion for summary judgment of invalidity. Since claim 1 is the '137 patent's sole independent claim, the court's grant of summary judgment of indefiniteness as to claim 1 invalidated each claim in the '137 patent.

DISCUSSION

* * *

B. The Law of Indefiniteness

Every patent's specification must "conclude with one or more claims particularly pointing out and distinctly claiming the subject matter which the applicant regards as his invention." 35 U.S.C. § 112, ¶2 (2000). Because the claims perform the fundamental function of delineating the scope of the invention, the purpose of the definiteness requirement is to ensure that the claims delineate the scope of the invention using language that adequately notifies the public of the patentee's right to exclude.

According to the Supreme Court, "[t]he statutory requirement of particularity and distinctness in claims is met only when [the claims] clearly distinguish what is claimed from what went before in the art and clearly circumscribe what is foreclosed from future enterprise." *United Carbon Co. v. Binney & Smith Co.*, 317 U.S. 228, 236 (1942). The definiteness requirement, however, does not compel absolute clarity. Only claims "not amenable to construction" or "insolubly ambiguous" are indefinite. Thus, the definiteness of claim terms depends on whether those terms can be given any reasonable meaning. Furthermore, a difficult issue of claim construction does not *ipso facto* result in a holding of indefiniteness. *Exxon Research & Eng'g*, 265 F.3d at 1375. "If the meaning of the claim is discernible, even though the task may be formidable and the conclusion may be one over which reasonable persons will disagree, we have held the claim sufficiently clear to avoid invalidity on indefiniteness grounds." *Id.* In this regard it is important to note that an issued patent is entitled to a statutory presumption of validity. *See* 35 U.S.C. § 282 (2000). "By finding claims indefinite only if reasonable efforts at claim construction prove futile, we accord respect to the statutory presumption of validity and we protect the inventive contribution of patentees, even when the drafting of their patents has been less than ideal." *Exxon Research & Eng'g*, 265 F.3d at 1375. In this way we also follow the requirement that clear and convincing evidence be shown to invalidate a patent.

In the face of an allegation of indefiniteness, general principles of claim construction apply. Intrinsic evidence in the form of the patent specification and file history should guide a court toward an acceptable claim construction. *Phillips v. AWH Corp.* And while "we have emphasized the importance of intrinsic evidence in claim construction, we have also authorized district courts to rely on extrinsic evidence," such as expert testimony. *Id.* at 18. In construing claims, "what matters is for the court to attach the appropriate weight to be assigned to those sources in light of the statutes and policies that inform patent law." *Id.* at 31.

C. Analysis

With these principles in mind, we proceed to the question at hand: whether the '137 patent's use of "aesthetically pleasing" meets the standards articulated in our case law concerning definiteness. We begin our analysis by noting our agreement with the district court's understanding that the ordinary meaning of "aesthetically pleasing" includes "having beauty that gives pleasure or enjoyment" or, in other words, "beautiful." We also recognize that the district court's opinion presents a reasoned and detailed analysis of both the intrinsic evidence, including the specification of the '137 patent and the prosecution history of the '040 patent, and the extrinsic evidence in the form of Datamize's expert testimony. Datamize, however, argues that the district court erred by considering the phrase "aesthetically pleasing" divorced from the context of claim 1.

Datamize is right to point out that the phrase "aesthetically pleasing" should be considered in the context of claim 1. "Aesthetically pleasing" is used three times in claim 1. The first use of "aesthetically pleasing" relates to the look and feel of custom interface screens on kiosks:

> providing a plurality of pre-defined interface screen element types, each element type defining a form of element available for presentation on said custom interface screens, wherein each said element type permits limited variation in its on-screen

characteristics in conformity with a desired uniform and *aesthetically pleasing* look and feel for said interface screens on all kiosks of said kiosk system.

'137 patent, col. 20, ll. 50-57 (emphasis added).

The second use relies on the first use for antecedent basis and similarly relates to the look and feel of interface screens:

each element type having a plurality of attributes associated therewith, wherein each said element type and its associated attributes are subject to pre-defined constraints providing element characteristics in conformance with said uniform and *aesthetically pleasing* look and feel for said interface screens.

Id. at col. 20, ll. 58-63 (emphasis added).

The third use provides a slightly different context, relating to the aggregate layout of elements on the interface screen:

assigning values to the attributes associated with each of said selected elements consistent with said pre-defined constraints, whereby the aggregate layout of said plurality of selected elements on said interface screen under construction will be *aesthetically pleasing* and functionally operable for effective delivery of information to a kiosk user.

Id. at col. 21, ll. 6-12 (emphasis added). Thus, in the context of claim 1, "aesthetically pleasing" relates to the look and feel of custom interface screens on kiosks, and the aggregate layout of elements on an interface screen is apparently one example or aspect of the interface screens that may be "aesthetically pleasing."

This context, while helpful in terms of identifying the components of the claimed invention that must be "aesthetically pleasing," does not suggest or provide any meaningful definition for the phrase "aesthetically pleasing" itself. Merely understanding that "aesthetically pleasing" relates to the look and feel of interface screens, or more specifically to the aggregate layout of elements on interface screens, fails to provide one of ordinary skill in the art with any way to determine whether an interface screen is "aesthetically pleasing."

Datamize, however, contends that when construed in the context of claim 1, the phrase "aesthetically pleasing" applies to the process of defining a "desired" result and not the actual result itself. Datamize believes a reasonable construction of "aesthetically pleasing" in the context of the claims involves the intent, purpose, wish, or goal of a person practicing the invention: that person simply must intend to create an "aesthetically pleasing" interface screen; whether that person actually succeeds is irrelevant. In other words, Datamize suggests we adopt a construction of "aesthetically pleasing" that only depends on the subjective opinion of a person selecting features to be included on an interface screen. Indeed, Datamize argues that the district court erred by requiring an objective definition for the phrase "aesthetically pleasing." Citing our decision in *Orthokinetics, Inc. v. Safety Travel Chairs, Inc.,* 806 F.2d 1565, 1575-76 (Fed. Cir. 1986), Datamize maintains that a claim term need not be subject to a single, objective definition to be definite but rather may include a subjective element. According to Datamize, subjective terms are permissible so long as one of ordinary skill in the art would understand their scope. In this regard, Datamize, citing *Seattle Box Co. v. Industrial Crate & Packing, Inc.,* 731 F.2d 818, 826 (Fed. Cir. 1984), implies that "aesthetically pleasing" includes "words of degree" that are not fatally imprecise. Datamize also contends that the existence of aesthetic constraints in a computer program, as opposed to purely functional constraints, would be circumstantial evidence of a person's subjective "desire" to achieve an "aesthetically pleasing" look and feel for an interface screen. Related to these arguments, Datamize believes that the person practicing the invention is the "system creator," defined by Datamize as the person who creates the authoring software. According to Datamize, the appropriate inquiry would focus on whether a system creator makes aesthetic choices to limit or constrain the possible on-screen characteristics of screen elements since these choices would reflect a subjective intent to create an "aesthetically pleasing" look and feel for an interface screen.

Datamize's proposed construction of "aesthetically pleasing" in the context of claim 1 is not reasonable for several reasons. First and foremost, the plain meaning of the claim language requires that the look and feel of interface screens actually be "aesthetically pleasing." The first use of "aesthetically pleasing" in claim 1 clearly sets forth two requirements for the look and feel of interface screens: the look and feel must be (1) uniform and (2) "aesthetically pleasing." That the uniform and "aesthetically pleasing" look and feel must also be "desired" does not alter that fact.

Furthermore, in *Orthokinetics* we did not conclude, as Datamize suggests, that the absence of an objective definition for a claim term does not render the phrase indefinite. In that case we concluded that the phrase "so dimensioned" in the following limitation is not indefinite: "wherein said front leg portion is *so dimensioned* as to be insertable through the space between the doorframe of an automobile and one of the seats thereof." *Orthokinetics*, 806 F.2d at 1575. We noted that based on expert testimony it was undisputed that one of ordinary skill in the art would easily have been able to determine the appropriate dimensions that the claim language required. *Id.* at 1576. One desiring to build and use the invention, a travel chair, "must measure the space between the selected automobile's doorframe and its seat and then dimension the front legs of the travel chair so they will fit in that particular space in that particular automobile." *Id.* The fact that the claims were intended to cover the use of the invention with various types of automobiles made no difference; we concluded that the phrase "so dimensioned" is as accurate as the subject matter permits since automobiles are of various sizes. *Id.* Thus, in *Orthokinetics* we recognized that an objective definition encompassed by the claim term "so dimensioned" could be applied to innumerable specific automobiles.

In stark contrast to *Orthokinetics*, here Datamize has offered no objective definition identifying a standard for determining when an interface screen is "aesthetically pleasing." In the absence of a workable objective standard, "aesthetically pleasing" does not just include a subjective element, it is completely dependent on a person's subjective opinion. To the extent Datamize argues that such a construction of "aesthetically pleasing" does not render the phrase indefinite, we disagree. The scope of claim language cannot depend solely on the unrestrained, subjective opinion of a particular individual purportedly practicing the invention. Some objective standard must be provided in order to allow the public to determine the scope of the claimed invention. Even if the relevant perspective is that of the system creator, the identity of who makes aesthetic choices fails to provide any direction regarding the relevant question of how to determine whether that person succeeded in creating an "aesthetically pleasing" look and feel for interface screens. A purely subjective construction of "aesthetically pleasing" would not notify the public of the patentee's right to exclude since the meaning of the claim language would depend on the unpredictable vagaries of any one person's opinion of the aesthetics of interface screens. While beauty is in the eye of the beholder, a claim term, to be definite, requires an objective anchor. Thus, even if we adopted a completely subjective construction of "aesthetically pleasing," this would still render the '137 patent invalid.

Furthermore, "aesthetically pleasing" does not exactly compare to words of degree such as "substantially equal to," *see Seattle Box Co.,* 731 F.2d at 826, "about," *see BJ Servs. Co. v. Halliburton Energy Servs., Inc.,* 338 F.3d 1368, 1372-73 (Fed. Cir. 2003), or "substantial absence," *see Exxon Research & Eng'g,* 265 F.3d at 1380-81. The language, however, invokes a similar analysis. "When a word of degree is used the district court must determine whether the patent's specification provides some standard for measuring that degree." *Seattle Box Co.,* 731 F.2d at 826. Similarly, when faced with a purely subjective phrase like "aesthetically pleasing," a court must determine whether the patent's specification supplies some standard for measuring the scope of the phrase. Thus, we next consult the written description. *See id.*

. . . [W]hile the description of an embodiment provides examples of aesthetic features of screen displays that can be controlled by the authoring system, it does not explain what selection of these features would be "aesthetically pleasing." Major aesthetic choices apparently may include some aspect of button styles and sizes, window borders, color combinations, and type fonts. The written description, however, provides no guidance to a person making aesthetic choices such that their choices will result in an "aesthetically pleasing" look and feel of an interface screen. For example, the specification does not explain what factors a person should consider when selecting a feature to include in the authoring system. Left unanswered are questions like: which color combinations would be "aesthetically pleasing" and which would not? And more generally, how does one determine whether a color combination is "aesthetically pleasing"? Again, one skilled in the art reading the specification is left with the unhelpful direction to consult the subjective opinions of aesthetic design specialists, database specialists, and academic studies.

Simply put, the definition of "aesthetically pleasing" cannot depend on an undefined standard. Reference to undefined standards, regardless of whose views might influence the formation of those standards, fails to provide any direction to one skilled in the art attempting to determine the scope of the claimed invention. In short, the definition of "aesthetically pleasing" cannot depend on the undefined views of unnamed persons, even if they are experts, specialists, or academics. Thus, the written description does not provide any reasonable, definite construction of "aesthetically pleasing."

STAR SCIENTIFIC, INC. v. R.J. REYNOLDS TOBACCO COMPANY

537 F.3d 1357 (Fed. Cir. 2008)

MICHEL, Chief Judge.

Plaintiff-Appellant Star Scientific, Inc. ("Star") appeals from a final judgment in favor of Defendants-Appellees R.J. Reynolds Tobacco Company (N.C.) and R.J. Reynolds Tobacco Company (N.J.) (collectively, "RJR"). The district court entered memoranda and orders . . . granting summary judgment of invalidity of all asserted claims of the 6,202,649 and 6,425,401 patents due to indefiniteness.

We . . . reverse the grant of summary judgment as to indefiniteness because we conclude that the claim term at issue, "anaerobic condition," is not indefinite, and we remand for further proceedings on infringement and validity.

I. BACKGROUND

A. Tobacco Curing Technology

Fresh tobacco ("green tobacco") must be dried in a process called "curing" before it is suitable for consumption as cigarettes or other such products. Curing is done in curing "barns," and commercial tobacco companies like RJR cure their tobacco in bulk-curing barns in which substantial quantities of harvested tobacco are cured together in large stacks. Smaller operations may use the older and long-used technology of "stick barns" in which much smaller quantities of tobacco are cured.

Four major mechanisms of curing have been used in the United States:

(1) air curing, where the tobacco is air-dried without the application of heat;

(2) radiant heat indirect-fired curing ("radiant heat curing"), where fuel (typically oil) is burned and the hot exhaust gases are passed through pipes running through the barn such that the hot pipes radiate heat into the barn to dry the tobacco, but the exhaust gases are then expelled outside the barn;

(3) direct-fired curing, where fuel (typically propane) is burned and the hot exhaust gases themselves are blown directly into the barn to dry the tobacco; and

(4) forced air indirect-fired curing, where fuel is burned to heat clean air that is then blown into the barn to dry the tobacco, while the exhaust gases from the fuel burning are expelled outside the barn.

In the 1960s, the primary method used by American tobacco companies was radiant heat curing. By the 1970s, most companies switched to direct-fired curing, which was the predominant method used until at least the late 1990s.

Cured tobacco contains a number of hazardous chemicals, including carcinogens known as tobacco specific nitrosamines ("TSNAs"), which are not present in green tobacco. In the 1990s, researchers began to explore TSNA formation in tobacco and discovered links between TSNAs and direct-fired curing. As a result, some researchers began to investigate how curing methods could be altered to minimize TSNA formation.

* * *

D. Claim Construction, Trial and Summary Judgment

Claim 4 of the '649 patent is representative of all of the asserted claims:

A process of substantially preventing the formation of at least one nitrosamine in a harvested tobacco plant, the process comprising:

drying at least a portion of the plant, while said portion is uncured, yellow, and in a state susceptible to having the formation of nitrosamines arrested, in a controlled environment and for a time sufficient to substantially prevent the formation of said at least one nitrosamine;

wherein said controlled environment comprises air free of combustion exhaust gases and an airflow sufficient to substantially prevent an *anaerobic condition* around the vicinity of said plant portion; and

wherein said controlled environment is provided by controlling at least one of humidity, temperature, and airflow.

. . . [T]he court construed "anaerobic condition" to mean "an oxygen deficient condition (such as is created by an atmosphere of combustion gases or from the release of carbon dioxide by the plant during cure) which promotes microbial nitrate reductase activity."[4]

* * *

II. Discussion

* * *

B. Indefiniteness

. . . The district court held that the term "anaerobic condition" is indefinite and thus, since it appears in every asserted independent claim, held that all asserted claims are invalid as indefinite. However, because the claim term "anaerobic condition" is not indefinite, we also reverse the grant of summary judgment.

The requirement of claim definiteness is set forth in 35 U.S.C. §112, ¶2, which requires claims "particularly pointing out and distinctly claiming the subject matter which the applicant regards as his invention." We have held that "[o]nly claims not amenable to construction or insolubly ambiguous are indefinite." *Datamize*, 417 F.3d at 1347. A claim term is not indefinite just because "it poses a difficult issue of claim construction." *Exxon Research & Eng'g Co. v. United States*, 265 F.3d 1371, 1375 (Fed. Cir. 2001). Rather, the standard is whether "the claims [are] amenable to construction, however difficult that task may be." *Id.* "By finding claims indefinite only if reasonable efforts at claim construction prove futile, we accord respect to the statutory presumption of patent validity. . . ." *Id.*

The parties do not dispute the claim constructions reached by the district court, and the district court did construe all terms relevant to this appeal. In and of itself, a reduction of the meaning of a claim term into words is not dispositive of whether the term is definite. *Halliburton Energy Serv., Inc. v. M-I LLC*, 514 F.3d 1244, 1251 (Fed. Cir. 2008). And if reasonable efforts at claim construction result in a definition that does not provide sufficient particularity and clarity to inform skilled artisans of the bounds of the claim, the claim is insolubly ambiguous and invalid for indefiniteness.

The district court construed the term "anaerobic condition" to mean "an oxygen deficient condition (such as is created by an atmosphere of combustion gases or from the release of carbon dioxide by the plant during cure) which promotes microbial nitrate reductase activity." Thus, a skilled artisan would know that the claim term contemplates only conditions where the dearth of oxygen promotes the activity of the nitrate reductase enzyme. It is undisputed

---

4. Nitrate reductase is the enzyme used by the microbes on the surface of curing tobacco leaves to catalyze some of the chemical reactions that ultimately produce TSNAs.

that those of ordinary skill would understand from the patents' specifications that the significance of nitrate reductase activity to the claimed invention is that it produces nitrites, which then form TSNAs. Therefore, from the claim term "anaerobic condition" and the intrinsic record, a skilled artisan would discern that the term delineates those conditions where the shortage of oxygen results in increased TSNA formation. This is further supported by statements to that effect in the patents' specifications. *See, e.g.,* '649 patent col. 4 ll. 36-39 ("For example, it is postulated that if the conditions [contemplated for the present invention] are made aerobic, the microbes will consume oxygen in the atmosphere for their energy source, and therefore no nitrites will form.").

We have stated that "[w]hen a word of degree is used . . . the patent's specification [must] provide[ ] some standard for measuring that degree" to be definite. *Datamize,* 417 F.3d at 1351. Here, the term "anaerobic condition" is in effect a term of degree because its bounds depend on the degree of oxygen deficiency. And as the district court determined in its claim construction, the intrinsic record provides a standard for measuring that degree and assessing the bounds of "anaerobic condition" as required by *Datamize,* namely the level of TSNA formation. In fact, the claims explicitly refer to the standard, requiring that the tobacco be cured in a "controlled environment" that prevents an "anaerobic condition" in order to "substantially prevent the formation of at least one nitrosamine." *See* '649 patent cl. 4.

The district court further determined that TSNA formation is itself a well-defined standard as disclosed by the asserted patents. It construed the term "substantially prevent the formation of at least one nitrosamine" to mean "the level of at least one of the nitrosamines falls within the following ranges: less than about 0.05 $\mu g/g$ for NNN, less than about 0.10 $\mu g/g$ for NAT plus NAG, and less than about 0.05 $\mu g/g$ for NNK." In other words, the district court was able to discern from the intrinsic record that TSNA formation, as contemplated by the asserted patents, is tied to highly specific measurements of four very specific chemical compounds. Far from being insolubly ambiguous, a skilled artisan could determine whether an "anaerobic condition" was present—or, rather, was prevented—simply by measuring the levels of NNN, NAT, NAG, and NNK.

The district court's contrary conclusion was based on its misunderstanding that claim definiteness requires that a potential infringer be able to determine if a process infringes before practicing the claimed process.[12] But we disclaimed any such approach in *Invitrogen Corp. v. Biocrest Manufacturing, L.P.,* 424 F.3d 1374, 1384 (Fed. Cir. 2005). We explained that Stratagene, in making a similar argument, was "really talking about the difficulty of avoiding infringement, not indefiniteness of the claim." *Id.* "The test for indefiniteness does not depend on a potential infringer's ability to ascertain the nature of its own accused product to determine infringement, but instead on whether the claim delineates to a skilled artisan the bounds of the invention." *Id. See also Datamize,* 417 F.3d at

---

12. The district court misunderstood our decision in *Geneva Pharmaceuticals, Inc. v. GlaxoSmithKline PLC,* 349 F.3d 1373, 1383-84 (Fed. Cir. 2003). There, we rejected a proposed construction that, if adopted, would have rendered the term indefinite because a given composition could both infringe and not infringe simultaneously. We did *not* hold the claim term at issue to be indefinite; in fact, after rejecting that proposed construction, we arrived at the correct construction which did not render the term indefinite. *Id.* at 1384. And while we emphasized that a claim is indefinite if a skilled artisan cannot determine if an accused product infringes or not, we did *not* hold that the infringement determination must be able to be made at any particular time.

1354 (holding that "indefiniteness does not depend on the difficulty experienced by a particular person in comparing the claims with the prior art or the claims with allegedly infringing products or acts"). As construed by the district court, the term "anaerobic condition" clearly delineates the bounds of claim scope and thus is not indefinite. The district court's grant of summary judgment of indefiniteness must therefore be reversed.

CONCLUSION

For the reasons provided above, we reverse the district court's judgment of unenforceability of both asserted patents due to inequitable conduct. We also reverse the district court's grant of summary judgment of invalidity of all asserted claims due to indefiniteness and remand for further proceedings on the infringement complaint consistent with this opinion.

Comments

1. *The Policies of Definiteness.* The policies underlying the definiteness requirement have been part of patent law jurisprudence since at least the late nineteenth century. *See Merrill v. Yeomans*, 94 U.S. 568, 573 (1876) (stating "[t]he growth of the patent system in the last quarter of a century in this country has reached a stage in its progress where the variety and magnitude of the interests involved require accuracy, precision, and care in the preparation of all the papers on which the patent is founded"). A few years after the *Merrill* decision, the Supreme Court in *Bates v. Coe*, 98 U.S. 31, 39 (1878), provided three policy reasons for clear claiming:

> Accurate description of the invention is required by law, for several important purposes: (1) That the government may know what is granted, and what will become public property when the term of the monopoly expires; (2) That licensed persons desiring to practice the invention may know during the term how to make, construct, and use the invention; [and] (3) That other inventors may know what part of the field of invention is unoccupied.

There are two important points to take away from this language. First, patents are written by and for persons of skill in the art, what *Bates* refers to as "inventors" and "persons desiring to practice the invention." Thus, when interpreting claims, it is the person of technical skill in the art whose perspective and understanding is relevant, not the layperson or judge. (The issue of claim interpretation is explored in detail in Chapter 7.) The key inquiry under definiteness "requires an analysis of whether those persons skilled in the art would understand the bounds of the claim when read in light of the specification," *Credle v. Bond*, 25 F.3d 1566, 1576 (Fed. Cir. 1994). Recall, this person with technical skill—what is referred to as the "person having ordinary skill in the art"—is central to determining compliance with the three disclosure requirements of §112, ¶1 and, as you will see, is equally central to several other important determinations in patent law.

The second point is that certainty and security in property rights are paramount concerns in any property rights regime, including patent law. *See* TERRY L. ANDERSON & PETER J. HILL, THE NOT SO WILD, WILD WEST 206 (2004) (stating "[w]ell-defined and secure property rights for intellectual property are a key to economic growth in the modern world"). Competitors of the patent owner should be provided with enough notice regarding the metes and bounds of the patent owner's property interest so that the competitor can make an informed decision as where he should and should not tread.

What then are we to make of the language in *Star Scientific* that the "test for indefiniteness does not depend on a potential infringer's ability to ascertain the nature of its own accused product to determine infringement, but instead on whether the claim delineates to a skilled artisan the bounds of the invention?" Is this language consistent with *Bates* and underlying policy of §112, ¶2?

2. ***The Elusive Nature of Certainty.*** Certainty is a virtue in numerous areas of law, and in our daily lives. Imagine driving on the interstate and coming across a sign that reads: "Drive at a Reasonable Speed." Would you prefer this standard to "Speed Limit—65 m.p.h."? Most of us (perhaps) would opt for the latter because it provides us with more certainty. Unfortunately, it is not that simple in patent law because language is an imperfect tool to describe a non-tangible object; some amount of ambiguity is always going to be present. (We will revisit this issue in Chapter 7 when the Doctrine of Equivalents is discussed.) Perhaps this is why, as Comment 3 explains, "mathematical precision" is not needed when drafting claims. Also, sometimes claims are drafted when the innovation is nascent, and the inventor's understanding of the discovery is less than complete. As time goes by, the technology matures and the claim language may not reflect the technological trends. One question to ponder is does patent counsel have an incentive to purposefully draft ambiguous claims when more precise language is available? Armed with ambiguous claim language (but clear enough to satisfy §112, ¶2), counsel has greater flexibility to develop arguments relating to claim scope.

3. ***An "Objective Anchor."*** The *Datamize* court stated that definiteness requires an "objective anchor" or a "workable objective standard." But the "purpose of the claims is not to explain the technology or how it works, but to state the legal boundaries of the patent grant." (Does this sound familiar? See Comment 6, below.) Accordingly, "[a] claim is not 'indefinite' simply because it is hard to understand when viewed without benefit of the specification." *S3 Inc. v. NVIDIA Corp.*, 259 F.3d 1364, 1369 (Fed. Cir. 2001). As the *Star Scientific* case demonstrates, a patentee does not have to "define his invention with mathematical precision" to comply with the definiteness requirement; indeed, terms of degree such as "substantially" or "about" are frequently and properly used in claim drafting. *See Power-One, Inc. v. Artesyn Technologies, Inc.*, 599 F.3d 1343, 1348 (Fed. Cir. 2010) (finding claim terms "near" and "adapted to" not indefinite "because the [textual] environment dictates the necessary preciseness of the terms"); *Acumed LLC v. Stryker Corporation*, 483 F.3d 800, 806 (Fed. Cir. 2007) (noting "a sound claim construction need not always purge every shred of ambiguity").

And "[i]f the meaning of the claim is discernible, even though the task may be formidable and the conclusion may be one over which reasonable persons will disagree, we have held the claim sufficiently clear to avoid invalidity on indefiniteness grounds." *Exxon Research & Eng'g Co. v. United States*, 265 F.3d 1371, 1375 (Fed. Cir. 2001). In short, only claims "not amenable to construction" or "insolubly ambiguous" are indefinite. The word "substantially" may be ambiguous to a layperson or a judge, but definite to a person of ordinary skill in the art. As the Federal Circuit stated, "when the term 'substantially' serves reasonably to describe the subject matter so that its scope would be understood by persons in the field of invention, and to distinguish the claimed subject matter form the prior art, it is not indefinite." *Verve, LLC v. Crane Cams, Inc.*, 311 F.3d 1116, 1120 (Fed. Cir. 2002).

It takes a special sort of ambiguity (e.g., "aesthetically pleasing") to run afoul of the definiteness requirement. Failure to comply with section 112, ¶2 is typically very difficult to prove. As the Federal Circuit has stated, because claim construction commonly presents difficult questions over which reasonable minds may disagree, proof of indefiniteness must meet an "exacting standard." *Halliburton Energy Servs., Inc. v. M-I LLC*, 514 F.3d 1244, 1249 (Fed. Cir. 2008). (Although, as discussed in Comment 4, this may be changing somewhat.) For example, in *Young v. Lumenis, Inc.*, 492 F.3d 1336 (Fed. Cir. 2007), Dr. Young invented a surgical method for declawing a domesticated cat. One claim limitation read: "forming a first circumferential incision in the epidermis *near* the edge of the ungual crest of the claw" (emphasis added). The district court found the word "near" to be indefinite under section 112, ¶2, and relied on *Amgen Inc. v. Chugai Pharm. Co., Ltd.*, 927 F.2d 1200, 1218 (Fed. Cir. 1991), for the "principle that a word of degree can be indefinite when it fails to distinguish the invention over the prior art and does not permit one of ordinary skill to know what activity constitutes infringement." The Federal Circuit reversed. The court cited *Datamize* for the proposition that claims are indefinite if they are "not amenable to construction or are insolubly ambiguous. . . . Thus, the definiteness of claim terms depends on whether those terms can be given any reasonable meaning." 417 F.3d at 1347. The court wrote: "As used in the claim, the term 'near' is not insolubly ambiguous and does not depart from the ordinary and customary meaning of the phrase 'near' as meaning 'close to or at' the edge of the ungual crest. Reference to the specification shows that it is consistent with that understanding of the term." 492 F.3d at 1346.

In *Bancorp Services, L.L.C. v. Hartford Life Insurance Co.*, 359 F.3d 1367 (Fed. Cir. 2004). Bancorp owned a patent related to a system for administering and tracking the value of life insurance policies in several accounts. All of the independent claims of the patent referred to "surrender value protected investment credits," and it is this phrase that Hartford asserted was indefinite. Hartford argued that the term was not defined in the patent and it does not have a commonly understood meaning by persons having ordinary skill in the art. The court agreed with Hartford that "surrender value protected investment credits" was not defined in the patent and Bancorp did not provide an industry publication that defines the term. Nevertheless, said the court, "the components of the term have well-recognized meanings, which allow the reader to infer the meaning of the entire phrase with reasonable confidence." The court, citing the presumption of validity that accompanies issued patents, expressed a reluctance to invalidate claims that are not "insolubly ambiguous."

Another case where the court was reluctant to invalidate a claim based on indefiniteness was *Athletic Alternatives v. Prince Mfg.*, 73 F.3d 1573 (Fed. Cir. 1996). There the court believed the claim language in question was subject to two interpretations, one narrower than the other, but both enabled by the specification. In this situation, the court adopted the narrower interpretation instead of invalidating the claim. The court based its decision on the notice function of the patent claim and created a canon of construction, as follows:

> Where there is an equal choice between a broader and a narrower meaning of a claim, and there is an enabling disclosure that indicates that the applicant is at least entitled to a claim having the narrower meaning, we consider the notice function of the claim to be best served by adopting the narrower meaning.

Id. at 1581. In a concurring opinion, Judge Nies argued this canon of construction is "illogical" because "[n]arrowness cannot be equated with definiteness." For Judge Nies, providing the patentee with a narrower meaning "eviscerates" the definiteness requirement "while purporting to rely on it." *Id.* at 1583.

4. *No Longer a Perfunctory Requirement?* For some time, the indefiniteness requirement had not been a significant hurdle for patentees requires, but in recent years, the requirement has acquired some bite. For example, in *Halliburton Energy Services, Inc. v. M-I LLC,* 514 F.3d 1244 (Fed. Cir. 2008), the court found the term "fragile gel" for drilling fluids to be indefinite under section 112, ¶2. The patentee (Halliburton) argued that "fragile gel" means either the "ability of the fluid to transition quickly from gel to liquid, and the ability of the fluid to suspend drill cuttings at rest." While these definitions were supported by the specification, this "does not end the inquiry. Even if a claim term's definition can be reduced to words, the claim is still indefinite if a person of ordinary skill in the art cannot translate the definition into meaningfully precise claim scope." *Id.* at 1251. Moreover, the court noted these proposed definitions are functional, meaning that the "fluid is defined by what it does, rather than what it is." The court noted while functional claim drafting is permissible, there are inherent dangers, citing *General Electric Co. v. Wabash Appliance Corp.,* 304 U.S. 364, 371 (1938) (holding claims invalid where the grains of the claimed lighting filament were distinguished from the prior art only because they were "of such size and contour as to prevent substantial sagging and offsetting" of the filament during the commercially useful life of the lamp). Accordingly, "in some instances, use of functional language can fail "to provide a clear-cut indication of the scope of subject matter embraced by the claim" and thus can be indefinite." 514 F.3d at 1355.

The court then provided some guidance for functional claim drafting in the context of section 112, ¶2:

> When a claim limitation is defined in purely functional terms, the task of determining whether that limitation is sufficiently definite is a difficult one that is highly dependent on context (e.g., the disclosure in the specification and the knowledge of a person of ordinary skill in the relevant art area). We note that the patent drafter is in the best position to resolve the ambiguity in the patent claims, and it is highly desirable that patent examiners demand that applicants do so in appropriate circumstances so that the patent can be amended during prosecution rather than attempting to resolve the ambiguity in litigation.

> A patent drafter could resolve the ambiguities of a functional limitation in a number of ways. For example, the ambiguity might be resolved by using a quantitative metric (e.g., numeric limitation as to a physical property [such as "how quickly the gel must break (time to break at given conditions) and how

strong the gel must be (strength at given conditions)]") rather than a qualitative functional feature. The claim term might also be sufficiently definite if the specification provided a formula for calculating a property along with examples that meet the claim limitation and examples that do not.

Id. at 1255-1256.

After *Halliburton*, the Federal Circuit handed down a series of software-related cases in which the patents were drafted in means-plus-function format (see Chapter 7.B.5 for a discussion of means-plus-function claims). In each of these cases, the Federal Circuit invalided the claims for indefiniteness because the specification did not disclose sufficient corresponding structure. *See Net MoneyIN Inc. v. Verisign Inc.*, 545 F.3d 1359 (Fed. Cir. 2008); *Aristocrat Technologies Australia Ltd. v. International Game Technology, Inc.*, 543 F.3d 657 (Fed. Cir. 2008); *Finisar Corp. v. DirectTV Group*, 523 F.3d 1323 (Fed. Cir. 2008). These cases prompted the USPTO to issue memoranda relating to the indefiniteness requirement. The first memorandum stated that a claim is indefinite if specification "is not clear and precise and one of ordinary skill in the art would consider the term indefinite (e.g., the definition's broadest reasonable interpretation results in more than one meaning and/or interpretation)." The second memo pertained to computer-implemented inventions drafted in means-plus-function format. This memo noted that the corresponding structure set forth in the specification must include not only the algorithm but also the general purpose microprocessor.

Building on this trend, the Board of Patent Appeals and Interferences issued a precedential opinion in *Ex parte Miyazaki*, 89 U.S.P.Q. 2d 1207 (Bd. App. and Interf. 2008), in which the five-member panel, citing *Halliburton*, held that indefiniteness is proper if the claim possesses multiple plausible interpretations. The Board also wrote that "we employ a lower threshold of ambiguity when reviewing a pending claim for indefiniteness that those used by post-issuance courts." According to the Board:

> [R]ather than requiring that the claims be insolubly ambiguous, we hold that if a claim is amenable to two or more plausible claim constructions, the USPTO is justified in requiring the applicant to more precisely define the metes and bounds of the claimed invention by holding the claim unpatentable under 35 U.S.C. §112, second paragraph, as indefinite.
>
> The USPTO, as the sole agency vested with the authority to grant exclusionary rights to inventors for patentable inventions, has a duty to guard the public against patents of ambiguous and vague scope. Such patents exact a cost on society due to their ambiguity that is not commensurate with the benefit that the public gains from disclosure of the invention. The USPTO is justified in using a lower threshold showing of ambiguity to support a finding of indefiniteness under 35 U.S.C. §112, second paragraph, because the applicant has an opportunity and a duty to amend the claims during prosecution to more clearly and precisely define the metes and bounds of the claimed invention and to more clearly and precisely put the public on notice of the scope of the patent.

5. *A Call for a More Definite Definiteness Requirement.* Despite the aforementioned cases in Comment 4, some commentators and at least one Federal Circuit judge would like to see a more robust definiteness requirement. For example, Senior Federal Circuit Judge Jay Plager wrote:

Despite the varying formulations that this court has used over the years in describing its "indefiniteness" jurisprudence . . . , the general conclusion from our law seems to be this: if a person of ordinary skill in the art can come up with a plausible meaning for a disputed claim term in a patent, that term, and therefore the claim, is not indefinite [under § 112, ¶2]. . . .

Judge Plager praised the USPTO's application of the indefiniteness requirement, citing *Ex parte Miyazaki, supra* Comment 4. He continued:

The United States Patent and Trademark Office ("PTO"), by contrast, appears to be taking steps to give the statutory requirement real meaning. . . . The court now spends a substantial amount of judicial resources trying to make sense of unclear, over-broad, and sometimes incoherent claim terms. It is time for us to move beyond sticking our fingers in the never-ending leaks in the dike that supposedly defines and figuratively surrounds a claimed invention. Instead, we might spend some time figuring out how to support the PTO in requiring that the walls surrounding the claimed invention be made of something other than quicksand.

Enzo Biochem, Inc. v. Applera Corp., 605 F.3d 1347, 1348 (Fed. Cir. 2010) (Plager, J., dissent from denial of rehearing *en banc*).

6. *Written Description Requirement and Definiteness.* The Federal Circuit has distinguished the definiteness requirement from the written description requirement based on both historical and policy grounds. The *Vas-Cath* court offered a historical explanation, noting "the 'written description' require-ment was a part of the patent statutes at a time before claims were required." 935 F.2d at 1560. But understanding the persistence of the written descrip-tion requirement in the light of section 112, ¶2 is more challenging. The *Vas-Cath* court, quoting *Rengo Co. v. Molins Mach. Co.*, noted the "subtle" and "complementary" relationship between the policies of the written descrip-tion and definiteness requirements, but also stressed how these two require-ments "approach a similar problem from different directions." According to the court, the written description requirement "guards against the inventor's overreaching by insisting that he recount his invention in such detail that his future claims can be determined to be encompassed within his original creation," whereas the "definiteness requirement shapes the future conduct of persons other than the inventor, by insisting that they receive notice of the scope of the patented device." While the issue of perspective may be accu-rate, perhaps a more convincing distinction is that the written description requirement is more informative than the claims. This point was made by Judge Lourie in *University of Rochester*:

The separate written description requirement poses no conflict with the role of the claims. It is well established that the specification teaches an invention, whereas the claims define the right to exclude. While claims must be supported by the written description, the latter contains much material that is not in the claims. The written description contains an elucidation of various aspects of an invention as well as material that is necessary for enablement. Moreover, the written description often contains material that an applicant intended to claim that has been rejected in examination. Thus, the written description and the claims do not duplicate each other.

University of Rochester, 373 F.3d 1303, 1306 (Fed. Cir. 2004) (refusal to hear *en banc*).

7. ***History of the Patent Claim.*** The claim is an early nineteenth-century innovation of patent attorneys that was developed to assist clients in proving validity and infringement. *See* John F. Duffy, *The* Festo *Decision and the Return of the Supreme Court to the Bar of Patents*, 2002 SUP. CT. REV. 273, 309 (stating the claim "arose not from any administrative, judicial, or legislative requirement. Instead, it was an innovation of patent attorneys, and it was formulated to protect and to expand the rights of patentees"). *See also* Karl B. Lutz, *Evolution of the Claims of U.S. Patents*, 20 J. PAT. OFF. SOC'Y 134 (1938); William Redin Woodward, *Definiteness and Particularity in Patent Claims*, 46 MICH. L. REV. 755 (1948).

E. BEST MODE

The best mode requirement of section 112, ¶1 dictates that in addition to providing an enabling disclosure, the patentee must disclose the best way (or mode) of practicing the claimed invention as contemplated by the inventor. (The best mode is sometimes referred to as the preferred embodiment.) The stated purpose of the best mode requirement is to prevent an inventor from obtaining patent protection while concealing (as a trade secret, for example) preferred embodiments of his claimed invention from the public. For example, an inventor claims "a method of making chemical X wherein A and B are heated between 100-110°C." If an *inventor* knows, *at the time of filing*, that heating at 107°C provides optimal results, he must disclose that information. An important distinction between the best mode requirement and the enablement requirement is that failure to comply with best mode requires subjective inventor knowledge of and concealment of a best mode.

There is no duty to update the best mode or add a best mode after the application has been filed. And for proceedings commenced on or after September 16, 2011, failure to comply with the best mode requirement cannot form the basis of a validity challenge. This compromise position—which was part of the America Invents Act—sought to maintain, on the one hand, the quid pro quo between the inventor and society by still requiring the inventor to disclose the best mode and, on the other hand, the perceived need to curtail best mode civil challenges (and associated litigation costs) that require the very difficult task of discerning inventor intent.[12]

The law and policy of the best mode requirement are discussed in *Young Dental.*

---

12. For a discussion of this compromise from someone who was "intimately involved in the machinations of the America Invents Act," *see* A. Christal Sheppard, *Because Inquiring Minds Want to Know—Best Mode—Why Is It One-Sided?*, available at http://www.patentlyo.com/patent/2011/09/guest-post-because-inquiring-minds-want-to-know-best-mode-why-is-it-one-sided-.html.

STATUTE: Specification

35 U.S.C. §112, ¶1

YOUNG DENTAL MANUFACTURING COMPANY, INC. v. Q3 SPECIAL PRODUCTS, INC.

112 F.3d 1137 (Fed. Cir. 1997)

CLEVENGER, Circuit Judge.

Young Dental Manufacturing Company (Young) appeals the judgment of the United States District Court for the Eastern District of Missouri in favor of Q3 Special Products and David G. Kraenzle (collectively Q3). The court upheld a jury verdict of invalidity of all asserted claims for violation of the best mode requirement of 35 U.S.C. §112.

I

Young's asserted patents, U.S. Patent Nos. 5,156,547 and 5,423,679 (the '547 and '679 patents), disclose an improved disposable prophy angle (DPA). A prophy angle is the small hand-held device used by dentists to polish teeth. It holds a rubber cup, known as a prophy cup, which the dentist dips into an abrasive paste and then holds against the patient's teeth as the cup rotates. Early prophy angles were not disposable; they were made entirely of metal and had to be sterilized in an autoclave between uses. In the 1970s, plastic DPAs were introduced which could be pushed onto the end of a metal handpiece and locked onto the handpiece's drive shaft. These early DPAs did not replace metal DPAs, however, largely because they often ran roughly, fell apart, and overheated.

In November 1990, Ronald Bailey, an employee of Young, filed a patent application for an improved DPA and assigned the application to Young. The application matured into the patents in suit. Fig. 1 of the '547 patent shows the components of Bailey's DPA in side cross-section.

The body **3** of the angle includes a sleeve **4**, a neck **5**, and a head **6** formed integrally with each other. The head is formed as a cylinder at right angles to the neck. The body and head have axial bores **7** and **9**, respectively, into which are placed drive shaft **15** and driven shaft **29**, respectively. To assemble the prophy angle, one inserts the drive shaft into the body bore from the distal end of the prophy angle through aperture **11**. One then inserts the driven shaft into the head bore, where the drive gear **17** meshes with the driven gear **27**. A snap cap **35** slides down into head bore **9** to lock the gears and shafts in place. At its front edge, the snap cap has a sheath **43** that covers the aperture and a latch **41** that locks the cap in place.

The '547 patent was the first to issue from Bailey's application. It claims the DPA and a method for assembling the DPA. The '547 patent was followed by the '679 patent, a divisional based on a continuation-in-part application of the '547 patent. . . .

Kraenzle worked as an engineer with Young from December 1990 until his resignation in March 1992. In April 1992, he designed the device accused here of infringing and in July 1992 filed the patent application that matured into the '859 patent. Kraenzle formed Q3 in July 1992 with Chris Carron, another former Young employee, and began selling the accused device in July 1993,

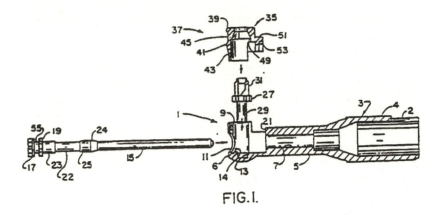

FIG. I.

the same month in which the '859 patent issued. Kraenzle is the president and majority shareholder of Q3. . . .

II

On November 1, 1993, Young sued Q3, Kraenzle, and Carron, alleging infringement of the '547 patent. . . . Young later added a count for infringement of the '679 patent. Q3 counterclaimed for a declaration of noninfringement and invalidity. . . . The jury returned a verdict in favor of Q3. The jury found . . . invalidity . . . for failure to comply with the best mode requirement for all asserted claims.

* * *

IV

Young asserts that the district court should not have submitted the best mode issue to the jury. On this point, we agree with Young. Section 112 requires that the specification "set forth the best mode contemplated by the inventor of carrying out his invention." 35 U.S.C. § 112 (1994). The purpose of this requirement is to restrain inventors from applying for a patent while at the same time concealing from the public preferred embodiments which the inventor has, in fact, conceived. To establish invalidity for failure to disclose the best mode, the party seeking to invalidate the patent must present clear and convincing evidence that the inventor both knew of and concealed a better mode of carrying out the claimed invention than was set forth in the specification.

Two factual inquiries underlie the determination of whether a patent complies with the best mode requirement. Under the first inquiry, which is entirely subjective, one must ask whether, at the time the patent application was filed, the inventor knew of a mode of practicing the claimed invention that he considered to be better than any other. *United States Gypsum Co. v. National Gypsum Co.,* 74 F.3d 1209, 1212 (Fed. Cir. 1996). If the inventor had a best mode of practicing the claimed invention, one proceeds to the second inquiry. That inquiry involves determining whether the specification adequately disclosed what the inventor contemplated as the best mode so that those having ordinary skill in the art could practice it. *Id.* This latter inquiry is "largely an objective inquiry that depends upon the scope of the claimed invention and the level of skill in the art." *Id.* (quoting *Chemcast Corp. v. Arco Indus.*, 913 F.2d 923, 928 (Fed. Cir. 1990)).

The best mode requirement does not apply to "production details." *Wahl Instruments, Inc. v. Acvious, Inc.*, 950 F.2d 1575, 1579-80 (Fed. Cir. 1991). Our precedent has applied the term "production details" in two senses, only one of which truly refers to production details as such. In the first sense, i.e., that of "true" production details, we have referred to commercial considerations that do not relate to the quality or nature of the invention, such as equipment on hand or prior relationships with suppliers. *Id.* In the second sense, under the rubric of production details, we have referred to what more properly are considered routine details. Routine details are details that are apparent to one of ordinary skill in the art. They are appropriately discussed separately from production details because routine details *do* relate to the quality or nature of the invention. Nevertheless, they need not be disclosed because, by definition, their disclosure is not required under the second inquiry of the best mode determination. In other words, to satisfy the second inquiry of the best mode test, an inventor need only disclose information about the best mode that would not have been apparent to one of ordinary skill in the art. Because routine details are apparent to one of ordinary skill, they need not be disclosed.

The details that Q3 asserts are missing from the '547 and '679 patents are such routine details. Q3 first asserts that Bailey failed to disclose the gear ratio between the drive gear and the driven gear in Bailey's DPA. The gear ratio does not escape scrutiny as a production detail because it relates to the quality and nature of the invention—i.e., it affects the stable operation of the DPA at high rotational speeds. However, there is no competent evidence of record indicating that one of skill in the art could not have readily selected a satisfactory gear ratio for this application based on the patent disclosure. Rather, the patent figures disclose the gear shapes and the general design of the gears, and the specification describes the structure of the gears. *See Amgen, Inc. v. Chugai Pharm. Co.*, 927 F.2d 1200, 1212 (Fed. Cir. 1991) ("What is required is an adequate disclosure of the best mode, not a guarantee that every aspect of the specification be precisely and universally reproducible."). We hold that there was no competent evidence to show that the disclosures of the '547 or '679 patent were inadequate to satisfy the best mode requirement.

Q3 also asserts that Bailey failed to disclose the grade of plastic used for the body (Lexan 141) and gears (Celcon M-90) of his preferred embodiment. In this regard, Bailey actually disclosed that he preferred that the parts be made from Lexan and Celcon; he merely failed to disclose the particular grades of these two plastics in his contemplated best mode. "A description of particular materials or sources or of a particular method or technique selected for manufacture may or may not be required as part of a best mode disclosure respecting a device." *Wahl Instruments*, 950 F.2d at 1579.

We do not find any competent evidence of record to show that such detailed disclosure was necessary in the '547 or '679 patent to inform one of skill in the art about the inventor's best mode. Rather, the evidence of record shows that, given the disclosure of the types of plastic, it would have been readily apparent to one of skill in the art to select the particular grade of plastic that would result in efficient DPA operation. In fact, Kraenzle also selected Lexan 141 and Celcon M-90 for use with his DPAs. He testified that he did so at the suggestion of his mold maker because the grades were "general purpose grades, which are right from the Lexan manual." In his '859 patent, Kraenzle, like Bailey, only disclosed the general types of plastics he used and not the particular grades. It thus seems rather curious for Q3 to argue here that disclosure of particular types of plastic are not routine details for purposes of Bailey's application when Kraenzle did not disclose such information in his own application.

Comments

1. *The Two-Part Test.* Compliance with the best mode requirement entails application of a two-part test whose application—since September 16, 2011—resides solely with the USPTO. But as one commentator noted, "the risk of rejection at the PTO for failure to disclose the best mode is almost nonexistent." Ryan Vacca, *Patent Reform and Best Mode: A Signal to the Patent Office or a Step Toward Elimination?*, 75 ALB. L. REV. 279, 295 (2011). The reason is because the first part of the test comprises a subjective component that asks whether at the time of filing the inventor knew of a mode of making and using his invention that he considered best. Importantly, the best mode requirement is not an issue if someone other than the inventor knew of a best mode at the time of filing, even if that other person was employed by the same company as the inventor and the company was the assignee. *See Glaxo, Inc. v Novopharm Ltd.*, 52 F.3d 1043, 1049 (Fed. Cir. 1995) ("The statutory language could not be clearer. The best mode of carrying out an invention, indeed if there is one, to be disclosed is that 'contemplated by the inventor.'"). This subjective prong of the best mode requirement is personal, and seeks to discern the inventor's state of mind. In contrast, the enablement requirement focuses on the objective knowledge of a person of ordinary skill in the art.

   If the answer to the first question is yes, the second part of test, which is objective, is reached. This part of the test compares what the inventor knew with what he disclosed by framing the question as follows: Is the disclosure adequate to enable one of ordinary skill in the art to practice the best mode or has the inventor "concealed" his preferred mode? *See Northern Telecom Ltd. v. Samsung Electronics Co., Ltd.*, 215 F.3d 1281, 1286 (Fed. Cir. 2000). Interestingly, there is no duty to update the best mode after the application has been filed. Arguably, this lack of duty to update is inconsistent with the underlying policies of the disclosure requirements. But requiring an inventor to update the application may lead to the introduction of "new matter," which is currently prohibited once the application is filed. *See* 35 U.S.C. §132(a) ("No amendment shall introduce new matter into the disclosure of the invention."). Of course, if a duty to update were introduced into the patent system, an amendment to section 132 could address the new matter issue by, for example, requiring the applicant to show that the new text pertains only to best mode compliance.

   Failure to comply with the best mode requirement typically occurs in two situations: first, when the patent specification does not adequately disclose a preferred embodiment of the claimed invention, and second, when the patentee fails "to disclose aspects of making or using the claimed invention and the undisclosed matter materially affected the properties of the claimed invention." *Bayer AG v. Schein Pharmaceuticals, Inc.*, 301 F.3d 1306, 1319 (Fed. Cir. 2002).

In addition, when an inventor uses a proprietary product in his preferred embodiment, he must "at a minimum, . . . provide supplier/trade name information in order to satisfy the best mode requirement." *U.S. Gypsum Co. v. Nat'l Gypsum Co.*, 74 F.3d 1209, 1214 (Fed. Cir. 1996) (citing *Chemcast*, 913 F.2d at 929). In *Green Edge Enterprises LLC v. Rubber Mulch Etc.*, 620 F.3d 1287, 2010 WL 3464414 (Fed. Cir. 2010), the patent claimed a synthetic mulch that is colored with a "water-based acrylic colorant" to imitate natural mulch. With respect to the colorant, the specification disclosed that "[t]he most preferred colorants are water-based acrylic systems such as the colorant systems sold under the name 'VISICHROME,' by Futura Coatings, Inc." Futura, however, did not sell a colorant under that name; rather, the inventor had used a Futura product sold under the product code "24009." But the inventor produced a letter it had received from the vice president of Futura, wherein the VP wrote "[t]he Futura 'Visichrome' colorant system is designed to be a user-friendly system. The infinite colors available are packaged as a single component water-based acrylic system." The VP did not remember why he used the term "Visichrome" in the letter.

The parties agreed that a best mode existed; therefore, only step two of the best mode inquiry was at issue. The district court granted the accused infringer's motion for summary judgment and held that the inventor violated the best mode requirement because "'Visichrome' is the only water-based acrylic colorant disclosed in the specification and it did not exist, despite have been referred to in Futura's letter to the patentee. The Federal Circuit reversed the district court's summary judgment ruling. The appellate court framed the issue as whether "the name 'Visichrome' was descriptive of a sufficiently specific product so that one seeking to obtain and practice the best mode of the invention, product number 24009, would have succeeded." According to the court, "despite the [Futura VP's] inability to remember why he used the term 'Visichrome' in his letter, it is at least possible, even likely, that . . . at the time of filing, someone contacting Futura to obtain the 'Visichrome' colorant system would have received a response similar to [the VP's] letter" to the inventor.

2. ***Production Details.*** Some information, commonly referred to as "production details," do not need to be disclosed. As noted in *Young Dental*, there are two types of production details. First, so-called commercial considerations such as the equipment on hand or prior relationships with suppliers are not required to be disclosed. These are considerations that do not relate to the quality of the claimed invention. The second type of production detail are qualitatively significant vis-à-vis the claimed invention, but are deemed routine, such as details of production of which those of ordinary skill in the art are aware. *See Great Northern Corp. v. Henry Molded Products, Inc.*, 94 F.3d 1569 (Fed. Cir. 1996).

3. ***Best Mode—An Uncommon Requirement.*** In addition to the difficulties associated with applying the best mode requirement, perhaps the AIA effectively eliminated the requirement because the United States is one of a very small minority of countries that has a best mode requirement. Other countries that have what can be characterized as a best mode requirement include Egypt, Brazil, and Colombia. The Egyptian *Law on Protection of Intellectual*

Property Rights, Book One, Part I, Article 13, states the "patent application shall be accompanied by a detailed description of the invention, including a full statement of the subject matter and the best way to enable a person of expertise to execute it." The Colombian provision, found in *The Andean Community, Decision 486, Article 28(e)* reads, the "description shall contain the name of the invention and . . . a description of the best method known to the applicant for carrying out the invention. . . ." And *Article 24 of the Brazilian Industrial Property Code* states the "specification shall clearly and sufficiently describe the object, so as to permit its reproduction by a technician versed in the subject, and shall indicate, when applicable, the best of doing it." Article 29 of TRIPS permits signatory countries to have a best mode requirement, but does not require such. Article 29.1 states:

Article 29

Conditions on Patent Applicants

1. Members . . . **may** require the applicant to indicate the best mode for carrying out the invention known to the inventor at the filing date. . . .

(Emphasis added.)

CHAPTER

3

Eligible Subject Matter and Utility

INTRODUCTION

The statutory subject matter requirement—which shares the same statutory section as utility—pertains to the kinds of inventions that are eligible for patent protection. The types of inventions set forth in section 101 of the patent code include a "process, machine, manufacture, or composition of matter, or any new and useful improvement thereof." These terms, characterized as the "great and distinct classes of invention,"[1] have been part of the American patent landscape for more than 200 years.[2] Like the utility requirement, statutory subject matter—despite the increased amount of attention it has received over the past few years by the courts—remains a relatively infrequent impediment to patent protection, the heavy lifting being done by sections 102, 103, and 112.

The utility requirement is, most fundamentally, based on the IP clause of the Constitution, which empowers Congress "to promote the progress of the *useful* arts." But beyond this single word in the Constitution and section 101,[3] Congress, as with much of patent doctrine, has left the development of what is "useful" to the courts. Judicial interpretation of the utility requirement has evolved to include an operability component and a substantiality component. Operability simply asks if the invention works as claimed and described in the patent. This form of utility is easily satisfied and is rarely a concern for patent applicants or patentees during litigation. Substantial utility is a more subjective and controversial inquiry focusing on the degree of usefulness or whether the claimed invention has *enough* utility given the polices of patent law. Substantial utility typically applies—if at all—to the life science and chemical industries, which commonly involve building blocks of research and upstream research tools.

1. *Ex parte Blythe*, 1885 Comm'n Dec. 82, 86 (Comm'r Pat. 1885).
2. *See In re Comiskey*, 499 F.3d 1365, 1375 (Fed. Cir. 2007) ("Beginning with the first patent act, the Patent Act of 1790, 'Congress responded to the bidding of the Constitution,' by including provisions limiting patentable subject matter."). The 1793 Act used the word "art" instead of "process," but the courts have commonly equated "process" and "art" or subsumed process within "art." It was not until the 1952 Patent Act, that Congress, for clarification, changed the word "art" to "process."
3. And a more indirect utility requirement in section 112, ¶ 1, which requires the specification enable a person having skill in the art to "make and use" the claimed invention.

STATUTE: **Inventions patentable**
35 U.S.C. § 101

A. ELIGIBLE SUBJECT MATTER

The statutory subject matter requirement is similar to the utility requirement in two ways. First, they both find a home in section 101 of Title 35, and second, neither of them has historically been a significant obstacle to patentability, despite the fact that the eligibility provision has attracted greater judicial attention in recent years. As Justice Kennedy wrote in *Bilski v. Kappos*, patent law's eligibility requirement should err on the side of inclusiveness because "times change" and "[t]echnology and other innovations progress in unexpected ways." Nonetheless, eligibility remains conceptually important to our understanding of what types of inventions we want to allow in and subject to the more rigorous requirements embodied in sections 102, 103, and 112. In this regard, section 101 can be viewed as the gateway to patentability.[4] But as the principal cases remind us, inclusiveness does not mean section 101 is without filters; namely, laws or products of nature, abstract ideas, and physical phenomena remain outside the realm of patentable subject matter. And these filters are most germane when applied to life science, business method, and software-related inventions.

It should come as no surprise then that of the four principal cases in this section, three relate to the life sciences (*Chakrabarty*, *Mayo*, and *Myriad*) and the other has implications for software and business methods (*Bilski*).

1. Biomedical-Related Inventions

DIAMOND v. CHAKRABARTY

447 U.S. 303 (1980)

Chief Justice BURGER delivered the opinion of the Court.

We granted certiorari to determine whether a live, human-made micro-organism is patentable subject matter under 35 U.S.C. § 101.

I

In 1972, respondent Chakrabarty, a microbiologist, filed a patent application, assigned to the General Electric Co. The application asserted 36 claims related to Chakrabarty's invention of "a bacterium". . . . This human-made, genetically engineered bacterium is capable of breaking down multiple components of

---

4. *See Comiskey, supra* note 2, at 1371 (stating "[o]nly if the requirements of §101 are satisfied is the inventor 'allowed to pass through to' the other requirements for patentability, such as novelty under §102 and, of pertinence to this case, non-obviousness under §103"); *In re Bergy*, 596 F.2d 952, 960 (CCPA 1979) (referring to section 101, the court stated "[t]he question here, as it has always been, is: are the inventions claimed of a *kind* contemplated by Congress as possibly patentable *if* they turn out to be new, useful, and unobvious within the meaning of those terms as used in the statute") (emphasis in original).

crude oil. Because of this property, which is possessed by no naturally occurring bacteria, Chakrabarty's invention is believed to have significant value for the treatment of oil spills.[2]

Chakrabarty's patent claims were of three types: first, process claims for the method of producing the bacteria; second, claims for an inoculum comprised of a carrier material floating on water, such as straw, and the new bacteria; and third, claims to the bacteria themselves. The patent examiner allowed the claims falling into the first two categories, but rejected claims for the bacteria. His decision rested on two grounds: (1) that micro-organisms are "products of nature," and (2) that as living things they are not patentable subject matter under 35 U.S.C. § 101.

Chakrabarty appealed the rejection of these claims to the Patent Office Board of Appeals, and the Board affirmed the Examiner on the second ground. Relying on the legislative history of the 1930 Plant Patent Act, in which Congress extended patent protection to certain asexually reproduced plants, the Board concluded that § 101 was not intended to cover living things such as these laboratory created micro-organisms.

The Court of Customs and Patent Appeals, by a divided vote, [in an opinion by Judge Rich,] reversed on the authority of its prior decision in *In re Bergy*, 563 F.2d 1031, 1038 (1977), which held that "the fact that microorganisms . . . are alive . . . [is] without legal significance" for purposes of the patent law. Subsequently, we granted the Acting Commissioner of Patents and Trademarks' petition for certiorari in *Bergy*, vacated the judgment, and remanded the case "for further consideration in light of *Parker v. Flook*." The Court of Customs and Patent Appeals then vacated its judgment in *Chakrabarty* and consolidated the case with *Bergy* for reconsideration. After re-examining both cases in the light of our holding in *Flook*, that court, with one dissent, [again through Judge Rich,] reaffirmed its earlier judgments.

The Commissioner of Patents and Trademarks again sought certiorari, and we granted the writ as to both *Bergy* and *Chakrabarty*. Since then, *Bergy* has been dismissed as moot, leaving only *Chakrabarty* for decision.

II

The Constitution grants Congress broad power to legislate to "promote the Progress of Science and useful Arts, by securing for limited Times to Authors and Inventors the exclusive Right to their respective Writings and Discoveries." Art. I, § 8, cl. 8. The patent laws promote this progress by offering inventors exclusive rights for a limited period as an incentive for their inventiveness and research efforts. *Kewanee Oil Co. v. Bicron Corp.*; *Universal Oil Co. v. Globe Co.* The authority of Congress is exercised in the hope that "[t]he productive effort thereby fostered will have a positive effect on society through the introduction of new products and processes of manufacture into the economy, and the emanations

---

2. At present, biological control of oil spills requires the use of a mixture of naturally occurring bacteria, each capable of degrading one component of the oil complex. In this way, oil is decomposed into simpler substances which can serve as food for aquatic life. However, for various reasons, only a portion of any such mixed culture survives to attack the oil spill. By breaking down multiple components of oil, Chakrabarty's micro-organism promises more efficient and rapid oil-spill control.

by way of increased employment and better lives for our citizens." *Kewanee*, 416 U.S. at 480.

The question before us in this case is a narrow one of statutory interpretation requiring us to construe 35 U.S.C. § 101, which provides:

> Whoever invents or discovers any new and useful process, machine, manufacture, or composition of matter, or any new and useful improvement thereof, may obtain a patent therefor, subject to the conditions and requirements of this title.

Specifically, we must determine whether respondent's micro-organism constitutes a "manufacture" or "composition of matter" within the meaning of the statute.

III

In cases of statutory construction we begin, of course, with the language of the statute. *Southeastern Community College v. Davis.* And "unless otherwise defined, words will be interpreted as taking their ordinary, contemporary common meaning." *Perrin v. United States*, 444 U.S. 37, 42 (1979). We have also cautioned that courts "should not read into the patent laws limitations and conditions which the legislature has not expressed." *United States v. Dubilier Condenser Corp.*, 289 U.S. 178, 199 (1933).

Guided by these canons of construction, this Court has read the term "manufacture" in § 101 in accordance with its dictionary definition to mean "the production of articles for use from raw or prepared materials by giving to these materials new forms, qualities, properties, or combinations, whether by hand-labor or by machinery." *American Fruit Growers, Inc. v. Brogdex Co.*, 283 U.S. 1, 11 (1931). Similarly, "composition of matter" has been construed consistent with its common usage to include "all compositions of two or more substances and . . . all composite articles, whether they be the results of chemical union, or of mechanical mixture, or whether they be gases, fluids, powders or solids." *Shell Development Co. v. Watson*, 149 F. Supp. 279, 280 (D.C. 1957). In choosing such expansive terms as "manufacture" and "composition of matter," modified by the comprehensive "any," Congress plainly contemplated that the patent laws would be given wide scope.

The relevant legislative history also supports a broad construction. The Patent Act of 1793, authored by Thomas Jefferson, defined statutory subject matter as "any new and useful art, machine, manufacture, or composition of matter, or any new or useful improvement [thereof]." Act of Feb. 21, 1793, § 1, 1 Stat. 319. The Act embodied Jefferson's philosophy that "ingenuity should receive a liberal encouragement." 5 Writings of Thomas Jefferson 75-76 (Washington ed. 1871). Subsequent patent statutes in 1836, 1870, and 1874 employed this same broad language. In 1952, when the patent laws were recodified, Congress replaced the word "art" with "process," but otherwise left Jefferson's language intact. The Committee Reports accompanying the 1952 Act inform us that Congress intended statutory subject matter to "include anything under the sun that is made by man." S. Rep. No. 1979, 82d Cong., 2d Sess., 5 (1952); H.R. Rep. No. 1923, 82d Cong., 2d Sess., 6 (1952).

This is not to suggest that § 101 has no limits or that it embraces every discovery. The laws of nature, physical phenomena, and abstract ideas have been held not patentable. Thus, a new mineral discovered in the earth or a new plant found in the wild is not patentable subject matter. Likewise, Einstein could not patent his celebrated law that E=mc²; nor could Newton have patented the law of gravity. Such discoveries are "manifestations of . . . nature, free to all men and reserved exclusively to none." *Funk Brothers, supra*, 333 U.S., at 130.

Judged in this light, respondent's micro-organism plainly qualifies as patentable subject matter. His claim is not to a hitherto unknown natural phenomenon, but to a nonnaturally occurring manufacture or composition of matter—a product of human ingenuity "having a distinctive name, character [and] use." *Hartranft v. Wiegmann*, 121 U.S. 609, 615 (1887). The point is underscored dramatically by comparison of the invention here with that in *Funk*. There, the patentee had discovered that there existed in nature certain species of root-nodule bacteria which did not exert a mutually inhibitive effect on each other. He used that discovery to produce a mixed culture capable of inoculating the seeds of leguminous plants. Concluding that the patentee had discovered "only some of the handiwork of nature," the Court ruled the product nonpatentable:

Each of the species of root-nodule bacteria contained in the package infects the same group of leguminous plants which it always infected. No species acquires a different use. The combination of species produces no new bacteria, no change in the six species of bacteria, and no enlargement of the range of their utility. Each species has the same effect it always had. The bacteria perform in their natural way. Their use in combination does not improve in any way their natural functioning. They serve the ends nature originally provided and act quite independently of any effort of the patentee. 333 U.S., at 131.

Here, by contrast, the patentee has produced a new bacterium with markedly different characteristics from any found in nature and one having the potential for significant utility. His discovery is not nature's handiwork, but his own; accordingly it is patentable subject matter under §101.

IV

Two contrary arguments are advanced, neither of which we find persuasive.

(A)

The petitioner's first argument rests on the enactment of the 1930 Plant Patent Act, which afforded patent protection to certain asexually reproduced plants, and the 1970 Plant Variety Protection Act, which authorized protection for certain sexually reproduced plants but excluded bacteria from its protection. In the petitioner's view, the passage of these Acts evidences congressional understanding that the terms "manufacture" or "composition of matter" do not include living things; if they did, the petitioner argues, neither Act would have been necessary.

We reject this argument. Prior to 1930, two factors were thought to remove plants from patent protection. The first was the belief that plants, even those artificially bred, were products of nature for purposes of the patent law. This position appears to have derived from the decision of the patent office in *Ex parte Latimer*, in which a patent claim for fiber found in the needle of the Pinus australis was rejected. The Commissioner reasoned that a contrary result would permit "patents [to] be obtained upon the trees of the forest and the plants of the earth, which of course would be unreasonable and impossible." Id., at 126. The *Latimer* case, it seems, came to "se[t] forth the general stand taken in these matters" that plants were natural products not subject to patent protection. The second obstacle to patent protection for plants was the fact that plants were thought not amenable to the "written description" requirement of the patent law. *See* 35 U.S.C. §112. Because new plants may differ from old only in color or perfume, differentiation by written description was often impossible.

In enacting the Plant Patent Act, Congress addressed both of these concerns. It explained at length its belief that the work of the plant breeder "in aid of nature" was patentable invention. S. Rep. No. 315, 71st Cong., 2d Sess., 6-8 (1930); H.R. Rep. No. 1129, 71st Cong., 2d Sess., 7-9 (1930). And it relaxed the written description requirement in favor of "a description . . . as complete as is reasonably possible." 35 U.S.C. §162. No Committee or Member of Congress, however, expressed the broader view, now urged by the petitioner, that the terms "manufacture" or "composition of matter" exclude living things. The sole support for that position in the legislative history of the 1930 Act is found in the conclusory statement of Secretary of Agriculture Hyde, in a letter to the Chairmen of the House and Senate Committees considering the 1930 Act, that "the patent laws . . . at the present time are understood to cover only inventions or discoveries in the field of inanimate nature." *See* S. Rep. No. 315, *supra*, at Appendix A; H.R. Rep. No. 1129, *supra*, at Appendix A. Secretary Hyde's opinion, however, is not entitled to controlling weight. His views were solicited on the administration of the new law and not on the scope of patentable subject matter—an area beyond his competence. Moreover, there is language in the House and Senate Committee Reports suggesting that to the extent Congress considered the matter it found the Secretary's dichotomy unpersuasive. The Reports observe:

> There is a clear and logical distinction *between the discovery of a new variety of plant and of certain inanimate things*, such, for example, as a new and useful natural mineral. The mineral is created wholly by nature unassisted by man. . . . On the other hand, a plant discovery resulting from cultivation is unique, isolated, and is not repeated by nature, nor can it be reproduced by nature unaided by man. . . . (emphasis added).

Congress thus recognized that the relevant distinction was not between living and inanimate things, but between products of nature, whether living or not, and human-made inventions. Here, respondent's micro-organism is the result of human ingenuity and research. Hence, the passage of the Plant Patent Act affords the Government no support.

Nor does the passage of the 1970 Plant Variety Protection Act support the Government's position. As the Government acknowledges, sexually reproduced plants were not included under the 1930 Act because new varieties could not be reproduced true-to-type through seedlings. By 1970, however, it was generally recognized that true-to-type reproduction was possible and that plant patent protection was therefore appropriate. The 1970 Act extended that protection. There is nothing in its language or history to suggest that it was enacted because §101 did not include living things.

In particular, we find nothing in the exclusion of bacteria from plant variety protection to support the petitioner's position. The legislative history gives no reason for this exclusion. As the Court of Customs and Patent Appeals suggested, it may simply reflect congressional agreement with the result reached by that court in deciding *In re Arzberger*, which held that bacteria were not plants for the purposes of the 1930 Act. Or it may reflect the fact that prior to 1970 the Patent Office had issued patents for bacteria under §101. In any event, absent some clear indication that Congress "focused on [the] issues . . . directly related to the one presently before the Court," *SEC v. Sloan*, 436 U.S. 103, 120-121 (1978), there is no basis for reading into its actions an intent to modify the plain meaning of the words found in §101.

(B)

The petitioner's second argument is that micro-organisms cannot qualify as patentable subject matter until Congress expressly authorizes such protection. His position rests on the fact that genetic technology was unforeseen when Congress enacted §101. From this it is argued that resolution of the patentability of inventions such as respondent's should be left to Congress. The legislative process, the petitioner argues, is best equipped to weigh the competing economic, social, and scientific considerations involved, and to determine whether living organisms produced by genetic engineering should receive patent protection. In support of this position, the petitioner relies on our recent holding in *Parker v. Flook*, and the statement that the judiciary "must proceed cautiously when . . . asked to extend patent rights into areas wholly unforeseen by Congress." *Id.*, at 596.

It is, of course, correct that Congress, not the courts, must define the limits of patentability; but it is equally true that once Congress has spoken it is "the province and duty of the judicial department to say what the law is." *Marbury v. Madison*, 1 Cranch 137, 177 (1803). Congress has performed its constitutional role in defining patentable subject matter in §101; we perform ours in construing the language Congress has employed. In so doing, our obligation is to take statutes as we find them, guided, if ambiguity appears, by the legislative history and statutory purpose. Here, we perceive no ambiguity. The subject-matter provisions of the patent law have been cast in broad terms to fulfill the constitutional and statutory goal of promoting "the Progress of Science and the useful Arts" with all that means for the social and economic benefits envisioned by Jefferson. Broad general language is not necessarily ambiguous when congressional objectives require broad terms.

Nothing in *Flook* is to the contrary. That case applied our prior precedents to determine that a "claim for an improved method of calculation, even when tied to a specific end use, is unpatentable subject matter under §101." 437 U.S., at 595, n.18. The Court carefully scrutinized the claim at issue to determine whether it was precluded from patent protection under "the principles underlying the prohibition against patents for 'ideas' or phenomena of nature." *Id.*, at 593. We have done that here. *Flook* did not announce a new principle that inventions in areas not contemplated by Congress when the patent laws were enacted are unpatentable per se.

To read that concept into *Flook* would frustrate the purposes of the patent law. This Court frequently has observed that a statute is not to be confined to the "particular application[s] . . . contemplated by the legislators." *Barr v. United States*, 324 U.S. 83, 90 (1945). This is especially true in the field of patent law. A rule that unanticipated inventions are without protection would conflict with the core concept of the patent law that anticipation undermines patentability. Mr. Justice Douglas reminded that the inventions most benefiting mankind are those that "push back the frontiers of chemistry, physics, and the like." *Great A. & P. Tea Co. v. Supermarket Equip. Corp.*, 340 U.S. 147, 154 (1950) (concurring opinion). Congress employed broad general language in drafting §101 precisely because such inventions are often unforeseeable.

To buttress his argument, the petitioner, with the support of *amicus,* points to grave risks that may be generated by research endeavors such as respondent's. The briefs present a gruesome parade of horribles. Scientists, among them Nobel laureates, are quoted suggesting that genetic research may pose a serious threat to the human race, or, at the very least, that the dangers are far too substantial to permit such research to proceed apace at this time. We are told that genetic research and related technological developments may spread pollution and disease, that it may result in a loss of genetic diversity, and that its practice may tend to depreciate the value of human life. These arguments are forcefully, even passionately, presented; they remind us that, at times, human ingenuity seems unable to control fully the forces it creates—that with Hamlet, it is sometimes better "to bear those ills we have than fly to others that we know not of."

It is argued that this Court should weigh these potential hazards in considering whether respondent's invention is patentable subject matter under § 101. We disagree. The grant or denial of patents on micro-organisms is not likely to put an end to genetic research or to its attendant risks. The large amount of research that has already occurred when no researcher had sure knowledge that patent protection would be available suggests that legislative or judicial fiat as to patentability will not deter the scientific mind from probing into the unknown any more than Canute could command the tides. Whether respondent's claims are patentable may determine whether research efforts are accelerated by the hope of reward or slowed by want of incentives, but that is all.

What is more important is that we are without competence to entertain these arguments—either to brush them aside as fantasies generated by fear of the unknown, or to act on them. The choice we are urged to make is a matter of high policy for resolution within the legislative process after the kind of investigation, examination, and study that legislative bodies can provide and courts cannot. That process involves the balancing of competing values and interests, which in our democratic system is the business of elected representatives. Whatever their validity, the contentions now pressed on us should be addressed to the political branches of the Government, the Congress and the Executive, and not to the courts.

We have emphasized in the recent past that "[o]ur individual appraisal of the wisdom or unwisdom of a particular [legislative] course . . . is to be put aside in the process of interpreting a statute." *TVA v. Hill,* 437 U.S., at 194. Our task, rather, is the narrow one of determining what Congress meant by the words it used in the statute; once that is done our powers are exhausted. Congress is free to amend § 101 so as to exclude from patent protection organisms produced by genetic engineering. Cf. 42 U.S.C. § 2181(a), exempting from patent protection inventions "useful solely in the utilization of special nuclear material or atomic energy in an atomic weapon." Or it may choose to craft a statute specifically designed for such living things. But, until Congress takes such action, this Court must construe the language of § 101 as it is. The language of that section fairly embraces respondent's invention.

Justice BRENNAN, with whom Justice WHITE, Justice MARSHALL, and Justice POWELL join, dissenting.

I agree with the Court that the question before us is a narrow one. Neither the future of scientific research, nor even, the ability of respondent Chakrabarty to reap some monopoly profits from his pioneering work, is at stake. Patents on the processes by which he has produced and employed the new living organism are not contested. The only question we need decide is whether Congress, exercising its authority under Art. I, §8, of the Constitution, intended that he be able to secure a monopoly on the living organism itself, no matter how produced or how used. Because I believe the Court has misread the applicable legislation, I dissent.

The patent laws attempt to reconcile this Nation's deep seated antipathy to monopolies with the need to encourage progress. Given the complexity and legislative nature of this delicate task, we must be careful to extend patent protection no further than Congress has provided. In particular, were there an absence of legislative direction, the courts should leave to Congress the decisions whether and how far to extend the patent privilege into areas where the common understanding has been that patents are not available.

In this case, however, we do not confront a complete legislative vacuum. The sweeping language of the Patent Act of 1793, as re-enacted in 1952, is not the last pronouncement Congress has made in this area. In 1930 Congress enacted the Plant Patent Act affording patent protection to developers of certain asexually reproduced plants. In 1970 Congress enacted the Plant Variety Protection Act to extend protection to certain new plant varieties capable of sexual reproduction. Thus, we are not dealing—as the Court would have it—with the routine problem of "unanticipated inventions." *Ante.* In these two Acts Congress has addressed the general problem of patenting animate inventions and has chosen carefully limited language granting protection to some kinds of discoveries, but specifically excluding others. These Acts strongly evidence a congressional limitation that excludes bacteria from patentability.[2]

First, the Acts evidence Congress' understanding, at least since 1930, that §101 does not include living organisms. If newly developed living organisms not naturally occurring had been patentable under §101, the plants included in the scope of the 1930 and 1970 Acts could have been patented without new legislation. Those plants, like the bacteria involved in this case, were new varieties not naturally occurring.[3] Although the Court, *ante*, rejects this line of argument, it does not explain why the Acts were necessary unless to correct a pre-existing situation.[4] I cannot share the Court's implicit assumption that Congress was

---

2. But even if I agreed with the Court that the 1930 and 1970 Acts were not dispositive, I would dissent. This case presents even more cogent reasons than *Deepsouth Packing Co.* not to extend the patent monopoly in the face of uncertainty. At the very least, these Acts are signs of legislative attention to the problems of patenting living organisms, but they give no affirmative indication of congressional intent that bacteria be patentable. The caveat of *Parker v. Flook*, 437 U.S. 584, 596 (1978), an admonition to "proceed cautiously when we are asked to extend patent rights into areas wholly unforeseen by Congress," therefore becomes pertinent. I should think the necessity for caution is that much greater when we are asked to extend patent rights into areas Congress has foreseen and considered but has not resolved.

3. The Court refers to the logic employed by Congress in choosing not to perpetuate the "dichotomy" suggested by Secretary Hyde. *Ante*, at 2209. But by this logic the bacteria at issue here are distinguishable from a "mineral . . . created wholly by nature" in exactly the same way as were the new varieties of plants. If a new Act was needed to provide patent protection for the plants, it was equally necessary for bacteria. Yet Congress provided for patents on plants but not on these bacteria. In short, Congress decided to make only a subset of animate "human-made inventions," *ibid.*, patentable.

4. If the 1930 Act's only purpose were to solve the technical problem of description referred to by the Court, *ante*, at 2209, most of the Act, and in particular its limitation to asexually reproduced plants, would have been totally unnecessary.

engaged in either idle exercises or mere correction of the public record when it enacted the 1930 and 1970 Acts. And Congress certainly thought it was doing something significant. The Committee Reports contain expansive prose about the previously unavailable benefits to be derived from extending patent protection to plants.[5] Because Congress thought it had to legislate in order to make agricultural "human-made inventions" patentable and because the legislation Congress enacted is limited, it follows that Congress never meant to make items outside the scope of the legislation patentable.

Second, the 1970 Act clearly indicates that Congress has included bacteria within the focus of its legislative concern, but not within the scope of patent protection. Congress specifically excluded bacteria from the coverage of the 1970 Act. 7 U.S.C. §2402(a). The Court's attempts to supply explanations for this explicit exclusion ring hollow. It is true that there is no mention in the legislative history of the exclusion, but that does not give us license to invent reasons. The fact is that Congress, assuming that animate objects as to which it had not specifically legislated could not be patented, excluded bacteria from the set of patentable organisms.

The Court protests that its holding today is dictated by the broad language of §101, which cannot "be confined to the 'particular application[s] . . . contemplated by the legislators.'" *Ante*, quoting *Barr v. United States*, 324 U.S. 83, 90 (1945). But as I have shown, the Court's decision does not follow the unavoidable implications of the statute. Rather, it extends the patent system to cover living material even though Congress plainly has legislated in the belief that §101 does not encompass living organisms. It is the role of Congress, not this Court, to broaden or narrow the reach of the patent laws. This is especially true where, as here, the composition sought to be patented uniquely implicates matters of public concern.

Comments

1. **Chakrabarty *and the Then-Nascent Biotechnology Industry.*** In *Chakrabarty*, the Court held that a living, genetically altered microorganism constituted patentable subject matter. The modified microorganism, due to human intervention, was not a product of nature and fell within the broadly defined concepts of manufacture or composition of matter. This decision was important because it held that life can be patented and, coupled with

---

5. Secretary Hyde's letter was not the only explicit indication in the legislative history of these Acts that Congress was acting on the assumption that legislation was necessary to make living organisms patentable. The Senate Judiciary Committee Report on the 1970 Act states the Committee's understanding that patent protection extended no further than the explicit provisions of these Acts:

Under the patent law, patent protection is limited to those varieties of plants which reproduce asexually, that is, by such methods as grafting or budding. No protection is available to those varieties of plants which reproduce sexually, that is, generally by seeds. S. Rep. No. 91-1246, p. 3 (1970).

Similarly, Representative Poage, speaking for the 1970 Act, after noting the protection accorded asexually developed plants, stated that "for plants produced from seed, there has been no such protection." 116 Cong. Rec. 40295 (1970).

Cohen and Boyer's breakthrough relating to recombinant DNA, gave a significant boost to the nascent biotechnology industry. *See* F.M. SCHERER, NEW PERSPECTIVES ON ECONOMIC GROWTH AND TECHNOLOGICAL INNOVATION 56 (1999) (stating the "Cohen-Boyer patents . . . set the stage for a whole new biotechnology industry"); Rebecca S. Eisenberg, *The Story of Diamond v. Chakrabarty*, in INTELLECTUAL PROPERTY STORIES 356-357 (Jane C. Ginsburg & Rochelle Cooper Dreyfuss eds., 2006) (stating *Chakrabarty* "was a watershed moment . . . for the biotechnology industry [and] investment in biotechnology R&D has flourished in [its] wake"). Indeed, genomic-related patent applications increased dramatically after *Chakrabarty*. *See* Andrew W. Torrance, *Biology & Genetics: Gene Concepts, Gene Talk, and Gene Patents*, 11 MINN. J.L. SCI. & TECH. 157, 177 (2010). Another contributing factor to the growth of the biotech industry was the passage of the Bayh-Dole Act, which permitted non-profit entities such as research universities to own patents resulting from federally funded research. *See* 35 U.S.C. §§ 200-205. *See also The Bayh-Dole Act: Selected Issues in Patent Policy and the Commercialization of Technology*, Congressional Research Service Report of Congress 8 (June 10, 2005) (stating the Bayh-Dole Act "appears to have met its expressed goals of using the patent system to promote the utilization of inventions arising from federally-supported research or development; . . . and to promote collaboration between commercial concerns and nonprofit organizations, including universities"). *Cf.* DEREK BOK, UNIVERSITIES IN THE MARKETPLACE 77 (2003) (while acknowledging Bayh-Dole is not without benefits, Bok states that "[u]niversities have paid a price for industry support through excessive secrecy, periodic exposés of financial conflict, and corporate efforts to manipulate or suppress research results."); DAVID C. MOWERY, RICHARD R. NELSON, BHAVEN N. SAMPAT & ARVIDS A. ZIEDONIS, IVORY TOWER AND INDUSTRIAL INNOVATION: UNIVERSITY-INDUSTRY TECHNOLOGY TRANSFER BEFORE AND AFTER THE BAYH-DOLE ACT IN THE UNITED STATES (2004) (arguing that Bayh-Dole has not been as successful as its advocates claim and cautioning against other countries' desire to replicate Bayh-Dole).

2. **The Chakrabarty Dissent.** The dissent in *Chakrabarty* offered a compelling legal argument that garnered four of the nine Justices. Perhaps the most persuasive argument from the dissent was based on the canon of claim construction known as *expressio unius est exclusio alterius*, which holds "to express or include one thing implies the exclusion of the other." BLACK'S LAW DICTIONARY (7th ed. 1999). The applicability of this doctrine to *Chakrabarty* was that living matter, namely plants in this instance, was not patentable until Congress enacted the 1930 and 1970 Plant Acts; and since Congress only spoke to plants, living matter other than plants, such as microorganisms, were not patentable. Did the majority adequately address this argument?

In addition, the majority's reliance on the "anything under the sun is made by man" language is not without controversy. The full sentence—which is part of the legislative history of the 1952 Patent Act—states: "A person may have 'invented' a machine or a manufacture, which may include anything under the sun that is made by man, but it is not necessarily patentable under section 101 unless the conditions of [this] title are fulfilled." S. Rep. 1979, at 5; H.R. Rep. 1923 at 6. Justice Stevens, in his concurrence in *Bilski v. Kappos*, asserted, "Viewed as a whole, it seems clear that this language does not purport to explain that 'anything under the sun is patentable. Indeed, the language may be understood to state the exact opposite: that '[a] person may have invented . . . anything under the sun,' but that thing is not necessarily patentable under Section 101." *Bilski v. Kappos,* 130 S. Ct. 3218, 3249 (2010) (Stevens J., concurring).

MAYO COLLABORATIVE SERVICES v. PROMETHEUS LABORATORIES, INC.

132 S. Ct. 1289 (2012)

BREYER, J., delivered the opinion for a unanimous Court.

Section 101 of the Patent Act defines patentable subject matter. It says:

> Whoever invents or discovers any new and useful process, machine, manufacture, or composition of matter, or any new and useful improvement thereof, may obtain a patent therefor, subject to the conditions and requirements of this title. 35 U.S.C. §101.

The Court has long held that this provision contains an important implicit exception. "[L]aws of nature, natural phenomena, and abstract ideas" are not patentable. *Diamond v. Chakrabarty,* 447 U.S. 303, 309 (1980). Thus, the Court has written that "a new mineral discovered in the earth or a new plant found in the wild is not patentable subject matter. Likewise, Einstein could not patent his celebrated law that E=mc²; nor could Newton have patented the law of gravity. Such discoveries are 'manifestations of . . . nature, free to all men and reserved exclusively to none.'" *Chakrabarty, supra,* at 309.

"Phenomena of nature, though just discovered, mental processes, and abstract intellectual concepts are not patentable, as they are the basic tools of scientific and technological work." *Gottschalk v. Benson,* 409 U.S. 63, 67 (1972). And monopolization of those tools through the grant of a patent might tend to impede innovation more than it would tend to promote it.

The Court has recognized, however, that too broad an interpretation of this exclusionary principle could eviscerate patent law. For all inventions at some level embody, use, reflect, rest upon, or apply laws of nature, natural phenomena, or abstract ideas. Thus, in *Diehr* the Court pointed out that "'a process is not unpatentable simply because it contains a law of nature or a mathematical algorithm.'" 450 U.S., at 187. It added that "an *application* of a law of nature or mathematical formula to a known structure or process may well be deserving of patent protection." *Diehr, supra,* at 187. And it emphasized Justice Stone's similar observation in *Mackay Radio & Telegraph Co. v. Radio Corp. of America,* 306 U.S. 86 (1939):

> While a scientific truth, or the mathematical expression of it, is not a patentable invention, a novel and useful structure created with the aid of knowledge of scientific truth may be.

Still, as the Court has also made clear, to transform an unpatentable law of nature into a patent-eligible *application* of such a law, one must do more than simply state the law of nature while adding the words "apply it."

The case before us lies at the intersection of these basic principles. It concerns patent claims covering processes that help doctors who use thiopurine drugs to treat patients with autoimmune diseases determine whether a given dosage level is too low or too high. The claims purport to apply natural laws describing the relationships between the concentration in the blood of certain thiopurine metabolites and the likelihood that the drug dosage will be ineffective or induce harmful side effects. We must determine whether the claimed processes have transformed these unpatentable natural laws into patent-eligible applications of those laws. We conclude that they have not done so and that therefore the processes are not patentable.

Our conclusion rests upon an examination of the particular claims before us in light of the Court's precedents. Those cases warn us against interpreting patent statutes in ways that make patent eligibility "depend simply on the draftsman's art" without reference to the "principles underlying the prohibition against patents for [natural laws]." *Parker v. Flook,* 437 U.S. 584, 593 (1978). They warn us against upholding patents that claim processes that too broadly preempt the use of a natural law. And they insist that a process that focuses upon the use of a natural law also contain other elements or a combination of elements, sometimes referred to as an "inventive concept," sufficient to ensure that the patent in practice amounts to significantly more than a patent upon the natural law itself.

We find that the process claims at issue here do not satisfy these conditions. In particular, the steps in the claimed processes (apart from the natural laws themselves) involve well-understood, routine, conventional activity previously engaged in by researchers in the field. At the same time, upholding the patents would risk disproportionately tying up the use of the underlying natural laws, inhibiting their use in the making of further discoveries.

I

A

The patents before us concern the use of thiopurine drugs in the treatment of autoimmune diseases, such as Crohn's disease and ulcerative colitis. When a patient ingests a thiopurine compound, his body metabolizes the drug, causing metabolites to form in his bloodstream. Because the way in which people metabolize thiopurine compounds varies, the same dose of a thiopurine drug affects different people differently, and it has been difficult for doctors to determine whether for a particular patient a given dose is too high, risking harmful side effects, or too low, and so likely ineffective.

At the time the discoveries embodied in the patents were made, scientists already understood that the levels in a patient's blood of certain metabolites, including, in particular, 6-thioguanine and its nucleotides (6-TG) and 6-methylmercaptopurine (6-MMP), were correlated with the likelihood that a particular dosage of a thiopurine drug could cause harm or prove ineffective. But those in the field did not know the precise correlations between metabolite levels and likely harm or ineffectiveness. The patent claims at issue here set forth processes embodying researchers' findings that identified these correlations with some precision.

More specifically, the patents—U.S. Patent No. 6,355,623 ('623 patent) and U.S. Patent No. 6,680,302 ('302 patent)—embody findings that concentrations in a patient's blood of 6-TG or of 6-MMP metabolite beyond a certain level (400 and 7000 picomoles per 8×10^8 red blood cells, respectively) indicate that the dosage is likely too high for the patient, while concentrations in the blood of 6-TG metabolite lower than a certain level (about 230 picomoles per 8×10^8 red blood cells) indicate that the dosage is likely too low to be effective.

The patent claims seek to embody this research in a set of processes. Like the Federal Circuit we take as typical claim 1 of the '623 Patent, which describes one of the claimed processes as follows:

A method of optimizing therapeutic efficacy for treatment of an immune-mediated gastrointestinal disorder, comprising:

(a) administering a drug providing 6-thioguanine to a subject having said immune-mediated gastrointestinal disorder; and

(b) determining the level of 6-thioguanine in said subject having said immune-mediated gastrointestinal disorder,

wherein the level of 6-thioguanine less than about 230 pmol per $8x10^8$ red blood cells indicates a need to increase the amount of said drug subsequently administered to said subject and

wherein the level of 6-thioguanine greater than about 400 pmol per $8x10^8$ red blood cells indicates a need to decrease the amount of said drug subsequently administered to said subject.

'623 patent, col.20, ll.10-20, 2 App. 16.

For present purposes we may assume that the other claims in the patents do not differ significantly from claim 1.

B

Respondent, Prometheus Laboratories, Inc. (Prometheus), is the sole and exclusive licensee of the '623 and '302 patents. It sells diagnostic tests that embody the processes the patents describe. For some time petitioners, Mayo Clinic Rochester and Mayo Collaborative Services (collectively Mayo), bought and used those tests. But in 2004 Mayo announced that it intended to begin using and selling its own test—a test using somewhat higher metabolite levels to determine toxicity (450 pmol per $8x10^8$ for 6-TG and 5700 pmol per $8x10^8$ for 6-MMP). Prometheus then brought this action claiming patent infringement.

The District Court found that Mayo's test infringed claim 7 of the '623 patent. In interpreting the claim, the court accepted Prometheus' view that the toxicity-risk level numbers in Mayo's test and the claim were too similar to render the tests significantly different. The number Mayo used (450) was too close to the number the claim used (400) to matter given appropriate margins of error. The District Court also accepted Prometheus' view that a doctor using Mayo's test could violate the patent even if he did not actually alter his treatment decision in the light of the test. In doing so, the court construed the claim's language, "indicates a need to decrease" (or "to increase"), as not limited to instances in which the doctor actually decreases (or increases) the dosage level where the test results suggest that such an adjustment is advisable.

Nonetheless the District Court ultimately granted summary judgment in Mayo's favor. The court reasoned that the patents effectively claim natural laws or natural phenomena—namely the correlations between thiopurine metabolite levels and the toxicity and efficacy of thiopurine drug dosages—and so are not patentable.

On appeal, the Federal Circuit reversed. It pointed out that in addition to these natural correlations, the claimed processes specify the steps of (1) "administering a [thiopurine] drug" to a patient and (2) "determining the [resulting metabolite] level." These steps, it explained, involve the transformation of the human body or of blood taken from the body. Thus, the patents satisfied the Circuit's "machine or transformation test," which the court thought sufficient to "confine the patent monopoly within rather definite bounds," thereby bringing the claims into compliance with §101.

We granted the petition, vacated the judgment, and remanded the case for reconsideration in light of *Bilski,* which clarified that the "machine or transformation test" is not a definitive test of patent eligibility, but only an important and useful clue. On remand the Federal Circuit reaffirmed its earlier conclusion. It thought that the "machine-or-transformation test," understood merely as an important and useful clue, nonetheless led to the "clear and compelling conclusion . . . that the . . . claims . . . do not encompass laws of nature or preempt natural correlations." Mayo again filed a petition for certiorari, which we granted.

II

Prometheus' patents set forth laws of nature — namely, relationships between concentrations of certain metabolites in the blood and the likelihood that a dosage of a thiopurine drug will prove ineffective or cause harm. Claim 1, for example, states that *if* the levels of 6-TG in the blood (of a patient who has taken a dose of a thiopurine drug) exceed about 400 pmol per 8×10^8 red blood cells, *then* the administered dose is likely to produce toxic side effects. While it takes a human action (the administration of a thiopurine drug) to trigger a manifestation of this relation in a particular person, the relation itself exists in principle apart from any human action. The relation is a consequence of the ways in which thiopurine compounds are metabolized by the body — entirely natural processes. And so a patent that simply describes that relation sets forth a natural law.

The question before us is whether the claims do significantly more than simply describe these natural relations. To put the matter more precisely, do the patent claims add *enough* to their statements of the correlations to allow the processes they describe to qualify as patent-eligible processes that *apply* natural laws? We believe that the answer to this question is no.

A

If a law of nature is not patentable, then neither is a process reciting a law of nature, unless that process has additional features that provide practical assurance that the process is more than a drafting effort designed to monopolize the law of nature itself. A patent, for example, could not simply recite a law of nature and then add the instruction "apply the law." Einstein, we assume, could not have patented his famous law by claiming a process consisting of simply telling linear accelerator operators to refer to the law to determine how much energy an amount of mass has produced (or vice versa). Nor could Archimedes have secured a patent for his famous principle of flotation by claiming a process consisting of simply telling boat builders to refer to that principle in order to determine whether an object will float.

What else is there in the claims before us? The process that each claim recites tells doctors interested in the subject about the correlations that the researchers discovered. In doing so, it recites an "administering" step, a "determining" step, and a "wherein" step. These additional steps are not themselves natural laws but neither are they sufficient to transform the nature of the claim.

First, the "administering" step simply refers to the relevant audience, namely doctors who treat patients with certain diseases with thiopurine drugs. That audience is a pre-existing audience; doctors used thiopurine drugs to treat patients suffering from autoimmune disorders long before anyone asserted these claims. In any event, the "prohibition against patenting abstract ideas 'cannot be circumvented by attempting to limit the use of the formula to a particular technological environment.'" *Bilski, supra,* at 3230.

Second, the "wherein" clauses simply tell a doctor about the relevant natural laws, at most adding a suggestion that he should take those laws into account when treating his patient. That is to say, these clauses tell the relevant audience about the laws while trusting them to use those laws appropriately where they are relevant to their decisionmaking (rather like Einstein telling linear accelerator operators about his basic law and then trusting them to use it where relevant).

Third, the "determining" step tells the doctor to determine the level of the relevant metabolites in the blood, through whatever process the doctor or the laboratory wishes to use. As the patents state, methods for determining metabolite levels were well known in the art. Indeed, scientists routinely measured metabolites as part of their investigations into the relationships between metabolite levels and efficacy and toxicity of thiopurine compounds. Thus, this step tells doctors to engage in well-understood, routine, conventional activity previously engaged in by scientists who work in the field. Purely "conventional or obvious" "[pre]-solution activity" is normally not sufficient to transform an unpatentable law of nature into a patent-eligible application of such a law. See *Bilski,* 130 S. Ct., at 3230 ("[T]he prohibition against patenting abstract ideas 'cannot be circumvented by' . . . adding 'insignificant post-solution activity.'")

Fourth, to consider the three steps as an ordered combination adds nothing to the laws of nature that is not already present when the steps are considered separately. See *Diehr, supra,* at 188 ("[A] new combination of steps in a process may be patentable even though all the constituents of the combination were well known and in common use before the combination was made"). Anyone who wants to make use of these laws must first administer a thiopurine drug and measure the resulting metabolite concentrations, and so the combination amounts to nothing significantly more than an instruction to doctors to apply the applicable laws when treating their patients.

The upshot is that the three steps simply tell doctors to gather data from which they may draw an inference in light of the correlations. To put the matter more succinctly, the claims inform a relevant audience about certain laws of nature; any additional steps consist of well-understood, routine, conventional activity already engaged in by the scientific community; and those steps, when viewed as a whole, add nothing significant beyond the sum of their parts taken separately. For these reasons we believe that the steps are not sufficient to transform unpatentable natural correlations into patentable applications of those regularities.

B

1

A more detailed consideration of the controlling precedents reinforces our conclusion. The cases most directly on point are *Diehr* and *Flook,* two cases in which the Court reached opposite conclusions about the patent eligibility of processes that embodied the equivalent of natural laws. The *Diehr* process (held patent eligible) set forth a method for molding raw, uncured rubber into various cured, molded products. The process used a known mathematical equation, the Arrhenius equation, to determine when (depending upon the temperature inside the mold, the time the rubber had been in the mold, and the thickness of the rubber) to open the press. It consisted in effect of the steps of: (1) continuously monitoring the temperature on the inside of the mold, (2) feeding the resulting numbers into a computer, which would use the Arrhenius equation to continuously recalculate the mold-opening time, and (3) configuring the computer so that at the appropriate moment it would signal "a device" to open the press. *Diehr,* 450 U.S., at 177-179.

The Court pointed out that the basic mathematical equation, like a law of nature, was not patentable. But it found the overall process patent eligible because of the way the additional steps of the process integrated the equation into the process as a whole. Those steps included "installing rubber in a press, closing the mold, constantly determining the temperature of the mold, constantly recalculating the appropriate cure time through the use of the formula and a digital computer, and automatically opening the press at the proper time." *Id.,* at 187. It nowhere suggested that all these steps, or at least the combination of those steps, were in context obvious, already in use, or purely conventional. And so the patentees did not "seek to pre-empt the use of [the] equation," but sought "only to foreclose from others the use of that equation in conjunction with all of the other steps in their claimed process." *Ibid.* These other steps apparently added to the formula something that in terms of patent law's objectives had significance—they transformed the process into an inventive application of the formula.

The process in *Flook* (held not patentable) provided a method for adjusting "alarm limits" in the catalytic conversion of hydrocarbons. Certain operating conditions (such as temperature, pressure, and flow rates), which are continuously monitored during the conversion process, signal inefficiency or danger when they exceed certain "alarm limits." The claimed process amounted to an improved system for updating those alarm limits through the steps of: (1) measuring the current level of the variable, *e.g.,* the temperature; (2) using an apparently novel mathematical algorithm to calculate the current alarm limits; and (3) adjusting the system to reflect the new alarm-limit values. 437 U.S., at 585-587.

The Court, as in *Diehr,* pointed out that the basic mathematical equation, like a law of nature, was not patentable. But it characterized the claimed process as doing nothing other than "provid[ing] a[n unpatentable] formula for computing an updated alarm limit." *Flook, supra,* at 586. Unlike the process in *Diehr,* it did not "explain how the variables used in the formula were to be selected, nor did the [claim] contain any disclosure relating to chemical processes at work or the means of setting off an alarm or adjusting the alarm limit." *Diehr, supra,* at 192, n.14. And so the other steps in the process did not limit the claim to a particular application. Moreover, "[t]he chemical processes involved in catalytic conversion of hydrocarbons[,] . . . the practice of monitoring the chemical process variables, the use of alarm limits to trigger alarms, the notion that alarm limit values must be recomputed and readjusted, and the use of computers for 'automatic monitoring-alarming' " were all "well known," to the point where, putting the formula to the side, there was no "inventive concept" in the claimed application of the formula. *Id.,* at 594. "[P]ost-solution activity" that is purely "conventional or obvious," the Court wrote, "can[not] transform an unpatentable principle into a patentable process." *Id.,* at 589, 590.

The claim before us presents a case for patentability that is weaker than the (patent-eligible) claim in *Diehr* and no stronger than the (unpatentable) claim in *Flook.* Beyond picking out the relevant audience, namely those who administer doses of thiopurine drugs, the claim simply tells doctors to: (1) measure (somehow) the current level of the relevant metabolite, (2) use particular (unpatentable) laws of nature (which the claim sets forth) to calculate the current toxicity/inefficacy limits, and (3) reconsider the drug dosage in light of the law. These instructions add nothing specific to the laws of nature other than what is well-understood, routine, conventional activity, previously engaged in by those in the field. And since they are steps that must be taken in order to apply the laws in question, the effect is simply to tell doctors to apply the law somehow when treating their patients. The process in *Diehr* was not so characterized; that in *Flook* was characterized in roughly this way.

***

In *Bilski* the Court considered claims covering a process for hedging risks of price changes by, for example, contracting to purchase commodities from sellers at a fixed price, reflecting the desire of sellers to hedge against a drop in prices, while selling commodities to consumers at a fixed price, reflecting the desire of consumers to hedge against a price increase. One claim described the process; another reduced the process to a mathematical formula. 130 S. Ct., at 3223-3224. The Court held that the described "concept of hedging" was "an unpatentable abstract idea." *Id.,* at 3239. The fact that some of the claims limited hedging to use in commodities and energy markets and specified that "well-known random analysis techniques [could be used] to help establish some of the inputs into the equation" did not undermine this conclusion, for "*Flook* established that limiting an abstract idea to one field of use or adding token postsolution components did not make the concept patentable." *Id.,* at 3231.

3

The Court has repeatedly emphasized this last mentioned concern, a concern that patent law not inhibit further discovery by improperly tying up the future use of laws of nature. Thus, in *Morse* the Court set aside as unpatentable Samuel Morse's general claim for "'the use of the motive power of the electric or galvanic current . . . however developed, for making or printing intelligible characters, letters, or signs, at any distances,'" 15 How., at 86. The Court explained:

> For aught that we now know some future inventor, in the onward march of science, may discover a mode of writing or printing at a distance by means of the electric or galvanic current, without using any part of the process or combination set forth in the plaintiff's specification. His invention may be less complicated—less liable to get out of order—less expensive in construction, and in its operation. But yet if it is covered by this patent the inventor could not use it, nor the public have the benefit of it without the permission of this patentee. *Id.,* at 113.

. . . These statements reflect the fact that, even though rewarding with patents those who discover new laws of nature and the like might well encourage their discovery, those laws and principles, considered generally, are "the basic tools of scientific and technological work." *Benson, supra,* at 253. And so there is a danger that the grant of patents that tie up their use will inhibit future innovation premised upon them, a danger that becomes acute when a patented process amounts to no more than an instruction to "apply the natural law," or otherwise forecloses more future invention than the underlying discovery could reasonably justify.

The laws of nature at issue here are narrow laws that may have limited applications, but the patent claims that embody them nonetheless implicate this concern. They tell a treating doctor to measure metabolite levels and to consider the resulting measurements in light of the statistical relationships they describe. In doing so, they tie up the doctor's subsequent treatment decision whether that treatment does, or does not, change in light of the inference he has drawn using the correlations. And they threaten to inhibit the development of more refined treatment recommendations (like that embodied in Mayo's test), that combine Prometheus' correlations with later discovered features of metabolites, human physiology or individual patient characteristics. The "determining" step too is set forth in highly general language covering all processes that make use of the correlations after measuring metabolites, including later discovered processes that measure metabolite levels in new ways.

We need not, and do not, now decide whether were the steps at issue here less conventional, these features of the claims would prove sufficient to invalidate them. For here, as we have said, the steps add nothing of significance to the natural laws themselves. Unlike, say, a typical patent on a new drug or a new way of using an existing drug, the patent claims do not confine their reach to particular applications of those laws. The presence here of the basic underlying concern that these patents tie up too much future use of laws of nature simply reinforces our conclusion that the processes described in the patents are not patent eligible, while eliminating any temptation to depart from case law precedent.

III

We have considered several further arguments in support of Prometheus' position. But they do not lead us to adopt a different conclusion. First, the Federal Circuit, in upholding the patent eligibility of the claims before us, relied on this Court's determination that "[t]ransformation and reduction of an article 'to a different state or thing' is *the clue* to the patentability of a process claim that does not include particular machines." *Benson, supra,* at 70-71. It reasoned that the claimed processes are therefore patent eligible, since they involve transforming the human body by administering a thiopurine drug and transforming the blood by analyzing it to determine metabolite levels.

The first of these transformations, however, is irrelevant. As we have pointed out, the "administering" step simply helps to pick out the group of individuals who are likely interested in applying the law of nature. And the second step could be satisfied without transforming the blood, should science develop a totally different system for determining metabolite levels that did not involve such a transformation. Regardless, in stating that the "machine-or-transformation" test is an *"important and useful clue"* to patentability, we have neither said nor implied that the test trumps the "law of nature" exclusion. *Bilski, supra,* at 3225-3227 (emphasis added). That being so, the test fails here.

Second, Prometheus argues that, because the particular laws of nature that its patent claims embody are narrow and specific, the patents should be upheld. Thus, it encourages us to draw distinctions among laws of nature based on whether or not they will interfere significantly with innovation in other fields now or in the future.

But the underlying functional concern here is a *relative* one: how much future innovation is foreclosed relative to the contribution of the inventor. A patent upon a narrow law of nature may not inhibit future research as seriously as would a patent upon Einstein's law of relativity, but the creative value of the discovery is also considerably smaller. And, as we have previously pointed out, even a narrow law of nature (such as the one before us) can inhibit future research.

In any event, our cases have not distinguished among different laws of nature according to whether or not the principles they embody are sufficiently narrow. And this is understandable. Courts and judges are not institutionally well suited to making the kinds of judgments needed to distinguish among different laws of nature. And so the cases have endorsed a bright-line prohibition against patenting laws of nature, mathematical formulas and the like, which serves as a somewhat more easily administered proxy for the underlying "building-block" concern.

Third, the Government argues that virtually any step beyond a statement of a law of nature itself should transform an unpatentable law of nature into a potentially patentable application sufficient to satisfy §101's demands. The Government does not necessarily believe that claims that (like the claims before us) extend just minimally beyond a law of nature should receive patents. But in its view, other statutory provisions—those that insist that a claimed process be novel, 35 U.S.C. §102, that it not be "obvious in light of prior art," §103, and that it be "full[y], clear[ly], concise[ly], and exact[ly]" described, §112—can perform this screening function. In particular, it argues that these claims likely fail for lack of novelty under §102.

This approach, however, would make the "law of nature" exception to §101 patentability a dead letter. The approach is therefore not consistent with prior law. The relevant cases rest their holdings upon section 101, not later sections.

We recognize that, in evaluating the significance of additional steps, the §101 patent-eligibility inquiry and, say, the §102 novelty inquiry might sometimes overlap. But that need not always be so. And to shift the patent-eligibility inquiry entirely to these later sections risks creating significantly greater legal uncertainty, while assuming that those sections can do work that they are not equipped to do.

What role would laws of nature, including newly discovered (and "novel") laws of nature, play in the Government's suggested "novelty" inquiry? Intuitively, one would suppose that a newly discovered law of nature is novel. The Government, however, suggests in effect that the novelty of a component law of nature may be disregarded when evaluating the novelty of the whole. But §§102 and 103 say nothing about treating laws of nature as if they were part of the prior art when applying those sections. Cf. *Diehr*, 450 U.S., at 188 (patent claims "must be considered as a whole"). And studiously ignoring *all* laws of nature when evaluating a patent application under §§102 and 103 would "make all inventions unpatentable because all inventions can be reduced to underlying principles of nature which, once known, make their implementation obvious." *Id.*, at 189, n.12.

Fourth, Prometheus, supported by several *amici,* argues that a principle of law denying patent coverage here will interfere significantly with the ability of medical researchers to make valuable discoveries, particularly in the area of diagnostic research. That research, which includes research leading to the discovery of laws of nature, is expensive; it "ha[s] made the United States the world leader in this field"; and it requires protection.

Other medical experts, however, argue strongly against a legal rule that would make the present claims patent eligible, invoking policy considerations that point in the opposite direction. The American Medical Association, the American College of Medical Genetics, the American Hospital Association, the American Society of Human Genetics, the Association of American Medical Colleges, the Association for Molecular Pathology, and other medical organizations tell us that if "claims to exclusive rights over the body's natural responses to illness and medical treatment are permitted to stand, the result will be a vast thicket of exclusive rights over the use of critical scientific data that must remain widely available if physicians are to provide sound medical care." Brief for American College of Medical Genetics et al. as *Amici Curiae* 7; see also App. to Brief for Association Internationale pour la Protection de la Propriete Intellectuelle et al. as *Amici Curiae* A6, A16 (methods of medical treatment are not patentable in most of Western Europe).

We do not find this kind of difference of opinion surprising. Patent protection is, after all, a two-edged sword. On the one hand, the promise of exclusive rights provides monetary incentives that lead to creation, invention, and discovery. On the other hand, that very exclusivity can impede the flow of information that might permit, indeed spur, invention, by, for example, raising the price of using the patented ideas once created, requiring potential users to conduct costly and time-consuming searches of existing patents and pending patent applications, and requiring the negotiation of complex licensing arrangements. At the same time, patent law's general rules must govern inventive activity in many different fields of human endeavor, with the result that the practical effects of rules that reflect a general effort to balance these considerations may differ from one field to another.

In consequence, we must hesitate before departing from established general legal rules lest a new protective rule that seems to suit the needs of one field produce unforeseen results in another. And we must recognize the role of Congress in crafting more finely tailored rules where necessary. Cf. 35 U.S.C. §§161-164 (special rules for plant patents). We need not determine here whether, from a policy perspective, increased protection for discoveries of diagnostic laws of nature is desirable.

* * *

For these reasons, we conclude that the patent claims at issue here effectively claim the underlying laws of nature themselves. The claims are consequently invalid. And the Federal Circuit's judgment is reversed.

Comments

1. ***"Laws of Nature, Physical Phenomena, and Abstract Ideas" Not Patentable.*** While § 101 is inclusive, the Supreme Court has repeatedly stated "laws of nature,

physical phenomena, and abstract ideas" are off limits. So why is it that E=mc², abstract ideas, and laws or products of nature are unpatentable under section 101? One common rationale posits that these types of subject matter represent "part of the storehouse of knowledge of all men . . . free to all men and reserved exclusively to none." *Funk Bros. Seed Co. v. Kalo Inoculant Co.*, 333 U.S. 127, 130 (1948). This rationale was lost on the businessman in *The Little Prince* who wanted to own the stars. Recall the colloquy that transpires between the little prince and the businessman:

> "How is it possible for one to own the stars?"
>
> "To whom do they belong?" the businessman retorted, peevishly.
>
> "I don't know. To nobody."
>
> "Then they belong to me, because I was the first person to think of it."
>
> "Is that all that is necessary?"
>
> "Certainly. When you find a diamond that belongs to nobody, it is yours. When you discover an island that belongs to nobody, it is yours. When you get an idea before any one else, you take out a patent on it: it is yours. So with me: I own the stars, because nobody else before me ever thought of owning them."

Antoine de Saint-Exupéry, THE LITTLE PRINCE (Chapter 13).

Another rationale states allowing patent protection on abstract ideas and laws of nature would lead to excessive rent seeking and enormous social costs. In a precursor to his opinion in *Mayo*, Justice Breyer wrote in 2006:

> The justification for the principle does not lie in any claim that "laws of nature" are obvious, or that their discovery is easy, or that they are not useful. To the contrary, research into such matters may be costly and time-consuming; monetary incentives may matter; and the fruits of those incentives and that research may prove of great benefit to the human race. Rather, the reason for the exclusion is that sometimes *too much* patent protection can impede rather than "promote the Progress of Science and useful Arts," the constitutional objective of patent and copyright protection.

* * *

> Patent law seeks to avoid the dangers of overprotection just as surely as it seeks to avoid the diminished incentive to invent that underprotection can threaten. One way in which patent law seeks to sail between these opposing and risky shoals is through rules that bring certain types of invention and discovery within the scope of patentability while excluding others.

LabCorp v. Metabolite Laboratories, Inc., 548 U.S. 124, 125 (2006) (dissenting from dismissal of certiorari). Consistent with his *LabCorp* dissent, Justice Breyer wrote in *Mayo*, "[M]onopolization of those tools through the grant of a patent might tend to impede innovation more than it would tend to promote it." *See also* WILLIAM M. LANDES & RICHARD A. POSNER, THE ECONOMIC STRUCTURE OF INTELLECTUAL PROPERTY LAW 305-306 (2004) (noting transaction costs would be "enormous because the scope" of protection "often is extremely difficult to pin down, and this would make it difficult for newcomers to know when they needed to get a license"); Michael J. Meurer & Katherine J. Strandburg, *Patent Carrots and Sticks: A Model of Nonobviousness*,

12 Lewis & Clark L. Rev. 547, 577 (2008) (stating "while offering patents
for the discovery of new laws of nature might well induce private investors
to fund more difficult research projects, the social cost of giving one entity
control over applications of that law of nature may simply be too great to be
offset by the increased investment in science that the possibility of a patent
attracts").

   But is the transaction/social costs argument more comfortably situated
in section 112 than in section 101? Is this argument reminiscent of Justice
Taney's concern about Morse's claim 8? Some commentators see a distinction in this regard between section 101 and section 112. *See* Mark A. Lemley,
Michael Risch, Ted Sichelman & R. Polk Wagner, *Life After Bilski*, 63 Stan. L.
Rev. 1315, 1330 (2011) (asserting that while "some claims may be too broad
in light of the [patent's] disclosure, they are not necessarily abstract ideas";
and, in addition, "enablement does not provide enough of a limitation on
scope as the level of skill in the art goes up," whereas section 101 "is primarily
concerned with removing obstructions to follow-on innovation"). Moreover,
there are definitional problems with respect to an "abstract idea," particularly as they relate to computer-implemented inventions. What is an "abstract
idea"? In *CLS Bank Int'l v. Alice Corp. Pty. Ltd.*, 685 F.3d 1341, 1348-1349 (Fed.
Cir. 2012) (panel decision), the Federal Circuit acknowledged this problem
when it wrote the "abstractness of the 'abstract ideas' test to patent eligibility
has become a serious problem, leading to great uncertainty and to the devaluing of inventions of practical utility and economic potential." This case was
taken *en banc* by the Federal Circuit and is discussed in the Comments following the principal case, *Bilski v. Kappos* in section A.2 below.

   Several commentators have also recognized the difficulties in defining
an "abstract idea." *See* Lemley et al., *Life After* Bilski, *supra* (arguing that the
abstract ideas filter should be recast from eligibility considerations to one
concerned with preventing a patentee from claiming too broadly). And
Michael Risch has argued for the elimination of the common law eligibility
filters. *See* Michael Risch, *Everything Is Patentable*, 75 Tenn. L. Rev. 591, 598
(stating "[v]irtually all of the important historical patentable subject matter cases may be explained by applying each of the other requirements for
patentability").

2. ***"Inventive Concept."*** The Court demanded the presence of an "inventive concept sufficient to ensure that the patent in practice amounts to significantly
   more than a patent upon the natural law itself." One can reasonably argue
   that patent law could make an objective distinction between the claimed
   invention in *Prometheus* and, say, the law of gravity. The former — as the Court
   acknowledged — is variable, that is, "the way in which people metabolize
   thiopurine compounds varies," whereas the law of gravity is universal and
   invariable. In the end, the Court concluded the patent claims do not "add
   enough to their statements of the correlations to allow the processes they
   describe to qualify as patent-eligible processes that *apply* natural laws." There
   was no "inventive concept" beyond what occurs naturally. What is enough?
   The Court also remarked how the additional steps recited in the claimed
   invention "consist of well-understood, routine, conventional activity already
   engaged in by the scientific community." Is this an eligibility or novelty/obvi-
   ousness argument? If a law of nature is part of a claim, *Prometheus* — despite
   its recognition that "all inventions can be reduced to underlying principles

of nature"—seems to suggest that eligibility requires the patentee to set forth the law's application in a novel and nonobvious manner. In *CLS Bank Int'l v. Alice Corp.*, 717 F.3d 1269 (Fed. Cir. 2013) (*en banc*), Judge Rader cautioned that the phrase "'inventive concept' should not be read to conflate principles of patent eligibility with those of validity, [n]or should it be read to instill an 'inventiveness' or 'ingenuity' component into the inquiry." And Judge Lourie wrote that "inventive concept" should not be read as requiring claim limitations to "exhibit inventiveness" in the same sense as novelty and nonobviousness; rather, the phrase "refers to a genuine human contribution to the claimed subject matter," as opposed to a mere discovery of an abstract idea or scientific truth.

3. **USPTO's Interim Guidelines for Process Claims Involving Laws of Nature.** In the light of *Mayo*, the USPTO issued examination guidelines for process claims in which a law of nature, a natural phenomenon, or naturally occurring relation or correlation is a limited element or step. (Process claims involving abstract ideas are to be examined under the guidelines issued after *Bilski.*) The guidelines set forth three inquiries:

> (1) is the claimed invention directed to a process, defined as an act, or a series of acts or steps

> (2) does the claim focus on use of a law of nature, a natural phenomenon, or naturally occurring relation or correlation (collectively referred to as a natural principle herein)? (Is the natural principle a limiting feature of the claim?)

> (3) Does the claim include additional elements/steps or a combination of elements/steps that integrate the natural principle into the claimed invention such that the natural principle is practically applied, and are sufficient to ensure that the claim amounts to significantly more than the natural principle itself? (Is it more than a law of nature + the general instruction to simply "apply it"?)

See casebook website (http://www.law.case.edu/lawofpatents) for a copy of the guidelines.

ASSOCIATION FOR MOLECULAR PATHOLOGY v. MYRIAD GENETICS, INC.

133 S. Ct. 2107 (2013)

Justice THOMAS delivered the opinion of the Court.

Respondent Myriad Genetics, Inc. (Myriad), discovered the precise location and sequence of two human genes, mutations of which can substantially increase the risks of breast and ovarian cancer. Myriad obtained a number of patents based upon its discovery. This case involves claims from three of them and requires us to resolve whether a naturally occurring segment of deoxyribonucleic acid (DNA) is patent eligible under 35 U.S.C. §101 by virtue of its isolation from the rest of the human genome. We also address the patent eligibility of synthetically created DNA known as complementary DNA (cDNA), which contains the same protein-coding information found in a segment of natural DNA but omits portions within the DNA segment that do not code for proteins. For the reasons that follow, we hold that a naturally occurring DNA segment is a product of nature and not patent eligible merely because it has been isolated, but that cDNA is patent eligible because it is not naturally occurring. We, therefore, affirm in part and reverse in part the decision of the United States Court of Appeals for the Federal Circuit.

I

A

Genes form the basis for hereditary traits in living organisms. See generally *Association for Molecular Pathology v. United States Patent and Trademark Office,* 702 F. Supp. 2d 181, 192-211 (S.D.N.Y. 2010). The human genome consists of approximately 22,000 genes packed into 23 pairs of chromosomes. Each gene is encoded as DNA, which takes the shape of the familiar "double helix" that Doctors James Watson and Francis Crick first described in 1953. Each "cross-bar" in the DNA helix consists of two chemically joined nucleotides. The possible nucleotides are adenine (A), thymine (T), cytosine (C), and guanine (G), each of which binds naturally with another nucleotide: A pairs with T; C pairs with G. The nucleotide cross-bars are chemically connected to a sugar-phosphate backbone that forms the outside framework of the DNA helix. Sequences of DNA nucleotides contain the information necessary to create strings of amino acids, which in turn are used in the body to build proteins. Only some DNA nucleotides, however, code for amino acids; these nucleotides are known as "exons." Nucleotides that do not code for amino acids, in contrast, are known as "introns."

Creation of proteins from DNA involves two principal steps, known as transcription and translation. In transcription, the bonds between DNA nucleotides separate, and the DNA helix unwinds into two single strands. A single strand is used as a template to create a complementary ribonucleic acid (RNA) strand. The nucleotides on the DNA strand pair naturally with their counterparts, with the exception that RNA uses the nucleotide base uracil (U) instead of thymine (T). Transcription results in a single strand RNA molecule, known as pre-RNA, whose nucleotides form an inverse image of the DNA strand from which it was created. Pre-RNA still contains nucleotides corresponding to both the exons and introns in the DNA molecule. The pre-RNA is then naturally "spliced" by the physical removal of the introns. The resulting product is a strand of RNA that contains nucleotides corresponding only to the exons from the original DNA strand. The exons-only strand is known as messenger RNA (mRNA), which creates amino acids through translation. In translation, cellular structures known as ribosomes read each set of three nucleotides, known as codons, in the mRNA. Each codon either tells the ribosomes which of the 20 possible amino acids to synthesize or provides a stop signal that ends amino acid production.

DNA's informational sequences and the processes that create mRNA, amino acids, and proteins occur naturally within cells. Scientists can, however, extract DNA from cells using well known laboratory methods. These methods allow scientists to isolate specific segments of DNA—for instance, a particular gene or part of a gene—which can then be further studied, manipulated, or used. It is also possible to create DNA synthetically through processes similarly well known in the field of genetics. One such method begins with an mRNA molecule and uses the natural bonding properties of nucleotides to create a new, synthetic DNA molecule. The result is the inverse of the mRNA's inverse image of the original DNA, with one important distinction: Because the natural creation of mRNA involves splicing that removes introns, the synthetic DNA created from mRNA also contains only the exon sequences. This synthetic DNA created in the laboratory from mRNA is known as complementary DNA (cDNA).

Changes in the genetic sequence are called mutations. Mutations can be as small as the alteration of a single nucleotide—a change affecting only one letter in the genetic code. Such small-scale changes can produce an entirely different amino acid or can end protein production altogether. Large changes, involving the deletion, rearrangement, or duplication of hundreds or even millions of nucleotides, can result in the elimination, misplacement, or duplication of entire genes. Some mutations are harmless, but others can cause disease or increase the risk of disease. As a result, the study of genetics can lead to valuable medical breakthrough.

B

This case involves patents filed by Myriad after it made one such medical breakthrough. Myriad discovered the precise location and sequence of what are now known as the BRCA1 and BRCA2 genes. Mutations in these genes can dramatically increase an individual's risk of developing breast and ovarian cancer. The average American woman has a 12- to 13-percent risk of developing breast cancer, but for women with certain genetic mutations, the risk can range between 50 and 80 percent for breast cancer and between 20 and 50 percent for ovarian cancer. Before Myriad's discovery of the BRCA1 and BRCA2 genes, scientists knew that heredity played a role in establishing a woman's risk of developing breast and ovarian cancer, but they did not know which genes were associated with those cancers.

Myriad identified the exact location of the BRCA1 and BRCA2 genes on chromosomes 17 and 13. Chromosome 17 has approximately 80 million nucleotides, and chromosome 13 has approximately 114 million. Within those chromosomes, the BRCA1 and BRCA2 genes are each about 80,000 nucleotides long. If just exons are counted, the BRCA1 gene is only about 5,500 nucleotides long; for the BRCA2 gene, that number is about 10,200. Knowledge of the location of the BRCA1 and BRCA2 genes allowed Myriad to determine their typical nucleotide sequence. That information, in turn, enabled Myriad to develop medical tests that are useful for detecting mutations in a patient's BRCA1 and BRCA2 genes and thereby assessing whether the patient has an increased risk of cancer.

Once it found the location and sequence of the BRCA1 and BRCA2 genes, Myriad sought and obtained a number of patents. Nine composition claims from three of those patents are at issue in this case. Claims 1, 2, 5, and 6 from the '282 patent are representative. The first claim asserts a patent on "[a]n isolated DNA coding for a BRCA1 polypeptide," which has "the amino acid sequence set forth in SEQ ID NO:2." SEQ ID NO:2 sets forth a list of 1,863 amino acids that the typical BRCA1 gene encodes. Put differently, claim 1 asserts a patent claim on the DNA code that tells a cell to produce the string of BRCA1 amino acids listed in SEQ ID NO:2.

Claim 2 of the '282 patent operates similarly. It claims "[t]he isolated DNA of claim 1, wherein said DNA has the nucleotide sequence set forth in SEQ ID NO:1." Like SEQ ID NO:2, SEQ ID NO:1 sets forth a long list of data, in this instance the sequence of cDNA that codes for the BRCA1 amino acids listed in claim 1. Importantly, SEQ ID NO:1 lists only the cDNA exons in the BRCA1 gene, rather than a full DNA sequence containing both exons and introns. As a result, the Federal Circuit recognized that claim 2 asserts a patent on the cDNA nucleotide sequence listed in SEQ ID NO:1, which codes for the typical BRCA1 gene.

Claim 5 of the '282 patent claims a subset of the data in claim 1. In particular, it claims "[a]n isolated DNA having at least 15 nucleotides of the DNA of claim 1." The practical effect of claim 5 is to assert a patent on any series of 15 nucleotides that exist in the typical BRCA1 gene. Because the BRCA1 gene is thousands of nucleotides long, even BRCA1 genes with substantial mutations are likely to contain at least one segment of 15 nucleotides that correspond to the typical BRCA1 gene. Similarly, claim 6 of the '282 patent claims "[a]n isolated DNA having at least 15 nucleotides of the DNA of claim 2." *Ibid.* This claim operates similarly to claim 5, except that it references the cDNA-based claim 2. The remaining claims at issue are similar, though several list common mutations rather than typical BRCA1 and BRCA2 sequences. See *ibid.* (claim 7 of the '282 patent); (claim 1 of the '473 patent); (claims 1, 6, and 7 of the '492 patent).

C

Myriad's patents would, if valid, give it the exclusive right to isolate an individual's BRCA1 and BRCA2 genes (or any strand of 15 or more nucleotides within the genes) by breaking the covalent bonds that connect the DNA to the rest of the individual's genome. The patents would also give Myriad the exclusive right to synthetically create BRCA cDNA. In Myriad's view, manipulating BRCA DNA in either of these fashions triggers its "right to exclude others from making" its patented composition of matter under the Patent Act. 35 U.S.C. §154(a)(1); see also §271(a) ("[W]hoever without authority makes . . . any patented invention . . . infringes the patent").

But isolation is necessary to conduct genetic testing, and Myriad was not the only entity to offer BRCA testing after it discovered the genes. The University of Pennsylvania's Genetic Diagnostic Laboratory (GDL) and others provided genetic testing services to women. Petitioner Dr. Harry Ostrer, then a researcher at New York University School of Medicine, routinely sent his patients' DNA samples to GDL for testing. After learning of GDL's testing and Ostrer's activities, Myriad sent letters to them asserting that the genetic testing infringed Myriad's patents. App. 94-95 (Ostrer letter). In response, GDL agreed to stop testing and informed Ostrer that it would no longer accept patient samples. Myriad also filed patent infringement suits against other entities that performed BRCA testing, resulting in settlements in which the defendants agreed to cease all allegedly infringing activity. Myriad, thus, solidified its position as the only entity providing BRCA testing.

Some years later, petitioner Ostrer, along with medical patients, advocacy groups, and other doctors, filed this lawsuit seeking a declaration that Myriad's patents are invalid under 35 U.S.C. §101. Citing this Court's decision in *MedImmune, Inc. v. Genentech, Inc.,* 549 U.S. 118 (2007), the District Court denied Myriad's motion to dismiss for lack of standing. The District Court then granted summary judgment to petitioners on the composition claims at issue in this case based on its conclusion that Myriad's claims, including claims related to cDNA, were invalid because they covered products of nature. The Federal Circuit reversed, and this Court granted the petition for certiorari, vacated the judgment, and remanded the case in light of *Mayo Collaborative Services v. Prometheus Laboratories, Inc.,* 566 U.S. ___ (2012).

On remand, the Federal Circuit affirmed the District Court in part and reversed in part, with each member of the panel writing separately. . . . With respect to the merits, the court held that both isolated DNA and cDNA were patent eligible under §101. The central dispute among the panel members was whether the act of *isolating* DNA—separating a specific gene or sequence of nucleotides from the rest of the chromosome—is an inventive act that entitles the individual who first isolates it to a patent. Each of the judges on the panel had a different view on that question. Judges Lourie and Moore agreed that Myriad's claims were patent eligible under §101 but disagreed on the rationale. Judge Lourie relied on the fact that the entire DNA molecule is held together by chemical bonds and that the covalent bonds at both ends of the segment must be severed in order to isolate segments of DNA. This process technically creates new molecules with unique chemical compositions. Judge Lourie found this chemical alteration to be dispositive, because isolating a particular strand of DNA creates a nonnaturally occurring molecule, even though the chemical alteration does not change the information-transmitting quality of the DNA. Accordingly, he rejected petitioners' argument that isolated DNA was ineligible for patent protection as a product of nature.

Judge Moore concurred in part but did not rely exclusively on Judge Lourie's conclusion that chemically breaking covalent bonds was sufficient to render isolated DNA patent eligible. Instead, Judge Moore also relied on the United States Patent and Trademark Office's (PTO) practice of granting such patents and on the reliance interests of patent holders. However, she acknowledged that her vote might have come out differently if she "were deciding this case on a blank canvas."

Finally, Judge Bryson concurred in part and dissented in part, concluding that isolated DNA is not patent eligible. As an initial matter, he emphasized that the breaking of chemical bonds was not dispositive: "[T]here is no magic to a chemical bond that requires us to recognize a new product when a chemical bond is created or broken." 689 F.3d at 1351. Instead, he relied on the fact that "[t]he nucleotide sequences of the claimed molecules are the same as the nucleotide sequences found in naturally occurring human genes." *Id.*, at 1355. . . .

Although the judges expressed different views concerning the patentability of isolated DNA, all three agreed that patent claims relating to cDNA met the patent eligibility requirements of §101.

II

A

Section 101 of the Patent Act provides:

"Whoever invents or discovers any new and useful . . . composition of matter, or any new and useful improvement thereof, may obtain a patent therefor, subject to the conditions and requirements of this title." 35 U.S.C. §101.

We have "long held that this provision contains an important implicit exception[:] Laws of nature, natural phenomena, and abstract ideas are not patentable." *Mayo.* Rather, "'they are the basic tools of scientific and technological work'" that lie beyond the domain of patent protection. *Id.* As the Court has explained, without this exception, there would be considerable danger that the grant of patents would "tie up" the use of such tools and thereby "inhibit future innovation premised upon them." *Id.* This would be at odds with the very point of patents, which exist to promote creation. *Diamond v. Chakrabarty,* 447 U.S. 303, 309 (1980) (Products of nature are not created, and "'manifestations . . . of nature [are] free to all men and reserved exclusively to none'").

The rule against patents on naturally occurring things is not without limits, however, for "all inventions at some level embody, use, reflect, rest upon, or apply laws of nature, natural phenomena, or abstract ideas," and "too broad an interpretation of this exclusionary principle could eviscerate patent law." *Mayo.* As we have recognized before, patent protection strikes a delicate balance between creating "incentives that lead to creation, invention, and discovery" and "imped[ing] the flow of information that might permit, indeed spur, invention." *Id.* We must apply this well-established standard to determine whether Myriad's patents claim any "new and useful . . . composition of matter," §101, or instead claim naturally occurring phenomena.

B

It is undisputed that Myriad did not create or alter any of the genetic information encoded in the BRCA1 and BRCA2 genes. The location and order of the nucleotides existed in nature before Myriad found them. Nor did Myriad create or alter the genetic structure of DNA. Instead, Myriad's principal contribution was uncovering the precise location and genetic sequence of the BRCA1 and BRCA2 genes within chromosomes 17 and 13. The question is whether this renders the genes patentable.

Myriad recognizes that our decision in *Chakrabarty* is central to this inquiry. In *Chakrabarty,* scientists added four plasmids to a bacterium, which enabled it to break down various components of crude oil. The Court held that the modified bacterium was patentable. It explained that the patent claim was "not to a hitherto unknown natural phenomenon, but to a nonnaturally occurring manufacture or composition of matter—a product of human ingenuity 'having a distinctive name, character [and] use.'" *Id.,* at 309-310. The *Chakrabarty* bacterium was new "with markedly different characteristics from any found in nature," 447 U.S., at 310, due to the additional plasmids and resultant "capacity for degrading oil." *Id.,* at 305, n.1. In this case, by contrast, Myriad did not create anything. To be sure, it found an important and useful gene, but separating that gene from its surrounding genetic material is not an act of invention.

Groundbreaking, innovative, or even brilliant discovery does not by itself satisfy the §101 inquiry. In *Funk Brothers Seed Co. v. Kalo Inoculant Co.,* 333 U.S. 127 (1948), this Court considered a composition patent that claimed a mixture of naturally occurring strains of bacteria that helped leguminous plants take nitrogen from the air and fix it in the soil. The ability of the bacteria to fix nitrogen was well known, and farmers commonly "inoculated" their crops with them to improve soil nitrogen levels. But farmers could not use the same inoculant for all crops, both because plants use different bacteria and because certain bacteria inhibit each other. Upon learning that several nitrogen-fixing bacteria did not inhibit each other, however, the patent applicant combined them into a single inoculant and obtained a patent. The Court held that the composition was not patent eligible because the patent holder did not alter the bacteria in any way. *Id.,* at 132 ("There is no way in which we could call [the bacteria mixture a product of invention] unless we borrowed invention from the discovery of the natural principle itself"). His patent claim thus fell squarely within the law of nature exception. So do Myriad's. Myriad found the location of the BRCA1 and BRCA2 genes, but that discovery, by itself, does not render the BRCA genes "new . . . composition[s] of matter," §101, that are patent eligible.

Indeed, Myriad's patent descriptions highlight the problem with its claims. For example, a section of the '282 patent's Detailed Description of the Invention indicates that Myriad found the location of a gene associated with increased risk of breast cancer and identified mutations of that gene that increase the risk.[4] In subsequent language Myriad explains that the location of the gene was unknown until Myriad found it among the approximately eight million nucleotide pairs contained in a subpart of chromosome 17. The '473 and '492 patents contain similar language as well. Many of Myriad's patent descriptions simply detail the "iterative process" of discovery by which Myriad narrowed the possible locations for the gene sequences that it sought. Myriad seeks to import these extensive research efforts into the §101 patent-eligibility inquiry. But extensive effort alone is insufficient to satisfy the demands of §101.

Nor are Myriad's claims saved by the fact that isolating DNA from the human genome severs chemical bonds and thereby creates a nonnaturally occurring molecule. Myriad's claims are simply not expressed in terms of chemical composition, nor do they rely in any way on the chemical changes that result from the isolation of a particular section of DNA. Instead, the claims understandably focus on the genetic information encoded in the BRCA1 and BRCA2 genes. If the patents depended upon the creation of a unique molecule, then a would-be infringer could arguably avoid at least Myriad's patent claims on entire genes (such as claims 1 and 2 of the '282 patent) by isolating a DNA sequence that included both the BRCA1 or BRCA2 gene and one additional nucleotide pair. Such a molecule would not be chemically identical to the molecule "invented" by Myriad. But Myriad obviously would resist that outcome because its claim is concerned primarily with the information contained in the genetic *sequence*, not with the specific chemical composition of a particular molecule.

Finally, Myriad argues that the PTO's past practice of awarding gene patents is entitled to deference, citing *J.E.M. Ag Supply, Inc. v. Pioneer Hi-Bred Int'l, Inc.*, 534 U.S. 124 (2001). We disagree. *J.E.M.* held that new plant breeds were eligible for utility patents under §101 notwithstanding separate statutes providing special protections for plants. After analyzing the text and structure of the relevant statutes, the Court mentioned that the Board of Patent Appeals and Interferences had determined that new plant breeds were patent eligible under §101 and that Congress had recognized and endorsed that position in a subsequent Patent Act amendment. In this case, however, Congress has not endorsed

---

4. The full relevant text of the Detailed Description of the Patent is as follows:

It is a discovery of the present invention that the BRCA1 locus which predisposes individuals to breast cancer and ovarian cancer, is a gene encoding a BRCA1 protein, which has been found to have no significant homology with known protein or DNA sequences. . . . It is a discovery of the present invention that mutations in the BRCA1 locus in the germline are indicative of a predisposition to breast cancer and ovarian cancer. Finally, it is a discovery of the present invention that somatic mutations in the BRCA1 locus are also associated with breast cancer, ovarian cancer and other cancers, which represents an indicator of these cancers or of the prognosis of these cancers. The mutational events of the BRCA1 locus can involve deletions, insertions and point mutations.

Notwithstanding Myriad's repeated use of the phrase "present invention," it is clear from the text of the patent that the various discoveries *are* the "invention."

the views of the PTO in subsequent legislation. While Myriad relies on Judge Moore's view that Congress endorsed the PTO's position in a single sentence in the Consolidated Appropriations Act of 2004, see Brief for Respondents 31, n.8; 689 F.3d, at 1346, that Act does not even mention genes, much less isolated DNA.

Further undercutting the PTO's practice, the United States argued in the Federal Circuit and in this Court that isolated DNA was *not* patent eligible under §101, and that the PTO's practice was not "a sufficient reason to hold that isolated DNA is patent-eligible." These concessions weigh against deferring to the PTO's determination.[7]

C

cDNA does not present the same obstacles to patentability as naturally occurring, isolated DNA segments. As already explained, creation of a cDNA sequence from mRNA results in an exons-only molecule that is not naturally occurring. Petitioners concede that cDNA differs from natural DNA in that "the non-coding regions have been removed." Brief for Petitioners 49. They nevertheless argue that cDNA is not patent eligible because "[t]he nucleotide sequence of cDNA is dictated by nature, not by the lab technician." *Id.*, at 51. That may be so, but the lab technician unquestionably creates something new when cDNA is made. cDNA retains the naturally occurring exons of DNA, but it is distinct from the DNA from which it was derived. As a result, cDNA is not a "product of nature" and is patent eligible under §101, except insofar as very short series of DNA may have no intervening introns to remove when creating cDNA. In that situation, a short strand of cDNA may be indistinguishable from natural DNA.[9]

III

It is important to note what is *not* implicated by this decision. First, there are no method claims before this Court. Had Myriad created an innovative method of manipulating genes while searching for the BRCA1 and BRCA2 genes, it could possibly have sought a method patent. But the processes used by Myriad to isolate DNA were well understood by geneticists at the time of Myriad's patents "were well understood, widely used, and fairly uniform insofar as any scientist engaged in the search for a gene would likely have utilized a similar approach," and are not at issue in this case.

Similarly, this case does not involve patents on new *applications* of knowledge about the BRCA1 and BRCA2 genes. Judge Bryson aptly noted that, "[a]s the first party with knowledge of the [BRCA1 and BRCA2] sequences, Myriad was in an excellent position to claim applications of that knowledge. Many of its unchallenged claims are limited to such applications." 689 F.3d, at 1349.

Nor do we consider the patentability of DNA in which the order of the naturally occurring nucleotides has been altered. Scientific alteration of the genetic code presents a different inquiry, and we express no opinion about the application of §101 to such endeavors. We merely hold that genes and the information

---

7. Myriad also argues that we should uphold its patents so as not to disturb the reliance interests of patent holders like itself. Concerns about reliance interests arising from PTO determinations, insofar as they are relevant, are better directed to Congress. See *Mayo*.

9. We express no opinion whether cDNA satisfies the other statutory requirements of patentability. *See, e.g.*, 35 U.S.C. §§102, 103, and 112.

they encode are not patent eligible under §101 simply because they have been isolated from the surrounding genetic material.

For the foregoing reasons, the judgment of the Federal Circuit is affirmed in part and reversed in part.

Comments

1. ***DNA and Patentability.*** In one of the most highly anticipated Supreme Court opinions in recent years, the Court held that an isolated DNA sequence (or genomic DNA) is ineligible for patent protection. At the time of the *Myriad* opinion, recent studies had shown that about 20 percent of human genes were patented. *See, e.g.,* Kyle Jensen & Fiona Murray, *Intellectual Property Landscape of the Human Genome,* 310 SCIENCE 239-240 (October 2005). There are approximately 22,000 genes, which make up about 2 percent of the human genome. Thus, only a small percentage of DNA actually codes for proteins; much of our DNA is comprised of regulatory regions such as promoters, enhancers, and activators that play an important role in transcription and gene expression. *See Human Genome Project Information* at http://www. ornl.gov/sci/techresources/Human_Genome/project/info.shtml ("Genes comprise only about 2% of the human genome; the remainder consists of noncoding regions, whose functions may include providing chromosomal structural integrity and regulating where, when, and in what quantity proteins are made.").

The question that had been percolating for some time is: If naturally occurring substances are not patentable, how is it that firms obtained patents on DNA sequences? The legal answer, prior to *Myriad,* had been human intervention, which allowed, for instance, one to claim an isolated DNA sequence that is markedly different from the naturally occurring DNA sequence. In other words, a DNA sequence as it exists in the human body is not subject to patent protection, but a sequence "isolated from its natural state" (i.e., isolated from other cellular components such as ribosomes) resulting in markedly different characteristics is eligible for patent protection under section 101. As Judge Lourie wrote in the *Myriad* Federal Circuit majority opinion (ultimately reversed by the Supreme Court), the "BRCA1 and 2 in their isolated state are not the same molecules as DNA as it exists in the body; human intervention in cleaving a portion of a native chromosomal DNA imparts on that isolated DNA a distinctive chemical identity from that possessed by native DNA." According to Judge Lourie, the DNA molecule is chemically manipulated "to produce a molecule that is markedly different from that which exists in the body." The majority's emphasis on "markedly different" characteristics—language from *Chakrabarty*—was fundamental to the Federal Circuit's analysis. To satisfy this test, the court relied heavily on the structural differences between the claimed DNA and native DNA, namely the cleaving of the covalent bonds. The fact that the information between the claimed and native DNA may be the same was "irrelevant" for the Federal Circuit. Rather, chemical entities such as DNA are "best described in patents by their structures rather than their functions."

Judge Bryson's dissent in Federal Circuit *Myriad* strongly challenged this characterization, stressing the majority's analysis would lead to the patenting of new minerals discovered in the earth or new plants found in the wild. According to the dissent, by relying so heavily on the structural differences between isolated and native DNA, the majority reveals the weakness of its argument and conveniently ignores the fact that both forms of DNA have "the same sequence, they code for the same proteins, and they represent the same units of heredity." Unlike the making of a baseball bat from an ash tree, which leads to a distinct product in terms of nature, form, and use, the very purpose of isolating DNA is to preserve its function and use.

The Supreme Court sided with Judge Bryson, stressing that the genetic *information* contained in the claimed DNA sequence and the naturally occurring sequence are the same, despite any chemical dissimilarities. As such, an isolated DNA sequence is a product of nature.

The Federal Circuit majority made a secondary argument, one based on social welfare and labor theory. The court asserted that isolating a DNA sequence that can provide important diagnostic tools and medicines is far more worthy of patent protection than snapping a leaf from a tree or removing an organ from a body, two examples used by the dissent. Indeed, "[s]napping a leaf from a tree is a physical separation, easily done by anyone" whereas "[c]reating a new chemical entity is the work of human transformation, requiring skill, knowledge, and effort."

This argument was also rejected by the Supreme Court. As the Court wrote, "[g]roundbreaking, innovative, or even brilliant discovery does not by itself satisfy the §101 inquiry." Patent law—like copyright law—is agnostic in this regard. From a normative perspective, one can ask if patent law should judge the relative social worthiness of, for example, a genetic diagnostic and a new and nonobvious pizza box? In the copyright context, Justice Holmes admonished his colleagues admonition that "[i]t would be a dangerous undertaking for persons trained only to the law to constitute themselves final judges of the worth of pictorial illustrations, outside of the narrowest and most obvious limits." *Bleistein v. Donaldson Lithographing Co.*, 188 U.S. 239, 251 (1903). Patent law has historically deferred to the market to make these judgments. (See the discussion in Chapter 1 on the relationship between patent and the market.) Beyond the normative question, are courts and patent offices institutionally capable to judge which inventive contributions benefit society the most? Moreover, with respect to "skill, knowledge, and effort," let's not forget that numerous noteworthy inventions are the result of fortuity. As Charles Slack writes regarding Goodyear's discovery of vulcanization:

> Sometime during the winter, . . . Goodyear accidentally dropped, placed, or spilled a quantity of rubber mixed with sulfur and white lead on a hot stove. When he retrieved the sample he discovered something remarkable: the sample had not melted, as he expected, but instead had hardened to the consistency of leather. Here, at last, was the final clue, the missing piece to the puzzle: heat.

CHARLES SLACK, NOBLE OBSESSION 84 (2002). Another notable example is penicillin. While Alexander Fleming is the name most commonly associated with the discovery of penicillin, it was not until Howard Florey came upon Fleming's writings several years later that the value of penicillin was truly appreciated. *See* ERIC LAX, THE MOLD IN DR. FLOREY'S COAT: THE STORY OF THE PENICILLIN MIRACLE (2004). Should it make a difference with respect to patentability that an inventor did not engage in purposeful labor or was simply lucky? At least since 1952, patent law has only cared about the claimed invention, not the path to invention. *See* 35 U.S.C. §103 (stating "[p]atentability shall not be negated by the manner in which the invention was made").

2. ***cDNA, Incentives, and Striking the Right Balance.*** The Court recognized there are limits to the prohibition against patenting laws of nature because all inventions "at some level" reflect a naturally occurring product. Thus, there is a need for "a delicate balance between creating 'incentives that lead to creation, invention, and discovery' and 'imped[ing] the flow of information that might permit, indeed spur, invention.'" The Court erred on the side of the latter with respect to naturally occurring DNA sequences. But it recognized the eligibility of cDNA (or complementary DNA), because, according to the Court, cDNA does not contain non-coding portions (or introns such as promoters and enhancers), which are present in naturally occurring DNA sequences. This distinction was a compromise position that reflects the balance inherent in the patent system. But why didn't the Court explicitly invoke *Prometheus*'s "inventive concept" principle when drawing this distinction? (See Comment 2 following *Prometheus.*) Was it implied that a patent on cDNA, in the words of *Prometheus*, "amounts to significantly more than a patent upon the natural law itself"?

By allowing patent protection on cDNA, the Court sought to retain sufficient incentives for biotechnology firms to invest in creating innovative research tools and diagnostics. For example, cDNA can be used to identify polymorphisms that are indicative of particular diseases; potentially patentable therapeutic proteins can then be designed to detect and treat these diseases. While the creation of cDNA and resulting treatments, of course, must satisfy additional patentability requirements such as nonobviousness, the Court at least gave firms the opportunity to make the case.

In addition, the Court was quick to point out that the possibility of patent protection remains for "innovative methods of manipulating genes"; "new applications of knowledge" about genes; and inventions that alter the naturally occurring nucleotide sequence of genes. Therefore, from a greater remove, it is difficult to discern the extent to which the Court's holding would dilute — if at all — the incentives that are at play in the biotechnology industry. (See Comment 3 on the relationship between patents and the biotech/pharma industries.) Indeed, a few weeks after the Supreme Court decision, Myriad sued Ambry Genetics for patent infringement alleging Ambry's process for determining mutations in BRCA 1 and 2 infringed claims in 10 patents owned or licensed by Myriad.

What if the Supreme Court affirmed the Federal Circuit? Would that mean if an individual undergoes a whole-genome sequence analysis, that individual (or the company that performs the analysis) may be liable for patent infringement? Of course, the answer to this question depends on what is claimed in the patent. Would an entire-genome analysis infringe a claim to an *isolated* DNA sequence? Recall that the Federal Circuit based its decision in large part on the structural dissimilarities between a native DNA sequence and an isolated DNA sequence. Nonetheless, DNA sequence patents could "have significant implications for the development of multigene (multiplex) genetic tests and the anticipated eventual development of whole-genome sequencing for clinical use." Secretary's Advisory Committee on Genetics, Health, and Society, *Public Consultation Draft Report on Gene Patents and Licensing Practices and Their Impact on Patient Access to Genetic Tests* 36 (2009). Thus, it would not be unreasonable for a company that provides whole-genome sequencing to seek a license.

3. *Patents and the Biotechnology/Pharma Industries.* Patents play an extremely important role in the biotechnology industry. As two economists observed, "[t]he collection of small and medium sized firms in the American biotechnology industry is . . . a striking example of enterprises that would not have come into existence without the prospect of a patent, and which depend on patent protection to make their profits, and to attract capital." Robert Mazzoleni & Richard Nelson, *The Benefits and Costs of Strong Patent Protection: A Contribution to the Current Debate*, 27 RESEARCH POLICY 273, 276 (1998). *See also* Stuart J.H. Graham et al., *High Technology Entrepreneurs and the Patent System: Results of the 2008 Berkeley Patent Study*, 24 BERKELEY TECH. L.J. 1255 (2009) (noting "investors of many types value patents as an input into their investment decision, particularly venture capital investors in the life sciences"); FED. TRADE COMM'N, TO PROMOTE INNOVATION: THE PROPER BALANCE OF COMPETITION AND PATENT LAW AND POLICY, ch. 3, at 15 (2003) ("The biotechnology industry also relies primarily on patents to provide incentives to invest in innovation. Biotechnology companies seek patent protection to appropriate the value of their inventions, to attract investment from capital markets, which funds their costly research, and to facilitate inter-firm relationships necessary for commercial development of their inventions.").

Patents are also extremely important to biotech's close cousin, the pharmaceutical industry. *See* Wesley M. Cohen et al., *Protecting Their Intellectual Assets: Appropriability Conditions and Why U.S. Manufacturing Firms Patent (or Not)*, Nat'l Bureau of Econ. Research, Working Paper No. 7552 (2004) (finding pharmaceutical industry relies heavily on the patent system). The principal reason for pharma's reliance on the patent system relates to the extremely high research and development costs associated with developing a new drug the low success rate, and relative ease associated with reverse engineering. *See* Bruce N. Kuhlik, *The Assault on Pharmaceutical Intellectual Property*, 71 U. CHI. L. REV. 93, 94 (2004) (discussing the risk associated with drug development and why patent protection is important to the pharmaceutical industry, particularly because "[i]t typically takes from ten to fifteen years from drug discovery to approval by the Food and Drug Administration" [and] "[o]f every five thousand medicines tested, only one ultimately receives FDA approval"). *See also* JOHN AVELLANET, GETTING TO MARKET NOW 44 (stating "[f]or every 1000 idea or product concepts that are created, less than 10 to 15 will make onto market," with respect to new medicine development, "the success rate is even lower. Only 1 out of every 250 new biologic and drug candidates will make it to market, and of those, only one-third will break even financially"); SHREEFAL S. MEHTA, COMMERCIALIZING SUCCESSFUL BIOMEDICAL TECHNOLOGIES 21 (2008) (stating "only an estimated 1% of compounds that enter early pre-clinical screening successfully becom[e] drugs for a given disease"); FED. TRADE COMM'N report, *supra*, at ch. 3, at 4 (stating "[r]epresentatives from the pharmaceutical industry stated that patent protection is indispensable in promoting pharmaceutical innovation for drug products containing new chemical entities. The sunk cost of engaging in research projects aimed toward the development of these drugs is extremely high. By preventing rival firms from free riding on the innovating firms' discoveries, patents can enable pharmaceutical firms to cover their fixed costs and regain the capital they invest in R&D efforts"). *See also PhRMA Statement on Patent Reform Act of 2009* ("A strong and reliable patent system provides American businesses with an incentive that spurs innovation across the country. It is especially important for pharmaceutical and biotechnology innovators that are faced with the daunting average investment of 10 to 15 years and roughly one billion dollars to develop a new drug.") at http://www.phrma.org/news_room/press_releases/phrma_statement_on_patent_reform_act_of_2009.

Interestingly, the cost and risk associated with developing new drugs was deemed irrelevant in a high-profile compulsory license case in India. In 2013, the Indian IP Appellate Board granted generic-maker Natco a compulsory license to make Bayer A.G.'s cancer drug Nexavar based on the Board's conclusion that Bayer did not make the drug sufficiently available at a reasonable price and that it failed to "work" the patent (i.e., did not "manufacture to a reasonable extent"). The Board dismissed Bayer's argument relating to the high cost and risk associated with drug development. As the company's vice president of global oncology marketing asserted in an affidavit, "[o]nly one out of 20 substances going into especially costly clinical testing with patients will actually be launched as a product." According to the Board, arguments based on R&D costs "do not assist in deciding what the public can afford reasonably."

Approximately $100 billion per year globally is devoted to pharmaceutical R&D, of which $30 billion comes from public sources such as the National Institutes of Health. These significant investments reflect the fact that the cost of developing a new drug is extremely expensive, although estimates vary. *Compare* AVELLANT, GETTING TO MARKET, *supra*, at 56 (stating "Phase III [FDA] trials can last up to 5 years and cost between $50 and $500 million . . . [and] there is still only at 58% chance of approval"); Kuhlik, *Pharmaceutical Intellectual Property*, *supra*, at 94 ("The average cost of developing a new drug has been estimated at $802 million."); Joseph A. DiMasi, Ronald W. Hansen & Henry G. Grabowski, *The Price of Innovation: New Estimates of Drug Development Costs*, 22 J. HEALTH ECON. 151, 180 (2003) (estimating new drug development cost at $802 million), *with* Public Citizen, *Tufts Drug Study Sample Is Skewed; True Figure of R&D Costs Likely Is 75 Percent Lower* (Dec. 4, 2001) (estimating figure to be much less); U.S. CONG. OFFICE OF TECH ASSESSMENT, PHARMACEUTICAL R&D: COSTS, RISKS, AND REWARDS 214 (1993) ("Total estimated preclinical pharmaceutical R&D constituted approximately $450 million in 1988"). Because of the high R&D costs, patent protection is essential, even though it contributes to the high costs of drugs. *See* ADAM B. JAFFE & JOSH LERNER, INNOVATION AND ITS DISCONTENTS: HOW OUR BROKEN PATENT SYSTEM IS ENDANGERING INNOVATION AND PROGRESS, AND WHAT TO DO ABOUT IT? 40-41 (2004) ("Patents make new drugs expensive, which is bad. But if they were not expensive, the revenue from selling them would not justify the large cost of developing them. So nobody would undertake such development. And expensive new drugs are better than no new drugs. This is the tradeoff at the heart of the patent system."). Thus, the issue for many commentators is not whether the patent system has a role to play in the pharmaceutical and biotechnology industries, but where on the developmental continuum patent law should be inserted. That is, is patent policy best served by allowing patent protection on upstream biotech research (e.g., cDNA, stem cells, and proteins) or downstream research (e.g., marketable therapeutics)? This issue is explored further in Comment 4, *infra.*

4. *Upstream-Downstream and In-Between.* Patent law's relationship with the biotechnology industry has not been without controversy, particularly in the context of patenting upstream research tools such as genes. The concern with patenting upstream is either a single patent owner will have broad patent rights or there will be numerous patent holders. The former may exercise his rights strategically as a holdout or may not be willing to engage in self-induced competition if he is also a developer, in both instances impeding innovation or downstream development. With many patent holders, the concern is one of thickets or an "anticommons," meaning that downstream developers will face insurmountable transactions costs when they seek to obtain permission to use upstream patented research. *See* Michael A. Heller & Rebecca S. Eisenberg, *Can Patents Deter Innovation? The Anticommons in Biomedical Research,* in 280 SCIENCE 698-701 (May 1998), at http://www.sciencemag.org/cgi/content/full/280/5364/698; Arti K. Rai, *Genome Patents: A Case Study in Patenting Research Tools,* 77 ACADEMIC MEDICINE 1368-1372 (Dec. 2002).

   In contrast, some commentators assert that upstream research is usually a product of biotechnology companies, many of which are small and in need of capital. Patenting upstream research may provide an important economic tool to recoup R&D costs or attract investment from downstream players so that development can continue. *See* Stuart J.H. Graham, Ted Sichelman, Robert P. Merges & Pamela Samuelson, *High Technology Entrepreneurs and the Patent System: Results from the 2008 Berkeley Patent Survey,* 24 BERKELEY TECH. L.J. 1255, 1290-1291 ("Among biotechnology companies, patenting is ranked the most important appropriability strategy"); F.M. Scherer, *The Economics of Human Gene Patents,* 77 ACADEMIC MEDICINE 1348-1367 (2002). Other commentators have questioned the anticommons scenario on empirical grounds. *See* David E. Adelman, *The Fallacy of the Commons,* 20 BERKELEY TECH. L.J. 985, 986 (2005) (concluding that "the threats to biomedical innovation posed by biotech patenting are generally modest"); David E. Adelman & Kathryn L. DeAngelis, *Patent Metrics: The Mismeasure of Innovation in the Biotech Patent Debate,* 85 TEX. L. REV. 1677, 1686 (2007) (asserting "[p]roponents of the generalized anticommons theory either ignore the characteristics of the scientific commons altogether or base their views on questionable assumptions about it, such as the assumption that upstream patents will inevitably restrict access to essential research tools for which no alternatives exist"). *See also* John P. Walsh, Ashish Arora & Wesley M. Cohen, *Effects of Research Tool Patents and Licensing on Biomedical Innovation,* in PATENTS IN THE KNOWLEDGE-BASED ECONOMY 285-340 (National Academies Press 2003):

[W]e report the results of 70 interviews with personnel at biotechnology and pharmaceutical firms and universities in considering the effects of research tool patents on industrial or academic biomedical research. . . . [W]e consider whether biomedical innovation has suffered because of either an anticommons or restrictions on the use of upstream discoveries in subsequent research. Notwithstanding the possibility of such impediments to biomedical innovation, there is still ample reason to suggest that patenting benefits biomedical innovation, especially via its considerable impact on R&D incentives or via its role in supporting an active market for technology. . . . To prefigure our result, we find little evidence of routine breakdowns in negotiations over rights, although research tool patents are observed to impose a range of social costs and there is some restriction of access.

Id. at 287-289. *See also* REAPING THE BENEFITS OF GENOMIC AND PROTEOMIC RESEARCH: INTELLECTUAL PROPERTY RIGHTS, INNOVATION, AND PUBLIC HEALTH 134 (National Research Council) (Steven A. Merrill & Anne-Marie Mazza eds., 2006) (concluding that while "there are reasons to be concerned about the future," for present purposes "the number of projects abandoned or delayed as a result of technology access difficulties is reported to be small, as is the number of occasions in which investigators revise their protocols to avoid intellectual property complications or pay high costs to obtain access to intellectual property").

5. *No Patents on Humans.* Section 33(a) of the AIA expressly prohibits the issuance of a patent "on a claim directed to or encompassing a human organism." *See* Leahy-Smith America Invents Act, Pub. L. No. 112-29, §4, 125 Stat. 284, 340 (2011). The USPTO viewed this provision as reflecting "longstanding USPTO policy." Memo from Robert W. Bahr, Senior Patent Counsel to the Patent Examining Corps (Sept. 20, 2011). *See also* MPEP §2105 ("If the broadest reasonable interpretation of the claimed invention as a whole encompasses a human being, then a rejection under 35 U.S.C. 101 must be made indicating that the claimed invention is directed to nonstatutory subject matter.").

HARVARD COLLEGE v. CANADA (COMMISSIONER OF PATENTS)

2002 Supreme Court of Canada 76, [2002] 4 S.C.R. 45

BASTARACHE, J.

I. INTRODUCTION

118 This appeal raises the issue of the patentability of higher life forms within the context of the *Patent Act*, R.S.C. 1985. The respondent, the President and Fellows of Harvard College, seeks to patent a mouse that has been genetically altered to increase its susceptibility to cancer, which makes it useful for cancer research. The patent claims also extend to all non-human mammals which have been similarly altered.

119 The Commissioner of Patents upheld the Patent Examiner's refusal to grant the patent. This decision was in turn upheld by the Federal Court, Trial Division, but was overturned by a majority of the Federal Court of Appeal. . . .

120 [T]he sole question is whether Parliament intended the definition of "invention", and more particularly the words "manufacture" or "composition

of matter", within the context of the *Patent Act*, to encompass higher life forms such as the oncomouse. In my opinion, Parliament did not intend higher life forms to be patentable. Had Parliament intended every conceivable subject matter to be patentable, it would not have chosen to adopt an exhaustive definition that limits invention to any "art, process, machine, manufacture or composition of matter". In addition, the phrases "manufacture" and "composition of matter" do not correspond to common understandings of animal and plant life. Even accepting that the words of the definition can support a broad interpretation, they must be interpreted in light of the scheme of the Act and the relevant context. The Act in its current form fails to address many of the unique concerns that are raised by the patenting of higher life forms, a factor which indicates that Parliament never intended the definition of "invention" to extend to this type of subject matter. Given the unique concerns associated with the grant of a monopoly right over higher life forms, it is my view that Parliament would not likely choose the *Patent Act* as it currently exists as the appropriate vehicle to protect the rights of inventors of this type of subject matter.

II. FACTUAL BACKGROUND

***

122 The technology by which a cancer-prone mouse ("oncomouse") is produced is described in the patent application disclosure. The oncogene (the cancer-promoting gene) is obtained from the genetic code of a non-mammal source, such as a virus. A vehicle for transporting the oncogene into the mouse's chromosomes is constructed using a small piece of bacterial DNA referred to as a plasmid. The plasmid, into which the oncogene has been "spliced", is injected into fertilized mouse eggs, preferably while they are at the one-cell stage. The eggs are then implanted into a female host mouse, or "foster mother", and permitted to develop to term. After the offspring of the foster mother are delivered, they are tested for the presence of the oncogene; those that contain the oncogene are called "founder" mice. Founder mice are mated with mice that have not been genetically altered. In accordance with Mendelian inheritance principles, 50 percent of the offspring will have all of their cells affected by the oncogene, making them suitable for the uses described above.

123 In its patent application, the respondent seeks to protect both the process by which the oncomice are produced and the end product of the process, i.e. the founder mice and the offspring whose cells are affected by the oncogene. The process and product claims also extend to all non-human mammals. . . .

III. RELEVANT STATUTORY PROVISIONS

124 *Patent Act*, R.S.C. 1985:

2. In this Act, except as otherwise provided, . . .

"invention" means any new and useful art, process, machine, manufacture or composition of matter, or any new and useful improvement in any art, process, machine, manufacture or composition of matter;

* * *

126 The Patent Examiner's rejection of claims 1 to 12 was based on his conclusion that higher life forms fall outside the definition of "invention" as given in s. 2 of the *Patent Act*, and therefore are not patentable subject matter. . . . In addition, the Patent Examiner noted that neither the Patent Appeal Board nor the courts have expressly stated that higher life forms constitute patentable subject matter.

B. Decision of the Commissioner of Patents (August 4, 1995)

* * *

130 Turning to the issue at hand, the Commissioner expressed the view that the words "manufacture" and "composition of matter" as found in s. 2 apply to something that has been made under the control of the inventor. At the same time, the resulting product must be reproducible in a consistent manner. Considering the invention in question, the Commissioner determines that there are two distinct phases. The first phase involves the preparation of the genetically engineered plasmid. The second involves the development of a genetically engineered mouse in the uterus of the host mouse. The Commissioner concluded that while the first phase is controlled by human intervention, in the second phase it is the laws of nature that take over to produce the mammalian end product. He was therefore unwilling to extend the meaning of "manufacture" or "composition of matter" to include a non-human mammal. In his view, the inventors do not have full control over all of the characteristics of the resulting mouse, and human intervention ensures that reproducibility extends only so far as the cancer-forming gene.

* * *

V. ANALYSIS

* * *

B. The Definition of "Invention": Whether a Higher Life Form Is a "Manufacture" or a "Composition of Matter"

153 The sole question in this appeal is whether the words "manufacture" and "composition of matter", in the context of the *Patent Act*, are sufficiently broad to include higher life forms. If these words are not sufficiently broad to include higher life forms, it is irrelevant whether this Court believes that higher life forms such as the oncomouse ought to be patentable. The grant of a patent reflects the interest of Parliament to promote certain manifestations of human ingenuity. As Binnie J. indicates in his reasons, there are a number of reasons why Parliament might want to encourage the sort of biomedical research that resulted in the oncomouse. But there are also a number of reasons why Parliament might want to be cautious about encouraging the patenting of higher life forms. In my view, whether higher life forms such as the oncomouse ought to be patentable is a matter for Parliament to determine. This Court's views as to the utility or propriety of patenting non-human higher life forms such as the oncomouse are wholly irrelevant.

***

155 Having considered the relevant factors, I conclude that Parliament did not intend to include higher life forms within the definition of "invention" found in the *Patent Act*. In their grammatical and ordinary sense alone, the words "manufacture" and "composition of matter" are somewhat imprecise and ambiguous. However, it is my view that the best reading of the words of the Act supports the conclusion that higher life forms are not patentable. . . . This conclusion is supported by the fact that the patenting of higher life forms raises unique concerns which do not arise in respect of non-living inventions and which are not addressed by the scheme of the Act. Even if a higher life form could, scientifically, be regarded as a "composition of matter", the scheme of the Act indicates that the patentability of higher life forms was not contemplated by Parliament. Owing to the fact that the patenting of higher life forms is a highly contentious and complex matter that raises serious practical, ethical and environmental concerns that the Act does not contemplate, I conclude that the Commissioner was correct to reject the patent application. . . .

(1) The Words of the Act

156 The definition of "invention" in s. 2 of the *Patent Act* lists five categories of invention: art (*réalisation*), process (*procédé*), machine (*machine*), manufacture (*fabrication*) or composition of matter (*composition de matières*). The first three, "art", "process" and "machine", are clearly inapplicable when considering claims directed toward a genetically engineered non-human mammal. If a higher life form is to fit within the definition of "invention", it must therefore be considered to be either a "manufacture" or a "composition of matter".

157 . . . In *Chakrabarty*, the majority attributed the widest meaning possible to the phrases "composition of matter" and "manufacture" for the reason that inventions are, necessarily, unanticipated and unforeseeable. Burger C.J., at p. 308, also referred to the fact that the categories of invention are prefaced by the word "any" ("*any* new and useful process, machine, manufacture, or composition of matter"). Finally, the Court referred to extrinsic evidence of Congressional intent to adopt a broad concept of patentability, noting at p. 309 that: "The Committee Reports accompanying the 1952 Act inform us that Congress intended statutory subject matter to 'include anything under the sun that is made by man.'"

158 I agree that the definition of "invention" in the *Patent Act* is broad. Because the Act was designed in part to promote innovation, it is only reasonable to expect the definition of "invention" to be broad enough to encompass unforeseen and unanticipated technology. I cannot however agree with the suggestion that the definition is unlimited in the sense that it includes "anything under the sun that is made by man". In drafting the *Patent Act*, Parliament chose to adopt an exhaustive definition that limits invention to any "art, process, machine, manufacture or composition of matter". Parliament did not define "invention" as "anything new and useful made by man". By choosing to define invention in this way, Parliament signaled a clear intention to include certain subject matter as patentable and to exclude other subject matter as being outside the confines of the Act. This should be kept in mind when determining whether the words "manufacture" and "composition of matter" include higher life forms.

159 With respect to the meaning of the word "manufacture" (*fabrication*), although it may be attributed a very broad meaning, I am of the opinion that the word would commonly be understood to denote a non-living mechanistic

product or process. . . . In my view, while a mouse may be analogized to a "manufacture" when it is produced in an industrial setting, the word in its vernacular sense does not include a higher life form. The definition in *Hornblower v. Boulton* (1799), 8 T.R. 95, 101 E.R. 1285 (K.B.), cited by the respondent, is equally problematic when applied to higher life forms. In that case, the English courts defined "manufacture" as "something made by the hands of man" (p. 1288). In my opinion, a complex life form such as a mouse or a chimpanzee cannot easily be characterized as "something made by the hands of man."

160 As regards the meaning of the words "composition of matter", I believe that they must be defined more narrowly than was the case in *Chakrabarty*, namely "all compositions of two or more substances and . . . all composite articles". If the words "composition of matter" are understood this broadly, then the other listed categories of invention, including "machine" and "manufacture", become redundant. This implies that "composition of matter" must be limited in some way. Although I do not express an opinion as to where the line should be drawn, I conclude that "composition of matter" does not include a higher life form such as the oncomouse.

* * *

164 Lastly, I wish also to address Rothstein J.A.'s assertion that "[t]he language of patent law is broad and general and is to be given wide scope because inventions are, necessarily, unanticipated and unforeseeable" (para. 116). In my view, it does not thereby follow that all proposed inventions are patentable. On the one hand, it might be argued that, in this instance, Parliament could foresee that patents might be sought in higher life forms. Although Parliament would not have foreseen the genetically altered mouse and the process of genetic engineering used to produce it, Parliament was well aware of animal husbandry or breeding. While the technologies used to produce a crossbred animal and a genetically engineered animal differ substantially, the end result, an animal with a new or several new features, is the same. Yet Parliament chose to define the categories of invention using language that does not, in common usage, refer to higher life forms. One might thus infer that Parliament did not intend to include higher life forms in the definition of "invention".

* * *

166 Patenting higher life forms would involve a radical departure from the traditional patent regime. Moreover, the patentability of such life forms is a highly contentious matter that raises a number of extremely complex issues. If higher life forms are to be patentable, it must be under the clear and unequivocal direction of Parliament. For the reasons discussed above, I conclude that the current Act does not clearly indicate that higher life forms are patentable. Far from it. Rather, I believe that the best reading of the words of the Act supports the opposite conclusion — that higher life forms such as the oncomouse are not currently patentable in Canada.

(2) *The Scheme of the Act*

167 This interpretation of the words of the Act finds support in the fact that the patenting of higher life forms raises unique concerns which do not arise with respect to non-living inventions and which cannot be adequately addressed by the scheme of the Act. . . . The patenting of higher life forms raises special

concerns that do not arise in respect of non-living inventions. Unlike other inventions, biologically based inventions are living and self-replicating. In addition, the products of biotechnology are incredibly complex, incapable of full description, and can contain important characteristics that have nothing to do with the invention. In my view, the fact that the *Patent Act* in its current state is ill-equipped to deal appropriately with higher life forms as patentable subject matter is an indication that Parliament never intended the definition of "invention" to extend to this type of subject matter.

168 The respondent argues that the concerns arising out of higher life forms as patentable subject matter are "external to the *Patent Act* and its jurisprudence" and that there is therefore no statutory basis to reject the patentability of higher life forms on moral, ethical or environmental grounds. I agree with the respondent that some of the policy concerns raised by the interveners are more appropriately dealt with outside the patent system. For example, some interveners expressed concern for the environmental and animal welfare implications of biotechnology. These issues are only tenuously linked to the patentability of higher life forms and are more directly related to the development and use of the technology itself. With regard to research and experimentation involving animals, by the time a researcher is in a position to file for a patent, any harm to the animal resulting from research will already have been done. Correspondingly, it is preferable to address this issue through existing or new regimes for protecting animal welfare. . . .

169 While the above-mentioned concerns are only indirectly related to the *Patent Act*, several of the issues raised by the interveners and in the literature are more directly related to patentability and to the scheme of the *Patent Act* itself. These issues, which pertain to the scope and content of the monopoly right accorded to the inventor by a patent, have been explored in depth by the Canadian Biotechnology Advisory Committee (CBAC), a body created in 1999 with a mandate to provide the government with advice on policy issues associated with biotechnology. In June 2002, the CBAC released its final report, *Patenting of Higher Life Forms and Related Issues: Report to the Government of Canada Biotechnology Ministerial Coordinating Committee*. The report recommends that higher life forms should be patentable. Nonetheless, it concludes, at p. 7, that given the importance of issues raised by the patenting of higher life forms and the significant "values" content of the issues raised, Parliament and not the courts should determine whether and to what degree patent rights ought to extend to plants and animals.

* * *

173 In its recommendations, the CBAC . . . deals with a concern that was raised before this Court by the intervener Canadian Environmental Law Association. The intervener submitted that patents on life forms may actually deter further innovation in the biomedical field by foreclosing opportunities for research and product development to those that do not hold the patent. Arguably, this potential is inherent in the nature of a patent system. Yet the impact may be more significant with respect to the products of biotechnology. As noted by the CBAC, at p. 14: "Access to basic or platform technology such as DNA sequences, cell lines, plants and animals at reasonable cost is crucial to research". High research costs can be expected to drive up the price of the end product, which in the case of biotechnology includes diagnostic tests and therapeutic agents important to the health of Canadians.

* * *

175 Perhaps the most significant issue addressed by the CBAC is the patentability of human life. The CBAC recommends that if Canada decides to permit patents over higher life forms, human bodies at all stages of development should be excluded. It observes in this regard that although humans are also animals, no country, including Canada, allows patents on the human body. According to the CBAC, this understanding derives from the universal principle of respect for human dignity, one element of which is that humans are not commodities (see CBAC, *supra*, at p. 8).

* * *

183 As noted earlier, the CBAC has recommended that higher life forms (i.e., plants, seeds and non-human animals) that meet the criteria of novelty, non-obviousness and utility be recognized as patentable. The concerns above therefore are not raised to justify a position that higher life forms should not be patentable, but rather serve to illustrate that the *Patent Act* in its current form is not well suited to address the unique characteristics possessed by higher life forms. The lack of direction currently in the *Patent Act* to deal with issues that might reasonably arise signals a legislative intention that higher life forms are currently not patentable. In addition, the discussion of the issues raised by the CBAC and other groups illustrates the complexity of the concerns. In my view, this Court does not possess the institutional competence to deal with issues of this complexity, which presumably will require Parliament to engage in public debate, a balancing of competing societal interests and intricate legislative drafting.

(3) The Object of the Act

184 The respondent submits that the object of the *Patent Act* is to encourage and reward the development of innovations and technology. In its view, this objective supports a broad reading of the definition of "invention" that does not exclude any area of technology save for the statutory exclusion in s. 27(3).

185 There is no doubt that two of the central objects of the Act are "to advance research and development and to encourage broader economic activity" (see *Free World Trust v. Électro Santé Inc.*, [2000] 2 S.C.R. 1024, 2000 SCC 66, at para. 42). As noted earlier, this does not, however, imply that "anything under the sun that is made by man" is patentable. Parliament did not leave the definition of "invention" open, but rather chose to define it exhaustively. Regardless of the desirability of a certain activity, or the necessity of creating incentives to engage in that activity, a product of human ingenuity must fall within the terms of the Act in order for it to be patentable. The object of the Act must be taken into account, but the issue of whether a proposed invention *ought* to be patentable does not provide an answer to the question of whether that proposed invention *is* patentable. In addition, the manner in which Canada has administered its patent regime in the past reveals that the promotion of ingenuity has at times been balanced against other considerations. For example, under the former provisions of the *Patent Act*, a licence could be granted to manufacture a patented medicine seven years after the patent first appeared on the market. The existence of this compulsory licence scheme demonstrates that other objectives, including fairness and the promotion of Canada's universal healthcare system,

have at times existed as part of the patent regime (see Chong, *supra*; see also Rudolph, *supra*, at p. 35, note 74).

186 Given the above, the respondent's argument that the object of the Act leads inexorably to the broadest reading of the definition of "invention" possible is problematic and is, in my view, based on an oversimplification of the patent regime. In the court below, Rothstein J.A. preferred the approach taken by the majority of the U.S. Supreme Court in *Chakrabarty, supra*. The majority read the language of the Act expansively on the basis that the Act embodied Thomas Jefferson's philosophy that "ingenuity should receive a liberal encouragement" (p. 308). The minority of the court did not wholly accept this characterization, commenting in respect to the objective of the Act, at p. 319 of the reasons:

> The patent laws attempt to reconcile this Nation's deep-seated antipathy to monopolies with the need to encourage progress. Given the complexity and legislative nature of this delicate task, we must be careful to extend patent protection no further than Congress has provided. In particular, were there an absence of legislative direction, the courts should leave to Congress the decisions whether and how far to extend the patent privilege into areas where the common understanding has been that patents are not available.

187 Based on the language and the scheme of the Act, both of which are not well accommodated to higher life forms, it is reasonable to assume that Parliament did not intend the monopoly right inherent in the grant of a patent to extend to inventions of this nature. It simply does not follow from the objective of promoting ingenuity that all inventions must be patentable, regardless of the fact that other indicators of legislative intention point to the contrary conclusion.

* * *

C. Drawing the Line: Is It Defensible to Allow Patents on Lower Life Forms While Denying Patents on Higher Life Forms

197 The respondent notes that the Commissioner of Patents has since 1982 accepted that lower life forms come within the definitions of "composition of matter" and "manufacture" and has granted patents on such life forms accordingly. It adds that the *Patent Act* does not distinguish, in its definition of "invention", between subject matter that is less complex (lower life forms) and subject matter that is more complex (higher life forms). It submits that there is therefore no evidentiary or legal basis for the distinction the Patent Office has made between lower life forms such as bacteria, yeast and moulds, and higher life forms such as plants and animals.

198 The patentability of lower life forms is not at issue before this Court, and was in fact never litigated in Canada. In *Abitibi, supra*, the Patent Appeal Board, the Commissioner concurring, rejected the prior practice of the Patent Office and issued a patent on a microbial culture that was used to digest, and thereby purify, a certain waste product that emanates from pulp mills. The decision, in this regard, was based largely on the U.S. Supreme Court's decision in *Chakrabarty, supra*, and on the practice in Australia, Germany and Japan. Having noted that judicial bodies in these countries altered their interpretation of patentable subject matter to include micro-organisms, the Board observed, at p. 88: "[o]bviously the answer to the question before us, which once had seemed so

clear and definite has become clouded and uncertain". The Board was careful to limit the subject matter to which the decision would apply (at p. 89):

> . . . this decision will extend to all micro-organisms, yeasts, moulds, fungi, bacteria, actinomycetes, unicellular algae, cell lines, viruses or protozoa; in fact to all new life forms which are produced *en masse* as chemical compounds are prepared, and are formed in such large numbers that any measurable quantity will possess uniform properties and characteristics.

199 Though this Court is not faced with the issue of the patentability of lower life forms, it must nonetheless address the respondent's argument that the line between higher and lower life forms is indefensible. As discussed above, I am of the opinion that the unique concerns and issues raised by the patentability of plants and animals necessitate a parliamentary response. Only Parliament has the institutional competence to extend patent rights or another form of intellectual property protection to plants and animals and to attach appropriate conditions to the right that is granted. In the interim, I see no reason to alter the line drawn by the Patent Office. The distinction between lower and higher life forms, though not explicit in the Act, is nonetheless defensible on the basis of common sense differences between the two. Perhaps more importantly, there appears to be a consensus that human life is not patentable; yet this distinction is also not explicit in the Act. If the line between lower and higher life forms is indefensible and arbitrary, so too is the line between human beings and other higher life forms.

200 The appellant submits that a fully developed non-human mammal is worlds apart from a yeast, a mould, or even the single-celled egg leading to its development. Whereas simple organisms are easily defined or identified by reference to a limited number of properties, complex life forms are not. In addition, simple organisms are often produced by processes similar to the manufacture of chemicals, while complex intelligent life forms are not.

201 As I stated above, the issue of whether a lower life form is a "composition of matter" or "manufacture" was never challenged in the courts in this country and it is difficult to say whether the Canadian courts would have followed the approach of the majority of the U.S. Supreme Court in *Chakrabarty*, or whether the approach of the minority would have been preferred. Regardless of the wisdom of the decision, it is now accepted in Canada that lower life forms are patentable. Nonetheless, I agree with the appellant that this does not necessarily lead to the conclusion that higher life forms are patentable, at least in part for the reasons that it is easier to conceptualize a lower life form as a "composition of matter" or "manufacture" than it is to conceptualize a higher life form in these terms.

* * *

BINNIE, J., dissenting.

1 The biotechnology revolution in the 50 years since discovery of the structure of DNA has been fuelled by extraordinary human ingenuity and financed in significant part by private investment. Like most revolutions, it has wide ramifications, and presents potential and serious dangers as well as past and future benefits. In this appeal, however, we are only dealing with a small corner of the biotechnology controversy. We are asked to determine whether the oncomouse, a genetically modified rodent with heightened genetic susceptibility to cancer,

is an invention. The legal issue is a narrow one and does not provide a proper platform on which to engage in a debate over animal rights, or religion, or the arrogance of the human race.

2 The oncomouse has been held patentable, and is now patented in jurisdictions that cover Austria, Belgium, Denmark, Finland, France, Germany, Greece, Ireland, Italy, Luxembourg, The Netherlands, Portugal, Spain, Sweden, the United Kingdom and the United States. A similar patent has been issued in Japan. New Zealand has issued a patent for a transgenic mouse that has been genetically modified to be susceptible to HIV infection. Indeed, we were not told of any country with a patent system comparable to Canada's (or otherwise) in which a patent on the oncomouse had been applied for and been refused.

3 If Canada is to stand apart from jurisdictions with which we usually invite comparison on an issue so fundamental to intellectual property law as what constitutes an "invention", the respondent, successful everywhere but in Canada, might expect to see something unique in our legislation. However, one looks in vain for a difference in definition to fuel the Commissioner's contention that, *as a matter of statutory interpretation*, the oncomouse is not an invention. The truth is that our legislation is not unique. The Canadian definition of what constitutes an invention, initially adopted in pre-Confederation statutes, was essentially taken from the United States *Patent Act* of 1793, a definition generally attributed to Thomas Jefferson. The United States patent on the oncomouse was issued 14 years ago. My colleague, Bastarache J., acknowledges that the fertilized, genetically altered oncomouse *egg* is an invention under our *Patent Act*, R.S.C. 1985, c. P-4 (para. 162). Thereafter, we part company, because my colleague goes on to conclude that the resulting *oncomouse*, that grows from the patented egg, is not itself patentable because it is not an invention. Subject matter patentability, on this view, is lost between two successive stages of a transgenic mouse's genetically pre-programmed growth. In my opinion, with respect, such a "disappearing subject-matter" exception finds no support in the statutory language.

4 A patent, of course, does not give its holder a license to practise the invention free of regulatory control (any more than an *un*patented invention enjoys such immunity). On the contrary, the grant of a patent simply reflects the public interest in promoting the disclosure of advancements in learning by rewarding human ingenuity. Innovation is said to be the lifeblood of a modern economy. We neglect rewarding it at our peril. Having disclosed to the public the secrets of how to make or use the invention, the inventor can prevent *unauthorized* people for a limited time from taking a "free ride" in exploiting the information thus disclosed. At the same time, persons skilled in the art of the patent are helped to further advance the frontiers of knowledge by standing on the shoulders of those who have gone before.

* * *

C. The Commercial and Scientific Context

16 Biotechnology is global in scope. Worldwide demand is expected to more than double from $20 billion in 1995 to $50 billion by 2005. Canada is a significant player. Statistics Canada reports that Canada's biotechnology sector in 1999 generated almost $2 billion in revenues, including $718 million in exports. These revenues are expected to exceed $5 billion in 2002. The Canadian Biotechnology Advisory Committee (CBAC), formed in 1999 to advise

the federal government on these matters, recently reported that Canada has more biotechnology companies *per capita* than any other country: *Patenting of Higher Life Forms and Related Issues: Report to the Government of Canada Biotechnology Ministerial Coordinating Committee,* June 2002, p. 2. It was calculated by Ernst & Young in its *Seventh Annual European Life Sciences Report 2000,* that Canada is second behind the U.S. in terms of number of companies, third behind the U.S. and U.K. in revenues, and first in R&D *per* employee.

* * *

18 This is not to suggest that because something is beneficial it is necessarily patentable. As stated, such value judgments have been excluded from the administration of the *Patent Act.* It is to say, however, that the massive investment of the private sector in biotechnical research is exactly the sort of research and innovation that the *Patent Act* was intended to promote.

* * *

F. Patenting of "Higher Life Forms" in Comparable Jurisdictions

33 In 1873, Louis Pasteur was granted a patent in the United States on a certain yeast, which is a living organism.

34 A patent for the Harvard oncomouse was issued by the United States Patent Office on April 12, 1988 and by the European Patent Office on May 13, 1992, despite the explicit power under the *European Patent Convention* to refuse a patent based on "morality" or "*ordre public*". As mentioned earlier, a similar patent has been issued in Japan, and New Zealand has issued a patent for a transgenic mouse.

35 The appellant Commissioner's principal argument is that to allow the oncomouse patent would be to "expand" the scope of the *Patent Act* (i.e., his factum, paras. 2, 3, 35 and 73), but the opposite conclusion reached in so many countries with comparable legislation suggests the contrary. In those jurisdictions, patents for the oncomouse have been issued without any need for legislative amendment, including the United States where the language of our definition of "invention" originated. The Commissioner seeks to *restrict* the legislative definition of invention, and he does so (in my view) for policy reasons unrelated to the *Patent Act* or to its legitimate role and function.

* * *

Comments

1. *The Influence (or Not) of* **Chakrabarty** *on the Canadian Supreme Court.* The *Chakrabarty* case has been very influential, not only within the United States, but in foreign jurisdictions. But the majority in the above Canadian Supreme Court case was not swayed by *Chakrabarty*'s reasoning. The Canadian Supreme Court considered and rejected the rationale in *Chakrabarty*. In particular, the Court refused to recognize that a higher life form is a "composition of matter." For the Canadian Justices, "anything under the sun that is made by man" is not eligible for patent protection.

2. *The European Approach to Transgenic Animals.* The genetically engineered mouse was a research tool, genetically designed to possess a predisposition

to breast cancer. While patenting the oncomouse was essentially uncontroversial in the United States, the same was not true during the European experience, which ultimately resulted in European Patent No. 0169672. The principal argument asserted by European opponents on patenting the oncomouse were grounded in public order and morality, two concepts finding textual support in Article 53(a) of the European Patent Convention. This argument was ultimately unsuccessful, as reflected in the following statement by the Examining Division of the European Patent Office (EPO):

> [The oncomouse] cannot be considered immoral or contrary to public order. The provision of a type of test animal useful in cancer research and giving rise to a reduction in the amount of testing on animals together with a low risk connected with the handling of the animals by qualified staff can generally be regarded as beneficial to mankind. A patent should therefore not be denied for the present invention on the ground of Article 53(a) EPC.

Harvard/Oncomouse, 1992 O.J. E.P.O. at 593 (Examining Div.).

3. *Patents Now Expired.* Harvard obtained three patents covering different aspects of the oncomouse—U.S. Patent Nos. 4,736,866, 5,087,571, and 5,925,803—that were all licensed to du Pont. The patents, which were filed prior to 1995 and, therefore, enjoy a 17-year term, have expired; but the term "OncoMouse®" remains a registered trademark of Dupont.

A Note on Patents, Biotechnology, and the Bayh-Dole Act

In addition to the *Chakrabarty* decision, another significant event occurred in 1980 that positively affected the biotechnology industry. In that year, Congress enacted the Bayh-Dole Act, which allows universities and other non-profit entities to "elect to retain title" for inventions that resulted from federal funding. *See* 35 U.S.C. §§ 200-205. The goal of this legislation was to encourage "private industry to utilize government funded inventions through the commitment of the risk capital necessary to develop such inventions to the point of commercial application." H.R. Rep. No. 96-1307, pt. 1, at 3 (1980). According to Rebecca Eisenberg, the "Act has been consistently hailed as an unqualified success in stimulating the commercial development of discoveries emerging from government-sponsored research in universities." Rebecca S. Eisenberg, *Public Research and Private Development: Patents and Technology Transfer in Government Sponsored Research*, 82 U. VA. L. REV. 1663, 1708-1709 (1996). *See also The Bayh-Dole Act: Selected Issues in Patent Policy and the Commercialization of Technology*, Congressional Research Service Report of Congress 8 (June 10, 2005) (stating the Bayh-Dole Act "appears to have met its expressed goals of using the patent system to promote the utilization of inventions arising from federally-supported research or development; . . . and to promote collaboration between commercial concerns and nonprofit organizations, including universities"). *But see* DAVID C. MOWERY, RICHARD R. NELSON, BHAVEN N. SAMPAT & ARVIDS A. ZIEDONIS, IVORY TOWER AND INDUSTRIAL INNOVATION: UNIVERSITY-INDUSTRY TECHNOLOGY TRANSFER BEFORE AND AFTER THE BAYH-DOLE ACT IN THE UNITED STATES (2004) (arguing that Bayh-Dole has not been as successful as its advocates claim and cautioning against other countries' desire to replicate Bayh-Dole); DEREK BOK, UNIVERSITIES IN THE MARKETPLACE 77 (2003) (while acknowledging Bayh-Dole is not without benefits, Bok states that "[u]niversities have paid a price for industry support through excessive secrecy, periodic exposés of financial conflict, and corporate efforts to manipulate or suppress research results"). *See also* Margo A. Bagley, *Academic Discourse and Proprietary Rights: Putting Patents in Their Proper Place*, 47 B.C. L. REV. 217 (2006).

Several noteworthy surveys have revealed that the biotechnology and pharmaceutical industries rely quite heavily on patents as a means of appropriation. *See* Wesley M. Cohen et al., *Protecting Their Intellectual Assets: Appropriability Conditions and Why U.S. Manufacturing Firms Patent (or Not)*, Nat'l Bureau of Econ. Research, Working Paper No. 7552 (2004); Robert Mazzoleni & Richard R. Nelson, *The Benefits and Costs of Strong Patent Protection: A Contribution to the Current Debate*, 27 RES. POL'Y 273, 276 (1998) (noting that small and medium size biotechnology firms provide "a striking example of enterprises that would not have come into existence without the prospect of a patent"). Much of the upstream research for these industries occurs in research universities.

In a higher-education setting, the University of Wisconsin was at the forefront of commercializing inventions. In the 1920s, Henry Steenbock, a UW scientist, discovered how to enrich milk with vitamin D. Once his research was published, Quaker Oats offered to purchase Steenbock's patented invention for $900,000. Steenbock declined this offer, instead proposing a foundation be established that would both hold title and license the patent to Quaker Oats. This foundation—named the Wisconsin Alumni Research Foundation (WARF)—was created in 1925 with the help of Quaker lawyers. Today, WARF is one of the giants of university technology-transfer.

COMPARATIVE PERSPECTIVE
Biotechnology Patents in Europe

The eligibility requirements in Europe and the United States provide an interesting point of comparison. In contrast to the American statutory approach, which defines what can be patented, the Europeans offer a negative expression of eligible subject matter. *See* EPC Article 57. Of note for biotech-related inventions, Article 53(a) denies patent protection for "inventions the publication or exploitation of which would be contrary to '*ordre public*' or morality. . . ."

Toward the end of the twentieth century, the European Parliament sought to provide a competitive boost to the European biotech industry by issuing a *directive* codifying patent protection for biotech-related inventions. *See* Directive 98/44/EC. Several concerns were raised about the Directive, and it "was a source of friction for a decade between the European Union and its Member States as a result of differences in the national law implementing it." Laurent Manderieux, *Europe's IP Architecture*, in THE HANDBOOK OF EUROPEAN INTELLECTUAL PROPERTY MANAGEMENT 3-10 (Jolly & Philpott eds., 2007). The aforementioned public morality provision in the EPC was used as tool to fight (ultimately unsuccessfully) the Directive by countries such as The Netherlands and political parties such as the Green Party. What is particularly interesting is that the European Patent Office issued biotech-related patents prior to the Directive, and certainly subsequent to its adoption.

2. Business Methods and Software-Related Inventions

BILSKI v. KAPPOS
130 S. Ct. 3218 (2010)

JUSTICE KENNEDY delivered the opinion of the Court.

The question in this case turns on whether a patent can be issued for a claimed invention designed for the business world. The patent application claims a procedure for instructing buyers and sellers how to protect against the risk of price fluctuations in a discrete section of the economy. Three arguments are advanced for the proposition that the claimed invention is outside the scope of patent law: (1) it is not tied to a machine and does not transform an article; (2) it involves a method of conducting business; and (3) it is merely an abstract idea. The Court of Appeals ruled that the first mentioned of these, the so-called machine-or-transformation test, was the sole test to be used for determining the patentability of a "process" under the Patent Act, 35 U.S.C. § 101.

I

Petitioners' application seeks patent protection for a claimed invention that explains how buyers and sellers of commodities in the energy market can protect, or hedge, against the risk of price changes. The key claims are claims 1 and 4. Claim 1 describes a series of steps instructing how to hedge risk. Claim 4 puts the concept articulated in claim 1 into a simple mathematical formula. Claim 1 consists of the following steps:

> (a) initiating a series of transactions between said commodity provider and consumers of said commodity wherein said consumers purchase said commodity at a fixed rate based upon historical averages, said fixed rate corresponding to a risk position of said consumers;
>
> (b) identifying market participants for said commodity having a counter-risk position to said consumers; and
>
> (c) initiating a series of transactions between said commodity provider and said market participants at a second fixed rate such that said series of market participant transactions balances the risk position of said series of consumer transactions.

The remaining claims explain how claims 1 and 4 can be applied to allow energy suppliers and consumers to minimize the risks resulting from fluctuations in market demand for energy. For example, claim 2 claims "[t]he method of claim 1 wherein said commodity is energy and said market participants are transmission distributors." Some of these claims also suggest familiar statistical approaches to determine the inputs to use in claim 4's equation. For example, claim 7 advises using well-known random analysis techniques to determine how much a seller will gain "from each transaction under each historical weather pattern."

The patent examiner rejected petitioners' application, explaining that it " 'is not implemented on a specific apparatus and merely manipulates [an] abstract idea and solves a purely mathematical problem without any limitation to a practical application, therefore, the invention is not directed to the technological arts.' " The Board of Patent Appeals and Interferences affirmed, concluding that the application involved only mental steps that do not transform physical matter and was directed to an abstract idea.

The United States Court of Appeals for the Federal Circuit heard the case en banc and affirmed. The case produced five different opinions. Students of patent law would be well advised to study these scholarly opinions.

Chief Judge Michel wrote the opinion of the court. The court rejected its prior test for determining whether a claimed invention was a patentable "process" under §101—whether it produces a "'useful, concrete, and tangible result'"—as articulated in *State Street Bank & Trust Co. v. Signature Financial Group, Inc.* and *AT&T Corp. v. Excel Communications, Inc.* The court held that "[a] claimed process is surely patent-eligible under §101 if: (1) it is tied to a particular machine or apparatus, or (2) it transforms a particular article into a different state or thing." The court concluded this "machine-or-transformation test" is "the sole test governing §101 analyses," and thus the "test for determining patent eligibility of a process under §101." Applying the machine-or-transformation test, the court held that petitioners' application was not patent eligible.

II

A

Section 101 defines the subject matter that may be patented under the Patent Act:

> Whoever invents or discovers any new and useful process, machine, manufacture, or composition of matter, or any new and useful improvement thereof, may obtain a patent therefor, subject to the conditions and requirements of this title.

Section 101 thus specifies four independent categories of inventions or discoveries that are eligible for protection: processes, machines, manufactures, and compositions of matter. "In choosing such expansive terms . . . modified by the comprehensive 'any,' Congress plainly contemplated that the patent laws would be given wide scope." *Diamond v. Chakrabarty*, 447 U.S. 303, 308 (1980). Congress took this permissive approach to patent eligibility to ensure that "'ingenuity should receive a liberal encouragement.'" *Id.*, at 308-309 (quoting 5 Writings of Thomas Jefferson 75-76 (H. Washington ed. 1871)).

The Court's precedents provide three specific exceptions to §101's broad patent-eligibility principles: "laws of nature, physical phenomena, and abstract ideas." *Chakrabarty, supra,* at 309. While these exceptions are not required by the statutory text, they are consistent with the notion that a patentable process must be "new and useful." And, in any case, these exceptions have defined the reach of the statute as a matter of statutory *stare decisis* going back 150 years. The concepts covered by these exceptions are "part of the storehouse of knowledge of all men . . . free to all men and reserved exclusively to none." *Funk Brothers Seed Co. v. Kalo Inoculant Co.*, 333 U.S. 127, 130 (1948).

The §101 patent-eligibility inquiry is only a threshold test. Even if an invention qualifies as a process, machine, manufacture, or composition of matter, in order to receive the Patent Act's protection the claimed invention must also satisfy "the conditions and requirements of this title." §101. Those requirements include that the invention be novel, see §102, nonobvious, see §103, and fully and particularly described, see §112.

The present case involves an invention that is claimed to be a "process" under §101. Section 100(b) defines "process" as:

process, art or method, and includes a new use of a known process, machine, manufacture, composition of matter, or material.

The Court first considers two proposed categorical limitations on "process" patents under § 101 that would, if adopted, bar petitioners' application in the present case: the machine-or-transformation test and the categorical exclusion of business method patents.

B

1

Under the Court of Appeals' formulation, an invention is a "process" only if: "(1) it is tied to a particular machine or apparatus, or (2) it transforms a particular article into a different state or thing." 545 F.3d, at 954. This Court has "more than once cautioned that courts 'should not read into the patent laws limitations and conditions which the legislature has not expressed.'" *Diamond v. Diehr*, 450 U.S. 175, 182 (1981) (quoting *Chakrabarty, supra*, at 308). In patent law, as in all statutory construction, "[u]nless otherwise defined, 'words will be interpreted as taking their ordinary, contemporary, common meaning.'" *Diehr, supra*, at 182. The Court has read the § 101 term "manufacture" in accordance with dictionary definitions, and approved a construction of the term "composition of matter" consistent with common usage.

Any suggestion in this Court's case law that the Patent Act's terms deviate from their ordinary meaning has only been an explanation for the exceptions for laws of nature, physical phenomena, and abstract ideas. See *Parker v. Flook*, 437 U.S. 584, 588-589 (1978). This Court has not indicated that the existence of these well-established exceptions gives the Judiciary *carte blanche* to impose other limitations that are inconsistent with the text and the statute's purpose and design. Concerns about attempts to call any form of human activity a "process" can be met by making sure the claim meets the requirements of § 101.

The Court of Appeals incorrectly concluded that this Court has endorsed the machine-or-transformation test as the exclusive test. *Gottschalk v. Benson*, 409 U.S. 63, 70 (1972), noted that "[t]ransformation and reduction of an article 'to a different state or thing' is the clue to the patentability of a process claim that does not include particular machines." At the same time, it explicitly declined to "hold that no process patent could ever qualify if it did not meet [machine or transformation] requirements." *Id.*, at 71.

This Court's precedents establish that the machine-or-transformation test is a useful and important clue, an investigative tool, for determining whether some claimed inventions are processes under § 101. The machine-or-transformation test is not the sole test for deciding whether an invention is a patent-eligible "process."

2

It is true that patents for inventions that did not satisfy the machine-or-transformation test were rarely granted in earlier eras, especially in the Industrial Age, as explained by Judge Dyk's thoughtful historical review. See 545 F.3d, at 966-976 (concurring opinion). But times change. Technology and other innovations progress in unexpected ways. For example, it was once forcefully argued that until recent times, "well-established principles of patent law probably would have prevented the issuance of a valid patent on almost any conceivable computer program." *Diehr*, 450 U.S., at 195 (Stevens, J., dissenting). But this fact does not mean that unforeseen innovations such as computer programs are always unpatentable. Section 101 is a "dynamic provision designed to encompass new and unforeseen inventions." *J.E.M. Ag. Supply, Inc. v. Pioneer Hi-Bred Int'l, Inc.*, 534 U.S. 124, 135 (2001). A categorical rule denying patent protection for "inventions in areas not contemplated by Congress . . . would frustrate the purposes of the patent law." *Chakrabarty*, 447 U.S., at 315.

The machine-or-transformation test may well provide a sufficient basis for evaluating processes similar to those in the Industrial Age—for example, inventions grounded in a physical or other tangible form. But there are reasons to doubt whether the test should be the sole criterion for determining the patentability of inventions in the Information Age. As numerous *amicus* briefs argue, the machine-or-transformation test would create uncertainty as to the patentability of software, advanced diagnostic medicine techniques, and inventions based on linear programming, data compression, and the manipulation of digital signals.

In the course of applying the machine-or-transformation test to emerging technologies, courts may pose questions of such intricacy and refinement that they risk obscuring the larger object of securing patents for valuable inventions without transgressing the public domain. As a result, in deciding whether previously unforeseen inventions qualify as patentable "process[es]," it may not make sense to require courts to confine themselves to asking the questions posed by the machine-or-transformation test. Section 101's terms suggest that new technologies may call for new inquiries. See *Benson, supra*, at 71 (to "freeze process patents to old technologies, leaving no room for the revelations of the new, onrushing technology[,] . . . is not our purpose").

It is important to emphasize that the Court today is not commenting on the patentability of any particular invention, let alone holding that any of the above-mentioned technologies from the Information Age should or should not receive patent protection. This Age puts the possibility of innovation in the hands of more people and raises new difficulties for the patent law. With ever more people trying to innovate and thus seeking patent protections for their inventions, the patent law faces a great challenge in striking the balance between protecting inventors and not granting monopolies over procedures that others would discover by independent, creative application of general principles. Nothing in this opinion should be read to take a position on where that balance ought to be struck.

C

1

Section 101 similarly precludes the broad contention that the term "process" categorically excludes business methods. The term "method," which is within §100(b)'s definition of "process," at least as a textual matter and before consulting other limitations in the Patent Act and this Court's precedents, may include at least some methods of doing business. *See, e.g.*, Webster's New International Dictionary 1548 (2d ed. 1954) (defining "method" as "[a]n orderly procedure or process . . . regular way or manner of doing anything; hence, a set form of procedure adopted in investigation or instruction"). The Court is unaware of any argument that the "'ordinary, contemporary, common meaning,'" *Diehr*, *supra*, at 182, of "method" excludes business methods. Nor is it clear how far a prohibition on business method patents would reach, and whether it would exclude technologies for conducting a business more efficiently.

The argument that business methods are categorically outside of §101's scope is further undermined by the fact that federal law explicitly contemplates the existence of at least some business method patents. Under 35 U.S.C. §273(b)(1), if a patent-holder claims infringement based on "a method in [a] patent," the alleged infringer can assert a defense of prior use. For purposes of this defense alone, "method" is defined as "a method of doing or conducting business." §273(a)(3). In other words, by allowing this defense the statute itself acknowledges that there may be business method patents. Section 273's definition of "method," to be sure, cannot change the meaning of a prior-enacted statute. But what §273 does is clarify the understanding that a business method is simply one kind of "method" that is, at least in some circumstances, eligible for patenting under §101.

2

Interpreting §101 to exclude all business methods simply because business method patents were rarely issued until modern times revives many of the previously discussed difficulties. At the same time, some business method patents raise special problems in terms of vagueness and suspect validity. The Information Age empowers people with new capacities to perform statistical analyses and mathematical calculations with a speed and sophistication that enable the design of protocols for more efficient performance of a vast number of business tasks. If a high enough bar is not set when considering patent applications of this sort, patent examiners and courts could be flooded with claims that would put a chill on creative endeavor and dynamic change.

In searching for a limiting principle, this Court's precedents on the unpatentability of abstract ideas provide useful tools. Indeed, if the Court of Appeals were to succeed in defining a narrower category or class of patent applications that claim to instruct how business should be conducted, and then rule that the category is unpatentable because, for instance, it represents an attempt to patent abstract ideas, this conclusion might well be in accord with controlling precedent. But beyond this or some other limitation consistent with the statutory text, the Patent Act leaves open the possibility that there are at least some processes that can be fairly described as business methods that are within patentable subject matter under §101.

Finally, even if a particular business method fits into the statutory definition of a "process," that does not mean that the application claiming that method should be granted. In order to receive patent protection, any claimed invention must be novel, §102, nonobvious, §103, and fully and particularly described, §112. These limitations serve a critical role in adjusting the tension, ever present in patent law, between stimulating innovation by protecting inventors and impeding progress by granting patents when not justified by the statutory design.

III

Even though petitioners' application is not categorically outside of §101 under the two broad and atextual approaches the Court rejects today, that does not mean it is a "process" under §101. Petitioners seek to patent both the concept of hedging risk and the application of that concept to energy markets. App. 19-20. Rather than adopting categorical rules that might have wide-ranging and unforeseen impacts, the Court resolves this case narrowly on the basis of this Court's decisions in *Benson, Flook,* and *Diehr,* which show that petitioners' claims are not patentable processes because they are attempts to patent abstract ideas. Indeed, all members of the Court agree that the patent application at issue here falls outside of § 101 because it claims an abstract idea.

In *Benson,* the Court considered whether a patent application for an algorithm to convert binary-coded decimal numerals into pure binary code was a "process" under § 101. 409 U.S., at 64-67. The Court first explained that " '[a] principle, in the abstract, is a fundamental truth; an original cause; a motive; these cannot be patented, as no one can claim in either of them an exclusive right.' " *Id.,* at 67. The Court then held the application at issue was not a "process," but an unpatentable abstract idea. "It is conceded that one may not patent an idea. But in practical effect that would be the result if the formula for converting . . . numerals to pure binary numerals were patented in this case." 409 U.S., at 71. A contrary holding "would wholly pre-empt the mathematical formula and in practical effect would be a patent on the algorithm itself." *Id.,* at 72.

In *Flook,* the Court considered the next logical step after *Benson.* The applicant there attempted to patent a procedure for monitoring the conditions during the catalytic conversion process in the petrochemical and oil-refining industries. The application's only innovation was reliance on a mathematical algorithm. *Flook* held the invention was not a patentable "process." The Court conceded the invention at issue, unlike the algorithm in *Benson,* had been limited so that it could still be freely used outside the petrochemical and oil-refining industries. Nevertheless, *Flook* rejected "[t]he notion that post-solution activity, no matter how conventional or obvious in itself, can transform an unpatentable principle into a patentable process." *Id.,* at 590. The Court concluded that the process at issue there was "unpatentable under § 101, not because it contain[ed] a mathematical algorithm as one component, but because once that algorithm [wa]s assumed to be within the prior art, the application, considered as a whole, contain[ed] no patentable invention." *Id.,* at 594. As the Court later explained, *Flook* stands for the proposition that the prohibition against patenting abstract ideas "cannot be circumvented by attempting to limit the use of the formula to a particular technological environment" or adding "insignificant postsolution activity." *Diehr,* 450 U.S., at 191-192.

Finally, in *Diehr,* the Court established a limitation on the principles articulated in *Benson* and *Flook.* The application in *Diehr* claimed a previously unknown method for "molding raw, uncured synthetic rubber into cured precision products," using a mathematical formula to complete some of its several steps by way of a computer. *Diehr* explained that while an abstract idea, law of nature, or mathematical formula could not be patented, "an *application* of a law of nature or mathematical formula to a known structure or process may well be deserving of patent protection." *Id.,* at 187. *Diehr* emphasized the need to consider the invention as a whole, rather than "dissect[ing] the claims into old and new elements and then . . . ignor[ing] the presence of the old elements in the analysis." *Id.,* at 188. Finally, the Court concluded that because the claim was not "an attempt to patent a mathematical formula, but rather [was] an industrial process for the molding of rubber products," it fell within § 101's patentable subject matter. *Id.,* at 192-193.

In light of these precedents, it is clear that petitioners' application is not a patentable "process." Claims 1 and 4 in petitioners' application explain the basic concept of hedging, or protecting against risk: "Hedging is a fundamental economic practice long prevalent in our system of commerce and taught in any introductory finance class." 545 F.3d, at 1013 (Rader, J., dissenting). The concept of hedging, described in claim 1 and reduced to a mathematical formula in claim 4, is an unpatentable abstract idea, just like the algorithms at issue in *Benson* and *Flook*. Allowing petitioners to patent risk hedging would pre-empt use of this approach in all fields, and would effectively grant a monopoly over an abstract idea.

Petitioners' remaining claims are broad examples of how hedging can be used in commodities and energy markets. *Flook* established that limiting an abstract idea to one field of use or adding token post-solution components did not make the concept patentable. That is exactly what the remaining claims in petitioners' application do. These claims attempt to patent the use of the abstract idea of hedging risk in the energy market and then instruct the use of well-known random analysis techniques to help establish some of the inputs into the equation. Indeed, these claims add even less to the underlying abstract principle than the invention in *Flook* did, for the *Flook* invention was at least directed to the narrower domain of signaling dangers in operating a catalytic converter.

* * *

Today, the Court once again declines to impose limitations on the Patent Act that are inconsistent with the Act's text. The patent application here can be rejected under our precedents on the unpatentability of abstract ideas. The Court, therefore, need not define further what constitutes a patentable "process," beyond pointing to the definition of that term provided in §100(b) and looking to the guideposts in *Benson, Flook,* and *Diehr.*

And nothing in today's opinion should be read as endorsing interpretations of §101 that the Court of Appeals for the Federal Circuit has used in the past. *See, e.g., State Street,* 149 F.3d, at 1373; *AT&T Corp.,* 172 F.3d, at 1357. It may be that the Court of Appeals thought it needed to make the machine-or-transformation test exclusive precisely because its case law had not adequately identified less extreme means of restricting business method patents, including (but not limited to) application of our opinions in *Benson, Flook,* and *Diehr.* In disapproving an exclusive machine-or-transformation test, we by no means foreclose the Federal Circuit's development of other limiting criteria that further the purposes of the Patent Act and are not inconsistent with its text.

The judgment of the Court of Appeals is affirmed.

JUSTICE STEVENS, with whom JUSTICE GINSBURG, JUSTICE BREYER, and JUSTICE SOTOMAYOR join, concurring in the judgment.

In the area of patents, it is especially important that the law remain stable and clear. The only question presented in this case is whether the so-called machine-or-transformation test is the exclusive test for what constitutes a patentable "process" under 35 U.S.C. §101. It would be possible to answer that question simply by holding, as the entire Court agrees, that although the machine-or-transformation test is reliable in most cases, it is not the *exclusive* test.

I agree with the Court that, in light of the uncertainty that currently pervades this field, it is prudent to provide further guidance. But I would take a different approach. Rather than making any broad statements about how to define the term "process" in § 101 or tinkering with the bounds of the category of unpatentable, abstract ideas, I would restore patent law to its historical and constitutional moorings.

For centuries, it was considered well established that a series of steps for conducting business was not, in itself, patentable. In the late 1990's, the Federal Circuit and others called this proposition into question. Congress quickly responded to a Federal Circuit decision with a stopgap measure designed to limit a potentially significant new problem for the business community. It passed the First Inventors Defense Act of 1999 (codified at 35 U.S.C. § 273), which provides a limited defense to claims of patent infringement. Following several more years of confusion, the Federal Circuit changed course, overruling recent decisions and holding that a series of steps may constitute a patentable process only if it is tied to a machine or transforms an article into a different state or thing. This "machine-or-transformation test" excluded general methods of doing business as well as, potentially, a variety of other subjects that could be called processes.

The Court correctly holds that the machine-or-transformation test is not the sole test for what constitutes a patentable process; rather, it is a critical clue. But the Court is quite wrong, in my view, to suggest that any series of steps that is not itself an abstract idea or law of nature may constitute a "process" within the meaning of § 101. The language in the Court's opinion to this effect can only cause mischief. The wiser course would have been to hold that petitioners' method is not a "process" because it describes only a general method of engaging in business transactions—and business methods are not patentable. More precisely, although a process is not patent-ineligible simply because it is useful for conducting business, a claim that merely describes a method of doing business does not qualify as a "process" under § 101.

II

Before explaining in more detail how I would decide this case, I will comment briefly on the Court's opinion. The opinion is less than pellucid in more than one respect, and, if misunderstood, could result in confusion or upset settled areas of the law. Three preliminary observations may be clarifying.

First, the Court suggests that the terms in the Patent Act must be read as lay speakers use those terms, and not as they have traditionally been understood in the context of patent law. [I]f this portion of the Court's opinion were taken literally, the results would be absurd: Anything that constitutes a series of steps would be patentable so long as it is novel, nonobvious, and described with specificity. But the opinion cannot be taken literally on this point. The Court makes this clear when it accepts that the "atextual" machine-or-transformation test, is "useful and important," even though it "violates" the stated "statutory interpretation principles;" and when the Court excludes processes that tend to pre-empt commonly used ideas.

Second, in the process of addressing the sole issue presented to us, the opinion uses some language that seems inconsistent with our centuries-old reliance on the machine-or-transformation criteria as clues to patentability. Most notably, the opinion for a plurality suggests that these criteria may operate differently when addressing technologies of a recent vintage. In moments of caution, however, the opinion for the Court explains—correctly—that the Court is merely restoring the law to its historical state of rest. Notwithstanding this internal tension, I understand the Court's opinion to hold only that the machine-or-transformation test remains an important test for patentability. Few, if any, processes cannot effectively be evaluated using these criteria.

Third, in its discussion of an issue not contained in the questions presented—whether the particular series of steps in petitioners' application is an abstract idea—the Court uses language that could suggest a shift in our approach to that issue. Although I happen to agree that petitioners seek to patent an abstract idea, the Court does not show how this conclusion follows "clear[ly]," *ante*, at 15, from our case law. The patent now before us is not for "[a] principle, in the abstract," or a "fundamental truth." *Parker v. Flook*, 437 U.S. 584, 589 (1978) (internal quotation marks omitted). Nor does it claim the sort of phenomenon of nature or abstract idea that was embodied by the mathematical formula at issue in *Gottschalk v. Benson*, 409 U.S. 63, 67 (1972), and in *Flook*.

The Court construes petitioners' claims on processes for pricing as claims on "the basic concept of hedging, or protecting against risk," and thus discounts the application's discussion of what sorts of data to use, and how to analyze those data, as mere "token post-solution components." In other words, the Court artificially limits petitioners' claims to hedging, and then concludes that hedging is an abstract idea rather than a term that describes a category of processes including petitioners' claims. Why the Court does this is never made clear. One might think that the Court's analysis means that any process that utilizes an abstract idea is *itself* an unpatentable, abstract idea. But we have never suggested any such rule, which would undermine a host of patentable processes. It is true, as the Court observes, that petitioners' application is phrased broadly. But claim specification is covered by § 112, not § 101; and if a series of steps constituted an unpatentable idea merely because it was described without sufficient specificity, the Court could be calling into question some of our own prior decisions. At points, the opinion suggests that novelty is the clue. See *ante*, at 14. But the fact that hedging is " 'long prevalent in our system of commerce,' " *ibid.*, cannot justify the Court's conclusion, as "the proper construction of § 101 . . . does not involve the familiar issu[e] of novelty" that arises under § 102. *Flook*, 437 U.S., at 588. At other points, the opinion for a plurality suggests that the analysis turns on the category of patent involved. But we have never in the past suggested that the inquiry varies by subject matter.

The Court, in sum, never provides a satisfying account of what constitutes an unpatentable abstract idea. Indeed, the Court does not even explain if it is using the machine-or-transformation criteria. The Court essentially asserts its conclusion that petitioners' application claims an abstract idea. This mode of analysis (or lack thereof) may have led to the correct outcome in this case, but it also means that the Court's musings on this issue stand for very little.

* * *

JUSTICE BREYER, with whom JUSTICE SCALIA joins as to Part II, concurring in the judgment.

I

I write separately in order to highlight the substantial *agreement* among many Members of the Court on many of the fundamental issues of patent law raised by this case. In light of the need for clarity and settled law in this highly technical area, I think it appropriate to do so.

II

In addition to the Court's unanimous agreement that the claims at issue here are unpatentable abstract ideas, it is my view that the following four points are consistent with both the opinion of the Court and Justice Stevens' opinion concurring in the judgment:

First, although the text of § 101 is broad, it is not without limit. "[T]he underlying policy of the patent system [is] that 'the things which are worth to the public the embarrassment of an exclusive patent,' . . . must outweigh the restrictive effect of the limited patent monopoly." *Graham v. John Deere Co.,* 383 U.S. 1, 10-11 (1966) (quoting Letter from Thomas Jefferson to Isaac McPherson (Aug. 13, 1813)). The Court has thus been careful in interpreting the Patent Act to "determine not only what is protected, but also what is free for all to use." *Bonito Boats, Inc. v. Thunder Craft Boats, Inc.,* 489 U.S. 141, 151 (1989). In particular, the Court has long held that "[p]henomena of nature, though just discovered, mental processes, and abstract intellectual concepts are not patentable" under § 101, since allowing individuals to patent these fundamental principles would "wholly pre-empt" the public's access to the "basic tools of scientific and technological work." *Gottschalk v. Benson,* 409 U.S. 63, 67, 72 (1972).

Second, in a series of cases that extend back over a century, the Court has stated that "[t]ransformation and reduction of an article to a different state or thing is *the clue* to the patentability of a process claim that does not include particular machines." *Diehr, supra,* at 184 (emphasis added). Application of this test, the so-called "machine-or-transformation test," has thus repeatedly helped the Court to determine what is "a patentable 'process.'" *Flook, supra,* at 589.

Third, while the machine-or-transformation test has always been a "useful and important clue," it has never been the "sole test" for determining patentability. Rather, the Court has emphasized that a process claim meets the requirements of § 101 when, "considered as a whole," it "is performing a function which the patent laws were designed to protect (*e.g.,* transforming or reducing an article to a different state or thing)." *Diehr, supra,* at 192. The machine-or-transformation test is thus an *important example* of how a court can determine patentability under § 101, but the Federal Circuit erred in this case by treating it as the *exclusive test.*

Fourth, although the machine-or-transformation test is not the only test for patentability, this by no means indicates that anything which produces a " 'useful, concrete, and tangible result,' " *State Street Bank & Trust Co.,* is patentable. "[T]his Court has never made such a statement and, if taken literally, the statement would cover instances where this Court has held the contrary." *Laboratory Corp. of America Holdings v. Metabolite Laboratories, Inc.,* 548 U.S. 124, 136 (2006) (Breyer, J., dissenting from dismissal of certiorari as improvidently granted). Indeed, the introduction of the "useful, concrete, and tangible result" approach to patentability, associated with the Federal Circuit's *State Street* decision, preceded the granting of patents that "ranged from the somewhat ridiculous to the truly absurd." *In re Bilski,* 545 F.3d 943, 1004 (CA Fed. 2008) (Mayer, J., dissenting) (citing patents on, *inter alia,* a "method of training janitors to dust and vacuum using video displays," a "system for toilet reservations," and a "method of using color-coded bracelets to designate dating status in order to limit 'the embarrassment of rejection' "). To the extent that the Federal Circuit's decision in this case rejected that approach, nothing in today's decision should be taken as disapproving of that determination.

In sum, it is my view that, in reemphasizing that the "machine-or-transformation" test is not necessarily the *sole* test of patentability, the Court intends neither to de-emphasize the test's usefulness nor to suggest that many patentable processes lie beyond its reach.

Comments

1. *Judicial Restraint and the Unexpected Nature of Innovation.* The *Bilski* opinion kept the doors of section 101 wide open; and, absent some textual indication from Congress, refused to find categorical exclusions beyond three traditional filters: laws of nature, abstract ideas, and physical phenomena. In this regard, *Bilski* is an exercise in judicial restraint. The *Bilski* Court could have, as Justice Stevens advocated for in his dissent, found certain types of inventions ineligible for patent protection. Compare *Bilski*'s restrained approach to *Chakrabarty*, whereby Chief Justice Burger rebuffed the petitioner's argument that microorganisms cannot qualify as eligible subject matter absent express Congressional authorization. Citing *Marbury v. Madison*, the Court stated that Congress had spoken (i.e., section 101), and that "it is the province and duty" of the Court to provide meaning to the relevant statutory text.

   Bilski was also sensitive to the role of incentives, noting that Congress assumed a "permissive approach to patent eligibility to ensure that 'ingenuity should receive a liberal encouragement'" (quoting *Chakrabarty*). Moreover, a restrictive reading of section 101 would be inconsistent with the nature of innovation because "times change" and "[t]echnology and other innovations progress in unexpected ways." As such, "[a] categorical rule denying patent protection for 'inventions in areas not contemplated by Congress . . . would frustrate the purposes of the patent law.'" *Cf. Chakrabarty*, 447 U.S. at 316 ("A rule that unanticipated inventions are without protection would conflict with the core concept of the patent law that anticipation undermines patentability. . . . Congress employed broad general language in drafting § 101 precisely because such inventions are often unforeseeable.").

   Similarly, the Federal Circuit *Bilski* opinion asserted that the core principle of its subject matter jurisprudence is inclusiveness, given the unpredictable nature and extraordinary diversity of technological innovation. The court refused to create categorical exclusions, but of course recognized that laws of nature, physical phenomena, and abstract ideas (or what, during oral argument, Chief Judge Michel referred to as "the three No No's") are not patentable. As the Federal Circuit wrote in footnote 23, "we decline to adopt a broad exclusion over software or any other such category of subject matter beyond the exclusion of claims drawn to fundamental principles set forth by the Supreme Court." *Bilski*, 545 F.3d at 960. For a discussion on the benefits and shortcomings of rules and standards in the context of patent law's eligibility requirement, *see* Craig Allen Nard, *Legal Forms and the Common Law of Patents*, 90 B.U. L. Rev. 51 (2010), and John F. Duffy, *Rules and Standards on the Forefront of Patentability*, 51 Wm. & Mary L. Rev. 609 (2009).

2. *What Is the Machine-Transformation Test?* In Federal Circuit *Bilski*, the court— purportedly based on Supreme Court precedent—erected what has come to

be known as the machine-transformation test. This test holds that a process is eligible for patent protection when "(1) it is tied to a particular machine or apparatus, or (2) it transforms a particular article into a different state or thing." 545 F.3d at 954. The court added two additional filters in unpacking this test, namely that the claimed machine or transformation of an article "must impose meaningful limits on the claim's scope" to satisfy section 101's eligibility requirements, and the specific machine or transformation "must not merely be insignificant extra-solution activity." Accordingly, the machine-transformation test can be viewed as a rule-like framework that is broad and inclusive, but not without underlying considerations that can inform the subject matter analysis. The question remains as to how aggressively the Federal Circuit and PTO will apply the machine-transformation framework. See Comment 3.

The Supreme Court faulted the Federal Circuit for identifying the machine-transformation rule as the *sole* test for what constitutes eligible subject matter, but the Court did not quibble with the Federal Circuit's description or characterization of the test. And the Court underscored that the machine-transformation test "is a useful and important clue, an investigative tool, for determining whether some claimed inventions are processes under §101." But what is this test?

a. *What Is a "Machine"?* The Federal Circuit did not elaborate on the machine component, but other case law have stated "a machine is a 'concrete thing, consisting of parts, or of certain devices and combination of devices,'" which "'includes every mechanical device or combination of mechanical powers and devices to perform some function and produce a certain effect or result.'" *See In re Nuijten*, 500 F.3d 1346, 1355 (Fed. Cir. 2007) (denying patent eligibility for a claim to an encoded signal used for reducing distortion in, for example, a digital audio file); *In re Ferguson*, 558 F.3d 1359, 1364 (Fed. Cir. 2009) (denying patent eligibility based on *Bilski* for a claim for marketing a product because "applicants' method claims are not tied to any concrete parts, devices, or combination of devices").

Bilski left open the question "whether or when recitation of a computer suffices to tie a process claim to a particular machine." In *Cybersource Corp. v. Retail Decisions, Inc.*, 654 F.3d 1366, 1375 (Fed. Cir. 2011), the Federal Circuit stated that programming a general purpose computer to perform an algorithm creates a new machine, because a general purpose computer in effect becomes a special purpose computer once it is programmed to perform particular functions pursuant to instructions from program software. In contrast, reciting the use of a computer to execute an algorithm that can be performed entirely in the human mind is not eligible. *See also Ultramercial, LLC v. Hulu, LLC*, 657 F.3d 1323, 1329 (Fed. Cir. 2011) (stating "a programmed computer contains circuitry unique to that computer" and a "new machine could be claimed in terms of a complex array of hardware circuits, or more efficiently, in terms of the programming that facilitates a unique function").

What is a "particular machine"? The common law will have to play itself out and draw the line at the appropriate level of abstraction, but one can plausibly argue that under *Benson,* a claimed process tied to a computer may not satisfy the machine prong unless the claim is geared toward a real-world application, something concrete, not overly abstract. In other words, a computer is not a "particular machine." As the Federal Circuit noted, in *Benson* "the limitations tying the process to a computer were not actually limiting because the fundamental principle at issue, a particular algorithm, had no utility other than operating on a digital computer."

But this may be too broad a reading of *Benson*. Federal Circuit *Bilski* recognized that "*Benson* presents a difficult case" because "the claimed process operated on a machine, a digital computer, but was still held to be ineligible subject matter." Thus, the claimed process in *Benson* arguably satisfies the machine-transformation test. One way to reconcile *Benson* with the machine-transformation test, therefore, is find another reason why the *Benson* claims were deemed ineligible. This other reason may be that Benson's claimed invention would have preempted a fundamental principle, particularly because the only use of the claimed algorithm was on a digital computer. *See* Federal Circuit *Bilski*, footnote 9. That is, the claims "purported to cover any use of the claimed method in a general-purpose digital computer of any type." *Id.* Thus, a claim to an algorithm tied to a computer may be eligible if the algorithm has additional computer-related uses beyond what is claimed.

For a discussion of preemption, abstract ideas, and "machine" claim limitations, in the context of software-related inventions, *see CLS Bank Int'l v. Alice Corp.*, 717 F.3d 1269 (Fed. Cir. 2013) (*en banc*) discussed in Comment 4, below.

b. *What Is a "Transformation"?* Regarding the transformation component, the Federal Circuit made clear that the transformation "must be central to the purpose of the claimed process" and must transform an "article." It is hard to know what the court meant by the former other than the transformation imposes "meaningful limits" on claim scope. Regarding the latter, the court endeavored to clarify "what sorts of things constitute 'articles.'" For instance, a claimed process directed toward "a chemical or physical transformation of *physical objects or substances*" (emphasis in original). And a claimed process that employs electronic signals and electronically manipulated data are eligible if the data represents physical or tangible objects. As an example, the court used the dependent claim in *Abele* wherein transformed data were represented in the form of bone structure and organs. The court added the "electronic transformation of the data itself into a visual depiction in *Abele* was sufficient." But the issue becomes more difficult as you move away from physicality. What about data transformations that do not represent physical or tangible information on a computer screen; in other words, the transformation of data that results in an intangible representation. Thus, the physicality of the representation seems to play an important role in the transformation test. *See Cybersource*, 654 F.3d at 1370 (stating "mere collection and organization of data regarding credit card numbers and Internet addresses is insufficient to meet the transformation prong of the test").

In a case issued by the Board of Patent Appeals and Interferences, *Ex parte Halligan*, 89 U.S.P.Q.2d 1355 (B.P.A.I. 2008), the inventor claimed a method for identifying a trade secret under the common law, particularly the First Restatement of Torts § 757. The Board began its analysis by noting Federal Circuit *Bilski*:

> Explained that transformation of data is sufficient to render a process patent-eligible if the data represents physical and tangible objects, i.e., transformation of such raw data into a particular visual depiction of a physical object on a

display. The court further noted that transformation of data is insufficient to render a process patent-eligible if the data does not specify any particular type or nature of data and does not specify how or where the data was obtained or what the data represented.

Id. Based on this understanding of Federal Circuit *Bilski*, the Board rejected claims 122 and 123 under the transformation prong "because the data does not represent physical and tangible objects. Rather, the data represents information about a trade secret, which is an intangible asset." As such, the Board further stated in footnote 3, "we need not reach the issue of whether mere calculation of a number based on inputs of other numbers is a sufficient 'transformation' of data to render a process patent-eligible under §101." Claims 122 and 123 were not tied to a machine, and therefore, the machine prong was not relevant to these claims.

The preamble of claims 119 and 120, however, did recite: "*A programmed computer method* based upon the six factors of a trade secret from the First Restatement of Torts for identifying trade secrets within a plurality of potential trade secrets of a business, where each of the plurality of potential trade secrets comprise information." (Emphasis added.) The issue for the Board was "whether recitation of a programmed computer suffices to tie the process claims to a particular machine." The Board acknowledged that while Federal Circuit *Bilski* did not expressly discuss this issue, the court "did provide some guidance when it explained that the use of a specific machine must impose meaningful limits on the claim's scope to impart patent-eligibility." With this is mind, the Board rejected claims 119 and 120:

> Claims 119 and 120 recite a method performed on a programmed computer. This recitation fails to impose any meaningful limits on the claim's scope as it adds nothing more than a general purpose computer that has been programmed in an unspecified manner to implement the functional steps recited in the claims. Were the recitation of a "programmed computer" in combination with purely functional recitations of method steps, where the functions are implemented using an unspecified algorithm, sufficient to transform otherwise unpatentable method steps into a patent eligible process, this would exalt form over substance and would allow pre-emption of the fundamental principle present in the non-machine implemented method by the addition of the mere recitation of a "programmed computer." Such a field-of-use limitation is insufficient to render an otherwise ineligible process claim patent eligible.

Id.

Needless to say, the machine-transformation test is an imperfect device to gauge eligibility. As several commentators have written, the test "contains a number of ambiguities, leads to some bizarre results, and poorly tracks the stated goal of preventing the patenting of abstract ideas." Mark A. Lemley, Michael Risch, Ted Sichelman & R. Polk Wagner, *Life After Bilski*, 63 STAN. L. REV. 1315, 1322 (2011). As you read Comment 3 and have an opportunity to read the cases in full, ask yourself if the courts have provided enough guidance in the eligibility space, particularly with respect to what constitutes an abstract idea and mental process.

3. *Post-***Bilski***: What Is the Test for Patent Eligibility?* Presumably, an invention can satisfy section 101 even though it fails the machine-or-transformation test and vice versa. The Court charged the Federal Circuit to develop "other limiting

criteria that further the purposes of the Patent Act and are not inconsistent with its text." Thus, the common law—as it typically does—will evolve to fill in the interstices of section 101. Several Federal Circuit cases post-*Bilski* are illustrative of this process, but also highlight the difficulty in drawing clear lines between what is and is not patentable subject matter.

In the first case following *Bilski*, *Research Corp. Technologies v. Microsoft Corp.*, 627 F.3d 859 (Fed. Cir. 2010), the court found that section 101 was satisfied for patents relating to digital imaging halftoning, which "allows computer displays and printers to render an approximation of an image by using fewer colors or shades of gray than the original image." *Id.* at 863. The court read *Bilski* as refocusing eligibility on the three traditional filters. As the alleged infringer in *Research Corp.* did not assert the patents in suit claimed laws of nature or physical phenomena, the court turned its attention to whether the claims captured abstract ideas. In addressing this question, the court noted the Supreme Court "did not presume to provide a rigid formula or definition for abstractness" and invited the Federal Circuit "to develop 'other limiting criteria that further the purposes of the Patent Act and are not inconsistent with its text.'" *Id.* Accordingly,

> With that guidance, this court also will not presume to define "abstract" beyond the recognition that this disqualifying characteristic should exhibit itself so manifestly as to override the broad statutory categories of eligible subject matter and the statutory context that directs primary attention on the patentability criteria of the rest of the Patent Act. . . .
>
> The invention presents *functional and palpable applications in the field of computer technology*. These inventions address "a need in the art for a method of and apparatus for the halftone rendering of gray scale images in which a digital data processor is utilized in a simple and precise manner to accomplish the halftone rendering." . . . Indeed, this court notes that *inventions with specific applications or improvements to technologies in the marketplace are not likely to be so abstract* that they override the statutory language and framework of the Patent Act.

Id. at 868-869 (emphasis added). What is particularly interesting about *Research Corp.* is the court's treatment of eligibility vis-à-vis the other patentability requirements. The court indicated that section 101 was merely a "threshold test," and noted *Bilski* admonished that eligibility should not become a substitute for a "patentability analysis related to prior art, adequate disclosure, or the other conditions and requirements." *Id.* at 868. Thus, "a patent that presents a process sufficient to pass the coarse eligibility filter may nonetheless be invalid as indefinite because the invention would not provide sufficient particularity and clarity to inform skilled artisans of the bounds of the claim." Indeed, section 112 "provides powerful tools to weed out claims that may present a vague or indefinite disclosure of the invention." *Id.* at 869.

This channeling from section 101 to sections 102, 103, and 112 is also reflected in *CLS Bank Int'l v. Alice Corp. Pty. Ltd.*, 685 F.3d 1341, 1348 (Fed. Cir. 2012) ("Although §101 has been characterized as a 'threshold test,' and certainly *can* be addressed before other matters touching the validity of patents, it need not *always* be addressed first, particularly when other sections might be discerned by the trial judge as having the promise to resolve a dispute more expeditiously or with more clarity and predictability.") (emphasis in original). *See* Comment 4 for more on *CLS. See also Classen Immunotherapies, Inc. v. Biogen IDEC*, 659 F.3d 1057, 1073 (Fed. Cir. 2011) (Rader, J., additional views) (arguing because a robust eligibility requirement adds cost and complexity to the patent system, and the patent code "already contains ample protections against vague claims," the Federal Court "should decline to accept invitations to restrict subject matter eligibility"), and Judge Plager's opinion in *Dealertrack v. Huber*, 674 F.3d 1315, 1335 (Fed. Cir. 2012) (Plager, J., concurring in part and dissenting in part) ("I believe that this court should exercise its inherent power to control the processes of litigation, and insist that litigants, and trial courts, initially address patent invalidity issues in infringement suits in terms of the defenses provided in the statute: 'conditions of patentability,' specifically §§102 and 103, and in addition §112, and not foray into the jurisprudential morass of §101 unless absolutely necessary."). USPTO Director Kappos wrote approvingly of *CLS Bank Int'l*'s approach to sequencing the patentability requirements, stating "[b]ased on my experience, I appreciate the wisdom of the court's discussion relating to resolving disputed claims by focusing initially on patentability requirements of §102, 103, and 112, rather than §101." *See Director Kappos: Some Thoughts on Patentability*, at Patently-O (Aug. 4, 2012) (http://www.patentlyo.com/patent/2012/08/director-kappos-some-thoughts-on-patentability.html).

Eligibility was also satisfied in *Ultramercial, LLC v. Hulu, LLC*, 657 F.3d 1323 (Fed. Cir. 2011). The invention related to a method for distributing copyrighted material (e.g., songs) over the Internet where the consumer receives a copyrighted product for free in exchange for viewing an advertisement, and the advertiser pays for the copyrighted work. The court held this method claimed in the '545 patent is eligible for patent protection. According to the court, "the '545 patent does not simply claim the age-old idea that advertising can serve as currency," but rather "discloses a practical application of this idea." *Id.* at 1328. The court noted that section 101 merely provides a "threshold check" and the patentability ultimately depends on novelty, nonobviousness, and disclosure determinations.

The court reached a different result in *CyberSource Corp. v. Retail Decisions, Inc.*, 654 F.3d 1366 (Fed. Cir. 2011), wherein the patent related to a "method and system for detecting fraud in a credit card transaction between [a] consumer and a merchant over the Internet" by relying on "Internet address" information to discern whether an IP address relating to the particular transaction "is consistent with other Internet addresses [that have been] used in transactions utilizing [the same] credit card." The court first analyzed the claimed invention under the machine-transformation test, and found that section 101 was not satisfied. Because the machine-transformation test is not dispositive, the court also found the claimed invention was an unpatentable mental process, which is a "subcategory of unpatentable abstract ideas." Mental processes are not patentable because the "application of [only] human intelligence to the solution of practical problems is no more than a claim to a fundamental principle." *Bilski*, 545 F.3d at 965.

4. **Bilski, CLS Bank *and Software-Related Patents.*** The Supreme Court refused to categorically preclude software patents. As the Court noted, "it was once forcefully argued that until recent times, 'well-established principles of patent law probably would have prevented the issuance of a valid patent on almost any conceivable computer program.' *Diehr*, (Stevens, J., dissenting). But this

fact does not mean that unforeseen innovations such as computer programs are always unpatentable. Section 101 is a 'dynamic provision designed to encompass new and unforeseen inventions.'" *J.E.M. Ag. Supply, Inc. v. Pioneer Hi-Bred Int'l, Inc.*, 534 U.S. 124, 135 (2001).

The Federal Circuit's *Bilski* opinion said very little about the patentability of software, or more generally, computers—other than—like the Supreme Court—refuse to recognize a categorical exclusion. Indeed, Supreme Court *Bilski*, as noted above, eschewed explicit subject matter exclusions in footnote 23. The Federal Circuit has, however, been sympathetic to software patents, recently noting that "[f]ar from abstract ideas, advances in computer technology—both hardware and software—drive innovation in every area of scientific and technical endeavor." *Ultramercial*, 657 F.3d at 1329.

Nonetheless, despite decades of case law and commentary, there remains a great deal of ambiguity and controversy relating to the patentability and analytical framework of software. In an attempt to add some certainty in this space, the Federal Circuit agreed to hear *en banc CLS Bank Int'l v. Alice Corp.*, 717 F.3d 1269 (Fed. Cir. 2013). The patents in this case were computer-implemented inventions—software—that concern "the management of risk relating to specified, yet unknown, future events." In particular, the patents claim subject matter relating to "a computerized trading platform used for conducting financial transactions in which a third party settles obligations between a first and a second party so as to eliminate 'counterparty' or 'settlement' risk."

The *CLS Bank* court presented the following questions as part of its *en banc* order:

a. What test should the court adopt to determine whether a computer-implemented invention is a patent ineligible "abstract idea"; and when, if ever, does the presence of a computer in a claim lend patent eligibility to an otherwise patent-ineligible idea?

b. In assessing patent eligibility under 35 U.S.C. §101 of a computer-implemented invention, should it matter whether the invention is claimed as a method, system, or storage medium; and should such claims at times be considered equivalent for §101 purposes?

The court, in a one-paragraph per curiam opinion, held that the computer method and computer-readable medium claims relating to trading risk management contracts were ineligible for patent protection under section 101. But there was a 5-5 split among the Federal Circuit judges with respect to the computer systems claims. Remarkably, the *en banc* decision yielded six separate opinions, none of which has precedential value. Therefore, the clarity and resolution the aforementioned questions sought to achieve remains elusive. Despite the lack of binding authority a few remarks about the opinions of Judges Lourie and Rader are in order.

Judge Lourie recognized that section 101's "proper application to computer-implemented inventions . . . has long vexed" the courts. *CLS Bank*, 717 F.3d at 1276. While section 101 is inclusive, it must accommodate the three traditional filters: laws of nature, natural phenomena, and abstract ideas. For Judge Lourie, adding consistency and predictability to when these filters apply is paramount. As he noted, what constitutes an abstract idea "can feel subjective and unsystematic, and the debate often trends toward the meta-physical." *Id.* at ___. Indeed, the panel opinion also expressed frustration at the lack of clarity in defining an "abstract idea," noting "[t]he abstractness of the 'abstract ideas' test to patent eligibility has become a serious problem, leading to great uncertainty and to the devaluing of inventions of practical utility and economic potential"; and "[n]otwithstanding . . . well-intentioned efforts and the great volume of pages in the Federal Reporters treating the abstract ideas exception, the dividing line between inventions that are directed to patent ineligible abstract ideas and those that are not remains elusive." 685 F.3d at 1348-1349. And recall Justice Stevens's remark about the majority opinion in *Bilski*: "The Court, in sum, never provides a satisfying account of what constitutes an unpatentable abstract idea."

To add clarity regarding the application of the three filters, Judge Lourie identified several common themes among Supreme Court patent eligibility jurisprudence and constructed an analysis that focuses on whether a claim preempts abstract ideas or, alternatively, whether the claim contains "additional substantive limitations that narrow, confine, or otherwise tie down the claim so that, in practical terms, it does not cover the full abstract idea itself." Citing *Mayo*, a substantive limitation "has 'sometimes' been referred to as an 'inventive concept.'" An inventive concept "refers to a genuine human contribution to the claimed subject matter," an invention that is "a product of human ingenuity." Moreover, the human contribution "must represent more than a trivial appendix to the underlying abstract idea," beyond mere "tangential, routine, well-understood, or conventional" limitations. An example, according to Judge Lourie, is the "administering" and "determining" steps in *Mayo*. While these steps could not be characterized as an abstract idea, "they were necessary to every practical use of what [the Supreme Court] found to be a natural law and therefore were not truly limiting." In this regard, "the preemption analysis centers on the practical, real-world effects of the claim." Sensitive to the charge that "inventive concept" is just another name for novelty and nonobviousness, Judge Lourie wrote, unlike these two patentability requirements, analyzing eligibility "considers whether steps combined with a natural law or abstract idea are so insignificant, conventional, or routine as to yield a claim that effectively covers the natural law or abstract idea."

Claim 26 is illustrative of the type of limitations (italicized) that Judge Lourie found wanting. The claim read:

> [A] *computer*, coupled to said *data storage* unit and said *communications controller*, that is configured to (a) receive a transaction from said first party device via said communications controller; (b) electronically adjust said first account and said third account . . . after ensuring that said first party and/or said second party have adequate value in said first account and/or said third account, respectively; and (c) generate an instruction to said first exchange institution and/or said second exchange institution to adjust said second account and/or said fourth account in accordance with the adjustment of said first account and/or said third account. . . .

(Emphasis added.) According to Judge Lourie:

> For all practical purposes, *every* general-purpose computer will include "a computer," "a data storage unit," and "a communications controller" that would be

capable of performing the same generalized functions required of the claimed systems to carry out the otherwise abstract methods recited therein.

Therefore, as with the asserted method claims, such limitations are not actually limiting in the sense required under §101; they provide no significant "inventive concept." The system claims are instead akin to stating the abstract idea of third-party intermediation and adding the words: "apply it" on a computer. *See Mayo.* That is not sufficient for patent eligibility, and the system claims before us fail to define patent-eligible subject matter under §101, just as do the method and computer-readable medium claims.

A particular computer system, composed of wires, plastic, and silicon, is no doubt a tangible machine. But that is not the question. The question we must consider is whether a *patent claim* that ostensibly describes such a system on its face represents something more than an abstract idea in legal substance. . . . No question should have arisen concerning the eligibility of claims to basic computer hardware. But we are living and judging now, and have before us not the patent eligibility of specific types of computers or computer components, but computers that have routinely been adapted by software consisting of abstract ideas, and claimed as such, to do all sorts of tasks that formerly were performed by humans. And the Supreme Court has told us that, while avoiding confusion between §101 and §§102 and 103, merely adding existing computer technology to abstract ideas—mental steps—does not as a matter of substance convert an abstract idea into a machine.

We are not here faced with a computer *per se*. Such are surely patent-eligible machines. We are faced with abstract methods coupled with computers adapted to perform those methods.

(Emphasis in original.)

Judge Rader expressed a divergent view of section 101, which he sees as broad in scope and receptive to inventions that fit into one of the defined statutory categories. Turning to the exceptions or filters, Judge Rader emphasized that courts must consider the claim language as a whole, because "[a]ny claim can be stripped down, simplified, generalized, or paraphrased to remove all of its concrete limitations, until at its core, something that could be characterized as an abstract idea is revealed." The key distinction is between a claim that seeks to patent an idea (ineligible) itself or the application of that idea (eligible). To assist in drawing this distinction, the "relevant inquiry must be whether a claim includes *meaningful* limitations restricting it to an application." (Emphasis in original.) Meaningful limitations include reference to "material objects or specific examples." For example, a claim that "merely describes an abstract idea" or "covers all practical applications" of the idea is ineligible for patent protection because the claim would preempt all uses of the idea. A claim will also be ineligible "if its purported limitations provide no real direction, cover all possible ways to achieve the provided result, or are overly-generalized." In contrast, a meaningful limitation is, for example, one that "requires a particular machine implementing a process or a particular transformation of matter." In addition, eligibility will obtain when a patent applicant adds "limitations which are essential to the invention."

With respect to computer-implemented inventions, more than recitation of a general purpose computer is needed to satisfy section 101. But a claim that "tie[s] the otherwise abstract idea to a *specific way* of doing something with a computer, or a *specific computer* for doing something" is likely patent eligible. Examples of meaningful limitations "may include the computer being part of the solution, being integral to the performance of the method, or containing an improvement in computer technology." Accordingly,

> [W]e must examine whether, despite falling within the plain language of Section 101, clear and convincing evidence shows that a claim to a computer-implemented invention is barred from patent eligibility by reason of the narrow judicial prohibition against claiming an abstract idea. In *Bilski* the Court analyzed whether, and under what circumstances, a method claim's tie to a machine could make it a practical application of the underlying idea, and thus patent-eligible. The Court explained that a machine tie, though not required, is a "useful and important clue" that a method claim is patent-eligible. *Bilski*, 130 S. Ct. at 3227. If tying a method to a machine can be an important indication of patent-eligibility, it would seem that a claim embodying the *machine itself*, with all its structural and functional limitations, would rarely, if ever, be an abstract idea.
>
> Indeed, in theory, an inventor could claim a machine combination with circuitry, transistors, capacitors, and other tangible electronic components precisely arrayed to accomplish the function of translating Chinese to English. These complex interrelated machine components would squarely fit within the terms of Section 101 and involve nothing theoretical, highly generalized, or otherwise abstract. The fact that innovation has allowed these machines to move from vacuum-tube-filled specialized mechanical behemoths, to generalized machines changed by punch cards, to electronically programmable machines that can fit in the palm of your hand, does not render them abstract.

(Emphasis in original.) Prior to oral arguments, then USPTO Commissioner David Kappos gave a keynote address to the Center for American Progress strongly defending software patents:

> Software patents, like all patents, are a form of innovation currency. They are also ecosystem enablers, and job creators. The innovation protected by software patents is highly integrated with hardware. All of it must remain eligible for protection. . . . You know, the history of software patents is not a perfect one, although things are improving. . . . But it's important to note that, during the so-called smartphone patent wars, innovation continues at breakneck pace. A system like ours, in which innovation is happening faster than consumers can keep up, cannot fairly be characterized as "broken." The fact is, the explosion of innovation—and follow-on litigation—that we see across consumer electronics hardware and software is a direct reflection of how our patent system wires us for innovation. It's both natural and reasonable that in a fast-growing, competitive market, innovators would seek to protect their breakthroughs using our patent system.

November 20, 2012. For a full version of the speech, *see* http://www.uspto.gov/news/speeches/2012/kappos_CAP.jsp.

5. *Software and Patents: A Complex and Controversial Relationship.* The patenting of software has always been controversial. Software firms, especially during the 1980s, turned to copyright law as a means of appropriating their innovations. Code was considered a form of expression. But by the early 1990s, copyrights became less important as courts began narrowly interpreting copyright law as applied to software. *See, e.g., Apple Computer, Inc. v. Microsoft,*

Inc., 35 F.3d 1435 (9th Cir. 1994) (denying copyright protection for Apple's graphical user interface); *Lotus Development Corp. v. Borland International, Inc.*, 49 F.3d 807 (1st Cir. 1995) (holding no copyright protection for pulldown menus). As such, copyright doctrine was seen as an increasingly poor fit for software. Copyright law protects the expression of the software code, not functional elements of the software. And reverse engineering is a rather straightforward means of obtaining access to software's functionality. Unlike a patent, a copyright does not protect its owner against reverse engineering, which is considered a form of fair use. *See Sony Computer Entertainment, Inc. v. Connectix Corp.*, 203 F.3d 596 (9th Cir. 2000). *See also* Robert J. Mann, *Do Patents Facilitate Financing in the Software Industry*, 83 Tex. L. Rev. 961, 1013, 1015 (2005) (stating "[t]he most obvious problem with copyright protection for software relates to reverse engineering" by competitors, but copyright law does have an important role in preventing piracy by customers and code "theft" from departing employees); Peter S. Menell, *Envisioning Copyright Law's Digital Future*, 36 N.Y.L. Sch. L. Rev. 63, 65-66 (2003) ("Copyright law provides a thin layer of protection for computer software, effectively prohibiting wholesale piracy of computer programs without affording control for interface specifications and other essential elements of computer functionality."). Thus, in many respects, patent law is a much more attractive option for software firms.

Diehr was decided in 1981, but it was not until the 1990s that software patents became more commonplace. *See, e.g., Arrhythmia Research Technology Inc. v. Corazonix Corp.*, 958 F.2d 1053 (Fed. Cir. 1992). In fact, the number of software patent applications and issued patents increased dramatically in the 1990s. *See* Stuart J.H. Graham & David C. Mowery, *Intellectual Property Protection in the U.S. Software Industry*, in Patents in the Knowledge-Based Economy 219 (Wesley A. Cohen & Stephen A. Merrill eds., 2003); James Bessen & Robert M. Hunt, *An Empirical Look at Software Patents*, 16 J. Econ. & Mgmt. Strategy 157 (2007). As Julie Cohen and Mark Lemley write, "the past three decades have witnessed an about-face on the question of software's eligibility for patent protection . . . [as] software's status as patentable subject matter was first doubted, then grudgingly admitted, and finally embraced." Julie E. Cohen & Mark A. Lemley, *Patent Scope and Innovation in the Software Industry*, 89 Cal. L. Rev. 1, 7 (2001).

But software patents remain controversial. Some economists have argued patents are not needed to incentivize software innovation, and indeed, are harmful to software innovation because the sheer number of software patents makes it difficult for innovators to obtain permission to pursue their research. *See* James Bessen & Michael J. Meurer, Patent Failure: How Judges, Bureaucrats, and Lawyers Put Innovators at Risk 96-146 (2008) (asserting that with the exception of chemical and pharmaceutical inventions, patents discourage innovation—particularly in the IT industry—because of the number of patents and rising costs of litigation). Software patents can present significant barriers to entry for small entities, imposing a tax of sorts, either in the form of due diligence (e.g., money spent on infringement studies of existing patents). As a group of economists recently wrote in opposition to the failed European Software Directive, "[s]oftware patents damage innovation by raising costs and uncertainties in assembling the many components needed for complex computer programs and constraining the speed and effectiveness of innovation." http://www.researchineurope.org/policy/pat-entdirltr.pdf. Moreover, large entities in the software industry have argued they are being plagued by low-quality patents owned by smaller entities. For criticisms of software patents, see JAMES BESSEN & MICHAEL J. MEURER, PATENT FAILURE: HOW JUDGES, BUREAUCRATS, AND LAWYERS PUT INNOVATORS AT RISK (2007); James Bessen & Eric Maskin, *Sequential Innovation, Patents and Imitation*, at http://ssrn.com/abstract=206189 (Jan. 2000); PATENTS IN THE KNOWLEDGE-BASED ECONOMY 2 (Wesley M. Cohen & Stephen A. Merrill eds., 2003); James Bessen, *Patent Thickets: Strategic Patenting of Complex Technologies*, available at http://papers.ssrn.com/sol3/papers.cfm?abstract_id=327760. The attitude within the IT industry generally has been described as one of mutually assured destruction, meaning that Firm 1 arms itself with patents because Firms 2, 3, and 4 have done the same. The first firm to sue another will be hit with counter-infringement suits. Of course, this can give rise to cross-licensing opportunities, assuming transaction costs are not prohibitive.

But other commentators have contested these claims. *See* Ted Sichelman, *Why* Bilski *Benefits Start-Up Companies*, at Patently-O Blog (June 29, 2010 at http://www.patentlyo.com) (stating "there is little evidence that these patent-holders required *startups* to license them in any significant numbers. The Berkeley Patent Survey found that only 8% of the population of respon-dent software companies and 12% of venture-backed software companies had licensed-in even one patent. In sum total, a relatively low percentage, 0.6% and 3%, respectively, reported licensing a patent solely to avoid a law-suit.") (The "Berkeley Patent Survey" can be found at Stuart J.H. Graham, Ted Sichelman, Robert P. Merges & Pamela Samuelson, *High Technology Entrepreneurs and the Patent System: Results of the 2008 Berkeley Patent Survey*, 24 BERKELEY TECH. L.J. 1248 (2010)). *See also* John R. Allison & Robert J. Mann, *The Disputed Quality of Software Patents*, at http://ssrn.com/abstract=970083 (March 2007) (disputing the notion that software patents are of a lower quality than other types of patents, and also stating that "the data substan-tially undermine the traditional story that large firms in the software indus-try are plagued by a large number of low-quality patents obtained by the smaller firms in the industry"). *See also* Mann, *Facilitate Financing, supra*, at 1004-1009 (rejecting software thicket thesis); Robert P. Merges, *Patents, Entry and Growth in the Software Industry*, at http://papers. ssrn.com/sol3/papers. cfm?abstract_id=926204 (asserting that patents have not damaged the soft-ware industry and new firm entry remains robust).

6. *Defining Software and the Software Patent.* It is common to think of software as part of a CD-ROM or that which forms part of a computer and provides it with functional applications. But it is more accurate to think of software as a series of instructions, known as source code and object code, "that directs a computer to perform specified functions or operations." *Fantasy Sports Props., Inc. v. Sportslines.com, Inc.*, 287 F.3d 1108, 1118 (Fed. Cir. 2002). Indeed, the PTO's Manual of Patent Examination Procedure (MPEP) states "a computer program is merely a set of instructions capable of being executed by a com-puter." MPEP §2106.IV.B.1(a) (8th ed. 2001).

It is particularly difficult to define a software patent and there is no univer-sally accepted definition. Perhaps the reason for this elusiveness has some-thing to do with software's pervasiveness across many industries that make categorization quite difficult. *See* Stuart J.H. Graham & David C. Mowery,

Software Patents: Good News or Bad News, http://tiger.gatech.edu/files/gt_tiger_software.pdf at 29 (May 2004) (stating "[o]ne of the thorniest problems in analyzing software patenting, of course, is defining and measuring software patents").

7. *The USPTO's Interim Guidelines.* On July 27, 2010, the USPTO issued interim examiner guidelines for determining eligible subject matter for process-related inventions. The guidelines incorporate four factors that are to be considered independently. The first two factors reflect the machine-transformation test:

   a. Whether the method involves or is executed by a particular machine or apparatus. If so, the claims are less likely to be drawn to an abstract idea; if not, they are more likely to be so drawn.

   b. Whether performance of the claimed method results in or otherwise involves a transformation of a particular article. If such a transformation exists, the claims are less likely to be drawn to an abstract idea; if not, they are more likely to be so drawn.

   c. Whether performance of the claimed method involves an application of a law of nature, even in the absence of a particular machine, apparatus, or transformation. If such an application exists, the claims are less likely to be drawn to an abstract idea; if not, they are more likely to be so drawn.

   d. Whether a general concept (which could also be recognized in such terms as a principle, theory, plan or scheme) is involved in executing the steps of the method. The presence of such a general concept can be a clue that the claim is drawn to an abstract idea.

   A subordinate factor within the first two factors relates to "the nature of the article transformed, i.e., whether it is an object or substance, weighing toward eligibility, compared to a concept such as a contractual obligation or mental judgment, which would weigh against eligibility." The guidelines do not address transformations of data. The "general concept" mentioned in the last factor is accompanied by a list of examples, including basic economic practices and theories (e.g., insurance, hedging); basic legal theories (e.g., contracts, dispute resolution); mathematical concepts (e.g., algorithms, geometry); mental activity (e.g., observation, opinion); interpersonal interactions or relationships (e.g., dating); teaching concepts (e.g., repetition, memorization); and human behavior (e.g., exercising, wearing clothing).

8. *Business Method and Other "Non-Traditional" Patents.* The *Bilski* opinion held that section 101 does not preclude the patentability of business methods. (Bilski's claimed invention was deemed ineligible because it was an abstract idea.) Thus, business method inventions remain viable as long as they satisfy the machine-transformation test (or some other yet to be constructed common law test) and do not fall into one of the three exclusionary categories. (Justice Stevens's dissent would have rendered business methods ineligible.)

   The *State Street Bank* case spurred patenting in business methods, financial tools, and the like. Indeed, the PTO was flooded with business method patents in the wake of *State Street Bank* and its rejection of the "ill-conceived exception." *But see* John F. Duffy, *Why Business Method Patents?,* at http://ssrn.

com/abstract=1501317 (arguing that the rise in business method patents is due to events outside the legal system, noting over "the last quarter of the twentieth century, the methods of business, finance and management underwent a tremendous transformation as vastly better information technologies and empirical tools became available").

The increase in patent applications posed problems for the PTO. *See* Robert P. Merges, *As Many as Six Possible Patents Before Breakfast: Property Rights for Business Concepts and Patent System Reform,* 14 BERKELEY TECH. L.J. 577 (1999). In addition, commentators have criticized business method patents. According to two commentators:

> Beyond the issue of permissible subject matter, settled by State Street, critics raise essentially two objections. First, some BMPs appear to be based on ideas that cannot reasonably be considered novel because similar methods have existed in various unprotected forms for some time. For example, Priceline. com's "reverse auction," in which purchasers list a maximum price and the software auctioneer finds a willing supplier, has antecedents in Dutch auctions and other selling methods. Similarly, Barnes & Noble contested the validity of Amazon's "one-click" patent on the grounds that other techniques involving a single operation by the consumer, contingent on the seller's ability to identify the consumer uniquely, were in operation prior to the patent's issuance in 1999. . . .
>
> Second, many patents cover remarkably broad claims that could permit patentees to exclude competition in a wide swath of Internet applications. . . . In brief, [business method patents] are controversial because they provide broad and lengthy exclusivity for inventions that may not be particularly novel or non-obvious.

Keith E. Maskus & Eina Vivian Wong, *Searching for Economic Balance in Business Method Patents,* 8 WASH. U. J.L. & POL'Y 289, 291-292 (2002). Rochelle Dreyfuss asserts that incentives other than patents are more germane to business method innovations:

> Business methods are . . . hard to free ride on. They depend in strong ways on the social structure within the firms utilizing compensation schemes, lines of reporting, supervising policies, and other business factors. Moreover, as we saw, sticky business methods are their own reward. With lock in, network effects, and even good old fashioned loyalty, lead time (the first mover advantage) goes a long way to assuring returns adequate to recoup costs and earn substantial profit. In sum, while business innovations are certainly desirable, it is not clear that business method patents are needed to spur people to create them.

Rochelle Cooper Dreyfuss, *Are Business Method Patents Bad for Business?,* 16 SANTA CLARA COMPUTER & HIGH TECH. L.J. 263, 274-275 (2000). *See also* Michael J. Meurer, *Business Method Patents and Patent Floods,* 8 WASH. U. J.L. & POL'Y 309 (2002); John R. Thomas, *Liberty and Property in Patent Law,* 39 HOUS. L. REV. 569 (2002). But some commentators have argued that the criticism of business method patents lacks empirical support, which has "led to undesirable results." *See, e.g.,* John R. Allison & Emerson H. Tiller, *The Business Method Patent Myth,* 18 BERKELEY TECH. L.J. 987, 990 (2003) (comparing Internet business method patents to large random sample of general patents and finding business method patents "actually fare quite well statistically").

Yet another concern about patenting business methods and financial tools is that these types of inventions are far removed from patent law's traditional technological subject matter. *See* John R. Thomas, *The Patenting of the Liberal Professions*, 40 B.C. L. REV. 1139 (1999) (criticizing the patenting of non-technological arts). Of course, *Bilski* rejected the technological arts test. For a lengthy debate on this issue, *see also Ex parte Lundgren*, 76 U.S.P.Q.2d 1385 (B.P.A.I. 2004).

One business method patent that received a great deal of publicity was Amazon.com's "one-click" ordering method. In fact, Amazon successfully obtained a preliminary injunction against Barnes & Noble, although the injunction was reversed on appeal. *See Amazon.com, Inc. v. Barnesandnoble.com, Inc.*, 239 F.3d 1343 (Fed. Cir. 2001). Other notable business method patents include Netflix.com's patent entitled "Method and Apparatus for Renting Items." *See* U.S. Patent No. 6584450 (from the Abstract: "According to a computer-implemented approach for renting items to customers, customers specify what items to rent using item selection criteria separate from deciding when to receive the specified items"); and also Amazon.com's "Internet-Based Customer Referral System." *See* U.S. Patent No. 6029141 (from the Abstract: "Disclosed is an Internet-based referral system that enables individuals and other business entities ("associates") to market products, in return for a commission, that are sold from a merchant's Web site").

COMPARATIVE PERSPECTIVE
Software and Business Method Patents in Europe

Compare *Bilski*'s "measured approach" with the European model. Article 52(2) of the European Patent Convention states: "The following . . . shall not be regarded as inventions—(a) discoveries, scientific theories and mathematical methods; (b) aesthetic creations; (c) schemes, rules and methods for performing mental acts, playing games or doing business, and programs for computers; (d) presentations of information." And Article 53 expressly excludes from patent protection:

(a) inventions the publication or exploitation of which would be contrary to "ordre public" or morality, provided that the exploitation shall not be deemed to be so contrary merely because it is prohibited by law or regulation in some or all of the Contracting States;

(b) plant or animal varieties or essentially biological processes for the production of plants or animals; this provision does not apply to microbiological processes or the products thereof.

Although there is substantive overlap regarding exclusions (e.g., scientific theories), there are important institutional differences and approaches to developing eligibility requirements.

Under Section 52(2)(c) of the European Patent Convention, methods of "doing business and programs for computers" are not eligible for patent protection. Article 52(3) states:

The provisions of paragraph 2 shall exclude patentability of the subject-matter or activities referred to in that provision only to the extent to which a European patent application or European patent relates to such subject-matter or activities as such.

Although the Europeans continue to view business method patents skeptically, the Patent Office in Europe has not shown the same skepticism toward software. The claimed invention satisfies the eligibility requirements as long as it reveals a "technical character." *See* EPO Guidelines for Substantive Examination, Part C, Chapter IV, §§2.1, 2.2. *See also Computer Program Product/IBM*, T 1173/97-3.5.1 (EPO Bd. of App. July 1, 1998). For instance, in 2005, 8,664 applications were filed in the "computing" field, doubling the amount of applications filed in 1999 (3,955), and doubling the number of applications in biochemistry/genetic engineering, which generated 4,098 applications in 2005. EPO 2005 ANNUAL REPORT (Business Report, p. 22). Indeed, Microsoft was a top-10 filer of applications in 2005 with 879.

While it is clear that the EPO issues patents on software-related inventions, despite Article 52 apparent prohibition, there remains a degree of uncertainty regarding enforcement as numerous national courts are less enthusiastic about software patents. Recall that there is no European-wide patent or community patent. Because of this disparate treatment of software-related patents among the EU member states, the software industry, much like the biotechnology industry before it, wanted to enhance certainty for software patents throughout Europe. To this end, the European Parliament considered a directive on European software patents in 2005, but rejected it overwhelmingly. In a study commissioned by the Parliament, the authors wrote that "conclusive evidence supporting a liberalization of existing European patent law and practice in respect of software . . . , on the basis of U.S. experience, does not exist." BNA Patent, Trademark & Copyright Law Daily (Sept. 26, 2003).

B. UTILITY

1. Operability and the Basic Utility Test

The utility requirement demands the invention be operable, that is, achieve some intended result. While there are examples of inoperable inventions (e.g., perpetual motion machines and the invention in *Swartz*), the operability requirement is easily satisfied.

IN RE SWARTZ
232 F.3d 862 (Fed. Cir. 2000)

PER CURIAM.

Mitchell R. Swartz appeals from the decision of the United States Patent and Trademark Office (PTO) Board of Patent Appeals and Interferences (Board), affirming the examiner's final rejection of claims 25-48 of application Serial No. 07/760,970 for lack of operability or utility under 35 U.S.C. § 101. . . .

The PTO has the initial burden of challenging a patent applicant's presumptively correct assertion of utility. If the PTO provides evidence showing that one of ordinary skill in the art would reasonably doubt the asserted utility, however, the burden shifts to the applicant to submit evidence sufficient to convince such a person of the invention's asserted utility. Here the PTO provided several references showing that results in the area of cold fusion were irreproducible. Thus the PTO provided substantial evidence that those skilled in the art would "reasonably doubt" the asserted utility and operability of cold fusion. *See In re Brana,* 51 F.3d 1560 (Fed. Cir. 1995). The examiner found that Mr. Swartz had not submitted evidence of operability that would be sufficient to overcome reasonable doubt. After its review of the evidence, the Board found that Mr. Swartz had "produced no persuasive objective evidence, in our view, that overcomes the examiner's position."

On this appeal, Mr. Swartz complains that the Board "ignored" evidence that he submitted and disregarded his arguments, and he invites this Court to examine voluminous record material that he urges supports his position on the issue of utility. Such conclusory allegations in an appeal brief are quite insufficient to establish that the Board's decision on the issue of utility is not supported by substantial evidence or to establish that the Board's ultimate conclusion of a lack of enablement is incorrect as a matter of law.

Finally, Mr. Swartz's attempt to show that his claims are directed to a process other than cold fusion must fail. In his written description and throughout prosecution of his application, Mr. Swartz continually represented his invention as relating to cold fusion.

For the reasons discussed above, the Board did not err in concluding that the utility of Mr. Swartz's claimed process had not been established and that his application did not satisfy the enablement requirement. Accordingly, the judgment of the Board is affirmed.

Comments

1. *The Utility of Fusion.* The utility requirement of *Swartz* looks to whether the claimed invention simply works; in other words, is the invention operable? The invention does not have to work perfectly or be better than the prior art. *See Brooktree Corp. v. Adv. Micro Devices, Inc.,* 977 F.2d 1555, 1571 (Fed Cir. 1992); *Stifbung v. Renishaw PLL,* 945 F.2d 1173, 1180 (Fed. Cir. 1991). Swartz's claims to cold fusion were not reproducible. Similarly, the Federal Circuit has affirmed utility rejections based on inoperability in *Newman v. Quigg,* 877 F.2d 1575 (Fed. Cir. 1989) (perpetual motion machine), and *Fregeau v. Mossinghoff,* 776 F.2d 1034 (Fed. Cir. 1985) (method for enhancing the flavor of a beverage by passing it through a magnetic field). In other words, the underlying scientific principle is implausible or inconsistent with what a skilled artisan would believe.

A great deal of money and time have been (and continues to be) expended on studying fusion, the process whereby heavy versions of hydrogen atoms (e.g., deuterium and tritium) fuse together to form helium. The reaction produces an immense amount of energy. Indeed, fusion occurs at the center of the sun, whereby hydrogen atoms collide under very high pressures resulting in intense light and heat of 30 million degrees Fahrenheit. The commercial benefit of fusion would be substantial because of the near limitless "clean" energy it would produce. But fusion, thus far, has not proven to be practical because of the enormous amount of energy required to begin the reaction. And although the International Thermonuclear Experimental Reactor Consortium is building the world's first large-scale nuclear fusion reactor in France, many advocates agree that practical application of fusion is not likely until 2040.

2. *Operability and Utility's Modern Application.* The *Swartz* case represents the modern analytical approach to utility that can be traced to *In re Brana.* In *Brana*, the Federal Circuit articulated a two-step test for determining whether the utility requirement has been met. First, the PTO "has the initial burden of challenging a *presumptively* correct assertion of utility in the disclosure." Second, "[o]nly after the PTO provides evidence showing that one of ordinary skill in the art would reasonably doubt the asserted utility does the burden shift to the applicant" to prove utility. *Brana*, 51 F.3d at 1566 (Fed. Cir. 1995) (emphasis added). The PTO may use peer-reviewed journals and anecdotal information. *See In re Dash*, 118 Fed. Appx. 488, 491 (Fed. Cir. 2004).

Under the operability requirement, the claim invention must be "capable of being used to effect the object proposed." *Mitchell v. Tilghman*, 86 U.S. (19 Wall.) 287, 396 (1873). But not every objective stated in the specification must be met before operability is satisfied. Indeed, "[w]hen a properly claimed invention meets at least one stated objective, utility under §101 is clearly shown." *Raytheon Co. v. Roper Corp.*, 724 F.2d 951, 958 (Fed. Cir. 1983). Moreover, the claimed invention need not be the best or only way to accomplish the stated objectives.

The operability prong of usefulness, according to one commentator, will typically disqualify inventions (1) "that violate the laws of nature" (e.g., perpetual motion machine); (2) that could possibly work, but that someone familiar with the subject matter would view as incredible" (e.g., cure for HIV/AIDS or Alzheimer's disease); and (3) "that cannot be implemented by following the patent's teachings" (e.g., insufficient detail in the specification or a misunderstanding of the nature of the invention). Michael Risch, *A Surprisingly Useful Requirement*, 19 GEO. MASON L. REV. 57, 65-66 (2011).

3. *Beneficial Utility and Patent Law's Erstwhile Morality Consideration.* In the nineteenth century, there was a morality component to the utility requirement, sometimes referred to as beneficial utility. Justice Story's opinion in *Bedford v. Hunt*, 3 F. Cas. 37, 37 (C.C.D. Mass. 1817) is largely considered the progenitor of the morality requirement. In *Hunt*, Justice Story wrote:

> By useful invention, in the statute, is meant such a one as may be applied to some beneficial use in society, in contradistinction to an invention, which is injurious to the morals, the health, or the good order of society.

Unlike the Europeans, the morality requirement is a relic of a bygone era, no longer a player in patent law. *See Juicy Whip, Inc. v. Orange Bang, Inc.*, 185 F.3d 1364, 1366 (Fed. Cir. 1999) ("To be sure, since Justice Story's opinion in *Lowell v. Lewis*, 15 F. Cas. 1018 (C.C.D. Mass. 1817), it has been stated that inventions that are 'injurious to the well-being, good policy, or sound morals of society' are unpatentable. . . . [But this principle] has not been applied broadly in recent years. . . . As the Supreme Court put the point more generally, 'Congress never intended that the patent laws should displace the police powers of the States, meaning by that term those powers by which the health, good order, peace and general welfare of the community are promoted.'"). For a discussion on the role of ethics and morality in patent law, *see* Cynthia M. Ho, *Splicing Morality and Patent Law: Issues Arising from Mixing Mice and Men*, 2 WASH. U. J.L. & POL'Y 247 (2000).

2. Substantial Utility

The most relevant and controversial aspect of the utility requirement relates to what is known as "substantial utility." It is in this form that the utility requirement retains practical significance, particularly as applied to chemical and biotechnology-related inventions. Over the past 10 years the PTO, although inconsistently, has turned to the utility requirement to cast doubt on the patentability of certain genomic-related inventions. The *In re Fisher* case, which relies on *Brenner v. Manson*, explores this issue.

BRENNER v. MANSON
383 U.S. 519 (1966)

Justice FORTAS delivered the opinion of the Court.

[Manson's request for an interference was denied by the examiner based on Manson's failure to comply with the utility requirement. The Court of Customs and Patent Appeals (CCPA) reversed, stating that "'where a claimed process produces a known product it is not necessary to show utility for the product.'" The Commissioner of Patents, Brenner, petitioned the Supreme Court—successfully—to grant certiorari.]

In December 1957, Howard Ringold and George Rosenkranz applied for a patent on an allegedly novel process for making certain known steroids. They claimed priority as of December 17, 1956, the date on which they had filed for a Mexican patent. . . .

In January 1960, Manson, a chemist engaged in steroid research, filed an application to patent precisely the same process described by Ringold and Rosenkranz. He asserted that it was he who had discovered the process, and that he had done so before December 17, 1956. Accordingly, he requested that an "interference" be declared in order to try out the issue of priority between his claim and that of Ringold and Rosenkranz.

A Patent Office examiner denied Manson's application, and the denial was affirmed by the Board of Appeals within the Patent Office. The ground for rejection was the failure "to disclose any utility for" the chemical compound produced by the process. This omission was not cured, in the opinion of the Patent

Office, by Manson's reference to an article in the November 1956 issue of the Journal of Organic Chemistry, 21 J. Org. Chem. 1333-1335, which revealed that steroids of a class which included the compound in question were undergoing screening for possible tumor-inhibiting effects in mice, and that a homologue adjacent to Manson's steroid had proven effective in that role. Said the Board of Appeals, "It is our view that the statutory requirement of usefulness of a product cannot be presumed merely because it happens to be closely related to another compound which is known to be useful."

The Court of Customs and Patent Appeals (hereinafter CCPA) reversed. The court held that "where a claimed process produces a known product it is not necessary to show utility for the product," so long as the product "is not alleged to be detrimental to the public interest." *Certiorari* was granted to resolve this running dispute over what constitutes "utility" in chemical process claims.

II.

Our starting point is the proposition, neither disputed nor disputable, that one may patent only that which is "useful." [U]tility has maintained a central place in all of our patent legislation, beginning with the first patent law in 1790 and culminating in the present law's provision that

> whoever invents or discovers any new and useful process, machine, manufacture, or composition of matter, or any new and useful improvement thereof, may obtain a patent therefor, subject to the conditions and requirements of this title.

As is so often the case, however, a simple, everyday word can be pregnant with ambiguity when applied to the facts of life. That this is so is demonstrated by the present conflict between the Patent Office and the CCPA over how the test is to be applied to a chemical process which yields an already known product whose utility—other than as a possible object of scientific inquiry—has not yet been evidenced. It was not long ago that agency and court seemed of one mind on the question. In *Application of Bremner,* 182 F.2d 216, 217, the court affirmed rejection by the Patent Office of both process and product claims. It noted that "no use for the products claimed to be developed by the processes had been shown in the specification." It held that "It was never intended that a patent be granted upon a product, or a process producing a product, unless such product be useful."

The Patent Office has remained stead-fast in this view. The CCPA, however, has moved sharply away from *Bremner.* The trend began in *Application of Nelson.* There, the court reversed the Patent Office's rejection of a claim on a process yielding chemical intermediates "useful to chemists doing research on steroids," despite the absence of evidence that any of the steroids thus ultimately produced were themselves "useful." The trend has accelerated, culminating in the present case where the court held it sufficient that a process produces the result intended and is not "detrimental to the public interest."

Respondent does not—at least in the first instance—rest upon the extreme proposition, advanced by the court below, that a novel chemical process is patentable so long as it yields the intended product and so long as the product is not itself "detrimental." Nor does he commit the outcome of his claim to the slightly more conventional proposition that any process is "useful" within the meaning of §101 if it produces a compound whose potential usefulness is under investigation by serious scientific researchers, although he urges this position, too, as an alternative basis for affirming the decision of the CCPA. Rather, he begins with the much more orthodox argument that his process has a specific utility which would entitle him to a declaration of interference even under the Patent Office's reading of §101. The claim is that the supporting affidavits filed pursuant to Rule 204(b), by reference to Ringold's 1956 article, reveal that an adjacent homologue of the steroid yielded by his process has been demonstrated to have tumor-inhibiting effects in mice, and that this discloses the requisite utility. We do not accept any of these theories as an adequate basis for overriding the determination of the Patent Office that the "utility" requirement has not been met.

Even on the assumption that the process would be patentable were respondent to show that the steroid produced had a tumor-inhibiting effect in mice, we would not overrule the Patent Office finding that respondent has not made such a showing. The Patent Office held that, despite the reference to the adjacent homologue, respondent's papers did not disclose a sufficient likelihood that the steroid yielded by his process would have similar tumor-inhibiting characteristics. Indeed, respondent himself recognized that the presumption that adjacent homologues have the same utility has been challenged in the steroid field because of "a greater known unpredictability of compounds in that field." In these circumstances and in this technical area, we would not overturn the finding of the Primary Examiner, affirmed by the Board of Appeals and not challenged by the CCPA.

The second and third points of respondent's argument present issues of much importance. Is a chemical process "useful" within the meaning of §101 either (1) because it works — i.e., produces the intended product — or (2) because the compound yielded belongs to a class of compounds now the subject of serious scientific investigation? These contentions present the basic problem for our adjudication. Since we find no specific assistance in the legislative materials underlying §101, we are remitted to an analysis of the problem in light of the general intent of Congress, the purposes of the patent system, and the implications of a decision one way or the other.

In support of his plea that we attenuate the requirement of "utility," respondent relies upon Justice Story's well-known statement that a "useful" invention is one "which may be applied to a beneficial use in society, in contradistinction to an invention injurious to the morals, health, or good order of society, or frivolous and insignificant" — and upon the assertion that to do so would encourage inventors of new processes to publicize the event for the benefit of the entire scientific community, thus widening the search for uses and increasing the fund of scientific knowledge. Justice Story's language sheds little light on our subject. Narrowly read, it does no more than compel us to decide whether the invention in question is "frivolous and insignificant" — a query no easier of application than the one built into the statute. Read more broadly, so as to allow the patenting of any invention not positively harmful to society, it places such a special meaning on the word "useful" that we cannot accept it in the absence of evidence that Congress so intended. There are, after all, many things in this world which may not be considered "useful" but which, nevertheless, are totally without a capacity for harm.

It is true, of course, that one of the purposes of the patent system is to encourage dissemination of information concerning discoveries and inventions. And it may be that inability to patent a process to some extent discourages disclosure and leads to greater secrecy than would otherwise be the case. The inventor of the process, or the corporate organization by which he is employed, has some incentive to keep the invention secret while uses for the product are searched out. However, in light of the highly developed art of drafting patent claims so that they disclose as little useful information as possible—while broadening the scope of the claim as widely as possible—the argument based upon the virtue of disclosure must be warily evaluated. Moreover, the pressure for secrecy is easily exaggerated, for if the inventor of a process cannot himself ascertain a "use" for that which his process yields, he has every incentive to make his invention known to those able to do so. Finally, how likely is disclosure of a patented process to spur research by others into the uses to which the product may be put? To the extent that the patentee has power to enforce his patent, there is little incentive for others to undertake a search for uses.

Whatever weight is attached to the value of encouraging disclosure and of inhibiting secrecy, we believe a more compelling consideration is that a process patent in the chemical field, which has not been developed and pointed to the degree of specific utility, creates a monopoly of knowledge which should be granted only if clearly commanded by the statute. Until the process claim has been reduced to production of a product shown to be useful, the metes and bounds of that monopoly are not capable of precise delineation. It may engross a vast, unknown, and perhaps unknowable area. Such a patent may confer power to block off whole areas of scientific development, without compensating benefit to the public. The basic *quid pro quo* contemplated by the Constitution and the Congress for granting a patent monopoly is the benefit derived by the public from an invention with substantial utility. Unless and until a process is refined and developed to this point—where specific benefit exists in currently available form—there is insufficient justification for permitting an applicant to engross what may prove to be a broad field.

These arguments for and against the patentability of a process which either has no known use or is useful only in the sense that it may be an object of scientific research would apply equally to the patenting of the product produced by the process. Respondent appears to concede that with respect to a product, as opposed to a process, Congress has struck the balance on the side of nonpatentability unless "utility" is shown. Indeed, the decisions of the CCPA are in accord with the view that a product may not be patented absent a showing of utility greater than any adduced in the present case. We find absolutely no warrant for the proposition that although Congress intended that no patent be granted on a chemical compound whose sole "utility" consists of its potential role as an object of use-testing, a different set of rules was meant to apply to the process which yielded the unpatentable product. That proposition seems to us little more than an attempt to evade the impact of the rules which concededly govern patentability of the product itself.

This is not to say that we mean to disparage the importance of contributions to the fund of scientific information short of the invention of something "useful," or that we are blind to the prospect that what now seems without "use" may tomorrow command the grateful attention of the public. But a patent is not a hunting license. It is not a reward for the search, but compensation for its successful conclusion. "(A) patent system must be related to the world of commerce rather than to the realm of philosophy. . . ."

The judgment of the CCPA is reversed.

Justice HARLAN, concurring in part and dissenting in part.

* * *

What I find most troubling about the result reached by the Court is the impact it may have on chemical research. Chemistry is a highly interrelated field and a tangible benefit for society may be the outcome of a number of different discoveries, one discovery building upon the next. To encourage one chemist or research facility to invent and disseminate new processes and products may be vital to progress, although the product or process be without "utility" as the Court defines the term, because that discovery permits someone else to take a further but perhaps less difficult step leading to a commercially useful item. In my view, our awareness in this age of the importance of achieving and publicizing basic research should lead this Court to resolve uncertainties in its favor and uphold the respondent's position in this case.

This position is strengthened, I think, by what appears to have been the practice of the Patent Office during most of this century. While available proof is not conclusive, the commentators seem to be in agreement that until *Application of Bremner,* 182 F.2d 216 in 1950, chemical patent applications were commonly granted although no resulting end use was stated or the statement was in extremely broad terms. Taking this to be true, *Bremner* represented a deviation from established practice which the CCPA has now sought to remedy in part only to find that the Patent Office does not want to return to the beaten track. If usefulness was typically regarded as inherent during a long and prolific period of chemical research and development in this country, surely this is added reason why the Court's result should not be adopted until Congress expressly mandates it, presumably on the basis of empirical data which this Court does not possess.

Comments

1. *Substantial Utility.* Justice Story famously wrote in 1817, "[t]he law . . . does not look to the degree of utility." *Bedford v. Hunt,* 3 F. Cas. 37, 37 (C.C.D. Mass. 1817). Similarly, the nineteenth-century treatise author, William Robinson, wrote, "[w]hen actual utility exists, its degree is unimportant. However, slight the advantage which the public have received from the inventor, it offers a sufficient reason for his compensation." WILLIAM C. ROBINSON, 1 THE LAW OF PATENTS 464-465 (1890). These statements reflect a discomfort with having the court (or PTO), acting on behalf of the public interest, determine how useful an invention must be. But the substantial utility doctrine as set forth in *Brenner* seems to do just that. The *Brenner* Court also uses language that appears to comingle the policies of sections 101 and 112. For instance, the Court employs phrases such as "basic quid pro quo" and "metes and bounds" of the claimed invention must be capable of "precise delineation." These words smack of section 112's enablement and definiteness requirements, respectively.

   What policies are served by adopting the *Brenner* Court's understanding of the utility doctrine? One commentator has asserted that substantial (or practical) utility can be seen as a way to "avoid inefficient blocking patents," facilitating the "development of useful technical and market information," and "limit[ing] commercialization of non-beneficial products." Michael Risch, *Reinventing Usefulness*, 2010 BYU L. REV. 1195, 1227. And Robert Merges asserts that "[t]he obvious rationale for this requirement is that it prevents the dissipation of legitimate rents by requiring those who obtain a patent to show real technological progress." In other words, awarding a patent at "too early a stage in the innovation process would clearly lead to excessive expenditures of resources in an attempt to draft an early and broad patent instrument." ROBERT P. MERGES, JUSTIFYING INTELLECTUAL PROPERTY LAW 175 (2011).

2. *Promoting the Useful Arts and Industry Norms.* Justice Harlan's dissent envisioned a utility requirement that is much more consistent and reflective of industry innovation norms. Recall, Harlan wrote: "What I find most troubling about the result reached by the Court is the impact it may have on chemical research. Chemistry is a highly interrelated field and a tangible benefit for society may be the outcome of a number of different discoveries, one discovery building upon the next." Judge Rich of the CCPA and then the Federal Circuit shared Justice Harlan's view of section 101 utility. For instance, in *In re Kirk*, 376 F.2d 936 (CCPA 1967), Judge Rich, in a powerful dissent, wrote:

> I believe . . . that usefulness, *to* chemists doing research on steroids, *as* intermediates to make other compounds they desire to make is sufficient [to satisfy the utility requirement]. I further believe that this is the law as to the meaning of "useful" in 35 U.S.C. § 101 as it was applied for decades and reaffirmed by the 1952 codification. . . . From a practical administrative standpoint, the best rule, which is what we had in substance until 1950, is that chemical compounds are per se "useful" within the meaning of 35 U.S.C. § 101. . . . [Such a rule] would have the salutary effects of . . . (5) increasing the incentives to produce and disclose new compounds, (6) encouraging the production and marketing of new compounds for experimental purposes which will develop new uses for them, thus advancing the art and advantaging the public.

In re Kirk, 376 F.2d at 946, 949, 957 (emphasis in original). In the context of the pharmaceutical industry, the Federal Circuit—in a manner that appears sensitive to industry practice—moved away somewhat from the substantial utility test by holding that the combination of in vitro and in vivo testing of structurally similar compounds complied with § 101's utility requirement. *See Cross v. Iizuka*, 753 F.2d 1040, 1050 (Fed. Cir. 1985) (noting in vitro data is "[p]resumably . . . the accepted practice in the pharmaceutical industry. . . . In vitro testing, in general, is relatively less complex, less time consuming, and less expensive than in vivo testing. Moreover, in vitro results with respect to the particular pharmacological activity are generally predictive of in vivo test results, i.e., there is reasonable correlation there between").

IN RE FISHER

421 F.3d 1365 (Fed. Cir. 2005)

MICHEL, Chief Judge.

Dane K. Fisher and Raghunath Lalgudi (collectively "Fisher") appeal from the decision of the U.S. Patent and Trademark Office ("PTO") Board of Patent Appeals and Interferences ("Board") affirming the examiner's final rejection of the only pending claim of application Serial No. 09/619,643 (the "'643 application"), entitled "Nucleic Acid Molecules and Other Molecules Associated with Plants," as unpatentable for lack of utility under 35 U.S.C. § 101. Because we conclude that substantial evidence supports the Board's findings that the claimed invention lacks a specific and substantial utility, we affirm.

I. BACKGROUND

A. Molecular Genetics and ESTs

The claimed invention relates to five purified nucleic acid sequences that encode proteins and protein fragments in maize plants. The claimed sequences are commonly referred to as "expressed sequence tags" or "ESTs." Before delving into the specifics of this case, it is important to understand more about the basic principles of molecular genetics and the role of ESTs.

Genes are located on chromosomes in the nucleus of a cell and are made of deoxyribonucleic acid ("DNA"). DNA is composed of two strands of nucleotides in double helix formation. The nucleotides contain one of four bases, adenine ("A"), guanine ("G"), cytosine ("C"), and thymine ("T"), that are linked by hydrogen bonds to form complementary base pairs (*i.e.*, A-T and G-C).

When a gene is expressed in a cell, the relevant double-stranded DNA sequence is transcribed into a single strand of messenger ribonucleic acid ("mRNA"). Messenger RNA contains three of the same bases as DNA (A, G, and C), but contains uracil ("U") instead of thymine. mRNA is released from the nucleus of a cell and used by ribosomes found in the cytoplasm to produce proteins.

Complementary DNA ("cDNA") is produced synthetically by reverse transcribing mRNA. cDNA, like naturally occurring DNA, is composed of nucleotides containing the four nitrogenous bases, A, T, G, and C. Scientists routinely compile cDNA into libraries to study the kinds of genes expressed in a certain tissue at a particular point in time. One of the goals of this research is to learn what genes and downstream proteins are expressed in a cell so as to regulate gene expression and control protein synthesis.[2]

An EST is a short nucleotide sequence that represents a fragment of a cDNA clone. It is typically generated by isolating a cDNA clone and sequencing a small number of nucleotides located at the end of one of the two cDNA strands. When an EST is introduced into a sample containing a mixture of DNA, the EST may hybridize with a portion of DNA. Such binding shows that the gene corresponding to the EST was being expressed at the time of mRNA extraction.

Claim 1 of the '643 application recites:

A substantially purified nucleic acid molecule that encodes a maize protein or fragment thereof comprising a nucleic acid sequence selected from the group consisting of SEQ ID NO: 1 through SEQ ID NO: 5.

The ESTs set forth in SEQ ID NO: 1 through SEQ ID NO: 5 are obtained from cDNA library LIB3115, which was generated from pooled leaf tissue harvested from maize plants (RX601, Asgrow Seed Company, Des Moines, Iowa,

---

2. We have discussed the basic principles of molecular genetics more extensively in prior cases. *See, e.g., In re Deuel,* 51 F.3d 1552, 1554-56 (Fed. Cir. 1995); *Amgen, Inc. v. Chugai Pharm. Co., Ltd.,* 927 F.2d 1200, 1207-08 (Fed. Cir. 1991); *In re O'Farrell,* 853 F.2d 894, 895-99 (Fed. Cir. 1988).

U.S.A.) grown in the fields at Asgrow research stations. SEQ ID NO: 1 through SEQ ID NO: 5 consist of 429, 423, 365, 411, and 331 nucleotides, respectively. When Fisher filed the '643 application, he claimed ESTs corresponding to genes expressed from the maize pooled leaf tissue at the time of anthesis. Nevertheless, Fisher did not know the precise structure or function of either the genes or the proteins encoded for by those genes.

The '643 application generally discloses that the five claimed ESTs may be used in a variety of ways, including: (1) serving as a molecular marker for mapping the entire maize genome, which consists of ten chromosomes that collectively encompass roughly 50,000 genes; (2) measuring the level of mRNA in a tissue sample via microarray technology to provide information about gene expression; (3) providing a source for primers for use in the polymerase chain reaction ("PCR") process to enable rapid and inexpensive duplication of specific genes; (4) identifying the presence or absence of a polymorphism; (5) isolating promoters via chromosome walking; (6) controlling protein expression; and (7) locating genetic molecules of other plants and organisms.

***

B. Final Rejection

In a final rejection, dated September 6, 2001, the examiner rejected claim 1 for lack of utility under §101. The examiner found that the claimed ESTs were not supported by a specific and substantial utility. She concluded that the disclosed uses were not specific to the claimed ESTs, but instead were generally applicable to any EST. . . . [T]he Board affirmed the examiner's rejection of the '643 application for lack of utility under §101. . . .

II. Discussion

Whether an application discloses a utility for a claimed invention is a question of fact. We consequently review the Board's determination that the '643 application failed to satisfy the utility requirement of §101 for substantial evidence.

A. Utility

1.

Fisher asserts that the Board unilaterally applied a heightened standard for utility in the case of ESTs, conditioning patentability upon "some undefined 'spectrum' of knowledge concerning the corresponding gene function." Fisher contends that the standard is not so high and that Congress intended the language of §101 to be given broad construction. In particular, Fisher contends that §101 requires only that the claimed invention "not be frivolous, or injurious to the well-being, good policy, or good morals of society," essentially adopting Justice Story's view of a useful invention from *Lowell v. Lewis,* 15 F.Cas. 1018, 1019 (No. 8568) (C.C.D. Mass. 1817). Under the correct application of the law, Fisher argues, the record shows that the claimed ESTs provide seven specific and substantial uses, regardless whether the functions of the genes corresponding to the claimed ESTs are known. Fisher claims that the Board's attempt to equate the claimed ESTs with the chemical compositions in *Brenner* was misplaced and that several decisions in the field of pharmaceuticals, namely, *Cross v. Iizuka,* 753 F.2d 1040 (Fed. Cir. 1985), *Nelson v. Bowler,* 626 F.2d 853 (C.C.P.A. 1980), and *In re Jolles,* 628 F.2d 1322 (C.C.P.A. 1980), are analogous and support finding utility of the claimed ESTs. Fisher likewise argues that the general commercial success of ESTs in the marketplace confirms the utility of the claimed ESTs. Hence, Fisher avers that the Board's decision was not supported by substantial evidence and should be reversed.

The government agrees with Fisher that the utility threshold is not high, but disagrees with Fisher's allegation that the Board applied a heightened utility standard. The government contends that a patent applicant need disclose only a single specific and substantial utility pursuant to *Brenner,* the very standard articulated in the PTO's "Utility Examination Guidelines" ("Utility Guidelines") and followed here when examining the '643 application. It argues that Fisher failed to meet that standard because Fisher's alleged uses are so general as to be meaningless. What is more, the government asserts that the same generic uses could apply not only to the five claimed ESTs but also to any EST derived from any organism. It thus argues that the seven utilities alleged by Fisher are merely starting points for further research, not the end point of any research effort. It further disputes the importance of the commercial success of ESTs in the marketplace, pointing out that Fisher's evidence involved only databases, clone sets, and microarrays, not the five claimed ESTs. Therefore, the government contends that we should affirm the Board's decision.

Several academic institutions and biotechnology and pharmaceutical companies write as amici curiae in support of the government. Like the government, they assert that Fisher's claimed uses are nothing more than a "laundry list" of research plans, each general and speculative, none providing a specific and substantial benefit in currently available form. The amici also advocate that the claimed ESTs are the objects of further research aimed at identifying what genes of unknown function are expressed during anthesis and what proteins of unknown function are encoded for by those genes. Until the corresponding genes and proteins have a known function, the amici argue, the claimed ESTs lack utility under § 101 and are not patentable.

We agree with both the government and the amici that none of Fisher's seven asserted uses meets the utility requirement of § 101. Section 101 provides: "Whoever invents . . . any new and *useful* . . . composition of matter . . . may obtain a patent therefor. . . ." (Emphasis added). In *Brenner,* the Supreme Court explained what is required to establish the usefulness of a new invention, noting at the outset that "a simple, everyday word ['useful,' as found in § 101] can be pregnant with ambiguity when applied to the facts of life." 383 U.S. at 529. Contrary to Fisher's argument that § 101 only requires an invention that is not "frivolous, injurious to the well-being, good policy, or good morals of society," the Supreme Court appeared to reject Justice Story's de minimis view of utility. *Id.* at 532-33. The Supreme Court observed that Justice Story's definition "sheds little light on our subject," on the one hand framing the relevant inquiry as "whether the invention in question is 'frivolous and insignificant'" if narrowly read, while on the other hand "allowing the patenting of any invention not positively harmful to society" if more broadly read. *Id.* at 533. In its place, the Supreme Court announced a more rigorous test, stating:

> The basic *quid pro quo* contemplated by the Constitution and the Congress for granting a patent monopoly is the benefit derived by the public from an invention with *substantial utility.* Unless and until a process is refined and developed to this point—where *specific benefit exists in currently available form*—there is insufficient

justification for permitting an applicant to engross what may prove to be a broad field.

Brenner, 383 U.S. at 534-35 (emphases added). Following *Brenner,* our predecessor court, the Court of Customs and Patent Appeals, and this court have required a claimed invention to have a specific and substantial utility to satisfy §101. *See, e.g., Fujikawa v. Wattanasin,* 93 F.3d 1559, 1563 (Fed. Cir. 1996) ("Consequently, it is well established that a patent may not be granted to an invention unless substantial or practical utility for the invention has been discovered and disclosed.").

The Supreme Court has not defined what the terms "specific" and "substantial" mean per se. Nevertheless, together with the Court of Customs and Patent Appeals, we have offered guidance as to the uses which would meet the utility standard of §101. From this, we can discern the kind of disclosure an application must contain to establish a specific and substantial utility for the claimed invention.

Courts have used the labels "practical utility" and "real world" utility interchangeably in determining whether an invention offers a "substantial" utility. Indeed, the Court of Customs and Patent Appeals stated that " '[p]ractical utility' is a shorthand way of attributing 'real-world' value to claimed subject matter. In other words, one skilled in the art can use a claimed discovery in a manner which provides some *immediate benefit to the public.*" *Nelson,* 626 F.2d at 856 (emphasis added).[4] It thus is clear that an application must show that an invention is useful to the public as disclosed in its current form, not that it may prove useful at some future date after further research. Simply put, to satisfy the "substantial" utility requirement, an asserted use must show that that claimed invention has a significant and presently available benefit to the public.

Turning to the "specific" utility requirement, an application must disclose a use which is not so vague as to be meaningless. Indeed, one of our predecessor courts has observed "that the nebulous expressions 'biological activity' or 'biological properties' appearing in the specification convey no more explicit indication of the usefulness of the compounds and how to use them than did the equally obscure expression 'useful for technical and pharmaceutical purposes' unsuccessfully relied upon by the appellant in *In re Diedrich.*" *In re Kirk,* 376 F.2d 936, 941 (1967). Thus, in addition to providing a "substantial" utility, an asserted use must also show that that claimed invention can be used to provide a well-defined and particular benefit to the public.

In 2001, partially in response to questions about the patentability of ESTs, the PTO issued Utility Guidelines governing its internal practice for determining whether a claimed invention satisfies §101. *See* Utility Examination Guidelines, 66 Fed. Reg. 1092 (Jan. 5, 2001). The PTO incorporated these guidelines into the Manual of Patent Examining Procedure ("MPEP"). *See* U.S. Pat. & Trademark Off., Manual of Patent Examining Procedure §2107 (8th ed. 2001, rev. May 2004). The MPEP and Guidelines "are not binding on this court, but may be given judicial notice to the extent they do not conflict with the statute." *Enzo Biochem v. Gen-Probe,* 323 F.3d 956, 964 (Fed. Cir. 2002). According to the Utility Guidelines, a specific utility is particular to the subject matter claimed

---

4. In *Cross,* this court considered the phrase "practical utility" to be synonymous with the phrase "substantial utility." 753 F.2d at 1047, n.13.

and would not be applicable to a broad class of invention. Manual of Patent Examining Procedure § 2107.01. The Utility Guidelines also explain that a substantial utility defines a "real world" use. In particular, "[u]tilities that require or constitute carrying out further research to identify or reasonably confirm a 'real world' context of use are not substantial utilities." *Id.* Further, the Utility Guidelines discuss "research tools," a term often given to inventions used to conduct research. The PTO particularly cautions that

> [a]n assessment that focuses on whether an invention is useful only in a research setting thus does not address whether the invention is in fact "useful" in a patent sense. [The PTO] must distinguish between inventions that have a specifically identified substantial utility and inventions whose asserted utility requires further research to identify or reasonably confirm.

Id. The PTO's standards for assessing whether a claimed invention has a specific and substantial utility comport with this court's interpretation of the utility requirement of § 101.

Turning to the parties' arguments, Fisher first raises a legal issue, charging that the Board applied a heightened standard for utility in the case of ESTs. Fisher apparently bases this argument on statements made by the Board in connection with its discussion of whether the claimed ESTs can be used to identify a polymorphism. In that context, the Board stated:

> Somewhere between having no knowledge (the present circumstances) and having complete knowledge of the gene and its role in the plant's development lies the line between "utility" and "substantial utility." We need not draw the line or further define it in this case because the facts in this case represent the lowest end of the *spectrum, i.e.,* an insubstantial use.

Board Decision, slip op. at 15 (emphasis added). Fisher reads the word "spectrum" out of context, claiming that the word somehow implies the application of a higher standard for utility than required by § 101. We conclude, however, that the Board did not apply an incorrect legal standard. In its decision, the Board made reference to a "spectrum" to differentiate between a substantial utility, which satisfies the utility requirement of § 101, and an insubstantial utility, which fails to satisfy § 101. The Board plainly did not announce or apply a new test for assessing the utility of ESTs. It simply followed the Utility Guidelines and MPEP, which mandate the specific and substantial utility test set forth in *Brenner.* Indeed, we note that Example 9 of the PTO's "Revised Interim Utility Guidelines Training Materials" is applicable to the facts here. *See* U.S. Pat. & Trademark Off., Revised Interim Utility Guidelines Training Materials 50-53 (1999), *available at* www.uspto.gov/web/menu/utility.pdf. In that example, a cDNA fragment disclosed as being useful as a probe to obtain the full length gene corresponding to a cDNA fragment was deemed to lack a specific and substantial utility. Additionally, the MPEP particularly explains that a claim directed to a polynucleotide disclosed to be useful as a "gene probe" or "chromosome marker," as is the case here, fails to satisfy the specific utility requirement unless a specific DNA target is also disclosed. Manual of Patent Examining Procedure § 2107.01.

Regarding the seven uses asserted by Fisher, we observe that each claimed EST uniquely corresponds to the single gene from which it was transcribed ("underlying gene"). As of the filing date of the '643 application, Fisher admits that the underlying genes have no known functions. Fisher, nevertheless, claims that this fact is irrelevant because the seven asserted uses are not related to the functions of the underlying genes. We are not convinced by this contention. Essentially, the claimed ESTs act as no more than research intermediates that may help scientists to isolate the particular underlying protein-encoding genes and conduct further experimentation on those genes. The overall goal of such experimentation is presumably to understand the maize genome—the functions of the underlying genes, the identity of the encoded proteins, the role those proteins play during anthesis, whether polymorphisms exist, the identity of promoters that trigger protein expression, whether protein expression may be controlled, etc. Accordingly, the claimed ESTs are, in words of the Supreme Court, mere "object[s] of use-testing," to wit, objects upon which scientific research could be performed with no assurance that anything useful will be discovered in the end. *Brenner*, 383 U.S. at 535.

Fisher compares the claimed ESTs to certain other patentable research tools, such as a microscope. Although this comparison may, on first blush, be appealing in that both a microscope and one of the claimed ESTs can be used to generate scientific data about a sample having unknown properties, Fisher's analogy is flawed. As the government points out, a microscope has the specific benefit of optically magnifying an object to immediately reveal its structure. One of the claimed ESTs, by contrast, can only be used to detect the presence of genetic material having the same structure as the EST itself. It is unable to provide any information about the overall structure let alone the function of the underlying gene. Accordingly, while a microscope can offer an immediate, real world benefit in a variety of applications, the same cannot be said for the claimed ESTs. Fisher's proposed analogy is thus inapt. Hence, we conclude that Fisher's asserted uses are insufficient to meet the standard for a "substantial" utility under §101.

Moreover, all of Fisher's asserted uses represent merely hypothetical possibilities, objectives which the claimed ESTs, or any EST for that matter, *could* possibly achieve, but none for which they have been used in the real world. Focusing on the two uses emphasized by Fisher at oral argument, Fisher maintains that the claimed ESTs could be used to identify polymorphisms or to isolate promoters. Nevertheless, in the face of a utility rejection, Fisher has not presented any evidence, as the Board well noted, showing that the claimed ESTs have been used in either way. That is, Fisher does not present either a single polymorphism or a single promoter, assuming at least one of each exists, actually identified by using the claimed ESTs. Further, Fisher has not shown that a polymorphism or promoter so identified would have a "specific and substantial" use. The Board, in fact, correctly recognized this very deficiency and cited it as one of the reasons for upholding the examiner's final rejection.

With respect to the remaining asserted uses, there is no disclosure in the specification showing that any of the claimed ESTs were used as a molecular marker on a map of the maize genome. There also is no disclosure establishing that any of the claimed ESTs were used or, for that matter, could be used to control or provide information about gene expression. Significantly, despite the fact that maize leaves produce over two thousand different proteins during anthesis, Fisher failed to show that one of the claimed ESTs translates into a portion of one of those proteins. Fisher likewise did not provide any evidence showing that the claimed ESTs were used to locate genetic molecules in other plants and organisms. What is more, Fisher has not proffered any evidence showing that any such generic molecules would themselves have a specific and substantial utility. Consequently, because Fisher failed to prove that its claimed ESTs can be successfully used in the seven ways disclosed in the '643 application, we have no choice but to conclude that the claimed ESTs do not have a "substantial" utility under § 101.

Furthermore, Fisher's seven asserted uses are plainly not "specific." Any EST transcribed from any gene in the maize genome has the potential to perform any one of the alleged uses. That is, any EST transcribed from any gene in the maize genome may be a molecular marker or a source for primers. Likewise, any EST transcribed from any gene in the maize genome may be used to measure the level of mRNA in a tissue sample, identify the presence or absence of a polymorphism, isolate promoters, control protein expression, or locate genetic molecules of other plants and organisms. Nothing about Fisher's seven alleged uses set the five claimed ESTs apart from the more than 32,000 ESTs disclosed in the '643 application or indeed from any EST derived from any organism. Accordingly, we conclude that Fisher has only disclosed general uses for its claimed ESTs, not specific ones that satisfy § 101.

We agree with the Board that the facts here are similar to those in *Brenner*. There, as noted above, the applicant claimed a process for preparing compounds of unknown use. Similarly, Fisher filed an application claiming five particular ESTs which are capable of hybridizing with underlying genes of unknown function found in the maize genome. The *Brenner* court held that the claimed process lacked a utility because it could be used only to produce a compound of unknown use. The *Brenner* court stated: "We find absolutely no warrant for the proposition that although Congress intended that no patent be granted on a chemical compound whose sole 'utility' consists of its potential role as an object of use-testing, a different set of rules was meant to apply to the process which yielded the unpatentable product." 383 U.S. at 535. Applying that same logic here, we conclude that the claimed ESTs, which do not correlate to an underlying gene of known function, fail to meet the standard for utility intended by Congress.

In addition to approving of the Board's reliance on *Brenner*, we observe that the facts here are even more analogous to those presented in *Kirk*, 376 F.2d 936, and *In re Joly*, 376 F.2d 906 (1967), two cases decided by our predecessor court shortly after *Brenner*. In *Kirk*, the applicant sought to patent new steroidal compounds disclosed as having two possible utilities. First, the applicant alleged that the claimed compounds were useful for their "biological activity" because "one skilled in the art would know how to use the compounds . . . to take advantage of their presently-existing biological activity." *Kirk*, 376 F.2d at 939. The court rejected this claimed utility on the ground that it was not sufficiently "specific," but was instead "nebulous." *Id.* at 941.

Second, the applicant asserted that the claimed compounds could be used by skilled chemists as intermediates in the preparation of final steroidal compounds of unknown use. Relying on *Brenner*, the court reasoned:

> It seems clear that, if a process for producing a product of only conjectural use is not itself "useful" within § 101, it cannot be said that the starting materials for such a process—*i.e.*, the presently claimed intermediates—are "useful." It is not enough that the specification disclose that the intermediate exists and that it

"works," reacts, or can be used to produce some intended product of no known use. Nor is it enough that the product disclosed to be obtained from the intermediate belongs to some class of compounds which now is, or in the future might be, the subject of research to determine some *specific use. Cf. Reiners v. Mehltretter*, 43 C.C.P.A. 1019, 236 F.2d 418, 421 [(C.C.P.A. 1956)] where compounds employed as intermediates to produce other directly useful compounds were found to be themselves useful.

Id. at 945-46 (emphasis added). Therefore, the court affirmed the Board's rejection of the claimed compounds for lack of utility.

The facts in *Joly* are nearly identical to the facts in *Kirk*. The *Joly* applicant filed an application claiming compounds useful as intermediates in preparing steroids that were themselves not shown or known to be useful, but that were similar in chemical structure to steroids of known pharmacological usefulness. The court adopted the reasoning of the *Kirk* court in its entirety and affirmed the Board's decision rejecting the claimed intermediates for failing to comply with §101. *Joly*, 376 F.2d at 908-09.

Just as the claimed compounds in *Kirk* and *Joly* were useful only as intermediates in the synthesis of other compounds of unknown use, the claimed ESTs can only be used as research intermediates in the identification of underlying protein-encoding genes of unknown function. The rationale of *Kirk* and *Joly* thus applies here. In the words of the *Kirk* court:

We do not believe that it was the intention of the statutes to require the Patent Office, the courts, or the public to play the sort of guessing game that might be involved if an applicant could satisfy the requirements of the statutes by indicating the usefulness of a claimed compound *in terms of possible use so general as to be meaningless* and then, after his research or that of his competitors has definitely ascertained an actual use for the compound, adducing evidence intended to show that a particular specific use would have been obvious to men skilled in the particular art to which this use relates.

376 F.2d at 942 (emphasis added).

That the *Kirk* and *Joly* decisions involved chemical compounds, while the present case involves biological entities, does not distinguish these decisions. The rationale presented therein, having been drawn from principles set forth by the Supreme Court in *Brenner*, applies with equal force in the fields of chemistry and biology as well as in any scientific discipline. In *Brenner*, the Supreme Court was primarily concerned with creating an unwarranted monopoly to the detriment of the public. . . . *Brenner*, 383 U.S. at 535-536. Here, granting a patent to Fisher for its five claimed ESTs would amount to a hunting license because the claimed ESTs can be used only to gain further information about the underlying genes and the proteins encoded for by those genes. The claimed ESTs themselves are not an end of Fisher's research effort, but only tools to be used along the way in the search for a practical utility. Thus, while Fisher's claimed ESTs may add a noteworthy contribution to biotechnology research, our precedent dictates that the '643 application does not meet the utility requirement of §101 because Fisher does not identify the function for the underlying protein-encoding genes. Absent such identification, we hold that the claimed ESTs have not been researched and understood to the point of providing an immediate, well-defined, real world benefit to the public meriting the grant of a patent.

* * *

3.

As a final matter, we observe that the government and its amici express concern that allowing EST patents without proof of utility would discourage research, delay scientific discovery, and thwart progress in the "useful Arts" and "Science." *See* U.S. Const. art. I, §8, cl. 8. The government and its amici point out that allowing EST claims like Fisher's would give rise to multiple patents, likely owned by several different companies, relating to the same underlying gene and expressed protein. Such a situation, the government and amici predict, would result in an unnecessarily convoluted licensing environment for those interested in researching that gene and/or protein.

The concerns of the government and amici, which may or may not be valid, are not ones that should be considered in deciding whether the application for the claimed ESTs meets the utility requirement of §101. The same may be said for the resource and managerial problems that the PTO potentially would face if applicants present the PTO with an onslaught of patent applications directed to particular ESTs. Congress did not intend for these practical implications to affect the determination of whether an invention satisfies the requirements set forth in 35 U.S.C. §§101, 102, 103, and 112. They are public policy considerations which are more appropriately directed to Congress as the legislative branch of government, rather than this court as a judicial body responsible simply for interpreting and applying statutory law. Under Title 35, an applicant is entitled to a patent if his invention is new, useful, nonobvious, and his application adequately describes the claimed invention, teaches others how to make and use the claimed invention, and discloses the best mode for practicing the claimed invention. What is more, when Congress enacted §101, it indicated that "anything under the sun that is made by man" constitutes potential subject matter for a patent. S. Rep. No. 82-1979, at 7 (1952), U.S. Code Cong. & Admin. News at 2394, 2399. Policy reasons aside, because we conclude that the utility requirement of §101 is not met, we hold that Fisher is not entitled to a patent for the five claimed ESTs.

* * *

RADER, Circuit Judge, dissenting.

This court today determines that expressed sequence tags (ESTs) do not satisfy 35 U.S.C. §101 unless there is a known use for the genes from which each EST is transcribed. While I agree that an invention must demonstrate utility to satisfy §101, these claimed ESTs have such a utility, at least as research tools in isolating and studying other molecules. Therefore, I respectfully dissent.

Several, if not all, of Fisher's asserted utilities claim that ESTs function to study other molecules. In simple terms, ESTs are research tools. Admittedly ESTs have use only in a research setting. However, the value and utility of research tools generally is beyond question, even though limited to a laboratory setting. Thus, if the claimed ESTs qualify as research tools, then they have a "specific" and "substantial" utility sufficient for §101. If these ESTs do not enhance research, then *Brenner v. Manson* controls and erects a §101 bar for lack of utility. For the following reasons, these claimed ESTs are more akin to patentable research tools than to the unpatentable methods in *Brenner.*

In *Brenner,* the Court confronted a growing conflict between this court's predecessor, the Court of Customs and Patent Appeals (CCPA), and the Patent Office over the patentability of methods of producing compounds with no known use. This conflict began with *In re Nelson,* the first in a series of cases wherein the CCPA reversed several Patent Office utility rejections. *Brenner* put an end to these cases because, in the 1960s, the Court could not distinguish between denying patents to compounds with no known use and denying patents to methods of producing those useless compounds. The Court commented:

> We find absolutely no warrant for the proposition that although Congress intended that no patent be granted on a chemical compound whose sole "utility" consists of its potential role as an object of use-testing, a different set of rules was meant to apply to the process which yielded the unpatentable product. That proposition seems to us little more than an attempt to evade the impact of the rules which concededly govern patentability of the product itself.

Id. at 535. This court's predecessor later extended *Brenner* to bar patents on compounds as intermediates in the preparation of other compounds having no known use. *See In re Kirk.*

This case is very different. Unlike the methods and compounds in *Brenner* and *Kirk,* Fisher's claimed ESTs *are* beneficial to society. As an example, these research tools "may help scientists to isolate the particular underlying protein-encoding genes . . . [with the] overall goal of such experimentation . . . presumably [being] to understand the maize genome[.]" *Majority Opinion,* at 1373. They also can serve as a probe introduced into a sample tissue to confirm "that the gene corresponding to the EST was being expressed in the sample tissue at the time of mRNA extraction." *Id.,* at 1367.

These research tools are similar to a microscope; both take a researcher one step closer to identifying and understanding a previously unknown and invisible structure. Both supply information about a molecular structure. Both advance research and bring scientists closer to unlocking the secrets of the corn genome to provide better food production for the hungry world. If a microscope has § 101 utility, so too do these ESTs.

The Board and this court acknowledge that the ESTs perform a function, that they have a utility, but proceed quickly to a value judgment that the utility would not produce enough valuable information. The Board instead complains that the information these ESTs supply is too "insubstantial" to merit protection. Yet this conclusion denies the very nature of scientific advance. Science always advances in small incremental steps. While acknowledging the patentability of research tools generally (and microscopes as one example thereof), this court concludes with little scientific foundation that these ESTs do not qualify as research tools because they do not "offer an immediate, real world benefit" because further research is required to understand the underlying gene. This court further faults the EST research for lacking any "assurance that anything useful will be discovered in the end." These criticisms would foreclose much scientific research and many vital research tools. Often scientists embark on research with no assurance of success and knowing that even success will demand "significant additional research."

Nonetheless, this court, oblivious to the challenges of complex research, discounts these ESTs because it concludes (without scientific evidence) that they do not supply enough information. This court reasons that a research tool has

a "specific" and "substantial" utility *only* if the studied object is readily understandable using the claimed tool—that no further research is required. Surely
this cannot be the law. Otherwise, only the final step of a lengthy incremental
research inquiry gets protection.

Even with a microscope, significant additional research is often required to
ascertain the particular function of a "revealed" structure. To illustrate, a cancerous growth, magnified with a patented microscope, can be identified and distinguished from other healthy cells by a properly trained doctor or researcher.
But even today, the scientific community still does not fully grasp the reasons
that cancerous growths increase in mass and spread throughout the body, or the
nature of compounds that interact with them, or the interactions of environmental or genetic conditions that contribute to developing cancer. Significant
additional research is required to answer these questions. Even with answers to
these questions, the cure for cancer will remain in the distance. Yet the microscope still has "utility" under §101. Why? Because it takes the researcher one
step closer to answering these questions. Each step, even if small in isolation, is
nonetheless a benefit to society sufficient to give a viable research tool "utility"
under §101. In fact, experiments that fail still serve to eliminate some possibilities and provide information to the research process.

The United States Patent Office, above all, should recognize the incremental
nature of scientific endeavor. Yet, in the interest of easing its administrative load,
the Patent Office will eliminate some research tools as providing "insubstantial"
advances. How does the Patent Office know which "insubstantial" research step
will contribute to a substantial breakthrough in genomic study? Quite simply, it
does not.

* * *

In truth, I have some sympathy with the Patent Office's dilemma. The Office
needs some tool to reject inventions that may advance the "useful arts" but not
sufficiently to warrant the valuable exclusive right of a patent. The Patent Office
has seized upon this utility requirement to reject these research tools as contributing "insubstantially" to the advance of the useful arts. The utility requirement
is ill suited to that task, however, because it lacks any standard for assessing
the state of the prior art and the contributions of the claimed advance. The
proper tool for assessing sufficient contribution to the useful arts is the obviousness requirement of 35 U.S.C. §103. Unfortunately this court has deprived the
Patent Office of the obviousness requirement for genomic inventions.

Comments

1. *Substantial and Specific Utility Defined.* A patent applicant must show both
   substantial and specific utility to satisfy section 101. The *Fisher* court initially
   noted that the Supreme Court has not defined substantial and specific utility. Beginning with substantial utility, the court noted that "practical utility"
   and "real world utility" have been used interchangeably with substantial
   utility, but they all require the claimed invention to provide "some immediate benefit to the public." The PTO's utility guidelines state "[u]tilities that

require or constitute carrying out further research to identify or reasonably confirm a 'real world' context of use are not substantial utilities." U.S. PTO, REVISED INTERIM UTILITY EXAMINATION GUIDELINES TRAINING MATERIALS, at 6. *See* http://www.uspto.gov/web/offices/pac/utility/utilityguide.pdf. This approach is consistent with *Brenner*.

The *Fisher* court also defined "specific utility" to mean that "an application must disclose a use which is not so vague as to be meaningless." That is, the claimed invention must provide the public with "a well-defined and particular benefit." In the biological realm, "nebulous expressions" such as "biological activity" or "biological properties" will not suffice. The 2001 PTO Utility Guidelines define specific utility as "utility that is specific to the subject matter claimed," in contrast to "a general utility that would be applicable to the broad class of the invention." *Id.* at 4.

2. ***The Utility Requirement and Genomics: The Upstream-Downstream Debate.*** There is little doubt that patents play an extremely important role in the biotechnology industry. To the extent there is controversy relating to patenting biotechnological inventions, it pertains to when (not if) patents should intervene. It is helpful to think of biomedical research on a developmental spectrum when thinking about the utility requirement, specifically, and the role of patent law, generally. Most commentators would agree that patents play an important role in downstream products (and processes), so-called small molecule drugs that are dominant in the pharmaceutical industry. But consensus dissipates somewhat as you move further upstream in the developmental spectrum, particularly into the realm of research tools that have foundational applicability, yet are far removed from the downstream product. Examples of research tools include polymerase chain reaction (PCR), used to replicate DNA; Express Sequence Tags (ESTs as in *Fisher*); DNA sequencing technology, Single Nucleotide Polymorphisms (SNPs), and even DNA sequences (i.e., genes). (Perhaps the most well-known research tool is the Cohen-Boyer technology relating to recombinant DNA.)

Note on Design Patents

Design patents, which are typically overshadowed by the more commercially powerful utility patents, enjoyed a great deal of publicity when a jury in August of 2012 found that Samsung infringed several Apple design patents relating the iPhone,[5] namely the "home button, rounded corners and tapered edges" in U.S. Patent No. D593087 and "On-Screen Icons" in U.S. Patent No. D604305. A design patent protects the ornamental features (e.g., shape or configuration) as embodied in or applied to a utilitarian or functional article. Design patents differ from utility patents in that the latter protects the functional features of the claimed article, the way it is used and how it works whereas a design patent simply covers the way in which the article looks. The design must be new, original, and ornamental. *See* 35 U.S.C. §§ 171-173. A design patent application has only one claim, which refers to the drawings. Because design patents are claimed as shown in the drawings, the Federal Circuit "has not required that the trial court

---

5. *See* http://cand.uscourts.gov/lhk/applevsamsung for information about the case.

attempt to provide a detailed verbal description of the claimed design, as is typically done in the case of utility patents." *Egyptian Goddess, Inc. v. Swisa, Inc.*, 543 F.3d 665, 679 (Fed. Cir. 2008) (*en banc*). A single article can be subject to both a utility and design patent. For instance, design patent number 500,000 covers a design of an automobile body. (Certainly, the automobile itself has several features eligible for utility patent protection.) Note on the cover page reproduced on the following page that the letter "D" precedes the patent number to indicate the patent is a design patent. The claim of the design patent reads: "An ornamental design for an automobile body, as shown and described."

The sole test for determining design patent infringement is the "ordinary observer" test. *See Egyptian Goddess*, 543 F.3d at 678. *See also Gorham Co. v. White*, 81 U.S. 511, 528 (1871) ("[I]f, in the eye of an ordinary observer, giving such attention as a purchaser usually gives, two designs are substantially the same, if the resemblance is such as to deceive such an observer, inducing him to purchase one supposing it to be the other, the first one patented is infringed by the other."). Under this test "infringement will not be found unless the accused article "embod[ies] the patented design or any colorable imitation thereof." *Id.*

---

(12) **United States Design Patent**   (10) Patent No.:   **US D500,000 S**
     Dyson et al.   (45) Date of Patent: ** **Dec. 21, 2004**

(54) **AUTOMOBILE BODY**

(75) Inventors: **Andrew P Dyson**, West Bloomfield, MI (US); **Joseph S Dehner**, Bloomfield, MI (US); **David C McKinnon**, Bloomfield, MI (US); **Glenn W Abbott**, West Bloomfield, MI (US)

(73) Assignee: **DaimlerChrysler Corporation**, Auburn Hills, MI (US)

(**) Term: **14 Years**

(21) Appl. No.: **29/201,094**

(22) Filed: **Mar. 10, 2004**

(51) LOC (7) Cl. **12-08**
(52) U.S. Cl. **D12/92**
(58) Field of Search D12/90–92, 86; D21/424, 433; 296/185

(56)   **References Cited**
               U.S. PATENT DOCUMENTS

D408,328 S * 4/1999 Ayoub et al. D12/92
D465,436 S * 11/2002 Dehner et al. D12/92
D476,601 S   7/2003 Stoddard et al. D12/92
D477,253 S * 7/2003 Minami et al. D12/92
D483,696 S * 12/2003 Howell et al. D12/92

* cited by examiner

Primary Examiner—Melody N. Brown
(74) *Attorney, Agent, or Firm*—Ralph E. Smith

(57)   **CLAIM**

The ornamental design for an automobile body, as shown and described.

                    DESCRIPTION

FIG. **1** is a front perspective view of an automobile body showing our new design;

FIG. **2** is a side view thereof;

FIG. **3** is a rear perspective view thereof;

FIG. **4** is a front view thereof;

FIG. **5** is a rear view thereof;

FIG. **6** is a front perspective view of an automobile body showing a second embodiment of our new design;

FIG. **7** is a side view of FIG. **6**;

FIG. **8** is a rear perspective view of FIG. **6**;

FIG. **9** is a front view of FIG. **6**; and,

FIG. **10** is a rear view of FIG. **6**.

It will be understood that the dashed lines presented in the drawings are for illustration only, and do not form a part of the claimed design.

1 Claim, 8 Drawing Sheets

According to the Federal Circuit:

> In some instances, the claimed design and the accused design will be sufficiently distinct that it will be clear without more that the patentee has not met its burden of proving the two designs would appear "substantially the same" to the ordinary observer, as required by *Gorham*. In other instances, when the claimed and accused designs are not plainly dissimilar, resolution of the question whether the ordinary observer would consider the two designs to be substantially the same will benefit from a comparison of the claimed and accused designs with the prior art, as in many of the cases discussed above and in the case at bar.

Egyptian Goddess, 543 F.3d at 678. One subtle difference from the *Gorham* case is that *Egyptian Goddess* highlighted the role of prior art in determining infringement. *Egyptian Goddess*, 543 F.3d at 676 ("When the differences between the claimed and accused design are viewed in light of the prior art, the attention of the hypothetical ordinary observer will be drawn to those aspects of the claimed design that differ from the prior art. And when the claimed design is close to the prior art designs, small differences between the accused design and the claimed design are likely to be important to the eye of the hypothetical ordinary observer.").

The *Egyptian Goddess* case did not address whether the "ordinary observer" test was also applicable to a design patent validity analysis. But in a subsequent case, the court held that the "ordinary observer" framework is the sole test for determining validity of design patents. *See International Seaway Trading Corp. v. Walgreens Corp.*, 589 F.3d 1233, 1240 (Fed. Cir. 2009) (stating "[i]n light of Supreme Court precedent and our precedent holding that the same tests must be applied to infringement and anticipation, and our holding in *Egyptian Goddess* that the ordinary observer test is the sole test for infringement, we now conclude that the ordinary observer test must logically be the sole test for anticipation as well").

Novelty and Priority

INTRODUCTION

The novelty and priority provisions of the patent code—embodied in section 102—were amended by the 2011 America Invents Act ("AIA") in important ways. But because these amendments only apply to patent applications filed on or after March 16, 2013, the pre-AIA law of novelty and priority will remain relevant for several years to come. Keep in mind, as well, that because of the prominent role of the common law in patent jurisprudence,[1] much (although certainly not all) of what you learn regarding the pre-AIA doctrine of novelty and priority will be relevant to the post-AIA statutory framework and applications filed thereunder. The reason for this carryover is that the AIA retained a good portion of the statutory language found in pre-AIA section 102,[2] and "a common law term in a statute comes with a common law meaning, absent anything pointing another way."[3]

Accordingly, although the AIA's amendments to section 102 will be discussed in detail, this chapter (beginning with the next paragraph) is devoted predominantly to pre-AIA section 102.

The novelty requirement—embodied in section 102(a), (e), and (g)(2)—guards the public domain, precluding a patent from issuing on claimed subject matter that is not new. Subsection (a) relates to whether someone other than the inventor knew, used, published, and patented the claimed invention

---

1. See Chapter 1, pages 5-6.

2. Terms such as "on sale" and "public use" —present in both the pre- and post-AIA section 102—will be explored in Chapter 6 when we cover Statutory Bars. This chapter will discuss "printed publication," which is also represented in both the "old" and "new" section 102. The post-AIA section 102 phrase "otherwise available to the public," however, is not found in the old section 102, and we will explore whether it at least covers the terms "known or used" that are part of the pre-AIA section 102.

3. *See Safeco Ins. Co. of America v. Burr*, 551 U.S. 47, 58 (2007); *Microsoft Corp. v. i4i Limited Partnership*, 131 S. Ct. 2238, 2245 (2011) (stating "where Congress uses a common law term in a statute, we assume the 'term . . . comes with a common law meaning, absent anything pointing another way'") (citing *Safeco*). One thing to ask, therefore, as you study the new section 102 is if there is indeed "anything pointing another way." *See also Payne v. Tennessee*, 501 U.S. 808, 828 (1991) ("Considerations in favor of *stare decisis* are at their acme in cases involving property and contract rights, where reliance interests are involved."). A patent is certainly a property right and has also been referred to as a contract between the patentee and society. *See, e.g., Robert Bosch, LLC v. Pylon Mfg. Corp.*, 659 F.3d 1142, 1149 (Fed. Cir. 2011) (referring to the "fundamental nature of patents as property rights"); *Markman v. Westview Instruments, Inc.*, 52 F.3d 967, 984 (Fed. Cir. 1995) (analogizing patents to contracts).

prior to the inventor's date of invention.[4] Under section 102(e), the focus is on third-party patent disclosures filed prior to the applicant's date of invention. And section 102(g)(2) pertains to third-party inventive activity prior to the applicant's date of invention. Under all three subsections, the issue is *not* which party is entitled to a patent; rather, the issue is whether someone other than the inventor knew, disclosed, or invented the claimed invention before the inventor himself invented, thereby defeating novelty. Sections A and B are devoted to novelty.

Section 102(g)(1) is the priority provision, which is invoked when two or more parties are claiming the same invention. Thus, unlike the novelty provisions where only one party is seeking patent protection on a given invention, each party involved in a priority contest is asserting he invented first,[5] and is therefore asking the USPTO or a court to award priority of invention to him. The process—within the USPTO—by which priority is determined is called an *interference*. Section C explores the issue of priority.

STATUTE: **Conditions for patentability; novelty and loss of right to patent**
35 U.S.C. § 102(a), (e) & (g)(2)

A. NOVELTY

The novelty requirement asks whether the claimed invention is new. If an invention is not new, it is said to be *anticipated* by the prior art. Think of this inquiry as focusing on just one inventor and asking whether, prior to the inventor's date of invention, someone other than the inventor, who is not seeking a patent, previously knew, disclosed, or invented what the inventor is seeking to patent. Thus, a threshold issue for a novelty analysis is determining date of invention. While this question is explored in detail in section C, below, a discussion here of a few fundamental principles would be helpful. Date of invention is measured by the date the claimed invention was *reduced to practice*. Reduction to practice can either be (1) constructive; or (2) actual. Constructive reduction to practice is the date on which the application is filed and satisfies section 112's disclosure requirements. Actual reduction to practice—which usually precedes the filing date—requires the inventor to prove that the claimed invention works for its intended purpose, which typically involves the inventor constructing and testing a prototype of the invention.[6]

---

4. Under the AIA, novelty is measured at the time of *filing*, not date of invention. See page 281 for a discussion of this change.

5. As with novelty, the AIA determines priority based on filing date—the first inventor to file a patent application claiming the invention is awarded the patent. See pages 281-285 for a discussion of this change.

6. As explored in section C, below, there can be several other relevant considerations such as *conception* date and whether the inventor was *diligent* in his efforts to reduce the invention to practice or filing an application with the USPTO.

1. Novelty's Doctrinal Framework

The *Atlas* case explores the doctrinal framework for proving anticipation (or lack of novelty). Proving anticipation requires the party challenging the patent's validity to show that each limitation of the claimed invention is disclosed—either expressly or inherently—in a single prior art reference prior to the inventor's date of invention.

ATLAS POWDER COMPANY v. IRECO INCORPORATED
190 F.3d 1342 (Fed. Cir. 1999)

RADER, Circuit Judge.

The United States District Court for the District of Wyoming determined that U.S. Patent No. 4,111,727 (the Clay patent) and its reissue, U.S. Patent No. RE 33,788 (the reissue patent) were invalid. Atlas Powder Company (Atlas), a licensee under those patents, sued IRECO Incorporated (IRECO) for infringement of the Clay patent. Following two bench trials, the district court concluded that both the original Clay patent and the reissue patent were invalid as anticipated by either U.S. Patent No. 3,161,551 (Egly) or U.K. Patent No. 1,306,546 (Butterworth). Because the district court correctly interpreted the claims and applied the law of anticipation, this court affirms the finding of invalidity.

I.

The Clay patent and its reissue both claim explosive compositions. To detonate, explosives require both fuel and oxidizers. The oxidizer rapidly reacts with the fuel to produce expanding gases and heat—an explosion. Composite explosives mix various sources of fuel and oxygen. The most widely used and economical composite explosive is ammonium nitrate and fuel oil (ANFO). ANFO explosives mix about 94% by weight of ammonium nitrate (AN), the oxidizer, with 6% by weight of fuel oil (FO). The AN may include porous prills, dense prills, Stengel flakes, or crystalline AN. ANFO explosives have two primary disadvantages. First, wet conditions dissolve the AN and make the explosive unusable in damp settings. Second, ANFO is a relatively weak explosive because interstitial air occupies considerable space in the mixture, thereby decreasing the amount of explosive material per unit of volume.

To address these shortcomings, explosive experts developed water-in-oil emulsions. These emulsions dissolved the oxidizer into water and then dispersed the solution in oil. Because oil surrounds the oxidizer, it is resistant to moisture, thus solving one of the problems with ANFO. Emulsions also increased the explosive's bulk strength by increasing the density of explosive material in the mixture. Emulsions, however, also have a disadvantage. Emulsions will not detonate unless sensitized. Sensitivity of a blasting composition refers to the ease of igniting its explosion. Experts generally sensitize emulsions by using gassing agents or adding microballoons throughout the mixture. The gassing agents or microballoons provide tiny gas or air bubbles throughout the mixture. Upon detonation, the gas pockets compress and heat up, thereby igniting the fuel around them. In other words, the tiny gas or air bubbles act as "hot spots" to propagate the explosion.

The Clay patent and its reissue both claim composite explosives made from the combination of an ANFO blasting composition and an unsensitized water-in-oil emulsion. Both patents claim essentially the same blasting composition. Claim one of the reissue patent recites:

1. A blasting composition consisting essentially of 10 to 40% by weight of a greasy water-in-oil emulsion and 60 to 90% of a substantially undissolved particulate solid oxidizer salt constituent, wherein the emulsion comprises about 3 to 15% by weight of water, about 2 to 15% of oil, 70 to 90% of powerful oxidizer salt comprising ammonium nitrate which may include other powerful oxidizer salts, wherein the solid constituent comprises ammonium nitrate and *in which sufficient aeration is entrapped to enhance sensitivity to a substantial degree,* and wherein the emulsion component is emulsified by inclusion of 0.1 to 5% by weight, based on the total composition, of an [oil-in-water] water-in-oil emulsifier to hold the aqueous content in the disperse or internal phase.

(Emphasis added.)

* * *

In its 1992 judgment, the district court found claims 1, 2, 3, 10, 12, 13, and 14 of the Clay patent invalid as anticipated by either one of two prior art references, Egly or Butterworth. Egly and Butterworth each disclose blasting compositions containing a water-in-oil emulsion and ANFO with ingredients identical to those of the Clay patents in overlapping amounts. The following chart illustrates the overlap between the explosive compositions disclosed in the prior art patents and the Clay reissue patent:

Composition Contents	Clay	Egly	Butterworth
Water-in-oil Emulsion	10-40%	20-67%	30-50%
Solid Ammonium Nitrate	60-90%	33-80%	50-70%
Emulsion Contents			
Ammonium Nitrate	70-90%	50-70%	65-85%
Water	about 3-15%	about 15-about 35%	7-27%
Fuel Oil	about 2-15%	about 5-about 20%	2-27%
Emulsifier	0.1-5%	about 1-5%	0.5-15%

The only element of the Clay patent claims which is arguably not present in the prior art compositions is "sufficient aeration . . . entrapped to enhance sensitivity to a substantial degree." The trial court determined that "sufficient aeration" was an inherent element in the prior art blasting compositions within the overlapping ranges. The district court also found that none of the accused products infringed any of the asserted claims. The 1992 judgment was not final, however, and specifically reserved a decision on the effect of the reissue patent for phase two of the case.

* * *

After the reissue patent issued, the district court conducted a second bench trial, in January 1996, on the issues of phase two. . . . Despite the PTO's consideration of the Egly and Butterworth references during prosecution of the reissue, the district court concluded that IRECO had overcome the Clay reissue patent's presumption of validity under 35 U.S.C. §282 (1994) by clear and convincing evidence. . . .

II.

Anticipation is a question of fact, including whether or not an element is inherent in the prior art. Therefore, this court reviews a finding of anticipation under the clearly erroneous standard.

"To anticipate a claim, a prior art reference must disclose every limitation of the claimed invention, either explicitly or inherently." *In re Schreiber,* 128 F.3d at 1477. Anticipation of a patent claim requires a finding that the claim at issue "reads on" a prior art reference. *See Titanium Metals Corp. v. Banner,* 778 F.2d 775, 781 (Fed. Cir. 1985). In other words, if granting patent protection on the disputed claim would allow the patentee to exclude the public from practicing the prior art, then that claim is anticipated, regardless of whether it also covers subject matter not in the prior art. *See id.* at 781. Specifically, when a patent claims a chemical composition in terms of ranges of elements, any single prior art reference that falls within each of the ranges anticipates the claim. *See id.* at 780-82 ("It is also an elementary principle of patent law that when, as by a recitation of ranges or otherwise, a claim covers several compositions, the claim is 'anticipated' if one of them is in the prior art."). In chemical compounds, a single prior art species within the patent's claimed genus reads on the generic claim and anticipates.

As noted previously, both Egly and Butterworth disclose blasting compositions with ingredients identical to those of the Clay patent and its reissue in overlapping amounts. The only element which is arguably missing from the prior art is the requirement that "sufficient aeration [be] entrapped to enhance sensitivity to a substantial degree." To decide the issue of anticipation, therefore, the district court examined whether "sufficient aeration . . . to enhance sensitivity" was inherently part of the prior art compositions. That decision, in turn, required the trial court to interpret the claim term "sufficient aeration." By looking at the express language of the claims and the patent's written description, the district court concluded that the claim term "sufficient aeration" included both interstitial air (between oxidizer particles) and porous air (within the pores of oxidizer particles).

The first task of this court on appeal is to construe independently the disputed claim term. This question requires this court to determine whether the claim term "sufficient aeration" includes porous air, as the trial court determined. The claim term "sufficient aeration" does not limit the air content of the composition to interstitial air. Rather, the broad term "aeration" contains no qualitative limits on the kind of air exposure, only the quantitative limit that the air exposure be "sufficient" to enhance sensitivity. If the inventor intended "sufficient aeration" to carry qualitative limits, he also did not express that intention in the patent's written description. The specification gives no explicit definition of the phrase "sufficient aeration . . . to enhance sensitivity," which appears in the patent for the first time in the claims.

It is, of course, possible that the inventor did not include qualitative limits on the term "sufficient aeration" in the specification because those of ordinary skill in the art understand that only interstitial air enhances sensitivity and satisfies the claim's language. *See Autogiro Co. of Am. v. U.S.,* 384 F.2d 391, 397 (Ct. Cl. 1967) ("Claims cannot be clear and unambiguous on their face."). The trial record, however, shows that those of ordinary skill in this art at the time the patent application was filed knew that both interstitial and porous air enhance sensitivity. Dr. Clay himself, the inventor of the patents in suit, testified that air from any source would contribute to the explosion of a heavy ANFO composition and, particularly, air trapped within the pores of porous prilled AN. Therefore, this court detects no error in the district court's conclusion that "sufficient aeration . . . to enhance sensitivity" is understood by those of ordinary skill in the art to include both interstitial and porous air. The district court appropriately construed the claims at issue to include aeration from both sources.

III.

Based on its correct interpretation of "sufficient aeration," the district court heard evidence on whether both interstitial and porous air were present and enhanced sensitivity in the prior art explosive compositions. Based on the evidence, the district court concluded that IRECO had shown the inherency of the disputed claim element in the prior art and overcome "the presumption of validity under 35 U.S.C. §282 by providing clear and convincing evidence of invalidity." This court must determine whether the district court committed clear error by determining that the evidence clearly and convincingly established that "sufficient aeration . . . to enhance sensitivity" was inherent in either Egly or Butterworth.

To invalidate a patent by anticipation, a prior art reference normally needs to disclose each and every limitation of the claim. However, a prior art reference may anticipate when the claim limitation or limitations not expressly found in that reference are nonetheless inherent in it. Under the principles of inherency, if the prior art necessarily functions in accordance with, or includes, the claimed limitations, it anticipates. Inherency is not necessarily coterminous with the knowledge of those of ordinary skill in the art. Artisans of ordinary skill may not recognize the inherent characteristics or functioning of the prior art. However, the discovery of a previously unappreciated property of a prior art composition, or of a scientific explanation for the prior art's functioning, does not render the old composition patentably new to the discoverer. *See Titanium Metals,* 778 F.2d at 782 ("Congress has not seen fit to permit the patenting of an old [composition], known to others . . . , by one who has discovered its . . . useful properties.").

This court's decision in *Titanium Metals* illustrates these principles. In *Titanium Metals,* the patent applicants sought a patent for a titanium alloy containing various ranges of nickel, molybdenum, iron, and titanium. The claims also required that the alloy be "characterized by good corrosion resistance in hot brine environments." *Titanium Metals,* 778 F.2d at 776. A prior art reference disclosed a titanium alloy falling within the claimed ranges, but did not disclose any corrosion-resistant properties. This court affirmed a decision of the PTO Board of Appeals finding the claimed invention unpatentable as anticipated. This court concluded that the claimed alloy was not novel, noting that "it is immaterial, on the issue of their novelty, what inherent properties the alloys have or whether these applicants discovered certain inherent properties." *Id.* at 782. This same reasoning holds true when it is not a property, but an ingredient, which is inherently contained in the prior art. The public remains free to make, use, or sell prior art compositions or processes, regardless of whether or not they understand their complete makeup or the underlying scientific principles which allow them to operate. The doctrine of anticipation by inherency, among other doctrines, enforces that basic principle.

The trial record contains exhaustive evidence regarding the inherency of both interstitial and porous air in the Egly and Butterworth compositions within the overlapping ranges. The testimony from expert witnesses for both parties established that whether sufficient air is present in the explosive composition to facilitate detonation is a function of the ratio of the emulsion to the solid constituent. Dr. Clay testified that "if you mix porous prills, for example, with 30% typical water-in-oil emulsions, you're going to have air in there and it will detonate." Another of Atlas' experts testified that a mixture of 30% of either an Egly or a Butterworth emulsion, mixed with 70% standard fertilizer grade porous AN would have interstitial air, assuming nothing was done to disturb the size distribution of the AN prills. The other experts agreed that the emulsions described in both Egly and Butterworth would inevitably and inherently have interstitial air remaining in the mixture up to a ratio of approximately 40% emulsion to 60% solid constituent. The expert testimony supports the district court's conclusion that "sufficient aeration" is inherent in both Egly and Butterworth.

The district court also relied on evidence from several tests which showed that "sufficient aeration . . . to enhance sensitivity" was inherently present within the overlapping ranges of the Clay patents and Egly and Butterworth. In tests conducted with porous prilled AN combined with FO, stable detonations were obtained in every 8" diameter bore hole test where the percentage of emulsion ranged from 30% to 42.5%. Butterworth specifically discloses the use of porous prilled AN. Butterworth, p. 3, ll. 35-50. These tests, therefore, support the finding that "[t]he emulsions described by Butterworth, combined with the ratios of ANFO disclosed by Butterworth, would inevitably and inherently have interstitial air remaining up to approximately 40% emulsion." The district court also found that the solid AN disclosed in Egly would have included porous prills. These tests, therefore, further support the court's finding that "emulsions described in the Egly Patent, combined with either AN or ANFO, would inevitably and inherently have interstitial air remaining in the mixture up to approximately 40% emulsion to 60% solid constituent." This court discerns no clear error in the district court's conclusion that "sufficient aeration" was inherent in each anticipating prior art reference.

Because "sufficient aeration" was inherent in the prior art, it is irrelevant that the prior art did not recognize the key aspect of Dr. Clay's alleged invention—that air may act as the sole sensitizer of the explosive composition. An inherent structure, composition, or function is not necessarily known. Once it is recognized that interstitial and porous air were inherent elements of the prior art compositions, the assertion that air may act as a sole sensitizer amounts to no more than a claim to the discovery of an inherent property of the prior art, not the addition of a novel element. Insufficient prior understanding of the inherent properties of a known composition does not defeat a finding of anticipation. In addition, there was evidence that Butterworth did recognize the functioning of interstitial and porous air in sensitizing the composition. Butterworth recognizes the need for a gaseous sensitizer. It teaches that the "sensitizer may be a gaseous sensitizer present in the composition in the form of gas bubbles or discrete particles containing an entrapped gas such as air." Although this typically suggests use of a gassing agent or microballoons, Butterworth expressly recognizes that in certain ranges (i.e., 50% to 70% by weight of ANFO) the mixture of porous prilled AN and FO alone provides the necessary sensitization. The district court found that Butterworth thus inherently appreciates that interstitial and porous air may serve as the necessary sensitizer. This court discerns no clear error in that finding.

In reaching this judgment, this court notes that Egly teaches away from air entrapment. Specifically, Egly teaches that it is desirable to "fill all spaces in between each particle to give added density." This statement in Egly, however, does not defeat the district court's finding of anticipation for several reasons. First, Egly's teaching does not in any way discredit the trial court's alternative reliance on Butterworth for invalidation of the Clay patent and its reissue. More important, the statement in Egly is, in fact, only a showing that Egly did not recognize the function of the inherently present interstitial air. As noted previously, an insufficient scientific understanding does not defeat a showing of inherency. In fact, even in Egly itself, the only way taught for removing interstitial air is the addition of more emulsion. Egly, however, teaches the use of a broad range—between 20% and 67% by weight—of water-in-oil emulsion. While Egly compositions containing amounts approaching 67% by weight of water-in-oil emulsions may have little or no entrapped air, the evidence established that at emulsion levels below 40%, Egly compositions 'inevitably and inherently" trap sufficient amounts of air to enhance sensitivity. This evidence included both substantial amounts of expert testimony and data showing extensive testing of Egly compositions.

Finally, although the record showed that special mixing techniques—such as grinding and screening the AN particles—remove interstitial air from the blasting compositions, Egly did not teach or suggest any such techniques. Thus, although Egly may have suggested removal of air, it nonetheless inherently contained interstitial aeration sufficient to enhance sensitivity when comprised of elements within the Clay patent ranges. Consequently, this court discerns no clear error in the district court's conclusion that Egly compositions within the range of the Clay patent claims inherently contain sufficient air to enhance sensitivity.

Based upon all the evidence, substantial amounts of which were not before the PTO in its reissue examination, the district court concluded that IRECO had proven

> clearly and convincingly that, unless extraordinary measures are taken to grind and screen ammonium nitrate, the existence of "interstitial air," or sufficient aeration to sustain a stable detonation, is a function of the ratios of emulsion to solid constituent. Specifically, at ratios of 30% emulsion and 70% solid constituent, which are common to the Clay Patent, the Egly Patent, and the Butterworth Patent, there is inherently sufficient aeration to sustain a stable detonation, barring extraordinary efforts to grind and screen the ammonium nitrate used in the solid constituent.

This court discerns no clear error in the district court's factual determination that the prior art inherently possesses sufficient aeration to enhance sensitivity to a substantial degree within the overlapping ranges. Nor does this court discern clear error in the district court's finding of anticipation based on either Egly or Butterworth. To uphold the Clay patent and its reissue would preclude the public from practicing the prior art.

Comments

1. *Identity of Invention, Anticipatory Enablement, and Arrangement.* A finding of anticipation requires each and every claim limitation to be disclosed in a single reference (identity of invention), and the reference must enable the claimed invention so as to place the invention in the possession of a person having ordinary skill in the art (anticipatory enablement). The reference does not have to explain every detail of the claimed invention because the reference is "considered together with the knowledge of one of ordinary skill in the pertinent art." *In re Samour*, 571 F.2d 559, 562 (CCPA 1978). But during prosecution of a patent application, an examiner can reject a patent claim as anticipated by a prior art reference "without conducting an inquiry into whether or not that prior art reference is enabling." In this regard, prior art references are presumed enabling, and once an examiner—"who has no access to experts or laboratories"—makes a prima facie case of anticipation, "the burden shifts to the applicant to submit rebuttal evidence of nonenablement." *In re Antor Media Corp.*, 689 F.3d 1282, 1289 (Fed. Cir. 2012).

In addition, anticipation requires that the reference reveal how the claim limitations are *arranged*. For example, a claim reciting limitations A, B, and C and the structural or interdependent relationship among A, B, and C will not be anticipated by a reference that merely recites A, B, and C without any mention of the aforementioned relationship. The case of *Net MoneyIN, Inc. v. Verisign, Inc.*, 545 F.3d 1359 (Fed. Cir. 2008) is illustrative. In *NetMoneyIN*, the patent-in-suit ('737 patent) related to a system for processing credit card transactions over the Internet. Claim 23 recited five limitations, what the claim referred to as "links" among various computers (including the customer's computer, vending computer, and payment processing computers) and how these links related to each other. The district court invalidated claim 23 based on a single prior art document referred to as the "iKP reference." According to the district court "[a]ll of the limitations of claim 23 can be found within the iKP reference. A simple combination would produce the system described in claim 23 of the '737 patent. That no specific example within iKP contains all five links does not preclude a finding of anticipation."

The Federal Circuit disagreed with this assessment, noting that the district court's "four corners" approach "does not tell the whole story." The prior art reference, wrote the court, "must not only disclose all elements of the claim within the four corners of the document, but must also disclose those elements 'arranged as in the claim.'" *Id.* at 1369. The Federal Circuit stated that the expression "arranged as in the claim" applies to all types of claims and is understood to mean that the prior art reference must show how the limitations are "arranged or combined in the same way as in the claim." *Id.* at 1370. In reversing the district court, the Federal Circuit noted "the iKP reference discloses two separate protocols for processing an Internet credit card transaction" and "[n]either of these protocols contains all five links arranged or combined in the same way as claimed in the '737 patent." Accordingly, "although the iKP reference might anticipate a claim directed to either of the two protocols disclosed, it cannot anticipate the system of claim 23." *Id.* at 1371.

2. *Inherency.* Anticipation is proven by showing that each limitation of the claimed invention is present, either expressly or under principles of inherency. While express disclosure is straightforward, the meaning of inherency is "perhaps the most elusive doctrine in all of patent law." Dan L. Burk & Mark A. Lemley, *Inherency*, 47 Wm. & Mary L. Rev. 371, 373 (2005). The Federal Circuit has held that a claim limitation is inherently anticipated if the limitation is necessarily present in or inevitably flows from the reference. *See Continental Can Co. USA v. Monsanto Co.*, 948 F.2d 1264, 1269 (Fed. Cir. 1991) (quoting *In re Oelrich*, 666 F.2d 578, 581 (CCPA 1981)) ("The mere fact that a certain thing may result from a given set of circumstances is not sufficient. If, however, the disclosure is sufficient to show that the natural result flowing from the operation as taught would result in the performance of the questioned function, it seems to be well settled that the disclosure should be regarded as sufficient."). And extrinsic evidence can be used to help discern if the claimed limitation is "present or inevitably flows from the reference." *Continental*, 948 F.2d at 1268 (stating "when the reference is silent about the asserted inherent characteristic, such gap in the reference may be filled with recourse to extrinsic evidence"). *See also* Timothy R. Holbrook, *Possession in Patent Law*, 59 S.M.U. L. Rev. 123, 172 n.273 (2006) (stating "[a] reference can be anticipatory even if part of the invention is not expressly disclosed but is inherently disclosed. Other prior art references can be used to show that the absent feature necessarily is present in the original piece of prior art").

But inherency does not require that a person of (having) ordinary skill in the art ("PHOSITA") appreciate or recognize the inherent disclosure *at the time of invention. See Schering Corporation v. Geneva Pharmaceuticals, Inc.*, 339 F.3d 1373, 1377 (Fed. Cir. 2003) (stating "inherent anticipation does not require that a person of ordinary skill in the art at the time would have recognized the inherent disclosure"); *Abbott Laboratories v. Baxter Pharmaceutical Products, Inc.*, 471 F.3d 1363, 1368 (Fed. Cir. 2006) ("'[I]nherent anticipation does not require that a person of ordinary skill in the art at the time would have recognized the inherent disclosure.'"). Not requiring PHOSITA knowledge at time of invention is logical. If the skilled artisan had knowledge of the inherent disclosure, the doctrine of inherency would be unnecessary because this knowledge would result in straightforward anticipation. Thus, inherency picks up where anticipation leaves off. But if knowledge is not a requirement, what is the basis for inherency? One rationale is to view inherency through the lens of public benefit. As Dan Burk and Mark Lemley point out:

> the inherency cases are all ultimately about whether the public already gets the benefit of the claimed element or invention. If the public already benefits from the invention, even if they don't know why, the invention is inherent in the prior art. If the public doesn't benefit from the invention, there is no inherency.

Burk & Lemley, *Inherency, supra,* at 374. Janice Mueller and Don Chisum build on the Burk-Lemley public benefit rationale by arguing that a finding of inherency should "demand[] that the prior art, which is relied upon to destroy novelty by establishing inherent anticipation . . . , satisfy a more rigorous standard of enablement than the level of enablement required" by section 112, ¶1. *See* Janice M. Mueller & Donald S. Chisum, *Enabling Patent Law's Inherency Anticipation Doctrine,* 45 HOUS. L. REV. 1101, 1103 (2008). Instead of permitting undue experimentation, which Mueller and Chisum regard as too liberal in the context of inherency, "no more than de minimis experimentation should be required to achieve a later-claimed invention." *Id.* at 1104.

An illustrative inherency case is *SmithKline Beecham Corp. v. Apotex Corp.,* 403 F.3d 1331 (Fed. Cir. 2005). In this case, SmithKline owned the '723 U.S. patent that claimed "crystalline paroxetine hydrochloride hemihydrate (PHC hemihydrate)," which was the active ingredient in SmithKline's antidepressant drug, Paxil. Shortly after Paxil hit the market, Apotex, a generic drug manufacture, initiated regulatory proceedings seeking FDA approval to market its own PHC antidepressant. Apotex asserted that its product would not infringe the '723 patent because Apotex's active ingredient was PHC anhydrate, not PHC hemihydrate. SmithKline sued Apotex under the theory PHC anhydrate tablets necessarily contain, by a manufacturing conversion process, at least trace amounts of PHC hemihydrate. Apotex responded by arguing that the '723 patent was inherently anticipated by the '196 patent, which expressly disclosed PHC anhydrate. The '196 patent did not expressly disclose PHC hemihydate—the active ingredient claimed in the '723 patent that was not discovered until five years after the '196 patent was filed. The district court held that the '723 patent was not inherently anticipated because Apotex "did not prove by clear and convincing evidence that it was impossible to make pure PHC anhydrate." *Id.* at 1342. The Federal Circuit found the district court's standard "too exacting." Instead, the court stated Apotex need only prove that the prior art disclosure " 'is sufficient to show that the natural result flowing from the operation as taught [in the prior art] would result in the claimed product.' " *Id.* at 1343. Applying this test, the court found that the '196 patent anticipates claim 1 of the '723 patent because the '196 patent inherently disclosed PHC hemihydrate; that is, "producing PHC anhydrate according to the '196 patent inevitably results in the production of at least trace amounts of anticipating PHC hemihydrate." *Id.* Thus, although not expressly disclosed, the '196 reference enabled a person of ordinary skill in the art to make PHC hemihydrate; indeed, one could say that PHC hemihydrate inevitably resulted from practicing the '196 patent.

2. "Known or Used" Under Section 102(a)

This section is devoted to the words "known" and "used" in section 102(a), which are not as straightforward as one may initially think. For instance, "known or used" by whom? And what exactly does it mean the invention was "known or used"? The *Gayler* and *Rosaire* cases and Comments that follow explore the nuances of this language in the context of patent law's policy objectives.

GAYLER v. WILDER
51 U.S. (10 How.) 477 (1850)

Chief Justice TANEY delivered the opinion of the court.

The [assignee, Wilder,] brought an action against Gayler and Brown, for an alleged infringement of a patent right for the use of plaster of Paris in the construction of fire-proof chests. In the declaration, it was averred that one Daniel Fitzgerald was the original and first inventor of a new and useful improvement in fire-proof chests or safes, and that letters patent were granted him therefor, bearing date the 1st day of June, 1843.

* * *

It appears that James Conner, who carried on the business of a stereotype founder in the city of New York, made a safe for his own use between the years 1829 and 1832, for the protection of his papers against fire; and continued to use it until 1838, when it passed into other hands. It was kept in his counting-room and known to the persons engaged in the foundery; and after it passed out of his hands, he used others of a different construction.

It does not appear what became of this safe afterwards. And there is nothing in the testimony from which it can be inferred that its mode of construction was known to the person into whose possession it fell, or that any value was attached to it as a place of security for papers against fire; or that it was ever used for that purpose.

Upon these facts the court instructed the jury, "that if Connor had not made his discovery public, but had used it simply for his own private purpose, and it had been finally forgotten or abandoned, such a discovery and use would be no obstacle to the taking out of a patent by Fitzgerald or those claiming under him, if he be an original, though not the first, inventor or discoverer."

The instruction assumes that the jury might find from the evidence that Conner's safe was substantially the same with that of Fitzgerald, and also prior in time. And if the fact was so, the question then was whether the patentee was "the original and first inventor or discoverer," within the meaning of the act of Congress.

The act of 1836, ch. 357, §6, authorizes a patent where the party has discovered or invented a new and useful improvement, "not known or used by others before his discovery or invention." And the 15th section provides that, if it appears on the trial of an action brought for the infringement of a patent that the patentee "was not the original and first inventor or discoverer of the thing patented," the verdict shall be for the defendant.

Upon a literal construction of these particular words, the patentee in this case certainly was not the original and first inventor or discoverer, if the Conner safe was the same with his, and preceded his discovery. But we do not think that this construction would carry into effect the intention of the legislature. It is not by detached words and phrases that a statute ought to be expounded. The whole act must be taken together, and a fair interpretation given to it, neither extending nor restricting it beyond the legitimate import of its language, and its obvious policy and object. And in the 15th section, after making the provision above mentioned, there is a further provision, that, if it shall appear that the patentee at the time of his application for the patent believed himself to be the first inventor, the patent shall not be void on account of the invention or discovery having been known or used in any foreign country, it not appearing that it had been before patented or described in any printed publication.

In the case thus provided for, the party who invents is not strictly speaking the first and original inventor. The law assumes that the improvement may have been known and used before his discovery. Yet his patent is valid if he discovered it by the efforts of his own genius, and believed himself to be the original inventor. The clause in question qualifies the words before used, and shows that by knowledge and use the legislature meant knowledge and use existing in a manner accessible to the public. If the foreign invention had been printed or patented, it was already given to the world and open to the people of this country, as well as of others, upon reasonable inquiry. They would therefore derive no advantage from the invention here. It would confer no benefit upon the community, and the inventor therefore is not considered to be entitled to the reward. But if the foreign discovery is not patented, nor described in any printed publication, it might be known and used in remote places for ages, and the people of this country be unable to profit by it. The means of obtaining knowledge would not be within their reach; and, as far as their interest is concerned, it would be the same thing as if the improvement had never been discovered. It is the inventor here that brings it to them, and places it in their possession. And as he does this by the effort of his own genius, the law regards him as the first and original inventor, and protects his patent, although the improvement had in fact been invented before, and used by others.

So, too, as to the lost arts. It is well known that centuries ago discoveries were made in certain arts the fruits of which have come down to us, but the means by which the work was accomplished are at this day unknown. The knowledge has been lost for ages. Yet it would hardly be doubted, if any one now discovered an art thus lost, and it was a useful improvement, that, upon a fair construction of the act of Congress, he would be entitled to a patent. Yet he would not literally be the first and original inventor. But he would be the first to confer on the public the benefit of the invention. He would discover what is unknown, and communicate knowledge which the public had not the means of obtaining without his invention.

Upon the same principle and upon the same rule of construction, we think that Fitzgerald must be regarded as the first and original inventor of the safe in question. The case as to this point admits, that, although Conner's safe had been kept and used for years, yet no test had been applied to it, and its capacity for resisting heat was not known; there was no evidence to show that any particular value was attached to it after it passed from his possession, or that it was ever afterwards used as a place of security for papers; and it appeared that he himself did not attempt to make another like the one he is supposed to have invented, but used a different one. And upon this state of the evidence the court put it to the jury to say, whether this safe had been finally forgotten or abandoned before Fitzgerald's invention, and whether he was the original inventor of the safe for which he obtained the patent; directing them, if they found these two facts, that their verdict must be for the plaintiff. We think there is no error in this instruction. For if the Conner safe had passed away from the memory of Conner himself, and of those who had seen it, and the safe itself had disappeared, the knowledge of the improvement was as completely lost as if it had never been discovered. The public could derive no benefit from it until it was discovered by another inventor. And if Fitzgerald made his discovery by his own efforts, without any knowledge of Conner's, he invented an improvement that was then new, and at that time unknown; and it was not the less new and unknown because Conner's safe was recalled to his memory by the success of Fitzgerald's.

We do not understand the Circuit Court to have said that the omission of Conner to try the value of his safe by proper tests would deprive it of its priority; nor his omission to bring it into public use. He might have omitted both, and also abandoned its use, and been ignorant of the extent of its value; yet, if it was the same with Fitzgerald's, the latter would not upon such grounds be entitled to a patent, provided Conner's safe and its mode of construction were still in the memory of Conner before they were recalled by Fitzgerald's patent.

The circumstances above mentioned, referred to in the opinion of the Circuit Court, appeared to have been introduced as evidence tending to prove that the Conner safe might have been finally forgotten, and upon which this hypothetical instruction was given. Whether this evidence was sufficient for that purpose or not, was a question for the jury, and the court left it to them. And if the jury found the fact to be so, and that Fitzgerald again discovered it, we regard him as standing upon the same ground with the discoverer of a lost art, or an unpatented and unpublished foreign invention, and like him entitled to a patent. For there was no existing and living knowledge of this improvement, or of its former use, at the time he made the discovery. And whatever benefit any individual may derive from it in the safety of his papers, he owes entirely to the genius and exertions of Fitzgerald.

Upon the whole, therefore, we think there is no error in the opinion of the Circuit Court, and the judgment is therefore affirmed.

ROSAIRE v. BAROID SALES DIVISION

218 F.2d 72 (5th Cir. 1955)

TUTTLE, Circuit Judge.

In this suit for patent infringement there is presented to us for determination the correctness of the judgment of the trial court, based on findings of fact and conclusions of law, holding that the two patents involved in the litigation were invalid and void and that furthermore there had been no infringement by defendant.

The Rosaire and Horvitz patents relate to methods of prospecting for oil or other hydrocarbons. The inventions are based upon the assumption that gases have emanated from deposits of hydrocarbons which have been trapped in the earth and that these emanations have modified the surrounding rock. The methods claimed involve the steps of taking a number of samples of soil from formations which are not themselves productive of hydrocarbons, either over a horizontal area or vertically down a well bore, treating each sample, as by grinding and heating in a closed vessel, to cause entrained or absorbed hydrocarbons therein to evolve as a gas, quantitatively measuring the amount of hydrocarbon gas so evolved from each sample, and correlating the measurements with the locations from which the samples were taken.

Plaintiff claims that in 1936 he and Horvitz invented this new method of prospecting for oil. In due course the two patents in suit, Nos. 2,192,525 and 2,324,085, were issued thereon. Horvitz assigned his interest to Rosaire. Appellant alleged that appellee Baroid began infringing in 1947; that he learned of this in 1949 and asked Baroid to take a license, but no license agreement was worked out, and this suit followed, seeking an injunction and an accounting.

In view of the fact that the trial court's judgment that the patents were invalid, would of course dispose of the matter if correct, we turn our attention to this issue. Appellee's contention is that the judgment of the trial court in this respect should be supported on two principal grounds. The first is that the prior art, some of which was not before the patent office, anticipated the two patents; the second is that work carried on by one Teplitz for the Gulf Oil Corporation invalidated both patents by reason of the relevant provisions of the patent laws which state that an invention is not patentable if it "was known or used by others in this country" before the patentee's invention thereof, 35 U.S.C.A. § 102(a). Appellee contends that Teplitz and his coworkers knew and extensively used in the field the same alleged inventions before any date asserted by Rosaire and Horvitz.

On this point appellant himself in his brief admits that "Teplitz conceived of the idea of extracting and quantitatively measuring entrained or absorbed gas from the samples of rock, rather than relying upon the free gas in the samples. We do not deny that Teplitz conceived of the methods of the patents in suit." And further appellant makes the following admission: "We admit that the Teplitz-Gulf work was done before Rosaire and Horvitz conceived of the inventions. We will show, however, that Gulf did not apply for patent until 1939, did not publish Teplitz's ideas, and did not otherwise give the public the benefit of the experimental work."

In support of their respective positions, both appellant and appellee stress the language in our opinion in the case of *Pennington v. National Supply Co.*, where, speaking through Judge Holmes, we said: "Appellant insists that the court erred in considering the prior use of the Texas machine, because that machine was abandoned by the Texas Company and was not successful until modified and rebuilt. As to this, it does not appear that the Texas machine was a failure, since it drilled three wells for the Texas Company, which was more than was usually accomplished by the rotary drilling machines then in use."

"An unsuccessful experiment which is later abandoned does not negative novelty in a new and successful device." *T.H. Symington Co. v. National Malleable Castings Co.*, 250 U.S. 383. Nevertheless, the existence and operation of a machine, abandoned after its completion and sufficient use to demonstrate its practicability, is evidence that the same ideas incorporated in a later development along the same line do not amount to invention. If the prior machine does not anticipate, it would not have done so if it had been neither unsuccessful nor abandoned. Novelty is ascribed to new things, without regard to the successful and continued use of old things. Correlatively, it is denied to old things, without regard to the circumstances which caused their earlier applications to be unsatisfactory or their use to be abandoned.

The question as to whether the work of Teplitz was "an unsuccessful experiment," as claimed by appellant, or was a successful trial of the method in question and a reduction of that method to actual practice, as contended by appellee, is, of course, a question of fact. On this point the trial court made the following finding of fact: "I find as a fact, by clear and substantial proof beyond a reasonable doubt, that Abraham J. Teplitz and his coworkers with Gulf Oil Corporation and its Research Department during 1935 and early 1936, before any date claimed by Rosaire, spent more than a year in the oil fields and adjacent territory around Palestine, Texas, taking and analyzing samples both over an area and down drill holes, exactly as called for in the claims of the patents which Rosaire and Horvitz subsequently applied for and which are here in suit. This Teplitz work was a successful and adequate field trial of the prospecting method involved and a reduction to practice of that method. The work was performed in the field under ordinary conditions without any deliberate attempt at concealment or effort to exclude the public and without any instructions of secrecy to the employees performing the work."

As we view it, if the court's findings of fact are correct then under the statute as construed by the courts, we must affirm the finding of the trial court that appellee's patents were invalid.

A close analysis of the evidence on which the parties rely to resolve this question clearly demonstrates that there was sufficient evidence to sustain the finding of the trial court that there was more here than an unsuccessful or incomplete experiment. It is clear that the work was not carried forward, but that appears to be a result of two things: (1) that the geographical area did not lend itself properly to the test, and (2) that the "entire gas prospecting program was therefore suspended in September of 1936, in order that the accumulated information might be thoroughly reviewed." It will be noted that the program was not suspended to test the worth of the method but to examine the data that was produced by use of the method involved. The above quotation came from one of the recommendations at the end of Teplitz's report, and was introduced on behalf of the appellant himself. Expert testimony presented by witnesses Rogers, Eckhardt and Weaver supported appellee's contention.

With respect to the argument advanced by appellant that the lack of publication of Teplitz's work deprived an alleged infringer of the defense of prior use, we find no case which constrains us to hold that where such work was done openly and in the ordinary course of the activities of the employer, a large producing company in the oil industry, the statute is to be so modified by construction as to require some affirmative act to bring the work to the attention of the public at large.

While there is authority for the proposition that one of the basic principles underlying the patent laws is the enrichment of the art, and that a patent is given to encourage disclosure of inventions, no case we have found requires a holding that, under the circumstances that attended the work of Teplitz, the fact of public knowledge must be shown before it can be urged to invalidate a subsequent patent. The case of *Corona Cord Tire Co. v. Dovan Chemical Corporation, supra,* is authority for the opposing view, that taken by the court below. In that case the Supreme Court said: "In 1916, while with the Norwalk Company, Kratz prepared D.P.G. and demonstrated its utility as a rubber accelerator by making test slabs of vulcanized or cured rubber with its use. Every time that he produced such a slab he recorded his test in cards which he left with the Norwalk Company and kept a duplicate of his own. . . . This work was known to, and was participated in, by his associate in the Norwalk Company, his immediate superior and the chief chemist of the company, Dr. Russell, who fully confirms Kratz's records and statement." *Corona Cord Tire,* 276 U.S. 358, 378, 379.

The court further states in the *Corona* case at page 382 of 276 U.S.: "But, even if we ignore this evidence of Kratz's actual use of D.P.G. in these rubber inner tubes which were sold, what he did at Norwalk, supported by the evidence of Dr. Russell, his chief, and by the indubitable records that are not challenged, leaves no doubt in our minds that he did discover in 1916 the strength of D.P.G. as an accelerator as compared with the then known accelerators, and that he then demonstrated it by a reduction of it to practice in production of cured or vulcanized rubber. This constitutes priority in this case."

The judgment of the trial court is affirmed.

Comments

1. *"Known or Used" by Whom?* The words "known or used" in section 102(a) refer to knowledge and use by someone other than the inventor. As Justice Story wrote, "known or used . . . cannot mean that the thing invented was not known or used . . . by the inventor himself, for that would prohibit him from the only means to obtain a patent." *Pennock v. Dialogue*, 27 U.S. (2 Pet.) 1, 18 (1829). In other words, an inventor cannot anticipate himself. *See Invitrogen Corp. v. Biocrest Mfg., L.P.*, 424 F.3d 1374, 1381 (Fed. Cir. 2005) (stating "an inventor's own work cannot be used to invalidate patents protecting his own later inventive activities unless . . . he places it on sale or uses it publicly more than a year before filing"); *In re Facius*, 408 F.2d 1396, 1406 (CCPA 1969) (noting "[c]ertainly one's own invention, whatever the form of disclosure to the public, may not be prior art against oneself, absent a statutory bar"). See Chapter 6 on statutory bars for a detailed discussion of potentially invalidating on-sale and public-use activity.

   And Congress used the disjunctive "or" when describing knowledge and use in section 102(a), which means that prior knowledge alone can defeat novelty. Recall the *Gayler* court noted Connor could have defeated novelty provided the safe's "mode of construction were still in the memory of Conner." Novelty, therefore, would be defeated in *Gayler* even if Connor abandoned the invention or never used it. This point raises an important distinction between sections 102(a) and (g), the latter requiring that to serve as prior art, the invention not be abandoned. See Comment 3 after the principal case of *Thomson v. Quixote*, below.

2. *"Known or Used" Where?* To serve as prior art, knowledge and use must be in the United States. Section 102(a) distinguishes knowledge and use from patents and printed publications, which can act as prior art if available in the United States "or a foreign country." (The AIA, as noted below, eliminated this geographic distinction for patent applications filed on or after March 16, 2013. *See* PATENT REFORM PERSPECTIVE after these Comments.) Prior to 1836, knowledge and use anywhere in the world defeated patent rights. But a geographic distinction was inserted in the 1836 Patent Act because, with the re-introduction of an examination system, it became clear that searching and finding foreign-based knowledge and use would be infeasible for examiners. *See* Mario Biagioli, *Patent Republic: Representing Inventions, Constructing Rights and Authors*, 73 SOCIAL RESEARCH 1129, 1152 (2007) (arguing that in 1836 "[n]ovelty . . . was redefined to conform to the less expansive notion of prior art that had to be introduced to make the examiners' job reasonable and to create politically defensible expectations about what the Patent Office could and could not do. Such an institutional decision, however, resulted from the consequences of the introduction of specification requirements. What

examiners could and could not do was what the specifications (as material inscriptions) allowed them to do. They could check a text against another text they could find in their library, but could not travel the world looking for machines"). The *Gayler* Court, in a slightly different context (namely, discussing information accessible to the public), stated:

> If the foreign invention had been printed or patented, it was already given to the world and open to the people of this country, as well as of others, upon reasonable inquiry. They would therefore derive no advantage from the invention here. It would confer no benefit upon the community, and the inventor therefore is not considered to be entitled to the reward. But if the foreign discovery is not patented, nor described in any printed publication, it might be known and used in remote places for ages, and the people of this country be unable to profit by it. The means of obtaining knowledge would not be within their reach.

51 U.S. at 497.

3. *How Public Must the Knowledge and Use Be?* It does not take much to satisfy the publicity requirement of section 102(a). Recall the work of Teplitz in *Rosaire*, which from a practical standpoint, was inaccessible to the public. So perhaps the publicity requirement of section 102(a) must be understood as the absence of secrecy or absence of active steps to maintain secrecy. As the *Rosaire* court expressly noted, Teplitz's work was "done openly and in the ordinary course" of business. In *Gayler*, the court sided with Fitzgerald because it was he who disclosed the invention to the public, or as the court stated, "[i]t is the inventor here that brings it to them." Yet Justice Taney's favorable statements about Fitzgerald are tempered by the court's recognition that if "Conner's safe and its mode of construction were still in the memory of Conner," Fitzgerald would be denied a patent even if Conner abandoned the invention and was "ignorant of the extent of its value." It was only because of the near total lack of evidence of prior knowledge of the safe that Fitzgerald's patent rights survive.

In both *Rosaire* and *Gayler*, the "public" is defined very inclusively; Teplitz and Conner were members of the public. A virtue of an inclusive definition is ease of application that results from a clear rule. If Conner is not the public, who is? How many people need to have access to the claimed invention before section 102(a)'s publicity requirement is triggered? A "reasonable" amount of people? How do we narrow the definition of public to exclude Teplitz and Conner without significantly sacrificing certainty in application of the rule?

Yet there are compelling arguments for a narrower definition of public. Are the actions of Conner and Teplitz on the one hand, or Fitzgerald, Rosaire, and Horvitz on the other hand, more consistent with patent law's constitutional purpose of "promot[ing] the progress of the useful arts? What did Teplitz's work bring to the public or what social benefits would result from a more detailed memory of Conner? It was Rosaire, Horvitz, and Fitzgerald who took the affirmative step of applying for a patent, and, by satisfying section 112's requirements, disclosed their respective inventions to the public, at least in a more extensive manner than those who came prior. As Judge Hand wrote of the *Gayler* holding, "what had not in fact enriched the art, should not count as prior art." *Gillman v. Stern*, 114 F.2d 28, 31 (2d Cir. 1940).

And Justice Grier, in *Adams v. Jones*, 1 F. Cas. 126 (1859), stated that "[i]t is only when some person, by labor and perseverance, has been successful in perfecting some valuable manufacture, by ingenious improvements, and labor-saving devices, that their patents are sought to be annulled by digging up some useless, musty, forgotten contrivances of unsuccessful experiments." (This statement reflects the Justice Grier we know from the *Morse* case.) *See also* ROBERT P. MERGES, JUSTIFYING INTELLECTUAL PROPERTY LAW 143 (2011) (stating that novelty rules relating to protecting the public domain "are so solicitous of preserving access to the prior art that they can seem almost absurd. There is no inquiry into the practical accessibility of the prior art; once it is public, even marginally, and only in one obscure place or one obscure form, the game is over — no patent. Period."). So ask yourself what makes more sense, a generous definition of public (e.g., *Gayler* and *Rosaire*) or a more restrictive definition?

Another interesting case is *Woodland Trust v. Flowertree Nursery, Inc.*, 148 F.3d 1368 (Fed. Cir. 1998). In *Woodland*, the '440 patent, owned by Woodland Trust, related to a method and apparatus for protecting a plot of foliage plants from freezing, by establishing an insulating covering of ice over ground level watering. The patent was filed on July 1, 1983 and issued on August 16, 1988. Flowertree asserted the '440 patent was invalid under section 102(a) because the invention was known and used prior to 1983 by Joseph Burke and William Hawkins, who owned Flowertree. Four witnesses, including the son of William Hawkins, testified that the claimed invention was known (and is still known) and in use in the 1960s and 1970s in Flowertree's Florida nurseries, but the use was discontinued in the late 1970s. The court did not find this evidence persuasive because it failed to prove that knowledge and use of the claimed invention was publicly accessible prior to Woodland Trust's date of invention. In particular, the court cited the lack of physical evidence of prior knowledge, the relationship of the witnesses, and the extensive passing of time (20 years) between the asserted prior uses and trial. *Id.* at 1373.

PATENT REFORM PERSPECTIVE
Novelty Under the AIA

The new section 102(a) reads in relevant part:

(a) NOVELTY; PRIOR ART.—A person shall be entitled to a patent unless—

(1) the claimed invention was patented, described in a printed publication, or in public use, on sale, or otherwise available to the public before the effective filing date of the claimed invention. . . .

(b) EXCEPTIONS—

(1) DISCLOSURES MADE 1 YEAR OR LESS BEFORE THE EFFECTIVE FILING DATE OF THE CLAIMED INVENTION—A disclosure made 1 year or less before the effective filing date of a claimed invention shall not be prior art to the claimed invention under subsection (a)(1) if—

(A) the disclosure was made by the inventor or joint inventor or by another who obtained the subject matter disclosed directly or indirectly from the inventor or a joint inventor; or

(B) the subject matter disclosed had, before such disclosure, been publicly disclosed by the inventor or a joint inventor or another who obtained the subject matter disclosed directly or indirectly from the inventor or a joint inventor. . . .

New section 102(a) collapses old sections 102(a) and (b) under the heading of "Novelty." There are several points that need to be addressed.

1. *Many Familiar Words.* Section 102(a)(1) retained many of the same words found in the old section 102(a), such as "patented," "printed publication," "public use," and "on sale." The AIA eliminated the words "known or used" and added the phrase "otherwise available to the public," which, although new to American patent law, should be given a meaning consistent with "known or used" as interpreted by the courts in *Gayler* and *Rosaire*. But it is unclear if the phrase "otherwise available to the public" modifies all that comes before it, or only the terms "public use" and "on sale," or is simply a catch-all phrase that expands the prior art world to include, for example, oral communications made at conferences. The Federal Circuit will no doubt have opportunities to address these questions.

While it is likely that the pre-AIA common law interpretation will apply to the other terms in section 102(a)(1), particularly "printed publication" (*see In re Klopfenstein* on page 310 of this chapter),[7] there is some debate as to whether the pre-AIA interpretation of "public use" and "on sale" will carry over into the post-AIA world. These terms and the case law relating to them will be explored in detail in Chapter 6, and, therefore, we will defer the exploration of this debate until then in another Patent Reform Perspective.

2. *Geographic Distinction Eliminated.* Section 102 eliminates the geographic distinction between knowledge and use, on the one hand, and patents and printed publications, on the other hand. (See Comment 2, above, for a discussion of why this distinction was created in the first place.) Prior art can now originate anywhere in the world. In this regard, the new section 102 tracks the European Patent Convention.

3. *Exceptions to Section 102(a)(1).* Section 102(b)(1) provides important exceptions to section 102(a)(1). The structure of these provisions parallel each other in that section 102(b)(1) provides exceptions to section 102(a)(1), and section 102(b)(2)'s exceptions map on to section 102(a)(2). (Subsections (b)(2) and (a)(2) will be explored after *Alexander Milburn*, a principal case in this chapter, on page 286)

Section 102(b)(1) creates two important exceptions—and an accompanying grace period —to the novelty principle set forth in section 102(a)(1).

a. *Inventor Was First to Disclose.* Under section 102(b)(1)(A), a disclosure of the claimed invention made one year or less before the

---

7. *See Safeco Ins. Co. of America v. Burr*, 551 U.S. 47, 58 (2007) (stating "a common law term in a statute comes with a common law meaning, absent anything pointing another way"); *Microsoft Corp. v. i4i Limited Partnership*, 131 S. Ct. 2238, 2245 (2011) (stating "where Congress uses a common law term in a statute, we assume the 'term . . . comes with a common law meaning, absent anything pointing another way'") (citing *Safeco*).

effective filing date will <u>not</u> be considered prior art under section 102(a)(1) *if* **the "disclosure was made by the inventor."** Note that the word "disclosure" is referring to prior art in section 102(a)(1). Therefore, any inventor-initiated disclosure as set forth in (a)(1) will trigger the grace period exception of section 102(b).[8] (As noted above, there is a debate—explored in Chapter 6—whether an *inventor's* non-public disclosure such as a confidential sale or non-informing use will qualify as a "public use" or "on-sale" against the *inventor*.)[9]

<u>Example 1</u>

Inventor publishes an article in the journal Nature on August 16, 2013, disclosing Invention ABC. Inventor has until August 16, 2014 to file a patent application in the United States claiming ABC. If Inventor fails to file before this date he is barred from obtaining patent protection under section 102(a)(1).[10]

<u>Example 2</u>

Inventor engages in a non-informing use of Invention ABC on March 5, 2013. ABC is a Process to make Product X, which is sold to the public. The use is commercial because Product X is being sold, but non-informing because the public cannot discern the Process from studying or using Product X. One school of thought holds this non-informing use is not prior art because the AIA requires greater publicity to qualify as a prior art event. In other words, non-informing uses and confidential sales—although both have a commercial component—are not prior art under section 102(a)(1).[11] Another school of thought asserts that based on pre-AIA precedent this use is a prior art even under section 102(a)(1)

---

8. Section 102(b)(1)(B) requires the disclosure to be "publicly disclosed," implying that private disclosures are prior art under section 102(a)(1)(A). This reading is consistent with the legislative history. According to Senator Leahy:

> We intend that if an inventor's actions are such as to constitute prior art under subsection 102(a), then those actions necessarily trigger subsection 102(b)'s protections for the inventor and, what would otherwise have been section 102(a) prior art, would be excluded as prior art by the grace period provided by subsection 102(b). . . . This means that any disclosure by the inventor whatsoever, whether or not in a form that resulted in the disclosure being available to the public, is wholly disregarded as prior art.

9. An example of a non-informing use is when an inventor secretly uses a process to produce a product that is commercially sold to the public. The use is non-informing because the public cannot discern the process based on simply analyzing the product.

10. While Inventor will not be barred from obtaining U.S. patent rights if he files in the United States within one year from the aforementioned disclosure, he may sacrifice foreign patent rights because most patent systems in Europe and the Japanese patent system provide grace periods under very limited circumstances. For example, under Article 55 of the European Patent Convention, an inventor will be entitled to a six-month grace period only if the disclosure "was due to, or in consequence of" either (1) "an evidence abuse in relation to the applicant or his legal predecessor" or the (2) "applicant or his legal predecessor displayed the invention at an officially recognized, international exhibition." See the Comparative Perspective in Chapter 6, page 480.

11. Proponents of this interpretation cite the legislative history, particularly Senator Leahy's statement that the new section 102(a) "was drafted in part to do away with precedent [e.g., *Metallizing*] under current law that private offers for sale or private uses or secret processes practiced in the United States that result in a product or service that is then made public may be deemed patent-defeating prior art."

and, therefore, triggers the one-year grace period.[12] As already noted, we will explore this issue in greater detail in Chapter 6 when we specifically discuss what constitutes a "public use" or "on-sale" event.

b. *Inventor Publicly Disclosed Prior to Third-Party Disclosure.* Under section 102(b)(1)(B), a disclosure of the claimed invention made one year or less before the effective filing date by **someone other** than the inventor will <u>not</u> be considered prior art against the inventor under section 102(a)(1) *if* "the subject matter disclosed had, before such disclosure, been "**publicly disclosed by the inventor**." But a third-party disclosure made **prior** to the inventor's public disclosure (even one day prior thereto) prevents the inventor from obtaining a patent under section 102(a)(1). This latter scenario represents a significant change from the 1952 Patent Act and reflects a European-style "absolute novelty" approach.

Thus, under section 102(b)(1)(B), the old grace period in the 1952 Patent Act remains for third-party disclosures only when the inventor **publicly** discloses the subject matter **before** the third party's disclosure and the inventor disclosure occurs one year or less before the effective filing date. An inventor who makes a non-public disclosure (e.g., confidential on-sale activity or non-informing use) will not be able to protect himself under section 102(b)(1)(B) because the disclosure is not public. Importantly, the third-party's disclosure—to serve as a bar to another—must be public, as well. The reason for this is that confidential sales or non-informing uses are prior art only against those who engage or perform them,[13] not against others.[14]

Questions remain on the preclusive effect of an inventor's public disclosure when a third party makes a subsequent disclosure that varies slightly (or is obvious) from the inventor's prior public disclosure. To have preclusive effect, do the third party and inventor's disclosures have to be identical?[15]

---

12. The case that is commonly cited for this proposition is *Metallizing Engineering Co. v. Kenyon Bearing & Auto Parts Co.*, 153 F.2d 516 (2d Cir. 1946). The advocates of this interpretation argue that *Metallizing* is based on sound policy, namely preventing an applicant from commercially exploiting his invention for more than one year while delaying filing a patent application. They also highlight the fact that legislative history is oftentimes an unreliable interpretive tool, particularly when it is being used to support a significant change in a long-standing common law interpretation.

13. *Metallizing Engineering, supra* note 12.

14. *See W.L. Gore & Assocs. v. Garlock, Inc.*, 721 F.2d 1540 (Fed. Cir. 1983). As noted in the text, there is debate as to whether the AIA overruled this long-standing principle. We explore this debate in greater detail in Chapter 6.

15. Jeff Lefstin has raised this issue in two essays published on the Patently-O website. *See* posts on September 22, 2011 and July 26, 2012. In particular, he points to language in the USPTO Guidelines on the implementation of the AIA:

[T]he exception in 35 U.S.C. 102(b)(1)(B) requires that the subject matter in the prior disclosure being relied upon under 35 U.S.C. 102(a) be the *same* "subject matter" as the subject matter publicly disclosed by the inventor before such prior art disclosure for the exception in 35 U.S.C. 102(b)(1)(B) to apply. Even if the only differences between the subject matter in the prior art disclosure that is relied upon under 35 U.S.C. 102(a) and the subject matter publicly disclosed by the inventor before such prior art disclosure are mere

Example 1

Inventor publishes an article in Science on July 9, 2013, disclosing ABC. Independent of Inventor, Competitor publishes an article in Discovery on December 29, 2013 disclosing ABC. Inventor can still obtain a patent on ABC if he files an application before July 9, 2014.

Example 2

Inventor enters into a confidential sale for Invention ABC on May 21, 2013. Competitor subsequently publishes an article in Science on December 29, 2013, disclosing ABC. Inventor is barred from obtaining patent protection. But Competitor can obtain a patent on ABC if he files an application before December 29, 2014.

Example 3

Inventor publishes an article in Science on July 9, 2013, disclosing ABC. Independent of Inventor, Competitor publishes an article in Discovery on December 29, 2013 disclosing ABX (an insubstantial or obvious variation of ABC). Under the USPTO guidelines, Inventor may not be able to obtain patent protection on ABC if the agency deems ABC obvious in the light of ABX.[16]

4. *Derivation and Disclosures in Patents/Patent Applications.* Section 102(b)(2)(A) incorporates the old derivation provision of section 102(f). A patent or patent application will not serve as prior art if the subject matter disclosed in the patent or patent application "was obtained directly or indirectly from the inventor." This provision reflects the long-standing patent law principle that someone who derived the invention from another cannot be an inventor.[17] Under section 100(f), an " 'inventor' means the individual or, if a joint invention, the individuals collectively who invented or discovered the subject matter of the invention." We discuss what it means to "invent" in section C of this chapter.

---

insubstantial changes, or only trivial or obvious variations, the exception under 35 U.S.C. 102(b)(1)(B) does not apply.

Examination Guidelines for Implementing the First-Inventor-to-File Provisions of the Leahy-Smith America Invents Act, Vol. 77 Fed. Reg. 43759, 43767 (July 26, 2012) (emphasis added). Based on this language, Lefstin asserts "the AIA's grace period with respect to later independent third-party disclosures would seem to be nearly eviscerated." *See* http://www.patentlyo.com/patent/2012/07/guest-post-by-dr-jeffrey-lefstin-on-pto-proposed-rules-on-first-to-file.html. Of course, the Federal Circuit will eventually weigh in, and may decide on a different interpretation.

16. *See id.*

17. An original inventor who believes his claimed invention was derived by another party—who in turn filed a patent application—must file a petition with the UPSTO to invoke a derivation proceeding. Under section 135(a), "The petition must set forth with particularity the basis for finding that an inventor named in an earlier application derived the claimed invention from the petitioner. The petition must be made under oath and supported by substantial evidence. The petition must be filed within 1 year of the date of the first publication of a claim to an invention that is the same or substantially the same as the earlier application's claim to the invention." *See* 35 U.S.C. §135(a). It remains an open question when the original inventor can prevent a deriver from obtaining a patent on an *obvious* variant of the original inventor's claimed invention. *See* Joshua Sarnoff, *Derivation and Prior Art Problems with the New Patent Act,* 2011 PATENTLY-O PATENT LAW REVIEW 12.

COMPARATIVE PERSPECTIVE
Defining Prior Art and Geographical Limitations

Under the pre-AIA, section 102(a)—for reasons discussed in Comment 2, above—precludes a patent from issuing on an invention if it was "known or used *in this country.*" This geographic constraint is at odds with the European Patent Convention (Article (2)) and the Japan Patent Law (Section 29(1)), both of which treat public knowledge and use anywhere as prior art. A noteworthy reason why this disparity is relevant relates to something called "bioprospecting," a process whereby companies (e.g., pharmaceutical) in developed countries learn of, for example, indigenous flora—used locally for medicinal purposes—or traditional knowledge (TK) from developing countries and thereafter obtain patent protection on the active ingredient contained in the flora or on information learned from the TK. Prominent examples include the need tree, turmeric, and basmati rice patent controversies. A great deal has been written on this issue and has captured the attention of the World Intellectual Property Organization. *See* http://www.wipo.int/tk/en. *See also* Margo A. Bagley, *Patently Unconstitutional: The Geographical Limitation on Prior Art in a Small World,* 87 MINN. L. REV. 679 (2003); Craig Allen Nard, *In Defense of Geographic Disparity,* 88 MINN. L. REV. 221 (2003); Keith Aoki, *Neocolonialism, Anticommons Property, and Biopiracy in the (Not-So-Brave) New World Order of International Intellectual Property Protection,* 6 IND. J. GLOBAL LEGAL STUD. 11 (1998) and sources cited therein.

3. Novelty-Defeating Patent Disclosures Under Section 102(e)

Section 102(e) embodies another novelty provision, but is limited to patent disclosures filed prior to the invention date. The typical scenario—as in *Alexander Milburn*—involves an inventor whose patent application is rejected (or invalidated) based on the disclosure (i.e., the specification) of a third party's earlier-filed patent application. Importantly, the prior disclosure of the third-party application can serve as a prior art reference only if the PTO publishes the application or issues the applicant a patent. Section 102(e) does not pertain to a situation where two or more parties claim the same invention. This scenario is the province of section 102(g)(1), which is explored in section C.

ALEXANDER MILBURN CO. v. DAVIS-BOURNONVILLE CO.
270 U.S. 390 (1926)

Justice HOLMES delivered the opinion of the Court.

This is a suit for the infringement of the plaintiff's patent for an improvement in welding and cutting apparatus alleged to have been the invention of one Whitford. The suit embraced other matters but this is the only one material here. The defense is that Whitford was not the first inventor of the thing patented, and the answer gives notice that to prove the invalidity of the patent evidence will be offered that one Clifford invented the thing, his patent being referred to and identified. The application for the plaintiff's patent was filed on March 4, 1911, and the patent was issued on June 4, 1912.

There was no evidence carrying Whitford's invention further back. Clifford's application was filed on January 31, 1911, before Whitford's, and his patent was issued on February 6, 1912. It is not disputed that this application gave a complete and adequate description of the thing patented to Whitford, but it did not claim it. The District Court gave the plaintiff a decree, holding that while Clifford might have added this claim to his application, yet as he did not, he was not a prior inventor. The decree was affirmed by the Circuit Court of Appeals.

The patent law authorizes a person who has invented an improvement like the present, "not known or used by others in this country, before his invention," etc., to obtain a patent for it. Rev. Sts. §4886, amended by Act March 3, 1897. Among the defences to a suit for infringement the fourth specified by the statute is that the patentee "was not the original and first inventor or discoverer of any material and substantial part of the thing patented." Rev. Sts. §4920, amended by Act March 3, 1897, c. 391, §2, 29 Stat. 692 (Comp. St. §9466). Taking these words in their natural sense as they would be read by the common man, obviously one is not the first inventor if, as was the case here, somebody else has made a complete and adequate description of the thing claimed before the earliest moment to which the alleged inventor can carry his invention back. But the words cannot be taken quite so simply. In view of the gain to the public that the patent laws mean to secure we assume for purposes of decision that it would have been no bar to Whitford's patent if Clifford had written out his prior description and kept it in his portfolio uncommunicated to anyone. More than that, since the decision in the case of the Cornplanter Patent, 23 Wall. 181, it is said, at all events for many years, the Patent Office has made no search among abandoned patent applications, and by the words of the statute a previous foreign invention does not invalidate a patent granted here if it has not been patented or described in a printed publication. These analogies prevailed in the minds of the courts below.

On the other hand publication in a periodical is a bar. This as it seems to us is more than an arbitrary enactment, and illustrates, as does the rule concerning previous public use, the principle that, subject to the exceptions mentioned, one really must be the first inventor in order to be entitled to a patent. We understand the Circuit Court of Appeals to admit that if Whitford had not applied for his patent until after the issue to Clifford, the disclosure by the latter would have had the same effect as the publication of the same words in a periodical, although not made the basis of a claim. The invention is made public property as much in the one case as in the other. But if this be true, as we think that it is, it seems to us that a sound distinction cannot be taken between that case and a patent applied for before but not granted until after a second patent is sought. The delays of the patent office ought not to cut down the effect of what has been done. The description shows that Whitford was not the first inventor. Clifford had done all that he could do to make his description public. He had taken steps that would make it public as soon as the Patent Office did its work, although, of course, amendments might be required of him before the end could be reached. We see no reason in the words or policy of the law for allowing Whitford to profit by the delay and make himself out to be the first inventor when he was not so in fact, when Clifford had shown knowledge inconsistent with the allowance of Whitford's claim, *Webster Loom Co. v. Higgins,*

105 U.S. 580, and when otherwise the publication of his patent would abandon the thing described to the public unless it already was old, *McClain v. Ortmayer,* 141 U.S. 419, 424.

The question is not whether Clifford showed himself by the description to be the first inventor. By putting it in that form it is comparatively easy to take the next step and say that he is not an inventor in the sense of the statute unless he makes a claim. The question is whether Clifford's disclosure made it impossible for Whitford to claim the invention at a later date. The disclosure would have had the same effect as at present if Clifford had added to his description a statement that he did not claim the thing described because he abandoned it or because he believed it to be old. It is not necessary to show who did invent the thing in order to show that Whitford did not.

It is said that without a claim the thing described is not reduced to practice. But this seems to us to rest on a false theory helped out by the fiction that by a claim it is reduced to practice. A new application and a claim may be based on the original description within two years, and the original priority established notwithstanding intervening claims. *Chapman v. Wintroath,* 252 U.S. 126, 137. A description that would bar a patent if printed in a periodical or in an issued patent is equally effective in an application so far as reduction to practice goes.

As to the analogies relied upon below, the disregard of abandoned patent applications however explained cannot be taken to establish a principle beyond the rule as actually applied. As an empirical rule it no doubt is convenient if not necessary to the Patent Office, and we are not disposed to disturb it, although we infer that originally the practice of the Office was different. The policy of the statute as to foreign inventions obviously stands on its own footing and cannot be applied to domestic affairs. The fundamental rule we repeat is that the patentee must be the first inventor. The qualifications in aid of a wish to encourage improvements or to avoid laborious investigations do not prevent the rule from applying here.

Comments

1. *Section 102(e)(1): Published Patent Applications as Prior Art.* Section 102(e)(1) states that a patent shall issue unless the applicant's invention was described in "an application for patent, published under section 122(b), by another filed in the United States before the invention by the applicant for patent." This revision to section 102(e) was part of the American Inventors Protection Act of 1999, which required applications filed on or after November 29, 2000 to be published "18 months after the earliest filing date." (An exception to this rule is when the applicant does not plan on filing outside the United States.) The effective prior art date of a published patent application is its filing date, even though the application was published 18 months thereafter.

2. *Section 102(e)(2):* **Milburn** *Codified and Then Some.* Section 102(e)(2) states that:

   a patent granted on an application for patent by another filed in the United States before the invention by the applicant for patent, except that an international application filed under the treaty defined in section 351(a) shall have the effects for the purposes of this subsection of an application filed in the

United States only if the international application designated the United States and was published under Article 21(2) of such treaty in the English language.

The first part of this section is a codification of *Milburn* and limits prior art to *United States* patent applications that *issue* as patents. Importantly, section 102(e)(2) applies to both non-provisional *and provisional* patent applications, which are filed without claims not more than one year earlier than the subsequent non-provisional application. *See In re Giacomini*, 612 F.3d 1380 (Fed. Cir. 2010) (holding provisional application filing date is prior art date under section 102(e)(2) provided the written description of the provisional supports the claimed invention).

The remaining part of section 102(e)(2) allows—under certain conditions—for international patent applications (i.e., non-U.S.) to serve as prior art. The conditions are that the applicant must designate the United States as a country in which it seeks protection and the application eventually be translated into English. (The AIA eliminated the requirement that foreign patent applications be published in English.) If these conditions are met the effective prior art date of the international patent application—filed pursuant to the Patent Cooperation Treaty (PCT)—will be its international filing date. The significance of this language in section 102(e)(2) is that a PCT application can serve as prior art even though the applicant never files in the United States. (Recall, the condition is that the applicant only *designate* the United States.)

The criticism, most often voiced, about section 102(e) prior art is that the prior art application is held in secret (by law) either until it is published—as in (e)(1)—or until it issues as a patent, as in the first clause of (e)(2). Justice Holmes's *Milburn* opinion provided an answer to this criticism. He wrote, "delays in the Patent Office ought not to cut down the effect of what has been done." What has been done? The prior applicant disclosed the invention before the subsequent applicant's date of invention. But for the delays in the patent office the prior applicant's application would issue the day it was filed, in which case its prior art effect under section 102(a) would be unquestioned. A billion-dollar prior art search would not turn up the prior applicant's patent application.

3. *Patent Disclosure as Prior Art.* Under section 102(e), a patent application is prior art for what it discloses, not for what it claims. If two or more applications claim the same subject matter then the relevant statutory section is 102(g)(1). The issue in this context is not one of prior art, but who is entitled to the patent. As Justice Holmes wrote in *Alexander Milburn*, "[i]t is not necessary to show who did invent the thing in order to show that Whitford did not." 270 U.S. at 401.

PATENT REFORM PERSPECTIVE
The AIA and Prior Art Patent Applications

The rule established in *Alexander Milburn* and subsequently codified in section 102(e)—including published patent applications—finds expression in the new section 102(a)(2), which applies to applications filed on or after March 16, 2013:

(a) NOVELTY; PRIOR ART.—A person shall be entitled to a patent unless . . .

(2) the claimed invention was described in a patent issued under section 151, or in an application for patent published or deemed published under section 122(b), in which the patent or application, as the case may be, names another inventor and was effectively filed before the effective filing date of the claimed invention.

(b) EXCEPTIONS. . . .

(2) DISCLOSURES APPEARING IN APPLICATIONS AND PATENTS.—A disclosure shall not be prior art to a claimed invention under subsection (a)(2) if—

(A) the subject matter disclosed was obtained directly or indirectly from the inventor or a joint inventor;

(B) the subject matter disclosed had, before such subject matter was effectively filed under subsection (a)(2), been publicly disclosed by the inventor or a joint inventor or another who obtained the subject matter disclosed directly or indirectly from the inventor or a joint inventor; or

(C) the subject matter disclosed and the claimed invention, not later than the effective filing date of the claimed invention, were owned by the same person or subject to an obligation of assignment to the same person.

According to the new section 102(a)(2), a patent shall issue if "the claimed invention was described in a patent issued under section 151, or in an application for patent published or deemed published under section 122(b), in which the patent or application, as the case may be, names another inventor and was effectively filed before the effective filing date of the claimed invention." The English language requirement has been eliminated for foreign applications that designate the U.S.

Section 102(b)(2) guards against derivation, and provides an exception to section 102(a)(2), stating that a patent or published application will not serve as prior art if the subject matter disclosed therein was first publicly disclosed by the inventor.

4. Novelty-Defeating Inventive Activity Under Section 102(g)(2)

The third (and final) novelty provision relates to prior-inventive activity. Under section 102(g)(2), a patent will not issue if the claimed invention was already "invented" in the United States. Unlike section 102(e), the prior art in this section is not a patent application, but rather inventive activity. The inventive activity must meet two conditions before it can qualify as prior art. First, the activity must occur in the United States, and second, it must be continuously used (not abandoned). The continuity-of-use requirement highlights an important distinction between sections 102(a) and (g)(2), provisions that otherwise look very similar. Another important difference is that section 102(g)(2) does not have a publicity requirement as does section 102(a). Thus, a trade secret can serve as section 102(g)(2) prior art. The Comments following *Thomson* explore the relationship of these two provisions in more detail.

THOMSON, S.A. v. QUIXOTE CORP.
166 F.3d 1172 (Fed. Cir. 1999)

RICH, Circuit Judge.

Thomson, S.A. ("Thomson") appeals from the June 24, 1997 order of the United States District Court for the District of Delaware in an action for patent infringement. The court sustained the jury verdict that U.S. Patent Nos. 4,868,808, 5,182,743, 4,961,183, and 5,175,725 are invalid for lack of novelty under 35 U.S.C. § 102(g). We affirm.

BACKGROUND

Plaintiff-Appellant Thomson is the assignee of the patents in suit, which are directed to optical information-storage devices, such as compact discs ("CDs"). Thomson makes and markets machines that "read" or "play" CDs, and grants licenses under the patents in suit to companies which produce CDs. Defendants-Appellees, Quixote Corp. and Disc Manufacturing, Inc. (collectively, "Quixote") make CDs.

Thomson sued Quixote for patent infringement. The parties agreed to base the outcome of the trial on three representative claims: claims 1 and 13 of U.S. Patent No. 4,868,808, and claim 1 of U.S. Patent No. 5,182,743.

At trial, the parties stipulated that Thomson's invention date for the patents in suit is August 25, 1972. Quixote's defense included evidence purporting to show that the representative claims are anticipated by an unpatented laser videodisc developed before August 1972 by a non-party, MCA Discovision, Inc. ("MCA"). After trial, the jury found in special verdicts that all of the representative claims were literally infringed, but that those claims are invalid due to lack of novelty (*i.e.*, anticipated) under 35 U.S.C. § 102(g).

Thomson submitted a motion requesting that the district court either set aside the jury's verdict of invalidity and enter Judgment as a Matter of Law ("JMOL") holding the patents not invalid, or grant a new trial on the lack of novelty issue.

In its opinion denying Thomson's motion, the district court described evidence in the record supporting the jury's finding of anticipation for each of the limitations that Thomson asserted had not been proven to be present in the MCA videodisc. The court noted that the evidence supporting the anticipation finding came from one or more sources: the live testimony of two people who had worked on the MCA laser videodisc project; an expert's report and portions of his deposition testimony, both of which were read into the record; the expert's exhibits; and certain MCA documents that the expert had reviewed. The court concluded that substantial evidence supports the jury's finding that Quixote had shown, by clear and convincing evidence, that every limitation in the representative claims was anticipated by the MCA device.

Thomson appeals the district court's denial of its motion for JMOL.

ANALYSIS

* * *

Thomson's core argument in support of reversing the district court's denial of its motion for JMOL is based on its assertions that (1) the jury verdict rests upon mere testimonial evidence by the two non-party MCA employees who worked on the videodisc project, and (2) this evidence is insufficient as a matter of law to support a holding of invalidity under subsection 102(g), because such testimonial evidence by inventors of their prior invention requires corroboration. Even if we accept Thomson's first assertion, and further assume that the MCA employees were acting as inventors in the laser videodisc project, Thomson's argument fails because this case does not present circumstances in which there is a need for corroboration, as hereinafter explained.

We begin with the language of 35 U.S.C. § 102(g):

> A person shall be entitled to a patent unless . . . before the applicant's invention thereof the invention was made in this country by another [inventor] who had not abandoned, suppressed, or concealed it. . . .*

We have interpreted [this] sentence . . . to permit qualifying art to invalidate a patent claim even if the same art may not qualify as prior art under other subsections of §102.[3] Art is not qualified under subsection 102(g) unless, viewed under a rule of reason, the totality of the evidence that the art satisfies the requirements of subsection 102(g) is clear and convincing. We have also often held, in both interference and infringement lawsuits, that an inventor's testimony alone respecting the facts surrounding a claim of derivation or priority of invention cannot satisfy the clear and convincing standard without corroboration. Although courts have reviewed infringement suits in which the defendant had attempted to prove subsection 102(g)-type anticipation by a non-party inventor at trial, neither the Supreme Court nor we have directly held whether the corroboration rule must be applied to testimony by non-party inventors that is directed to establishing their invention as anticipating the claims at issue.

The cases that discuss skepticism of uncorroborated inventor testimony directed to establishing priority over an opponent's patent claim involve situations where the inventor is self-interested in the outcome of the trial and is thereby tempted to "remember" facts favorable to his or her case. *See, e.g.,*

---

* [This statutory language has been slightly revised and forms part of what is now section 102(g) (2), which reads in relevant part: "A person shall be entitled to patent unless . . . before such person's invention thereof, the invention was made in this country by another inventor who had not abandoned, suppressed, or concealed it. . . ." —ED.]

3. The interpretation of subsection 102(g) to provide a prior art basis for invalidating a patent claim in infringement litigation was not intended by the drafters of the 1952 Patent Act. As the second sentence in the subsection indicates, 102(g) was written merely to provide a statutory basis for determining priority of invention in the context of interference proceedings before what was then the United States Patent Office. See P.J. Federico, Commentary on the New Patent Act at 19, in 35 U.S.C.A. (1954 ed., discontinued in subsequent volumes) (reprinted in 75 J. Pat. Trademark Off. Soc'y 161, 180 (1993)). Nevertheless, the first sentence is clear and, as the cases show, has been taken to have independent significance as a basis for prior art outside of the interference context.

This result makes sense. The first to invent who has invested time and labor in making and using the invention—but who might have opted not to apply for a patent—will not be liable for infringing another's patent on that same invention, while the public will have benefited because the invention was not abandoned, suppressed or concealed.

Barbed-Wire, 143 U.S. at 284-85 (indicating that testifying non-party inventors' patents would increase in value if patent claims at issue were invalidated).

The clear and convincing standard of proof required to establish priority, along with the numerous methods in the Federal Rules of Civil Procedure and Evidence by which a party may test, challenge, impeach, and rebut oral testimony, normally protects patentees from erroneous findings of invalidity. Thus, the corroboration rule is needed only to counterbalance the self-interest of a testifying inventor against the patentee. We therefore hold that corroboration is required only when the testifying inventor is asserting a claim of derivation or priority of his or her invention and is a named party, an employee of or assignor to a named party, or otherwise is in a position where he or she stands to directly and substantially gain by his or her invention being found to have priority over the patent claims at issue.

In the current case, the purported inventors who testified were non-parties and their testimony concerned an unpatented prior invention. Although Thomson argues that the corroboration rule is justified here because both testifying witnesses were involved in businesses that supplied goods and services to Quixote, this does not rise to the level of self-interest required to justify triggering application of the corroboration rule. In fact, Thomson's only reference to the record showing this potential source of bias is a transcript of Thomson's cross examination of one of the witnesses, which means that the jury had the necessary facts to assess the credibility of the witnesses.

We therefore conclude that the district court was correct in holding that substantial evidence supports the jury's finding that Quixote showed, by clear and convincing evidence, that every limitation in the representative claims was anticipated, and that the district court was correct in denying Thomson's motion for JMOL.

Comments

1. *Original Intent of Section 102(g).* Using section 102(g) as a prior art provision was a dubious proposition prior to *Thomson*. The intent of this provision was to "codify the law on determining priority" and "preserve[] in the statutes a basis for interferences." Giles S. Rich, Speech to the New York Patent Law Association (Nov. 6, 1951). *See also* P.J. Federico, *Commentary on the New Patent Act* at 19, 35 U.S.C. §§ 1 et seq. (1954 ed., discontinued in subsequent volumes) (reprinted in 75 J. PAT. TRADEMARK OFF. SOC'Y 161, 180 (1993)) (stating section (g) "relates to prior inventorship"). Federico's commentary is one of the most cited secondary sources by the Federal Circuit.

   With section 102(g)'s origins in mind, the court in *Thomson* stated in footnote 3, "[n]evertheless, the first sentence [of section 102(g)] is clear and . . . has been taken to have independent significance as a basis for prior art outside of the interference context." This statement is significant because of its author — Judge Giles Rich, who had a deep understanding of patent law and the history of the 1952 Patent Act. Since *Thomson*, section 102(g) has been split into two subsections, one for interferences (section 102(g)(1)) and one for prior art (section 102(g)(2)). *See also New Idea Farm Equipment Corp. v. Sperry Corp.*, 916 F.2d 1561, 1565 (Fed. Cir. 1990) (stating "[w]hile more commonly applied to interferences, section 102(g) is indeed applicable to prior invention situations other than in the context of an interference"); *Teva Pharmaceutical Industries, Ltd. v. Astrazeneca Pharmaceuticals LP*, 661 F.3d 1378, 1384 (Fed. Cir. 2011) (invalidating patent based on section 102(g)(2) prior art and stating "[t]o establish prior invention, the party asserting it must prove that it appreciated what it had made. The prior inventor does not need to know everything about how or why its invention worked. Nor must it conceive of its invention using the same words as the patentee would later use to claim it").

2. ***Distinguishing Between Section 102(g)(1) and (2).*** When an application is made for a patent claiming the same subject matter as another application or an issued patent, section 102(g)(1) governs, and an interference may be declared by the Patent & Trademark Office. An interference is a procedural mechanism to determine who is the first inventor (i.e., who has priority of invention). Priority is discussed in section C, *infra*. Section 102(g)(2) provides a novelty-based statutory foundation for so-called secret prior art. Under this section, a patent will not issue if the claimed invention "was made in this country by another inventor who had not abandoned, suppressed, or concealed it" before the patent applicant's date of invention. Unlike section 102(g)(1), section 102(g)(2) contemplates a scenario whereby the first inventor has opted *not* to pursue a patent, but is making or using the claimed invention. *See Corona Cord Tire Co. v. Dovan Chemical Corp.*, 276 U.S. 358, 384 (1928) (noting that first inventor who decides not to pursue a patent may still use his inventive activity as prior art). See Comment 5, below, for a discussion on the relationship between "concealment" and section 102(g)(2) "inventive activity." But it is important to note that prior inventive activity will not serve as prior art under section 102(g)(2) unless the prior inventor possessed "contemporaneous recognition and appreciation of the invention." *Estee Lauder, Inc. v. L'Oreal, S.A.*, 129 F.3d 588, 593 (Fed. Cir. 1997).

3. ***The Relationship Between Section 102(a) and Section 102(g).*** What is the relationship between section 102(a) and (g)? It appears that (g) eviscerates (a) because the former incorporates public and "secret" knowledge and use. But there are important distinctions. Unlike section 102(g), section 102(a) has a publicity requirement. Moreover, section 102(a) does not require continued use like section 102(g); that is, under section 102(g), to serve as prior art, the invention may be held in secret, but cannot be abandoned, suppressed or concealed. Recall in *Rosaire* that Teplitz's use served as prior art under section 102(a) because, while the work was ultimately suspended, it nonetheless was "successful" and "done openly and in the ordinary course of the activities of the employer." And in *Gayler*, remember the Court wrote:

> We do not understand the Circuit Court to have said that the omission of Conner to try the value of his safe by proper tests would deprive it of its priority; nor his omission to bring it into public use. He might have omitted both, and also abandoned its use, and been ignorant of the extent of its value; yet, if it was the same with Fitzgerald's, the latter would not upon such grounds be entitled to a patent, provided Conner's safe and its mode of construction were still in the memory of Conner before they were recalled by Fitzgerald's patent.

In other words, as long as Connor had knowledge of the invention, novelty may be defeated even if he abandoned or never used the invention. MCA's inventive activity in *Thomson*, in contrast, qualified for section 102(g) prior art, but may not satisfy section 102(a)'s requirements due to lack of public accessibility. As the *Thomson* court wrote, "We have interpreted . . . 102(g) to permit qualifying art to invalidate a patent claim even if the same art may not qualify as prior art under other subsections of § 102." *See also International Glass Co. v. United States*, 408 F.2d 395, 402 (Ct. Cl. 1969) (discussing differences between section 102(a) and section 102(g)).

Lastly, for inventive activity to serve as prior art under section 102(g)(2), the activity must occur within the United States. In contrast, prior publications and patents published outside the United States are eligible to serve as prior art under section 102(a). But section 102(g)(1) does allow USPTO patent applicants—in the context of an interference proceeding—to use inventive activity abroad (in any WTO country) to prove date of invention.

4. ***Why Isn't Section 102(g) Activity Considered Concealment?*** Prior art under section 102(g)(2) is thought of as "secret" because it is very difficult to uncover, particularly process-related inventions. But at what point does the secrecy of the prior use become so extensive as to constitute concealment under section 102(g)? Does it matter if the first inventor commercially exploits the secret invention (e.g., a secret process from which products are sold)? The circumstances and rationale have yet to be fully developed by the courts and have been treated somewhat inconsistently. But there are certain principles and distinctions that can be discerned from the case law.

For instance, in *Gillman v. Stern*, 114 F.2d 28 (2d Cir. 1940), plaintiff Gillman sued Stern and others for infringement of a patent related to a pneumatic puffing machine for quilting. The defendants asserted the patent was invalid based on prior activity of Haas, who took great measures to maintain the secrecy of his puffing machine. According to the court, Haas's machine:

> was always kept as strictly secret as was possible, consistently with its exploitation. In general, everybody was carefully kept out of Haas' shop where the four machines were used. He testified that "no one was allowed to enter but my employees, [who were instructed] that if anybody should ask to get any kind of information simply tell them you don't know. In fact I have my shop door so arranged that it could only be opened from the inside." He also enjoined secrecy on his wife who testified "no one ever got into the place and no one ever saw the machine. He made everything himself." . . . It does not appear that [Hass's employees] knew how the machines which they used were made, or how they operated.

Id. at 30. Judge Learned Hand held that Haas's prior use could not be used to defeat patent rights. Haas was a third party (not the inventor) who "kept his machine absolutely secret from the outside world." After discussing *Gayler v. Wilder*, Judge Hand wrote, "[j]ust as a secret use is not a 'public use,' so a secret inventor is not a 'first inventor.' Haas' use was one where 'the machine, process, and product were not well known to the employees in the plant,' and where 'efforts were made to conceal them from anyone who had a legitimate interest in understanding them,' if by 'legitimate interest' one means something more than curiosity or mischief." *Gillman*, 114 F.2d at 31.

Judge Hand then wrote of non-informing public uses and secret uses, and somewhat reluctantly embraced the notion that non-informing public uses, unlike secret uses, can serve as prior art. *Id.* Judge Hand was apparently dissatisfied with this distinction, but felt constrained by the statute:

> It is true that in each case the fund of common knowledge is not enriched, and that might indeed have been good reason originally for throwing out each as anticipations. But when the statute made any "public use" fatal to a patent, and when thereafter the court held that it was equally fatal, whether or not the patentee had consented to it, there was no escape from holding—contrary to the underlying theory of the law—that it was irrelevant whether the use informed the public so that they could profit by it.

Id. at 31.

The non-informing public use/secret use distinction was applied by the Seventh Circuit in *Dunlop Holdings, Ltd. v. Ram Golf Corp.*, 524 F.2d 33 (7th Cir. 1975), where the court found that an inventor's non-informing public use precluded a finding of concealment under section 102(g). Dunlop held a patent on a highly durable golf ball, which was made of a synthetic material called "Surlyn" that possessed improved cut-resistant properties. Prior to Dunlop's invention date, Butch Wagner began experimenting with Surlyn-covered golf balls, which led to his developing a formula that adjusted the weight and texture of the golf ball cover. Although Wagner was careful to keep his formula secret, he sold thousands of golf balls covered with Surlyn. The accused infringer, Ram, asserted that Dunlop's patent was invalid in the light of Wagner's prior inventive activity. The court, in an opinion by then-Judge Stevens, held that Wagner's inventive activity was a non-informing public use, and therefore, invalidating prior art. Judge Stevens distinguished *Gillman* by noting that "Haas had used the machine in his own factory under tight security" and although "the output from the machine had been sold, the public had not been given access to the machine itself." *Id.* at 36. In contrast, "the evidence clearly demonstrates that Wagner endeavored to market his golf balls as promptly and effectively as possible. . . . Therefore, at best, the evidence establishes a non-informing public use of the subject matter of the invention." *Dunlop*, 524 F.2d at 36. The court concluded by offering an explanation as to why Wagner's non-informing public use forecloses a finding of concealment. The court explained that even though Wagner's use does not disclose his discovery to the public, he nonetheless gave "the public the benefit of the invention" by introducing the discovery into the marketplace, a fact that militates against a finding of suppression "in an economic sense." *Id.* at 37. Building upon the marketplace rationale, the court stated that despite a lack of express disclosure "when the article itself is freely accessible to the public at large, it is fair to presume that its secret will be uncovered by potential competitors long before the time when a patent would have expired if the inventor had made a timely application and disclosure to the Patent Office." *Id.* In a footnote to this point, the court stressed that it is likely that a competitor would soon reverse engineer the golf ball covering revealing its "secret ingredient."

The case of *Friction Division Products Inc. v. E.I. du Pont de Nemours & Co.*, 658 F. Supp. 998 (D. Del. 1987), also involved an invalidating non-informing use. The claimed invention related to the use of Kelvar pulp in friction products. du Pont, the alleged infringer, provided evidence that its prior inventive activity anticipated the claimed invention. The patentee, in contrast, asserted that du Pont abandoned, suppressed, or concealed the invention. The district court, relying heavily on *Dunlop Holdings*, sided with du Pont. According to the court:

> In order to avoid a finding that a prior invention was abandoned, suppressed or concealed, under 35 U.S.C. §102(g), the prior inventor must take affirmative steps to make the invention publicly known. Making the invention publicly known requires only that the public enjoy the *benefits* or the use of the prior invention. Public use of the invention, without disclosing the details of it, is sufficient to negate any intention to abandon, suppress or conceal. Engaging in activities designed to bring about public or commercial use of the invention is also sufficient.
>
> There can be no question but that du Pont has been actively disclosing its knowledge on the use of Kevlar pulp in friction products. In fact, du Pont has done nothing but promote Kevlar pulp throughout the industry since it first realized its potential as an asbestos replacement. du Pont's visits to [companies within the industry] are all evidence of its efforts to bring about the public or commercial use of its invention.

658 F. Supp. at 1013-1014 (emphasis in original). Thus, a non-informing prior use "that gives the public the benefit of the invention" will most likely not lead to a finding of concealment under section 102(g)(2). A key point of distinction, therefore, between non-informing public use (*Dunlop* and *Friction*) and secret use (*Gillman*) seems to be whether the prior user commercialized the invention. Although in *Gillman* the output of Haas's machine was sold to the public, he "kept his machine in absolute secret from the outside world." In contrast, Wagner sold thousands of surlyn-covered golf balls and du Pont made efforts to publicly disclose its invention relating to the use of Kevlar pulp in friction products.

Are you persuaded by the rationale distinguishing non-informing public use and secret use? What other factors would you consider?

PATENT REFORM PERSPECTIVE
The AIA, Section 102(g) Prior Art, and Prior User Rights

In footnote 3 of *Thomson*, the court acknowledged the historical ambiguity surrounding section 102(g)'s prior art status, and concluded that allowing section 102(g) prior art "makes sense" because "[t]he first to invent who has invested time and labor in making and using the invention—but who might have opted not to apply for a patent—will not be liable for infringing another's patent on that same invention, while the public will have benefited because the invention was not abandoned, suppressed or concealed."

This footnote portrays a zero-sum game. A court can, on the one hand, invalidate the patent based on prior art—a process—that even an exceedingly extensive prior art search would not uncover, or, on the other hand, find the patent not invalid, thus rendering the prior user an infringer, even though there is no duty to obtain a patent and the prior user was producing a product from the process. Faced with this dilemma, the *Thomson* court invalidated the patent under section 102(g), stating that while the drafters of the 1952 Patent Act did not intend section 102(g) to used in this manner, the "result makes sense." According to the court, the "first to invent who has invested time and labor in making and using the invention—but who might have opted not to apply for a patent—will not be liable for infringing another's patent on that same invention, while the public will have benefited because the invention was not abandoned, suppressed or concealed." *Id.* at n.3. The court did not discuss the social good the patentee did by actually disclosing the invention to the public via a patent application. (Do you agree with the court's statement that MCA's testimony "does not rise to the level of self-interest required to justify triggering application of the corroboration rule"?) Subsequent Federal Circuit cases have created distance from this statement. *See Finnigan Corp. v. ITC,* 180 F.3d 1354, 1368-1369 (Fed. Cir. 1999) (stating corroborating testimony is required for testimony relating to invalidating prior art).

The AIA seeks to avoid the zero-sum game by eliminating section 102(g) prior art (secret prior invention), which means that secret prior invention like MCA's will not qualify as prior art. But the AIA also created a prior user right, which, if he qualifies under the statute, will enable the secret prior inventor/user to continue commercially exploiting his invention. Thus, the prior user provision allows courts to find a patent not invalid, while also protecting the secret prior inventor/user from an infringement finding. According to the USPTO Report on Prior User Rights:

> Providing limited prior user rights in a first-inventor-to-file system addresses the inherent inequity such a system creates between an earlier commercial user of the subject matter and a later patentee. A prior user rights defense is pro-manufacturing and pro-jobs, as it rewards businesses that put new technology promptly into commercial use, and provides protection for early commercial use when challenged by the later filing of patent applications by other entities.

REPORT ON THE PRIOR USER RIGHTS DEFENSE 3 (Recommendation 9) (USPTO Jan. 2012). The prior user provision became effective on January 16, 2011.

Specifically, the AIA amends section 273 and expands the prior user right to include any "process, or consisting of a machine, manufacture, or composition of matter used in a manufacturing or other commercial process." To take advantage of the prior user right, a party must prove that it commercially used the patented invention for at least one year prior to the earlier of the (1) "effective filing date of the claimed invention"; or (2) "the date on which the claimed invention was disclosed to the public in a manner that qualified for the exception from prior art under section 102(b)." The commercial use has to be in the United States and "either in connection with an internal commercial use or an actual arm's length sale or other arm's length commercial transfer of a useful end result of such commercial use." §273(a)(1).

The one-year requirement seeks to prevent prior users from learning of an imminent patent filing and racing to establish a prior user right. The one-year timeframe was also a compromise with universities who see the prior user right as a threat. *See* 157 Cong. Rec. S5430 (daily ed. Sept. 8, 2011) (statement of Sen. Kyl) ("The compromise reached in the House of Representatives addresses university concerns by requiring a defendant to show that he commercially used the subject matter that infringes the patent at least 1 year before the patent owner either filed an application or disclosed the invention to the public."). But does the one-year commercial use requirement favor only those prior users (who are also oftentimes prior inventors) who have the foresight to opt for a long-term commercialization plan based on trade secret protection. In other words, a prior user/inventor who does not engage in commercial use prior to the specified timeframe will be an overnight infringer because he does not qualify for the prior user defense; and the AIA eliminates section 102(g) prior art that the defendant was able to take advantage of in *Thomson v. Quixote*. Additional questions include whether the prior user will be less inclined to seek patent protection (thus disclosing the invention), knowing it can seek refuge as a prior user? Relatedly, would the second inventor also be disinclined to file for patent protection because the prior user would be beyond his legal grasp? In other words, is the prior user defense simply a compulsory, royalty-free license by another name? Would a prior user defense disproportionately favor larger entities at the expense of smaller concerns and individuals?

Importantly, the prior user defense only removes infringement liability; it cannot be the basis for invalidating a patent. 35 U.S.C. §273(g). (Recall section 102(g) prior art is eliminated under the AIA.) The right is only applicable to prior, *non-public* activity (namely a "process, or . . . a machine, manufacture, or composition of matter used in a manufacturing or other commercial process"), as public commercial use would serve as prior art under section 102(a), rendering the prior user exception to infringement liability unnecessary. Further, the right only covers specific claims and not the entire patent. *Id.* at §273(e)(3). Thus, a prior user practicing just one claim of a patent does not gain a prior user right to the patent's other claims. But the defense does extend to "variations in quantity or volume or use" and "to improvements . . . that do not infringe additional specifically claimed subject matter of the patent." *Id.* Another limitation relates to transferability. Specifically, the right cannot be "licensed or assigned or transferred to another person except as an ancillary and subordinate part of a good-faith assignment or transfer for other reasons of the entire enterprise or line of business to which the defense relates." *Id.* at §273(e)(1)(B). Lastly, to address concerns raised by university tech-transfer offices, a prior user cannot assert the defense against a university-owned or assigned patent. *Id.* at §273(e)(5)(A).

5. Foreign-Based Activity as Prior Art Under Sections 102(e) and (g)

Patent law is a global affair. Multinational companies typically seek patent protection in several countries, and have R&D facilities throughout the world. When filing outside the United States, various international treaties come into play. Under the Paris Convention of 1883, for instance, a party who files for patent protection in a Paris Convention member country, say Spain, can receive the benefit of the Spanish filing date when he subsequently files—within 12 months—in another member country.[18] For example, IBM files a patent application in Spain claiming ABC on May 2, 2007. If IBM files other applications (claiming the same subject matter) in other member states within 12 months, each application will be accorded the Spanish filing date, as if they were all filed on May 2, 2007. *See* 35 U.S.C. §119. Thus, the Paris Convention provides a significant procedural advantage for applicants with a global patent strategy.

This common scenario is uncontroversial, but only applies when one is *obtaining* patent rights. What is the prior art effect of IBM's filing in Spain? That is, under section 102(e), can IBM's patent *application* in Spain, as described above, serve as a prior art as of May 2, 2007 against a U.S. patent application filed thereafter? Is *Milburn* applicable? What about inventive activity abroad? Does the reasoning in *Thomson* apply? This section and the *Hilmer* cases address these questions.

The AIA overruled the *Hilmer* cases—see the Patent Reform Perspective following *Hilmer II*. But the *Hilmer* doctrine remains good law for applications filed on or before March 16, 2013.

IN RE HILMER (*HILMER I*)
359 F.2d 859 (CCPA 1966)

RICH, Judge.

The sole issue is whether a majority of the Patent Office Board of Appeals erred in overturning a consistent administrative practice and interpretation of the law of nearly forty years standing by giving a United States patent effect as prior art as of a foreign filing date to which the *patentee* of the reference was entitled under 35 U.S.C. §119.

Because it held that a U.S. patent, cited as a prior art reference under 35 U.S.C. §102(e) and §103, is effective as of its foreign "convention" filing date, relying on 35 U.S.C. §119, the board affirmed the rejection of claims 10, 16, and 17 of application serial No. 750,887, filed July 25, 1958, for certain sulfonyl ureas.

This opinion develops the issue, considers the precedents, and explains why, on the basis of legislative history, we hold that section 119 does not modify the express provision of section 102(e) that a reference patent is effective as of the date the application for it was "filed in the United States."

---

18. The full title of the treaty is the "Paris Convention for the Protection of Industrial Property," signed in Paris on March 20, 1883. The treaty entered into force in 1884 with 14 member states. As of March 2010, there were 173 contracting states. *See* http://www.wipo.int/treaties/en/ShowResults.jsp?lang=en&treaty_id=2.

The two "references" relied on are: Habicht 2,962,530 Nov. 29, 1960 (filed in the United States January 23, 1958, found to be entitled to priority as of the date of filing in Switzerland on January 24, 1957) and Wagner et al. 2,975,212 March 14, 1961 (filed in the United States May 1, 1957).

The rejection here is the aftermath of an interference (No. 90,218) between appellants and Habicht, a *priority* dispute in which Habicht was the winning party on a single count. He won because appellants conceded priority of the invention *of the count* to him. The earliest date asserted by appellants for their invention is their German filing date, July 31, 1957, which, we note, is a few months later than Habicht's priority date of January 24, 1957.

After termination of the interference and the return of this application to the examiner for further ex parte prosecution,* the examiner rejected the appealed claims on Habicht, as a primary reference, in view of Wagner *et al.*, as a secondary reference, holding the claimed compounds to be "unpatentable over the primary reference in view of the secondary reference which renders them obvious to one of ordinary skill in the art."

Appellants appealed to the board contending that "The Habicht disclosure cannot be utilized as anticipatory art." They said, "The rejection has utilized . . . the disclosure of the winning party as a basis for the rejection. The appellants insist that this is contrary to the patent statutes." Explaining this they said:

> . . . the appellants' German application was filed subsequent to the Swiss filing date (of Habicht) *but prior to the U.S. filing date of the Habicht application.* The appellants now maintain that the Habicht disclosure *cannot* be utilized as anticipatory in view of 35 U.S.C. 119 which is entitled "Benefit of Earlier Filing Date in Foreign Countries: Right of Priority." This section defines the rights of foreign applicants and more specifically defines those rights with respect to dates to which they are entitled if this same privilege is awarded to citizens of the United States. There is no question (but) that Section 119 only deals with "right of priority." The section does not provide for the use of a U.S. patent as an anticipatory reference as of its foreign filing date. . . .

* * *

The second restriction in the board's fourth statement of the issue is that "the reference patent is found to be entitled to the date of a prior foreign application under 35 USC 119. . . ." To some degree this loads the question. There is in it an implicit assumption that if the patent is "entitled to the date of a prior foreign application," it is entitled to it, and that is that. But one must examine closely into what is meant by the word "entitled." In essence, that is the problem in this appeal and we wish to point to it at the outset to dispel any mistaken assumptions. A patent may be "entitled" to a foreign filing date for some purposes and not for others, just as a patent may be "used" in two ways. A patent owner uses his patent as a legal right to exclude others, granted to him under 35 U.S.C. § 154. Others, wholly unrelated to the patentee, use a patent, not as a legal right, but simply as evidence of prior invention or prior art, *i.e.*, as a "reference." This is not an exercise of the patent right. This is how the Patent Office is "using" the Habicht patent. These are totally different things, governed by

---

* [After losing the interference, Hilmer returned to the USPTO claiming a *variation* of the invention that was subject to the interference proceeding with Habicht—Ed.]

different law, founded on different theories, and developed through different histories.

* * *

We can now summarize the issue and simultaneously state the board's decision. Continuing the above quotation, the board said:

> The Examiner insists, however, that the effective date of the Habicht patent is January 24, 1957, the date of an application filed in Switzerland which is claimed by Habicht under 35 USC 119. Appellants have not overcome this earlier date of Habicht. The issue is hence presented of whether the foreign priority date of a United States patent can be used as the effective filing date of the patent *when it is used as a reference.* (And this is the second statement of the issue by the board.) Our conclusion is that the priority date governs.

This is the decision alleged to be in error. We think it was error.

* * *

Turning from the general to the specific, we will now consider our specific reasons for construing the applicable statutes as they have for so long been construed, contrary to the recent innovation of the Patent Office.

OPINION

* * *

The board's construction is based on the idea that the language of the statute is plain, that it means what it says, and that what it says is that the application filed abroad is to have the same *effect* as though it were filed here—*for all purposes.* We can reverse the statement to say that the actual U.S. application is to have the same effect as though it were filed in the U.S. on the day when the foreign application was filed, the whole thing being a question of effective date. We take it either way because it makes no difference here.

Before getting into history, we note first that there is in the very words of the statute a refutation of this literalism. It says "shall have the same effect" and it then says "but" for several situations it shall not have the same effect, namely, it does not enjoy the foreign date with respect to any of the patent-defeating provisions based on publication or patenting anywhere in the world or public use or being on sale in this country *more than one year before the date of actual filing in this country.*

As to the other statute involved, we point out that the words of section 102(e), which the board "simply" reads together with section 119, also seem plain. Perhaps they mean precisely what they say in specifying, as an express patent-defeating provision, an application by another describing the invention but only as of the date it is "filed *in the United States.*"

The great logical flaw we see in the board's reasoning is in its premise (or is it an *a priori* conclusion?) that "these two provisions must be read together." Doing so, it says 119 in effect destroys the plain meaning of 102(e) but the board will not indulge the reverse construction in which the plain words of 102(e) limit the apparent meaning of 119. We see no reason for reading these two provisions together and the board has stated none. We believe, with the dissenting board member, that 119 and 102(e) deal with unrelated concepts and further that the historical origins of the two sections show neither was intended to affect the other, wherefore they should not be read together in violation of the most basic rule of statutory construction, the "master rule," of carrying out the legislative intent. Additionally, we have a long and consistent administrative practice in applying an interpretation contrary to the new view of the board, confirmed by legislation ratification in 1952. . . .

Section 119

* * *

This priority right was a protection to one who was trying to *obtain* patents in foreign countries, the protection being against patent-defeating provisions of national laws based on events intervening between the time of filing at home and filing abroad. . . .

* * *

We need not guess what Congress has since believed to be the meaning of the disputed words in section 119, for it has spoken clearly. Section 1 of the bill, the report says, was to extend "the so-called period of priority," which then existed under R.S. 4887. On p. 3 the report says:

> In this connection, it may be observed that the portion of the statute which provides that the filing of a foreign application—shall have the same force and effect as the same application would have if filed in this country on the date on which the application for patent for the same invention, discovery, or design was first filed in such foreign country—is intended to mean "shall have the same force and effect," etc., insofar as applicant's right to a patent is concerned. This statutory provision has no bearing upon the right of another party to a patent except in the case of an interference where the two parties are claiming the same patentable invention. U.S. Code Congressional Service 1946, p. 1493.

We emphasize none of those words because we wish to emphasize them all. We cannot readily imagine a clearer, more definitive statement as to the legislature's own view of the words "same effect," which now appear in section 119. This statement flatly contradicts the board's views. The board does not mention it.

* * *

For the foregoing reasons, we are clearly of the opinion that section 119 is not to be read as anything more than it was originally intended to be by its drafters, the Commission appointed under the 1898 Act of Congress, namely, a revision of our statutes to provide for a right of priority in conformity with the International Convention, for the benefit of United States citizens, by creating the necessary reciprocity with foreign members of the then Paris Union.

* * *

Section 102(e)

We have quoted this section above and pointed out that it is a patent-defeating section, by contrast with section 119 which gives affirmative "priority" rights *to applicants* notwithstanding it is drafted in terms of "An application." The priority right is to save the applicant (or his application if one prefers to say it that way) *from patent-defeating provisions* such as 102(e); and of course it has the same effect in guarding the validity of the patent when issued.

Section 102(e), on the other hand, is one of the provisions which defeats applicants and invalidates patents and is closely related in fact and in history to the requirement of section 102(a) which prohibits a patent if

> (a) the invention was known or used by others in this country, or patented or described in a printed publication in this or a foreign country, *before* the *invention* thereof by the applicant for patent. . . .

We will not undertake to trace the ancestry of 102(e) back of its immediate parentage but clearly it had ancestors or it would never have come to the Supreme Court. We will regard its actual birth as the case of *Alexander Milburn Co. v. Davis-Bournonville Co.*, 270 U.S. 390 (March 8, 1926), which we shall call *Milburn*. It is often called the *Davis-Bournonville* case. It was an infringement suit on a patent to Whitford and the defense, under R.S. 4920, was that he was not the first inventor. . . .

We need not go into the reasoning of the *Milburn* case, which has its weaknesses, because all that matters is the rule of law it established: That a complete description of an invention in a U.S. patent application, filed before the date of invention of another, if it matures into a patent, may be used to show that that other was not the first inventor. This was a patent-defeating, judge-made rule and now is section 102(e). The rule has been expanded somewhat subsequent to 1926 so that the reference patent may be used as of its U.S. filing date as a general prior art reference. . . .

What has always been pointed out in attacks on the *Milburn* rule, or in attempts to limit it, is that it uses, as prior knowledge, information which was secret at the time *as of which* it is used—the contents of U.S. patent applications which are preserved in secrecy, generally speaking, 35 U.S.C. 122. This is true, and we think there is some validity to the argument that that which is secret should be in a different category from knowledge which is public. Nevertheless we have the rule. However, we are not disposed to extend that rule, which applies to the date of filing applications *in the United States*, the actual filing date when the disclosure is on deposit in the U.S. Patent Office and on its way, in due course, to publication in an issued patent.

The board's new view, as expressed in this case . . . has the practical potential effect of pushing back the date of the unpublished, secret disclosures, which ultimately have effect as prior art references in the form of U.S. patents, by the full one-year priority period of section 119. We think the *Milburn* rule, as codified in section 102(e), goes far enough in that direction. We see no valid reason to go further, certainly no compelling reason.

* * *

Section 104

This brings us to another related section of the statute. We noted above that section 102(a) refers to knowledge of an invention *in this country* as a patent-defeating provision. This had been interpreted, long before the 1952 codification, to mean public knowledge. . . .

* * *

The "elsewhere" is section 104 which has also superseded section 9 of the 1946 Boykin act, above discussed. Before quoting it, we will mention another patent-defeating provision, 102(g) which says a patent may not be obtained on an invention if "before the applicant's invention thereof the invention was made *in this country* by another who had not abandoned, suppressed, or concealed it." The first sentence of section 104 reads:

§ 104, Inventions made abroad.

Inventions made abroad and in the courts, an applicant for a patent, or a patentee, may not establish a date of invention by reference to knowledge or use thereof, or other activity with respect thereto, in a foreign country, except as provided in section 119 of this title.

The second sentence is an exception not relevant here.

It seems clear to us that the prohibitions of 104, the limitations in sections 102(a) and 102(g) to "in this country," and the specifying in 102(e) of an application filed "in the United States" clearly demonstrates a policy in our patent statutes to the effect that knowledge and acts in a foreign country are not to defeat the rights of applicants for patents, except as applicants may become involved in *priority* disputes. We think it follows that section 119 must be interpreted as giving only a positive right or benefit to an applicant who has first filed abroad to *protect him* against possible intervening patent-defeating events in *obtaining* a patent. Heretofore it has always been so interpreted with the minor exceptions, of little value as precedents, hereinafter discussed. So construed, it has no effect on the effective date of a U.S. patent as a reference under section 102(e).

* * *

The simple observable fact, therefore, is that the effect of section 102(e) is to make a U.S. patent *available* as a reference, as of its U.S. filing date, and that thereafter the rejection of an application, or the holding of invalidity in the case of a patent, is *predicated on* some other section of the statute containing a patent-defeating provision to which the reference applies. Much confused thinking could be avoided by realizing that rejections are based on statutory provisions, not on references, and that the references merely supply the evidence of lack of novelty, obviousness, loss of right or whatever may be the ground of rejection of the board's decision.

Section 120

At oral argument the Patent Office Solicitor argued by "analogy" from 35 U.S.C. § 120 (a section which he said gives one U.S. application the benefit of an earlier U.S. application under specified circumstances *for all purposes*) that section 119 should similarly give to a patent, used as a reference under section 102(e), effect as of an earlier *foreign* filing date.

* * *

We find no substance in this argument because: (1) as above pointed out, our statute law makes a clear distinction between acts abroad and acts here except for patents and printed publications. Section 120, following policy in sections 102(a), (e) and (g) and 104, contains the limitation to applications "filed in the

United States," excluding foreign applications from its scope. (2) Use of the same expression is mere happenstance and no reason to transfer the meaning and effect of section 120 as to U.S. filing dates to section 119 with respect to foreign filing dates. Section 120 was not drafted until 49 years after the predecessor of section 119 was in the statute.

* * *

The decision of the board is reversed and the case is remanded for further proceedings consistent herewith.

IN RE HILMER (*HILMER II*)
424 F.2d 1108 (CCPA 1970)

RICH, Acting Chief Judge.

This is a sequel to our opinion in *In re Hilmer* (herein "*Hilmer I*"), familiarity with which is assumed.

* * *

In *Hilmer I*, the question we decided was whether the Habicht patent was effective as a prior art reference under 35 U.S.C. §102(e) as of the Swiss filing date. We held that it was not and that it was "prior art" under 102(e) only as of the U.S. filing date, which date Hilmer could overcome by being entitled to rely on the filing date of his German application to show his date of invention. This disposed of a rejection predicated on the disclosure of the Habicht patent, as a primary reference, coupled with a secondary prior art patent to *Wagner et al.*, No. 2,975,212, issued March 14, 1961, filed May 1, 1957 (herein "Wagner").

* * *

The board's conclusion was that the subject matter of claim 1, the compound claimed, is prior art against Hilmer. As to the basis on which it can be considered to be, or treated as, prior art, the board divided. Two members stated that the statutory basis is 35 U.S.C. §102(g) combined with §119 and read in the light of §104.

Note must be taken of the fact that the rejection here is under 103 for obviousness wherefore it is clear that the subject matter of the appealed claims is different from the subject matter of Habicht's claim 1, allegedly, however, only in an obvious way by reason of the further disclosures of Wagner. Were the appealed claims to the *same* subject matter, it seems clear that Hilmer, because he conceded *priority* to Habicht, would not be entitled to them and Hilmer appears to have admitted as much throughout this appeal. But, it is contended, the situation is different when the claims on appeal are to different subject matter. We confess to some difficulty in determining just what appellants' view is but it seems to come down to this:

> Appellants are entitled to the benefit of their German filing date and this antedates Habicht's U.S. filing date, which is the earliest date as of which Habicht's claim 1 invention can be "prior art." The words appellants use, referring to Habicht's U.S. filing date, are, "the only possible date that can be considered for anticipation purposes." Appellants appear to use the term "anticipation" in the broad sense to mean "prior."

We turn now to the reasoning by which the board majority arrived at the conclusion that the compound of Habicht claim 1 is in the prior art—*i.e.,* ahead of Hilmer's German filing date—and usable with the Wagner patent to support a section 103 obviousness rejection. We note at the outset that the board majority in no way relied on what occurred in the interference, on the concession of priority, or on any estoppel growing out of the interference.

Before examining the board majority's statutory theory, we will recall the fact that in *Hilmer I* we dealt with another statutory theory that by combining §102(e) and §119 a U.S. patent had an effective date as a prior art reference for all it discloses as of its foreign convention filing date. We reversed that holding and remanded. We now are presented with another theory that by combining §102(g) with §119 at least the claimed subject matter of a U.S. patent is prior art as of the convention filing date. The crux of the matter lies in §102(g), which we must have before us.

*   *   *

The board majority's rationalization begins thus:

Section 102(g) of the statute refers to the prior invention of another as a basis for refusing a patent. Inasmuch as the subject matter of the claim of the Habicht patent is patented to another, it must be recognized as an invention of another, and being the invention of another, some date of invention must be ascribed to it. When nothing else is available, the date of filing the application [in the United States] is by law taken as the date of invention since the invention obviously must have been made on or before the day the application for a patent for it was filed.

But this much, assuming its correctness, would not sustain the rejection because appellants are entitled to a date of invention which is earlier than the day the Habicht application was filed in the United States, the date obviously referred to in the above quotation. To sustain the rejection it was necessary for the board to accord an earlier date to Habicht's invention, the only such date available being the date Habicht filed his application in *Switzerland.* This, however, is not in compliance with the provision of 102(g) that the invention be "made" (or at the very least *be*) "in this country." The board majority attempted to vault this hurdle as follows:

While Section 102(g) refers to the prior invention as made "in this country," this limitation is removed as to application filing date by Section 119 of the statute which provides that an application for a patent for an invention shall have the same effect as though filed in this country on the date a prior application was filed in a foreign country, under the conditions prescribed. That this is the effect of Section 119 is also evident from Section 104. . . . The Habicht invention is . . . entitled to the filing date of the application in Switzerland as its date of invention in this country. Hence, we conclude on the basis of Section 102(g) and Section 119 that the claimed subject matter of the Habicht patent is available for use against the present application (as patent-defeating prior art) as of the date of the application filed in Switzerland.

We disagree with this line of reasoning.

In *Hilmer I* we explained at length why we could not accept similar reasoning about §119 which was there alleged to remove or qualify the limitation in §102(e) to the date when an application was filed "in the United States." For the same reasons we hold, contrary to the *ipse dixit* of the board, that § 119 does not remove the limitation of § 102(g) found in the phrase "in this country."

We disagree with the board that such an effect "is also evident from Section 104." Section 104 merely states that, except as provided by § 119, an applicant or patentee may not establish a date of invention "by reference to knowledge or use thereof, or other activity" in a foreign country. Thus § 119 and § 104 relate, respectively, only to what an applicant or patentee may and may not do to protect himself against patent-defeating events occurring between his invention date and his U.S. filing date. Moreover, we discussed § 104 and § 102(a), (e), and (g) in *Hilmer I* and there showed that they indicate an intention on the part of Congress that knowledge and acts in a foreign country are not to defeat the rights of an applicant for a patent, except as the applicant may become involved in a priority dispute with another applicant entitled to § 119 benefits. The present appeal does not involve a priority dispute. We repeat what we said at the end of that discussion in *Hilmer I*:

> We think it follows that section 119 must be interpreted as giving only a positive right or benefit to an applicant who has first filed abroad to protect *him* against possible intervening patent-defeating events in obtaining a patent.

That Habicht, as an applicant, was entitled to the benefit of his Swiss filing date does not mean that his invention acquires that same date under § 102(g) as patent-defeating prior art, in direct contravention of the "in this country" limitation of the section.

* * *

As we understand the meaning of the term "priority," it refers either (a) to the issue which exists in the interference proceedings, namely, which of two or more rival inventors *attempting to patent* the *same* invention shall be deemed prior or first in law and *entitled to the patent* or (b) preservation of an effective filing date during a period such as the "convention" year as against acts which would otherwise bar the grant of a patent, for the protection *of an applicant* against loss of right *to a patent*. Nothing we have seen tends to indicate that this matter of "priority" has ever been intended to modify the long-standing provisions of our statutes as to what shall be deemed "prior art" under § 103.

Comments

1. **Hilmer I** *and the* **Milburn** *Rule.* The *Hilmer* decisions make a clear distinction between obtaining patent rights and defeating patent rights. Despite the "same effect" language of section 119, the *Hilmer I* decision stands for the proposition that a foreign filing date (unlike a domestic filing date) cannot be used as a foreign-application prior art date in determining the patentability of later inventions by others. Given the policy of *Milburn*, what is the difference between Habicht filing his application in Switzerland or the United States? Certainly patent offices outside the United States have inefficiencies and experience delays; or as Justice Holmes put it, "[t]he delays of the patent office ought not to cut down the effect of what has been done." The answer may simply be a matter of statutory construction in that section 102(e)(2) requires the earlier application be filed in United States. And the

court expressed skepticism of the *Milburn* rule because of the secret nature of the earlier-filed application. Moreover, what is particularly troublesome from Habicht's perspective is that his U.S. patent is — as a result of the *Hilmer* decisions — not as commercially significant because it is competing with Hilmer's arguably obvious variation.

2. **Hilmer II** *and Foreign-Based Inventive Activity.* According to *Hilmer II*, inventive activity *outside* the United States cannot be used as prior art to defeat patent rights under section 102(g)(2). In *Hilmer II*, the court stated that Congress intended that "knowledge and acts in a foreign country are not to defeat the rights of an applicant for a patent, except as the applicant may become involved in a priority dispute with another applicant." Thus, as discussed in the Comments following the *Mahurkar* case in section C, foreign-based inventive activity can only be used in the context of a priority dispute (interference) when two or more parties are vying for the patent. As in *Hilmer I*, the *Hilmer II* court was very skeptical of so-called secret prior art. It is one thing to allow inventive acts in the United States to qualify as prior art to defeat patent rights; but it is an entirely different matter to permit acts outside the U.S. to defeat patents, acts that are arguably more difficult to find or appreciate. This geographical distinction is analogous to the geographical distinction in section 102(a). In that section, it is thought that knowledge and use are more difficult to find or locate than patents and publications.

3. *The* **Hilmer** *Rules and International Obligations.* The United States is a signatory member of both the Paris Convention and the Trade Related Aspects of Intellectual Property Rights (TRIPS). Of note, Article 27(1) of TRIPS sets forth the non-discrimination principle and states that "patents shall be available and patent rights enjoyable without discrimination as to the place of invention." Article 4 of TRIPS states that "With regard to the protection of intellectual property, any advantage, favour, privilege or immunity granted by a Member to the nationals of any other country shall be accorded immediately and unconditionally to the nationals of all other Members." Article 4 of the Paris Convention's priority provision entitles a U.S. patent applicant to a filing date of up to 12 months earlier than its U.S. filing date.

   Hilmer I and *Hilmer II* are arguably inconsistent with international obligations, specifically *Hilmer's* distinction between patent-obtaining activity and patent-defeating activity. Recall, the *Hilmer* rules prevent a foreign-filed application and foreign-based inventive activity to be used as prior art to defeat patent rights. Non-U.S. inventors who file in the U.S. typically first file outside of the United States and take advantage of the 12-month priority period under section 119 of the patent code when subsequently filing in the United States. So the question is do the *Hilmer* rules discriminate against non-U.S. applicants by preventing them from using their foreign-filing dates and inventive activity defensively? Some commentators think so. *See* Toshiko Takenaka, *Rethinking the United States First-to-Invent Principle from a Comparative Law Perspective: A Proposal to Restructure § 102 Novelty and Priority Provisions*, 39 HOUS. L. REV. 621, 659 (2002) ("The *Hilmer* doctrine . . . has been extensively criticized by foreign legal commentators for violating the priority right provision under the Paris Convention, as well as the non-discrimination policy provision regarding the place of invention under the TRIPS Agreement"); Heinz Bardehle, *A New Approach to Worldwide Harmonization of Patent Law*, 81 J.

PAT. & TRADEMARK OFF. SOC'Y 303 (1999) (arguing that *Hilmer* is inconsistent with TRIPS).

PATENT REFORM PERSPECTIVE
AIA Overrules **Hilmer I** *and* **II**

Section 102(d) allows the foreign priority date to serve as the **effective prior art date** of a foreign application. This provision, therefore, overrules *In re Hilmer,* which held that a foreign filing date can serve as a priority date for purposes of obtaining a patent, but the same filing date could not be used for prior art purposes to defeat patent rights—only the application's U.S. filing date could serve that function. Under section 102(d), if an inventor files a foreign application and claims priority to that filing date, the U.S. patent's effective date as prior art will be the filing date of the foreign patent application, not the U.S. filing date.

B. "PRINTED PUBLICATION"

The phrase "printed publication" appears in both sections 102(a) and (b), and its meaning is the same for both. At one level, a printed publication is easy to identify; for instance, a scholarly article published in the journal Nature or a book published by Oxford University Press. But what about unpublished materials such as a Ph.D. thesis indexed in a university library or a slide presentation at a professional conference? Are these "printed publications" in the eyes of patent law? The focus of the inquiry, as discussed in *In re Klopfenstein*, is on public accessibility and dissemination.

IN RE KLOPFENSTEIN
380 F.3d 1345 (Fed. Cir. 2004)

PROST, Circuit Judge.

Carol Klopfenstein and John Brent appeal a decision from the Patent and Trademark Office's Board of Patent Appeals and Interferences ("Board") upholding the denial of their patent application. The Board upheld the Patent and Trademark Office's ("PTO's") initial denial of their application on the ground that the invention described in the patent application had already been described in a printed publication more than one year before the date of the patent application. We affirm.

BACKGROUND
A.

The appellants applied for a patent on October 30, 2000. Their patent application, Patent Application Serial No. 09/699,950 ("the '950 application"), discloses methods of preparing foods comprising extruded soy cotyledon fiber ("SCF"). The '950 application asserts that feeding mammals foods containing extruded SCF may help lower their serum cholesterol levels while raising HDL cholesterol levels. The fact that extrusion reduces cholesterol levels was already known by those of ordinary skill in the art that worked with SCF. What was not known at the time was that double extrusion increases this effect and yielded even stronger results.

In October 1998, the appellants, along with colleague M. Liu, presented a printed slide presentation ("Liu" or "the Liu reference") entitled "Enhancement of Cholesterol-Lowering Activity of Dietary Fibers By Extrusion Processing" at a meeting of the American Association of Cereal Chemists ("AACC"). The four-teen-slide presentation was printed and pasted onto poster boards. The printed slide presentation was displayed continuously for two and a half days at the AACC meeting.

In November of that same year, the same slide presentation was put on dis-play for less than a day at an Agriculture Experiment Station ("AEs") at Kansas State University.

Both parties agree that the Liu reference presented to the AACC and at the AES in 1998 disclosed every limitation of the invention disclosed in the '950 patent application. Furthermore, at neither presentation was there a disclaimer or notice to the intended audience prohibiting note-taking or copying of the presentation. Finally, no copies of the presentation were disseminated either at the AACC meeting or at the AES, and the presentation was never catalogued or indexed in any library or database.

B.

On October 24, 2001, nearly one year after its filing, the '950 patent application was rejected by the PTO examiner. The examiner found all of the application's claims anticipated by the Liu reference or obvious in view of Liu and other refer-ences. Shortly thereafter, the appellants amended the claims of the '950 patent and described the circumstances under which the Liu reference had been displayed to the AACC and at the AES. The appellants argued that the Liu reference was not a "printed publication" because no copies were distributed and because there was no evidence that the reference was photographed. The examiner rejected these arguments and issued a final office action on April 10, 2002 rejecting the claims of the '950 application. The appellants then appealed to the Board.

Before the Board, the appellants again advanced their argument that the lack of distribution and lack of evidence of copying precluded the Liu refer-ence from being considered a "printed publication." The appellants further contended that the Liu reference was also not a "printed publication" because it was not catalogued or indexed in any library or database. The Board rejected the appellants' arguments and affirmed the decision of the PTO examiner, find-ing the Liu reference to be a "printed publication." The Board affirmed on the grounds that the full invention of the '950 application was made publicly accessible to those of ordinary skill in the art by the Liu reference and that this introduction into the public domain of disclosed material via printed display represented a "printed publication" under 35 U.S.C. § 102(b).

DISCUSSION

A.

The only question in this appeal is whether the Liu reference constitutes a "printed publication" for the purposes of 35 U.S.C. § 102(b). As there are no factual disputes between the parties in this appeal, the legal issue of whether the Liu reference is a "printed publication" will be reviewed de novo.

B.

The appellants argue on appeal that the key to establishing whether or not a reference constitutes a "printed publication" lies in determining whether or not it had been disseminated by the distribution of reproductions or copies and/or indexed in a library or database. They assert that because the Liu reference was not distributed and indexed, it cannot count as a "printed publication" for the purposes of 35 U.S.C. §102(b). To support their argument, they rely on several precedents from this court and our predecessor court on "printed publications." They argue that *In re Cronyn, In re Hall, Massachusetts Institute of Technology v. AB Fortia* ("*MIT*"), and *In re Wyer,* among other cases, all support the view that distribution and/or indexing is required for something to be considered a "printed publication."[2]

We find the appellants' argument unconvincing and disagree with their characterization of our controlling precedent. Even if the cases cited by the appellants relied on inquiries into distribution and indexing to reach their holdings, they do not limit this court to finding something to be a "printed publication" *only* when there is distribution and/or indexing. Indeed, the key inquiry is whether or not a reference has been made "publicly accessible." As we have previously stated,

> The statutory phrase "printed publication" has been interpreted to mean that before the critical date the reference must have been sufficiently accessible to the public interested in the art; dissemination and public accessibility are the keys to the legal determination whether a prior art reference was "published."

In re Cronyn, 890 F.2d at 1160.[3] For example, a public billboard targeted to those of ordinary skill in the art that describes all of the limitations of an invention and that is on display for the public for months may be neither "distributed" nor "indexed"—but it most surely is "sufficiently accessible to the public interested in the art" and therefore, under controlling precedent, a "printed publication." Thus, the appellants' argument that "distribution and/or indexing" are the key components to a "printed publication" inquiry fails to properly reflect what our precedent stands for.

Furthermore, the cases that the appellants rely on can be clearly distinguished from this case. *Cronyn* involved college students' presentations of their undergraduate theses to a defense committee made up of four faculty members. Their theses were later catalogued in an index in the college's main library. The index

---

2. Appellants acknowledge that our precedent considers the term "printed publication" to be a unitary concept that may not correspond exactly to what the term "printed publication" meant when it was introduced into the patent statutes in 1836. *In re Wyer,* 655 F.2d at 226. Indeed, the question to be resolved in a "printed publication" inquiry is the extent of the reference's "accessibility to at least the pertinent part of the public, of a perceptible description of the invention, in whatever form it may have been recorded." *Id.*

3. While the *Cronyn* court held "dissemination" to be necessary to finding something to be a "printed publication," the court there used the word "disseminate" in its literal sense, i.e. "make widespread" or "to foster general knowledge of." *Webster's Third New International Dictionary* 656 (1993). The court did not use the word in the narrower sense the appellants have employed it, which requires distribution of reproductions or photocopies.

was made up of thousands of individual cards that contained only a student's name and the title of his or her thesis. The index was searchable by student name and the actual theses themselves were neither included in the index nor made publicly accessible. We held that because the theses were only presented to a handful of faculty members and "had not been cataloged [sic] or indexed in a meaningful way," they were not sufficiently publicly accessible for the purposes of 35 U.S.C. § 102(b). *In re Cronyn*, 890 F.2d at 1161.

In *Hall*, this court determined that a thesis filed and indexed in a university library did count as a "printed publication." The *Hall* court arrived at its holding after taking into account that copies of the indexed thesis itself were made freely available to the general public by the university more than one year before the filing of the relevant patent application in that case. But the court in *Hall* did not rest its holding merely on the indexing of the thesis in question. Instead, it used indexing as a factor in determining "public accessibility." As the court asserted:

> The ["printed publication"] bar is grounded on the principle that once an invention is in the public domain, it is no longer patentable by anyone.... Because there are many ways in which a reference may be disseminated to the interested public, "public accessibility" has been called the touchstone in determining whether a reference constitutes a "printed publication" bar under 35 U.S.C. § 102(b).

In re Hall, 781 F.2d at 898-99.

In *MIT*, a paper delivered orally to the First International Cell Culture Congress was considered a "printed publication." In that case, as many as 500 persons having ordinary skill in the art heard the presentation, and at least six copies of the paper were distributed. The key to the court's finding was that actual copies of the presentation were distributed. The court did not consider the issue of indexing. The *MIT* court determined the paper in question to be a "printed publication" but did not limit future determinations of the applicability of the "printed publication" bar to instances in which copies of a reference were actually offered for distribution. *MIT*, 774 F.2d at 1108-10.[4]

Finally, the *Wyer* court determined that an Australian patent application kept on microfilm at the Australian Patent Office was "sufficiently accessible to the public and to persons skilled in the pertinent art to qualify as a 'printed publication.'" *In re Wyer*, 655 F.2d at 226. The court so found even though it did not determine whether or not there was "actual viewing or dissemination" of the patent application. *Id.* It was sufficient for the court's purposes that the records of the application were kept so that they could be accessible to the public. *Id.*[5] According to the *Wyer* court, the entire purpose of the "printed publication"

---

4. With regard to scientific presentations, it is important to note than an entirely oral presentation at a scientific conference that includes neither slides nor copies of the presentation is without question not a "printed publication" for the purposes of 35 U.S.C. § 102(b). Furthermore, a presentation that includes a transient display of slides is likewise not necessarily a "printed publication." *See, e.g., Regents of the Univ. of Cal. v. Howmedica, Inc.*, 530 F. Supp. 846, 860 (D.N.J. 1981). While *Howmedica* is not binding on this court, it stands for the important proposition that the mere presentation of slides accompanying an oral presentation at a professional conference is not per se a "printed publication" for the purposes of § 102(b).

5. Unlike in *Cronyn*, it was the actual patent application—and not just an index card searchable by author name only—that was made publicly accessible.

bar was to "prevent withdrawal" of disclosures "already in the possession of the public" by the issuance of a patent. *Id.*

Thus, throughout our case law, public accessibility has been the criterion by which a prior art reference will be judged for the purposes of §102(b). Oftentimes courts have found it helpful to rely on distribution and indexing as proxies for public accessibility. But when they have done so, it has not been to the exclusion of all other measures of public accessibility. In other words, distribution and indexing are not the only factors to be considered in a §102(b) "printed publication" inquiry.

C.

In this case, the Liu reference was displayed to the public approximately two years before the '950 application filing date. The reference was shown to a wide variety of viewers, a large subsection of whom possessed ordinary skill in the art of cereal chemistry and agriculture. Furthermore, the reference was prominently displayed for approximately three cumulative days at AACC and the AES at Kansas State University. The reference was shown with no stated expectation that the information would not be copied or reproduced by those viewing it. Finally, no copies of the Liu display were distributed to the public and the display was not later indexed in any database, catalog or library.

Given that the Liu reference was never distributed to the public and was never indexed, we must consider several factors relevant to the facts of this case before determining whether or not it was sufficiently publicly accessible in order to be considered a "printed publication" under §102(b). These factors aid in resolving whether or not a temporarily displayed reference that was neither distributed nor indexed was nonetheless made sufficiently publicly accessible to count as a "printed publication" under §102(b). The factors relevant to the facts of this case are: the length of time the display was exhibited, the expertise of the target audience, the existence (or lack thereof) of reasonable expectations that the material displayed would not be copied, and the simplicity or ease with which the material displayed could have been copied. Only after considering and balancing these factors can we determine whether or not the Liu reference was sufficiently publicly accessible to be a "printed publication" under §102(b).

The duration of the display is important in determining the opportunity of the public in capturing, processing and retaining the information conveyed by the reference. The more transient the display, the less likely it is to be considered a "printed publication." *See, e.g., Howmedica,* 530 F. Supp. at 860 (holding that a presentation of lecture slides that was of limited duration was insufficient to make the slides "printed publications" under §102(b)). Conversely, the longer a reference is displayed, the more likely it is to be considered a "printed publication." In this case, the Liu reference was displayed for a total of approximately three days. It was shown at the AACC meeting for approximately two and a half days and at the AES at Kansas State University for less than one day.

The expertise of the intended audience can help determine how easily those who viewed it could retain the displayed material. As Judge Learned Hand explained in *Jockmus v. Leviton,* 28 F.2d 812, 813-14 (2d Cir. 1928), a reference, "however ephemeral its existence," may be a "printed publication" if it "goes direct to those whose interests make them likely to observe and remember whatever it may contain that is new and useful." In this case, the intended target audience at the AACC meeting was comprised of cereal chemists and others having ordinary skill in the art of the '950 patent application. The intended viewers at the AES most likely also possessed ordinary skill in the art.

Whether a party has a reasonable expectation that the information it displays to the public will not be copied aids our § 102(b) inquiry. Where professional and behavioral norms entitle a party to a reasonable expectation that the information displayed will not be copied, we are more reluctant to find something a "printed publication." This reluctance helps preserve the incentive for inventors to participate in academic presentations or discussions. Where parties have taken steps to prevent the public from copying temporarily posted information, the opportunity for others to appropriate that information and assure its widespread public accessibility is reduced. These protective measures could include license agreements, non-disclosure agreements, anti-copying software or even a simple disclaimer informing members of the viewing public that no copying of the information will be allowed or countenanced. Protective measures are to be considered insofar as they create a reasonable expectation on the part of the inventor that the displayed information will not be copied. In this case, the appellants took no measures to protect the information they displayed—nor did the professional norms under which they were displaying their information entitle them to a reasonable expectation that their display would not be copied. There was no disclaimer discouraging copying, and any viewer was free to take notes from the Liu reference or even to photograph it outright.

Finally, the ease or simplicity with which a display could be copied gives further guidance to our § 102(b) inquiry. The more complex a display, the more difficult it will be for members of the public to effectively capture its information. The simpler a display is, the more likely members of the public could learn it by rote or take notes adequate enough for later reproduction. The Liu reference was made up of 14 separate slides. One slide was a title slide; one was an acknowledgement slide; and four others represented graphs and charts of experiment results. The other eight slides contained information presented in bullet point format, with no more than three bullet points to a slide. Further, no bullet point was longer than two concise sentences. Finally, as noted earlier, the fact that extrusion lowers cholesterol levels was already known by those who worked with SCF. The discovery disclosed in the Liu reference was that double extrusion increases this effect. As a result, most of the eight substantive slides only recited what had already been known in the field, and only a few slides presented would have needed to have been copied by an observer to capture the novel information presented by the slides.

Upon reviewing the above factors, it becomes clear that the Liu reference was sufficiently publicly accessible to count as a "printed publication" for the purposes of 35 U.S.C. § 102(b). The reference itself was shown for an extended period of time to members of the public having ordinary skill in the art of the invention behind the '950 patent application. Those members of the public were not precluded from taking notes or even photographs of the reference. And the reference itself was presented in such a way that copying of the information it contained would have been a relatively simple undertaking for those to whom it was exposed—particularly given the amount of time they had to copy the information and the lack of any restrictions on their copying of the information. For these reasons, we conclude that the Liu reference was made sufficiently publicly accessible to count as a "printed publication" under § 102(b).

Comments

1. *"Public Accessibility."* Public accessibility is the key to determining whether a reference constitutes a printed publication. *See In re Hall*, 781 F.2d 897, 899 (Fed. Cir. 1986) (referring to public accessibility as the "touchstone" for printed publication determinations). A reference is considered publicly accessible if it was "disseminated or otherwise made available to the extent that persons interested and ordinarily skilled in the subject matter or art exercising reasonable diligence, can locate it." *Kyocera Wireless Corp. v. Int'l Trade Comm'n*, 545 F.3d 1340, 1350 (Fed. Cir. 2008). Accessibility focuses on the public interested in the art, so that by examining the reference, one could make the claimed invention without further research or experimentation. There is no requirement that particular members of the public actually receive the printed publication or the information be disseminated. *See In re Wyer*, 655 F.2d 221, 226 (CCPA 1981) (Australian patent application kept on microfilm at the Australian Patent Office was "sufficiently accessible to the public and to persons skilled in the pertinent art to qualify as a 'printed publication'" even though court did not determine whether there was "actual viewing or dissemination" of the patent application). And the public accessibility requirement may be satisfied even though access is "restricted to a part of the public, so long as accessibility is sufficient 'to raise a presumption that the public concerned with the art would know of'" the invention. *In re Bayer*, 568 F.2d 1357, 1361 (CCPA 1978). A case where access was too restricted, thus rendering section 102(b) inapplicable, was *Northern Telecom, Inc. v. Datapoint Corp.*, 908 F.2d 931 (Fed. Cir. 1990). In this case, the documents were housed within the library at Mitre Corporation, and "[a]ccess to the library was restricted to persons authorized by Mitre." *Id.* at 936.

In *In re Hall*, which was discussed in the principal case, the Federal Circuit held that a single doctoral thesis deposited and indexed in a German library was sufficiently accessible to be a "printed publication." But the "indexing" system in *In re Cronyn*, 890 F.2d 1158 (Fed. Cir. 1989), was not sufficient. In *Cronyn*, the alleged printed publication were student theses filed in Reed College's main library and in the library of the particular department in which the student's work was done. The theses were listed on individual cards that displayed the student's name and the title of the thesis. The cards were filed alphabetically by the author's name, and the titles were sometimes descriptive. The Federal Circuit held the theses were not publicly accessible because, unlike *In re Hall*, the theses were not indexed, catalogued, or shelved in "a meaningful way." The court continued: "Although the titles of the theses were listed on 3 out of 450 cards filed alphabetically by author in a shoebox in the chemistry department library, such "availability" was not sufficient to make them reasonably accessible to the public. Here, the only research aid was the student's name, which, of course, bears no relationship to the subject of the student's thesis." *Id.* at 1161.

Accessibility was given a generous definition in *Bruckelmyer v. Ground Heaters*, 445 F.3d 1374 (Fed. Cir. 2006). The patentee owned two patents for a method of thawing frozen ground. Thawing was important to enable concrete to be poured. The patentee stipulated that if a Canadian patent *application* were deemed a printed publication, it would render the patentee's patents invalid. The application, as filed, contained drawings that were not included in the issued patent because they were deleted during prosecution; but the drawings were key to a finding of invalidity. The issue on appeal was whether the published application, which contained the drawings, was a printed publication under section 102(b). Relying on *Klopfenstein* and *Cronyn*, the patentee argued that the drawings were not printed publications because they were not publicly accessible, which, according to the patentee, requires the reference to "either (1) be published to those interested in the art for a sufficient amount of time to allow them to 'captur[e], process[] and retain[] the information conveyed by the reference, or (2) those interested must be able to locate the material in a meaningful way." *Id.* at 1377. The Federal Circuit disagreed because the patent application was laid open for inspection, which allowed persons of ordinary skill in the art exercising reasonable diligence to locate the application. The court relied on *In re Wyer*, 655 F.2d 221 (CCPA 1981), which involved an Australian patent application laid open for public inspection and an abstract of the application that was published by the Australian Patent Office more than two years before the filing date of the corresponding U.S. patent application. According to court in *Bruckelmyer*, "the existence of a published abstract that would have allowed one skilled in the art exercising reasonable diligence to locate the foreign patent application and the fact that the application was classified and indexed in the patent office, were central to the *Wyer* court's conclusion that the application was 'publicly accessible.'" *Bruckelmyer*, 445 F.3d at 1379. A petition for *en banc* review was denied, but prompted a dissent from Judge Newman. In focusing on the importance of public accessibility, she wrote:

> It is undisputed that these cancelled drawings are not available in any database or any library, and that no index, no catalog, no abstract suggests their existence or their content. It is not contested that the only way to obtain these drawings (although their existence was unknown) is to personally go to the Canadian Patent Office in Hull, Quebec, and ask to examine the file wrapper (the prosecution history) of this particular patent.

453 F.3d 1352, 1353 (Fed. Cir. 2006) (Newman, J., dissenting from denial of petition to hear *en banc*). For a discussion of the implications of *Klopfenstein* on the academic community and scientists, *see* Sean B. Seymore, *The "Printed Publication" Bar After* Klopfenstein: *Has the Federal Circuit Changed the Way Professors Should Talk About Science?*, 40 AKRON L. REV. 493 (2007).

Public accessibility was also at issue in *In re Lister*, 583 F.3d 1307 (Fed. Cir. 2009). Lister filed a patent application claiming a method of playing golf and also registered a copyright on his manuscript, which disclosed the claimed method. The PTO rejected the application under section 102(b) based on the manuscript's "printed publication" status in the Library of Congress, which is where the Copyright Office is located. According to the PTO, an interested researcher would be able to view the manuscript by visiting the Copyright Office and a "researcher would have been able to find the manuscript by searching the Copyright Office's catalog by title for the word 'golf' in combination with the word 'handicap.'" The Federal Circuit reversed. The records at the Library of Congress were not searchable by subject or keyword, as opposed to author's last name or title. And therefore, an interested researcher would not be able to access the manuscript in the Library of Congress by "exercising reasonable diligence." But the Library of Congress's records are searchable via Westlaw and Lexis, which offered search features that satisfy the "public accessibility" test. Nonetheless, the court found that there was insufficient evidence that Lister's manuscript was available and listed in the Westlaw and Lexis databases before the critical date.

2. **Klopfenstein** *and Presentations*. Would an oral presentation satisfy the "public accessibility" requirement? What if the audience members comprised of persons of ordinary skill in the art took copious notes? What about a PowerPoint presentation? Would it matter how long each PowerPoint slide was projected? What if the presentation was recorded?

3. *What Does "Printed" Mean?* Technology, as it typically does, has outpaced the term "printed publication." Historically, dissemination relied on a document being printed. But today, there is the Internet and digital technology. Judge Newman provides a helpful explanation of the terms "printed" and "publication" as used in sections 102(a) and (b):

> [I]n the case of "printed" publications, Congress no doubt reasoned that one would not go to the trouble of printing a given description of a thing unless it was desired to print a number of copies of it.
>
> Printing alone, of course, would be insufficient to reasonably assure that the public would have access to the work, for the possibility always exists that the printed matter may be suppressed and might never reach the public. Then too, there are time lapses between the printing and the publishing of a given work, and the public is not to be charged with knowledge of a subject until such time as it is available to it. For this reason, it is required that the description not only be printed but be published as well.
>
> But though the law has in mind the probability of public knowledge of the contents of the publication, the law does not go further and require that the probability must have become an actuality. In other words, once it has been established that the item has been both printed and published, it is not necessary to further show that any given number of people actually saw it or that any specific number of copies have been circulated. The law sets up a conclusive presumption to the effect that the public has knowledge of the publication when a single printed copy is proved to have been so published.
>
> The earlier cases decided by the CCPA interpreted "printed" as Congress no doubt understood the term: multiple copies that were made in order to disseminate the information. The idea was that there must be some likelihood that the information would, at least in principle, be available to interested persons in the United States. We need not consider the role in section 102 of today's searchable electronic data bases and other media, for in this case the subject matter entered no searchable library. The policy consideration for foreign prior art remains the same as when the statute was enacted—a requirement that the information be reasonably available in this country. The decisions developed the criterion that a "publication" must be "publicly accessible," as in *In re Wyer*, 655 F.2d 221, 226 (CCPA 1981), where the court defined "publicly accessible" as meaning "disseminated or otherwise made available to the extent that persons interested and ordinarily skilled in the subject matter or art, exercising reasonable diligence, can locate it and recognize and comprehend therefrom the essentials of the claimed invention without need of further research or experimentation."

Bruckelmyer v. Ground Heaters, 453 F.3d 1352, 1354 (Fed. Cir. 2006) (Newman, J., dissenting from denial of petition to hear *en banc*).

COMPARATIVE PERSPECTIVE
Novelty and State of the Art Under the European Patent Convention

Article 54 of the European Patent Convention defines both novelty and prior art. Article 54(1) states that an "invention shall be considered new if it does not form part of the state of the art." State of the art is defined as "everything made available to the public by means of a written or oral description, by use, or in any other way, before the date of filing of the European patent application." Article 54(2) EPC. (Although information made available to the public on the *same* day of filing is not considered state of the art.) This conception of prior art is known as "absolute novelty," which is considerably broader than the American conception embodied in 35 U.S.C. §102. Indeed, the examination guidelines of the European Patent Office state under Article 54 there "are no restrictions whatever as to the geographical location where or the language or manner in which the relevant information was made available to the public." C-IV-5.1 European Patent Office Guidelines for Examination. The concept of absolute novelty was first adopted in Article 4 of the Strasbourg Convention of 1963. *See* The Strasbourg Convention of 1963: Convention on the Unification of Certain Points of Substantive Law on Patents for Invention of 27 November 1963.

Thus, there are three important distinctions between Article 54 and section 102. First, the critical date under Article 54 is the date of filing of the European patent application, not the date of invention or one year from the date of filing. (Importantly, under the EPC, the date of priority can act as the filing date for prior art purposes assuming the applicant complies with the priority procedures of Articles 87-89. *See* Article 89 EPC and C-IV-5.3 European Patent Office Guidelines for Examination.) Second, there is no geographical restriction under Article 54 as there is under 35 U.S.C. §102(a) and (b); and third, Article 54 does not permit a universal grace period that applies to all forms of public disclosures and uses, although there are limited exceptions. See the Comparative Perspective on Prejudicial Disclosures in Chapter 6.

1. Available to the Public and the Person Skilled in the Art

State of the art information can take many forms, including *documentation.* A published document is deemed a part of the state of the art as of its publication date. *See* C-IV-7.3 European Patent Office Guidelines for Examination. A trade journal article is available when it is delivered to subscribers, not when it is sent to the journal. 1 EUROPEAN PATENT CONVENTION: A COMMENTARY 109 (M. Singer & D. Stauder eds., 2003); *oral recitation. See* D-V-3.21 European Patent Office Guidelines for Examination ("The state of the art is made available to the public by oral description when facts are unconditionally brought to the knowledge of members of the public in the course of a conversation or a lecture or by means of radio, television or sound reproduction equipment (tapes and records)"; *public use of a product or process. See* D-V-3.11 European Patent Office Guidelines for

Examination ("Use may be constituted by producing, offering, marketing or otherwise exploiting a product, or by offering or marketing a process or its application or by applying the process. Marketing may be affected, for example, by sale or exchange. The state of the art may also be made available to the public in other ways, as for example by demonstrating an object or process in specialist training courses or on television."); and *commercial sales*. Even a single use or sale will render the article used or sold available to the public under 54(2). *See* EPO Board of Appeals T0482/89 (stating that "in accordance with principles well-established in the case law of the majority of Contracting States, that a single sale is sufficient to render the article sold available to the public within the meaning of Article 54(2) EPC, provided the buyer is not bound by an obligation to maintain secrecy").

All that is required is that the information be made available to a single member of the public without a confidentiality requirement and that the information be enabling to a person skilled in the art. *See* European Patent Office Guidelines for Examination C-IV 5.2 ("Subject-matter can only be regarded as having been made available to the public, and therefore as comprised in the state of the art pursuant to Art. 54(1), if the information given to the skilled person is sufficient to enable him, at the relevant date, to practise the technical teaching which is the subject of the disclosure, taking into account also the general knowledge at that time in the field to be expected of him."). The person skilled in the art is not expressly mentioned in Article 54, but is regarded as "the decisive factor for the understanding of the technical teaching" not only for purposes of novelty, but also inventive step and adequacy of disclosure. *See* 1 EUROPEAN PATENT CONVENTION: A COMMENTARY 110 (M. Singer & D. Stauder eds., 2003). Unlike EPC Article 54, Articles 56 (Inventive Step) and 83 (Disclosure of Invention) expressly mention "person skilled in the art."

2. Novelty

Information that forms part of the state of the art does not necessarily mean that information is novelty defeating. The information must anticipate the claimed invention. In the important *Mobil Oil III* case, the Enlarged EPO Board of Appeals stated:

> Article 54(2) EPC defines the state of the art as comprising "everything made available to the public by means of a written or oral description, by use, or in any other way." . . . The word "available" carries with it the idea that, for lack of novelty to be found, all the technical features of the claimed invention in combination must have been communicated to the public, or laid open for inspection. . . . A claimed invention lacks novelty unless it includes at least one essential technical feature which distinguishes it from the state of the art. When deciding upon the novelty of a claim, a basic initial consideration is therefore to construe the claim in order to determine its technical features.

Enlarged EPO Board of Appeals G 0002/88. The prior art must contain "a clear and unmistakable disclosure of the subject matter of the later invention" to defeat novelty. EPO Board of Appeals T 450/89. *See also* T0661/97

("The Board concurs with the decision T 450/89 . . . that novelty should be affirmed if the prior art document does not comprise clear and unmistakable disclosure for the subject-matter of the later invention."); T1261/01 (lack of novelty requires "clear and unambiguous disclosure in the prior art of all features of the claim"). The European Examination Guidelines state novelty is defeated if the claimed subject matter can be derived "directly and unambiguously" from the prior art. C-IV-7.2.

A little background on what constitutes a "technical feature" may be helpful. The EPC and its implementing regulations require that claims be drafted in terms of technical features of the invention. For instance, Article 84 of the EPC requires that claims "define the matter for which protection is sought" and "be clear and concise and be supported by the description." EPC Implementing Regulation 29 builds on Article 84, by requiring that claims "define the matter for which protection is sought in terms of the technical features of the invention." A technical feature has been defined as "anything that is necessary to solve the technical problem under consideration." 1 EUROPEAN PATENT CONVENTION: A COMMENTARY 116 (M. Singer & D. Stauder eds., 2003). According to the EPO Board of Appeals,

> It follows that the technical features of the invention are the physical features which are essential to it. When considering the two basic types of claim . . . the technical features of a claim to a physical entity [i.e., product or apparatus claim] are the physical parameters of the entity, and the technical features of a claim to an activity [i.e., process or method claim] are the physical steps which define such activity.

Enlarged EPO Board of Appeals G 0002/88.

When comparing the claimed invention's technical features to the prior art, it is important to keep in mind that, as under American patent law, prior art references cannot be combined to defeat novelty, although combination is permissible when determining inventive step. *See* T1261/01 (noting "the lack-of-novelty objection fails because it relies on combining features taken from various parts" of the prior art). *See also* European Patent Office Guidelines for Examination C-IV-7.1 ("It should be noted that in considering novelty (as distinct from inventive step), it is not permissible to combine separate items of prior art together."). And when a single reference discloses "scattered elements" that form part of different embodiments, the EPO Board of Appeals requires the reference to disclose a "specific combination" to be novelty-defeating. For instance, in *Grehal* the applicant invented a shear that incorporated a stirrup. The party opposing the patent application, Diener, cited as prior art a catalogue that disclosed the features of the claimed invention, although these prior art features were disclosed in two different embodiments. According to Diener, the prior art features "were described in one and the same technical context and in one and the same document (the catalogue)," and therefore, "when taken as a whole, this set of known features anticipated the invention." The EPO disagreed:

> [W]hen assessing novelty it was not enough only to consider the content of a single document: each entity described in the document also had to be examined separately. It is not permissible to combine separate items belonging to different embodiments described in one and the same document

merely because they are disclosed in that one document, unless of course such combination has been specifically suggested therein. In other words, when the content of a single prior art document (in this case, a catalogue disclosing various types of shear) is considered in isolation when contesting the novelty of a claim, the said content must not be treated as something in the nature of a reservoir from which it would be permissible to draw features pertaining to separate embodiments in order to create artificially a particular embodiment which would destroy novelty, unless the document itself suggests such a combination of features. In the present case, apart from the fact that it is open to question whether a catalogue can be treated as a single document rather than as a selection of documents, the [prior art] shears are two completely separate items from the catalogue, shown on two different pages under different order numbers. They are therefore definitely two separate entities forming two independent bases for comparison which should be considered in isolation when assessing novelty, and it is not admissible to piece together artificially a more relevant state of the art from features belonging to one or both of these entities, even if they are both disclosed in one and the same document.

EPO Board of Appeals T 305/87. *Accord* T 166/01 (noting these "'scattered elements' [disclosed in the prior art] are not disclosed as a specific combination, contrary to the requirements set out in . . . T 305/87 that a specific combination has to be pointed out by a prior art document for it to be novelty-destroying"). *See also* European Patent Office Guidelines for Examination C-IV-7.1 ("It is . . . not permissible to combine separate items belonging to different embodiments described in one and the same document, unless such combination has specifically been suggested.").

The state of the art does not need to reveal the claimed invention expressly. Rather, claimed subject matter that can be implicitly derived from the prior art will also defeat novelty. *See* European Patent Office Guidelines for Examination C-IV-7.2 ("A document takes away the novelty of any claimed subject-matter derivable directly and unambiguously from that document including any features implicit to a person skilled in the art in what is expressly mentioned in the document, *e.g.* a disclosure of the use of rubber in circumstances where clearly its elastic properties are used even if this is not explicitly stated takes away the novelty of the use of an elastic material.") Implicit derivation should not be confused with inherency. An inherent feature under the EPC does not constitute state of the art. Enlarged EPO Board of Appeals G 0002/88. According to the Enlarged Board of Appeals:

> [U]nder Article 54(2) EPC the question to be decided is what has been "made available" to the public: the question is not what may have been "inherent" in what was made available (by a prior written description, or in what has previously been used (prior use), for example). Under the EPC, a hidden or secret use, because it has not been made available to the public, is not a ground of objection to validity of a European patent. . . . Thus, the question of "inherency" does not arise as such under Article 54 EPC.

Id.

C. PRIORITY

Perhaps the most significant change brought about by the AIA is the adoption of a first-inventor-to-file system. Under new section 102, the first inventor to submit an application to the patent office has priority of invention. The relevant question under the new regime is who *filed* first; not who invented first. Accordingly, section 102(g) has been eliminated.[19]

But since these AIA amendments only apply to patent applications filed on or after March 16, 2013, the pre-AIA priority rules remain relevant for patents based on applications filed before March 16, 2013. For these applications, the United States adheres to a first-to-invent principle, to which the remainder of this chapter is devoted unless otherwise indicated. The first party to invent is said to have priority of invention over other inventors who are also seeking a patent on the same invention. This seemingly simple doctrine is governed by several complex rules that play out in an interference proceeding,[20] and oftentimes in federal court.

The question of priority is governed by section 102(g)(1) of the patent code, which reads in relevant part:

> A person shall be entitled to a patent unless . . . during the course of an *interference* . . . , another inventor involved therein establishes, to the extent permitted in section 104, that before such person's invention thereof the invention was made by such other inventor and not *abandoned, suppressed, or concealed.* . . . In determining priority of invention under this subsection, there shall be considered not only the respective dates of *conception* and *reduction to practice* of the invention, but also the *reasonable diligence* of one who was first to conceive and last to reduce to practice, from a time prior to conception by the other.

Thus, there are numerous terms that must be defined and addressed: (1) abandoned, suppressed, or concealed; (2) conception; (3) reduction to practice; and (4) reasonable diligence. Importantly, while the AIA eliminated section 102(g) and adopted new priority rules, the aforementioned terms remain relevant in the derivation context. Under section 102(d) as amended by the AIA, a patent or patent application will not serve as prior art if the subject matter disclosed in the patent or patent application "was obtained directly or indirectly from the inventor." Under section 100(f), an "'inventor' means the individual or, if a joint invention, the individuals collectively who *invented* or discovered the

---

19. The USPTO issued final rules and guidelines relating to the first-inventor-to-file regime. *See* https://www.federalregister.gov/articles/2013/02/14/2013-03453/changes-to-implement-the-first-inventor-to-file-provisions-of-the-leahy-smith-america-invents-act and https://www.federalregister.gov/articles/2013/02/14/2013-03450/examination-guidelines-for-implementing-the-first-inventor-to-file-provisions-of-the-leahy-smith.

20. An interference is an *inter partes* administrative proceeding (within the USPTO), that seeks to determine who should be awarded priority of invention. There are complex procedural rules that accompany interference practice. *See* 35 U.S.C. §135 (2006); 37 C.F.R. §§41.200 et seq.; and Chapter 2300 of the MANUAL OF PATENT EXAMINATION PROCEDURE. The term "interference" can be gleaned from §135(a) of the patent code, which reads:

> Whenever an application is made for a patent which, in the opinion of the Director, would interfere with any pending application, or with any unexpired patent, an interference may be declared and the Director shall give notice of such declaration to the applicants, or applicant and patentee, as the case may be.

subject matter of the invention." (Emphasis added.) Thus, while these terms will have no applicability for determining *priority* for patent applications filed on or after March 16, 2013, they are relevant to discerning who *invented* "the subject matter of the invention" in a *derivation* context.

The general rule for awarding priority in a first-to-invent system is as follows: The first party (say Party A) to reduce to practice is the first to invent and, therefore, is awarded the patent, *unless* the party (say Party B) who was last to reduce to practice was also the first to conceive, in which case Party B is awarded priority if he can show that he exercised reasonable diligence from just prior to Party A's conception date until Party B's reduction to practice.

The principal cases below and comments that follow unpack this rule and define the various terms therein. The *Mahurkar* case explores the terms "conception" and "reduction to practice" in the context of proving date of invention. And the *Griffith* and *Fujikawa* cases explore "reasonable diligence" and "abandonment, suppression, and concealment."

1. Proving Date of Invention

The *Mahurkar* case explores how date of invention is proven. While *Mahurkar* is not a section 102(g) priority case, the opinion borrows from section 102(g) jurisprudence to determine Mahurkar's date of invention. (Indeed, the meaning of "invention" as used in section 102(a), (e), and (g) is the same throughout section 102.) The *Mahurkar* case explores the importance concepts of "conception" and "reduction to practice."

MAHURKAR v. C.R. BARD, INC.
79 F.3d 1572 (Fed. Cir. 1996)

RADER, Circuit Judge.

Dr. Sakharam D. Mahurkar sued C.R. Bard, Inc., Davol Inc., and Bard Access Systems, Inc. (Bard) for infringing U.S. Patent No. 4,808,155 (the '155 patent).

On appeal, the parties raised numerous issues to which this court gave full consideration. Because the district court correctly granted Dr. Mahurkar's motion on anticipation, this court affirms in part.

The '155 patent discloses a simple double-lumen catheter. A double-lumen catheter simultaneously removes and restores fluids to the human body during a transfusion. To accomplish this mission, this flexible surgical instrument uses two channels—one to withdraw fluids, another to inject fluids.

Dr. Mahurkar created the claimed invention to treat chronic dialysis patients whose veins usually will no longer tolerate acute catheters. Dr. Mahurkar's invention does not traumatize sensitive veins, yet still supports maximum blood flow with a minimum catheter cross section. After a chronic patient's veins have deteriorated from frequent transfusions, this catheter permits insertion into a major vein—percutaneous insertion—without expensive cut-down surgery.

Dr. Mahurkar filed an initial patent application on his invention on October 24, 1983. After two continuations, the United States Patent and Trademark Office (PTO) issued the '155 patent on February 28, 1989.

In May 1990, Dr. Mahurkar granted Bard a limited license under the '155 patent. This license limited Bard to non-hemodialysis applications. Dr. Mahurkar asserts that Bard made and sold infringing hemodialysis catheters in violation of that license. Specifically, Dr. Mahurkar claims that Bard's "Hickman I" and "Hickman II" hemodialysis catheters infringe the '155 patent.

Bard argues that the '155 patent is invalid under 35 U.S.C. § 102(a). In July 1983, Cook, Inc. published a nationwide catalog (the Cook catalog) disclosing a Cook Double Lumen Subclavian Hemodialysis Catheter. At the conclusion of the evidence at trial, Bard moved for judgment as a matter of law (JMOL) that the Cook catalog anticipated the '155 patent. Dr. Mahurkar cross-moved. The district court granted Dr. Mahurkar's motion for JMOL. According to the district court, no reasonable jury could find the Cook catalog anticipated claim 1 of the '155 patent.

* * *

At trial, Bard sought to show that the Cook catalog anticipated claim 1 of the '155 patent. The catalog's July 1983 publication date preceded the filing of the '155 patent by about three months. The parties disputed only the status of the Cook catalog as prior art under 35 U.S.C. § 102(a). By challenging the validity of the '155 patent, Bard bore the burden of persuasion by clear and convincing evidence on all issues relating to the status of the Cook catalog as prior art.

Section 102(a) of Title 35 defines one class of prior art. As a printed publication, the Cook catalog fits within some terms of 35 U.S.C. § 102(a). Section 102(a) also requires, however, that the catalog description appear before the invention.

In *ex parte* patent prosecution, an examiner may refer to a document published within one year before the filing date of a patent application as prior art. However, this label only applies until the inventor comes forward with evidence showing an earlier date of invention. Once the inventor shows an earlier date of invention, the document is no longer prior art under section 102(a).

Any suggestion that a document is prior art because it appears before the filing date of a patent ignores the requirements of section 102(a). Section 102(a) explicitly refers to invention dates, not filing dates. Thus, under section 102(a), a document is prior art only when published before the invention date. For the Cook catalog to constitute prior art, therefore, it must have been published before Dr. Mahurkar's invention date.

Resolution of this point turns on procedural rules regarding burdens of proof as well as several rules of law borrowed from the interference context. Bard offered into evidence at trial a document published about three months before the filing date of Dr. Mahurkar's patent disclosing each and every element of the claimed invention. Dr. Mahurkar then had the burden to offer evidence showing he invented the subject matter of his patent before the publication date of the document. Had Dr. Mahurkar not come forward with evidence of an earlier date of invention, the Cook catalog would have been anticipatory prior art under section 102(a) because Dr. Mahurkar's invention date would have been the filing date of his patent.

However, Dr. Mahurkar offered evidence at trial to show that he invented the subject matter of the patent before publication of the Cook reference. He met his burden of production. Consequently, this court turns to an evaluation of the evidence offered by Dr. Mahurkar under the proper burden of persuasion in this infringement action and the rules of law relating to invention dates.*

Section 102(g) of Title 35 contains the basic rule for determining priority. 35 U.S.C. §102(g). Section 102(g) also provides basic protection for the inventive process, shielding in particular the creative steps of conception and reduction to practice. In the United States, the person who first reduces an invention to practice is "prima facie the first and true inventor." *Christie v. Seybold*, 55 F. 69, 76 (6th Cir. 1893) (Taft, J.). However, the person "who first conceives, and, in a mental sense, first invents . . . may date his patentable invention back to the time of its conception, if he connects the conception with its reduction to practice by reasonable diligence on his part, so that they are substantially one continuous act." *Id.* Stated otherwise, priority of invention "goes to the first party to reduce an invention to practice unless the other party can show that it was the first to conceive the invention and that it exercised reasonable diligence in later reducing that invention to practice." *Price v. Symsek*, 988 F.2d 1187, 1190 (Fed. Cir. 1993).

To have conceived of an invention, an inventor must have formed in his or her mind "a definite and permanent idea of the complete and operative invention, as it is hereafter to be applied in practice." *Burroughs Wellcome Co. v. Barr Labs., Inc.*, 40 F.3d 1223, 1228 (Fed. Cir. 1994). The idea must be "so clearly defined in the inventor's mind that only ordinary skill would be necessary to reduce the invention to practice, without extensive research or experimentation." *Id.*

This court has developed a rule requiring corroboration where a party seeks to show conception through the oral testimony of an inventor. This requirement arose out of a concern that inventors testifying in patent infringement cases would be tempted to remember facts favorable to their case by the lure of protecting their patent or defeating another's patent. *Eibel Process Co. v. Minnesota & Ontario Paper Co.*, 261 U.S. 45 (1923). While perhaps prophylactic in application given the unique abilities of trial court judges and juries to assess credibility, the rule provides a bright line for both district courts and the PTO to follow in addressing the difficult issues related to invention dates.

In assessing corroboration of oral testimony, courts apply a rule of reason analysis. Under a rule of reason analysis, "[a]n evaluation of all pertinent evidence must be made so that a sound determination of the credibility of the inventor's story may be reached."

This court does not require corroboration where a party seeks to prove conception through the use of physical exhibits. The trier of fact can conclude for itself what documents show, aided by testimony as to what the exhibit would mean to one skilled in the art.

Reduction to practice follows conception. To show actual reduction to practice, an inventor must demonstrate that the invention is suitable for its intended purpose. *Scott v. Finney*, 34 F.3d 1058, 1061 (Fed. Cir. 1994). Depending on the

---

* [The burden of persuasion—also known as the burden of proof—is an "obligation which rests on one of the parties to an action to persuade the trier of the facts, generally the jury, of the truth of a proposition which he has affirmatively asserted by the pleadings." *Director, Office of Workers' Compensation Program, Dep't of Labor v. Greenwich Collieries*, 512 U.S. 267, 275 (1994). The burden of production, a distinct burden, refers to "a party's obligation to come forward with evidence to support its claim." *Id.* at 272.—Ed.]

character of the invention and the problem it solves, this showing may require test results. *Id.* at 1062. Less complicated inventions and problems do not demand stringent testing. In fact, some inventions are so simple and their purpose and efficacy so obvious that their complete construction is sufficient to demonstrate workability.

Where a party is first to conceive but second to reduce to practice, that party must demonstrate reasonable diligence toward reduction to practice from a date just prior to the other party's conception to its reduction to practice. *Griffith v. Kanamaru*, 816 F.2d 624, 625-26 (Fed. Cir. 1987).

Bard bears the burden of persuasion on the status of the Cook catalog as prior art. Bard must persuade the trier of fact by clear and convincing evidence that the Cook catalog was published prior to Dr. Mahurkar's invention date.

At trial, Dr. Mahurkar offered evidence to demonstrate prior invention in two ways. He offered evidence to show he conceived and reduced to practice his invention before publication of the catalog. He also offered evidence to show that he conceived of his invention prior to the date of publication of the Cook catalog and that he proceeded with reasonable diligence from a date just prior to publication of the catalog to his filing date. Bard, in turn, challenged Dr. Mahurkar's evidence.

With all of the evidence from both sides before the jury, Bard must persuade the jury by clear and convincing evidence that its version of the facts is true. In other words, Bard must persuade the jury that Dr. Mahurkar did not invent prior to publication of the catalog. This is because (1) he did not conceive and reduce his invention to practice before the publication date and (2) he did not conceive and thereafter proceed with reasonable diligence as required to his filing date. If Bard fails to meet this burden, the catalog is not prior art under section 102(a).

Viewing the evidence of record below in the light most favorable to Bard, this court concludes that no reasonable jury could have found clear and convincing evidence that the Cook catalog was prior art. Dr. Mahurkar testified that he conceived and began work on dual-lumen, flexible, hemodialysis catheters, including the '155 catheter, in 1979. From late 1980 through early 1981, Dr. Mahurkar constructed polyethylene prototype catheters in his kitchen. He bought tubing and various machines for making and testing his catheters.

During this time period, he also tested polyethylene prototypes and used them in flow and pressure drop tests in his kitchen. These tests used glycerine to simulate blood. These tests showed, to the limit of their design, the utility of his claimed invention. Dr. Mahurkar designed these tests to show the efficiency of his structure knowing that polyethylene catheters were too brittle for actual use with humans. But, he also knew that his invention would become suitable for its intended purpose by simple substitution of a soft, biocompatible material. Dr. Mahurkar adequately showed reduction to practice of his less complicated invention with tests which "[did] not duplicate all of the conditions of actual use." *Gordon v. Hubbard*, 347 F.2d 1001, 1006 (CCPA 1965).

Dr. Mahurkar provided corroboration for his testimony. Dr. Mahurkar confidentially disclosed the catheter prototype tips of his '155 invention to Geoffrey Martin, President of Vas-Cath Inc. in 1981, and Brian L. Bates of Cook, Inc. Mr. Martin testified that he received the polyethylene prototype tips from Dr. Mahurkar in 1981. Dr. Mahurkar also produced a letter from Stephen Brushey, an employee of Vas-Cath, dated April 21, 1981, that described several of his catheters. Additionally, Dr. Mahurkar presented a letter from Brian L. Bates of Cook, Inc., dated October 23, 1981. In this letter, Cook was "impressed with the thought and technology which has gone into the fabrication of the prototype material."

In addition to evidence of actual reduction to practice before publication of the Cook catalog, Dr. Mahurkar also showed reasonable diligence from his conception date through the filing of his patent application. From conception to filing, Dr. Mahurkar continuously sought to locate companies capable of extruding his tubing with the soft, flexible materials necessary for human use.

On this record and with the applicable burden of persuasion, no reasonable jury could have found that Bard proved the Cook catalog was prior art. Consequently, the court properly granted Dr. Mahurkar's motion for JMOL of non-anticipation of claim 1 of the '155 patent.

Comments

1. ***Proving Date of Invention.*** Although *Mahurkar* was a section 102(a) novelty case, the court borrowed extensively from section 102(g) interference practice. In doing so, the court provided a nice discussion of the various components involved in proving date of invention. To summarize, (1) the prima facie first inventor is the party who first reduced to practice, but a party who was second to reduce to practice will be considered the first inventor if he can show that he was the first to conceive and exercised reasonable diligence in reducing his invention to practice; (2) reduction to practice is proven when the invention works for its intended purpose and there is a contemporaneous appreciation of such; and (3) conception is shown through the presentation of corroborated evidence that the inventor formed in his mind "a definite and permanent idea of the complete and operative invention, as it is thereafter applied in practice." For a discussion of the differences between burden of production and burden of persuasion, *see Dep't of Labor v. Greenwich Collieries*, 512 U.S. 267, 272-276 (1994).

   a. ***Reduction to Practice.*** Why does patent law require an invention to be reduced to practice? To answer this question, it is instructive to read the words of Charles Goodyear on the nature of the inventive process:

      It is a mistaken idea with many, that the invention of an improvement consists in the first vague idea of it. It takes far more than that to entice one to the merit of an invention, for between the bare conception of an idea, and the demonstration of the practicability and utility of the thing conceived, there is almost always a vast amount of labor to be performed, time and money to be spent, and innumerable difficulties and prejudices to be encountered, before the work is accomplished.

      CHARLES SLACK, NOBLE OBSESSION 199 (2002) (quoting from Goodyear's 1853 book, *Gum-Elastic and Its Varieties, With a Detailed Account of Its Applications and Uses, and of the Discovery of Vulcanization*). Viewed in this light, the reduction to practice requirement offers greater confidence, something concrete, that an *invention* has obtained.

      Reduction to practice ("RTP") can either be (1) constructive; or (2) actual. Constructive RTP is the date on which the application is filed.

Actual RTP requires the inventor "prove that: (1) he constructed an embodiment or performed a process that met all the limitations . . . and (2) he determined that the invention would work for its intended purpose." *Cooper v. Goldfarb*, 154 F.3d 1321, 1327 (Fed. Cir. 1998). And whether actual testing is required to prove the invention works for its intended purpose depends on the character and complexity of the invention and the problem it addresses. *See Mahurkar*, 79 F.3d at 1578. Indeed, some inventions may be "so simple and their purpose and efficacy so obvious that their complete construction is sufficient to demonstrate workability." *Id.* And "there is no requirement . . . [of] repeatedly," *Fox Group, Inc. v. Cree, Inc.*, 700 F.3d 1300, 1305 (Fed. Cir. 2012); that is, once the product is reduced to practice there is no need to show that it could done again. Lastly, "conception and reduction to practice cannot be established nunc pro tunc"; rather, "[t]here must be contemporaneous recognition and appreciation of the invention represented by the counts." *Breen v. Henshaw*, 472 F.2d 1398, 1401 (CCPA 1973).

If testing is required, actual working conditions may not be necessary. Laboratory tests may be sufficient if they simulate actual working conditions. Neither perfection nor commercial viability is required to show actual RTP. In the Federal Circuit case of *Scott v. Finney*, 34 F.3d 1058 (Fed. Cir. 1994), the court stated that cases dealing with the sufficiency of testing in proving actual RTP "share a common theme." The court wrote:

> In tests showing the invention's solution of a problem, the courts have not required commercial perfection nor absolute replication of the circumstances of the invention's actual use. Rather, they have instead adopted a common sense assessment. This common sense approach prescribes more scrupulous testing under circumstances approaching actual use conditions when the problem includes many uncertainties. On the other hand, when the problem to be solved does not present myriad variables, common sense similarly permits little or no testing to show the soundness of the principles of operation of the invention.

Id. at 1063. Not unlike proving conception, the inventor must corroborate his actual reduction to practice.

b. **Conception.** An inventor may be able to move the date of invention date back further than his RTP if he can show he conceived of the invention prior to his reducing it to practice. Conception is a term of art in patent law and means the inventor had in his mind "a definite and permanent idea of the complete and operative invention, as it is hereafter to be applied in practice." *Burroughs Wellcome Co. v. Barr Labs., Inc.*, 40 F.3d 1223, 1228 (Fed. Cir. 1994). That is, the inventive idea was be "so clearly defined in the inventor's mind that only ordinary skill would be necessary to reduce the invention to practice, without extensive research or experimentation." *Id. See also Kridl v. McCormick*, 105 F.3d 1446, 1449 (Fed. Cir. 1997) ("Conception is the formation 'in the mind of the inventor of a definite and permanent idea of the complete and operative invention, as it is therefore to be applied in practice.'"); *Mergenthaler v. Scudder*, 1897 C.D. 724, 731 (1897) (setting forth the classic definition of conception). And corroboration is required if the inventor is only relying on oral testimony to prove conception, rather than documentation or physical exhibits. *See Mahurkar*, 79 F.3d at 1577-1578. Indeed, the *Mergenthaler* court stated that without such a requirement, there would be a "great temptation to perjury." 1897 C.D. at 732.

Moreover, conception requires "more than unrecognized accidental creation." In fact, "an accidental and unappreciated duplication of an invention does not defeat the patent right of one who, though later in time, was the first to recognize that which constitutes the inventive subject matter." *Silvestri v. Grant*, 496 F.2d 593, 597 (CCPA 1974). Thus, "[t]he date of conception of a prior inventor's invention is the date the inventor first appreciated the fact of what he made." *Dow Chem. Co. v. Astro-Valcour, Inc.*, 267 F.3d 1334, 1341 (Fed. Cir. 2001).

In *University of Pittsburgh v. Hedrick*, 573 F.3d 1290 (Fed. Cir. 2009), the issue was inventorship (something we take up in detail in Chapter 8). Hedrick argued that he should be named a co-inventor of the '231 patent, which related to creating stem cells from adipose-tissue. Hedrick argued that the work of the two listed co-inventors, Katz and Llull, "remained highly speculative" and "that Katz and Llull were required to 'know' that the invention contained every limitation of each claim at the time of conception." *Id.* at 1299. The Federal Circuit was not persuaded, and characterized Hedrick's argument as "premised upon a misapprehension of what it means to 'know' the limitations of the claims." *Id.* The court wrote:

> Knowledge in the context of a possessed, isolated biological construct does not mean proof to a scientific certainty that the construct is exactly what a scientist believes it is. Conception requires a definite and permanent idea of the operative invention, and "necessarily turns on the inventor's ability to describe his invention." Proof that the invention works to a scientific certainty is reduction to practice. . . . The district court found that Katz's laboratory notebooks sufficiently described to those skilled in the art how to isolate the cells from adipose-tissue, at which point they would be in possession of the invention. Thus, they had disclosed a "completed thought expressed in such clear terms as to enable those skilled in the art to make the invention."

Id.

2. ***Economic Nationalism, Foreign Inventive Activity, and Sections 102(g) and 104.*** Historically, American patent law has projected economic nationalism. The early patent acts (e.g., 1793 Act) prohibited foreigners from obtaining patents in the United States or required foreign inventors to pay a higher filing fee than American inventors (e.g., 1836 Act). In addition, until the mid-1990s, inventive activity—namely conception and reduction to practice—outside the United States could not be used to prove date of invention under section 104. But these statutory provisions were amended with the ratification of North American Free Trade Agreement (NAFTA) and the Trade-Related Aspects of Intellectual Property Rights (TRIPS) that formed part of the General Agreement on Tariffs and Trade (GATT). Now inventive activity in any NAFTA or WTO country can be used to show date of invention. (The amendment to section 104 became effective on December 8, 1993 for NAFTA countries and January 1, 1996 for WTO countries, of which there are 151 member states as of this writing.) In 1999, section 102(g) was amended as part of the American Inventors Protection Act, to reflect the changes made to section 104. Section 102(g) was bifurcated into two subsections, and now reads:

A person shall be entitled to a patent unless —

(g)(1) during the course of an interference conducted under section 135 or section 291, another inventor involved therein establishes, to the extent permitted in section 104, that before such person's invention thereof the invention was made by such other inventor and not abandoned, suppressed, or concealed, or (2) before such person's invention thereof, the invention was made in this country by another inventor who had not abandoned, suppressed, or concealed it. . . .

Subsection (g)(1)'s language "to the extent permitted in section 104" permits inventors to use foreign-based inventive activity to prove date of invention in the context of an interference — that is, when obtaining patent rights. But, as we saw in *Hilmer II* (in section A.5, above), foreign-based inventive activity cannot be used as prior art to defeat patent rights — thus, section 102(g)(2)'s language "made in this country." There remains a distinction between using foreign-based inventive activity to obtains patent rights in the context of an interference proceeding — the province of section 102(g)(1); and using foreign-based inventive activity to defeat patent rights, which is prohibited under section 102(g)(2).

The AIA has eliminated both sections 102(g) and 104.

2. Diligence and Abandonment

Diligence and abandonment are terms of art in patent that come into play in the context of determining priority of invention — that is, who invented the claimed invention first. Both diligence and abandonment have distinct temporal applicability. The issue of diligence is relevant prior to reduction to practice, whereas abandonment is something that occurs, if at all, after reduction to practice. Diligence becomes an issue when one party is the last to reduce to practice, but the first to conceive. For instance, Inventor 1 reduces to practice November 1, 2006 and conceives January 1, 2005. Inventor 2 reduces to practice August 1, 2006, but conceives April 1, 2005. Patent law wants to know why Inventor 1 reduced to practice after Inventor 2 when Inventor 1 conceived first, implying that Inventor 1 may not have sufficiently pursued reducing his invention to practice. To prevent the patent being awarded to Inventor 2, Inventor 1 must show that he was reasonably diligent in reducing his invention to practice from just prior to Inventor 2's conception to Inventor 1's reduction to practice. The question of abandonment arises when there is a relatively long gap between reduction to practice and filing date. The policy of diligence and abandonment — as is much of the policy throughout patent law — is to induce early disclosure of the invention or, at least, disclosure sooner than later. The *Griffith* and *Fujikawa* cases explore these important issues.

GRIFFITH v. KANAMARU

816 F.2d 624 (Fed. Cir. 1987)

NICHOLS, Senior Circuit Judge.

Owen W. Griffith (Griffith) appeals the decision of the Board of Patent Appeals and Interferences (board) (Patent Interference No. 101,562) that

Griffith failed to establish a *prima facie* case that he is entitled to an award of priority against the filing date of Tsuneo Kanamaru, *et al.* (Kanamaru) for a patent on aminocarnitine compounds. We affirm.

BACKGROUND

This patent interference case involves the application of Griffith, an Associate Professor in the Department of Biochemistry at Cornell University Medical College, for a patent on an aminocarnitine compound, useful in the treatment of diabetes, and a patent issued for the same invention to Kanamaru, an employee of Takeda Chemical Industries.

Griffith had established conception by June 30, 1981, and reduction to practice on January 11, 1984. Kanamaru filed for a United States patent on November 17, 1982. The board found, however, that Griffith failed to establish reasonable diligence for a *prima facie* case of prior invention and issued an order to show cause as to why summary judgment should not be issued.

The board considered the additional evidence submitted by Griffith pursuant to the show cause order and decided that Griffith failed to establish a *prima facie* case for priority against Kanamaru's filing date. This result was based on the board's conclusion that Griffith's explanation for inactivity between June 15, 1983, and September 13, 1983, failed to provide a legally sufficient excuse to satisfy the "reasonable diligence" requirement of 35 U.S.C. § 102(g). Griffith appeals on the issue of reasonable diligence.

ANALYSIS

I

This is a case of first impression and presents the novel circumstances of a university suggesting that it is reasonable for the public to wait for disclosure until the most satisfactory funding arrangements are made. The applicable law is the "reasonable diligence" standard contained in 35 U.S.C. § 102(g) and we must determine the appropriate role of the courts in construing this exception to the ordinary first-in-time rule.

Griffith must establish a *prima facie* case of reasonable diligence, as well as dates of conception and reduction to practice, to avoid summary judgment on the issue of priority. As a preliminary matter we note that, although the board focused on the June 1983 to September 1983 lapse in work, and Griffith's reasons for this lapse, Griffith is burdened with establishing a *prima facie* case of reasonable diligence from immediately before Kanamaru's filing date of November 17, 1982, until Griffith's reduction to practice on January 11, 1984. 35 U.S.C. § 102(g).

On appeal, Griffith presents two grounds intended to justify his inactivity on the aminocarnitine project between June 15, 1983, and September 13, 1983. The first is that, notwithstanding Cornell University's extraordinary endowment, it is reasonable, and as a policy matter desirable, for Cornell to require Griffith and other research scientists to obtain funding from outside the university. The second reason Griffith presents is that he reasonably waited for Ms. Debora Jenkins to matriculate in the Fall of 1983 to assist with the project. He had promised her she should have that task which she needed to qualify for her degree. We reject these arguments and conclude that Griffith has failed to establish grounds to excuse his inactivity prior to reduction to practice.

II

The reasonable diligence standard balances the interest in rewarding and encouraging invention with the public's interest in the earliest possible disclosure of innovation. Griffith must account for the entire period from just before Kanamaru's filing date until his reduction to practice. As one of our predecessor courts has noted:

> Public policy favors the early disclosure of inventions. This underlies the requirement for "reasonable diligence" in reducing an invention to practice, not unlike the requirement that, to avoid a holding of suppression or concealment, there be no unreasonable delay in filing an application once there has been a reduction to practice.

Naber v. Cricchi, 567 F.2d 382, 385 n.5 (CCPA 1977).

The board in this case was, but not properly, asked to pass judgment on the reasonableness of Cornell's policy regarding outside funding of research. The correct inquiry is rather whether it is reasonable for Cornell to require the public to wait for the innovation, given the well settled policy in favor of early disclosure. As the board notes, Chief Judge Markey has called early public disclosure the "linchpin of the patent system." *Horwath v. Lee,* 564 F.2d 948, 950 (CCPA 1977). A review of caselaw on excuses for inactivity in reduction to practice reveals a common thread that courts may consider the reasonable everyday problems and limitations encountered by an inventor. *See, e.g., Bey v. Kollonitsch,* 806 F.2d 1024 (Fed. Cir. 1986) (delay in filing excused where attorney worked on a group of related applications and other applications contributed substantially to the preparation of Bey's application); *Reed v. Tornqvist,* 436 F.2d 501 (CCPA 1971) (concluding it is not unreasonable for inventor to delay completing a patent application until after returning from a three week vacation in Sweden, extended by illness of inventor's father); *Keizer v. Bradley,* 270 F.2d 396 (1959) (delay excused where inventor, after producing a component for a color television, delayed filing to produce an appropriate receiver for testing the component); *Courson v. O'Connor,* 227 F. 890, 894 (7th Cir. 1915) ("exercise of reasonable diligence . . . does not require an inventor to devote his entire time thereto, or to abandon his ordinary means of livelihood"); *De Wallace v. Scott,* 15 App. D.C. 157 (1899) (where applicant made *bona fide* attempts to perfect his invention, applicant's poor health, responsibility to feed his family, and daily job demands excused his delay in reducing his invention to practice); *Texas Co. v. Globe Oil & Refining Co.,* 112 F. Supp. 455 (N.D. Ill. 1953) (delay in filing application excused because of confusion relating to war).

Griffith argues that the admitted inactivity of three months between June 15, 1983, and September 13, 1983, which he attributes to Cornell's "reasonable" policy requiring outside funding and to Griffith's "reasonable" decision to delay until a graduate student arrived, falls within legal precedent excusing inactivity in the diligence context. We disagree. We first note that, in regard to waiting for a graduate student, Griffith does not even suggest that he faced a genuine shortage of personnel. He does not suggest that Ms. Jenkins was the *only* person capable of carrying on with the aminocarnitine experiment. We can see no application of precedent to suggest that the convenience of the timing of the semester schedule justifies a three-month delay for the purpose of reasonable diligence. Neither do we believe that this excuse, absent even a suggestion by Griffith that Jenkins was uniquely qualified to do his research, is reasonable.

Griffith's second contention that it was reasonable for Cornell to require outside funding, therefore causing a delay in order to apply for such funds, is also insufficient to excuse his inactivity. The crux of Griffith's argument is that outside funding is desirable as a form of peer review, or monitoring of the worthiness of a given project. He also suggests that, as a policy matter, universities should not be treated as businesses, which ultimately would detract from scholarly inquiry. Griffith states that these considerations, if accepted as valid, would fit within the scope of the caselaw excusing inactivity for "reasonable" delays in reduction to practice and filing.

These contentions on delay do not fit within the texture and scope of the precedent cited by the parties or discussed in this opinion. Griffith argues this case is controlled by the outcome of *Litchfield v. Eigen,* 535 F.2d 72 (CCPA 1976). We disagree. In *Litchfield,* Judge Rich held that the inventors failed to establish due diligence because of their inactivity between April 1964 and September 1965. *Id.* at 76-77. The court based this conclusion on the finding that the inventors possessed the capacity to test the invention and chose instead to test other compounds. *Id.* Judge Rich did not reach the issue of the alleged budgetary limitations imposed by the sponsor and stated that the inventors failed to show any evidence of such financial limitations and that, therefore, the court could not consider this contention. *Id.*

Griffith's excuses sound more in the nature of commercial development, not accepted as an excuse for delay, than the "hardship" cases most commonly found and discussed *supra.* Delays in reduction to practice caused by an inventor's efforts to refine an invention to the most marketable and profitable form have not been accepted as sufficient excuses for inactivity. Griffith's case is analogous to that in *Seeberger v. Dodge,* 24 App. D.C. 476 (1905). In that case, the inventor was the first to conceive of an improvement in an escalator and was attempting to show diligence. The court noted:

> The testimony shows that he [Seeberger] was a man of means, and might have constructed an escalator had he undertaken to do so. Instead of this, his constant effort was to organize corporations, or to interest capital in other ways, for the purpose of engaging in the general manufacture of escalators.

Id. at 484-85.

The court held this unacceptable:

> One having the first complete conception of an invention cannot hold the field against all comers by diligent efforts, merely, to organize and procure sufficient capital to engage in the manufacture of his device or mechanism for commercial purposes. This is a different thing from diligence in actual reduction to practice.

Id. at 485.

The comparison we draw is that Cornell University, like Seeberger, has made a clear decision against funding Griffith's project in order to avoid the risks and distractions, albeit different in each case, that would result from directly financing these inventions. Griffith has placed in the record, and relies on, an able article by President Bok of Harvard, *Business and the Academy, Harvard Magazine,* May-June 1981, 31, App. at 81. Bok is explaining the policy issues respecting academic funding of scientific research, for the benefit of Harvard's alumni who must, of course, make up by their contributions the University's annual deficit. While much academic research could produce a profit, pursuit of such profit may be business inappropriate for a university though it would be right and proper for a commercial organization. For example, it might produce conflicts between the roles of scientists as inventors and developers against their roles as members of the university faculty. However large the university's endowment may be, it may be better to enlist private funding and let this source of funds develop the commercial utilization of any invention as perhaps, the beneficial owner. If there is a patent, the source of funds may end up assignee of the patent. It seems also implicit in this policy choice that faculty members may not be allowed single-minded pursuit of reduction to practice whenever they conceive some idea of value, and at times the rights of other inventors may obtain a priority that a single-minded pursuit would have averted. Bok says diligent reduction to practice, to satisfy the patent laws, may interfere with a faculty member's other duties. Bok is asking the approval of his alumni, not of the courts. The management of great universities is one thing, at least, the courts have not taken over and do not deem themselves qualified to undertake. Bok does not ask that the patent laws or other intellectual property law be skewed or slanted to enable the university to have its cake and eat it too, *i.e.*, to act in a noncommercial manner and yet preserve the pecuniary rewards of commercial exploitation for itself.

If, as we are asked to assume, Cornell also follows the policy Bok has so well articulated, it seems evident that Cornell has consciously chosen to assume the risk that priority in the invention might be lost to an outside inventor, yet, having chosen a noncommercial policy, it asks us to save it the property that would have inured to it if it had acted in single-minded pursuit of gain.

III

The board in this case considered primarily Griffith's contention that the Cornell policy was reasonable and therefore acceptable to excuse his delay in reduction to practice. Although we agree with the board's conclusion, it is appropriate to go further and consider other circumstances as they apply to the reasonable diligence analysis of 35 U.S.C. § 102(g). The record reveals that from the relevant period of November 17, 1982 (Kanamaru's filing date), to September 13, 1983 (when Griffith renewed his efforts towards reduction to practice), Griffith interrupted and often put aside the aminocarnitine project to work on other experiments. Between June 1982 and June 1983 Griffith admits that, at the request of the chairman of his department, he was primarily engaged in an unrelated research project on mitochondrial glutathione metabolism. Griffith also put aside the aminocarnitine experiment to work on a grant proposal on an unrelated project. Griffith's statement in the record that his unrelated grant application, if granted, might "support" a future grant request directed to the aminocarnitine project does not overcome the conclusion that he preferred one project over another and was not "continuously" or "reasonably" diligent. Griffith made only minimal efforts to secure funding directly for the aminocarnitine project.

The conclusion we reach from the record is that the aminocarnitine project was second and often third priority in laboratory research as well as the solicitation of funds. We agree that Griffith failed to establish a *prima facie* case of reasonable diligence or a legally sufficient excuse for inactivity to establish priority over Kanamaru.

FUJIKAWA v. WATTANASIN
93 F.3d 1559 (Fed. Cir. 1996)

CLEVENGER, Circuit Judge.

Yoshihiro Fujikawa *et al.* (Fujikawa) appeal from two decisions of the Board of Patent Appeals and Interferences of the United States Patent & Trademark Office (Board) granting priority of invention in two related interferences to Sompong Wattanasin, and denying Fujikawa's motion to add an additional subgenus count to the interferences. We affirm.

I.

These interferences pertain to a compound and method for inhibiting cholesterol biosynthesis in humans and other animals. The compound count recites a genus of novel mevalonolactones. The method count recites a method of inhibiting the biosynthesis of cholesterol by administering to a "patient in need of said treatment" an appropriate dosage of a compound falling within the scope of the compound count.

The real parties in interest are Sandoz Pharmaceuticals Corporation (Sandoz), assignee of Wattanasin, and Nissan Chemical Industries, Ltd. (Nissan), assignee of Fujikawa.

The inventive activity of Fujikawa, the senior party, occurred overseas. Fujikawa can thus rely only on his filing date, August 20, 1987, to establish priority. 35 U.S.C. §102(g) (1994). Whether Wattanasin is entitled to priority as against Fujikawa therefore turns on two discrete questions. First, whether Wattanasin has shown conception coupled with diligence from just prior to Fujikawa's effective filing date until reduction to practice. *Id.* Second, whether Wattanasin suppressed or concealed the invention between reduction to practice and filing. *Id.* With respect to the first question, Fujikawa does not directly challenge the Board's holdings on Wattanasin's conception or diligence, but rather contends that the Board incorrectly fixed the date of Wattanasin's reduction to practice. As for the second question, Fujikawa contends that the Board erred in concluding that Wattanasin had not suppressed or concealed the invention. Fujikawa seeks reversal, and thus to establish priority in its favor, on either ground.

II.

The Board divided Wattanasin's inventive activity into two phases. The first phase commenced in 1979 when Sandoz began searching for drugs which would inhibit the biosynthesis of cholesterol. Inventor Wattanasin was assigned to this project in 1982, and during 1984-1985 he synthesized three compounds falling within the scope of the compound count. When tested *in vitro*, each of these compounds exhibited some cholesterol-inhibiting activity, although not all the chemicals were equally effective. Still, according to one Sandoz researcher, Dr. Damon, these test results indicated that, to a high probability, the three compounds "would be active when administered *in vivo* to a patient to inhibit cholesterol biosynthesis, *i.e.* for the treatment of hypercholesteremia or atherosclerosis." Notwithstanding these seemingly positive results, Sandoz shelved Wattanasin's project for almost two years, apparently because the level of *in vitro* activity in two of the three compounds was disappointingly low.

By January 1987, however, interest in Wattanasin's invention had revived, and the second phase of activity began. Over the next several months, four more compounds falling within the scope of the compound count were synthesized. In October, these compounds were tested for *in vitro* activity, and each of the four compounds yielded positive results. Again, however, there were significant differences in the level of *in vitro* activity of the four compounds. Two of the compounds in particular, numbered 64-935 and 64-936, exhibited *in vitro* activity significantly higher than that of the other two compounds, numbered 64-933 and 64-934.

Soon after, in December 1987, the three most active compounds *in vitro* were subjected to additional *in vivo* testing. For Sandoz, one primary purpose of these tests was to determine the *in vivo* potency of the three compounds relative to that of Compactin, a prior art compound of known cholesterol-inhibiting potency. From the results of the *in vivo* tests, reproduced in the margin, Sandoz calculated an ED50 for each of the compounds and compared it to the ED50 of Compactin. Only one of the compounds, compound 64-935, manifested a better ED50 than Compactin: an ED50 of 0.49 as compared to Compactin's ED50 of 3.5. All of the tests performed by Sandoz were conducted in accordance with established protocols.

During this period, Sandoz also began to consider whether, and when, a patent application should be filed for Wattanasin's invention. Several times during the second phase of activity, the Sandoz patent committee considered the question of Wattanasin's invention but decided that it was too early in the invention's development to file a patent application. Each time, however, the patent committee merely deferred decision on the matter and specified that it would be taken up again at subsequent meetings. Finally, in January 1988, with the *in vivo* testing completed, the Committee assigned Wattanasin's invention an "A" rating which meant that the invention was ripe for filing and that a patent application should be prepared. The case was assigned to a Ms. Geisser, a young patent attorney in the Sandoz patent department with little experience in the pharmaceutical field.

Over the next several months the Sandoz patent department collected additional data from the inventor which was needed to prepare the patent application. This data gathering took until approximately the end of May 1988. At that point, work on the case seems to have ceased for several months until Ms. Geisser began preparing a draft sometime in the latter half of 1988. The parties dispute when this preparation began. Fujikawa contends that it occurred as late as October, and that Ms. Geisser was spurred to begin preparing the draft application by the discovery that a patent to the same subject matter had been issued to a third party, Picard. Fujikawa, however, has no evidence to support that contention. In contrast, Sandoz contends that Ms. Geisser began the draft as early as August, and that she was already working on the draft when she first heard of Picard's patent. The evidence of record, and in particular the testimony of Ms. Geisser, supports that version of events. In any event, the draft was completed in November and, after several turn-arounds with the inventor, ultimately filed in March of 1989.

Both Wattanasin and Fujikawa requested an interference with Picard. The requests were granted and a three-party interference between Picard, Fujikawa, and Wattanasin was set up. Early in the proceedings, however, Picard filed a request for an adverse judgment presumably because he could not antedate Fujikawa's priority date. What remained was a two-party interference between Fujikawa and Wattanasin. Ultimately, for reasons not significant to this appeal, the interference was divided into two interferences: one relating to the method count and one relating to the compound count. The Board decided each of these interferences adverse to Fujikawa.

With respect to the compound count, the Board made two alternative findings regarding reduction to practice. First, it found that the *in vitro* results in October 1987 showed sufficient practical utility for the compound so as to constitute a reduction to practice as of the date of those tests. In the alternative, the Board held, the in vivo tests which showed significant activity in the 64-935 compound at doses of 1.0 and 0.1 mg were sufficient to show practical utility. Consequently, Wattanasin had reduced the compound to practice, at the latest, as of December 1987. Since Fujikawa did not challenge Wattanasin's diligence for the period between Fujikawa's effective filing date of August 20, 1987 and Wattanasin's reduction to practice in either October or December 1987, the Board held that Wattanasin was de facto the first inventor of the compound count. Finally, the Board found that the seventeen month period (counting from the *in vitro* testing) or fifteen month period (counting from the *in vivo* testing) between Wattanasin's reduction to practice and filing was not sufficient to raise an inference of suppression or concealment given the complexity of the invention, and therefore awarded priority of the compound count to Wattanasin. In reaching this conclusion, the Board rejected Fujikawa's argument that Wattanasin was spurred to file by Picard because it held that spurring by Picard, a third party, had no legal effect in a priority dispute between Fujikawa and Wattanasin.

With respect to the method count, the Board determined that Wattanasin reduced to practice in December 1987 on the date that *in vivo* testing of the 64-935 compound was concluded. In reaching that conclusion, the Board first noted that a reduction to practice must include every limitation of the count. Consequently, Wattanasin's early *in vitro* testing could not constitute a reduction to practice of the method count, since that count recites administering the compound to a "patient." The *in vivo* testing, however, met the limitations of the count since the word "patient" was sufficiently broad to include the laboratory rats to whom the compounds were administered. The *in vivo* testing also proved that 64-935 had practical utility because the compound displayed significant cholesterol inhibiting activity at doses of 1.0 and 0.1 mg. Given this date of reduction to practice, the Board again held that Wattanasin was the *de facto* first inventor of the count and that the delay in filing of fifteen months was not sufficient to trigger an inference of suppression or concealment. The Board therefore awarded priority of the method count to Wattanasin.

III.

* * *

B.

Turning to the method count, the Board found that Wattanasin reduced the method to practice in December 1987 when successful *in vivo* testing of the compound was completed. This finding, too, was based on testimony that the *in vivo* data for one of the compounds tested, 64-935, showed significant cholesterol inhibiting activity in the laboratory rats tested.

Fujikawa challenges the Board's holding by referring to an anomaly in the test data of the 64-935 compound which it contends undercuts the reliability of the *in vivo* tests. In particular, Fujikawa points to the fact that the compound's potency was less at a dosage of 0.3 mg than it was at a dosage of 0.1 mg. On the basis of this aberration, Fujikawa's expert, Dr. Holmlund, testified that this test data was unreliable and could not support a finding that the compound was pharmacologically active.

It is clear from the Board's opinion, however, that to the extent Dr. Holmlund was testifying that this aberration would lead one of ordinary skill to completely reject these test results, the Board did not accept his testimony. This decision of the Board was not clear error. Admittedly, the decreased potency at 0.3 mg is curious. The question remains, however, as to how much this glitch in the data would undercut the persuasiveness of the test results as a whole in the mind of one of ordinary skill. Each party presented evidence on this point and the Board resolved this disputed question of fact by finding that the test results as a whole were sufficient to establish pharmacological activity in the minds of those skilled in the art. In doing so, the Board properly exercised its duty as fact finder, and we therefore affirm its finding on this point.

As noted above, Fujikawa does not challenge the Board's conclusions that Wattanasin conceived prior to Fujikawa's effective date or that Wattanasin pursued his invention with diligence prior to Fujikawa's date until his reductions to practice in October and December 1987. Consequently, we affirm the Board's finding that Wattanasin has shown conception coupled with diligence from just prior to Fujikawa's effective date of August 20, 1987 up to the date he reduced the invention to practice in October 1987, for the compound, or December 1987, for the method.

IV.

Having determined that Wattanasin was the *de facto* first inventor, the remaining question before the Board was whether Wattanasin had suppressed or concealed the invention between the time he reduced to practice and the time he filed his patent application. Suppression or concealment of the invention by Wattanasin would entitle Fujikawa to priority. 35 U.S.C. § 102(g).

Suppression or concealment is a question of law which we review *de novo*. Our case law distinguishes between two types of suppression and concealment: cases in which the inventor deliberately suppresses or conceals his invention, and cases in which a legal inference of suppression or concealment is drawn based on "too long" a delay in filing a patent application.

Fujikawa first argues that there is evidence of intentional suppression or concealment in this case. Intentional suppression refers to situations in which an inventor "designedly, and with the view of applying it indefinitely and exclusively for his own profit, withholds his invention from the public." *Id.* (*quoting Kendall v. Winsor*, 62 U.S. (21 How.) 322, 328 (1858)). Admittedly, Sandoz was not overly efficient in preparing a patent application, given the time which elapsed between its reduction to practice in late 1987 and its ultimate filing in March 1989. Intentional suppression, however, requires more than the passage of time. It requires evidence that the inventor intentionally delayed filing in order to prolong the period during which the invention is maintained in secret. Fujikawa presented no evidence that Wattanasin delayed filing for this purpose. On the contrary, all indications are that throughout the period between reduction to practice and filing, Sandoz moved slowly (one might even say fitfully), but inexorably, toward disclosure. We therefore hold that Wattanasin did not intentionally suppress or conceal the invention in this case.

Absent intentional suppression, the only question is whether the 17 month period between the reduction to practice of the compound, or the 15 month period between reduction to practice of the method, and Wattanasin's filing justify an inference of suppression or concealment. *See id.* The Board held that these facts do not support such an inference. As the Board explained: "In our view, this hiatus in time is not sufficiently long to raise the inference that Wattanasin suppressed or concealed the invention considering the nature and complexity of the invention here."

Fujikawa attacks this finding of the Board on two grounds. First, it contends that the Board should not have held that a 15 or 17 month delay is *per se* insufficient to raise an inference of suppression or concealment without examining the circumstances surrounding the delay and whether, in view of those circumstances, Wattanasin's delay was reasonable. Second, Fujikawa argues that the Board failed to consider evidence that Wattanasin was spurred to file by the issuance of a patent to a third party, Picard, directed to the same genus of compounds invented by Wattanasin. Evidence that a first inventor was spurred to disclose by the activities of a second inventor has always been an important factor in priority determinations because it creates an inference that, but for the efforts of the second inventor, "the public would never have gained knowledge of [the invention]." *Brokaw*, 429 F.2d at 480. Here, however, the Board expressly declined to consider the evidence of spurring because it held that spurring by a third party who is not a party to the interference is irrelevant to a determination of priority as between Wattanasin and Fujikawa. We first address Fujikawa's arguments concerning spurring.

A.

We are not certain that the Board is correct that third party spurring is irrelevant in determining priority. After all, "[w]hat is involved here is a policy question as to which of the two rival inventors has the greater right to a patent." *Brokaw*, 429 F.2d at 480. Resolution of this question could well be affected by the fact that one of the inventors chose to maintain his invention in secrecy until disclosure by another spurred him to file, even when the spurrer was a third party not involved in the interference. We need not resolve that question here, however, because we hold that no reasonable fact finder could have found spurring on the facts of this case. The only evidence in the record on the question of spurring is the testimony of Ms. Geisser who expressly testified that she had already begun work on the Wattanasin draft application before she learned of Picard's patent, in other words, that she had not been spurred by Picard. Consequently, we leave the question of the relevance of third-party spurring for another case.

B.

Fujikawa's other argument also requires us to examine the evidence of record in this case. As Fujikawa correctly notes, this court has not set strict time limits regarding the minimum and maximum periods necessary to establish an inference of suppression or concealment. Rather, we have recognized that "it is not the time elapsed that is the controlling factor but the total conduct of the first inventor." *Young v. Dworkin*, 489 F.2d 1277, 1285 (CCPA 1974) (Rich, J., concurring). Thus, the circumstances surrounding the first inventor's delay and the reasonableness of that delay are important factors which must be considered in deciding questions of suppression or concealment.

Fujikawa again correctly notes that the Board's opinion gives short shrift to the question of whether this delay on the facts of this case was reasonable. In seeking reversal of the Board's decision, Fujikawa asks us to assess the factual record for ourselves to determine whether Wattanasin engaged in sufficient disclosure-related activity to justify his 17-month delay in filing.

The facts of record, however, do not support Fujikawa's position.

In our view, the circumstances in this case place it squarely within the class of cases in which an inference of suppression or concealment is not warranted. We acknowledge, of course, that each case of suppression or concealment must be decided on its own facts. Still, the rich and varied case law which this court has developed over many years provides some guidance as to the type of behavior which warrants an inference of suppression or concealment. In this case Wattanasin delayed approximately 17 months between reduction to practice and filing. During much of that period, however, Wattanasin and Sandoz engaged in significant steps towards perfecting the invention and preparing an application. For example, we do not believe any lack of diligence can be ascribed to Wattanasin for the period between October and December 1987 when *in vivo* testing of the invention was taking place. *See Young.* Similarly, at its first opportunity following the *in vivo* testing, the Sandoz patent committee approved Wattanasin's invention for filing. This takes us up to the end of January 1988.

Over the next several months, until May 1988, the Sandoz patent department engaged in the necessary collection of data from the inventor and others in order to prepare Wattanasin's patent application. We are satisfied from the record that this disclosure-related activity was sufficient to avoid any inference of suppression or concealment during this period. Also, as noted above, the record indicates that by August 1988, Ms. Geisser was already at work preparing the application, and that work continued on various drafts until Wattanasin's filing date in March 1989. Thus, the only real period of unexplained delay in this case is the approximately three month period between May and August of 1988.

Given a total delay of 17 months, an unexplained delay of three months, the complexity of the subject matter at issue, and our sense from the record as a whole that throughout the delay Sandoz was moving, albeit slowly, towards filing an application, we conclude that this case does not warrant an inference of suppression or concealment. Consequently, we affirm the Board on this point.

C.

Finally, Fujikawa contends that assuming *in vitro* tests are sufficient to establish reduction to practice, Wattanasin reduced the compound count to practice in 1984 when he completed in vitro testing of his first three compounds falling within the scope of the count. If so, Fujikawa argues, the delay between reduction to practice and filing was greater than four years, and an inference of suppression or concealment is justified.[9]

---

9. This argument, of course, relates only to the compound count, since, as explained above, the method count was not reduced to practice until the *in vivo* testing in December 1987.

We reject this argument in view of *Paulik v. Rizkalla*. In *Paulik*, we held that a suppression or concealment could be negated by renewed activity prior to an opposing party's effective date. There, inventor Paulik reduced his invention to practice and submitted an invention disclosure to his employer's patent department. For four years the patent department did nothing with the disclosure. Then, just two months before Rizkalla's effective date, the patent department allegedly picked up Paulik's disclosure and worked diligently to prepare a patent application which it ultimately filed. *See id.* We held that although Paulik could not rely on his original date of reduction to practice to establish priority, he could rely on the date of renewed activity in his priority contest with Rizkalla. In large measure, this decision was driven by the court's concern that denying an inventor the benefit of his renewed activity, might "discourage inventors and their supporters from working on projects that had been 'too long' set aside, because of the impossibility of relying, in a priority contest, on either their original work or their renewed work." *Id.* at 1275-76.

Paulik's reasoning, if not its holding, applies squarely to this case. A simple hypothetical illustrates why this is so. Imagine a situation similar to the one facing Sandoz in early 1987. A decisionmaker with limited funds must decide whether additional research funds should be committed to a project which has been neglected for over two years. In making this decision, the decisionmaker would certainly take into account the likelihood that the additional research might yield valuable patent rights. Furthermore, in evaluating the probability of securing those patent rights, an important consideration would be the earliest priority date to which the research would be entitled, especially in situations where the decisionmaker knows that he and his competitors are "racing" toward a common goal. Thus, the right to rely on renewed activity for purposes of priority would encourage the decisionmaker to fund the additional research. Conversely, denying an inventor the benefit of renewed activity would discourage the decisionmaker from funding the additional research.

Here, Wattanasin returned to his abandoned project well before Fujikawa's effective date and worked diligently towards reducing the invention to practice a second time. For the reasons explained above, we hold that, on these facts, Wattanasin's earlier reduction to practice in 1984 does not bar him from relying on his earliest date of renewed activity for purposes of priority.

Comments

1. *Diligence.* Diligence is not always relevant when proving date of invention. It becomes important when a party is the first to conceive, but the second to reduce practice. (Recall, Griffith conceived first, but reduced to practice after Kanamaru, and therefore was required to prove diligence.) The diligence requirement wants to know what the party (e.g., Griffith)—who was first to conceive—was doing between his conception and reduction to practice.

   Diligence is measured from the time just prior to conception of the party who first reduced to practice (Party B) and ends at the reduction to practice date of the party who first conceived (Party A), i.e., the party attempting to prove diligence. Oftentimes, Party B cannot prove a conception date. In this situation, Party B's conception date is merged into its reduction to practice date, which can be either actual or constructive reduction to practice (the application filing date). And diligence is measured just prior to reduction to practice of Party B. The inventor does not need to show a continuous effort; he must provide an explanation for the entire period in question. There are a variety of ways to prove diligence, including ongoing laboratory experimentation. The question is whether the applicant was pursuing his goal in a reasonable manner.

2. *Abandonment.* As shown in *Mahurkar,* a party who is the first to reduce to practice is considered the first to invent. But an inventor who abandons his invention—even though he is the first to reduce to practice—may lose his right of priority. Abandonment is consistent with the foundational policy of early disclosure that is built into several other patent law doctrines. As the Federal Circuit has noted, while section 102(g) does not require an explicit disclosure, "the spirit and policy of the patent laws encourage an inventor to take steps to ensure that the public has gained knowledge of the invention which will insure its preservation in the public domain or else run the risk of being dominated by the patent of another." *Apotex USA, Inc. v. Merck & Co.,* 254 F.3d 1031, 1038 (Fed. Cir. 2001). An applicant can abandon either explicitly or the court could infer abandonment if the applicant was dilatory. Importantly, delay (unless extremely excessive) alone is typically not enough to infer abandonment.

In *Fox Group, Inc. v. Cree, Inc.,* 700 F.3d 1300 (Fed. Cir. 2012), Cree successfully argued that its prior invention—a low-defect silicon carbide crystal—was prior art under section 102(g). A sample of Cree's invention was sent to a university researcher and a Cree researcher published an article that included an X-ray topography of the crystal, but the article was not enabling (i.e., it did not demonstrate how the crystal was made). The patentee asserted that Cree's invention was abandoned because Cree never provided an enabling disclosure of its invention to the public. Under section 102(g), to serve as prior art, an invention must be disclosed to the public in some fashion. An inference of abandonment can be drawn from "[t]he failure to file a patent application, to describe the invention in a published document, or to use the invention publicly, within a reasonable time after first making the invention. . . ." *Dow Chem. Co. v. Astro-Valcour, Inc.,* 267 F.3d 1334, 1342 (Fed. Cir. 2001). Fox based its abandonment argument on Cree's failure (1) to file a patent application claiming the low-defect silicon carbide invention; (2) to commercialize the invention; and (3) "otherwise provide adequate disclosure." *Fox Group,* 700 F.3d at 1306. The court noted that "[f]iling a patent application and commercializing a product are only two convenient ways of proving an invention has been disclosed to the public." There are other means of disclosure, such as a printed publication. In response to Fox Group's non-enabling argument, the court stated that the precedent upon which Fox Group relies applies to process patents, not product patents. *Id.* at 1307 ("As Fox effectively admits, all of the cases it cites to support its assertion that §102(g) requires an enabling disclosure are process claims. [Fox's] patent [is] directed to a product, a silicon wafer comprising SiC material with specific low defect densities, but Fox argues that any distinction between product and process claims is irrelevant. We disagree.") For the court, Cree satisfied section 102(g)'s disclosure requirement because

"Cree promptly and publicly disclosed its findings concerning the low defect properties of the SiC material from which the [Kyoto Wafer] was cut through a presentation at the 1995 International Conference and a published paper on the subject." *Id.*

This reading of section 102(g) prompted a vigorous dissent that accused the majority of rendering the abandonment language of section 102(g) meaningless. Our precedent, wrote the dissent:

> makes clear that a prior inventor must show that the public was clearly given the benefit of an invention, via reverse-engineering, a detailed disclosure, or otherwise, if it wants to rely on §102(g) to invalidate a patent. Despite the majority's finding to the contrary, simply disclosing the existence of the product, without more, is insufficient to make an invention publicly known. There must be something more.

Neither Cree nor the majority point to any case law where §102(g) was used to invalidate a patent even though the prior inventor did not commercialize the product, make it available to the public so that reverse-engineering was possible, or provide some other detailed disclosure giving the public the benefit of the invention.

> The majority's approach cannot be the law. If a prior inventor could disclose the mere existence of a product and take no further action for nine years, the concept of abandonment, suppression, or concealment would be rendered meaningless. Consistent with our prior case law, where there is no enabling written disclosure, there must be evidence that the prior inventor timely made its invention available to the public in some other way— *e.g.,* through public use, commercialization, or filing a patent application claiming the invention. Such a requirement is consistent with §102(g)'s 's general goal of giving the public the benefit of the invention.

Id. at 1312-1313.

3. ***Foreign-Based Inventive Activity.*** In the *Fujikawa* case, note that Fujikawa's earliest invention date is the date he filed his application in the United States. This is because, as discussed in the Comments following *Mahurkar*, at the time the case was decided, U.S. patent law, namely section 104, did not allow for foreign inventive activity such as conception and reduction to practice to be used to prove an earlier date of invention; conception and reduction to practice had to occur in the United States for it to be used as proof of date of invention. This is also the most likely explanation as to why Kanamaru relied on his U.S. filing date, rather than earlier conception and actual reduction to practice—both of which likely occurred in Japan.

COMPARATIVE PERSPECTIVE
First-to-File vs. First-to-Invent

Until the enactment of the AIA, the United States was the only country in the world that subscribed to a first-to-invent system of priority. The pros and cons of the first-to-invent vis-à-vis a first-to-file system have been well mined. *See* Margo A. Bagley, *The Need for Speed (and Grace): Issues in a First-Inventor-to-File World*, 22 BERKELEY TECH. L.J. 1035, 1037-1047 (2008) (exploring the comparative costs and benefits of each priority system). Those who advocate a first-to-invent approach frequently assert that it provides a more equitable basis for giving rewards and fear a first-to-file system would unfairly burden the independent and small inventor class, those individuals who do not have the resources to file as promptly as larger entities. Moreover, first-to-invent advocates assert that a first-to-file system would encourage the filing of sloppy or incomplete patent applications. The first-to-file devotees point out that a first-to-file system is cleaner and does not subject the parties to the burdens and arcana associated with interferences. Moreover, a majority of the interferences (i.e., procedural mechanism for determining priority of invention) are won by the party who was the first-to-file, and therefore, the United States already has a *de facto* first-to-file system.

Some commentators have questioned the notion that a first-to-file system would harm small entities and independent inventors. *See* Gerald J. Mossinghoff, *The U.S. First-to-Invent System Has Provided No Advantage to Small Entities*, 84 J. PAT. & TRADEMARK OFF. SOC'Y 425 (2002) (arguing that many small entities benefit from a first-to-file system). *Cf.* James E. White, *The U.S. First-to-Invent System, the Mossinghoff Conclusion, and Statistics*, 85 J. PAT. & TRADEMARK OFF. SOC'Y 357 (2003) (questioning Mossinghoff's methodology). What is clear is that there are both advantages and disadvantages relating to a move from first-to-invent to first-to-file. For example, a study for priority disputes found that while a majority of parties who filed first also invented first, a considerable amount of these priority disputes — 43 percent — the party who invented first, but filed last, won. *See* Mark A. Lemley & Colleen V. Chien, *Are the U.S. Patent Priority Rules Really Necessary?*, 54 HASTINGS L.J. 1299, 1308-1309 (2003).

Nonobviousness

INTRODUCTION

An invention must be nonobvious to be patentable. The nonobvious inquiry—set forth in section 103—asks whether the claimed invention would have been obvious to a person of ordinary skill in the art. This inquiry has a temporal dimension. For applications filed before March 16, 2013, the timeframe for an obviousness analysis is *"at the time the invention was made."* For applications filed on or after March 16, 2013, the relevant timeframe is *"before the effective filing date of the claimed invention."* This change reflects the adoption of a first-inventor-to-file regime of the America Invents Act.

The novelty and nonobviousness requirements work together. The former seeks to assure the public domain remains undisturbed, while the latter demands that the claimed invention be sufficiently removed from the prior art, meaning in most cases the invention reflects a leap forward. Thus, while both sections 102 and 103 are designed to guard the public domain, section 103 is a more aggressive sentry.[1] Moreover, section 103 is a richer policy tool that allows for the combination of prior art references, and demands more complex rules. Therefore, as you work your way through this chapter, keep in mind that the nonobviousness requirement not only seeks to prevent the issuance of a patent that would withdraw "'what is already known'"[2] but also to "weed[] out those inventions which would not be disclosed or devised but for the inducement of a patent."[3]

The first significant judicial recognition that something more than novelty is required for patentability can be traced to *Hotchkiss v. Greenwood.*[4] The invention

---

1. For a discussion of the differences between the novelty and nonobviousness requirements, see Comment 1 following *United States v. Adams* in section B.

2. *KSR International Co. v. Teleflex, Inc.*, 550 U.S. 398, 416 (2007) (quoting *Great Atlantic & Pacific Tea Co. v. Supermarket Equip. Corp.*, 340 U.S. 147, 152 (1950)).

3. *Graham v. John Deere Co.*, 383 U.S. 1, 11 (1966). *See* ROBERT P. MERGES, JUSTIFYING INTELLECTUAL PROPERTY 155 (2011) (stating the nonobviousness requirement "conserves social resources" because "[a]n obvious invention will likely soon be made even without the award of a patent right").

4. 52 U.S. 248 (1851). The idea, however, of requiring something beyond novelty can be traced to the late eighteenth century. For instance, as Friedrich-Karl Beier reminds us, Thomas Jefferson unsuccessfully sought to insert language in the 1790 Patent Act that would have denied patents on inventions that were "so unimportant and obvious." Friedrich-Karl Beier, *The Inventive Step in Its Historical Development*, 17 INT'L REV. INDUS. PROP. & COPYRIGHT L. 301, 305 (1986). And John Duffy notes that the doctrine of nonobviousness can be traced to the 1793 Act, specifically the language in section 2: "that simply changing the form or the proportions of any machine, or composition of matter, in any degree, shall not be deemed a discovery." Act of Feb. 21, 1793, ch. 11, §2. *See* John F. Duffy, *Inventing Invention: A Case Study of Legal Innovation*, 86 TEX. L. REV. 1, 37 (2007). The

in *Hotchkiss* related to an old method of making doorknobs, but the only difference between the patented invention and the prior art was that the inventor substituted a clay or porcelain knob for a metallic knob. The invention was novel, but the Court nonetheless invalidated the patent because "there was an absence of that degree of skill and ingenuity, which constitute essential elements of every invention" beyond that which is "possessed by an ordinary mechanic."[5]

While an additional requirement, something above and beyond novelty, has been part of the patent law landscape since the mid-nineteenth century, its application had been inconsistent, in part because defining the requisite amount of "skill and ingenuity" is highly subjective and in part because its analytical framework did not adequately cabin judicial discretion. Over time, the unfettered decision-making that accompanied what became known as the "invention requirement" prompted concern—particularly during the 1940s—among members of the patent bar. According to one prominent patent lawyer, the "invention requirement . . . left every judge practically scot-free to decide this often controlling factor according to his personal philosophy of what inventions should be patented, whether or not he had any competence to do so or any knowledge of the patent system as an operative socioeconomic force."[6] This view gathered consensus and provided an impetus for the creation of section 103, which was designed to foster consistency and stability, as well as establish parameters for obviousness determinations. Section 103, therefore, was not a codification of the invention requirement; in fact, the "first policy decision underlying Section 103 was to cut loose altogether the century-old term 'invention.' "[7] Yet although the obviousness inquiry is more structured and particularized than it was prior to 1952, inconsistency remains simply because of the nature of what is being determined. No matter how many layers of fact-finding are established to cabin discretion, the ultimate inquiry remains whether the claimed invention is

---

1836 Act repealed this language, but "the concept continued to thrive" thereafter because of the common law's embrace of section 2's language in constructing a general doctrine, namely that, in addition to utility and novelty, a "change in principle" over the prior art was a requirement for patentability. *Hotchkiss* was the first significant opinion in this area and departed from the "change in principle" language, but, according to Duffy, is properly viewed as a continuation of the common law's interpretation of section 2 of the 1793 Act. *See Evans v. Eaton*, 20 U.S. 356 (1822).

5. *Hotchkiss*, 52 U.S. at 266.

6. Giles S. Rich, *The Vague Concept of "Invention" as Replaced by Section 103 of the Patent Act*, in NONOBVIOUSNESS: THE ULTIMATE CONDITION OF PATENTABILTY (J. Witherspoon ed., 1980), at 1:409.

7. *See* Giles S. Rich, *Laying the Ghost of the "Invention" Requirement*, in NONOBVIOUSNESS, *supra* note 6, at 1:508 ("The first policy decision underlying Section 103 was to cut loose altogether the century-old term 'invention.' So Section 103 speaks of a condition of *patentability* instead of 'invention.' The condition is unobviousness, but that is not all. The unobviousness is *as of a particular time* and *to a particular* legally fictitious, technical *person*, analogous to the 'ordinary reasonable man' so well known to courts as a legal concept. To protect the inventor from hindsight reasoning, the time is specified to be *the time when the invention was made*. To prevent the use of too high a standard—which would exclude inventors as a class and defeat the whole patent system—the invention must have been obvious at that time to 'a person having ordinary skill in the art to which said subject matter (*i.e.*, the invention) pertains.' But *that* is not all; *what* must have been obvious is '*the subject matter as a whole*.' That, of course, is the invention as defined by each patent claim."); P.J. Federico, *Commentary on the New Patent Act*, 75 J. PAT. TRADEMARK OFF. SOC'Y 160, 181 (1993) (stating section 103 "is added to the statute for uniformity and definiteness . . . and with the view that an explicit statement in the statute may have some stabilizing effect"). *See generally* George M. Siralla & Hon. Giles S. Rich, *35 U.S.C. 103: From Hotchkiss to Hand to Rich, the Obvious Patent Law Hall-of-Famers*, 32 J. MARSHALL L. REV. 437 (1999) (discussing the "invention requirement" and the creation of section 103).

obvious. As the Supreme Court noted in *Graham v. John Deere,*[8] while section 103 was an improvement over the invention requirement, "[w]hat is obvious is not a question upon which there is likely to be uniformity of thought in every given factual context."[9] Indeed, nonobviousness is frequently litigated, and is the most common basis for invalidating patent rights.[10]

Hotchkiss and *Graham* are the two great cases of the nineteenth and twentieth centuries, respectively, that stand for the proposition that something more than novelty is needed to obtain a patent and, in the case of *Graham,* what section 103's enactment in 1952 means for this heretofore common law requirement. And their influence remains, as evidenced by the first significant twenty-first century obviousness case, *KSR v. Teleflex,* the principal case following *Graham.*

STATUTE: **Conditions for patent ability; non-obvious subject matter**
35 U.S.C. § 103

A. THE HISTORICAL FOUNDATION OF SECTION 103 AND THE NONOBVIOUSNESS REQUIREMENT

The *Hotchkiss* case is widely regarded as creating an additional patentability hurdle, above and beyond novelty and utility. This common law development predated section 103 by 100 years, yet exerted significant influence on the drafters of the 1952 patent code and continues to play an important role in the common law development of the nonobviousness inquiry.

HOTCHKISS v. GREENWOOD
52 U.S. (11 How.) 248 (1851)

Justice NELSON delivered the opinion of the court.

The suit was brought against the defendants for the alleged infringement of a patent for a new and useful improvement in making door and other knobs of all kinds of clay used in pottery, and of porcelain.

The improvement consists in making the knobs of clay or porcelain, and in fitting them for their application to doors, locks, and furniture, and various other uses to which they may be adapted; but more especially in this, that of having the cavity in the knob in which the screw or shank is inserted, and by which it is fastened, largest at the bottom and in the form of dovetail, or wedge reversed, and a screw formed therein by pouring in metal in a fused state; and,

---

8. 383 U.S. 1 (1966).

9. *Id.* at 17.

10. *See* John R. Allison & Mark A. Lemley, *Empirical Evidence on the Validity of Litigated Patents,* 26 AM. INTELL. PROP. L.Q. 185 (1998) (finding that when asserted nonobviousness accounted for 42% of invalidity judgments at the appellate and trial levels, but also frequently failed as a defense 63.7% of the time); Gregory N. Mandel, *Patently Non-Obvious: Empirical Demonstration That the Hindsight Bias Renders Patent Decisions Irrational,* 67 OHIO ST. L.J. 1391, 1398 (2006) (stating "the non-obvious requirement is both the most commonly litigated patent validity issue") (citing Allison & Lemley).

after referring to drawings [see below] of the article thus made, the patentees conclude as follows:

> What we claim as our invention, and desire to secure by letters patent, is the manufacturing of knobs, as stated in the foregoing specifications, of potter's clay, or any kind of clay used in pottery, and shaped and finished by moulding, turning, burning, and glazing; and also of porcelain.

On the trial evidence was given on the part of the plaintiffs tending to prove the originality and usefulness of the invention, and also the infringement by the defendants; and on the part of the defendants, tending to show the want of originality; and that the mode of fastening the shank to the knob, as claimed by the plaintiffs, had been known and used before, and had been used and applied to the fastening of the shanks to metallic knobs.

And upon the evidence being closed, the counsel for the plaintiffs prayed the court to instruct the jury that, although the clay knob, in the form in which it was patented, may have been before known and used, and also the shank and spindle by which it is attached may have been before known and used, yet if such shank and spindle had never before been attached in this mode to a knob of potter's clay, and it required skill and invention to attach the same to a knob of this description, so that they would be firmly united, and make a strong and substantial article, and which, when thus made, would become an article much better and cheaper than the knobs made of metal or other materials, the patent was valid, and the plaintiffs would be entitled to recover.

The court refused to give the instruction, and charged the jury that, if knobs of the same form and for the same purposes as that claimed by the patentees, made of metal or other material, had been before known and used; and if the spindle and shank, in the form used by them, had been before known and used, and had been attached to the metallic knob by means of a cavity in the form of dovetail and infusion of melted metal, the same as the mode claimed by the

Hotchkiss, Davenport & Quincy,
Knob.
N° 2,197.   Patented July 29, 1841.

Witnesses: *Inventor:*
Samuel Longyear   *Davenport & Quincy*

patentees, in the attachment of the shank and spindle to their knob; and the knob of clay was simply the substitution of one material for another, the spindle and shank being the same as before in common use, and also the mode of connecting them by dovetail to the knob the same as before in common use, and no more ingenuity or skill required to construct the knob in this way than that possessed by an ordinary mechanic acquainted with the business, the patent was invalid, and the plaintiffs were not entitled to a verdict.

This instruction, it is claimed, is erroneous, and one for which a new trial should be granted.

The instruction assumes, and, as was admitted on the argument, properly assumes, that knobs of metal, wood, &c., connected with a shank and spindle, in the mode and by the means used by the patentees in their manufacture, had been before known, and were in public use at the date of the patent; and hence the only novelty which could be claimed on their part was the adaptation of this old contrivance to knobs of potter's clay or porcelain; in other words, the novelty consisted in the substitution of the clay knob in the place of one made of metal or wood, as the case might be. And in order to appreciate still more clearly the extent of the novelty claimed, it is proper to add, that this knob of potter's clay is not new, and therefore constitutes no part of the discovery. If it was, a very different question would arise; as it might very well be urged, and successfully urged, that a knob of a new composition of matter, to which this old contrivance had been applied, and which resulted in a new and useful article, was the proper subject of a patent.

The novelty would consist in the new composition made practically useful for the purposes of life, by the means and contrivances mentioned. It would be a new manufacture, and none the less so, within the meaning of the patent law, because the means employed to adapt the new composition to a useful purpose was old, or well known.

But in the case before us, the knob is not new, nor the metallic shank and spindle, nor the dovetail form of the cavity in the knob, nor the means by which the metallic shank is securely fastened therein. All these were well known, and in common use; and the only thing new is the substitution of a knob of a different material from that heretofore used in connection with this arrangement.

Now it may very well be, that, by connecting the clay or porcelain knob with the metallic shank in this well-known mode, an article is produced better and cheaper than in the case of the metallic or wood knob; but this does not result from any new mechanical device or contrivance, but from the fact, that the material of which the knob is composed happens to be better adapted to the purpose for which it is made. The improvement consists in the superiority of the material, and which is not new, over that previously employed in making the knob.

But this, of itself, can never be the subject of a patent. No one will pretend that a machine, made, in whole or in part, of materials better adapted to the purpose for which it is used than the materials of which the old one is constructed, and for that reason better and cheaper, can be distinguished from the old one; or, in the sense of the patent law, can entitle the manufacturer to a patent.

The difference is formal, and destitute of ingenuity or invention. It may afford evidence of judgment and skill in the selection and adaptation of the materials in the manufacture of the instrument for the purposes intended, but nothing more.

I remember having tried an action in the Circuit in the District of Connecticut some years since, brought upon a patent for an improvement in manufacturing buttons. The foundation of the button was wood, and the improvement consisted in covering the face with tin, and which was bent over the rim so as to be firmly secured to the wood. Holes were perforated in the centre, by which the button could be fastened to the garment. It was a cheap and useful article for common wear, and in a good deal of demand.

On the trial, the defendant produced a button, which had been taken off a coat on which it had been worn before the Revolution, made precisely in the same way, except the foundation was bone. The case was given up on the part of the plaintiff. Now the new article was better and cheaper than the old one; but I did not then suppose, nor do I now, that this could make any difference, unless it was the result of some new contrivance or arrangement in the manufacture. Certainly it could not, for the reason that the materials with which it was made were of a superior quality, or better adapted to the uses to which the article is applied.

It seemed to be supposed, on the argument, that this mode of fastening the shank to the clay knob produced a new and peculiar effect upon the article, beyond that produced when applied to the metallic knob, inasmuch as the fused metal by which the shank was fastened to the knob prevented the shank from acting immediately upon the knob, it being enclosed and firmly held by the metal; that for this reason the clay or porcelain knob was not so liable to crack or be broken, but was made firm and strong, and more durable.

This is doubtless true. But the peculiar effect thus referred to is not distinguishable from that which would exist in the case of the wood knob, or one of bone or ivory, or of other materials that might be mentioned.

Now if the foregoing view of the improvement claimed in this patent be correct, it is quite apparent that there was no error in the submission of the questions presented at the trial to the jury; for unless more ingenuity and skill in applying the old method of fastening the shank and the knob were required in the application of it to the clay or porcelain knob than were possessed by an ordinary mechanic acquainted with the business, there was an absence of that degree of skill and ingenuity which constitute essential elements of every invention. In other words, the improvement is the work of the skilful mechanic, not that of the inventor.

We think, therefore, that the judgment is, and must be, affirmed.

Comments

1. **Hotchkiss *and the "Invention" Requirement.*** The *Hotchkiss* decision is viewed today as a foundational case in obviousness jurisprudence. Yet until the patent act of 1952 and the *Graham* decision in 1966, *Hotchkiss*'s esteemed status in patent law history was uncertain. This is largely because of the divergent interpretations engendered by the opinion. One school of interpretation led to the so-called invention requirement; in short, to be patentable, there had to be an "invention." This view has been characterized as a vague and malleable standard that judges could manipulate to mean whatever they wanted it to mean. Indeed, it had been called the "plaything of the judiciary." *See* Giles S. Rich, *Why and How Section 103 Came to Be*, in NONOBVIOUSNESS: THE ULTIMATE CONDITION OF PATENTABILITY 1:208 (John Witherspoon ed.,

1980). From 1940 to 1950, some members of the Supreme Court, relying on *Hotchkiss*, embraced the invention requirement to further what many in the patent community viewed as an anti-patent attitude. *See, e.g., Cuno Engineering Corp. v. Automatic Devices Corp.*, 314 U.S. 84 (1941) (holding to be patentable, an invention had to be the result of a "flash of genius"); *Great Atlantic & Pacific Tea Co. v. Supermarket Equipment Corp.*, 340 U.S. 147 (1950) (creating "synergism requirement").

2. **Hotchkiss *and the "Ordinary Mechanic."*** After *Great Atlantic*—viewed by some as reflecting the Court's anti-patent attitude—a group of prominent patent professionals seized upon the "ordinary mechanic" language of *Hotchkiss* and sought to foster an alternative interpretative of *Hotchkiss*. The goal was to draft a "statutory substitute that would make more sense, would apply to all kinds of inventions, would restrict the court in their arbitrary, a priori judgments on patentability, and that, above all, would serve as a uniform *standard of patentability*." Giles S. Rich, *Laying the Ghost of the "Invention" Requirement*, in NONOBVIOUSNESS, *supra*, at 1:508 (emphasis in original). Thus, section 103 was born. Section 103, in many ways, formed the heart of the 1952 Act, and was a direct response to the "invention" requirement. The "ordinary mechanic" of *Hotchkiss* is the precursor to the "person having ordinary skill in the art" that today pervades patent law jurisprudence. By doing away with the "invention" test and requiring obviousness to be determined through the eyes of the skilled artisan, section 103 sought to encourage greater stability and consistency. *See* P.J. Federico, *Commentary on the New Patent Act*, 75 J. PAT. TRADEMARK OFF. SOC'Y 160, 181 (1993) (stating section 103 "is added to the statute for uniformity and definiteness . . . and with the view that an explicit statement in the statute may have some stabilizing effect").

But section 103 received an inconsistent judicial reception. Some circuit courts viewed section 103 as a codification of the "requirement for invention," even though it was clear the text of the statute omitted the word "invention." Other circuits recognized that section 103 was drafted to "restore the law to what it had been 20 or 30 years earlier and . . . to change the slow but steady drift of judicial decisions that had been hostile to patents." Giles S. Rich, *The Vague Concept of "Invention" as Replaced by Section 103 of the 1952 Patent Act*, in NONOBVIOUSNESS, *supra*, at 1:412.

In the light of this circuit conflict, the Supreme Court—14 years after the 1952 Patent Act—decided to weigh in, which is the subject of section B.

B. THE *GRAHAM* TEST

In 1965, the United States Supreme Court granted certiorari in *Graham v. John Deere* (as well as two companion cases) to consider (1) "what effect the 1952 act had upon traditional statutory and judicial tests of patentability," and (2) "what definitive tests are now required." The *Graham* framework has been at the core of nonobviousness determinations to the present day. Importantly, *Graham* notes—in section II of the opinion—that the obviousness requirement flows directly from the IP clause of the Constitution, thus implying that section 103 embodies a constitutional requirement.

GRAHAM v. JOHN DEERE CO.
383 U.S. 1 (1966)

Justice CLARK delivered the opinion of the Court.

After a lapse of 15 years, the Court again focuses its attention on the patentability of inventions under the standard of Art. I, §8, cl. 8, of the Constitution and under the conditions prescribed by the laws of the United States. Since our last expression on patent validity, *Great A. & P. Tea Co. v. Supermarket Equip. Corp.*, the Congress has for the first time expressly added a third statutory dimension to the two requirements of novelty and utility that had been the sole statutory test since the Patent Act of 1793. This is the test of obviousness, *i.e.*, whether "the subject matter sought to be patented and the prior art are such that the subject matter as a whole would have been obvious at the time the invention was made to a person having ordinary skill in the art to which said subject matter pertains. Patentability shall not be negatived by the manner in which the invention was made." §103 of the Patent Act of 1952.

The questions, involved in each of the companion cases before us, are what effect the 1952 Act had upon traditional statutory and judicial tests of patentability and what definitive tests are now required. We have concluded that the 1952 Act was intended to codify judicial precedents embracing the principle long ago announced by this Court in *Hotchkiss v. Greenwood*, and that, while the clear language of §103 places emphasis on an inquiry into obviousness, the general level of innovation necessary to sustain patentability remains the same.

* * *

II.

At the outset it must be remembered that the federal patent power stems from a specific constitutional provision which authorizes the Congress "To promote the Progress of . . . useful Arts, by securing for limited Times to . . . Inventors the exclusive Right to their . . . Discoveries." Art. I, §8, cl. 8. The clause is both a grant of power and a limitation. This qualified authority, unlike the power often exercised in the sixteenth and seventeenth centuries by the English Crown, is limited to the promotion of advances in the "useful arts." It was written against the backdrop of the practices—eventually curtailed by the Statute of Monopolies—of the Crown in granting monopolies to court favorites in goods or businesses which had long before been enjoyed by the public. The Congress in the exercise of the patent power may not overreach the restraints imposed by the stated constitutional purpose. Nor may it enlarge the patent monopoly without regard to the innovation, advancement or social benefit gained thereby. Moreover, Congress may not authorize the issuance of patents whose effects are to remove existent knowledge from the public domain, or to restrict free access to materials already available. Innovation, advancement, and things which add to the sum of useful knowledge are inherent requisites in a patent system which by constitutional command must "promote the Progress of . . . useful Arts." This is the standard expressed in the Constitution and it may not be ignored. And it is in this light that patent validity "requires reference to a standard written into the Constitution." *Great A. & P. Tea Co. v. Supermarket Equipment Corp.*, 340 U.S. at 154 (concurring opinion).

Within the limits of the constitutional grant, the Congress may, of course, implement the stated purpose of the Framers by selecting the policy which in its judgment best effectuates the constitutional aim. This is but a corollary to the grant to Congress of any Article I power. Within the scope established by the Constitution, Congress may set out conditions and tests for patentability. It is the duty of the Commissioner of Patents and of the courts in the administration of the patent system to give effect to the constitutional standard by appropriate application, in each case, of the statutory scheme of the Congress.

* * *

III.

The difficulty of formulating conditions for patentability was heightened by the generality of the constitutional grant and the statutes implementing it, together with the underlying policy of the patent system that "the things which are worth to the public the embarrassment of an exclusive patent," as Jefferson put it, must outweigh the restrictive effect of the limited patent monopoly. The inherent problem was to develop some means of weeding out those inventions which would not be disclosed or devised but for the inducement of a patent.

This Court formulated a general condition of patentability in 1851 in *Hotchkiss v. Greenwood. . . . Hotchkiss,* by positing the condition that a patentable invention evidence more ingenuity and skill than that possessed by an ordinary mechanic acquainted with the business, merely distinguished between new and useful innovations that were capable of sustaining a patent and those that were not. The *Hotchkiss* test laid the cornerstone of the judicial evolution suggested by Jefferson and left to the courts by Congress. The language in the case, and in those which followed, gave birth to "invention" as a word of legal art signifying patentable inventions. Yet, as this Court has observed, "[t]he truth is, the word ['invention'] cannot be defined in such manner as to afford any substantial aid in determining whether a particular device involves an exercise of the inventive faculty or not." *McClain v. Ortmayer,* 141 U.S. 419, 427 (1891). Its use as a label brought about a large variety of opinions as to its meaning both in the Patent Office, in the courts, and at the bar. The *Hotchkiss* formulation, however, lies not in any label, but in its functional approach to questions of patentability. In practice, *Hotchkiss* has required a comparison between the subject matter of the patent, or patent application, and the background skill of the calling. It has been from this comparison that patentability was in each case determined.

IV.

The 1952 Patent Act

The pivotal section around which the present controversy centers is §103. It provides:

§103. *Conditions for patentability; non-obvious subject matter*

A patent may not be obtained though the invention is not identically disclosed or described as set forth in section 102 of this title, if the differences between the subject matter sought to be patented and the prior art are such that the subject matter as a whole would have been obvious at the time the invention was made to a person having ordinary skill in the art to which said subject matter pertains. Patentability shall not be negatived by the manner in which the invention was made.

The section is cast in relatively unambiguous terms. Patentability is to depend, in addition to novelty and utility, upon the "non-obvious" nature of the "subject matter sought to be patented" to a person having ordinary skill in the pertinent art.

The first sentence of this section is strongly reminiscent of the language in *Hotchkiss*. Both formulations place emphasis on the pertinent art existing at the time the invention was made and both are implicitly tied to advances in that art. The major distinction is that Congress has emphasized "nonobviousness" as the operative test of the section, rather than the less definite "invention" language of *Hotchkiss* that Congress thought had led to "a large variety" of expressions in decisions and writings. In the title itself the Congress used the phrase "Conditions for patentability; *non-obvious subject matter*" (italics added), thus focusing upon "nonobviousness" rather than "invention."

* * *

It is undisputed that this section was, for the first time, a statutory expression of an additional requirement for patentability, originally expressed in *Hotchkiss*. It also seems apparent that Congress intended by the last sentence of §103 to abolish the test it believed this Court announced in the controversial phrase "flash of creative genius," used in *Cuno Engineering Corp. v. Automatic Devices Corp.*

V.

While the ultimate question of patent validity is one of law, *A. & P. Tea Co. v. Supermarket Equipment Corp.*, the §103 condition, which is but one of three conditions, each of which must be satisfied, lends itself to several basic factual inquiries. Under §103, the scope and content of the prior art are to be determined; differences between the prior art and the claims at issue are to be ascertained; and the level of ordinary skill in the pertinent art resolved. Against this background, the obviousness or nonobviousness of the subject matter is determined. Such secondary considerations as commercial success, long felt but unsolved needs, failure of others, etc., might be utilized to give light to the circumstances surrounding the origin of the subject matter sought to be patented. As indicia of obviousness or nonobviousness, these inquiries may have relevancy.

This is not to say, however, that there will not be difficulties in applying the nonobviousness test. What is obvious is not a question upon which there is likely to be uniformity of thought in every given factual context. The difficulties, however, are comparable to those encountered daily by the courts in such frames of reference as negligence and scienter, and should be amenable to a case-by-case development. We believe that strict observance of the requirements laid down here will result in that uniformity and definiteness which Congress called for in the 1952 Act.

Although we conclude here that the inquiry which the Patent Office and the courts must make as to patentability must be beamed with greater intensity on the requirements of §103, it bears repeating that we find no change in the general strictness with which the overall test is to be applied. We have been urged to find in §103 a relaxed standard, supposedly a congressional reaction to the "increased standard" applied by this Court in its decisions over the last 20 or 30 years. The standard has remained invariable in this Court. Technology, however, has advanced, and with remarkable rapidity in the last 50 years. Moreover, the ambit of applicable art in given fields of science has widened by disciplines unheard of a half century ago. It is but an evenhanded application to require that those persons granted the benefit of a patent monopoly be charged with an awareness of these changed conditions. The same is true of the less technical, but still useful arts. He who seeks to build a better mousetrap today has a long path to tread before reaching the Patent Office.

VI.

* * *

Graham v. John Deere Co., an infringement suit by petitioners, presents a conflict between two Circuits over the validity of a single patent on a "Clamp for vibrating Shank Plows." The invention, a combination of old mechanical elements, involves a device designed to absorb shock from plow shanks as they plow through rocky soil and thus to prevent damage to the plow. . . .

This patent, No. 2,627,798 (hereinafter called the '798 patent) relates to a spring clamp which permits plow shanks to be pushed upward when they hit obstructions in the soil, and then springs the shanks back into normal position when the obstruction is passed over. The device, which we show diagrammatically in the accompanying sketches (see Fig. 1), is fixed to the plow frame as a unit. The mechanism around which the controversy center is basically a hinge. The top half of it, known as the upper plate (marked 1 in the sketches), is a

FIGURE 1

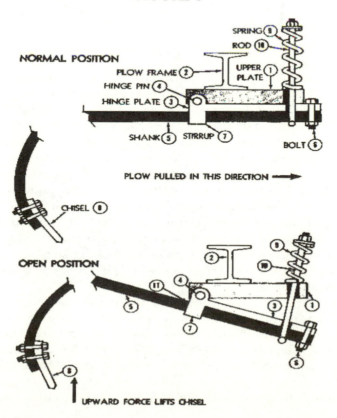

FIGURE 2

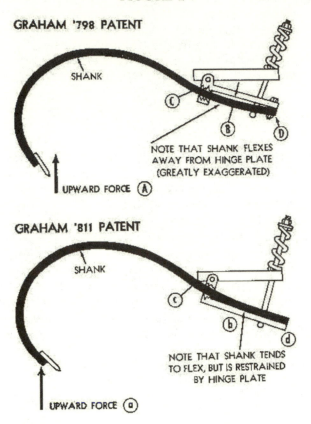

heavy metal piece clamped to the plow frame (2) and is stationary relative to the plow frame. The lower half of the hinge, known as the hinge plate (3), is connected to the rear of the upper plate by a hinge pin (4) and rotates downward with respect to it. The shank (5), which is bolted to the forward end of the hinge plate (at 6), runs beneath the plate and parallel to it for about nine inches, passes through a stirrup (7), and then continues backward for several feet curving down toward the ground. The chisel (8), which does the actual plowing, is attached to the rear end of the shank. As the plow frame is pulled forward, the chisel rips through the soil, thereby plowing it. In the normal position, the hinge plate and the shank are kept tight against the upper plate by a spring (9), which is atop the upper plate. A rod (10) runs through the center of the spring, extending down through holes in both plates and the shank. Its upper end is bolted to the top of the spring while its lower end is hooked against the underside of the shank.

When the chisel hits a rock or other obstruction in the soil, the obstruction forces the chisel and the rear portion of the shank to move upward. The shank is pivoted (at 11) against the rear of the hinge plate and pries open the hinge against the closing tendency of the spring. (See sketch labeled "Open Position," Fig. 1.) This closing tendency is caused by the fact that, as the hinge is opened, the connecting rod is pulled downward and the spring is compressed. When the obstruction is passed over, the upward force on the chisel disappears and the spring pulls the shank and hinge plate back into their original position. The lower, rear portion of the hinge plate is constructed in the form of a stirrup (7) which brackets the shank, passing around and beneath it. The shank fits loosely into the stirrup (permitting a slight up and down play). The stirrup is designed to prevent the shank from recoiling away from the hinge plate, and thus prevents excessive strain on the shank near its bolted connection. The stirrup also girds the shank, preventing it from fishtailing from side to side.

In practical use, a number of spring-hinge-shank combinations are clamped to a plow frame, forming a set of ground-working chisels capable of withstanding the shock of rocks and other obstructions in the soil without breaking the shanks. . . .

We confine our discussion to the prior patent of Graham, '811, and to the Glencoe clamp device, both among the references asserted by respondents. The Graham '811 and '798 patent devices are similar in all elements, save two: (1) the stirrup and the bolted connection of the shank to the hinge plate do not appear in '811; and (2) the position of the shank is reversed, being placed in patent '811 above the hinge plate, sandwiched between it and the upper plate. The shank is held in place by the spring rod which is hooked against the bottom of the hinge plate passing through a slot in the shank. Other differences are of no consequence to our examination. In practice the '811 patent arrangement permitted the shank to wobble or fishtail because it was not rigidly fixed to the hinge plate; moreover, as the hinge plate was below the shank, the latter caused wear on the upper plate, a member difficult to repair or replace. . . .

The contention is that this arrangement—which petitioners claim is not disclosed in the prior art—permits the shank to flex under stress for its entire length. As we have sketched (see sketch, "Graham '798 Patent" in Fig. 2), when the chisel hits an obstruction the resultant force (A) pushes the rear of the shank upward and the shank pivots against the rear of the hinge plate at (C). The natural tendency is for that portion of the shank between the pivot point and the bolted connection (i.e., between C and D) to bow downward and away from the hinge plate. The maximum distance (B) that the shank moves away from the plate is slight—for emphasis, greatly exaggerated in the sketches. This is so because of the strength of the shank and the short—nine inches or so—length of that portion of the shank between (C) and (D). On the contrary, in patent '811 (see sketch, "Graham '811 Patent" in Fig. 2), the pivot point is the upper plate at point (c); and while the tendency for the shank to bow between points (c) and (d) is the same as in '798, the shank is restricted because of the underlying hinge plate and cannot flex as freely. In practical effect, the shank flexes only between points (a) and (c), and not along the entire length of the shank, as in '798. Petitioners say that this difference in flex, though small, effectively absorbs the tremendous forces of the shock of obstructions whereas prior art arrangements failed. . . .

If free-flexing, as petitioners now argue, is the crucial difference above the prior art, then it appears evident that the desired result would be obtainable by not boxing the shank within the confines of the hinge. The only other effective place available in the arrangement was to attach it below the hinge plate and run it through a stirrup or bracket that would not disturb its flexing qualities. Certainly a person having ordinary skill in the prior art, given the fact that the flex in the shank could be utilized more effectively if allowed to run the entire length of the shank, would immediately see that the thing to do was what Graham did, i.e., invert the shank and the hinge plate.

UNITED STATES v. ADAMS

383 U.S. 39 (1966)

Justice CLARK delivered the opinion of the Court.

The United States seeks review of a judgment of the Court of Claims, holding valid and infringed a patent on a wet battery issued to Adams. This suit under 28 U.S.C. § 1498 (1964 ed.) was brought by Adams and others holding an interest in the patent against the Government charging both infringement and breach of an implied contract to pay compensation for the use of the invention. The Government challenged the validity of the patent, denied that it had been infringed or that any contract for its use had ever existed. The Trial Commissioner held that the patent was valid and infringed in part but that no contract, express or implied, had been established. The Court of Claims adopted these findings, initially reaching only the patent questions, but subsequently, on respondents' motion to amend the judgment, deciding the contract claims as well. The United States sought *certiorari* on the patent validity issue only. We granted the writ, along with the others, in order to settle the important issues of patentability. We affirm.

* * *

II.

The Patent in Issue and Its Background

The patent under consideration, U.S. No. 2,322,210, was issued in 1943 upon an application filed in December 1941 by Adams. It relates to a nonrechargeable, as opposed to a storage, electrical battery. Stated simply, the battery comprises two electrodes — one made of magnesium, the other of cuprous chloride — which are placed in a container. The electrolyte, or battery fluid, used may be either plain or salt water.

The specifications of the patent state that the object of the invention is to provide constant voltage and current without the use of acids, conventionally employed in storage batteries, and without the generation of dangerous fumes. Another object is "to provide a battery which is relatively light in weight with respect to capacity" and which "may be manufactured and distributed to the trade in a dry condition and rendered serviceable by merely filling the container with water." Following the specifications, which also set out a specific embodiment of the invention, there appear 11 claims. Of these, principal reliance has been placed upon Claims 1 and 10, which read:

1. A battery comprising a liquid container, a magnesium electropositive electrode inside the container and having an exterior terminal, a fused cuprous chloride electronegative electrode, and a terminal connected with said electronegative electrode.

10. In a battery, the combination of a magnesium electropositive electrode, and an electronegative electrode comprising cuprous chloride fused with a carbon catalytic agent.

For several years prior to filing his application for the patent, Adams had worked in his home experimenting on the development of a wet battery. He found that when cuprous chloride and magnesium were used as electrodes in an electrolyte of either plain water or salt water an improved battery resulted.

The Adams invention was the first practical, water-activated, constant potential battery which could be fabricated and stored indefinitely without any fluid in its cells. It was activated within 30 minutes merely by adding water. Once activated, the battery continued to deliver electricity at a voltage which remained essentially constant regardless of the rate at which current was withdrawn. Furthermore, its capacity for generating current was exceptionally large in comparison to its size and weight. The battery was also quite efficient in that substantially its full capacity could be obtained over a wide range of currents. One disadvantage, however, was that once activated the battery could not be shut off; the chemical reactions in the battery continued even though current was not withdrawn. Nevertheless, these chemical reactions were highly exothermic, liberating large quantities of heat during operation. As a result, the battery performed with little effect on its voltage or current in very low temperatures. Relatively high temperatures would not damage the battery. Consequently, the battery was operable from 65° below zero Fahrenheit to 200° Fahrenheit.

Less than a month after filing for his patent, Adams brought his discovery to the attention of the Army and Navy. Arrangements were quickly made for demonstrations before the experts of the United States Army Signal Corps. The Signal Corps scientists who observed the demonstrations and who conducted further tests themselves did not believe the battery was workable. Almost a year later, in December 1942, Dr. George Vinal, an eminent government expert with the National Bureau of Standards, still expressed doubts. He felt that Adams was making "unusually large claims" for "high watt hour output per unit weight," and he found "far from convincing" the graphical data submitted by the inventor showing the battery's constant voltage and capacity characteristics. He recommended, "Until the inventor can present more convincing data about the performance of his [battery] cell, I see no reason to consider it further."

However, in November 1943, at the height of World War II, the Signal Corps concluded that the battery was feasible. The Government thereafter entered into contracts with various battery companies for its procurement. The battery was found adaptable to many uses. Indeed, by 1956 it was noted that "[t]here can be no doubt that the addition of water activated batteries to the family of power sources has brought about developments which would otherwise have been technically or economically impractical."

Surprisingly, the Government did not notify Adams of its changed views nor of the use to which it was putting his device, despite his repeated requests. In 1955, upon examination of a battery produced for the Government by the Burgess Company, he first learned of the Government's action. His request for compensation was denied in 1960, resulting in this suit.

III.

The Prior Art

The basic idea of chemical generation of electricity is, of course, quite old. Batteries trace back to the epic discovery by the Italian scientist Volta in 1795, who found that when two dissimilar metals are placed in an electrically conductive fluid an electromotive force is set up and electricity generated. Essentially, the basic elements of a chemical battery are a pair of electrodes of different electrochemical properties and an electrolyte which is either a liquid (in "wet" batteries) or a moist paste of various substances (in the so-called "dry-cell" batteries). Various materials which may be employed as electrodes, various electrolyte possibilities and many combinations of these elements have been the object of considerable experiment for almost 175 years.

At trial, the Government introduced in evidence 24 patents and treatises as representing the art as it stood in 1938, the time of the Adams invention. Here, however, the Government has relied primarily upon only six of these references which we may summarize as follows.

The Niaudet treatise describes the Marie Davy cell invented in 1860 and De La Rue's variations on it. The battery comprises a zinc anode and a silver chloride cathode. Although it seems to have been capable of working in an electrolyte of pure water, Niaudet says the battery was of "little interest" until De La Rue used a solution of ammonium chloride as an electrolyte. Niaudet also states that "[t]he capital advantage of this battery, as in all where zinc with sal ammoniac [ammonium chloride solution] is used, consists in the absence of any local or internal action as long as the electric circuit is open; in other words, this battery does not work upon itself."

The Wood patent is relied upon by the Government as teaching the substitution of magnesium, as in the Adams patent, for zinc. Wood's patent, issued in 1928, states: "It would seem that a relatively high voltage primary cell would be obtained by using . . . magnesium as the . . . [positive] electrode and I am aware that attempts have been made to develop such a cell. As far as I am aware, however, these have all been unsuccessful, and it has been generally accepted that magnesium could not be commercially utilized as a primary cell electrode." Wood recognized that the difficulty with magnesium electrodes is their susceptibility to chemical corrosion by the action of acid or ammonium chloride electrolytes. Wood's solution to this problem was to use a "neutral electrolyte containing a strong soluble oxidizing agent adapted to reduce the rate of corrosion of the magnesium electrode on open circuit." There is no indication of its use with cuprous chloride, nor was there any indication that a magnesium battery could be water-activated.

The Codd treatise is also cited as authority for the substitution of magnesium. However, Codd simply lists magnesium in an electromotive series table, a tabulation of electrochemical substances in descending order of their relative electropositivity. He also refers to magnesium in an example designed to show that various substances are more electropositive than others, but the discussion involves a cell containing an acid which would destroy magnesium within minutes. In short, Codd indicates, by inference, only that magnesium is a theoretically desirable electrode by virtue of its highly electropositive character. He does not teach that magnesium could be combined in a water-activated battery or that a battery using magnesium would have the properties of the Adams device. Nor does he suggest, as the Government indicates, that cuprous chloride could be substituted for silver chloride. He merely refers to the cuprous ion—a generic term which includes an infinite number of copper compounds—and in no way suggests that cuprous chloride could be employed in a battery.

The Government then cites the Wensky patent which was issued in Great Britain in 1891. The patent relates to the use of cuprous chloride as a depolarizing agent. The specifications of his patent disclose a battery comprising zinc and copper electrodes, the cuprous chloride being added as a salt in an electrolyte solution containing zinc chloride as well. While Wensky recognized that cuprous chloride could be used in a constant-current cell, there is no indication that he taught a water-activated system or that magnesium could be incorporated in his battery.

Finally, the Skrivanoff patent depended upon by the Government relates to a battery designed to give intermittent, as opposed to continuous, service. While the patent claims magnesium as an electrode, it specifies that the electrolyte to be used in conjunction with it must be a solution of "alcoline, chloro-chromate, or a permanganate strengthened with sulphuric acid." The cathode was a copper or carbon electrode faced with a paste of "phosphoric acid, amorphous phosphorous, metallic copper in spangles, and cuprous chloride." This paste is to be mixed with hot sulfuric acid before applying to the electrode. The Government's expert testified in trial that he had no information as to whether the cathode, as placed in the battery, would, after having been mixed with the other chemicals prescribed, actually contain cuprous chloride. Furthermore, respondents' expert testified, without contradiction, that he had attempted to assemble a battery made in accordance with Skrivanoff's teachings, but was met first with a fire when he sought to make the cathode, and then with an explosion when he attempted to assemble the complete battery.

IV.

The Validity of the Patent

The Government challenges the validity of the Adams patent on grounds of lack of novelty under 35 U.S.C. § 102(a) as well as obviousness under 35 U.S.C. § 103. As we have seen in *Graham v. John Deere Co.*, novelty and nonobviousness—as well as utility—are separate tests of patentability and all must be satisfied in a valid patent.

The Government concludes that wet batteries comprising a zinc anode and silver chloride cathode are old in the art; and that the prior art shows that magnesium may be substituted for zinc and cuprous chloride for silver chloride. Hence, it argues that the "combination of magnesium and cuprous chloride in the Adams battery was not patentable because it represented either no change or an insignificant change as compared to prior battery designs." And, despite "the fact that, wholly unexpectedly, the battery showed certain valuable operating advantages over other batteries [these advantages] would certainly not justify a patent on the essentially old formula."

There are several basic errors in the Government's position. First, the fact that the Adams battery is water-activated sets his device apart from the prior art. It is true that Claims 1 and 10, do not mention a water electrolyte, but, as we have noted, a stated object of the invention was to provide a battery rendered serviceable by the mere addition of water. While the claims of a patent limit the invention, and specifications cannot be utilized to expand the patent monopoly, it is fundamental that claims are to be construed in the light of the specifications and both are to be read with a view to ascertaining the invention. Taken together with the stated object of disclosing a water-activated cell, the lack of reference to any electrolyte in Claims 1 and 10 indicates that water alone could be used. Furthermore, of the 11 claims in issue, three of the narrower ones include references to specific electrolyte solutions comprising water and certain salts. The obvious implication from the absence of any mention of an electrolyte— a necessary element in any battery—in the other eight claims reinforces this conclusion. It is evident that respondents' present reliance upon this feature was not the afterthought of an astute patent trial lawyer. In his first contact with the Government less than a month after the patent application was filed, Adams pointed out that "no acids, alkalines or any other liquid other than plain water is used in this cell. Water does not have to be distilled. . . ." The findings, approved and adopted by the Court of Claims, also fully support this conclusion.

Nor is *Sinclair & Carroll Co. v. Interchemical Corp.*, 325 U.S. 327 (1945), apposite here. There the patentee had developed a rapidly drying printing ink. All that was needed to produce such an ink was a solvent which evaporated quickly upon heating. Knowing that the boiling point of a solvent is an indication of its rate of evaporation, the patentee merely made selections from a list of solvents and their boiling points. This was no more than "selecting the last piece to put into the last opening in a jig-saw puzzle." 325 U.S., at 335. Indeed, the Government's reliance upon *Sinclair & Carroll* points up the fallacy of the underlying premise of its case. The solvent in *Sinclair & Carroll* had no functional relation to the printing ink involved. It served only as an inert carrier. The choice of solvent was dictated by known, required properties. Here, however, the Adams battery is shown to embrace elements having an interdependent functional relationship. It begs the question, and overlooks the holding of the Commissioner and the Court of Claims, to state merely that magnesium and cuprous chloride were individually known battery components. If such a combination is novel, the issue is whether bringing them together as taught by Adams was obvious in the light of the prior art.

We believe that the Court of Claims was correct in concluding that the Adams battery is novel. Skrivanoff disclosed the use of magnesium in an electrolyte completely different from that used in Adams. As we have mentioned, it is even open to doubt whether cuprous chloride was a functional element in Skrivanoff. In view of the unchallenged testimony that the Skrivanoff formulation was both dangerous and inoperable, it seems anomalous to suggest that it is an anticipation of Adams. An inoperable invention or one which fails to achieve its intended result does not negative novelty. That in 1880 Skrivanoff may have been able to convince a foreign patent examiner to issue a patent on his device has little significance in the light of the foregoing.

Nor is the Government's contention that the electrodes of Adams were mere substitutions of pre-existing battery designs supported by the prior art. If the use of magnesium for zinc and cuprous chloride for silver chloride were merely equivalent substitutions, it would follow that the resulting device—Adams'—would have equivalent operating characteristics. But it does not. The court below found, and the Government apparently admits, that the Adams battery "wholly unexpectedly" has shown "certain valuable operating advantages over other batteries" while those from which it is claimed to have been copied were long ago discarded. Moreover, most of the batteries relied upon by the Government were of a completely different type designed to give intermittent power and characterized by an absence of internal action when not in use. Some provided current at voltages which declined fairly proportionately with time. Others were so-called standard cells which, though producing a constant voltage, were of use principally for calibration or measurement purposes. Such cells cannot be used as sources of power. For these reasons we find no equivalency.

We conclude the Adams battery was also nonobvious. As we have seen, the operating characteristics of the Adams battery have been shown to have been unexpected and to have far surpassed then-existing wet batteries. Despite the fact that each of the elements of the Adams battery was well known in the prior art, to combine them as did Adams required that a person reasonably skilled in the prior art must ignore that (1) batteries which continued to operate on an open circuit and which heated in normal use were not practical; and (2) water-activated batteries were successful only when combined with electrolytes detrimental to the use of magnesium. These long-accepted factors, when taken together, would, we believe, deter any investigation into such a combination as is used by Adams. This is not to say that one who merely finds new uses for old inventions by shutting his eyes to their prior disadvantages thereby discovers a patentable innovation. We do say, however, that known disadvantages in old devices which would naturally discourage the search for new inventions may be taken into account in determining obviousness.

Nor are these the only factors bearing on the question of obviousness. We have seen that at the time Adams perfected his invention noted experts expressed disbelief in it. Several of the same experts subsequently recognized the significance of the Adams invention, some even patenting improvements on the same system. Fischbach *et al.*, U.S. Patent No. 2,636,060 (1953). Furthermore, in a crowded art replete with a century and a half of advancement, the Patent Office found not one reference to cite against the Adams application. Against the subsequently issued improvement patents to Fischbach, *supra*, and to Chubb, U.S. Reissue Patent No. 23,883 (1954), it found but three references prior to Adams—none of which are relied upon by the Government.

We conclude that the Adams patent is valid. The judgment of the Court of Claims is affirmed.

Comments

1. ***Nonobviousness as a Constitutional Requirement.*** One of the most important aspects of the *Graham* opinion is its explicit linking of the nonobviousness requirement with Article I, Section 8, Clause 8 of the Constitution. For the Court, "[i]nnovation, advancement, and things which add to the sum of useful knowledge are inherent requisites in a patent system which by constitutional command must 'promote the Progress of . . . useful Arts.' This is the standard in the Constitution and it may not be ignored." Thus, patent validity must be viewed through a constitutional lens, namely the preamble of the IP clause. But at the same time, by citing the preamble as the "constitutional standard," the Court "permits a goodly amount of congressional latitude in legislating on intellectual property." *See* John F. Duffy & Robert P. Merges, *The Story of* Graham v. John Deere Company: *Patent Law's Evolving Standard of Creativity (Patents)*, in Intellectual Property Stories 156 (J. Ginsburg & R. Dreyfuss eds., 2006).

2. ***Obviousness Is a Legal Determination.*** The *Graham* Court explicitly stated that "the ultimate question of patent validity is one of law." Just over 40 years later, the Court reaffirmed that while there are underlying factual considerations, "the ultimate judgment of obviousness is a legal determination." *KSR Co. v.*

Teleflex, Inc., 550 U.S. 398, 427 (2007) (citing *Graham*). Characterizing obviousness as a legal determination (with underlying factual findings) means that the ultimate decision under section 103 is more policy-laden in nature, particularly as it relates to how a person having ordinary skill in the art is constructed. See section C.2. See also the Policy Perspective following the principal case of *Procter & Gamble* in section C.1.

But a policy-driven obviousness determination is difficult to achieve as juries — rather than judges — routinely decide obviousness. Jurors typically check "yes" or "no" when asked whether the party asserting invalidity has proved by clear and convincing evidence that the claim in issue is obvious. The Federal Circuit has sanctioned this practice and relegated the court's role to reviewing the verdict on the legal determination of obviousness. In this context, for a patentee to "prevail it must establish that the jury's actual or inferred factual findings were not supported by substantial evidence, or that the evidence was not sufficient to support the findings and conclusions necessarily drawn by the jury on the way to its verdict." *Spectralytics, Inc. v. Cordis Corp.*, 649 F.3d 1336, 1342 (Fed. Cir. 2011). With respect to the jury's role in deciding obviousness, the Federal Circuit has stated:

> [I]t is neither error nor dangerous to justice to submit legal issues to juries, *the submission being accompanied by appropriate instructions on the law from the trial judge.* The rules relating to interrogatories, jury instructions, motions for directed verdict, JNOV, and new trial, and the rules governing appeals following jury trials, are fully adequate to provide for interposition of the judge as guardian of the law at the proper point and when necessary.

Railroad Dynamics, Inc. v. A. Stucki Co., 727 F.2d 1506 (Fed. Cir. 1984) (emphasis in original). In *Spectralytics, supra,* the district court judge asked the jury to decide whether the accused infringer (Cordis) "prove[d] by clear and convincing evidence that claim 1 of" the patent-in-suit "is invalid for obviousness." The jury answered "No" in a "black box" verdict. The district court let the jury decision stand, but noted "if this case had been tried to the Court, the Court likely would have found the" patent-in-suit obvious. On appeal, the accused infringer asserted, "[T]he district court abdicated its role as the ultimate decisionmaker [on the question of obviousness], in relying on the presumed jury findings." 649 F.3d at 1342. The Federal Circuit disagreed, noting "the Court cannot, on a post-trial motion, substitute its view of the evidence for the jury's." In the context of a jury's obviousness determination, "[w]e first presume that the jury resolved the underlying factual disputes in favor of the verdict winner and leave those presumed findings undisturbed if they are supported by substantial evidence. Then we examine the legal conclusion *de novo* to see whether it is correct in light of the presumed jury fact findings." *Id.*

While the jury's conclusion should be treated as a "nonbinding advisory opinion," it is rare for the jury to employ, for example, detailed special interrogatories, thereby precluding an independent judicial review of the jury's analysis. Is the "black box" approach inconsistent with Justice Breyer's concurrence in *Microsoft Corp. v. i4i Limited Partnership*, 131 S. Ct. 2238 (2011), wherein he recommended that on questions of patent validity district court judges should provide jurors with "interrogatories and special verdicts to make clear which specific factual findings underlie the jury's conclusions" and help to keep "separate[] factual and legal aspects of an invalidity claim." *Id.* at 2253. *See also In re Lockwood,* 50 F.3d 966, 990 (Fed. Cir. 1995) (Nies, J., dissenting from denial of rehearing *en banc*) (stating "[i]t is my understanding that the denomination of an issue as one of law represents a policy decision that a judge is more appropriate than a jury to make the decision. As a matter of policy for reasoned and uniform decisions, this is true of patent validity").

3. *The* **Graham** *Factors and Rules Versus Standards.* The *Graham* Court tracked the "relatively unambiguous terms" of section 103, noting there are several underlying factual determinations. These include: (1) the scope and content of the prior art; (2) differences between the prior art and the claims at issue; and (3) the level of ordinary skill in the pertinent art. Once these facts are ascertained, the decision-maker cast his mind back to "the time of invention" to determine obviousness. It is important to remember, however, that section 103 is a standard (or standard-like), not a rule for determining obviousness. In fact, the Court compared the nonobviousness test to the reasonable person test in negligence law—the quintessential standard—stating the "difficulties" in applying the section 103 inquiry "are comparable to those encountered daily by the courts in such frames of reference as negligence . . . and should be amenable to a case-by-case development." And the drafters "knew they were not making a *definition* but rather a *statement of policy,* a *specific approach* to a difficult problem." Giles S. Rich, *The Vague Concept of "Invention" as Replaced by §103 of the 1952 Patent Act,* 14 FED. CIRCUIT B.J. 147, 159 (2004-2005) (taken from the Kettering Award Address, The Patent, Trademark, and Copyright Research Institute 144-145 (1964)) (emphasis in original). Deciding whether to adopt a rule or standard is dependent on several factors and the nature of the legal regime in question. (A rules-based approach may be good for tax law, but ill suited for constitutional law.) Rules and standards each have their respective strengths and weaknesses, and "[n]o sensible person supposes that rules are always superior to standards, or vice versa." *MindGames, Inc. v. Western Publ'g Co., Inc.,* 218 F.3d 652, 657 (7th Cir. 2000) (Posner, J.). As the *MindGames* court explains:

> A rule singles out one or a few facts and makes it or them conclusive of legal liability; a standard permits consideration of all or at least most facts that are relevant to the standard's rationale. A speed limit is a rule; negligence is a standard. Rules have the advantage of being definite and of limiting factual inquiry but the disadvantage of being inflexible, even arbitrary, and thus overinclusive, or of being underinclusive and thus opening up loopholes. . . . Standards are flexible, but vague and open-ended; they make business planning difficult, invite the sometimes unpredictable exercise of judicial discretion, and are more costly to adjudicate—and yet when based on lay intuition they may actually be more intelligible, and thus in a sense clearer and more precise, to the persons whose behavior they seek to guide than rules would be.

Id. Importantly, while there are differences between a rule and a standard, they more often than not reside on a continuum, where legal forms can be characterized as either "rule-like" or "standard-like." *See* Kathleen M. Sullivan, *Foreword: The Justices of Rules and Standards,* 106 HARV. L. REV. 22, 61 (1992) (noting "distinctions between rules and standards . . . mark a continuum, not a divide. A rule may be corrupted by exceptions to the point where it resembles a standard; likewise, a standard may attach such fixed weights to the multiple factors it considers that it resembles a rule"). For example, exceptions may be carved into a rule, application of a standard may demand consideration of certain pre-fixed factors, or presumptions may be used. *See* Russell B. Korobkin, *Behavioral Analysis and Legal Form: Rules vs. Standards Revisited*, 79 OR. L. REV. 23, 26-28 (2000). *See also* Cass R. Sunstein, *Problems with Rules*, 83 CAL. L. REV. 953, 964 (1995) (describing a number of legal "devices" that operate as intermediaries between rules and standards, such as presumptions, factors, and principles).

The *Graham* Court expressly noted the unpredictability associated with applying the nonobviousness test, stating "[w]hat is obvious is not a question upon which there is likely to be uniformity of thought in every given factual context." But positioning the nonobviousness determination on the standard side of the continuum is understandable because given the infinite variety and unpredictable nature of innovation, Congress could not enact a rule that would include or foresee when any given invention would satisfy the obviousness requirement. An objective rule was, therefore, not only infeasible and costly, but would have exacerbated the over/underinclusive problem associate typically associated with rules.

In contrast to the "invention requirement," which is a pure standard, section 103 seeks to strike a balance between predictability and flexibility by establishing parameters—or pre-fixed factors—that contextualize an obviousness determination. These parameters require the decisionmaker to engage in factual findings relating to "scope and content of the prior art" (technology factor); "differences between the prior art and the claims at issue are to be ascertained" (comparative factor); "the level of ordinary skill in the pertinent art" (knowledge factor); and "at the time of the invention" (temporal factor). While these factual determinations do not unambiguously reveal what is and is not obvious, they do provide boundaries within which the section 103 decisionmaker must stay. (But see Comment 2 and the role of juries.) Reflecting this cabining approach, the principal architect of section 103 wrote, the obviousness determination "is *as of a particular time* and *to a particular* legally fictitious, technical *person.* . . . But *that* is not all; *what* must have been obvious is *the subject matter as a whole.* That, of course, is the invention as defined by each patent claim." Giles S. Rich, *Laying the Ghost of the "Invention" Requirement*, in NONOBVIOUSNESS: THE ULTIMATE CONDITION OF PATENTABILTY (J. Witherspoon ed., 1980), at 1:508 (emphasis in original). *See also* P.J. Federico, *Commentary on the New Patent Act*, 75 J. PAT. TRADEMARK OFF. SOC'Y 160, 181 (stating section 103 "is added to the statute for uniformity and definiteness . . . and with the view that an explicit statement in the statute may have some stabilizing effect"). For a discussion of rules and standards in the context of section 103, *see* Craig Allen Nard, *Legal Forms and the Common Law of Patents*, 90 B.U. L. REV. 51, 72 (2010).

This form of decision-making framework is common throughout the legal system. For instance, in discussing constitutional interpretation and the generality of constitutional clauses, Frederick Schauer writes:

> [L]inguistically articulated rules . . . exclude[] wrong answers rather than point[] to right ones. . . . Since no clause can generate a uniquely correct answer, at least in the abstract rather than in the context of a specific question,

the best view of the specific clauses is that they are merely less vague than the general clauses. The language of a clause, whether seemingly general or seemingly specific, establishes a boundary, or a frame, albeit a frame with fuzzy edges. Even though the language itself does not tell us what goes within the frame, it does tell us when we have gone outside it.

Frederick Schauer, *Easy Cases*, 58 S. Cal. L. Rev. 399, 430 (1985). The rule versus standard debate applies to many areas of the law and has produced a rich literature. *See, e.g.,* Daniel A. Crane, *Rules Versus Standards in Antitrust Adjudication*, 64 Wash. & Lee L. Rev. 49 (2007); Edward Lee, *Rules and Standards for Cyberspace*, 77 Notre Dame L. Rev. 1275 (2002); Thomas W. Merrill, *The Mead Doctrine: Rules and Standards, Meta-Rules and Meta-Standards*, 54 Admin. L. Rev. 807 (2002); Clayton P. Gillette, *Rules, Standards, and Precautions in Payment Systems*, 82 Va. L. Rev. 181 (1996); Louis Kaplow, *Rules Versus Standards: An Economic Analysis*, 42 Duke L.J. 557 (1992).

4. ***The Relationship Between the Nonobviousness and Novelty Requirements.*** It is important to understand that the novelty and nonobviousness requirements are distinct. For example, obviousness can be satisfied by combining references, but anticipation demands all claim limitations be disclosed in a single prior art reference. In addition, "secondary considerations" (discussed in section D, *infra*) can play an important role in a section 103 analysis, but are irrelevant under section 102. And lastly, anticipation can be proven inherently, which is not the same as proof of obviousness.

While it is exceedingly common for an invention that is deemed anticipated to also be regarded as obvious, there are occasions where an invention can be nonobvious yet anticipated. *See Cohesive Technologies, Inc. v. Water Corp.*, 543 F.3d 1351, 1364 (Fed. Cir. 2008). The *Cohesive* court provided the following example:

> Consider, for example, a claim directed toward a particular alloy of metal. The claimed metal alloy may have all the hallmarks of a nonobvious invention—there was a long felt but unresolved need for an alloy with the properties of the claimed alloy, others may have tried and failed to produce such an alloy, and, once disclosed, the claimed alloy may have received high praise and seen commercial success. Nevertheless, there may be a centuries-old alchemy textbook that, while not describing any metal alloys, describes a method that, if practiced precisely, actually produces the claimed alloy. While the prior art alchemy textbook inherently anticipates the claim under §102, the claim may not be said to be obvious under §103.

Id. at n.2.

5. **Graham *and the Rejection of the "Requirement for Invention."*** Consistent with section 103 and the intent of its drafters, the *Graham* Court rejected the confusing phrase "requirement for invention" as the operative test—what Judge Learned Hand referred to as a "fugitive, impalpable, wayward, and vague a phantom as exists in the whole paraphernalia of legal concepts." *Harries v. Air King Products Co.*, 183 F.2d 158, 162 (2d Cir. 1950) (Hand, J.). But the Court did not alter the objective level of creativity required to obtain a patent. Indeed, *Graham* recognized the similarities between *Hotchkiss* and section 103, stating the "first sentence of [section 103] is strongly reminiscent of the language in *Hotchkiss*" and both are "implicitly tied to advances in

that art." The Court also appreciated the basis and motivation behind section 103, namely the emphasis on "'nonobviousness' as the operative test . . . rather than the less definite 'invention' language of *Hotchkiss* that Congress thought had led to 'a large variety' of expressions in decisions and writings." According to the Court, patentability determinations by judges and examiners "must be beamed with greater intensity on the requirements of § 103." Interestingly, initial drafts of Justice Clark's opinion reveal a much more candid rejection of the invention requirement, referring to it as "elusive" and a "gossamer" concept. Only after receiving considerable pushback from Justice Black did Justice Clark tone down the opinion. For a discussion of *Graham*'s internal deliberations, *see* Duffy & Merges, *The Story of* Graham, *supra* Comment 1, at 134-141.

6. *Teaching Away.* An applicant or patentee has several arguments he can make to counter a finding or allegation of obviousness or simply to bolster the likelihood a court or examiner will find the claimed invention nonobviousness. Perhaps the strongest argument is that the prior art actually teaches away from the claimed invention or execution of the prior art resulted in a failure. The teaching away argument proved helpful to Adams. Recall the Court stated "that known disadvantages in old devices which would naturally discourage the search for new inventions may be taken into account in determining obviousness." The Federal Circuit has embraced the teaching away rationale. *See Boehringer Ingelheim Vetmedica, Inc. v. Schering-Plough Corp.,* 320 F.3d 1339, 1354 (Fed. Cir. 2003) (stating "[w]hile absolute certainty is not necessary to establish a reasonable expectation of success, there can be little better evidence negating an expectation of success than actual reports of failure"); *In re Gurley,* 27 F.3d 551, 553 (Fed. Cir. 1994) ("A reference may be said to teach away when a person of ordinary skill, upon reading the reference, would be discouraged from following the path set out in the reference or would be led in a direction divergent from the path that was taken by the applicant."). And, after *KSR* (the principal case in section C.1), evidence of teaching away has become more important.

Evidence of teaching away was helpful to the patentee in *Crocs, Inc. v. International Trade Comm'n,* 598 F.3d 1294 (Fed. Cir. 2010). The Federal Circuit faulted the Commission for discounting Crocs' expert testimony that at the time of invention, "foam shoe components connected through perforations such as by stitching or riveting were excessively prone to tearing." *Id.* at 1308. According to the Commission, "known or obvious composition does not become patentable simply because it has been described as somewhat inferior to some other product for the same use." *Id.* But the court noted "[a]lthough known in the art, foam was known as unsuitable" and "the Commission unreasonably determined that foam straps were known in the art without acknowledging that those prior art references rendered the material out of place for use as a strap." *Id.* at 1309. This evidence of teaching away strongly suggested to the court that a person of ordinary skill in the art "would have no reason to use foam straps in combination with a foam base portion." *Id. See also Spectralytics v. Cordis,* 649 F.3d 1336, 1343 (Fed. Cir. 2011) (stating "'[t]eaching away' does not require that the prior art foresaw the specific invention that was later made, and warned against taking that path. It is indeed of interest if the prior art warned against the very modification made by the patentee, but it is not the sole basis on which a trier of fact could find that the prior art led away from the direction taken by the patentee").

7. *Suing the U.S. Government for Patent Infringement.* A patentee may sue the United States government for patent infringement. Under 28 U.S.C. § 1498 — which is the only avenue to enforce U.S. government infringement — a patentee (like Adams) must bring suit in the Court of Federal Claims, not U.S. District Court. *See De Graffenried v. United States*, 29 Fed. Cl. 384, 391 (Fed. Cl. 1993) (stating "the government's sole liability for the unauthorized use of a patented invention is set forth in 28 U.S.C. § 1498(a)"). Section 1498(a) provides, in relevant part:

> Whenever an invention described in and covered by a patent of the United States is used or manufactured by or for the United States without license of the owner thereof or lawful right to use or manufacture the same, the owner's remedy shall be by action against the United States in the United States Court of Federal Claims for the recovery of his reasonable and entire compensation for such use and manufacture.

This statute acts as a waiver of the government's sovereign immunity with respect to "direct governmental infringement of a patent." *Decca Ltd. v. United States*, 640 F.2d 1156, 1167 (Ct. Cl. 1980). *See Crozier v. Fried, Krupp Aktiengesellschaft*, 224 U.S. 290, 304 (1912) (discussing the history of the statute). Section 1498 is "linked to the scope of the patent holder's rights as granted by the patent grant title 35 U.S.C. section 154(a)(1)," which includes infringing activity not only under section 271(a) but also 271(g). *Zoltek Corp. v. United States*, 672 F.3d 1309, 1323 (Fed. Cir. 2012) (*en banc*).

When the alleged infringer is a non-government entity (e.g., contractor), the Federal Circuit has held under section 1498(a), "the accused activity is 'for the United States' if it is conducted 'for the Government' and 'with the authorization or consent of the Government.'" *See Advanced Software Design v. Federal Reserve Bank of St. Louis*, 583 F.3d 1371, 1376 (Fed. Cir. 2009). And the authorization does not need to be particular or explicit. *Id.* at 1377. *See also Hughes Aircraft Co. v. United States*, 534 F.2d 889, 901 (Ct. Cl. 1976) (stating there is no requirement "that authorization or consent necessarily appear on the face of a particular contract. On the contrary, 'authorization or consent' on the part of the Government may be given in many ways other than by letter or other direct form of communication").

The courts have distinguished between Titles 28 and 35 in the context of patent infringement remedies. According to the Court of Federal Claims, while the "two titles are analogous, . . . Title 35 is premised on the notion that absent appropriate authorization, a private party generally cannot use a patented invention and is subject to injunction for any such unauthorized use," whereas section 1498(a) "is founded on the premise that, although the government is obliged to pay a patent holder reasonable and entire compensation for use of his or her patent, the government can never be denied such use." *De Graffenried, supra*, at 391. *See also Leesona Corp. v. United States*, 599 F.2d 958, 968-969 (Ct. Cl. 1979) (distinguishing recovery permitted under section 1498(a) from the patent infringement remedies of Title 35). Thus, injunctive relief is not available under section 1498, which means that, as a practical matter, the government can indirectly invoke a compulsory license. *See*

Motorola, Inc. v. United States, 729 F.2d 765, 768 n.3 (Fed. Cir. 1984) (injunctive relief is unavailable against the United States under section 1498).

8. ***Flash of Genius Rejected.*** One of the pre-1952 doctrines the drafters of section 103 rejected was the "flash of genius" test of *Cuno Engineering Corp. v. Automatic Devices Corp.*, 314 U.S. 84 (1941). The last sentence of section 103, which reads, "Patentability shall not be negatived by the manner in which the invention was made," specifically addressed *Cuno.* The *Graham* Court expressly adopted section 103's approach when it wrote, "It . . . seems apparent that Congress intended by the last sentence of § 103 to abolish the test it believed this Court announced in the controversial phrase 'flash of creative genius,' used in *Cuno.*" This approach is consistent with Justice Story's view of patentability, set forth in *Earle v. Sawyer,* 8 F. Cas. 254, 256 (C.C. Mass. 1825):

> It is of no consequence, whether the thing be simple or complicated; whether it be by accident, or by long, laborious thought, or by an instantaneous flash of mind, that it is first done. The law looks to the fact, and not to the process by which it is accomplished. It gives the first inventor, or discoverer of the thing, the exclusive right, and asks nothing as to the mode or extent of the application of his genius to conceive or execute it.

C. APPLICATION OF THE *GRAHAM* TEST

Application of the *Graham* framework gets to the heart of an obviousness inquiry. In the principal case of *KSR v. Teleflex,* the Supreme Court—working within and building on *Graham*—identified several considerations that are relevant to an obviousness determination. In short, *KSR* explores how a court determines whether an invention is obvious.

As you will recall from *Graham* and revisit in *KSR,* section 103 asks whether the claimed invention would have been obvious to a *person having ordinary skill in the art,* sometimes referred to as a PHOSITA.[11] Who this person is and what is considered "ordinary skill" are addressed in the principal case of *Daiichi Sankyo* and the Comments that follow the case. Moreover, recall under section 102 an invention is anticipated if a *single* prior art reference discloses each and every limitation of the claimed invention; in contrast, references can be combined under section 103. But a nonobvious inquiry is also more restrictive than section 102 in that prior art must be *analogous* before it can be used under section 103. The doctrine of analogous art is a filter, although less so after *KSR,* sifting out references that are too far afield from the claimed invention. The issue of analogous art is discussed in *In re Icon Health & Fitness* and *In re Klein.*

11. The acronym PHOSITA was coined by Cyril A. Soans in his article *Some Absurd Presumptions in Patent Cases,* 10 IDEA 433, 436 (1966). Soans referred to the person having ordinary skill in the art as "Mr. Phosita."

1. Determining Obviousness (or Not)

An overwhelming majority of obviousness decisions involve more than one prior art reference. Since the mid-1980s the Federal Circuit and its predecessor, the CCPA, have required that before prior art references can be combined under section 103, the references must *teach*, *suggest*, or *motivate* (TSM) a person of ordinary skill in the art to make the claimed invention. In other words, there had to be a reason to combine. Whether the TSM requirement is consistent with Supreme Court precedent was addressed in *KSR*, one of the most significant Supreme Court cases involving patent law in the past 50 years. A few years after *KSR* was decided, the Federal Circuit applied its teachings in *Perfect Web*, the principal case after *KSR* that involved an invention for managing bulk e-mail distributions. And in *Procter & Gamble*, which follows *Perfect Web*, the Federal Circuit applied the *Graham/KSR* framework in the pharmaceutical context.

KSR INTERNATIONAL v. TELEFLEX, INC.

550 U.S. 398 (2007)

Justice KENNEDY delivered the opinion of the Court.

Teleflex Incorporated and its subsidiary Technology Holding Company—both referred to here as Teleflex—sued KSR International Company for patent infringement. The patent at issue, United States Patent No. 6,237,565 B1, is entitled "Adjustable Pedal Assembly With Electronic Throttle Control." The patentee is Steven J. Engelgau, and the patent is referred to as "the Engelgau patent." Teleflex holds the exclusive license to the patent.

Claim 4 of the Engelgau patent describes a mechanism for combining an electronic sensor with an adjustable automobile pedal so the pedal's position can be transmitted to a computer that controls the throttle in the vehicle's engine. When Teleflex accused KSR of infringing the Engelgau patent by adding an electronic sensor to one of KSR's previously designed pedals, KSR countered that claim 4 was invalid under the Patent Act, 35 U.S.C. §103, because its subject matter was obvious.

Section 103 forbids issuance of a patent when "the differences between the subject matter sought to be patented and the prior art are such that the subject matter as a whole would have been obvious at the time the invention was made to a person having ordinary skill in the art to which said subject matter pertains."

In *Graham v. John Deere Co.*, 383 U.S. 1 (1966), the Court set out a framework for applying the statutory language of §103, language itself based on the logic of the earlier decision in *Hotchkiss v. Greenwood*, 11 How. 248 (1851), and its progeny. The analysis is objective:

> Under §103, the scope and content of the prior art are to be determined; differences between the prior art and the claims at issue are to be ascertained; and the level of ordinary skill in the pertinent art resolved. Against this background the obviousness or nonobviousness of the subject matter is determined. Such secondary considerations as commercial success, long felt but unsolved needs, failure of others, etc., might be utilized to give light to the circumstances surrounding the origin of the subject matter sought to be patented.

Id., at 17-18.

While the sequence of these questions might be reordered in any particular case, the factors continue to define the inquiry that controls. If a court, or patent examiner, conducts this analysis and concludes the claimed subject matter was obvious, the claim is invalid under §103.

Seeking to resolve the question of obviousness with more uniformity and consistency, the Court of Appeals for the Federal Circuit has employed an approach referred to by the parties as the "teaching, suggestion, or motivation" test (TSM test), under which a patent claim is only proved obvious if "some motivation or suggestion to combine the prior art teachings" can be found in the prior art, the nature of the problem, or the knowledge of a person having ordinary skill in the art. KSR challenges that test, or at least its application in this case. Because the Court of Appeals addressed the question of obviousness in a manner contrary to §103 and our precedents, we granted certiorari. We now reverse.

I

A

In car engines without computer-controlled throttles, the accelerator pedal interacts with the throttle via cable or other mechanical link. The pedal arm acts as a lever rotating around a pivot point. In a cable-actuated throttle control the rotation caused by pushing down the pedal pulls a cable, which in turn pulls open valves in the carburetor or fuel injection unit. The wider the valves open, the more fuel and air are released, causing combustion to increase and the car to accelerate. When the driver takes his foot off the pedal, the opposite occurs as the cable is released and the valves slide closed.

In the 1990's it became more common to install computers in cars to control engine operation. Computer-controlled throttles open and close valves in response to electronic signals, not through force transferred from the pedal by a mechanical link. Constant, delicate adjustments of air and fuel mixture are possible. The computer's rapid processing of factors beyond the pedal's position improves fuel efficiency and engine performance.

For a computer-controlled throttle to respond to a driver's operation of the car, the computer must know what is happening with the pedal. A cable or mechanical link does not suffice for this purpose; at some point, an electronic sensor is necessary to translate the mechanical operation into digital data the computer can understand.

Before discussing sensors further we turn to the mechanical design of the pedal itself. In the traditional design a pedal can be pushed down or released but cannot have its position in the footwell adjusted by sliding the pedal forward or back. As a result, a driver who wishes to be closer or farther from the pedal must either reposition himself in the driver's seat or move the seat in some way. In cars with deep footwells these are imperfect solutions for drivers of smaller stature. To solve the problem, inventors, beginning in the 1970's, designed pedals that could be adjusted to change their location in the footwell. Important for this case are two adjustable pedals disclosed in U.S. Patent Nos. 5,010,782 (filed July 28, 1989) (Asano) and 5,460,061 (filed Sept. 17, 1993) (Redding). The Asano patent reveals a support structure that houses the pedal so that even when the pedal location is adjusted relative to the driver, one of the pedal's pivot points stays fixed. The pedal is also designed so that the force necessary to push the pedal down is the same regardless of adjustments to its location. The

Redding patent reveals a different, sliding mechanism where both the pedal and the pivot point are adjusted.

We return to sensors. Well before Engelgau applied for his challenged patent, some inventors had obtained patents involving electronic pedal sensors for computer-controlled throttles. These inventions, such as the device disclosed in U.S. Patent No. 5,241,936 (filed Sept. 9, 1991) ('936), taught that it was preferable to detect the pedal's position in the pedal assembly, not in the engine. The '936 patent disclosed a pedal with an electronic sensor on a pivot point in the pedal assembly. U.S. Patent No. 5,063,811 (filed July 9, 1990) (Smith) taught that to prevent the wires connecting the sensor to the computer from chafing and wearing out, and to avoid grime and damage from the driver's foot, the sensor should be put on a fixed part of the pedal assembly rather than in or on the pedal's footpad.

In addition to patents for pedals with integrated sensors inventors obtained patents for self-contained modular sensors. A modular sensor is designed independently of a given pedal so that it can be taken off the shelf and attached to mechanical pedals of various sorts, enabling the pedals to be used in automobiles with computer-controlled throttles. One such sensor was disclosed in U.S. Patent No. 5,385,068 (filed Dec. 18, 1992) ('068). In 1994, Chevrolet manufactured a line of trucks using modular sensors "attached to the pedal support bracket, adjacent to the pedal and engaged with the pivot shaft about which the pedal rotates in operation." 298 F. Supp. 2d 581, 589 (ED Mich. 2003).

The prior art contained patents involving the placement of sensors on adjustable pedals as well. For example, U.S. Patent No. 5,819,593 (filed Aug. 17, 1995) (Rixon) discloses an adjustable pedal assembly with an electronic sensor for detecting the pedal's position. In the Rixon pedal the sensor is located in the pedal footpad. The Rixon pedal was known to suffer from wire chafing when the pedal was depressed and released.

This short account of pedal and sensor technology leads to the instant case.

B

KSR, a Canadian company, manufactures and supplies auto parts, including pedal systems. Ford Motor Company hired KSR in 1998 to supply an adjustable pedal system for various lines of automobiles with cable-actuated throttle controls. KSR developed an adjustable mechanical pedal for Ford and obtained U.S. Patent No. 6,151,976 (filed July 16, 1999) ('976) for the design. In 2000, KSR was chosen by General Motors Corporation (GMC or GM) to supply adjustable pedal systems for Chevrolet and GMC light trucks that used engines with computer-controlled throttles. To make the '976 pedal compatible with the trucks, KSR merely took that design and added a modular sensor.

Teleflex is a rival to KSR in the design and manufacture of adjustable pedals. As noted, it is the exclusive licensee of the Engelgau patent. Engelgau filed the patent application on August 22, 2000 as a continuation of a previous application for U.S. Patent No. 6,109,241, which was filed on January 26, 1999. He has sworn he invented the patent's subject matter on February 14, 1998. The Engelgau patent discloses an adjustable electronic pedal described in the specification as a "simplified vehicle control pedal assembly that is less expensive, and which uses fewer parts and is easier to package within the vehicle." Engelgau, col. 2, lines 2-5. Claim 4 of the patent, at issue here, describes:

A vehicle control pedal apparatus [12] comprising:

> a support [18] adapted to be mounted to a vehicle structure [20];
>
> an adjustable pedal assembly [22] having a pedal arm [14] moveable in for[e] and aft directions with respect to said support [18];
>
> a pivot [24] for pivotally supporting said adjustable pedal assembly [22] with respect to said support [18] and defining a pivot axis [26]; and
>
> an electronic control [28] attached to said support [18] for controlling a vehicle system;
>
> said apparatus [12] characterized by said electronic control [28] being responsive to said pivot [24] for providing a signal [32] that corresponds to pedal arm position as said pedal arm [14] pivots about said pivot axis [26] between rest and applied positions wherein the position of said pivot [24] remains constant while said pedal arm [14] moves in fore and aft directions with respect to said pivot [24].

Id., col. 6, lines 17-36.

We agree with the District Court that the claim discloses "a position-adjustable pedal assembly with an electronic pedal position sensor attached to the support member of the pedal assembly. Attaching the sensor to the support member allows the sensor to remain in a fixed position while the driver adjusts the pedal." 298 F. Supp. 2d, at 586-587.

Before issuing the Engelgau patent the U.S. Patent and Trademark Office (PTO) rejected one of the patent claims that was similar to, but broader than, the present claim 4. The claim did not include the requirement that the sensor be placed on a fixed pivot point. The PTO concluded the claim was an obvious combination of the prior art disclosed in Redding and Smith, explaining:

> Since the prior ar[t] references are from the field of endeavor, the purpose disclosed . . . would have been recognized in the pertinent art of Redding. Therefore it would have been obvious . . . to provide the device of Redding with the . . . means attached to a support member as taught by Smith.

Id., at 595.

In other words Redding provided an example of an adjustable pedal and Smith explained how to mount a sensor on a pedal's support structure, and the rejected patent claim merely put these two teachings together.

Although the broader claim was rejected, claim 4 was later allowed because it included the limitation of a fixed pivot point, which distinguished the design from Redding's. *Ibid.* Engelgau had not included Asano among the prior art references, and Asano was not mentioned in the patent's prosecution. Thus, the PTO did not have before it an adjustable pedal with a fixed pivot point. The patent issued on May 29, 2001 and was assigned to Teleflex.

Upon learning of KSR's design for GM, Teleflex sent a warning letter informing KSR that its proposal would violate the Engelgau patent. "'Teleflex believes that any supplier of a product that combines an adjustable pedal with an electronic throttle control necessarily employs technology covered by one or more'" of Teleflex's patents. *Id.*, at 585. KSR refused to enter a royalty arrangement with Teleflex; so Teleflex sued for infringement, asserting KSR's pedal infringed the Engelgau patent and two other patents. *Ibid.* Teleflex later abandoned its claims regarding the other patents and dedicated the patents to the public. The remaining contention was that KSR's pedal system for GM infringed claim 4 of the Engelgau patent. Teleflex has not argued that the other three claims of the patent are infringed by KSR's pedal, nor has Teleflex argued that the mechanical adjustable pedal designed by KSR for Ford infringed any of its patents.

C

The District Court granted summary judgment in KSR's favor. After reviewing the pertinent history of pedal design, the scope of the Engelgau patent, and the relevant prior art, the court considered the validity of the contested claim. By direction of 35 U.S.C. § 282, an issued patent is presumed valid. The District Court applied *Graham*'s framework to determine whether under summary-judgment standards KSR had overcome the presumption and demonstrated that claim 4 was obvious in light of the prior art in existence when the claimed subject matter was invented.

The District Court determined, in light of the expert testimony and the parties' stipulations, that the level of ordinary skill in pedal design was "'an undergraduate degree in mechanical engineering (or an equivalent amount of industry experience) [and] familiarity with pedal control systems for vehicles.'" 298 F. Supp. 2d, at 590. The court then set forth the relevant prior art, including the patents and pedal designs described above.

Following *Graham*'s direction, the court compared the teachings of the prior art to the claims of Engelgau. It found "little difference." 298 F. Supp. 2d, at 590. Asano taught everything contained in claim 4 except the use of a sensor to detect the pedal's position and transmit it to the computer controlling the throttle. That additional aspect was revealed in sources such as the '068 patent and the sensors used by Chevrolet.

Under the controlling cases from the Court of Appeals for the Federal Circuit, however, the District Court was not permitted to stop there. The court was required also to apply the TSM test. The District Court held KSR had satisfied the test. It reasoned (1) the state of the industry would lead inevitably to combinations of electronic sensors and adjustable pedals, (2) Rixon provided the basis for these developments, and (3) Smith taught a solution to the wire chafing problems in Rixon, namely locating the sensor on the fixed structure of

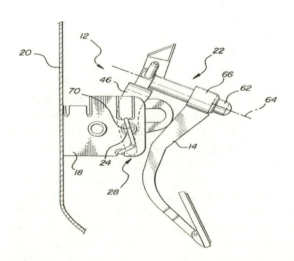

the pedal. This could lead to the combination of Asano, or a pedal like it, with a pedal position sensor.

The conclusion that the Engelgau design was obvious was supported, in the District Court's view, by the PTO's rejection of the broader version of claim 4. Had Engelgau included Asano in his patent application, it reasoned, the PTO would have found claim 4 to be an obvious combination of Asano and Smith, as it had found the broader version an obvious combination of Redding and Smith. As a final matter, the District Court held that the secondary factor of Teleflex's commercial success with pedals based on Engelgau's design did not alter its conclusion. The District Court granted summary judgment for KSR.

With principal reliance on the TSM test, the Court of Appeals reversed. It ruled the District Court had not been strict enough in applying the test, having failed to make " 'finding[s] as to the specific understanding or principle within the knowledge of a skilled artisan that would have motivated one with no knowledge of [the] invention . . . to attach an electronic control to the support bracket of the Asano assembly.' " 119 Fed. Appx., at 288 (brackets in original) (quoting *In re Kotzab*, 217 F.3d 1365, 1371 (CA Fed. 2000)). The Court of Appeals held that the District Court was incorrect that the nature of the problem to be solved satisfied this requirement because unless the "prior art references address[ed] the precise problem that the patentee was trying to solve," the problem would not motivate an inventor to look at those references. 119 Fed. Appx., at 288.

Here, the Court of Appeals found, the Asano pedal was designed to solve the " 'constant ratio problem' " — that is, to ensure that the force required to depress the pedal is the same no matter how the pedal is adjusted — whereas Engelgau sought to provide a simpler, smaller, cheaper adjustable electronic pedal. *Ibid.* As for Rixon, the court explained, that pedal suffered from the problem of wire chafing but was not designed to solve it. In the court's view Rixon did not teach anything helpful to Engelgau's purpose. Smith, in turn, did not relate to adjustable pedals and did not "necessarily go to the issue of motivation to attach the electronic control on the support bracket of the pedal assembly." *Ibid.* When the patents were interpreted in this way, the Court of Appeals held, they would not have led a person of ordinary skill to put a sensor on the sort of pedal described in Asano.

That it might have been obvious to try the combination of Asano and a sensor was likewise irrelevant, in the court's view, because " '[o]bvious to try" has long been held not to constitute obviousness.' " *Id.*, at 289 (quoting *In re Deuel*, 51 F.3d 1552, 1559 (CA Fed. 1995)).

The Court of Appeals also faulted the District Court's consideration of the PTO's rejection of the broader version of claim 4. The District Court's role, the Court of Appeals explained, was not to speculate regarding what the PTO might have done had the Engelgau patent mentioned Asano. Rather, the court held, the District Court was obliged first to presume that the issued patent was valid and then to render its own independent judgment of obviousness based on a review of the prior art. The fact that the PTO had rejected the broader version of claim 4, the Court of Appeals said, had no place in that analysis.

The Court of Appeals further held that genuine issues of material fact precluded summary judgment. Teleflex had proffered statements from one expert that claim 4 " 'was a simple, elegant, and novel combination of features,' " 119 Fed. Appx., at 290, compared to Rixon, and from another expert that claim 4 was nonobvious because, unlike in Rixon, the sensor was mounted on the support bracket rather than the pedal itself. This evidence, the court concluded, sufficed to require a trial.

II

A

We begin by rejecting the rigid approach of the Court of Appeals. Throughout this Court's engagement with the question of obviousness, our cases have set forth an expansive and flexible approach inconsistent with the way the Court of Appeals applied its TSM test here. To be sure, *Graham* recognized the need for "uniformity and definiteness." 383 U.S., at 18. Yet the principles laid down in *Graham* reaffirmed the "functional approach" of *Hotchkiss*, 11 How. 248. See 383 U.S., at 12. To this end, *Graham* set forth a broad inquiry and invited courts, where appropriate, to look at any secondary considerations that would prove instructive. *Id.*, at 17.

Neither the enactment of §103 nor the analysis in *Graham* disturbed this Court's earlier instructions concerning the need for caution in granting a patent based on the combination of elements found in the prior art. For over a half century, the Court has held that a "patent for a combination which only unites old elements with no change in their respective functions . . . obviously withdraws what is already known into the field of its monopoly and diminishes the resources available to skillful men." *Great Atlantic & Pacific Tea Co. v. Supermarket Equipment Corp.*, 340 U.S. 147, 152 (1950). This is a principal reason for declining to allow patents for what is obvious. The combination of familiar elements according to known methods is likely to be obvious when it does no more than yield predictable results. Three cases decided after *Graham* illustrate the application of this doctrine.

In *United States v. Adams*, 383 U.S. 39, 40 (1966), a companion case to *Graham*, the Court considered the obviousness of a "wet battery" that varied from prior designs in two ways: It contained water, rather than the acids conventionally employed in storage batteries; and its electrodes were magnesium and cuprous chloride, rather than zinc and silver chloride. The Court recognized that when a patent claims a structure already known in the prior art that is altered by the mere substitution of one element for another known in the field, the combination must do more than yield a predictable result. 383 U.S., at 50-51. It nevertheless rejected the Government's claim that Adams's battery was obvious. The Court relied upon the corollary principle that when the prior art teaches away from combining certain known elements, discovery of a successful means of combining them is more likely to be nonobvious. *Id.*, at 51-52. When Adams designed his battery, the prior art warned that risks were involved in using the types of electrodes he employed. The fact that the elements worked together in an unexpected and fruitful manner supported the conclusion that Adams's design was not obvious to those skilled in the art.

In *Anderson's-Black Rock, Inc. v. Pavement Salvage Co.*, 396 U.S. 57 (1969), the Court elaborated on this approach. The subject matter of the patent before the Court was a device combining two pre-existing elements: a radiant-heat burner and a paving machine. The device, the Court concluded, did not create some new synergy: The radiant-heat burner functioned just as a burner was expected to function; and the paving machine did the same. The two in combination did no more than they would in separate, sequential operation. *Id.*, at 60-62. In those circumstances, "while the combination of old elements performed a useful function, it added nothing to the nature and quality of the radiant-heat burner already patented," and the patent failed under §103. *Id.*, at 62.

Finally, in *Sakraida v. AG Pro, Inc.*, 425 U.S. 273 (1976), the Court derived from the precedents the conclusion that when a patent "simply arranges old elements with each performing the same function it had been known to perform" and yields no more than one would expect from such an arrangement, the combination is obvious. *Id.*, at 282.

The principles underlying these cases are instructive when the question is whether a patent claiming the combination of elements of prior art is obvious. When a work is available in one field of endeavor, design incentives and other market forces can prompt variations of it, either in the same field or a different one. If a person of ordinary skill can implement a predictable variation, §103 likely bars its patentability. For the same reason, if a technique has been used to improve one device, and a person of ordinary skill in the art would recognize that it would improve similar devices in the same way, using the technique is obvious unless its actual application is beyond his or her skill. *Sakraida* and *Anderson's-Black Rock* are illustrative—a court must ask whether the improvement is more than the predictable use of prior art elements according to their established functions.

Following these principles may be more difficult in other cases than it is here because the claimed subject matter may involve more than the simple substitution of one known element for another or the mere application of a known technique to a piece of prior art ready for the improvement. Often, it will be necessary for a court to look to interrelated teachings of multiple patents; the effects of demands known to the design community or present in the marketplace; and the background knowledge possessed by a person having ordinary skill in the art, all in order to determine whether there was an apparent reason to combine the known elements in the fashion claimed by the patent at issue. To facilitate review, this analysis should be made explicit. See *In re Kahn*, 441 F.3d 977, 988 (CA Fed. 2006) ("[R]ejections on obviousness grounds cannot be sustained by mere conclusory statements; instead, there must be some articulated reasoning with some rational underpinning to support the legal conclusion of obviousness"). As our precedents make clear, however, the analysis need not seek out precise teachings directed to the specific subject matter of the challenged claim, for a court can take account of the inferences and creative steps that a person of ordinary skill in the art would employ.

B

When it first established the requirement of demonstrating a teaching, suggestion, or motivation to combine known elements in order to show that the combination is obvious, the Court of Customs and Patent Appeals captured a helpful insight. See *Application of Bergel*, 292 F.2d 955, 956-957 (1961). As is clear from cases such as *Adams*, a patent composed of several elements is not proved obvious merely by demonstrating that each of its elements was, independently, known in the prior art. Although common sense directs one to look with care at a patent application that claims as innovation the combination of two known devices according to their established functions, it can be important to identify a reason that would have prompted a person of ordinary skill in the relevant field to combine the elements in the way the claimed new invention does. This is so because inventions in most, if not all, instances rely upon building blocks long since uncovered, and claimed discoveries almost of necessity will be combinations of what, in some sense, is already known.

Helpful insights, however, need not become rigid and mandatory formulas; and when it is so applied, the TSM test is incompatible with our precedents. The obviousness analysis cannot be confined by a formalistic conception of the words teaching, suggestion, and motivation, or by overemphasis on the importance of published articles and the explicit content of issued patents. The diversity of inventive pursuits and of modern technology counsels against limiting the analysis in this way. In many fields it may be that there is little discussion of obvious techniques or combinations, and it often may be the case that market demand, rather than scientific literature, will drive design trends. Granting patent protection to advances that would occur in the ordinary course without real innovation retards progress and may, in the case of patents combining previously known elements, deprive prior inventions of their value or utility.

In the years since the Court of Customs and Patent Appeals set forth the essence of the TSM test, the Court of Appeals no doubt has applied the test in accord with these principles in many cases. There is no necessary inconsistency between the idea underlying the TSM test and the *Graham* analysis. But when a court transforms the general principle into a rigid rule that limits the obviousness inquiry, as the Court of Appeals did here, it errs.

C

The flaws in the analysis of the Court of Appeals relate for the most part to the court's narrow conception of the obviousness inquiry reflected in its application of the TSM test. In determining whether the subject matter of a patent claim is obvious, neither the particular motivation nor the avowed purpose of the patentee controls. What matters is the objective reach of the claim. If the claim extends to what is obvious, it is invalid under §103. One of the ways in which a patent's subject matter can be proved obvious is by noting that there existed at the time of invention a known problem for which there was an obvious solution encompassed by the patent's claims.

The first error of the Court of Appeals in this case was to foreclose this reasoning by holding that courts and patent examiners should look only to the problem the patentee was trying to solve. The Court of Appeals failed to recognize that the problem motivating the patentee may be only one of many addressed by the patent's subject matter. The question is not whether the combination was obvious to the patentee but whether the combination was obvious to a person with ordinary skill in the art. Under the correct analysis, any need or problem known in the field of endeavor at the time of invention and addressed by the patent can provide a reason for combining the elements in the manner claimed.

The second error of the Court of Appeals lay in its assumption that a person of ordinary skill attempting to solve a problem will be led only to those elements of prior art designed to solve the same problem. *Ibid.* The primary purpose of Asano was solving the constant ratio problem; so, the court concluded, an inventor considering how to put a sensor on an adjustable pedal would have no reason to consider putting it on the Asano pedal. *Ibid.* Common sense teaches, however, that familiar items may have obvious uses beyond their primary purposes, and in many cases a person of ordinary skill will be able to fit the teachings of multiple patents together like pieces of a puzzle. Regardless of

Asano's primary purpose, the design provided an obvious example of an adjust-able pedal with a fixed pivot point; and the prior art was replete with patents indicating that a fixed pivot point was an ideal mount for a sensor. The idea that a designer hoping to make an adjustable electronic pedal would ignore Asano because Asano was designed to solve the constant ratio problem makes little sense. A person of ordinary skill is also a person of ordinary creativity, not an automaton.

The same constricted analysis led the Court of Appeals to conclude, in error, that a patent claim cannot be proved obvious merely by showing that the combi-nation of elements was "obvious to try." When there is a design need or market pressure to solve a problem and there are a finite number of identified, predict-able solutions, a person of ordinary skill has good reason to pursue the known options within his or her technical grasp. If this leads to the anticipated suc-cess, it is likely the product not of innovation but of ordinary skill and common sense. In that instance the fact that a combination was obvious to try might show that it was obvious under § 103.

The Court of Appeals, finally, drew the wrong conclusion from the risk of courts and patent examiners falling prey to hindsight bias. A factfinder should be aware, of course, of the distortion caused by hindsight bias and must be cautious of arguments reliant upon *ex post* reasoning. *See Graham*, 383 U.S., at 36 (warning against a "temptation to read into the prior art the teachings of the invention in issue" and instructing courts to " 'guard against slipping into the use of hindsight' " (quoting *Monroe Auto Equipment Co. v. Heckethorn Mfg. & Supply Co.*, 332 F.2d 406, 412 (CA6 1964))). Rigid preventative rules that deny factfinders recourse to common sense, however, are neither necessary under our case law nor consistent with it.

We note the Court of Appeals has since elaborated a broader conception of the TSM test than was applied in the instant matter. *See, e.g., Dystar Textilfarben GmbH & Co. Deutschland KG v. C.H. Patrick Co.*, 464 F.3d 1356, 1367 (2006) ("Our suggestion test is in actuality quite flexible and not only permits, but *requires*, consideration of common knowledge and common sense."); *Alza Corp. v. Mylan Labs., Inc.*, 464 F.3d 1286, 1291 (2006) ("There is flexibility in our obviousness jurisprudence because a motivation may be found *implicitly* in the prior art. We do not have a rigid test that requires an actual teaching to combine. . . ."). Those decisions, of course, are not now before us and do not correct the errors of law made by the Court of Appeals in this case. The extent to which they may describe an analysis more consistent with our earlier precedents and our deci-sion here is a matter for the Court of Appeals to consider in its future cases. What we hold is that the fundamental misunderstandings identified above led the Court of Appeals in this case to apply a test inconsistent with our patent law decisions.

III

When we apply the standards we have explained to the instant facts, claim 4 must be found obvious. We agree with and adopt the District Court's recitation of the relevant prior art and its determination of the level of ordinary skill in the field. As did the District Court, we see little difference between the teachings of Asano and Smith and the adjustable electronic pedal disclosed in claim 4 of the Engelgau patent. A person having ordinary skill in the art could have combined

Asano with a pedal position sensor in a fashion encompassed by claim 4, and would have seen the benefits of doing so.

* * *

B

The District Court was correct to conclude that, as of the time Engelgau designed the subject matter in claim 4, it was obvious to a person of ordinary skill to combine Asano with a pivot-mounted pedal position sensor. There then existed a marketplace that created a strong incentive to convert mechanical pedals to electronic pedals, and the prior art taught a number of methods for achieving this advance. The Court of Appeals considered the issue too narrowly by, in effect, asking whether a pedal designer writing on a blank slate would have chosen both Asano and a modular sensor similar to the ones used in the Chevrolet truckline and disclosed in the '068 patent. The District Court employed this narrow inquiry as well, though it reached the correct result nevertheless. The proper question to have asked was whether a pedal designer of ordinary skill, facing the wide range of needs created by developments in the field of endeavor, would have seen a benefit to upgrading Asano with a sensor.

In automotive design, as in many other fields, the interaction of multiple components means that changing one component often requires the others to be modified as well. Technological developments made it clear that engines using computer-controlled throttles would become standard. As a result, designers might have decided to design new pedals from scratch; but they also would have had reason to make pre-existing pedals work with the new engines. Indeed, upgrading its own pre-existing model led KSR to design the pedal now accused of infringing the Engelgau patent.

For a designer starting with Asano, the question was where to attach the sensor. The consequent legal question, then, is whether a pedal designer of ordinary skill starting with Asano would have found it obvious to put the sensor on a fixed pivot point. The prior art discussed above leads us to the conclusion that attaching the sensor where both KSR and Engelgau put it would have been obvious to a person of ordinary skill.

The '936 patent taught the utility of putting the sensor on the pedal device, not in the engine. Smith, in turn, explained to put the sensor not on the pedal's footpad but instead on its support structure. And from the known wire-chafing problems of Rixon, and Smith's teaching that "the pedal assemblies must not precipitate any motion in the connecting wires," Smith, col. 1, lines 35-37, the designer would know to place the sensor on a nonmoving part of the pedal structure. The most obvious nonmoving point on the structure from which a sensor can easily detect the pedal's position is a pivot point. The designer, accordingly, would follow Smith in mounting the sensor on a pivot, thereby designing an adjustable electronic pedal covered by claim 4.

Just as it was possible to begin with the objective to upgrade Asano to work with a computer-controlled throttle, so too was it possible to take an adjustable electronic pedal like Rixon and seek an improvement that would avoid the wire-chafing problem. Following similar steps to those just explained, a designer would learn from Smith to avoid sensor movement and would come, thereby, to Asano because Asano disclosed an adjustable pedal with a fixed pivot.

Teleflex indirectly argues that the prior art taught away from attaching a sensor to Asano because Asano in its view is bulky, complex, and expensive. The only evidence Teleflex marshals in support of this argument, however, is the Radcliffe declaration, which merely indicates that Asano would not have solved Engelgau's goal of making a small, simple, and inexpensive pedal. What the declaration does not indicate is that Asano was somehow so flawed that there was no reason to upgrade it, or pedals like it, to be compatible with modern engines. Indeed, Teleflex's own declarations refute this conclusion. Dr. Radcliffe states that Rixon suffered from the same bulk and complexity as did Asano. Teleflex's other expert, however, explained that Rixon was itself designed by adding a sensor to a pre-existing mechanical pedal. If Rixon's base pedal was not too flawed to upgrade, then Dr. Radcliffe's declaration does not show Asano was either. Teleflex may have made a plausible argument that Asano is inefficient as compared to Engelgau's preferred embodiment, but to judge Asano against Engelgau would be to engage in the very hindsight bias Teleflex rightly urges must be avoided. Accordingly, Teleflex has not shown anything in the prior art that taught away from the use of Asano.

Like the District Court, finally, we conclude Teleflex has shown no secondary factors to dislodge the determination that claim 4 is obvious. Proper application of *Graham* and our other precedents to these facts therefore leads to the conclusion that claim 4 encompassed obvious subject matter. As a result, the claim fails to meet the requirement of § 103.

We need not reach the question whether the failure to disclose Asano during the prosecution of Engelgau voids the presumption of validity given to issued patents, for claim 4 is obvious despite the presumption. We nevertheless think it appropriate to note that the rationale underlying the presumption—that the PTO, in its expertise, has approved the claim—seems much diminished here.

IV

A separate ground the Court of Appeals gave for reversing the order for summary judgment was the existence of a dispute over an issue of material fact. We disagree with the Court of Appeals on this point as well. To the extent the court understood the *Graham* approach to exclude the possibility of summary judgment when an expert provides a conclusory affidavit addressing the question of obviousness, it misunderstood the role expert testimony plays in the analysis. In considering summary judgment on that question the district court can and should take into account expert testimony, which may resolve or keep open certain questions of fact. That is not the end of the issue, however. The ultimate judgment of obviousness is a legal determination. *Graham*, 383 U.S., at 17. Where, as here, the content of the prior art, the scope of the patent claim, and the level of ordinary skill in the art are not in material dispute, and the obviousness of the claim is apparent in light of these factors, summary judgment is appropriate. Nothing in the declarations proffered by Teleflex prevented the District Court from reaching the careful conclusions underlying its order for summary judgment in this case.

* * *

We build and create by bringing to the tangible and palpable reality around us new works based on instinct, simple logic, ordinary inferences, extraordinary ideas, and sometimes even genius. These advances, once part of our shared knowledge, define a new threshold from which innovation starts once more. And as progress beginning from higher levels of achievement is expected in the normal course, the results of ordinary innovation are not the subject of exclusive rights under the patent laws. Were it otherwise patents might stifle, rather than promote, the progress of useful arts. See U.S. Const., Art. I, §8, cl. 8. These premises led to the bar on patents claiming obvious subject matter established in *Hotchkiss* and codified in §103. Application of the bar must not be confined within a test or formulation too constrained to serve its purpose.

KSR provided convincing evidence that mounting a modular sensor on a fixed pivot point of the Asano pedal was a design step well within the grasp of a person of ordinary skill in the relevant art. Its arguments, and the record, demonstrate that claim 4 of the Engelgau patent is obvious. In rejecting the District Court's rulings, the Court of Appeals analyzed the issue in a narrow, rigid manner inconsistent with §103 and our precedents. The judgment of the Court of Appeals is reversed, and the case remanded for further proceedings consistent with this opinion.

PERFECT WEB TECHNOLOGIES, INC. v. INFOUSA, INC.

587 F.3d 1324 (Fed. Cir. 2009)

LINN, Circuit Judge.

Perfect Web Technologies, Inc. ("Perfect Web") appeals a summary judgment order holding that the asserted claims of its U.S. Patent No. 6,631,400 ("'400 patent") are invalid. Because we agree with the district court that the asserted claims would have been obvious, we *affirm*.

BACKGROUND

The '400 patent claims methods of managing bulk e-mail distribution to groups of targeted consumers. The '400 patent's application was filed on April 13, 2000, at a time when, according to the specification, the Internet was at an "early and fervent stage of development." '400 patent col.1 ll.25-27. The patent recognizes that "electronic mail (email) is an often used component of the Internet." *Id.* col.1 ll.27-28. In describing "opt-in bulk e-mailing services," the patent explains that distributors access lists of customers who express subject matter preferences for commercial e-mail. *Id.* col.1 l.56. The patented invention involves comparing the number of successfully delivered e-mail messages in a delivery against a predetermined desired quantity, and if the delivery does not reach the desired quantity, repeating the process of selecting and e-mailing a group of customers until the desired number of delivered messages has been achieved.

Perfect Web asserted claims 1, 2, 5, 11, 12, and 15 against InfoUSA, Inc. Independent claim 1 represents the asserted claims:

1. A method for managing bulk e-mail distribution comprising the steps:

   (A) matching a target recipient profile with a group of target recipients;

   (B) transmitting a set of bulk e-mails to said target recipients in said matched group;

   (C) calculating a quantity of e-mails in said set of bulk e-mails which have been successfully received by said target recipients; and

(D) if said calculated quantity does not exceed a prescribed minimum quantity of successfully received e-mails, repeating steps (A)-(C) until said calculated quantity exceeds said prescribed minimum quantity.

DISCUSSION

Obviousness

Obviousness is a question of law based on underlying findings of fact. The underlying factual inquiries are: (1) the scope and content of the prior art, (2) the differences between the prior art and the claims at issue, (3) the level of ordinary skill in the pertinent art, and (4) secondary considerations of nonobviousness. *KSR Int'l Co. v. Teleflex Inc.*, 550 U.S. 398 (2007) (citing *Graham v. John Deere Co.*, 383 U.S. 1, 17-18 (1966)).

The district court began its obviousness analysis by stating that the relevant art in the '400 patent is "the art of e-mail marketing," and that the person of ordinary skill in that art possessed "at least a high school diploma, one year of experience in the industry, and proficiency with computers and e-mail programs." It then found that the prior art and '400 patent specification showed that steps (A)-(C) of the claim 1 method were previously known. According to the court, "[t]he question then becomes whether e-mail marketers of ordinary skill would have repeated the first three steps to deliver a prescribed quantity of e-mail to targeted recipients," as called for in step (D). Citing the Supreme Court's teaching in KSR that "[a] person of ordinary skill is also a person of ordinary creativity, not an automaton," the court found step (D) obvious: "the final step is merely the logical result of common sense application of the maxim 'try, try again.'"

* * *

Perfect Web argues . . . that common sense or knowledge "must be rooted in evidence and factual findings," because they play "the same role as the inquiry into whether the prior art contains any teaching, suggestion or motivation ('TSM') that would have led a person of ordinary skill to produce the claimed invention." Perfect Web contends that the district court improperly viewed the invention through a hindsight-tinted lens, misconstrued step (D) to mean "try, try again," and discounted expert testimony that the patent was not a common-sense advance.

A. "COMMON SENSE"

In rejecting rigid application of the "teaching, suggestion, or motivation" test for obviousness, the Supreme Court observed that common sense can be a source of reasons to combine or modify prior art references to achieve the patented invention. In *KSR*, the Court offered guidance that has now been cited repeatedly:

> When there is a design need or market pressure to solve a problem and there are a finite number of identified, predictable solutions, a person of ordinary skill has good reason to pursue the known options within his or her technical grasp. If this leads to the anticipated success, it is likely the product not of innovation but of ordinary skill and *common sense*. In that instance the fact that a combination was obvious to try might show that it was obvious under § 103.

550 U.S. at 421 (emphasis added). While the Court warned against "the distortion caused by hindsight bias and . . . *ex post* reasoning," it also noted: "Common sense teaches . . . that familiar items may have obvious uses beyond their primary purposes, and in many cases a person of ordinary skill will be able to fit the teachings of multiple patents together like pieces of a puzzle." *Id.* at 420-21.

Common sense has long been recognized to inform the analysis of obviousness if explained with sufficient reasoning. . . . We explained that when the PTO rejects a patent for obviousness, it "must not only assure that the requisite findings are made, based on evidence of record, but must also explain the reasoning by which the findings are deemed to support the agency's conclusion." *In re Lee*, 277 F.3d 1338, 1344 (Fed. Cir. 2002). *Lee* recognized that even though common knowledge and common sense do not substitute for facts, "they may be applied to analysis of the evidence." *Id.* at 1345. At the time, we required the PTO to identify record evidence of a teaching, suggestion, or motivation to combine references because "[o]mission of a relevant factor required by precedent is both legal error and arbitrary agency action." *Id.* at 1344. However, this did not preclude examiners from employing common sense. More recently, we explained that that use of common sense does not require a "specific hint or suggestion in a particular reference," only a reasoned explanation that avoids conclusory generalizations. *DyStar Textilfarben GmbH v. C.H. Patrick Co.*, 464 F.3d 1356, 1366 (Fed. Cir. 2006); *see also In re Kahn*, 441 F.3d 977, 987 (Fed. Cir. 2006) (requiring "some rationale, articulation, or reasoned basis to explain why the conclusion of obviousness is correct"). And since *KSR*, this court has recognized that obviousness is not subject to a "rigid formula," and that "common sense of those skilled in the art demonstrates why some combinations would have been obvious where others would not." *Leapfrog Enters. v. Fisher-Price, Inc.*, 485 F.3d 1157, 1161 (Fed. Cir. 2007).

In counseling that courts "need not seek out precise teachings directed to the specific subject matter of the challenged claim," the Supreme Court clarified that courts may look to a wider diversity of sources to bridge the gap between the prior art and a conclusion of obviousness. *KSR*. We previously noted that "[t]he reason, suggestion, or motivation to combine may be found explicitly or implicitly: 1) in the prior art references themselves; 2) in the knowledge of those of ordinary skill in the art that certain references, or disclosures in those references, are of special interest or importance in the field; or 3) from the nature of the problem to be solved. . . ." *Ruiz v. A.B. Chance Co.*, 234 F.3d 654, 665 (Fed. Cir. 2000). *KSR* expanded the sources of information for a properly flexible obviousness inquiry to include market forces; design incentives; the "interrelated teachings of multiple patents"; "any need or problem known in the field of endeavor at the time of invention and addressed by the patent"; and the background knowledge, creativity, and common sense of the person of ordinary skill. 550 U.S. at 418-21.

When considering these sources, the Supreme Court remarked that "[r]igid preventative rules that deny factfinders recourse to common sense, however, are neither necessary under our case law nor consistent with it." *Id.* at 421. Thus, the Supreme Court instructed that factfinders may use common sense in addition to record evidence. As an example of this flexibility, *KSR* noted that courts should avoid "overemphasis on the importance of published articles and the explicit content of issued patents." *Id.* at 419. Nor are expert opinions always a prerequisite, for "[i]n many patent cases expert testimony will not be necessary because the technology will be easily understandable without the need for expert explanatory testimony." *Centricut, LLC v. Esab Group, Inc.*, 390 F.3d 1361, 1369 (Fed. Cir. 2004) (quotation omitted). We therefore hold that while an analysis of obviousness always depends on evidence that supports the required *Graham* factual findings, it also may include recourse to logic, judgment, and common sense available to the person of ordinary skill that do not necessarily require explication in any reference or expert opinion.

Although the obviousness analysis should "take account of the inferences and creative steps that a person of ordinary skill in the art would employ," the Supreme Court emphasized that this evidentiary flexibility does not relax the requirement that, "[t]o facilitate review, this analysis should be made explicit." *Id.* at 418 (citing *Kahn*). "[T]he analysis that 'should be made explicit' refers not to the teachings in the prior art of a motivation to combine, but to the court's analysis." *Ball Aerosol & Specialty Container, Inc. v. Ltd. Brands, Inc.*, 555 F.3d 984, 993 (Fed. Cir. 2009). We reiterate that, on summary judgment, to invoke "common sense" or any other basis for extrapolating from prior art to a conclusion of obviousness, a district court must articulate its reasoning with sufficient clarity for review.

In this case, we find that the predicate evidence on which the district court based its "common sense" reasoning appears in the record, namely the facts that step (D) merely involves repeating earlier steps, and that a marketer could repeat those steps, if desired. The district court also adequately explained its invocation of common sense. In claim 1, steps (A)-(C) involve targeting a group of recipients, sending e-mail to those recipients, and calculating the number of successfully delivered e-mails. Perfect Web concedes that prior art references disclose these three steps. Step (D), the only remaining step, recites "repeating steps (A)-(C) until said calculated quantity exceeds said prescribed minimum quantity." Thus, this last step, and the claim as a whole, simply recites repetition of a known procedure until success is achieved. Recognizing this, the district court explained: "If 100 e-mail deliveries were ordered, and the first transmission delivered only 95, common sense dictates that one should try again. One could do little else." If the relevant technology were complex, the court might require expert opinions. *E.g., Procter & Gamble Co. v. Teva Pharms. USA, Inc.*, 566 F.3d 989, 996-98 (Fed. Cir. 2009) (crediting expert testimony of unexpected results). Here, however, the parties agreed that ordinary skill in the relevant art required only a high school education and limited marketing and computer experience. No expert opinion is required to appreciate the potential value to persons of such skill in this art of repeating steps (A)-(C).

Comments

1. *An "Expansive and Flexible Approach" to the Obviousness Inquiry.* KSR is a cautious, although loosely structured, opinion that recalibrates the obviousness inquiry, rather than offering a new and sweeping articulation of obviousness jurisprudence. The principal concern the Supreme Court expressed with the Federal Circuit's TSM test was not the test itself, but the inflexible and formalistic manner in which the appeals court applied the test. As the

Court wrote, "[W]hen a court transforms the general principle into a rigid rule that limits the obviousness inquiry, as the Court of Appeals did here, it errs."

The Supreme Court stressed that it had consistently adopted an "expansive and flexible approach" to the obviousness inquiry and, interestingly, seemed to implicitly endorse the Federal Circuit's *Dystar* and *Alza* opinions (cited in *Perfect Web*), both of which touted the flexibility built into the TSM test. In *Dystar*, for instance, the Federal Circuit wrote "[o]ur suggestion test is in actuality quite flexible and not only permits, but *requires,* consideration of common knowledge and common sense." 464 F.3d at 1367 (emphasis in original). And in *Alza*, the court pointed out "[w]e do not have a rigid test that requires an actual teaching to combine before concluding that one of ordinary skill in the art would know to combine references." 464 F.3d 1291.* And the *Perfect Web* case fully embraces *KSR*'s "expansive and flexible" approach.

The prominent role played by the *Great Atlantic* case in *KSR* is also noteworthy as section 103 was a response—in part—to *Great Atlantic*, which was decided in 1950. *See* Comment 2 following *Hotchkiss* and Giles S. Rich, *Laying the Ghost of "Invention" Requirement,* in NONOBVIOUSNESS: THE ULTIMATE CONDITION OF PATENTABILTY (J. Witherspoon ed., 1980), at 1:508 (asserting "what persuaded [the drafters of section 103] to replace the case law with a statutory provision was the Supreme Court's opinion, and Mr. Justice Douglas' concurring opinion," in *Great Atlantic*). Indeed, as the introductory remarks in the beginning of this chapter note, section 103 was seen as cabining judicial authority. Yet the *KSR* Court explicitly stated "[n]either the enactment of §103 nor the analysis in *Graham* disturbed this Court's earlier instructions concerning the need for caution in granting a patent based on the combination of elements found in the prior art." 550 U.S. at 415. The Court, quoting from *Great Atlantic*, wrote, "For over a half century, the Court has held that a patent for a combination which only unites old elements with no change in their respective functions . . . obviously withdraws what is already known into the field of its monopoly and diminishes the resources available to skillful men." *Great Atlantic*, 340 U.S. at 152. Thus, according to *KSR*, a combination of known elements is likely to be obvious if the elements do "no more than yield predictable results." In this regard, is the TSM test arguably inapplicable? Does the Supreme Court imply a presumption of obviousness? Not necessarily.

The Court recognized that obviousness cannot be proved "merely by demonstrating that each of its elements was, independently, known in the prior art." Indeed, identifying the reason for the combination can be important "because inventions in most, if not all, instances rely upon building blocks long since uncovered, and claimed discoveries almost of necessity will be combinations of what, in some sense, is already known." (See Comment 3

---

* Both *Dystar* and *Alza* were decided after the Supreme Court granted certiorari in *KSR*. This fact was not lost on Justice Scalia, who during oral argument stated "in the last year or so, after we granted cert in this case after these decades of thinking about [the nonobviousness doctrine, the Federal Circuit] suddenly decides to polish it up." *KSR* Transcript of Oral Argument at 53; *see also id.* (setting forth Justice Breyer's comment suggesting that, in its recent case law, the Federal Circuit "so quickly modified itself" after it had decades to elaborate a standard of obviousness).

below for more on this point.) As the Federal Circuit noted in a post-*KSR* decision, "[a]s long as the [TSM] test is not applied as a 'rigid and mandatory' formula, that test can provide 'helpful insight' to an obviousness inquiry." *Takeda Chem. Indus. v. Alphapharm Pty., Ltd.*, 492 F.3d 1350, 1357 (Fed. Cir. 2007) (quoting *KSR*, 550 U.S. at 401).

2. ***So What Is the Test for Obviousness?*** The *Graham* factors, of course, provide the conceptual framework for an obviousness analysis, and the TSM test is viewed by the Federal Circuit as fitting comfortably within the fabric of *Graham*. And as the last paragraph of Comment 1 discusses, TSM still has an important role as long as its application is not rigidly applied. The *KSR* Court focused on broad themes such as the role of common sense, predictability, and the importance of the person having ordinary skill in the art (discussed in Comment 6 and section C.2, *infra*) that all form part of the "expansive and flexible approach" to section 103. But what is the test for obviousness after *KSR?*

The Federal Circuit captured the test this way: "Obviousness requires more than a mere showing that the prior art includes separate references covering each separate limitation in a claim under examination. *KSR*, 550 U.S. at 418. Rather, obviousness demands the additional showing that a person of ordinary skill at the time of the invention would have selected and combined those prior art elements in the normal course of research and development to yield the claimed invention. *Id.* at 421." *Unigene Laboratories, Inc. v. Apotex, Inc.*, 655 F.3d 1352, 1360 (Fed. Cir. 2011).

In *Perfect Web*, the court—while stressing the need for a district court to "articulate its reasoning with sufficient clarity for review"—noted that the examiner's analysis "may include recourse to logic, judgment, and common sense available to a person of ordinary skill that do not necessarily require explication in any reference or expert opinion." 587 F.3d at 1329. But the Federal Circuit has also cautioned against the "mere recitation of the words 'common sense' without any support." The term "common sense" as employed within the section 103 statutory framework "is a shorthand label for knowledge so basic that it certainly lies within the skill set of an ordinary artisan," and, therefore, an obviousness determination based on common sense knowledge must be grounded in evidence "showing that this knowledge would reside in the ordinarily skilled artisan." *Mintz v. Dietz & Watson, Inc.*, 679 F.3d 1372, 1377 (Fed. Cir. 2012). Common sense was at issue in *C.W. Zumbiel Co. v. Kappos*, 702 F.3d 1371 (Fed. Cir. 2012). In *Zumbiel*, the claimed invention related to a carton for dispensing cans by locating and engaging "finger flaps" at certain locations on the carton. The cans are dispensed one by one. The court held that while the independent claims were obvious, the dependent claims reciting a specific location of the finger flap on the carton was not taught by the prior art. The dissent criticized the majority for ignoring "pragmatic and common sense considerations that are so essential to the obviousness inquiry" as set forth by *KSR*. According to the dissent, "somebody else beat the patentee to his idea by almost fifty years."

And in *TriMed, Inc. v. Stryker Corp.*, 608 F.3d 1333 (Fed. Cir. 2010), the Federal Circuit described the obviousness test by noting *KSR* requires that we "ask whether the improvement is more than the predictable use of prior art elements according to their established functions." *Id.* at 1341. To answer this question necessitates several factual inquiries, such as the "interrelated teachings of multiple patents; the effects of demands known to the design community or present in the marketplace; and the background knowledge possessed by a person having ordinary skill in the art, all in order to determine whether there was an apparent reason to combine the known elements in the fashion claimed by the patent at issue." *Id.* Predictability was also a relevant factor in *Tokai Corp. v. Easton Enterprises, Inc.*, 632 F.3d 1358 (Fed. Cir. 2011). The patents related to safety utility lighters with extended lighting rods (think lighting BBQ). Specifically, the claims related to "automatic child-safety mechanisms for preventing accidental ignition," which was part of a crowded prior art field. In invalidating the patent, the court noted, "the components required to assemble the claimed inventions are 'simple mechanical parts that are well known in the art,'" and that the limitation not expressly recited in the prior art was "nothing more than a predictable variation." *Id.* at 1371. Citing *KSR*, the court wrote, "the nature of the mechanical arts is such that 'identified, predictable solutions' to known problems may be within the technical grasp of a skilled artisan." *Id.* The dissent, written by Judge Newman, stressed that "[i]n a crowded and competitive field . . . a modification that achieves a valuable improvement is of significance in view of the many entrants seeking commercial advantage. . . . [I]ncremental but unobvious improvements serve the public interest, and are included in the purpose of the patent incentive," citing *In re Hummer*, 241 F.2d 742, 744 (1957) ("[A]pplicant seeks a patent on only a narrow improvement. Progress is as important, however, in crowded arts as well as in those which are in the pioneer stage.").

Another factor weighing in favor of an obviousness finding is "simultaneous invention" by another party. In *Geo. M. Martin Co. v. Alliance Machine Systems International LLC*, 618 F.3d 1394 (Fed. Cir. 2010), the court—to support a finding of obviousness—relied on a third party's development of the claimed invention "only a year later than the earliest possible reduction-to-practice date of the claimed invention." According to the court, "[i]ndependently made, simultaneous inventions, made 'within a comparatively short space of time,' are persuasive evidence that the claimed apparatus 'was the product only of ordinary mechanical or engineering skill." *Id.* at 1305. The claimed invention was reduced to practice in 2001. There were three prior art references —Pallmac, Visy, and Tecasa—that were combined to invalidate the patent-in-suit. The Pallmac and Visy machines were in use in 1998 and 1996. But the Tecasa machine was first known in June 2002, and therefore, the patentee asserted the Tecasa machine was not a simultaneous invention. The Federal Circuit disagreed, stating the "district court was correct to conclude that the invention of the Tecasa machine, occurring only a year later than the earliest possible reduction-to-practice date of the claimed invention, qualified as a simultaneous invention." *Id.* at 1306.

The implications of using "simultaneous invention" as a basis for obviousness are potentially profound because there is evidence showing that an "overwhelming majority of inventions, including the overwhelming majority of so-called 'pioneering' inventions, are in fact developed by individuals or groups independently at roughly the same time." Mark A. Lemley, *The Myth of the Sole Inventor*, 110 MICH. L. REV. 709, 712 (2012) (discussing "multiple studies" showing prevalence of simultaneous invention). As William Robinson wrote in his well-known nineteenth-century treatise on patent law, "[m]en of the same genius, recognizing the same wants, skilled in the same arts, and familiar with the same defects in present methods of supply, might naturally be expected to arrive, at nearly the same time, at the same means of answering the public need; and experience amply justifies this expectation." WILLIAM C. ROBINSON, THE LAW OF PATENTS §29 (1890).

An inventor may also face section 103 challenges when the prior art identifies the problem addressed by the claimed invention. As *KSR* noted, "any need or problem known in the field of endeavor at the time of invention and addressed by the patent can provide a reason for combining the elements in the manner claimed." 550 U.S. at 421. In *Bayer Healthcare Pharmaceuticals, Inc. v. Watson Pharmaceuticals, Inc.*, 713 F.3d 1369 (Fed. Cir. 2013), the patent was invalidated based on prior art that identified the problem the patentee was attempting to solve. Indeed, it was the identification of the problem that provided the motivation to combine the prior art references.

3. *"Articulated Reasoning" for Obviousness Rejection Still Required.* While *KSR* found fault in the Federal Circuit's application of the TSM test, "[i]t remains necessary to show 'some articulated reasoning with some rational underpinning to support the legal conclusion of obviousness,' but such reasoning 'need not seek out precise teachings directed to the specific subject matter of the challenged claim.'" *Aventis Pharma Deutschland GmbH v. Lupin, Ltd.*, 499 F.3d 1293, 1301 (Fed. Cir. 2007). *See also In re Ravi Vaidyanathan*, ___ F.3d ___, 381 Fed. Appx. 985 (Fed. Cir. 2010) (stating "while *KSR* relaxed some of the formalism of earlier decisions requiring a 'teaching, suggestion, or motivation' to combine prior art references, it did not remove the need to anchor the analysis in explanation of how a person of ordinary skill would select and apply the teachings of the references").

When common sense, for instance, provides the basis for an obviousness finding on summary judgment, *Perfect Web* made clear that "a district court must articulate its reasoning with sufficient clarity for review." The *Perfect Web* court also held that expert testimony is not required to prove obviousness when technology is easily accessible and an obviousness finding based on "logic, judgment, and common sense" of a PHOSITA. When expert testimony is required, however, the testimony must provide enough detail and analysis to support an obviousness finding. In *Innogenetics, N.V. v. Abbott Laboratories*, 512 F.3d 1363 (Fed. Cir. 2008), the Federal Circuit held the accused infringer's expert testimony was insufficient to support a finding of obviousness. The court noted that the expert, Dr. Patterson, "merely lists a number of prior art references and then concludes with the stock phrase 'to one skilled in the art it would have been obvious to perform the genotyping method'" set forth in the patent-in-suit. *Id.* at 1373. After emphasizing the need for an "articulated reasoning" underlying an obviousness finding, the court stated "[n]owhere does Dr. Patterson state how or why a person ordinarily skilled in the art would have found the claims of the [patent-in-suit] obvious in light of some combination of those particular references." *Id.*

4. *"Reasonable Expectation of Success."* Another consideration embraced by the Federal Circuit, but not mentioned in *KSR*, is the "reasonable expectation of success" requirement. This requirement usually goes hand in hand with TSM. In numerous cases, the Federal Circuit has not only required a motivation to combine references, but once combined, has asked whether a person of ordinary skill in the art would have a reasonable expectation of success.

See Dystar, 464 F.3d at 1360. *See also Pfizer, Inc. v. Apotex, Inc.,* 480 F.3d 1348, 1361 (Fed. Cir. 2007) ("Subsumed within the *Graham* factors is a subsidiary requirement articulated by this court that where, as here, all claim limitations are found in a number of prior art references, the burden falls on the challenger of the patent to show by clear and convincing evidence that a skilled artisan would have been motivated to combine the teachings of the prior art references to achieve the claimed invention, and that the skilled artisan would have had a reasonable expectation of success in doing so."); *PharmaStem Therapeutics, Inc. v. ViaCell, Inc.,* 491 F.3d 1342 (Fed. Cir. 2007) (holding patent-in-suit obvious because the prior art would have given rise to reasonable expectation of success for person having ordinary skill in the art).

5. ***Hindsight and the Rationale of the TSM Test.*** Just as historians caution us not to read history backward or to contemporize historical figures and decisions, so too with an obviousness determination. Section 103 demands the decisionmaker to cast its mind back to the state of the art at the time the invention was made, and prevent its current familiarity with the invention from biasing the section 103 analysis. The TSM test was created by the Federal Circuit and the Court of Customs and Patent Appeals to guard against the use of hindsight reasoning by forcing this temporal shift. As such, the court views TSM as consistent with *Graham* and the Supreme Court's "recognition of 'the importance of guarding against hindsight.'" *Dystar,* 464 F.3d at 1361 (quoting *Graham,* 383 U.S. at 36). *See In re Dembiczak,* 175 F.3d 994, 999 (Fed. Cir. 1999) (stating "the best defense against the subtle but powerful attraction of hindsight-based obviousness analysis is the rigorous application of the requirement for a showing of the teaching or motivation to combine prior art references"). *See also* Gregory Mandel, *Patently Non-Obvious: Empirical Demonstration That the Hindsight Bias Renders Patent Decisions Irrational,* 67 OHIO ST. L.J. 1691 (2006) (finding substantial hindsight bias of mock jurors in nonobviousness determinations based on actually litigated patents). *Cf.* Glynn S. Lunney, Jr. & Christian Johnson, *Not So Obvious After All: Patent Law's Nonobviousness Requirement, KSR, and the Fear of Hindsight,* 47 GA. L. REV. 41 (2012) (questioning Mandel's findings of "bias"). For another interesting empirical study relating to hindsight and obviousness determinations, *see* Christopher A. Cotropia, *Nonobviousness and the Federal Circuit: An Empirical Analysis of Recent Case Law,* 82 NOTRE DAME L. REV. 911 (2007).

But *KSR* viewed the hindsight rationale skeptically, criticizing the Federal Circuit for drawing "the wrong conclusion from the risk of courts and patent examiners falling prey to hindsight bias." Interestingly, the Court did not elaborate a great deal on the hindsight issue even though it forms the basis for the TSM test. The Court simply wrote, "[r]igid preventative rules that deny factfinders recourse to common sense, however, are neither necessary under our case law nor consistent with it." *KSR* did not give the hindsight issue significant attention, or certainly, the attention it deserves. As noted above, the rationale for TSM was to guard against the 20-20 vision that accompanies hindsight. And this rationale still holds true in the post-*KSR* world, although the TSM doctrine is more flexibly applied. *See Ortho-McNeil Pharm., Inc. v. Mylan Laboratories, Inc.,* 520 F.3d 1358, 1354-1365 (Fed. Cir. 2008) ("[A] flexible TSM test remains the primary guarantor against a non-statutory hindsight analysis. . . ."); *In re Translogic Tech., Inc.,* 504 F.3d 1249,

1257 (Fed. Cir. 2007) ("[A]s the Supreme Court suggests, a flexible approach to the TSM test prevents hindsight and focuses on evidence before the time of invention.").

6. *The Creative (and Resuscitated) PHOSITA.* Of the criticisms commentators have levied against TSM, perhaps the most pronounced was the mechanical role assumed by the person having ordinary skill in the art. The *KSR* Court breathed new life into the PHOSITA, twice referring to the creativity of this skilled artisan. Recall, the Court stated a determination of obviousness should "take account of the inferences and creative steps that a person of ordinary skill in the art would employ," and that the "person of ordinary skill is also a person of ordinary creativity, not an automaton."

Indeed, two of the three appeals court errors identified by *KSR* related to the Federal Circuit's narrow conception of the skilled artisan. First, the Federal Circuit erred by focusing on the problem the patentee was trying to solve. The focus should not be on the patentee. Rather, the question is "whether the combination was obvious to a person with ordinary skill in the art. Under the correct analysis, any need or problem known in the field of endeavor at the time of invention and addressed by the patent can provide a reason for combining the elements in the manner claimed." The second error was the Federal Circuit's assumption that a PHOSITA, confronted with a problem, will only consult the prior art designed to solve the same problem. According to the Court, "[c]ommon sense teaches . . . that familiar items may have obvious uses beyond their primary purposes, and in many cases a person of ordinary skill will be able to fit the teachings of multiple patents together like pieces of a puzzle."

But the Court did not provide much guidance about how to construct the skilled artisan, and the Federal Circuit's pronouncements in this regard are few and far between. Perhaps the appeals court will now devote more attention to this issue, given PHOSITA's newfound star power. *See* Jonathan J. Darrow, *The Neglected Dimension of Patent Law's PHOSITA Standard*, 23 HARV. J.L. & TECH. 227 (2009) (discussing the evolving role of the PHOSITA in patent law). *See also* the *Daiichi* case in section C.2, for a more detailed discussion of the PHOSITA.

7. *The USPTO's Response to* **KSR**. Reflecting *KSR*'s decision and rationale, the USPTO's Manual of Patent Examining Procedure section 2141 cites the following as "exemplary rationales" upon which to base obviousness rejections:

> (A) Combining prior art elements according to known methods to yield predictable results;
>
> (B) Simple substitution of one known element for another to obtain predictable results;
>
> (C) Use of known technique to improve similar devices (methods, or products) in the same way;
>
> (D) Applying a known technique to a known device (method, or product) ready for improvement to yield predictable results;
>
> (E) "Obvious to try"—choosing from a finite number of identified, predictable solutions, with a reasonable expectation of success;

(F) Known work in one field of endeavor may prompt variations of it for use in either the same field or a different one based on design incentives or other market forces if the variations are predictable to one of ordinary skill in the art;

(G) Some teaching, suggestion, or motivation in the prior art that would have led one of ordinary skill to modify the prior art reference or to combine prior art reference teachings to arrive at the claimed inventions.

See http://www.uspto.gov/web/offices/pac/mpep/s2141.html. As part of these Guidelines, the agency created an updated version of its 2010 *KSR* Guidelines that contains a helpful table of cases that set forth "teaching points" for each post-*KSR* case. *See* http://www.uspto.gov/patents/law/exam/ksr_training_materials.jsp.

8. ***"Obvious to Try" Doctrine Discredited.*** The *KSR* Court was highly skeptical of the Federal Circuit's "obvious to try" jurisprudence. Comment 2 following *Teva* explores *KSR*'s skepticism and the Federal Circuit's response, particularly as expressed in the closely watched biotechnology case, *In re Kubin*.

For present purposes, it is important to note that the Federal Circuit has absorbed *KSR*'s skepticism, but situated the "obvious to try" doctrine in the context of the nature of science and technology at issue. For example, in *Abbott Laboratories v. Sandoz, Inc.*, 544 F3d 1341 (Fed. Cir. 2008), the court emphasized "*KSR* did not create a presumption that all experimentation in fields where there is already a background of useful knowledge is 'obvious to try.'" *Id.* at 1352. As such, "[e]ach case must be decided in its particular context, including the characteristics of the science or technology, its state of advance, the nature of the known choices, the specificity or generality of the prior art, and the predictability of results in the area of interest." *Id.*

9. ***Criticisms of* KSR.** Some commentators have questioned *KSR*'s disregard of Federal Circuit jurisprudence and have criticized the Court for dismantling the structural constraints of section 103 as envisioned by its drafters. *See* Rebecca Eisenberg, *The Supreme Court and the Federal Circuit: Visitation and Custody of Patent Law*, 106 Mich. L. Rev. First Impressions 28, 31 (2007) (stating "[b]y ignoring close to a quarter century of Federal Circuit decisions, the Court's *KSR* decision undermined the stability and predictability in patent law that Congress sought to achieve through the [creation of the Federal Circuit]. Moreover, by failing to situate its own decisions against a broader backdrop of Federal Circuit authorities, the Court missed an opportunity to clarify the implications of its decisions in a field of law that it visits infrequently"); Peter Lee, *Patent Law and Two Cultures*, 120 Yale L.J. 2, 66 (2010) (stating *KSR* "offers a smorgasbord of factors to consider in the nonobviousness determination, but it does not present them in a systematic, prioritized, or weighted manner"); Gregory N. Mandel, *Another Missed Opportunity: The Supreme Court's Failure to Define Nonobviousness or Combat Hindsight Bias in* KSR v. Teleflex, 12 Lewis & Clark L. Rev. 323, 326 (2008) (noting "[d]espite issuing eight opinions on the nonobviousness requirement, the Court has provided almost no guidance concerning the degree of ingenuity necessary to meet the . . . non-obvious standard or how a decision-maker is supposed to evaluate whether the differences between the invention and the prior art meet this degree"). *But see* Lee Petherbridge & R. Polk Wagner, *The Federal Circuit and Patentability: An Empirical Assessment of the Law of Obviousness*, 85

TEX. L. REV. 2051, 2106-2107 (2007) (stating "[o]n its face . . . the [*KSR*] opinion preserves the core principle that already guides the Federal Circuit's case law [and] [t]hus, while the . . . *KSR* . . . opinion may well muddy the waters of patentability for a time as the early obviousness cases work their way through the Federal Circuit, we do not expect that the case will work a serious upset to the settled expectations of the innovation community in the United States").

PROCTER & GAMBLE COMPANY v. TEVA PHARMACEUTICALS USA, INC.

566 F.3d 989 (Fed. Cir. 2009)

HUFF, District Judge.*

Teva Pharmaceuticals USA, Inc. ("Teva") appeals from a final judgment of the United States District Court for the District of Delaware in favor of The Procter & Gamble Company ("P&G") in three cases upholding the validity of P&G's U.S. Patent 5,583,122 (the "'122 patent"). After a bench trial and a stipulation for judgment in the related cases, the district court rejected Teva's invalidity defenses of obviousness. We affirm.

I. BACKGROUND

The '122 patent claims the compound risedronate, the active ingredient of P&G's osteoporosis drug Actonel®. In August 2004, P&G sued Teva for infringement of the '122 patent after Teva notified P&G that it planned to market risedronate as a generic equivalent of Actonel®. Specifically, P&G alleged that Teva's proposed drug infringed claim 4 of the '122 patent for the compound risedronate, claim 16 for pharmaceutical compositions containing risedronate, and claim 23 for methods of treating diseases using risedronate. In its defense, Teva argued that the '122 patent was invalid as obvious in light of P&G's expired U.S. Patent 4,761,406 (the "'406 patent"), filed on June 6, 1985 and issued on August 2, 1988.

Risedronate, the subject of the contested claims, is a member of a group of compounds referred to as bisphosphonates. Bisphosphonates, in general, are active in inhibiting bone resorption. The first two promising bisphosphonates studied for the treatment of metabolic bone diseases, etidronate (EHDP) and clodronate, had clinical problems which prevented their commercialization. P&G conducted a significant amount of experimentation involving hundreds of different bisphosphonate compounds, but could not predict the efficacy or toxicity of the new compounds. Eventually, researchers at P&G identified risedronate as a promising drug candidate.

On December 6, 1985, risedronate's inventors applied for a patent on the compound. P&G is the owner by assignment of the '122 patent, entitled "Pharmaceutical Compositions Containing Geminal Diphosphonates," which issued on December 10, 1996.

---

* Honorable Marilyn L. Huff, District Judge, United States District Court for the Southern District of California, sitting by designation.

Risedronate is neither claimed nor disclosed in the '406 patent. Instead, the '406 patent, entitled "Regimen for Treating Osteoporosis," claims an intermittent dosing method for treating osteoporosis. As the trial court noted, the '406 patent "addresses the central problem seen in bisphosphonates at the time, namely that they inhibited bone mineralization, by teaching the use of a cyclic administrative regimen to achieve a separation of the benign effect of anti-resorption from the unwanted side effect of anti-mineralization in patients." *Procter & Gamble*, 536 F. Supp. 2d at 492. The '406 patent lists thirty-six polyphosphonate molecules as treatment candidates and eight preferred compounds for intermittent dosing, including 2-pyr EHDP. Teva contends that the structural similarities between risedronate and 2-pyr EHDP render the challenged claims of the '122 patent obvious.

From the testimony at trial, the district court concluded that the '406 patent would not have led a person of ordinary skill in the art to identify 2-pyr EHDP as the lead compound. In light of the extremely unpredictable nature of bisphosphonates at the time of the invention, the district court also found that a person of ordinary skill in the art would not have been motivated to make the specific molecular modifications to make risedronate. The district court concluded that unexpected results of risedronate's potency and toxicity rebut a claim of obviousness. The district court found that secondary considerations of non-obviousness supported its conclusions.

II. Discussion

* * *

B. Patent Obviousness-Legal Standard

Under the U.S. Patent Act, an invention cannot be patented if "the subject matter as a whole would have been obvious at the time the invention was made to a person having ordinary skill in the art to which said subject matter pertains." 35 U.S.C. § 103(a). Patents are presumed to be valid. A party seeking to invalidate a patent based on obviousness must demonstrate "by clear and convincing evidence that a skilled artisan would have been motivated to combine the teachings of the prior art references to achieve the claimed invention, and that the skilled artisan would have had a reasonable expectation of success in doing so." *Pfizer, Inc. v. Apotex, Inc.*, 480 F.3d 1348, 1361 (Fed. Cir. 2007). Clear and convincing evidence places in the fact finder "an abiding conviction that the truth of [the] factual contentions are highly probable." *Colorado v. New Mexico*, 467 U.S. 310, 316 (1984).

The obviousness determination turns on underlying factual inquiries involving: (1) the scope and content of prior art, (2) differences between claims and prior art, (3) the level of ordinary skill in pertinent art, and (4) secondary considerations such as commercial success and satisfaction of a long-felt need. *Graham v. John Deere Co.* The Supreme Court has explained that the Federal Circuit's "teaching, suggestion or motivation" test provides helpful insight into the obviousness question as long as it is not applied rigidly. *KSR Int'l Co. v. Teleflex Inc.* Accordingly, under *KSR*, "it remains necessary to identify some reason that would have led a chemist to modify a known compound in a particular manner to establish prima facie obviousness of a new claimed compound." *Takeda Chem. Indus., Ltd. v. Alphapharm Pty., Ltd.*, 492 F.3d 1350, 1357 (Fed. Cir. 2007).

If a patent challenger makes a prima facie showing of obviousness, the owner may rebut based on "unexpected results" by demonstrating "that the claimed invention exhibits some superior property or advantage that a person of ordinary skill in the relevant art would have found surprising or unexpected." *In re Soni*, 54 F.3d 746, 750 (Fed. Cir. 1995). We consider the relevant factors in turn.

C. Identification of a Lead Compound

An obviousness argument based on structural similarity between claimed and prior art compounds "clearly depends on a preliminary finding that one of ordinary skill in the art would have selected [the prior art compound] as a lead compound." *Takeda*, 492 F.3d at 1359; *see also Eisai Co. Ltd. v. Dr. Reddy's Labs., Ltd.*, 533 F.3d 1353, 1359 (Fed. Cir. 2008) (stating that "post-*KSR*, a prima facie case of obviousness for a chemical compound still, in general, begins with the reasoned identification of a lead compound" in the prior art). Teva argues that the '406 patent identifies 2-pyr EHDP as the most promising molecule for the inhibition of bone resorption. The trial court disagreed and concluded from the evidence that a person of ordinary skill in the art would not have identified 2-pyr EHDP as a lead compound for the treatment of osteoporosis.

We need not reach this question because we conclude that even if 2-pyr EHDP was a lead compound, the evidence does not establish that it would have been obvious to a person of ordinary skill at the time of the invention to modify 2-pyr EHDP to create risedronate.

D. Obviousness of Risedronate in Light of the Prior Art

To decide whether risedronate was obvious in light of the prior art, a court must determine whether, at the time of invention, a person having ordinary skill in the art would have had "reason to attempt to make the composition" known as risedronate and "a reasonable expectation of success in doing so." *PharmaStem Therapeutics, Inc. v. ViaCell, Inc.*, 491 F.3d 1342, 1360 (Fed. Cir. 2007).

The district court concluded that, even if 2-pyr EHDP were a lead compound, it would not render the '122 patent's claims on risedronate obvious because a person having ordinary skill in the art would not have had reason to make risedronate based on the prior art. The district court's findings also support the conclusion that there could have been no reasonable expectation as to risedronate's success.

The question of obviousness "often turns on the structural similarities and differences between the claimed compound and the prior art compound[ ]." *Eisai Co. Ltd. v. Dr. Reddy's Labs., Ltd.*, 533 F.3d 1353, 1356-57 (Fed. Cir. 2008); *see also Sanofi-Synthelabo v. Apotex, Inc.*, 550 F.3d 1075, 1086 (Fed. Cir. 2008) ("Precedent establishes the analytical procedure whereby a close structural similarity between a new chemical compound and prior art compounds is generally deemed to create a prima facie case of obviousness. . . ."); *In re Mayne*, 104 F.3d 1339, 1343 (Fed. Cir. 1997) ("Structural relationships often provide the requisite motivation to modify known compounds to obtain new compounds."). In this case, risedronate and 2-pyr EHDP are positional isomers; they each contain the same atoms arranged in different ways. In risedronate, the hydroxy-ethanediphosphonate group is connected to the # 3 carbon of a pyridine ring, while in 2-pyr EHDP, the hydroxy-ethane-diphosphonate group is connected to the # 2 carbon. Because the nitrogen atom is in a different position in the two molecules, they differ in three dimensional shape, charge distribution and hydrogen bonding properties.

To successfully argue that a new compound is obvious, the challenger may show "that the prior art would have suggested making the specific molecular modifications necessary to achieve the claimed invention." *Takeda*, 492 F.3d at 1356. "In keeping with the flexible nature of the obviousness inquiry, the requisite motivation [to modify] can come from any number of sources." *Eisai*, 533 F.3d at 1357. Thus, in addition to structural similarity between the compounds, a prima facie case of obviousness may be shown by "adequate support in the prior art" for the change in structure. As we noted in *Takeda*:

> A known compound may suggest its homolog, analog, or isomer because such compounds often have similar properties and therefore chemists of ordinary skill would ordinarily contemplate making them to try to obtain compounds with improved properties. . . . [However,] it remains necessary to identify some reason that would have led a chemist to modify a known compound in a particular manner to establish prima facie obviousness of a new claimed compound.

492 F.3d at 1356-57.

At trial, P&G's expert witnesses testified that, in 1985, a person having ordinary skill in the art realized that the properties of bisphosphonates could not be anticipated based on their structure. Additionally, the trial court relied on contemporaneous writings from Herbert Fleisch, the preeminent authority on bisphosphonates during the relevant time period. Dr. Fleisch wrote in 1984 that "every compound, while remaining a bisphosphonate, exhibits its own physical-chemical, biological and therapeutic characteristics, so that each bisphosphonate has to be considered on its own. To infer from one compound the effects in another is dangerous and can be misleading." Herbert Fleisch, *Chemistry and Mechanisms of Action of Bisphosphonates*, in Bone Resorption, Metastasis, and Diphosphonates 33-40 (S. Garattini ed., 1985). In this case, P&G synthesized and tested 2-pyr EHDP, risedronate (3-pyr EHDP) and 4-pyr EHDP, another structural isomer. Confirming the unpredictability of bisphosphonates, test results for 4-pyr EHDP revealed that it was not active in inhibiting bone resorption despite its close relationship with potent compounds. In light of the Supreme Court's instruction in *KSR*, the Federal Circuit has stated that, "[t]o the extent an art is unpredictable, as the chemical arts often are, *KSR*'s focus on 'identified, predictable solutions' may present a difficult hurdle because potential solutions are less likely to be genuinely predictable." *Eisai*, 533 F.3d 1353, 1359 (quoting *KSR*). The district court found that Teva failed to clear that hurdle, establishing insufficient motivation for a person of ordinary skill to synthesize and test risedronate. This finding was not clearly erroneous.

Additionally, there was an insufficient showing that a person of ordinary skill in the art would have had a "reasonable expectation of success" in synthesizing and testing risedronate. In *KSR*, the Supreme Court stated that when an obvious modification "leads to the anticipated success," the invention is likely the product of ordinary skill and is obvious under 35 U.S.C. §103. "[O]bviousness cannot be avoided simply by a showing of some degree of unpredictability in the art so long as there was a reasonable probability of success." *Pfizer*, 480 F.3d at 1364. Here, the district court's findings indicate that there was no reasonable expectation in 1985 that risedronate would be a successful compound.

Cases following *KSR* have considered whether a given molecular modification would have been carried out as part of routine testing. *See, e.g., Takeda,* 492 F.3d at 1360 (discussing the district court's finding that a modification was not known to be beneficial and was not considered "routine"). When a person of ordinary skill is faced with "a finite number of identified, predictable solutions" to a problem and pursues "the known options within his or her technical grasp," the resulting discovery "is likely the product not of innovation but of ordinary skill and common sense." *KSR,* 127 S. Ct. at 1742. So too, "[g]ranting patent protection to advances that would occur in the ordinary course without real innovation retards progress." *Id.* at 1741. In other cases, though, researchers can only "vary all parameters or try each of numerous possible choices until one possibly arrive[s] at a successful result, where the prior art [gives] either no indication of which parameters [are] critical or no direction as to which of many possible choices is likely to be successful." *In re O'Farrell,* 853 F.2d 894, 903 (Fed. Cir. 1988). In such cases, "courts should not succumb to hindsight claims of obviousness." *In re Kubin,* 561 F.3d 1351 (Fed. Cir. 2009). Similarly, patents are not barred just because it was obvious "to explore a new technology or general approach that seemed to be a promising field of experimentation, where the prior art gave only general guidance as to the particular form of the claimed invention or how to achieve it." *In re O'Farrell,* 853 F.2d at 903.

In this case, there is no credible evidence that the structural modification was routine. The district court found that the appellee's expert was evasive on this topic, stating that the witness "did not directly respond to most questions posed to him about whether it would be common for a chemist who develops a pyridine compound to conceive of and make [2-pyr EHDP, 3-pyr EHDP, and 4-pyr EHDP] isomers." *Procter & Gamble,* 536 F. Supp. 2d at 486. But evidence of evasion is not necessarily evidence that the testimony would otherwise have been favorable. The only direct evidence that the structural modification was routine was presented by an expert witness that the district court judge discredited.[1]

Accordingly, we conclude that the district court did not clearly err in finding that Teva had not established a prima facie case of obviousness as to the challenged claims of the '122 patent.

E. Unexpected Results

The district court found that, even if Teva could establish a prima facie case of obviousness, P&G had introduced sufficient evidence of unexpected results to rebut such a showing. Such evidence included "test data showing that the claimed composition[ ] possess[es] unexpectedly improved properties or properties that the prior art does not have." *In re Dillon,* 919 F.2d 688, 692-93 (Fed. Cir. 1990). Because Teva did not establish a prima facie case of obviousness, P&G need not rely on this evidence to defend the '122 patent.

Nonetheless, we note that P&G's witnesses consistently testified that the properties of risedronate were not expected. For example, Dr. Benedict testified that

---

1. Appellant's expert testified that "if someone was aware that [2-pyr EHDP] was safe and effective, they would immediately in terms of the drug discovery effort, make the [3-pyr EHDP]." However, the district court concluded that this witness "had no specialized experience in the area of bisphosphonates" aside from his preparation to testify in the litigation. *Procter & Gamble,* 536 F. Supp. 2d at 480. Additionally, the expert prepared his opinion by reviewing drug profiles in the current version of the Physician's Desk Reference instead of drug profiles from the relevant time, causing his opinions to be "marred by hindsight." *Id.* at 495.

he and other researchers did not predict the potency of risedronate. Ms. McOsker testified that she was "very surprised" by the low dose at which risedronate was effective. Dr. Miller stated that the superior properties of risedronate were unexpected and could not have been predicted. In a test to determine the lowest dose at which these compounds caused toxic reactions, risedronate outperformed 2-pyr EHDP by a substantial margin. Risedronate showed no observable toxic effect at a dose of 0.75 mg P/kg/day, while 2-pyr EHDP's "no observable effect level" was only 0.25 mg P/kg/day. In another test involving live animals, 2-pyr EHDP was lethal at a dose of 1.0 mg P/kg/day while risedronate was not. Ultimately, the district court weighed the evidence and evaluated the credibility of the witnesses in concluding that P&G had introduced sufficient evidence of unexpected results to rebut any finding of obviousness.

* * *

Comments

1. *Obviousness and Structural Similarity.* P&G, the patentee in *Teva*, claimed the compound risedronate, which was the active ingredient of P&G's osteoporosis drug Actonel®. Pharmaceuticals are small-molecule compounds; and small-molecule chemistry (and chemistry more broadly, particularly organic chemistry) implicates the doctrine of structural similarity in the context of nonobviousness jurisprudence. In the chemical arts, structural similarity between a prior art compound and the claimed compound may lead to a prima facie case of obviousness because structurally similar compounds (e.g., homologs, analogs, and isomers to the prior art) usually possess similar properties. *See In re Payne*, 606 F.2d 303, 313 (CCPA 1979) ("An obviousness rejection based on similarity in chemical structure and function entails the motivation of one skilled in the art to make a claimed compound, in the expectation that compounds similar in structure will have similar properties."); *Sanofi-Synthelabo v. Apotex, Inc.*, 550 F.3d 1075, 1086 (Fed. Cir. 2008) ("Precedent establishes the analytical procedure whereby a close structural similarity between a new chemical compound and prior art compounds is generally deemed to create a prima facie case of obviousness.").

   As *Teva* illustrates, the role of "predictability" is particularly relevant when determining obviousness of chemical inventions. This is because the combination of chemicals can yield unpredictable results, in contrast to, for example, mechanical inventions. In *Takeda Chemical Industries, Ltd. v. Alphapharm Pty., Ltd.*, 492 F.3d 1350 (Fed. Cir. 2007), the court noted that "normally a prima facie case of obviousness is based on structural similarity," yet despite the existence of structural similarity between the claimed compound and a prior art compound, the court held the claimed compound was nonobvious. This decision was based on a lack of motivation for a PHOSITA to select and modify the compound as claimed. In other words, the claimed invention functioned in an unpredictable manner (the lead compound had toxic properties and a PHOSITA would have no reason to select it). And in *Eisai Co. v. Dr. Reddy's Laboratories, Ltd.*, 533 F.3d 1353 (Fed. Cir. 2008), the court focused on the unpredictability of the chemical arts in finding the claimed invention nonobvious. As the court noted, "[t]o the extent an art is unpredictable, as the chemical arts often are, *KSR*'s focus on these 'identified, predictable solutions' may present a difficult hurdle because potential solutions are less likely to be genuinely predictable." *Id.* at 1359. *See also Ortho-McNeil Pharmaceutical, Inc. v. Teva Pharmaceutical Industries, Ltd.,* 344 Fed. Appx. 595, 601 (Fed. Cir. 2009) (stating the patentee "can rebut the prima facie case if it can show that the prior art teaches away from the claimed range, or the claimed range produces new and unexpected properties").

   Teva relied on both *Takeda* and *Eisai.* In *Teva,* the risedronate compound differed structurally from the prior art 2-pyr EHDP in "three dimensional shape, charge distribution and hydrogen bonding properties." Bisphosphonates are unpredictable, and the "properties of bisphosphonates could not be anticipated based on their structure." Moreover, the prior art did not suggest to a person of ordinary skill in the art to modify the prior art compound; and therefore, a PHOSITA would not have a reasonable expectation of success in synthesizing and testing risedronate. In other words, contrary to "a finite number of identified, predictable solutions" as noted in *KSR,* there was nothing in *Teva* to suggest that molecular modification was routine or susceptible to common sense. In fact, Dr. Benedict testified that the potency of risedronante was unpredictable and unexpected. And Ms. McOsker asserted she was "very surprised" at the efficacy of the low dosage risedronate.

2. ***Biotechnology and the "Obvious to Try" Doctrine After* KSR.** Prior to *KSR,* the Federal Circuit repeatedly held that "obvious to try" is not the standard under section 103. This position held true in all technological fields, but has had a particular salience in biotechnology. For instance, in *In re Deuel,* 51 F.3d 1552 (Fed. Cir. 1995), the Federal Circuit reversed the decision of the Board of Patent Appeals and Interferences that found obvious a claim to a DNA molecule encoding a particular protein. The Board based its decision on a prior art reference teaching a method of gene cloning, together with a reference disclosing a partial amino acid sequence of a protein. According to the Federal Circuit:

> A prior art disclosure of the amino acid sequence of a protein does not necessarily render particular DNA molecules encoding the protein obvious . . . ; and the existence of a general method of isolating cDNA or DNA molecules is essentially irrelevant to the question whether the specific molecules themselves would have been obvious, in the absence of other prior art that suggests the claimed DNAs.

Deuel, 51 F.3d at 1559.

   In *KSR,* however, the Supreme Court cast doubt on the Federal Circuit's "obvious to try" standard. This skepticism is reflected in the important post-*KSR* Federal Circuit biotechnology case, *In re Kubin,* 561 F.3d 1351 (Fed. Cir. 2009). In *Kubin,* the claimed invention related to DNA molecules encoding for the protein known as the Natural Killer Cell Activation Inducing Ligand ("NAIL")—a protein that plays a role in immunological responses. *Kubin* represents "a classic biotechnology invention—the isolation and sequencing of a human gene that encodes for a particular . . . protein." 561 F.3d at 1352. Knowledge of a DNA sequence (i.e., gene) provides the blue print for a particular protein, which is comprised of a series of amino acids; but the reverse is not always true. That is, knowledge of the amino acid sequence does not correspond directly to a singular DNA sequence. As such, a given protein can be encoded by several DNA sequences whereas a given DNA sequence only encodes for a singular protein. This phenomenon is known as "degeneracy." But through the use of recombinant DNA and cloning technologies, a person of ordinary skill in the art may isolate (although not predict because of the "degenerate" genetic code) the protein's encoding DNA molecule.

In *Kubin*, the specification recited an amino acid sequence of the NAIL protein. The issue the court addressed was whether it was obvious to a person of ordinary skill in the art to isolate the gene that encoded for the NAIL protein. There were two principal prior art references. The Valiante reference disclosed what was deemed to be the same protein as NAIL, and, while not disclosing the amino acid sequence, taught that the DNA and protein sequences of the claimed invention "may be obtained by resort to conventional methodologies known to one of skill in the art." The other significant reference was a book by Sambrook that—while not disclosing any particular gene—provided detailed instructions on cloning materials and techniques.

The Board rejected Kubin's claims as obvious based on the combined teachings of the Valiante patent and the Sambrook book. According to the Board, Kubin used "conventional techniques 'such as those outlined in Sambrook' to isolate and sequence the gene that codes for NAIL." *Id.* at 1354. Moreover, because the NAIL protein plays an important role in the human immune response, "the Board further found that 'one of ordinary skill in the art would have recognized the value of isolating NAIL cDNA, and would have been motivated to apply conventional methodologies, such as those disclosed in Sambrook and utilized in Valiante, to do so.'" *Id.* at 1355.

The Federal Circuit affirmed the Board. The court expressly noted that *KSR* "unambiguously discredited" *Deuel*'s understanding of the "obvious to try" doctrine. *Id.* at 1358. Recall, *KSR* wrote:

> When there is a design need or market pressure to solve a problem and there are a finite number of identified, predictable solutions, a person of ordinary skill has good reason to pursue the known options within his or her technical grasp. If this leads to the anticipated success, it is likely the product not of innovation but of ordinary skill and common sense. In that instance the fact that a combination was obvious to try might show that it was obvious under § 103.

KSR, 550 U.S. at 421. With this language in mind, the Federal Circuit looked to its 1988 decision in *In re O'Farrell*, 853 F.2d 894, 903 (Fed. Cir. 1988), and the question posed by that court: "When is an invention that was obvious to try nevertheless nonobvious?"

Relying on *O'Farrell*, the *Kubin* court provided an answer to this question by identifying four "obvious to try" scenarios: two of which where the "obvious to try" doctrine may not be applied (as in *Teva*), and two where application is permissible to support an obviousness rejection. For example:

> [1] what would have been "obvious to try" would have been to vary all parameters or try each of numerous possible choices until one possibly arrived at a successful result, where the prior art gave either no indication of which parameters were critical or no direction as to which of many possible choices is likely to be successful; [or]

> [2] what was "obvious to try" was to explore a new technology or general approach that seemed to be a promising field of experimentation, where the

prior art gave only general guidance as to the particular form of the claimed invention or how to achieve it.

Kubin, 561 F.3d at 1360 (quoting *In re O'Farrell*). According to the court, the aforementioned scenarios are akin to throwing "metaphorical darts at a board filled with combinatorial prior art possibilities." *Id.*

In contrast, an obviousness finding is appropriate where the

> [1] prior art "contained *detailed enabling methodology* for practicing the claimed invention, [2] a suggestion to modify the prior art to practice the claimed invention, and [3] evidence suggesting that [a person of ordinary skill in the art would have] *a reasonable expectation of success.*"

Id. (quoting *In re O'Farrell*) (emphasis in original). According to the *Kubin* court, "*KSR* reinvigorated this perceptive analysis." *Id.* As such, from a broader doctrinal perspective, the Federal Circuit sought to marry the rationales of *KSR* and *O'Farrell.*

The *Teva* court expressly relied on *O'Farrell* in finding "there is no credible evidence that the structural modification was routine," and therefore, the claimed invention was nonobvious. But in *Kubin*, the court noted the routine nature of isolating and sequencing a DNA molecule that encodes for a particular protein. In fact, Kubin employed a conventional technique; and the NAIL protein was known in the prior art as playing an important role in human immune response. *See* Rebecca S. Eisenberg, *Pharma's Nonobvious Problem*, 12 LEWIS & CLARK L. REV. 375, 404 (2008) (stating "[w]ith knowledge of even a partial amino acid sequence and standard cloning techniques, a geneticist would have constructed nucleotide probes to find a corresponding cDNA molecule in a cDNA library, with a great expectation of success").

What are the implications of *Kubin*? What advice would you provide to a client who was claiming an invention relating to DNA sequencing of a known protein? Why didn't an "obvious to try" argument work for Teva in *Procter & Gamble*? Did the USPTO lawyers do something right in *Kubin* that the Teva's lawyers failed to do? Or was the procedural posture determinative; namely, Procter & Gamble enjoyed a presumption of validity, whereas Kubin's patent application did not?

Kubin represents the evolving nature of biotechnology. The nonobvious hurdle will become increasingly more difficult to surmount as biotechnological techniques become more sophisticated and knowledge more nuanced. *See In re Droge*, 695 F.3d 1334, 1338 (Fed. Cir. 2012) (affirming USPTO rejection of patent application claiming methods for sequencing specific recombination of DNA in eukaryotic cell based on prior art related to bacteria cells, citing *Kubin* for the proposition, "[o]bviousness does not require absolute predictability of success . . . all that is required is a reasonable expectation of success"). Indeed, this holds true for all technologies, as what constitutes a sufficient leap from the prior art will always be in flux. Recall the Federal Circuit's remarks in *Abbott Laboratories* (Comment 8 following *Perfect Web*) that the "obvious to try" doctrine must be considered in the light of "the nature of the science or technology." 544 F.3d at 1352.

But in *Unigene Laboratories, Inc. v. Apotex, Inc.*, 655 F.3d 1352 (Fed. Cir. 2011), the Federal Circuit relied on the aforementioned *KSR* language about design need and market pressure in finding a patent on a pharmaceutical product not invalid. The court began by noting that "most inventions that are obvious were also obvious to try." *Id.* at 1361. Only if a PHOSITA has "a good reason to pursue the known options" will the combination be obvious to try. *Id.* (citing *KSR,* 550 U.S. at 421). Relying on *O'Farrell,* as the court did in *Kubin,* the court wrote: "When a field is 'unreduced by direction of the prior art,' and when prior art gives 'no indication of which parameters were critical or no direction as to which of many possible choices is likely to be successful,' an invention is not obvious to try." *Bayer Schering Pharma AG v. Barr Laboratories, Inc.,* 575 F.3d 1341, 1347 (Fed. Cir. 2009) (citing *In re O'Farrell*).

The patents in *Unigene* related to oral salmon calcitonin products ('014 patent) and a nasal spray formulation with the same active ingredient ('392 patent). The patentee, Unigene, also received a reissue patent of the '392. Unigene obtained FDA approval to market Fortical, a product based on the '392 and reissue patents. The approval was based, in part, on Unigene's claiming bioequivalency with Miacalcin, a product marketed by Novartis since 1995. The bioequivalency resulted from both drugs having the same active ingredient (salmon calcitonin) in the same concentration. But there was an important difference between Fortical and Miacalcin, namely the latter used benzalkonium chloride (BZK) as a preservative, absorption enhancer, and surfactant, whereas Fortical used three separate ingredients to achieve the same purposes, including 20mM citric acid as the absorption enhancer, pH stabilizer, and buffer.

The court noted that bioequivalency encourages replication of active ingredients, but stressed the "significant differences" in the prior art that would not lead a PHOSITA to use citric acid. *Id.* at 1363. In fact, some prior art taught away from the use of citric acid for absorption and stabilizing purposes. According to the court, while "design need and market pressure may dictate a commonsensical path using a finite number of identified predictable solutions to one of ordinary skill, deviations from that path are likely products of innovations." *Id.* at 1361. Although "the patent claims a new composition or formulation to deliver an FDA-approved active ingredient, . . . the claimed invention is not obvious if a person of ordinary skill would not select and combine the prior art references to reach the claimed composition or formulation." *Id.* Using citric acid was a sufficient deviation to support a finding of nonobviousness.

POLICY PERSPECTIVE
Using Section 103 as a Policy Tool

Within the parameters established by section 103, there resides a significant subjective component. As the *Graham* Court observed, "[w]hat is obvious is not a question upon which there is likely to be uniformity of thought in every given factual context." This subjectivity, however, allows section 103 to be used as a policy instrument to further the constitutional goal of promoting the progress of the useful arts. In this regard, the nonobviousness inquiry can be viewed as serving a "gatekeeper function," suggesting section 103 has a policy richness that is absent from section 102 and many other Title 35 statutory sections.

Some commentators see in section 103 fertile ground to further important functions of the patent system based on costs and uncertainly of invention. For instance, in an influential article, Edmund Kitch — concerned about over-rewarding inventive activity — suggested section 103 should reward patents for those innovations that would not have been developed "absent the protection of a patent." *See* Edmund W. Kitch, *Graham v. John Deere: New Standards for Patents*, 1966 SUP. CT. REV. 293, 301. As the Court in *Graham* noted, the nonobviousness requirement is designed to limit patent protection to those inventions "which would not be disclosed or devised but for the inducement of a patent." *Graham v. John Deere Co.*, 383 U.S. 1, 11 (1966). Kitch is not only concerned with costs of invention, but also a lack of value in the invented item. Once the market signals value, the idea in waiting may "be discovered more or less simultaneously by a number of those who can exploit it." WILLIAM M. LANDES & RICHARD A. POSNER, THE ECONOMIC STRUCTURE OF INTELLECTUAL PROPERTY LAW 304 (2003). In addition (and related) to costs, uncertainty plays an important role in invention, particularly if tackling uncertainty is a costly endeavor. Robert Merges, whose work builds on Kitch's insights, has argued that the nonobviousness requirement should act "as a legal rule that influences behavior" and "encourage[] researchers to pursue projects whose success appears highly uncertain at the outset." *See* Robert P. Merges, *Uncertainty and the Standard of Patentability*, 7 BERKELEY HIGH TECH. L.J. 1, 2 (1992). *See also* Kenneth J. Arrow, *Economic Welfare and the Allocation of Resources for Invention*, in THE RATE AND DIRECTION OF INVENTIVE ACTIVITY: ECONOMIC AND SOCIAL FACTORS 609, 610-614 (1962). Thus, Merges views section 103 as a tool to focus on those inventors who need the inducement of the patent system the most — to develop and disclose innovations whose success is rife with early-stage uncertainty. As Landes and Posner note, "[u]ncertainty implies the likelihood of failure en route to success. Those failures are costly, and since the costs are incurred before the successful invention can be patented and marketed, they are additional costs that the inventor must recover in the revenues generated by his patent." LANDES & POSNER, ECONOMIC STRUCTURE, *supra*, at 304.

Lastly, Dan Burk and Mark Lemley have advocated using the flexibility inherent in constructing the level of skill in the art possessed by a PHOSITA as a "policy lever" to tailor §103 (and other statutory sections) to the needs of divergent industries. *See* Dan L. Burk & Mark A. Lemley, *Policy Levers in Patent Law*, 89 VA. L. REV. 1575, 1648-1652 (2003). It is indeed somewhat surprising that there are very few judicial opinions that offer a detailed analysis of level of ordinary skill in the art, but this may all change in the light of *KSR*.

COMPARATIVE PERSPECTIVE
Section 103's European Counterpart— "Inventive Step"

The notion that something more than novelty is required for purposes of patentablity is shared by several patent systems throughout the world. In Europe, it is called "inventive step," and finds expression in Article 56 of the European Patent Convention:

> An invention shall be considered as involving an inventive step if, having regard to the state of the art, it is not obvious to a person skilled in the art. If the state of the art also includes documents within the meaning of Article 54, paragraph 3, these documents are not to be considered in deciding whether there has been an inventive step.

The European Patent Office ("EPO") defines "obvious" in Art. 56 as "that which does not go beyond the normal progress of technology but merely follows plainly or logically from the prior art, i.e., something which does not involve the exercise of any skill or ability beyond that to be expected of the person skilled in the art." EPO Guidelines for Examination on § 11.4 (April 11, 2010). The doctrines of nonobviousness and inventive step naturally have much in common, but there are also differences. Most notably, the Europeans and European Patent Office have adopted what is referred to as the "problem and solution approach" to Article 56. As Lionel Bently and Brad Sherman write:

> [R]ather than asking whether an invention is obvious, the European Patent Office asks whether the solution that an invention provides to the problem being addressed would have been obvious to the person skilled in the art. In more positive terms, this means that for an invention to be patentable, the solution must *not* have been obvious to the person skilled in the art at the priority date of the invention in question.

LIONEL BENTLY & BRAD SHERMAN, INTELLECTUAL PROPERTY LAW 440-441 (Oxford 2001) (emphasis in original). The EPO Guidelines set forth "three main stages" of the problem and solution approach: "(i) determining the 'closest prior art'; (ii) establishing the 'objective technical problem' to be solved; and (iii) considering whether or not the claimed invention, starting from the closest prior art and the objective technical problem, would have been obvious to the skilled person," EPO Guidelines for Examination § 11.5. For this approach to be applied properly, the inventor is required to disclose his claimed invention "in such a way that the technical problem or problems, with which it deals can be appreciated and the solution can be understood." *Id* at § 4.5.

In section 3 of the U.K. Patent Act, "[a]n invention shall be taken to involve an inventive step if it is not obvious to a person skilled in the art." The U.K. has developed a four-part obviousness test that resembles the U.S. approach:

> The first is to identify the inventive concept embodied in the patent in suit. Thereafter, the court has to assume the mantle of the normally skilled but unimaginative addressee in the art at the priority date and to impute to him

what was, at that date, common general knowledge in the art in question. The third step is to identify what, if any, differences exist between the matter cited as being "known or used" and the alleged invention. Finally, the court has to ask itself whether, viewed without any knowledge of the alleged invention, those differences constitute steps which would have been obvious to the skilled man or whether they require any degree of invention.

Windsurfing International Inc. v. Tabur Marine (Great Britain) Ltd., [1985] R.P.C. 59, 73-74. In *Haberman v. Jackal*, [1999] FSR 685, J. Laddie refined the analysis by adding several questions to the obviousness analysis, including (1) What was the problem which the patented development addressed; (2) How long had that problem existed; (3) How significant was the problem seen to be; and (4) How widely known was the problem and how many were likely to be seeking a solution. *Id.* at 699-701.

After *KSR*, the European problem and solution approach becomes problematic, because under *KSR* an applicant citing a problem opens himself up a section 103 rejection. Recall the Court stated, "any need or problem known in the field of endeavor at the time of invention and addressed by the patent can provide a reason for combining the elements in the manner claimed." During the European prosecution process, will applicants feel comfortable emphasizing the claimed invention solved a particular problem, knowing that the U.S. employs a broader scope of inquiry?

2. Constructing the Person Having Ordinary Skill in the Art

The person having ordinary skill in art is one of the cynosures of the American patent system and is valued, particularly after *KSR*, for his technical knowledge and the underlying assumptions and problems present in his technological community. How the PHOSITA is constructed and his level of skill in the art as determined by the court can greatly affect validity determinations and, as noted in the prior Policy Perspective—Using Section 103 as a Policy Tool, can be a valuable policy tool for courts. The *Daiichi* case reflects just how important the PHOSITA issue can be to an obviousness inquiry.

DAIICHI SANKYO CO., LTD. v. APOTEX, INC.

501 F.3d 1254 (Fed. Cir. 2007)

ARCHER, Senior Circuit Judge.

Apotex, Inc. and Apotex Corp. (collectively "Apotex") appeal the judgment of the United States District Court for the District of New Jersey that Apotex infringes U.S. Pat. No. 5,401,741 ("the '741 patent") and that the '741 patent is not invalid. Because the invention of the '741 patent would have been obvious in view of the prior art, we reverse.

I

The '741 patent is drawn to a method for treating bacterial ear infections by topically administering the antibiotic ofloxacin into the ear. Claim 1 is representative and states "[a] method for treating otopathy which comprises the topical otic administration of an amount of ofloxacin or a salt thereof effective to treat otopathy in a pharmaceutically acceptable carrier to the area affected with otopathy." '741 patent, col. 6 ll. 36-39.

Apotex [sought] approval to manufacture a generic ofloxacin ear drop [by filing an Abbreviated New Drug Application, or ANDA]. Following receipt of the ANDA, Daiichi, owner of the '741 patent, sued Apotex for infringement. [F]ollowing a bench trial, the court concluded that the '741 patent was not invalid. . . . Apotex appeals, and we have jurisdiction pursuant to 28 U.S.C. 1295(a)(1).

II

Obviousness is a question of law based on underlying questions of fact. Thus, we review the ultimate determination of obviousness by a district court de novo and the underlying factual inquiries for clear error.

The underlying factual inquiries in an obviousness analysis include: "(1) the scope and content of the prior art; (2) the level of ordinary skill in the prior art; (3) the differences between the claimed invention and the prior art; and (4) objective evidence of nonobviousness." *In re Dembiczak*, 175 F.3d 994, 998 (Fed. Cir. 1999). In this case, we begin our analysis with the question of the level of ordinary skill in the prior art.

The district court concluded that the ordinary person skilled in the art pertaining to the '741 patent "would have a medical degree, experience treating patients with ear infections, and knowledge of the pharmacology and use of antibiotics. This person would be . . . a pediatrician or general practitioner—those doctors who are often the 'first line of defense' in treating ear infections and who, by virtue of their medical training, possess basic pharmacological knowledge." *Daiichi Pharm. Co. v. Apotex, Inc.*, 380 F. Supp. 2d 478, 485 (D.N.J. 2005) ("Claim Construction Order"). Apotex argues that the district court clearly erred in this determination and that one having ordinary skill in the relevant art is properly defined as "a person engaged in developing new pharmaceuticals, formulations and treatment methods, or a specialist in ear treatments such as an otologist, otolaryngologist, or otorhinolaryngologist who also has training in pharmaceutical formulations."

"Factors that may be considered in determining level of ordinary skill in the art include: (1) the educational level of the inventor; (2) type of problems encountered in the art; (3) prior art solutions to those problems; (4) rapidity with which innovations are made; (5) sophistication of the technology; and (6) educational level of active workers in the field." *Envtl. Designs, Ltd. v. Union Oil Co.*, 713 F.2d 693, 696 (Fed. Cir. 1983) (citing *Orthopedic Equip. Co., Inc. v. All Orthopedic Appliances, Inc.*, 707 F.2d 1376, 1381-82 (Fed. Cir. 1983)). These factors are not exhaustive but are merely a guide to determining the level of ordinary skill in the art.

In making its determination regarding the level of skill in the art, the district court noted that the parties had provided "little more than conclusory arguments concerning this issue in their briefs." As a result, the court looked to other decisions involving patents for a method of treating a physical condition for guidance. Only one case cited by the district court is binding on us, *Merck & Co., Inc. v. Teva Pharms. USA, Inc.*, 347 F.3d 1367 (Fed. Cir. 2003). The district court was correct that in that case we affirmed the trial court's conclusion that a person having ordinary skill in the relevant art was a person having a medical degree, experience treating patients with osteoporosis, and knowledge of the pharmacology and usage of biphosponates—the compounds at issue in *Merck*. However, in *Merck* the level of skill in the art was not disputed by the parties. Thus, we simply accepted the district court's finding. That clearly is not the case before us. Therefore, the district court's reliance on the level of skill in the art stated in *Merck* was improper.

The art involved in the '741 patent is the creation of a compound to treat ear infections without damaging a patient's hearing. The inventors of the '741 patent were specialists in drug and ear treatments—not general practitioners or pediatricians. At the time of the invention, Inventor Sato was a university professor specializing in otorhinolaryngology; Inventor Handa was a clinical development department manager at Daiichi, where he was involved with new drug development and clinical trials; and Inventor Kitahara was a research scientist at Daiichi engaged in the research and development of antibiotics. Additionally, others working in the same field as the inventors of the '741 patent were of the same skill level. *See* Daiichi Material for [C]onference on Development, Nov. 11, 1987 (stating that "there are many voices among medical persons concerned with otorhinolaryngology for demanding development of an otic solution making use of [ofloxacin]").

Further, the problem the invention of the '741 patent was trying to solve was to create a topical antibiotic compound to treat ear infections (otopathy) that did not have damage to the ear as a side effect. '741 patent, col. 1 ll. 23-34. Indeed, most of the written description details the inventors' testing ofloxacin on guinea pigs and their findings that ototoxicity did not result from the use of their compound. Such animal testing is traditionally outside the realm of a general practitioner or pediatrician. Finally, while a general practitioner or pediatrician could (and would) prescribe the invention of the '741 patent to treat ear infections, he would not have the training or knowledge to develop the claimed compound absent some specialty training such as that possessed by the '741 patent's inventors. Accordingly, the level of ordinary skill in the art of the '741 patent is that of a person engaged in developing pharmaceutical formulations and treatment methods for the ear or a specialist in ear treatments such as an otologist, otolaryngologist, or otorhinolaryngologist who also has training in pharmaceutical formulations. Thus, the district court clearly erred in finding otherwise.

Comments

1. ***Level of Skill Matters.*** In *Daiichi*, the level of ordinary skill in the art was determinative on the issue of obviousness. According to the court, the PHOSITA was not a pediatrician or general practitioner as the district court found, but rather, "a person engaged in developing pharmaceutical formulations and treatment methods for the ear or a specialist in ear treatments such as an otologist, otolaryngologist, or otorhinolaryngologist who also has training in pharmaceutical formulations." In *Tokai Corp. v. Easton Enterprises, Inc.*, 632 F.3d 1358 (Fed. Cir. 2011), the Federal Circuit affirmed the district court's finding that the level of skill in the art—for

safety utility lighters with automatic child-safety mechanisms for preventing accidental ignition—was "an individual showing aptitude in high school shop class, or someone who builds, takes apart, or repairs basic mechanical toys/devices." *Id.* at 1369.

2. ***Constructing Level of Skill.*** George Will wrote, "To really see what a painter has put on canvas requires learning to think the way the painter thought." GEORGE F. WILL, MEN AT WORK 3 (1990). And so it is with constructing a PHOSITA, someone who understands the art in question and its context. How do we construct such a person? The *KSR* Court stated a determination of obviousness should "take account of the inferences and creative steps that a person of ordinary skill in the art would employ," and that the "person of ordinary skill is also a person of ordinary creativity, not an automaton." With that in mind, the six factors cited in *Daaichi* are considered in constructing the level of ordinary skill (although the Court's heavy reliance on the inventors' skill level is questionable). And according to the Manual of Patent Examining Procedure, the skilled artisan must "of necessity have the capability of understanding the scientific and engineering principles applicable to the pertinent art." *Ex parte Hiyamizu,* 10 U.S.P.Q.2d 1393, 1394 (Bd. Pat. App. & Inter. 1988) (the Board disagreed with the examiner's definition of one of ordinary skill in the art (a doctorate level engineer or scientist working at least 40 hours per week in semiconductor research or development), finding that the hypothetical person is not definable by way of credentials, and that the evidence in the application did not support the conclusion that such a person would require a doctorate or equivalent knowledge in science or engineering.). For a discussion of the relationship between a PHOSITA and patent drawings, *see* William J. Rankin, *The "Person Skilled in the Art" Is Really Quite Conventional: U.S. Patent Drawings and the Persona of the Inventor, 1870-2005,* in MAKING AND UNMAKING OF INTELLECTUAL PROPERTY 57 (Woodmansee et al. eds., 2001) (stating "patent drawings provide great insight to the identity of the (fictional) person to whom the patent specification is addressed—the ideal 'person skilled in the art.' . . . Like the implied reader of a text, every drawing creates a rhetorical reader often quite different from its actual audience").

3. ***PHOSITA's New Lease on Life.*** *KSR* breathed new life into the PHOSITA. A prominent role for the PHOSITA is understandable given that a section 103 obviousness determination is a question of law, based on whether a person having ordinary skill in the art, to which the claimed invention pertains, would have found the claimed invention obvious. Thus, constructing a PHOSITA is of crucial importance; indeed, this artisan of ordinary skill is one of the cynosures of the patent system, playing a prominent role in determining not only obviousness, but, for example, sufficiency of disclosure and claim interpretation.

But prior to *KSR*, the Federal Circuit adopted what has been characterized as a mechanical application of the PHOSITA, relegating the artisan to a relatively unimportant and unimaginative player in the patent system. The PHOSITA, according to the Federal Circuit, is "presumed to be one who thinks along the line of conventional wisdom in the art and is not one who undertakes to innovate, whether by patient, and often expensive, systematic research or by extraordinary insights, it makes no difference which." *Standard Oil Co. v. American Cyanamid Co.*, 774 F.2d 448, 454 (Fed. Cir. 1985). The Federal Circuit has noted that a PHOSITA is not the inventor or any particular expert or handyman, but rather a hypothetical person, which renders immaterial the subjective motivations of inventors. *See Kimberly-Clark Corp. v. Johnson & Johnson Co.*, 745 F.2d 1437, 1453 (Fed. Cir. 1984) ("The inventor, for purposes of legal reasoning, has been replaced, as some courts have discovered, by the statutory hypothetical 'person of ordinary skill in the art' who has been provided by 35 U.S.C. § 103. Since that date, there has been no need to presume that the inventor knows anything about the prior art.").

This construction of the PHOSITA has been criticized by commentators. As Rebecca Eisenberg states, the Federal Circuit "has all but ignored the statutory directive that judgments of nonobviousness be made from the perspective of PHOSITA. . . . The resulting analysis excludes from consideration the judgment, intuition and tacit knowledge of ordinary practitioners in the field that cannot be documented in the written record." Rebecca A. Eisenberg, *Obvious to Whom? Evaluating Inventions from the Perspective of PHOSITA*, 19 BERKELEY TECH. L.J. 885, 888 (2004). *See also* ROGER SCHECHTER & JOHN R. THOMAS, PRINCIPLES OF PATENT LAW 161 (2d ed. 2004) (stating "[i]n most fields, practitioners are seldom such dullards as to require detailed step-by-step instructions to accomplish basic tasks. Yet here, and in other cases, the Federal Circuit seems to state that an invention would not have been obvious unless its precise recipe existed in the prior art.").

4. ***What About Inventive Teams?*** How patent law views innovation has come a long way from the *Hotchkiss* framework. Recall the Supreme Court spoke of the "ingenuity and skill of the ordinary mechanic," a precursor to the PHOSITA. Throughout patent law doctrine, including section 103, the *person* having ordinary skill in the art plays a prominent role. But a great deal of innovation today is the product of inventive teams comprised of PHOSITAs with diverse backgrounds. How can one hypothetical person's ordinary knowledge capture the collective skill of a team? The United Kingdom — the Royal Court of Justice in particular — has adopted a "skilled team" approach, although the text of its patent law is quite similar to section 103 in referring to a "person skilled in the art." *See MedImmune v. Novartis*, [2012] EWCA Civ. 1234 (Kitchen, L.J.); *Schlumberger Holdings Ltd. v. Electromagnetic Geoservices AS* [2010] EWCA Civ. 819 (Jacob, L.J.) at 42 (stating "the court will have regard to the reality of the position at the time and the combined skills of real research teams in the art. . . . Where the invention involves the use of more than one skill, if it is obvious to a person skilled in the art of any one of those skills, then the invention is obvious"). *See also* Dennis Crouch, *Person(s) Skilled in the Art: Should the Now Established Model of Team-Based Inventing Impact the Obviousness Analysis?*, Patently-O (2011).

Tom Hartsfield, in the excerpt below, reminds us, however, that while major discoveries are often made by large teams of researchers, the individual working alone or with a partner has made — and continues to make — significant contributions.

TOM HARTSFIELD, HAS "BIG SCIENCE" PUSHED ASIDE THE LITTLE GUY?

RealClearScience, September 18, 2012*

Are we now living in an era where big, important scientific discoveries are predominantly made by enormous far-flung teams of researchers? This is the conclusion of Professor Athene Donald, a physicist at Cambridge.

It is true that the experimental collaboration running the LHC, which triumphantly announced the discovery of the Higgs boson last summer, altogether involves more than 10,000 scientists. But, how about the physicists who worked on the theory behind the Higgs boson? One worked alone, another (separately) with a single coworker, and the biggest collaboration (separate as well) was three people.

The importance of teams, collaborations and multi-national super-experiments in science is undeniable. Some projects simply require many minds to plan, many backs to build and many dollars to support.

However, the role of individuals and very small groups, and their work using hand-built and often single-operator experiments, is still every bit as important.

Just two years ago, the Nobel Prize in Physics was awarded to two researchers who made an entirely new kind of material, graphene, almost completely alone. How many millions of dollars did it cost? Andre Geim and Konstantin Novoselov made the graphene themselves using Scotch Tape. That's right. Their massive breakthrough was powered by simple creative ingenuity and a two dollar roll of tape.

This is not an isolated example. The 2009 prize was also awarded to two scientists who invented the CCD, the device which powers digital cameras. Two separate researchers, working alone, won the 2007 prize. This is not to even mention the theorists honored with the prize, many of whom worked alone or in very small groups.

The Nobel Prize is just one metric. However, analysis by any standard still leads to the same conclusion. There is no "age of the enormous team" sweeping aside an "age of the lonely genius." Both processes flourish in harmony.

For every major discovery that requires billions of dollars and an enormous team, there is another breakthrough made entirely by one, two, or three people, using means entirely of their own devising.

Some projects require enormous investments of manpower and resources. Right alongside these projects, others bare fruit in the hands of solitary scientists and tiny teams.

Sometimes the most brilliant ideas do not come from committees and billion-dollar budgets produced over years of negotiations. Instead, they spring from that amazing fountain of innovation within the human mind.

3. Available Prior Art and the Analogous Art Doctrine

Only "analogous" prior art can be used for a section 103 inquiry. Unlike section 102, which does not have an analogous art component, the courts have required art for an obviousness inquiry to come from "the same field of endeavor" as the

* http://www.realclearscience.com/blog/2012/09/science-has-room-for-the-little-guy-too.html. Reprinted with permission.

claimed invention or be "reasonably pertinent to the particular problem with which the inventor is involved." The latter prong of the analogous art doctrine has arguably been broadened by *KSR*, a point we take up in the Comments after *Icon Health* and *In re Klein*.

IN RE ICON HEALTH & FITNESS, INC.
496 F.3d 1374 (Fed. Cir. 2007)

PROST, Circuit Judge.

ICON Health & Fitness, Inc. ("Icon") appeals from a decision by the Board of Patent Appeals and Interferences ("Board") during reexamination of Icon's U.S. Patent No. 5,676,624 ("the '624 patent"). Finding no error in the Board's decision, we affirm its decision holding Icon's claims unpatentable as obvious.

BACKGROUND

Icon owns the '624 patent, issued October 14, 1997, and sought reexamination by the Patent and Trademark Office ("PTO"). The '624 patent claims a treadmill with a folding base, allowing the base to swivel into an upright storage position. Claim 1, from which all other claims on appeal depend, recites:

1. A treadmill comprising:

* * *

a gas spring connected between the tread base and the upright structure to assist in stably retaining said tread base in said second position relative to said upright structure with said tread base in said second position.

(emphasis added).

The present dispute involves only the final limitation, requiring a gas spring "to assist in stably retaining" the tread base in the upright position. On reexamination, the examiner rejected Icon's claims as obvious under 35 U.S.C. § 103, based on the combination of an advertisement by Damark International, Inc. ("Damark") and U.S. Patent No. 4,370,766 to Teague, Jr. ("Teague").

Damark consists of an advertisement for a folding treadmill; Icon does not challenge the Board's finding that Damark demonstrates all claim elements other than the gas spring. The present inquiry, therefore, focuses on Teague's disclosure of gas springs and the applicability of Teague to Icon's invention. Teague describes a bed that folds up into a cabinet or recess. It purports to improve on prior art counterbalancing mechanisms by using a novel dual-action spring rather than the prior single-action springs. Single-action springs provide a force pushing the bed closed at all times. Teague's dual-action spring, on the other hand, reverses its force as the mechanism passes a neutral position; the neutral position in Teague occurs when the center of gravity of the bed aligns vertically with the pivot point. As the bed moves past the neutral position to the closed position, the mechanism opposes continued motion. The bed moves into the closed position under the pull of gravity. When fully closed, therefore, the mechanism in Teague provides an opening force, but not one sufficient to counteract the force of gravity. Essentially, Teague's dual-action spring partially supports the weight of the bed in both the closed and open positions. This provides the benefit of reducing the force required to open the bed from the closed position, while still reducing the force required to lift the bed from the open position.

The Board affirmed the examiner's determination that the combination of Teague and Damark rendered claim 1 obvious. First, the Board rejected Icon's argument that Teague does not provide analogous art. Specifically, because Teague and the current application both address the need to stably retain a folding mechanism, the Board found Teague reasonably pertinent to the current application. Further, it found that discussion of a lifting force in the present application paralleled Teague's mechanism for creating a lifting force.

DISCUSSION

* * *

II

A

Icon disputes the Board's conclusion that one skilled in the art would have found it obvious to combine the teachings of Teague and Damark. As the first of its two major arguments on appeal, Icon argues that Teague falls outside the "treadmill art" and addresses a different problem than the present application, removing it from the relevant prior art. We agree that, describing a folding bed, Teague comes from a different field than Icon's application. We disagree, however, that Teague addresses a different problem.

If reasonably pertinent to the problem addressed by Icon, Teague may serve as analogous art. *Paulsen,* 30 F.3d at 1481. "A reference is reasonably pertinent if, even though it may be in a different field from that of the inventor's endeavor, it is one which, because of the matter with which it deals, logically would have commended itself to an inventor's attention in considering his problem." *In re Clay,* 966 F.2d 656, 659 (Fed. Cir. 1992). In other words, "familiar items may have obvious uses beyond their primary purposes." *KSR Int'l Co. v. Teleflex, Inc.,* 127 S. Ct. 1727, 1742. We therefore have concluded, for example, that an inventor considering a hinge and latch mechanism for portable computers would naturally look to references employing other "housings, hinges, latches, springs, etc.," which in that case came from areas such as "a desktop telephone directory, a piano lid, a kitchen cabinet, a washing machine cabinet, a wooden furniture cabinet, or a two-part housing for storing audio cassettes." *Paulsen,* 30 F.3d at 1481-82.

Icon's invention provides a treadmill with a folding mechanism and a means for retaining that mechanism in the folded position. The application specifically discusses the gas spring as part of a "lift assistance assembly . . . to apply a force or torque urging the tread base" towards the closed position. '624 patent, col. 15, ll. 3-5. Nothing about Icon's folding mechanism requires any particular focus on treadmills; it generally addresses problems of supporting the weight of such a mechanism and providing a stable resting position. Analogous art to Icon's application, when considering the folding mechanism and gas spring limitation, may come from any area describing hinges, springs, latches, counterweights, or other similar mechanisms—such as the folding bed in Teague. Accordingly, we conclude that substantial evidence supports the Board's finding that Teague provides analogous art.

B

Several factors support the Board's conclusion of obviousness. When analyzing Icon's application, we consider a variety of sources that may have led one skilled in the art to combine the teachings of Damark and Teague. Indeed, "any need or problem known in the field of endeavor at the time of invention and addressed by the patent can provide a reason for combining the elements in the manner claimed." *KSR,* 127 S. Ct. at 1742.

First, Teague discusses prior art, single-action coil springs that always push the bed towards the closed position. As Teague recites, in those beds, "the coil springs also exert forces holding the bed in the fully closed position." Teague, col. 1, ll. 51-55. Such springs, in this application, would produce a force always urging the tread base towards the closed position—exactly the type of mechanism that Icon argues its claims require. While the passage concerns coil springs rather than gas springs, Teague explicitly discusses the interchangeability of gas springs and coil springs. Teague, col. 3, ll. 61-65. Therefore, Teague provides an example of a mechanism clearly satisfying Icon's claim limitation.

Next, Icon's application discusses the gas spring in connection with a "lift assistance assembly." '624 patent, col. 15, ll. 3-25. Similarly, Teague is directed at a "counterbalancing mechanism," intended to support the weight of a bed as it opens and closes. Teague, col. 1, ll. 5-34. One skilled in the art would naturally look to prior art addressing the same problem as the invention at hand, and in this case would find an appropriate solution. Indeed, while perhaps not dispositive of the issue, the finding that Teague, by addressing a similar problem, provides analogous art to Icon's application goes a long way towards demonstrating a reason to combine the two references. Because Icon's broad claims read on embodiments addressing that problem as described by Teague, the prior art here indicates a reason to incorporate its teachings.

Finally, Teague provides a mechanism such that the bed "has two stable rest positions." Teague, col. 1, ll. 35-38. It describes, "as the center of gravity of the bed passes over the pivot axis . . . gravity tends to hold the bed in its fully closed position." Teague, col. 1, ll. 47-51. When folding the treadmill described in Icon's application, "[t]he tread base 434 is rotated until the center of gravity 440 is displaced clockwise past the vertical 446 a distance 448 selected to stably retain the tread base 434 in the second position." '624 patent, col. 12, ll. 29-32. The striking similarity between Icon's application and Teague clearly illustrates the similarity of problems they address and solutions to that problem, further supporting the idea that one skilled in the art would combine Teague with Damark.

The aforementioned connections between Teague and Icon's application provide a sufficient basis to conclude that one skilled in the art would combine the teachings of Teague and Damark. . . .

IN RE KLEIN

647 F.3d 1343 (Fed. Cir. 2011)

Schall, Circuit Judge.

Arnold G. Klein appeals the final decision of the Board of Patent Appeals and Interferences ("Board") affirming the rejection of certain claims of U.S. Patent

Application No. 10/200,747 ("'747 application") as obvious under 35 U.S.C.
§103. Because the Board's finding that five references at issue are analogous art
is not supported by substantial evidence, the obviousness rejections cannot be
sustained and, accordingly, we reverse.

BACKGROUND

I.

Mr. Klein filed the '747 application, titled "Convenience Nectar Mixing and
Storage Devices," on July 24, 2002. The '747 application concerns a mixing
device for use in preparation of sugar-water nectar for certain bird and butterfly
feeders. According to the specification, the device has a series of rails that, when
engaged with a divider, allow for the creation of two compartments for separating sugar and water within the device. The rails are located to divide the device
into proportionate volumes of one part sugar to four parts water (to make hum-
mingbird nectar), one part sugar to six parts water (to make oriole nectar), and
one part sugar to nine parts water (to make butterfly nectar). Once the respective compartments have been filled to the same level with sugar and water, the
divider is removed, allowing the sugar and water to mix and be stirred. The
specification does not suggest that the sugar to water ratios are novel, instead
disclosing in the "Background of the Invention" that these ratios are "currently
recognized as being proportionally equivalent in sugar content as the birds, and
butterflies [sic] natural nectar food sources."

Figures 1, 2A-2B, and 4 of the '747 application, shown below, illustrate device
11, divider 21, and rails 15, 16, and 17:

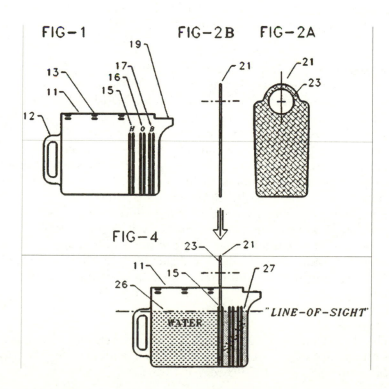

The sole independent claim at issue, claim 21, recites:

21. A convenience nectar mixing device for use in preparation of sugar-water nectar for feeding hummingbirds, orioles or butterflies, said device comprising:

> a container that is adapted to receive water,

> receiving means fixed to said container, and

> a divider movably held by said receiving means for forming a compartment within said container, wherein said compartment has a volume that is proportionately less than a volume of said container, by a ratio established for the formulation of sugar-water nectar for hummingbirds, orioles or butterflies, wherein said compartment is adapted to receive sugar, and wherein removal of said divider from said receiving means allows mixing of said sugar and water to occur to provide said sugar-water nectar.

The remaining claims at issue, claims 22-25, 29, and 30, each depend from claim 21.

In a final rejection dated September 24, 2007, the examiner made five separate rejections under 35 U.S.C. §103(a): (1) a rejection of claims 21, 22, and 30 over U.S. Patent No. 580,899 ("Roberts") in view of the prior art sugar to water ratios discussed in the Klein specification; (2) a rejection of claims 21, 22, and 30 over U.S. Patent No. 1,523,136 ("O'Connor") in view of the prior art sugar to water ratios discussed in the Klein specification; (3) a rejection of claims 21, 22, and 30 over U.S. Patent No. 2,985,333 ("Kirkman") in view of the prior art sugar to water ratios discussed in the Klein specification; (4) a rejection of claims 21-25 and 29 over U.S. Patent No. 2,787,268 ("Greenspan") in view of the prior art sugar to water ratios discussed in the Klein specification; and (5) a rejection of claims 21 and 29 over U.S. Patent No. 3,221,917 ("De Santo") in view of the prior art sugar to water ratios discussed in the Klein specification. Mr. Klein appealed the final rejection to the Board.

II.

The Board affirmed each of the five obviousness rejections. The Board described Roberts, O'Connor, Kirkman, Greenspan, and De Santo as each "teach[ing] a device with a container having a movable divider held in place by a 'receiving means,' such as slots, grooves, or threads, which could be used to divide ingredients in specific ratios." In addition, the Board pointed to the Klein specification's own statement that the sugar-water ratios were known. According to the Board, "[t]hose of skill in the art would have had reason to use the known ratios with the available containers having movable dividers to achieve the correct proportions of water and sugar and to mix the ingredients for different nectars." The Board rejected Mr. Klein's argument that the five cited references are non-analogous art. In doing so, the Board found that the prior art was properly relied upon by the examiner because it is reasonably pertinent to the problem Mr. Klein addresses, which the Board found to be "making a nectar feeder with a movable divider to prepare different ratios of sugar and water for different animals."

Mr. Klein appealed.

DISCUSSION

. . . The Board's determination that a prior art reference is analogous art presents an issue of fact, reviewed for substantial evidence. *In re Icon Health & Fitness, Inc.*, 496 F.3d 1374, 1378 (Fed. Cir. 2007).

I.

On appeal, Mr. Klein argues that the Board erred when it summarily concluded that the five cited references are "reasonably pertinent to the problem addressed by Klein." Although the Board made a finding of fact as to the particular problem that Mr. Klein was addressing, specifically, "making a nectar feeder with a movable divider to prepare different ratios of sugar and water for different animals," Mr. Klein contends that the Board failed to make any finding that any of the cited references are "reasonably pertinent" to that problem. Further, Mr. Klein argues, the Board identified no evidence that suggests that an inventor seeking to solve the problem Mr. Klein was addressing, which Mr. Klein characterizes as a "multiple ratio mixing problem," would look to any of the references to address the problem of preparing different ratios.

The government responds that the Board correctly found that the prior art references were directed toward the same problem Mr. Klein sought to solve with his device, which the government characterizes as a "compartment separation problem." Because "[t]he problem of keeping things separated is not unique to nectar mixing and storage devices," and "nothing about the prior art containers with adjustable, removable dividers is unique to their particular applications," the government contends that "[o]ne confronted with Klein's desire to keep two ingredients separated and also allow for them to be mixed together would have readily consulted these references to discover the broad solution therein employed, and applied it to his particular application with no more than ordinary skill required."

II.

A reference qualifies as prior art for an obviousness determination under §103 only when it is analogous to the claimed invention. "Two separate tests define the scope of analogous prior art: (1) whether the art is from the same field of endeavor, regardless of the problem addressed and, (2) if the reference is not within the field of the inventor's endeavor, whether the reference still is reasonably pertinent to the particular problem with which the inventor is involved." *In re Bigio*, 381 F.3d 1320, 1324 (Fed. Cir. 2004). Here, the Board focused exclusively on the "reasonably pertinent to the particular problem" test. "A reference is reasonably pertinent if, even though it may be in a different field from that of the inventor's endeavor, it is one which, because of the matter with which it deals, logically would have commended itself to an inventor's attention in considering his problem." *In re Clay*, 966 F.2d at 659. "If a reference disclosure has the same purpose as the claimed invention, the reference relates to the same problem, and that fact supports use of that reference in an obviousness rejection." *Id.*

Mr. Klein does not challenge the Board's factual finding of the problem he was addressing, namely "making a nectar feeder with a movable divider to prepare different ratios of sugar and water for different animals." Mr. Klein argues, however, that Roberts, O'Connor, Kirkman, Greenspan, and De Santo are each directed to a wholly different problem than the one he faced. We examine each reference in turn.

Roberts is directed to an "Apparatus for Keeping Accounts." The apparatus of Roberts includes receptacles, such as receptacles 1 and 2 (shown in dotted lines in Figure 1 below), having a "series of vertical channels 11, adapted to receive removable partitions 12, by means of which the receptacle[s] may be subdivided into compartments." Roberts col.1 ll.41-46, col.2 ll.53-56. According to Roberts, the receptacles are "designed to receive . . . statement-cards," and each includes a hand-hole 10 to assist in removing the receptacle from a drawer. Roberts col.1 ll.34-39, col.2 ll.53-56. Figure 1 of Roberts is shown below:

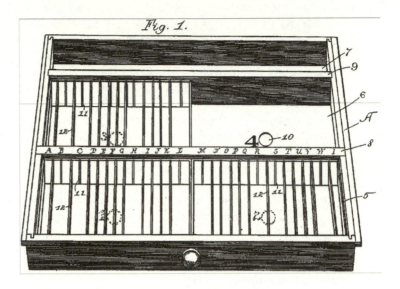

O'Connor is directed to a tool tray having dividers that are "readily movable" and that is "adapted to contain comparatively small articles, for example, drills, reamers, bits, etc., or hardware supplies such as bolts, nuts and the like." O'Connor col.1 ll.8-27. As shown in Figure 1 of O'Connor, reproduced below, divider 8 is not positioned flush with the bottom of the tray:

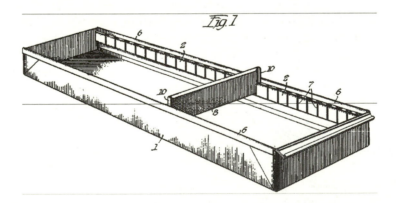

Kirkman is directed to a "Plastic Cabinet Drawer with Removable Partitions." Kirkman explains that it "relates to drawers for relatively small cabinets for containing various types of small articles, and more particularly to a drawer of this type provided with removable partitions or dividers, for dividing the drawer into two or more compartments of varying size, with means for frictionally holding the partitions in adjusted position [sic] within the drawer." Kirkman col.1 ll.15-21. As shown in Figure 1 of Kirkman below, the lower edge of partition 9 has a small notch:

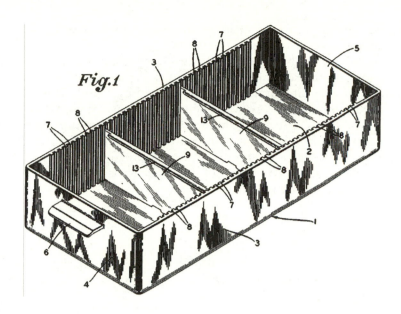

Fig.1

Mr. Klein argues that, consistent with the Board's own express findings, Roberts, O'Connor, and Kirkman are each directed to a container designed to *separate* its contents, as opposed to one designed to facilitate the *mixing* of those contents. ("Roberts teaches a container, in particular a drawer for keeping accounts, which has removable partitions for forming compartments *for the purpose of keeping statement and account cards separated*.") (emphasis added) (citing Roberts col.1 ll.7-13); *id.* ("O'Connor teaches a container, in particular a tool tray, with removable dividers that may be placed in the tray for forming compartments *for the purpose of keeping tools and other construction items (e.g., bolts, nuts) separated*.") (emphasis added) (citing O'Connor col.1 ll.8-20); *id.* ("Kirkman teaches a container, in particular a cabinet drawer, with removable dividers that may be placed in the drawer for forming compartments *for the purpose of keeping small household articles (e.g., hardware, cosmetics, and paperclips) separated*.") (emphasis added) (citing Kirkman col.1 ll.20-30). Mr. Klein also argues that, in view of (1) the hand-hole 10 of Roberts, (2) how divider 8 of O'Connor is positioned to not be flush with the bottom of the tray, and (3) the notch in the lower edge of partition 9 of Kirkman, none of these three references is "adapted to receive water," as is required by claim 21 of the '747 application.

We agree with Mr. Klein that the Board's conclusory finding that Roberts, O'Connor, and Kirkman are analogous is not supported by substantial evidence. The purpose of each of Roberts, O'Connor, or Kirkman is to separate solid objects. An inventor considering the problem of "making a nectar feeder with a movable divider to prepare different ratios of sugar and water for different animals," would not have been motivated to consider any of these references when making his invention, particularly since none of these three references shows a partitioned container that is adapted to receive water or contain it long enough to be able to prepare different ratios in the different compartments. *See Clay,* 966 F.2d at 659 ("If [a reference] is directed to a different purpose, the inventor would accordingly have had less motivation or occasion to consider it.").[1]

Turning to the remaining two references, Greenspan is directed to a "Blood Plasma Bottle" having a compartment for dried plasma and a compartment for water, where the compartments are separated by a "wall which is normally plugged during transportation of the bottle." Greenspan col.2 ll.12-17. When the plasma is going to be used, the plasma compartment is unplugged, the plug becomes the cap for the bottle, and the bottle is shaken to dissolve the plasma. *Id.* col.2 ll.17-23. As shown in Figure 2 of Greenspan, below, the wall 24 cannot be moved to adjust the relative sizes of the lower (plasma) compartment 30 or upper (water) compartment 28:

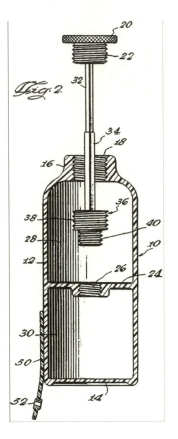

See Greenspan col.2 ll.37-39.

De Santo's "Fluid Container" has two compartments designed to hold two different types of fluid, which can be "rapidly and thoroughly mixed together at the desired time without opening the container externally" to make, for example, hair rinses. De Santo col.1 ll.8-17, 23-28. Compartments 24 and 26 are

1. We agree with Mr. Klein that, to the extent the government attempts to do so, it cannot redefine the problem Mr. Klein was addressing as a "compartment separation problem" on appeal. See Sec. & Exch. Comm'n v. Chenery Corp., 318 U.S. 80, 94 (1943) ("[A]n administrative order cannot be upheld unless the grounds upon which the agency acted in exercising its powers were those upon which its action can be sustained.").

separated by partition 28, which is "provided with a central opening 32 defining an annular valve seat 34 which is engageable with a valve member 36 to open and close the partition as desired." *Id.* col.2 ll.44-48, 55-58. As shown below in Figure 5, partition 28 is in a fixed location.

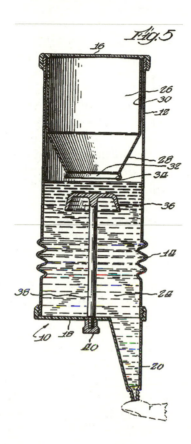

Greenspan and De Santo are not analogous, Mr. Klein argues, because they do not address multiple ratios or have a "movable divider." We agree. While Greenspan and De Santo are each directed to containers that facilitate the mixing of two separated substances together, an inventor considering the problem of "making a nectar feeder with *a movable divider to prepare different ratios of sugar and water for different animals*," would not have been motivated to consider either of these references since neither of the references shows a movable divider or the ability to prepare different ratios.[2] In the *Decision*, the Board did not set forth any reasoning in support of its finding that Greenspan and De Santo are analogous, and thus, this finding is also not supported by substantial evidence.

---

2. As noted above, we agree with Mr. Klein that the government cannot now redefine the problem Mr. Klein was addressing as a "compartment separation problem."

Comments

1. **KSR *and the Analogous Art Doctrine.*** Under Federal Circuit law, there are two distinct tests for defining the scope of analogous art: (1) whether the art is from the same field of endeavor, regardless of the problem addressed, and (2) if the reference is not within the field of the inventor's endeavor, whether the reference still is reasonably pertinent to the particular problem with which the inventor is involved. *In re Bigio*, 381 F.3d 1320, 1325 (Fed. Cir. 2004) (finding toothbrush art analogous to Bigio's hairbrush). A reference is reasonably pertinent if it, as a result of its subject matter, "logically would have commended itself to an inventor's attention in considering his problem." *Innovention Toys, LLC v. MGA Entm't, Inc.*, 637 F.3d 1314, 1321 (Fed. Cir. 2011). What is interesting about *Klein* and *Innovention* is their focus on whether the reference would have commended itself to the "inventor" rather than a person having ordinary skill in the art. The inventor-centric approach is particularly curious in the light of *KSR* and its emphasis on the PHOSITA. Ironically, pre-*KSR* Federal Circuit case law did approach the issue from the PHOSITA's perspective. *See, e.g., In re Kahn*, 441 F.3d 977, 987 (Fed. Cir. 2006) (stating "[r]eferences are selected as being reasonably pertinent to the problem based on the judgment of a person having ordinary skill in the art. It is necessary to consider 'the reality of the circumstances,'—in other words, common sense—in deciding in which fields a person of ordinary skill would reasonably be expected to look for a solution to the problem facing the inventor." (quoting *In re Wood*, 599 F.2d 1032, 1036 (CCPA 1979)).

2. ***Defining the Problem.*** With respect to the second prong, defining the problem—as reflected in the principal cases of *Icon Health* and *Klein*—is most likely determinative of the decision whether prior art is analogous. The *Klein* decision is particularly interesting in this regard. The Federal Circuit defined the problem narrowly, namely "making a nectar feeder with a movable divider to prepare different rations of sugar and water for different animals." 647 F.3d at 1348. As defined, the court found the prior art nonanalogous because none of the five references addressed the entire problem. Is a reference required to address the entire problem—rather than partially as in *Klein*—to be analogous? If yes, is *Klein* consistent with *KSR*, although, interestingly, the court did not cite *KSR*?

In *KSR*, the Supreme Court expressly stated the Federal Circuit erred "by holding that courts and patent examiners should look only to the problem the patentee was trying to solve." According to the Court, the Federal Circuit "failed to recognize that the problem motivating the patentee may be only one of many addressed by the patent's subject matter." It is arguable that *KSR* expanded the scope of the analogous art doctrine. In *Icon Health*, a principal case, the court, quoting *KSR*, stated "familiar items may have obvious uses beyond their primary purposes," and that "any need or problem known in the field of endeavor at the time of invention and addressed by the patent can provide a reason for combining the elements in the manner claimed." *KSR*, 127 S. Ct. at 1742. *Klein* arguably reigned in this expansive approach. *See also K-Tec, Inc. v. Vita-Mix Corp.*, 696 F.3d 1364 (Fed. Cir. 2012) (finding art non-analogous based on defined problem).

3. **Pre-*KSR* *Analogous Art Doctrine*.** Prior to *KSR*, the Federal Circuit noted, "[a] reference is reasonably pertinent if, even though it may be in a different field from that of the inventor's endeavor, it is one which, because of the matter with which it deals, logically would have commended itself to an inventor's attention in considering his problem." *In re Clay*, 966 F.2d 656, 659 (Fed. Cir. 1992). In *In re Kahn*, 441 F.3d 977, 986-987 (Fed. Cir. 2006), the court wrote, "References are selected as being reasonably pertinent to the problem based on the judgment of a" PHOSITA; and this judgment should be grounded on the "reality of the circumstances—in other words, common-sense—in deciding in which fields a person of ordinary skill would reasonably be expected to look for a solution to the problem facing the inventor." (quoting *In re Wood*, 599 F.2d 1032, 1036 (CCPA 1979)). In short, "familiar items may have obvious uses beyond their primary purposes." *KSR*, 127 S. Ct. at 1742.

   For example, *In re Paulsen*, 30 F.3d 1475 (Fed. Cir. 1994), cited by *Icon Health*, involved prior art that was not within the same field of endeavor of the claimed invention. In *Paulsen*, the patent related to a portable computer contained within a compact metal case. An important feature of the invention was the "claim shell" design. This configuration connected the display of the computer to the computer's midsection by a hinge assembly, which in turn allowed for the display to move from a closed position to an open position. In other words, the patent claimed the design of a "laptop" computer. During a reexamination, the PTO rejected the claims under section 103 in the light of references directed to hinges and latches as used in a desktop telephone directory, a piano lid, a kitchen cabinet, a washing machine cabinet, a wooden furniture cabinet, or a two-part housing for storing audiocassettes. The Federal Circuit, in affirming the PTO, rejected the applicant's argument that the prior art was non-analogous. The court agreed that the prior art was not in the same field of endeavor as computers, but the "problems encountered by the inventors of the '456 patent were problems that were not unique to portable computers." *Id.* at 1482.

   > They concerned how to connect and secure the computer's display housing to the computer while meeting certain size constraints and functional requirements. The prior art cited by the examiner discloses various means of connecting a cover (or lid) to a device so that the cover is free to swing radially along the connection axis, as well as means of securing the cover in an open or closed position. We agree with the Board that given the nature of the problems confronted by the inventors, one of ordinary skill in the art "would have consulted the mechanical arts for housings, hinges, latches, springs, etc."

   Id.

4. **What Constitutes Prior Art Under Section 103?** Section 103 refers to the differences between the claimed invention and the "prior art." The source of prior art for section 103 purposes comes from section 102. This sounds confusing, but think of section 102 as having a dual function, defining both (1) novelty (as well as priority and statutory bars) and (2) what constitutes prior art. Regarding the former, both sections 102 and 103 can be seen as guarding the public domain, but section 103 is more aggressive, preventing a patent from issuing on "concepts within the public grasp, or so obvious that they readily could be." *Bonito Boats, Inc. v. Thunder Craft Boats, Inc.*, 489 U.S. 141, 156 (1989).

Regarding the latter, section 102(a) prior art comprises patents and printed publications anywhere in the world, and public knowledge and use in the United States. (Of course, to constitute *prior* art, this information must be available before the date of invention.) Once identified, prior art can be used to defeat novelty under section 102 or be used to prove obviousness under section 103. A considerable majority of prior art used for obviousness is based on section 102(a). *See Ormco Corp. v. Align Technology, Inc.,* 463 F.3d 1299, 1305 (Fed. Cir. 2006) ("'Prior art' in the obviousness context includes the material identified in section 102(a)."); *In re Mulder,* 716 F.2d 1542, 1545 (Fed. Cir. 1983) ("[P]rinted publication . . . is prior art under [section] 102(a), . . . and thus also 'prior art' under [section] 103."). Prior art and activity under the section 102(b) on-sale and public-use bars and section 102(e) patent disclosures and (g) inventive activity can also serve as prior art for purposes of obviousness under section 103. *See LaBounty Mfg. v. Int'l Trade Comm'n,* 958 F.2d 1066, 1071 (Fed. Cir. 1992) ("Section 102(b) may create a bar to patentability . . . in conjunction with [section 103], if the claimed invention would have been obvious from the on-sale device in conjunction with the prior art."); *Netscape Communications Corp. v. Konrad,* 295 F.3d 1315, 1321 (Fed. Cir. 2002) (stating a "device used in public includes every limitation of the later claimed invention, or by obviousness if the differences between the claimed invention and the device used would have been obvious to one of ordinary skill in the art"); *Hazeltine Research, Inc. v. Brenner,* 382 U.S. 252 (1965) (§§ 102(e)-103); *In re Bass,* 474 F.2d 1276 (CCPA 1973) (§§ 102(g)-103).

5. *No Analogous Art Doctrine Under Section 102.* You may recall there is no analogous art doctrine for the novelty requirement. Any single prior art reference that discloses each limitation of the claimed invention is sufficient under the novelty inquiry. What is different about section 103? Because section 103 references by definition do not disclose each limitation and can be combined, it becomes more difficult for inventors through searching to fully appreciate the full scope of the prior art. Patent law requires the art to be "analogous" to ease the inventor's burden. Thus, the analogous art doctrine "more closely approximates the reality of the circumstances surrounding the making of an invention by only presuming knowledge by the inventor of prior art in the field of his endeavor and in analogous arts." *In re Wood,* 599 F.2d 1032, 1036 (CCPA 1979).

D. SECONDARY CONSIDERATIONS

Recall in *Graham,* the Supreme Court stated "[s]uch secondary considerations as commercial success, long felt but unsolved needs, failure of others, etc., might be utilized to give light to the circumstances surrounding the origin of the subject matter sought to be patented." 383 U.S. at 17-18. The *Transocean* case provides a nice discussion of these considerations.

TRANSOCEAN OFFSHORE DEEPWATER DRILLING, INC. v. MAERSK DRILLING USA, INC.

699 F.3d 1340 (Fed. Cir. 2012)

MOORE, Circuit Judge.

Transocean Offshore Deepwater Drilling, Inc. (Transocean) appeals from the decision of the U.S. District Court for the Southern District of Texas granting judgment as a matter of law (JMOL) that (1) the asserted claims of U.S. Patent Nos. 6,047,781 ('781 patent), 6,085,851 ('851 patent), and 6,068,069 ('069 patent) are invalid for obviousness. . . . Transocean also appeals from the district court's conditional grant of a new trial. For the reasons set forth below, we *reverse*.

BACKGROUND

The patents-in-suit, which share a common specification, are directed to an improved apparatus for conducting offshore drilling. . . . The process of creating a borehole in the seafloor requires lowering several components to the seabed from a derrick on the ocean surface. These include the drill bit, the casings that form the wall of the borehole, and a device called a blowout preventer. The components are lowered on a "drill string," which is made up of a series of pipe sections ("tubular members"). The drill string is assembled on the derrick, with pipe sections being added to the top of the string one by one to extend it to the seafloor.

The drill bit is the first component to be lowered. Once enough pipe sections have been added to the drill string to lower the drill bit to the seabed, a "top drive" on the derrick rotates the drill string to create a borehole. Additional pipe sections are added to the drill string as the bit drills deeper into the seabed. Once the drill creates a portion of the borehole, the derrick retracts the drill bit to the surface, removing each section of the drill string piece by piece. A section of casing is then lowered into the borehole, with the drill string again being constructed on the derrick, one pipe section at a time. The next step is lowering the blowout preventer to the seabed, again with the drill string being assembled piece by piece. The process of drilling and lowering casing into the borehole then repeats until the hole is the desired depth. Each time a component is lowered to the seafloor, a drill string must be assembled and disassembled.

Conventional drilling rigs use a derrick with a single drawworks and thus can only raise or lower one component at a time. Transocean sought to improve the efficiency of this time-consuming process using the "dual-activity" drilling apparatus disclosed in the patents-in-suit. The patents recite a derrick with both a main and an auxiliary advancing station, each of which can separately assemble drill strings and lower components to the seafloor. Each advancing station has a drawworks for raising and lowering the drill string and a top drive for rotating the drill string. While the auxiliary advancing station drills and cases the first portion of the borehole, the main advancing station lowers the blowout preventer. The auxiliary advancing station then retracts the drill string and supports the main advancing station by preparing lengths of drill string in advance. Transocean's patents disclose a pipe handling system, also called a transfer assembly, which allows the transfer of casing, drill string, and other components between the two advancing stations and from the advancing stations to storage areas.

Transocean asserted claims 10-13 and 30 of the '781 patent, claim 10 of the '851 patent, and claim 17 of the '069 patent against Maersk. Transocean alleged that Maersk infringed the claims by entering into a contract with Statoil Gulf of Mexico LLC (Statoil), which granted Statoil the right to use an allegedly infringing drilling rig. In *Transocean I,* the district court granted Maersk's motion for summary judgment of obviousness, concluding that the asserted claims would have been obvious over the combination of two prior art references: U.K. patent application GB 2 041 836 (Horn) and U.S. Patent No. 4,850,439 (Lund).

On appeal, we reversed its grant of summary judgment of invalidity for obviousness. On remand, a jury found that Maersk failed to prove that the asserted claims would have been obvious. The jury made specific findings that the prior art failed to disclose every element of the asserted claims and that each of seven objective factors indicated nonobviousness. The district court, however, granted Maersk's motions for judgment as a matter of law (JMOL) that the asserted claims are invalid as obvious. Transocean now appeals from these rulings. We have jurisdiction under 28 U.S.C. §1295(a)(1).

Discussion

* * *

I. Obviousness

A patent is invalid as obvious "if the differences between the subject matter sought to be patented and the prior art are such that the subject matter as a whole would have been obvious at the time the invention was made to a person having ordinary skill in the art to which said subject matter pertains." 35 U.S.C. §103(a). Obviousness is a question of law with several underlying factual inquiries: (1) the scope and content of the prior art; (2) the differences between the prior art and the claims at issue; (3) the level of ordinary skill in the field of the invention; and (4) objective considerations such as commercial success, long felt but unsolved need, and the failure of others. *Graham v. John Deere Co. of Kan. City,* 383 U.S. 1, 17-18 (1966); *see also KSR Int'l Co. v. Teleflex, Inc.* Patent invalidity must be established by clear and convincing evidence. *Microsoft Corp. v. i4i Ltd.,* 131 S. Ct. 2238, 2242 (2011).

A. Prima Facie Case

. . . In *Transocean I,* we expressly held that the Horn and Lund references teach every limitation of the asserted claims. . . .

The establishment of a prima facie case, however, is *not* a conclusion on the ultimate issue of obviousness. By definition, the existence of a prima facie case simply means that the party challenging a patent has presented evidence "sufficient to establish a fact or raise a presumption [of obviousness] unless disproved or rebutted." Black's Law Dictionary (9th ed. 2009). The prima facie inquiry is based on the first three *Graham* factors—the scope and content of the prior art, the differences between the prior art and the claims, and the level of ordinary skill in the art—which the Supreme Court described as the background against which the obviousness or nonobviousness of the subject matter is determined. 383 U.S. at 17. A party is also free to introduce evidence relevant to the fourth *Graham* factor, objective evidence of nonobviousness, which may be sufficient to disprove or rebut a prima facie case of obviousness.

As we have repeatedly held, "evidence rising out of the so-called 'secondary considerations' must always when present be considered en route to a determination of obviousness." *Stratoflex, Inc. v. Aeroquip Corp.*, 713 F.2d 1530, 1538 (Fed. Cir. 1983). Objective evidence of nonobviousness is an important component of the obviousness inquiry because "evidence of secondary considerations may often be the most probative and cogent evidence in the record. It may often establish that an invention appearing to have been obvious in light of the prior art was not." *Id.* This objective evidence must be "considered as part of all the evidence, not just when the decisionmaker remains in doubt after reviewing the art." *Id.* at 1538-39. Thus, in order to determine obviousness, the decisionmaker must be able to consider all four *Graham* factors. Although we held in *Transocean I* that Maersk presented a prima facie case of obviousness, it was not error to allow the jury to consider the strength of that prima facie case in making the ultimate determination of obviousness. When the ultimate question of obviousness is put to the jury, the jury must be able to review all of the evidence of obviousness. *Id.* Hence it was not error for the court to allow the jury to weigh the strength of the prima facie case together with the objective evidence in order to reach a conclusion on the ultimate question of obviousness.

B. Objective Evidence

Although we held in *Transocean I* that Horn and Lund establish a prima facie case that the asserted claims would have been obvious, we reversed the district court's grant of summary judgment because the court failed to consider Transocean's objective evidence of nonobviousness. On the summary judgment record, Transocean presented evidence of industry praise, commercial success, industry skepticism, and copying. We stated that, "[i]f all of the factual disputes regarding the objective evidence resolve in favor of Transocean, it has presented a strong basis for rebutting the *prima facie* case" of obviousness.

On remand, the jury made express findings on seven types of objective evidence of nonobviousness: commercial success, industry praise, unexpected results, copying, industry skepticism, licensing, and long-felt but unsolved need. The jury found that each of these considerations supported the nonobviousness of Transocean's claims. In granting Maersk's motion for JMOL of obviousness, however, the district court concluded that the record evidence fails to support these findings. We disagree. As detailed below, Transocean presented substantial evidence from which a reasonable jury could find that each of the seven objective factors supports the nonobviousness of Transocean's claims.

1. Commercial Success

The district court rejected the jury's finding that commercial success supports nonobviousness. The court found that sales of Transocean's dual-activity rigs are "due primarily to various litigation[s]," and thus they "are not a result of a free market." The court also found that, at the time Transocean's patents issued, the drilling industry was "fully aware of the possibilities of a dual string rig as prior art" and that Transocean's patent application on this technology had been rejected in Europe as lacking inventiveness. Maersk contends that Transocean failed to tie its commercial success evidence to the claimed combination of two advancing stations with a pipe transfer assembly. Maersk also argues that unclaimed features of Transocean's rigs, such as increased size and capacity, are responsible for any commercial success.

As an initial matter, the district court erred by considering proceedings before the European Patent Office in its commercial success analysis. Transocean needed to show both commercial success and that a nexus exists between that success and the merits of the claimed invention. It is irrelevant to the commercial success analysis, however, that a foreign patent office rejected Transocean's patent application on the dual-activity technology. The district court's analysis seems to have been clouded by its view that the asserted claims would have been obvious over the prior art. This is precisely the sort of hindsight bias that evaluation of objective evidence is intended to avoid.

Transocean presented sufficient evidence of both commercial success and nexus to the features of the claimed invention. It showed, for example, that its dual-activity drilling rigs commanded a market premium over single-activity rigs. Transocean points to two contracts it signed on the same day with Anadarko Petroleum Corporation, one for a dual-activity drilling rig and one for a single-activity rig. Transocean charged a roughly 12% premium for the dual-activity rig. Transocean introduced other contracts that provided for reduced daily rates if the dual-activity feature on the rig was not available. Transocean's damages expert, Mr. Bratic, testified that the average reduction in this circumstance is 10%.

Transocean also presented evidence that some customers expressly require dual-activity rigs. For example, a Maersk employee testified at trial that Maersk added dual-activity to its new drilling rig design based on market surveys showing customer demand for this feature. Testimony by Maersk's own employee shows that customers request the dual-activity feature specifically based on the efficiency gains it provides by "involving two well centers in drilling the wells." The Maersk employee stated that "[m]any operators do require dual activity . . . for flexibility and for improved efficiency." Maersk sought to "incorporate the same efficiency improvement features as used by our competition" by incorporating Transocean's "dual-activity" technology, which Maersk distinguished from the "dual drilling" disclosed in the prior art. Transocean also offered testimony that dual-activity rigs account for an increasing percentage of the rigs sold and that they have become the industry standard.

From this evidence, a reasonable jury could conclude that Transocean's dual-activity rigs have been a commercial success and that this success has a nexus to the features claimed in the patents. We thus conclude that substantial evidence supports the jury's finding that commercial success weighs in favor of nonobviousness.

2. Industry Praise and Unexpected Results

The jury found that Transocean's dual-activity rigs received industry praise and achieved unexpectedly superior results, and that these factors supported nonobviousness. The district court rejected the jury's findings, reasoning that Transocean presented no statistical data to support these conclusions.

Maersk contends that any praise or unexpected and superior results are due to unclaimed features of Transocean's rig or elements from the prior art. Maersk argues that Transocean's evidence of praise for dual-activity rigs is no different from praise for the dual-drilling technology taught in the prior art. With dual-activity rigs, only one of two advancing stations actually drills, whereas dual-drilling involves using both advancing stations to simultaneously drill two wells.

We conclude that substantial evidence supports the jury's findings on industry praise and unexpected results. Transocean presented numerous documents showing industry praise for the unexpected increase in drilling efficiency made possible using Transocean's patented dual-activity technology. For example, Transocean cited a position paper written by a competitor stating that its own deepwater rig:

> must, at the least, include the most effective drilling cost reductions achieved by the new deepwater units. . . . Drilling cost reduction through technology advances pushed forward by the deepwater demands are *typified by innovations such as Transoceans [sic] dual-derrick concept,* designed to enable continuous drilling, potentially improving productive time by 25% to 40%.

J.A. 11505 (emphasis added).

Transocean also relied on an article in Offshore Magazine stating that multi-functionality (i.e., dual-activity) is "critical to [the] future." J.A. 13370. This article specifically describes the features of Transocean's dual-activity rigs: "a modified derrick and drill floor will allow for the makeup of drill-string and bottom hole assemblies separate from the drilling line where other functions such as casing installation may be underway." *Id.* The article states that the dual-activity operation will "allow for 20-40% faster tripping of drill-strings." *Id.* Transocean cites a second Offshore Magazine article, which praises the development of Transocean's dual-activity drillship as one of the fifty key events or technologies in history that shaped the offshore drilling industry. The article notes the ability of the rig to reduce drilling time and costs by "conduct[ing] drilling operations simultaneously rather than sequentially via two full capability drilling rigs." *Id.* This is quite an impressive accolade, and the jury was free to credit it as such.

Additionally, one of the named inventors of the patents-in-suit, Mr. Scott, testified that industry members doubted whether the claimed dual-activity feature would increase drilling efficiency. BP, for example, doubted whether dual-activity would cut costs so it had its own efficiency engineers analyze one of Transocean's dual-activity drilling rigs. *Id.* BP concluded that the rig could lead to even greater efficiency and cost savings than Transocean suggested.

This is substantial evidence from which the jury could reasonably conclude that Transocean's claimed dual-activity apparatus produced unexpected efficiency gains and that this benefit garnered praise in the drilling industry. Transocean's evidence also links both the industry praise and the unexpected efficiency gains directly to the claimed dual-activity feature. The first Offshore Magazine article, for example, expressly attributes improved efficiency to a derrick that can prepare drill string *separate from the drilling line,* as described in Transocean's patents. This description clearly distinguishes Transocean's dual-activity technology from the dual-drilling technology described in the prior art. *Id.* We conclude that the district court erred by determining that the jury lacked substantial evidence to find that industry praise and unexpected results support nonobviousness.

3. Copying

The district court failed to address the jury's finding that copying of the claimed invention supported nonobviousness. Maersk argues that Transocean's copying evidence is not tied to the novel features of its invention. We disagree.

Transocean points to an internal Maersk document stating "we have to incorporate the same efficiency improvement features as used by our competition," and that "[t]his feature is generally described as 'dual-activity.'" The Maersk document describes the features of dual-activity drilling, which it distinguishes from the "dual drilling" disclosed by Horn. The document states that Transocean's drill-ships are probably the "best known examples of dual activity vessels."

Transocean also presented evidence that Maersk was aware of Transocean's patents during the time Maersk was designing its accused rig. For example, a Maersk employee testified that he became aware of Transocean's patents "early on in the design development phase" of building the accused rig. Another Maersk employee stated that he became aware of the patents-in-suit during the design of the accused rig, but concluded that the patents were "not necessarily something that could be seen as protected" based on the prior art. A third Maersk employee stated that Maersk discussed Transocean's patents with customers in the United States and told them that Maersk did not infringe because the patents are invalid in view of the prior art.

This evidence shows that Maersk was aware of Transocean's patents and its drill-ships embodying the patents while Maersk designed its accused rig. The evidence also shows that Maersk decided to incorporate the claimed dual-activity feature anyway because it believed Transocean's patents were invalid over the prior art. Moreover, Maersk's internal document expressly ties its copying to the novel "dual-activity" features of Transocean's invention, which it distinguishes from the "dual drilling" taught in the prior art. This is substantial evidence that supports the jury's finding of copying.

4. Industry Skepticism

The jury found that industry skepticism supports nonobviousness. Although the district court admitted that "[i]t may be argued that a few in the market were skeptical," the court nonetheless concluded that Transocean presented insufficient evidence of industry skepticism to support the jury's finding. The court did not credit Transocean's evidence that people in the industry were skeptical of dual-activity rigs due to fears of "clashing," which occurs when the two drill strings collide with one another. The court reasoned that literature predating the filing of the patents-in-suit stated that concerns over clashing were unfounded. Maersk echoes this argument, pointing to a brochure by Horn dismissing concerns about clashing.

We conclude that the jury's fact finding was supported by substantial evidence. Transocean proffered testimony regarding skepticism by two named inventors of the patents-in-suit, Mr. Scott and Mr. Herrmann. They testified that even though they personally did not believe clashing was a concern, industry experts and Transocean's customers were skeptical of the claimed dual-activity feature due to fears of clashing. Mr. Herrmann recounted several occasions when industry experts stated that clashing would prevent dual-activity drilling from working, and he stated that some people are still concerned with clashing even today, Mr. Scott recounted similar experiences.

This evidence is sufficient for a reasonable jury to conclude that members of the drilling industry were skeptical of Transocean's dual-activity rigs. Although Maersk presented evidence that it contends dispels concerns over clashing, Transocean's evidence indicates that skepticism persists nonetheless. A reasonable jury could accept Transocean's evidence of skepticism even if the evidence could also support a contrary conclusion. We thus conclude that the district court erred by rejecting the jury's finding that skepticism supports nonobviousness.

5. Licensing

The jury found that Transocean established that its licenses to customers and competitors were due to the merits of the claimed invention and thus support nonobviousness. The district court did not directly address licensing, but found that Transocean's sales of its dual-activity technology were due primarily to litigation or threat of litigation, and thus seems not to have credited Transocean's licensing evidence. Maersk similarly contends that Transocean's licenses do not support nonobviousness because they are attributable to the threat of litigation. Maersk also argues that Transocean's licenses are not tied to the asserted claims because they convey rights not only to the patents-in-suit, but also to foreign counterparts and other patents that are not part of this case.

Transocean counters that the royalties paid under the licenses exceed any litigation costs, and thus are an accurate reflection of the value of the claimed invention. For example, Transocean introduced evidence at trial of a royalty payment by Noble Drilling (U.S.) Inc. totaling nearly $500,000 for one month of operations for one dual-activity rig. Transocean contends that large, sophisticated companies would not pay royalties exceeding the cost of litigation if the royalty did not reflect the value of the licensed technology. Transocean also offered testimony that at least three companies licensed its dual-activity drilling patents despite being under no threat of litigation. For example, Transocean's in-house counsel testified that both Shell and Pride Global, Limited, approached Transocean seeking to license its dual-activity technology.

We conclude that Transocean presented sufficient evidence for the jury to find that Transocean's licensing supports nonobviousness. From Transocean's testimony regarding the value of the licenses relative to litigation costs and regarding licenses with companies under no apparent threat of litigation, a reasonable jury could have found that the licenses reflect the value of the claimed invention and are not solely attributable to litigation. As a result, the district court erred by holding that the jury lacked substantial evidence to support its finding regarding licensing.

6. Long-Felt But Unsolved Need

The jury found that Transocean's invention provided a solution to a long-felt but unsolved need, and that this supports nonobviousness. The district court disagreed, finding that there was no long-felt but unresolved need because the prior art already disclosed dual string drilling technology. According to the court, no substantial demand existed for dual string drilling technology until deepwater drilling became more prevalent around the year 2000. On appeal, Maersk similarly argues that Transocean failed to present evidence linking any unmet need to the claimed features of the asserted claims.

We disagree. Transocean presented evidence at trial that its dual-activity technology satisfied a long-felt need for greater drilling efficiency. Transocean proffered testimony by two of the named inventors that the drilling industry had been operating in deepwater since the 1970s. One of Transocean's expert witnesses similarly testified that companies began to move towards deepwater drilling in the 1970s and that the drilling industry is always seeking greater efficiency from its rigs. The expert concluded that Transocean's dual-activity technology thus fulfilled a long-felt but unsolved need for a drilling rig that could operate efficiently in deep water.

Two of the named inventors testified that, prior to the claimed invention, the industry had been searching for ways to increase efficiency by building sections of drill string "offline," out of the path of the well conducting the drilling. These efforts were unsuccessful, however, and left an unsolved need for an efficient method of building the long drill strings needed for deepwater drilling without interrupting operations on the drilling well.

We conclude that substantial evidence supports the jury's finding that long-felt but unsolved need supports nonobviousness. From this testimony, a reasonable jury could conclude that Transocean's patents fulfilled a need in the drilling industry for a more efficient way to drill in deep water by allowing offline building of drill string and also including an auxiliary advancing station capable of lowering drilling components to the seabed. The district court erred by concluding that the jury lacked substantial evidence to support its finding on long-felt need.

C. Conclusion

We held in *Transocean I* that Horn and Lund teach each limitation of the asserted claims, provide a motivation to combine their teachings, and thus make out a prima facie case of obviousness. In granting Maersk's motion for JMOL of obviousness, the district court concluded that the objective evidence of nonobviousness was "insufficient, as a matter of law, to overcome Maersk['s] *prima facie* case of obviousness." We disagree.

On remand, Transocean presented compelling objective evidence of nonobviousness. We stated in *Transocean I* that, "[i]f all of the factual disputes regarding the objective evidence resolve in favor of Transocean, it has presented a strong basis for rebutting the *prima facie* case." 617 F.3d at 1305. Not only did the jury find for Transocean on the objective factors we noted in *Transocean I,* but it also found that three additional objective factors weighed in favor of nonobviousness.

Few cases present such extensive objective evidence of nonobviousness, and thus we have rarely held that objective evidence is sufficient to overcome a prima facie case of obviousness. *But see Tec Air, Inc. v. Denso Mfg. Mich. Inc.,* 192 F.3d 1353, 1361 (Fed. Cir. 1999) ("Alternatively, even assuming that [the accused infringer] established a *prima facie* case of obviousness, [the patentee] presented sufficient objective evidence of nonobviousness to rebut it.").

This, however, is precisely the sort of case where the objective evidence "establish[es] that an invention appearing to have been obvious in light of the prior art was not." *Stratoflex,* 713 F.2d at 1538. The jury found that seven distinct objective factors support nonobviousness and, as discussed above, these findings are all supported by substantial evidence. Weighing this objective evidence along with all the other evidence relevant to obviousness, we conclude that Maersk failed to prove by clear and convincing evidence that the asserted claims would have been obvious. We therefore reverse the district court's grant of JMOL of obviousness.

* * *

Comments

1. *Commercial Success as Proof of Nonobviousness.* Commercial success of an invention—the most commonly asserted secondary consideration—is relevant to nonobviousness because it assumes that if the invention were obvious, competitors of the inventor would have produced the invention given its significant consumer demand. *See Merck & Co., Inc. v. Teva Pharmaceuticals USA, Inc.*, 395 F.3d 1364, 1376 (Fed. Cir. 2005) ("Commercial success is relevant because the law presumes an idea would successfully have been brought to market sooner, in response to market forces, had the idea been obvious to persons skilled in the art."). At the same time, if an invention does not enjoy commercial success, it does not necessarily follow that the invention is obvious.

   A patent product's success in the market, however, may be the result of factors that have very little to do with the product's technical quality. In fact, there are many products on the market that prompt consumer attention and devotion because of aggressive advertising or clever marketing. For this reason, a party asserting commercial success must link up its technical innovation with the ultimate purchase. In other words, there must be a nexus or causal relationship between the commercial success of the product and the technical merits of the claimed invention. *See Ormco Corp. v. Align Technology, Inc.*, 463 F.3d 1299, 1311-1312 (Fed. Cir. 2006) (stating "[e]vidence of commercial success, or other secondary considerations, is only significant if there is a nexus between the claimed invention and the commercial success" and "[t]hus, if the commercial success is due to an unclaimed feature of the device, the commercial success is irrelevant").

2. *Additional Thoughts on Commercial Success.* The Federal Circuit's receptivity of secondary considerations was particularly pronounced in the early 1980s, soon after the court's creation and its mandate to strengthen patent rights was fresh. *See, e.g., Stratoflex, Inc. v. Aeroquip Corp.*, 713 F.2d 1530, 1538-1539 (Fed. Cir. 1983) (stating "evidence of secondary considerations may often be the most probative and cogent evidence in the record. It may often establish that an invention appearing to have been obvious in light of the prior art was not. It is to be considered as part of all the evidence, not just when the decisionmaker remains in doubt after reviewing the art"); *W.L. Gore & Associates, Inc. v. Garlock, Inc.*, 721 F.2d 1540 (Fed. Cir. 1983) (stating that secondary considerations can "often serve as insurance against the insidious attraction of the siren hindsight when confronted with a difficult task of evaluating the prior art"). The court's emphasis on commercial success has prompted some commentators to express doubts about the value of commercial success. For example, Robert Merges offered a thorough criticism of the commercial success doctrine, stating that it "is a poor indicator of patentability because it is indirect; it depends for its effectiveness on a long chain of inferences, and the links in the chain are often subject to doubt." Robert P. Merges, *Commercial Success and Patent Standards: Economic Perspectives on Innovation*, 76 CAL. L. REV. 803, 838-839 (1988). But Edmund Kitch has noted that using success in the marketplace as an indicator of patentability allows for greater "security in the investment process necessary to maximize the value of the patent." Edmund W. Kitch, *The Nature and Function of the Patent System*, 20 J.L. & ECON. 265, 283 (1977).

3. **Long-Felt Need and Failure of Others.** A patentee may also argue that his invention is not obvious because he developed what was considered a long-felt need in the industry, a solution competitors unsuccessfully were trying to develop as well. As Judge Easterbrook wrote, "If people are clamoring for a solution, and the best minds do not find it for years, that is practical evidence . . . of the state of knowledge." *In re Mahurkar Patent Litigation*, 831 F. Supp. 1354, 1377-1378 (N.D. Ill. 1993), *aff'd*, 71 F.3d 1573 (Fed. Cir. 1995). Yet, as with commercial success, there is a counterargument. For example, competitors of the patentee may have had different R&D priorities, decided to spend precious research dollars on other projects or not at all, or simply been content with the existing state of affairs.

4. **Licensing/Acquiescence.** Yet another secondary consideration relates to the patentee's assertion that his patent is not obvious because he enjoyed a successful licensing strategy. In other words, a party's willingness to license his patent is an implicit admission of nonobviousness. Why would a competitor pay a royalty on an invalid patent? Well, as any business person knows, litigation is quite expensive and results in high opportunity costs. Thus, it is oftentimes rational from a business perspective for a competitor to license a patent—even if he doubts its validity—rather than challenge its validity in court. As the defendant, in a patent litigation suit responded when asked why he settled, "It was a nuisance lawsuit, and it was the most efficient decision to settle it for a minimal amount." N.Y. TIMES, Business Section (Dec. 25, 2004).

CHAPTER

6

Statutory Bars

INTRODUCTION

This chapter is concerned with *statutory bars*. Prior to the enactment of the America Invents Act ("AIA"), statutory bars were embodied in section 102(b). The AIA eliminated this section as a stand-alone statutory bar provision, but retained key language—in particular, the words "on sale" and "public use"—that is now part of the new section 102(a)(1). Therefore, as with our discussion of novelty in Chapter 4, much of what you learn regarding pre-AIA statutory bar doctrine will apply to the post-AIA statutory framework.[1] And, again as with novelty jurisprudence, the AIA amendments relating to statutory bars only apply to patent applications filed on or after March 16, 2013, making pre-AIA law of statutory bars relevant for several years to come.

Accordingly, although the AIA's amendments to section 102 will be discussed in detail, this chapter (beginning with the next paragraph) is devoted predominantly to pre-AIA statutory bar jurisprudence and understanding the aforementioned phrases "on sale" and "public use." The issue we explore is: Irrespective of whether the claimed invention is novel, did the inventor or some third party use the invention publicly or offer the invention for sale before a certain date, commonly known as the critical date? What it means to engage in "public use" and "on sale" activity is the subject of this chapter.

Under the pre-AIA section 102(b), an inventor will be barred from obtaining a patent if, more than one year before the filing date of his patent application, he or a third party sells, offers for sale, or publicly uses the claimed invention (or an obvious variation thereof) in the United States, or patents, or describes in a printed publication the claimed invention (or an obvious variation thereof) anywhere in the world. The relevant timeframe for statutory bars is one year before the application is filed; this date is known as the *critical date* and the one-year period between the triggering event (e.g., public use) and the filing date is commonly referred to as the *grace period*. (The AIA retained the one-year grace period in section 102(b)(1).)

Statutory bars operate independently of novelty, and thus can attach even if an inventor satisfies the novelty requirement. Statutory bars and novelty differ in two important ways. First, statutory bars focus on activity of both the inventor

---

1. *See Safeco Ins. Co. of America v. Burr*, 551 U.S. 47, 58 (2007); *Microsoft Corp. v. i4i Limited Partnership*, 131 S. Ct. 2238, 2245 (2011) (stating "where Congress uses a common law term in a statute, we assume the 'term . . . comes with a common law meaning, absent anything pointing another way'") (citing *Safeco*).

and third parties; and second, as noted above, the critical date for statutory bars is one year before the application was filed; novelty focuses on activity before the date of invention.

The idea that an inventor can engage in activity that defeats his patent rights dates back to the late eighteenth century. Under Section 1 of the Patent Act of 1793, an inventor was entitled to a patent if, among other things, his invention was not in use before the date of application. In the historically important case of *Pennock v. Dialogue*,[2] Justice Story—patent law's great nineteenth-century jurist—gave meaning to this language and identified its underlying policies, thus providing a rationale for what is today section 102(b) and statutory bars. Justice Story expressed a utilitarian view of the patent system, one designed primarily to promote the public good.[3] And this goal could be furthered by disclosing to the public innovations "at as early a period as possible, having a due regard to the rights of the inventor."[4] With this premise, Justice Story stressed that an inventor should not be "permitted to hold back from the knowledge of the public the secrets of his invention," while also commercially exploiting his invention, because:

> if he should for a long period of years retain the monopoly, and make, and sell his invention publicly, and thus gather the whole profits of it, relying upon his superior skill and knowledge of the structure; and then, and then only, when the danger of competition should force him to secure the exclusive right, he should be allowed to take out a patent, and thus exclude the public from any farther use than what should be derived under it during his fourteen years; it would materially retard the progress of science and the useful arts, and give a premium to those who should be least prompt to communicate their discoveries.[5]

Promoting early disclosure, preventing the removal of inventions from the public that the public have justifiably come to expect are freely available, and preventing the inventor from commercially exploiting the exclusivity of his invention beyond the statutory term are policies underlying section 102(b), are as relevant today as they were in the nineteenth century. In addition to the public welfare rationale, Justice Story also noted that the policy underlying prompt disclosure should be balanced with "a due regard to the rights of the inventor." To this end, the Court of Claims, a Federal Circuit predecessor court, has identified an additional policy, namely giving "the inventor a reasonable amount of time following sales activity (set by statute as 1 year) to determine whether a patent is a worthwhile investment." *General Electric Co. v. United States*, 654 F.2d 55, 61 (Ct. Cl. 1981).

Keep these policies in mind as you proceed through the materials in this chapter. The two principal statutory bars under section 102(b) are on sale and public use, addressed in sections A and B, respectively.

---

2. 27 U.S. (2 Pet.) 1 (1829).

3. In cases prior to *Pennock*, Justice Story expressed more of a natural rights theory. In *Lowell v. Lewis*, for example, he wrote that "let the damages be estimated as high as they can be, consistently with the rule of law on this subject, if the plaintiff's patent has been violated; wrongdoers may not reap the fruits of the labor and genius of other men." 15 F. Cas. 1018, 1019 (C.C. Mass. 1817). *See also Ex parte Wood*, 22 U.S. 603, 608 (1824) (stating "[t]he inventor has . . . a property in his inventions; a property which is often of very great value, and of which the law intended to give him the absolute enjoyment and possession").

4. *Id*. at 19.

5. *Id*.

STATUTE: **Conditions for patentability; novelty and loss of right to patent**
35 U.S.C. § 102(b)

A. ON-SALE BAR

Under section 102(b), an inventor will be barred from obtaining patent rights if he or a third party sold or offered for sale the claimed invention more than one year before the patent application is filed. This is known as the "on-sale" bar, which, while easy enough to state, contains numerous sub-issues that have been the subject of extensive litigation. For instance, what constitutes an "offer"? Does the offer have to be "accepted" for the bar to apply? How are licenses and assignments treated? These questions are addressed in the principal case, *Plumtree*, and the Comments that follow.

An additional issue—and perhaps the most difficult—is, assuming an offer is made, at what developmental stage must an invention be before the one-year clock is triggered? Does the invention have to be built and work for its intended purpose; a mere conception; or somewhere in between? The issue of developmental stage of invention and why it is important are explored in *Pfaff, Space Systems*, and the Comments thereafter.

1. Developmental Stage of the Claimed Invention

PFAFF v. WELLS ELECTRONICS

525 U.S. 55 (1998)

STEVENS, J., delivered the opinion for a unanimous Court.

Section 102(b) of the Patent Act of 1952 provides that no person is entitled to patent an "invention" that has been "on sale" more than one year before filing a patent application. We granted certiorari to determine whether the commercial marketing of a newly invented product may mark the beginning of the 1-year period even though the invention has not yet been reduced to practice.

I

On April 19, 1982, petitioner, Wayne Pfaff, filed an application for a patent on a computer chip socket. Therefore, April 19, 1981, constitutes the critical date for purposes of the on-sale bar of 35 U.S.C. § 102(b); if the 1-year period began to run before that date, Pfaff lost his right to patent his invention.

Pfaff commenced work on the socket in November 1980, when representatives of Texas Instruments asked him to develop a new device for mounting and removing semiconductor chip carriers. In response to this request, he prepared detailed engineering drawings that described the design, the dimensions, and the materials to be used in making the socket. Pfaff sent those drawings to a manufacturer in February or March 1981.

Prior to March 17, 1981, Pfaff showed a sketch of his concept to representatives of Texas Instruments. On April 8, 1981, they provided Pfaff with a written confirmation of a previously placed oral purchase order for 30,100 of his new sockets for a total price of $91,155. In accord with his normal practice, Pfaff did not make and test a prototype of the new device before offering to sell it in commercial quantities.[3]

The manufacturer took several months to develop the customized tooling necessary to produce the device, and Pfaff did not fill the order until July 1981. The evidence therefore indicates that Pfaff first reduced his invention to practice in the summer of 1981. The socket achieved substantial commercial success before Patent No. 4,491,377 (the '377 patent) issued to Pfaff on January 1, 1985.[4]

After the patent issued, petitioner brought an infringement action against respondent, Wells Electronics, Inc., the manufacturer of a competing socket. Wells prevailed on the basis of a finding of no infringement. When respondent began to market a modified device, petitioner brought this suit, alleging that the modifications infringed six of the claims in the '377 patent.

After a full evidentiary hearing before a Special Master, the District Court held that two of those claims (1 and 6) were invalid because they had been anticipated in the prior art. Nevertheless, the court concluded that four other claims (7, 10, 11, and 19) were valid and three (7, 10, and 11) were infringed by various models of respondent's sockets. Adopting the Special Master's findings, the District Court rejected respondent's §102(b) defense because Pfaff had filed the application for the '377 patent less than a year after reducing the invention to practice.

The Court of Appeals reversed, finding all six claims invalid. Four of the claims (1, 6, 7, and 10) described the socket that Pfaff had sold to Texas Instruments prior to April 8, 1981. Because that device had been offered for sale on a commercial basis more than one year before the patent application was filed on April 19, 1982, the court concluded that those claims were invalid under §102(b). That conclusion rested on the court's view that as long as the invention was "substantially complete at the time of sale," the 1-year period began to run, even though the invention had not yet been reduced to practice.

Because other courts have held or assumed that an invention cannot be "on sale" within the meaning of §102(b) unless and until it has been reduced to practice, *see, e.g., Timely Products Corp. v. Arron*, 523 F.2d 288, 299-302 (C.A.2 1975), and because the text of §102(b) makes no reference to "substantial completion" of an invention, we granted *certiorari*.

---

3. At his deposition, respondent's counsel engaged in the following colloquy with Pfaff:
   Q: Now, at this time [late 1980 or early 1981] did we [sic] have any prototypes developed or anything of that nature, working embodiment?
   A: No.
   Q: It was in a drawing. Is that correct?
   A: Strictly in a drawing. Went from the drawing to the hard tooling. That's the way I do my business.
   Q: "Boom boom"?
   A: You got it.
   Q: You are satisfied, obviously, when you come up with some drawings that it is going to go—"it works"?
   A: I know what I'm doing, yes, most of the time.
4. Initial sales of the patented device were:
1981 $350,000
1982 $937,000
1983 $2,800,000
1984 $3,430,000

II

The primary meaning of the word "invention" in the Patent Act unquestionably refers to the inventor's conception rather than to a physical embodiment of that idea. The statute does not contain any express requirement that an invention must be reduced to practice before it can be patented. Neither the statutory definition of the term in §100 nor the basic conditions for obtaining a patent set forth in §101 make any mention of "reduction to practice." The statute's only specific reference to that term is found in §102(g), which sets forth the standard for resolving priority contests between two competing claimants to a patent. That subsection provides:

> In determining priority of invention there shall be considered not only the respective dates of conception and reduction to practice of the invention, but also the reasonable diligence of one who was first to conceive and last to reduce to practice, from a time prior to conception by the other.

Thus, assuming diligence on the part of the applicant, it is normally the first inventor to conceive, rather than the first to reduce to practice, who establishes the right to the patent.

It is well settled that an invention may be patented before it is reduced to practice. In 1888, this Court upheld a patent issued to Alexander Graham Bell even though he had filed his application before constructing a working telephone. Chief Justice Waite's reasoning in that case merits quoting at length:

> It is quite true that when Bell applied for his patent he had never actually transmitted telegraphically spoken words so that they could be distinctly heard and understood at the receiving end of his line, but in his specification he did describe accurately and with admirable clearness his process, that is to say, the exact electrical condition that must be created to accomplish his purpose, and he also described, with sufficient precision to enable one of ordinary skill in such matters to make it, a form of apparatus which, if used in the way pointed out, would produce the required effect, receive the words, and carry them to and deliver them at the appointed place. The particular instrument which he had, and which he used in his experiments, did not, under the circumstances in which it was tried, reproduce the words spoken, so that they could be clearly understood, but the proof is abundant and of the most convincing character, that other instruments, carefully constructed and made exactly in accordance with the specification, without any additions whatever, have operated and will operate successfully. A good mechanic of proper skill in matters of the kind can take the patent and, by following the specification strictly, can, without more, construct an apparatus which, when used in the way pointed out, will do all that it is claimed the method or process will do. . . .
>
> The law does not require that a discoverer or inventor, in order to get a patent for a process, must have succeeded in bringing his art to the highest degree of perfection. It is enough if he describes his method with sufficient clearness and precision to enable those skilled in the matter to understand what the process is, and if he points out some practicable way of putting it into operation. *The Telephone Cases*, 126 U.S. 1, 535-536 (1888).

When we apply the reasoning of *The Telephone Cases* to the facts of the case before us today, it is evident that Pfaff could have obtained a patent on his novel socket when he accepted the purchase order from Texas Instruments for 30,100 units. At that time he provided the manufacturer with a description and drawings that had "sufficient clearness and precision to enable those skilled in the matter" to produce the device. The parties agree that the sockets manufactured to fill that order embody Pfaff's conception as set forth in claims 1, 6, 7, and 10 of the '377 patent. We can find no basis in the text of § 102(b) or in the facts of this case for concluding that Pfaff's invention was not "on sale" within the meaning of the statute until after it had been reduced to practice.

III

Pfaff nevertheless argues that longstanding precedent, buttressed by the strong interest in providing inventors with a clear standard identifying the onset of the 1-year period, justifies a special interpretation of the word "invention" as used in § 102(b). We are persuaded that this nontextual argument should be rejected.

As we have often explained, most recently in *Bonito Boats, Inc. v. Thunder Craft Boats, Inc.*, 489 U.S. 141, 151 (1989), the patent system represents a carefully crafted bargain that encourages both the creation and the public disclosure of new and useful advances in technology, in return for an exclusive monopoly for a limited period of time. The balance between the interest in motivating innovation and enlightenment by rewarding invention with patent protection on the one hand, and the interest in avoiding monopolies that unnecessarily stifle competition on the other, has been a feature of the federal patent laws since their inception.

Consistent with these ends, § 102 of the Patent Act serves as a limiting provision, both excluding ideas that are in the public domain from patent protection and confining the duration of the monopoly to the statutory term.

We originally held that an inventor loses his right to a patent if he puts his invention into public use before filing a patent application. "His voluntary act or acquiescence in the public sale and use is an abandonment of his right." *Pennock v. Dialogue*, 2 Pet. 1, 24 (1829) (Story, J.). A similar reluctance to allow an inventor to remove existing knowledge from public use undergirds the on-sale bar.

Nevertheless, an inventor who seeks to perfect his discovery may conduct extensive testing without losing his right to obtain a patent for his invention—even if such testing occurs in the public eye. The law has long recognized the distinction between inventions put to experimental use and products sold commercially. In 1878, we explained why patentability may turn on an inventor's use of his product.

> It is sometimes said that an inventor acquires an undue advantage over the public by delaying to take out a patent, inasmuch as he thereby preserves the monopoly to himself for a longer period than is allowed by the policy of the law; but this cannot be said with justice when the delay is occasioned by a bona fide effort to bring his invention to perfection, or to ascertain whether it will answer the purpose intended. His monopoly only continues for the allotted period, in any event; and it is the interest of the public, as well as himself, that the invention should be perfect and properly tested, before a patent is granted for it. *Any attempt to use it for a profit, and not by way of experiment, for a longer period than two years before the application, would deprive the inventor of his right to a patent. Elizabeth v. American Nicholson Pavement Co.,* 97 U.S. 126, 137 (1877) (emphasis added).

The patent laws therefore seek both to protect the public's right to retain knowledge already in the public domain and the inventor's right to control whether and when he may patent his invention. The Patent Act of 1836, 5 Stat. 117, was the first statute that expressly included an on sale bar to the issuance of a patent. Like the earlier holding in *Pennock*, that provision precluded patentability if the invention had been placed on sale at any time before the patent application was filed. In 1839, Congress ameliorated that requirement by enacting a 2-year grace period in which the inventor could file an application.

In *Andrews v. Hovey*, 123 U.S. 267, 274 (1887), we noted that the purpose of that amendment was "to fix a period of limitation which should be certain"; it required the inventor to make sure that a patent application was filed "within two years from the completion of his invention," *ibid*. In 1939, Congress reduced the grace period from two years to one year.

Petitioner correctly argues that these provisions identify an interest in providing inventors with a definite standard for determining when a patent application must be filed. A rule that makes the timeliness of an application depend on the date when an invention is "substantially complete" seriously undermines the interest in certainty.[11] Moreover, such a rule finds no support in the text of the statute. Thus, petitioner's argument calls into question the standard applied by the Court of Appeals, but it does not persuade us that it is necessary to engraft a reduction to practice element into the meaning of the term "invention" as used in § 102(b).

The word "invention" must refer to a concept that is complete, rather than merely one that is "substantially complete." It is true that reduction to practice ordinarily provides the best evidence that an invention is complete. But just because reduction to practice is sufficient evidence of completion, it does not follow that proof of reduction to practice is necessary in every case. Indeed, both the facts of *The Telephone Cases* and the facts of this case demonstrate that one can prove that an invention is complete and ready for patenting before it has actually been reduced to practice.

We conclude, therefore, that the on sale bar applies when two conditions are satisfied before the critical date. First, the product must be the subject of a commercial offer for sale. An inventor can both understand and control the timing of the first commercial marketing of his invention. The experimental use doctrine, for example, has not generated concerns about indefiniteness, and we perceive no reason why unmanageable uncertainty should attend a rule that measures the application of the on sale bar of § 102(b) against the date when an invention that is ready for patenting is first marketed commercially. In this case the acceptance of the purchase order prior to April 8, 1981, makes it clear that such an offer had been made, and there is no question that the sale was commercial rather than experimental in character.

---

11. The Federal Circuit has developed a multifactor, "totality of the circumstances" test to determine the trigger for the on sale bar. *See, e.g., Micro Chemical, Inc. v. Great Plains Chemical Co.*, 103 F.3d 1538, 1544 (C.A. Fed. 1997) (stating that, in determining whether an invention is on sale for purposes of 102(b), "'all of the circumstances surrounding the sale or offer to sell, including the stage of development of the invention and the nature of the invention, must be considered and weighed against the policies underlying section 102(b)'"); *see also UMC Electronics Co. v. United States*, 816 F.2d 647, 656 (1987) (stating the on sale bar "does not lend itself to formulation into a set of precise requirements"). As the Federal Circuit itself has noted, this test "has been criticized as unnecessarily vague." *Seal-Flex, Inc. v. Athletic Track & Court Construction*, 98 F.3d 1318, 1323, n.2 (C.A. Fed. 1996).

Second, the invention must be ready for patenting. That condition may be satisfied in at least two ways: by proof of reduction to practice before the critical date; or by proof that prior to the critical date the inventor had prepared drawings or other descriptions of the invention that were sufficiently specific to enable a person skilled in the art to practice the invention.[14] In this case the second condition of the on sale bar is satisfied because the drawings Pfaff sent to the manufacturer before the critical date fully disclosed the invention.

The evidence in this case thus fulfills the two essential conditions of the on sale bar. As succinctly stated by Learned Hand:

> [I]t is a condition upon an inventor's right to a patent that he shall not exploit his discovery competitively after it is ready for patenting; he must content himself with either secrecy, or legal monopoly. *Metallizing Engineering Co. v. Kenyon Bearing & Auto Parts Co.*, 153 F.2d 516, 520 (C.A. 2 1946).

The judgment of the Court of Appeals finds support not only in the text of the statute but also in the basic policies underlying the statutory scheme, including § 102(b). When Pfaff accepted the purchase order for his new sockets prior to April 8, 1981, his invention was ready for patenting. The fact that the manufacturer was able to produce the socket using his detailed drawings and specifications demonstrates this fact. Furthermore, those sockets contained all the elements of the invention claimed in the '377 patent. Therefore, Pfaff's '377 patent is invalid because the invention had been on sale for more than one year in this country before he filed his patent application. Accordingly, the judgment of the Court of Appeals is affirmed.

SPACE SYSTEMS/LORAL, INC. v. LOCKHEED MARTIN CORP.

271 F.3d 1076 (Fed. Cir. 2001)

NEWMAN, Circuit Judge.

Space Systems/Loral, Inc. (herein "SSL") appeals the decision of the United States District Court for the Northern District of California, granting summary judgment in favor of Lockheed Martin Corporation based on the court's ruling of invalidity of SSL's United States Patent No. 4,537,375. Because the district court misapplied the law of "on sale," 35 U.S.C. § 102(b), we reverse the summary judgment and remand for further proceedings.

BACKGROUND

The '375 patent is directed to an attitude control system for maintaining the position and orientation of a satellite. A satellite in orbit may drift out of

---

14. The Solicitor General has argued that the rule governing on sale bar should be phrased somewhat differently. In his opinion, "if the sale or offer in question embodies the invention for which a patent is later sought, a sale or offer to sell that is primarily for commercial purposes and that occurs more than one year before the application renders the invention unpatentable. *Seal-Flex, Inc. v. Athletic Track and Court Constr.*, 98 F.3d 1318, 1325 (Fed. Cir. 1996) (Bryson, J., concurring in part and concurring in the result)." It is true that evidence satisfying this test might be sufficient to prove that the invention was ready for patenting at the time of the sale if it is clear that no aspect of the invention was developed after the critical date. However, the possibility of additional development after the offer for sale in these circumstances counsels against adoption of the rule proposed by the Solicitor General.

position due to influences such as gravitational effects of the sun and moon and pressure from the solar wind, generally called "disturbance transients." To return the satellite to its correct orbit and orientation various on-board devices are employed, such as momentum/reaction wheels or thrusters, which are small rocket engines. Such corrective maneuvers are called "station keeping." Imbalances in thruster power or misalignments with respect to the satellite's center of mass, which may change as fuel is consumed, tend to introduce new errors in position or orientation during station keeping maneuvers. Such new errors require further correction after the primary correcting maneuver is made. The novel method of station keeping described in the '375 patent is called the "prebias" technique. By this technique a correction for thruster imbalances is made before the primary station keeping maneuver is performed, using data stored from previous maneuvers. If any attitude inaccuracies remain they are subjected to a further correction, but as a result of the prebias step substantially less fuel is required overall than would be consumed without the prebias compensatory action. Conservation of on-board fuel prolongs the effective life of a satellite. . . . The district court held that the invention claimed in the '375 patent was on sale more than one year before the patent application was filed, rendering the patent invalid pursuant to §102(b). Since the '375 application date is April 21, 1983, the "critical date" for the on sale bar is April 21, 1982.

The relevant events are not in dispute. Ford Aerospace and Communications Corp., a predecessor of SSL and the initial assignee of the '375 patent, entered into a contract with Société Nationale Industrielle Aerospatiale, a French company that had contracted with the Arab Satellite Communications Organization to develop the "Arabsat" satellite system. Ford was responsible for several aspects of the Arabsat system, including the satellite attitude control system.

Dr. Fred Chan, a Ford employee, conceived of the prebias method of satellite station keeping as a potential improvement over the design that was originally intended to be used. On March 19, 1982 Ford sent Aerospatiale a document entitled "Engineering Change Proposal" (ECP) which described the prebiasing idea and how Dr. Chan proposed to achieve it, by the steps of storing an estimated disturbance torque, performing a first thruster modulation in response to the stored value, detecting the net position error, and then performing a second modulation in response to the net position error and the stored value. Included were Dr. Chan's rough drawings, along with an estimate of the cost of developing the system. The district court held that this submission was an invalidating on sale event. Applying *Pfaff v. Wells Electronics, Inc.*, 525 U.S. 55, (1998), the court ruled that the ECP was a commercial offer of sale, and that the invention was ready for patenting because "SSL admitt[ed] that Dr. Chan had legal conception of every element of every claim of the '375 patent at the time the ECP was submitted to Aerospatiale." The court held that it was irrelevant that the inventor was uncertain whether the system could be made to work.

DISCUSSION

In this case there was no dispute as to what transpired; the issue was whether the criteria of the on sale bar were met. In *Pfaff, supra,* the Supreme Court held that the on sale bar arises when the invention is both (1) ready for patenting and (2) the subject of a commercial offer for sale. SSL states that neither of these criteria was met. SSL states that at the time the engineering proposal was sent to Aerospatiale and for many months thereafter, Dr. Chan's idea was not ready for patenting for its feasibility was not yet known and it had not been enabled. Dr. Chan testified that at the time he sent the proposal to Aerospatiale he had conceived of the idea but he did not know whether he could make it work. He testified that the method for generating a value had to be developed, and that he was not sure he could establish a stable control loop. He stated that it was not until many months later, after development and testing of an engineering model, that he determined that the idea would work.

Lockheed presented no evidence disputing Dr. Chan's testimony, and does not assign error to the district court's statement that it could not conclude as a matter of law that the engineering proposal was an "enabling disclosure." Instead, Lockheed states that the bar arises, as a matter of law, "if an inventor offers for sale a product which has reached the 'conception stage.'" Lockheed stresses that "Because SSL had conceived the invention as of March 19, 1982, it could have filed a patent application—the invention was ready for patenting." Lockheed states that conception embraces enablement, and since SSL conceded conception at the time of the Engineering Change Proposal, it also conceded enablement. Thus Lockheed led the district court into error, for the district court ruled that all that is required for an invention to be ready for patenting is "legal conception of every element of every claim." The court described "legal conception" as a mental act, and held that it is not necessary to enable an invention that is fully conceived, in order for the invention to be ready for patenting. Lockheed states that this is the law of *Pfaff*. That is incorrect.

In *Pfaff* the Court explained that two ways to show that an invention is ready for patenting are if it has been actually reduced to practice, or if "prior to the critical date the inventor had prepared drawings or other descriptions of the invention that were sufficiently specific to enable a person skilled in the art to practice the invention." 525 U.S. at 67-68. The Court noted that it must be "clear that no aspect of the invention was developed after the critical date." *Id.* at 68 n.14.

Lockheed argues that Dr. Chan's rough drawings showed the essential principles of the invention, although in lesser detail than was later available and included in the patent application. SSL responds that many months of development were required in order to learn the information that was essential to an operable invention, and that the drawings do not show an enabled invention. Lockheed states that its position that conception alone suffices in order to satisfy the *Pfaff* requirement of ready for patenting is supported by the Court's statements in *Pfaff* that "invention . . . refers to the inventor's conception rather than to a physical embodiment of [the] idea," 525 U.S. at 60. However, the Court in defining "invention" was not saying that conception alone equals "ready for patenting." The Court later explained that "The word 'invention' must refer to a concept that is complete, rather than merely one that is 'substantially complete.' It is true that reduction to practice ordinarily provides the best evidence that an invention is complete . . . it does not follow that proof of reduction to practice is necessary in every case." 525 U.S. at 66.

The Court thus held that reduction to practice was not necessary in every case; but the Court did not hold that a conception, having neither a reduction to practice nor an enabling description, is ready for patenting as a matter of law. To be "ready for patenting" the inventor must be able to prepare a patent application, that is, to provide an enabling disclosure as required by 35 U.S.C. §112. For a complex concept such as the prebias technique, wherein the inventor himself was uncertain whether it could be made to work, a bare conception that has not been enabled is not a completed invention ready for patenting. Although conception can occur before the inventor has verified that his idea will work, *see Burroughs Wellcome Co. v. Barr Labs., Inc.,* 40 F.3d 1223, 1228 (Fed. Cir. 1994), when development and verification are needed in order to prepare a patent application that complies with § 112, the invention is not yet ready for patenting.

Lockheed argues that since Dr. Chan's proposal included the system's four steps that are set forth in the claim, the idea was "ready for patenting" as a matter of law, even if it were not then enabled. However, the patent statute requires an enabling disclosure of how to make and use the invention. The fact that a concept is eventually shown to be workable does not retrospectively convert the concept into one that was "ready for patenting" at the time of conception. As we have observed, the Court recognized this distinction when it stated in *Pfaff* that the on sale bar does not arise when there is "additional development after the offer for sale." 525 U.S. at 68 n.14. The district court erred in ruling that the prebias invention was ready for patenting upon conception as communicated in the engineering proposal. The judgment based thereon can not stand; thus we need not reach the question of whether a commercial offer of sale was made.

Comments

1. *"Ready for Patenting."* The second part of the *Pfaff* test focused on the developmental stage of the invention at the time of the offer for sale. (The first prong of *Pfaff* is explored in the next subsection and *Plumtree*.) By rejecting the "substantially complete" test, the Supreme Court situated the on-sale bar within the more familiar patent law principles embodied in sections 102(g) and 112. Accordingly, the *Pfaff* Court held that the invention must be "ready for patenting" to trigger the one-year clock at the time of an offer for sale. An invention will be deemed "ready for patenting" if either it was reduced to practice (see Chapter 4) or subject to an enabling disclosure—such as engineering drawings or other documented evidence—consistent with section 112. *See Space Systems* (stating to be "ready for patenting the inventor must be able to prepare a patent application, that is, to provide an enabling disclosure as required by 35 U.S.C. § 112"); *Robotic Vision Systems, Inc. v. View Engineering, Inc.,* 249 F.3d 1307, 1312, 1314 (Fed. Cir. 2001) (affirming district court finding that "the invention was ready for patenting because the inventor's disclosure was also an enabling disclosure, i.e., one that was sufficiently specific to enable his co-worker, who was a person skilled in the art, to practice the invention").

In *Honeywell Int'l, Inc. v. Universal Avionics Systems, Inc.,* 488 F.3d 982 (Fed. Cir. 2007), the patented technology related to "terrain warning systems," which help prevent pilots from flying into mountains or hillsides. Prior to the critical date, Honeywell entered into negotiations with Gulfstream and Canadair, two commercial aircraft manufacturers, to test its system with human pilots in an actual cockpit setting. Honeywell used design notes, computer simulations, test aircraft, and demonstrations to those with expertise in air safety such as pilots. There was also a videotape of the invention in use aboard an actual aircraft, which shows the invention in operation. Nonetheless, the Federal Circuit held Honeywell did not violate the on-sale bar because the developmental stage of the invention was not ready for patenting, and therefore, step two of *Pfaff* was not satisfied.

2. ***Why Isn't Conception Conclusive Evidence of "Ready for Patenting"?*** The Federal Circuit rejected Lockheed's argument that a proper reading of *Pfaff* would support an argument that conception alone is sufficient evidence of "ready for patenting." According to the court, this was not *Pfaff*'s holding; rather, while evidence of reduction to practice is not needed, "[t]o be 'ready for patenting' the inventor must be able to prepare a patent application, that is, to provide an enabling disclosure as required by 35 U.S.C. § 112." But isn't this statement a description of conception? Consider the court's statement in *University of Pittsburgh v. Hedrick*, wherein the court wrote, in the context of an inventorship dispute, that conception does not require "scientific certainty." Rather,

> [c]onception requires a definite and permanent idea of the operative invention, and necessarily turns on the inventor's ability to describe his invention. Proof that the invention works to a scientific certainty is reduction to practice. . . . [The inventors] had disclosed a completed thought expressed in such clear terms as to enable those skilled in the art to make the invention.

573 F.3d 1290, 1299 (Fed. Cir. 2009). Does this definition of conception sounds like "ready for patenting"?

3. ***Why Do We Care About Developmental Stage of the Invention?*** One reason developmental stage is important is to provide the inventor with some certainty regarding when his attempted commercial activity triggers the one-year clock. Consider Judge Smith's dissent in *UMC Electronics Co. v. United States*, 816 F.2d 647, 664 (Fed. Cir. 1987), wherein he expressed concerns about the majority's holding that something less than reduction to practice ("RTP") of the claimed invention will suffice to trigger the clock:

> It is the users of the patent system who will suffer the impact of the panel majority decision. The question is not theoretical; it is of great practical importance.
>
> Those inventors who have sought financing, or who have contacted potential customers, or who have engaged in other normal business activities before they have made a workable device will not know how the time limit for filing a patent application will be measured or where the line will be drawn between raw idea and proved invention. Inventors do not normally try to patent something they have not yet found workable. The patent law, and particularly section 112, does not favor it. Most inventors do not hire a patent lawyer until they have something that works, by which time, according to the panel majority, it may be too late.
>
> * * *
>
> It is not clear why this change is being wrought on the community of inventors and the public without providing some alternative measure of certainty. The "all circumstances" rule evoked by the panel majority means that the critical question in more and more cases can only be answered with finality by a judicial determination in which there is no further appeal.

Reduction to practice lends itself to greater certainty, but it can arguably be manipulated by inventors, who could just stop short of RTP, yet engage in commercially exploitative conduct. But once you allow something less than RTP, such as conception, certainty is sacrificed. Perhaps the *Pfaff* Court, as discussed in *Space Systems*, thought "ready for patenting" was a viable compromise.

4. **Seller's Knowledge and Time of Offer.** The *Space Systems* court seemed to rely in part on the fact that at the time the alleged offer was made, Dr. Chan was uncertain about whether the claimed invention worked. But other cases suggest a more objective test with respect to the inventor's (or seller's) knowledge of the product offered for sale. For instance, the court has held a section 102(b) offer will exist even though the offer does not specifically identify the characteristics of the claimed invention or the seller and buyer do not recognize the significance of the characteristics at the time of the offer. *See Abbott Laboratories v. Geneva Pharmaceuticals, Inc.*, 182 F.3d 1315, 1318-1319 (Fed. Cir. 1999). The underlying point of the on-sale bar is that the seller attempted to commercially exploit the claimed invention, and the potential buyer's understanding of the invention is irrelevant in this regard. Indeed, the inventor is not required to have "complete confidence" in the operability of his invention for the on-sale bar to apply. *See also Scaltech Inc. v. Retec/Tetra LLC*, 178 F.3d 1378, 1383 (Fed. Cir. 1999) (stating "[w]e note that there is no requirement that the offer specifically identify these [claim] limitations. . . . Nor is there a requirement that Scaltech must have recognized the significance of these limitations at the time of offer"); *Robotic Vision Systems, Inc. v. View Engineering, Inc.*, 249 F.3d 1307, 1312 (Fed. Cir. 2001) (stating "[n]otably absent from [the *Pfaff*] test is a requirement that an inventor have complete confidence that his invention work will work for its intended purpose. . . . We did not hold that lack of skepticism regarding the 'workability of an invention' was an evidentiary requirement. It will be a rare case indeed in which an inventor has no uncertainty concerning the workability of his invention before he has reduced it to practice").

An objective approach seems to make more sense. Consider an inventor who offers his invention for sale, but expresses deep skepticism about its functionality. Yet PHOSITAs in the inventor's art collectively believe the invention will work for its intended purpose. Isn't the PHOSITA's objective belief evidence of ready for patenting? Why should the inventor's subjective belief be a factor in determining whether the invention were "ready for patenting"? Should the converse lead to a different result? That is, the PHOSITAs were skeptical, but the inventor was optimistic of the invention's operability. Should the PHOSITA's skepticism weigh against a finding of ready for patenting?

2. What Constitutes an Offer for Sale?

PLUMTREE SOFTWARE, INC. v. DATAMIZE, LLC

473 F.3d 1152 (Fed. Cir. 2006)

DYK, Circuit Judge.

Plumtree Software, Inc. ("Plumtree") filed this declaratory judgment action against Datamize, LLC ("Datamize") in the United States District Court for the

Northern District of California. The district court . . . granted summary judgment in favor of Plumtree on the ground that Datamize's patents were invalid under the on sale bar doctrine, 35 U.S.C. §102(b). Datamize now appeals. We vacate and remand for further proceedings on the merits.

BACKGROUND

I

This case involves two Datamize patents, U.S. Patent Nos. 6,460,040 ("'040 patent") and 6,658,418 ("'418 patent"). Datamize principal Kevin Burns is the named inventor of the patents, which were continuations of his U.S. Patent No. 6,014,137 ("'137 patent"). The patents are entitled "Authoring System for Computer-based Information Delivery System" and share a common specification.

The patented invention is a computer program that is used to create other computer programs (an "authoring tool"). The invention encompasses both the method of creating the computer program and the software for creating the computer program. The '040 patent contains method claims, and the '418 patent is asserted to contain both method and apparatus claims. The authoring tool may be used to create customized kiosks. As an example, the patents explain the authoring tool might be used to create electronic kiosks used at ski resorts to provide information to customers about ski conditions, local hotels, and restaurants through a touch screen or key pad. The patented invention is not the kiosk itself, but is the software for, and the method of, creating the kiosk.

Plumtree is a computer software company that produces "corporate portal" software. The corporate portal is web-based software that brings together various applications and information into a customized desktop screen that employees of an organization can separately access. Plumtree primarily markets its corporate portal software to companies that want to organize their corporate intranet sites.

* * *

DISCUSSION

* * *

II

A claimed invention is considered to be on sale under §102(b) if the invention is sold or offered for sale more than one year before the filing date of the patent application. Here the '040 and '418 patents claim priority to a provisional application that was filed on February 27, 1996. Thus, for purposes of the on sale bar, the critical date is February 27, 1995.

The facts pertinent to the on sale bar issue are as follows. By December 1994 Kevin Burns, the inventor of the '040 and '418 patents, had completed development of the authoring tool ultimately reflected in the patent claims. In the winter of 1994 his company, MA, learned that the SIA was going to hold a trade show in Las Vegas, Nevada in March 1995. As part of the show, SIA planned to include an example of a "ski store of the future" called the "Mountain Visions" store.

On January 17, 1995, representatives from MA gave a presentation to the representatives from SIA at SIA's headquarters in Virginia. At the time of the presentation, the authoring tool had been reduced to practice, but MA had not yet used the authoring tool to create a kiosk product. The slides used during MA's presentation refer to "proprietary authoring tools" that "allow rapid updating" and "support new technologies as they appear." However, Emmett Burns later testified that he could not "recall telling SIA any of the particulars of the authoring tool at the SIA meeting." He stated that he did not explain how the authoring tool allowed for "rapid updating" because "even if [h]e explained any of it[,] [t]hese people . . . are not technology people; and they go into a different space if you start to get into that." Rather, Emmett Burns testified that the purpose of the presentation was to show SIA what the ultimate kiosk product, entitled "SkiPath," "would be like."

On January 25, 1995, SIA sent a letter to MA confirming the agreement that MA would "participat[e] as [a] sponsor of the 'interactive' portion of the electronic information center of Mountain Visions at SIA." The letter stated that in exchange for SIA "waiving the $10,000 sponsorship fee associated with participation in the electronic information center," MA agreed to:

1. Provide software/hardware package necessary to produce the interactive touch-screen information center as presented to SIA on January 17, 1995 in McLean, VA.
2. Provide multiples of this software/hardware package to allow for multiple customer access in the information center.
3. Work to the best of their ability to put the other product sponsors participating in the concept store on the interactive system, as presented [] January 17th, at no charge to these companies. SIA will work to facilitate this effort wherever possible.
4. Provide looped advertising/entertainment video on 3/4 inch VHS for the overhead monitor system. SIA would help to acquire entertainment segments if necessary.
5. Exhibit within the trade show. SIA will facilitate getting Multimedia Adventures an appropriate booth space to exhibit and sell your products.

On January 26, 1995, Kevin Burns "filled out an exhibit space contract for [MA's] exhibit space at the tradeshow" and paid $2,430 in exhibit space fees. The exhibit space contract stated that "the type of product" MA would display was a "computer kiosk." Emmett Burns later testified that the agreement between SIA and MA was that in exchange for space at the trade show, MA would "put the system in the store." He explained that "the system" was "the multimedia kiosk" (SkiPath).

The trade show was held on March 3-7, 1995 (after the February 27, 1995, critical date) in Las Vegas, NV. Kevin Burns testified that "a Mulitmedia Adventures product" was demonstrated and that there was a demonstration of the "kiosk system," which was called "SkiPath." The record establishes that "SkiPath [was] created with the authoring system" and that the authoring system embodied all the claims of all three of Datamize's patents. Kevin Burns also testified, somewhat confusingly, that "the network kiosk system that was demonstrated in March of 1995 at the Las Vegas show embod[ied] all the claims" of the '040 and '418 patents. Although Kevin Burns began creating SkiPath before the January 17 meeting, the programming and testing of the SkiPath product was not completed until the end of the first day of the trade show. Thus, the record is not clear whether the patented process was used before the critical date.

[T]he district court considered Plumtree's motion for summary judgment. The court held both the '040 and '418 patents invalid under the on sale bar rule. The court concluded that "the on sale bar [was] triggered by the facts of this case" because there was "an agreement to 'perform' a method claim" before the critical date. The basis for this holding was the fact that "[a]t the January 17, 1995, meeting, MA offered to provide its interactive electronic kiosk system during the March 1995 trade show." The court found that MA received consideration because "MA was granted a 'prime location' and its fee was waived in exchange for the display of MA's kiosk." *Id.* The court noted that MA's meeting with SIA on January 17, 1995, and the subsequent agreement both occurred before the February 27, 1995, critical date. The court then stated that "the agreement with SIA embodied all of the claims of the '040 and '418 patents" because "the kiosk at the trade show embodied all of the claims." Accordingly, the court granted summary judgment in favor of Plumtree.

III

The Supreme Court in *Pfaff v. Wells Electronics, Inc.* has set forth a two-part test for determining whether there was a sale or offer for sale for purposes of §102(b). First, "the product must be the subject of a commercial [sale or] offer for sale." *Id.* Second, "the invention must be ready for patenting." *Id.* The second condition is met by "proof of reduction to practice before the critical date." *Id.* Here the parties agree that the authoring tool was reduced to practice in the winter of 1994. Accordingly, we need only consider the first prong of the *Pfaff* test.

A commercial sale or offer for sale necessarily involves consideration. *See Group One, Ltd. v. Hallmark Cards, Inc.*; Restatement (Second) of Contracts §71 (1981). We agree with the district court that MA received valid consideration. SIA awarded MA floor space at the trade show and waived $10,000 sponsorship fee normally charged to show participants. Datamize argues that waiver of the $10,000 sponsorship fee did not constitute consideration because Plumtree did not demonstrate that the fee waiver was "somehow due to the invention." We do not find this argument persuasive.

However, on this record, we cannot sustain the district court's conclusion that the method claims are invalid under the on sale bar rule. The district court reasoned that "the agreement with SIA embodied all of the claims of the '040 and '418 patents" because "the kiosk at the trade show embodied all of the claims." In so holding, the district court relied on Kevin Burns's testimony that "the network kiosk system that was demonstrated in March of 1995 at the Las Vegas show embod[ied] all the claims" of the '040 and '418 patents. These statements reflect confusion as to the nature of the patented product. Here the invention reflected in the method claims is a process for creating a kiosk system, not the kiosk system itself. The kiosk system itself is not patented. The court's focus on whether the kiosk system somehow embodied the claims of the patent was misplaced, and the district court's reasoning does not support a grant of summary judgment. Nor does the record support the ultimate result reached by the district court.

In our view, Plumtree could meet the first prong of the *Pfaff* test under either of two alternative theories. First, Plumtree could demonstrate that before the critical date MA made a commercial offer to perform the patented method (even if the performance itself occurred after the critical date). Second, Plumtree could demonstrate that before the critical date MA in fact performed the patented method for a promise of future compensation. Under the second theory, Plumtree would not need to prove that the contract itself required performance of the patented method. We address these alternative theories in turn.

Under the first theory, Plumtree would have to demonstrate that before the critical date MA made a commercial offer to perform the patented method. A commercial offer is "one which the other party could make into a binding contract by simple acceptance (assuming consideration)." *Group One*, 254 F.3d at 1048. Under this standard, it is clear that the offeror must be legally bound to perform the patented method if the offer is accepted. *See Linear Tech. Corp. v. Micrel, Inc.*, 275 F.3d 1040, 1050 (Fed. Cir. 2001) (stating that there was no offer where communication did not "indicate LTC's intent to be bound" (citing Restatement (Second) of Contracts § 26 (1981)). Whether there has been a commercial offer is governed by federal common law.

Whether MA made a commercial offer to perform the patented method is governed by our decision in *Scaltech, Inc. v. Retec/Tetra, LLC,* 269 F.3d 1321, 1327 (Fed. Cir. 2001), where before the critical date Scaltech made a commercial offer to perform a patented method. There we stated that "the fact that the process itself was not offered for sale but only offered to be used by the patentee . . . does not take it outside the on sale bar rule." *Id.* at 1328. We reasoned that "[t]he on sale bar rule applies to the sale of an 'invention,' and in this case, the invention was a process." *Id.* We then asked whether there was a "commercial offer" and whether the offer was "of the patented invention." *Id.* We concluded that Scaltech's offer before the critical date to perform the patented method implicated the on sale bar because the commercial "offer for sale . . . satisf[ied] each claim limitation of the patent." *Id.* at 1329-30.

Here, as in *Scaltech*, there has been a commercial offer before the critical date of February 27, 1995, because there was a binding contract between MA and SIA. The more difficult question is whether the commercial offer was "of the patented invention." We have stated that "the invention that is the subject matter of the offer for sale must satisfy each claim limitation of the patent." *Id.* at 1329. Datamize admits that "SkiPath [was] created with the authoring system" and that the authoring system "embodied all the claims of all three of Datamize's patents." On its face, however, the written agreement between MA and SIA did not unambiguously require use of the patented method. The agreement did require MA to "provide the software/hardware package necessary to produce the interactive touch-screen information center as presented to SIA on January 17, 1995 in McLean, Virginia." This reference to the software/hardware package is ambiguous as to whether it required MA to provide the kiosk system software or to perform the patented method. Moreover, Plumtree has made no showing that extrinsic evidence would compel an interpretation that MA was bound to perform the patented method. Therefore, the record does not provide a basis for summary judgment on this issue.

We now turn to the second possible theory. Even if Plumtree did not agree before the critical date to perform the patented process, Plumtree could prevail on summary judgment if it demonstrated that MA in fact performed each of the steps of the patented process before the critical date pursuant to the contract. In *In re Kollar*, 286 F.3d 1326 (Fed. Cir. 2002), this court considered whether

granting a license to perform a patented method violated the on sale bar. After
concluding that there was no sale under the particular facts of that case, we
noted that "[a]ctually performing the process itself for consideration would . . .
trigger the application of §102(b)." *Id.* We have explained that "the intent of
[§102(b)] is to preclude attempts by the inventor or his assignee to profit from
commercial use of an invention for more than a year before an application for
patent is filed." *D.L. Auld Co. v. Chroma Graphics Corp.,* 714 F.2d 1144, 1147 (Fed.
Cir. 1983); *see also In re Kollar,* 286 F.3d at 1333 ("Surely a sale by the patentee . . .
of a product made by the claimed process would constitute . . . a sale because
that party is commercializing the patented process in the same sense as would
occur when the sale of a tangible patented item takes place."). Performing the
steps of the patented method for a commercial purpose is clearly an attempt to
profit from the commercial use of an invention. Consequently, performing the
patented method for commercial purposes before the critical date constitutes
a sale under §102(b).

However, Plumtree has not on this record established that MA actually performed all of the patented steps before the critical date pursuant to the contract. While it is apparent that Kevin Burns used the authoring tool to create
the kiosk system, the kiosk system was not finished until after the critical date,
and it is unclear whether Burns performed each of the patented method steps
before the critical date. Accordingly, summary judgment was not appropriate in
this case.

CONCLUSION

For the foregoing reasons, we conclude that the district court erred in granting summary judgment pursuant to §102(b) because the record contains insufficient facts to determine whether the patented process was sold or offered for
sale before the critical date. Accordingly, we vacate the district court's summary
judgment ruling and remand for further proceedings.

Comments

1. ***"Commercial Offer for Sale" vs. Assignments and Licenses.*** Unlike *Space Systems,*
the *Plumtree* court did not have to decide if the invention was "ready for patenting" because it was already reduced to practice at the time of the alleged
offer. But the court did have to decide whether a commercial offer for sale
was made. Prior to *Pfaff,* it was not entirely clear what constituted an offer
under section 102(b), and the *Pfaff* court did not address the issue. But,
as noted in *Plumtree,* the Federal Circuit has subsequently defined commercial offer for sale by applying traditional contract principles. The court held
that "the offer must meet the level of an offer for sale in the contract sense
as understood by the commercial community." *Group One, Ltd. v. Hallmark
Cards, Inc.,* 254 F.3d 1041, 1046-1047 (Fed. Cir. 2001).

This test needs to be placed in context. For example, an on-sale bar does
not arise from assignment that is executed to raise funds to be used to further
develop or refine the invention. *See Moleculon Research Corp. v. CBS, Inc.,* 793
F.2d 1261, 1267 (Fed. Cir. 1986) (assignment does not violate section 102(b)).
There is a distinction between offering the patent itself for sale and what is

claimed in the patent. The former, which provides its owner with the right to exclude (the property right), does not invoke section 102(b). This rule reflects the business realities ordinarily surrounding the selling of business assets, including patent rights. Also, because section 102(b) relates to a sale of a product, not prospective licensing activity, an offer to license or a mere transfer of know-how will not invoke section 102(b). *See In re Kollar*, 286 F.3d 1326, 1331 (Fed. Cir. 2002) (holding an offer to license a patent claiming an invention after future research and development had occurred, without more, is not an offer to sell the invention). Of course, just calling something a "license" does not make it so, particularly if the "license" masks a sale that would immediately transfer the product to the "buyer" as if it were sold.

This distinction between license and sell was at issue in *Elan Corp. v. Andrx Pharmaceuticals, Inc.*, 366 F.3d 1336 (Fed. Cir. 2004). Elan owned a patent on a formulation of naproxen, an anti-inflammatory drug. Prior to the critical date, Elan wrote a letter regarding the patented naproxen formulation to a prospective licensee, Lederle Laboratories, stating:

> On the licensing side, we are actively seeking a partner and believe Lederle's marketing strengths make you ideal in this respect. Ideally, we want to have our partner determined this year so that they can actively participate in the planning of the clinical studies, even though Elan would remain responsible for conducting them. As I indicated to you, we see any license as involving two types of payment—a licensing fee in the form of recoverable advance royalties and a charge for the clinical program as patients become enrolled. On the former, the total licensing fee would be $2.75 million dollars, payable: (i) $500,000 on contract signature, (ii) $500,000 on I.N.D. filing, (iii) 750,000 on N.D.A. filing, and (iv) $1,000,000 on N.D.A. approval, all recoverable against a 5% running royalty by withholding one-third of each payment due. On the clinical side, we would ask for a payment of $250,000 upon enrollment of each 50 new patients, up to a maximum of $2.5 million dollars.

The Federal Circuit held this language did not constitute an offer for sale under section 102(b) because the letter did not offer naproxen tablets for sale, but only granted a license under the patent and offered an opportunity to be a partner in the clinical test and marketing of the naproxen at some indefinite point in the future. Regarding the language in the letter, the court stated while no particular language is required to transform an offer to license to an offer for sale, "a communication that fails to constitute a definite offer to sell the product and to include material terms is not an 'offer' in the contract sense. *Restatement (Second) of Contracts* § 33(3) (1981)." *Id.* at 1341. According to the court, Elan's "letter lacked any mention of quantities, time of delivery, place of delivery, or product specifications beyond the general statement that the potential product would be a 500 mg once-daily tablet containing naproxen." *Id.* In addition, "the dollar amounts recited in the fourth paragraph of the letter are clearly not price terms for the sale of tablets, but rather the amount that Elan was requesting to form and continue a partnership. Indeed, the letter explicitly refers to the total as a 'licensing fee.'" *Id.* The court concluded by warning that "if Elan had simply disguised a sales price as a licensing fee it would not avoid triggering the on sale bar." *Id.*

2. *Subject Matter of the Sale.* Whatever is offered for sale must be compared with what is ultimately claimed. Consistent with the policies underlying section

102(b), the subject matter of the offer for sale must either fully anticipate or render obvious what is eventually claimed. *See Scaltech, Inc. v. Retec/Tetra LLC*, 178 F.3d 1378, 1383 (Fed. Cir. 1999) (stating the "'invention' which has been offered for sale must, of course, be something within the scope of the claim"); *Minnesota Mining & Mfg. Co. v. Chemque, Inc.*, 303 F.3d 1294, 1301 (Fed. Cir. 2002) (stating on-sale bar applies if "the product sold or offered for sale anticipated the claimed invention or rendered it obvious"). In other words, an inventor does not run afoul of section 102(b) if he offered for sale something significantly different than what he claimed. This was Plumtree's problem. But wasn't MA's offer to provide a kiosk at the trade show tantamount to promising to practice the claimed invention? Although the contract "did not unambiguously require use of the patented method," didn't the patented method have to be performed to make the kiosk? What about the following example? Inventor has a patent on a process of making a chair having elements ABC. There is no patent on the chair. Prior to the critical date, Inventor agrees with a trade show host to display the Inventor's chair at an upcoming trade show, and consideration is forthcoming. Although the contract with the trade show host "did not unambiguously require use of the patented method," the only way to produce the chair was to practice the patented method. Is this scenario different from *Plumtree?*

In *Sparton v. United States*, 399 F.3d 1321 (Fed. Cir. 2005), the Navy entered into a contract with Sparton for the procurement of a sonobuoy, a device that is used to detect, locate, and classify the source of underwater sounds, such as those generated by submarines. Sparton subsequently submitted an Engineering Change Proposal ("ECP") to the Navy under its existing contract, proposing to incorporate dual depth operating capability into the existing sonobuoy by modifying the design. The sonobuoy device described in the ECP included a *multi-piece release plate* for either retaining or deploying the sonobuoy internal components within or from the sonobuoy housing. But shortly after the ECP was issued, Sparton developed, and later tested, a sonobuoy having a *single-piece release plate*. This single-piece release plate performed better than previous release plates and was ultimately used in the sonobuoy Sparton delivered to the Navy under the contract.

Sparton obtained two patents that each contained claim limitations drawn to a single piece release plate for a sonobuoy. In 1992, Sparton filed suit in the Claims Court against the United States to recover money damages for the government's unlicensed use of Sparton's patented inventions. The government maintained that the patents were invalid under section 102(b)'s on sale bar. The Federal Circuit held that the patented invention was not the subject of the offer for sale prior to the critical date. According to the court, the offer for sale was the submission of an ECP incorporating dual depth operating capability. The ECP included a description of the dual depth sonobuoy deployment design, including drawings. This description and drawings contained a release plate mechanism. But the court noted that:

> [t]he parties disagree as to what type of release plate was identified. The specific release plate mechanism proposed in the ECP is not relevant to our analysis, because, as the Claims Court noted, the government concedes, and the parties do not dispute, the release plate mechanism described in the [patents-

in-suit] is not the release plate that was part of the original design proposed in the ECP; in other words, the . . . contract does not include a release plate that meets the description of the release plate limitation of the claimed inventions. This fact is of utmost importance, as both sides agree that what was offered in the ECP was not the patented invention. . . . Accordingly, there is nothing to suggest that prior to the critical date of March 29, 1972, Sparton made an offer for anything other than dual-depth sonobuoys having the release plate mechanism described in the ECP.

Id. at 1323.

3. ***Timing of the Commercial Offer.*** The Federal Circuit has held that a commercial offer can take place once the invention is conceived, although not yet "ready for patenting." Ready for patenting remains a requirement for ultimate application of the on-sale bar, but the timing of a commercial offer can be locked in at conception. *See August Technology Corp. v. Camtek, Ltd.,* 655 F.3d 1278 (Fed. Cir. 2011). For example, Inventor offers to sell Product X prior to the critical date and prior to conception. At this point there is no *commercial* offer for sale because Inventor "was merely offering to sell an idea for" Product X. Assuming the offer is not retracted, once conception occurs—again before the critical date—the offer is transformed into a commercial offer for sale, thus meeting the first prong of *Pfaff;* and if Product subsequently becomes ready for patenting before the critical date, the on-sale bar attaches. The only way to avoid the on-sale bar in this scenario is to retract the offer prior to conception taking hold. The *August* court explained:

> Under *Pfaff,* the invention must be ready for patenting prior to the critical date. But to conclude that it must also be ready for patenting at the time of the offer would render the second prong of the *Pfaff* test superfluous. . . . While the invention need not be ready for patenting at the time of the offer, consistent with our cases, we hold that there is no offer for sale until such time as the invention is conceived. *Pfaff* states that the "word 'invention' in the Patent Act unquestionably refers to the inventor's conception." 525 U.S. at 60. . . . Hence, if an offer for sale is made and retracted prior to conception, there has been no offer for sale of the invention. In contrast, if an offer for sale is extended and remains open, a subsequent conception will cause it to become an offer for sale of the invention as of the conception date. In such a case, the seller is offering to sell *the invention* once he has conceived of it. Before that time, he was merely offering to sell an idea for a product.

Id. at 1289.

B. PUBLIC-USE BAR

The public-use bar, like its neighbor, the on-sale bar, focuses on inventor and third-party activity. A "public use" more than one year before the filing date will defeat patent rights, but what actually constitutes a "public use" is an inquiry not free from difficulty. As you will see in *Egbert* and *Motionless,* the threshold for "public use" is quite low.

EGBERT v. LIPPMANN

104 U.S. 333 (1882)

Mr. Justice WOODS.

This suit was brought for an alleged infringement of the complainant's patent, No. 5216, dated Jan. 7, 1873, for an improvement in corset-springs.

The original letters bear date July 17, 1866, and were issued to Samuel H. Barnes. The reissue was made to the complainant, under her then name, Frances Lee Barnes, executrix of the original patentee.

* * *

The evidence on which the defendants rely to establish a prior public use of the invention consists mainly of the testimony of the complainant.

She testifies that Barnes invented the improvement covered by his patent between January and May, 1855; that between the dates named the witness and her friend Miss Cugier were complaining of the breaking of their corset-steels. Barnes, who was present, and was an intimate friend of the witness, said he thought he could make her a pair that would not break. At their next interview he presented her with a pair of corset-steels which he himself had made. The witness wore these steels a long time. In 1858 Barnes made and presented to her another pair, which she also wore a long time. When the corsets in which these steels were used wore out, the witness ripped them open and took out the steels and put them in new corsets. This was done several times.

. . . [T]hese steels embodied the invention afterwards patented by Barnes and covered by the reissued letters-patent on which this suit is brought.

Joseph H. Sturgis, another witness for complainant, testifies that in 1863 Barnes spoke to him about two inventions made by himself, one of which was a corset-steel, and that he went to the house of Barnes to see them. Before this time, and after the transactions testified to by the complainant, Barnes and she had intermarried. Barnes said his wife had a pair of steels made according to his invention in the corsets which she was then wearing, and if she would take them off he would show them to witness. Mrs. Barnes went out, and returned with a pair of corsets and a pair of scissors, and ripped the corsets open and took out the steels. Barnes then explained to witness how they were made and used.

* * *

We observe, in the first place, that to constitute the public use of an invention it is not necessary that more than one of the patented articles should be publicly used. The use of a great number may tend to strengthen the proof, but one well-defined case of such use is just as effectual to annul the patent as many. . . .

We remark, secondly, that, whether the use of an invention is public or private does not necessarily depend upon the number of persons to whom its use is known. If an inventor, having made his device, gives or sells it to another, to be used by the donee or vendee, without limitation or restriction, or injunction of secrecy, and it is so used, such use is public, even though the use and knowledge of the use may be confined to one person.

We say, thirdly, that some inventions are by their very character only capable of being used where they cannot be seen or observed by the public eye. An invention may consist of a lever or spring, hidden in the running gear of a watch, or of a rachet, shaft, or cog-wheel covered from view in the recesses of a machine for spinning or weaving. Nevertheless, if its inventor sells a machine of which his invention forms a part, and allows it to be used without restriction of any kind, the use is a public one. So, on the other hand, a use necessarily open to public view, if made in good faith solely to test the qualities of the invention, and for the purpose of experiment, is not a public use within the meaning of the statute.

Tested by these principles, we think the evidence of the complainant herself shows that for more than two years before the application for the original letters there was, by the consent and allowance of Barnes, a public use of the invention, covered by them. He made and gave to her two pairs of corset-steels, constructed according to his device, one in 1855 and one in 1858. They were presented to her for use. He imposed no obligation of secrecy, nor any condition or restriction whatever. They were not presented for the purpose of experiment, nor to test their qualities. No such claim is set up in her testimony. The invention was at the time complete, and there is no evidence that it was afterwards changed or improved. The donee of the steels used them for years for the purpose and in the manner designed by the inventor. They were not capable of any other use. She might have exhibited them to any person, or made other steels of the same kind, and used or sold them without violating any condition or restriction imposed on her by the inventor.

According to the testimony of the complainant, the invention was completed and put into use in 1855. The inventor slept on his rights for eleven years. Letters-patent were not applied for till March, 1866. In the mean time, the invention had found its way into general, and almost universal, use. A great part of the record is taken up with the testimony of the manufacturers and venders of corset-steels, showing that before he applied for letters the principle of his device was almost universally used in the manufacture of corset-steels. It is fair to presume that having learned from this general use that there was some value in his invention, he attempted to resume, by his application, what by his acts he had clearly dedicated to the public.

* * *

We are of opinion that the defense of two years' public use, by the consent and allowance of the inventor, before he made application for letters-patent, is satisfactorily established by the evidence.

Mr. Justice MILLER, dissenting.

The sixth section of the act of July 4, 1836, c. 357, makes it a condition of the grant of a patent that the invention for which it was asked should not, at the time of the application for a patent, "have been in public use or on sale with the consent or allowance" of the inventor or discoverer. Section fifteen of the same act declares that it shall be a good defense to an action for infringement of the patent, that it had been in public use or on sale with the consent or allowance of the patentee before his application. This was afterwards modified by the seventh section of the act of March 3, 1839, c. 88, which declares that no patent shall be void on that ground unless the prior use has been for more than two years before the application.

This is the law under which the patent of the complainant is held void by the opinion just delivered. The previous part of the same section requires that the invention must be one "not known or used by others" before the discovery or invention made by the applicant. In this limitation, though in the same sentence as the other, the word "public" is not used, so that the use by others which would defeat the applicant, if without his consent, need not be public; but where the use of his invention is by his consent or allowance, it must be public or it will not have that affect.

The reason of this is undoubtedly that, if without his consent others have used the machine, composition, or manufacture, it is strong proof that he was not the discoverer or first inventor. In that case he was not entitled to a patent. If the use was with his consent or allowance, the fact that such consent or allowance was first obtained is evidence that he was the inventor, and claimed to be such. In such case, he was not to lose his right to a patent, unless the use which he permitted was such as showed an intention of abandoning his invention to the public. It must, in the language of the act, be in public use or on sale.

The word public is, therefore, an important member of the sentence. A private use with consent, which could lead to no copy or reproduction of the machine, which taught the nature of the invention to no one but the party to whom such consent was given, which left the public at large as ignorant of this as it was before the author's discovery, was no abandonment to the public, and did not defeat his claim for a patent. If the little steep spring inserted in a single pair of corsets, and used by only one woman, covered by her outer-clothing, and in a position always withheld from public observation, is a public use of that piece of steel, I am at a loss to know the line between a private and a public use.

The opinion argues that the use was public, because, with the consent of the inventor to its use, no limitation was imposed in regard to its use in public. It may be well imagined that a prohibition to the party so permitted against exposing her use of the steel spring to public observation would have been supposed to be a piece of irony. An objection quite the opposite of this suggested by the opinion is, that the invention was incapable of a public use. That is to say, that while the statute says the right to the patent can only be defeated by a use which is public, it is equally fatal to the claim, when it is permitted to be used at all, that the article can never be used in public. . . .

MOTIONLESS KEYBOARD CO. v. MICROSOFT CORP.

486 F.3d 1376 (Fed. Cir. 2007)

RADER, Circuit Judge.

[T]he U.S. District Court for the District of Oregon determined . . . on summary judgment . . . that the 5,178,477 and 5,332,322 patents were invalid based on public use under 35 U.S.C. § 102(b). . . . Because the trial court misapplied the concept of public use . . . this court reverses its invalidity rulings.

I

MKC owns the '477 and '322 patents. The '477 patent, entitled "Ergonomic Keyboard Input Device," claims an ergonomic keyboard designed to accommodate the architecture of the human hand. According to the invention, the keyboard requires only slight finger gestures to actuate the keys. The '322 patent, entitled "Ergonomic Thumb-Actuable Keyboard for Hand-Grippable Device," issued as a continuation-in-part of the '477 patent. [Figure 1 of the '322 patent is below.] This patent claims a hand-held device that frees the thumb to actuate the keys in multiple and differentiated ways.

Thomas L. Gambaro is the sole inventor of both the '477 and the '322 patents. Mr. Gambaro invented the novel ergonomic keyboard technology on a part-time basis while also working in other jobs such as graphic artist and dishwasher. In fact, Mr. Gambaro developed some of the ergonomic keyboard technology while he lived in a friend's attic. As an independent inventor, Mr. Gambaro developed his technology advances without the benefit of a well-funded laboratory and then traversed the patent system on a limited budget.

During his inventive work, Mr. Gambaro developed different prototype models of his keyboard technology. Eventually, on February 22, 1987, Mr. Gambaro developed the Cherry Model 5. Shortly after developing the Cherry Model 5, Mr. Gambaro entered into a business partnership with Mr. Keith Coulter. Thereafter, Mr. Gambaro and Mr. Coulter set out to gain financial support to further develop and patent the keyboard technology.

Thus, Mr. Gambaro began to demonstrate the Cherry Model 5 to potential investors. He also demonstrated the device to a friend, Ms. Kathie Roberts. While the potential investors signed two-year non-disclosure agreements (NDAs), Ms. Roberts did not. Mr. Gambaro entered into some of the NDAs with potential investors in 1987, meaning those agreements expired in 1989. Additionally, Mr. Gambaro disclosed the Cherry Model 5 to Ms. Sheila Lanier on June 25, 1990 to conduct typing tests. While Mr. Gambaro showed the Cherry Model 5 to his business partner, numerous potential investors, a friend and a typing tester, according to the record, only Ms. Lanier used the device to transmit data to a computer. In due course, Mr. Gambaro assigned both patents to MKC.

MKC sued Microsoft, Nokia, and Saitek for infringement of the '477 and '322 patents in the U.S. District Court for the District of Oregon. Specifically, MKC alleged that Microsoft's "Strategic Commander" game controller infringed claims 1, 2, 5, 6, and 8 of the '477 patent. MKC also alleged that Microsoft's

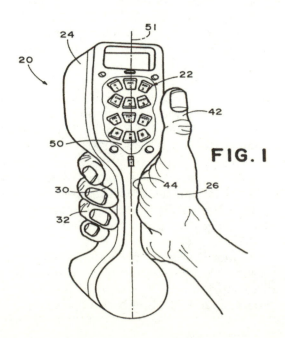

FIG. I

"Sidewinder Precision 2," "Sidewinder Force Feedback 2," and various Saitek game joysticks infringed claims 1, 2, 3 and 5 of the '322 patent.

The defendants collectively moved for summary judgment of invalidity of both patents based on public use under 35 U.S.C § 102(b). The District Court entered summary judgment construing the claims of the '477 and '322 patents. Based on its reading of the patents, the trial court . . . invalidated the '477 and '322 patents based on public use under 35 U.S.C. § 102(b).

* * *

IV

MKC appeals the district court grant of summary judgment that the '477 and '322 patents are invalid for public use under 35 U.S.C. § 102(b):

> A person shall be entitled to a patent unless—
>> (b) the invention was patented or described in a printed publication in this or a foreign country or *in public use* or on sale in this country, more than one year prior to the date of the application for patent in the United States.

35 U.S.C. § 102(b) (emphasis added). Because the applicant filed the '477 patent on June 6, 1991, the critical date for the invalidity analysis is June 6, 1990. The critical date for the '322 patent is January 11, 1992. To sustain the invalidity determination, the record must show that an embodiment of the patented invention was in public use as defined by the statute before the critical date.

The district court found that MKC admitted that the Cherry Model 5 embodied the '477 patent and the '322 patent as of February 22, 1987. Even assuming that MKC admitted that the Cherry Model 5 embodied each claim of the '477 and '322 patents—a question this court need not decide—this court concludes that there was no "public use" under 35 U.S.C. § 102(b). Therefore, the district court's grant of summary judgment of invalidity for public use was improper.

The record shows that the inventor disclosed the Cherry Model 5 to his business partner, potential investors, a friend, and a typing tester before the critical date. While the potential investors signed NDAs, some of the NDAs expired in 1989—again prior to the critical dates for each patent. Thus, this court must examine, in the context of the district court's summary judgment ruling of invalidity, whether these disclosures and demonstrations were public uses within the meaning of the statutory bar.

Public use includes "any [public] use of [the claimed] invention by a person other than the inventor who is under no limitation, restriction or obligation of secrecy to the inventor." *In re Smith*, 714 F.2d 1127, 1134 (Fed. Cir. 1983) (citing *Egbert v. Lippmann*, 104 U.S. 333, 336 (1881)). In *Pfaff v. Wells Elecs., Inc.*, the Supreme Court noted that both the "on sale" and "public use" bars were based on the same policy considerations. *Pfaff v. Wells Elecs., Inc.*, 525 U.S. 55, 64 (1998). Specifically, "[t]he [Supreme] Court noted that both the on sale and public use bars of § 102(b) stem from the same 'reluctance to allow an inventor to remove existing knowledge from public use.'" *Invitrogen Corp. v. Biocrest Mfg., L.P.*, 424 F.3d 1374, 1379 (Fed. Cir. 2005).

The district court found that Mr. Gambaro had disclosed the Cherry Model 5 to potential investors in order to obtain capital. As such, the district court reasoned that these disclosures showed the invention entered the public domain prior to the critical date because Mr. Gambaro's business partner was under no

obligation to keep the Cherry Model 5 secret. Further, the disclosures to potential investors showed that Mr. Gambaro attempted to obtain capital to develop
his invention. The district court found the NDAs inconsequential because "a
confidentiality agreement will not preclude application of the public use doctrine, if the device was disclosed for commercial purposes." *Id.* (citing *Kinzenbaw
v. Deere & Co.,* 741 F.2d 383, 390 (Fed. Cir. 1984)). MKC admits to a series of
limited disclosures to potential investors to raise capital to develop the invention and prosecute the patent application. However, MKC further contends that
the disclosures did not involve the Cherry Model 5 or its use as claimed in the
'477 or '322 patents.

"The classical standard for assessing the public nature of a use was established in *Egbert v. Lippmann* 104 U.S. 333 (1881). In *Egbert,* the inventor of a
corset spring gave two samples of the invention to a lady friend, who used them
for more than two years before the inventor applied for a patent." *Invitrogen,*
424 F.3d at 1382. Although the inventor in *Egbert* did not obtain any commercial advantage, the Court determined that the invention had been used for its
intended purpose for over a decade without limitation or confidentiality requirements. Thus, even though not in public view, the invention was in public use. *Id.*
In *Electric Storage Battery Co. v. Shimadzu,* 307 U.S. 5 (1939), the Court found "the
ordinary use of a machine or the practice of a process in a factory in the usual
course of producing articles for commercial purposes is a public use." *Id.* at 20.
On the other hand, in *TP Laboratories, Inc. v. Professional Positioners, Inc.,* 724 F.2d
965 (Fed. Cir. 1984), this court found that premature installation of an inventive orthodontic appliance in several patients without a written confidentiality
agreement was not a public use due to the expectation of confidentiality inherent in the dentist-patient relationship. This case again presents the question of
the meaning of public use under 35 U.S.C. §102(b).

In this case, Mr. Gambaro disclosed his Cherry Model 5 to his business partner, a friend, potential investors, and a typing tester (Ms. Lanier). In all these
disclosures, except in the case of Ms. Lanier, however, the Cherry Model 5 was
not connected to a computer or any other device. In the case of Ms. Lanier, the
Cherry Model 5 was used to conduct typing tests on July 25, 1990, and thereby
connected to a computer for its intended purpose. With respect to the '477 patent, the typing test occurred after the critical date of June 6, 1990. With respect
to the '322 patent, Ms. Lanier appears to have performed a one-time typing test
to assess typing speed. The typing test by Ms. Lanier was allegedly performed
on July 25, 1990 and, according to a synopsis of NDAs in the record, Ms. Lanier
signed an NDA on the same day. The critical date for the '322 patent is January
11, 1992. In this case, the one time typing test coupled with a signed NDA and
no record of continued use of the Cherry Model 5 by Ms. Lanier after July 25,
1990 did not elevate to the level of public use. Thus, the Cherry Model 5 was
never in public use. All disclosures, except for the one-time typing test, only
provided a visual view of the new keyboard design without any disclosure of the
Cherry Model 5's ability to translate finger movements into actuation of keys
to transmit data. In essence, these disclosures visually displayed the keyboard
design without putting it into use. In short, the Cherry Model 5 was not in public use as the term is used in section 102(b) because the device, although visually
disclosed and only tested one time with a NDA signed by the typing tester, was
never connected to be used in the normal course of business to enter data into
a system.

Unlike the situations in *Egbert* and *Electric Storage Battery*, where the inventions were used for their intended purpose, neither the inventor nor anyone else ever used the Cherry Model 5 to transmit data in the normal course of business. The entry of data did not ever occur outside of testing and the tester signed an NDA. The Cherry Model 5 was not used in public, for its intended purpose, nor was the Cherry Model 5 ever given to anyone for such public use. Thus, the disclosures in this record do not rise to the level of public use.

Comments

1. *How Public Is "Public Use" and What Is "Use"?* The public-use bar applies when the "device used in public includes every limitation of the later claimed invention, or by obviousness if the differences between the claimed invention and the device used would have been obvious to one of ordinary skill in the art." *Netscape Communications Corp. v. Konrad*, 295 F.3d 1315, 1321 (Fed. Cir. 2002). But the use need not be enabling. *See In re Epstein*, 32 F.3d 1559, 1568 (Fed. Cir. 1994) (stating "there is no requirement for an enablement-type inquiry" with respect to public use or on sale). Rather, the public use must simply relate to a device that embodied the invention. Moreover, the *Motionless* court made clear that to constitute public use, the invention must be used for its intended purpose. The court was able to distinguish *Egbert* and *Electric Storage Battery* on this basis, because "neither the inventor nor anyone else ever used the Cherry Model 5 to transmit data in the normal course of business." By requiring actual use the *Motionless* court gave meaning to the statutory language "in public use." In this sense, *Motionless* can be seen through the lens of statutory interpretation. Moreover, the actual use requirement of *Motionless* arguably better serves one of the policies underlying the public-use bar, namely preventing the removal of inventions from the public that the public have justifiably come to expect are freely available.

But given that the policies for the on-sale and public-use bars are the same, can the actual use requirement be easily manipulated and potentially frustrate these policies? For example, what if Gambro displayed the Cherry 5 in an enabling manner, and a PHOSITA had a complete understanding of how the Cherry 5 worked and operated for its intended use? Would this disclosure qualify as a public use under *Motionless*? Consider the compromise position taken in *Pfaff*. The "ready for patenting" standard can be seen as providing enough certainty for inventors while also being less manipulable. From a policy perspective, why is a use requirement—as described in *Motionless*—needed if a PHOSITA is enabled by a visual demonstration or verbal description? Can an inventor simply describe or display (without using) his invention?

In addition, how public must the use be? The *Egbert* Court assumed a minimalist approach to public use. The public use was by Samuel Barnes's wife, Frances, of apparently a single embodiment of the invention that could not be seen by the "public eye." Frances was the public. (Sturgis's involvement just made it easier to prove public use, yet Frances alone was enough for the majority.) Thus, *Egbert* established that public use will be found when one person other than the inventor engages in one non-private use of one article. The public-use threshold is low, but clean and easier to apply than a test requiring, for example, an "unreasonable number of people or articles" before the public-use bar attaches. Once you move beyond one person, one article, the test becomes more difficult to apply. But ease of application can lead to potentially harsh results. Also, Samuel and Frances were romantically involved (or, as the court said, were "intimate friend[s]") and eventually married. Should the nature of their relationship make it easier or more difficult to prove public use?

2. *Non-Commercial Private Activity.* A patentee can take precautions against application of the public-use bar. For instance, a *non-commercial* private use, under the inventor's control, will not invoke section 102(b). As Judge Learned Hand wrote in *Metallizing Engineering Co. v. Kenyon Bearing & Auto Parts Co.*, 153 F.2d 516 (2d Cir. 1946), "[i]t is indeed true that an inventor may continue for more than a year to practice his invention for his private purposes of his own enjoyment and later patent it. But that is, properly considered, not an exception to the doctrine, for he is not then making use of his secret to gain a competitive advantage over others; he does not thereby extend the period of his monopoly." Applying this principle to *Egbert,* it may have been deemed a private use if Frances (instead of Samuel) were the inventor in *Egbert,* told no one of the corset, and simply used the corset for its intended purpose. What if Frances were the inventor and told Samuel about her corset invention? Would such a disclosure count as a public use under *Motionless?*

Recall, the patentee in *Motionless* avoided a finding of public use by employing NDA agreements. And in *Moleculon Research Corp. v. CBS, Inc.,* 793 F.2d 1261 (Fed. Cir. 1986), the invention was the "Rubik's Cube," the popular puzzle of years ago. The inventor was a graduate student who built several embodiments of the invention, and displayed them to his roommates and another graduate student. He also revealed the invention to his employer. The Federal Circuit held this was not a public use because they were under the control of the inventor who did not allow unrestricted use and "at all times retained control over the [invention]'s use and the distribution of information concerning it." *Id.* at 1266.

The role of confidentiality was at issue in *American Seating Co. v. USSC Group, Inc.,* 514 F.3d 1262 (Fed. Cir. 2008). The inventors invented a tie-down restraint system for wheelchair bound passengers on public transportation such as buses. As the inventors improved their invention, they "placed evolving prototypes in an out-of-service bus for the purpose of soliciting feedback from friends and colleagues who to varying degrees assisted in the invention's development." *Id.* at 1267. The accused infringer argued that this introduction of the inventors' prototype was an invalidating public use under section 102(b) because there was no written confidentiality agreement. The Federal Circuit disagreed, noting that "[w]hen access to an invention is clearly limited and controlled by the inventor, depending upon the relationships of the observers and the inventor, an understanding of confidentiality can be implied." *Id.* at 1268. According to the court, the inventors and the limited amount of people who viewed the invention "shared a general understanding of confidentiality." For example, the inventors "demonstrated the prototype on an out-of-service bus, solicited feedback, and removed the invention to store under his control" and "[t]here was no evidence that the prototype was placed in service before [the critical date], and no evidence that an unrestricted number of people unconnected with the development of the invention observed the invention in use." *Id.*

In *Invitrogen v. Biocrest*, 424 F.3d 1374 (Fed. Cir. 2005), the patentee used the claimed process before the critical date, in its own laboratories, to produce cells that would be used within the company for other projects. The record also showed that the patentee kept its use of the claimed process confidential. The process was known only within the company. The patentee did not sell the claimed process or any products made with it. Nonetheless, the district court determined that use of the claimed invention in the patentee's general business of widespread research generated commercial benefits, and therefore, section 102(b) applied. The patentee argued, however, that its secret internal use was not "public use" because it neither sold nor offered for sale the claimed process or any product derived from the process, nor did it otherwise place into the public domain either the process or any product derived from it. The Federal Circuit agreed, stating the "fact that Invitrogen secretly used cells internally to develop future products that were never sold, without more, is insufficient to create a public use bar to patentability." *Id.* at 1383. *Cf. Baxter Int'l, Inc. v. Cobe Labs, Inc.*, 88 F.3d 1054 (Fed. Cir. 1996), in which the Federal Circuit invalidated the patent under section 102(b) public use based on testimony by the inventor that he demonstrated the claimed invention to co-workers and visitors who were under no duty to maintain its confidentiality. In particular, the inventor in *Baxter* failed "to maintain the [invention] as confidential coupled with the free flow into his laboratory of people . . . who were under no duty of confidentiality." *Id.* at 1059. And in *Beachcombers v. Wildewood Creative Prods., Inc.*, 31 F.3d 1154 (Fed. Cir. 1994), the inventor disclosed her invention at a house party she hosted for 20 to 30 guests. At the party, the inventor testified that "she personally demonstrated the device to some of the guests for the purpose of getting feedback on the device; and that she made no efforts to conceal the device or keep anything about it secret." *Id.* at 1160. A friend of the inventor's also testified that she (the friend) observed the invention at the party and "that a lot of other guests were present at the time she observed the device; that other guests were looking at the device and picking it up; and that Bennett never asked her to maintain in secrecy any information about the device." *Id.*

3. ***Secret Commercial Activity by Inventor and Third Party.*** While a secret *non-commercial* activity is not a triggering event, an inventor who engages in a secret *commercial* activity more than one year before filing his patent application is barred from obtaining a patent under section 102(b). The commercial activity can take the form of either a non-informing public use, *see Metallizing Eng'g Co. v. Kenyon Bearing & Auto Parts Co.*, 153 F.2d 516 (2d Cir. 1946), or a confidential sale of the claimed invention, *see In re Caveney*, 761 F.2d 671, 675-676 (Fed. Cir. 1985). *See also W.L. Gore & Assocs., Inc. v. Garlock, Inc.*, 721 F.2d 1540 (Fed. Cir. 1983). A common example of a non-informing public use is when an inventor uses his inventive process in secret (inside his factory) to make a product that he subsequently sells to the public. The product

does not reveal anything about the process (non-informing), but the inventor is commercially benefitting from the sale. This scenario was present in *Metallizing*, and the court invalidated the patent on the process. As Judge Learned Hand famously wrote:

> it is a condition upon an inventor's right to a patent that he shall not exploit his discovery competitively after it is ready for patenting; he must content himself with either secrecy, or legal monopoly. But if he goes beyond that period of probation, he forfeits his right regardless of how little the public may have learned about the invention.

153 F.3d at 520. *See also Pennock v. Dialogue*, 27 U.S. (2 Pet.) 1, 18 (1829) (stating "[i]f an inventor should be permitted to hold back from the knowledge of the public the secrets of his invention; if he should, for a long period of years, retain the monopoly, and make and sell his invention publicly, and thus gather the whole profits of it, relying upon his superior skill and knowledge of the structure; and then, and then only, when the danger of competition should force him to secure the exclusive right, he should be allowed to take out a patent, . . . it would materially retard the progress of science and the useful arts, and give a premium to those who should be least prompt to communicate their discoveries"). *Cf. Invitrogen*, discussed in Comment 2, *supra*. For a critique of *Metallizing*, *see* Dmitry Karshtedt, *Did Learned Hand Get It Wrong? The Questionable Patent Forfeiture Rule of* Metallizing Engineering, 57 VILL. L. REV. 261 (2012).

Interestingly, the courts have distinguished between inventor and third-party non-informing public use. For example, in *W.L. Gore & Assoc. v. Garlock, Inc.*, 721 F.2d 1540 (Fed. Cir. 1983), the patentee, Gore, claimed a process for stretching Teflon tape. Prior to Gore's critical date, a third party—Budd—secretly used the claimed process to manufacture tape similar to the new tape made by Gore. But the court held Budd's secret use did not invalidate Gore's patented process. As the court wrote, "[t]here is no reason or statutory basis . . . on which Budd's . . . secret commercialization of a process, if established, could be held a bar to the grant of a patent to Gore on that process." *Id.* at 1550. Why allow a patent to escape section 102(b) based on third-party secret commercial use, when the same type of use by an inventor would be a statutory bar? A rationale was provided in *Gore*: "As between a prior inventor who benefits from a process by selling its product but suppresses, conceals, or otherwise keeps the process from the public, and a later inventor who promptly files a patent application from which the public will gain a disclosure of the process, the law favors the latter." *Id.* Thus, as an equitable consideration, courts preclude alleged infringers from using third-party secret commercial use to invalidate a patent that disclosed to the public what the third party purposefully did not. The patentee, in this instance, is rewarded for acting consistently with patent law's policy of encouraging technological dissemination.

One of the most debated topics relating to the AIA is whether a non-informing public use or confidential offer for sale (e.g., *Metallizing* and *Caveney*) remain triggering events under new section 102(a)(1). For a discussion of this debate, see the Patent Reform Perspective immediately below.

PATENT REFORM PERSPECTIVE
Statutory Bars and Exceptions Under the AIA

The new section 102(a) reads in relevant part:

(a) NOVELTY; PRIOR ART.—A person shall be entitled to a patent unless—

(1) the claimed invention was patented, described in a printed publication, or in **public use, on sale**, or otherwise available to the public before the effective filing date of the claimed invention . . .

(b) EXCEPTIONS.—

(1) DISCLOSURES MADE 1 YEAR OR LESS BEFORE THE EFFECTIVE FILING DATE OF THE CLAIMED INVENTION.—A disclosure made 1 year or less before the effective filing date of a claimed invention shall not be prior art to the claimed invention under subsection (a)(1) if—

(A) the disclosure was made by the inventor or joint inventor or by another who obtained the subject matter disclosed directly or indirectly from the inventor or a joint inventor; or

(B) the subject matter disclosed had, before such disclosure, been publicly disclosed by the inventor or a joint inventor or another who obtained the subject matter disclosed directly or indirectly from the inventor or a joint inventor. . . .

New section 102(a) collapses old sections 102(a) and (b) under the heading of "Novelty." There are several points that need to be addressed.

1. *Many Familiar Words.* Section 102(a)(1) retained many of the same words found in the old section 102(b), such as "patented," "printed publication," "public use," and "on sale." As discussed in Chapter 4, the AIA added the phrase "otherwise available to the public," which is new statutory language. For purposes relevant to this chapter, it is unclear if the phrase "otherwise available to the public" modifies all that comes before it, or only the terms "public use" and "on sale" or is simply a catchall phrase that expands the prior art world to include, for example, oral communications made at conferences. Comment 3, below, addresses this issue.

2. *Exceptions to Section 102(a)(1).* Section 102(b)(1) creates two important exceptions—and an accompanying grace period—to the novelty principle set forth in section 102(a)(1). What are the exceptions?

   a. *Inventor Was First to Disclose.* First, under section 102(b)(1)(A), a disclosure of the claimed invention made one year or less before to the effective filing date will <u>not</u> be considered prior art under section 102(a)(1) *if the "disclosure was made by the inventor."* Note that the word "disclosure" is referring to prior art in section 102(a)(1). Therefore, any inventor-initiated disclosure as set forth in (a)(1) will trigger the grace period exception of section 102(b).

   b. *Inventor Publicly Disclosed Prior to Third-Party Disclosure.* Second, under section 102(b)(1)(B), a disclosure of the claimed invention made one year or less before the effective filing date by **someone other** than the inventor will <u>not</u> be considered prior art against the inventor under section 102(a)(1) *if* "the subject matter disclosed had, before such disclosure, been "**publicly disclosed by the inventor.**" A third-party disclosure made **prior** to the inventor's public disclosure—even one day prior thereto—would prevent the inventor from obtaining a patent under section 102(a)(1). This scenario represents a significant change from the 1952 Patent Act and reflects a European-style "absolute novelty" approach.

Thus, the old grace period in the 1952 Patent Act remains for third-party disclosures only when the inventor **publicly** discloses **before** the third party's disclosure. An inventor who makes a non-public disclosure (e.g., confidential on-sale activity or non-informing use) will not be able to protect himself under section 102(b)(1)(B). Importantly, the third party's disclosure—to serve as a bar to another—must be public, as well. The reason for this is that confidential sales or non-informing uses are prior art only for those who engage or perform them, not against others.

3. *Is Secret Commercialization by Patentee Prior Art Under Section 102(a)(1)?*
A key question relating to the AIA is whether an *inventor's* secret commercial use such as a confidential offer for sale or non-informing public use will still qualify as a "public use" or "on-sale" event that will trigger the one-year grace period.

Commentators disagree on the answer to this question; and the Federal Circuit will, of course, eventually address the issue.

Those who argue that the AIA overruled *Metallizing* (and *Caveney*) point to the statutory language and the legislative history of the AIA. With respect to the former, the phrase "otherwise available to the public" modifies "on sale" and "public use" such that these events, unlike the non-informing public use of *Metallizing*, must be public or publicly accessible. Moreover, the two uses of the alternative conjunction "or" suggests the phrase "or in public use, on sale, or otherwise available to the public" are three related categories that have public accessibility as a common thread. The legislative history supports this view. Senator Kyl, speaking before the Senate vote, said, "[W]hen the committee included the words 'or otherwise available to the public' in section 102(a), the word 'otherwise' made clear that the preceding items are things that are of the same quality or nature. As a result, the preceding events and things are limited to those that make the invention 'available to the public.'" 157 Cong. Rec. S1370 (daily ed. Mar. 8, 2011). And Senator Leahy remarked that section 102(a) was drafted "to do away with precedent under current law that private offers for sale or private uses or secret processes practiced in the United States that result in a product or service that is then made public may be deemed patent-defeating prior art." S. Rep. No. 111-118 at 6 (2009) (statement of Sen. Leahy).

The position is reflected in the USPTO's "Examination Guidelines for Implementing the First-Inventor-to-File Provisions of the Leahy-Smith America Invents Act." The agency writes that section "102(a)(1), unlike pre-AIA . . . [section] 102(b), contains the residual clause 'otherwise available to the public,'" and "[t]he legislative history of the

AIA indicates that the inclusion of this clause . . . should be viewed as indicating that [section] 102(a)(1) does not cover non-public uses or non-public offers for sale." Federal Register, v. 77, No. 144, 43759, 43765, n.29 (July 26, 2012). Several intellectual property organizations also support this view, citing policy considerations that are served by this interpretation. For example, the Section of Intellectual Property of the ABA argued that "[s]uch accessibility is critical to provide a simpler, more predictable and fully transparent patent system." Letter to USPTO from ABA Section on IP, page 4 (Oct. 1, 2012). And the American Intellectual Property Association wrote that greater public accessibility "would further the goal of increasing objectivity in the identification of prior art." Letter to USPTO from AIPLA, page 8 (Oct. 5, 2012).

Commentators who support the position that non-informing public uses (*Metallizing*) and confidential sales (*Caveney*) survive the AIA and remain prior art or triggering events point to the well-known doctrine that holds "where Congress uses a common-law term in a statute, we assume the 'term . . . comes with a common law meaning, absent anything pointing another way.'" *Microsoft Corp. v. i4i Limited Partnership*, 131 S. Ct. 2238, 2245 (2011). In addition, the use of term "*public* disclosure" in section 102(b)(1)(B) implies that "disclosures" under section 102(a)(1) includes private disclosures. Why else would Congress include the word "public" to modify "disclosure" in section 102(b)(1)(B)? Lastly, relying on statements in the legislative history is suspect because "[w]here the mind labours to discover the design of the legislature, it seizes every thing from which aid can be derived." *United States v. Fisher*, 6 U.S. 358, 2 Cranch 358, 386 (1805) (Marshall, C.J.). Or as Judge Leventhal is credited with saying—somewhat more colloquially—examining legislative history is "the equivalent of entering a crowded cocktail party and looking over the heads of the guests for one's friends." *Conroy v. Aniskoff*, 507 U.S. 511, 519 (1993) (Justice Scalia attributes this line to Judge Leventhal). Accordingly, it takes more than select statements from the legislative history to overturn decades of common law.

This interpretive camp also argues *Metallizing* and its progeny are based on "impeccable policy reasons," namely preventing "an applicant from making a secret commercial use for more than a year while delaying the filing of a patent application." Comments of Professor Mark Lemley at www.uspto.gov/patents/law/comments/fitf_guidance.jsp. Moreover, Lemley sees the abrogation of *Metallizing* and *Gore* as having a "more pernicious effect" in that allowing for a reinterpretation of "public use"—a term that "appears unchanged in the new section 102"—would "open the door to reinterpretation of the settled meaning of terms present in both the old and new statutes." *Id.*

C. THIRD-PARTY ACTIVITY

In addition to inventor activity (so-called self-induced statutory bars), third-party actions can defeat patent rights, even if the third party has no legal relationship with the inventor. In fact, as held in *Lorenz* and *Evans*, a statutory bar will be found when the invention was obtained through improper means or arguably unethical commercial behavior. When reading these cases, ask yourself which section 102(b) policy is served by permitting third-party activity to bar patent rights.

LORENZ v. COLGATE-PALMOLIVE-PEET CO.
167 F.2d 423 (3d Cir. 1948)

BIGGS, Circuit Judge.

. . . In the District Court Lorenz and Wilson (Lorenz), persons interested in Lorenz Patent No. 2,084,446, one of two interfering patents, brought suit under R.S. Sec. 4918, 35 U.S.C.A. §66, against Colgate-Palmolive-Peet Company (Colgate), the owner of the other interfering patent, Ittner, No. 1,918,603. . . . Both patents cover a process for the manufacture of soap and the recovery of glycerine. . . .

The interference between Lorenz and Ittner in the Patent Office arose under the following circumstances. Lorenz had filed an application for his process in the Patent Office on January 24, 1920. Shortly thereafter he communicated the substance of the disclosures of his application to Ittner, who was Colgate's chief chemist, in order that Colgate might exploit the process if it so desired. After examination Ittner expressed himself as uninterested in the process. Next, the Patent Office rejected Lorenz's application and he abandoned the prosecution of the application. On July 18, 1933, Patent No. 1,918,603 was issued to Ittner on an application filed by him on February 19, 1931. Lorenz, learning of the Ittner patent, filed a petition in the Patent Office to revive his original application. This petition was rejected. On November 8, 1934, more than a year after the issuance of the Ittner patent, Lorenz filed a new application in which he adopted as his own nineteen claims of Ittner's patent, asserting that the subject matter of Ittner's patent had been disclosed by him to Ittner in 1920. The Patent Office declared an interference. The examiner of interferences decided in Lorenz's favor and for reasons which need not be gone into here no appeal was taken.

* * *

We proceed immediately to an examination of the defense of prior public use. . . .

The court below found that:

> It clearly appears from the undisputed testimony and the documentary evidence offered in support thereof that the process of the patent was in public use in the factory of the defendant from November 1931 until November 1932, approximately one year, but more than two years prior to the Lorenz application of November 8, 1934. This use was preceded by several months of experimentation,

but commercial production of soap and glycerine by the process of the patent was accomplished in November of 1931 and continued thereafter until 1932, when the use of the process was either discontinued or abandoned. This public use, although it did not enrich the art, was sufficient under the statute to preclude the issuance of a valid patent. . . .

. . . Agreeing with Lorenz that under the peculiar circumstances of this case an unusually heavy burden rests upon Colgate in order to prove prior public use, we have made generous allowance for the difficulties which Lorenz encountered in procuring evidence to rebut Colgate's proof of prior public use. But we cannot say that the court below erred in finding that the process of Lorenz's patent was in public use in Colgate's plant for a period of a year more than two years preceding the filing of Lorenz's second patent application on November 8, 1934. . . .

We come then to the question whether the public use under the circumstances was such as to be within the purview of R.S. Sec. 4886. Lorenz contends that it was not such a use; that Congress did not intend the provision of the statute to bar the grant of a valid monopoly to an inventor whose disclosures have been "pirated" by the person to whom he confided them. . . .

Colgate asserts that its use was neither fraudulent nor piratical and that the disclosures made by Lorenz to Ittner in 1920 carried no pledge, express or implied, that Ittner or Colgate should not make use of Ittner's invention; that Lorenz had filed a patent application and that Ittner knew this and that otherwise Ittner would have refused to receive the disclosures; that since these were made under a then pending application Ittner and Colgate were at liberty to make use of Lorenz's process and answer to Lorenz in a patent infringement suit for profits or damages; that no confidential or trust relationship in Lorenz's favor was or could be imposed on either Ittner or Colgate under the circumstances. We are aware of the ordinary practice under which manufacturers refuse to receive an inventor's disclosures unless there is a pending patent application which covers the discovery. This proper practice is one which usually inures to the benefit of both inventor and manufacturer since it settles in written terms the nature of the disclosure and lessens the probability of future disputes. In the case at bar, however, Ittner immediately rejected Lorenz's disclosures as commercially impractical only to make substantial commercial use of them some eleven years later. The circumstances of the instant case are therefore unusual and reflect a very different pattern from that which customarily ensues when an inventor makes a disclosure to a manufacturer. Usually if the manufacturer declares himself interested in the process a contract is drawn up whereby the rights of the parties are fixed for the periods of manufacture both prior to the issuance of the patent as well as thereafter. No such opportunity was given to Lorenz in the case at bar because of Ittner's rejection of the process as soon as it had been disclosed to him.

We do not doubt that Lorenz's disclosures were made to Ittner with the implicit understanding that if Ittner was to make use of them an arrangement was to be effected whereby Lorenz was to be compensated. Certainly Lorenz was not offering his process to Ittner gratis. Under these circumstances we cannot say that an inventor may not invoke the aid of a court of equity to impose an accounting on the manufacturer, provided the inventor moves to protect his rights with reasonable promptness. We think it clear that Ittner received the disclosures *cum onere* and that Colgate cannot now be heard to assert that it owes no duty to Lorenz.

But Colgate's position in this regard is not really an issue in the instant case. The scope which Congress intended the public use statute to have is the important question. Here the defense of prior public use in reality is asserted on behalf of the public, albeit by Colgate. Was it the intention of Congress that public use by one who employs a process in breach of a fiduciary relationship, who tortiously appropriates it or who pirates it, should bar the inventor from the fruits of his monopoly? Lorenz asserts that there is no case in point and that the question is an original one. He relies on certain cases beginning with *Pennock v. Dialogue.*

* * *

On consideration of these authorities, and we can find no others even as pertinent, and weighing the policy embodied in the statute we are forced to the conclusion that the decisions of the Supreme Court in *Klein v. Russell* and in *Andrews v. Hovey* on rehearing, and that of the Circuit Court of Appeals for the Second Circuit in *Eastman v. Mayor of New York* point the way to the ruling which we must make on this point. The prior public use proviso of R.S. Sec. 4886 was enacted by Congress in the public interest. It contains no qualification or exception which limits the nature of the public use. We think that Congress intended that if an inventor does not protect his discovery by an application for a patent within the period prescribed by the Act, and an intervening public use arises from any source whatsoever, the inventor must be barred from a patent or from the fruits of his monopoly, if a patent has issued to him. There is not a single word in the statute which would tend to put an inventor, whose disclosures have been pirated, in any different position from one who has permitted the use of his process. . . . As Judge Coxe said in the *Eastman* case, isolated instances of injustice may result if the law be strictly applied, but the inventor's remedy is sure. He is master of the situation and by prompt action can protect himself fully and render the defense of prior public use impossible: "If (the inventor) fails to take so simple and reasonable a precaution why should it not be said that the risk is his own and that he cannot complain of the consequences of his own supineness?" Moreover, it is apparent that if fraud or piracy be held to prevent the literal application of the prior-public-use provision a fruitful field for collusion will be opened and the public interest which [the statute] is designed to protect will suffer. While we cannot fail to view Lorenz's predicament with sympathy, we may not render our decision on such a basis. For these reasons we hold, as did the court below, that the Lorenz patent is void by reason of prior public use.

EVANS COOLING SYSTEMS, INC. v. GENERAL MOTORS CORP.
125 F.3d 1448 (Fed. Cir. 1997)

MICHEL, Circuit Judge.

Evans Cooling Systems, Inc. and Patent Enforcement Fund, Inc. (collectively, "Evans") appeal the September 30, 1996 order of the United States District Court for the District of Connecticut granting summary judgment to General Motors Corporation ("GM") of invalidity based on the "on sale" bar under 35 U.S.C. §102(b). Because there were no materially disputed questions of fact regarding whether the patented invention was offered for sale more than one year prior to the critical date and because we decline to create an exception to the on sale bar for those instances in which a third party misappropriates the invention and later places the invention on sale or causes an innocent third party to place the invention on sale, we affirm.

BACKGROUND

United States Patent Number 5,255,636 ("the '636 patent") issued on October 26, 1993 and claims an aqueous reverse flow cooling system for internal combustion engines. An understanding of the technology is not necessary to this appeal and we therefore do not discuss it. John Evans, the named inventor, admits he conceived the patented invention in 1984 and reduced it to practice in 1986. Mr. Evans did not file a patent application, however, until July 1, 1992.

In early 1994, Evans filed the present lawsuit alleging that GM infringed the '636 patent by the manufacture and sale of cars having GM's "LT1" and "L99" engines. GM counterclaimed for a declaration of invalidity and non-infringement. GM asserted that the '636 patent was invalid because GM and its independent dealers had placed the patented invention on sale prior to the critical date with the introduction of its 1992 Corvette. Specifically, GM sent an "Order Guide" for the 1992 Corvette to its independent dealers in late April or early May, 1991 to be used for ordering the vehicle described in the Order Guide. At about the same time, GM sent its dealers a supplemental brochure that provided additional ordering information for the 1992 Corvette, specifically stating that the car had reverse flow engine cooling. A representative of GM testified that it expected the dealers would start ordering the vehicles as soon as the Order Guide was sent to them. A sales representative at a GM dealership also testified that it was the dealership's common practice to order new cars and enter into agreements to sell new cars shortly after receiving the Guide. GM produced computer records documenting over 2000 orders placed by dealers around the country for the 1992 Corvette before the critical date. The orders, over 300 of which were placed on behalf of specific retail customers, were placed through a computer network and GM transmitted an acknowledgment back to the dealer after receiving the order. As a specific example, GM introduced evidence regarding a retail customer named Aram Najarian who visited a Corvette dealer in West Bloomfield, Michigan, in June, 1991. Mr. Najarian entered into a contract with a GM dealer on June 13, 1991 in which GM agreed to sell and Mr. Najarian agreed to buy a Corvette with an LT1 engine. Although a firm price was not established at that time, Mr. Najarian was informed that the price would be up to $2000 higher than the 1991 model and he placed a deposit on the car at that time. The order was transmitted to GM, and GM sent back an acknowledgment on June 14, 1991.

Evans asserted before the trial court that GM should not be allowed to invalidate the '636 patent because GM, in fact, stole the invention from Evans. Specifically, GM allegedly requested that Evans demonstrate its aqueous reverse flow cooling system at GM's test facility in the spring of 1989, and Evans alleges that GM stole the invention during this demonstration.

The district court granted summary judgment in favor of GM on September 30, 1996, because the record established that GM and its dealers placed the 1992 Corvette with the LT1 engine on sale prior to the critical date. The district court relied on the facts that Mr. Najarian entered into a contract with a GM dealer, the dealer agreed to sell and Mr. Najarian agreed to buy a 1992 Corvette, and Mr. Najarian paid a deposit and the dealer transmitted the order to GM. The court also noted that even an offer to sell will raise the on sale bar and that this transaction went beyond mere indefinite discussions about a possible sale. Turning to the policies underlying the on sale bar, the district court noted that John Evans claimed he reduced the invention to practice in 1986 but failed to file an application for some six years.

DISCUSSION

A person is not entitled to a patent if "the invention was . . . on sale in this country, more than one year prior to the date of the application for patent in the United States." 35 U.S.C. § 102(b). . . .

I.

[The court held the order entered into by Najarian and Cauley Chevrolet on June 13, 1991 was an offer for sale that invalidates the '636 patent.]

II.

Although our analysis would normally be complete once we had concluded there was an invalidating offer for sale, Evans urges this court to create a new exception to the on sale bar. Specifically, Evans asks us to rule that an otherwise invalidating offer for sale does not invalidate a patent "where a third party surreptitiously steals an invention while it is a trade secret and then, unbeknownst to the inventor, allegedly puts the invention on sale [more than one year] before the inventor files a patent application covering the stolen invention."

Evans cites three Supreme Court cases and asserts that they state that prior use of an invention by one who misappropriates the invention cannot invalidate a patent. *See Pennock v. Dialogue*, 27 U.S. (2 Pet.) 1, 19-20 (1829) ("[i]f before his application for a patent his invention should be pirated by another, or used without his consent; it can scarcely be supposed, that the legislature had within its contemplation such knowledge or use. . . . The use here referred to has always been understood to be a public use, and not a private or surreptitious use in fraud of the inventor."); *Shaw v. Cooper*, 32 U.S. (7 Pet.) 292, 319-20 (1833) ("But there may be cases, in which a knowledge of the invention may be surreptitiously obtained, and communicated to the public, that do not affect the right of the inventor. . . . If the right were asserted by him who fraudulently obtained it, perhaps no lapse of time could give it validity."); *Kendall v. Winsor*, 62 U.S. (21 How.) 322, 329 (1859) (affording immunity from suit to prior third party users of a patented invention but refusing to extend such immunity to those who received knowledge of the patented invention through fraud). Evans argues that these Supreme Court cases have never been expressly overruled and, in fact, the one time the Court of Customs and Patent Appeals addressed the issue it expressly left it open, stating:

> We do not find it here necessary to decide whether a fraudulent use of an invention for more than two years [then the bar period] prior to an application for a patent therefor bars the issue of the patent upon such application. . . . It may be that . . . said Minerals Separation should have been held to be estopped to bring a public use proceeding. But even so, as to this we express no opinion. . . .

In re Martin, 22 C.C.P.A. 891 (CCPA 1935).

We, however, do not find any of these cases dispositive of the issue presented by this case. In *Pennock,* the Supreme Court actually invalidated the patents in suit under the public use bar, and in that case the use had been with the permission of the patentee, thereby rendering any statements regarding piracy mere dicta. Likewise, the statements relied on by Evans in *Shaw* are dicta, as there too the patent was invalidated because the innocent public had come to know and use the invention, although there was some evidence that the invention had first become known to the public by fraudulent means. The statutory on sale bar wasn't even in issue in *Kendall.* Rather, the issue was whether the defendant had the right to continue to use the invention after the patent issued. *See also Eastman v. Mayor of N.Y.,* 134 F. 844, 852-55 (2d Cir. 1904) (discussing whether "fraudulent, surreptitious, or piratical" use of an invention could raise the public use bar and rejecting statements in above Supreme Court cases as dicta).

We note as well that the one other court that has addressed this precise issue has rejected arguments similar to Evans' arguments. *See Lorenz v. Colgate-Palmolive-Peet Co.,* 167 F.2d 423 (3d Cir. 1948). There, the court addressed the following question: "Was it the intention of Congress that public use by one who employs a process in breach of a fiduciary relationship, who tortiously appropriates it or who pirates it, should bar the inventor from the fruits of his monopoly?" 167 F.2d at 426. Lorenz had disclosed his invention to Colgate. Although Colgate told Lorenz the idea was rejected, it later made substantial commercial use of Lorenz's invention and then sought to invalidate Lorenz's patent based on this use. *Id.* at 424-25. After reviewing the Supreme Court and other relevant case law, the court rejected an exception to the statutory bar, stating:

> The prior-public-use proviso . . . contains no qualification or exception which limits the nature of the public use. We think that Congress intended that if an inventor does not protect his discovery by an application for a patent within the period prescribed by the Act, and an intervening public use arises from any source whatsoever, the inventor must be barred from a patent or from the fruits of his monopoly, if a patent has issued to him. There is not a single word in the statute which would tend to put an inventor, whose disclosures have been pirated, in any different position from one who has permitted the use of his process. . . . [I]solated instances of injustice may result if the law be strictly applied, but the inventor's remedy is sure. He is master of the situation and by prompt action [in filing a patent application] can protect himself fully and render the defense of prior public use impossible.

Id. at 429-30. Although this decision is not binding on this court, it is persuasive.

Even if we were to create an exception to the on sale bar such that third parties accused of misappropriating an invention could not invalidate a patent based upon sales by the guilty third party, GM correctly asserts that *Martin* squarely holds that activities of third parties uninvolved in the alleged misappropriation raise the statutory bar, even if those activities are instigated by the one who allegedly misappropriated the invention. In *Martin,* Martin's employer stole Martin's invention and filed an application on it and disclosed it to a third party. 74 F.2d at 952-53. After learning of his employer's activities, Martin filed his own application. After an interference was declared, the employer argued Martin's application was barred based on the activities of the third party. Martin conceded his invention had been in public use, but argued that the bar should not apply because the third party's use was "instigated by [his] employer and was a surreptitious and fraudulent public use against him." *Id.* at 953. After reviewing the Supreme Court and other relevant case law, the Court of Customs and Patent Appeals noted it had "been unable to find any authoritative decisions upon the question of whether a fraudulent public use of an invention . . . prior to the filing of an application . . . , or such public use of an invention instigated by fraud, bars the issuance of a patent. . . ." *Id.* at 955. Although the Court of Customs and Patent Appeals did not address that precise issue, the Court of Customs and Patent Appeals did hold that allowance of the application was barred because the third party's public use had been innocent, even though it had obtained the technology from the employer. *Id.*

As discussed below, this holding is dispositive here because, although Evans has charged GM with misappropriation, it has never contended that the independent dealers had any participation in or knowledge of the alleged theft; nor is there any indication that Mr. Najarian had such knowledge. Thus, the independent dealers are innocent users who put the invention on sale by placing orders for innocent retail customers like Najarian.

While such a result may not seem fair, Evans is not without recourse if GM in fact misappropriated his invention. Evans would have an appropriate remedy in state court for misappropriation of a trade secret. We note as well that the facts Evans alleges in support of its misappropriation claim demonstrate that Evans knew GM stole the invention at the very time it was allegedly stolen because during the demonstration GM employees allegedly told Mr. Evans they intended to steal the invention and a sealed room was unsealed during the night between the tests. Evans' patent rights would have nevertheless been protected if Mr. Evans had filed a patent application no more than one year from the date of the demonstration. This he did not do; instead Mr. Evans waited for more than two years after the demonstration and some six years after it was reduced to practice.

CONCLUSION

The '636 patent is invalid due to the pre-critical date contract entered into between the independent GM dealership and Mr. Najarian whereby the dealership offered to sell and Mr. Najarian agreed to buy a 1992 Corvette containing the LT1 engine. Even if GM misappropriated the idea behind the LT1 engine cooling system from Mr. Evans, the invention was nevertheless on sale and we decline to create the suggested new exception to the 102(b) bar which has no basis in the language of the statute. The trial court's decision is therefore affirmed.

Comments

1. ***The Policy Behind Allowing Third-Party Activity to Defeat Patent Rights?*** Despite the 1839 Act, and the 1870 Act, which is consistent with the 1839 Act in this regard, the policy considerations identified in *Pennock*, such as the policy of not allowing undue extension of the patent term or public dedication by the inventor, arguably do not apply in the same way to third-party activity. Characterizing the case law that permitted third-party barring activity,

William Robinson, the influential nineteenth-century treatise author, stated, "[t]his new position harmonizes with the tendency of modern judicial authority to discourage, as far as possible, any delay of the inventor in applying for a patent after his invention is complete, but is not consistent with the theory of dedication to the public, which always involves knowledge and consent" of the inventor. *See* WILLIAM C. ROBINSON, THE LAW OF PATENTS 501-506 (1890).

Modern case law, however, has cited public dedication as a reason for allowing third-party barring activity. For example, in *General Electric v. United States*, 654 F.2d 55, 61 (Ct. Cl. 1981), the court stated, "Congress should be held to have concluded, at the least, that the policy against removing inventions from the public domain and the policy favoring early patent filing are of sufficient importance in and of themselves to invalidate a patent where the invention is sold by one other than the inventor or one under his control." *Id.* at 62. And in *Baxter International, Inc. v. Cobe Laboratories, Inc.*, 88 F.3d 1054 (Fed. Cir. 1996), Judge Lourie wrote that "the most applicable policy underlying the public use bar here is discouraging removal from the public domain of inventions that the public reasonably has come to believe are freely available." In *Baxter*, Cullis invented a sealless centrifuge for separating blood into its components and obtained a patent. Dr. Jacques Suaudeau, a researcher at the NIH, was the alleged prior user. Dr. Suaudeau used a centrifuge that damaged platelets in the blood. According to his analysis, this damage was caused by the centrifuge's rotating seals. Dr. Suaudeau consulted with his colleague at the NIH, Dr. Yoichiro Ito, who advised Suaudeau to use a sealless centrifuge designed by Dr. Ito himself. Suaudeau tested his centrifuge for as long as forty-three hours, all of which in his NIH laboratory. Baxter, the assignee, argued Suaudeau's use of the centrifuge was not publicly known or accessible. The court disagreed, and found Suaudeau engaged in "public use" under section 102(b).

One could understandably ask whether Suaudeau's invention was in public use or whether the public came to believe that the invention was in the public domain. Moreover, did the court give insufficient weight to section 102(b)'s other underlying policies such as prompt disclosure and providing the inventor with an economic/marketing trial period? In her dissent, Judge Newman wrote that the majority created "a new and mischievous category of 'secret' prior art" that is "immune to the most painstaking documentary search."

2. ***Third-Party Use and the Public Interest.*** The issue of whether a third-party act can be a public-use or on-sale event can be traced back to the nineteenth century. In *Pennock v. Dialogue*, 27 U.S. 1 (1829), Justice Story noted that an inventor would be barred from obtaining a patent if the inventor made or authorized any public use or sale of an embodiment of his invention (except possibly for purposes of experimentation) even one day before the inventor filed an application for a patent. But, in discussing the nature of the disclosure, Justice Story added: "But how known or used? If it were necessary, as it well might be, to employ others to assist in the original structure or use by the inventor himself; or if before his application for a patent his invention should be pirated by another, or used without his consent; it can scarcely be supposed, that the legislature had within its contemplation such knowledge or use." *Id.* at 19.

Pennock was codified in the 1836 Act, which prevented an inventor from receiving a patent on his invention if "at the time of his application" the invention was "in public use or on sale with consent or allowance." 5 Stat. 117. Three years later, the 1839 Act introduced a "grace period." As such, pre-application public-use and on-sale activity did not preclude a patent from issuing "except on proof of abandonment of such invention to the public; or that such purchase, sale, or prior use has been for more than two years prior to such application for a patent." 5 Stat. 353. Presumably, a sale or use without the inventor's "consent or allowance" would not be a barring event under the 1836 Act. The 1839 Act eliminated any reference to "consent or allowance," but added a two-year grace period. Subsequent to the 1839 Act, the Supreme Court has indicated that the statutory bar standards are the same, whether the use or sale is by the inventor or a third party acting without the inventor's consent or allowance. In *Andrews v. Hovey*, 123 U.S. 267 (1887), for example, the Court wrote:

> It is very plain that under the act of 1836, if the thing patented had been in public use or on sale, with the consent or allowance of the applicant, for anytime, however short, prior to his application, the patent issued to him was invalid. Then came section 7 of the act of 1839, which was intended as an amelioration in favor of the inventor, in this respect, of the strict provisions of the act of 1836 [because it introduced a two-year grace period]. . . .
>
> [But deleting the "consent or allowance" language,] [t]he evident intention of congress was to take away the right (which existed under the act of 1836) to obtain a patent after an invention had for a long period of time been in public use, without the consent or allowance of the inventor; it limited that period to two years, whether the inventor had or had not consented to or allowed the public use. The right of an inventor to obtain a patent was in this respect narrowed, and the rights of the public as against him were enlarged, by the act of 1839.

Id. at 274. Which approach is more consistent with the policies of patent law: A grace period or inventor consent? Whom are you trying to protect: the inventor, the public, or both? Which approach is more easily administered in terms of certainty? The Federal Circuit case law is consistent with *Andrews. See Zacharin v. United States*, 213 F.3d 1366, 1371 (Fed. Cir. 2000) (stating "it is of no consequence that the sale was made by a third party, not the inventor").

3. ***Stolen or Pirated Inventions.*** It seems odd to allow use or on-sale activity resulting from theft to constitute a barring event. Is the public harmed in the absence of a statutory bar? The *Lorenz* court placed emphasis on the inventor, stating that "he is master of the situation," and "by prompt action can protect himself fully and render the defense of prior public use impossible." The prompt disclosure rationale is consistent with Professor Robinson's understanding of third-party activity, noted in Comment 1, *supra.* But note that Lorenz did file a timely application, although it did not issue into a patent. (The reasons behind his abandonment are unclear.) Perhaps *Lorenz* is best read as a statutory interpretation case. Recall the court emphasized that Congress's intent was that if an inventor does not protect himself by applying for a patent, and "an intervening public use arises from any source whatsoever, the inventor must be barred from a patent." According to the court, "[t]here is not a single word in the statute which would tend to put an inventor,

whose disclosures have been pirated, in any different position from one who has permitted the use of his process." The *Evans* case involves another misappropriation—although more blatant—and reaches the same result. *See also Abbott Laboratories v. Geneva Pharmaceuticals, Inc.*, 182 F.3d 1315, 1318 (Fed. Cir. 1999) (stating "the statutory on sale bar is not subject to exceptions for sales made by third parties either innocently or fraudulently").

COMPARATIVE PERSPECTIVE
Prejudicial Disclosures Under the European Patent Convention

The EPC is less generous to the patent applicant than American patent law in terms of types of disclosures that can defeat patent rights. Under Article 55, novelty will not be defeated if the invention was disclosed "no earlier than six months" before the European patent application was filed *and* the disclosure "was due to, or in consequence of" either (1) "an evident abuse in relation to the applicant or his legal predecessor" or the (2) "applicant or his legal predecessor displayed the invention at an officially recognized, international exhibition." Under American patent law, the grace period is one year and any type of activity within that one-year grace period cannot defeat patent rights.

The temporal condition of Article 55 requires a disclosure of the invention six months prior to the filing of the European patent application. This clause does not expressly address the question of what happens when priority applications are in play, namely, is it six months prior to the actual filing of the European application or six months prior to the filing of a priority application upon which the European application relies. The Enlarged Board of Appeal sided with the former, stating: "For the calculation of the six-month period referred to in Article 55 EPC, the relevant date is the date of the actual filing of the European patent application; the date of priority is not to be taken account of in calculating this period." *University Patents*, G03/98. The Board provided several reasons. First, Article 89, which governs priority, only expressly mentions Articles 54 and 60, not Article 55. Thus, said the Board, "neither the wording of Article 55 EPC nor that of Article 89 EPC provides for the period for non-prejudicial disclosures to be calculated from the priority date." The Board rejected the argument that Article 89 implicitly refers to Article 55. This argument is based on Article 89's express mention of Article 54(2) and (3), which in turn expressly mentions Article 55. According to the Board, this argument is unpersuasive because "Article 89 EPC associates the effect of the priority right not with the state of the art but with three specifically named provisions, which do not include Article 55 EPC. That is where it differs from Article 56, which refers generically to the notion of the state of the art for the purpose of deciding whether there has been an inventive step." Lastly, the Board rejected the argument that it is "unreasonable that the fate of an application should be conditional on whether it was originally filed with a national office or with the EPO." The Board thought this argument was "beside the point" and stated "on the assumption that a provision in line with Article 55 EPC applies to the national office, all that matters is whether the application being assessed is a first filing or a subsequent application filed more than six months after the disclosure. Only the first filing enjoys protection against abusive disclosure, not the subsequent application, regardless of whether it is filed with the EPO or with a national office." (The Board did note that the national courts of Switzerland and Germany are in accord with the Board's interpretation, but the Netherlands dates the six-month period from date of priority.)

An "evident abuse in relation to the application" requires the existence of a confidential relationship or one based on trust, either as part of an express written agreement or implicitly formed based on the relationship or business dealings of the relevant parties. *See* European Patent Office Guidelines for Examination D-V 3.1.3.2 ("The basic principle to be adopted is that subject-matter has not been made available to the public by use or in any other way if there is an express or tacit agreement on secrecy which has not been broken (reference should be made to the particular case of a non-prejudicial disclosure arising from an evident abuse in relation to the applicant, in accordance with Art. 55(1)(a)), or if the circumstances of the case are such that such secrecy derives from a relationship of good faith or trust. Good faith and trust are factors which may occur in contractual or commercial relationships."). For instance, negotiations between parties related to an inchoate or unpatented invention will likely lead to a finding of implied confidentiality. The abuse in question refers to a breach of this relationship, but the focus of the breach is not on the intent of the breaching party, but rather the effect of the breach "unjustifiably injuring the rights of the actual person entitled." 1 EUROPEAN PATENT CONVENTION: A COMMENTARY 139 (M. Singer & D. Stauder eds., 2003). Moreover, an abuse can occur if the invention was obtained unlawfully (e.g., theft) from the inventor or a third party who was in a confidential relationship with the inventor. The United Kingdom Patent Act of 1977 assumes this position more explicitly than the EPC. *See* §2(4)(a). But the U.K. Patent Act expressly notes that section 2 (and many other sections) "are so framed as to have, as nearly as practicable, the same effects in the United Kingdom as the corresponding provisions of the European Patent Convention." In this particular instance, the EPC is more generous to the inventor than the American patent code. Under 35 U.S.C. §102, not only is independent third-party disclosure capable of defeating patent rights, but a third party who steals (or pirates) the invention or obtains it by fraud and subsequently discloses can defeat patent rights.

The second form of non-prejudicial disclosure relates to inventions disclosed at officially recognized conventions (or exhibitions). The exhibition must be recognized by the Convention on International Exhibitions ("CIE"). *See* http://www.bie-paris.org/main/index.php?p=214&m2=227 (last visited March 13, 2007). This provision of Article 55 is seldom used, because, according to Singer and Stauder, "[e]xhibitions that satisfy the requirements specified in the [CIE] are extremely rare." 1 EUROPEAN PATENT CONVENTION: A COMMENTARY 140 (M. Singer & D. Stauder eds., 2003).

D. EXPERIMENTAL USE

A patentee may rebut a finding of public use by asserting he was engaged in experimental use, an argument frequently employed by patentees in the face of a public-use or on-sale allegation. An invention cannot be in public use or on sale in the legal sense of these terms if it were subject to ongoing experimentation. The factors that comprise an experimental use defense are explored in the following principal cases.

CITY OF ELIZABETH v. AMERICAN NICHOLSON PAVEMENT CO.
97 U.S. (7 Otto) 126 (1878)

Justice BRADLEY delivered the opinion of the court.

This suit was brought by the American Nicholson Pavement Company against the city of Elizabeth, N.J., George W. Tubbs, and the New Jersey Wood-Paving Company, a corporation of New Jersey, upon a patent issued to Samuel Nicholson, . . . for a new and improved wooden pavement. . . . [I]n the specification, it is declared that the nature and object of the invention consists in providing a process or mode of constructing wooden block pavements upon a foundation along a street or roadway with facility, cheapness, and accuracy, and also in the creation and construction of such a wooden pavement as shall be comparatively permanent and durable, by so uniting and combining all its parts, both superstructure and foundation, as to provide against the slipping of the horses' feet, against noise, against unequal wear, and against rot and consequent sinking away from below. . . . The patent has four claims, the first two of which, which are the only ones in question, are as follows:

I claim as an improvement in the art of constructing pavements:

1. Placing a continuous foundation or support, as above described, directly upon the roadway; then arranging thereon a series of blocks, having parallel sides, endwise, in rows, so as to leave a continuous narrow groove or channel-way between each row, and then filling said grooves or channel-ways with broken stone, gravel, and tar, or other like materials.

2. I claim the formation of a pavement by laying a foundation directly upon the roadway, substantially as described, and then employing two sets of blocks: one a principal set of blocks, that shall form the wooden surface of the pavement when completed, and an auxiliary set of blocks or strips of board, which shall form no part of the surface of the pavement, but determine the width of the groove between the principal blocks, and also the filling of said groove, when so formed between the principal blocks, with broken stone, gravel, and tar, or other like material.

The bill charges that the defendants infringed this patent by laying down wooden pavements in the city of Elizabeth, N.J., constructed in substantial conformity with the process patented, and prays an account of profits, and an injunction.

* * *

They averred that the alleged invention of Nicholson was in public use, with his consent and allowance, for six years before he applied for a patent, on a certain avenue in Boston called the Mill-dam; and contended that said public use worked an abandonment of the pretended invention.

* * *

To determine this question, it is necessary to examine the circumstances under which this pavement was put down, and the object and purpose that Nicholson had in view. It is perfectly clear from the evidence that he did not intend to abandon his right to a patent. He had filed a caveat in August, 1847, and he constructed the pavement in question by way of experiment, for the purpose of testing its qualities. The road in which it was put down, though a public road, belonged to the Boston and Roxbury Mill Corporation, which received toll for its use; and Nicholson was a stockholder and treasurer of the corporation. The pavement in question was about seventy-five feet in length, and was laid adjoining to the toll gate and in front of the toll-house. It was constructed by Nicholson at his own expense, and was placed by him where it was, in order to see the effect upon it of heavily loaded wagons, and of varied and constant use; and also to ascertain its durability, and liability to decay. Joseph L. Lang, who was toll-collector for many years, commencing in 1849, familiar with the road before that time, and with this pavement from the time of its origin, testified as follows:

> Mr. Nicholson was there almost daily, and when he came he would examine the pavement, would often walk over it, cane in hand, striking it with his cane, and making particular examination of its condition. He asked me very often how people liked it, and asked me a great many questions about it. I have heard him say a number of times that this was his first experiment with this pavement, and he thought that it was wearing very well. The circumstances that made this locality desirable for the purpose of obtaining a satisfactory test of the durability and value of the pavement were: that there would be a better chance to lay it there; he would have more room and a better chance than in the city; and, besides, it was a place where most everybody went over it, rich and poor. It was a great thoroughfare out of Boston. It was frequently traveled by teams having a load of five or six tons, and some larger. As these teams usually stopped at the toll-house, and started again, the stopping and starting would make as severe a trial to the pavement as it could be put to.

This evidence is corroborated by that of several other witnesses in the cause; the result of the whole being that Nicholson merely intended this piece of pavement as an experiment, to test its usefulness and durability. Was this a public use, within the meaning of the law?

An abandonment of an invention to the public may be evinced by the conduct of the inventor at any time, even within the two years named in the law. The effect of the law is, that no such consequence will necessarily follow from the invention being in public use or on sale, with the inventor's consent and allowance, at any time within two years before his application; but that, if the invention is in public use or on sale prior to that time, it will be conclusive evidence of abandonment, and the patent will be void.

But, in this case, it becomes important to inquire what is such a public use as will have the effect referred to. That the use of the pavement in question was public in one sense cannot be disputed. But can it be said that the invention was in public use? The use of an invention by the inventor himself, or of any other person under his direction, by way of experiment, and in order to bring the invention to perfection, has never been regarded as such a use.

Now, the nature of a street pavement is such that it cannot be experimented upon satisfactorily except on a highway, which is always public.

When the subject of invention is a machine, it may be tested and tried in a building, either with or without closed doors. In either case, such use is not a public use, within the meaning of the statute, so long as the inventor is engaged, in good faith, in testing its operation. He may see cause to alter it and improve it, or not. His experiments will reveal the fact whether any and what alterations may be necessary. If durability is one of the qualities to be attained, a long period, perhaps years, may be necessary to enable the inventor to discover whether his purpose is accomplished. And though, during all that period, he may not find that any changes are necessary, yet he may be justly said to be using his machine only by way of experiment; and no one would say that such a use, pursued with a bona fide intent of testing the qualities of the machine, would be a public use, within the meaning of the statute. So long as he does not voluntarily allow others to make it and use it, and so long as it is not on sale for general use, he keeps the invention under his own control, and does not lose his title to a patent.

It would not be necessary, in such a case, that the machine should be put up and used only in the inventor's own shop or premises. He may have it put up and used in the premises of another, and the use may inure to the benefit of the owner of the establishment. Still, if used under the surveillance of the inventor, and for the purpose of enabling him to test the machine, and ascertain whether it will answer the purpose intended, and make such alterations and improvements as experience demonstrates to be necessary, it will still be a mere experimental use, and not a public use, within the meaning of the statute.

Whilst the supposed machine is in such experimental use, the public may be incidentally deriving a benefit from it. If it be a grist-mill, or a carding-machine, customers from the surrounding country may enjoy the use of it by having their grain made into flour, or their wool into rolls, and still it will not be in public use, within the meaning of the law.

But if the inventor allows his machine to be used by other persons generally, either with or without compensation, or if it is, with his consent, put on sale for such use, then it will be in public use and on public sale, within the meaning of the law.

If, now, we apply the same principles to this case, the analogy will be seen at once. Nicholson wished to experiment on his pavement. He believed it to be a good thing, but he was not sure; and the only mode in which he could test it was to place a specimen of it in a public roadway. He did this at his own expense, and with the consent of the owners of the road. Durability was one of the qualities to be attained. He wanted to know whether his pavement would stand, and whether it would resist decay. Its character for durability could not be ascertained without its being subjected to use for a considerable time. He subjected it to such use, in good faith, for the simple purpose of ascertaining whether it was what he claimed it to be. Did he do any thing more than the inventor of the supposed machine might do, in testing his invention? The public had the incidental use of the pavement, it is true; but was the invention in public use, within the meaning of the statute? We think not. The proprietors of the road alone used the invention, and used it at Nicholson's request, by way of experiment. The only way in which they could use it was by allowing the public to pass over the pavement.

Had the city of Boston, or other parties, used the invention, by laying down the pavement in other streets and places, with Nicholson's consent and allowance, then, indeed, the invention itself would have been in public use, within the meaning of the law; but this was not the case. Nicholson did not sell it, nor allow others to use it or sell it. He did not let it go beyond his control. He did nothing that indicated any intent to do so. He kept it under his own eyes, and never for a moment abandoned the intent to obtain a patent for it.

In this connection, it is proper to make another remark. It is not a public knowledge of his invention that precludes the inventor from obtaining a patent for it, but a public use or sale of it. In England, formerly, as well as under our Patent Act of 1793, if an inventor did not keep his invention secret, if a knowledge of it became public before his application for a patent, he could not obtain one. To be patentable, an invention must not have been known or used before the application; but this has not been the law of this country since the passage of the act of 1836, and it has been very much qualified in England. Therefore, if it were true that during the whole period in which the pavement was used, the public knew how it was constructed, it would make no difference in the result.

It is sometimes said that an inventor acquires an undue advantage over the public by delaying to take out a patent, inasmuch as he thereby preserves the monopoly to himself for a longer period than is allowed by the policy of the law; but this cannot be said with justice when the delay is occasioned by a bona fide effort to bring his invention to perfection, or to ascertain whether it will answer the purpose intended. His monopoly only continues for the allotted period, in any event; and it is the interest of the public, as well as himself, that the invention should be perfect and properly tested, before a patent is granted for it. Any attempt to use it for a profit, and not by way of experiment, for a longer period than two years before the application, would deprive the inventor of his right to a patent. . . .

ELECTROMOTIVE DIVISION OF GENERAL MOTORS CORP. v. TRANSPORTATION SYSTEMS DIVISION OF GENERAL ELECTRIC CO.

417 F.3d 1203 (Fed. Cir. 2005)

MICHEL, Chief Judge.

The Electromotive Division of General Motors Corporation ("EMD") appeals the United States District Court for the Eastern District of Michigan's grant of summary judgment of invalidity of United States Patent Nos. 5,169,242 and 5,567,056 ("the '242 and '056 patents," respectively) under the on sale bar of 35 U.S.C. § 102(b). The '242 patent is generally directed to compressor bearings for use in turbochargers for diesel locomotive engines. The '056 patent relates generally to planetary bearings for use in turbocharger planetary drive trains. Because the patented compressor and planetary bearings were subject to pre-critical date sales that were commercial and not primarily experimental, we agree with the district court that the '242 and '056 patents have been proven invalid as a matter of law under the on sale bar of § 102(b). Accordingly, we affirm the district court's grant of summary judgment of invalidity of both patents in favor of the Transportation Systems Division of General Electric Company and Daido Industrial Bearings, Ltd.

I. Background

A. EMD's General Design and Testing Procedures

EMD is a division of General Motors Corporation focused on the design and production of locomotives. As part of that business, EMD designs and manufactures component parts for locomotive engines, including the two kinds of bearings at issue in this case. Both types of bearings are embedded in turbochargers, which are in turn embedded in the engines of locomotives that EMD sells.

After developing a new bearing, EMD typically initiates a two-phase testing program before releasing the new bearing for commercial production. In the first phase, termed Reliability Growth Testing, EMD tests its new bearings indoors at its engineering facilities on multiple unit turbocharger cells ("in-house program"). The purpose of the in-house program is to ascertain the durability and reliability of the new bearings.

Upon completion of the in-house program, EMD commences the second phase of testing, termed Reliability Verification Testing ("field program"). This testing occurs outdoors under actual use conditions. That is, after EMD integrates the new bearings into existing orders, the customer railroads use the new bearings in their routine operations. The purpose of this second phase is to verify durability.

During the field program, EMD does not engage in ongoing monitoring or periodic inspections of its new bearings because they are buried inside turbochargers and cannot readily be examined by visual inspection. Rather, EMD inspects the new bearings only if a particular turbocharger fails and is sent back to EMD. In such case, EMD disassembles the failed turbocharger to assess whether the failure was caused by the new bearings or some other part.

B. Events Involving the New Compressor Bearings

In the late 1980s, EMD developed a new compressor bearing for use in diesel locomotive turbochargers. On July 17, 1989, James L. Blase, an EMD employee and one of the named inventors on the two asserted patents, reported during an internal meeting that he had tested the new compressor bearings for approximately 3000 hours in a twelve-cylinder multiple unit locomotive engine. The minutes of that meeting document that the in-house program had been completed. Thus, EMD decided to proceed with the field program by substituting the new compressor bearings into locomotive orders previously placed by Norfolk Southern, Go Transit, and LXO railroads.[1]

EMD contacted Norfolk Southern, Go Transit, and LXO for permission to substitute the prior art bearings, originally to be used in the purchased locomotives, with the new compressor bearings. According to Mr. Blase, the three railroads agreed to accept the new bearings. None of the three companies, however, signed a confidentiality agreement or any other contract consenting to participate in the field program. They likewise were not given any design details or other documentation regarding the new compressor bearings. Further, Norfolk Southern, Go Transit, and LXO were not restricted or supervised in their use of

---

1. In the fall of 1988 and spring of 1989, EMD sold a total of forty-six locomotives to Norfolk Southern, Go Transit, and LXO, scheduling delivery for late 1989 and early 1990. Norfolk Southern ordered thirty-three locomotives, Go Transit ordered twelve locomotives, and LXO ordered one locomotive.

the new compressor bearings and were not under any obligation to collect data, keep progress records, or even operate the subject locomotives during the time of the field program.

After arranging for the substitution, EMD prepared internal memos documenting the change to be made in the Norfolk Southern, Go Transit, and LXO orders. For example, a July 19, 1989 internal memo stated: "Orders 887007 [for Norfolk Southern], C484 [for Go Transit], and 899110 [for LXO] are to have Turbocharger 40014638 replaced by Turbocharger 40021524. . . . The turbocharger and EMD make component schedules must be revised to reflect this change." A different July 19, 1989 memo stated that "the drawings and bills of material for these orders must be changed to include this new bearing. This will be accomplished with an expedited RFC. Jim Korenchan will write this RFC and get it to the drafting room by 7-19-89." Similarly, a July 25, 1989 internal memo stated: "This new bearing addresses all known failure modes and MUST be included in upcoming 12-710GA engines. The orders affected are the [Norfolk Southern] GP59 order No. 887007, Go Transit order no. C484, and LXO no. 899110."

On August 28, 1989, EMD modified its original specification of February 1, 1989 for the Norfolk Southern order, agreeing to supply more new compressor bearings to Norfolk Southern than originally planned for in its prior locomotive order. In particular, EMD noted that it "will provide spare parts for [Norfolk Southern]'s GP59 loco motives," including the "Turbo" of part number 40021531. The specified Turbo included the new compressor bearings.

Between January 1989 and November 1989, EMD purchased a total of 303 new compressor bearings from Allison Gas & Turbine ("Allison"), another division of General Motors Corporation, for a price of $298.80 each. Allison manufactured these bearings according to specifications provided by EMD. After receiving the new compressor bearings from Allison, EMD substituted them into locomotives previously sold to Norfolk Southern, Go Transit, and LXO. Thereafter, EMD shipped the subject locomotives to the three railroads.

On November 27, 1990, EMD filed a patent application for its new compressor bearings. Based upon this filing date, the critical date for applying the on sale bar for the '242 patent is November 27, 1989. The '242 patent issued on December 8, 1992. Claims 1 through 7 of the '242 patent are directed to a turbocharger assembly, and claims 8 through 18 are directed to the new compressor bearings.

On August 19, 1991, EMD released the new compressor bearings for production. All locomotive sales involving diesel engines after August 1991 included the new compressor bearings. Before this release, however, EMD employed prior art bearings in all customer orders, except the Norfolk Southern, Go Transit, and LXO orders discussed above. EMD likewise did not advertise, market, or create promotional materials for the new compressor bearings prior to the August 1991 release.

C. Events Involving the New Planetary Bearings

In September 1992, EMD designed a new planetary bearing for use in turbocharger planetary drive trains. In January 1993, EMD initiated the in-house program for this new bearing type. In March 1993, EMD decided to proceed with the field program. To do so, EMD approached Union Pacific railroad for permission to substitute its new planetary bearings for prior art bearings in an order for two locomotives that Union Pacific placed earlier in 1992. Union Pacific allegedly agreed. Nevertheless, it did not sign a confidentiality agreement or any other type of a contract consenting to participate in the field program. Union Pacific also was not placed under any restrictions or supervision regarding the use of the locomotives containing new planetary bearings. Nor was Union Pacific given any design details for the new planetary bearings or required to monitor or document its usage of the subject locomotives during the field program.

On July 6, 1993, EMD ordered 105 new planetary bearings at $88.87 per bearing from its supplier Glacier, now Daido Industrial Bearings, Ltd. ("Daido"). On August 6, 1993, EMD installed six planetary bearings that it had purchased from Daido into turbochargers for the two locomotives destined for Union Pacific. EMD shipped those locomotives to Union Pacific that same day. On September 7, 1994, EMD released the planetary bearings for production, meaning that the new planetary bearings were included in all future locomotive sales involving turbocharger planetary drive trains.

On September 29, 1994, EMD filed a patent application for its new planetary bearings. Based upon this filing date, the critical date for the '056 patent is September 29, 1993. The '056 patent issued on October 22, 1996. Claims 1 through 6 of the '056 patent are directed to the new planetary bearings, while claim 7 is directed to a turbocharger planetary drive train.

* * *

II. DISCUSSION

* * *

B. Evidence of Experimentation

GE contends that EMD's sale of spare compressor bearings cannot be the subject of experimentation. We are persuaded by this contention, noting in particular that the record does not reveal when or how Norfolk Southern intended to use the spare compressor bearings. There also was no evidence showing that Norfolk Southern replaced even one of the compressor bearings found in locomotives that EMD considered part of its field program with one of the spare compressor bearings. Such replacement must have occurred prior to the production release of the new compressor bearings in August 1991. Any replacement after that date certainly could not qualify as experimentation because EMD incorporated the new compressor bearings into all diesel engine locomotive orders following production release. Therefore, for the reasons set forth below, we conclude that EMD's sale of spare compressor bearings to Norfolk Southern was not primarily for experimentation and thus that the district court did not err in holding the '242 patent invalid under § 102(b).

Regarding planetary bearings, EMD argues that, at a minimum, a genuine issue of fact exists as to whether the sale of the new planetary bearings was primarily for experimentation, pointing out that (1) completion of the field program was required under EMD's policy before releasing a new bearing for production; (2) neither monitoring nor inspection was necessary because the purpose of the field program was merely to verify durability; (3) inspection was not even possible because the new planetary bearings were embedded in the turbochargers housed inside locomotive engines; and (4) failed turbochargers were returned to EMD for teardown and inspection. EMD also analogizes the facts here to those in *Manville Sales Corp. v. Paramount Systems, Inc.*, 917 F.2d 544 (Fed. Cir. 1990), and *EZ Dock*, 276 F.3d 1347. In both cases, which involved durability testing, we rejected an assertion of the on sale bar.

GE responds that the field program was unnecessary because the new planetary bearings had already been shown to work for their intended purpose during the in-house program. GE also asserts that durability testing under actual use conditions was not required because durability is not a claim limitation in the '056 patent. Additionally, GE contends that the district court correctly found, despite EMD's subjective intent to experiment, that the objective evidence revealed that EMD's sale to Union Pacific was not primarily for experimentation, noting, inter alia, that EMD did not control Union Pacific's use of the new planetary bearings and that the field program lacked the customary objective indicia associated with experimentation such as test records.

* * *

It is important to recognize that this court has limited experimentation sufficient to negate a pre-critical date public use or commercial sale to cases where the testing was performed to perfect claimed features, or, in a few instances like the case here, to perfect features inherent to the claimed invention. *See, e.g.*, *EZ Dock*, 276 F.3d at 1353 (experimentation focused on durability of claimed polyethylene floating dock in turbulent water of the Mississippi River, although durability was not a claim limitation); *Seal-Flex, Inc. v. Athletic Track & Court Constr.*, 98 F.3d 1318, 1320 (Fed. Cir. 1996) (experimentation focused on durability of claimed all-weather activity mat under harsh weather conditions, but durability was not a claim limitation); *Manville*, 917 F.2d at 550-551 (experimentation focused on durability of claimed self-centering, lightpole luminaire under severe winter conditions in Wyoming, even though durability was not a claim limitation). Here, EMD designed its field program to verify durability, a feature, although unclaimed, we hold is inherent to the new planetary bearings. Hence, evidence showing that EMD's field program has the requisite objective indicia of experimentation may negate EMD's pre-critical date sale of the new planetary bearings to Union Pacific.[2]

Few decisions address how to determine if a pre-critical date public use or sale is experimental rather than a public use or sale under §102(b), even though the doctrine has been in existence since *City of Elizabeth v. Pavement Co.*[3] But certain things are settled. Significantly, an inventor's subjective intent to experiment cannot establish that his activities are, in fact, experimental.

> When sales are made in an ordinary commercial environment and the goods are placed outside the inventor's control, an inventor's secretly held subjective intent to "experiment," even if true, is unavailing without objective evidence to support

2. It is well-settled that an accused infringer carries the burden of proving invalidity by clear and convincing evidence. When the accused infringer alleges invalidity under §102(b) based upon a pre-critical date public use or commercial sale, however, an inventor may introduce evidence showing that his public use or sale was primarily for purposes of experimentation, thus neutralizing the accused infringer's showing.

3. Although *City of Elizabeth* involved a pre-critical date public use of the claimed invention, we have applied experimentation not only in that context but also in the on sale context. *See In re Hamilton*, 882 F.2d 1576, 1580 (Fed. Cir. 1989).

the contention. Under such circumstances, the customer at a minimum must be made aware of the experimentation.

LaBounty Mfg. v. United States ITC, 958 F.2d 1066, 1072 (Fed. Cir. 1992). Thus, while EMD officials may have subjectively believed they were conducting experimentation under actual use conditions, their beliefs cannot establish that EMD's sales were primarily for experimentation.

We have generally looked to objective evidence to show that a pre-critical date sale was primarily for experimentation. For example, in *TP Laboratories, Inc. v. Professional Positioners, Inc.,* 724 F.2d 965, 972 (Fed. Cir. 1984), we indicated that various objective indicia may be considered in determining whether the inventors engaged in experimentation:

> The length of the test period is merely a piece of evidence to add to the evidentiary scale. The same is true with respect to whether payment is made for the device, whether a user agreed to use secretly, whether records were kept of progress, whether persons other than the inventor conducted the asserted experiments, how many tests were conducted, how long the testing period was in relationship to tests of other similar devices.

Id. at 971-72.

Recently, we catalogued and consolidated all these considerations into a list of thirteen objective factors: (1) the necessity for public testing; (2) the amount of control over the experiment retained by the inventor; (3) the nature of the invention; (4) the length of the test period; (5) whether payment was made; (6) whether there was a secrecy obligation; (7) whether records of the experiment were kept; (8) who conducted the experiment; (9) the degree of commercial exploitation during testing; (10) whether the invention reasonably requires evaluation under actual conditions of use; (11) whether testing was systematically performed; (12) whet her the inventor continually monitored the invention during testing; and (13) the nature of the contacts made with potential customers. *Allen Eng'g,* 299 F.3d at 1353. This list is not exhaustive, and all of the experimentation factors may not apply in a particular case. They simply represent various kinds of evidence relevant to the question of whether pre-critical date activities involving the patented invention—either public use or sale—were primarily experimental and not commercial.

This court, however, has held or at least suggested that certain evidentiary showings can be dispositive of the question of experimentation. In *In re Hamilton,* 882 F.2d 1576 (Fed. Cir. 1989), we stated:

> First, we may agree with [the inventor] that control is not the "lodestar" test in all cases involving experimental use. It is nonetheless an important factor. The experimental use doctrine operates in the inventor's favor to allow the inventor to refine his invention or to assess its value relative to the time and expense of prosecuting a patent application. If it is not the inventor or someone under his control or "surveillance" who does these things, there appears to us no reason why he should be entitled to rely upon them to avoid the statute.

Id. at 1581 (emphasis in original). We observed that nothing in the record showed that the *Hamilton* inventor knew what, if anything, the customer was doing in terms of testing the invention. As a result, we concluded that the inventor's purpose in making the sale was not primarily experimental.

Following *Hamilton*, this court again emphasized the importance of control in *Lough v. Brunswick Corp.*, 86 F.3d 1113 (Fed. Cir. 1996). In particular, this court said that an inventor must show control over the alleged testing to establish experimentation. *Id.* at 1120. Additionally, the *Lough* court placed critical emphasis on experimental records. After listing various objective indicia of experimentation, which included both whether records or progress reports were made concerning the testing and the extent of control the inventor maintained over the testing, this court stated: "The last factor of control is critically important, because, if the inventor has no control over the alleged experiments, he is not experimenting. If he does not inquire about the testing or receive reports concerning the results, similarly, he is not experimenting." *Id.* The *Lough* court also stated: "When one distributes his invention to members of the public under circumstances that evidence a near total disregard for supervision and control concerning its use, the absence of these minimal indicia of experimentation require a conclusion that the invention was in public use." *Id.* at 1122 (emphasis added). Hence, this court held, based primarily upon the absence of control and records, that the inventor's public use of the claimed invention was not experimental.

Two years after *Lough*, in a concurring opinion in *C.R. Bard, Inc. v. M3 Systems, Inc.*, 157 F.3d 1340 (Fed. Cir. 1998), Judge Bryson urged that control and record-keeping are vital to a showing of experimentation. "Certain factors, such as the requirement that the inventor control the testing, that detailed progress records be kept, and that the purported testers know that testing is occurring, are critical to proving experimental purpose." *Id.* at 1380 (citing *Lough*, 86 F.3d at 1120). Judge Bryson stressed awareness by the purported testers that testing is occurring. He suggested or at least implied that consideration of these three factors form the first, and potentially decisive, step in determining whether a public use or sale was primarily experimental. Indeed, we discern that Judge Bryson applied only these three factors to conclude that the on sale bar applied.

> The facts of this case are analogous to those in *U.S. Environmental Products, Inc. v. Westall*, 911 F.2d 713 (Fed. Cir. 1990). In *Westall*, this court affirmed a district court's conclusion that a patent was invalidated by a sale more than one year before the filing date. That conclusion was based primarily on (1) the lack of written progress records and the failure to adhere to a testing schedule; (2) the inventor's failure to maintain control over the testing; and (3) promotion of the invention during the testing. In this case, as in *Westall*, the evidence shows that neither the in-house tests . . . nor the field tests . . . were under the control of the inventor or his company. There is little or no evidence of any written progress records; indeed, the inventor was apparently never provided with any test results. Finally, the communications between [a company with which the inventor was associated] and [the customer] throughout the purported testing period emphasized commercial sales and projections, not controlled experimentation.

Id. at 1381 (internal citation omitted).

We agree with Judge Bryson that a customer's awareness of the purported testing in the context of a sale is a critical attribute of experimentation. If an inventor fails to communicate to a customer that the sale of the invention was made in pursuit of experimentation, then the customer, as well as the general public, can only view the sale as a normal commercial transaction. Indeed, our predecessor court recognized in *In re Dybel*, 524 F.2d 1393, 1401 (C.C.P.A. 1975), that "[an inventor's] failure to communicate to any of the purchasers or prospective purchasers of his device that the sale or offering was for experimental use is fatal to his case." And, "we have held that the assertion of experimental sales, at a minimum, requires that customers must be made aware of the experimentation." *Paragon Podiatry Lab., Inc. v. KLM Labs., Inc.*, 984 F.2d 1182, 1186 (Fed. Cir. 1993). Accordingly, we hold not only that customer awareness is among the experimentation factors, but also that it is critical.

Our precedent has treated control and customer awareness of the testing as especially important to experimentation. Indeed, this court has effectively made control and customer awareness dispositive. *See, e.g., Lough*, 86 F.3d at 1120; *Hamilton*, 882 F.2d at 1581. Accordingly, we conclude that control and customer awareness ordinarily must be proven if experimentation is to be found.

We now consider the facts of this case. First, the record, as the district court noted, is devoid of any evidence that EMD, or Union Pacific under EMD's direction, controlled the field program for its new planetary bearings. EMD did not provide any protocols to Union Pacific directing their use of locomotives containing the new planetary bearings. EMD likewise neither supervised nor restricted Union Pacific's use of the new planetary bearings in any way. Mr. Blase testified that the railroads involved in the field testing were not required to run the subject locomotives under any specific conditions.

The record also shows that EMD made no attempt to monitor the conditions under which Union Pacific used the "test" locomotives. EMD explains away its lack of oversight by arguing that the field program was conducted solely to verify the durability of its new planetary bearings as measured by the number of turbocharger failures, not by the daily use of its new planetary bearings. Such an argument is, however, unconvincing. EMD did not request or receive any comments or data from Union Pacific concerning the operation or durability of its new planetary bearings. Without obligating Union Pacific to provide such feedback, it cannot be reasonably said that EMD exercised any monitoring over the field program.

That Union Pacific returned failed turbochargers to EMD for teardown and inspection is insufficient to establish EMD's control over the field program. Union Pacific voluntarily returned failed turbochargers under the basic warranty given by EMD to all of its customers. It was not, however, under any obligation to do so. Mr. Blase testified that EMD requested the return of failed components from all customers in the ordinary course of business. Union Pacific thus would have returned all failed turbochargers whether it was participating in experimentation or was merely an ordinary customer. What is more, EMD's teardown reports focused only on the appearance and features of the new planetary bearings without any correlation to the field conditions. Nothing in the teardown reports thus distinguish them from any other failure reports prepared outside the field program. Accordingly, the district court did not err in finding that EMD exercised no control over Union Pacific's use of the new bearings.

Second, the record is insufficient, even on summary judgment, to objectively establish Union Pacific's awareness of the field program. The only evidence regarding communications with Union Pacific concerning the field program comes from Mr. Blase's deposition testimony and an internal memo he prepared. In his deposition, Mr. Blase testified:

Q: Okay. Now when you would generally send out or do field verification or reliability verification in the field, were there agreements that customers entered into in connection with those?

A: The customer would understand that—that the—that what they were receiving would be a reliability verification test.

Q: Would you tell them which components were associated with that?

A: We would indicate to them which components are under reliability—reliability verification test, yes.

Q: You would tell them that.

A: Sure.

Q: Okay. Did they sign any type of secrecy agreement or confidentiality agreement in connection with that?

A: I do not know that.

Q: Okay. Who would know that?

A: The—the correspondence with the customer would be handled through the sales department as far as I know.

Q: And who was in the sales department during this timeframe?

A: I don't recall.

Similarly, in his memo, Mr. Blase stated under the heading "Status of Public Disclosure" that "upon applying for field test on a customer's locomotive, the customer is made aware that there is an experimental part in the turbochargers they are receiving, yet details of the part are not fully disclosed." Apart from this single sentence, Mr. Blase did not otherwise describe EMD's communications with any customer or state exactly what Union Pacific was told, if anything.

Neither Mr. Blase's testimony nor his memo establishes awareness by Union Pacific that the new planetary bearings were substituted into their pre-existing order for the purpose of testing those bearings in actual use rather than as part of a commercial sale. Mr. Blase's testimony simply suggests the possibility that an unidentified EMD employee may have engaged in a conversation with one or more unidentified employees of Union Pacific about substituting the new planetary bearings.

Further, the record fails to show any objective evidence supporting Mr. Blase's inference that Union Pacific was "aware" of the field testing. It does not contain even the hint of a written agreement with Union Pacific, testimony from any representative of Union Pacific describing the railroad's awareness of the field program, or any other form of corroborating documentation held by Union Pacific regarding the field program. The lack of such evidence to corroborate Mr. Blase's conclusory testimony and memo thus validates the lack of customer awareness.

The facts here are closely analogous to those in *Lough*, where, as noted above, this court rejected an inventor's claim that a pre-critical date public use of his liquid seal assembly invention was made for experimentation. In *Lough*, the inventor distributed six prototypes of his liquid seal assembly invention to his friends for use in their boats. After distribution, the *Lough* inventor did not maintain any supervision over his friends' use of the liquid seal assemblies or follow-up with them for comments as to the operability of the liquid seal assemblies. Similarly, EMD allowed Union Pacific unsupervised use of the new planetary bearings. EMD neither monitored the conditions under which Union Pacific used the new planetary bearings nor solicited any feedback from Union Pacific regarding the bearings' performance. What is more, EMD, like the inventor in *Lough*, did not maintain any records of the alleged testing or require Union Pacific to do so. As we stated in *Lough*, "Lough's failure to monitor the use of his prototypes by his acquaintances, in addition to the lack of records or reports from those acquaintances concerning the operability of the devices, compel the conclusion that, as a matter of law, he did not engage in experimental use." 86 F.3d at 1122. We are equally compelled to conclude as a matter of law that EMD did not engage in any experimentation on its new planetary bearings.

* * *

Because the facts do not show the existence of control or customer awareness, we do not consider the other experimentation factors. We conclude, as a matter of law, that EMD's sale to Union Pacific of the new planetary bearings was not made primarily for experimentation. We, therefore, conclude that Daido's sale to EMD could not have been made primarily for experimentation, since the purpose for the upstream sale was to make the downstream sale possible. Accordingly, the district court did not err in holding the '056 patent invalid under the on sale bar of § 102(b).

LISLE CORP. v. A.J. MANUFACTURING CO.

398 F.3d 1306 (Fed. Cir. 2005)

LOURIE, Circuit Judge.

A.J. Manufacturing Company ("A.J.") appeals from the decision of the United States District Court for the Northern District of Illinois denying A.J.'s motion for judgment as a matter of law ("JMOL") after a jury found the '776 patent was not shown to be invalid for public use. We affirm.

BACKGROUND

The patent in this appeal relates to an inner tie rod tool. Most automobiles today are equipped with a rack and pinion steering control system. A component of the rack and pinion steering control system is the inner tie rods. As the patent explains, "[s]ervicing of such a rack and pinion steering system often requires removal and replacement of the tie rods." Due to the location of the tie rods and the variety of nut shapes holding the tie rods in place, removal of that component can be tedious with prior art tools. The patented invention alleviates the need for automobile mechanics to completely dismantle steering control systems and keep multiple prior art tie rod tools for various inner tie rod designs.

* * *

Lisle and A.J., the parties to this dispute, are manufacturers and competitors in the field of automotive tools. Lisle owns the '776 patent, and on October 1, 2002, Lisle filed suit accusing A.J. of infringing the patent by manufacturing and selling its YA3000A tool. In its Answer, A.J. denied infringing the patent and asserted that the patent was invalid.

[After ruling on summary judgment motions relating to infringement,] a jury trial was held on the single issue of whether the '776 patent was invalid on the ground of public use under 35 U.S.C. § 102(b). On February 12, 2004, the jury found the '776 patent was not shown to be invalid on the ground of public use. The district court denied A.J.'s motion for JMOL of invalidity of the '776 patent after the jury rendered its verdict.

DISCUSSION

A patent is presumed to be valid. 35 U.S.C. § 282 (2000). Nonetheless, a patent can be found invalid if "the invention was in . . . public use . . . in this country more than one year prior to the date of the application for patent in the United States." 35 U.S.C. § 102(b). Experimental use negates patent invalidity for public use; when proved, it may show that particular acts do not constitute a public use within the meaning of § 102. Although the determination of whether a patent is invalid for public use is a question of law that we review *de novo,* the disputed facts found to support that determination are reviewed for substantial evidence.

* * *

II. Invalidity

A.J. appeals from the denial of its motion for JMOL of invalidity of the '776 patent on the ground of public use and requests that we overturn a jury verdict concluding otherwise. The undisputed facts are that sometime in May 1989 Lisle became interested in developing an improved tie rod tool. The early prototype tool was similar to A.J.'s product, and Lisle does not dispute that the prototype tool would have fallen within the scope of the claims of the '776 patent. It is established law that that which infringes, if later, anticipates if earlier. However, on or about December 12, 1989, Lisle delivered the prototype tool to four different automobile repair shops in Omaha, Nebraska. Lisle did not receive any payment for those tools. Upon distributing the tool, Lisle also did not require any of the mechanics to enter into a formal confidentiality agreement. On June 26, 1992, over thirty months after the first prototype tool was delivered, Lisle filed the application leading to the '776 patent.

A.J. asserts that based on the substantial evidence it presented at trial, the district court should have set aside as a matter of law the jury's verdict that the '776 patent was not shown to be invalid for public use. A.J.'s primary argument for reversing the jury's verdict is that Lisle failed to demonstrate the requisite level of control over the work of the mechanics with the prototype tool to support an experimental use defense. To support its position, A.J. cites the lack of a formal confidentiality agreement, the lack of restrictions placed on the use of the prototype tool by the mechanics, and the absence of any documentary evidence regarding the actual testing of the prototype tool. A.J. also contends that the district court erred by providing a jury instruction with an erroneous standard for rebutting a *prima facie* case of invalidity for public use. Based on that purported legal error, A.J. seeks a new trial on the issue of invalidity for public use.

We affirm the district court's denial of A.J.'s motion for JMOL of invalidity. The parties accept that, were the deliveries of the prototype tools to the automobile repair shops not to constitute experimental use, they would be evidence of public use. After all, the mechanics were members of the relevant public. However, substantial evidence supports the jury's findings of fact in favor of Lisle on the question of experimental use, and those findings support the conclusion of lack of public use. To counter A.J.'s attempt to show public use, Lisle relies on the testimony of Mr. Danny Williams, co-inventor of the '776 patent and an engineer for Lisle, which was presented to the jury. Williams testified that he needed to know how well the wrench disc would fit on the inner tie rod socket and whether the prototype tool would fit in the confined location of the tie rod in different automobile models. Williams also stated that, under company protocol, he and other engineers at Lisle would have contacted the mechanics who were given the prototype tool every two to four weeks by telephone or in person to receive testing feedback. Williams further testified that he modified the design of the retainer in the prototype tool and added additional wrench disc sizes based on comments he received from the outside mechanics. Finally, Williams explained that although there was no formal confidentiality agreement between Lisle and the mechanics who were given the prototype tools, Lisle had prior working relationships with those mechanics. Williams also believed that the mechanics knew that the prototype tool was given to them for experimental purposes.

The jury was also presented with "General Meeting Reports" that were drafted by the president of Lisle, Mr. John Lisle. The reports gave updates on the then-current status of the tie rod tool project, plans for future testing, concerns regarding the commercial viability of the tools, and suggestions from outside mechanics regarding how to improve the design of the tool. Mr. Marvin Negley, Manager of Engineering at Lisle, also testified that those reports were based on information that Mr. Lisle received during weekly management meetings. While we express no view as to whether we as fact-finders might have concluded that this evidence was sufficient to rebut a *prima facie* case of public use, we agree with Lisle that the submitted testimony and reports do constitute substantial evidence from which a reasonable jury could find that Lisle rebutted the *prima facie* case of public use and thus A.J. failed to prove by facts supported by clear and convincing evidence that the '776 patent was invalid for public use. . . .

Comments

1. *The Policies of Experimental Use.* The common law experimental use doctrine can be traced to the early nineteenth century. *See* REPORT FROM THE HON. HENRY L. ELLSWORTH TO THE SECRETARY OF STATE AND TRANSMITTED TO THE SELECT COMMITTEE ON THE PATENT LAWS 175, 179 (1836) (comparing the American and the British approach toward public use, stating "[o]ur courts have adopted a more liberal policy, and very justly decided that public experiments to test the value of the invention, do not destroy the right on the ground of publicity").

   The first policy underlying the experimental use doctrine is to provide the inventor with time to test his invention. This policy results in social benefits (society receives a more refined and commercially ready invention) and permits inventors to determine if the invention is worth the time and expense of preparing and prosecuting a patent application. An additional policy seeks to preclude an inventor from extending the term of the patent's statutory life while commercially exploiting the invention. It is important to emphasize that activity that would typically result in a finding of public use must be experimental in nature and, the scope and length of the activity must be reasonable in terms of that purpose. If the purpose was experimental and the activity reasonable, it is not legally significant that the inventor benefits incidentally from the activity. *See In re Hamilton*, 882 F.2d 1576, 1581 (Fed. Cir. 1989) ("The experimental use doctrine operates in the inventor's favor to allow *the inventor* to refine his invention or to assess its value relative to the time and expense of prosecuting a patent application. If it is not the inventor or someone under his control or 'surveillance' who does these things, there appears to us no reason why he should be entitled to rely upon them to avoid the statute.") (emphasis in original).

2. *Experimental Use's Multi-Factor Test.* The courts have adopted a multi-factored approach to experimental use. Consider the 13 factors set forth in *Allen Eng'g Corp. v. Bartell Indus., Inc.*, 299 F.3d 1336, 1353 (Fed. Cir. 2002): (1) the necessity for public testing; (2) the amount of control over the experiment retained by the inventor; (3) the nature of the invention; (4) the length of the test period; (5) whether payment was made; (6) whether there was a secrecy obligation; (7) whether records of the experiment were kept; (8) who conducted the experiment; (9) the degree of commercial exploitation during testing; (10) whether the invention reasonably requires evaluation under actual conditions of use; (11) whether testing was systematically performed; (12) whether the inventor continually monitored the invention during testing; and (13) the nature of the contacts made with potential customers. While no one factor is dispositive, control is an extremely important consideration. The *Electromotive* court, citing Judge Bryson's concurrence in *C.R. Bard*, also highlighted the importance of detailed progress records and knowledge by the purported testers that testing is occurring. In fact, Judge Bryson went so far as to suggest that these three factors (including control) form the first, and potentially decisive, step in determining whether a public use or sale was primarily experimental. *See Clock Spring LP v. Wrapmaster, Inc.*, 560 F.3d 1317 (Fed. Cir. 2009) (finding no experimental use because three of eleven demonstrations of claimed invention were outside of inventor's "control or surveillance").

In *City of Elizabeth*, the duration of the test period was due to the nature of the invention and Nicholson exercised the requisite amount of control during the experimental period. Recall Mr. Lang's testimony: "Mr. Nicholson was there almost daily, and when he came he would examine the pavement, would often walk over it, cane in hand, striking it with his cane, and making particular examination of its condition. He asked me very often how people liked it, and asked me a great many questions about it." In *Lisle Corp.*, the patentee was able to show sufficient control. The court affirmed a finding of experimental use even though there was no formal confidentiality agreement between Lisle and the mechanics. Williams, whose testimony was crucial, noted that Lisle and the mechanics had prior working relationships, and that Lisle would have contacted the mechanics every two to four weeks for testing feedback. There were also "General Meeting Reports" drafted by the president of Lisle, which provided updates of "tie rod" project. The relationship between Lisle and the mechanics was informal, not the formal or highly structured arrangements you would see in larger corporate entities. The Federal Circuit has stated "less formal and seemingly casual experiments can be expected" with individual or small business units," and that these types of experiments "may be deemed legally sufficient to avoid the public use bar, but only if they demonstrate the presence of the same basic elements that are required to validate experimental use." *Lough v. Brunswick Corp.*, 86 F.3d 1113, 1121 (Fed. Cir. 1996).

The patentees in *Electromotive* and *Lough* (cited in *Electromotive*) were not as fortunate. Lough was a repairman at a marina who designed a new upper seal assembly on a Brunswick indoor/outdoor motor. Lough made six prototypes, installing one in his own boat and gave the rest away, but with no provision or contract for follow-up involvement during the alleged experimentation. More than one year before filing a patent application, he gave one prototype to a friend who installed it in his own boat. He also installed a prototype in the dealership owner's boat and one in the boat of a customer. And he gave the remaining two prototypes to friends who were employees at another marina, who in turn installed one on the boat of someone unknown to Lough. Lough neither monitored the alleged experiments, nor kept records or reports from his friends and acquaintances concerning how well his invention operated. Even though Lough was an individual inventor who never commercialized his invention, the court found public use:

> Lough in effect provided the prototype seal assemblies to members of the public for their free and unrestricted use. The law does not waive statutory requirements for inventors of lesser sophistication. When one distributes his invention to members of the public under circumstances that evidence a near total disregard for supervision and control concerning its use, the absence of these minimal indicia of experimentation require a conclusion that the invention was in public use.

Lough, 86 F.3d at 1122. Mr. Lough did not exert the requisite control, the most important factor in proving experimental use. In dissent, Judge Plager wrote "[t]he record in this case is undisputed that Lough made no sales of his invention until after his patent application was filed. Nor was this simply market testing, rather than product testing." *Id.* at 1125. There is abundant Federal Circuit precedent, according to Judge Plager, "in which inventors tested their products in various ways before various audiences, and in which we have held that such testing, when it made sense in light of the circumstances, did not constitute public use under." *Id.* For Judge Plager, Lough was an individual inventor, someone who "failed to conduct his testing, his experiments, with the careful attention we lawyers, with our clean and dry hands, have come to prefer." *Id.* at 1124. Does the majority or dissent provide more certainty to individual inventors?

3. **When Is Experimental Use No Longer Experimental?** Experimental use ends when the invention is either reduced to practice or is ready for patenting, which is the test formulated in *Pfaff. See Invitrogen Corp. v. Biocrest Mfg. L.P.*, 424 F.3d 1374, 1379-1380 (Fed. Cir. 2005) (stating "[t]his court notes that in applying the *Pfaff* two-part test in the context of a public use bar, evidence of experimental use may negate either the 'ready for patenting' or 'public use' prong"); *Allen Eng'g Corp. v. Bartell Indus. Inc.*, 299 F.3d 1336, 1354 (Fed. Cir. 2002) (stating "once the invention is reduced to practice, there can be no experimental use negation"). As explored in *Pfaff* and subsequent comments, the ready for patenting test embraces an enablement standard. Reduction to practice requires more, namely proof that the inventor (1) "constructed an embodiment or performed a process that met all the limitations" and (2) "determined that the invention would work for its intended purpose." *Z4*

Techs., Inc. v. Microsoft Corp., 507 F.3d 1340, 1352 (Fed. Cir. 2007). For example, in *In re Omeprazole Litigation*, 536 F.3d 1361 (Fed. Cir. 2008), the claimed invention (a drug for treating gastrointestinal disorders) was undergoing a phase III clinical trial as required by the Food and Drug Administration. The issue was whether this use—a clinical trial—constituted public use under section 102(b) or was experimental use. The Federal Circuit held the invention was not in public use because the accused infringer "has not demonstrated that, without conducting the Phase III clinical tests, the inventors knew that the Phase III formulation would achieve the goals of long-term stability and in vivo stability such that it would be effective as a treatment for gastrointestinal disease." *Id.* at 1375.

When issues of durability are relevant, an inventor may have to test his invention in its intended environment for several years, such as Mr. Nicholson. And even if no improvements are needed after this period, the inventor will still be deemed to have engaged in experimental use. *See City of Elizabeth*, 97 U.S. 126, 135 (1877) ("If durability is one of the qualities to be attained, a long period, perhaps years, may be necessary to enable the inventor to discover whether his purpose is accomplished. And though, during all that period, he may not find that any changes are necessary, yet he may be justly said to be using his machine only by way of experiment; and no one would say that such a use, pursued with a bona fide intent of testing the qualities of the machine, would be a public use, within the meaning of the statute."). *See also Aerovox Corp. v. Polymet Mfg.*, 67 F.2d 860, 863 (2d Cir. 1933) (Hand, J.) (stating "it did not appear that Nicholson, the inventor, delayed for any other reason than to learn how well his pavement would wear; apparently it was already as good as he hoped to make it"); *Manville Sales Corp. v. Paramount Systems, Inc.*, 917 F.2d 544, 551 (Fed. Cir. 1990) (noting "[w]hen durability in an outdoor environment is inherent to the purpose of an invention, then further testing to determine the invention's ability to serve that purpose will not subject the invention to a section 102(b) bar").

Enforcing Patent Rights

INTRODUCTION

A patent owner has numerous rights. The most fundamental right is found in section 154 of the patent code, which provides the patent owner with the "right to exclude others from making, using, offering for sale, or selling the invention throughout the United States or importing the invention into the United States."[1] In addition, section 271 states "whoever without authority makes, uses, offers to sell, or sells any patented invention, within the United States or imports into the United States any patented invention during the term of the patent therefor, infringes the patent." Reverse engineering, independent creation, and lack of intent are not defenses to patent infringement.[2]

---

1. Section 154 continues to provide "if the invention is a process," the patentee is granted "the right to exclude others from using, offering for sale or selling throughout the United States, or importing into the United States, products made by that process, referring to the specification for the particulars thereof."

2. Accordingly, patent infringement has been characterized as a strict liability regime. *See In re Seagate Tech., LLC*, 497 F.3d 1360, 1368 (Fed. Cir. 2007) (*en banc*) (referring to patent infringement as "a strict liability offense"). *See also* Mark A. Lemley, *Should Patent Infringement Require Proof of Copying*, 105 MICH. L. REV. 1525, 1525 (2007) (stating "[p]atent infringement is a strict liability offense"); Christopher A. Cotropia & Mark A. Lemley, *Copying in Patent Law*, 87 N.C. L. REV. 1421, 1425 (2009) (noting "copying is irrelevant to the issue of liability"). Indeed, direct infringement has traditionally been understood to require nothing more than unauthorized use of a patented invention. *See Aro Mfg. Co. v. Convertible Top Replacement*, 377 U.S. 476, 484 (1964) (discussing section 271(a) and stating "[n]ot only does that provision explicitly regard an unauthorized user of a patented invention as an infringer, but it has often and clearly been held that unauthorized use, without more, constitutes infringement"), *cf.* Roger D. Blair & Thomas F. Cotter, *Strict Liability and Its Alternatives in Patent Law*, 17 BERKELEY TECH. L.J. 799 (2002) (arguing that patent law is best conceived as a modified strict liability regime). In this regard, patent law is distinct from trade secret and copyright law where independent creation is a defense. *See Blair v. Westinghouse Elec. Corp.*, 291 F. Supp. 664, 670 (D.D.C. 1968) (stating "[i]t is, of course, elementary, that an infringement may be entirely inadvertent and unintentional and without knowledge of the patent. In this respect the law of patents is entirely different from the law of copyright"); Stephen M. Maurer & Suzanne Scotchmer, *The Independent Invention Defense in Intellectual Property*, 69 ECONOMICA 535, 535 (2002) (stating "[p]erhaps the most basic difference between patents and other intellectual property such as trade secrets and copyright is that independent invention is not a defense to infringement"). Importantly, however, a patentee will not be able to recover damages until the alleged infringer has actual or constructive notice, and then damages will be available only for subsequent infringing activity. *See* 35 U.S.C. § 287(a). *See also Maxwell v. J. Baker, Inc.*, 86 F.3d 1098, 1111 (Fed. Cir. 1996) (stating "the statute defines that [a patentee] is entitled to damages from the time when it either began marking its product in compliance with section 287(a) [constructive notice,] or when it actually notified [the accused infringer] of its infringement, whichever was earlier"). But process patent holders are an exception to the notice requirement because of the practical difficulty of marking process inventions. *See American Medical Systems, Inc. v. Medical Engineering Corp.*, 6 F.3d 1523 (Fed. Cir. 1993). Marking and section 287 are discussed in Chapter 9.

As discussed in Chapter 1, a patent confers on its owner the *right to exclude*; it does not provide the right to make, use, and sell the patented invention.[3] With this in mind, it follows that one may obtain a patent on an invention and still infringe a preexisting patent. To illustrate this point, let's revisit the chair hypothetical we saw in Chapter 2, Comment 1, following the *Incandescent Lamp* case. Inventor 1 obtains a patent on a chair and claims a seat portion, a back portion, and four legs. Subsequently, Inventor 2 invents and secures a patent on a chair having a seat portion, a back portion *that reclines* and four legs. Although Inventor 2 received a patent (say, because the reclining feature in combination with the other features were novel and not obvious), he cannot practice the commercial embodiment of his claimed invention because it would infringe Inventor 1's patent. Infringement exists here because Inventor 2's chair has all of the limitations of Inventor 1's patent claim (i.e., a seat portion, a back portion, and four legs). While the reclining feature may have allowed Inventor 2 to patent his chair, this feature does not save Inventor 2 from infringement. But, by the same token, Inventor 1 cannot practice Inventor 2's claimed invention. As the Supreme Court recognized in *Smith v. Nichols*,

> [A] new idea may be ingrafted upon an old invention, be distinct from the conception which preceded it, and be an improvement. In such case it is patentable. The prior patentee cannot use it without the consent of the improver, and the latter cannot use the original invention without the consent of the former.[4]

But there is a way out of this "blocking patent" congestion.[5] Assuming Inventor 2's invention is an improvement with greater commercial potential, each party has the motivation to enter into a cross-licensing agreement permitting each to practice their respective claimed inventions.[6] Matters become more complex when multiple parties and patent rights are involved,[7] which can lead to large-scale cross-licensing or pooling arrangements.[8] These private ordering

---

3. See Chapter 1, pages 1-2.

4. 88 U.S. 112, 118-119 (1874).

5. A similar situation would exist if an improver developed a new use of a patented product. For example, Inventor 1 patents a composition of matter that is used for shining shoes. Inventor 2 subsequently discovers that Inventor 1's patent composition can be used to treat burns. Inventor 2 can obtain a patent on the new use, but must still obtain a license from Inventor 1 to make or use the composition. Likewise, Inventor 1 must obtain a license from Inventor 2 if the former wants to use his patented composition to treat burns. Importantly, a patentee of a product or composition patent can exclude others from any use of the product or composition even if the patentee did not envision or disclose the use.

6. For a good discussion of blocking patents, *see* Mark A. Lemley, *The Economics of Improvement in Intellectual Property Law*, 75 TEX. L. REV. 989, 1000-1013 (1997); Robert P. Merges, *Intellectual Property Rights and Bargaining Breakdown: The Case of Blocking Patents*, 62 TENN. L. REV. 75 (1994).

7. This scenario is sometimes referred to as a "patent thicket," which Carl Shapiro defined as a "dense web of overlapping intellectual property rights that a company must hack its way through in order to actually commercialize new technology." Carl Shapiro, *Navigating the Patent Thicket: Cross-Licenses, Patent Pools, and Standard Setting*, in 1 INNOVATION POLICY & THE ECONOMY 118, 120 (Adam B. Jaffe, Josh Lerner & Scott Stern eds., 2001). To successfully navigate this thicket requires good lawyering and attentive due diligence. *See* James E. Bessen, *Patent Thickets: Strategic Patenting of Complex Technologies* (Boston Univ. Sch. of Law, Research on Innovation 2003), available at http://ssrn.com/abstract=327760.

8. Cross-licensing and pooling arrangements have been defined as "agreements of two or more owners of different items of intellectual property to license one another or third parties." ANTITRUST GUIDELINES FOR THE LICENSING OF INTELLECTUAL PROPERTY §5.5 (Department of Justice and Federal Trade Commission, April 6, 1995). Cross-licensing and patent pooling have been part of the patent landscape for several years. For example, in the early part of the twentieth century

responses are common in cumulative technology industries such as telecommunications and information technology,[9] and are consistent with patent law's disseminative function. And, as noted by the Department of Justice and Federal Trade Commission IP-Antitrust Guidelines, while pooling and cross-licensing arrangements may have anticompetitive effects, they may also "provide procompetitive benefits by integrating complementary technologies, reducing transaction costs, clearing blocking positions, and avoiding costly infringement litigation."[10]

A patent is enforceable from the date it issues[11] and is presumed valid under 35 U.S.C. § 282, which places the "burden of establishing invalidity" on "the party asserting such invalidity."[12] To meet this burden, the challenger "must persuade the factfinder of its invalidity defense by clear and convincing evidence."[13] While this standard of proof is unwavering throughout the patent's life,[14] evidence of invalidity not before the PTO during prosecution of the patent may " 'carry more weight' in an infringement action than evidence previously considered by the PTO";[15] and, in contrast, when the evidence was considered by

---

Standard Oil Company and The Texas Company cross-licensed each other in an agreement that came to be known as the "Patent Club," *see* PAUL H. GIDDENS, STANDARD OIL COMPANY: OIL PIONEER OF THE MIDDLE WEST 258 (1955); and in the nineteenth century, the "sewing machine war" led to the first privately formed patent pool in 1856, called the "Sewing Machine Combination." *See* Adam Mossoff, *The Rise and Fall of the First American Patent Thicket: The Sewing Machine War of the 1850s*, 53 ARIZ. L. REV. 165 (2011).

9. Cumulative technology is usually contrasted to discrete technology. According to Robert Merges and Richard Nelson, discrete technologies do "not point the way to wide ranging subsequent technical advances" and "do not typically incorporate a large number of interrelated components; they stand more or less alone" and "tend not to comprise integral components of some larger product or system." Examples include chemicals and pharmaceuticals where the patent is on a specific compound that did not form part of a larger product. In contrast, cumulative technologies "build on and interact with many other features of existing technology" . . . and "[i]n many cases the technology in question defines a complex system with many components, subcomponents and parts, and technical advance may proceed on a number of different fronts at once." Robert P. Merges & Richard R. Nelson, *On Complex Economics of Patent Scope*, 90 COLUM. L. REV. 839, 881 (1990). Some commentators have suggested the pharmaceutical and biotechnology industries are becoming more cumulative in nature. *See* Testimony of Richard C. Levin, FTC/DOJ Hearings on Competition and Intellectual Property Law (Washington D.C. February 6, 2002) (stating "with the widespread use of patented research tools and the attendant need for cross-licensing, the pharmaceutical and biotechnology industries are moving closer to the cumulative technology paradigm"). The phrase "complex technology" has also been used to describe a product or process "comprised of numerous, separately patentable elements." Wesley M. Cohen, Richard R. Nelson & John P. Walsh, *Protecting Their Intellectual Assets: Appropriability Conditions and Why U.S. Manufacturing Firms Patent (or Not)* 11 (NBER Working Paper No. W7552, May 2004).

10. ANTITRUST GUIDELINES, *supra* note 8, at § 5.5.

11. There is one notable exception. For applications filed on or after November 29, 2000, the patent applicant enjoys provisional rights beginning on the date the application is published and ending on the date the patent issues. But enforcement is only available upon issuance of the patent application. Thus, the remedy is retroactive; but no injunctive relief is available during the period of time between publication and issuance. *See* 35 U.S.C. § 154(d).

12. 35 U.S.C. § 282(a).

13. *See Microsoft Corp. v. i4i Limited Partnership*, 131 S. Ct. 2238, 2243 (2011) (" '[O]ne otherwise an infringer who assails the validity of a patent fair upon its face bears a heavy burden of persuasion, and fails unless his evidence has more than a dubious preponderance.' ") (quoting Justice Cardozo in *RCA v. Radio Engineering Laboratories*, 293 U.S. 1, 8 (1934)).

14. *Sciele Pharma Inc. v. Lupin, Ltd.*, 684 F.3d 1253 (Fed. Cir. 2012) (stating "the burden is always the same, clear and convincing evidence").

15. *Microsoft*, 131 S. Ct at 2251. This "commonsense principle" has been recognized by the Federal Circuit. *See American Hoist & Derrick Co. v. Sowa & Sons, Inc.*, 725 F.2d 1350, 1360 (Fed. Cir. 1984) ("When new evidence touching validity of the patent not considered by the PTO is relied on, the tribunal considering it is not faced with having to disagree with the PTO or with deferring

the PTO, the challenger "bears the added burden of overcoming the deference that is due to a qualified government agency presumed to have done its job."[16]

Patent law is exclusively federal; thus, a patentee may enforce his patent rights only by filing suit in federal district court.[17] Litigation may also commence when a potential infringer takes the initiative and files a declaratory judgment action (a "DJ") in district court alleging either, or both, patent invalidity and noninfringement.[18] In either case, the Court of Appeals for the Federal Circuit, with rare exception, has exclusive appellate jurisdiction.[19] And, as in other areas of the law, the Supreme Court has jurisdiction to hear Federal Circuit appeals, if it so chooses.

The total number of patent cases filed in 2012 was 5,189, a 29 percent increase from 2011.[20] Empirical scholarship on patent litigation suggests that only about 1.5 percent of patents are ever litigated,[21] and these patents tend to be (1) the most "valuable,"[22] and (2) owned by entities that do not manufacture

---

to its judgment or with taking its expertise into account. The evidence may, therefore, carry more weight and go further toward sustaining the attacker's unchanging burden.").

16. *PharmaStem Therapeutics, Inc. v. ViaCell, Inc.*, 491 F.3d 1342, 1366 (Fed. Cir. 2007).

17. *See* 28 U.S.C. § 1338(a): "The district courts shall have original jurisdiction of any civil action arising under any Act of Congress relating to patents, plant variety protection, copyrights and trademarks. Such jurisdiction shall be exclusive of the courts of the states in patent, plant variety protection and copyright cases."

18. *See* Declaratory Judgment Act, 28 U.S.C. §§ 2201-02. Declaratory judgment actions are discussed in Chapter 8, section A.3.

19. *See* 28 U.S.C. § 1295(a): "The United States Court of Appeals for the Federal Circuit shall have exclusive jurisdiction (1) of an appeal from a final decision of a district court of the United States, . . . if the jurisdiction of that court was based, in whole or in part, on section 1338 of this title." Section 1338 states, in relevant part, that "district courts shall have original jurisdiction of any civil action arising under any Act of Congress relating to patents." Importantly, regional circuits may hear cases with patent law issues if the patent issue is raised in a counterclaim. *See Holmes Group, Inc. v. Vornado Air Circulation Systems, Inc.*, 539 U.S. 826 (2002). See Chapter 1 for a discussion of the Federal Circuit's jurisdiction and docket.

20. 2013 PATENT LITIGATION STUDY 6 (PRICEWATERHOUSECOOPERS). The average time to trial from 2005-2012 is 2.5 years. *Id.* at 21 Chart 7(b). But this rise in filed cases can be attributed in part to the anti-joinder provisions of the AIA, which prevents the joinder of multiple defendants just because they allegedly infringe the same patent. To join multiple defendants they must allegedly infringe using the same product or process. *See* 35 U.S.C. §299. In 2012, the top five district courts in terms of patent filings were: (1) Eastern District, Texas; (2) Delaware; (3) Central District, California; (4) Northern District, Illinois; and (5) Northern District, California. Judicial Business of the United States Courts: 2012 Annual Report of the Director, Table C-7, available at http://www.uscourts. gov/uscourts/Statistics/JudicialBusiness/2012/appendices/C07Sep12.pdf. Delaware, the favored state of incorporation for so many businesses, may assume the top spot in 2013 because of the aforementioned changes to the joinder provisions.

21. *See* Mark A. Lemley, *Rational Ignorance at the Patent Office*, 95 Nw. L. REV. 1495, 1501 (2001). Some scholars have suggested that the small number of patents being litigated is because "[m]any patents are not worth enforcing—either because the inventions they cover turn out to be worthless, or because even if the invention has economic value the patent does not." John R. Allison, Mark A. Lemley, Kimberly A. Moore & R. Derek Trunkey, *Valuable Patents*, 92 GEO. L.J. 435, 436 (2004). Of course, many patents are licensed (or subject to cross-licensing) agreements, can be used to intimidate competitors, or be useful in attracting capital investment. *See* Shubha Ghosh & Jay Kesan, *What Do Patents Purchase? In Search of Optimal Ignorance in the Patent Office*, 40 HOUS. L. REV. 1219 (2004). *But see* Lemley, *Rational Ignorance, supra* (estimating only 3.5% of patents are licensed for a royalty).

22. *See* John R. Allison et al., *Valuable Patents, supra* note 21 (identifying "valuable patents" as having different characteristics from other patents, such as more claims, citation to more prior art, cited more by later issued patents, and are part of a series of continuation applications). *See also* John R. Allison & Thomas W. Sager, *Valuable Patents Redux: On the Enduring Merit of Using Patent Characteristics to Identify Valuable Patents*, 85 TEX. L. REV. 1769 (2007) (asserting statistics measuring patent value set forth in *Valuable Patents* article have significant explanatory power); John A. Allison, Mark A. Lemley & Joshua Walker, *Extreme Value or Trolls on Top? The Characteristics of the Most-*

the patented invention (typically, but not exclusively, brought by so-called Patent Assertion Entities or Non-Practicing Entities).[23] Of this small percentage, Paul Janicke's empirical work on patent litigation reveals that 13 percent of patent cases in 2012 were adjudicated[24] — summary judgment (7.9%), bench trial (2.2%), or jury trial (2.5%).[25] The remaining (nearly 85%) resulted in some form of settlement.[26] Mark Lemley has studied patent litigation in the busiest 33 district courts from 2000 to March 2010. Over this 10-year period, he found that 75.5 percent of the patent cases were settled and 15 percent went to judgment.[27] And of those cases that went to judgment, the patentee's success rate varied depending on where the case was filed.[28]

One of the more prominent incentives driving settlement is the high cost of patent litigation. One survey showed that 2012 median litigation fees, inclusive of all costs, through trial were $350,000 when less than $1 million was at risk; $1,000,000 when $1-10 million was at risk; and $2,000,000 when $10-25 million was at stake.[29] Many commentators have expressed concern about the rising litigation costs, suggesting the high costs are beginning to outweigh the commercial benefits of the patent system.[30] Moreover, patent litigation has risen

---

Litigated Patents, 158 U. Pa. L. Rev. 1, 28 (2009) (confirming Allisons, findings on characteristics of valuable patents).

23. *See* Allison et al., *Extreme Value or Trolls on Top? supra* note 22, at 3-4. *See also* 2013 Patent Litigation Study, *supra* note 20, at 3 (noting non-practicing entities accounted for a majority of patent filings in 2012).

24. These statistics are available at *PatentStats.org*, sponsored by the University of Houston Law Center. Getting to trial (surviving summary judgment) is important to patentees as they tend to fare better when the case reaches the jury. For instance, a study by Mark Lemley shows that patent cases filed in the District of Delaware from 2000 to March 2010 go to trial 11.8% of the time, the highest rate among district courts. The patentee wins 45.3% of these cases, which is well above the national average win rate for patentees. *See* Mark A. Lemley, *Where to File Your Patent Case*, available at http://papers.ssrn.com/sol3/papers.cfm?abstract_id=1597919. This study is based on data from the Stanford IP Litigation Clearinghouse (IPLC), which can be found at lexmachina.org.

25. *See* Janicke, *PatentStats.org, supra* note 24.

26. *Id.* Janicke defines "settlement" cases that resulted in a "consent judgment," "voluntary dismissal," "dismissal stating settlement," and "other dismissals." In testimony on patent reform before the House Subcommittee on Courts, the Internet, and Intellectual Property, an Apple Computer representative stated: "[F]or every lawsuit that goes to final judgment, there is 25 more that don't go to final judgment, that get adjudicated or settled ahead of time, and for every one of those, there's 25 [cease and desist] letters that were written that never made it to a lawsuit at all." H.R. Rep. 109-11, pt. 1, at 122 (2005).

27. *See* Lemley, *Where to File Your Patent Case, supra* note 24. Lemley's dataset includes pending cases, which may explain why his settlement figure is lower than Janicke's. For other noteworthy studies on patent litigation, *see* PricewaterhouseCoopers 2013 Patent Litigation Study, *Supra* note 20. For a study of patent litigation statistics in the context of the pharmaceutical industry, *see* the report by RBC Capital Markets, *Pharmaceuticals: Analyzing Litigation Success Rates* (January 15, 2010), available at http://amlawdaily.typepad.com/pharmareport.pdf. Interestingly, a sizeable percentage of litigated patents are held invalid. *See* John R. Allison & Mark A. Lemley, *Empirical Evidence on the Validity of Litigated Patents*, 26 AIPLA Q.J. 185 (1998) (finding 46% litigated patents are invalidated).

28. Lemley, *Where to File Your Patent Case, supra* note 24. From 1995-2012, the top five district courts most favorable to patentees with respect to "median time-to-trial, median damages awarded, and overall success rates" include: (1) E.D. Virginia; (2) District of Delaware; (3) E.D. Texas; (4) Western District of Wisconsin; and (5) D. New Jersey. 2013 Patent Litigation Study, *supra* note 20, at 23 Chart 8. Lemley notes that he is not making a causal claim, as the variation may be a result of "the nature of the cases, the lawyers" or other factors. *Id.* at n.12.

29. American Intellectual Property Law Association, Report of the Economic Survey 29 (2013), available at http://www.patentinsurance.com/iprisk/aipla-survey/.

30. *See* James Bessen & Michael J. Meurer, Patent Failure: How Judges, Bureaucrats, and Lawyers Put Innovators at Risk (2008).

dramatically over the past 20 years (although not uniformly), with patents in some industries much more likely to be litigated than in other industries. The top five industries from 2007-2012 with respect to patent infringement federal court decisions were (1) consumer products; (2) biotech/pharma; (3) computer hardware/electronics; (4) industrial/construction; and (5) medical devices.[31]

In a patent infringement suit, a patentee asserts that the patent *claims* are infringed, not the commercial embodiment of the claimed invention or what is set forth in the specification. As explored in Chapter 2, patent claims are the touchstone of patent protection, and it is the claims that set forth the patentee's proprietary boundaries. Claim interpretation precedes a determination of validity and infringement, and is a crucial and oftentimes determinative aspect of patent litigation.

This chapter focuses on infringement. The first significant issue in the context of litigation is claim interpretation. The *Markman* case, the first principal case below, directly addresses the question of who—judge or jury—interprets claim language. (The evidentiary sources of interpretation were covered in Chapter 2.) The Supreme Court, based on historical and functional considerations, held claim interpretation is solely for the judge.

The causes of action for patent infringement can be divided into two categories: (1) *direct infringement*; and (2) *indirect infringement*. Under the theory of direct infringement, the patentee brings an action against a defendant who himself is committing acts (e.g., making a product or practicing a process) that infringe one or more patent claims. Direct patent infringement comprises both (1) literal infringement; and (2) non-literal infringement, commonly referred to as the *doctrine of equivalents* (or "DOE"). Literal infringement is straightforward and occurs when every limitation recited in the claim is found in the accused device. Consider again the chair example:

> Inventor 1 obtains a patent on a chair and claims a seat portion, a back portion, and four legs. Subsequently, Competitor makes and uses a competing chair having a seat portion, a back portion and four legs.

Competitor literally infringes Inventor 1's patent claim, because Competitor practices each and every limitation set forth in Inventor 1's claim. Sometimes patent professionals would say that Inventor 1's claim "reads on" Competitor's product. Literal infringement is discussed in section B.1, below.

The common law doctrine of equivalents ("DOE") comes into play when there is no literal infringement, and allows liability when an accused infringing device (or process) is an "equivalent" to the claimed invention. For example:

> Inventor 1 claims a chair frame made of *titanium* and having a seat portion, a back portion, and four legs. Competitor makes a chair having a seat portion, a back portion, four legs, and a chair frame made of *aluminum*.

There is no literal infringement because Competitor's product does not have each and every limitation of Inventor 1's claim, but Competitor may still infringe under the DOE if it is determined that aluminum is an "equivalent" to

---

31. *See* PWC PATENT LITIGATION STUDY, *supra* note 20, at 14, Chart 6b. Rounding out the top ten from 2007-2012 in descending order are software; telecommunications; business/consumer services; automotive/transportation; and chemicals/synthetic materials. *Id.*

titanium. How that determination is made, and the analytical structure of the DOE are explored in section B.2, below.

There are four important limitations on the DOE: (1) *prosecution history estoppel*; (2) the *public dedication* rule; (3) *all-limitations/specific exclusion rule*; and (4) *prior art*. Prosecution History Estoppel ("PHE") precludes a patent owner in an infringement proceeding from obtaining broader claim scope than the issued claims (as construed), when the original claims in the application would have encompassed the equivalent at issue and where the claim was narrowed to exclude the equivalent, which was foreseeable at the time of such narrowing. For instance, Inventor initially claims three legs as part of his invention. The patent examiner rejects the application because there is prior art that discloses a chair having three legs. In response, Inventor amends the claim by deleting "three legs" and adding "four legs." The patent issues. When Inventor tries to enforce his patent (based on the DOE) against Competitor's three-legged chair, Competitor can invoke the doctrine of prosecution history estoppel and argue, successfully, that Inventor surrendered "three legs" to obtain a patent and, therefore, the DOE cannot extend the claim scope to capture three legs. A chair with three legs was certainly foreseeable at the time Inventor amended his claim; in fact, PHE would apply even if Inventor did not initially claim three legs as long as a three-legged chair was foreseeable at the time Inventor narrowed his claim through amendment. The PHE and its relationship with the DOE will become clearer after you read *Festo Corp.* (*Festo VIII*), the principal case in section B.3.a, below.

The *public dedication rule* holds that subject matter disclosed in the specification, but not claimed is dedicated to the public domain. So, assume Inventor claims a chair having a seat portion *made of cotton*, a back portion and four legs, but the specification reveals to a PHOSITA that the chair can be made of either cotton or wool. Competitor makes a chair with every limitation in Inventor's claim, but instead of cotton, uses wool. The public dedication rule can be used by Competitor during litigation to argue that Inventor dedicated wool to the public domain because Inventor, while expressly disclosing both wool and cotton in the specification, only claimed cotton. This doctrine is explored in the principal case of *Johnston Associates* in section B.3.b, below.

The *all-limitations rule* holds that each limitation of a patent claim is material to defining the scope of the patented invention and must not be vitiated or rendered meaningless. Thus, for there to be infringement under the DOE an equivalent of each claim limitation must be found in the accused device. In other words, the DOE is applied to each limitation, not to the invention as a whole. The related *specific exclusion rule*, a corollary to the all-limitations rule, holds that the DOE is unavailable to capture subject matter that the claim specifically excludes. The reasoning behind this rule is that by defining a claim in a way that specifically excludes certain subject matter, the patentee implicitly disclaimed the subject matter and is therefore prevented from invoking the DOE. *See* the principal case of *SciMed Life Systems* in section B.3.c, below.

The role of *prior art* as a limitation on the DOE is straightforward. Claim scope cannot extend to include subject matter that forms part of the prior art. The reason is claims that read on the prior art do not satisfy the patentability requirements, and therefore, the PTO would never have issued the patent. *See* the principal case of *Wilson Sporting Goods* in section B.3.d, below.

COMPARATIVE PERSPECTIVE
Enforcing Patents in Europe

While it is common to refer to patents that issue from the European Patent Office ("EPO") as "European Patents," there is no such thing as a European patent that provides a unitary right in all member states of the European Patent Convention ("EPC") or European Union. While the EPC contains substantive laws relating to patentability, these laws are almost exclusively applicable to the process of obtaining patent rights. A patent issuing from the EPO eventually becomes a bundle of individual national patents based on the countries designated by the applicant. Thus, while the process of obtaining rights is centralized, enforcement is a matter of national law. As Article 64(3) of the EPC states, "[a]ny infringement of a European patent shall be dealt with by national law." This disparate enforcement structure is of particular concern within the European patent community and beyond. As noted in a report produced by the EPO in 2006, the present enforcement structure:

> Is a *fragmentation of the European market*, as it is impossible to ensure that a European patent yields a uniform level of protection throughout all states. The disparities between the national systems as regards the litigation of European patents are thus prejudicial to the free movement of goods in Europe and counteract progress towards the creation of an environment conducive to free competition.

Assessment of the Impact of the European Patent Litigation Agreement (EPLA) on Litigation of European Patents (EPO 2006), para. 8 (emphasis in original).

There have been two noteworthy responses to these concerns. First, the idea of a community wide patent was first raised at the Luxembourg Community Patent Convention in 1975, which would create a unitary patent right within the European Union. Although this idea sounds attractive, it has been mired in difficulty from the very beginning, despite several attempts to revisit the proposal. The principal failure to adopt a community patent regime relates to difficulties on a common language(s) for the patent and the fact that the role of national patent offices would be diminished as well as that of translators. Under the current system, once a patent is granted by the EPO, the patent must be translated in an official language of each designated country (i.e., country where the patentee wants protection). If translation is not forthcoming within a prescribed time frame, the patent "shall be deemed to be void ab initio in that State." EPC Article 65. As Laurent Manderieux explains, until recently there was no effective EU consensus on the community patent because:

> Several countries want their language to be an official one for patents, and at the same time, if too many translations are compulsory, operators would find no cost advantage over the present system, and thus they would show no interest in the new system. Also several stages have reservations on how to establish an EU-wide jurisdiction which could decide on questions regarding an EU-wide patent right.

Laurent Manderieux, *Europe's IP Architecture*, in THE HANDBOOK OF EUROPEAN INTELLECTUAL PROPERTY MANAGEMENT 3-10 (Jolly & Philpott eds., 2007). Indeed, because of translation costs, a "European patent" costs considerably more to obtain than an American patent. To address these concerns, in December 2012, 25 member states of the EU—in a noteworthy development—adopted a unitary patent regime and unitary patent court. The unitary patent can be filed in any of the EU's 23 official languages, but thereafter *only* need be translated into English, French, or German for the patent to apply to the 25 participating states. (Spain and Italy did not participate because of objections to the final language regime.) According to the EPO, the "unitary patent will be a European patent granted by the EPO under the provisions of the [EPC] to which unitary effect for the territory of the 25 participating states is given after grant." The unified patent court will have a central division in Paris, with two sections, one in London for disputes involving chemistry and pharmaceuticals, and one in Munich for mechanical engineering disputes. The Paris, London, and Munich courts will have jurisdiction over revocation actions (invalidity) and declarations of noninfringement. In addition, there are local or regional divisions (also courts of first instance) that will hear infringement and counter-revocation claims. Revocation proceedings commenced in the central division or its two sections will be stayed if a subsequent infringement action has been filed with a local or regional court. The appellate court is located in Luxembourg. For more on both, *see* http://www.epo.org/law-practice/unitary.html.

A. CLAIM INTERPRETATION

The principal case of *Markman v. Westview Instruments, Inc.* is arguably the most well-known case in patent law because its holding gave birth to the *Markman* hearing, a staple of almost every patent litigation. (The *Markman* hearing is discussed in Comment 1 immediately following case.) The Supreme Court was asked in *Markman* to address whether the act of interpreting claims—claim interpretation—is a matter for the jury as of right or for the court. The Supreme Court affirmed the Federal Circuit and held claim interpretation is solely for the judge. But the Court neither directly address what standard of review the Federal Circuit should use when reviewing district court claim interpretations, nor directly rule on whether claim interpretation is a question of law, fact, or both—although the Federal Circuit held claim interpretation is a question of law to be reviewed *de novo*. *See Markman*, 52 F.3d 967, 979, 983-984 (Fed. Cir. 1995) (*Markman I*). The Supreme Court's treatment, or lack thereof, of the standard of review prompted the Federal Circuit to sit *en banc* to resolve this issue, but the standard of review remains a point of contention among the judges. See Comment 2 following *Markman* for a discussion of the Federal Circuit's *en banc* ruling and underlying policy considerations relating to the standard of review of district court claim interpretations.

MARKMAN v. WESTVIEW INSTRUMENTS, INC. (*MARKMAN II*)

517 U.S. 370 (1996)

Justice SOUTER delivered the opinion of the Court.

The question here is whether the interpretation of a so-called patent claim, the portion of the patent document that defines the scope of the patentee's rights, is a matter of law reserved entirely for the court, or subject to a Seventh Amendment guarantee that a jury will determine the meaning of any disputed term of art about which expert testimony is offered. We hold that the construction of a patent, including terms of art within its claim, is exclusively within the province of the court.

* * *

III

[The Court initially applied its Seventh Amendment "historical test" to determine whether a right to a jury trial on the issue claim interpretation "existed under the English common law when the Amendment was adopted." This test did not yield a definitive answer, forcing the Court to look "elsewhere" to answer the question presented.]

Since evidence of common law practice at the time of the Framing does not entail application of the Seventh Amendment's jury guarantee to the construction of the claim document, we must look elsewhere to characterize this determination of meaning in order to allocate it as between court or jury. We accordingly consult existing precedent and consider both the relative interpretive skills of judges and juries and the statutory policies that ought to be furthered by the allocation.

A

The two elements of a simple patent case, construing the patent and determining whether infringement occurred, were characterized by the former patent practitioner, Justice Curtis. "The first is a question of law, to be determined by the court, construing the letters-patent, and the description of the invention and specification of claim annexed to them. The second is a question of fact, to be submitted to a jury." *Winans v. Denmead,* 15 How., at 338.

In arguing for a different allocation of responsibility for the first question, Markman relies primarily on two cases, *Bischoff v. Wethered,* 19 L. Ed. 829 (1870), and *Tucker v. Spalding,* 20 L. Ed. 515 (1872). These are said to show that evidence of the meaning of patent terms was offered to 19th-century juries, and thus to imply that the meaning of a documentary term was a jury issue whenever it was subject to evidentiary proof. That is not what Markman's cases show, however. . . . [N]either *Bischoff* nor *Tucker* indicates that juries resolved the meaning of terms of art in construing a patent, and neither case undercuts Justice Curtis's authority.

B

Where history and precedent provide no clear answers, functional considerations also play their part in the choice between judge and jury to define terms of art. We said in *Miller v. Fenton,* 474 U.S. 104 (1985), that when an issue "falls somewhere between a pristine legal standard and a simple historical fact, the fact/law distinction at times has turned on a determination that, as a matter of the sound administration of justice, one judicial actor is better positioned than another to decide the issue in question." So it turns out here, for judges, not juries, are the better suited to find the acquired meaning of patent terms.

The construction of written instruments is one of those things that judges often do and are likely to do better than jurors unburdened by training in exegesis. Patent construction in particular "is a special occupation, requiring, like all others, special training and practice. The judge, from his training and discipline, is more likely to give a proper interpretation to such instruments than a jury; and he is, therefore, more likely to be right, in performing such a duty, than a jury can be expected to be." *Parker v. Hulme*, 18 F. Cas., at 1140. Such was the understanding nearly a century and a half ago, and there is no reason to weigh the respective strengths of judge and jury differently in relation to the modern claim; quite the contrary, for "the claims of patents have become highly technical in many respects as the result of special doctrines relating to the proper form and scope of claims that have been developed by the courts and the Patent Office." Woodward, *Definiteness and Particularity in Patent Claims*, 46 MICH. L. REV. 755, 765 (1948).

Markman would trump these considerations with his argument that a jury should decide a question of meaning peculiar to a trade or profession simply because the question is a subject of testimony requiring credibility determinations, which are the jury's forte. It is, of course, true that credibility judgments have to be made about the experts who testify in patent cases, and in theory there could be a case in which a simple credibility judgment would suffice to choose between experts whose testimony was equally consistent with a patent's internal logic. But our own experience with document construction leaves us doubtful that trial courts will run into many cases like that. In the main, we expect, any credibility determinations will be subsumed within the necessarily sophisticated analysis of the whole document, required by the standard construction rule that a term can be defined only in a way that comports with the instrument as a whole. Thus, in these cases a jury's capabilities to evaluate demeanor, to sense the "mainsprings of human conduct," or to reflect community standards, are much less significant than a trained ability to evaluate the testimony in relation to the overall structure of the patent. The decisionmaker vested with the task of construing the patent is in the better position to ascertain whether an expert's proposed definition fully comports with the specification and claims and so will preserve the patent's internal coherence. We accordingly think there is sufficient reason to treat construction of terms of art like many other responsibilities that we cede to a judge in the normal course of trial, notwithstanding its evidentiary underpinnings.

C

Finally, we see the importance of uniformity in the treatment of a given patent as an independent reason to allocate all issues of construction to the court. As we noted in *General Elec. Co. v. Wabash Appliance Corp.*, 304 U.S. 364, 369 (1938), "[t]he limits of a patent must be known for the protection of the patentee, the encouragement of the inventive genius of others and the assurance that the subject of the patent will be dedicated ultimately to the public." Otherwise, a "zone of uncertainty which enterprise and experimentation may enter only at the risk of infringement claims would discourage invention only a little less than unequivocal foreclosure of the field," *United Carbon Co. v. Binney & Smith*

Co., 317 U.S. 228, 236 (1942), and "[t]he public [would] be deprived of rights supposed to belong to it, without being clearly told what it is that limits these rights." *Merrill v. Yeomans*, 94 U.S. 568, 573 (1877). It was just for the sake of such desirable uniformity that Congress created the Court of Appeals for the Federal Circuit as an exclusive appellate court for patent cases, observing that increased uniformity would "strengthen the United States patent system in such a way as to foster technological growth and industrial innovation." H.R. Rep. No. 97-312, pp. 20-23 (1981).

Uniformity would, however, be ill served by submitting issues of document construction to juries. Making them jury issues would not, to be sure, necessarily leave evidentiary questions of meaning wide open in every new court in which a patent might be litigated, for principles of issue preclusion would ordinarily foster uniformity. *Cf. Blonder-Tongue Laboratories, Inc. v. University of Ill. Foundation*, 402 U.S. 313 (1971). But whereas issue preclusion could not be asserted against new and independent infringement defendants even within a given jurisdiction, treating interpretive issues as purely legal will promote (though it will not guarantee) intrajurisdictional certainty through the application of *stare decisis* on those questions not yet subject to interjurisdictional uniformity under the authority of the single appeals court.

* * *

Accordingly, we hold that the interpretation of the word "inventory" in this case is an issue for the judge, not the jury, and affirm the decision of the Court of Appeals for the Federal Circuit.

Comments

1. *The* **Markman** *Hearing.* The Supreme Court's *Markman* decision and subsequent Federal Circuit case law led to the creation of what eventually became known as the *Markman* hearing, a procedural device employed by district court judges designed to determine the meaning of the claim language at issue. District court judges have broad discretion in how they structure the hearing, and are faced with common procedural questions. For instance, (1) When during the trial should the court construe the patent claim? (2) What input may the court properly receive to help in claim construction? and (3) How may the court use this input? Questions 2 and 3 were explored in Chapter 2. With respect to timing, then Judge McKelvie stated in *Elf Atochem North America, Inc. v. Libbey-Owens-Ford Co., Inc.*, 894 F. Supp. 844, 850 (D. Del. 1995): "The 'obligation' created by the Federal Circuit to instruct the jury on the meaning of the words used by an inventor in a claim basically leaves a district court with three options. The court can attempt to resolve these disputes on the paper record. Second, the court can hold a trial to resolve the disputes. Finally, the court can wait until trial and attempt to resolve claim disputes the evening before the jury must be instructed." Given the determinative nature of claim construction, most courts opt to hold a pre-trial *Markman* hearing, typically followed by the "winning" party filing summary judgment motions on validity and/or infringement.

   It has been several years since the *Markman* decision, and courts have developed established structures for *Markman* hearings, particularly in jurisdictions that have crowded patent dockets (e.g., C.D. and N.D. California). For example, the Northern District of California (and several other jurisdictions) has adopted special local rules for patent cases, which, in effect, impose more detailed pleading and disclosure requirements than are generally mandated by the Federal Rules of Civil Procedure. (See the casebook website at http://law.case.edu/lawofpatents/ under Chapter 7 for the N.D. California's "Patent Local Rules.")

2. *Standard of Appellate Review and Claim Interpretation.* The grant of certiorari in *Markman* focused on the Seventh Amendment right to a jury trial in the context of claim construction. While the Court held that claim construction is "is an issue for the judge, not the jury," the Justices did not expressly discuss the proper standard of review of district court judge claim interpretations, or rule whether an interpretive analysis is one of fact, law, or a mixture thereof.

But, in what turned out to be controversial dicta, the Court characterized claim construction as a "mongrel practice" that "falls somewhere between a pristine legal standard and a simple historical fact." 517 U.S. at 378, 388. This language is noteworthy because the categorization of claim construction as one of law and/or fact may determine whether a claim construction ruling is reviewed *de novo* (as a legal question), for clear error (as fact finding in a bench trial), or some mixed review.

Failure to expressly address this issue prompted a minority of Federal Circuit judges, sympathetic to a more deferential standard of review, to assert that *de novo* review was not endorsed by the Supreme Court, and claim interpretation is a mixed question of law and fact. *See, e.g., Fromson v. Anitec Printing Plates, Inc.*, 132 F.3d 1437 (Fed. Cir. 1997). Other judges disagreed, and continued to stress that claim interpretation is a question of law subject to *de novo* review. *See, e.g., Phonometrics, Inc. v. N. Telecom, Inc.*, 133 F.3d 1359 (Fed. Cir. 1998). This intra-circuit conflict led to *Cybor Corp. v. FAS Technologies, Inc.*, 138 F.3d 1448, 1456 (Fed. Cir. 1998), an *en banc* decision that unequivocally held claim construction is "a purely legal question" that is reviewed "de novo on appeal including any allegedly fact based questions relating to claim construction."

One could argue that *Cybor* is understandable if the predominant policy consideration is uniformity. Consider the following hypothetical litigation scenario:

> The '123 patent is owned by patentee A. A files a patent infringement suit in the Northern District of Ohio asserting that defendant B is infringing the '123 patent. Shortly thereafter, patentee A files another patent infringement action in the Northern District of California claiming that defendant C is infringing the '123 patent. Each district court judge—allowing and relying on expert testimony—interpret the same claim language differently. These divergent interpretations lead to the '123 patent being held invalid by the Ohio judge, and not invalid by the California judge.

It is plausible that under a standard of review that is more deferential than *de novo*, the Federal Circuit would affirm both district court interpretations, resulting in disuniformity.

But uniformity in claim representation is only one policy objective; certainty is another, particularly *early* certainty. An appellate standard of review that is more deferential may lead to greater affirmance rates of district court claim construction rulings. A higher affirmance rate will inject certainty earlier in the litigation, and arguably promote more settlement activity. In his *Cybor* dissent, Judge Rader wrote "this court's enthusiastic assertion of its unfettered review authority has the potential to undercut the benefits of *Markman I*," namely "early certainty about the meaning of a patent claim," which, "in turn, would prompt early settlement of many, if not most, patent suits." 138 F.3d at 1475.

Indeed, the *de novo* review standard has resulted in a relatively high reversal rate of district court claim constructions. In a comprehensive study, Kimberly A. Moore (now Federal Circuit Judge Moore) looked at Federal Circuit cases from 1996-2003 and found that the Federal Circuit held district court judges wrongly construed 34.5 percent of claim terms; 29.7 percent led to reversals. *See* Kimberly A. Moore, Markman *Eight Years Later: Is Claim Construction More Predictable?*, 9 Lewis & Clark L. Rev. 231 (2005). *See also* Christian A. Chu, *Empirical Analysis of the Federal Circuit's Claim Construction Trends*, 16 Berkeley Tech. L.J. 1075, 1104 (2001) (finding between January 1998 and April 2000, the Federal Circuit changed district court claim constructions in 44 percent of the 179 appellate cases). *But see* Jeffrey A. Lefstin, *Claim Construction, Appeal, and the Predictability of Interpretive Regimes*, 61 U. Miami L. Rev. 1033, 1038 (2007) (asserting "there is almost no evidence showing that the claim construction reversal rate is 'high' relative to anything else"). A recent empirical study by Jonas Anderson and Peter Menell found that the average reversal rate has "dropped precipitously" after *Phillips* was decided (see Chapter 2) "from 37.6 percent to 23.8 percent on a per claim term basis," and "[r]eversal rates have fallen for all members of the Federal Circuit and across all technology fields except business methods." Indeed, "[d]uring 2011, the average reversal rate dipped to 17%." *See* J. Jonas Andersen & Peter S. Menell, *From De Novo Review to Informal Deference: An Historical, Empirical, and Normative Analysis of the Standard of Appellate Review for Patent Claim Construction* (2012), 108 Nw. U. L. Rev. ___ (2013) (forthcoming), available at http://papers.ssrn.com/sol3/papers.cfm?abstract_id=2150360&download=yes, at 8-9.

3. ***Perspective of District Court Judges.*** The issue of standard of review in the context of claim interpretation jurisprudence has arguably been the most significant and relevant patent law issue for district court judges. *See* Hon. Kathleen O'Malley, *The Past, Present and Future of the Federal Circuit*, 54 Case W. Res. L. Rev. 671, 673 (2004) (discussing significance of standard of review and Federal Circuit claim construction jurisprudence). Judge Patti Saris of the U.S. District Court in Massachusetts views *de novo* review as a "key legal development," but is critical of the standard because it does not reflect the comparative institutional advantages district court judges possess:

> According to the literature, over fifty percent of all *Markman* hearings now involve the taking of evidence. Even in those cases where I do not hear evidence, I see terrific demonstratives. Because I am a visual learner, I understand evidence presented to me better when I receive a tutorial by live or video testimony, rather than by a cold affidavit. This is important because a de novo standard of review by definition is a fresh look by three people on an appellate level who did not have an opportunity to attend the hearing. . . . My perspective . . . is that there should be more deference given to the interpretation of the trial judge who had the opportunity to see, hear, and look at evidence.

Construction from the Perspective of the District Judge, 54 Case W. Res. L. Rev. 671, 679 (2004). And Judge Marsha J. Pechman of the U.S. District Court for the

Western District of Washington put it this way: Given the high reversal rate on claim construction, "you might as well throw darts." BNA PTCJ Daily, Sept. 14, 2005.

In addition, some judges sit on courts with busy patent dockets, and therefore, hear considerably more patent cases than judges in other districts. But according to a study by David Schwartz, there is no correlation between various measures of experience and likelihood of affirmance at the Federal Circuit. *See* David L. Schwartz, *Practice Makes Perfect? An Empirical Study of Claim Construction Reversal Rates in Patent Cases*, 107 MICH. L. REV. 223 (2008). For instance, the Central District of California — the second busiest district court in terms of patent cases—had the highest claim construction reversal rate (43.5%), whereas the reversal rate of the thirteenth busiest docket — the Western District of Wisconsin—was 21.1 percent. *Id.* at 246. Schwartz also looked at experience levels of individual judges and found that the "claim construction reversal rate varies little with the total number of patent lawsuits handled." *Id.* at 256. Possible explanations for these results, according to Schwartz, are the indeterminacy of language, complexity of the patent cases, and *de novo* review. *Id.* at 259-266.

4. *Are* **Cybor's** *Days Numbered?* The Federal Circuit has begun to openly question the wisdom of *Cybor*. For instance, in a petition for rehearing (ultimately denied) in *Amgen v. Hoechst Marion Roussel, Inc.*, 469 F.3d 1039 (Fed. Cir. 2006), six dissenting and concurring opinions were filed revealing the internal division relating to *Cybor* and the court's standard of review for claim construction. Judge Michel wrote:

> I have come to believe that reconsideration is appropriate and revision may be advisable. In my view, four practical problems have emerged under the *Markman-Cybor* regime: (1) a steadily high reversal rate; (2) a lack of predictability about appellate outcomes, which may confound trial judges and discourage settlements; (3) loss of the comparative advantage often enjoyed by the district judges who heard or read all of the evidence and may have spent more time on the claim constructions than we ever could on appeal; and (4) inundation of our court with the minutia of construing numerous disputed claim terms (in multiple claims and patents) in nearly every patent case.

Id. at 1040. And more recently, Judge O'Malley of the Federal Circuit urged her colleagues to reconsider *Cybor*, stating that it "was ill considered thirteen years ago and has not proven beneficial to patent jurisprudence in the long run." *Retractable Techs. v. Becton Dickinson & Co.*, 659 F.3d 1369, 1374 (Fed. Cir. 2011) (O'Malley, J., dissenting from denial of petition for rehearing *en banc*). Interestingly, Judge O'Malley, who has served as a judge on the Federal Circuit since 2010, was a federal district court judge (N.D. Ohio) from 1994-2010. *See also Flo Healthcare v. Kappos and Rioux Vision*, 697 F.3d 1367 (Fed. Cir. 2012) (discussing the need for judicial clarity on standard of review with respect to decisions from Board of Patent Appeals and Interferences and district court claim constructions). On March 15, 2013, the Federal Circuit decided to hear *en banc* the standard of review issue. *See Lighting Ballast Control LLC v. Philips Electronics North America Corp.*, 500 Fed. Appx. 951 (Fed. Cir. 2013). The court asked the parties to brief whether *Cybor* should be overruled, and whether the appellate court should give deference to any aspect of the district court's claim interpretation. Oral arguments were held on September 13, 2013.

5. *Procedural Devices to Enhance Predictability.* There are also procedural devices available to district court judges that would foster uniformity. For instance, the doctrine of issue preclusion, when available, addresses, at least partially, the uniformity issue at the district court level. *See, e.g., TM Patents v. IBM Corp.,* 72 F. Supp. 2d 370 (S.D.N.Y. 1999) (applying issue preclusion against plaintiff-patentee); *Abbott Labs. v. Day,* 110 F. Supp. 2d 667 (N.D. Ill. 2000) (same). But some district courts have refused to apply issue preclusion against plaintiff-patentees based on finality concerns. *See, e.g., Graco Children's Products, Inc. v. Regalo Int'l,* 77 F. Supp. 2d 660 (E.D. Pa. 1999) (issue preclusion does not apply to patentee because case settled and, therefore, not appealed); *Kollmorgen Corp. v. Yaskawa Elec. Corp.,* 147 F. Supp. 2d 464, 468 (W.D. Va. 2002) (stating "[a]s more than forty percent of all *Markman* Orders are reversed by the Federal Circuit, logic dictates that for these claim constructions to have a preclusive effect, the litigants must first have an opportunity to seek Federal Circuit review"). The Federal Circuit was prepared to weigh in on the role of issue preclusion, but the case was dismissed under Fed. R. App. P. 42(b). *See Shire LLP v. Sandoz, Inc.,* 2009 WL 5948890 (Fed. Cir. 2009).

Lastly, the Federal Circuit could apply *stare decisis* as a basis for adopting the prior claim construction. While the court has hinted *stare decisis* may apply to claim construction, *see Key Pharm. v. Hercon Labs Corp.,* 161 F.3d 709, 716 (Fed. Cir. 1998) (noting that the Federal Circuit does not take "lightly" the task of claim interpretation "as we recognize the national stare decisis effect that this court's decisions on claim construction have"), thus far there is no Federal Circuit decision that has employed the principle, despite the Supreme Court's acknowledgement of the doctrine's applicability:

> [W]hereas issue preclusion could not be asserted against new and independent infringement defendants even within a given jurisdiction, treating interpretive issues as purely legal will promote . . . intrajurisdictional certainty through the application of stare decisis on those questions not yet subject to interjurisdictional uniformity under the authority of the single appeals court.

Markman, 517 U.S. at 391. *See also Cybor,* 138 F.3d at 1479 (Newman, J., dissenting) (stating "[t]he promise of uniformity and finality, flowing from decisions of national effect, is a failed promise if we are not bound by stare decisis in our own claim interpretation"). While *stare decisis* may foster uniformity, it is not without problems. Most notably it denies a new defendant his day in court, although this concern is more pronounced in the issue preclusion context. *See Texas Instruments v. Linear Tech. Corp.,* 182 F. Supp. 2d 580, 585-589 (E.D. Tex. 2002) (rejecting applicability of *stare decisis* in context of claim construction).

6. *Interlocutory Appeal.* Given the high reversal rate of district court claim constructions, and accompanying waste of judicial resources and significant private legal costs, perhaps there should be an interlocutory route to review. A central question in this regard is whether a claim construction ruling is a final judgment because appeals can only be entertained from final judgments. *See* Craig Allen Nard, *Process Considerations in the Age of* Markman *and Mantras,* 2001 U. ILL. L. REV. 101 (exploring interlocutory review of district court claim constructions). The Federal Circuit—"in its discretion"—may grant interlocutory review, but has thus far refused. *See Cybor,* 138 F.3d at 1479 (Newman, J., dissenting) (stating "[a]lthough the district courts have extended themselves, and so-called '*Markman* hearings' are common, this

has not been accompanied by interlocutory review of the trial judge's claim interpretation. The Federal Circuit has thus far declined all such certified questions"). Practically, interlocutory review would greatly increase the Federal Circuit's patent.

For their part, trial judges may be more inclined to dispose of cases on summary judgment. As then district court (now circuit court) judge, Kent Jordan, stated upon ruling in favor of defendant's motion for summary judgment of noninfringement, "[i]t may be cold comfort, but at least [patentee] now has the prospect of obtaining a definitive ruling on the disputed claim construction without first having to incur the considerable expense of a full trial on the merits. Should the Federal Circuit alter the claim construction on appeal, the parties may then proceed to trial, confident that they have the correct claim construction in hand." *Chimie v. PPG Industries, Inc.*, 303 F. Supp. 2d 502, 509 (D. Del. 2004). *See also* Kimberly A. Moore, *Are District Court Judges Equipped to Decide Patent Cases*, 15 HARV. J.L. & TECH. 1, 33 (2001) (asserting "[s]ummary judgment on the issue of infringement will likely increase after *Markman*"); William F. Lee & Anita K. Krug, *Still Adjusting to Markman: A Prescription for the Timing of Claim Construction Hearings*, 13 HARV. J.L. & TECH. 55, 59 (1999) (stating an "expected result of *Markman* has been an increase in the number of motions for summary judgment and partial summary judgment on matters of claim construction and infringement").

B. INFRINGEMENT

1. Literal Infringement

Literal infringement is a straightforward doctrine that forms an important part of the patentee's enforcement rights. An accused device will be found to literally infringe when the device possesses each and every limitation recited in at least one patent claim. Sometimes patent professionals say the patentee's claim "reads on" the accused device. The principal case of *Larami Corporation v. Amron* explores literal infringement.

LARAMI CORPORATION v. AMRON

27 U.S.P.Q.2d 1280 (E.D. Pa. 1993)*

MEMORANDUM

REED, J.

This is a patent case concerning toy water guns manufactured by plaintiff Larami Corporation ("Larami"). Currently before me is Larami's motion for partial summary judgment of noninfringement of United States Patent No. 4,239,129 ("the '129 patent").

---

* [The Federal Circuit affirmed, 91 F.3d 166 (Fed. Cir. 1996), in an unpublished "table" decision, which is a non-precedential decision without explanation. — ED.]

I. Background

Larami manufactures a line of toy water guns called "SUPER SOAKERS." This line includes five models: SUPER SOAKER 20, SUPER SOAKER 30, SUPER SOAKER 50, SUPER SOAKER 100, and SUPER SOAKER 200. All use a hand-operated air pump to pressurize water and a "pinch trigger" valve mechanism for controlling the ejection of the pressurized water. All feature detachable water reservoirs prominently situated outside and above the barrel of the gun. The United States Patent and Trademark Office has issued patents covering four of these models. Larami does not claim to have a patent which covers SUPER SOAKER 20.

Defendants Alan Amron and Talk To Me Products, Inc. (hereinafter referred to collectively as "TTMP") claim that the SUPER SOAKER guns infringe on the '129 patent which TTMP obtained by assignment from Gary Esposito ("Esposito"), the inventor. The '129 patent covers a water gun which, like the SUPER SOAKERS, operates by pressurizing water housed in a tank with an air pump. In the '129 patent, the pressure enables the water to travel out of the tank through a trigger-operated valve into an outlet tube and to squirt through a nozzle. Unlike the SUPER SOAKERS, the '129 patent also contains various electrical features to illuminate the water stream and create noises. Also, the water tank in the '129 patent is not detachable, but is contained within a housing in the body of the water gun.

The "Background of the Invention" contained in the '129 patent reads as follows:

> Children of all ages, especially boys, through the years have exhibited a fascination for water, lights and noise and the subject invention deals with these factors embodied in a toy simulating a pistol.
>
> An appreciable number of U.S. patents have been issued which are directed to water pistols but none appear to disclose a unique assemble of components which can be utilized to simultaneously produce a jet or stream of water, means for illuminating the stream and a noise, or if so desired, one which can be operated without employing the noise and stream illuminating means. A reciprocal pump is employed to obtain sufficient pressure whereby the pistol can eject a stream an appreciable distance in the neighborhood of thirty feet and this stream can be illuminated to more or less simulate a lazer [sic] beam.

Larami brought this action seeking a declaration that the "SUPER SOAKER" does not infringe the '129 patent (Count I). TTMP counterclaimed for infringement of the '129 patent. Larami has moved for partial summary judgment of noninfringement of the '129 patent (Count I) and for partial summary judgment on TTMP's counterclaim for infringement of the '129 patent.

II. Discussion

* * *

B. *Infringement and Claim Interpretation*

A patent owner's right to exclude others from making, using or selling the patented invention is defined and limited by the language in that patent's claims. Thus, establishing infringement requires the interpretation of the "elements" or "limitations" of the claim and a comparison of the accused product with those elements as so interpreted. . . .

A patent holder can seek to establish patent infringement in either of two ways: by demonstrating that every element of a claim (1) is literally infringed or (2) is infringed under the doctrine of equivalents. To put it a different way, because every element of a claim is essential and material to that claim, a patent owner must, to meet the burden of establishing infringement, "show the presence of every element *or* its substantial equivalent in the accused device." *Key Mfg. Group, Inc.,* 925 F.2d at 1447 (emphasis added). If even *one* element of a patent's claim is missing from the accused product, then "[t]here can be no infringement as a matter of law. . . ." *London v. Carson Pirie Scott & Co.,* 946 F.2d 1534, 1538-39 (Fed. Cir. 1991).

Larami contends, and TTMP does not dispute, that twenty-eight (28) of the thirty-five (35) claims in the '129 patent are directed to the electrical components that create the light and noise. Larami's SUPER SOAKER water guns have no light or noise components. Larami also contends, again with no rebuttal from TTMP, that claim 28 relates to a "poppet valve" mechanism for controlling the flow of water that is entirely different from Larami's "pinch trigger" mechanism. Thus, according to Larami, the six remaining claims (claims 1, 5, 10, 11, 12 and 16) are the only ones in dispute. Larami admits that these six claims address the one thing that the SUPER SOAKERS and the '129 patent have in common—the use of air pressure created by a hand pump to dispense liquid. Larami argues, however, that the SUPER SOAKERS and the '129 patent go about this task in such fundamentally different ways that no claim of patent infringement is sustainable as a matter of law.

In its memorandum of law in opposition to Larami's motion for partial summary judgment, TTMP points to evidence to support its assertion that only SUPER SOAKER 20 literally infringes claim 1. TTMP has neither produced nor referred to evidence contradicting facts averred by Larami on all other claims of the '129 patent.

1. Literal Infringement of Claim 1

TTMP claims that SUPER SOAKER 20 literally infringes claim 1 of the '129 patent. Claim 1 describes the water gun as:

> [a] toy comprising an elongated housing [case] having a chamber therein for a liquid [tank], a pump including a piston having an exposed rod [piston rod] and extending rearwardly of said toy facilitating manual operation for building up an appreciable amount of pressure in said chamber for ejecting a stream of liquid therefrom an appreciable distance substantially forwardly of said toy, and means for controlling the ejection.

U.S. Patent No. 4,239,129 (bracketed words supplied; [*see* Figure 5 of the '129 patent].

[The specification reads (emphasis added):

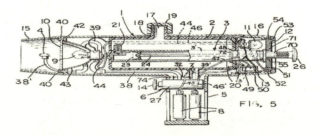

FIG. 5

Referring to the drawings . . . the device or toy includes, among other things, wall structure forming an elongated barrel generally designated **1** and *a chamber or tank* **2** *for liquid within the confines of the barrel,* a pump generally designated **3** in the tank, for applying pressure to the liquid, for ejecting a jet stream of water through a nozzle **4** and a hollow handle **5** disposed intermediate the extremities of the barrel for containing a valve means generally designated **6**, a switch **7** carried by the tank and a source of electricity preferably comprising a pair of batteries **8**. The toy or device also includes a lamp **9** and a light responsive means **10** located at the front extremity of the barrel, a lamp **11**, light responsive means or lens **12** and a buzzer **13** at its rear extremity and a trigger **14** for controlling the operation of the valve means **6** and the switch **7**. . . . The tank **2** [is] located in the barrel].

Claim 1 requires, among other things, that the toy gun have "an elongated housing having a chamber therein for a liquid." The SUPER SOAKER 20 water gun, in contrast, has an external water reservoir (chamber) that is detachable from the gun housing, and not contained within the housing. TTMP argues that SUPER SOAKER 20 contains a "chamber therein for a liquid" *as well as* a detachable water reservoir. It is difficult to discern from TTMP's memorandum of law exactly where it contends the "chamber therein" is located in SUPER SOAKER 20. Furthermore, after having examined SUPER SOAKER 20, I find that it is plain that there is no "chamber" for liquid contained within the housing of the water gun. The only element of SUPER SOAKER 20 which could be described as a "chamber" for liquid is the external water reservoir located atop the housing. Indeed, liquid is located within the housing only when the trigger causes the liquid to pass from the external water reservoir through the tubing in the housing and out of the nozzle at the front end of the barrel. SUPER SOAKER 20 itself shows that such a transitory avenue for the release of liquid is clearly not a "chamber therein for liquid." Therefore, because the absence of even one element of a patent's claim from the accused product means there can be no finding of literal infringement, *London,* 946 F.2d at 1538-39, I find that SUPER SOAKER 20 does not infringe claim 1 of the '129 patent as a matter of law.

Accordingly, I conclude that the SUPER SOAKER 20 water gun does not literally infringe claim 1 of the '129 patent.

Comments

1. *Each and Every Limitation Matters.* Literal infringement demands that the accused product possess each and every limitation of at least one of the patent claims in suit. The *Larami* case highlights this rule as well as the importance of claim drafting, particularly drafting with an eye toward litigation and competitor conduct. Recall, claim 1 read: "[a] toy comprising an elongated housing [case] *having a chamber therein* for a liquid [tank]." The court found that the accused product—the SUPER SOAKER 20—did not have a "chamber therein," and therefore, there was no literal infringement. Rather, the accused device comprised an external, detachable chamber "not contained within the housing." Why was the word "therein" included? Perhaps to distinguish the claimed invention from the prior art or in response to the prosecuting examiner's office action, which could be discerned from studying the '129 patent's prosecution history. (In case you're wondering, the patentee also lost his doctrine of equivalents argument.)

Literal infringement was found to be lacking in *Felix v. American Honda Motor*, 562 F.3d 1167 (Fed. Cir. 2009). In *Felix*, the patent described an arrangement that included a pickup truck and what would be considered the trunk of a conventional car. In particular, the patent related to "a built-in storage compartment for a pickup truck bed." The claims included a "storage system for a vehicle including a vehicle bed," comprising:

a lid assembly

a channel formed at the rim of a bed opening and including an inner flange;

a weathertight gasket mounted on said flange and engaging said lid in its closed position.

(emphasis added). The gasket on the accused product was mounted on the lid of the storage system, not the flange. Therefore, Honda did not literally infringe. As the court noted, "Because the gasket of the In-Bed Trunk is not securely affixed or fastened to the flange (as is apparent when the lid of the In-Bed Trunk is open), the In-Bed Trunk does not literally infringe." *Id.* at 1181.

Literal infringement may also be found indirectly when, for example, the patent-in-suit reads on part of an industry standard, and the accused product meets the requirements for the standard. In this scenario, a patentee may not have to compare its patent claims to the accused product because "if an accused product operates in accordance with a standard, then comparing the claims to the standard is the same as comparing the claims to the accused product." *Fujitsu Ltd. v. Netgear, Inc.*, 620 F.3d 1321, 1327 (Fed. Cir. 2010). This approach is based on the public policy that "[i]f a court determines that all implementations of a standard infringe the claims of a patent, then it would be a waste of judicial resources to separately analyze every accused product that undisputedly practices the standard." *Id.* The *Fujitsu* court did note, however, that to take advantage of this indirect route to showing infringement, the standard must "provide a level of specificity." *Id.* at 1328. The patent-in-suit in *Fujitsu*—the '952 patent— claimed methods of segmenting and transmitting a message, something known as "fragmentation," which is a feature of the 802.11 industry standard. But because fragmentation was an *optional* feature in the standard, the court held the patentee could not take advantage of the aforementioned indirect proof—that is, simply comparing the accused product to the standard—and was required to compare the patent claims to the accused product. *Id.*

2. ***Literal Infringement, Claim Scope, and Section 112.*** Let's change one of the key facts of *Larami*. Suppose TTMP's '129 patent claim did not include the word "therein," so that the claim would read: "[a] toy comprising an elongated housing [case] having a chamber for a liquid [tank]." And let's assume the specification and the drawings remain the same. Would Larami's SuperSoaker still literally infringe? This hypothetical brings into play the *BMW* case (and *Liebel-Flarsheim*, which is discussed in *BMW*) we covered in Chapter 2. Recall in both cases the patentee argued for broad claim scope because the respective claims covered both mechanical and electronic side impact sensors (*BMW*) and injectors that were either jacketless or had jackets (*Liebel-Flarsheim*). In both cases, the court emphasized that the *full scope* of the claimed invention must be enabled. As the *BMW* court wrote, while every embodiment of the

claimed invention does not have to be disclosed in the specification to satisfy the enablement requirement, the "disclosure must teach the full range of embodiments in order for the claims to be enabled." And what about the claim construction tenet that holds claims are to be interpreted in the light of the specification, but it is improper to import a limitation from the specification into the claims? As the Federal Circuit noted, "even where a patent describes only a single embodiment, claims will not be read restrictively unless the patentee has demonstrated a clear intention to limit the claim scope using words or expressions of manifest exclusion or restriction." *Innova/Pure Water, Inc. v. Safari Water Filtration Sys.*, 381 F.3d 1111, 1117 (Fed. Cir. 2004). With these doctrines in mind, would TTMP have an enablement problem if it argued that claim 1 reads on a device that has either an internal *or* an external water chamber? What claim scope would you allow? Would TTMP have a written description problem under *Gentry Gallery*, where the Federal Circuit limited claim scope in the light of a narrow disclosure (see Chapter 2)? The court justified this approach because "the disclosure unambiguously limited the location of the controls to the console" and the inventor considered the location of the "controls on the console to be an essential element of his invention." Thus, the key question for TTMP would be whether the location of the chamber is "essential element of the invention."

3. *Infringement of Method Claims.* The law distinguishes between method claims, on the one hand, and product or apparatus claims, on the other hand. *See NTP, Inc. v. Research in Motion Ltd.*, 418 F.3d 1282, 1317 (Fed. Cir. 2005) (stating "the concept of 'use' of a patented method or process is fundamentally different from the use of a patented system or device"). For infringement of a method claim, the patentee must prove that the accused infringer performs each and every step of the claimed method. *See Joy Technologies, Inc. v. Flakt, Inc.*, 6 F.3d 770, 773 (Fed. Cir. 1993). Thus, "the sale of equipment to perform a process is not a sale of the process within the meaning of section 271(a)." *Id. See also Fromson v. Advance Offset Plate, Inc.*, 720 F.2d 1565, 1568 (Fed. Cir. 1983) (finding no direct infringement by manufacturer who performed the first step of a process claim even where its customer performed the other step of the claim); *Cross Med. Prods. v. Medtronic Sofamor Danek*, 424 F.3d 1293, 1311 (rejecting patentees' efforts to combine the acts of surgeons with those of a medical device manufacturer to find direct infringement of an apparatus claim).

Nonetheless, a party who performs fewer than the claimed steps may be liable for direct infringement if the party exercises "control and direction" of the infringing activity. *See BMC Resources, Inc. v. Paymentech L.P.*, 498 F.3d 1373, 1381 (Fed. Cir. 2007) (stating "[a] party cannot avoid infringement, however, simply by contracting out steps of a patented process to another entity. . . . It would be unfair indeed for the mastermind in such situations to escape liability."). The *BMC* court acknowledged that requiring "control and direction . . . for a finding of joint infringement may in some circumstances allow parties to enter into arms-length agreements to avoid infringement." *Id.* Nevertheless, "expanding the rules governing direct infringement to reach independent conduct of multiple actors would subvert the statutory scheme for indirect infringement," which, unlike the strict liability offense of direct infringement, requires as an inquiry into the accused infringer's state of mind. *Id.*

4. *Additional Elements and the Importance of Transition Terms.* Literal infringement cannot be avoided if the accused device contains additional elements not found in the claim. For example, Inventor claims a widget, comprising A, B, and C; an accused device would still infringe if it possessed A, B, C, and D. There is one important caveat regarding this scenario. For literal infringement to hold, the claim must employ the open-ended transition word, "comprising," which has legal significance. The term comprising "raises a presumption that the list of elements is nonexclusive." *Dippin' Dots, Inc. v. Mosey,* 476 F.3d 1337, 1343 (Fed. Cir. 2007); *CollegeNet, Inc. v. ApplyYourself, Inc.,* 418 F.3d 1225, 1235 (Fed. Cir. 2005) ("The transitional term 'comprising' . . . is inclusive or open-ended and does not exclude additional, unrecited elements or method steps."). So, in the above example, the addition of "D" would not preclude a finding of literal infringement.

   In contrast, use of the transition phrase "consisting of" indicates that the claim is closed (that is, that invention is limited to no more and no fewer than the listed limitations). *See, e.g., In re Gray,* 53 F.2d 520 (CCPA 1931). Thus, a claim that reads a "widget consisting of A, B, and C" will not read on a device that contains A, B, C, and D. Moreover, the phrase "consisting essentially of" has been interpreted to exclude "ingredients that would materially affect the basic and novel characteristics of the claimed composition." *Atlas Powder Co. v. E.I. du Pont de Nemours & Co.,* 750 F.2d 1569, 1574 (Fed. Cir. 1984). Yet another phrase, "composed of," has been construed to be synonymous with either "consisting of" or "consisting essentially of," depending upon the written disclosure. *See AFG Indus., Inc. v. Cardinal IG Co., Inc.,* 239 F.3d 1239, 1244-1245 (Fed. Cir. 2001).

5. *Practical Significance of Literal Infringement.* Literal infringement has considerable practical significance. While there are relatively few published opinions, literal infringement is a common occurrence in practice, largely because of the uncertainties relating to claim interpretation, namely, "the pre-litigation ambiguity of the literal scope of the claims." JANICE M. MUELLER, AN INTRODUCTION TO PATENT LAW 287 (2006). Moreover, as explored in the next section, the doctrine of equivalents has, in the past several years, been reined in, making literal infringement a more reliable enforcement tool.

2. The Doctrine of Equivalents

The origins of the doctrine of equivalents (DOE) date to the early nineteenth century when courts assumed a generous posture toward the scope of the patentee's protection. The patent claim was an innovation of the patent bar in the early nineteenth century, and was not instituted formally into the statutory framework until 1836.[32] As such, prior to 1836, juries determined infringement based on what can be characterized as a "substantiality" test, not unlike modern copyright law. The jury would compare the patentee's invention as set forth

---

32. *See* John F. Duffy, *The* Festo *Decision and the Return of the Supreme Court to the Bar of Patents,* 2002 SUP. CT. REV. 273, 309 (stating the claim "arose not from any administrative, judicial, or legislative requirement. Instead, it was an innovation of patent attorneys, and it was formulated to protect and to expand the rights of patentees").

in the specification with the accused device. For example, Justice Story charged the jury in *Odiorne v. Winkley*,[33] "[t]he first question for consideration is, whether the machines used by the defendant are substantially, in their principles and mode of operation, like the plaintiff's machines"; and adding, "[m]ere colorable alterations of a machine are not sufficient to protect the defendant."[34]

By the mid-nineteenth century, the fundamental tension between the DOE and providing clear notice in one's property right became apparent.[35] This tension remains in contemporary patent law.[36] On the one hand, there is an interest—primarily governed by section 112—in providing a clear definition of the scope of the patent right because lack of clarity can impede legitimate investment in technology-based products and services. Certainty is the key in any property-rights system. On the other hand, strict and literal adherence to the written claim in determining the scope of protection ignores the imprecise nature of language and can invite unfair subversion of a valuable right, which would substantially diminish the economic value of patents. As Judge Learned Hand noted, courts "resort to the 'doctrine of equivalents' to temper unsparing logic and prevent an infringer from stealing the benefit of the invention." *Royal Typewriter Co. v. Remington Rand, Inc.*, 168 F.2d 691, 692 (2d Cir. 1948).

Somewhere beyond the literal claim language resides an "optimal" claim scope in any given case, and where exactly to strike this optimal balance is one of the most, if not the most, important and difficult questions in patent law. Using the DOE to strike an optimal balance has proved challenging because there are different views of what "optimal" means. (Recall the *Morse* case in Chapter 2.) As Justice Robin Jacob of the Court of Appeals in England and Wales stated, "[t]here is no general 'doctrine of equivalents'; any student of patent law knows that various legal systems allow for such a concept, but that none of them can agree what it is or should be." *Rockwater Ltd. v. Technip France SA*, [2004] EWCA Civ 381 ¶41.

---

33. 18 F. Cas. 581 (C.C.D. Mass. 1814).

34. *Id.* at 582. The use of the word "substantially" in the context of patent infringement can be traced to the 1817 cases of *Gray v. James*, 10 F. Cas. 1015, 1016 (C.C.D. Pa. 1817), and *Lowell v. Lewis*, 15 F. Cas. 1018, 1021 (C.C. Mass. 1817). In the former, Circuit Judge Washington charged the jury that discerning differences in principle between two machines can be difficult, "[b]ut we think it may safely be laid down as a general rule, that where the machines are substantially the same, and operate in the same manner, to produce the same result, they must be in principle the same." *Id.* In *Lowell*, Circuit Justice Story instructed the jury that "whether the defendant has violated the patent-right of the plaintiff . . . depends upon the fact, whether the pumps of Mr. Perkins and of Mr. Baker are substantially the same invention. I say substantially the same invention, because a mere change of the form or proportions of any machine cannot, per se, be deemed a new invention."

35. For instance, in *Winans v. Denmead*, a noteworthy nineteenth-century DOE case, four justices dissented to an infringement finding under the DOE. In an opinion by Justice Campbell, the dissent emphasized that the patentee confined his claim to the conical form and may have been "unwilling to expose the validity of his patent, by the assertion of a right to any other." The Patent Act required patentees to "specify and point out" what they claim as an invention. Requiring less than precision and particularity in claims would be "mischievous" and "productive of oppressive and costly litigation, of exorbitant and unjust pretensions and vexatious demands." 56 U.S. (15 How.) 330, 347 (1853).

36. Indeed, some commentators have argued for the abolishment of the DOE. *See, e.g.,* Joshua D. Sarnoff, *Abolishing the Doctrine of Equivalents and Claiming the Future After* Festo, 19 BERKELEY TECH. L.J. 1157 (2004).

COMPARATIVE PERSPECTIVE
Non-Literal Infringement in Europe

Non-literal infringement is part of the European patent law fabric. Article 69 of the European Patent Convention reflects a compromise between the U.K., which emphasized claim language, and Germany, which focused more on the nature of the underlying invention. Under Article 69, the "extent of the protection conferred by a European patent . . . shall be determined by the terms of the claims." But "the description and drawings shall [also] be used to interpret the claims." The U.K./German compromise is also reflected in the "Protocol on the Interpretation of Article 69," which reads:

Article 1
General Principles

Article 69 should not be interpreted in the sense that the extent of the protection conferred by a European patent is to be understood as that defined by the strict literal meaning of the wording used in the claim, the description and drawings being employed only for the purpose of resolving an ambiguity found in the claims. Neither should it be interpreted in the sense that the claims serve only as a guideline and that the actual protection conferred may extend to what from a consideration of the description and drawings by a person skilled in the art, the patentee has contemplated. On the contrary, it is to be interpreted as defining a position between these extremes which combines a fair protection for the patentee with a reasonable degree of certainty for third parties.

Article 2
Equivalents

For the purpose of determining the extent of protection conferred by a European patent, due account shall be taken of any element which is equivalent to an element specified in the claims.

Two important cases issued by the House of Lords interpreted Article 69. In *Catnic Components Ltd. v. Hill and Smith*, [1982] RPC 183 (HL), Lord Diplock stressed that a patent's specification should be given a purposive, rather than a literal, interpretation, which meant that a patent should be construed through the eyes of a person skilled in the art. In a more recent House of Lords case, *Kirin-Amgen, Inc. v. Hoechst Marion Roussel Ltd.*, [2004] UKHL 46, [2004] All ER (D) 286 (Oct. 1, 2004), Lord Hoffmann provides an excellent discussion of *Catnic* and Article 69. *Kirin-Amgen* is a principal case, below. But first we turn to two prominent American Supreme Court cases that established the current parameters of the DOE: *Graver Tank* and *Warner-Jenkinson*.

GRAVER TANK & MFG. CO. v. LINDE AIR PRODS. CO.
339 U.S. 605 (1950)

Justice JACKSON delivered the opinion of the Court.

[The patent-in-suit, owned by Linde Air Products, related to fluxes that were compositions used in electric welding and assisted in the fusing of metals. The patent had two sets of claims, one of which described a major element as any "silicate," and the other set described the element as any "alkaline earth metal silicate." The first set—"silicate"—was held invalid as too broad. The validity of the "alkaline earth metal silicate" set was upheld and the question became whether this set of claims was infringed.]

* * *

At the outset it should be noted that the single issue before us is whether the trial court's holding that the four flux claims have been infringed will be sustained.

In determining whether an accused device or composition infringes a valid patent, resort must be had in the first instance to the words of the claim. If accused matter falls clearly within the claim, infringement is made out and that is the end of it.

But courts have also recognized that to permit imitation of a patented invention which does not copy every literal detail would be to convert the protection of the patent grant into a hollow and useless thing. Such a limitation would leave room for—indeed encourage—the unscrupulous copyist to make unimportant and insubstantial changes and substitutions in the patent which, though adding nothing, would be enough to take the copied matter outside the claim, and hence outside the reach of law. One who seeks to pirate an invention, like one who seeks to pirate a copyrighted book or play, may be expected to introduce minor variations to conceal and shelter the piracy. Outright and forthright duplication is a dull and very rare type of infringement. To prohibit no other would place the inventor at the mercy of verbalism and would be subordinating substance to form. It would deprive him of the benefit of his invention and would foster concealment rather than disclosure of inventions, which is one of the primary purposes of the patent system.

The doctrine of equivalents evolved in response to this experience. The essence of the doctrine is that one may not practice a fraud on a patent. Originating almost a century ago in the case of *Winans v. Denmead*, it has been consistently applied by this Court and the lower federal courts, and continues today ready and available for utilization when the proper circumstances for its application arise. "To temper unsparing logic and prevent an infringer from stealing the benefit of the invention" a patentee may invoke this doctrine to proceed against the producer of a device "if it performs substantially the same function in substantially the same way to obtain the same result." *Sanitary Refrigerator Co. v. Winters*, 280 U.S. 30, 42. The theory on which it is founded is that "if two devices do the same work in substantially the same way, and accomplish substantially the same result, they are the same, even though they differ in name, form or shape." *Union Paper-Bag Machine Co. v. Murphy*, 97 U.S. 120, 125. The doctrine operates not only in favor of the patentee of a pioneer or primary invention, but also for the patentee of a secondary invention consisting of a combination of old ingredients which produce new and useful results, *Imhaeuser v. Buerk*, although the area of equivalence may vary under the circumstances. *See Continental Paper Bag Co. v. Eastern Paper Bag Co.*, 210 U.S. 405, 414-415, and cases cited; *Seymour v. Osborne*, 11 Wall. 516, 556. The wholesome realism of this doctrine is not always applied in favor of a patentee but is sometimes used against him. Thus, where a device is so far changed in principle from a patented article that it performs the same or a similar function in a substantially different way, but nevertheless falls within the literal words of the claim, the doctrine of equivalents may be used to restrict the claim and defeat the patentee's action for infringement. *Westinghouse v. Boyden Power-Brake Co.*, 170 U.S. 537, 568. In its early development, the doctrine was usually applied in cases involving devices where there was equivalence in mechanical components. Subsequently, however, the same principles were also applied to compositions, where there was equivalence between chemical ingredients. Today the doctrine is applied to mechanical or chemical equivalents in compositions or devices.

What constitutes equivalency must be determined against the context of the patent, the prior art, and the particular circumstances of the case. Equivalence, in the patent law, is not the prisoner of a formula and is not an absolute to be considered in a vacuum. It does not require complete identity for every purpose and in every respect. In determining equivalents, things equal to the same thing may not be equal to each other and, by the same token, things for most purposes different may sometimes be equivalents. Consideration must be given to the purpose for which an ingredient is used in a patent, the qualities it has when combined with the other ingredients, and the function which it is intended to perform. An important factor is whether persons reasonably skilled in the art would have known of the interchangeability of an ingredient not contained in the patent with one that was.

A finding of equivalence is a determination of fact. Proof can be made in any form: through testimony of experts or others versed in the technology; by documents, including texts and treatises; and, of course, by the disclosures of the prior art. Like any other issue of fact, final determination requires a balancing of credibility, persuasiveness and weight of evidence. It is to be decided by the trial court and that court's decision, under general principles of appellate review, should not be disturbed unless clearly erroneous. Particularly is this so in a field where so much depends upon familiarity with specific scientific problems and principles not usually contained in the general storehouse of knowledge and experience.

In the case before us, we have two electric welding compositions or fluxes: the patented composition, Unionmelt Grade 20, and the accused composition, Lincolnweld 660. The patent under which Unionmelt is made claims essentially a combination of alkaline earth metal silicate and calcium fluoride; Unionmelt actually contains, however, silicates of calcium and magnesium, two alkaline earth metal silicates. Lincolnweld's composition is similar to Unionmelt's, except that it substitutes silicates of calcium and manganese—the latter not an alkaline earth metal—for silicates of calcium and magnesium. In all other respects, the two compositions are alike. The mechanical methods in which these compositions are employed are similar. They are identical in operation and produce the same kind and quality of weld.

The question which thus emerges is whether the substitution of the manganese which is not an alkaline earth metal for the magnesium which is, under the circumstances of this case, and in view of the technology and the prior art, is a change of such substance as to make the doctrine of equivalents inapplicable; or conversely, whether under the circumstances the change was so insubstantial that the trial court's invocation of the doctrine of equivalents was justified.

Without attempting to be all-inclusive, we note the following evidence in the record: Chemists familiar with the two fluxes testified that manganese and magnesium were similar in many of their reactions. There is testimony by a metallurgist that alkaline earth metals are often found in manganese ores in their natural state and that they serve the same purpose in the fluxes; and a chemist testified that "in the sense of the patent" manganese could be included as an alkaline earth metal. Much of this testimony was corroborated by reference to recognized texts on inorganic chemistry. Particularly important, in addition, were the disclosures of the prior art, also contained in the record. The Miller patent, No. 1,754,566, which preceded the patent in suit, taught the use of manganese silicate in welding fluxes. Manganese was similarly disclosed in the Armor patent, No. 1,467,825, which also described a welding composition. And the record contains no evidence of any kind to show that Lincolnweld was developed as the result of independent research or experiments.

It is not for this Court to even essay an independent evaluation of this evidence. This is the function of the trial court. And, as we have heretofore observed, "To no type of case is this . . . more appropriately applicable than to the one before us, where the evidence is largely the testimony of experts as to which a trial court may be enlightened by scientific demonstrations. This trial occupied some three weeks, during which, as the record shows, the trial judge visited laboratories with counsel and experts to observe actual demonstrations of welding as taught by the patent and of the welding accused of infringing it, and of various stages of the prior art. He viewed motion pictures of various welding operations and tests and heard many experts and other witnesses."

The trial judge found on the evidence before him that the Lincolnweld flux and the composition of the patent in suit are substantially identical in operation and in result. He found also that Lincolnweld is in all respects equivalent to Unionmelt for welding purposes. And he concluded that "for all practical purposes, manganese silicate can be efficiently and effectively substituted for calcium and magnesium silicates as the major constituent of the welding composition." These conclusions are adequately supported by the record; certainly they are not clearly erroneous.

It is difficult to conceive of a case more appropriate for application of the doctrine of equivalents. The disclosures of the prior art made clear that manganese silicate was a useful ingredient in welding compositions. Specialists familiar with the problems of welding compositions understood that manganese was equivalent to and could be substituted for magnesium in the composition of the patented flux and their observations were confirmed by the literature of chemistry. Without some explanation or indication that Lincolnweld was developed by independent research, the trial court could properly infer that the accused flux is the result of imitation rather than experimentation or invention. Though infringement was not literal, the changes which avoid literal infringement are colorable only. We conclude that the trial court's judgment of infringement respecting the four flux claims was proper, and we adhere to our prior decision on this aspect of the case.

Justice BLACK, with whom Justice DOUGLAS concurs, dissenting.

I heartily agree with the Court that "fraud" is bad, "piracy" is evil, and "stealing" is reprehensible. But in this case, where petitioners are not charged with any such malevolence, these lofty principles do not justify the Court's sterilization of Acts of Congress and prior decisions, none of which are even mentioned in today's opinion.

R.S. §4888, as amended, 35 U.S.C. §33, 35 U.S.C.A. §33, provides that an applicant "shall particularly point out and distinctly claim the part, improvement, or combination which he claims as his invention or discovery." We have held in this very case that this statute precludes invoking the specifications to alter a claim free from ambiguous language, since "it is the claim which measures the grant to the patentee." *Graver Mfg. Co. v. Linde Co.*, 336 U.S. 271, 277. What is not specifically claimed is dedicated to the public. *See, e.g., Miller v. Bridgeport Brass Co.*, 104 U.S. 350, 352. For the function of claims under R.S. §4888, as we have frequently reiterated, is to exclude from the patent monopoly field all that is not specifically claimed, whatever may appear in the specifications. Today the Court tacitly rejects those cases. It departs from the underlying principle which, as the Court pointed out in *White v. Dunbar*, 119 U.S. 47, 51, forbids treating a patent claim "like a nose of wax, which may be turned and twisted in any direction, by merely referring to the specification, so as to make it include something more than, or something different from, what its words express. . . . The claim is a statutory requirement, prescribed for the very purpose of making the patentee define precisely what his invention is; and it is unjust to the public, as well as an evasion of the law, to construe it in a manner different from the plain import of its terms." Giving this patentee the benefit of a grant that it did not precisely claim is no less "unjust to the public" and no less an evasion of R.S. §4888 merely because done in the name of the "doctrine of equivalents."

In seeking to justify its emasculation of R.S. §4888 by parading potential hardships which literal enforcement might conceivably impose on patentees who had for some reason failed to claim complete protection for their discoveries, the Court fails even to mention the program for alleviation of such hardships which Congress itself has provided. 35 U.S.C. §64, 35 U.S.C.A. §64, authorizes reissue of patents where a patent is "wholly or partly inoperative" due to certain errors arising from "inadvertence, accident, or mistake" of the patentee. And while the section does not expressly permit a patentee to expand his claim, this Court has reluctantly interpreted it to justify doing so. *Miller v. Bridgeport Brass Co.*, 104 U.S. 350, 353-354. That interpretation, however, was accompanied by a warning that "Reissues for the enlargement of claims should be the exception and not the rule." 104 U.S. at page 355. And Congress was careful to hedge the privilege of reissue by exacting conditions. It also entrusted the Patent Office, not the courts, with initial authority to determine whether expansion of a claim was justified,[3] and barred

---

3. This provision was inserted in the law for the purpose of relieving the courts from the duty of ascertaining the exact invention of the patentee by inference and conjecture, derived from a laborious examination of previous inventions, and a comparison thereof with that claimed by him. This duty is now cast upon the Patent Office. There his claim is, or is supposed to be, examined, scrutinized, limited, and made to conform to what he is entitled to. If the office refuses to allow him all that he asks, he has an appeal. But the courts have no right to enlarge a patent beyond the scope of its claim as allowed by the Patent Office, or the appellate tribunal to which contested applications are referred. When the terms of a claim in a patent are clear and distinct (as they always should be), the patentee, in a suit brought upon the patent, is bound by it. *Merrill v. Yeomans*, 94 U.S. 568.

suits for retroactive infringement based on such expansion. Like the Court's opinion, this congressional plan adequately protects patentees from "fraud," "piracy," and "stealing." Unlike the Court's opinion, it also protects business men from retroactive infringement suits and judicial expansion of a monopoly sphere beyond that which a patent expressly authorizes. The plan is just, fair, and reasonable. In effect it is nullified by this decision undercutting what the Court has heretofore recognized as wise safeguards. One need not be a prophet to suggest that today's rhapsody on the virtue of the "doctrine of equivalents" will, in direct contravention of the *Miller* case *supra*, make enlargement of patent claims the "rule" rather than the "exception."

Comments

1. *Some Thoughts on* **Graver Tank.** Prior to *Warner-Jenkinson* (the next principal case), *Graver Tank* was the most significant Supreme Court opinion on the doctrine of equivalents. Justice Jackson's opinion is replete with equitable considerations relating to the patentee's property right. For example, he stated "to permit imitation of a patented invention which does not copy every literal detail would be to convert the protection of the patent grant into a hollow and useless thing" and limiting the patentee to his literal claim scope would encourage skullduggery—namely an "unscrupulous copyist" who would "make unimportant and insubstantial changes and substitutions in the patent." But did the majority opinion adequately address Justice Black's dissent and his unease with non-literal infringement? What about the importance of certainty and ex post innovation?

   For the dissent, the notice function is disserved by venturing beyond the claim. Indeed, as Justice Black wrote, "What is not specifically claimed is dedicated to the public." This point of view has been embraced by the Federal Circuit. *See Johnson & Johnston Associates, Inc. v. R.E. Service Co.*, 285 F.3d 1046, 1054 (Fed. Cir. 2002) ("[W]hen a patent drafter discloses but declines to claim a subject matter, . . . this action dedicates that unclaimed subject matter to the public"). (The public dedication rule is discussed in section B.3.b, below.) Interestingly, *Johnson & Johnston* distinguished *Graver Tank*, noting that the patentee in *Graver Tank*—unlike the patentee in *Johnston & Johnston*— "initially claimed the 'equivalent' subject matter." *Id.* at 1053.

   Perhaps Justice Black's most trenchant argument is the availability of reissue. The reissue proceeding was an innovation of the patent bar, and codified in 1832. *See Grant v. Raymond*, 31 U.S. 218 (1832) (recognizing the power of the patent office (more accurately, the Secretary of State) to cancel and reissue patents). The modern statutory reissue provision expressly allows for claim broadening if done within two years from issuance. According to §251:

   > Whenever any patent is, through error without any deceptive intention, deemed wholly or partly inoperative or invalid, by reason of a defective specification or drawing, or by reason of the patentee claiming more or less than he had a right to claim in the patent, the Director shall, on the surrender of such patent and the payment of the fee required by law, reissue the patent for the invention disclosed in the original patent, and in accordance with a new and amended

application, for the unexpired part of the term of the original patent. No new matter shall be introduced into the application for reissue.

The reissue proceeding has been cited by several commentators—who view the DOE as an erosive force on patent law's notice function—as a viable alternative to the doctrine of equivalents. *See, e.g.,* Paul M. Janicke, *Heat of Passion: What Really Happened in* Graver Tank, 24 AIPLA Q.J. 1 (1997) (suggesting reissue-like procedures for use in enlarging the scope of claims under certain circumstances as an alternative to the doctrine of equivalents); Michael J. Meurer & Craig Allen Nard, *Invention, Refinement, and Patent Claim Scope: A New Perspective on the Doctrine of Equivalents*, 93 GEO. L.J. 1947 (2005) (embracing reissue as an alternative to DOE).

2. **Graver** *Establishes the DOE Debate for 60 years.* The arguments put forth by the majority and dissent remain as relevant today as when *Graver* was decided. Justice Jackson's argument envisioned a world without the DOE, one where a patent would be converted "into a hollow and useless thing" subjected to the mercy of the "unscrupulous copyist." 339 U.S. at 617. This equitable argument is consistent with nineteenth-century justifications for non-literal infringement. For example, in the famous nineteenth-century case of *Winans v. Denmead*, 56 U.S. (15 How.) 330 (1853), Justice Curtis, writing for the majority, focused on the merit of the patentee/inventor and the bad motives of the defendant. Curtis highlighted the minor change made by the defendant, what he characterized as the "work of a constructor, not of an inventor," and wrote to allow the defendant to escape infringement with such a minor change would render the property of inventors "valueless." *Id.* at 341. For a thorough historical treatment of the DOE, *see* Joshua D. Sarnoff, *The Historic and Modern Doctrines of Equivalents and Claiming the Future: Part I (1790-1870)*, 87 J. PAT. & TRADEMARK OFF. SOC'Y 371 (2005); Joshua D. Sarnoff, *The Historic and Modern Doctrines of Equivalents and Claiming the Future: Part II (1870-1952)*, 87 J. PAT. & TRADEMARK OFF. SOC'Y 441 (2005).

But the role of the patent claim as guidepost has become increasingly important since *Graver* was decided. The claim was emphasized by Justice Black in his dissent, and has become the center of attention as the Federal Circuit and Supreme Court continue to wrestle with a way to, on the one hand, retain the DOE and, on the other hand, address the social costs associated with non-literal infringement. In *Warner-Jenkinson*, the Supreme Court visited the DOE for the first time since *Graver Tank* and acknowledged the doctrine had "taken on a life of its own, unbounded by the patent claims." In cases decided after *Warner-Jenkinson*, the Supreme Court and the Federal Circuit emphasized the primacy of the notice function of the claim and placed several limitations on the DOE.

WARNER-JENKINSON CO., INC. v. HILTON DAVIS CHEMICAL CO.
520 U.S. 17 (1997)

Justice THOMAS delivered the opinion of the Court.

Nearly 50 years ago, this Court in *Graver Tank & Mfg. Co. v. Linde Air Products Co.* set out the modern contours of what is known in patent law as the "doctrine of equivalents." Under this doctrine, a product or process that does not literally infringe upon the express terms of a patent claim may nonetheless be found to infringe if there is "equivalence" between the elements of the accused product or process and the claimed elements of the patented invention. . . . Petitioner, which was found to have infringed upon respondent's patent under the doctrine of equivalents, invites us to speak the death of that doctrine. We decline that invitation. The significant disagreement within the Court of Appeals for the Federal Circuit concerning the application of *Graver Tank* suggests, however, that the doctrine is not free from confusion. We therefore will endeavor to clarify the proper scope of the doctrine.

I

The essential facts of this case are few. Petitioner Warner-Jenkinson Co. and respondent Hilton Davis Chemical Co. manufacture dyes. Impurities in those dyes must be removed. Hilton Davis holds United States Patent No. 4,560,746 ('746 patent), which discloses an improved purification process involving "ultra-filtration." The '746 process filters impure dye through a porous membrane at certain pressures and pH levels,[1] resulting in a high purity dye product.

The '746 patent issued in 1985. As relevant to this case, the patent claims as its invention an improvement in the ultrafiltration process as follows:

> In a process for the purification of a dye . . . the improvement which comprises: subjecting an aqueous solution . . . to ultrafiltration through a membrane having a nominal pore diameter of 5-15 Angstroms under a hydrostatic pressure of approximately 200 to 400 p.s.i.g., *at a pH from approximately 6.0 to 9.0*, to thereby cause separation of said impurities from said dye. . . . App. 36-37 (emphasis added).

The inventors added the phrase "at a pH from approximately 6.0 to 9.0" during patent prosecution. At a minimum, this phrase was added to distinguish a previous patent (the "Booth" patent) that disclosed an ultrafiltration process operating at a pH above 9.0. The parties disagree as to why the low-end pH limit of 6.0 was included as part of the claim.[2]

In 1986, Warner-Jenkinson developed an ultrafiltration process that operated with membrane pore diameters assumed to be 5-15 Angstroms, at pressures of 200 to nearly 500 p.s.i.g., and at a pH of 5.0. Warner-Jenkinson did not learn of the '746 patent until after it had begun commercial use of its ultrafiltration process. Hilton Davis eventually learned of Warner-Jenkinson's use of ultrafiltration and, in 1991, sued Warner-Jenkinson for patent infringement.

---

1. The pH, or power (exponent) of Hydrogen, of a solution is a measure of its acidity or alkalinity. A pH of 7.0 is neutral; a pH below 7.0 is acidic; and a pH above 7.0 is alkaline. Although measurement of pH is on a logarithmic scale, with each whole number difference representing a ten-fold difference in acidity, the practical significance of any such difference will often depend on the context. Pure water, for example, has a neutral pH of 7.0, whereas carbonated water has an acidic pH of 3.0, and concentrated hydrochloric acid has a pH approaching 0.0. On the other end of the scale, milk of magnesia has a pH of 10.0, whereas household ammonia has a pH of 11.9. 21 Encyclopedia Americana 844 (Int'l ed. 1990).

2. Petitioner contends that the lower limit was added because below a pH of 6.0 the patented process created "foaming" problems in the plant and because the process was not shown to work below that pH level. Brief for Petitioner 4, n. 5, 37, n. 28. Respondent counters that the process was successfully tested to pH levels as low as 2.2 with no effect on the process because of foaming, but offers no particular explanation as to why the lower level of 6.0 pH was selected. Brief for Respondent 34, n.34.

As trial approached, Hilton Davis conceded that there was no literal infringement, and relied solely on the doctrine of equivalents. Over Warner-Jenkinson's objection that the doctrine of equivalents was an equitable doctrine to be applied by the court, the issue of equivalence was included among those sent to the jury. The jury found that the '746 patent was not invalid and that Warner-Jenkinson infringed upon the patent under the doctrine of equivalents. The jury also found, however, that Warner-Jenkinson had not intentionally infringed, and therefore awarded only 20% of the damages sought by Hilton Davis. The District Court denied Warner-Jenkinson's post-trial motions, and entered a permanent injunction prohibiting Warner-Jenkinson from practicing ultrafiltration below 500 p.s.i.g. and below 9.01 pH. A fractured *en banc* Court of Appeals for the Federal Circuit affirmed.

The majority below held that the doctrine of equivalents continues to exist and that its touchstone is whether substantial differences exist between the accused process and the patented process. The court also held that the question of equivalence is for the jury to decide and that the jury in this case had substantial evidence from which it could conclude that the Warner-Jenkinson process was not substantially different from the ultrafiltration process disclosed in the '746 patent.

There were three separate dissents, commanding a total of 5 of 12 judges. Four of the five dissenting judges viewed the doctrine of equivalents as allowing an improper expansion of claim scope, contrary to this Court's numerous holdings that it is the claim that defines the invention and gives notice to the public of the limits of the patent monopoly. *Id.* at 1537-1538 (Plager, J., dissenting). The fifth dissenter, the late Judge Nies, was able to reconcile the prohibition against enlarging the scope of claims and the doctrine of equivalents by applying the doctrine to each element of a claim, rather than to the accused product or process "overall." *Id.*, at 1574 (Nies, J., dissenting). As she explained it, "[t]he 'scope' is not enlarged if courts do not go beyond the substitution of equivalent elements." *Ibid.* All of the dissenters, however, would have found that a much narrowed doctrine of equivalents may be applied in whole or in part by the court. *Id.*, at 1540-1542 (Plager, J., dissenting); *id.*, at 1579 (Nies, J., dissenting).

We granted *certiorari*, and now reverse and remand.

II

* * *

A

Petitioner's primary argument in this Court is that the doctrine of equivalents, as set out in *Graver Tank* in 1950, did not survive the 1952 revision of the Patent Act, 35 U.S.C. §100 *et seq.*, because it is inconsistent with several aspects of that Act. In particular, petitioner argues: (1) the doctrine of equivalents is inconsistent with the statutory requirement that a patentee specifically "claim" the invention covered by a patent, 35 U.S.C. §112; (2) the doctrine circumvents the patent reissue process—designed to correct mistakes in drafting or the like—and avoids the express limitations on that process, 35 U.S.C. §§251-252; (3) the doctrine is inconsistent with the primacy of the Patent and Trademark Office (PTO) in setting the scope of a patent through the patent prosecution process; and (4) the doctrine was implicitly rejected as a general matter by Congress' specific and limited inclusion of the doctrine in one section regarding "means" claiming, 35 U.S.C. § 112, ¶6. All but one of these arguments were made in *Graver Tank* in the context of the 1870 Patent Act, and failed to command a majority.[3]

The 1952 Patent Act is not materially different from the 1870 Act with regard to claiming, reissue, and the role of the PTO. Compare, *e.g.*, 35 U.S.C. § 112 ("The specification shall conclude with one or more claims particularly pointing out and distinctly claiming the subject matter which the applicant regards as his invention") with The Consolidated Patent Act of 1870, ch. 230, § 26, 16 Stat. 198, 201 (the applicant "shall particularly point out and distinctly claim the part, improvement, or combination which he claims as his invention or discovery"). Such minor differences as exist between those provisions in the 1870 and the 1952 Acts have no bearing on the result reached in *Graver Tank*, and thus provide no basis for our overruling it. In the context of infringement, we have already held that pre-1952 precedent survived the passage of the 1952 Act. We see no reason to reach a different result here.

Petitioner's fourth argument for an implied congressional negation of the doctrine of equivalents turns on the reference to "equivalents" in the "means" claiming provision of the 1952 Act. . . . Because § 112, ¶6 was enacted as a targeted cure to a specific problem, and because the reference in that provision to "equivalents" appears to be no more than a prophylactic against potential side effects of that cure, such limited congressional action should not be overread for negative implications. Congress in 1952 could easily have responded to *Graver Tank* as it did to the *Halliburton* decision. But it did not. Absent something more compelling than the dubious negative inference offered by petitioner, the lengthy history of the doctrine of equivalents strongly supports adherence to our refusal in *Graver Tank* to find that the Patent Act conflicts with that doctrine. Congress can legislate the doctrine of equivalents out of existence any time it chooses. The various policy arguments now made by both sides are thus best addressed to Congress, not this Court.

B

We do, however, share the concern of the dissenters below that the doctrine of equivalents, as it has come to be applied since *Graver Tank*, has taken on a life of its own, unbounded by the patent claims. There can be no denying that the doctrine of equivalents, when applied broadly, conflicts with the definitional and public-notice functions of the statutory claiming requirement. Judge Nies identified one means of avoiding this conflict:

---

3. *Graver Tank* was decided over a vigorous dissent. In that dissent, Justice Black raised the first three of petitioner's four arguments against the doctrine of equivalents. *See* 339 U.S., at 613-614 (doctrine inconsistent with statutory requirement to "distinctly claim" the invention); *id.*, at 614-615 (patent reissue process available to correct mistakes); *id.*, at 615, n.3 (duty lies with the Patent Office to examine claims and to conform them to the scope of the invention; inventors may appeal Patent Office determinations if they disagree with result). Indeed, petitioner's first argument was not new even in 1950. Nearly 100 years before *Graver Tank*, this Court approved of the doctrine of equivalents in *Winans v. Denmead*, 15 How. 330, 14 L. Ed. 717 (1854). The dissent in *Winans* unsuccessfully argued that the majority result was inconsistent with the requirement in the 1836 Patent Act that the applicant "particularly 'specify and point' out what he claims as his invention," and that the patent protected nothing more. Id., 15 How. at 347 (Campbell, J., dissenting).

[A] distinction can be drawn that is not too esoteric between substitution of an equivalent for a component *in* an invention and enlarging the metes and bounds of the invention *beyond* what is claimed.

* * *

Where a claim to an invention is expressed as a combination of elements, as here, "equivalents" in the sobriquet "Doctrine of Equivalents" refers to the equivalency of an *element* or *part* of the invention with one that is substituted in the accused product or process.

* * *

This view that the accused device or process must be more than "equivalent" *overall* reconciles the Supreme Court's position on infringement by equivalents with its concurrent statements that "the courts have no right to enlarge a patent beyond the scope of its claims as allowed by the Patent Office." The "scope" is not enlarged if courts do not go beyond the substitution of equivalent elements. 62 F.3d, at 1573-1574 (Nies, J., dissenting) (emphasis in original).

We concur with this apt reconciliation of our two lines of precedent. Each element contained in a patent claim is deemed material to defining the scope of the patented invention, and thus the doctrine of equivalents must be applied to individual elements of the claim, not to the invention as a whole. It is important to ensure that the application of the doctrine, even as to an individual element, is not allowed such broad play as to effectively eliminate that element in its entirety. So long as the doctrine of equivalents does not encroach beyond the limits just described, or beyond related limits to be discussed infra, we are confident that the doctrine will not vitiate the central functions of the patent claims themselves.

III

Understandably reluctant to assume this Court would overrule *Graver Tank*, petitioner has offered alternative arguments in favor of a more restricted doctrine of equivalents than it feels was applied in this case. We address each in turn.

A

Petitioner first argues that *Graver Tank* never purported to supersede a well-established limit on non-literal infringement, known variously as "prosecution history estoppel" and "file wrapper estoppel." According to petitioner, any surrender of subject matter during patent prosecution, regardless of the reason for such surrender, precludes recapturing any part of that subject matter, even if it is equivalent to the matter expressly claimed. Because, during patent prosecution, respondent limited the pH element of its claim to pH levels between 6.0 and 9.0, petitioner would have those limits form bright lines beyond which no equivalents may be claimed. Any inquiry into the reasons for a surrender, petitioner claims, would undermine the public's right to clear notice of the scope of the patent as embodied in the patent file.

We can readily agree with petitioner that *Graver Tank* did not dispose of prosecution history estoppel as a legal limitation on the doctrine of equivalents. But petitioner reaches too far in arguing that the reason for an amendment during patent prosecution is irrelevant to any subsequent estoppel. In each of our cases cited by petitioner and by the dissent below, prosecution history estoppel was tied to amendments made to avoid the prior art, or otherwise to address a specific concern—such as obviousness—that arguably would have rendered the claimed subject matter unpatentable. Thus, in *Exhibit Supply Co. v. Ace Patents Corp.*, Chief Justice Stone distinguished inclusion of a limiting phrase in an original patent claim from the "very different" situation in which "the applicant, in order to meet objections in the Patent Office, *based on references to the prior art*, adopted the phrase as a substitute for the broader one" previously used. 315 U.S. 126, 136 (1942) (emphasis added). Similarly, in *Keystone Driller Co. v. Northwest Engineering Corp.*, 294 U.S. 42 (1935), estoppel was applied where the initial claims were "rejected on the prior art," *id.*, at 48, n.6, and where the allegedly infringing equivalent element was outside of the revised claims and within the prior art that formed the basis for the rejection of the earlier claims.

It is telling that in each case this Court probed the reasoning behind the Patent Office's insistence upon a change in the claims. In each instance, a change was demanded because the claim as otherwise written was viewed as not describing a patentable invention at all—typically because what it described was encompassed within the prior art. But, as the United States informs us, there are a variety of other reasons why the PTO may request a change in claim language. Brief for United States as Amicus Curiae 22-23 (counsel for the PTO also appearing on the brief). And if the PTO has been requesting changes in claim language without the intent to limit equivalents or, indeed, with the expectation that language it required would in many cases allow for a range of equivalents, we should be extremely reluctant to upset the basic assumptions of the PTO without substantial reason for doing so. Our prior cases have consistently applied prosecution history estoppel only where claims have been amended for a limited set of reasons, and we see no substantial cause for requiring a more rigid rule invoking an estoppel regardless of the reasons for a change.[6]

In this case, the patent examiner objected to the patent claim due to a perceived overlap with the Booth patent, which revealed an ultrafiltration process operating at a pH above 9.0. In response to this objection, the phrase "at a pH from approximately 6.0 to 9.0" was added to the claim. While it is undisputed that the upper limit of 9.0 was added in order to distinguish the Booth patent, the reason for adding the lower limit of 6.0 is unclear. The lower limit certainly did not serve to distinguish the Booth patent, which said nothing about pH levels below 6.0. Thus, while a lower limit of 6.0, by its mere inclusion, became a material element of the claim, that did not necessarily preclude the application of the doctrine of equivalents as to that element. *See Hubbell v. United States*, 179 U.S. 77, 82 (1900) (" '[A]ll [specified elements] must be regarded as material,' " though it remains an open " 'question whether an omitted part is supplied by an equivalent device or instrumentality.' " Where the reason for the change was not

---

6. That petitioner's rule might provide a brighter line for determining whether a patentee is estopped under certain circumstances is not a sufficient reason for adopting such a rule. This is especially true where, as here, the PTO may have relied upon a flexible rule of estoppel when deciding whether to ask for a change in the first place. To change so substantially the rules of the game now could very well subvert the various balances the PTO sought to strike when issuing the numerous patents which have not yet expired and which would be affected by our decision.

related to avoiding the prior art, the change may introduce a new element, but it does not necessarily preclude infringement by equivalents of that element.

We are left with the problem, however, of what to do in a case like the one at bar, where the record seems not to reveal the reason for including the lower pH limit of 6.0. In our view, holding that certain reasons for a claim amendment may avoid the application of prosecution history estoppel is not tantamount to holding that the absence of a reason for an amendment may similarly avoid such an estoppel. Mindful that claims do indeed serve both a definitional and a notice function, we think the better rule is to place the burden on the patent-holder to establish the reason for an amendment required during patent prosecution. The court then would decide whether that reason is sufficient to overcome prosecution history estoppel as a bar to application of the doctrine of equivalents to the element added by that amendment. Where no explanation is established, however, the court should presume that the PTO had a substantial reason related to patentability for including the limiting element added by amendment. In those circumstances, prosecution history estoppel would bar the application of the doctrine equivalents as to that element. The presumption we have described, one subject to rebuttal if an appropriate reason for a required amendment is established, gives proper deference to the role of claims in defining an invention and providing public notice, and to the primacy of the PTO in ensuring that the claims allowed cover only subject matter that is properly patentable in a proffered patent application. Applied in this fashion, prosecution history estoppel places reasonable limits on the doctrine of equivalents, and further insulates the doctrine from any feared conflict with the Patent Act.

Because respondent has not proffered in this Court a reason for the addition of a lower pH limit, it is impossible to tell whether the reason for that addition could properly avoid an estoppel. Whether a reason in fact exists, but simply was not adequately developed, we cannot say. On remand, the Federal Circuit can consider whether reasons for that portion of the amendment were offered or not and whether further opportunity to establish such reasons would be proper.

B

Petitioner next argues that even if *Graver Tank* remains good law, the case held only that the absence of substantial differences was a necessary element for infringement under the doctrine of equivalents, not that it was sufficient for such a result. Relying on *Graver Tank*'s references to the problem of an "unscrupulous copyist" and "piracy," 339 U.S., at 607, petitioner would require judicial exploration of the equities of a case before allowing application of the doctrine of equivalents. To be sure, *Graver Tank* refers to the prevention of copying and piracy when describing the benefits of the doctrine of equivalents. That the doctrine produces such benefits, however, does not mean that its application is limited only to cases where those particular benefits are obtained.

Elsewhere in *Graver Tank* the doctrine is described in more neutral terms. And the history of the doctrine as relied upon by *Graver Tank* reflects a basis for the doctrine not so limited as petitioner would have it. In *Winans v. Denmead*, 15 How. 330, 343 (1854), we described the doctrine of equivalents as growing out of a legally implied term in each patent claim that "the claim extends to the thing patented, however its form or proportions may be varied." Under that view, application of the doctrine of equivalents involves determining whether a particular accused product or process infringes upon the patent claim, where the claim takes the form—half express, half implied—of "X and its equivalents."

If the essential predicate of the doctrine of equivalents is the notion of identity between a patented invention and its equivalent, there is no basis for treating an infringing equivalent any differently than a device that infringes the express terms of the patent. Application of the doctrine of equivalents, therefore, is akin to determining literal infringement, and neither requires proof of intent.

Petitioner also points to *Graver Tank*'s seeming reliance on the absence of independent experimentation by the alleged infringer as supporting an equitable defense to the doctrine of equivalents. The Federal Circuit explained this factor by suggesting that an alleged infringer's behavior, be it copying, designing around a patent, or independent experimentation, indirectly reflects the substantiality of the differences between the patented invention and the accused device or process. According to the Federal Circuit, a person aiming to copy or aiming to avoid a patent is imagined to be at least marginally skilled at copying or avoidance, and thus intentional copying raises an inference —rebuttable by proof of independent development—of having only insubstantial differences, and intentionally designing around a patent claim raises an inference of substantial differences. This explanation leaves much to be desired. At a minimum, one wonders how ever to distinguish between the intentional copyist making minor changes to lower the risk of legal action, and the incremental innovator designing around the claims, yet seeking to capture as much as is permissible of the patented advance.

But another explanation is available that does not require a divergence from generally objective principles of patent infringement. In both instances in *Graver Tank* where we referred to independent research or experiments, we were discussing the known interchangeability between the chemical compound claimed in the patent and the compound substituted by the alleged infringer. The need for independent experimentation thus could reflect knowledge—or lack thereof—of interchangeability possessed by one presumably skilled in the art. The known interchangeability of substitutes for an element of a patent is one of the express objective factors noted by *Graver Tank* as bearing upon whether the accused device is substantially the same as the patented invention. Independent experimentation by the alleged infringer would not always reflect upon the objective question whether a person skilled in the art would have known of the interchangeability between two elements, but in many cases it would likely be probative of such knowledge.

Although *Graver Tank* certainly leaves room for petitioner's suggested inclusion of intent-based elements in the doctrine of equivalents, we do not read it as requiring them. The better view, and the one consistent with *Graver Tank*'s predecessors and the objective approach to infringement, is that intent plays no role in the application of the doctrine of equivalents.

C

Finally, petitioner proposes that in order to minimize conflict with the notice function of patent claims, the doctrine of equivalents should be limited to equivalents that are disclosed within the patent itself. A milder version of this argument, which found favor with the dissenters below, is that the doctrine should be limited to equivalents that were known at the time the patent was issued, and should not extend to after-arising equivalents.

As we have noted . . . with regard to the objective nature of the doctrine, a skilled practitioner's knowledge of the interchangeability between claimed and accused elements is not relevant for its own sake, but rather for what it tells the fact-finder about the similarities or differences between those elements. Much as the perspective of the hypothetical "reasonable person" gives content to concepts such as "negligent" behavior, the perspective of a skilled practitioner provides content to, and limits on, the concept of "equivalence." Insofar as the question under the doctrine of equivalents is whether an accused element is equivalent to a claimed element, the proper time for evaluating equivalency —and thus knowledge of interchangeability between elements—is at the time of infringement, not at the time the patent was issued. And rejecting the milder version of petitioner's argument necessarily rejects the more severe proposition that equivalents must not only be known, but must also be actually disclosed in the patent in order for such equivalents to infringe upon the patent.

IV

The various opinions below, respondents, and amici devote considerable attention to whether application of the doctrine of equivalents is a task for the judge or for the jury. However, despite petitioner's argument below that the doctrine should be applied by the judge, in this Court petitioner makes only passing reference to this issue. *See* Brief for Petitioner 22, n.15 ("If this Court were to hold in *Markman v. Westview Instruments, Inc.*, that judges rather than juries are to construe patent claims, so as to provide a uniform definition of the scope of the legally protected monopoly, it would seem at cross-purposes to say that juries may nonetheless expand the claims by resort to a broad notion of 'equivalents'"); Reply Brief for Petitioner 20 (whether judge or jury should apply the doctrine of equivalents depends on how the Court views the nature of the inquiry under the doctrine of equivalents).

Petitioner's comments go more to the alleged inconsistency between the doctrine of equivalents and the claiming requirement than to the role of the jury in applying the doctrine as properly understood. Because resolution of whether, or how much of, the application of the doctrine of equivalents can be resolved by the court is not necessary for us to answer the question presented, we decline to take it up. The Federal Circuit held that it was for the jury to decide whether the accused process was equivalent to the claimed process. There was ample support in our prior cases for that holding. Nothing in our recent *Markman* decision necessitates a different result than that reached by the Federal Circuit. Indeed, *Markman* cites with considerable favor, when discussing the role of judge and jury, the seminal *Winans* decision. *Markman v. Westview Instruments, Inc.* Whether, if the issue were squarely presented to us, we would reach a different conclusion than did the Federal Circuit is not a question we need decide today.[8]

---

8. With regard to the concern over unreviewability due to black-box jury verdicts, we offer only guidance, not a specific mandate. Where the evidence is such that no reasonable jury could determine two elements to be equivalent, district courts are obliged to grant partial or complete summary judgment. *See* Fed. Rule Civ. Proc. 56. If there has been a reluctance to do so by some courts due to unfamiliarity with the subject matter, we are confident that the Federal Circuit can remedy the problem. Of course, the various legal limitations on the application of the doctrine of equivalents are to be determined by the court, either on a pretrial motion for partial summary judgment or on a motion for judgment as a matter of law at the close of the evidence and after the jury verdict. Fed. Rule Civ. Proc. 56; Fed. Rule Civ. Proc. 50. Thus, under the particular facts of a

V

All that remains is to address the debate regarding the linguistic framework under which "equivalence" is determined. Both the parties and the Federal Circuit spend considerable time arguing whether the so-called "triple identity" test—focusing on the function served by a particular claim element, the way that element serves that function, and the result thus obtained by that element — is a suitable method for determining equivalence, or whether an "insubstantial differences" approach is better. There seems to be substantial agreement that, while the triple identity test may be suitable for analyzing mechanical devices, it often provides a poor framework for analyzing other products or processes. On the other hand, the insubstantial differences test offers little additional guidance as to what might render any given difference "insubstantial."

In our view, the particular linguistic framework used is less important than whether the test is probative of the essential inquiry: Does the accused product or process contain elements identical or equivalent to each claimed element of the patented invention? Different linguistic frameworks may be more suitable to different cases, depending on their particular facts. A focus on individual elements and a special vigilance against allowing the concept of equivalence to eliminate completely any such elements should reduce considerably the imprecision of whatever language is used. An analysis of the role played by each element in the context of the specific patent claim will thus inform the inquiry as to whether a substitute element matches the function, way, and result of the claimed element, or whether the substitute element plays a role substantially different from the claimed element. With these limiting principles as a backdrop, we see no purpose in going further and micro-managing the Federal Circuit's particular word-choice for analyzing equivalence. We expect that the Federal Circuit will refine the formulation of the test for equivalence in the orderly course of case-by-case determinations, and we leave such refinement to that court's sound judgment in this area of its special expertise.

* * *

Comments

1. ***DOE's Temporal Dimension and After-Arising Technology.*** Unlike literal infringement, which is measured at the time of filing, *Warner-Jenkinson* made clear that equivalents are measured at the "time of infringement," which implies that the DOE can capture after-arising technologies (i.e., technologies that were developed after the patent was filed). *See SmithKline Beecham Corp. v. Excel Pharmaceuticals, Inc.*, 356 F.3d 1357, 1363-1364 (Fed. Cir. 2004) (stating that after-arising technology is the "quintessential example of an enforceable

---

case, if prosecution history estoppel would apply or if a theory of equivalence would entirely vitiate a particular claim element, partial or complete judgment should be rendered by the court, as there would be no further material issue for the jury to resolve. Finally, in cases that reach the jury, a special verdict and/or interrogatories on each claim element could be very useful in facilitating review, uniformity, and possibly post verdict judgments as a matter of law. *See* Fed. Rule Civ. Proc. 49; Fed. Rule Civ. Proc. 50. We leave it to the Federal Circuit how best to implement procedural improvements to promote certainty, consistency, and reviewability to this area of the law.

equivalent," and noting further "[u]sually, if the alleged equivalent represents later-developed technology (e.g., transistors in relation to vacuum tubes, or Velcro® in relation to fasteners) or technology that was not known in the relevant art, then it would not have been foreseeable. In contrast, old technology, while not always foreseeable, would more likely have been foreseeable"); *Pennwalt Corp. v. Durand-Wayland, Inc.*, 833 F.2d 931, 941-942 (Fed. Cir. 1987) (*en banc*) ("It is clear that an equivalent can be found in subsequently developed technology"); *Chiuminatta Concrete Concepts, Inc. v. Cardinal Industries*, 145 F.3d 1303, 1310 (Fed. Cir. 1998) ("The doctrine of equivalents is necessary because one cannot predict the future. Due to technological advances, a variant of an invention may be developed after the patent is granted, and that variant may constitute so insubstantial a change from what is claimed in the patent that it should be held to be an infringement. Such a variant, based on after-developed technology, could not have been disclosed in the patent."). This doctrine was fully endorsed in the *Festo* opinion (next principal case), where the Supreme Court limited the patentee's ability to prove equivalence to "unforeseeable" technologies, that is, after-arising technologies.

The DOE is applied at the time of infringement, in part, to address the temporal constraints of literal infringement. Another reason is that the cumulative and unforeseeable nature of complex and ramified technologies, whereby the patentee opens a door for a subsequent improver-inventor, permitting the improver-inventor to benefit from the patentee's disclosure, thereby lowering the costs, accelerating the development, or simply making possible subsequent inventive activities. The DOE allows the patentee to capture some of this improvement activity; the difficult question is how big of a net should the patentee be permitted to cast. As we saw in Chapter 2 and the *Morse* case, allowing a patentee to capture after-arising technologies may provide an additional ex ante incentive, but may also negatively affect incentives associated with improvement activity—ex post incentives. *See* Suzanne Scotchmer, *Standing on the Shoulders of Giants: Cumulative Research and the Patent Law*, in J. ECON. PERSP., Vol. 5, No. 1, 29-41 (1991).

The relationship between after-arising technology and the DOE was discussed by Judge Rader in his concurring opinion in *Festo Corp. v. Shoketsu Kinzoku Kogyo Kabushiki Co., Ltd.*:

> A primary justification for the doctrine of equivalents is to accommodate after-arising technology. Without a doctrine of equivalents, any claim drafted in current technological terms could be easily circumvented after the advent of an advance in technology. A claim using the terms "anode" and "cathode" from tube technology would lack the "collectors" and "emitters" of transistor technology that emerged in 1948. Thus, without a doctrine of equivalents, infringers in 1949 would have unfettered license to appropriate all patented technology using the out-dated terms "cathode" and "anode." Fortunately, the doctrine of equivalents accommodates that unforeseeable dilemma for claim drafters. Indeed, in *Warner-Jenkinson*, the Supreme Court acknowledged the doctrine's role in accommodating after-arising technology.

234 F.3d 558, 619 (*en banc*) (Rader, J., concurring).

An after-arising technology was present in *Hughes Aircraft Co. v. United States*, 717 F.2d 1351 (Fed. Cir. 1983). In *Hughes*, the invention related to satellite technology, particularly controlling the attitude of a communications satellite. The inventor was a Hughes employee named Williams. The patent claimed the attitude was adjusted by communication between the satellite and a ground control station. As satellite technology evolved, self-contained, on-board computations using microprocessors would supplant the need for ground control communication to adjust the satellite's attitude. These types of microprocessors were unknown at the time the Hughes patent was filed. Nonetheless, the Federal Circuit held the on-board microprocessor technology infringed the Hughes patent. According to the court, "partial variation in technique, an embellishment made possible by post-Williams technology, does not allow the accused spacecraft to escape the web of infringement." *Id.* at 1365. In other words, the inventor can capture after-arising technologies and is not required to predict all future developments that enable the practice of his invention in substantially the same way.

And in *Energy Transportation Group, Inc. v. William Demant Holding A/S*, 697 F.3d 1342 (Fed. Cir. 2012), the Federal Circuit relied on *Hughes Aircraft* in affirming a $31 million award for infringement of patents on technology for reducing acoustic feedback in a programmable digital hearing aid related to hearing aid technology. In particular, the patents, particularly the '850 patent, describe a method of programming coefficients for the acoustic feedback filter with the use of a "host controller." The host controller calculates optimum coefficients for cancellation of acoustic feedback. Then, according to the patents, those coefficients are programmed into the filter. The claims recited either a "programmable filter," a "programmable delay line filter," or a filter that is "programmed" to reduce acoustic feedback. *Id.* at 1348. The accused product employs an adaptive filter that is repeatedly programed in the feedback path of the circuit with new coefficients to cancel and eliminate feedback. In particular, unlike what is disclosed in the specification, the accused devices relocated the calculation and programming of filter coefficients from an external host controller into the hearing aid itself.

Because of this difference, the district court found no literal infringement. But the court did find infringement under the DOE. The Federal Circuit affirmed. Beginning with claim construction, the Federal Circuit held that nothing in the '850 patent "claims indicate the plain and ordinary meaning of 'programmed' should be limited to external or fixed programming. The claims do not specify where the programming occurs, how frequently it occurs, or what structure provides the programming"; and "the specification gives no reason to construe the claims to require that an external computer calculate the values programmed into the filter." *Id.* at 1349. With this claim construction in hand, the court turned to infringement under the DOE and analogized the case to *Hughes Aircraft*:

> [In *Hughes*], [d]ue to vast reduction in the size and vast improvement in the capacity of computer components, the accused devices were able to calculate the ISA position onboard the satellite. The accused satellites transferred different information to the ground station because the onboard computer calculated ISA position. Despite this "missing limitation" from the claims, the after arising technology still permitted the ground crew to control the satellite. The result was an insubstantial change in the way the satellites performed the claimed function.

> In this case as well, advances in computer technology allowed the accused devices to relocate calculation and programming of filter coefficients from an external host controller into the hearing aid itself. The accused devices "determin[e] the effect on the amplitude and phase" of acoustic feedback using onboard calculations. '850 patent, co. 14, ll. 8-10. While the improvement in technology allows Defendants' products to constantly recalculate filter coefficients using electronics located on the hearing aid, the accused devices nonetheless perform the same function in substantially the same way, with substantially the same result claimed by the '850 patent, thus providing substantial evidence for the jury's infringement verdict.

697 F.3d at 1353-1354.

In addition, the United States added its weight to this issue in its amicus brief in *Warner-Jenkinson*:

> Of course, when an accused equivalent (meeting the objective standard of insubstantiality) could not have been known because it was developed or discovered only after the patent issued, the case for application of the doctrine of equivalents becomes especially clear. For example, a claim to a chemical composition might include an inactive filler as a minor, unimportant ingredient. After the patent issues, a competitor of the patentee might manufacture a composition exactly as claimed but use a different, inactive filler, unknown in the art at the time the patent application was filed, that performs exactly as those literally covered by the claim. Such a substitution, once it became available, might be known to persons of skill in the relevant art to be interchangeable with the claimed filler, and yet it would not have been possible to include the accused element in the patent because it did not exist at the time of issue.

1996 WL 172221, at *23 n.8.

Some commentators, such as Timothy Holbrook, have argued that "[n]either the courts nor commentators have provided an adequate explanation for why the patentee is entitled to protection under the doctrine of equivalents for a device that she never invented." Timothy R. Holbrook, *Equivalency and Patent Law's Possession Paradox*, 23 HARV. J.L. & TECH. 1, 36 (2009). Holbrook offers two justifications. First, he asserts it is fair to permit a patentee to capture after-arising technology "when a change outside of the patentee's field affects that field and her invention in a way that allows others to capture the essence of the invention by making trivial changes." *Id.* Second, Holbrook argues that an after-arising alleged equivalent may be captured under the DOE if the patentee's "disclosure enables the asserted equivalent at the time of infringement." *Id.* at 37. This theory, notes Holbrook, "ties the availability of equivalents to the disclosure of the patent document, but allows those teachings to grow over time." *Id.* For additional perspectives on the DOE and after-arising technologies, *see* Christopher A. Cotropia, *"After-Arising" Technologies and Tailoring Patent Scope*, 61 N.Y.U. ANN. SURV. AM. L. 151 (2005); Kevin Emerson Collins, *Enabling After-Arising Technology*, 34 J. CORP. L. 1083 (2009); Kevin Emerson Collins, *The Reach of Literal Claim Scope Into After-Arising Technology: On Thing Construction and the Meaning of Meaning*, 41 CONN. L. REV. 493 (2008).

Interestingly, despite the DOE's role in expanding claim scope and the ability of patentee's to capture after-arising technology, two commentators have observed that "patentees rarely win doctrine of equivalents cases." *See* John R. Allison & Mark A. Lemley, *The (Unnoticed) Demise of the Doctrine of*

Equivalents, 59 STAN. L. REV. 955, 966 (2007) (finding "patentees won only 24% of the doctrine of equivalents cases decided in the last eight years [c]ompared to the overall patentee win rates on other issues—54% on validity alone in cases at various stages of litigation, and 58% overall in cases that make it to trial"). *See also* Lee Petherbridge, *On the Decline of the Doctrine of Equivalents*, 31 CARDOZO L. REV. 1371 (2010) (providing empirical support for the reasons behind the DOE's decline). But recent Federal Circuit cases suggest the DOE is very much alive. *See, e.g., Deere & Co. v. Bush Hog, LLC*, 703 F.3d 1349 (Fed. Cir. 2012), and *Brilliant Instruments, Inc. v. GuideTech, LLC*, 703 F.3d 1342 (Fed. Cir. 2013).

2. *Timing Is Everything: The DOE's Relationship with Section 112?* How can a patent claim be interpreted to capture after-arising technology when the technology did not exist at the time the patent was filed? Another way of asking this question is: Isn't there a conflict between satisfying the disclosure requirements and the DOE? The key to this apparent conflict is the *timing* of the inquiry. Recall from Chapter 2 that enablement is measured at the time of filing. In contrast, equivalents are measured at the time of infringement.

An illustrative case on time-shifting between enablement and DOE infringement is *In re Hogan*, 559 F.2d 595 (CCPA 1977). In *Hogan*, the issue involved the PTO's use of "later state of the art" to support a section 112 rejection based on lack of commensurability. The appellant filed several continuations, all of which, appellant argued, enjoyed the filing date of the original application filed in 1953.

The PTO relied on numerous references that had an effective date prior to 1971, but after 1953. The PTO argued that the claims of the 1971 application covered both crystalline polymers and amorphous polymers. Since amorphous polymers did not exist in 1953, the PTO argued, the disclosure of the 1971 application "is not commensurate in scope with the breadth of the claims." *Id.* at 605. The PTO pointed to the Edwards reference (filed in 1962)—which first disclosed amorphous polymers—as evidence that amorphous polymers did not exist in 1953.

The CCPA reversed the rejection. First, the court stated it was improper for the PTO to use later state of the art (i.e., Edwards) to prove that amorphous polymers did not exist in 1953. As the court noted, "if appellants' 1953 application provided sufficient enablement, considering all available evidence of the 1953 state of the art, then the fact of that enablement was established for all time and a later change in the state of the art cannot change it." *Id.* at 605. In other words, the filing date (assuming a sufficient disclosure) locks in compliance with the enablement requirement, and it is impermissible to use later state of the art to prove non-compliance.

The court then discussed claim scope, asking "[t]o what scope of protection is this applicant's particular contribution to the art entitled?" According to the court:

> The PTO position, that claim 13 is of sufficient breadth to cover the later state of the art (amorphous polymers) shown in the "references," reflects a concern that allowance of claim 13 might lead to enforcement efforts against the later developers. Any such conjecture, if it exists, is both irrelevant and unwarranted. The business of the PTO is patentability, not infringement. . . . The courts have consistently considered subsequently existing states of the art as raising questions of infringement, but never validity. It is, of course, a major

and infinitely important function of the PTO to insure that those skilled in the art are enabled, as of the filing date, to practice the invention claimed. If, in the light of all proper evidence, the invention claimed be clearly enabled as of that date, the inquiry under §112, first paragraph, is at an end.

Id. at 607.

3. ***Patenting the Accused Device.*** *Warner-Jenkinson* did not directly address the related issue of whether the patentability of a later-developed, accused device or method is relevant to equivalency. It is well-settled that a patent on an accused product or process does not give the owner of the patent a right to exploit the product or process. Existence of a patent provides no defense to literal infringement of a claim. For example, in *Bio-Technology General Corp. v. Genentech, Inc.*, 80 F.3d 1553 (Fed. Cir. 1996), Genentech's patent claiming a recombinant process for producing a hormone read literally on the accused infringer's process. The accused infringer argued that its process involved a unique, patented purification method. The court dismissed the argument: "That [the accused infringer] patented its unique purification method is irrelevant: '[T]he existence of one's own patent does not constitute a defense to infringement of someone else's patent. It is elementary that a patent grants only the right *to exclude others* and confers no right on its holder to make, use, or sell.'" 80 F.3d at 1559.

But some Federal Circuit decisions suggest that a patent on the accused device may be relevant to the substantiality of the difference between the patent claim and the accused device, at least when the patent in suit was cited and considered by the PTO in issuing the subsequent patent. *See Zygo Corp. v. Wyko Corp.*, 79 F.3d 1563, 1570 (Fed. Cir. 1996) (stating the accused device is "presumed nonobvious" when it is patented, and "[t]he nonobviousness . . . is relevant to the issue of whether the change therein is substantial"); *Hoganas AB v. Dresser Industries, Inc.*, 9 F.3d 948, 954 (Fed. Cir. 1993) (stating "the PTO must have considered the accused product to be nonobvious with respect to the patented composition. Accordingly, the issuance of that patent is relevant to the equivalence issue"). In addition, a patent on an accused product prompts a comparison between the nonobviousness test and the insubstantial differences framework of the doctrine of equivalents. *See Roton Barrier, Inc. v. Stanley Works*, 79 F.3d 1112, 1128 (Fed. Cir. 1996) (Nies, J. additional views: "If the second patent requires practice of the first i.e., the second merely adds an element 'D' to a patented combination A+B+C, the combination A+B+C+D clearly infringes. Conversely, if the second patent is granted for A+B+D over one claiming A+B+C, the change from C to D must not have been obvious to be validly patented. Evidence of a patent covering the change, in my view, is clearly relevant unless the patent is invalid. A substitution in a patented invention cannot be both nonobvious and insubstantial. I would apply nonobviousness as the test for the 'insubstantial change' requirement of *Hilton Davis*.").

The Federal Circuit rejected an *en banc* petition to clarify this interplay by a vote of 8-3. *See Siemens Medical Solutions USA, Inc. v. Saint-Gobain Ceramics & Plastics, Inc.*, 647 F.3d 1373 (Fed. Cir. 2011) (denial of petition to hear *en banc*). The petitioner argued there was an inconsistency between, on the one hand, the court's requiring a showing of clear and convincing evidence to prove invalidity based on obviousness and, on the other hand, application of the lower preponderance of the evidence to prove an independently patented accused product infringes the patent-in-suit under the DOE. For the majority, the petitioner sought to overturn a "well-established" rule "that a patent can cover, or dominate, separately patented subject matter," and stressed the basic point that a patent grants a right to exclude, not the "right to make or use or sell." *Id.* at 1374-1375. As such, "[i]nventing an improvement to patented inventions . . . does not entitle such an inventor to infringe the underlying patented technology." *Id.* at 1375. In contrast, for the dissent, "just as the doctrine of equivalents cannot extend a patent's scope to cover prior art, it should not permit patents to be extended to cover new and nonobvious inventions." *Id.* at 1379. Accordingly, "a purported equivalent cannot be both insubstantially different and nonobvious, and in no event should the doctrine of equivalents permit a patent to capture another's subsequent invention that is novel and nonobvious." *Id.* at 1380. For more on this issue, *see* Alan Durham, *Patent Symmetry*, 87 B.U. L. Rev. 969 (2007) (exploring the relationship between equivalents and obviousness).

4. ***The Linguistic Framework.*** The Federal Circuit devoted a great deal of text to the proper linguistic framework for the DOE and the role of the jury in deciding equivalence infringement. Regarding the former, the debate at the Federal Circuit centered on the respective benefits and drawbacks between *Graver Tank*'s tripartite test and the "insubstantial differences" test. The Federal Circuit adopted "insubstantial differences" as the "ultimate test," retaining the tripartite function-way-result test as a permissible formulation in particular cases. The Supreme Court expressed concern with each linguistic test, stating "[t]here seems to be substantial agreement that, while the triple identity test may be suitable for analyzing mechanical devices, it often provides a poor framework for analyzing other products or processes. On the other hand, the insubstantial differences test offers little additional guidance as to what might render any given difference "insubstantial." The Court neither adopted a new linguistic framework, nor endorsed the two existing frameworks. Rather, the Court thought that focusing on individual claim elements during an equivalency determination and assuring against vitiation of claim elements would "reduce considerably the imprecision of whatever language is used." In the end, the Court left to the Federal Circuit to "refine the formulation of the test for equivalence in the orderly course of case-by-case determinations." Indeed, the Federal Circuit continues to use both linguistic tests, and, at times, conflates the two. *See, e.g., Searfoss v. Pioneer Consol. Corp.*, 374 F.3d 1142, 1150 (Fed. Cir. 2002) ("'An element in the accused product is equivalent to a claim limitation if the differences between the two are "insubstantial" to one of ordinary skill in the art.' In determining whether the differences between the accused product and the claim limitation are 'insubstantial,' it is axiomatic that we may determine whether the accused product performs the same function, in the same way with the same result.").

5. ***The Growing Emphasis on Patent Law's Notice Function.*** The patent law landscape had changed a great deal since the Supreme Court decided *Graver Tank*. In the mid-1990s, the Federal Circuit began to place greater emphasis on certainty and the notice function. One way to pursue these policy goals was to limit the role of juries in patent litigation and rein in the DOE, which some thought was becoming increasingly unruly. Recall, the role of the jury

in claim construction was eliminated in *Markman*; was the DOE next? When the Supreme Court agreed to hear *Warner-Jenkinson*, many in the patent community thought the viability of *Graver* was in danger and that the respective roles of judge and jury in the context of the DOE would be modified in a manner consistent with *Markman*. But, despite the "considerable attention" given to the judge-jury issue, the Court "decline[d] to take it up."

The Court did, however, recognize that the DOE had "taken on a life of its own, unbounded by the patent claims." In addressing this concern, the Court adopted the all-limitations rule advocated by the late Judge Nies. Under the all-limitations rule, "the patentee has the burden to present particularized evidence that links the accused products to the patent on a limitation by limitation basis." *Motionless Keyboard Co. v. Microsoft Corp.*, 486 F.3d 1376 (Fed. Cir. 2007). *See also PC Connector Solutions LLC v. SmartDisk Corp.*, 406 F.3d 1359, 1364 (Fed. Cir. 2005) (stating the patentee must present "particularized evidence and linking argument as to the 'insubstantiality of the differences' between the claimed invention and the accused device, or with respect to the 'function, way, result' test"). The "all-limitations rule" is discussed below in section B.3.c.

Moreover, the Court constructed a rebuttable presumption, barring application of the DOE, when a patentee is unable to provide a reason for a narrowing amendment. Lastly, a strict liability framework was reaffirmed for patent infringement; as the Court stated, "intent plays no role in the application of the doctrine of equivalents." All of these moves were grounded in the desire for greater certainty and notice.

But the Court would only go so far, rebuffing Petitioner's argument that the DOE should be limited to equivalents disclosed in the patent specification or, at least, to equivalents known at the time the patent issued. Has the Court reconsidered this position in *Festo*, the next principal case?

3. Limitations on the Doctrine of Equivalents

There are four limitations to the DOE that are explored in this section. They include (1) prosecution history estoppel; (2) public dedication rule; (3) all-limitations and specific exclusion rule; and (4) prior art. Each of these limitations is explored in the following four subsections.

a. Prosecution History Estoppel

In its traditional setting, *prosecution history estoppel* ("PHE") applies when a patentee attempts to acquire a claim scope during litigation that it surrendered during prosecution. For instance, PHE estops a patentee who narrowed his claim during prosecution to overcome a prior art rejection from recapturing—during litigation—the surrendered claim breadth. Thus, the PHE acts as a limitation on the DOE.

The Supreme Court *Festo* case (*Festo VIII*) reveals a broader and more rigorous application of PHE. *Festo VIII* held that a patentee who, during prosecution, narrowed his claim scope by amendment is presumed to have surrendered the "the territory between the original claim and the amended claim," unless the patentee can show (1) the equivalent that he is seeking to capture was unforeseeable at the time of the amendment; (2) the rationale underlying the amendment bears no more than a tangential relation to the equivalent in question; or (3) some other reason suggesting that the patentee could not reasonably be expected to have described the insubstantial substitute in question.

FESTO CORP. v. SHOKETSU KINZOKU KOGYO KABUSHIKI CO., LTD. (*FESTO VIII*)
535 U.S. 722 (2002)

Justice KENNEDY delivered the opinion of the Court.

This case requires us to address once again the relation between two patent law concepts, the doctrine of equivalents and the rule of prosecution history estoppel. The Court considered the same concepts in *Warner-Jenkinson Co. v. Hilton Davis Chemical Co.*, and reaffirmed that a patent protects its holder against efforts of copyists to evade liability for infringement by making only insubstantial changes to a patented invention. At the same time, we appreciated that by extending protection beyond the literal terms in a patent the doctrine of equivalents can create substantial uncertainty about where the patent monopoly ends. If the range of equivalents is unclear, competitors may be unable to determine what is a permitted alternative to a patented invention and what is an infringing equivalent.

To reduce the uncertainty, *Warner-Jenkinson* acknowledged that competitors may rely on the prosecution history, the public record of the patent proceedings. In some cases the Patent and Trademark Office (PTO) may have rejected an earlier version of the patent application on the ground that a claim does not meet a statutory requirement for patentability. When the patentee responds to the rejection by narrowing his claims, this prosecution history estops him from later arguing that the subject matter covered by the original, broader claim was nothing more than an equivalent. Competitors may rely on the estoppel to ensure that their own devices will not be found to infringe by equivalence.

In the decision now under review the Court of Appeals for the Federal Circuit held that by narrowing a claim to obtain a patent, the patentee surrenders all equivalents to the amended claim element. Petitioner asserts this holding departs from past precedent in two respects. First, it applies estoppel to every amendment made to satisfy the requirements of the Patent Act and not just to amendments made to avoid pre-emption by an earlier invention, *i.e.,* the prior art. Second, it holds that when estoppel arises, it bars suit against every equivalent to the amended claim element. The Court of Appeals acknowledged that this holding departed from its own cases, which applied a flexible bar when considering what claims of equivalence were estopped by the prosecution history. Petitioner argues that by replacing the flexible bar with a complete bar the Court of Appeals cast doubt on many existing patents that were amended during the application process when the law, as it then stood, did not apply so rigorous a standard.

We granted certiorari to consider these questions.

I

Petitioner Festo Corporation owns two patents for an improved magnetic rodless cylinder, a piston-driven device that relies on magnets to move objects in a conveying system. The device has many industrial uses and has been employed in machinery as diverse as sewing equipment and the Thunder Mountain ride at Disney World. Although the precise details of the cylinder's operation are not essential here, the prosecution history must be considered.

Petitioner's patent applications, as often occurs, were amended during the prosecution proceedings. The application for the first patent, the Stoll Patent (U.S. Patent No. 4,354,125), was amended after the patent examiner rejected the initial application because the exact method of operation was unclear and some claims were made in an impermissible way. (They were multiply dependent.) 35 U.S.C. §112. The inventor, Dr. Stoll, submitted a new application designed to meet the examiner's objections and also added certain references to prior art. The second patent, the Carroll Patent (U.S. Patent No. 3,779,401), was also amended during a reexamination proceeding. The prior art references were added to this amended application as well. Both amended patents added a new limitation—that the inventions contain a pair of sealing rings, each having a lip on one side, which would prevent impurities from getting on the piston assembly. The amended Stoll Patent added the further limitation that the outer shell of the device, the sleeve, be made of a magnetizable material.

After Festo began selling its rodless cylinder, respondents (whom we refer to as SMC) entered the market with a device similar, but not identical, to the ones disclosed by Festo's patents. SMC's cylinder, rather than using two one-way sealing rings, employs a single sealing ring with a two-way lip. Furthermore, SMC's sleeve is made of a nonmagnetizable alloy. SMC's device does not fall within the literal claims of either patent, but petitioner contends that it is so similar that it infringes under the doctrine of equivalents.

SMC contends that Festo is estopped from making this argument because of the prosecution history of its patents. The sealing rings and the magnetized alloy in the Festo product were both disclosed for the first time in the amended applications. In SMC's view, these amendments narrowed the earlier applications, surrendering alternatives that are the very points of difference in the competing devices—the sealing rings and the type of alloy used to make the sleeve. As Festo narrowed its claims in these ways in order to obtain the patents, says SMC, Festo is now estopped from saying that these features are immaterial and that SMC's device is an equivalent of its own.

The United States District Court for the District of Massachusetts disagreed. It held that Festo's amendments were not made to avoid prior art, and therefore the amendments were not the kind that give rise to estoppel. A panel of the Court of Appeals for the Federal Circuit affirmed. We granted certiorari, vacated, and remanded in light of our intervening decision in *Warner-Jenkinson v. Hilton Davis Chemical Co.* After a decision by the original panel on remand, the Court of Appeals ordered rehearing en banc to address questions that had divided its judges since our decision in *Warner-Jenkinson*.

The en banc court reversed, holding that prosecution history estoppel barred Festo from asserting that the accused device infringed its patents under the doctrine of equivalents. The court held, with only one judge dissenting, that estoppel arises from any amendment that narrows a claim to comply with the Patent Act, not only from amendments made to avoid prior art. More controversial in the Court of Appeals was its further holding: When estoppel applies, it stands as a complete bar against any claim of equivalence for the element that was amended. The court acknowledged that its own prior case law did not go so far. Previous decisions had held that prosecution history estoppel constituted a flexible bar, foreclosing some, but not all, claims of equivalence, depending on the purpose of the amendment and the alterations in the text. The court concluded, however, that its precedents applying the flexible-bar rule should be overruled because this case-by-case approach has proved unworkable. In the court's view a complete-bar rule, under which estoppel bars all claims of equivalence to the narrowed element, would promote certainty in the determination of infringement cases.

We granted certiorari.

II

The patent laws "promote the Progress of Science and useful Arts" by rewarding innovation with a temporary monopoly. U.S. Const., Art. I, §8, cl. 8. The monopoly is a property right; and like any property right, its boundaries should be clear. This clarity is essential to promote progress, because it enables efficient investment in innovation. A patent holder should know what he owns, and the public should know what he does not. For this reason, the patent laws require inventors to describe their work in "full, clear, concise, and exact terms," 35 U.S.C. §112, as part of the delicate balance the law attempts to maintain between inventors, who rely on the promise of the law to bring the invention forth, and the public, which should be encouraged to pursue innovations, creations, and new ideas beyond the inventor's exclusive rights.

Unfortunately, the nature of language makes it impossible to capture the essence of a thing in a patent application. The inventor who chooses to patent an invention and disclose it to the public, rather than exploit it in secret, bears the risk that others will devote their efforts toward exploiting the limits of the patent's language:

> An invention exists most importantly as a tangible structure or a series of drawings. A verbal portrayal is usually an afterthought written to satisfy the requirements of patent law. This conversion of machine to words allows for unintended idea gaps which cannot be satisfactorily filled. Often the invention is novel and words do not exist to describe it. The dictionary does not always keep abreast of the inventor. It cannot. Things are not made for the sake of words, but words for things. *Autogiro Co. of America v. United States*, 181 Ct. Cl. 55 (1967).

The language in the patent claims may not capture every nuance of the invention or describe with complete precision the range of its novelty. If patents were always interpreted by their literal terms, their value would be greatly diminished. Unimportant and insubstantial substitutes for certain elements could defeat the patent, and its value to inventors could be destroyed by simple acts of copying. For this reason, the clearest rule of patent interpretation, literalism, may conserve judicial resources but is not necessarily the most efficient rule. The scope of a patent is not limited to its literal terms but instead embraces all equivalents to the claims described. See *Winans v. Denmead*, 56 U.S. (15 How.) 330, 347 (1854). It is true that the doctrine of equivalents renders the scope of patents less certain. It may be difficult to determine what is, or is not, an equivalent to a particular element of an invention. If competitors cannot be certain about a patent's extent, they may be deterred from engaging in legitimate manufactures outside its limits, or they may invest by mistake in competing products that the patent secures. In addition the uncertainty may lead to wasteful litigation between competitors, suits that a rule of literalism might avoid. These concerns with the doctrine of equivalents, however, are not new. Each time the Court has considered the doctrine, it has acknowledged this uncertainty as the price of ensuring the appropriate incentives for innovation, and it has affirmed the doctrine over dissents that urged a more certain rule. When the Court in *Winans v. Denmead, supra,* first adopted what has become the doctrine of equivalents, it stated that "[t]he exclusive right to the thing patented is not secured, if the public are at liberty to make substantial copies of it, varying its form or proportions." *Id.,* at 343. The dissent argued that the Court had sacrificed the objective of "[f]ul[l]ness, clearness, exactness, preciseness, and particularity, in the description of the invention." *Id.,* at 347 (opinion of Campbell, J.).

The debate continued in *Graver Tank & Mfg. Co. v. Linde Air Products Co.,* 339 U.S. 605 (1950), where the Court reaffirmed the doctrine. *Graver Tank* held that patent claims must protect the inventor not only from those who produce devices falling within the literal claims of the patent but also from copyists who "make unimportant and insubstantial changes and substitutions in the patent which, though adding nothing, would be enough to take the copied matter outside the claim, and hence outside the reach of law." *Id.* at 607. Justice Black, in dissent, objected that under the doctrine of equivalents a competitor "cannot rely on what the language of a patent claims. He must be able, at the peril of heavy infringement damages, to forecast how far a court relatively unversed in a particular technological field will expand the claim's language. . . ." *Id.,* at 617.

Most recently, in *Warner-Jenkinson,* the Court reaffirmed that equivalents remain a firmly entrenched part of the settled rights protected by the patent. A unanimous opinion concluded that if the doctrine is to be discarded, it is Congress and not the Court that should do so:

> [T]he lengthy history of the doctrine of equivalents strongly supports adherence to our refusal in *Graver Tank* to find that the Patent Act conflicts with that doctrine. Congress can legislate the doctrine of equivalents out of existence any time it chooses. The various policy arguments now made by both sides are thus best addressed to Congress, not this Court. 520 U.S., at 28.

III

Prosecution history estoppel requires that the claims of a patent be interpreted in light of the proceedings in the PTO during the application process. Estoppel is a "rule of patent construction" that ensures that claims are interpreted by reference to those "that have been cancelled or rejected." *Schriber-Schroth Co. v. Cleveland Trust Co.,* 311 U.S. 211, 220-221 (1940). The doctrine of equivalents allows the patentee to claim those insubstantial alterations that were not captured in drafting the original patent claim but which could be created through trivial changes. When, however, the patentee originally claimed the subject matter alleged to infringe but then narrowed the claim in response to a rejection, he may not argue that the surrendered territory comprised unforeseen subject matter that should be deemed equivalent to the literal claims of the issued patent. On the contrary, "[b]y the amendment [the patentee] recognized and emphasized the difference between the two phrases[,] . . . and [t]he difference which [the patentee] thus disclaimed must be regarded as material." *Exhibit Supply Co. v. Ace Patents Corp.,* 315 U.S. 126, 136-137 (1942).

A rejection indicates that the patent examiner does not believe the original claim could be patented. While the patentee has the right to appeal, his decision to forgo an appeal and submit an amended claim is taken as a concession that the invention as patented does not reach as far as the original claim. See *Goodyear Dental Vulcanite Co. v. Davis*, 102 U.S. 222, 228 (1880) ("In view of [the amendment] there can be no doubt of what [the patentee] understood he had patented, and that both he and the commissioner regarded the patent to be for a manufacture made exclusively of vulcanites by the detailed process"); *Wang Laboratories, Inc. v. Mitsubishi Electronics America, Inc.*, 103 F.3d 1571, 1577-1578 (C.A. Fed. 1997) ("Prosecution history estoppel . . . preclud[es] a patentee from regaining, through litigation, coverage of subject matter relinquished during prosecution of the application for the patent"). Were it otherwise, the inventor might avoid the PTO's gatekeeping role and seek to recapture in an infringement action the very subject matter surrendered as a condition of receiving the patent.

Prosecution history estoppel ensures that the doctrine of equivalents remains tied to its underlying purpose. Where the original application once embraced the purported equivalent but the patentee narrowed his claims to obtain the patent or to protect its validity, the patentee cannot assert that he lacked the words to describe the subject matter in question. The doctrine of equivalents is premised on language's inability to capture the essence of innovation, but a prior application describing the precise element at issue undercuts that premise. In that instance the prosecution history has established that the inventor turned his attention to the subject matter in question, knew the words for both the broader and narrower claim, and affirmatively chose the latter.

A

The first question in this case concerns the kinds of amendments that may give rise to estoppel. Petitioner argues that estoppel should arise when amendments are intended to narrow the subject matter of the patented invention, for instance, amendments to avoid prior art, but not when the amendments are made to comply with requirements concerning the form of the patent application. In *Warner-Jenkinson* we recognized that prosecution history estoppel does not arise in every instance when a patent application is amended. Our "prior cases have consistently applied prosecution history estoppel only where claims have been amended for a limited set of reasons," such as "to avoid the prior art, or otherwise to address a specific concern—such as obviousness—that arguably would have rendered the claimed subject matter unpatentable." 520 U.S., at 30-32. While we made clear that estoppel applies to amendments made for a "substantial reason related to patentability," *id.*, at 33, we did not purport to define that term or to catalog every reason that might raise an estoppel. Indeed, we stated that even if the amendment's purpose were unrelated to patentability, the court might consider whether it was the kind of reason that nonetheless might require resort to the estoppel doctrine. *Id.*, at 40-41.

Petitioner is correct that estoppel has been discussed most often in the context of amendments made to avoid the prior art. Amendment to accommodate prior art was the emphasis, too, of our decision in *Warner-Jenkinson, supra*, at 30. It does not follow, however, that amendments for other purposes will not give rise to estoppel. Prosecution history may rebut the inference that a thing not described was indescribable. That rationale does not cease simply because the narrowing amendment, submitted to secure a patent, was for some purpose other than avoiding prior art.

We agree with the Court of Appeals that a narrowing amendment made to satisfy any requirement of the Patent Act may give rise to an estoppel. As that court explained, a number of statutory requirements must be satisfied before a patent can issue. The claimed subject matter must be useful, novel, and not obvious. 35 U.S.C. §§ 101-103. In addition, the patent application must describe, enable, and set forth the best mode of carrying out the invention. § 112. These latter requirements must be satisfied before issuance of the patent, for exclusive patent rights are given in exchange for disclosing the invention to the public. What is claimed by the patent application must be the same as what is disclosed in the specification; otherwise the patent should not issue. The patent also should not issue if the other requirements of § 112 are not satisfied, and an applicant's failure to meet these requirements could lead to the issued patent being held invalid in later litigation.

Petitioner contends that amendments made to comply with § 112 concerns the form of the application and not the subject matter of the invention. The PTO might require the applicant to clarify an ambiguous term, to improve the translation of a foreign word, or to rewrite a dependent claim as an independent one. In these cases, petitioner argues, the applicant has no intention of surrendering subject matter and should not be estopped from challenging equivalent devices. While this may be true in some cases, petitioner's argument conflates the patentee's reason for making the amendment with the impact the amendment has on the subject matter.

Estoppel arises when an amendment is made to secure the patent and the amendment narrows the patent's scope. If a § 112 amendment is truly cosmetic, then it would not narrow the patent's scope or raise an estoppel. On the other hand, if a § 112 amendment is necessary and narrows the patent's scope—even if only for the purpose of better description—estoppel may apply. A patentee who narrows a claim as a condition for obtaining a patent disavows his claim to the broader subject matter, whether the amendment was made to avoid the prior art or to comply with § 112. We must regard the patentee as having conceded an inability to claim the broader subject matter or at least as having abandoned his right to appeal a rejection. In either case estoppel may apply.

B

Petitioner concedes that the limitations at issue—the sealing rings and the composition of the sleeve—were made for reasons related to § 112, if not also to avoid the prior art. Our conclusion that prosecution history estoppel arises when a claim is narrowed to comply with § 112 gives rise to the second question presented: Does the estoppel bar the inventor from asserting infringement against any equivalent to the narrowed element or might some equivalents still infringe? The Court of Appeals held that prosecution history estoppel is a complete bar, and so the narrowed element must be limited to its strict literal terms. Based upon its experience the Court of Appeals decided that the flexible-bar rule is unworkable because it leads to excessive uncertainty and burdens legitimate innovation. For the reasons that follow, we disagree with the decision to adopt the complete bar.

Though prosecution history estoppel can bar challenges to a wide range of equivalents, its reach requires an examination of the subject matter surrendered by the narrowing amendment. The complete bar avoids this inquiry by establishing a *per se* rule; but that approach is inconsistent with the purpose of applying the estoppel in the first place—to hold the inventor to the representations made during the application process and to the inferences that may reasonably be drawn from the amendment. By amending the application, the inventor is deemed to concede that the patent does not extend as far as the original claim. It does not follow, however, that the amended claim becomes so perfect in its description that no one could devise an equivalent. After amendment, as before, language remains an imperfect fit for invention. The narrowing amendment may demonstrate what the claim is not; but it may still fail to capture precisely what the claim is. There is no reason why a narrowing amendment should be deemed to relinquish equivalents unforeseeable at the time of the amendment and beyond a fair interpretation of what was surrendered. Nor is there any call to foreclose claims of equivalence for aspects of the invention that have only a peripheral relation to the reason the amendment was submitted. The amendment does not show that the inventor suddenly had more foresight in the drafting of claims than an inventor whose application was granted without amendments having been submitted. It shows only that he was familiar with the broader text and with the difference between the two. As a result, there is no more reason for holding the patentee to the literal terms of an amended claim than there is for abolishing the doctrine of equivalents altogether and holding every patentee to the literal terms of the patent.

This view of prosecution history estoppel is consistent with our precedents and respectful of the real practice before the PTO. While this Court has not weighed the merits of the complete bar against the flexible bar in its prior cases, we have consistently applied the doctrine in a flexible way, not a rigid one. We have considered what equivalents were surrendered during the prosecution of the patent, rather than imposing a complete bar that resorts to the very literalism the equivalents rule is designed to overcome.

The Court of Appeals ignored the guidance of *Warner-Jenkinson*, which instructed that courts must be cautious before adopting changes that disrupt the settled expectations of the inventing community. In that case we made it clear that the doctrine of equivalents and the rule of prosecution history estoppel are settled law. The responsibility for changing them rests with Congress. *Ibid.* Fundamental alterations in these rules risk destroying the legitimate expectations of inventors in their property. The petitioner in *Warner-Jenkinson* requested another bright-line rule that would have provided more certainty in determining when estoppel applies but at the cost of disrupting the expectations of countless existing patent holders. We rejected that approach: "To change so substantially the rules of the game now could very well subvert the various balances the PTO sought to strike when issuing the numerous patents which have not yet expired and which would be affected by our decision." *Id.,* at 32, n.6; see also *id.,* at 41 (Ginsburg, J., concurring) ("The new presumption, if applied woodenly, might in some instances unfairly discount the expectations of a patentee who had no notice at the time of patent prosecution that such a presumption would apply"). As *Warner-Jenkinson* recognized, patent prosecution occurs in the light of our case law. Inventors who amended their claims under the previous regime had no reason to believe they were conceding all equivalents. If they had known, they might have appealed the rejection instead. There is no justification for applying a new and more robust estoppel to those who relied on prior doctrine.

In *Warner-Jenkinson* we struck the appropriate balance by placing the burden on the patentee to show that an amendment was not for purposes of patentability:

> Where no explanation is established, however, the court should presume that the patent application had a substantial reason related to patentability for including the limiting element added by amendment. In those circumstances, prosecution history estoppel would bar the application of the doctrine of equivalents as to that element. *Id.* at 33.

When the patentee is unable to explain the reason for amendment, estoppel not only applies but also "bar[s] the application of the doctrine of equivalents as to that element." *Ibid.* These words do not mandate a complete bar; they are limited to the circumstance where "no explanation is established." They do provide, however, that when the court is unable to determine the purpose underlying a narrowing amendment — and hence a rationale for limiting the estoppel to the surrender of particular equivalents — the court should presume that the patentee surrendered all subject matter between the broader and the narrower language.

Just as *Warner-Jenkinson* held that the patentee bears the burden of proving that an amendment was not made for a reason that would give rise to estoppel, we hold here that the patentee should bear the burden of showing that the amendment does not surrender the particular equivalent in question. This is the approach advocated by the United States, see Brief for United States as *Amicus Curiae* 22-28, and we regard it to be sound. The patentee, as the author of the claim language, may be expected to draft claims encompassing readily known equivalents. A patentee's decision to narrow his claims through amendment may be presumed to be a general disclaimer of the territory between the original claim and the amended claim. *Exhibit Supply,* 315 U.S., at 136-137 ("By the amendment [the patentee] recognized and emphasized the difference between the two phrases and proclaimed his abandonment of all that is embraced in that difference"). There are some cases, however, where the amendment cannot reasonably be viewed as surrendering a particular equivalent. The equivalent may have been unforeseeable at the time of the application; the rationale underlying the amendment may bear no more than a tangential relation to the equivalent in question; or there may be some other reason suggesting that the patentee could not reasonably be expected to have described the insubstantial substitute in question. In those cases the patentee can overcome the presumption that prosecution history estoppel bars a finding of equivalence.

This presumption is not, then, just the complete bar by another name. Rather, it reflects the fact that the interpretation of the patent must begin with its literal claims, and the prosecution history is relevant to construing those claims. When the patentee has chosen to narrow a claim, courts may presume the amended text was composed with awareness of this rule and that the territory surrendered is not an equivalent of the territory claimed. In those instances, however, the patentee still might rebut the presumption that estoppel bars a claim of equivalence. The patentee must show that at the time of the amendment one skilled in the art could not reasonably be expected to have drafted a claim that would have literally encompassed the alleged equivalent.

IV

On the record before us, we cannot say petitioner has rebutted the presumptions that estoppel applies and that the equivalents at issue have been surrendered. Petitioner concedes that the limitations at issue—the sealing rings and the composition of the sleeve—were made in response to a rejection for reasons under §112, if not also because of the prior art references. As the amendments were made for a reason relating to patentability, the question is not whether estoppel applies but what territory the amendments surrendered. While estoppel does not effect a complete bar, the question remains whether petitioner can demonstrate that the narrowing amendments did not surrender the particular equivalents at issue. On these questions, respondents may well prevail, for the sealing rings and the composition of the sleeve both were noted expressly in the prosecution history. These matters, however, should be determined in the first instance by further proceedings in the Court of Appeals or the District Court.

The judgment of the Federal Circuit is vacated, and the case is remanded for further proceedings consistent with this opinion.

Comments

1. ***Limiting and Tolerating Uncertainty.*** The Supreme Court rejected the complete bar approach of the Federal Circuit, although it did acknowledge the importance of certainty in a property rights-based system such as patent law. In adopting its framework of presumptions and burdens (see Comment 2, below), the Court recognized the inherent limitations of language in describing an invention. (For example, how would you describe something as simple as a pizza box or a pencil?). But it also candidly acknowledged that the patent system has tolerated "uncertainty as the price of ensuring the appropriate incentives for innovation." This sentiment was echoed by Lord Hoffmann in *Kirin-Amgen*: "[U]ncertainty is inherent in any rule which involves the construction of any document. It afflicts the whole of the law of contract, to say nothing of legislation. In principle it is without remedy." *Kirin-Amgen, Inc. v. Hoechst Marion Roussel Ltd* [2004] All ER (D) 286 (Oct. 1, 2004), ¶48. *Kirin-Amgen* is discussed at the end of this section.

2. ***The Age of Presumptions and Burdens.*** The *Festo* Court, consistent with *Warner-Jenkinson*, favored the creation of a rebuttable presumption. Recall, in *Warner-Jenkinson*, the Court wrote, "[w]hen the patentee is unable to explain the reason for amendment, estoppel not only applies but also 'bar[s] the application of the doctrine of equivalents as to that element.'" In *Festo*, the Supreme Court expanded this presumption, noting that a narrowing of claim scope during prosecution "may be presumed to be a general disclaimer of the territory between the original and the amended claim"; that is, "the territory surrendered is not an equivalent of the territory claimed." This presumption led the Court to impose a burden on the patentee "of showing that the amendment does not surrender the particular equivalent in question." According to the Court:

   > The patentee must show that at the time of the amendment one skilled in the art could not reasonably be expected to have drafted a claim that would have literally encompassed the alleged equivalent.

In particular, to rebut the presumption, the patentee must show (1) the equivalent was unforeseeable at the time of amendment; (2) the rationale underlying the amendment was tangentially related to the equivalent; or (3) some other reason suggesting that the patentee could not reasonably be expected to have described the insubstantial substitute in question.

Recall also that the petitioner in *Warner-Jenkinson* argued, unsuccessfully, that the DOE should be "limited to equivalents that were known at the time the patent was issued, and should not extend to after-arising technologies." 520 U.S. at 30. The Court rejected this argument because equivalents are measured at the time of infringement, implying that not only can the patentee capture technology that existed at the time the patent issued, but also after-arising technology. The *Festo* Court, however, prevents patentees from capturing extant technologies because what is known at the time of issuance is obviously foreseeable. Under *Festo*, only unforeseeable equivalents are eligible to be captured by the DOE, a position that is consistent with measuring equivalents at the time of infringement.

3. *Recognizing a "Narrowing" Amendment Made for "Reasons Related to Patentability."* For the *Festo* presumption to apply, an amendment must have narrowed the claim and have been filed for substantial reasons related to patentability. Any amendment made in response to prior art based on sections 102 and 103 would certainly be related to patentability. Indeed, most amendments filed in response to section 112 rejections would also satisfy this prong of *Festo*. The question of what constitutes a narrowing of claim scope is not as straightforward as it seems. For instance, in *Honeywell Int'l, Inc. v. Hamilton Sundstrand Corp.*, 370 F.3d 1131 (Fed. Cir. 2004), the patentee rewrote a dependent claim into an independent claim and cancelled the original independent claim, which was rejected by the Examiner as obvious under section 103. In rejecting the independent claim (and the dependent claim because it was dependent on an obvious independent claim), the Examiner indicated that the dependent claim would be allowable if written in independent form. Importantly, the dependent claim contained an additional limitation not present in the original independent claim. The Federal Circuit held that this action constituted a narrowing of claim scope, and therefore, the *Festo* presumption applied. According to the court:

> The fact that the scope of the rewritten claim has remained unchanged will not preclude the application of prosecution history estoppel if, by canceling the original independent claim and rewriting the dependent claims into independent form, the scope of the subject matter claimed in the independent claim has been narrowed to secure the patent.

Id. at 1142.

4. *Defining and Refining Foreseeability.* The *Festo* saga had worked its way through the courts for 20 years, and has gone through—according to the Federal Circuit's count—13 rounds. In *Festo VIII*, the Supreme Court constructed the foreseeability test as a means of rebutting application of PHE. Defining foreseeability is, of course, quite challenging whether the subject is tort law or patent law. In *Festo XIII*, the Federal Circuit added resolution to this standard, and held that the DOE may be barred even if the function of the

equivalent was unforeseeable. A PHOSITA, according to the court, does not have to foresee that an equivalent would perform the same function, in the same way, to achieve the same result. While use of a non-magnetizeable aluminum alloy was known at the time of the patentee's amendment, the ability of the alloy to serve magnetic shielding function as set forth in the specification was unknown. As the court wrote, "[a]n equivalent is foreseeable if one skilled in the art would have known that the alternative existed in the field of art as defined by the original claim scope, even if the suitability of the alternative for the particular purposes defined by the amended claim scope were unknown."

In another *Festo* iteration, the Federal Circuit in *Festo IX*, decided immediately after the Supreme Court decision, emphasized the objective nature of the foreseeability inquiry:

> This criterion presents an objective inquiry, asking whether the alleged equivalent would have been unforeseeable to one of ordinary skill in the art at the time of the amendment. Usually, if the alleged equivalent represents later-developed technology (e.g., transistors in relation to vacuum tubes, or Velcro® in relation to fasteners) or technology that was not known in the relevant art, then it would not have been foreseeable. In contrast, old technology, while not always foreseeable, would more likely have been foreseeable. Indeed, if the alleged equivalent were known in the prior art in the field of the invention, it certainly should have been foreseeable at the time of the amendment. By its very nature, objective unforeseeability depends on underlying factual issues relating to, for example, the state of the art and the understanding of a hypothetical person of ordinary skill in the art at the time of the amendment. Therefore, in determining whether an alleged equivalent would have been unforeseeable, a district court may hear expert testimony and consider other extrinsic evidence relating to the relevant factual inquiries.

Festo IX, 344 F.3d at 1369. The 2007 *Festo* decision further refined the foreseeability component by holding that "[a]n equivalent is foreseeable if one skilled in the art would have known that the alternative existed in the field of art as defined by the original claim scope, even if the suitability of the alternative for the particular purposes defined by the amended claim scope were unknown." *Festo X*, 493 F.3d 1368, 1382 (Fed. Cir. 2007).

Foreseeability was at issue in *SmithKline Beecham Corp. v. Excel Pharaceuticals, Inc.*, 356 F.3d 1357 (Fed. Cir. 2004). In *SmithKline*, the patent related to an antidepressant, particularly "controlled sustained release tablets" containing bupropion hydrochloride, which were developed to avoid multiple dosages. The key ingredient for obtaining sustained release was hydroxypropyl methylcellulose (HPMC). But the claims in question did not originally recite HPMC. Rather, HPMC was added through a narrowing amendment in response to a section 112 enablement rejection. The accused product, made by Excel, did not literally infringe the patent because the accused product used polyvinyl alcohol or PVA (not HPMC) as its release agent. And Excel argued that the patentee is precluded from arguing that PVA is equivalent to HPMC because the patentee narrowed its claim to add HPMC. The patentee argued that it could not have claimed PVA because its patent disclosure only recited HPMC, and therefore, asserted (correctly) that there was no support in the specification as required by section 112 for PVA. The Federal Circuit rejected this argument because it did not fit into one of the three *Festo* exceptions. PVA was not an unforeseeable equivalent at the time of amendment, and the rationale underlying the amendment was germane to the equivalent in question—in other words, not tangentially related. As the court stated, "the Supreme Court in *Festo* neither excuses an applicant from failing to claim 'readily known equivalents' at the time of application nor allows a patentee to rebut the *Festo* presumption by invoking its own failure to include a known equivalent in its original disclosure." *Id.* at 1364. *See also Glaxo Wellcome, Inc. v. Impax Labs., Inc.*, 356 F.3d 1348 (Fed. Cir. 2004) (same); *Ranbaxy Pharm., Inc. v. Apotex, Inc.*, 350 F.3d 1235, 1241 (Fed. Cir. 2003) (holding that if an allegedly infringing product was readily known by those of skill in the art to be equivalent to the claim limitation, "it would have been foreseeable to literally include [it] in the claim").

5. ***Clarification and Elaboration.*** The Federal Circuit has clarified and added resolution to the Supreme Court's *Festo* decision.

   a.   ***Time of Amendment or Application.*** The timeframe for the foreseeability inquiry was identified by the Supreme Court—somewhat confusingly—as time of application and time of amendment. The Federal Circuit subsequently held the relevant time period for evaluating unforeseeability is time of amendment.

   b.   ***Retroactivity.*** The *Festo* presumption applies to extant patents and patents in litigation. *See Festo IX,* 344 F.3d at 1370 n.4 ("Consistent with Supreme Court precedent, the holdings of that Court and our own regarding the *Festo* presumption of surrender and its rebuttal apply to all granted patents and to all pending litigation that has not been concluded with a final judgment, including appeals").

6. ***Estoppel by Argument.*** Prosecution history estoppel can be invoked by arguments made during prosecution regardless of whether claim language is amended. *See Medtronic, Inc. v. Guidant Corp.,* 465 F.3d 1360, 1373 (Fed. Cir. 2006) ("A surrender can occur by argument as well as by amendment.").

7. ***The Tangential-Relation Principle.*** Another way to rebut the *Festo* presumption is to prove that the rationale underlying the narrowing amendment was "tangentially related to the equivalent in question"; that is, the amendment "was peripheral, or not directly relevant, to the alleged equivalent." *Festo IX,* 344 F.3d at 1369. This principle has been narrowly construed by the Federal Circuit. *See Cross Med. Prods., Inc. v. Medtronic Sofamor Danek, Inc.,* 480 F.3d 1335, 1342 (Fed. Cir. 2007).

8. **Festo *Loses on Remand.*** Ten years after the trial and Supreme Court intervention, District Court Judge Patti Saris, who wrote the original *Festo* opinion, held June 10, 2005 that SMC did not infringe Festo's '125 patent, thus reversing the originally jury verdict. The sole issue on remand was whether Festo could rebut the *Festo* presumption, something it was unable to do. The accused product did not have a single sealing ring and non-magnetizable sleeve, two elements, which, according to Judge Saris, were foreseeable to a person having ordinary skill in the art at the time the patent application were amended in November of 1981.

Festo – Warner-Jenkinson **Flow Chart**

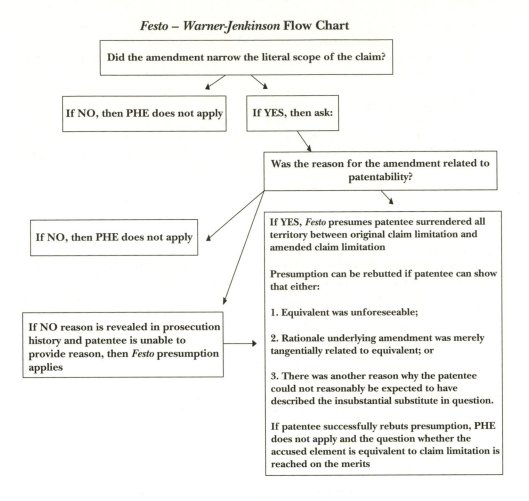

Did the amendment narrow the literal scope of the claim?

If NO, then PHE does not apply

If YES, then ask:

Was the reason for the amendment related to patentability?

If NO, then PHE does not apply

If YES, *Festo* presumes patentee surrendered all territory between original claim limitation and amended claim limitation

Presumption can be rebutted if patentee can show that either:

1. Equivalent was unforeseeable;

2. Rationale underlying amendment was merely tangentially related to equivalent; or

3. There was another reason why the patentee could not reasonably be expected to have described the insubstantial substitute in question.

If patentee successfully rebuts presumption, PHE does not apply and the question whether the accused element is equivalent to claim limitation is reached on the merits

If NO reason is revealed in prosecution history and patentee is unable to provide reason, then *Festo* presumption applies

---

POLICY PERSPECTIVE

Festo and the Devolution of Responsibility

The *Festo* decision can be viewed as re-focusing the temporal dimension of the patent game, what can be characterized as a devolution of responsibility. Although not expressly stating as much, the Court emphasized the decentralized nature of information, a central tenet of the Austrian school of economic thought. For instance, nearly 60 years ago, Friedrich Hayek wrote of the decentralized nature of knowledge, stating that "[t]he economic problem of society is . . . how to secure the best use of resources known to any of the members of society, for ends whose relative importance only these individuals know." Friedrich A. Hayek, *The Use of Knowledge in Society*, in INDIVIDUALISM AND ECONOMIC ORDER 78 (1948). For Hayek,

> [t]he peculiar character of the problem of a rational economic order is determined precisely by the fact that the knowledge of the circumstances of which we must make use never exists in concentrated or integrated form but solely as the dispersed bits of incomplete and frequently contradictory knowledge which all the separate individuals possess. Or, to put it briefly, it is a problem of the utilization of knowledge which is not given to anyone in its totality.

Id. at 77-78.

Hayek's insight is that the information about social wants and capabilities is naturally dispersed because it involves all of society. *See* Andrew P. Morriss & Susan E. Dudley, *Defining What to Regulate: Silica and the Problem of Regulatory Categorization*, 58 ADMIN. L. REV. 259, 281 (2006) (stating "Hayek's central point was that decentralized markets focus dispersed information—information that no one individual . . . can obtain—and convey it efficiently to market participants"); Maxwell L. Stearns, *Appellate Courts Inside and Out*, 101 MICH. L. REV. 1764, 1777 (2002) (noting "[o]ne major benefit of generating information as to value in this decentralized and uncoordinated manner is that countless subjective valuation measures—reflected in the individual transactions—produce an objective valuation that can be tested in the marketplace").

By emphasizing foreseeability, the *Festo* Court understood that the inventor—not the centralized PTO or the courts—is in the best position (and is the most highly motivated) to comprehend and understand the state of art and technologic trends relating to his claimed invention. The same point can be made regarding *Warner-Jenkinson's* presumption that the DOE is unavailable to a patentee who fails to provide a reason why he amended his claim. And it is the patentee who should bear the costs of a narrow claim scope. As the Federal Circuit noted in *Freedman Seating Co. v. Am. Seating Co.*, 420 F.3d 1350, 1361 (Fed. Cir. 2005), "as between the patentee who had a clear opportunity to negotiate broader claims but did not do so, and the public at large, it is the patentee who must bear the cost of its failure to seek protection for [a] foreseeable alteration of its claimed structure." *See also SmithKline Beecham Corp. v. Excel Pharaceuticals, Inc.*, 356 F.3d 1357, 1364 (Fed. Cir. 2004) (stating "the Supreme Court in *Festo* neither excuses an applicant from failing to claim 'readily known equivalents' at the time of application nor allows a patentee to rebut the *Festo* presumption by invoking its own failure to include a known equivalent in its original disclosure").

b. Disclosure-Dedication Rule

The "Disclosure-Dedication Rule" has its basis in the nineteenth-century Supreme Court case of *Miller v. Bridgeport Brass Co.*, cited by the *Graver* dissent. The *Miller* Court held that subject matter disclosed in the patent specification, but not claimed, is dedicated to the public.

JOHNSON & JOHNSTON ASSOCS., INC. v. R.E. SERVICE CO., INC.

285 F.3d 1046 (Fed. Cir. 2002) (*en banc*)

PER CURIAM.

Johnson and Johnston Associates (Johnston) asserted United States Patent No. 5,153,050 (the '050 patent) against R.E. Service Co. and Mark Frater (collectively RES). A jury found that RES willfully infringed claims 1 and 2 of the patent under the doctrine of equivalents and awarded Johnston $1,138,764 in damages. After a hearing before a three-judge panel on December 7, 1999, this court ordered *en banc* rehearing of the doctrine of equivalents issue. Because this court concludes that RES, as a matter of law, could not have infringed the '050 patent under the doctrine of equivalents, this court reverses the district court's judgment of infringement under the doctrine of equivalents, willfulness, damages, attorneys fees, and expenses.

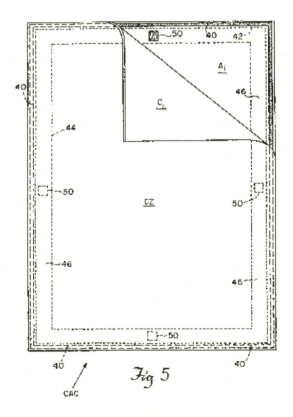

Fig. 5

I.

The '050 patent, which issued October 6, 1992, relates to the manufacture of printed circuit boards. Printed circuit boards are composed of extremely thin sheets of conductive copper foil joined to sheets of a dielectric (nonconductive) resin-impregnated material called "prepreg." The process for making multi-layered printed circuit boards stacks sheets of copper foil and prepreg in a press, heats them to melt the resin in the prepreg, and thereby bonds the layers.

In creating these circuit boards, workers manually handle the thin sheets of copper foil during the layering process. Without the invention claimed in the '050 patent, stacking by hand can damage or contaminate the fragile foil, causing discontinuities in the etched copper circuits. The '050 patent claims an assembly that prevents most damage during manual handling. The invention adheres the fragile copper foil to a stiffer substrate sheet of aluminum. With the aluminum substrate for protection, workers can handle the assembly without damaging the fragile copper foil. After the pressing and heating steps, workers can remove and even recycle the aluminum substrate. Figure 5 of the '050 patent shows the foil-substrate combination, with the foil layer peeled back at one corner for illustration:

Surface C_i is the protected inner surface of the copper foil; A_i is the inner surface of the aluminum substrate. A band of flexible adhesive 40 joins the substrate and the foil at the edges, creating a protected central zone CZ. The specification explains:

> Because the frail, thin copper foil C was adhesively secured to its aluminum substrate A, the [laminate] is stiffer and more readily handled resulting in far fewer spoils due to damaged copper foil. The use of the adhered substrate A, regardless of what material it is made of, makes the consumer's (manufacturer's) objective of using thinner and thinner foils and ultimately automating the procedure more realistic since the foil, by use of the invention, is no longer without the much needed physical support.

'050 patent, col. 8, ll. 21-30.

The specification further describes the composition of the substrate sheet:

> While aluminum is currently the preferred material for the substrate, other metals, such as stainless steel or nickel alloys, may be used. In some instances . . . polypropelene [sic] can be used.

'050 patent, col. 5, ll. 5-8.

As noted, the jury found infringement of claims 1 and 2:

> Claim 1. A component for use in manufacturing articles such as printed circuit boards comprising:
>
> > a laminate constructed of a sheet of copper foil which, in a finished printed circuit board, constitutes a functional element and a sheet of *aluminum* which constitutes a discardable element;
> >
> > one surface of each of the copper sheet and the *aluminum* sheet being essentially uncontaminated and engageable with each other at an interface;
> >
> a band of flexible adhesive joining the uncontaminated surfaces of the sheets together at their borders and defining a substantially uncontaminated central zone inwardly of the edges of the sheets and unjoined at the interface;

'050 patent, Claim 1, col. 8, ll. 47-60 (emphasis supplied). Claim 2 defines a similar laminate having sheets of copper foil adhered to both sides of the aluminum sheet.

* * *

In 1997, RES began making new laminates for manufacture of printed circuit boards. The RES products, designated "SC2" and "SC3," joined copper foil to a sheet of steel as the substrate instead of a sheet of aluminum. Johnston filed a suit for infringement. In this case, the district court granted RES's motion for summary judgment of no literal infringement. With respect to the doctrine of equivalents, RES argued, citing *Maxwell v. J. Baker, Inc.,* that the '050 specification, which disclosed a steel substrate but did not claim it, constituted a dedication of the steel substrate to the public. Johnston argued that the steel substrate was not dedicated to the public, citing *YBM Magnex, Inc. v. Int'l Trade Comm'n.* On cross-motions for summary judgment, the district court ruled that the '050 patent did not dedicate the steel substrate to the public, and set the question of infringement by equivalents for trial, along with the issues of damages and willful infringement.

* * *

II.

On appeal, RES does not challenge the jury's factual finding of equivalency between the copper-steel and copper-aluminum laminates. Instead, citing *Maxwell,* RES argues that Johnston did not claim steel substrates, but limited its patent scope to aluminum substrates, thus dedicating to the public this unclaimed subject matter. On this ground, RES challenges the district court's denial of its motion for summary judgment that RES's copper-steel laminates are not equivalent, as a matter of law, to the claimed copper-aluminum laminates. Johnston responds that the steel substrates are not dedicated to the public, citing *YBM Magnex.* In other words, the two parties dispute whether *Maxwell* or *YBM Magnex* applies in this case with regard to infringement under the doctrine of equivalents.

In *Maxwell,* the patent claimed a system for attaching together a mated pair of shoes. Maxwell claimed fastening tabs between the inner and outer soles of the attached shoes. Maxwell disclosed in the specification, but did not claim, fastening tabs that could be "stitched into a lining seam of the shoes." Based on the "well-established rule that 'subject matter disclosed but not claimed in a patent application is dedicated to the public,'" this court held that Baker could not, as a matter of law, infringe under the doctrine of equivalents by using the disclosed but unclaimed shoe attachment system. *Maxwell,* 86 F.3d at 1106 (quoting *Unique Concepts, Inc. v. Brown,* 939 F.2d 1558, 1562-63 (Fed. Cir. 1991)). This court stated further:

> By [Maxwell's failure] to claim these alternatives, the Patent and Trademark Office was deprived of the opportunity to consider whether these alternatives were patentable. A person of ordinary skill in the shoe industry, reading the specification and prosecution history, and interpreting the claims, would conclude that Maxwell, by failing to claim the alternate shoe attachment systems in which the tabs were attached to the inside shoe lining, dedicated the use of such systems to the public.

Maxwell, 86 F.3d at 1108.

In *YBM Magnex,* the patent claimed a permanent magnet alloy comprising certain elements, including "6,000 to 35,000 ppm oxygen." The accused infringer used similar magnet alloys with an oxygen content between 5,450 and 6,000 ppm (parts per million), which was allegedly disclosed but not claimed in the '439 patent. In *YBM Magnex,* this court stated that *Maxwell* did not create a new rule of law that doctrine of equivalents could never encompass subject matter disclosed in the specification but not claimed. Distinguishing *Maxwell,* this court noted:

> Maxwell avoided examination of the unclaimed alternative, which was distinct from the claimed alternative. In view of the distinctness of the two embodiments, both of which were fully described in the specification, the Federal Circuit denied Maxwell the opportunity to enforce the unclaimed embodiment as an equivalent of the one that was claimed.

145 F.3d at 1320. In other words, this court in *YBM Magnex* purported to limit *Maxwell* to situations where a patent discloses an unclaimed alternative distinct from the claimed invention. Thus, this court must decide whether a patentee can apply the doctrine of equivalents to cover unclaimed subject matter disclosed in the specification.

III.

Both the Supreme Court and this court have adhered to the fundamental principle that claims define the scope of patent protection. *See, e.g., Aro Mfg. v. Convertible Top Replacement Co.,* 365 U.S. 336, 339 (1961) ("[T]he claims made in the patent are the sole measure of the grant. . . . "); *Atl. Thermoplastics Co. v. Faytex Corp.,* 974 F.2d 1299, 1300 (Fed. Cir. 1992) ("The claims alone define the patent right"). The claims give notice both to the examiner at the U.S. Patent and Trademark Office during prosecution, and to the public at large, including potential competitors, after the patent has issued. Consistent with its scope definition and notice functions, the claim requirement presupposes that a patent applicant defines his invention in the claims, not in the specification. After all, the claims, not the specification, provide the measure of the patentee's right to exclude. Moreover, the law of infringement compares the accused product with the claims as construed by the court. Infringement, either literally or under the doctrine of equivalents, does not arise by comparing the accused product "with a preferred embodiment described in the specification, or with a commercialized embodiment of the patentee." *SRI Int'l,* 775 F.2d at 1121.

Even as early as the 1880s, the Supreme Court emphasized the predominant role of claims. For example, in *Miller v. Bridgeport Brass Co.,* a case addressing a reissue patent filed fifteen years after the original patent, the Supreme Court broadly stated: "[T]he claim of a specific device or combination, and an omission to claim other devices or combinations apparent on the face of the patent, are, in law, a dedication to the public of that which is not claimed." 104 U.S. 350, 352 (1881). Just a few years later, the Court repeated that sentiment in another reissue patent case: "[T]he claim actually made operates in law as a disclaimer of what is not claimed; and of all this the law charges the patentee with the fullest notice." *Mahn,* 112 U.S. at 361. The Court explained further:

> Of course, what is not claimed is public property. The presumption is, and such is generally the fact, that what is not claimed was not invented by the patentee, but

was known and used before he made his invention. But, whether so or not, his own act has made it public property if it was not so before. The patent itself, as soon as it is issued, is the evidence of this. The public has the undoubted right to use, and it is to be presumed does use, what is not specifically claimed in the patent.

Id. at 361.

The doctrine of equivalents extends the right to exclude beyond the literal scope of the claims. The Supreme Court first applied the modern doctrine of equivalents in *Graver Tank & Mfg. Co. v. Linde Air Prods. Co.* (*Graver Tank II*). In that case, the Court explained: "equivalency must be determined against the context of the patent, the prior art, and the particular circumstances of the case." 339 U.S. 605, 609 (1950). In *Graver I*, a predecessor case addressing the validity of the claims at issue, the Court held invalid composition claims 24 and 26 comprising "silicates" and "metallic silicates." *Graver Tank & Mfg. v. Linde Air Prods. Co.*, 336 U.S. 271, 276-77 (1949) (*Graver I*). Specifically, the Court found those claims too broad because they encompassed some inoperative silicates along with the nine operative metallic silicates in the specification. The Court did not hold invalid narrower claims comprising "alkaline earth metals."

Thus, in the infringement action of *Graver II*, the Supreme Court addressed only the narrower claims comprising "alkaline earth metals." The alleged infringing compositions in *Graver II* are similar to the compositions of the narrower claims, except that they substitute silicate of manganese—a metallic silicate such as in the earlier invalidated claims—for silicates of "alkaline earth metals" (*e.g.*, magnesium or calcium) claimed in the narrower claims. Because the Court determined that "under the circumstances the change was so insubstantial," and because the accused compositions "perform[ed] substantially the same function in substantially the same way to obtain the same result," the Court upheld the finding of infringement under the doctrine of equivalents. *Graver II*. The Court's holding and the history of *Graver II* show that the patentee had not dedicated unclaimed subject matter to the public. In fact, the patentee had claimed the "equivalent" subject matter, even if the Court eventually held the relevant claims too broad.

In 1997, less than a year after this court decided *Maxwell*, the Supreme Court addressed the doctrine of equivalents again in *Warner-Jenkinson v. Hilton Davis*. In that case, Warner-Jenkinson invited the Court "to speak the death" of the doctrine of equivalents. 520 U.S. at 21. The Court declined that invitation. In *Warner-Jenkinson*, the patentee added the phrase "at a pH from approximately 6.0 to 9.0" to claim 1 during prosecution. The alleged infringer operated its ultrafiltration process at a pH of 5.0. The Supreme Court stated that "while a lower limit of [pH] 6.0, by its mere inclusion, became a material element of the claim, that did not necessarily preclude the application of the doctrine of equivalents as to that element." *Id.* at 32. On remand, the Supreme Court instructed this court to determine the patentee's reason, if any, for adding the lower pH limit of 6.0 during prosecution.

The patent at issue in *Warner-Jenkinson* did not disclose or suggest an ultrafiltration process where the pH of the reaction mixture was 5.0. In fact, the specification practically repeated the claim language: "it is preferred to adjust the *pH to approximately 6.0 to 8.0* before passage through the ultrafiltration membrane." U.S. Patent No. 4,560,746, col. 7, ll. 59-61 (emphasis added). Thus, *Warner-Jenkinson* did not present an instance of the patentee dedicating subject matter to the public in its specification. In 1998, less than a year later, this court decided *YBM Magnex*.

IV.

As stated in *Maxwell*, when a patent drafter discloses but declines to claim subject matter, as in this case, this action dedicates that unclaimed subject matter to the public. Application of the doctrine of equivalents to recapture subject matter deliberately left unclaimed would "conflict with the primacy of the claims in defining the scope of the patentee's exclusive right." *Sage Prods. Inc. v. Devon Indus., Inc.*, 126 F.3d 1420, 1424 (Fed. Cir. 1997) (citing *Warner-Jenkinson*, 520 U.S. at 29).

Moreover, a patentee cannot narrowly claim an invention to avoid prosecution scrutiny by the PTO, and then, after patent issuance, use the doctrine of equivalents to establish infringement because the specification discloses equivalents. "Such a result would merely encourage a patent applicant to present a broad disclosure in the specification of the application and file narrow claims, avoiding examination of broader claims that the applicant could have filed consistent with the specification." *Maxwell*, 86 F.3d at 1107 (citing *Genentech, Inc. v. Wellcome Found. Ltd.*, 29 F.3d 1555, 1564 (Fed. Cir. 1994)). By enforcing the *Maxwell* rule, the courts avoid the problem of extending the coverage of an exclusive right to encompass more than that properly examined by the PTO. *Keystone Bridge Co. v. Phoenix Iron Co.*, 95 U.S. 274, 278 (1877) ("[T]he courts have no right to enlarge a patent beyond the scope of its claim as allowed by the Patent Office, or the appellate tribunal to which contested applications are referred.").

V.

In this case, Johnston's '050 patent specifically limited the claims to "a sheet of aluminum" and "the aluminum sheet." The specification of the '050 patent, however, reads: "While aluminum is currently the preferred material for the substrate, other metals, such as stainless steel or nickel alloys may be used." Col. 5, ll. 5-10. Having disclosed without claiming the steel substrates, Johnston cannot now invoke the doctrine of equivalents to extend its aluminum limitation to encompass steel. Thus, Johnston cannot assert the doctrine of equivalents to cover the disclosed but unclaimed steel substrate. To the extent that *YBM Magnex* conflicts with this holding, this *en banc* court now overrules that case.

A patentee who inadvertently fails to claim disclosed subject matter, however, is not left without remedy. Within two years from the grant of the original patent, a patentee may file a reissue application and attempt to enlarge the scope of the original claims to include the disclosed but previously unclaimed subject matter. 35 U.S.C. §251 (2000). In addition, a patentee can file a separate application claiming the disclosed subject matter under 35 U.S.C. §120 (2000) (allowing filing as a continuation application if filed before all applications in the chain issue). Notably, Johnston took advantage of the latter of the two options by filing two continuation applications that literally claim the relevant subject matter.

PAULINE NEWMAN, Circuit Judge, dissenting.

Patentees often must draw lines in order to claim their invention with specificity. *See* 35 U.S.C. §112 (the claims must "particularly point[] out and distinctly claim[] the subject matter which the applicant regards as his invention.") The establishment of a *per se* rule so heavily weighted against disclosure is not only inappropriately simplistic, but is contrary to the policy of the patent law.

* * *

The public interest in fostering innovation and technological advance is not served by a judicial decision that imposes legal obstacles to the disclosure of scientific and technologic information. Information dissemination is a critical purpose of the patent system. By penalizing the inclusion of information in the specification the patent becomes less useful as a source of knowledge, and more a guarded legal contract.

No patentee deliberately chooses the doctrine of equivalents to protect commercial investment. Yet every patentee must guard against infringement at the edges of the invention. After today, whenever a patentee draws a line in a disclosed continuum, the copier who simply crosses the line can avoid even the charge of equivalency; a safe and cheap way to garner the successes of another. Each new pitfall for inventors simply diminishes the value of the patent incentive, and ultimately inhibits technological innovation. Concern for the effectiveness of the patent system has always been a factor in innovation activity. A study by Wesley M. Cohen et al., *Protecting Their Intellectual Assets: Appropriability Conditions and Why U.S. Manufacturing Firms Patent (Or Not)*, Nat'l Bureau of Econ. Research Working Paper 7552, at 14 (2000), reported that in a 1994 survey of R & D managers 65% of the respondents cited the ease of avoiding patent claims as the main deterrent to patent-based investment in technology, and 47% also cited concern for disclosing technical information without adequate protection.

Discovery of and commercialization of new things is notoriously risk-laden, yet it is the inventor and the innovator, those whose ingenuity and ambition create new things while taking the risk of loss, who provide the basis of industrial advance and economic growth.

* * *

A judicial change in the balance between innovator and imitator should not be made in disregard of the consequences. The neatness of a *per se* rule is not necessarily sound legal or economic policy. Nor is it sound judicial policy, for in addition to issues of commerce and technology-based industry, this case raises questions of fundamental fairness as to disputes that will now be excluded from judicial review. Fairness is the foundation of due process; it is superior to, not subordinate to, *per se* rules.

Comments

1. *Sufficiency of the Disclosure.* How specific must the disclosure be to dedicate subject matter to the public? Does the disclosure have to be enabling or simply mention the equivalent? The Federal Circuit addressed these questions in *PSC Computer Products, Inc. v. Foxconn Int'l, Inc.*, 355 F.3d 1353 (Fed. Cir. 2004). According to the court, a mere "generic reference in a written specification" does not "necessarily dedicate[] all members of that particular

genus to the public." *Id.* at 1360. Rather, for subject matter to be dedicated to the public, a PHOSITA must be able to "understand the unclaimed disclosed teaching upon reading the written description." The court also added that the "disclosure must be of such specificity that one of ordinary skill in the art could identify the subject matter that had been disclosed and not claimed," but this standard "does not impose a §112 [enablement] requirement on the disclosed but unclaimed subject matter." *Toro Co. v. White Consolidated Industries, Inc.*, 383 F.3d 1326 (Fed. Cir. 2004).

In *Pfizer, Inc. v. Teva Pharmaceuticals, USA, Inc.*, 429 F.3d 1364, 1379 (Fed. Cir. 2005), the Federal Circuit seems to have required more express language to invoke the public dedication rule, stating that "in *PSC Computer Products* the driving force behind the court's holding was the public notice function of patents. And in our view, the public notice function of patents suggests that before unclaimed subject matter is deemed to have been dedicated to the public, that unclaimed subject matter must have been identified by the patentee as an alternative to a claim limitation."

2. ***Distinguishing* Graver.** In *Johnston* and *Maxwell*, the court tried to distinguish *Graver Tank*. Recall in *Graver*, manganese silicate was set forth in the specification and the patent claimed manganese silicates (the broad claim) and also claimed alkaline earth silicates, of which manganese was not a part (the narrow claim). Unlike the narrow claim, which was valid and infringed, the broad claim was invalidated as too broad. So why weren't manganese silicates dedicated to the public according to *Johnston* and *Maxwell*? Because manganese silicates were originally claimed. The fact that this claim was later invalidated is irrelevant.

3. ***The Revenge of Justice Black's* Graver Dissent.** The public dedication rule is reminiscent of Justice Black's dissent in *Graver*. Recall Justice Black's statement, "[w]hat is not specifically claimed is dedicated to the public." 339 U.S. at 614. Compare the language in *Johnston*, "when a patent drafter discloses but declines to claim subject matter, as in this case, this action dedicates that unclaimed subject matter to the public." 285 F.3d at 1054. In addition, Justice Black highlighted the availability of reissue for patentees "who had for some reason failed to claim complete protection for their discoveries." 339 U.S. at 614. Similarly, in *Johnston*, the court wrote, "[a] patentee who inadvertently fails to claim disclosed subject matter . . . is not left without remedy" because "[w]ithin two years from the grant of the original patent, a patentee may file a reissue application and attempt to enlarge the scope of the original claims to include the disclosed but previously unclaimed subject matter." 285 F.3d at 1055.

4. ***Beyond* Warner-Jenkinson.** In *Warner-Jenkinson*, the Court rejected Petitioner's argument that the DOE should be "limited to equivalents that are disclosed within the patent itself." The public dedication rule, however, holds unclaimed subject matter disclosed in the specification is surrendered to the public, as long as the language in the specification satisfies *PSC* and *Pfizer* (see Comment 1, above). Is the public dedication rule inconsistent with *Warner-Jenkinson*? The rule is consistent with *Festo* because disclosed, yet unclaimed subject matter is foreseeable.

5. ***Public Dedication in English Common Law.*** Prior to the European Patent Convention of 1977, English common law principles placed a great deal of emphasis on the patent claim, and embraced what can be characterized as

a "public dedication rule." For instance, Lord Russell in *Electric and Musical Industries Ltd. v. Lissen Ltd.* (1938) 56 RPC 23, 29, wrote of patent claims:

> Their primary object is to limit and not to extend the monopoly. What is not claimed is disclaimed. The claims must undoubtedly be read as part of the entire document and not as a separate document; but the forbidden field must be found in the language of the claims and not elsewhere.

c. All-Limitations Rule and Specific Exclusion

The *all-limitations rule* demands that each limitation of a patent claim is material to defining the scope of the patented invention and must not be vitiated or rendered meaningless. For there to be infringement under the DOE an equivalent of each claim limitation must be found in the accused device. In other words, the DOE is applied to each limitation, not to the invention as a whole. The *specific exclusion rule*, which is a corollary to the all-limitations rule, holds that the DOE is unavailable to capture subject matter that the claim specifically excludes. The reasoning behind this rule is that by defining a claim in a way that specially excludes certain subject matter, the patentee implicitly disclaimed the subject matter and is therefore prevented from invoking the DOE. The principal case of *SciMed Life Systems* provides a discussion of these two related principles.

SCIMED LIFE SYSTEMS, INC. v. ADVANCED CARDIOVASCULAR SYSTEMS, INC.

242 F.3d 1337 (Fed. Cir. 2001)

BRYSON, Circuit Judge.

SciMed Life Systems, Inc. (SciMed) owns three U.S. patents drawn to features of balloon dilatation catheters: U.S. Patent Nos. 5,156,594 (the '594 patent), 5,217,482 (the '482 patent), and 5,395,334 (the '334 patent). SciMed filed suit against Advanced Cardiovascular Systems, Inc. (ACS) in the United States District Court for the Northern District of California, charging ACS with infringement of each of the three patents. On ACS's motion for summary judgment, the district court ruled that ACS had not infringed the disputed patents. The district court's ruling was based on the court's conclusion that the asserted claims were limited to a structure not found in ACS's accused devices and on the court's conclusion that ACS's devices did not infringe SciMed's patents under the doctrine of equivalents. We agree with the district court's claim construction and its ruling on the equivalents issue. We therefore affirm the summary judgment of non-infringement.

I

Balloon dilatation catheters are used in coronary angioplasty procedures to remove restrictions in coronary arteries. The SciMed patents describe catheters having three sections: a first shaft section, a second shaft section, and a transition section between the two. The first shaft section is long, relatively stiff, and generally tubular. The second shaft section is relatively flexible and contains a balloon at the end, which is inflated to relieve the arterial restriction. The transition section connects the first and second shaft sections and provides a gradual transition in stiffness between the two shaft sections.

The catheters claimed in the SciMed patents contain two passageways, or lumens. The first lumen, the guide-wire lumen, is used to guide the catheter through a patient's arteries to the site of the arterial restriction. A guide wire is first inserted into one of the patient's arteries. The guide-wire lumen is then threaded over the guide wire to guide the catheter through the patient's arteries until the catheter reaches the coronary restriction. In the invention recited in the SciMed patents, the guide wire does not enter the catheter at the proximal end of the catheter, *i.e.*, the end closer to the surgeon, but at a point nearer to the distal end of the catheter, *i.e.*, the leading end of the catheter as it is inserted into the patient. The guide-wire lumen is present only in the distal portion of the catheter and does not extend the entire length of the catheter. The second lumen is the inflation lumen. It extends through all sections of the catheter and terminates in a connection with the balloon. The balloon is inflated by forcing fluid into the inflation lumen. The balloon then compresses the material restricting the artery, thereby relieving the restriction.

The parties agree that only two arrangements of the two lumens are known and practiced in the art. In the dual (or adjacent) lumen configuration, the two lumens are positioned side-by-side within the catheter. In the coaxial lumen configuration, the guide wire lumen runs inside the inflation lumen; in that configuration the inflation lumen, viewed in cross-section, is annular in shape. The parties also agree that the accused ACS devices employ only the dual lumen configuration and that the preferred embodiment described in the SciMed patents employs the coaxial lumen configuration.

Based on language in the common written description portion of the three SciMed patents, the district court construed the asserted claims of the patents to be limited to catheters with coaxial lumens, and not to read on catheters with a dual lumen configuration. The court noted that "the language contained in SciMed's specifications *expressly* limits all embodiments of the claimed invention to a coaxial structure." The court focused in particular on language from the common specification describing the coaxial lumen structure as the "basic sleeve structure for all embodiments of the present invention contemplated and disclosed herein." That language, the court concluded, "leaves no doubt that a person skilled in the art would conclude that the inventor envisioned only one design for the catheters taught in SciMed's patents—an intermediate sleeve section containing two . . . lumens arranged coaxially."

In light of the district court's construction of the asserted claims, SciMed conceded that ACS's accused catheters did not literally infringe any of the asserted claims. In addition, the court held on summary judgment that the two lumen arrangements were sufficiently different that no reasonable jury could find the accused catheters to infringe the SciMed patents under the doctrine of equivalents. SciMed appeals the claim construction and the summary judgment based on that construction.

II

The principal question in this case is a narrow one: whether the common specification of the three patents limits the scope of the asserted claims to catheters with coaxial lumens. There is nothing pertinent to this issue in the prosecution history of the three patents; the case turns entirely on an interpretation of the asserted claims in light of the specification, which is essentially identical for each of the three patents. Like the district court, we interpret the specification to disclaim the dual lumen configuration and to limit the scope of the asserted claims to catheters with coaxial lumen structures having annular inflation lumens. We therefore construe the asserted claims to read only on catheters with coaxial lumens, and not on catheters with dual or side-by-side lumens.

Claim 19 of the '594 patent is representative of the asserted claims of the three patents in suit. It claims the following:

> In an elongate dilatation catheter of the type that can be slidably moved along a guide wire that can extend past a distal end of the catheter, wherein the guide wire is received in a guide wire lumen of the catheter, the guide wire extending from a distal guide wire lumen opening to a proximal guide wire lumen opening disposed in a portion of the catheter that is spaced distally from a proximal end of the catheter, the dilatation catheter including an inflatable balloon and an inflation lumen extending through the catheter separate from the guide wire lumen, an improvement comprising:
>
>> a first proximal shaft section of the catheter defined by a relatively rigid metallic tube;
>>
>> a second shaft section disposed distally of the first shaft section, the second shaft section being relatively more flexible than the first shaft section; and
>>
>> a transition section disposed between the first shaft section and the second shaft section, the transition section including a transition member comprising a metallic element of gradually diminished dimension, the transition member extending adjacent to the proximal guide wire lumen opening, and the transition member having gradually decreasing rigidity in the distal direction to provide a relatively smooth transition between the first shaft section and the second shaft section.

SciMed argues at length that in construing the claims based on the written description, the district court has committed one of the cardinal sins of patent law — reading a limitation from the written description into the claims. But that is not an accurate characterization of what the district court did. Instead, the district court properly followed the invocation that "[c]laims must be read in view of the specification, of which they are a part." *Markman v. Westview Instruments,* 52 F.3d 967, 979-980 (Fed. Cir. 1995).

As this court has recently explained, "[o]ne purpose for examining the specification is to determine if the patentee has limited the scope of the claims." *Watts v. XL Sys., Inc.,* 232 F.3d 877, 882 (Fed. Cir. 2000). Where the specification makes clear that the invention does not include a particular feature, that feature is deemed to be outside the reach of the claims of the patent, even though the language of the claims, read without reference to the specification, might be considered broad enough to encompass the feature in question. Thus, in the *Watts* case, the claim in dispute recited pipe joints that could be "sealingly connected." The court noted that the specification described only one method to achieve the sealing connection, that is, to misalign the taper angles of the respective threads of the joined pipes. The court pointed out that the specification "actually limits the invention to structures that utilize misaligned taper angles, stating that 'the present invention utilizes [the varying taper angle] feature.'" 232 F.3d at 883. In light of that statement, the court construed the claim language as "limited to connections effected by misaligned taper angles. . . ."

Finally, we find instructive the analysis in *Toro Co. v. White Consolidated Industries, Inc.,* 199 F.3d 1295 (Fed. Cir. 1999). The patent at issue described and claimed a hand-held convertible vacuum-blower for vacuuming and blowing leaves and yard debris. In the claimed device, the cover was fitted with a ring that restricted the size of the air inlet when the device was being used in blower mode. One of the questions before the court was whether the cover, which the claim characterized as "including" a restriction ring, had to be permanently attached to the restriction ring. To answer that question the court looked to the specification. The court observed that the specification and drawings showed the ring as part of and permanently attached to the cover, and did not illustrate or describe any other structure. Indeed, the court pointed out, the specification described the advantages of the unitary structure as important to the invention. Based on the specification, the court construed the term "including" in the asserted claims as requiring that the restriction ring be attached to the cover.

The analysis in these cases is directly applicable to the claim construction issue presented here. At various points, the common specification of the three patents indicates that the claimed invention uses coaxial, rather than side-by-side lumens, *i.e.*, that the guide wire lumen is contained within the inflation lumen and that the inflation lumen is annular. Read together, these portions of the common specification lead to the inescapable conclusion that the references in the asserted claims to an inflation lumen "separate from" the guide wire lumen must be understood as referring to coaxial lumens, and thus that the asserted claims read only on catheters having coaxial lumens.

First, the abstract of each of the patents refers to the intermediate sleeve section of the invention as including "an inner core tube which defines a guide wire lumen." The abstract adds that the inflation lumen is "continued as an annular inflation lumen" through the sleeve section of the catheter. Thus, from the outset the specification identifies the inflation lumen, as that term is used in the SciMed patents, as annular, *i.e.*, coaxial rather than dual in structure.

Second, in discussing the disadvantages of certain prior art structures, the written description of each of the patents explains that the prior art catheters with shortened guide wire lumens "suffer from several disadvantages." The first cited disadvantage is that "[s]uch catheters have been one piece polyethylene catheters having dual lumen configurations adjacent their distal regions. Typically, such catheters have larger than necessary shaft sizes and are stiffer in their distal regions than would be desired. . . ." Thus, the SciMed patents distinguish the prior art on the basis of the use of dual lumens and point out the advantages of the coaxial lumens used in the catheters that are the subjects of the SciMed patents. That discussion in the written description supports the district court's conclusion that the claims should not be read so broadly as to encompass the distinguished prior art structure.

Third, the "Summary of the Invention" portion of the patents describes "the present invention" as having a sleeve section with an inner core tube [80 in Fig. 3 below] having a guide wire lumen [52 in Fig. 3] extending through it and an outer sleeve [82 in Fig. 3] defining "a longitudinally extending annular inflation lumen." The characterization of the "present invention" includes several more references to the "annular inflation lumen" as well, and the "Conclusion" section of the written description again refers to the "guide wire lumen and annular inflation lumen" in the distal portions of the catheter. As in *Wang Labs*, the characterization of the coaxial configuration as part of the "present invention" is strong evidence that the claims should not be read to encompass the opposite structure.

The most compelling portion of the specification, and the portion on which the district court principally focused, is the passage in the section entitled "Catheter Intermediate Sleeve Section" in which the inflation lumen is described as annular in structure, being formed from an outer sleeve or tube (the inflation lumen) and an inner core tube (the guide wire lumen). The patents then recite:

> The intermediate sleeve structure defined above is the basic sleeve structure for *all embodiments of the present invention contemplated and disclosed herein*—namely, an inner core tube [80] bonded to a distal portion of the main catheter shaft, with an outer sleeve [82] forming an annular continuation of the inflation lumen through the main shaft between the core tube and outer sleeve. As discussed below and illustrated herein, various configurations of the connections and components relative to the formation of the distal guide wire lumen, including the coupling of the main shaft to the intermediate sleeve section, are contemplated.

(emphasis added).

This language defines SciMed's invention in a way that excludes the dual, or side-by-side, lumen arrangement. SciMed argues that the references to the

U.S. Patent   Oct. 20, 1992   Sheet 3 of 6   5,156,594

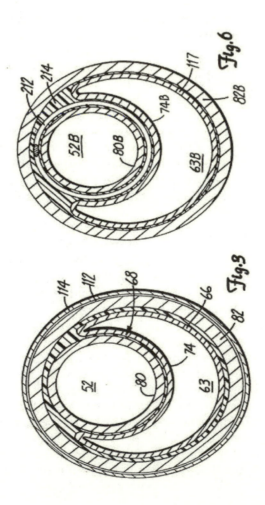

annular inflation lumen are meant only to refer to the preferred embodiment of the invention, and not to indicate that the claims should be construed as limited to a structure employing coaxial lumens. That argument, however, flies in the face of the many statements in the written description that define "the invention" as employing a coaxial lumen structure and distinguish the prior art in part on the ground that it used a dual lumen structure, which had the disadvantage of making the shaft sizes of the catheters larger than necessary and making the catheters "stiffer in their distal regions than would be desired." SciMed's argument is particularly unconvincing in the face of its own statement in the written description that the structure containing coaxial lumens ("namely, an inner core tube bonded to a distal portion of the main catheter shaft, with an outer sleeve forming an annular continuation of the inflation lumen through the main shaft between the core tube and the outer sleeve") is "the basic sleeve structure for all embodiments of the present invention contemplated and disclosed herein." That characterization of the invention cannot reasonably be interpreted as limited to the preferred embodiment, as SciMed argues, but is expressly made applicable to "all embodiments of the present invention."

The words "all embodiments of the present invention" are broad and unequivocal. It is difficult to imagine how the patents could have been clearer in making the point that the coaxial lumen configuration was a necessary element of every variant of the claimed invention. Moreover, there is no suggestion that the patentee made that statement unaware of the alternative dual lumen configuration, because earlier in the patent the patentee had distinguished the dual lumen configuration used in prior art devices as having disadvantages that the coaxial lumens used in the patented invention had overcome. This is therefore a clear case of disclaimer of subject matter that, absent the disclaimer, could have been considered to fall within the scope of the claim language.

. . . In this case, the written description makes clear that when the asserted claims refer to the respective locations of the guide wire and inflation lumens, and in particular when the claims refer to the inflation lumen as "extending through the catheter separate from" the guide wire lumen, the claim language refers to coaxial lumens. Because the three SciMed patents make clear that the lumens referred to in the claims are all coaxial in structure, the district court was correct to construe the patents as disclaiming the dual lumen configuration. Under such a construction, SciMed concedes that no literal infringement can be found. The district court therefore properly entered summary judgment in favor of ACS on the issue of literal infringement.

III

[T]he district court rejected SciMed's argument that ACS's accused devices infringed the three asserted patents under the doctrine of equivalents. We agree with the court that the doctrine of equivalents is inapplicable in this case and that the district court properly granted summary judgment to ACS on that issue.

As noted above, the common specification of SciMed's patents referred to prior art catheters, identified them as using the dual lumen configuration, and criticized them as suffering from the disadvantages of having "larger than necessary shaft sizes" and being "stiffer in their distal regions than would be desired." That criticism of the dual lumen configuration was consistent with the evidence from SciMed witnesses and documents, which noted the advantages of the coaxial lumen configuration in increasing the flexibility of catheters and their ability to track through the coronary arterial system. The disclaimer of dual lumens was made even more explicit in the portion of the written description in which the patentee identified coaxial lumens as the configuration used in "all embodiments of the present invention."

Having specifically identified, criticized, and disclaimed the dual lumen configuration, the patentee cannot now invoke the doctrine of equivalents to "embrace a structure that was specifically excluded from the claims." *Dolly, Inc. v. Spalding & Evenflo Cos.*, 16 F.3d 394, 400 (Fed. Cir. 1994). A particular structure can be deemed outside the reach of the doctrine of equivalents because that structure is clearly excluded from the claims whether the exclusion is express or implied. In *Moore, U.S.A., Inc. v. Standard Register Co.*, 229 F.3d 1091 (Fed. Cir. 2000), for example, the court considered a claim to a mailer-type business form in which the longitudinal strips of adhesive extend "the majority of the lengths" of the longitudinal margins of the form. The patentee argued that the accused form, in which the longitudinal strips of adhesive extended a minority of the length of the longitudinal margin of the form, infringed under the doctrine of equivalents. The court rejected the argument, holding that "it would defy logic to conclude that a minority—the very antithesis of a majority—could be insubstantially different from a claim limitation requiring a majority, and no reasonable juror could find otherwise." 229 F.3d at 1106. Similarly, in *Eastman Kodak Co. v. Goodyear Tire & Rubber Co.*, 114 F.3d 1547 (Fed. Cir. 1997), the patent claimed a process that included crystallizing a particular substance at high temperature "under an inert gas atmosphere." The patentee argued that certain of the accused processes, which used "heated air" rather than "an inert gas atmosphere" infringed under the doctrine of equivalents. The court rejected that argument, explaining that "the claim language specifically excludes reactive gases—such as 'heated air'—from the scope of the claims" and in light of that specific exclusion, the accused processes could not infringe under the doctrine of equivalents. 114 F.3d at 1561. In each of these cases, by defining the claim in a way that clearly excluded certain subject matter, the patent implicitly disclaimed the subject matter that was excluded and thereby barred the patentee from asserting infringement under the doctrine of equivalents.

The court did effectively the same thing in *Sage Products, Inc. v. Devon Industries, Inc.*, 126 F.3d 1420 (Fed. Cir. 1997). In that case, the claim was to a syringe disposal container having an elongated slot at the top of the container body and a "first constriction extending over said slot." Although those limitations did not literally read on the accused device, the patentee argued that the device infringed under the doctrine of equivalents. The court rejected that argument, noting that the claim

> defines a relatively simple structural device. No subtlety of language or complexity of the technology, nor any subsequent change in the state of the art, such as later-developed technology, obfuscated the significance of this limitation at the time of its incorporation into the claim. . . . If Sage desired broad patent protection for any container that performed a function similar to its claimed container, it could

have sought claims with fewer structural encumbrances. . . . [A]s between the patentee who had a clear opportunity to negotiate broader claims but did not do so, and the public at large, it is the patentee who must bear the cost of its failure to seek protection for this foreseeable alteration of its claimed structure.

126 F.3d at 1425. Thus, the court determined that because the scope of the claim was limited in a way that plainly and necessarily excluded a structural feature that was the opposite of the one recited in the claim, that different structure could not be brought within the scope of patent protection through the doctrine of equivalents.

The principle articulated in these cases is akin to the familiar rule that the doctrine of equivalents cannot be employed in a manner that wholly vitiates a claim limitation. *See Warner-Jenkinson Co. v. Hilton Davis Chem. Co.*, 520 U.S. 17, 29-30 (1997). Thus, if a patent states that the claimed device must be "non-metallic," the patentee cannot assert the patent against a metallic device on the ground that a metallic device is equivalent to a non-metallic device. The unavailability of the doctrine of equivalents could be explained either as the product of an impermissible vitiation of the "non-metallic" claim limitation, or as the product of a clear and binding statement to the public that metallic structures are excluded from the protection of the patent. As the court made clear in *Sage*, the foreclosure of reliance on the doctrine of equivalents in such a case depends on whether the patent clearly excludes the asserted equivalent structure, either implicitly or explicitly.

Each of the SciMed patents specifically recognized and disclaimed the dual lumen structure, making clear that the patentee regarded the dual lumen configuration as significantly inferior to the coaxial lumen configuration used in the invention. Where such an explicit disclaimer is present, the principles of those cases apply *a fortiori*, and the patentee cannot be allowed to recapture the excluded subject matter under the doctrine of equivalents without undermining the notice function of the patent. As the court observed in *Sage*, the patentee had an opportunity to draft the patent in a way that would make clear that dual lumens as well as coaxial lumens were within the scope of the invention, but the patentee did just the opposite, leaving competitors and the public to draw the reasonable conclusion that the patentee was not seeking patent protection for catheters that used a dual lumen configuration. Under these circumstances, the district court was justified in concluding that a reasonable jury could not find that the accused devices infringe the SciMed patents under the doctrine of equivalents.

Comments

1. *The Specific-Exclusion Rule.* Specific-exclusion is very similar to the vitiation principle. A recent example can be found in *Cook Biotech Inc. v. ACell, Inc.*, 460 F.3d 1365 (Fed. Cir. 2006). In *Cook*, the patentee claimed "[a] composition comprising *urinary bladder submucosa* delaminated from both the abluminal muscle layers and at least the luminal portion of the tunica mucosa of a segment of a urinary bladder of a warm blooded vertebrate." The accused infringer, ACell, argued that the "all limitations rule" bars the capture of equivalents specifically excluded by the claims at issue. Specifically, because

the patent claims a composition comprising urinary bladder submucosa, and such submucosa must have been delaminated from "the luminal portion of the tunica mucosa," an accused product that contains some or all of "the luminal portion of the tunica mucosa" cannot infringe under the doctrine of equivalents. The Federal Circuit agreed with ACell, noting that the patentee's "theory of equivalence with respect to asserted claims would violate a corollary to the all limitations rule . . . that 'the concept of equivalency cannot embrace a structure that is specifically excluded from the scope of the claims.'" The accused product consists of two tissue layers specifically excluded from the claimed composition by delaminating the luminal portion of the tunica mucosa. The court stated:

> A claim that specifically excludes an element cannot through a theory of equivalence be used to capture a composition that contains that expressly excluded element without violating the "all limitations rule." Permitting appellees to assert such a theory of equivalence would effectively remove the requirement that the urinary bladder submucosa be delaminated from "the luminal portion of the tunica mucosa." *See Warner-Jenkinson.*

Id. at 1379.

2. ***The All-Limitations Rule.*** The court in *SciMed* referred "to the familiar rule that the doctrine of equivalents cannot be employed in a manner that wholly vitiates a claim limitation." This rule is known as the all-limitations rule. In *Warner-Jenkinson* the Court, relying on the late Judge Nies's dissent, adopted an all-limitations rule when applying the DOE. According to the Court, this rule "reconcile[s] the prohibition against enlarging the scope of claims and the doctrine of equivalents by applying the doctrine to each element of a claim, rather than to the accused product or process 'overall.'" *Warner-Jenkinson,* 517 U.S. at 25. Recall the Court's language:

> Each element contained in a patent claim is deemed material to defining the scope of the patented invention, and thus the doctrine of equivalents must be applied to individual elements of the claim, not to the invention as a whole. It is important to ensure that the application of the doctrine, even as to an individual element, is not allowed such broad play as to effectively eliminate that element in its entirety.

Warner-Jenkinson, 520 U.S. at 29. Thus, each claim limitation must not be vitiated or read completely out of the claim. *See Bell Atlantic Network Services, Inc. v. Covad Communications Group, Inc.,* 262 F.3d 1258, 1279-1280 (Fed. Cir. 2001) (stating "if a court determines that a finding of infringement under the doctrine of equivalents 'would entirely vitiate a particular claim element,' then the court should rule that there is no infringement under the doctrine of equivalents") (citing *Warner-Jenkinson*). Thus, for there to be infringement under the DOE, "the patentee has the burden to present particularized evidence that links the accused products to the patent on a limitation by limitation basis." *Motionless Keyboard Co. v. Microsoft Corp.,* 486 F.3d 1376 (Fed. Cir. 2007).

In *Depuy Spine, Inc. v. Medtronic Sofamor Danek, Inc.,* 469 F.3d 1005, 1017 (Fed. Cir. 2006), the Federal Circuit, informed by *Warner-Jenkinson,* elaborated on the all-limitations rule:

[W]e have held that in certain instances, the "all elements" rule* forecloses resort to the doctrine of equivalents because, on the facts or theories presented in a case, a limitation would be read completely out of the claim—*i.e.*, the limitation would be effectively removed or "vitiated." For instance, we have concluded that in some cases, the evidence was such that no reasonable jury could determine a proffered equivalent to be insubstantially different from the claimed limitation. *See, e.g., Freedman Seating,* 420 F.3d at 1361 (holding that a limitation was vitiated in part because the structural difference in the accused device "is not a 'subtle difference in degree,' but rather 'a clear, substantial difference or difference in kind'"; *Ethicon,* 149 F.3d 1309, 1319 (Fed. Cir. 1998) (holding that the "all elements" rule barred application of the doctrine of equivalents because, on the facts presented, no reasonable jury could find the differences to be insubstantial). We have also concluded that in some cases, the patentee's theory of equivalence was legally insufficient because, rather than demonstrate an insubstantial difference between a limitation and an element in the accused device, the theory effectively eliminated a limitation in its entirety. *See, e.g., Tronzo,* 156 F.3d at 1160 (holding that the patentee's theory of equivalence—that "*any* shape would be equivalent to the conical limitation"—would write such a limitation out of the claims (emphasis in original)); *Forest Labs., Inc. v. Abbott Labs.,* 239 F.3d 1305, 1313 (Fed. Cir. 2001) (holding that the patentee's theory of equivalence—that a limitation on the percentages of water in a composition was "irrelevant" when compared to the accused composition—vitiated such a limitation). Thus, the "all elements" rule generally is not met—and therefore a claim limitation can be said to be vitiated—if the theory or evidence of equivalence is legally incapable of establishing that the differences between the limitation in the claim and the accused device are insubstantial; *i.e.*, if the theory or evidence is so legally insufficient as to warrant a holding of non-infringement as a matter of law.

3. ***Identifying Vitiation.*** Identifying what exactly constitutes a limitation, and when a claim limitation is vitiated are questions that are sometimes difficult to answer. For example, in *Corning Glass Works v. Sumitomo Electric U.S.A.,* 868 F.2d 1251 (Fed. Cir. 1989), the court recognized that the all-limitations rule has led to "confusion . . . because of misunderstanding or misleading uses of the term 'element' in discussing claims." According to the court, an "'[e]lement' may be used to mean a single limitation, but it has also been used to mean a series of limitations which, taken together, make up a component of the claimed invention." *Id.* at 1259. The court continued, stating that under the all-limitations rule, "[a]n equivalent must be found for every

---

* [The Federal Circuit has expressed a preference, although inconsistently applied, for the word "limitation" (instead of "element") when referring to claim language, and "element" when referring to the accused device. *See Festo Corp. v. Shoketsu Kinzoku Kogyo Kabushiki Co., Inc.,* 234 F.3d 558, 563 n.1 (Fed. Cir. 2000) (*en banc*) ("In our prior cases, we have used both the term 'element' and the term 'limitation' to refer to words in a claim. It is preferable to use the term 'limitation' when referring to claim language and the term 'element' when referring to the accused device"). In fact, one member of the court stated that he prefers to call the "all-elements rule" the "all-limitations rule." *See* Raj S. Dav, *A Mathematical Approach to Claim Elements and the Doctrine of Equivalents,* 16 HARV. J.L. & TECH. 507, 532 n.133, quoting Judge Paul Michel as follows:

> I like to call it [referring to the "all-elements rule"] the "all-limitations rule," because I don't know what an element is. And every time I've had to debate with someone, it's clear that they have a slightly different idea of what an element is than what I think it is. Once you get past atomic elements, I don't think it's a useful word.

Nonetheless, as *Depuy* reveals, the court continues to use the phrase "all-elements rule." —ED.]

limitation of the claim somewhere in an accused device, but not necessarily in a corresponding component, although that is generally the case." *Id.* This language suggests the all-limitations rule is more flexible than a one-to-one correspondence that demands each claim limitation to have a corresponding equivalent in the accused device.

But subsequent decisions sought to clarify *Corning Glass.* In *Dolly, Inc. v. Spalding & Evenflo Companies, Inc.,* 16 F.3d 394 (Fed. Cir. 1994), for instance, the Federal Circuit, referring to the *Corning Glass* language noted above, stated the "language in *Corning Glass* did not substitute a broader limitation-by-limitation comparison for the doctrine of equivalents than the element-by-element comparison in *Pennwalt.* Rather, . . . *Corning Glass* reaffirmed that the rule requires an equivalent for every limitation of the claim, even though the equivalent may not be present in the corresponding component of the accused device." *Id.* at 399. *See also Forest Labs. v. Abbott Labs.,* 239 F.3d 1305, 1313 (Fed. Cir. 2001) (noting *Corning Glass* "did not dispense with the need for one-to-one correspondence of limitations and elements"). Thus, the court remarked that equivalency will result "when two components of the accused device perform a single function of the patented invention" or "when separate claim limitations are combined into a single component of the accused device." *Dolly,* 16 F.3d at 398. A recent example of the latter can be found in *Eagle Comtronics, Inc. v. Arrow Communication Laboratories, Inc.,* 305 F.3d 1303 (Fed. Cir. 2002). In *Eagle,* the invention related to an improved cable filter structure used to decode or unscramble protected television signals. Claim 1, the only independent claim, recited several limitations, three of which included a (1) front cap, (2) a rear insert body including a rear end portion, and (3) a seal located between the front cap and the rear insert body. The accused products did not have separate elements corresponding to the front cap and rear insert body limitations, but did have a seal located along the periphery of the accused products. The patentee conceded there was no literal infringement, but argued infringement under the DOE. The accused infringer asserted because the accused devices do not possess a corresponding element to the aforementioned claim limitations, therefore, applying of the DOE would impermissibly vitiate these limitations. The Federal Circuit disagreed, stating:

> While a claim limitation cannot be totally missing from an accused device, whether or not a limitation is deemed to be vitiated must take into account that when two elements of the accused device perform a single function of the patented invention, or when separate claim limitations are combined into a single element of the accused device, a claim limitation is not necessarily vitiated, and the doctrine of equivalents may still apply if the differences are insubstantial.

Id. at 1317.

In *Sage Prods. v. Devon Indus.,* 126 F.3d 1420 (Fed. Cir. 1997), however, vitiation was a concern and led to a finding of no infringement under the DOE. In *Sage,* the invention was a container for disposing of hazardous medical waste. The relevant claim language stated the invention comprised a container body with "an elongated slot at the top of the container body. . . ." *Id.* at 1422. The defendant made a similar container, but the slot for disposing the waste was within the container body. *Id.* at 1423. Both containers featured two constrictions that kept the waste securely within the container.

The plaintiff argued "having two constrictions below the top of the container is the same, for purposes of infringement, as having one constriction above and one constriction below." *Id.* at 1424. The court found no literal infringement and ruled the all-limitations rule would be violated if the patentee were allowed to show the slot within the container was equivalent to a slot at the top of the container.

The Federal Circuit sought to clarify the relationship between vitiation and the DOE in *Deere & Co. v. Bush Hog LLC,* 703 F.3d 1349 (Fed. Cir. 2012). The court noted that "the doctrine of equivalents, by its very nature, assumes that some element is missing from the literal claim language but may be supplied by an equivalent substitute." *Id.* at 1356. And the court cautioned, therefore:

> Courts should be cautious not to shortcut this inquiry by identifying a "binary" choice in which an element is either present or "not present." Stated otherwise, the vitiation test cannot be satisfied by simply noting that an element is missing from the claimed structure or process because the doctrine of equivalents, by definition, recognizes that an element is missing that must be supplied by the equivalent substitute. If mere observation of a missing element could satisfy the vitiation requirement, this "exception" would swallow the rule. And, the Supreme Court declined to let numerous contentions bury the doctrine.

Id. at 1356-1357. And in *Brilliant Instruments, Inc. v. GuideTech, LLC,* 703 F.3d 1342 (Fed. Cir. 2013), the court elaborated on *Deere*:

> The vitiation test cannot be satisfied merely by noting that the equivalent substitute is outside the claimed limitation's literal scope. Rather, vitiation applies when one of skill in the art would understand that the literal and substitute limitations are not interchangeable, not insubstantially different, and when they do not perform substantially the same function in substantially the same way, to accomplish substantially the same result. In short, saying that a claim element would be vitiated is akin to saying that there is no equivalent to the claim element in the accused device based on the well-established "function-way-result" or "insubstantial differences" tests.

d. Prior Art

Claim coverage under the DOE cannot extend to include subject matter that forms part of the prior art. The reason for this limitation is straightforward: Claims that read on the prior art do not satisfy the patentability requirements, and therefore, the PTO would never have issued the patent of such claim breadth. Indeed, it is not uncommon for a party accused of infringement to assert that it is merely practicing the prior art, thus implying that a finding of infringement leads to a finding of invalidity. The principal case of *Wilson Sporting Goods Co.* explores the role of prior art as a limitation on the DOE.

WILSON SPORTING GOODS CO. v. DAVID GEOFFREY & ASSOCIATES
904 F.2d 677 (Fed. Cir. 1990)

RICH, Circuit Judge.

These appeals, consolidated by agreement, are from judgments of the United States District Court for the District of South Carolina in two actions brought by

Wilson Sporting Goods Co. (Wilson) for infringement of United States Patent 4,560,168 ('168), entitled "Golf Ball." In the first action, the magistrate entered judgment of liability against Dunlop Slazenger Corporation (Dunlop) upon jury verdicts of patent validity and willful infringement.

BACKGROUND

A. The Proceedings

Wilson is a full-line sporting goods company and is one of about six major competitors in the golf ball business. Among its well-known balls are the ProStaff and Ultra. Dunlop is also a major player in the golf ball business. It competes head-to-head with Wilson by selling the Maxfli Tour Limited and Slazenger balls. It sells the Maxfli Tour Limited ball to numerous distributors, but sells the Slazenger ball only to DGA, which distributes the ball to U.S. customers.

Wilson accused Dunlop of infringing claims 1, 7, 15-16, and 19-22 of its '168 patent, and made a general accusation of infringement against DGA.

After a five day jury trial on the issue of liability, the jury returned special interrogatories finding the asserted claims "valid" (i.e., not proved invalid) and willfully infringed. Judgment was entered upon the verdict, Dunlop's motion for JNOV was denied, and Dunlop appealed.

B. The Technology

For more than a century, golfers have been searching for a "longer" ball. As one of the parties put it, "distance sells." Inventors have experimented with numerous aspects of ball design over the years, but as United States Golf Association (U.S.G.A.) rules began to strictly control ball size, weight, and other parameters, inventors focused their efforts on the "dimples" in the ball's surface. According to one witness, new dimple designs provide the only real opportunity for increasing distance within the confines of U.S.G.A. rules.

Dimples create surface turbulence around a flying ball, lessening drag and increasing lift. In lay terms, they make the ball fly higher and farther. While this much is clear, "dimple science" is otherwise quite complicated and inexact: dimples can be numerous or few, and can vary as to shape, width, depth, location, and more.

Wilson's '168 patent claims a certain configuration of dimples on a golf ball cover. The shape and width of the dimples in the '168 patent is for the most part immaterial. What is critical is their location on the ball. The goal is to create a more symmetrical distribution of dimples.

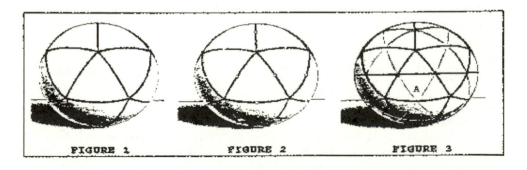

FIGURE 1   FIGURE 2   FIGURE 3

Generally speaking, the dimples in the patent are arranged by dividing the cover of a spherical golf ball into 80 imaginary spherical triangles and then placing the dimples (typically several hundred) into strategic locations in the triangles. The triangles are constructed as follows. First, the ball is divided into an imaginary "icosahedron," as shown in Figure 1. An icosahedral golf ball is completely covered by 20 imaginary equilateral triangles, 5 of which cover each pole of the ball and ten of which surround its equator. Second, the midpoints of each of the sides of each of the 20 icosahedral triangles are located, as shown in Figure 2. Third, the midpoints are joined, thus subdividing each icosahedral triangle into four smaller triangles.

The resulting 80 imaginary triangles are shown in Figure 3. Critically important are the light lines which join the midpoints. As can be seen from Figure 3, they form the arcs of circles which pass completely around the widest part of the ball. There are six such circles, referred to in the patent as "great circles."

All of the claims of the '168 patent require this basic golf ball having eighty sub-triangles and six great circles. Particular claims require variations on the placement of dimples in the triangles, with one common theme — the dimples must be arranged on the surface of the ball so that no dimple intersects any great circle. Equivalently stated, the dimples must be arranged on the surface of the ball so that no dimple intersects the side of any central triangle. *See* Figure 4, below. When the dimples are arranged in this manner, the ball has six axes of symmetry, compared to prior balls which had only one axis of symmetry.

C. Patent and Trademark Office (PTO) Proceedings

Wilson employee Steven Aoyama filed his patent application on April 27, 1984. Twenty seven claims were presented. All were allowed on the first action without comment by the examiner. The patent issued on December 24, 1985, to Wilson as assignee of Aoyama.

Claim 1, the only independent claim, reads:

1. A golf ball having a spherical surface with a plurality of dimples formed therein and six great circle paths which do not intersect any di[m]ples, the dimples being arranged by dividing the spherical surface into twenty spherical triangles corresponding to the faces of a regular icosahedron, each of the twenty triangles being sub-divided into four smaller triangles consisting of a central triangle and three apical triangles by connecting the midpoints [of the sides] of each of said twenty triangles along great circle paths, said dimples being arranged so that the dimples do not intersect the sides of any of the central triangles. [Bracketed insertions ours.]

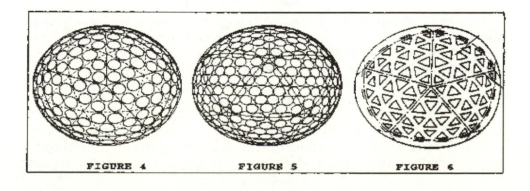

FIGURE 4   FIGURE 5   FIGURE 6

The remaining 26 claims are dependent upon claim 1. They contain further limitations as to the number and location of dimples in the sub-triangles. Claim 7, for example, requires that all "central triangles [have] the same number of dimples." Other dependent claims locate dimples on the perimeter of the apical triangles, so that dimples are shared by adjacent apical triangles. *See* Figure 5.

D. The Prior Art

* * *

The prior art . . . includes several patents to Uniroyal and a Uniroyal golf ball sold in the 1970's. The Uniroyal ball is an icosahedral ball having six great circles with 30 or more dimples intersecting the great circles by about 12-15 thousandths of an inch. We discuss it extensively below.

E. The Accused Balls

There are four accused products, all of which the jury found to infringe. . . . The accused balls (collectively "Dunlop's balls") have dimples which are arranged in an icosahedral pattern having six great circles, but the six great circles are not dimple-free as the claims literally require. The number of dimples which intersect great circles and the extent of their intersection were disputed by the parties, but the evidence most favorable to appellee Wilson can be summarized as follows (units of last two columns are 0.001"):

Ball	Dimples	Dimples Intersected	Dimple Radius	Extent of Intersection
Maxfli Tour MD	432	60	60-80	7.5
Maxfli Tour HT	432	60	60-80	8.7
Interlock (S)	480	60	60-80	4.0
Interlock (B)	480	60	60-80	4.0

OPINION

* * *

B. Denial of JNOV on Infringement

1. Dunlop's Argument

The only theory of liability presented to the jury by Wilson was infringement under the doctrine of equivalents. Dunlop's argument for reversal is straightforward. It contends that there is no principled difference between the balls which the jury found to infringe and the prior art Uniroyal ball; thus to allow the patent to reach Dunlop's balls under the doctrine of equivalents would improperly ensnare the prior art Uniroyal ball as well.

2. Independent Claim 1

Infringement *may* be found under the doctrine of equivalents if an accused product "performs substantially the same overall function or work, in substantially the same way, to obtain substantially the same overall result as the claimed invention." *Pennwalt Corp. v. Durand-Wayland, Inc.,* 833 F.2d 931, 934 (Fed. Cir. 1987) (en banc). Even if this test is met, however, there can be no infringement if the asserted scope of equivalency of what is literally claimed would encompass the prior art. *Id.* This issue—whether an asserted range of equivalents would cover what is already in the public domain—is one of law, which we review *de novo,* but we presume that the jury resolved underlying evidentiary conflicts in Wilson's favor.

This court on occasion has characterized claims as being "expanded" or "broadened" under the doctrine of equivalents. Precisely speaking, these characterizations are inaccurate.

To say that the doctrine of equivalents extends or enlarges *the claims* is a contradiction in terms. The claims—i.e., the scope of patent protection *as defined by* the claims—remain the same and application of the doctrine *expands the right to exclude* to "equivalents" of what is claimed.

The doctrine of equivalents, by definition, involves going beyond any permissible interpretation of the claim language; i.e., it involves determining whether the accused product is "equivalent" to what is described by the claim language.

This distinction raises an interesting question: If the doctrine of equivalents does not involve expanding the claims, why should the *prior art* be a limitation on the range of permissible equivalents? It is *not* because we construe claims narrowly if necessary to sustain their validity. As we have said, the doctrine of equivalents does not involve expansion of the *claims.* Nor is it because to hold otherwise would allow the patentee to preempt a product that was in the public domain prior to the invention. The accused products here, as in most infringement cases, were never "in the public domain." They were developed long after the invention and differ in several respects from the prior art.

The answer is that a patentee should not be able to obtain, under the doctrine of equivalents, coverage which he could not lawfully have obtained from the PTO by literal claims. The doctrine of equivalents exists to prevent a fraud on a patent, *Graver Tank, not* to give a patentee something which he could not lawfully have obtained from the PTO had he tried. Thus, since prior art always limits what an inventor could have claimed, it limits the range of permissible equivalents of a claim.

Whether prior art restricts the range of equivalents of what is literally claimed can be a difficult question to answer. To simplify analysis and bring the issue onto familiar turf, it may be helpful to conceptualize the limitation on the scope of equivalents by visualizing a *hypothetical* patent claim, sufficient in scope to *literally* cover the accused product. The pertinent question then becomes whether that hypothetical claim could have been allowed by the PTO over the prior art. If not, then it would be improper to permit the patentee to obtain that coverage in an infringement suit under the doctrine of equivalents. If the hypothetical claim could have been allowed, then *prior art* is not a bar to infringement under the doctrine of equivalents.

Viewing the issue in this manner allows use of traditional patentability rules and permits a more precise analysis than determining whether an *accused product* (which has no claim limitations on which to focus) would have been obvious in view of the prior art. In fact, the utility of this hypothetical broader claim may explain why "expanded claim" phraseology, which we now abandon, had crept into our jurisprudence. Finally, it reminds us that Wilson is seeking patent coverage beyond the limits considered by the PTO examiner.

In this context it is important to remember that the burden is on Wilson to prove that the range of equivalents which it seeks would not ensnare the prior art Uniroyal ball. The patent owner has always borne the burden of proving infringement, and there is no logical reason why that burden should shift to the accused infringer simply because infringement in this context might require an inquiry into the patentability of a *hypothetical* claim. Any other approach would ignore the realities of what happens in the PTO and violate established patent law. Leaving this burden on Wilson does not, of course, in any way undermine the presumed validity of Wilson's actual patent claims. In the present situation, Wilson's claims will remain valid whether or not Wilson persuades us that it is entitled to the range of equivalents sought here.

The specific question before us, then, is whether Wilson has proved that a hypothetical claim, similar to claim 1 but broad enough to literally cover Dunlop's balls, could have been patentable. As we have explained above, Dunlop's balls are icosahedral balls with six great circles, five of which are intersected by dimples. The balls contain 432 to 480 dimples, 60 of which intersect great circles in amounts from 4 to 9 thousandths of an inch. In order for a hypothetical claim to cover Dunlop's balls, its limitations must permit 60 dimples to intersect the great circles by at least 9 thousandths of an inch. Thus, the issue is whether a hypothetical claim directed to an icosahedral ball having six great circles intersected by 60 dimples in amounts up to 9 thousandths of an inch could have been patentable in view of the prior art Uniroyal ball.

On the Uniroyal ball, the extent to which the dimples intersect the great circles is from 12 to 15 thousandths of an inch. Stated as a percentage of dimple radius, the intersection permitted in the hypothetical claim is 13% or less, and the dimples on the Uniroyal ball intersect by 17% to 21%. The number of dimples which intersect the great circles is also similar for the hypothetical claim and the prior art Uniroyal ball. The pertinent hypothetical claim limitation reads on any ball having 60 or less intersecting dimples. This limitation reads on the prior art Uniroyal ball, which has 30 intersecting dimples. If viewed in relative terms, the hypothetical claim limitation reads on any ball which has less than 14% of its dimples intersecting great circles. Roughly 12% of the dimples on the Uniroyal ball intersect great circles.

We hold that these differences are so slight and relatively minor that the hypothetical claim—which permits twice as many intersecting dimples, but with slightly smaller intersections—viewed as a whole would have been obvious in view of the Uniroyal ball. As Dunlop puts it, there is simply "no principled difference" between the hypothetical claim and the prior art Uniroyal ball. Accordingly, Wilson's claim 1 cannot be given a range of equivalents broad enough to encompass the accused Dunlop balls.

3. Dependent Claims

Before separately analyzing the asserted dependent claims, we should first explain why we are bothering to do so. This court has stated: "It is axiomatic that dependent claims cannot be found infringed unless the claims from which they depend have been found to have been infringed." *Wahpeton Canvas Co., Inc. v. Frontier, Inc.,* 870 F.2d 1546, 1553 & n. 9 (Fed. Cir. 1989). While this proposition is no doubt generally correct, it does not apply in the circumstances of this case.

Here, we have reversed the judgment of infringement of independent claim 1 solely because the asserted range of equivalents of the claim limitations would encompass the prior art Uniroyal ball. The dependent claims, of course, are *narrower* than claim 1; therefore, it does not automatically follow that the ranges of equivalents of these narrower claims would encompass the prior art, because of their added limitations. In contrast, in *Wahpeton Canvas* the court affirmed the judgment of noninfringement of the independent claims because the accused products did not include particular claim limitations or their substantial equivalents. Where that is the reason for noninfringement of the independent claim, it follows that, for the same reason, the dependent claims will not be infringed. But that is not true here and we therefore turn to the asserted dependent claims, to determine whether they can be infringed under the doctrine of equivalents.

Implicit in the jury's conclusion that the Dunlop balls infringe the asserted dependent claims is a finding that the Dunlop balls have, in addition to the features we have described above, the further limitations of the dependent claims. Each dependent claim contains a small variation on the theme of an icosahedral ball having six great circles. We have considered each asserted dependent claim and conclude that none could be given a range of equivalents broad enough to encompass Dunlop's balls because that would extend Wilson's patent protection beyond hypothetical claims it could lawfully have obtained from the PTO. . . .

Conclusion

We conclude that the magistrate erred in denying Dunlop's motion for JNOV on infringement, because, as a matter of law, a range of equivalents broad enough to cover Dunlop's balls would also have encompassed the prior art. Accordingly, we reverse the judgment of infringement by Dunlop.

Comments

1. *The Hypothetical Claim: Back to the Future.* The *Wilson* court asks us to cast our minds back to the prosecution phase to determine if the hypothetical claim, "sufficient in scope to literally cover the accused product," would have been allowed to issue by the PTO over the prior art. *Wilson* was based on "the fundamental principle that no one deserves an exclusive right to technology already in the public domain." *Marquip, Inc. v. Fosber America, Inc.*, 198 F.3d 1363, 1366 (Fed. Cir. 1999). The hypothetical claim construct is not obligatory, but a methodology to help "define the limits imposed by the prior art on the range of equivalents." *Key Mfg. Group, Inc. v. Microdot, Inc.*, 925 F.2d 1444, 1449 (Fed. Cir. 1991).

2. *Applying* **Wilson.** The *Wilson* framework has generated a great deal of commentary, and has been applied in numerous cases. *See, e.g., Streamfeeder LLC v. Sure-Feed Systems, Inc.*, 175 F.3d 974 (Fed. Cir. 1999) (holding hypothetical claim would not have issued over prior art, and therefore no infringement); *Key Manufacturing, supra* (same); *Abbott Laboratories v. Dey LP*, 287 F.3d 1097 (Fed. Cir. 2002) (applying *Wilson* and holding prior art does not preclude application of DOE). One particular difficulty in applying *Wilson* is defining the breadth of a hypothetical claim that includes the equivalent in question.

COMPARATIVE PERSPECTIVE
Claim Interpretation and Non-Literal Infringement in the United Kingdom

In the following opinion, Lord Hoffmann explores claim interpretation and the role of non-literal infringement under U.K. law. He also discusses the American approach to claim interpretation and the DOE. As you read the opinion, ask yourself what are the differences between the U.S. and U.K. approaches to claim interpretation and the DOE, and how these approaches further the policies of patent law.

KIRIN-AMGEN, INC. v. HOECHST MARION ROUSSEL LTD.

[2004] UKHL 46, [2004] All ER (D) 286 (Oct. 1, 2004)

LORD HOFFMANN.

[The patent-in-suit related to the production of erythropoietin ("EPO") by recombinant DNA technology. The Court discussed the technology and the claim language in question.]

Extent of Protection: The Statutory Provisions

18. Until the Patents Act 1977, which gave effect to the European Patent Convention ("EPC") there was nothing in any UK statute about the extent of protection conferred by a patent. It was governed by the common law, the terms of the royal grant and general principles of construction. It was these principles which Lord Diplock expounded in the leading case of *Catnic Components Ltd v Hill & Smith Ltd* [1982] RPC 183, which concerned a patent granted before 1977. But the EPC and the Act deal expressly with the matter in some detail. Article 84 specifies the role of the claims in an application to the European Patent Office for a European patent:

> The claims shall define the matter for which protection is sought. They shall be clear and concise and be supported by the description.

19. For present purposes, the most important provision is article 69 of the EPC, which applies to infringement proceedings in the domestic courts of all Contracting States:

> The extent of the protection conferred by a European patent or a European patent application shall be determined by the terms of the claims. Nevertheless, the description and drawings shall be used to interpret the claims.

20. In stating unequivocally that the extent of protection shall be "determined" (in German, "bestimmt") by the "terms of the claims" (den Inhalt der Patentansprüche) the Convention followed what had long been the law in the United Kingdom. During the course of the 18th and 19th centuries, practice and common law had come to distinguish between the part of the specification in which the patentee discharged his duty to disclose the best way of performing the invention and the section which delimited the scope of the monopoly which he claimed: *see* Fletcher-Moulton LJ in *British United Shoe Machinery Co Ltd v A. Fussell & Sons Ltd* (1908) 25 RPC 631, 650. The best-known statement of

the status of the claims in UK law is by Lord Russell of Killowen in *Electric and Musical Industries Ltd v Lissen Ltd* (1938) 56 RPC 23, 39:

> The function of the claims is to define clearly and with precision the monopoly claimed, so that others may know the exact boundary of the area within which they will be trespassers. Their primary object is to limit and not to extend the monopoly. What is not claimed is disclaimed. The claims must undoubtedly be read as part of the entire document and not as a separate document; but the forbidden field must be found in the language of the claims and not elsewhere.

21. The need to set clear limits upon the monopoly is not only, as Lord Russell emphasised, in the interests of others who need to know the area "within which they will be trespassers" but also in the interests of the patentee, who needs to be able to make it clear that he lays no claim to prior art or insufficiently enabled products or processes which would invalidate the patent.

22. In Germany, however, the practice before 1977 in infringement proceedings (validity is determined by a different court) was commonly to treat the claims as a point of departure ("Ausgangspunkt") in determining the extent of protection, for which the criterion was the inventive achievement ("erfinderische Leistung") disclosed by the specification as a whole. Likewise in the Netherlands, Professor Jan Brinkhof, former Vice-President of the Hague Court of Appeals, has written that the role of the claims before 1977 was "extremely modest": see Is there a European Doctrine of Equivalence? (2002) 33 IIC 911, 915. What mattered was the "essence of the invention" or what we would call the inventive concept.

The Protocol

23. Although the EPC thus adopted the United Kingdom principle of using the claims to determine the extent of protection, the Contracting States were unwilling to accept what were understood to be the principles of construction which United Kingdom courts applied in deciding what the claims meant. These principles, which I shall explain in greater detail in a moment, were perceived as having sometimes resulted in claims being given an unduly narrow and literal construction. The Contracting Parties wanted to make it clear that legal technicalities of this kind should be rejected. On the other hand, it was accepted that countries which had previously looked to the "essence of the invention" rather than the actual terms of the claims should not carry on exactly as before under the guise of giving the claims a generous interpretation.

24. This compromise was given effect by the "Protocol on the Interpretation of Article 69":

> Article 69 should not be interpreted in the sense that the extent of the protection conferred by a European patent is to be understood as that defined by the strict, literal meaning of the wording used in the claims, the description and drawings being employed only for the purpose of resolving an ambiguity found in the claims. Neither should it be interpreted in the sense that the claims serve only as a guideline and that the actual protection conferred may extend to what, from a consideration of the description and drawings by a person skilled in the art, the patentee has contemplated. On the contrary, it is to be interpreted as defining a position between these extremes which combines a fair protection for the patentee with a reasonable degree of certainty for third parties.

25. It is often said, on the basis of the words "a position between these extremes," that the Protocol represents a compromise between two different approaches to the interpretation of claims. But that is not quite accurate. It is a protocol on the interpretation of article 69, not a protocol on the interpretation of claims. The first sentence does deal with interpretation of the claims and, to understand it, one needs to know something about the rules which English courts used to apply, or impose on themselves, when construing not merely patents but documents in general. The second sentence does not deal with the interpretation of claims. Instead, it makes it clear that one cannot go beyond the claims to what, on the basis of the specification as a whole, it appears that "the patentee has contemplated." But the last sentence indicates that, in determining the extent of protection according to the content of the claims but avoiding literalism, the courts of the Contracting States should combine "a fair protection for the patentee with a reasonable degree of certainty for third parties."

26. Both article 69 and the Protocol are given effect in United Kingdom law, in relation to infringement, by sections 60 and 125 of the Act. Section 60 provides that a person infringes a patent if he does various things in the United Kingdom "in relation to the invention" without the consent of the proprietor of the patent. Section 125 defines the extent of "the invention":

> (1) For the purpose of this Act an invention for a patent for which an application has been made or for which a patent has been granted shall, unless the context otherwise requires, be taken to be that specified in a claim of the specification of the application or patent, as the case may be, as interpreted by the description and any drawings contained in that specification, and the extent of the protection conferred by a patent or application for a patent shall be determined accordingly.

> (3) The Protocol on the Interpretation of Article 69 of the European Patent Convention (which Article contains a provision corresponding to subsection (1) above) shall, as for the time being in force, apply for the purposes of subsection (1) above as it applies for the purposes of that Article.

The English Rules of Construction

27. As I indicated a moment ago, it is impossible to understand what the first sentence of the Protocol was intending to prohibit without knowing what used to be the principles applied (at any rate in theory) by an English court construing a legal document. These required the words and grammar of a sentence to be given their "natural and ordinary meaning," that is to say, the meanings assigned to the words by a dictionary and to the syntax by a grammar. This meaning was to be adopted regardless of the context or background against which the words were used, unless they were "ambiguous," that is to say, capable of having more than one meaning. As Lord Porter said in *Electric & Musical Industries Ltd v Lissen Ltd* (1938) 56 RPC 23, 57:

> If the Claims have a plain meaning in themselves, then advantage cannot be taken of the language used in the body of the Specification to make them mean something different.

28. On the other hand, if the language of the claim "in itself" was ambiguous, capable of having more than one meaning, the court could have regard to the context provided by the specification and drawings. If that was insufficient to resolve the ambiguity, the court could have regard to the background, or what

was called the "extrinsic evidence" of facts which an intended reader would reasonably have expected to have been within the knowledge of the author when he wrote the document.

29. These rules, if remorselessly applied, meant that unless the court could find some ambiguity in the language, it might be obliged to construe the document in a sense which a reasonable reader, aware of its context and background, would not have thought the author intended. Such a rule, adopted in the interests of certainty at an early stage in the development of English law, was capable of causing considerable injustice and occasionally did so. The fact that it did not do so more often was because judges were generally astute to find the necessary "ambiguity" which enabled them to interpret the document in its proper context. Indeed, the attempt to treat the words of the claim as having meanings "in themselves" and without regard to the context in which or the purpose for which they were used was always a highly artificial exercise.

30. It seems to me clear that the Protocol, with its reference to "resolving an ambiguity," was intended to reject these artificial English rules for the construction of patent claims. As it happens, though, by the time the Protocol was signed, the English courts had already begun to abandon them, not only for patent claims, but for commercial documents generally. The speeches of Lord Wilberforce in *Prenn v Simmonds* [1971] 1 WLR 1381 and *Reardon Smith Line Ltd v Yngvar Hansen-Tangen* [1976] 1 WLR 989 are milestones along this road. It came to be recognised that the author of a document such as a contract or patent specification is using language to make a communication for a practical purpose and that a rule of construction which gives his language a meaning different from the way it would have been understood by the people to whom it was actually addressed is liable to defeat his intentions. It is against that background that one must read the well known passage in the speech of Lord Diplock in *Catnic Components Ltd v Hill & Smith Ltd* [1982] RPC 183, 243 when he said that the new approach should also be applied to the construction of patent claims:

> A patent specification should be given a purposive construction rather than a purely literal one derived from applying to it the kind of meticulous verbal analysis in which lawyers are too often tempted by their training to indulge.

31. This was all of a piece with Lord Diplock's approach a few years later in *The Antaios* [1985] AC 191, 201 to the construction of a charterparty:

> I take this opportunity of re-stating that if detailed semantic and syntactical analysis of words in a commercial contract is going to lead to a conclusion that flouts business commonsense, it must be made to yield to business commonsense.

32. Construction, whether of a patent or any other document, is of course not directly concerned with what the author meant to say. There is no window into the mind of the patentee or the author of any other document. Construction is objective in the sense that it is concerned with what a reasonable person to whom the utterance was addressed would have understood the author to be using the words to mean. Notice, however, that it is not, as is sometimes said, "the meaning of the words the author used," but rather what the notional addressee would have understood the author to mean by using those words. The meaning of words is a matter of convention, governed by rules, which can be found in dictionaries and grammars. What the author would have been understood to mean by using those words is not simply a matter of rules. It is highly sensitive to

the context of and background to the particular utterance. It depends not only upon the words the author has chosen but also upon the identity of the audience he is taken to have been addressing and the knowledge and assumptions which one attributes to that audience. I have discussed these questions at some length in *Mannai Investment Co Ltd v Eagle Star Life Assurance Co Ltd* [1997] AC 749 and *Investors Compensation Scheme Ltd v West Bromwich Building Society* [1998] 1 WLR 896.

33. In the case of a patent specification, the notional addressee is the person skilled in the art. He (or, I say once and for all, she) comes to a reading of the specification with common general knowledge of the art. And he reads the specification on the assumption that its purpose is to both to describe and to demarcate an invention—a practical idea which the patentee has had for a new product or process—and not to be a textbook in mathematics or chemistry or a shopping list of chemicals or hardware. It is this insight which lies at the heart of "purposive construction." If Lord Diplock did not invent the expression, he certainly gave it wide currency in the law. But there is, I think, a tendency to regard it as a vague description of some kind of divination which mysteriously penetrates beneath the language of the specification. Lord Diplock was in my opinion being much more specific and his intention was to point out that a person may be taken to mean something different when he uses words for one purpose from what he would be taken to mean if he was using them for another. The example in the Catnic case was the difference between what a person would reasonably be taken to mean by using the word "vertical" in a mathematical theorem and by using it in a claimed definition of a lintel for use in the building trade. The only point on which I would question the otherwise admirable summary of the law on infringement in the judgment of Jacob LJ in *Rockwater Ltd v Technip France SA* (unreported) [2004] EWCA Civ 381, at paragraph 41, is when he says in sub-paragraph (e) that to be "fair to the patentee" one must use "the widest purpose consistent with his teaching." This, as it seems to me, is to confuse the purpose of the utterance with what it would be understood to mean. The purpose of a patent specification, as I have said, is no more nor less than to communicate the idea of an invention. An appreciation of that purpose is part of the material which one uses to ascertain the meaning. But purpose and meaning are different. If, when speaking of the widest purpose, Jacob LJ meant the widest meaning, I would respectfully disagree. There is no presumption about the width of the claims. A patent may, for one reason or another, claim less than it teaches or enables.

34. "Purposive construction" does not mean that one is extending or going beyond the definition of the technical matter for which the patentee seeks protection in the claims. The question is always what the person skilled in the art would have understood the patentee to be using the language of the claim to mean. And for this purpose, the language he has chosen is usually of critical importance. The conventions of word meaning and syntax enable us to express our meanings with great accuracy and subtlety and the skilled man will ordinarily assume that the patentee has chosen his language accordingly. As a number of judges have pointed out, the specification is a unilateral document in words of the patentee's own choosing. Furthermore, the words will usually have been chosen upon skilled advice. The specification is not a document inter rusticos for which broad allowances must be made. On the other hand, it must be recognised that the patentee is trying to describe something which, at any rate in his

opinion, is new; which has not existed before and of which there may be no generally accepted definition. There will be occasions upon which it will be obvious to the skilled man that the patentee must in some respect have departed from conventional use of language or included in his description of the invention some element which he did not mean to be essential. But one would not expect that to happen very often.

35. One of the reasons why it will be unusual for the notional skilled man to conclude, after construing the claim purposively in the context of the specification and drawings, that the patentee must nevertheless have meant something different from what he appears to have meant, is that there are necessarily gaps in our knowledge of the background which led him to express himself in that particular way. The courts of the United Kingdom, the Netherlands and Germany certainly discourage, if they do not actually prohibit, use of the patent office file in aid of construction. There are good reasons: the meaning of the patent should not change according to whether or not the person skilled in the art has access to the file and in any case life is too short for the limited assistance which it can provide. It is however frequently impossible to know without access, not merely to the file but to the private thoughts of the patentee and his advisors as well, what the reason was for some apparently inexplicable limitation in the extent of the monopoly claimed. One possible explanation is that it does not represent what the patentee really meant to say. But another is that he did mean it, for reasons of his own; such as wanting to avoid arguments with the examiners over enablement or prior art and have his patent granted as soon as possible. This feature of the practical life of a patent agent reduces the scope for a conclusion that the patentee could not have meant what the words appear to be saying. It has been suggested that in the absence of any explanation for a restriction in the extent of protection claimed, it should be presumed that there was some good reason between the patentee and the patent office. I do not think that it is sensible to have presumptions about what people must be taken to have meant but a conclusion that they have departed from conventional usage obviously needs some rational basis.

The Doctrine of Equivalents

36. At the time when the rules about natural and ordinary meanings were more or less rigidly applied, the United Kingdom and American courts showed understandable anxiety about applying a construction which allowed someone to avoid infringement by making an "immaterial variation" in the invention as described in the claims. In England, this led to the development of a doctrine of infringement by use of the "pith and marrow" of the invention (a phrase invented by Lord Cairns in *Clark v Adie* (1877) 2 App Cas 315, 320) as opposed to a "textual infringement." The pith and marrow doctrine was always a bit vague ("necessary to prevent sharp practice" said Lord Reid in *C Van Der Lely NV v Bamfords Ltd* [1963] RPC 61, 77) and it was unclear whether the courts regarded it as a principle of construction or an extension of protection outside the claims.

37. In the United States, where a similar principle is called the "doctrine of equivalents," it is frankly acknowledged that it allows the patentee to extend his monopoly beyond the claims. In the leading case of *Graver Tank & Manufacturing Co Inc v Linde Air Products Company* 339 US 605, 607 (1950), Jackson J said that the American courts had recognised:

that to permit imitation of a patented invention which does not copy every literal detail would be to convert the protection of the patent grant into a hollow and useless thing. Such a limitation would leave room for—indeed encourage—the unscrupulous copyist to make unimportant and insubstantial changes and substitutions in the patent which, though adding nothing, would be enough to take the copied matter outside the claim, and hence outside the reach of law.

38. In similar vein, Learned Hand J (a great patent lawyer) said that the purpose of the doctrine of equivalents was "to temper unsparing logic and prevent an infringer from stealing the benefit of the invention": *Royal Typewriter Co v Remington Rand Inc* (CA2nd Conn) 168 F2nd 691, 692. The effect of the doctrine is thus to extend protection to something outside the claims which performs substantially the same function in substantially the same way to obtain the same result.

39. However, once the monopoly had been allowed to escape from the terms of the claims, it is not easy to know where its limits should be drawn. In *Warner-Jenkinson Co v Hilton Davis Chemical Co* 520 US 17, 28-29 (1997) the United States Supreme Court expressed some anxiety that the doctrine of equivalents had "taken on a life of its own, unbounded by the patent claims." It seems to me, however, that once the doctrine is allowed to go beyond the claims, a life of its own is exactly what it is bound to have. The American courts have restricted the scope of the doctrine by what is called prosecution history or file wrapper estoppel, by which equivalence cannot be claimed for integers restricting the monopoly which have been included by amendment during the prosecution of the application in the patent office. The patentee is estopped against the world (who need not have known of or relied upon the amendment) from denying that he intended to surrender that part of the monopoly. File wrapper estoppel means that the true scope of patent protection often cannot be established without an expensive investigation of the patent office file. Furthermore, the difficulties involved in deciding exactly what part of the claim should be taken to have been withdrawn by an amendment drove the Federal Court of Appeals in *Festo Corporation v Shoketsu Kinzoku Kogyo Kabushiki Co Ltd* 234 F3rd 558 (2000) to declare that the law was arbitrary and unworkable. Lourie J said:

> The only settled expectation currently existing is the expectation that clever attorneys can argue infringement outside the scope of the claims all the way through this Court of Appeals.

40. In order to restore some certainty, the Court of Appeals laid down a rule that any amendment for reasons of patent validity was an absolute bar to any extension of the monopoly outside the literal meaning of the amended text. But the Supreme Court reversed this retreat to literalism on the ground that the cure was worse than the disease: see *Festo Corporation v Shoketsu Kinzoku Kogyo Kabushiki Co Ltd* (28 May 2002) US Supreme Court.

41. There is often discussion about whether we have a European doctrine of equivalents and, if not, whether we should. It seems to me that both the doctrine of equivalents in the United States and the pith and marrow doctrine in the United Kingdom were born of despair. The courts felt unable to escape from interpretations which "unsparing logic" appeared to require and which prevented them from according the patentee the full extent of the monopoly

which the person skilled in the art would reasonably have thought he was claiming. The background was the tendency to literalism which then characterised the approach of the courts to the interpretation of documents generally and the fact that patents are likely to attract the skills of lawyers seeking to exploit literalism to find loopholes in the monopoly they create. (Similar skills are devoted to revenue statutes).

42. If literalism stands in the way of construing patent claims so as to give fair protection to the patentee, there are two things that you can do. One is to adhere to literalism in construing the claims and evolve a doctrine which supplements the claims by extending protection to equivalents. That is what the Americans have done. The other is to abandon literalism. That is what the House of Lords did in the *Catnic* case, where Lord Diplock said (at [1982] RPC 183, 242):

> Both parties to this appeal have tended to treat "textual infringement" and infringement of the "pith and marrow" of an invention as if they were separate causes of action, the existence of the former to be determined as a matter of construction only and of the latter upon some broader principle of colourable evasion. There is, in my view, no such dichotomy; there is but a single cause of action and to treat it otherwise . . . is liable to lead to confusion.

43. The solution, said Lord Diplock, was to adopt a principle of construction which actually gave effect to what the person skilled in the art would have understood the patentee to be claiming.

44. Since the *Catnic* case we have article 69 which, as it seems to me, firmly shuts the door on any doctrine which extends protection outside the claims. I cannot say that I am sorry because the *Festo* litigation suggests, with all respect to the courts of the United States, that American patent litigants pay dearly for results which are no more just or predictable than could be achieved by simply reading the claims.

Is *Catnic* Consistent with the Protocol?

45. In *Improver Corp v Remington Consumer Products Ltd* [1989] RPC 69 the Court of Appeal said that Lord Diplock's speech in *Catnic* advocated the same approach to construction as is required by the Protocol. (*See also Southco Inc v Dzus Fastener Europe Ltd* [1992] RPC 299.) But in *PLG Research Ltd v Ardon International Ltd* [1995] RPC 287, 309 Millett LJ said:

> Lord Diplock was expounding the common law approach to the construction of a patent. This has been replaced by the approach laid down by the Protocol. If the two approaches are the same, reference to Lord Diplock's formulation is unnecessary, while if they are different it is dangerous.

46. This echoes, perhaps consciously, the famous justification said to have been given by the Caliph Omar for burning the library of Alexandria: "If these writings of the Greeks agree with the Book of God, they are useless and need not be preserved: if they disagree, they are pernicious and ought to be destroyed" —a story which Gibbon dismissed as Christian propaganda. But I think that the Protocol can suffer no harm from a little explanation and I entirely agree with the masterly judgment of Aldous J in *Assidoman Multipack Ltd v The Mead Corporation* [1995] RPC 321, in which he explains why the *Catnic* approach accords with the Protocol.

47. The Protocol, as I have said, is a Protocol for the construction of article 69 and does not expressly lay down any principle for the construction of claims. It does say what principle should not be followed, namely the old English literalism, but otherwise it says only that one should not go outside the claims. It does however say that the object is to combine a fair protection for the patentee with a reasonable degree of certainty for third parties. How is this to be achieved? The claims must be construed in a way which attempts, so far as is possible in an imperfect world, not to disappoint the reasonable expectations of either side. What principle of interpretation would give fair protection to the patentee? Surely, a principle which would give him the full extent of the monopoly which the person skilled in the art would think he was intending to claim. And what principle would provide a reasonable degree of protection for third parties? Surely again, a principle which would not give the patentee more than the full extent of the monopoly which the person skilled in the art would think that he was intending to claim. Indeed, any other principle would also be unfair to the patentee, because it would unreasonably expose the patent to claims of invalidity on grounds of anticipation or insufficiency.

48. The *Catnic* principle of construction is therefore in my opinion precisely in accordance with the Protocol. It is intended to give the patentee the full extent, but not more than the full extent, of the monopoly which a reasonable person skilled in the art, reading the claims in context, would think he was intending to claim. Of course it is easy to say this and sometimes more difficult to apply it in practice, although the difficulty should not be exaggerated. The vast majority of patent specifications are perfectly clear about the extent of the monopoly they claim. Disputes over them never come to court. In borderline cases, however, it does happen that an interpretation which strikes one person as fair and reasonable will strike another as unfair to the patentee or unreasonable for third parties. That degree of uncertainty is inherent in any rule which involves the construction of any document. It afflicts the whole of the law of contract, to say nothing of legislation. In principle it is without remedy, although I shall consider in a moment whether uncertainty can be alleviated by guidelines or a "structured" approach to construction.

Equivalents as a Guide to Construction

49. Although article 69 prevents equivalence from extending protection outside the claims, there is no reason why it cannot be an important part of the background of facts known to the skilled man which would affect what he understood the claims to mean. That is no more than common sense. It is also expressly provided by the new article 2 added to the Protocol by the Munich Act revising the EPC, dated 29 November 2000 (but which has not yet come into force):

> For the purpose of determining the extent of protection conferred by a European patent, due account shall be taken of any element which is equivalent to an element specified in the claims.

50. In the *Catnic* case [1982] RPC 183, 243 Lord Diplock offered some observations on the relevance of equivalence to the question of construction:

> The question in each case is: whether persons with practical knowledge and experience of the kind of work in which the invention was intended to be used, would

understand that strict compliance with a particular descriptive word or phrase appearing in a claim was intended by the patentee to be an essential requirement of the invention so that any variant would fall outside the monopoly claimed, even though it could have no material effect upon the way the invention worked.

The question, of course, does not arise where the variant would in fact have a material effect upon the way the invention worked. Nor does it arise unless at the date of publication of the specification it would be obvious to the informed reader that this was so. Where it is not obvious, in the light of then-existing knowledge, the reader is entitled to assume that the patentee thought at the time of the specification that he had good reason for limiting his monopoly so strictly and had intended to do so, even though subsequent work by him or others in the field of the invention might show the limitation to have been unnecessary. It is to be answered in the negative only when it would be apparent to any reader skilled in the art that a particular descriptive word or phrase used in a claim cannot have been intended by a patentee, who was also skilled in the art, to exclude minor variants which, to the knowledge of both him and the readers to whom the patent was addressed, could have no material effect upon the way in which the invention worked.

51. In *Improver Corporation v Remington Consumer Products Ltd* [1990] FSR 181, 189 I tried to summarise this guidance:

If the issue was whether a feature embodied in an alleged infringement which fell outside the primary, literal or acontextual meaning of a descriptive word or phrase in the claim ("a variant") was nevertheless within its language as properly interpreted, the court should ask itself the following three questions:

(1) Does the variant have a material effect upon the way the invention works? If yes, the variant is outside the claim. If no?

(2) Would this (ie that the variant had no material effect) have been obvious at the date of publication of the patent to a reader skilled in the art? If no, the variant is outside the claim. If yes?

(3) Would the reader skilled in the art nevertheless have understood from the language of the claim that the patentee intended that strict compliance with the primary meaning was an essential requirement of the invention? If yes, the variant is outside the claim.

On the other hand, a negative answer to the last question would lead to the conclusion that the patentee was intending the word or phrase to have not a literal but a figurative meaning (the figure being a form of synecdoche or metonymy) denoting a class of things which include the variant and the literal meaning, the latter being perhaps the most perfect, best-known or striking example of the class.

52. These questions, which the Court of Appeal in *Wheatly v Drillsafe Ltd* [2001] RPC 133, 142 dubbed "the Protocol questions" have been used by English courts for the past fifteen years as a framework for deciding whether equivalents fall within the scope of the claims. On the whole, the judges appear to have been comfortable with the results, although some of the cases have exposed the limitations of the method. When speaking of the "*Catnic* principle" it is important to distinguish between, on the one hand, the principle of purposive construction which I have said gives effect to the requirements of the Protocol, and on the other hand, the guidelines for applying that principle to equivalents, which are encapsulated in the Protocol questions. The former is the bedrock of patent construction, universally applicable. The latter are only guidelines, more useful in some cases than in others. I am bound to say that the cases show a tendency

for counsel to treat the Protocol questions as legal rules rather than guides which will in appropriate cases help to decide what the skilled man would have understood the patentee to mean.

* * *

69. I shall say in a moment why I agree with the Court of Appeal, but I want first to emphasise a point I have already made about the use of the Protocol questions. The determination of the extent of protection conferred by a European patent is an examination in which there is only one compulsory question, namely that set by article 69 and its Protocol: what would a person skilled in the art have understood the patentee to have used the language of the claim to mean? Everything else, including the Protocol questions, is only guidance to a judge trying to answer that question. But there is no point in going through the motions of answering the Protocol questions when you cannot sensibly do so until you have construed the claim. In such a case—and the present is in my opinion such a case—they simply provide a formal justification for a conclusion which has already been reached on other grounds.

70. I agree with the Court of Appeal that the invention should normally be taken as having been claimed at the same level of generality as that at which it is defined in the claims. It would be unusual for the person skilled in the art to understand a specification to be claiming an invention at a higher level of generality than that chosen by the patentee. That means that once the judge had construed the claims as he did, he had answered the question of infringement. It could only cause confusion to try to answer the Protocol questions as well.

71. No doubt there will be patent lawyers who are dismayed at the notion that the Protocol questions do not provide an answer in every case. They may feel cast adrift on a sea of interpretative uncertainty. But that is the fate of all who have to understand what people mean by using language. The Protocol questions are useful in many cases, but they are not a substitute for trying to understand what the person skilled in the art would have understood the patentee to mean by the language of the claims.

72. This is perhaps an appropriate point at which to mention what may appear to be a difference between the German, United Kingdom and Netherlands approach to these questions. It used to be thought that despite article 69 and the Protocol, there remained serious differences between the approaches to construction of the United Kingdom on the one hand and Germany and the Netherlands on the other. And it is true that in the early years of the EPC, there was a view in the German and Netherlands courts that the Convention had made no difference and that the Protocol entitled the courts of Contracting States to go on deciding the extent of protection exactly as before. The position in the Netherlands is described by Professor Brinkhof in the article *Is there a European Doctrine of Equivalence?* (2002) IIC 911 to which I have already referred.

73. But I do not think that this is any longer true. The highest courts in both Germany (see Batteriekastenschnur [1989] GRUR 903, 904) and the Netherlands (see Ciba-Geigy/Ot Optics (1995) Nederlandse Jurisprudentie 39) have said that the effect of article 69 is to give the claims what the European Patent Office has called a "central role": see BAYER/Plant growth regulating agent [1990] EPOR 257, 261. The Bundesgerichtshof said in the Batteriekastenschnur case that the claims are no longer merely a point of departure but the decisive basis (massgebliche Grundlage) for determining the extent of protection.

* * *

75. The German courts have their own guidelines for dealing with equivalents, which have some resemblance to the Protocol questions. In the "quintet" of cases before the Bundesgerichtshof (see, for example, Kunstoffrohrteil [2002] GRUR 511 and Schneidemesser 1 [2003] ENPR 12 309) which concerned questions of whether figures or measurements in a claim allow some degree of approximation (and, if so, what degree), the court expressly said that its approach was similar to that adopted in *Catnic*. But there are differences from the Protocol questions which are lucidly explained by Dr Peter Meier-Beck (currently a judge of the 10th Senate) in a paper to be published in the International Review of Intellectual Property and Competition Law (IIC). For example, German judges do not ask whether a variant "works in the same way" but whether it solves the problem underlying the invention by means which have the same technical effect. That may be a better way of putting the question because it avoids the ambiguity illustrated by American Home Products Corporation v Novartis Pharmaceuticals UK Ltd [2001] RPC 159 over whether "works in the same way" involves an assumption that it works at all. On the other hand, as is illustrated by the present case, everything will depend upon what you regard as "the problem underlying the invention." It seems to me, however, that the German courts are also approaching the question of equivalents with a view to answering the same ultimate question as that which I have suggested is raised by Article 69, namely what a person skilled in the art would have thought the patentee was using the language of the claim to mean.

The Decision of the Court of Appeal

* * *

77. . . . An invention is a practical product or process, not information about the natural world. That seems to me to accord with the social contract between the state and the inventor which underlies patent law. The state gives the inventor a monopoly in return for an immediate disclosure of all the information necessary to enable performance of the invention. That disclosure is not only to enable other people to perform the invention after the patent has expired. If that were all, the inventor might as well be allowed to keep it secret during the life of the patent. It is also to enable anyone to make immediate use of the information for any purpose which does not infringe the claims. The specifications of valid and subsisting patents are an important source of information for further research, as is abundantly shown by a reading of the sources cited in the specification for the patent in suit. Of course a patentee may in some cases be able to frame his claim to a product or process so broadly that in practice it will be impossible to use the information he has disclosed, even to develop important improvements, in a way which does not infringe. But it cannot be right to give him a monopoly of the use of the information as such.

New Technology

* * *

80. I do not dispute that a claim may, upon its proper construction, cover products or processes which involve the use of technology unknown at the time

the claim was drafted. The question is whether the person skilled in the art would understand the description in a way which was sufficiently general to include the new technology. There is no difficulty in principle about construing general terms to include embodiments which were unknown at the time the document was written. One frequently does that in construing legislation, for example, by construing "carriage" in a 19th century statute to include a motor car. In such cases it is particularly important not to be too literal. It may be clear from the language, context and background that the patentee intended to refer in general terms to, for example, every way of achieving a certain result, even though he has used language which is in some respects inappropriate in relation to a new way of achieving that result: compare *Regina (Quintavalle) v Secretary of State for Health* [2003] 2 AC 687. In the present case, however, I agree with the Court of Appeal (and with the judge, before he came to apply the Protocol questions) that the man skilled in the art would not have understood the claim as sufficiently general to include gene activation. He would have understood it to be limited to the expression of an exogenous DNA sequence which coded for EPO.

81. The argument over whether the claim can include the new technology is linked to a dispute over the meaning of the second Protocol question. When one asks whether it would have been obvious to the person skilled in the art that the variant worked in the same way as the invention, does one assume that it works? Otherwise, in the case of a technology which was unknown at the priority date, the person skilled in the art would probably say that it was by no means obvious that it would work in the same way because it was not obvious that it would work at all.

82. Some might say, in answer to this question, that it depends on the nature of the invention. For example, in *American Home Products Corporation v Novartis Pharmaceuticals UK Ltd* [2001] RPC 159 the alleged invention was a second medical use for the known drug rapamycin, which was found to have an immuno-suppressive effect. The question was whether a claim to rapamycin should be construed as including derivatives of rapamycin. The evidence was that the person skilled in the art would be unable to say without experimentation that any particular derivative would have an immuno-suppressive effect. In applying the second Protocol question, it would have been absurd to ask whether, assuming that a derivative "worked" in the sense of having an immuno-suppressive effect, it worked "in the same way." That would really be to beg the question. Neither the product nor the process was new: the whole point of the invention was the newly discovered immuno-suppressive effect.

83. On the other hand, in *Improver Corporation v Remington Consumer Products Ltd* [1990] FSR 181 the invention was based upon the discovery that an arcuate rod with slits, when rotated at high speed, would take the hair off the skin by means of the opening and closing of the slits. The claim was to a rod in the form of an "helical spring" but the alleged infringer had found that an arcuate rod of vulcanised rubber with slits would do just as well. In answering the second Protocol question, I said that it did not matter that it would not have been obvious to the person skilled in the art to substitute a rubber rod. The question was whether such a rod would work in the same way as an helical spring. I went on, however, to say (in answer to the third question) that "helical spring" could not be generalised to mean any arcuate rod with slits. It meant an helical spring.

84. So perhaps a better answer to the dispute over the second Protocol question is that new technology is another situation in which the Protocol questions may be unhelpful. On the other hand, if the claim can properly be construed in a way which is sufficiently general to include the new technology, the Protocol questions tend to answer themselves.

Comments

1. **Catnic, *"Purposive Construction," and Equivalents.*** Lord Hoffmann was clear to distinguish between principles of claim construction and the "Protocol questions" relating to non-literal infringement. The *Catnic* principle of purposive construction gives effect to the protocol of Article 69, and is considered a "bedrock of patent construction." In contrast, the protocol questions of *Improver* and *Catnic* are "only guidelines, more useful in some cases than in others."

   Regarding purposive construction, Lord Hoffmann was clear in his emphasis on the importance of objective interpretation. For him, "[t]here is no window into the mind of the patentee or the author of any other document." Rather, "[c]onstruction is objective in the sense that it is concerned with what a reasonable person to whom the utterance was addressed would have understood the author to be using the words to mean." This approach is similar to the American approach to claim construction and the central role of the person of ordinary skill in the art. One important difference, however, is the effect given to prosecution history estoppel, a prominent doctrine in American patent law. (See Comment 3, below.)

   In addition, in discussing equivalents, Lord Hoffmann views Article 69 as "firmly shut[ting] the door on any doctrine which extends protection outside the claims." He asks how can a rule be constructed that satisfies Article 69's compromise, namely to "combine fair protection for the patentee with a reasonable degree of certainty for third parties." As with claim construction, Lord Hoffmann turns to the skilled artisan in his discussion of non-literal infringement. Citing the *Catnic* principle and its accordance with the Protocol, he states the principle is "intended to give the patentee the full extent, but not more than the full extent, of the monopoly which a reasonable person skilled in the art, reading the claims in context, would think he was intending to claim."

2. *Language and Context.* The meaning of language and context are extremely important to Lord Hoffmann. For example, in ¶29, he states "the attempt to treat the words of the claim as having meanings 'in themselves' and without regard to the context in which or the purpose for which they were used was always a highly artificial exercise." And in ¶32, he notes,

   > What the author would have been understood to mean by using those words is not simply a matter of rules. It is highly sensitive to the context of and background to the particular utterance. It depends not only upon the words the author has chosen but also upon the identity of the audience he is taken to have been addressing and the knowledge and assumptions which one attributes to that audience.

   Of course, the importance of context in understanding linguistic meaning has relevance beyond the law. Indeed, Lord Hoffmann has noted elsewhere his views on interpretation are influenced by the philosophy of language and the work of John Searle and Ludwig Wittgenstein. *See, e.g.,* JOHN R. SEARLE, THE CONSTRUCTION OF SOCIAL REALITY (1995), and LUDWIG WITTGENSTEIN, PHILOSOPHICAL INVESTIGATIONS (G.E.M. Anscombe trans., 1953).

3. *"Life Is Too Short" for the Use of Prosecution History in the U.K.* Unlike the United States, the U.K. views prosecution history as having little value for purposes of claim interpretation or infringement analysis. According to *Kirin-Amgen,* "[t]here are good reasons" for discouraging the use of prosecution history, namely "the meaning of the patent should not change according to whether or not the person skilled in the art has access to the file and in any case life is too short for the limited assistance which it can provide." Indeed, under U.K. law, a party cannot make reference to the prosecution history unless the patentee puts it into evidence and relies on it.

4. *Article 69 and U.K.-Germany Compromise.* The U.K. has traditionally placed a great deal of emphasis on the patent claim, which was viewed as a self-contained device that was used "to limit and not to extend the monopoly." In contrast, the German practice historically used the claim as a "point of departure in determining the extent of protection." Article 69, and more accurately, its protocol, sought a compromise position between these two views. And, according to *Kirin-Amgen* and Lord Hoffmann, Germany (and the Netherlands) has now trended toward the traditional U.K. position that the claim plays a "central role."

5. *Penicillin and the U.K.-Germany Approach to the Value of Patents.* The divergent views of the U.K. and Germany were not limited to claim interpretation and non-literal infringement. These competing views can be seen in how the countries viewed the value of patents during the first half of the twentieth century, as reflected in the history of penicillin. Howard Florey of England and Ernst Chain of Germany (he moved to England when he was 27), two scientists instrumental to the development of penicillin at Oxford, debated whether they should seek a patent. Florey, steeped in the scientific culture of England, "believed it was odious for a scientist to claim a gain as his own." But Chain was adamant that a patent should be obtained. As Eric Lax writes, "[f]rom his father's and own experiences as a scientist in Germany, Chain knew firsthand how in the competitive world outside Britain patents leveraged economic advantage." ERIC LAX, THE MOLD IN DR. FLOREY'S COAT 162 (2004). Lax continues that, "[o]ne of the many differences between the German and the British approaches to science in the early twentieth century was the importance of patents. In Germany, a patent was a natural and valued part of scientific advance; in Britain it was a repugnant sign of commercialism." *Id.* at 163. Much to the chagrin of Chain, a decision was made at Oxford University not to seek patent protection. But Florey, Chain, and Alexander Fleming would go on to receive the Nobel Prize in 1945 for Physiology or Medicine. Consistent with the German view, patents also played in important role in Germany's dominance of the synthetic dye industry in the late 19th and early 20th centuries at the expense of British and American companies. *See* JOHANN PETER MURMANN, KNOWLEDGE AND COMPETITIVE ADVANTAGE: THE COEVOLUTION OF FIRMS, TECHNOLOGY, AND NATIONAL INSTITUTIONS 86-93, 179-192 (2003).

4. Indirect Infringement

Indirect infringement has, in recent years, assumed great importance in copyright law, particularly in the context of peer-to-peer networks, and it was at the heart of the famous "Betamax case." *See Sony Corp. v. Universal City Studio, Inc.*, 464 U.S. 417 (1984). But indirect infringement is equally important in patent law and has a richer historical presence. (Indeed, *Sony* relied on patent law's indirect infringement jurisprudence.) The doctrine of indirect infringement allows patentees to capture actors who, while not directly infringing, aid and abet the direct infringer by, for example, supplying an individual component of a patent invention (contributing to infringement) or providing instruction that facilitates direct infringement (inducing infringement). The rationale for the doctrine of indirect infringement was aptly described by the Supreme Court in *Dawson Chemical Co. v. Rohm & Haas Co.*:

> [It] exists to protect patent rights from subversion by those who, without directly infringing the patent themselves, engage in acts designed to facilitate infringement by others. This protection is of particular importance in situations . . . where enforcement against direct infringers would be difficult, and where the technicalities of patent law make it relatively easy to profit from another's invention without risking a charge of direct infringement.

448 F.3d 176, 188 (1980).

The statutory authority for inducement and contributory infringement is in section 271(b) and (c), respectively. In addition to these sections, there are common law requirements that must be satisfied. The principal cases, *Lucent*, *Global-Tech*, and *Akamai*, explore both the statutory and common law requirements of inducement and contributory infringement.

LUCENT TECHNOLOGIES, INC. v. GATEWAY, INC.

580 F.3d 1301 (Fed. Cir. 2009)

MICHEL, Chief Judge.

Microsoft Corporation appeals the denial of post-trial motions concerning a jury verdict that Microsoft indirectly infringed U.S. Patent No. 4,763,356 (the "Day patent" [assigned to Lucent]). Because the infringement decision was not contrary to law and supported by substantial evidence, we affirm.

BACKGROUND

In December 1986, three computer engineers at AT&T filed a patent application, which eventually issued as the Day patent. The patent is generally directed to a method of entering information into fields on a computer screen without using a keyboard. A user fills in the displayed fields by choosing concurrently displayed, predefined tools adapted to facilitate the inputting of the information in a particular field, wherein the predefined tools include an on-screen graphical keyboard, a menu, and a calculator. The system may display menus of information for filling in a particular field and may also be adapted to communicate with a host computer to obtain the information that is inserted into the fields. In addition, one of the displayed fields can be a bit-mapped graphics field, which the user fills in by writing on the touch screen using a stylus.

In 2002, Lucent initiated the present action against Gateway, and Microsoft subsequently intervened. At trial, Lucent charged infringement by Microsoft of claims 19 and 21, among others, of the Day patent. Lucent alleged indirect infringement of claim 19 based on the sales and use of Microsoft Money, Microsoft Outlook, and Windows Mobile. As to claim 21, Lucent asserted that the use of Windows Mobile infringed. Microsoft challenged Lucent's infringement contentions, contending . . . Microsoft's sales of its products did not infringe the Day patent.

The jury found Microsoft liable on claim 19 as to all three products and on claim 21 as to Windows Mobile. The parties filed numerous post-trial motions, including Microsoft's renewed motion challenging the jury's finding of infringement. Microsoft has timely appealed the district court's decision. We have jurisdiction pursuant to 28 U.S.C. §1295(a)(1).

ANALYSIS

* * *

III. Infringement

The jury found indirect infringement by Microsoft. Claims 19 and 21 are method claims; thus, Microsoft's sales of its software alone cannot infringe the patent. Infringement occurs only when someone performs the method using a computer running the necessary software. Thus, Microsoft can only be liable for infringement of claims 19 and 21 as a contributor and/or an inducer.

* * *

B. Contributory Infringement

Under 35 U.S.C. §271(c), a party is liable for infringement if he "offers to sell or sells within the United States or imports into the United States . . . a material or apparatus for use in practicing a patented process, constituting a material part of the invention, knowing the same to be especially made or especially adapted for use in an infringement of such patent, and not a staple article or commodity of commerce suitable for substantial noninfringing use." "In order to succeed on a claim of contributory infringement, in addition to proving an act of direct infringement, plaintiff must show that defendant 'knew that the combination for which its components were especially made was both patented and infringing' and that defendant's components have 'no substantial non-infringing uses.'" *Cross Med. Prods., Inc. v. Medtronic Sofamor Danek, Inc.*, 424 F.3d 1293, 1312 (Fed. Cir. 2005).

According to Microsoft, Lucent did not prove contributory infringement because the products have substantial noninfringing uses. Lucent counters that the date-picker tool does not have any noninfringing uses. Thus, as framed by the parties, the main issue reduces to whether the "material or apparatus" is the entire software package or just the particular tool (e.g., the calendar date-picker) that performs the claimed method. If the former, then Microsoft prevails because the entire software package has substantial noninfringing uses. If the material or apparatus is the specific date-picker tool, then Lucent wins because that tool was "especially made or especially adapted for" practicing the claimed method.

One example illustrates the problem with Microsoft's approach. Consider a software program comprising five—and only five—features. Each of the five features is separately and distinctly patented using a method claim. That is, the first feature infringes a method claim in a first patent, the second feature infringes a method claim in a second patent, and so forth. Assume also that the company selling the software doesn't provide specific instructions on how to use the five features, thus taking potential liability outside the realm of §271(b). In this scenario, under Microsoft's position, the software seller can never be liable for contributory infringement of any one of the method patents because the entire software program is capable of substantial noninfringing use. This seems both untenable as a practical outcome and inconsistent with both the statute and governing precedent.

Similarly, if, instead of selling Outlook with the date-picker, Microsoft had offered the date-picker for sale as a separate download to be used with Outlook, there would be little dispute that Microsoft was contributing to infringement of the Day patent. As we explained in *Ricoh Co. v. Quanta Computer Inc.,* 550 F.3d 1325, 1337 (Fed. Cir. 2008), an infringer "should not be permitted to escape liability as a contributory infringer merely by embedding [the infringing apparatus] in a larger product with some additional, separable feature before importing and selling it."

Microsoft puts much reliance on *Hodosh v. Block Drug Co.,* 833 F.2d 1575 (Fed. Cir. 1987). Microsoft understands *Hodosh* to require "a focus on the product actually sold, not on a mere ingredient." Under this view, Microsoft didn't contribute to infringement because "[e]ach accused product had substantial noninfringing uses." Instead, according to Microsoft, the district court "eviscerate[d] *Hodosh* and read[ ] 'substantial noninfringing use' out of the statute."

But our court has previously rejected the interpretation of *Hodosh* urged by Microsoft on appeal:

> [T]his reading of *Hodosh* divorces the court's holding from the facts upon which it was rendered. In focusing on "what was actually sold," the *Hodosh* court rejected the argument that an otherwise *infringing* product may automatically escape liability merely because it contains a *noninfringing* staple ingredient. . . . It does not follow from *Hodosh* that the inclusion of a component with substantial noninfringing uses in a product that contains *other* components useful only to infringe a process patent can or should defeat liability for contributory infringement under §271(c).

Ricoh, 550 F.3d at 1339-40.

More importantly, Microsoft fails to appreciate the factual basis for *Hodosh*'s holding. In *Hodosh,* the patent at issue claimed "a method for desensitizing teeth with a composition containing an alkali metal nitrate." 833 F.2d at 1576. The accused infringer sold toothpaste, e.g., "Sensodyne-F," containing potassium nitrate, an alkali metal nitrate. *Id.* The accused infringer argued that the sale of the toothpaste, which itself was not patented, could not constitute contributory infringement because the toothpaste contained a staple article, i.e., potassium nitrate. *Hodosh,* 833 F.2d at 1578. The court rejected this argument. While potassium nitrate, when sold in bulk form, was "a staple article or commodity of commerce suitable for substantial noninfringing use," it was suitable only for the infringing use when sold as an ingredient in the toothpaste specially made to perform the patented method of desensitizing teeth.

Here, the infringing feature for completing the forms, i.e., the date-picker tool, is suitable only for an infringing use. Inclusion of the date-picker feature within a larger program does not change the date-picker's ability to infringe. Because Microsoft included the date-picker tool in Outlook, the jury could reasonably conclude, based on the evidence presented, that Microsoft intended computer users to use the tool—perhaps not frequently—and the only intended use of the tool infringed the Day patent. *See Metro-Goldwyn-Mayer Studios Inc. v. Grokster, Ltd.*, 545 U.S. 913, 932 (2005) (explaining that the contributory infringement doctrine "was devised to identify instances in which it may be presumed from distribution of an article in commerce that the distributor intended the article to be used to infringe another's patent, and so may justly be held liable for that infringement"). . . .

Comments

1. *Contributory Infringement.* The *Lucent* case identified the requirements that must obtain before contributory infringement can be found. The patentee must show (1) there was an act of direct infringement; (2) the defendant sold or offered to sell a component that is a "material part of the [patented] invention"; (3) knew that the combination for which its components were especially made was both patented and infringing; and (4) that defendant's components have "no substantial non-infringing uses." The doctrine of contributory infringement was originally a common law creation that was codified in section 271(c) in 1952. The legislative history of section 271(c) captures the goal of this doctrine: "One who makes a special device constituting the heart of a patented machine and supplies it to others with directions (specific or implied) to complete the machine is obviously appropriating the benefit of the patented invention." H.R. Rep. No. 82-1923, at 9 (1952).

2. *The Non-Staple Article Requirement.* This requirement goes to the heart of contributory infringement. There can be no contributory infringement if an article is capable of substantial noninfringing use. This requirement is made express in section 271(c), which states the article must be "especially made or especially adapted for use in an infringement of such patent, and not a staple article or commodity of commerce suitable for substantial noninfringing use." The sell of a non-staple article is tantamount to direct infringement because the article has no other plausible use. And merely adding separable, noninfringing components to an accused device—that standing alone satisfies the non-staple article requirement—does not avoid indirect infringement. *See Ricoh Co., Ltd. v. Quanta Computer, Inc.*, 550 F.3d 1325, 1337-1338 (Fed. Cir. 2008) (accused infringer should not "escape" contributory infringement by "embedding the microcontroller in a larger product with some additional, separable feature").

   In *C.R. Bard, Inc. v. Advanced Cardiovascular Systems, Inc.*, 911 F.2d 670 (Fed. Cir. 1990), the patentee's contributory infringement claim failed because of the staple article doctrine. In *Bard*, the patentee held a patent on a method for using a catheter in coronary angioplasty. The patentee alleged the defendant's (ACS) sale of catheters for use by surgeons was an act of contributory infringement. The court disagreed because there were three possible ways to use the ACS catheter, only one of which resulted in direct infringement. The catheters were staple articles, capable of substantial noninfringing use. The court stated that "'[w]hen a charge of contributory infringement is predicated entirely on the sale of an article of commerce that is used by the purchaser to infringe a patent, the public interest in access to that article is necessarily implicated.'" In other words, the patentee should not be permitted to impede access to articles that have substantial noninfringing use.

The non-staple requirement was also at issue in *Dawson Chemical Co. v. Rohm & Haas Co.*, 448 U.S. 176 (1980), but in the context of the relationship between contributory infringement under section 271(c) and patent misuse under section 271(d). In *Dawson*, Rohm & Haas owned a patent on a method for applying propanil, which was not subject to patent protection. Rohm & Haas agreed to license its patent only to those who also purchased propanil from Rohm & Haas. Propanil was commercially available from other sources, but formed a "material part of the claimed invention" and had "no use except through practice of the patented method." In other words, propanil was a non-staple article, not subject to substantial noninfringing uses. Dawson asserted Rohm & Haas was misusing the patent by conditioning a license on the purchase of propanil. The Court, in a lengthy opinion, disagreed with Dawson based on propanil's non-staple status. According to the court,

> The provisions of §271(d) effectively confer upon the patentee, as a lawful adjunct of his patent rights, a limited power to exclude others from competition in nonstaple goods. A patentee may sell a nonstaple article himself while enjoining others from marketing that same good without his authorization. . . . To be sure, the sum effect of Rohm & Haas' actions is to suppress competition in the market for an unpatented commodity. But . . . this conduct is no different from that which the statute [§271(c)] expressly protects. . . . If [Dawson's] argument were accepted, it would force patentees either to grant licenses or to forfeit their statutory protection against contributory infringement.

Id. at 201, 215. (The doctrine of patent misuse is explored in Chapter 8.)

3. *Contributory Infringement's Knowledge Requirement.* Section 271(c) has a knowledge requirement: "[w]hoever offers to sell or sells . . . *knowing* the same to be especially made or especially adapted for use in an infringement of such patent." 35 U.S.C. §271(c) (2000) (emphasis added). Does this requirement mean the alleged infringer intended to make the article that led to direct infringement, or knew of the patent's existence, or had knowledge that the article would be used to infringe? In discussing this requirement, the *DSU* court (cited in *Lucent*) quoted the Supreme Court's *Grokster* decision relating to peer-to-peer networks:

> One who makes and sells articles which are only adapted to be used in a patented combination will be presumed to intend the natural consequences of his acts; he will be presumed to intend that they shall be used in the combination of the patent.

Thus, if one makes a non-staple article, knowledge of the article's use to infringe will be presumed, apparently because the article has no other substantial commercial use. This language suggests knowledge of the patent and use of the article for infringement is not required under section 271(c).

4. *No Geographic Limitation in Section 271(b).* Unlike section 271(c), the active inducement statutory provision does not include a geographic limitation. This means that section 271(b) can apply to inducement activity in the United States and abroad. Section 271(c), in contrast, is limited to contributory infringement activity within the United States.

GLOBAL-TECH APPLIANCES, INC. v. SEB S.A.
131 S. Ct. 2060 (2011)

Justice ALITO delivered the opinion of the Court.

We consider whether a party who "actively induces infringement of a patent" under 35 U.S.C. §271(b) must know that the induced acts constitute patent infringement.

I

This case concerns a patent for an innovative deep fryer designed by respondent SEB S.A., a French maker of home appliances. In the late 1980's, SEB invented a "cool-touch" deep fryer, that is, a deep fryer for home use with external surfaces that remain cool during the frying process. The cool-touch deep fryer consisted of a metal frying pot surrounded by a plastic outer housing. Attached to the housing was a ring that suspended the metal pot and insulated the housing from heat by separating it from the pot, creating air space between the two components. SEB obtained a U.S. patent for its design in 1991, and sometime later, SEB started manufacturing the cool-touch fryer and selling it in this country under its well-known "T-Fal" brand. Superior to other products in the American market at the time, SEB's fryer was a commercial success.

In 1997, Sunbeam Products, Inc., a U.S. competitor of SEB, asked petitioner Pentalpha Enterprises, Ltd., to supply it with deep fryers meeting certain specifications. Pentalpha is a Hong Kong maker of home appliances and a wholly owned subsidiary of petitioner Global-Tech Appliances, Inc.

In order to develop a deep fryer for Sunbeam, Pentalpha purchased an SEB fryer in Hong Kong and copied all but its cosmetic features. Because the SEB fryer bought in Hong Kong was made for sale in a foreign market, it bore no U.S. patent markings. After copying SEB's design, Pentalpha retained an attorney to conduct a right-to-use study, but Pentalpha refrained from telling the attorney that its design was copied directly from SEB's.

The attorney failed to locate SEB's patent, and in August 1997 he issued an opinion letter stating that Pentalpha's deep fryer did not infringe any of the patents that he had found. That same month, Pentalpha started selling its deep fryers to Sunbeam, which resold them in the United States under its trademarks. By obtaining its product from a manufacturer with lower production costs, Sunbeam was able to undercut SEB in the U.S. market.

After SEB's customers started defecting to Sunbeam, SEB sued Sunbeam in March 1998, alleging that Sunbeam's sales infringed SEB's patent. Sunbeam notified Pentalpha of the lawsuit the following month. Undeterred, Pentalpha went on to sell deep fryers to Fingerhut Corp. and Montgomery Ward & Co., both of which resold them in the United States under their respective trademarks.

SEB settled the lawsuit with Sunbeam, and then sued Pentalpha, asserting two theories of recovery: First, SEB claimed that Pentalpha had directly infringed

SEB's patent in violation of 35 U.S.C. §271(a), by selling or offering to sell its deep fryers; and second, SEB claimed that Pentalpha had contravened §271(b) by actively inducing Sunbeam, Fingerhut, and Montgomery Ward to sell or to offer to sell Pentalpha's deep fryers in violation of SEB's patent rights.

Following a 5-day trial, the jury found for SEB on both theories and also found that Pentalpha's infringement had been willful. Pentalpha filed post-trial motions seeking a new trial or judgment as a matter of law on several grounds. As relevant here, Pentalpha argued that there was insufficient evidence to support the jury's finding of induced infringement under §271(b) because Pentalpha did not actually know of SEB's patent until it received the notice of the Sunbeam lawsuit in April 1998.

The District Court rejected Pentalpha's argument, as did the Court of Appeals for the Federal Circuit, which affirmed the judgment. Summarizing a recent en banc decision, the Federal Circuit stated that induced infringement under §271(b) requires a "plaintiff [to] show that the alleged infringer knew or should have known that his actions would induce actual infringements" and that this showing includes proof that the alleged infringer knew of the patent. Although the record contained no direct evidence that Pentalpha knew of SEB's patent before April 1998, the court found adequate evidence to support a finding that "Pentalpha deliberately disregarded a known risk that SEB had a protective patent." Such disregard, the court said, "is not different from actual knowledge, but is a form of actual knowledge."

II

Pentalpha argues that active inducement liability under §271(b) requires more than deliberate indifference to a known risk that the induced acts may violate an existing patent. Instead, Pentalpha maintains, actual knowledge of the patent is needed.

A

In assessing Pentalpha's argument, we begin with the text of §271(b)—which is short, simple, and, with respect to the question presented in this case, inconclusive. Section 271(b) states: "Whoever actively induces infringement of a patent shall be liable as an infringer."

Although the text of §271(b) makes no mention of intent, we infer that at least some intent is required. The term "induce" means "[t]o lead on; to influence; to prevail on; to move by persuasion or influence." Webster's New International Dictionary 1269 (2d ed. 1945). The addition of the adverb "actively" suggests that the inducement must involve the taking of affirmative steps to bring about the desired result, see *id.,* at 27.

When a person actively induces another to take some action, the inducer obviously knows the action that he or she wishes to bring about. If a used car salesman induces a customer to buy a car, the salesman knows that the desired result is the purchase of the car. But what if it is said that the salesman induced the customer to buy a *damaged* car? Does this mean merely that the salesman induced the customer to purchase a car that happened to be damaged, a fact of which the salesman may have been unaware? Or does this mean that the salesman knew that the car was damaged? The statement that the salesman induced the customer to buy a damaged car is ambiguous.

So is §271(b). In referring to a party that "induces infringement," this provision may require merely that the inducer lead another to engage in conduct that happens to amount to infringement, *i.e.,* the making, using, offering to sell, selling, or importing of a patented invention. See §271(a). On the other hand, the reference to a party that "induces infringement" may also be read to mean that the inducer must persuade another to engage in conduct that the inducer knows is infringement. Both readings are possible.

B

Finding no definitive answer in the statutory text, we turn to the case law that predates the enactment of §271 as part the Patent Act of 1952. As we recognized in *Aro Mfg. Co. v. Convertible Top Replacement Co.,* 377 U.S. 476 (1964) (*Aro II*), "[t]he section was designed to 'codify in statutory form principles of contributory infringement' which had been 'part of our law for about 80 years.'" *Id.,* at 485-486, n. 6, 84 S. Ct. 1526 (quoting H.R. Rep. No. 1923, 82d Cong., 2d Sess., 9 (1952)).

Unfortunately, the relevant pre-1952 cases are less clear than one might hope with respect to the question presented here. Before 1952, both the conduct now covered by §271(b) (induced infringement) and the conduct now addressed by §271(c) (sale of a component of a patented invention) were viewed as falling within the overarching concept of "contributory infringement." Cases in the latter category—*i.e.,* cases in which a party sold an item that was not itself covered by the claims of a patent but that enabled another party to make or use a patented machine, process, or combination—were more common. . . .

While both the language of §271(b) and the pre-1952 case law that this provision was meant to codify are susceptible to conflicting interpretations, our decision in *Aro II* resolves the question in this case. In *Aro II,* a majority held that a violator of §271(c) must know "that the combination for which his component was especially designed was both patented and infringing," 377 U.S., at 488, and as we explain below, that conclusion compels this same knowledge for liability under §271(b).

C

As noted above, induced infringement was not considered a separate theory of indirect liability in the pre-1952 case law. Rather, it was treated as evidence of "contributory infringement," that is, the aiding and abetting of direct infringement by another party. When Congress enacted §271, it separated what had previously been regarded as contributory infringement into two categories, one covered by §271(b) and the other covered by §271(c).

Aro II concerned §271(c), which states in relevant part:

> Whoever offers to sell or sells . . . a component of a patented [invention] . . . , constituting a material part of the invention, *knowing the same to be especially made or especially adapted for use in an infringement* of such patent, and not a staple article or commodity of commerce suitable for substantial noninfringing use, shall be liable as a contributory infringer." (Emphasis added.)

This language contains exactly the same ambiguity as §271(b). The phrase "knowing [a component] to be especially made or especially adapted for use in an infringement" may be read to mean that a violator must know that the component is "especially adapted for use" in a product that happens to infringe a patent. Or the phrase may be read to require, in addition, knowledge of the patent's existence.

This question closely divided the *Aro II* Court. In a badly fractured decision, a majority concluded that knowledge of the patent was needed. 377 U.S., at 488, and n.8. Four Justices disagreed with this interpretation and would have held that a violator of §271(c) need know only that the component is specially adapted for use in a product that happens to infringe a patent. These Justices thought that this reading was supported by the language of §271(c) and the pre-1952 case law, and they disagreed with the inference drawn by the majority from the amendment of §271(c)'s language.

While there is much to be said in favor of both views expressed in *Aro II*, the "holding in *Aro II* has become a fixture in the law of contributory infringement under [section] 271(c),"—so much so that SEB has not asked us to overrule it. Nor has Congress seen fit to alter §271(c)'s intent requirement in the nearly half a century since *Aro II* was decided. In light of the "'special force'" of the doctrine of *stare decisis* with regard to questions of statutory interpretation, we proceed on the premise that §271(c) requires knowledge of the existence of the patent that is infringed.

Based on this premise, it follows that the same knowledge is needed for induced infringement under §271(b). As noted, the two provisions have a common origin in the pre-1952 understanding of contributory infringement, and the language of the two provisions creates the same difficult interpretive choice. It would thus be strange to hold that knowledge of the relevant patent is needed under §271(c) but not under §271(b).

Accordingly, we now hold that induced infringement under §271(b) requires knowledge that the induced acts constitute patent infringement.

III

Returning to Pentalpha's principal challenge, we agree that deliberate indifference to a known risk that a patent exists is not the appropriate standard under §271(b). We nevertheless affirm the judgment of the Court of Appeals because the evidence in this case was plainly sufficient to support a finding of Pentalpha's knowledge under the doctrine of willful blindness.

A

The doctrine of willful blindness is well established in criminal law. Many criminal statutes require proof that a defendant acted knowingly or willfully, and courts applying the doctrine of willful blindness hold that defendants cannot escape the reach of these statutes by deliberately shielding themselves from clear evidence of critical facts that are strongly suggested by the circumstances. The traditional rationale for this doctrine is that defendants who behave in this manner are just as culpable as those who have actual knowledge. It is also said that persons who know enough to blind themselves to direct proof of critical facts in effect have actual knowledge of those facts.

Given the long history of willful blindness and its wide acceptance in the Federal Judiciary, we can see no reason why the doctrine should not apply in civil lawsuits for induced patent infringement under 35 U.S.C. §271(b).

Pentalpha urges us not to take this step, arguing that §271(b) demands more than willful blindness with respect to *the induced acts* that constitute infringement.

This question, however, is not at issue here. There is no need to invoke the doctrine of willful blindness to establish that Pentalpha knew that the retailers who purchased its fryer were selling that product in the American market; Pentalpha was indisputably aware that its customers were selling its product in this country.

B

While the Courts of Appeals articulate the doctrine of willful blindness in slightly different ways, all appear to agree on two basic requirements: (1) the defendant must subjectively believe that there is a high probability that a fact exists and (2) the defendant must take deliberate actions to avoid learning of that fact. We think these requirements give willful blindness an appropriately limited scope that surpasses recklessness and negligence. Under this formulation, a willfully blind defendant is one who takes deliberate actions to avoid confirming a high probability of wrongdoing and who can almost be said to have actually known the critical facts. By contrast, a reckless defendant is one who merely knows of a substantial and unjustified risk of such wrongdoing, and a negligent defendant is one who should have known of a similar risk but, in fact, did not, see §2.02(2)(d).

The test applied by the Federal Circuit in this case departs from the proper willful blindness standard in two important respects. First, it permits a finding of knowledge when there is merely a "known risk" that the induced acts are infringing. Second, in demanding only "deliberate indifference" to that risk, the Federal Circuit's test does not require active efforts by an inducer to avoid knowing about the infringing nature of the activities.

In spite of these flaws, we believe that the evidence when viewed in the light most favorable to the verdict for SEB is sufficient under the correct standard. The jury could have easily found that before April 1998 Pentalpha willfully blinded itself to the infringing nature of the sales it encouraged Sunbeam to make.

SEB's cool-touch fryer was an innovation in the U.S. market when Pentalpha copied it. As one would expect with any superior product, sales of SEB's fryer had been growing for some time. Pentalpha knew all of this, for its CEO and president, John Sham, testified that, in developing a product for Sunbeam, Pentalpha performed "market research" and "gather[ed] information as much as possible." Pentalpha's belief that SEB's fryer embodied advanced technology that would be valuable in the U.S. market is evidenced by its decision to copy all but the cosmetic features of SEB's fryer.

Also revealing is Pentalpha's decision to copy an overseas model of SEB's fryer. Pentalpha knew that the product it was designing was for the U.S. market, and Sham—himself a named inventor on numerous U.S. patents—was well aware that products made for overseas markets usually do not bear U.S. patent markings. Even more telling is Sham's decision not to inform the attorney from whom Pentalpha sought a right-to-use opinion that the product to be evaluated was simply a knockoff of SEB's deep fryer. On the facts of this case, we cannot fathom what motive Sham could have had for withholding this information other than to manufacture a claim of plausible deniability in the event that his company was later accused of patent infringement. Nor does Sham's testimony on this subject provide any reason to doubt that inference. Asked whether the attorney would have fared better had he known of SEB's design, Sham was nonresponsive. All he could say was that a patent search is not an "easy job" and that is why he hired attorneys to perform them.

Taken together, this evidence was more than sufficient for a jury to find that Pentalpha subjectively believed there was a high probability that SEB's fryer was patented, that Pentalpha took deliberate steps to avoid knowing that fact, and that it therefore willfully blinded itself to the infringing nature of Sunbeam's sales.

AKAMAI TECHNOLOGIES, INC. v. LIMELIGHT NETWORKS, INC.

692 F.3d 1301 (Fed. Cir. 2012)

PER CURIAM.

When a single actor commits all the elements of infringement, that actor is liable for direct infringement under 35 U.S.C. §271(a). When a single actor induces another actor to commit all the elements of infringement, the first actor is liable for induced infringement under 35 U.S.C. §271(b). But when the acts necessary to give rise to liability for direct infringement are shared between two or more actors, doctrinal problems arise. In the two cases before us, we address the question whether a defendant may be held liable for induced infringement if the defendant has performed some of the steps of a claimed method and has induced other parties to commit the remaining steps (as in the *Akamai* case), or if the defendant has induced other parties to collectively perform all the steps of the claimed method, but no single party has performed all of the steps itself (as in the *McKesson* case).

The problem of divided infringement in induced infringement cases typically arises only with respect to method patents. When claims are directed to a product or apparatus, direct infringement is always present, because the entity that installs the final part and thereby completes the claimed invention is a direct infringer. But in the case of method patents, parties that jointly practice a patented invention can often arrange to share performance of the claimed steps between them. In fact, sometimes that is the natural way that a particular method will be practiced, as the cases before us today illustrate. Recent precedents of this court have interpreted section 271(b) to mean that unless the accused infringer directs or controls the actions of the party or parties that are performing the claimed steps, the patentee has no remedy, even though the patentee's rights are plainly being violated by the actors' joint conduct. We now conclude that this interpretation of section 271(b) is wrong as a matter of statutory construction, precedent, and sound patent policy.

Much of the briefing in these cases has been directed to the question whether direct infringement can be found when no single entity performs all of the claimed steps of the patent. It is not necessary for us to resolve that issue today because we find that these cases and cases like them can be resolved through an application of the doctrine of induced infringement. In doing so, we reconsider and overrule the 2007 decision of this court in which we held that in order for a party to be liable for induced infringement, some other single entity must be liable for direct infringement. *BMC Resources, Inc. v. Paymentech, L.P.*, 498 F.3d 1373 (Fed. Cir. 2007). To be clear, we hold that all the steps of a claimed method must be performed in order to find induced infringement, but that it is not necessary to prove that all the steps were committed by a single entity.

I

The essential facts of the cases before us are as follows:

Akamai Technologies, Inc., owns a patent that covers a method for efficient delivery of web content. The claimed method consists of placing some of a content provider's content elements on a set of replicated servers and modifying the content provider's web page to instruct web browsers to retrieve that content from those servers. Akamai filed a complaint against Limelight Networks, Inc., alleging infringement of the patent. In its complaint, Akamai alleged both direct and induced infringement. Limelight maintains a network of servers and, as in the patented method, it allows for efficient content delivery by placing some content elements on its servers. Limelight, however, does not modify the content providers' web pages itself. Instead, Limelight instructs its customers on the steps needed to do that modification.

McKesson Information Solutions LLC owns a patent covering a method of electronic communication between healthcare providers and their patients. McKesson filed a complaint against Epic Systems Corp. alleging that Epic induced infringement of the patent. Epic is a software company that licenses its software to healthcare organizations. The licensed software includes an application called "MyChart," which permits healthcare providers to communicate electronically with patients. McKesson alleged that Epic induced Epic's customers to infringe McKesson's patent. Epic does not perform any steps of the patent. Instead, those steps are divided between patients, who initiate communications, and healthcare providers, who perform the remainder of the steps.

In the respective district court cases, Limelight and Epic were held not to infringe the patents asserted against them. In *Akamai*, because Limelight's customers (and not Limelight itself) performed one of the steps of the claimed method, the district court granted Limelight's motion for judgment as a matter of law based on this court's opinions in *BMC* and *Muniauction, Inc. v. Thomson Corp.*, 532 F.3d 1318 (Fed. Cir. 2008). In *McKesson,* the district court relied on the same cases to grant summary judgment of noninfringement on the ground that the patients (and not Epic's direct customers) performed the step of initiating the communication.

II

A

This court has held that for a party to be liable for direct patent infringement under 35 U.S.C. §271(a), that party must commit all the acts necessary to infringe the patent, either personally or vicariously. In the context of a method claim, that means the accused infringer must perform all the steps of the claimed method, either personally or through another acting under his direction or control. Direct infringement has not been extended to cases in which multiple independent parties perform the steps of the method claim. Because direct infringement is a strict liability tort, it has been thought that extending liability in that manner would ensnare actors who did not themselves commit all the acts necessary to constitute infringement and who had no way of knowing that others were acting in a way that rendered their collective conduct infringing. *See In re Seagate Tech., LLC,* 497 F.3d 1360, 1368 (Fed. Cir. 2007) (en banc) ("Because patent infringement is a strict liability offense, the nature of the offense is only relevant in determining whether enhanced damages are warranted."). For that reason, this court has rejected claims of liability for direct infringement of method claims in cases in which several parties have collectively committed the acts necessary to constitute direct infringement, but no single party has committed all of the required acts. *See BMC,* 498 F.3d at 1381 ("Direct infringement is a strict-liability offense, but it is limited to those who practice each and every element of the claimed invention.").

To be sure, the court has recognized that direct infringement applies when the acts of infringement are committed by an agent of the accused infringer or a party acting pursuant to the accused infringer's direction or control. Absent an agency relationship between the actors or some equivalent, however, a party that does not commit all the acts necessary to constitute infringement has not been held liable for direct infringement even if the parties have arranged to "divide" their acts of infringing conduct for the specific purpose of avoiding infringement liability.

Because the reasoning of our decision today is not predicated on the doctrine of direct infringement, we have no occasion at this time to revisit any of those principles regarding the law of divided infringement as it applies to liability for direct infringement under 35 U.S.C. §271(a).

B

The induced infringement provision of the Patent Act, 35 U.S.C. §271(b), provides that "[w]hoever actively induces infringement of a patent shall be liable as an infringer." Because section 271(b) extends liability to a party who advises, encourages, or otherwise induces others to engage in infringing conduct, it is well suited to address the problem presented by the cases before us, i.e., whether liability should extend to a party who induces the commission of infringing conduct when no single "induced" entity commits all of the infringing acts or steps but where the infringing conduct is split among more than one other entity.

Induced infringement is in some ways narrower than direct infringement and in some ways broader. Unlike direct infringement, induced infringement is not a strict liability tort; it requires that the accused inducer act with knowledge that the induced acts constitute patent infringement. *See Global-Tech Appliances, Inc. v. SEB S.A.,* 131 S. Ct. 2060, 2068 (2011). In fact, this court has described the required intent as follows: "[I]nducement requires that the alleged infringer knowingly induced infringement and possessed specific intent to encourage another's infringement." *DSU Med. Corp. v. JMS Co.,* 471 F.3d 1293, 1306 (Fed. Cir. 2006) (en banc).[1] On the other hand, inducement does not require that the induced party be an agent of the inducer or be acting under the inducer's direction or control to such an extent that the act of the induced party can be attributed to the inducer as a direct infringer. It is enough that the inducer "cause[s], urge[s], encourage[s], or aid[s]" the infringing conduct and that the induced conduct is carried out.

---

1. Because liability for inducement, unlike liability for direct infringement, requires specific intent to cause infringement, using inducement to reach joint infringement does not present the risk of extending liability to persons who may be unaware of the existence of a patent or even unaware that others are practicing some of the steps claimed in the patent.

An important limitation on the scope of induced infringement is that inducement gives rise to liability only if the inducement leads to actual infringement. That principle, that there can be no indirect infringement without direct infringement, is well settled. The reason for that rule is simple: There is no such thing as attempted patent infringement, so if there is no infringement, there can be no indirect liability for infringement.

That much is uncontroversial. In *BMC*, however, this court extended that principle in an important respect that warrants reconsideration. In that case, the court ruled that in order to support a finding of induced infringement, not only must the inducement give rise to direct infringement, but in addition the direct infringement must be committed by a single actor. The court reached that conclusion based on the propositions that (1) liability for induced infringement requires proof of direct infringement and (2) liability for direct infringement requires that a single party commit all the acts necessary to constitute infringement. While those two propositions were well supported in this court's law, the conclusion that the court drew from them was not.

Requiring proof that there *has been* direct infringement as a predicate for induced infringement is not the same as requiring proof that a single party would be *liable* as a direct infringer. If a party has knowingly induced others to commit the acts necessary to infringe the plaintiff's patent and those others commit those acts, there is no reason to immunize the inducer from liability for indirect infringement simply because the parties have structured their conduct so that no single defendant has committed all the acts necessary to give rise to liability for direct infringement.

A party who knowingly induces others to engage in acts that collectively practice the steps of the patented method—and those others perform those acts—has had precisely the same impact on the patentee as a party who induces the same infringement by a single direct infringer; there is no reason, either in the text of the statute or in the policy underlying it, to treat the two inducers differently. In particular, there is no reason to hold that the second inducer is liable for infringement but the first is not.

Likewise, a party who performs some of the steps itself and induces another to perform the remaining steps that constitute infringement has precisely the same impact on the patentee as a party who induces a single person to carry out all of the steps. It would be a bizarre result to hold someone liable for inducing another to perform all of the steps of a method claim but to hold harmless one who goes further by actually performing some of the steps himself. The party who actually participates in performing the infringing method is, if anything, more culpable than one who does not perform any steps.

The text of the induced infringement statute is entirely consistent with this analysis. While the direct infringement statute, section 271(a), states that a person who performs the acts specified in the statute "infringes the patent," section 271(b) is structured differently. It provides that whoever "actively induces infringement of a patent shall be liable as an infringer." Nothing in the text indicates that the term "infringement" in section 271(b) is limited to "infringement" by a single entity. Rather, "infringement" in this context appears to refer most naturally to the acts necessary to infringe a patent, not to whether those acts are performed by one entity or several.

C

The legislative history of the 1952 Patent Act provides strong support for interpreting induced infringement not to require that a single entity—as opposed to multiple entities—commit all the acts necessary to constitute infringement. . . . Although less was said about induced infringement than about contributory infringement in the legislative history, what was said was significant. Giles Rich, one of the principal drafters of the statute, and a frequent witness at hearings on the legislation, made clear in the course of his statement during an early House hearing on contributory infringement that the revised provisions on infringement were intended to reach cases of divided infringement, even when no single entity would be liable for direct infringement. In the course of his statement commenting on the proposed version of what was to become section 271(b) of the 1952 Act, Judge (then Mr.) Rich addressed the problem of "combination patents" and stated the following:

> Improvements in such arts as radio communication, television, etc., sometimes involve the new combinations of elements which in use are normally owned by different persons. Thus, a new method of radio communication may involve a change in the transmitter and a corresponding change in the receiver. To describe such an invention in patent claims, it is necessary either to specify *a new method which involves both transmitting and receiving*, or a new combination of an element in the receiver and an element in the transmitter. There are patents with such claims covering television inventions of importance.

> The recent decisions of the Supreme Court [the cases targeted by the statutory changes] appear to make it impossible to enforce such patents in the usual case where a radio transmitter and a radio receiver are owned and operated by different persons, *for, while there is obvious infringement of the patent, there is no direct infringer of the patent but only two contributory infringers.*

Contributory Infringement of Patents: Hearings Before the Subcomm. on Patents, Trade-marks, and Copyrights of the H. Comm. on the Judiciary, 80th Cong. 5 (1948) ("1948 Hearing") (statement of G. Rich on behalf of the New York Patent Law Association) (emphasis added).

Judge Rich's statement makes clear that he saw no anomaly in finding liability for indirect infringement when there was "obvious infringement of the patent" even though there was "no direct infringer of the patent." In the hypothetical case that he described, involving a claim to a method in which changes would be made in both a transmitter and a receiver, he expressly stated that the "obvious infringement" should be remediable, even though "there is no direct infringer" of the patent, a description that perfectly fits the two cases before us.

As if to lay to rest any doubts as to his views of the proper scope of indirect infringement under the new statute, Judge Rich added, in response to questioning, that "contributory infringement [apparently referring to both contributory infringement and induced infringement] is a specific application to patent law of the law of joint tort feasor where two people somehow together create an infringement which neither one of them individually or independently commits." *Id.* at 12.

In summing up its objections to this court's ruling, Judge Linn's dissent argues that the court today is making a "sweeping change to the nation's patent policy" that goes beyond the proper scope of the court's authority and that a step such as the one taken by the en banc court today should be left to

Congress. Of course, the question whether the majority's position constitutes a change in the law, or whether the dissent's position would constitute a change, depends on what one thinks the prior rule was. Based on the legislative history, general tort principles, and prior case law, including this court's decision in *Fromson*, we believe that *BMC* and the cases that have followed it changed the pre-existing regime with respect to induced infringement of method claims, although admittedly at that time there were relatively few cases in which that issue had arisen. In either event, the court's task is to attempt to determine what Congress had in mind when it enacted the induced infringement statute in 1952. At the end of the day, we are persuaded that Congress did not intend to create a regime in which parties could knowingly sidestep infringement liability simply by arranging to divide the steps of a method claim between them. And we have found no evidence to suggest that Congress intended to create different rules for method claims than for other types of claims. While we believe that our interpretation of section 271(b) represents sound policy, that does not mean that we have adopted that position as a matter of policy preference. In the process of statutory interpretation, it is relevant to ask what policy Congress was attempting to promote and to test each party's proposed interpretation by asking whether it comports with that policy. In these cases, we conclude that it is unlikely that Congress intended to endorse the "single entity rule," at least for the purpose of induced infringement, advocated by Epic and Limelight, which would permit ready evasion of valid method claims with no apparent countervailing benefits.

III

In the *McKesson* case, Epic can be held liable for inducing infringement if it can be shown that (1) it knew of McKesson's patent, (2) it induced the performance of the steps of the method claimed in the patent, and (3) those steps were performed. McKesson preserved its claim of induced infringement, even though this court's decisions in *BMC* and *Muniauction* made the inducement claim difficult to maintain. McKesson is entitled to litigate that issue on remand to the district court.

In the *Akamai* case, although the jury found that the content providers acted under Limelight's direction and control, the trial court correctly held that Limelight did not direct and control the actions of the content providers as those terms have been used in this court's direct infringement cases. Notwithstanding that ruling, under the principles of inducement laid out above, Limelight would be liable for inducing infringement if the patentee could show that (1) Limelight knew of Akamai's patent, (2) it performed all but one of the steps of the method claimed in the patent, (3) it induced the content providers to perform the final step of the claimed method, and (4) the content providers in fact performed that final step.

Although the patentee in *Akamai* did not press its claim of induced infringement at trial, it argues this court should overrule "the mistaken view that only a single entity can infringe a method claim." That argument, while focused on direct infringement, is critical to the conclusion that divided infringement can give rise to liability, whether under a theory of direct infringement or induced infringement. While we do not hold that Akamai is entitled to prevail on its theory of direct infringement, the evidence could support a judgment in its favor on a theory of induced infringement. For that reason, we conclude that

Akamai should be given the benefit of this court's ruling disapproving the line of divided infringement cases that the district court felt compelled to follow. We therefore reverse the judgment in both cases and remand in both cases for further proceedings on the theory of induced infringement.

REVERSED and REMANDED.

LINN, Circuit Judge, dissenting.

In its opinion today, this court assumes the mantle of policy maker. It has decided that the plain text of §271(a) and (b) fails to accord patentees certain extended rights that a majority of this court's judges would prefer that the statute covered. To correct this situation, the majority effectively rewrites these sections, telling us that the term "infringement" was not, as was previously thought, defined by Congress in §271(a), but instead can mean different things in different contexts.

The majority's approach is contrary to both the Patent Act and to the Supreme Court's longstanding precedent that "if there is no direct infringement of a patent there can be no contributory infringement." *Aro Mfg. Co. v. Convertible Top Replacement Co.*, 365 U.S. 336, 341 (1961). In 1952, Congress removed joint-actor patent infringement liability from the discretion of the courts, defining "infringement" in §271(a) and expressly defining the *only* situations in which a party could be liable for something less than an infringement in §271(b) and (c) — clearing away the morass of multi-actor infringement theories that were the unpredictable creature of common law. Since that time, Congress has on three occasions made policy choices to treat certain special circumstances as tantamount to "infringement." *See* 35 U.S.C. §271(e)(2), (f), and (g). In doing so, Congress did not give the courts blanket authority to take it upon themselves to make further policy choices or define "infringement."

The majority opinion is rooted in its conception of what Congress ought to have done rather than what it did. It is also an abdication of this court's obligation to interpret Congressional policy rather than alter it. When this court convenes en banc, it frees itself of the obligation to follow its own prior precedential decisions. But it is beyond our power to rewrite Congress's laws. Similarly, we are obliged to follow the pronouncements of the Supreme Court concerning the proper interpretation of those acts.

On this unsound foundation, the majority holds that in the present appeals there has been predicate "infringement" even though §271(a)'s requirements are not satisfied. On that basis, the majority vacates the contrary judgments of the district courts and remands for further proceedings concerning liability under §271(b). In my view, the plain language of the statute and the unambiguous holdings of the Supreme Court militate for adoption en banc of the prior decisions of the court in *BMC Resources* and *Muniauction*, which hold that liability under §271(b) requires the existence of an act of direct infringement under §271(a), meaning that all steps of a claimed method be practiced, alone or vicariously, by a single entity or joint enterprise. For these reasons, I respectfully dissent.

Comments

1. *Inducement.* An infringement theory based on active inducement is statutorily grounded in section 271(b), which states "[w]hoever actively induces

infringement of a patent shall be liable as an infringer." This provision was added to the patent code in 1952, but the inducement as a theory of infringement has a rich common law history. As the Federal Circuit noted, "[t]he statutory liability for inducement of infringement derives from the common law, wherein acts that the actor knows will lead to the commission of a wrong by another, place shared liability for the wrong on the actor." *National Presto Indus., Inc. v. West Bend Co.*, 76 F.3d 1185, 1194 (Fed. Cir. 1996). The most common analogy resides in tort or criminal law, a joint tortfeasor or one who aids and abets a wrongful act. *See* H.R. Rep. No. 82-1923, at 9 (1952) (stating section 271(b) "recites in broad terms that one who aids and abets an infringement is likewise an infringer"). Examples of acts that can constitute "active inducement" include providing instructions, demonstrations, or training on how to practice the claimed invention.

2. ***Inducement's Knowledge Requirement.*** The nature of the knowledge requirement for active inducement has not been without confusion. For instance, in *Insituform Technologies, Inc. v. CAT Contracting, Inc.*, 385 F.3d 1360, 1377 (Fed. Cir. 2004), the Federal Circuit conceded "there is a lack of clarity concerning whether the required intent must be merely to induce the specific acts or additionally to cause an infringement." The Court in *Global-Tech* sought to clarify "the legal standard for the state of mind element of a claim for actively inducing infringement."

Relying on *Aro Manufacturing Co.* and its contributory infringement jurisprudence, the Court in *Global-Tech* held that knowledge that the induced acts constitute infringement is required. Thus, knowledge of the existence of the infringed patent is required. This knowledge can be shown through, of course, actual knowledge or, more importantly, willful blindness, that is, when an accused infringer "who takes deliberate actions to avoid confirming a high probability of wrongdoing and who can almost be said to have actually known the critical facts." This threshold is higher than negligence, recklessness, and what the Federal Circuit called "deliberate indifference," all of which are insufficient for induced infringement because they do "not require active efforts by an inducer to avoid knowing about the infringing nature of the activities."

In *Global-Tech*, the "active efforts" included Pentalpha's knowledge that its fryers would be sold in the United States, and yet it copied the design of a SEB fryer purchased in Hong Kong. Moreover, Pentalpha did not reveal to its attorney that it was designing a knock-off fryer. As Justice Alito wrote, "we cannot fathom what motive Sham could have had for withholding this information other than to manufacture a claim of plausible deniability in the event that his company was later accused of patent infringement."

3. ***"Non-Infringement" Opinion Letters and the AIA.*** Section 298 of the America Invents Act states the "failure of an infringer to obtain the advice of counsel with respect to any allegedly infringed patent, or the failure of the infringer to present such advice to the court or jury, may not be used to prove that the accused infringer . . . intended to induce infringement of the patent." In the light of this statutory provision and difficulties associated with proving willful blindness, the question remains whether a competitor (potential alleged infringer) of the patentee should nonetheless obtain a freedom to operate

("non-infringement") opinion? What are the costs and benefits of such an opinion in the light of section 298 and *Global-Tech*?

There are both financial costs, which can be considerable, as well as strategic costs, which, for example, can arise from an incompetent letter. Such a letter may lead to a finding of willful ignorance or, at least, deliberate shielding. Lastly, there is the issue of waiver of privilege that may accompany a letter. While this risk has been diminished since *In re Seagate Technology, LLC,* 497 F.3d 1360 (Fed. Cir. 2007) (see Chapter 9), addressing the waiver issue diverts resources and attention away from the merits of the defendant's case. The benefits of obtaining a letter, however, are potentially significant. Most importantly, a competent letter directly and powerfully counters the patentee's claim that the defendant had the requisite intent to induce infringement, even if the defendant had actual notice of the patent. *See DSU Med. Corp. v. JMS Co.,* 471 F.3d 1293 (Fed. Cir. 2006) (court's finding of no specific intent was based in part on the existence of a noninfringement letter); and an absence of a letter may be evidence of intent. *See Broadcom v. Qualcomm,* 543 F.3d 683, 699 (Fed. Cir. 2008) (holding "failure to procure [noninfringement] opinion may be probative of intent in th[e] context" of inducement to infringe). Another benefit of an opinion—assuming infringement is found—is that while it is impermissible to draw an adverse inference of willful infringement in the absence of an opinion, the presence of a competent opinion is strong evidence against any plausible claim of willful infringement. (More on this point in Chapter 9.)

4. ***Multiple Actors and Direct Infringement of Method Claims.*** Section 271(a) has been interpreted as requiring a single actor to perform all of the steps in a claimed process. There is no such thing as *joint direct* infringement in and of itself, and the *Akamai* court did nothing to change this rule. But the *en banc* court—by a vote of 6-5—made an exception to the single-actor rule in the context of an allegation of active inducement, which, like contributory infringement, requires proof of direct infringement. Under the *Akamai* holding, a patentee can prove active inducement when (1) an alleged inducer possesses knowledge of the patent (*see Global-Tech* for knowledge standard); (2) has induced multiple parties to perform different steps of the claimed process; and (3) those steps were performed by the induced parties. Because of the intent prong associated with indirect infringement, innocent downstream parties who perform one of the steps of the claimed process will not be liable (see footnote 1 of the opinion). In contrast, direct infringement is a strict liability tort.

Akamai certainly renders method patents stronger, and closes a loophole that permitted would-be infringers to circumvent infringement by manipulating the single-actor direct infringement rule of *BMC*. But did the Federal Circuit deploy its common law powers too aggressively; or, as Judge Linn wrote, perhaps the "majority opinion is rooted in its conception of what Congress ought to have done rather than what it did." Re-read section 271(a) and (b), and ask yourself if you agree with Judge Linn's assessment. What about the majority's statement that at the "end of the day, we are persuaded that Congress did not intend to create a regime in which parties could knowingly sidestep infringement liability simply by arranging to divide the steps of a method claim between them."

5. Infringement of Means-Plus-Function Claims

Under section 112, ¶6, patent claims may be drafted in means-plus-function format—a means for performing a particular function (e.g., means for attaching A to B). This format permits patentees to draft claims using functional language while disclosing structural aspects—that correspond to the "means" —in the specification. A principal advantage of a means-plus-function claim is efficiency because one does not need to recite in the claim every possible means of achieving the claimed function. Although courts have taken a narrow interpretation of means-plus-function claims, they remain useful, particularly for software and electrical inventions. Software programs are typically subdivided into modules each having a specific function that a means-plus-function claim can capture. Electrical (or electronic) devices usually possess functional circuitry that can be constructed in numerous ways and with myriad components, which can be set forth in the specification.

The infringement analysis for means-plus-function claims can be confusing. Infringement of a means-plus-function claim is deemed literal infringement, but section 112, ¶6 provides a patentee to capture not only the means disclosed in the specification, but "equivalents thereof." The courts use the term "literal" infringement because the accused product must perform the identical function of the claim, and "equivalents" are limited to the disclosed structure, not to all possible structures or acts that might perform the claimed function. Identity of function is a threshold requirement, meaning that an analysis of structural equivalence is conditioned on a finding of identical function. Infringement of means-plus-function claims is explored in *Odetics*, the principal case.

ODETICS, INC. v. STORAGE TECHNOLOGY CORP.

185 F.3d 1259 (Fed. Cir. 1999)

CLEVENGER, Circuit Judge.

On March 27, 1998, a jury impaneled in the United States District Court for the Eastern District of Virginia concluded that automated storage library systems manufactured and sold by Storage Technology Corporation, and used by Visa International Service Association, Inc., Visa USA, Inc., and Crestar Bank, Inc. (collectively, "STK") literally infringed United States Patent No. 4,779,151 ("the '151 patent") owned by the plaintiff, Odetics, Inc. ("Odetics"). After initially denying STK's renewed motion for Judgment as a Matter of Law ("JMOL"), the district court sua sponte reconsidered, granting the JMOL and ordering that judgment be entered in favor of STK. The district court deemed its reconsidered decision to be "mandat[ed]" by "the analytical framework established" by this court's opinion in *Chiuminatta Concrete Concepts, Inc. v. Cardinal Indus., Inc.*, Odetics appeals the reconsideration judgment.

Because *Chiuminatta* did not mark a change in the proper infringement analysis under §112, ¶6, and the jury's verdict is supported by substantial evidence, we reverse the grant of JMOL and order the jury's verdict reinstated.

I

This patent infringement action concerns robotic tape storage systems, which are typically used to store, organize, and retrieve videotapes or computer data tapes. The storage systems generally consist of a large, generally cylindrical housing with a pivoting retrieval mechanism, such as a robotic arm, located in the center of the housing. Acting on commands to retrieve certain tapes, the robotic arm can selectively grip the desired tape, removing it from its storage shelf and placing it on another shelf or in a tape player/recorder. These systems are highly automated and are especially useful in situations where large quantities of data must be easily and quickly retrieved from storage.

A

At issue are claims 9 and 14 of the '151 patent. Claim 9 reads as follows (emphasis supplied to highlight disputed limitation):

> 9. A tape cassette handling system comprising:
>
> a plurality of tape transports;
> a housing including a cassette storage library having a plurality of storage bins and at least one cassette access opening for receiving cassettes to be moved to the storage bins or to the tape transports, or for receiving cassettes to be removed from the library or from the tape transports;
> a *rotary means* rotatably mounted within the library adjacent the access opening for providing access to the storage library, the rotary means having one or more holding bins each having an opening for receiving a cassette, wherein the rotary means is rotatable from a first position in which the opening of at least one holding bin is accessible from outside of the housing to a second position in which the opening of at least one holding bin is accessible from inside of the housing; and
> cassette manipulator means located within the housing for selectively moving cassettes between the rotary means, said storage bins and said tape transports.

Claim 14 is identical in all relevant aspects.

The critical "rotary means" claim element is in means-plus-function form, requiring that it "be construed to cover the corresponding structure, material, or acts described in the specification and equivalents thereof." 35 U.S.C. § 112, ¶ 6. In *Odetics II,* this court held that the structure corresponding to the "rotary means" element was "the components that receive the force and rotate as a result of that force (*i.e.,* the rod, gear, and rotary loading and loading mechanisms)." This court noted that this structure could be seen in Fig. 3 of the '151 patent, except that the structure did not include the motor (52) or its gear (54).

Thus, the structure corresponding to the "rotary means" element, as depicted in Fig. 3 of the '151 patent, is a set of tape holders or bins, a rod providing the axis of rotation, and a gear capable of receiving a force sufficient to cause the structure to accomplish the claimed "rotary" function.

STK manufactures and sells Library Storage Modules ("libraries") to companies, such as Visa and Crestar, that require large quantities of automated data storage. Library systems sold by STK are scaleable: that is, additional libraries may be added to increase the amount of storage space. When libraries are added, STK uses a device known as a "pass-thru port" to link the libraries, allowing data tapes to be passed from library to library. The pass-thru ports bridge the gaps between the libraries using a "bin array"—a box-like set of tape slots or holders—that slides linearly along a short track. As the bin arrays move from library to library, they rotate to allow tapes to be manipulated from within the library housings. This rotation is accomplished by the use of "cam followers," or pins, that are affixed to the bottom of the bin array. As a bin array moves along

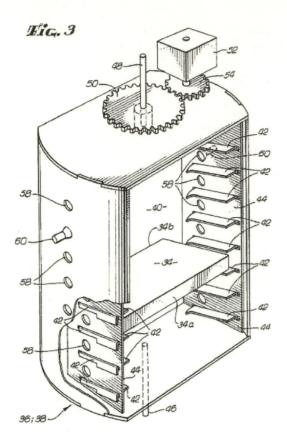

Fig. 3

its track, the pins come into contact with angled structures, or "cams," that exert force against the pins, causing the bin array to rotate about a rod that forms its axis. The "bin array" in the accused devices, then, comprises a set of tape holders or bins, a rod, and pins.

* * *

II

* * *

A

Because the district court explicitly premised its grant of STK's JMOL motion on the "mandate" resulting from its review of the *Chiuminatta* opinion, we must first decide whether, in the words of the district court, *Chiuminatta* "announced a significant change in the proper mode of infringement analysis under §112, ¶6." Indeed, the crux of the district court's reading of *Chiuminatta* is that statutory equivalence under §112, ¶6 requires "component by component" equivalence between the relevant structure identified in the patent and the portion of the accused device asserted to be structurally equivalent. This reading of *Chiuminatta* misapprehends §112, ¶6 infringement analysis and is therefore incorrect.

A claim limitation written in means-plus-function form, reciting a function to be performed rather than definite structure, is subject to the requirements of 35 U.S.C. §112, ¶6. As such, the limitation must be construed "to cover the corresponding structure, material, or acts described in the specification and equivalents thereof." *See* 35 U.S.C. §112, ¶6. Literal infringement of a §112, ¶6 limitation requires that the relevant structure in the accused device perform the identical function recited in the claim and be identical or equivalent to the corresponding structure in the specification. Functional identity and either structural identity or equivalence are *both* necessary.

Structural equivalence under §112, ¶6 is, as noted by the Supreme Court, "an application of the doctrine of equivalents . . . in a restrictive role." *Warner-Jenkinson Co., Inc. v. Hilton Davis Chem. Co.*, 520 U.S. 17, 28 (1997). As such, "their tests for equivalence are closely related," *Chiuminatta*, 145 F.3d at 1310, involving "similar analyses of insubstantiality of differences." *Al-Site* [*v. VSI Int'l, Inc.*], 174 F.3d at 1321 (quoting *Chiuminatta*, 145 F.3d at 1310. In the doctrine of equivalents context, the following test is often used: if the "function, way, or result" of the assertedly substitute structure is substantially different from that described by the claim limitation, equivalence is not established. As we have noted, this tripartite test developed for the doctrine of equivalents is not wholly transferable to the §112, ¶6 statutory equivalence context. Instead, the statutory equivalence analysis, while rooted in similar concepts of insubstantial differences as its doctrine of equivalents counterpart, is narrower. This is because, under §112, ¶6 equivalence, functional *identity* is required; thus the equivalence (indeed, identity) of the "function" of the assertedly substitute structure, material, or acts must be first established in order to reach the statutory equivalence analysis. *See* 35 U.S.C. §112, ¶6. The content of the test for insubstantial differences under §112, ¶6 thus reduces to "way" and "result." That is, the statutory equivalence analysis requires a determination of whether the "way" the assertedly substitute structure performs the claimed function, and the "result" of that performance, is substantially different from the "way" the claimed function is performed by the "corresponding structure, acts, or materials described in the specification," or its "result." Structural equivalence under §112, ¶6 is met only if the differences are insubstantial; that is, if the assertedly equivalent structure performs the claimed function in substantially the same way to achieve substantially the same result as the corresponding structure described in the specification. *See* 35 U.S.C. §112, ¶6 (means-plus-function claim literally covers "the corresponding structure, material, or acts described in the specification *and equivalents thereof*" (emphasis supplied)).

The similar analysis of equivalents under §112, ¶6 and the doctrine of equivalents does not, however, lead to the conclusion that *Pennwalt* and *Warner-Jenkinson* command a component-by-component analysis of structural equivalence under §112, ¶6. It is of course axiomatic that "[e]ach element contained in a patent claim is deemed material to determining the scope of the patented invention." *Warner-Jenkinson*, 520 U.S. at 29. Thus a claim limitation written in §112, ¶6 form, like all claim limitations, must be met, literally or equivalently, for infringement to lie. As we noted above, such a limitation is literally met by structure, materials, or acts in the accused device that perform the claimed function in substantially the same way to achieve substantially the same result. The individual components, if any, of an overall structure that corresponds to the claimed function are not claim limitations. Rather, the claim limitation is the overall structure corresponding to the claimed function. This is why structures with different numbers of parts may still be equivalent under §112, ¶6, thereby meeting the claim limitation. *See, e.g., Al-Site,* 174 F.3d at 1321-22 (upholding jury verdict of § 112, ¶6 equivalence between "a mechanically-fastened loop . . . includ[ing] either the rivet fastener or the button and hole fastener" and "holes in the arms [of an eyeglass hanger tag]"). The appropriate degree of specificity is provided by the statute itself; the relevant structure is that which "corresponds" to the claimed function. *See, e.g., Chiuminatta,* 145 F.3d at 1308-09 (structure "unrelated to the recited function" disclosed in the patent is irrelevant to § 112, ¶6). Further deconstruction or parsing is incorrect.

Rather than altering this well-worn path of the law, *Chiuminatta* confirms it. After determining that the structure corresponding to the "means . . . for supporting the surface of the concrete" was a "skid plate" or "generally rectangular strip of metal having rounded ends between which is a flat piece," the court proceeded to analyze the differences between the skid plate and the assertedly equivalent structure in the accused device, a set of soft rubber wheels. In finding "not insubstantial" differences between the wheels and skid plate, the court noted that the *way* the structures performed the claimed function were substantially different: while the wheels roll or rotate across the surface, the skid plate "skid[s] as the saw moves across the concrete and thus ha[s] a different impact on the concrete." At no point did the *Chiuminatta* court deconstruct the skid plate structure into component parts in order to analyze equivalence. Instead, *Chiuminatta* simply applied the well-established law of insubstantial differences to the particular structures at issue. The component-by-component analysis used by the district court finds no support in the law.

B

Although we have determined that the premise of the district court's reconsidered grant of JMOL is incorrect, our inquiry is not at an end. STK argues that the grant of JMOL can be upheld on alternative grounds. We disagree.

First, STK contends that the jury's verdict of infringement was unsupported by substantial evidence. Whether an accused device infringes a § 112, ¶6 claim as an equivalent is a question of fact. STK asserts that Odetics did not present substantial evidence that the "bin array" of the accused device is equivalent to the '151 patent's "rotary means" claim element and corresponding structure in the specification. A review of the record, however, overwhelmingly proves otherwise. [T]he jury was instructed that "'a rotary means rotatably mounted' could be what is depicted in Figure 3 [of the '151 patent], less elements 52 and 54, or the equivalent. In other words, [the rotary means structure is] depicted in Figure 3, less elements 52 and 54, that figure, or the equivalent." [T]he district court noted to the jury that the structure corresponding to the claimed function was "rotatable" as a result of receiving a rotary force. The "bin array" in the accused device contains a rod, bins for holding the cassettes, and pins or "cam followers" protruding from the bottom of the cassette bin. Odetics's theory of equivalence was to point out the parallels between the claimed and accused structures, noting that rotation is accomplished in the '151 patent by exerting force against the teeth of the gear, thereby turning the bin about the rod, and that rotation is accomplished in the accused device by exerting force against the cam followers, also turning the bin about the rod. Thus Odetics argued to the jury that the structures were equivalent "rotary means" within the meaning of § 112, ¶6. To prove its case, Odetics introduced documentary and testimonial evidence of structural equivalence, including diagrams, claim charts, computer animation sequences, and the opinions of its expert, Dr. John M. McCarthy, whom the parties agree is a specialist in robotics. Dr. McCarthy specifically and clearly testified—on at least eight occasions during the trial—that the "rotary means" structure was equivalent to the "bin array" in the accused devices and why this was so. Indeed, he described the "bin array" structure in the accused devices and the rotary means structure in the '151 patent as "nearly identical," possible to "match directly," "completely equivalent," having "almost identical correspondence," "literally equivalent," and that they "correspond so completely, that I could match every element one-for-one." When pressed to describe specifically why the presence of pins or cam followers in the accused devices rather than the gear depicted in the '151 patent did not affect his equivalence analysis, Dr. McCarthy first noted that "you can push on a pin as well as you can push on a gear tooth. . . . For this application, this is completely equivalent, pushing on these pins and pushing on these gear teeth, particularly from [the perspective of] one of ordinary skill in the art." On cross-examination, Dr. McCarthy further explained that one could "[t]ake that gear off, put those pins on. . . . [The accused "bin array" structure] is completely equivalent, completely identical."

Given the clear, consistent, and oft-repeated evidence that the "rotary means" structure in the '151 patent and the "bin array" structure in the accused devices were equivalent, the district court, announcing its initial ruling against JMOL, stated: "the jury could find infringement, as it did, based on Dr. McCarthy's testimony of literal infringement. So STK's motion for Judgment as a Matter of Law must be denied." We agree. Odetics introduced substantial evidence that the rotary means and bin array structures were equivalent; a reasonable jury was therefore entitled to find infringement. *See, e.g., Al-Site,* 174 F.3d at 1316, 50 U.S.P.Q.2d at 1165 (expert testimony that an "'equivalent fastening means could be a rivet, glue, or staple . . .' constitutes sufficient evidence to sustain the jury's verdict").

STK's argument that the testimony of Dr. McCarthy relates only to the functional identity of the two structures—and is thus insufficient to demonstrate structural equivalence—is unavailing. Dr. McCarthy testified repeatedly about the *structural* similarities, noting that, overall, the two structures "match directly," and that "the entire [bin array] structure surely is equivalent." Dr. McCarthy also stated that the *way* that the two structures accomplish the claimed "rotary" function, and the *result* of that function, is substantially equivalent: "[the depiction of the rotary means structure] represents the way this system is actuated. That's the point [at which] the force is applied to rotat[e]. Any equivalent way of rotating, is what's captured in this drawing." Therefore, when the question is whether substantial evidence supports the jury verdict, Dr. McCarthy's testimony answers that question against STK, as the district court correctly noted in the initial denial of the renewed motion for JMOL.

Contrary to STK's argument, the "bin array" structure (the rod, bin, and pins) is not precluded from being equivalent, under § 112, ¶6, to the '151 patent's "rotary means" structure (the rod, bin, and gear) by the fact that the "bin array" structure would not be able to perform unrelated functions, such as "meshing with a gear motor." A claim limitation written according to § 112, ¶6 recites a function to be performed. *See* 35 U.S.C. § 112, ¶6. The scope of that functional limitation is, of course, limited to the "corresponding structure, material, or acts described in the specification and equivalents thereof." *Id.* The "corresponding" structure is the structure disclosed as performing the function. That two structures may perform unrelated—and, more to the point, unclaimed—functions differently or not at all is simply not pertinent to the measure of §112, ¶6 equivalents. *See Chiuminatta,* 145 F.3d at 1308 (structure that "reduce[s] wobbling" and "support[s] the weight of the cutting blade" is unrelated to the claimed function of "'support[ing] the surface of the concrete' and accordingly are not to be read as limiting the scope of the means clause"). In this case, Dr. McCarthy testified that the structural equivalence between the "rotary means" and the "bin array" derives from the capacity of both structures to perform the identical function in the same way: to receive the force necessary to accomplish the "rotary" function.

* * *

For the reasons stated above, we reverse the grant of JMOL in favor of STK and order the jury's verdict reinstated.

Comments

1. ***Pre-1952 Prohibition.*** Prior to the 1952 Patent Act, functionally defined claims were prohibited because of fear of excessive ambiguity and scope. *See Halliburton Oil Well Cementing Co. v. Walker,* 329 U.S. 1 (1946). The 1952 Act overruled *Halliburton,* "but provided a standard to make the broad claim language more definite" by requiring the applicant to "describe in the patent specification some structure which performs the specified function" and stating "a court must construe the functional claim language 'to cover the corresponding structure, material, or acts described in the specification and equivalents thereof.'" *Valmont Industries, Inc. v. Reinke Manufacturing Co., Inc.,* 983 F.2d 1039, 1041 (Fed. Cir. 1993).

2. ***Infringement Under Section 112, ¶6: Statutory and Common Law Equivalents.*** A means-plus-function claim is literally infringed if the accused device possesses a structure that performs the identical function set forth in the claim *and* the structure is identical or equivalent to the structure set forth in the patent specification. *See Intellectual Science & Technology, Inc. v. Sony Electronics, Inc.,* 589 F.3d 1179, 1183 (Fed. Cir. 2009) (stating a means-plus-function claim term "literally covers an accused device if the relevant structure in the accused device performs the identical function recited in the claim and that structure is identical or equivalent to the corresponding structure in the specification"). The infringement is deemed "literal" because the functions are the same. If there is "identity of function," an equivalents analysis is limited to the structure disclosed in the specification.

    As *Odetics* discusses, section 112, ¶6 statutory equivalence is essentially a common law equivalence analysis (i.e., insubstantial differences) in a limited role because the identity of function is a prerequisite to application of a statutory equivalence analysis to determine if the accused structure and disclosed structure are equivalent. In determining equivalence, the Federal Circuit has noted that "evidence of known interchangeability between structure in the accused device and the disclosed structure has . . . been considered an important factor." *Hearing Components, Inc. v. Shure, Inc.,* 600 F.3d 1357, 1371 (Fed. Cir. 2010). Interestingly, section 112, ¶6 says nothing about structural equivalence. The statute states the "claim shall be construed to cover the corresponding structure, material, or acts described in the specification and equivalents thereof." This view is reflected in *de Graffenried*, 20 Cl. Ct. 458, 479-480 (1980) (noting the "the term 'equivalent' in Section 112 should not be interpreted as being limited to structures that are 'equivalent' to the physical structure of the 'means' disclosed in a patent. The literal wording of Section 112 contains no such requirement. The statute merely refers to structures 'described in the specification and equivalents thereof.' It does not state that the only possible 'equivalents' to the structures described in the specification are devices with equivalent physical structures, i.e., it does not provide structures 'described in the specification and *structural* equivalents thereof' ").

Because infringement under section 112, ¶6 is deemed literal infringement, the structural equivalent must exist at the time the patent issued. (Recall, literal infringement is measured at the time of issuance and does not apply to after-arising technology.) In contrast, under the common law DOE, equivalence is measured at the time of infringement, and therefore, applies to after-arising technology. In both instances, an equivalency analysis will apply, but whether the resulting infringement (assuming there is infringement) is called literal or non-literal depends on when the accused equivalent became available. This temporal distinction was discussed in *Al-Site Corp. v. VSI Int'l, Inc.*, 174 F.3d 1308, 1321 n.2 (Fed. Cir. 1999):

> A proposed equivalent must have arisen at a definite period in time, i.e., either before or after patent issuance. If before, a §112, ¶6 structural equivalents analysis applies and any analysis for equivalent structure under the doctrine of equivalents collapses into the §112, ¶6 analysis. If after, a non-textual infringement analysis proceeds under the doctrine of equivalents. Patent policy supports application of the doctrine of equivalents to a claim element expressed in means-plus-function form in the case of "after-arising" technology because a patent draftsman has no way to anticipate and account for later developed substitutes for a claim element. Therefore, the doctrine of equivalents appropriately allows marginally broader coverage than §112, ¶6.

One final point: if the accused structure does not literally perform the claimed function, "§112, ¶6 plays no role in determining whether an equivalent function is performed by the accused device under the doctrine of equivalents." *Pennwalt Corp. v. Durand-Wayland, Inc.*, 833 F.2d 931, 934 (Fed. Cir. 1987) (en banc).

3. ***Constructing a Section 112, ¶6 Claim.*** The easiest way to invoke section 112, ¶6 is to use "means for" language. The use of the word "means" creates a rebuttable presumption that section 112, ¶6 applies; conversely, the failure to use "means" invokes a presumption that section 112, ¶6 does not apply. *See CCS Fitness v. Brunswick Corp.*, 288 F.3d 1359, 1369 (Fed. Cir. 2002). But use of the word "means" does not guarantee ¶6 will apply; nor is it necessary to use "means" to qualify for a means-plus-function claim. The key is not to recite a definite structure that performs the described function. *See Apex, Inc. v. Raritan Computer, Inc.*, 325 F.3d 1364, 1373 (Fed. Cir. 2003). *See also Greenberg v. Ethicon Endo-Surgery, Inc.*, 91 F.3d 1580, 1584 (Fed. Cir. 1996) ("We do not mean to suggest that section 112(6) is triggered only if the claim uses the word 'means.' . . . Nonetheless, the use of the term 'means' has come to be so

closely associated with 'means-plus-function' claiming that it is fair to say that the use of the term 'means' (particularly as used in the phrase 'means for') generally invokes section 112(6) and that the use of a different formulation generally does not.").

C. DEFINING THE GEOGRAPHIC SCOPE OF THE PATENT RIGHT

Territoriality is a fundamental principle of American patent law. As the Supreme Court stated at the beginning of the twentieth century, "[t]he right conferred by a patent under our law is confined to the United States and its territories . . . and infringement of this right cannot be predicated of acts wholly done in a foreign country." *Dowagiac Mfg. Co. v. Minnesota Moline Plow Co.*, 235 U.S. 641, 650 (1915). The territoriality principle, however, has been altered by statute to capture certain forms of export and import activity. *See* section 271(f) and (g) and the principal cases of *Microsoft* and *Eli Lilly*. But before export and import issues are addressed, we must first understand the geographic scope of infringement that occurs "within the United States" under section 271(a).

1. The Parameters of Section 271(a): Defining "Within the United States"

Section 271(a) of title 35 sets forth the requirements for a claim of direct infringement of a patent. It provides:

> Except as otherwise provided in this title, whoever without authority makes, uses, offers to sell, or sells any patented invention, *within the United States or imports into the United States* any patented invention during the term of the patent therefor, infringes the patent.

Section 154(a)(1) grants a patentee the right to exclude others from making, using, offering for sale, or selling the claimed invention "within the United States" or importing the invention "into" the United States. Thus, activity in a foreign country, *in and of itself*, does not constitute an infringing act. But the statutory term "within the United States" is not as straightforward as initially appears, as illustrated by *NTP, Inc. v. Research in Motion*, the well-known Blackberry® case.

NTP, INC. v. RESEARCH IN MOTION, LTD.
418 F.3d 1282 (Fed. Cir. 2005)

LINN, Circuit Judge.

Research In Motion, Ltd. ("RIM") appeals from a judgment of the U.S. District Court for the Eastern District of Virginia ("district court") entered in favor of NTP, Inc. ("NTP") following a jury verdict that RIM's BlackBerry TM system infringed NTP's patents . . . and awarding damages to NTP in the amount of $53,704,322.69. The court, in a final order also appealed by RIM, permanently enjoined any further infringement by RIM, but stayed the injunction pending this appeal. . . .

I. BACKGROUND

The technology at issue relates to systems for integrating existing electronic mail systems ("wireline" systems) with radio frequency ("RF") wireless communication networks, to enable a mobile user to receive email over a wireless network.

* * *

C. The Patents-in-Suit

Inventors Thomas J. Campana, Jr.; Michael P. Ponschke; and Gary F. Thelen (collectively "Campana") developed an electronic mail system that was claimed in the '960, '670, '172, '451, and '592 patents. . . .

Campana's particular innovation was to integrate existing electronic mail systems with RF wireless communications networks. In simplified terms, the Campana invention operates in the following manner: A message originating in an electronic mail system may be transmitted not only by wireline but also via RF, in which case it is received by the user and stored on his or her mobile RF receiver. The user can view the message on the RF receiver and, at some later point, connect the RF receiver to a fixed destination processor, i.e., his or her personal desktop computer, and transfer the stored message. Intermediate transmission to the RF receiver is advantageous because it "eliminat[es] the requirement that the destination processor [be] turned on and carried with the user" to receive messages. Instead, a user can access his or her email stored on the RF receiver and "review . . . its content without interaction with the

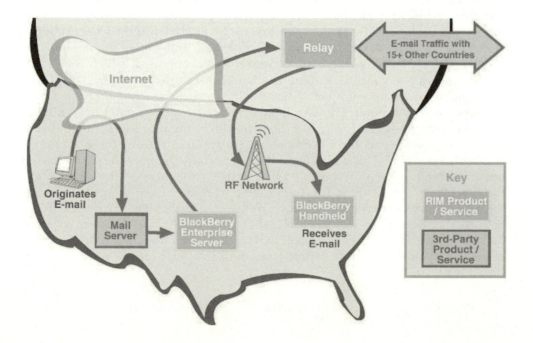

destination processor," while reserving the ability to transfer the stored messages automatically to the destination processor. The patents-in-suit do not disclose a method for composing and sending messages from the RF receiver. [The graphic below illustrates the above description.]*

D. The Accused System

RIM is a Canadian corporation with its principal place of business in Waterloo, Ontario. RIM sells the accused BlackBerry system, which allows out-of-office users to continue to receive and send electronic mail, or "email" communications, using a small wireless device. The system utilizes the following components: (1) the BlackBerry handheld unit (also referred to as the "BlackBerry Pager"); (2) email redirector software (such as the BlackBerry Enterprise Server ("BES"), the Desktop Redirector, or the Internet Redirector); and (3) access to a nationwide wireless network (such as Mobitex, DataTAC, or GPRS).

The BlackBerry system uses "push" email technology to route messages to the user's handheld device without a user-initiated connection. There are multiple BlackBerry email "solutions" that interface with different levels of the user's email system. In the Desktop solution, the BlackBerry email redirector software, the Desktop Redirector, is installed on the user's personal computer. In the Corporate solution, different BlackBerry email redirector software, the BES program, is installed on the organizational user's mail server, where it can function for the benefit of the multiple users of that server. Also at issue in this case is RIM's Internet solution of the BlackBerry system. The Internet solution operates in a manner similar to the Corporate solution, but it executes a different email redirector software, Internet Redirector. In either version, the BlackBerry email redirector software merges seamlessly with the user's existing email system. The operation of the email redirector software is transparent to the user's desktop email client and the organizational user's mail server. That is, the user's email system does not recognize or incorporate the BlackBerry wireless system into its operation. No modification of the underlying email system is required to run RIM's wireless email extension. When new mail is detected in the Desktop solution, the Desktop Redirector is notified and retrieves the message from the mail server. It then copies, encrypts, and routes the message to the BlackBerry "Relay" component of RIM's wireless network, which is located in Canada. In the Corporate solution, the BES software performs this same function but intercepts the email before the message reaches the individual user's personal computer. The individual user's personal computer need not be turned on for the BES software to properly redirect the user's emails. However, the user retains some control over message forwarding by using the BlackBerry "Desktop Manager." This additional software permits the user to specify his or her email redirection preferences. In both systems, the message travels through the BlackBerry Relay, where it is translated and routed from the processors in the user's email system to a partner wireless network. That partner network delivers the message to the user's BlackBerry handheld, and the user is "notified virtually instantly" of new email messages. *White Paper* at 6. This process, accomplished without any command from the BlackBerry user, is an example of

---

* [This graphic appeared in RIM's brief before the Federal Circuit and is reproduced here with permission from RIM's counsel.—ED.]

"push" email architecture. *Id.* There are significant advantages to "push" email architecture. Most importantly, the user is no longer required to initiate a connection with the mail server to determine if he or she has new email. As RIM's technical literature explains, "[b]y having the desktop connect to the user, time spent dialing-up and connecting to the desktop (possibly to find that there is no new email) is eliminated as users . . . are notified virtually instantly of important messages, enabling the user to respond immediately." *Id.*

RIM's system also permits users to send email messages over the wireless network from their handhelds. This functionality is achieved through the integration of an RF transmitter and a processor in the BlackBerry handheld unit. The processor allows the user to manipulate, view, and respond to email on his or her BlackBerry handheld. Sending a message from the handheld requires the same steps as the process for receiving email, only in reverse. When the user composes a message on his or her handheld, it is sent back to that user's desktop machine over the partner and BlackBerry wireless networks. The BlackBerry email redirector software then retrieves the outgoing message from the user's mail server and places it in the user's desktop email software, where it is dispersed through normal channels. In this way, messages sent from the BlackBerry handheld are identical to messages sent from the user's desktop email—they originate from the same address and also appear in the "sent mail" folder of the user's email client.

* * *

II. ANALYSIS

* * *

B. Infringement

. . . RIM contends that because the BlackBerry Relay is located in Canada, as a matter of law RIM cannot be held liable for infringement under 35 U.S.C. §271.

* * *

2. *Section 271(a)*

Section 271(a) of title 35 sets forth the requirements for a claim of direct infringement of a patent. It provides:

> Except as otherwise provided in this title, whoever without authority makes, uses, offers to sell, or sells any patented invention, within the United States or imports into the United States any patented invention during the term of the patent therefor, infringes the patent.

35 U.S.C. §271(a)(2000). The territorial reach of section 271 is limited. Section 271(a) is only actionable against patent infringement that occurs within the United States. *See Pellegrini v. Analog Devices, Inc.*, 375 F.3d 1113, 1117 (Fed. Cir. 2004) ("[As] the U.S. Supreme Court explained nearly 150 years ago in *Brown v. Duchesne*, the U.S. patent laws 'do not, and were not intended to, operate beyond the limits of the United States.'").

Ordinarily, whether an infringing activity under section 271(a) occurs within the United States can be determined without difficulty. This case presents an added degree of complexity, however, in that: (1) the "patented invention" is not one single device, but rather a system comprising multiple distinct components or a method with multiple distinct steps; and (2) the nature of those components or steps permits their function and use to be separated from their physical location.

In its complaint, NTP alleged that RIM had infringed its patents by "making, using, selling, offering to sell and importing into the United States products and services, including the Defendant's BlackBerry™ products and their related software. . . ." NTP's theory of infringement tracks the language of section 271(a). In the district court, RIM moved for summary judgment of non-infringement, arguing that it could not be held liable as a direct infringer under section 271(a). According to RIM, the statutory requirement that the allegedly infringing activity occur "within the United States" was not satisfied because the BlackBerry Relay component of the accused system is located in Canada. The Relay component is alleged to meet the "interface" or the "interface switch" limitation in the '960, '670, '172, and '451 patents. RIM's argument based on the location of its Relay outside the United States does not apply to the asserted claims of the '592 patent (claims 40, 150, 278, 287, 653, and 654) because those claims do not include the "interface" or "interface switch" limitation.

[D]uring trial, the court . . . held that "the fact that the BlackBerry relay is located in Canada is not a bar to infringement in this matter." The court therefore instructed the jury that "the location of RIM's Relay in Canada does not preclude infringement." In the district court, the jury found direct, induced, and contributory infringement by RIM on all asserted claims. The asserted claims included both systems and methods for transmitting an email message between an originating processor and a destination processor. By holding RIM liable for contributory infringement and inducing infringement, the jury necessarily found that its customers are direct infringers of the claimed systems and methods.

On appeal, RIM argues that the district court erred in its interpretation of the infringement statute. RIM does not appeal the jury's finding that its customers use, *i.e.*, put into service, its systems and methods for transmitting email messages. RIM has, however, appealed whether any direct infringement, by it or its customers, can be considered "within the United States" for purposes of section 271(a). Citing the Supreme Court's decision in *Deepsouth* [*Packing Co. v. Laitram Corp.*, 406 U.S. 518 (1972)], RIM contends that an action for infringement under section 271(a) may lie only if the allegedly infringing activity occurs within the United States. RIM urges that, in this case, that standard is not met because the BlackBerry Relay component, described by RIM as the "control point" of the accused system, is housed in Canada. For section 271(a) to apply, RIM asserts that the entire accused system and method must be contained or conducted within the territorial bounds of the United States. RIM thus contends that there can be no direct infringement as a matter of law because the location of RIM's Relay outside the United States precludes a finding of an infringing act occurring within the United States.

The question before us is whether the using, offering to sell, or selling of a patented invention is an infringement under section 271(a) if a component or step of the patented invention is located or performed abroad. Pursuant to section 271(a), whoever without authority "uses, offers to sell, or sells any patented invention, within the United States . . . during the term of the patent therefor, infringes the patent." 35 U.S.C. §271(a). The grammatical structure of the statute indicates that "within the United States" is a separate requirement from the infringing acts clause. Thus, it is unclear from the statutory language how the territoriality requirement limits direct infringement where the location of at least a part of the "patented invention" is not the same as the location of the infringing act.

RIM argues that *Deepsouth* answers this question. However, *Deepsouth* did not address this issue. In *Deepsouth*, the Supreme Court considered whether section 271(a) prevented, as direct infringement, the domestic production of all component parts of a patented combination for export, assembly, and use abroad. The Court held that the export of unassembled components of an invention could not infringe the patent. The Court said that it could not "endorse the view that the 'substantial manufacture of the constituent parts of a machine' constitutes direct infringement when we have so often held that a combination patent protects only against the operable assembly of the whole and not the manufacture of its parts." *Id.* at 528. Thus, the Court concluded that the complete manufacture of the operable assembly of the whole within the United States was required for infringement by making under section 271(a). In that case, however, both the act of making and the resulting patented invention were wholly outside the United States. By contrast, this case involves a system that is partly within and partly outside the United States and relates to acts that may be occurring within or outside the United States.

Although *Deepsouth* does not resolve these issues, our predecessor court's decision in *Decca Ltd. v. United States*, 544 F.2d 1070 (1976), is instructive. In *Decca*, the plaintiff sued the United States for use and manufacture of its patented invention under 28 U.S.C. § 1498. The claimed invention was a radio navigation system requiring stations transmitting signals that are received by a receiver, which then calculates position by the time difference in the signals. At the time of the suit, the United States was operating three such transmitting stations, one of which was located in Norway and thus was outside the territorial limits of the United States. Only asserted claim 11 required three transmitting stations. Thus, in considering infringement of claim 11, the court considered the extraterritorial reach of the patent laws as applied to a system in which a component was located outside the United States. The court recognized that *Deepsouth* did not address this issue. In analyzing whether such a system was "made" in the United States, however, the court focused on the "operable assembly of the whole" language from *Deepsouth* and concluded that "[t]he plain fact is that one of the claimed elements is outside of the United States so that the combination, as an operable assembly, simply is not to be found solely within the territorial limits of this country." *Id.* at 1082. The court recognized that what was located within the United States was as much of the system as was possible, but the court reached no clear resolution of whether the accused system was "made" within the United States. Nevertheless, the court said, "[a]nalyzed from the standpoint of a use instead of a making by the United States, a somewhat clearer picture emerges." *Id.* The court concluded that "it is obvious that, although the Norwegian station is located on Norwegian soil, a navigator employing signals from that station is, in fact, 'using' that station and such use occurs wherever the signals are received and used in the manner claimed." *Id.* at 1083. In reaching its decision, the court found particularly significant "the ownership of the equipment by the United States, the control of the equipment from the United States and . . . the actual beneficial use of the system within the United States." *Id.* Although *Decca* was decided within the context of section 1498, which raises questions of use *by* the United States, the question of use *within* the United States also was implicated because direct infringement under section 271(a) is a necessary predicate for government liability under section 1498.

Decca provides a legal framework for analyzing this case. As our predecessor court concluded, infringement under section 271(a) is not necessarily precluded even though a component of a patented system is located outside the United States. However, as is also evident from *Decca,* the effect of the extraterritorial component may be different for different infringing acts. In *Decca,* the court found it difficult to conclude that the system had been made within the United States but concluded that the system had been used in the United States even though one of the claim limitations was only met by including a component located in Norway. Not only will the analysis differ for different types of infringing acts, it will also differ as the result of differences between different types of claims. Because the analytical frameworks differ, we will separately analyze the alleged infringing acts, considering first the system claims and then the claimed methods.

a. "uses . . . within the United States"

The situs of the infringement "is wherever an offending act [of infringement] is committed." *N. Am. Philips Corp. v. Am. Vending Sales, Inc.,* 35 F.3d 1576, 1579 (Fed. Cir. 1994) ("[Section 271] on its face clearly suggests the conception that the 'tort' of patent infringement occurs where the offending act is committed and not where the injury is felt."). The situs of the infringing act is a "purely physical occurrence[]." *Id.* In terms of the infringing act of "use," courts have interpreted the term "use" broadly. In *Bauer & Cie v. O'Donnell,* 229 U.S. 1 (1913), the Supreme Court stated that "use," as used in a predecessor to title 35, is a "comprehensive term and embraces within its meaning the right to put into service any given invention." *Id.* at 10-11. The ordinary meaning of "use" is to "put into action or service." *Webster's Third New International Dictionary* 2523 (1993).

The use of a claimed system under section 271(a) is the place at which the system as a whole is put into service, *i.e.,* the place where control of the system is exercised and beneficial use of the system obtained. Based on this interpretation of section 271(a), it was proper for the jury to have found that use of NTP's asserted system claims occurred within the United States. RIM's customers located within the United States controlled the transmission of the originated information and also benefited from such an exchange of information. Thus, the location of the Relay in Canada did not, as a matter of law, preclude infringement of the asserted system claims in this case.

RIM argues that the BlackBerry system is distinguishable from the system in *Decca* because the RIM Relay, which controls the accused systems and is necessary for the other components of the system to function properly, is not located within the United States. While this distinction recognizes technical differences between the two systems, it fails to appreciate the way in which the claimed NTP system is actually used by RIM's customers. When RIM's United States customers send and receive messages by manipulating the handheld devices in their possession in the United States, the location of the use of the communication system as a whole occurs in the United States. This satisfactorily establishes that the situs of the "use" of RIM's system by RIM's United States customers for purposes of section 271(a) is the United States. Therefore, we conclude that the jury was properly presented with questions of infringement as to NTP's system claims containing the "interface" or "interface switch" limitation; namely, claim 15 of the '960 patent; claim 8 of the '670 patent; and claims 28 and 248 of the '451 patent.

We reach a different conclusion as to NTP's asserted method claims. Under section 271(a), the concept of "use" of a patented method or process is fundamentally different from the use of a patented system or device. *See In re Kollar,* 286 F.3d 1326, 1332 (Fed. Cir. 2002) (recognizing "the distinction between a claim to a product, device, or apparatus, all of which are tangible items, and a claim to a process, which consists of a series of acts or steps. . . . [A process] consists of doing something, and therefore has to be carried out or performed."). Although the Supreme Court focused on the whole operable assembly of a system claim for infringement in *Deepsouth,* there is no corresponding whole operable assembly of a process claim. A method or process consists of one or more operative steps, and, accordingly, "[i]t is well established that a patent for a method or process is not infringed unless all steps or stages of the claimed process are utilized." *Roberts Dairy Co. v. United States,* 530 F.2d 1342, 1354 (1976).

Because a process is nothing more than the sequence of actions of which it is comprised, the use of a process necessarily involves doing or performing each of the steps recited. This is unlike use of a system as a whole, in which the components are used collectively, not individually. We therefore hold that a process cannot be used "within" the United States as required by section 271(a) unless each of the steps is performed within this country. In the present case, each of the asserted method claims of the '960, '172, and '451 patents recites a step that utilizes an "interface" or "interface switch," which is only satisfied by the use of RIM's Relay located in Canada. Therefore, as a matter of law, these claimed methods could not be infringed by use of RIM's system.

Thus, we agree with RIM that a finding of direct infringement by RIM's customers under section 271(a) of the method claims reciting an "interface switch" or an "interface" is precluded by the location of RIM's Relay in Canada. As a consequence, RIM cannot be liable for induced or contributory infringement of the asserted method claims, as a matter of law.

b. "offers to sell, or sells"

Because we conclude that RIM's customers could not have infringed the asserted method claims of the '960, '172, and '451 patents under the "use" prong of section 271(a), and thus, could not have provided the necessary predicate for the charges of induced or contributory infringement of those claims, we must consider whether RIM could have directly infringed the method claims under the "sell" or "offer to sell" prongs of section 271(a). The cases cited by RIM are concerned primarily with the "use" and "make" prongs of section 271(a) and do not directly address the issue of whether a method claim may be infringed by selling or offering to sell within the meaning of section 271(a).

Because the relevant precedent does not address the issue of whether a sale of a claimed method can occur in the United States, even though the contemplated performance of that method would not be wholly within the United States, the issue is one of first impression. We begin with the language of the statute. Section 271(a) does not define "sells" or "offers to sell," nor does the statute specify which infringing acts apply to which types of claims. Section 271(a) was merely a codification of the common law of infringement that had developed up to the time of passage of the 1952 Patent Act. It was not meant to change the law of infringement. A claim directed to a method or process, although some-what controversial in the Nineteenth Century, is now a well-established form of claiming. Nevertheless, the precise contours of infringement of a method claim have not been clearly established.

In *Enercon GmbH v. International Trade Commission*, 151 F.3d 1376 (Fed. Cir. 1998), this court considered the meaning of the phrase "sale for importation" in the International Trade Commission's governing statute, 19 U.S.C. § 1337. Because the term "sale" was not defined in the statute, we assumed that Congress intended to give the term its ordinary meaning. In considering the ordinary meaning, we looked to dictionaries and to the Uniform Commercial Code. We employ a similar methodology here, looking to the ordinary meaning of the term "sale." The definition of "sale" is: "1. The transfer of property or title for a price. 2. The agreement by which such a transfer takes place. The four elements are (1) parties competent to contract, (2) mutual assent, (3) a thing capable of being transferred, and (4) a price in money paid or promised." *Black's Law Dictionary* 1337 (7th ed. 1999). Thus, the ordinary meaning of a sale includes the concept of a transfer of title or property. The definition also requires as the third element "a thing capable of being transferred." It is difficult to apply this concept to a method claim consisting of a series of acts. It is difficult to envision what property is transferred merely by one party performing the steps of a method claim in exchange for payment by another party. Moreover, per-formance of a method does not necessarily require anything that is capable of being transferred.

Congress has consistently expressed the view that it understands infringe-ment of method claims under section 271(a) to be limited to use. The com-mittee reports surrounding the passage of the Process Patents Amendments Act of 1987 indicate that Congress did not understand all of the infringing acts in section 271(a) to apply to method claims. The Senate Report explains, "Under our current patent laws, a patent on a process gives the patentholder the right to exclude others from using that process in the United States without authorization from the patentholder. The other two standard aspects of the pat-ent right—the exclusive right to make or sell the invention—are not directly applicable to a patented process." S. Rep. No. 100-83, at 30 (1987). The House Report expresses a similar view: "With respect to process patents, courts have reasoned that the only act of infringement is the act of making through the use of a patented process. . . ." H.R. Rep. No. 99-807, at 5 (1986). Although this issue has not been directly addressed, this court expressed a similar view in *Joy Technologies, Inc. v. Flakt, Inc.*, 6 F.3d 770 (Fed. Cir. 1993). In that case, we said, "A method claim is *directly* infringed only by one practicing the patented method." *Id.* at 775.

In 1994, Congress passed legislation to implement the Uruguay Round of the General Agreement on Tariffs and Trade. Uruguay Round Agreements Act, Pub. L. No. 103-465, 108 Stat. 4809 (1994). That legislation modified section 271(a) to include the infringing acts of offering to sell and importing into the United States. *Id.* § 533, 108 Stat. at 4988. The portion of the Uruguay Round being implemented in the modification of section 271(a) was the Agreement on Trade-Related Aspects of Intellectual Property Rights. That agreement clearly spells out the rights to be protected. It states:

1. A patent shall confer on its owner the following exclusive rights:

    (a) where the subject matter of a patent is a product, to prevent third parties not having the owner's consent from the acts of: making, using, offering for sale, selling or importing for these purposes that product;

    (b) where the subject matter of a patent is a process, to prevent third parties not having the owner's consent from the act of using the process, and from the acts of: using, offering for sale, selling, or importing for these purposes at least the product obtained directly by that process.

Agreement on Trade-Related Aspects of Intellectual Property Rights, Apr. 15, 1994, art. 28, H.R. Doc. No. 103-316, at 1634 (1994) (footnote omitted). The agreement makes clear that claimed processes are to be directly protected only from "the act of using the process." The joint committee report from the Senate reflects the same understanding: "The list of exclusive rights granted to patent owners is expanded to preclude others from offering to sell or importing products covered by a U.S. patent or offering to sell the products of patented processes." S. Rep. 103-412, at 230 (1994), U.S. Code Cong. & Admin. News 1994 at pp. 3773, 4002. Thus, the legislative history of section 271(a) indicates Congress's understanding that method claims could only be directly infringed by use.

In the context of the on sale bar, we have held that a method claim may be invalid if an offer to perform the method was made prior to the critical date. Nevertheless, we have previously "decline[d] to import the authority construing the 'on sale' bar of §102(b) into the 'offer to sell' provision of §271(a)." *3D Sys., Inc. v. Aarotech Labs., Inc.,* 160 F.3d 1373, 1379 n. 4 (Fed. Cir. 1998). As the Supreme Court cautioned in *Deepsouth,* 406 U.S. at 531: "We would require a clear and certain signal from Congress before approving the position of a litigant who, as respondent here, argues that the beachhead of privilege is wider, and the area of public use narrower, than courts had previously thought." The indication we have from Congress on infringement by selling or offering to sell method claims shows that it believes the beachhead is narrow.

In this case, we conclude that the jury could not have found that RIM infringed the asserted method claims under the "sells" or "offers to sell" prongs of section 271(a). We need not and do not hold that method claims may not be infringed under the "sells" and "offers to sell" prongs of section 271(a). Rather, we conclude only that RIM's performance of at least some of the recited steps of the asserted method claims as a service for its customers cannot be considered to be selling or offering to sell the invention covered by the asserted method claims. The sale or offer to sell handheld devices is not, in and of itself, enough. Thus, we conclude as a matter of law that RIM did not sell or offer to sell the invention covered by NTP's method claims within the United States.

Comments

1. *"Control" and "Beneficial Use."* The following passage in *NTP* reflects the expansive approach the court took in interpreting section 271(a):

> The use of a claimed system under section 271(a) is the place at which the system as a whole is put into service, *i.e.,* the place where *control* of the system is exercised and *beneficial use* of the system obtained. Based on this interpretation

of section 271(a), it was proper for the jury to have found that use of NTP's asserted system claims occurred within the United States. RIM's customers located within the United States controlled the transmission of the originated information and also benefited from such an exchange of information. Thus, the location of the Relay in Canada did not, as a matter of law, preclude infringement of the asserted system claims in this case.

(emphasis added). The *NTP* court held that the geographic test for infringement was whether "control and beneficial use" of RIM's system was within the United States; not whether the actual infringement occurs in the United States. Some commentators have suggested *NTP* and *Decca*—which *NTP* relied on—have embraced a "locus of infringement" posture when interpreting section 271(a). *See* Mark Lemley, David O'Brien, Ryan M. Kent, Ashok Ramani & Robert Van Nest, *Divided Infringement Claims*, 33 AIPLA Q.J. 255, 269 (2005) (stating *NTP* and *Decca* "have adopted a 'locus of infringement' approach, under which the invention is deemed to exist in the country with the strongest connection to the invention").

In addition, a contract executed outside of the United States that provides for an "offer for sale" of a patented product in the United States invokes the "within the United States" language of section 271(a), even though the actual product eventually sold did not infringe the patent. In *Transocean Offshore Deepwater Drilling, Inc. v. Maersk Contractors USA, Inc.*, 617 F.3d 1296 (Fed. Cir. 2010), two U.S. companies executed a contract in Norway that called for the delivery and installation of a potentially infringing oil rig in U.S. waters. But the rig that was ultimately delivered embodied a "work-around" design that differed from the rig set forth in the contract. The court nonetheless held that the contract constituted an "offer for sale within the United States," thus distinguishing between the offer to sale and the actual sale itself. According to the court, "[t]he focus should not be on the location of the offer, but rather the location of the future sale that would occur pursuant to the offer." *Id.* at *9. Accordingly, the "potentially infringing article is the rig sold in the contract, not the altered rig that Maersk USA delivered to the U.S." *Id.* at *11.

2. **Deepsouth** *and Congress's Response.* The *RIM* court discussed the *Deepsouth* case and rejected RIM's reliance on *Deepsouth*'s holding. The court distinguished *Deepsouth* because in *RIM* "the *location* of the infringement is within United States territory, not abroad as in *Deepsouth*." In *Deepsouth*, the defendant made the components of the patented device and transported them to foreign-based customers. The components were thereafter assembled outside of the United States. The Supreme Court held for the accused infringer, noting "a combination patent protects only against the operable assembly of the whole and not the manufacture of its parts." Deepsouth Packing Co. v. Laitram Corp., 406 U.S. 518, 528 (1972). While one who manufactures unassembled components may be liable of contributory infringement, there must first be direct infringement. Activity that would otherwise constitute direct infringement if done in the United States (e.g., making and using), is not direct infringement if performed abroad.

Several years after *Deepsouth*, Congress responded with section 271(f), which was enacted in 1984. Under this statutory provision, one who supplies unassembled parts of a patented device is an infringer. The policies underlying section 271(f) are explained in the legislative history:

The . . . change . . . will prevent copiers from avoiding U.S. patents by supplying components of a patented product in this country so that the assembly of the components may be completed abroad. This proposal responds to the United States Supreme Court decision in *Deepsouth Packing Co. v. Laitram Corp.*, 406 U.S. 518 (1972), concerning the need for a legislative solution to close a loophole in patent law.

In this regard, section 101 adds a new subsection 271(f) to the patent law. Subsection 271(f) makes it an infringement to supply components of a patented invention, or to cause components to be supplied, that are to be combined outside the United States. In order to be liable as an infringer under paragraph (f)(1), one must supply or cause to be supplied "all or a substantial portion" of the components in a manner that would infringe the patent if such a combination occurred in the United States. The term "actively induce" is drawn from existing subsection 271(b) of the patent law, which provides that whoever actively induces patent infringement is liable as an infringer.

Under paragraph (f)(1) the components may be staple articles or commodities of commerce which are also suitable for substantial non-infringing use, but under paragraph (f)(2) the components must be especially made or adapted for use in the invention. The passage in paragraph (f)(2) reading "especially adapted for use in an infringement of such patent, and not a staple article or commodity of commerce suitable for substantial non-infringing use" comes from existing section 271(c) of the patent law, which governs contributory infringement. Paragraph (f)(2), like existing subsection 271(c), requires the infringer to have knowledge that the component is especially made or adapted. Paragraph (f)(2) also contains a further requirement that infringers must have an intent that the components will be combined outside of the United States in a manner that would infringe if the combination occurred within the United States.

Section-by-Section Analysis of H.R. 6286, Patent Law Amendments Act of 1984, Congressional Record, Oct. 1, 1984, H10525-26. *Deepsouth* is also explored in the next principal case, immediately below.

2. The Parameters of Section 271(f): Export Activity

It is axiomatic that someone who makes and uses a patented invention in the United States without permission of the patent owner engages in patent infringement. But what about a situation where a third party makes an incomplete version of the patented product in the United States for export or only makes a component of a patented machine and thereafter exports it for assembly abroad with other components that ultimately form the patented device? There is no infringement under section 271(a) because the assembly was outside the United States. But there may be infringement under section 271(f), which was drafted with this type of scenario in mind. The principal case of *Microsoft v. AT&T* explores the reach and parameters of section 271(f).

MICROSOFT CORP. v. AT&T CORP.

550 U.S. 437 (2007)

Justice GINSBURG delivered the opinion of the Court.

It is the general rule under United States patent law that no infringement occurs when a patented product is made and sold in another country. There is an exception. Section 271(f) of the Patent Act, adopted in 1984, provides that infringement does occur when one "supplies . . . from the United States," for "combination" abroad, a patented invention's "components." 35 U.S.C. §271(f)(1). This case concerns the applicability of §271(f) to computer software first sent from the United States to a foreign manufacturer on a master disk, or by electronic transmission, then copied by the foreign recipient for installation on computers made and sold abroad.

AT&T holds a patent on an apparatus for digitally encoding and compressing recorded speech. Microsoft's Windows operating system, it is conceded, has the potential to infringe AT&T's patent, because Windows incorporates software code that, when installed, enables a computer to process speech in the manner claimed by that patent. It bears emphasis, however, that uninstalled Windows software does not infringe AT&T's patent any more than a computer standing alone does; instead, the patent is infringed only when a computer is loaded with Windows and is thereby rendered capable of performing as the patented speech processor. The question before us: Does Microsoft's liability extend to computers made in another country when loaded with Windows software copied abroad from a master disk or electronic transmission dispatched by Microsoft from the United States? Our answer is "No."

The master disk or electronic transmission Microsoft sends from the United States is never installed on any of the foreign-made computers in question. Instead, copies made abroad are used for installation. Because Microsoft does not export from the United States the copies actually installed, it does not "suppl[y] . . . from the United States" "components" of the relevant computers, and therefore is not liable under §271(f) as currently written.

Plausible arguments can be made for and against extending §271(f) to the conduct charged in this case as infringing AT&T's patent. Recognizing that §271(f) is an exception to the general rule that our patent law does not apply extraterritorially, we resist giving the language in which Congress cast §271(f) an expansive interpretation. Our decision leaves to Congress' informed judgment any adjustment of §271(f) it deems necessary or proper.

I

Our decision some 35 years ago in *Deepsouth Packing Co. v. Laitram Corp.*, 406 U.S. 518 (1972), a case about a shrimp deveining machine, led Congress to enact §271(f). In that case, Laitram, holder of a patent on the time-and-expense-saving machine, sued Deepsouth, manufacturer of an infringing deveiner. Deepsouth conceded that the Patent Act barred it from making and selling its deveining machine in the United States, but sought to salvage a portion of its business: Nothing in United States patent law, Deepsouth urged, stopped it from making in the United States the *parts* of its deveiner, as opposed to the machine itself, and selling those *parts* to foreign buyers for assembly and use abroad. *Id.*, at 522-524.[1] We agreed.

Interpreting our patent law as then written, we reiterated in *Deepsouth* that it was "not an infringement to make or use a patented product outside of the

---

1. Deepsouth shipped its deveining equipment "to foreign customers in three separate boxes, each containing only parts of the 1-ton machines, yet the whole [was] assemblable in less than one hour." *Deepsouth Packing Co. v. Laitram Corp.*, 406 U.S. 518, 524 (1972).

United States." *Id.*, at 527; see 35 U.S.C. § 271(a) (1970 ed.) ("[W]hoever without authority makes, uses or sells any patented invention, within the United States during the term of the patent therefor, infringes the patent."). Deepsouth's foreign buyers did not infringe Laitram's patent, we held, because they assembled and used the deveining machines outside the United States. Deepsouth, we therefore concluded, could not be charged with inducing or contributing to an infringement. Nor could Deepsouth be held liable as a direct infringer, for it did not make, sell, or use the patented invention—the fully assembled deveining machine—within the United States. The parts of the machine were not themselves patented, we noted, hence export of those parts, unassembled, did not rank as an infringement of Laitram's patent.

Laitram had argued in *Deepsouth* that resistance to extension of the patent privilege to cover exported parts "derived from too narrow and technical an interpretation of the [Patent Act]." *Id.*, at 529. Rejecting that argument, we referred to prior decisions holding that "a combination patent protects only against the operable assembly of the whole and not the manufacture of its parts." *Id.*, at 528. Congress' codification of patent law, we said, signaled no intention to broaden the scope of the privilege. *Id.*, at 530 ("When, as here, the Constitution is permissive, the sign of how far Congress has chosen to go can come only from Congress."). And we again emphasized that

> [o]ur patent system makes no claim to extraterritorial effect; these acts of Congress do not, and were not intended to, operate beyond the limits of the United States; and we correspondingly reject the claims of others to such control over our markets.

Id., at 531 (quoting *Brown v. Duchesne*, 19 How. 183, 195 (1857)).

Absent "a clear congressional indication of intent," we stated, courts had no warrant to stop the manufacture and sale of the parts of patented inventions for assembly and use abroad. 406 U.S., at 532.

Focusing its attention on *Deepsouth*, Congress enacted § 271(f).[3] The provision expands the definition of infringement to include supplying from the United States a patented invention's components:

> (1) Whoever without authority supplies or causes to be supplied in or from the United States all or a substantial portion of the components of a patented invention, where such components are uncombined in whole or in part, in such manner as to actively induce the combination of such components outside of the United States in a manner that would infringe the patent if such combination occurred within the United States, shall be liable as an infringer.
>
> (2) Whoever without authority supplies or causes to be supplied in or from the United States any component of a patented invention that is especially made or especially adapted for use in the invention and not a staple article or commodity of commerce suitable for substantial noninfringing use, where such component is uncombined in whole or in part, knowing that such component is so made

---

3. See also, *e.g.*, Patent Law Amendments of 1984, S. Rep. No. 98-663, pp. 2-3 (1984) (describing § 271(f) as "a response to the Supreme Court's 1972 *Deepsouth* decision which interpreted the patent law not to make it infringement where the final assembly and sale is abroad"); Section-by-Section Analysis of H.R. 6286, 130 Cong. Rec. 28069 (1984) ("This proposal responds to the United States Supreme Court decision in *Deepsouth* . . . concerning the need for a legislative solution to close a loophole in [the] patent law.").

or adapted and intending that such component will be combined outside of the United States in a manner that would infringe the patent if such combination occurred within the United States, shall be liable as an infringer.

35 U.S.C. § 271(f).

II

Windows is designed, authored, and tested at Microsoft's Redmond, Washington, headquarters. Microsoft sells Windows to end users and computer manufacturers, both foreign and domestic. Purchasing manufacturers install the software onto the computers they sell. Microsoft sends to each of the foreign manufacturers a master version of Windows, either on a disk or via encrypted electronic transmission. The manufacturer uses the master version to generate copies. Those copies, not the master sent by Microsoft, are installed on the foreign manufacturer's computers. Once assembly is complete, the foreign-made computers are sold to users abroad.

AT&T's patent ('580 patent) is for an apparatus (as relevant here, a computer) capable of digitally encoding and compressing recorded speech. Windows, the parties agree, contains software that enables a computer to process speech in the manner claimed by the '580 patent. In 2001, AT&T filed an infringement suit in the United States District Court for the Southern District of New York, charging Microsoft with liability for domestic and foreign installations of Windows.

Neither Windows software (*e.g.*, in a box on the shelf) nor a computer standing alone (*i.e.*, without Windows installed) infringes AT&T's patent. Infringement occurs only when Windows is installed on a computer, thereby rendering it capable of performing as the patented speech processor. Microsoft stipulated that by installing Windows on its own computers during the software development process, it directly infringed the '580 patent. Microsoft further acknowledged that by licensing copies of Windows to manufacturers of computers sold in the United States, it induced infringement of AT&T's patent.

Microsoft denied, however, any liability based on the master disks and electronic transmissions it dispatched to foreign manufacturers, thus joining issue with AT&T. By sending Windows to foreign manufacturers, AT&T contended, Microsoft "supplie[d] . . . from the United States," for "combination" abroad, "components" of AT&T's patented speech processor; accordingly, AT&T urged, Microsoft was liable under § 271(f). Microsoft responded that unincorporated software, because it is intangible information, cannot be typed a "component" of an invention under § 271(f). In any event, Microsoft urged, the foreign-generated copies of Windows actually installed abroad were not "supplie[d] . . . from the United States." Rejecting these responses, the District Court held Microsoft liable under § 271(f). On appeal, a divided panel of the Court of Appeals for the Federal Circuit affirmed. We granted certiorari, and now reverse.

III

A

This case poses two questions: First, when, or in what form, does software qualify as a "component" under § 271(f)? Second, were "components" of the foreign-made computers involved in this case "supplie[d]" by Microsoft "from the United States"?[7]

As to the first question, no one in this litigation argues that software can *never* rank as a "component" under §271(f). The parties disagree, however, over the stage at which software becomes a component. Software, the "set of instructions, known as code, that directs a computer to perform specified functions or operations," *Fantasy Sports Properties, Inc. v. Sportsline.com, Inc.*, 287 F.3d 1108, 1118 (CA Fed. 2002), can be conceptualized in (at least) two ways. One can speak of software in the abstract: the instructions themselves detached from any medium. (An analogy: The notes of Beethoven's Ninth Symphony.) One can alternatively envision a tangible "copy" of software, the instructions encoded on a medium such as a CD-ROM. (Sheet music for Beethoven's Ninth.) AT&T argues that software in the abstract, not simply a particular copy of software, qualifies as a "component" under §271(f). Microsoft and the United States argue that only a copy of software, not software in the abstract, can be a component.[8]

The significance of these diverse views becomes apparent when we turn to the second question: Were components of the foreign-made computers involved in this case "supplie[d]" by Microsoft "from the United States"? If the relevant components are the copies of Windows actually installed on the foreign computers, AT&T could not persuasively argue that those components, though generated abroad, were "supplie[d] . . . from the United States" as §271(f) requires for liability to attach.[9] If, on the other hand, Windows in the abstract qualifies as a component within §271(f)'s compass, it would not matter that the master copies of Windows software dispatched from the United States were not themselves installed abroad as working parts of the foreign computers.[10]

With this explanation of the relationship between the two questions in view, we further consider the twin inquiries.

B

First, when, or in what form, does software become a "component" under §271(f)? We construe §271(f)'s terms "in accordance with [their] ordinary or natural meaning." *FDIC v. Meyer*, 510 U.S. 471, 476 (1994). Section 271(f) applies to the supply abroad of the "components of a patented invention, where *such*

---

7. The record leaves unclear which paragraph of §271(f) AT&T's claim invokes. While there are differences between §271(f)(1) and (f)(2), the parties do not suggest that those differences are outcome determinative. Cf. *infra*, at 14-15, n.16 (explaining why both paragraphs yield the same result). For clarity's sake, we focus our analysis on the text of §271(f)(1).

8. Microsoft and the United States stress that to count as a component, the copy of software must be expressed as "object code." "Software in the form in which it is written and understood by humans is called 'source code.' To be functional, however, software must be converted (or 'compiled') into its machine-usable version," a sequence of binary number instructions typed "object code." It is stipulated that object code was on the master disks and electronic transmissions Microsoft dispatched from the United States.

9. On this view of "component," the copies of Windows on the master disks and electronic transmissions that Microsoft sent from the United States could not themselves serve as a basis for liability, because those copies were not installed on the foreign manufacturers' computers. See §271(f)(1) (encompassing only those components "combin[ed] . . . outside of the United States in a manner that would infringe the patent if such combination occurred within the United States").

10. The Federal Circuit panel in this case, relying on that court's prior decision in *Eolas Technologies Inc. v. Microsoft Corp.*, 399 F.3d 1325 (2005), held that software qualifies as a component under §271(f). We are unable to determine, however, whether the Federal Circuit panels regarded as a component software in the abstract, or a copy of software.

components are uncombined in whole or in part, in such manner as to actively induce the combination of *such components.*" §271(f)(1) (emphasis added). The provision thus applies only to "such components"[11] as are combined to form the "patented invention" at issue. The patented invention here is AT&T's speech-processing computer.

Until it is expressed as a computer-readable "copy," *e.g.*, on a CD-ROM, Windows software—indeed any software detached from an activating medium—remains uncombinable. It cannot be inserted into a CD-ROM drive or downloaded from the Internet; it cannot be installed or executed on a computer. Abstract software code is an idea without physical embodiment, and as such, it does not match §271(f)'s categorization: "components" amenable to "combination." Windows abstracted from a tangible copy no doubt is information—a detailed set of instructions—and thus might be compared to a blueprint (or anything containing design information, *e.g.*, a schematic, template, or prototype). A blueprint may contain precise instructions for the construction and combination of the components of a patented device, but it is not itself a combinable component of that device. AT&T and its *amici* do not suggest otherwise. Cf. *Pellegrini v. Analog Devices, Inc.*, 375 F.3d 1113, 1117-1119 (CA Fed. 2004) (transmission abroad of instructions for production of patented computer chips not covered by §271(f)).

AT&T urges that software, at least when expressed as machine-readable object code, is distinguishable from design information presented in a blueprint. Software, unlike a blueprint, is "modular"; it is a stand-alone product developed and marketed "for use on many different types of computer hardware and in conjunction with many other types of software." Software's modularity persists even after installation; it can be updated or removed (deleted) without affecting the hardware on which it is installed. Software, unlike a blueprint, is also "dynamic." After a device has been built according to a blueprint's instructions, the blueprint's work is done (as AT&T puts it, the blueprint's instructions have been "exhausted."). Software's instructions, in contrast, are contained in and continuously performed by a computer. See also *Eolas Technologies Inc. v. Microsoft Corp.*, 399 F.3d 1325, 1339 (CA Fed. 2005) ("[S]oftware code . . . drives the functional nucleus of the finished computer product.)"

The distinctions advanced by AT&T do not persuade us to characterize software, uncoupled from a medium, as a combinable component. Blueprints too, or any design information for that matter, can be independently developed, bought, and sold. If the point of AT&T's argument is that we do not see blueprints lining stores' shelves, the same observation may be made about software in the abstract: What retailers sell, and consumers buy, are *copies* of software. Likewise, before software can be contained in and continuously performed by a computer, before it can be updated or deleted, an actual, physical copy of the software must be delivered by CD-ROM or some other means capable of interfacing with the computer.[12]

11. "Component" is commonly defined as "a constituent part," "element," or "ingredient." Webster's Third New International Dictionary of the English Language 466 (1981).

12. The dissent, embracing AT&T's argument, contends that, "unlike a blueprint that merely instructs a user how to do something, software actually causes infringing conduct to occur." (Stevens, J., dissenting). We have emphasized, however, that Windows can "caus[e] infringing conduct to occur"—*i.e.*, function as part of AT&T's speech-processing computer-only when expressed

Because it is so easy to encode software's instructions onto a medium that can be read by a computer, AT&T intimates, that extra step should not play a decisive role under §271(f). But the extra step is what renders the software a usable, combinable part of a computer; easy or not, the copy-producing step is essential. Moreover, many tools may be used easily and inexpensively to generate the parts of a device. A machine for making sprockets might be used by a manufacturer to produce tens of thousands of sprockets an hour. That does not make the machine a "component" of the tens of thousands of devices in which the sprockets are incorporated, at least not under any ordinary understanding of the term "component." Congress, of course, might have included within §271(f)'s compass, for example, not only combinable "components" of a patented invention, but also "information, instructions, or tools from which those components readily may be generated." It did not. In sum, a copy of Windows, not Windows in the abstract, qualifies as a "component" under §271(f).

C

The next question, has Microsoft "supplie[d] . . . from the United States" components of the computers here involved? Under a conventional reading of §271(f)'s text, the answer would be "No," for the foreign-made copies of Windows actually installed on the computers were "supplie[d]" from places outside the United States. The Federal Circuit majority concluded, however, that "for software 'components,' the act of copying is subsumed in the act of 'supplying.'" 414 F.3d, at 1370. A master sent abroad, the majority observed, differs not at all from the exact copies, easily, inexpensively, and swiftly generated from the master; hence "sending a single copy abroad with the intent that it be replicated invokes §271(f) liability for th[e] foreign-made copies." *Ibid.;* cf. (Stevens, J., dissenting) ("[A] master disk is the functional equivalent of a warehouse of components . . . that Microsoft fully expects to be incorporated into foreign-manufactured computers.").

Judge Rader, dissenting, noted that "supplying" is ordinarily understood to mean an activity separate and distinct from any subsequent "copying, replicating, or reproducing-in effect manufacturing." 414 F.3d, at 1372-1373 ("[C]opying and supplying are separate acts with different consequences—particularly when the 'supplying' occurs in the United States and the copying occurs in Dusseldorf or Tokyo. As a matter of logic, one cannot supply one hundred components of a patented invention without first making one hundred copies of the component. . . ."). He further observed: "The only true difference between making and supplying software components and physical components [of other patented inventions] is that copies of software components are easier to make and transport." *Id.,* at 1374. But nothing in §271(f)'s text, Judge Rader maintained, renders ease of copying a relevant, no less decisive, factor in triggering liability for infringement. See *ibid.* We agree.

Section 271(f) prohibits the supply of components "from the United States . . . in such manner as to actively induce the combination of *such components.*" §271(f)(1) (emphasis added). Under this formulation, the very components

---

as a computer-readable copy. Abstracted from a usable copy, Windows code is intangible, uncombinable information, more like notes of music in the head of a composer than "a roller that causes a player piano to produce sound." *Ibid.*

supplied from the United States, and not copies thereof, trigger §271(f) liability when combined abroad to form the patented invention at issue. Here, as we have repeatedly noted, the copies of Windows actually installed on the foreign computers were not themselves supplied from the United States. Indeed, those copies did not exist until they were generated by third parties outside the United States. Copying software abroad, all might agree, is indeed easy and inexpensive. But the same could be said of other items: "Keys or machine parts might be copied from a master; chemical or biological substances might be created by reproduction; and paper products might be made by electronic copying and printing." Section 271(f) contains no instruction to gauge when duplication is easy and cheap enough to deem a copy in fact made abroad nevertheless "supplie[d] . . . from the United States." The absence of anything addressing copying in the statutory text weighs against a judicial determination that replication abroad of a master dispatched from the United States "supplies" the foreign-made copies from the United States within the intendment of §271(f).

D

Any doubt that Microsoft's conduct falls outside §271(f)'s compass would be resolved by the presumption against extraterritoriality, on which we have already touched. The presumption that United States law governs domestically but does not rule the world applies with particular force in patent law. The traditional understanding that our patent law "operate[s] only domestically and d[oes] not extend to foreign activities," is embedded in the Patent Act itself, which provides that a patent confers exclusive rights in an invention within the United States. 35 U.S.C. §154(a)(1) (patentee's rights over invention apply to manufacture, use, or sale "throughout the United States" and to importation "into the United States"). See *Deepsouth*, 406 U.S., at 531 ("Our patent system makes no claim to extraterritorial effect"; our legislation "d[oes] not, and [was] not intended to, operate beyond the limits of the United States, and we correspondingly reject the claims of others to such control over our markets." (quoting *Brown*, 19 How., at 195)).

As a principle of general application, moreover, we have stated that courts should "assume that legislators take account of the legitimate sovereign interests of other nations when they write American laws." *F. Hoffmann-La Roche Ltd v. Empagran S.A.*, 542 U.S. 155, 164 (2004). Thus, the United States accurately conveyed in this case: "Foreign conduct is [generally] the domain of foreign law," and in the area here involved, in particular, foreign law "may embody different policy judgments about the relative rights of inventors, competitors, and the public in patented inventions." Applied to this case, the presumption tugs strongly against construction of §271(f) to encompass as a "component" not only a physical copy of software, but also software's intangible code, and to render "supplie[d] . . . from the United States" not only exported copies of software, but also duplicates made abroad.

AT&T argues that the presumption is inapplicable because Congress enacted §271(f) specifically to extend the reach of United States patent law to cover certain activity abroad. But as this Court has explained, "the presumption is not defeated . . . just because [a statute] specifically addresses [an] issue of extraterritorial application," *Smith v. United States*, 507 U.S. 197, 204 (1993); it remains instructive in determining the *extent* of the statutory exception. See *Empagran*, 542 U.S., at 161-162, 164-165.

AT&T alternately contends that the presumption holds no sway here given that §271(f), by its terms, applies only to domestic conduct, *i.e.*, to the supply of a patented invention's components "from the United States." §271(f)(1). AT&T's reading, however, "converts a single act of supply from the United States into a springboard for liability each time a copy of the software is subsequently made [abroad] and combined with computer hardware [abroad] for sale [abroad.]" Brief for United States as *Amicus Curiae* 29; see 414 F.3d, at 1373, 1375 (Rader, J., dissenting). In short, foreign law alone, not United States law, currently governs the manufacture and sale of components of patented inventions in foreign countries. If AT&T desires to prevent copying in foreign countries, its remedy today lies in obtaining and enforcing foreign patents.

IV

AT&T urges that reading §271(f) to cover only those copies of software actually dispatched from the United States creates a "loophole" for software makers. Liability for infringing a United States patent could be avoided, as Microsoft's practice shows, by an easily arranged circumvention: Instead of making installation copies of software in the United States, the copies can be made abroad, swiftly and at small cost, by generating them from a master supplied from the United States. The Federal Circuit majority found AT&T's plea compelling:

> Were we to hold that Microsoft's supply by exportation of the master versions of the Windows software—specifically for the purpose of foreign replication—avoids infringement, we would be subverting the remedial nature of §271(f), permitting a technical avoidance of the statute by ignoring the advances in a field of technology—and its associated industry practices—that developed after the enactment of §271(f). . . . Section §271(f), if it is to remain effective, must therefore be interpreted in a manner that is appropriate to the nature of the technology at issue. 414 F.3d, at 1371.

While the majority's concern is understandable, we are not persuaded that dynamic judicial interpretation of §271(f) is in order. The "loophole," in our judgment, is properly left for Congress to consider, and to close if it finds such action warranted.

There is no dispute, we note again, that §271(f) is inapplicable to the export of design tools—blueprints, schematics, templates, and prototypes—all of which may provide the information required to construct and combine overseas the components of inventions patented under United States law. We have no license to attribute to Congress an unstated intention to place the information Microsoft dispatched from the United States in a separate category.

Section 271(f) was a direct response to a gap in our patent law revealed by this Court's *Deepsouth* decision. The facts of that case were undeniably at the fore when §271(f) was in the congressional hopper. In *Deepsouth*, the items exported were kits containing all the physical, readily assemblable parts of a shrimp deveining machine (not an intangible set of instructions), and those parts themselves (not foreign-made copies of them) would be combined abroad by foreign buyers. Having attended to the gap made evident in *Deepsouth*, Congress did not address other arguable gaps: Section 271(f) does not identify as an infringing act conduct in the United States that facilitates making a component of a patented invention outside the United States; nor does the provision check "suppl[ying] . . . from the United States" information, instructions, or other materials needed to make copies abroad. Given that Congress did not home in on the loophole AT&T describes, and in view of the expanded extraterritorial thrust AT&T's reading of §271(f) entails, our precedent leads us to leave in Congress' court the patent-protective determination AT&T seeks.

Congress is doubtless aware of the ease with which software (and other electronic media) can be copied, and has not left the matter untouched. In 1998, Congress addressed "the ease with which pirates could copy and distribute a copyrightable work in digital form." *Universal City Studios, Inc. v. Corley*, 273 F.3d 429, 435 (CA2 2001). The resulting measure, the Digital Millennium Copyright Act, 17 U.S.C. § 1201 *et seq.*, "backed with legal sanctions the efforts of copyright owners to protect their works from piracy behind digital walls such as encryption codes or password protections." *Universal City Studios*, 273 F.3d, at 435. If the patent law is to be adjusted better "to account for the realities of software distribution," 414 F.3d, at 1370, the alteration should be made after focused legislative consideration, and not by the Judiciary forecasting Congress' likely disposition.

For the reasons stated, the judgment of the Court of Appeals for the Federal Circuit is reversed.

Justice STEVENS, dissenting.

As the Court acknowledges, "[p]lausible arguments can be made for and against extending §271(f) to the conduct charged in this case as infringing AT&T's patent." Strong policy considerations, buttressed by the presumption against the application of domestic patent law in foreign markets, support Microsoft Corporation's position. I am, however, persuaded that an affirmance of the Court of Appeals' judgment is more faithful to the intent of the Congress that enacted §271(f) than a reversal.

The provision was a response to our decision in *Deepsouth Packing Co. v. Laitram Corp.*, 406 U.S. 518 (1972), holding that a patent on a shrimp deveining machine had not been infringed by the export of components for assembly abroad. Paragraph (1) of §271(f) would have been sufficient on its own to overrule *Deepsouth*, but it is paragraph (2) that best supports AT&T's position here. It provides:

> Whoever without authority supplies or causes to be supplied in or from the United States any component of a patented invention that is especially made or especially adapted for use in the invention and not a staple article or commodity of commerce suitable for substantial noninfringing use, where such component is uncombined in whole or in part, knowing that such component is so made or adapted and intending that such component will be combined outside of the United States in a manner that would infringe the patent if such combination occurred within the United States, shall be liable as an infringer.

§271(f)(2).

Under this provision, the export of a specially designed knife that has no use other than as a part of a patented deveining machine would constitute infringement. It follows that §271(f)(2) would cover the export of an inventory of such knives to be warehoused until used to complete the assembly of an infringing machine.

The relevant component in this case is not a physical item like a knife. Both Microsoft and the Court think that means it cannot be a "component." But if a disk with software inscribed on it is a "component," I find it difficult to understand why the most important ingredient of that component is not also a component. Indeed, the master disk is the functional equivalent of a warehouse of components — components that Microsoft fully expects to be incorporated into foreign-manufactured computers. Put somewhat differently: On the Court's view, Microsoft could be liable under §271(f) only if it sends individual copies of its software directly from the United States with the intent that each copy would be incorporated into a separate infringing computer. But it seems to me that an indirect transmission via a master disk warehouse is likewise covered by §271(f).

I disagree with the Court's suggestion that because software is analogous to an abstract set of instructions, it cannot be regarded as a "component" within the meaning of §271(f). Whether attached or detached from any medium, software plainly satisfies the dictionary definition of that word. See *ante*, at 9, n.11 (observing that "'[c]omponent' is commonly defined as 'a constituent part,' 'element,' or 'ingredient'"). And unlike a blueprint that merely instructs a user how to do something, software actually causes infringing conduct to occur. It is more like a roller that causes a player piano to produce sound than sheet music that tells a pianist what to do. Moreover, it is surely not "a staple article or commodity of commerce suitable for substantial noninfringing use" as that term is used in §271(f)(2). On the contrary, its sole intended use is an infringing use.

I would therefore affirm the judgment of the Court of Appeals.

Comments

1. **Patent Rights Are Territorial.** There is no such thing as a worldwide patent. To say that patent rights are territorial means that "the right conferred by a patent under [U.S. law] is confined to the United States and its Territories." Accordingly, "infringement of this right cannot be predicated [on] acts wholly done in a foreign country." *Dowagiac Mfg. Co. v. Minnesota Moline Plow Co.*, 235 U.S. 641, 650 (1915). The *Microsoft* Court placed particular emphasis on the territoriality aspect of patent rights:

   > Any doubt that Microsoft's conduct falls outside §271(f)'s compass would be resolved by the presumption against extraterritoriality. . . . The presumption that United States law governs domestically but does not rule the world applies with particular force in patent law. The traditional understanding that our patent law "operate[s] only domestically and d[oes] not extend to foreign activities," is embedded in the Patent Act itself, which provides that a patent confers exclusive rights in an invention within the United States. 35 U.S.C. §154(a)(1).

   For a detailed discussion of the *Microsoft* case and, more generally, issues relating to territoriality, *see* Timothy R. Holbrook, *Extraterritoriality in U.S. Patent Law*, 49 WM. & MARY L. REV. 2119 (2008).

2. **Federal Circuit's View of Section 271(f) Prior to Microsoft.** In recent years, section 271(f) has been the subject of a small, but important group of cases. In *Pellegrini v. Analog Devices, Inc.*, 375 F.3d 1113 (Fed. Cir. 2004), for example, the patent related to brushless motor drive circuits that used integrated circuit chips. It was undisputed that the accused infringer, Analog, manufactured and sold the circuit chips outside the United States. The chips in

question—the ADMC chips—were manufactured in Ireland by two independent contractors hired by Analog in Taiwan. Also, most of the chips were shipped and sold to customers outside the United States. Pellegrini sued Analog for direct and indirect infringement, asserting that certain claims of its patent read on a combination of ADMC chips and other components in brushless motors. The district court granted Analog's motion for summary judgment of noninfringement because U.S. patent laws do not have extraterritorial effect. The court rejected Pellegrini's argument that, because Analog's headquarters are located in the United States and instructions for the production and disposition of the ADMC chips emanate from the United States, the chips should be regarded as having been "supplie[d] or cause[d] to be supplied in or from the United States" and Analog should be liable as an infringer under 35 U.S.C. §271(f)(1).

The Federal Circuit affirmed the district court, and characterized the issue—one of first impression—as "whether components that are manufactured outside the United States and never physically shipped to or from the United States may nonetheless be "supplie[d] or cause[d] to be supplied in or from the United States" within the meaning of 35 U.S.C. §271(f)(1) if those components are designed within the United States and the instructions for their manufacture and disposition are transmitted from within the United States." *Id.* at 1115-1116. According to the court, section 271(f) was inapplicable because "Analog did not make, use, sell, or offer to sell ADMC products in the United States, and it did not import ADMC products into the United States. Analog also does not supply ADMC chips in or from the United States, and does not cause ADMC chips to be supplied in or from the United States." *Id.* at 1118. The court wrote:

> §271(f) applies only where components of a patent invention are physically present in the United States and then either sold or exported "in such a manner as to actively induce the combination of such components outside the United States in a manner that would infringe the patent if such combination occurred within the United States." ... The plain language of §271(f)(1) focuses on the location of the accused components, not the accused infringer. Pellegrini contends that it is irrelevant that the chips within the scope of the partial summary judgment never enter the United States, because to impose a location requirement would lead to a "seemingly contradictory construction of §271(f)(1)." According to Pellegrini, "it is difficult to understand how the combination of such components outside the United States can occur if they are inside the United States." However, the language of §271(f) clearly contemplates that there must be an intervening sale or exportation; there can be no liability under §271(f)(1) unless components are shipped from the United States for assembly.

Id. at 1117.

Pellegrini was distinguished in *Eolas Techs., Inc. v. Microsoft Corp*, 399 F.3d 1325 (Fed. Cir. 2005) (now overruled—see Comment 4), which seemingly eliminated the physicality requirement under section 271(f) as interpreted by *Pellegrini*. The *Eolas* case is factually similar to *Microsoft v. AT&T*. In *Eolas*, the licensee sued Microsoft under section 271(f)(1) based on Microsoft's export to foreign manufacturers of its "golden master" disks that contained code for Windows. The code was replicated by the foreign manufactures outside of the United States and, as in *AT&T*, the master disk did not form a physical part of infringing product. The court held Microsoft infringed, stating "*Pellegrini* requires only that components are physically *supplied* from the United States," implying that what is actually shipped (i.e., the components themselves) need not be tangible or physical.

3. *Section 271(f) at the Supreme Court.* The Supreme Court addressed two questions in *Microsoft v. AT&T*: Was the software a "component" under section 271(f), and, were "components" of a foreign-made computer "supplied" by Microsoft "from the United States"?

In interpreting the term "components" in section 271, the Court noted that the statute refers to components that are combined to form the patented invention, which is AT&T's speech-processing computer. As such, "[u]ntil [the software] is expressed as a computer-readable 'copy,' e.g., on a CD-ROM, Windows software—indeed any software detached from an activating medium—remains uncombinable." The Court also rejected AT&T's argument that "[b]ecause it is so easy to encode software's instructions onto a medium that can be read by a computer, that extra step should not play a decisive role under §271(f)." But, wrote the Court, the extra step is what renders the software a usable, combinable part of a computer; easy or not." In short, "copy-producing step is essential." Justice Stevens, in his dissent, was not persuaded of the importance of "copy-producing step." For him, "if a disk with software inscribed on it is a 'component,' I find it difficult to understand why the most important ingredient of that component is not also a component." That the majority opinion was too formalistic was implicit in Justice Stevens's dissent. As he wrote, liability under section 271(f) would attached only if Microsoft "sends individual copies of its software directly from the United States with the intent that each copy would be incorporated into a separate infringing computer."

In addressing whether Microsoft "supplied" components, the Court refused to read section 271(f) expansively. For example, the Court expressly rejected the "easy" to copy argument, stating "[s]ection 271(f) contains no instruction to gauge when duplication is easy and cheap enough to deem a copy in fact made abroad nevertheless 'supplie[d] . . . from the United States.'" This reasoning eschews, absent Congressional intervention, a technology-specific approach to patent law, at least with regard to section 271(f). In an exercise of judicial restraint, the Court stated "[o]ur decision leaves to Congress' informed judgment any adjustment of §271(f) it deems necessary or proper."

The Court's reading of section 271(f) permits a U.S. producer to evade liability by shipping components abroad to have them copied, and thereafter have the copies used or installed by a foreign entity to create another product. But lurking behind the legal issues and questions of statutory construction, was whether an affirmance of the Federal Circuit would induce software companies (and companies in other industries) to move their manufacturing facilities outside the United States. This argument was raised in the briefs, including amici briefs. In addition, *Microsoft* also highlights the importance of obtaining foreign patent protection; section 271(f) can be circumvented if the actual production occurs abroad, even though the product design occurred in the United States or if instructions on how to produce the product were shipped from the United States. Perhaps the lack of patent protection in Europe reflects the less than sympathetic environment in Europe vis-à-vis the United States for software patents.

4. *Section 271(f) Does Not Apply to Method Claims.* In *Microsoft v. AT&T*, the Supreme Court reserved judgment on whether "an intangible method or process . . . qualifies as a 'patented invention' under §271(f)." 550 U.S. at 452 n.13. In *Cardiac Pacemakers, Inc. v. St. Jude Medical, Inc.*, 576 F.3d 1348 (Fed. Cir. 2009) (*en banc*), the Federal Circuit held that section 271(f) does not apply to method patents, thus overruling *Eolas* (see Comment 2) and like-minded cases. The court disagreed with Cardiac's position that section 271(f) applies to all classes of invention. The Federal Circuit noted when interpreting the statutory term "patented invention" in section 271(f), there exists a critical distinction between, on the one hand, components of a tangible product, device, and apparatus; and, on the other hand, a method or process, which consists of a series of acts or steps. *Id.* at 1362. According to the court, "method patents do have 'components,' *viz.*, the steps that comprise the method, and thus they meet that definitional requirement of Section 271(f), but the steps are not the physical components used in performance of the method." *Id.* at 1363.

Moreover, section 271(f) requires "components" to be "supplied," which implies the component have a physicality. The definition of "supply" — according to the court — "is to 'provide that which is required,' or 'to furnish with . . . supplies, provisions, or equipment . . .' meanings [that] imply the transfer of a physical object. Supplying an intangible step is thus a physical impossibility." *Id.* at 1364.

Lastly, argued the court, holding the section 271(f) does not apply to method patents is consistent with the section's legislation history. Section 271(f) was explicitly enacted to overrule *Deepsouth*, which involved a product patent. *Id.* ("The legislative history of Section 271(f) is almost completely devoid of any reference to the protection of method patents and the Supreme Court has advised us that it is Congress's right, not the courts', to extend the statute beyond the *Deepsouth* problem it was designed to fix.").

5. *Section 271(f)'s Structure.* Sections 271(f)(1) and (2) mirror the inducement and contributory infringement provisions of sections 271(b) and (c), respectively. For example, §271(f)(1) reads, in relevant part, "[w]hoever without authority supplies or causes to be supplied in or from the United States all or a substantial portion of the components of a patented invention . . . in such a manner as to actively induce the combination of such components" resulting in infringement "shall be liable as an infringer." And §271(f)(2) reads, in relevant part, "[w]hoever without authority supplies or causes to be supplied in or from the United States all or a substantial portion of the components of a patented invention that is especially made or especially adapted for use in the invention and not a staple article . . . suitable for substantial non-infringement use . . . knowing that such component is so made or adapted and intending that such component will be combined outside the United States" resulting in infringement "shall be liable as an infringer." Thus, §271(f)(2), like §271(c), has an intent component.

Section 271(f), as discussed in *Microsoft*, was a direct response to the Supreme Court case of *Deepsouth Packing Co. v. Laitram Corp.*, 406 U.S. 518 (1972). See Comment 2 after the *RIM* case. But contributory infringement can be found only if there is direct infringement, which did not exist in *Deepsouth* because the manufacture and use was outside the United States.

3. The Parameters of Section 271(g): Import Activity

It is an act of infringement to import a patented product into the United States. Under section 271(g), it is also an act of infringement to import an unpatented product into the United States if that product was "made by" a patented process—even though the process was practiced outside of the United States. This form of importation became an infringing act only after the enactment of the Patent Process Amendments Act of 1988, which became effective of February 23, 1989. There are important conditions associated with this right. For instance, the imported, unpatented product must be "made by" the patented process. According to section 271(g), "[a] product which is made by a patented process will . . . not be considered to be so made after—(1) it is materially changed by subsequent processes; or (2) it becomes a trivial and nonessential component of another product." The *Eli Lilly* case explores the phrase "materially changed."

ELI LILLY & CO. v. AMERICAN CYANAMID CO.
82 F.3d 1568 (Fed. Cir. 1996)

BRYSON, Circuit Judge.

The ongoing struggle between "pioneer" drug manufacturers and generic drug distributors has once more come before our court. Eli Lilly and Company (Lilly), the "pioneer" drug manufacturer in this case, has filed suit for patent infringement against the appellees, who are involved in various ways in the distribution of a particular generic drug. Lilly sought a preliminary injunction, arguing that the importation and sale of the generic drug in this country infringed Lilly's patent on a process for making a related compound. After a hearing, the United States District Court for the Southern District of Indiana denied Lilly's request for a preliminary injunction. The court found that Lilly had failed to show that it was likely to prevail on the merits of its infringement claim and had failed to show that it would suffer irreparable harm in the absence of preliminary injunctive relief. *Eli Lilly & Co. v. American Cyanamid Co.* Because Lilly has failed to overcome the substantial hurdle faced by a party seeking to overturn the denial of a preliminary injunction, we affirm.

I

The pharmaceutical product at issue in this case is a broad-spectrum antibiotic known as "cefaclor." Cefaclor is a member of the class of cephalosporin antibiotics, all of which are based on the cephem nucleus. Although there are many different cephem compounds, only a few have utility as antibiotic drugs. Each of the known commercial methods for producing cefaclor requires the production of an intermediate cephem compound known as an enol. Once the desired enol cephem intermediate is obtained, it is then subjected to several processing steps in order to produce cefaclor.

A

Lilly developed cefaclor and patented it in 1975. Until recently, Lilly has been the exclusive manufacturer and distributor of cefaclor in this country. In addition to its product patent on cefaclor, Lilly obtained several patents covering different aspects of the manufacture of cefaclor, including processes for producing enol cephem intermediates. Many of those patents have now expired.

In 1995, Lilly purchased the patent at issue in this case, U.S. Patent No. 4,160,085 (the '085 patent). Claim 5 of that patent defines a method of producing enol cephem compounds, including what is called "compound 6," an enol cephem similar to the one Lilly uses in its process for manufacturing cefaclor. The '085 patent will expire on July 3, 1996.

Compound 6 differs from cefaclor in three respects. Although both compound 6 and cefaclor are based on the cephem nucleus, compound 6 has a hydroxy group at the 3-position on the cephem nucleus, a para-nitrobenzyl carboxylate ester at the 4-position, and a phenylacetyl group at the 7-position. Cefaclor has different groups at each of those positions: it has a chlorine atom at the 3-position, a free carboxyl group at the 4-position, and a phenylglycyl group at the 7-position. Each of those differences between compound 6 and cefaclor contributes to the effectiveness of cefaclor as an orally administered antibiotic drug. The free carboxyl group at the 4-position is believed important for antibacterial activity; the chlorine increases cefaclor's antibiotic potency; and the phenylglycyl group enables cefaclor to be effective when taken orally.

To produce cefaclor from compound 6 requires four distinct steps. First, the hydroxy group is removed from the 3-position and is replaced by a chlorine atom, which results in the creation of "compound 7." Second, compound 7 is subjected to a reaction that removes the phenylacetyl group at the 7-position, which results in the creation of "compound 8." Third, a phenylglycyl group is added at the 7-position, which results in the creation of "compound 9." Fourth, the para-nitrobenzyl carboxylate ester is removed from the 4-position, which results in the creation of cefaclor.

B

On April 27, 1995, defendants Zenith Laboratories, Inc. (Zenith) and American Cyanamid Company (Cyanamid) obtained permission from the Food and Drug Administration to distribute cefaclor in this country. Defendant Biocraft Laboratories, Inc. (Biocraft) had applied for FDA approval to manufacture and sell cefaclor in the United States but had not yet obtained that approval. All three have obtained large quantities of cefaclor that were manufactured in Italy by defendant Biochimica Opos, S.p.A. (Opos).

On the same day that Zenith and Cyanamid obtained FDA approval to sell cefaclor in this country, Lilly obtained the rights to the '085 patent and filed suit against Zenith, Cyanamid, Biocraft, and Opos. In its complaint, Lilly sought a declaration that the domestic defendants' importation of cefaclor manufactured by Opos infringed Lilly's rights under several patents, including the '085 patent. Lilly also requested a preliminary injunction, based on the alleged infringement of claim 5 of the '085 patent, to bar the defendants from importing or inducing the importation of cefaclor manufactured by Opos.

The district court held a three-day hearing on the motion for a preliminary injunction. Following the hearing, the court denied the motion in a comprehensive opinion. The court devoted most of its attention to the question whether Lilly had met its burden of showing that it was likely to prevail on the merits of its claim that the defendants were liable for infringing claim 5 of the '085 patent.

Based on the evidence presented at the hearing, the district court concluded that Lilly had shown that it was likely to prevail on the issue of the validity of the

'085 patent. With respect to the infringement issue, however, the court held that Lilly had not met its burden of showing that it was likely to prevail.

The district court correctly framed the issue as whether, under the Process Patent Amendments Act of 1988, Pub. L. No. 100-418, §§ 9001-07, the importers of cefaclor infringed claim 5 of the '085 patent, which granted U.S. patent protection to the process that Opos used to make compound 6. The Process Patent Amendments Act makes it an act of infringement to import, sell, offer to sell, or use in this country a product that was made abroad by a process protected by a U.S. patent. 35 U.S.C. § 271(g). The Act, however, does not apply if the product made by the patented process is "materially changed by subsequent processes" before it is imported. 35 U.S.C. § 271(g)(1).

The district court found that compound 6 and cefaclor differ significantly in their structure and properties, including their biological activity. Citing the Senate Report on the Process Patent Amendments Act, the district court found that, because the processing steps necessary to convert compound 6 to cefaclor "'change the physical or chemical properties of the product in a manner which changes the basic utility of the product,'" 896 F. Supp. at 857 (citing S. Rep. No. 83, 100th Cong., 1st Sess. 50 (1987)), Lilly was not likely to succeed on its claim that the defendants infringed Lilly's rights under claim 5 of the '085 patent by importing and selling cefaclor.

The district court also found that Lilly had failed to prove that it would suffer irreparable harm in the absence of a preliminary injunction. The presumption of irreparable harm that is available when a patentee makes a strong showing of likelihood of success on the merits was not available here, the court held, because of Lilly's failure to make such a showing on the issue of infringement. In addition, the court was not persuaded by Lilly's arguments that it faced irreparable economic injury if it were not granted immediate equitable relief. Under the circumstances of this case, the district court found that an award of money damages would be an adequate remedy in the event that Lilly ultimately proves that the importation of cefaclor made by the Opos process infringes the '085 patent. In light of Lilly's failure to establish either a likelihood of success on the merits or irreparable harm, the court found it unnecessary to articulate findings regarding the other factors bearing on the propriety of preliminary injunctive relief—the balance of the hardships and the effect of the court's action on the public interest.

II

The Process Patent Amendments Act of 1988 was enacted to close a perceived loophole in the statutory scheme for protecting owners of United States patents. Prior to the enactment of the 1988 statute, a patentee holding a process patent could sue for infringement if others used the process in this country, but had no cause of action if such persons used the patented process abroad to manufacture products, and then imported, used, or sold the products in this country. In that setting, the process patent owner's only legal recourse was to seek an exclusion order for such products from the International Trade Commission under section 337a of the Tariff Act of 1930, 19 U.S.C. § 1337a (1982). By enacting the Process Patent Amendments Act, the principal portion of which is codified as 35 U.S.C. § 271(g), Congress changed the law by making it an act of infringement to import into the United States, or to sell or use within the United States "a product which is made by a process patented in the

United States . . . if the importation, sale, or use of the product occurs during the term of such process patent."

A concern raised during Congress's consideration of the process patent legislation was whether and to what extent the new legislation would affect products other than the direct and unaltered products of patented processes—that is, whether the new statute would apply when a product was produced abroad by a patented process but then modified or incorporated into other products before being imported into this country. Congress addressed that issue by providing that a product that is "made by" a patented process within the meaning of the statute "will . . . not be considered to be so made after—(1) it is materially changed by subsequent processes; or (2) it becomes a trivial and nonessential component of another product." 35 U.S.C. § 271(g).

That language, unfortunately, is not very precise. Whether the product of a patented process is a "trivial and nonessential component" of another product is necessarily a question of degree. Even less well defined is the question whether the product of a patented process has been "materially changed" before its importation into this country. While applying that statutory language may be relatively easy in extreme cases, it is not at all easy in a closer case such as this one.

A

Lilly argues that the "materially changed" clause of section 271(g) must be construed in light of its underlying purpose, which is to protect the economic value of U.S. process patents to their owners. Prior to the enactment of the Process Patent Amendments Act, the value of a U.S. process patent could be undermined by a manufacturer who used the process abroad and then imported the product into this country. Because the purpose of the process patent legislation was to protect against such subversion of protected economic rights, Lilly argues that the statute should be read to apply to any such scheme that undercuts the commercial value of a U.S. process patent. In Lilly's view, the product of a patented process therefore should not be considered "materially changed" if the principal commercial use of that product lies in its conversion into the product that is the subject of the infringement charge. Because cefaclor is the only product of compound 6 that is sold in the United States market, Lilly argues, the change in compound 6 that results in cefaclor—no matter how significant as a matter of chemical properties or molecular structure—is not a "material change" for purposes of section 271(g).

Although we are not prepared to embrace Lilly's argument, we acknowledge that it has considerable appeal. Congress was concerned with the problem of the overseas use of patented processes followed by the importation of the products of those processes, and a grudging construction of the statute could significantly limit the statute's effectiveness in addressing the problem Congress targeted. That is especially true with respect to chemical products, as to which simple, routine reactions can often produce dramatic changes in the products' structure and properties.

Nonetheless, while the general purpose of the statute informs the construction of the language Congress chose, purpose cannot displace language, and we cannot stretch the term "materially changed" as far as Lilly's argument would require. The problem is that the language of the statute refers to changes in the product; the statute permits the importation of an item that is derived from a product made by a patented process as long as that product is "materially changed" in the course of its conversion into the imported item. The reference to a "changed" product is very hard to square with Lilly's proposed test, which turns on the quite different question of whether the use or sale of the imported item impairs the economic value of the process patent.

The facts of this case demonstrate how far Lilly's test strays from the statutory text. While Lilly notes that there are only four steps between compound 6 and cefaclor, and that all four steps involve relatively routine chemical reactions, Lilly does not suggest any limiting principle based on the structure of the intermediate product or the nature of the steps necessary to produce the imported product. Thus, even if there were ten complex chemical reactions that separated compound 6 from cefaclor, Lilly's test would characterize the two compounds as not "materially" different as long as the primary commercial use of compound 6 in this country was to produce cefaclor.

Besides not responding to the natural meaning of the term "changed," Lilly's construction of the "materially changed" clause would create a curious anomaly. Lilly's value-based construction of the clause turns in large measure on Lilly's contention that the only commercial use for compound 6 in this country is to produce cefaclor; that is, Lilly views compound 6 and cefaclor as essentially the same product because compound 6 has no commercial use in the U.S. market except to produce cefaclor. Under that approach, however, the question whether compound 6 was "materially changed" in the course of its conversion to cefaclor would depend on whether and to what extent other derivative products of compound 6 are marketed in this country. Thus, under Lilly's theory compound 6 would become materially different from cefaclor if and when compound 6 came to have other commercial uses in the United States, even though the respective structures and properties of the two compounds remained unchanged.

That is asking the statutory language to do too much work. We cannot accept the argument that the question whether one compound is "materially changed" in the course of its conversion into another depends on whether there are other products of the first compound that have economic value. We therefore do not adopt Lilly's proposed construction of section 271(g). We look instead to the substantiality of the change between the product of the patented process and the product that is being imported.

In the chemical context, a "material" change in a compound is most naturally viewed as a significant change in the compound's structure and properties. Without attempting to define with precision what classes of changes would be material and what would not, we share the district court's view that a change in chemical structure and properties as significant as the change between compound 6 and cefaclor cannot lightly be dismissed as immaterial. Although compound 6 and cefaclor share the basic cephem nucleus, which is the ultimate source of the antibiotic potential of all cephalosporins, the cephem nucleus is common to thousands of compounds, many of which have antibiotic activity, and many of which are dramatically different from others within the cephem family. Beyond the cephem nucleus that they have in common, compound 6 and cefaclor are different in four important structural respects, corresponding to the four discrete chemical steps between the two compounds. While the addition or removal of a protective group, standing alone, might not be sufficient to constitute a "material change" between two compounds (even though it could dramatically affect certain of their properties), the conversion process between compound 6 and cefaclor involves considerably more than the removal of a protective group. We therefore conclude that the statutory text of section 271(g) does not support Lilly's contention that it is likely to prevail on the merits of its infringement claim.

B

In aid of their differing approaches to the issue of statutory construction, both sides in this dispute seek support for their positions in the legislative history of the 1988 statute. As is often the case, there is something in the legislative history for each side. On Lilly's side, for example, are characterizations of the legislation as creating process patent protection that is "meaningful and not easily evaded," H.R. Rep. No. 60, 100th Cong., 1st Sess. 13 (1987), and as excluding products only if they "cease to have a reasonable nexus with the patented process," S. Rep. No. 83, 100th Cong., 1st Sess. 36 (1987). On the other side are directions for applying the statute to chemical intermediates—directions that suggest a narrower construction of the statute than Lilly proposes. On balance, while we do not find the legislative history dispositive, we conclude that it does not unequivocally favor Lilly's position and thus does not raise doubts about the district court's statutory analysis as applied to the facts of this case.

* * *

RADER, Circuit Judge, concurring.

I depart from the court's reasoning and conclusion about the "material change" standard under 35 U.S.C. § 271(g).

I

The court's majority places great emphasis on the legislative history to resolve the meaning of "material change"—a curious approach given its recognition that the legislative history contains "something . . . for each side." The enactment history is far from dispositive in this case. The record of the enactment of this provision evinces a bitter battle between the pharmaceutical industry and its generic industry competitors.

* * *

II

Sadly this decision will create another massive loophole in the protection of patented processes. This decision will, in effect, deny protection to holders of process patents on intermediates as opposed to "final" products. This decision denies protection to a patented process anytime it is not the only way to make an intermediate, even if it is the most economically efficient way to produce the intermediate.

In view of the purpose of the statute, compound 6 and cefaclor are essentially the same product. Compound 6 has no commercial use in the U.S. market except to make cefaclor. The patented process is thus in use to make compound 6-a product only four simple, well-known steps from cefaclor. The record shows no other current commercial use of compound 6. Rather than attempting to distill an elixir from this intoxicating witches brew of enactment history, this court should interpret "material change" consistent with the overriding purpose of the Act—to provide protection to process patent holders. With its eye firmly fixed on the purpose of the Act, this court would avoid eliminating processes for intermediates from the protections of the 1988 Act.

Comment

Why Was the PPAA Needed? Process patents—particularly in certain industries such as biotechnology and pharmaceutical—are not without economic value. This fact was reflected in the following memorandum, which also nicely captures the rationale for enacting the PPAA:

> The extension (to product of the process) seems to be an exception to the principle that the protection conferred by a patent or another title of protection for an invention is defined by the object of the invention. In the case of a process invention, a strict application of the said principle would mean that the owner of a process patent could only exclude others from using the patented process. The legal provisions which extend process protection to products obtained by the patented process are based on practical economic considerations. A process which leads to a specific product presents an economic value only through the product. However, it is not always possible to obtain a patent for the product; for example, the product may not be new or may—although new—lack inventive step [i.e., the invention is obvious]. The invention of a new and inventive process for the production of such a product which is not patentable constitutes an important technological advance but the reward granted through a process patent is not important because—without an extension to the product—the process patent would be difficult to enforce (since infringement of the process is difficult to prove) and could even be circumvented by use of the process in another country where the process is not protected. In order to make patent protection of a process meaningful, it is therefore necessary to consider the patented process and the resulting product as a whole, with the consequence that process protection is automatically extended to the resulting product even if the said product has not been claimed.

S. Rep. No. 100-83, at 30-31.

8

Defenses to Patent Infringement

INTRODUCTION

This chapter explores defenses that are available to alleged infringers. The most common defenses are noninfringement and invalidity, both of which have a statutory basis. *See* 35 U.S.C. §282.[1] As issues of infringement and validity were previously covered, however, the following materials are devoted to other defenses, including (A) the patent exhaustion doctrine, repair-reconstruction, and defenses related to the role of contract in exploiting patent rights, namely patent misuse; (B) antitrust counterclaims; (C) inequitable conduct; (D) experimental use; (E) inventorship; and (F) preemption.

A. THE RIGHTS AND LIMITATIONS ON THE USE OF CONTRACT IN EXPLOITING PATENT RIGHTS

A third-party purchaser of a patented product enjoys certain rights with respect to the product. Under the principle of *patent exhaustion* (sometimes referred to as the first-sale doctrine) the patentee is stripped of his rights *in the product* that embodies the claimed invention once he (or his licensee acting within the scope of his license) sells the product.[2] Importantly, the exhaustion

---

1. Specifically, §282(b) states:

> The following shall be defenses in any action involving the validity or infringement of a patent and shall be pleaded:
> (1) Noninfringement, absence of liability for infringement, or unenforceability.
> (2) Invalidity of the patent or any claim in suit on any ground specified in part II as a condition for patentability, patentability.
> (3) Invalidity of the patent or any claim in suit for failure to comply with—
> (A) any requirement of section 112, except that the failure to disclose the best mode shall not be a basis on which any claim of a patent may be canceled or held invalid or otherwise unenforceable; or
> (B) any requirement of section 251.
> (4) Any other fact or act made a defense by this title.

Note that consistent with our discussion in Chapter 2, failure to comply with the best mode requirement is not longer available as a defense for proceedings commenced on or after September 16, 2011.

2. *See Intel Corp. v. USLI System Technology, Inc.*, 955 F.2d 1566, 1568 (Fed. Cir. 1993) (stating "[t]he law is well settled that an authorized sale of a patented product places that product beyond

principle only applies to the product sold, and does not affect (or exhaust) the patentee's statutory right to exclude. The rationale for this principle is that the patentee presumably received consideration, which includes remuneration for the use and resale of the product, and therefore, should not be permitted to exercise control over the sold product. As the Supreme Court stated in *United States v. Univis Lens Co.*,[3] "[o]ur decisions have uniformly recognized that the purpose of the patent law is fulfilled with respect to any particular article when the patentee has received his reward for the use of his invention by the sale of the article, and that once that purpose is realized the patent law affords no basis for restraining the use and enjoyment of the thing sold."[4]

Once a product is sold, therefore, it becomes the personal property (or tangible property) of its owner. In *Bloomer v. McQuewan*,[5] the Supreme Court recognized that "when the machine passes to the hands of the purchaser, it is no longer within the limits of the monopoly. It passes outside of it, and is not longer under the protection of the act of Congress."[6] What exactly can the purchaser—absent an express contract—do with the product? It is clear that while the patent rights are naturally retained by the patentee, the purchaser can use and resell the product as purchased. But what if the product needs to be fixed or modified in some way? The answer to this question is the domain of the *repair-reconstruction doctrine*, which can be viewed as attempting to define the scope of patent exhaustion. The repair-reconstruction doctrine holds that a purchaser of a patented product may repair the product, but may not reconstruct it. Where to draw the line between permissible repair and impermissible reconstruction has perpetually vexed courts. The repair-reconstruction doctrine and the issues associated therewith are explored in the principal case of *Jazz Photo* in A.1, below.

In addition to the patentee's statutory rights as constrained by the exhaustion doctrine, it is quite common for a patentee to turn to private law, namely contract, to exploit his patent rights in a manner consistent with the patent code and traditional contract principles. A patentee may contractually restrict a licensee's or purchaser's use of the product, and therefore render irrelevant the default rule embodied in the repair-reconstruction doctrine. The restriction may include geographic restrictions; limits on how many times the licensee or purchaser can use the product; define the particular purposes for which the product can be used; or condition access to the patented product on the purchase of an unpatented article—a practice commonly referred to as "tying."

---

the reach of the patent. The patent owner's rights with respect to the product end with its sale, and a purchaser of such a product may use or resell the product free of the patent"). The counterpart provision in copyright law is found in 17 U.S.C. §109(a) (stating "the owner of a particular copy or phonorecord lawfully made under this title, or any person authorized by such owner, is entitled, without the authority of the copyright owner, to sell or otherwise dispose of the possession of that copy or phonorecord").

3. 316 U.S. 241 (1942).

4. *Id.* at 251. *See also B. Braun Med., Inc. v. Abbott Labs.*, 124 F.3d 1419, 1426 (Fed. Cir. 1997) (stating "[t]he theory behind [exhaustion] is that in such a transaction [i.e., unconditional sale of a patented device], the patentee has bargained for, and received, an amount equal to the full value of the goods"). Of course, exhaustion attaches only if the product sold is covered by the patent claims. *See Bandag v. Al Bolser's Tire Stores, Inc.*, 750 F.2d 903, 924 (Fed. Cir. 1984) (finding no exhaustion because method claims did not cover product that was sold).

5. 55 U.S. (14 How.) 539 (1852).

6. *Id.* at 549.

But the patentee must be careful not to be overly restrictive, lest he be found to have "misused" his patent right. The misuse doctrine—which is different from antitrust—seeks to prevent a patentee from obtaining market benefit from leveraging his patent right beyond what the patent statute provides. To what extent a patentee can contractually limit a third party's use of the patented invention without engaging in patent misuse or other forms of anti-competitive misconduct is an issue addressed by the five principal cases in section A.2, *Philips, Morton Salt, Mallinckrodt, Quanta* and *Bowman*.

The last subsection, A.3, discusses the ability of licensees to challenge the validity of the licensed patent. The principal cases of *Lear, MedImmune,* and *SanDisk* explore this issue. The remaining principal cases in this subsection analyze the legal appropriateness of license provisions that relate to how royalties should be paid. In *Brulotte,* the license required the licensee to pay royalties beyond the term of the patent; *Scheiber* provides a contemporary analysis of the *Brulotte* court's reasoning.

1. The Scope of Patent Exhaustion and the Repair-Reconstruction Doctrine

The doctrine of repair-reconstruction can be thought of as providing contract default rules in the absence of a license or an express contract setting forth the particulars of how the purchased or licensed patented product can be used.[7] In this regard, the repair-reconstruction rule, as explored in *Jazz Photo*, defines the scope of the patent exhaustion doctrine.

JAZZ PHOTO CORP. v. INTERNATIONAL TRADE COMMISSION
264 F.3d 1094 (Fed. Cir. 2001)

PAULINE NEWMAN, Circuit Judge.

In an action brought under section 337 of the Tariff Act of 1930 as amended, 19 U.S.C. §337, Fuji Photo Film Co. charged twenty-seven respondents, including the appellants Jazz Photo Corporation, Dynatec International, Inc., and Opticolor, Inc., with infringement of fifteen patents owned by Fuji. The charge was based on the respondents' importation of used "single-use" cameras called "lens-fitted film packages" (LFFP's), which had been refurbished[1] for reuse in various overseas facilities. Section 337 makes unlawful "[t]he importation into the United States . . . of articles that . . . infringe a valid and enforceable United States patent . . . [or that] are made, produced, processed, . . . under, or by means of, a process covered by the claims of a valid and enforceable United States patent." 19 U.S.C. §1337(a)(1)(B).

---

7. *See* WILLIAM M. LANDES & RICHARD A. POSNER, THE ECONOMIC STRUCTURE OF INTELLECTUAL PROPERTY 381-382 (2003) (stating the "repair-reconstruction distinction has nothing to do with patent policy"; rather, "[i]t is solely a matter of interpreting the license").

1. We use "refurbish" as a convenient neutral term without legal significance, intended to connote neither "repair" nor "reconstruction" of the used cameras.

The Commission determined that twenty-six respondents, including the appellants, had infringed all or most of the claims in suit of fourteen Fuji United States patents, and issued a General Exclusion Order and Order to Cease and Desist.

The Commission's decision rests on its ruling that the refurbishment of the used cameras is prohibited "reconstruction," as opposed to permissible "repair." On review of the law and its application, we conclude that precedent does not support the Commission's application of the law to the facts that were found. We conclude that for used cameras whose first sale was in the United States with the patentee's authorization, and for which the respondents permitted verification of their representations that their activities were limited to the steps of (1) removing the cardboard cover, (2) cutting open the plastic casing, (3) inserting new film and a container to receive the film, (4) replacing the winding wheel for certain cameras, (5) replacing the battery for flash cameras, (6) resetting the counter, (7) resealing the outer case, and (8) adding a new cardboard cover, the totality of these procedures does not satisfy the standards required by precedent for prohibited reconstruction; precedent requires, as we shall discuss, that the described activities be deemed to be permissible repair.

For those cameras that meet the criteria outlined above, the Commission's ruling of patent infringement is reversed and the Commission's exclusion and cease and desist orders are vacated. For all other cameras, the Commission's orders are affirmed.

DISCUSSION

* * *

I

The Patented Inventions

The LFFP is a relatively simple camera, whose major elements are an outer plastic casing that holds a shutter, a shutter release button, a lens, a viewfinder, a film advance mechanism, a film counting display, and for some models a flash assembly and battery. The casing also contains a holder for a roll of film, and a container into which the exposed film is wound. At the factory a roll of film is loaded into the camera. The casing is then sealed by ultrasonic welding or light-tight latching, and a cardboard cover is applied to encase the camera.

LFFPs are intended by the patentee to be used only once. After the film is exposed the photo-processor removes the film container by breaking open a pre-weakened portion of the plastic casing which is accessed by removal of the cardboard cover. Discarded LFFPs, subsequently purchased and refurbished by the respondents, are the subject of this action.

The parts of an LFFP are illustrated in Figure 8 of the '087 patent:

Claim 1 of the '087 patent is representative of claims directed to the entire LFFP:

1. A lens-fitted photographic film package having an externally operable member for effecting an exposure, comprising:

a light-tight film casing which must be destroyed to open the same, having an opening through which said exposure is made when said externally operable member is operated;

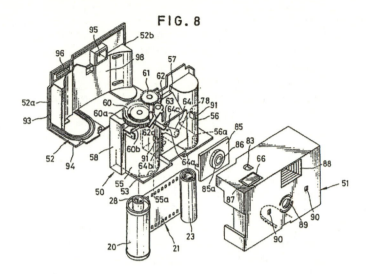

FIG. 8

an unexposed rolled film disposed on one side of said opening in said light-tight casing;

a removable light-tight film container having a film winding spool therein disposed on the opposite side of said opening in said light-tight casing from said rolled film, one end of said rolled film being attached to said film winding spool;

means for winding said rolled film into said light-tight film container and around said film winding spool;

and winding control means responsive to operation of said externally operable member for allowing said film winding spool to rotate so as to enable said rolled film to be advanced by only one frame after every exposure;

said winding control means including: a sprocket wheel driven by movement of said rolled film;

and a frame counter driven by said sprocket wheel, said frame counter being provided with indications designating a series of frame numbers and means for disabling said winding control means responsive to said frame counter indicating there remains on said unexposed film no film frame capable of being exposed.

* * *

It is not disputed that the imported refurbished cameras contain all of the elements of all or most of the claims in suit.

The Accused Activities

The appellants import used LFFPs that have been refurbished by various overseas entities (called "remanufacturers" in the ITC proceeding). Some of the remanufacturers refused discovery entirely or in part, and some presented evidence that the ALJ found incomplete or not credible. The Commission explains: "Since so little was known about the accused infringing processes, the ALJ considered the common steps that each participating respondent admitted during the hearing were part of their processes." The ALJ summarized these common steps as follows:

- removing the cardboard cover;
- opening the LFFP body (usually by cutting at least one weld);
- replacing the winding wheel or modifying the film cartridge to be inserted;
- resetting the film counter;
- replacing the battery in flash LFFPs;
- winding new film out of a canister onto a spool or into a roll;
- resealing the LFFP body using tape and/or glue;
- applying a new cardboard cover.

The Commission held that these activities constitute prohibited reconstruction. In view of this holding, it was not material to the Commission's ruling that the full extent of various respondents' activities was not made known, for in all events the importation would be infringing and unlawful.

The appellants argue that they are not building new LFFPs, but simply replacing the film in used cameras. They argue that the LFFPs have a useful life longer than the single use proposed by Fuji, that the patent right has been exhausted as to these articles, and that the patentee cannot restrict their right to refit the cameras with new film by the procedures necessary to insert the film and reset the mechanism. Unless these activities are deemed to be permissible, infringement of at least some of the patents in suit is conceded.

Burden and Standard of Proof

On this appeal there is much argument as to the burden and standard of proof. The administrative law judge ruled that the respondents must prove that their remanufactured cameras meet the criteria of permissible repair by clear and convincing evidence. The Commission held that this was not the correct standard, and that the respondents were required to prove the affirmative defense of permissible repair by no more than a preponderance of the evidence. However, the Commission found that this error did not change the correctness of the ALJ's conclusion that the respondents' actions were impermissible reconstruction of the patented articles.

While it is not disputed that repair is an affirmative defense, the parties disagree as to the order of coming forward with evidence, as well as the placement of the burden of proving that the accused activities are infringing reconstruction. The appellants state that the burden of proving infringement does not leave the patentee, and thus that the Commission incorrectly placed upon the appellants the burden of proving noninfringement. The appellants also argue that Fuji's unrestricted first sale of the patented cameras satisfied *prima facie* the appellants' burden on the affirmative defense of repair, for it established that the patent right had been exhausted; they state that this shifted to the patentee the burden of proving that the accused activities were not repair. In support the appellants cite *General Electric Co. v. United States*, 572 F.2d 745, 783 n.17 (1978), where the court noted that "Plaintiff, of course, has the burden of proof on issues relating to infringement (including 'reconstruction')."

The Commission ruled that "Once Fuji carried its burden of proof that its claims covered the remanufactured cameras, it was up to appellants to prove their affirmative defense that they were only repairing the cameras, not reconstructing them." The Commission has correctly described this evidentiary sequence. The initial burden is upon the complainant to establish its cause of action, here patent infringement; the patentee must present evidence sufficient to establish that one or more patent claims are infringed. The respondents did not dispute that many or most of the claims in suit read literally on their refurbished cameras. Thus Fuji met its initial burden of showing infringement.

The burden of establishing an affirmative defense is on the party raising the defense. The Commission correctly held that the respondents had the burden of establishing this defense by a preponderance of the evidence, including the burden of coming forward with evidence to show that the activities performed in processing the used cameras constituted permissible repair.

The Law of Permissible Repair and Prohibited Reconstruction

The distinction between permitted and prohibited activities, with respect to patented items after they have been placed in commerce by the patentee, has been distilled into the terms "repair" and "reconstruction." The purchaser of a patented article has the rights of any owner of personal property, including the right to use it, repair it, modify it, discard it, or resell it, subject only to overriding conditions of the sale. Thus patented articles when sold "become the private individual property of the purchasers, and are no longer specifically protected by the patent laws." *Mitchell v. Hawley,* 83 U.S. (16 Wall.) 544, 548 (1872). The fact that an article is patented gives the purchaser neither more nor less rights of use and disposition. However, the rights of ownership do not include the right to construct an essentially new article on the template of the original, for the right to make the article remains with the patentee.

While the ownership of a patented article does not include the right to make a substantially new article, it does include the right to preserve the useful life of the original article. It is readily apparent that there is a continuum between these concepts; precedent demonstrates that litigated cases rarely reside at the poles wherein "repair" is readily distinguished from "reconstruction." Thus the law has developed in the body of precedent, illustrating the policy underlying the law as it has been applied in diverse factual contexts.

The principle of the distinction between permissible and prohibited activities was explained in *Wilson v. Simpson,* 50 U.S. (9 How.) 109 (1850), where the Court distinguished the right of a purchaser of a patented planing machine to replace the machine's cutting-knives when they became dull or broken, from the patentee's sole right to make or renew the entire machine. The Court observed that the knives had to be replaced every 60-90 days whereas the machines would last for several years, explaining, "what harm is done to the patentee in the use of his right of invention, when the repair and replacement of a partial injury are confined to the machine which the purchaser has bought?" *Id.* at 123.

This principle underlies the application of the law. It was elaborated by the Court in *Aro Manufacturing Co. v. Convertible Top Replacement Co.,* 365 U.S. 336 (1961), where the patented combination was a fabric convertible top and the associated metal support structure. The Court explained that replacement of the worn fabric top constituted permissible repair of the patented combination, and could not be controlled by the patentee. The Court restated the principles that govern the inquiry as applied to replacement of unpatented parts of a patented article:

> The decisions of this Court require the conclusion that reconstruction of a patented entity, comprised of unpatented elements, is limited to such a true reconstruction of the entity as to "in fact make a new article," *United States v. Aluminum*

Co. of America, [148 F.2d 416, 425 (2d Cir. 1945)], after the entity, viewed as a whole, has become spent. In order to call the monopoly, conferred by the patent grant, into play for a second time, it must, indeed, be a second creation of the patented entity, as, for example, in *American Cotton Tie Co. v. Simmons,* [106 U.S. 89 (1882)]. Mere replacement of individual unpatented parts, one at a time, whether of the same part repeatedly or different parts successively, is no more than the lawful right of the owner to repair his property.

365 U.S. at 346.

This right of repair, provided that the activity does not "in fact make a new article," accompanies the article to succeeding owners. In *Wilbur-Ellis Co. v. Kuther,* 377 U.S. 422 (1964), the Court dealt with the refurbishing of patented fish-canning machines by a purchaser of used machines. The Court held that the fairly extensive refurbishment by the new owner, including modification and resizing of six separate parts of the machine, although more than customary repair of spent or broken components, was more like repair then reconstruction, for it extended the useful life of the original machine. *See id.* at 425 ("Petitioners in adapting the old machines to a related use were doing more than repair in the customary sense; but what they did was kin to repair for it bore on the useful capacity of the old combination, on which the royalty had been paid.").

Precedent has classified as repair the disassembly and cleaning of patented articles accompanied by replacement of unpatented parts that had become worn or spent, in order to preserve the utility for which the article was originally intended. In *General Electric Co. v. United States,* 572 F.2d 745 (1978), the court held that the Navy's large scale "overhauling" of patented gun mounts, including disassembly into their component parts and replacement of parts that could not be repaired with parts from other gun mounts or new parts, was permissible repair of the original gun mounts. The court explained that the assembly-line method of reassembly, without regard to where each component had originated, was simply a matter of efficiency and economy, with the same effect as if each gun mount had been refurbished individually by disassembly and reassembly of its original components with replacement of a minor amount of worn elements. *Id.* at 780-86.

Similarly, in *Dana Corp. v. American Precision Co.,* 827 F.2d 755 (Fed. Cir. 1987), the court held that the "rebuilding" of worn truck clutches, although done on a commercial scale, was permissible repair. The defendants in *Dana Corp.* acquired worn clutches that had been discarded by their original owners, disassembled them, cleaned and sorted the individual parts, replaced worn or defective parts with new or salvaged parts, and reassembled the clutches. Although the patentee stressed that some new parts were used and that the rebuilding was a large scale commercial operation, the activity was held to be repair. *Id.* at 759. The court also observed that in general the new parts were purchased from Dana, the original manufacturer of the patented clutches, and that repair of used clutches was contemplated by the patentee. The court rejected the argument that the complete disassembly and production-line reassembly of the clutches constituted a voluntary destruction followed by a "second creation of the patented entity," invoking the phrase of *Aro Manufacturing,* 365 U.S. at 346.

"Reconstruction," precedent shows, requires a more extensive rebuilding of the patented entity than is exemplified in *Aro Manufacturing, Wilbur-Ellis, General*

Electric, and *Dana Corp.* In contrast, in *Sandvik Aktiebolag v. E.J. Co.,* 121 F.3d 669 (Fed. Cir. 1997), reconstruction was held to apply when a patented drill bit was "recreated" by construction of an entirely new cutting tip after the existing cutting tip could no longer be resharpened and reused. The court explained that it was not dispositive that the cutting tip was the "novel feature" of the invention, but that prohibited reconstruction occurred because a "new article" was made after the patented article, "viewed as a whole, has become spent."

Underlying the repair/reconstruction dichotomy is the principle of exhaustion of the patent right. The unrestricted sale of a patented article, by or with the authority of the patentee, "exhausts" the patentee's right to control further sale and use of that article by enforcing the patent under which it was first sold. In *United States v. Masonite Corp.,* 316 U.S. 265, 278 (1942), the Court explained that exhaustion of the patent right depends on "whether or not there has been such a disposition of the article that it may fairly be said that the patentee has received his reward for the use of the article." *See, e.g., Intel Corp. v. USLI Sys. Tech., Inc.,* 995 F.2d 1566, 1568 (Fed. Cir. 1993) ("The law is well settled that an authorized sale of a patented product places that product beyond the reach of the patent."). Thus when a patented device has been lawfully sold in the United States, subsequent purchasers inherit the same immunity under the doctrine of patent exhaustion. However, the prohibition that the product may not be the vehicle for a "second creation of the patented entity" continues to apply, for such re-creation exceeds the rights that accompanied the initial sale.

Fuji states that some of the imported LFFP cameras originated and were sold only overseas, but are included in the refurbished importations by some of the respondents. The record supports this statement, which does not appear to be disputed. United States patent rights are not exhausted by products of foreign provenance. To invoke the protection of the first sale doctrine, the authorized first sale must have occurred under the United States patent. *See Boesch v. Graff,* 133 U.S. 697, 701-703 (1890) (a lawful foreign purchase does not obviate the need for license from the United States patentee before importation into and sale in the United States). Our decision applies only to LFFPs for which the United States patent right has been exhausted by first sale in the United States. Imported LFFPs of solely foreign provenance are not immunized from infringement of United States patents by the nature of their refurbishment.

Application of the Law

In the Commission's Initial Determination the administrative judge, applying the four factors discussed in *Sandvik Aktiebolag,* 121 F.3d at 673, held that the remanufacturers had made a new LFFP after the useful life of the original LFFP had been spent. Thus, the ALJ ruled that the remanufacturers were engaged in prohibited reconstruction. The Commission adopted the ALJ's findings and conclusions that the remanufacturers were not simply repairing an article for which either the producer or the purchaser expected a longer useful life, pointing out that the purchaser discarded the camera after use. The Commission ruled that the respondents were not simply repairing the LFFP in order to achieve its intended life span, but created a new single use camera that would again be discarded by its purchaser after use.

Although the Commission's conclusion is supported by its reasoning and reflects concern for the public interest, for there was evidence of imperfections and failures of some refurbished cameras, precedent requires that these cameras be viewed as repaired, not reconstructed. In *Dana Corp.*, for example, the truck clutches had lived their intended lives as originally produced, yet the court ruled that the "rebuilding" of the used clutches was more akin to repair than to reconstruction. The activities of disassembly and rebuilding of the gun mounts of *General Electric* were similarly extensive, yet were deemed to be repair. *Aro Manufacturing* and the other Supreme Court decisions which underlie precedent require that infringing reconstruction be a "second creation" of the patented article. Although the Commission deemed this requirement met by the "remanufactured" LFFPs, precedent places the acts of inserting new film and film container, resetting the film counter, and resealing the broken case — the principal steps performed by the remanufacturers — as more akin to repair.

The Court has cautioned against reliance on any specific set of "factors" in distinguishing permissible from prohibited activities, stating in *Aro Manufacturing* that "While there is language in some lower court opinions indicating that 'repair' or 'reconstruction' depends on a number of factors, it is significant that each of the three cases of this Court, cited for that proposition, holds that a license to use a patented combination includes the right 'to preserve its fitness for use. . . .'" 365 U.S. at 345. Indeed, this criterion is the common thread in precedent, requiring consideration of the remaining useful capacity of the article, and the nature and role of the replaced parts in achieving that useful capacity. The appellants stress that all of the original components of the LFFP except the film and battery have a useful remaining life, and are reused. The appellants state that but for the exposed roll of film and its container, any portion of the case that was broken by the photo processor, and the winding wheel in certain cameras, the refurbished LFFP is substantially the original camera, for which the patent right has been exhausted.

The Commission placed weight on Fuji's intention that the LFFP not be reused. The '087 patent specification states that

> forming an opening in the film package makes it impossible to reuse the film package. Therefore, it will be impossible to refill a new film into the used film package in order to reclaim a film package for reuse.

'087 patent, col. 6, lines 14-18. However, the patentee's unilateral intent, without more, does not bar reuse of the patented article, or convert repair into reconstruction. *See Hewlett-Packard*, 123 F.3d at 1453 ("a seller's intent, unless embodied in an enforceable contract, does not create a limitation on the right of a purchaser to use, sell, or modify a patented product so long as a reconstruction of the patented combination is avoided").

Claim 7 of the '087 patent is representative of those claims that specifically recite the film container and unexposed film roll, elements that are replaced by the remanufacturers:

> 7. A lens-fitted photographic film package comprising:
>
> a light-tight film casing which must be destroyed to open the same, having an opening through which an exposure is made;
>
> a light-tight film container having a film winding spool therein disposed on one side of said opening in said light-tight film casing;
>
> a rotatable spool disposed on the opposite side of said opening in said light-tight film casing from said light-tight film container;

one end of said spool being exposed outside said light-tight film casing;

a film roll of unexposed film of which one end is attached to said film winding spool in said light-tight film container and which is rolled around said rotatable spool.

The appellants state that the film and its removable container are commercial items, and that their replacement in a camera cannot be deemed to be reconstruction. As discussed in *Aro Manufacturing*, the replacement of unpatented parts, having a shorter life than is available from the combination as a whole, is characteristic of repair, not reconstruction. On the totality of the circumstances, the changes made by the remanufacturers all relate to the replacement of the film, the LFFP otherwise remaining as originally sold.

* * *

License

Fuji alternatively contends that the right to repair the patented cameras is impliedly limited by the circumstances of sale, pointing to the instructions and warnings printed on the covers of the LFFPs, and arguing that these constituted a license limited to a single use. *See Mallinckrodt, Inc. v. Medipart, Inc.*, 976 F.2d 700, 709 (Fed. Cir. 1992) (the conditions of sale of a "single-use" medical device may contractually restrict further use). The administrative law judge found that:

A Fuji flash QuickSnap single use camera is in a box and each of the box and the outer cardboard cover of the camera has statements instructing the purchaser to not remove the film and return the camera to the photoprocessor and further cautioning the purchaser about the risk of electrical shock if opened by the purchaser. . . . [The packaging also] instructs the purchaser that the single use camera will not be returned to the purchaser after processing. Similar notations are on [other cameras].

Initial Determination at 141.

A license is governed by the laws of contract. *See McCoy v. Mitsuboshi Cutlery, Inc.*, 67 F.3d 917, 920 (Fed. Cir. 1995) ("Whether express or implied, a license is a contract governed by ordinary principles of state contract law."). It was undisputed that no express conditions of sale, license terms or restrictions attended the sale of these cameras. There was no express contractual undertaking by the purchaser. The administrative judge observed that any issue of implied contract or license was mooted by the finding of infringement based on reconstruction, *see* Initial Determination at 165, and made no findings on the issues of contract or license.

Determinations of express or implied license or contract are matters of law. As stated in *Hewlett-Packard*, "A seller's intent, unless embodied in an enforceable contract, does not create a limitation on the right of a purchaser to use, sell, or modify a patented product as long as a reconstruction of the patented combination is avoided." 123 F.3d at 1453. We do not discern an enforceable restriction on the reuse of these cameras based on the package statements. These statements are instructions and warnings of risk, not mutual promises or a condition placed upon the sale.

These package instructions are not in the form of a contractual agreement by the purchaser to limit reuse of the cameras. There was no showing of a "meeting of the minds" whereby the purchaser, and those obtaining the purchaser's discarded camera, may be deemed to have breached a contract or violated a license limited to a single use of the camera. We conclude that no license limitation may be implied from the circumstances of sale.

* * *

CONCLUSION

The judgment of patent infringement is reversed with respect to LFFPs for which the patent right was exhausted by first sale in the United States, and that were permissibly repaired. Permissible repair is limited, as discussed herein, to the steps of removing the cardboard cover, cutting open the casing, inserting new film and film container, resetting the film counter, resealing the casing, and placing the device in a new cardboard cover. Included in permissible repair is replacement of the battery in flash cameras and the winding wheel in the cameras that so require. For these products the Commission's orders are vacated.

LFFPs whose prior sale was not in the United States . . . remain subject to the Commission's orders. For these products the Commission's orders are affirmed.

Comments

1. ***Repair-Reconstruction and Patent Exhaustion.*** The principle of patent exhaustion applies when there is no express contractual restriction on the use of the patented product. In this scenario, the repair-reconstruction doctrine can be seen as providing default rules for filling in the interstices of the exhaustion principle. As the *Jazz Photo* court stated, "[u]nderlying the repair/reconstruction dichotomy is the principle of exhaustion of the patent right." *See* Mark D. Janis, *A Tale of the Apocryphal Axe: Repair, Reconstruction, and the Implied License in Intellectual Property Law*, 58 MD. L. REV. 423, 427 (1999) (referring to the exhaustion doctrine as the "organizing principle" for repair-reconstruction). (We revisit exhaustion in the context of "field-of-use" contractual restrictions in section A.2.b, below.)

2. ***Distinguishing Between Repair and Reconstruction.*** In *Goodyear Shoe Machinery Co. v. Jackson*, 112 U.S. 146, 150 (1901), the Court asked the following questions: "What is legitimate repair, and what is reconstruction or reproduction as applied to a particular patented device or machine? When does repair destroy the identity of such device or machine and encroach upon invention? At what point does the legitimate repair of such device or machine end, and illegitimate reconstruction begin?" These questions are as relevant and perplexing today as they were at the turn of the twentieth century. Indeed, courts continue to struggle with defining the boundary between permissible repair and impermissible reconstruction. This difficulty arises, according to the Federal Circuit, because "[i]t is impracticable, as well as unwise, to attempt to lay down any rule on this subject, owing to the number and infinite variety of patented inventions." *FMC Corp. v. Up-Right, Inc.*, 21 F.3d 1073, 1079 (Fed. Cir. 1994).

   But the situation is not hopeless. Indeed, prior cases can provide context and add resolution to this issue. For instance, the Federal Circuit, one year after *Jazz Photo*, identified "three primary repair and reconstruction situations." In *Husky Injection Molding Systems Ltd. v. R & D Tool & Engineering Co.,* 291 F.3d 780, 786-787 (Fed. Cir. 2002), the court wrote:

> First, there is the situation in which the entire patented item is spent, and the alleged infringer reconstructs it to make it useable again. Second, there is the situation in which a spent part is replaced. . . . [T]he Supreme Court set forth a definitive test in *Aro I*. Third, there is the situation in which a part is not spent but is replaced to enable the machine to perform a different function. This is a situation "kin to repair."
>
> Despite the number of cases concerning repair and reconstruction, difficult questions remain. One of these arises from the necessity of determining what constitutes replacement of a part of the device, which is repair or akin to repair, and what constitutes reconstruction of the entire device, which would not be repair or akin to repair. Some few situations suggest an obvious answer. For example, if a patent is obtained on an automobile, the replacement of the spark plugs would constitute permissible repair, but few would argue that the retention of the spark plugs and the replacement of the remainder of the car at a single stroke was permissible activity akin to repair. Thus, there may be some concept of proportionality inherent in the distinction between repair and reconstruction.

3. ***International Exhaustion.*** Can a patentee block the importation of his patented product that was manufactured and sold outside the United States by the patentee or someone with his authorization? The *Jazz Photo* court stated, "United States patent rights are not exhausted by products of foreign provenance. To invoke the protection of the first sale doctrine, the authorized first sale must have occurred under the United States patent." 264 F.3d at 1105. *See also Fuji Photo Film Co., Ltd. v. Jazz Photo Corp.,* 394 F.3d 1368, 1376 (Fed. Cir. 2005) (stating first-sale doctrine is limited to sales occurring in the United States); *Boesch v. Graff,* 133 U.S. 697, 702 (1890) (holding that a "dealer residing in the United States" cannot "purchase in another country articles patented there, from a person authorized to sell them, and import them to and sell them in the United States, without the license or consent of the owners of the United States patent"). *Cf. Curtiss Aeroplane & Motor Corp. v. United Aircraft Engineering Corp.,* 266 F. 71, 78 (2d Cir. 1920) (stating "[t]he purchaser of a patented article from a territorial licensee (one whose rights are limited to a restricted territory) may, unless there is a specific agreement to the contrary, use the article so purchased outside of the territory without interference from the patentee. The article is no longer within the monopoly of the patentee, and the purchaser can use it anywhere"). The Europeans have adopted the principle of community-wide exhaustion. The European Court of Justice has held a lawful first sale of a patented product within the European Union exhausts patent rights within the EU. *See Centrafarm BV v. Sterling Drug Incorporated,* 2 C.M.L.R. 480 (1974); *Merck v. Stephar,* 3 C.M.L.R. 463 (1981). Exhaustion does not apply, however, for sales outside the EU.

4. ***Implied License.*** An implied license defense differs from patent exhaustion in that the former is concerned with the conduct of the patentee (or someone acting with his authorization), rather than on the actual sale of the patented product. Accordingly, "'[a]ny language used by the *owner* of the patent, or any conduct on his part exhibited to another from which that other may *properly infer that the owner consents* to his use of the patent [*i.e.,* patented invention]

. . . constitutes a license. . . .' (emphasis added)." *Stickle v. Heublein, Inc.*, 716 F.2d 1550, 1559 (Fed. Cir. 1983). As this language indicates, the implied license defense is grounded in the doctrine of equitable estoppel, and "cannot arise out of the unilateral expectations or even reasonable hopes of one party. One must have been led to take action by the conduct of the other party." *Id. See Bandag, Inc. v. Al Bolser's Tire Stores, Inc.*, 750 F.2d 903 (Fed. Cir. 1984) (court refused to imply a license because alleged infringer's behavior was not in response to patentee's conduct). The implied license defense is rarely invoked successfully. But for a case where the defense was successfully asserted, *see Anton/Bauer, Inc. v. PAG, Ltd.*, 329 F.3d 1343 (Fed. Cir. 2003).

2. Contractual Limitations and the Misuse Doctrine

The use of contract in patent law is quite common, particularly in the form of patent licenses. A license that centers on the use of a patented product is typically negotiated between private parties, and therefore, as in other matters of commerce, the parties can choose the terms of the contract consistent with other areas of the law (e.g., antitrust). For instance, a patentee and his licensee may agree on terms that restrict the use of the patented product, such as how many times the licensee can use the product and the manner and place in which the product can be used or produced; condition access to the patented product on the purchase of an unpatented product; or agree to structure royalty payments based on various conditions and criteria. Contractual restrictions on use can be viewed as modifying the default rules embodied in the repair/reconstruction doctrine.

In these types of restrictive contracts, the issue is to what extent can a patentee restrict the use of the patented product or structure the terms of royalty payments without running afoul of patent law's misuse doctrine? (Antitrust implications and other forms of licensing are explored in section B, below.) The misuse doctrine is designed to prevent a patentee from exploiting his patent rights beyond what the patent code provides. What this means and the relationship between restrictive contracting and the misuse doctrine are explored in the principal cases of *Morton Salt, Philips, Mallinckrodt, Quanta* and *Bowman*. The *Brulotte* and *Scheiber* cases discuss legal issues associated with how parties contractually structure royalty payments.

a. Package Licenses and Tying Arrangements

MORTON SALT CO. v. G.S. SUPPIGER CO.
314 U.S. 488 (1942)

Mr. Chief Justice STONE delivered the opinion of the Court.

Respondent (Suppiger Co.) brought this suit in the district court for an injunction and an accounting for infringement of its Patent No. 2,060,645, of November 10, 1936, on a machine for depositing salt tablets, a device said to be useful in the canning industry for adding predetermined amounts of salt in tablet form to the contents of the cans.

[T]he trial court, without passing on the issues of validity and infringement, granted summary judgment dismissing the complaint. It took the ground that respondent was making use of the patent to restrain the sale of salt tablets in competition with its own sale of unpatented tablets, by requiring licensees to use with the patented machines only tablets sold by respondent. The Court of Appeals for the Seventh Circuit reversed, as it did not appear that the use of its patent substantially lessened competition or tended to create a monopoly in salt tablets. We granted certiorari because of the public importance of the question presented.

The Clayton Act authorizes those injured by violations tending to monopoly to maintain suit for treble damages and for an injunction in appropriate cases. But the present suit is for infringement of a patent. The question we must decide is not necessarily whether respondent has violated the Clayton Act, but whether a court of equity will lend its aid to protect the patent monopoly when respondent is using it as the effective means of restraining competition with its sale of an unpatented article.

Both respondent's wholly owned subsidiary and the petitioner manufacture and sell salt tablets used and useful in the canning trade. The tablets have a particular configuration rendering them capable of convenient use in respondent's patented machines. Petitioner makes and leases to canners unpatented salt deposition machines, charged to infringe respondent's patent. For reasons we indicate later, nothing turns on the fact that petitioner also competes with respondent in the sale of the tablets, and we may assume for purposes of this case that petitioner is doing no more than making and leasing the alleged infringing machines. The principal business of respondent's subsidiary, from which its profits are derived, is the sale of salt tablets. In connection with this business, and as an adjunct to it, respondent leases its patented machines to commercial canners, some two hundred in all, under licenses to use the machines upon condition and with the agreement of the licensees that only the subsidiary's salt tablets be used with the leased machines.

It thus appears that respondent is making use of its patent monopoly to restrain competition in the marketing of unpatented articles, salt tablets, for use with the patented machines, and is aiding in the creation of a limited monopoly in the tablets not within that granted by the patent. A patent operates to create and grant to the patentee an exclusive right to make, use and vend the particular device described and claimed in the patent. But a patent affords no immunity for a monopoly not within the grant, and the use of it to suppress competition in the sale of an unpatented article may deprive the patentee of the aid of a court of equity to restrain an alleged infringement by one who is a competitor. It is the established rule that a patentee who has granted a license on condition that the patented invention be used by the licensee only with unpatented materials furnished by the licensor, may not restrain as a contributory infringer one who sells to the licensee like materials for like use.

The grant to the inventor of the special privilege of a patent monopoly carries out a public policy adopted by the Constitution and laws of the United States, "to promote the Progress of Science and useful Arts, by securing for limited Times to . . . Inventors the exclusive Right. . . ." to their "new and useful" inventions. But the public policy which includes inventions within the granted monopoly excludes from it all that is not embraced in the invention. It equally forbids the use of the patent to secure an exclusive right or limited monopoly not granted by the Patent Office and which it is contrary to public policy to grant.

It is a principle of general application that courts, and especially courts of equity, may appropriately withhold their aid where the plaintiff is using the right asserted contrary to the public interest. Respondent argues that this doctrine is limited in its application to those cases where the patentee seeks to restrain contributory infringement by the sale to licensees of a competing unpatented article, while here respondent seeks to restrain petitioner from a direct infringement, the manufacture and sale of the salt tablet depositor. It is said that the equitable maxim that a party seeking the aid of a court of equity must come into court with clean hands applies only to the plaintiff's wrongful conduct in the particular act or transaction which raises the equity, enforcement of which is sought; that where, as here, the patentee seeks to restrain the manufacture or use of the patented device, his conduct in using the patent to restrict competition in the sale of salt tablets does not foreclose him from seeking relief limited to an injunction against the manufacture and sale of the infringing machine alone.

Undoubtedly "equity does not demand that its suitors shall have led blameless lives," but additional considerations must be taken into account where maintenance of the suit concerns the public interest as well as the private interests of suitors. Where the patent is used as a means of restraining competition with the patentee's sale of an unpatented product, the successful prosecution of an infringement suit even against one who is not a competitor in such sale is a powerful aid to the maintenance of the attempted monopoly of the unpatented article, and is thus a contributing factor in thwarting the public policy underlying the grant of the patent. Maintenance and enlargement of the attempted monopoly of the unpatented article are dependent to some extent upon persuading the public of the validity of the patent, which the infringement suit is intended to establish. Equity may rightly withhold its assistance from such a use of the patent by declining to entertain a suit for infringement, and should do so at least until it is made to appear that the improper practice has been abandoned and that the consequences of the misuse of the patent have been dissipated.

The reasons for barring the prosecution of such a suit against one who is not a competitor with the patentee in the sale of the unpatented product are fundamentally the same as those which preclude an infringement suit against a licensee who has violated a condition of the license by using with the licensed machine a competing unpatented article, *Motion Picture Patents Co. v. Universal Film Mfg. Co.*, or against a vendee of a patented or copyrighted article for violation of a condition for the maintenance of resale prices. It is the adverse effect upon the public interest of a successful infringement suit in conjunction with the patentee's course of conduct which disqualifies him to maintain the suit, regardless of whether the particular defendant has suffered from the misuse of the patent. Similarly equity will deny relief for infringement of a trademark where the plaintiff is misrepresenting to the public the nature of his product either by the trademark itself or by his label. The patentee, like these other holders of an exclusive privilege granted in the furtherance of a public policy, may not claim protection of his grant by the courts where it is being used to subvert that policy.

It is unnecessary to decide whether respondent has violated the Clayton Act, for we conclude that in any event the maintenance of the present suit to restrain petitioner's manufacture or sale of the alleged infringing machines is contrary to public policy and that the district court rightly dismissed the complaint for want of equity.

U.S. PHILIPS CORP. v. INTERNATIONAL TRADE COMMISSION
424 F.3d 1179 (Fed. Cir. 2005)

BRYSON, Circuit Judge.

U.S. Philips Corporation appeals from a final order of the United States International Trade Commission, in which the Commission held six of Philips's patents for the manufacture of compact discs to be unenforceable because of patent misuse. The Commission ruled that Philips had employed an impermissible tying arrangement because it required prospective licensees to license packages of patents rather than allowing them to choose which individual patents they wished to license and making the licensing fee correspond to the particular patents designated by the licensees. We reverse and remand.

I

Philips owns patents to technology for manufacturing recordable compact discs ("CD-Rs") and rewritable compact discs ("CD-RWs") in accordance with the technical standards set forth in a publication called the Recordable CD Standard (the "Orange Book"), jointly authored by Philips and Sony Corporation. Since the 1990s, Philips has been licensing those patents through package licenses. Philips specified that the same royalty was due for each disc manufactured by the licensee using patents included in the package, regardless of how many of the patents were used. Potential licensees who sought to license patents to the technology for manufacturing CD-Rs or CD-RWs were not allowed to license those patents individually and were not offered a lower royalty rate for licenses to fewer than all the patents in a package.

Initially, Philips offered four different pools of patents for licensing: (1) a joint CD-R patent pool that included patents owned by Philips and two other companies (Sony and Taiyo Yuden); (2) a joint CD-RW patent pool that included patents owned by Philips and two other companies (Sony and Ricoh); (3) a CD-R patent pool that included only patents owned by Philips; and (4) a CD-RW patent pool that included only patents owned by Philips. After 2001, Philips offered additional package options by grouping its patents into two categories, which Philips denominated "essential" and "nonessential" for producing compact discs compliant with the technical standards set forth in the Orange Book.

In the late 1990s, Philips entered into package licensing agreements with Princo Corporation and Princo America Corporation (collectively, "Princo"); GigaStorage Corporation Taiwan and GigaStorage Corporation USA (collectively, "GigaStorage"); and Linberg Enterprise Inc. ("Linberg"). Soon after entering into the agreements, however, Princo, GigaStorage, and Linberg stopped paying the licensing fees. Philips filed a complaint with the International Trade Commission that Princo, GigaStorage, and Linberg, among others, were violating section 337(a)(1)(B) of the Tariff Act of 1930, 19 U.S.C. § 1337(a)(1)(B), by importing into the United States certain CD-Rs and CD-RWs that infringed six of Philips's patents.

The Commission instituted an investigation and identified 19 respondents, including GigaStorage and Linberg. Additional respondents, including Princo, were added through intervention. In the course of the proceedings before an administrative law judge, the respondents raised patent misuse as an affirmative defense, alleging that Philips had improperly forced them, as a condition of licensing patents that were necessary to manufacture CD-Rs or CD-RWs, to take licenses to other patents that were not necessary to manufacture those products. In particular, the respondents argued that a number of the patents that Philips had included in the category of "essential" patents were actually not essential for manufacturing compact discs compliant with the Orange Book standards, because there were commercially viable alternative methods of manufacturing CD-Rs and CD-RWs that did not require the use of the technology covered by those patents. The allegedly nonessential patents included U.S. Patent Nos. 5,001,692 ("the Farla patent"), 5,740,149 ("the Iwasaki patent"), Re. 34,719 ("the Yamamoto patent"), and 5,060,219 ("the Lokhoff patent").

The administrative law judge ruled that the intervenors had infringed various claims of the six asserted Philips patents. The administrative law judge further ruled, however, that all six of the asserted patents were unenforceable by reason of patent misuse. Among the grounds invoked by the administrative law judge for finding patent misuse was his conclusion that the package licensing arrangements constituted tying arrangements that were illegal under analogous antitrust law principles and thus rendered the subject patents unenforceable.

Philips petitioned the Commission for review of the administrative law judge's decision. In an order that addressed only the findings concerning patent misuse, the Commission affirmed the administrative law judge's ruling that Philips's package licensing practice "constitutes patent misuse per se as a tying arrangement between (1) licenses to patents that are essential to manufacture CD-Rs or CD-RWs according to Orange Book standards and (2) licenses to other patents that are not essential to that activity." The Commission found that the Farla, Iwasaki, Yamamoto, and Lokhoff patents were not essential to manufacturing CD-Rs or CD-RWs. Specifically, the Commission found that the Farla and Lokhoff patents were nonessential with respect to the Philips-only CD-RW and CD-R licenses, and that the Farla, Iwasaki, Yamamoto, and Lokhoff patents were nonessential with respect to the joint CD-RW license. The Commission concluded that the four nonessential patents were impermissibly tied to patents that were essential to manufacturing CD-Rs and CD-RWs, because "none of the so-called essential patents could be licensed individually for the manufacture of CD-RWs and CD-Rs apart from the package" that Philips denominated as "essential." The Commission also found, based on the administrative law judge's findings and analysis, that the joint license for CD-R and CD-RW technology unlawfully tied patents for CD-Rs and CD-RWs in accordance with the Orange Book standards to patents that were not essential to manufacture such discs.

The Commission explained why it concluded that each of the four patents was nonessential. According to the Commission, the Farla and Iwasaki patents were not essential because there was an economically viable alternative method of writing information to discs that did not require the producer to practice those patents; the Yamamoto patent was not essential because there was a potential alternative method of creating master discs that did not require the producer to practice that patent; and the Lokhoff patent was not essential because there were alternative possible methods of accomplishing copy protection that did not require the producer to practice that patent. Based on those findings, the Commission concluded that the four "nonessential" patents constituted separate products from the patents that were essential to the manufacture of the subject discs.

The Commission ruled that Philips's patent package licensing arrangement constituted per se patent misuse because Philips did not give prospective licensees the option of licensing individual patents (presumably for a lower fee) rather than licensing one or more of the patent packages as a whole. The Commission took no position on the administrative law judge's ruling that patent pooling arrangements between Philips and its co-licensors constituted patent misuse per se based on the theories of price fixing and price discrimination, and it took no position on the administrative law judge's conclusion that the royalty structure of the patent pools was an unreasonable restraint of trade.

As an alternative ground, the Commission concluded that even if Philips's patent package licensing practice was not per se patent misuse, it constituted patent misuse under the rule of reason. Adopting the administrative law judge's findings, the Commission ruled that the anticompetitive effects of including nonessential patents in the packages of so-called essential patents outweighed the pro-competitive effects of that practice. In particular, the Commission held that including such nonessential patents in the licensing packages could foreclose alternative technologies and injure competitors seeking to license such alternative technologies to parties who needed to obtain licenses to Philips's "essential" patents. The Commission took no position with respect to the portion of the administrative law judge's rule of reason analysis in which the administrative law judge concluded that the royalty rate structure of the patent pooling arrangements constituted an unreasonable restraint on competition.

II

Patent misuse is an equitable defense to patent infringement. It "arose to restrain practices that did not in themselves violate any law, but that drew anticompetitive strength from the patent right, and thus were deemed to be contrary to public policy." *Mallinckrodt, Inc. v. Medipart, Inc.,* 976 F.2d 700, 704 (Fed. Cir. 1992). The purpose of the patent misuse defense "was to prevent a patentee from using the patent to obtain market benefit beyond that which inheres in the statutory patent right." *Id.* As the Supreme Court has explained, the doctrine of patent misuse bars a patentee from using the "patent's leverage" to "extend the monopoly of his patent to derive a benefit not attributable to the use of the patent's teachings," such as requiring a licensee to pay a royalty on products that do not use the teaching of the patent. *Zenith Radio Corp. v. Hazeltine Research, Inc.,* 395 U.S. 100, 135-36 (1969). The "key inquiry is whether, by imposing conditions that derive their force from the patent, the patentee has impermissibly broadened the scope of the patent grant with anticompetitive effect." *C.R. Bard, Inc. v. M3 Sys., Inc.,* 157 F.3d 1340, 1372 (Fed. Cir. 1998).

This court summarized the principles of patent misuse as applied to "tying" arrangements in *Virginia Panel Corp. v. MAC Panel Co.,* 133 F.3d 860, 868-69 (Fed. Cir. 1997). The court there explained that because of the importance of anticompetitive effects in shaping the defense of patent misuse, the analysis of tying arrangements in the context of patent misuse is closely related to the analysis of tying arrangements in antitrust law. The court further explained that, depending on the circumstances, tying arrangements can be viewed as per se patent misuse or can be analyzed under the rule of reason. *Id.* The court noted that certain specific practices have been identified as constituting per se patent misuse, "including so-called 'tying' arrangements in which a patentee conditions a license under the patent on the purchase of a separable, staple good, and arrangements in which a patentee effectively extends the term of its patent by requiring post-expiration royalties." *Id.* at 869 (citations omitted). If the particular licensing arrangement in question is not one of those specific practices that has been held to constitute per se misuse, it will be analyzed under the rule of reason. *Id.* We have held that under the rule of reason, a practice is impermissible only if its effect is to restrain competition in a relevant market. *Monsanto Co. v. McFarling*, 363 F.3d 1336, 1341 (Fed. Cir. 2004).

The Supreme Court's decisions analyzing tying arrangements under antitrust law principles are to the same effect. The Court has made clear that tying arrangements are deemed to be per se unlawful only if they constitute a "naked restrain[t] of trade with no purpose except stifling of competition" and "always or almost always tend to restrict competition and decrease output" in some substantial portion of a market. *Broad. Music, Inc. v. Columbia Broad. Sys., Inc.*, 441 U.S. 1, 19-20 (1979). The Supreme Court has applied the per se rule only when "experience with a particular kind of restraint enables the Court to predict with confidence that the rule of reason will condemn it." *Arizona v. Maricopa County Med. Soc'y*, 457 U.S. 332, 344 (1982). *See also Jefferson Parish Hosp. Dist. v. Hyde*, 466 U.S. 2, 14 (1983) ("[T]he law draws a distinction between the exploitation of market power by merely enhancing the price of the tying product, on the one hand, and by attempting to impose restraints on competition in the market for a tied product, on the other."). Conduct is not considered per se anticompetitive if it has "redeeming competitive virtues and . . . the search for those values is not almost sure to be in vain." *Broad. Music*, 441 U.S. at 13.

While the doctrine of patent misuse closely tracks antitrust law principles in many respects, Congress has declared certain practices not to be patent misuse even though those practices might otherwise be subject to scrutiny under antitrust law principles. In 35 U.S.C. §271(d), Congress designated several specific practices as not constituting patent misuse. The designated practices include "condition[ing] the license of any rights to the patent or the sale of the patented product on the acquisition of a license to rights in another patent or purchase of a separate product," unless, in view of the circumstances, the patent owner "has market power for the patent or patented product on which the license or sale is conditioned." *Id.* §271(d)(5). Because the statute is phrased in the negative, it does not require that patent misuse be found in the case of all such conditional licenses in which the patent owner has market power; instead, the statute simply excludes such conditional licenses in which the patent owner lacks market power from the category of arrangements that may be found to constitute patent misuse. To establish the defense of patent misuse, the accused infringer must show that the patentee has power in the market for the tying product. *See id.* at 1349 n.7.

Philips argues briefly that it lacks market power and that it is thus shielded from liability by section 271(d)(5). Based on detailed analysis by the administrative law judge, however, the Commission found that Philips has market power in the relevant market and that section 271(d)(5) is therefore inapplicable to this case. We sustain that ruling. Philips contends that at the time Philips and Sony first created their package license arrangements, CDs had significant competition among computer data storage devices and thus Philips lacked market power in the market for computer data storage discs. However, Philips first created the package licenses long before GigaStorage and Princo entered into their agreements. According to the administrative law judge, the patent package arrangements were instituted in the early 1990s. Yet Princo did not enter into its agreement until June of 1997, and GigaStorage did not enter into its licensing agreement until October of 1999. Thus, any lack of market power that Philips and its co-licensors may have had in the early 1990s is irrelevant to the situation in the late 1990s, when the parties entered into the agreements at issue in this case. At that time, according to the administrative law judge's well-supported finding, compact discs had become "unique products [with] no close practice substitutes." Philips's argument about lack of market power is therefore unpersuasive, and for that reason section 271(d)(5) does not provide Philips a statutory safe haven from the judicially created defense of patent misuse.

Apart from its specific challenge to the Commission's ruling on the market power issue, Philips launches a more broad-based attack on the Commission's conclusion that Philips's patent licensing policies constitute per se patent misuse. In so doing, Philips makes essentially two arguments: first, that the Commission was wrong as a legal matter in ruling that the package licensing arrangements at issue in this case are among those few practices that the courts have identified as so clearly anticompetitive as to warrant being condemned as per se illegal; and second, that the Commission erred as a factual matter in concluding that Philips's package licensing arrangements reflect the use of market power in one market to foreclose competition in a separate market. We address the two arguments separately.

A

In its brief, the Commission argues that it is "hornbook law" that mandatory package licensing has been held to be patent misuse. Philips invites us to consider whether that broad proposition is sound. Upon consideration, we conclude that the proposition as applied to the circumstances of this case is not supported by precedent or reason.

In its opinion, the Commission acknowledged that the *Virginia Panel* case and many other patent tying cases "involve a tying patent and a tied *product,* rather than a tying patent and a tied *patent.*" (emphasis in original). The Commission nonetheless concluded that "finding patent misuse based on a tying arrangement between patents in a mandatory package license is a reasonable application of Supreme Court precedent." In so ruling, the Commission relied primarily on two Supreme Court cases: *United States v. Paramount Pictures, Inc.,* 334 U.S. 131, 156-59 (1948), and *United States v. Loew's, Inc.,* 371 U.S. 38, 44-51 (1962). Those cases condemned the practice of "block-booking" movies to theaters (in the *Paramount* case) and to television stations (in the *Loew's* case) as antitrust violations.

Block-booking is the practice in which a distributor licenses one feature or group of features to exhibitors on the condition that the exhibitors agree to license another (presumably inferior) feature or group of features released by the distributor during a given period. In *Paramount* and *Loew's,* the Court held that block-booking, as practiced in those cases, was per se illegal. The

Commission reasoned that the practice of block-booking that was the focus of the Court's condemnation in *Paramount* and *Loew's* is similar to the package licensing agreements at issue in this case and that under the analysis employed in *Paramount* and *Loew's,* Philips's package licensing agreements must be condemned as per se patent misuse.

We do not agree with the Commission that the decisions in *Paramount* and *Loew's* govern this case. In *Paramount,* the district court held that the defendant movie distributor had engaged in unlawful conduct because it offered to permit exhibitors to show the films they wished to license only if they agreed to license and exhibit other films that they were not interested in licensing. The Supreme Court affirmed that ruling. The Court held that block-booking was illegal because it "prevents competitors from bidding for single features on their individual merits," and because it "adds to the monopoly of a single copyrighted picture that of another copyrighted picture which must be taken and exhibited in order to secure the first." 334 U.S. at 156-57. The result, the Court explained, "is to add to the monopoly of the copyright in violation of the principle of the patent cases involving tying clauses." *Id.* at 158. Because the block-booking arrangement at issue in *Paramount* required the licensee to exhibit all of the films in the group for which a license was taken, the *Paramount* block-booking was more akin to a tying arrangement in which a patent license is tied to the purchase of a separate product, rather than to an arrangement in which a patent license is tied to another patent license. Indeed, all of the patent tying cases to which the Supreme Court referred in *Paramount* involved tying arrangements in which, as the Court described them, "the owner of a patent [conditioned] its use on the purchase or use of patented or unpatented materials." 334 U.S. at 157. Because the arrangement in the *Paramount* case was equivalent in substance to a patent-to-product tying arrangement, *Paramount* does not stand for the proposition that a pure patent-to-patent tying arrangement, such as Philips's package licensing agreement, is per se unlawful.

Philips gives its licensees the option of using any of the patents in the package, at the licensee's option. Philips charges a uniform licensing fee to manufacture discs covered by its patented technology, regardless of which, or how many, of the patents in the package the licensee chooses to use in its manufacturing process. In particular, Philips's package licenses do not require that licensees actually use the technology covered by any of the patents that the Commission characterized as nonessential. In that respect, Philips's licensing agreements are different from the agreements at issue in *Paramount,* which imposed an obligation on the purchasers of package licenses to exhibit films they did not wish to license. That obligation not only extended the exclusive right in one product to products in which the distributor did not have exclusive rights, but it also precluded exhibitors, as a practical matter, from exhibiting other films that they may have preferred over the tied films they were required to exhibit. Because Philips's package licensing agreements do not compel the licensees to use any particular technology covered by any of the licensed patents, the *Paramount* case is not a sound basis from which to conclude that the package licensing arrangements at issue in this case constitute patent misuse per se.

In the case of patent-to-product tying, the patent owner uses the market power conferred by the patent to compel customers to purchase a product in a separate market that the customer might otherwise purchase from a competitor. The patent owner is thus able to use the market power conferred by the patent to foreclose competition in the market for the product. By contrast, a package licensing agreement that includes both essential and nonessential patents does not impose any requirement on the licensee. It does not bar the licensee from using any alternative technology that may be offered by a competitor of the licensor. Nor does it foreclose the competitor from licensing his alternative technology; it merely puts the competitor in the same position he would be in if he were competing with unpatented technology.

A package license is in effect a promise by the patentee not to sue his customer for infringing any patents on whatever technology the customer employs in making commercial use of the licensed patent. That surrender of rights might mean that the customer will choose not to license the alternative technology offered by the patentee's competition, but it does not compel the customer to use the patentee's technology. The package license is thus not anticompetitive in the way that a compelled purchase of a tied product would be.

Contrary to the Commission's characterization, the intervenors were not "forced" to "take" anything from Philips that they did not want, nor were they restricted from obtaining licenses from other sources to produce the relevant technology. Philips simply provided that for a fixed licensing fee, it would not sue any licensee for engaging in any conduct covered by the entire group of patents in the package. By analogy, if Philips had decided to surrender its "nonessential" patents or had simply announced that it did not intend to enforce them, there would have been no way for the manufacturers to decline or reject Philips's decision. Yet the economic effect of the package licensing arrangement for Philips's patents is not fundamentally different from the effect that such decisions would have had on third parties seeking to compete with the technology covered by those "nonessential" patents. Thus, we conclude that the Commission erred when it characterized the package license agreements as a way of forcing the intervenors to license technology that they did not want in order to obtain patent rights that they did.

The Commission stated that it would not have found the package licenses to constitute improper tying if Philips had offered to license its patents on an individual basis, as an alternative to licensing them in packages. The Commission's position, however, must necessarily be based on an assumption that, if the patents were offered on an individual basis, individual patents would be offered for a lower price than the patent packages as a whole. If that assumption were not implicit in the Commission's conclusion, the Commission would be saying in effect that it would be unlawful for Philips to charge the same royalty for its essential patents that it charges for its patent packages and to offer the nonessential patents for free. Yet that sort of pricing policy plainly would not be unlawful.

[T]he Commission's assumption that a license to fewer than all the patents in a package would presumably carry a lower fee than the package itself ignores the reality that the value of any patent package is largely, if not entirely, based on the patents that are essential to the technology in question. A patent that is nonessential because it covers technology that can be fully replaced by alternative technology that is available for free is essentially valueless. A patent that is nonessential because it covers technology that can be fully replaced by alternative technology that is available through a license from another patent owner has value, but its value is limited by the price of the alternative technology. Short of imposing an obligation on the licensor to make some sort of allocation of fees across a group of licenses, there is no basis for the Commission to conclude that a smaller group of the licenses—the so-called "essential" licenses—would have been available for a lower fee if they had not been "tied to" the so-called nonessential patents.

It is entirely rational for a patentee who has a patent that is essential to particular technology, as well as other patents that are not essential, to charge what the market will bear for the essential patent and to offer the others for free. Because a license to the essential patent is, by definition, a prerequisite to practice the technology in question, the patentee can charge whatever maximum amount a willing licensee is able to pay to practice the technology in question. If the patentee allocates royalty fees between its essential and nonessential patents, it runs the risk that licensees will take a license to the essential patent but not to the nonessential patents. The effect of that choice will be that the patentee will not be able to obtain the full royalty value of the essential patent. For the patentee in this situation to offer its nonessential patents as part of a package with the essential patent at no additional charge is no more anticompetitive than if it had surrendered the nonessential patents or had simply announced a policy that it would not enforce them against persons who licensed the essential patent. In either case, those offering technology that competed with the nonessential patents would be unhappy, because they would be competing against free technology. But the patentee would not be using his essential patent to obtain power in the market for the technology covered by the nonessential patents. This package licensing arrangement cannot fairly be characterized as an exploitation of power in one market to obtain a competitive advantage in another.[5]

Aside from the absence of evidence that the package licensing arrangements in this case had the effect of impermissibly broadening the scope of the "essential" patents with anticompetitive effect, Philips argues that the Commission failed to acknowledge the unique pro-competitive benefits associated with package licensing. Philips points to the federal government's guidelines for licensing intellectual property, which recognize that patent packages "may provide pro-competitive benefits by integrating complementary technologies, reducing transaction costs, clearing blocking positions, and avoiding costly infringement litigation. By promoting the dissemination of technology, cross-licensing and pooling arrangements are often pro-competitive." U.S. Department of Justice and Federal Trade Commission, *Antitrust Guidelines for the Licensing of Intellectual Property* §5.5 (1995).

Philips introduced evidence that package licensing reduces transaction costs by eliminating the need for multiple contracts and reducing licensors' administrative and monitoring costs. *See Tex. Instruments, Inc. v. Hyundai Elecs.*, 49 F. Supp. 2d 893, 901 (E.D. Tex. 1999) (describing how "extremely expensive and time-consuming" it is for parties to license and manage the licensing of technology by using individual patents and how it is preferable to employ a patent

---

5. The implication of the Commission's decision is that a party with both an essential patent and a nonessential patent is not allowed to package the two together and only offer the package for a single price. That would have the perverse effect of potentially putting a party owning both an essential patent and a nonessential but related patent in a worse position than a party owning only the essential patent. The party owning only the essential patent would be free to charge any licensing fee up to the maximum that a manufacturer would be willing to pay to practice the patented technology, while a party owning both the essential patent and a nonessential patent would be barred from extracting that maximum licensing fee for its essential patent and assuring the manufacturer that it would not be subject to suit on the nonessential patent.

portfolio). Package licensing can also obviate any potential patent disputes between a licensor and a licensee and thus reduce the likelihood that a licensee will find itself involved in costly litigation over unlicensed patents with potentially adverse consequences for both parties, such as a finding that the licensee infringed the unlicensed patents or that the unlicensed patents were invalid. Thus, package licensing provides the parties a way of ensuring that a single licensing fee will cover all the patents needed to practice a particular technology and protecting against the unpleasant surprise for a licensee who learns, after making a substantial investment, that he needed a license to more patents than he originally obtained. Finally, grouping licenses in a package allows the parties to price the package based on their estimate of what it is worth to practice a particular technology, which is typically much easier to calculate than determining the marginal benefit provided by a license to each individual patent. In short, package licensing has the pro-competitive effect of reducing the degree of uncertainty associated with investment decisions.

The package licenses in this case have some of the same advantages as the package licenses at issue in the *Broadcast Music* case. The Supreme Court determined in that case that the blanket copyright package licenses at issue had useful, pro-competitive purposes because they gave the licensees "unplanned, rapid, and indemnified access to any and all of the repertory of [musical] compositions, and [they gave the owners] a reliable method of collecting for the use of the their copyrights." While "[i]ndividual sales transactions [would be] quite expensive, as would be individual monitoring and enforcement," a package licensing agreement would ensure access and save costs. *Id.* Hence, the Supreme Court determined that such conduct should fall under "a more discriminating examination under the rule of reason." *Id.* at 24. In light of the efficiencies of package patent licensing and the important differences between product-to-patent tying arrangements and arrangements involving group licensing of patents, we reject the Commission's conclusion that Philips's conduct shows a "lack of any redeeming virtue" and should be "conclusively presumed to be unreasonable and therefore illegal without elaborate inquiry as to the precise harm they have caused or the business excuse for their use." *N. Pac. Ry. Co. v. United States*, 356 U.S. 1, 5 (1958). We therefore hold that the analysis that led the Commission to apply the rule of per se illegality to Philips's package licensing agreements was legally flawed.

Comments

1. **Philips *and the Role of Efficiency and Transaction Costs.*** In *Philips*, the Federal Circuit affirmed the International Trade Commission's finding that Philips had market power (a rare instance, see Comment 1 after *Illinois Tool* in section B.1 on patents and market power), and therefore, Philips was not statutorily protected by section 271(d)(5). But the court nonetheless reversed the Commission's holding that Philips's package license was an illegal tying arrangement. Judge Bryson, in an opinion consistent with recent economic thinking about licensing arrangements, focused on the pro-competitive nature of the package license as well as efficiency considerations. For example, Judge Bryson noted that packaging the licenses is no worse than an

unpackaged arrangement. In fact, it is more efficient because it leads to fewer transaction costs (*see* next to last paragraph of the opinion). And a package license does not impose an obligation on the licensee to use the patentee's technology. Rather, the licenses are merely a guarantee that the licensee will not be sued for engaging in conduct that would otherwise infringe. *See* HERBERT HOVENKAMP, MARK D. JANIS, MARK A. LEMLEY & CHRISTOPHER R. LESLIE, IP AND ANTITRUST: AN ANALYSIS OF ANTITRUST PRINCIPLES APPLIED TO INTELLECTUAL PROPERTY LAW 3-27 (2012) (stating "[t]he *Philips* reasoning is largely persuasive, though as with all ties, the fact that the licensee takes the nonessential patents for free at least raises the risk that competition in that technology will suffer"; but further noted, "[f]oreclosure is hardly inevitable . . . and so the Court's rejection of per se condemnation is appropriate"). But why, as Judge Bryson notes, would a patentee be unable to "obtain the full royalty value of the essential patents" if he is forced to license the essential and non-essential patents separately? In other words, if the entire value, as Judge Bryson asserts, resides in the essential patents, why would the patentee run the risk of not realizing the full royalty value of these patents? How do the non-essential patents add any value to the package, if indeed they have no commercial value?

The Federal Circuit had an opportunity to revisit the *Philips* case, but in the context of a specific feature of the technology, namely the identification of disc positioning. *See Princo Corp. v. International Trade Commission*, 616 F.3d 1318 (Fed. Cir. 2010) (*en banc*). In *Princo*, Philips and Sony formed a patent license package that included Philips's "Raaymakers" technology, which was part of the "Orange Book" standard and Sony's "Lagadec" patent, which was not part of the Orange Book. (In fact, the Raaymakers and Lagadec technologies were incompatible.) The license prohibited a licensee from using non–Orange Book patents, which meant that Philips and Sony sought to suppress the Lagadec technology. Princo argued that the suppression of a competitive technology (Lagadec patent) constituted misuse, and Philips "'leveraged' its patents . . . because it used the proceeds of its highly successful licensing program to fund royalty payments to Sony and because those payments gave Sony the incentive to enter into the alleged agreement to suppress the Lagadec patent."

The court in an opinion written by Judge Bryson rejected this argument, stating that misuse is about patent leverage, but leverage "requires, at minimum, that the patent in suit must itself significantly contribute to the practice under attack." *Id.* at 1331. According to the court, "[p]atent misuse will not be found when there is no connection between the patent right and the misconduct in question, or no use of the patent. In this case, there is no such link between the putative misconduct and the Raaymakers patents." *Id.* Moreover, with respect to Princo's argument that Philips funded Sony, thus inducing Sony to agree to suppress the Lagadec patent, the court noted that using funds from a lawful licensing program to support anticompetitive behavior is not the kind of "leveraging" that the Supreme Court and this court have referred to in discussing the leveraging of a patent that constitutes patent misuse." *Id.* at 1332. In fact, "[e]ven if such use of funds were to be deemed misconduct, it does not place any conditions on the availability of Philips's patents to any potential licensees, so it is not the power of Philips's patent right that is being misused." *Id.* Lastly, as he did in the 2004 *Philips* case, Judge Bryson cited efficiency considerations that arise from collaboration and joint ventures:

> Collaboration for the purpose of developing and commercializing new technology can result in economies of scale and integrations of complementary capacities that reduce costs, facilitate innovation, eliminate duplication of effort and assets, and share risks that no individual member would be willing to undertake alone, thereby "promot[ing] rather than hinder[ing] competition." Dep't of Justice & FTC, *Antitrust Guidelines for the Licensing of Intellectual Property* §§ 5.1, at 24; 5.5, at 28 (Apr. 6, 1995). . . . In particular, as we explained in *Philips I*, research joint ventures that seek to develop industry-wide standards for new technology can have decidedly procompetitive effects. The absence of standards for new technology can easily result in a "Tower of Babel" effect that increases costs, reduces utility, and frustrates consumers. As a leading treatise has noted, cooperation by competitors in standard-setting "can provide procompetitive benefits the market would not otherwise provide, by allowing a number of different firms to produce and market competing products compatible with a single standard."

Id. at 1335. Do you agree with the majority's characterization of patent misuse? Judge Dyk, in his dissent, would have adopted a more robust misuse doctrine, one that is broader than antitrust doctrine and does not require leveraging.

2. *Tying Arrangements.* One of the earliest and well-known cases dealing with misuse is *Morton Salt Co. v. G.S. Suppiger Co.*, which involved a tying arrangement. The Supreme Court did not decide if Suppiger violated the antitrust laws, yet nonetheless asked "whether a court of equity will lend its aid to protect the patent monopoly when respondent is using it as the effective means of restraining competition with its sale of an unpatented article." *Id.* at 490. The court viewed the patent grant as imbued with the public interest and held Suppiger was "making use of its patent monopoly to restrain competition in the marketing of unpatented articles, salt tablets, for use with the patented machines, and is aiding in the creation of a limited monopoly in the tablets not within that granted by the patent." *Id.* at 491. In other words, Suppiger was improperly attempting to extend his patent rights beyond what is statutorily permissible, and "courts, and especially courts of equity, may appropriately withhold their aid where the plaintiff is using the right asserted contrary to the public interest." *Id.* at 492.

Section 271(d)(5) states a tying arrangement will not lead to misuse if the patentee lacks market power "for the patent or patented product on which the license or sale is conditioned." (In this regard, section 271(d)(5) overruled *Morton Salt's* per se prohibition of tying agreements.) Market power is an important condition because it is a rare case that a patent confers market power. (Section B.1 explores patents and market power in more detail.) Indeed, there are almost always viable substitutes to the patented product. *See* Edmund W. Kitch, *Elementary and Persistent Errors in the Economic Analysis of Intellectual Property*, 53 VAND. L. REV. 1727, 1730 (2000) (explaining why "patents that confer monopoly market power are rare"). *See also Illinois Tool Works, Inc. v. Independent Ink, Inc.*, 547 U.S. 28, 31 (2006) (referring to the presumption of market power and patents, the court stated "when a seller conditions its sale of a patented product (the 'tying' product) on the purchase of a second product (the 'tied' product), [the presumption of market power] has its foundation in the judicially created patent misuse doctrine" and "[i]n 1988, Congress substantially undermined that foundation, amending the Patent Act to eliminate the market power presumption in patent misuse cases").

Section 271(d)(5) embraces the notion that it is difficult to leverage through tying or bundling arrangements market power from a patented product into a separate market, usually a market for the tied, unpatented good. In *Scheiber v. Dolby Laboratories, Inc.*, Judge Posner writes, "[t]he naive objection [to tying or bundling arrangements] is that they extend monopoly; the sophisticated objection is that they facilitate price discrimination." He continues:

> The traditional objection to tying is that by telling the buyer that he can't buy the tying product unless he agrees to buy a separate product from the seller as well, the seller is trying to "lever" or "extend" his monopoly to the market for that separate product. Yet if the seller tries to charge a monopoly price for that separate product, the buyer will not be willing to pay as much for the tying product as he would if the separate product, which he has to buy also, were priced at a lower rate. Acquiring monopoly power in the tied-product market comes at the expense of losing it in the tying-product market. Thus, as these cases and a tidal wave of legal and economic scholarship point out, the idea that you can use tying to lever your way to a second monopoly is economic nonsense, imputing systematic irrationality to businessmen. Congress seems to have recognized this in the 1988 amendment.

293 F.3d 1014, 1020 (7th Cir. 2002). *See also* ROBERT H. BORK, THE ANTITRUST PARADOX: A POLICY AT WAR WITH ITSELF 372-381 (1978) (discussing why tying arrangements do not injure competition). This approach should be contrasted with the more traditional notion that tying is a means of leveraging to restrain competition, and therefore should be deemed illegal per se. *See* Donald Turner, *The Validity of Tying Arrangements Under the Antitrust Laws*, 58 HARV. L. REV. 50, 62 (1958) (stating "it is a reasonable assumption that the purpose of the seller in using a tie-in is to restrain competition in the tied product"); *Times-Picayune Publishing Co. v. United States*, 345 U.S. 594, 611 (1953) (stating tying arrangements allow a seller to leverage "his dominant position in one market to expand his empire into the next").

It should be apparent that the law's treatment of tying arrangements involving patents as evolved a great deal. As the 2007 Department of Justice and FTC study on antitrust and IP stated, "[o]nce thought to be worthy of judicial condemnation without examination of any actual competitive effects, tying currently is deemed per se illegal under U.S. Supreme Court rulings only if specific conditions are met, including proof that the defendant has market power over the tying product." ANTITRUST ENFORCEMENT AND INTELLECTUAL PROPERTY RIGHTS: PROMOTING INNOVATION AND COMPETITION 104 (Dep't of Justice and Federal Trade Commission 2007).

3. ***The Benefits of Patent Licensing and Patent Pools.*** Patent licensing is a very common activity and typically leads to efficiency gains and pro-competitive effects. Patent owners are not always in the best position to exploit their patent rights or have the means to commercialize their inventions or otherwise capture the return on their investment. Licensing provides the patent owner with an opportunity to integrate various complementary factors related to

production, such as manufacturing and distribution, thus putting the patented invention to the most efficient and productive use. As a government report on antitrust and licensing of intellectual property stated, integration through licensing "can lead to more efficient exploitation of the intellectual property, benefiting consumers through the reduction of costs and the introduction of new products," and also "increase the value of intellectual property to consumers and to the developers of the technology." ANTITRUST GUIDELINES FOR THE LICENSING OF INTELLECTUAL PROPERTY §2.3 (Dep't of Justice and Federal Trade Commission 1995). *See also* WILLIAM J. BAUMOL, THE FREE-MARKET INNOVATION MACHINE: ANALYZING THE GROWTH MIRACLE OF CAPITALISM 77-91 (2002) (discussing the economic incentives and benefits of licensing); ANTITRUST ENFORCEMENT AND INTELLECTUAL PROPERTY RIGHTS: PROMOTING INNOVATION AND COMPETITION (Dep't of Justice and Federal Trade Commission 2007).

In addition to the typical patentee/licensee arrangement, it is common for patent holders in some industries, particularly information technology and telecommunications, to pool their patents. (The first modern patent pool was pioneered by MPEG LA relating to the MPEG-2 standard.) Patent pools are seen as a means for reducing transaction costs and deterring litigation. With respect to the latter, one often hears employed in this context the Cold War phrase "mutually assured destruction" (MAD) — "if you sue me, I'll sue you." In exceedingly crowded patent spaces, where each player has its own arsenal of IP, patent pools can lead to efficiency and social welfare gains by allowing patentees to focus on innovation instead of litigation while also enhancing consumer access to patented technology. As the DOJ/FTC Antitrust Licensing Guidelines state, pooling arrangements "may provide procompetitive benefits by integrating complementary technologies, reducing transaction costs, clearing blocking positions, and avoiding costly infringement litigation. By promoting the dissemination of technology, cross-licensing and pooling arrangements are often procompetitive." ANTITRUST GUIDELINES FOR THE LICENSING OF INTELLECTUAL PROPERTY §5.5 (Dep't of Justice and Federal Trade Commission 1995). Yet, the terms of these arrangements may also give rise to antitrust concerns if they involve price fixing, market division, or coordinated output restrictions. *Id. See also United States v. Singer Manufacturing Co.*, 374 U.S. 174 (1963). For more on the competitive concerns of patent pools, *see* ANTITRUST ENFORCEMENT AND INTELLECTUAL PROPERTY RIGHTS: PROMOTING INNOVATION AND COMPETITION 74-85 (Dep't of Justice and Federal Trade Commission 2007).

For scholarly commentary on patent pools, *see* Richard J. Gilbert, *Ties That Bind: Policies to Promote (Good) Patent Pools*, 77 ANTITRUST L.J. 1 (2010); Steven C. Carlson, *Patent Pools and the Antitrust Dilemma*, 16 YALE J. ON REG. 359 (1999). For a discussion of patent pools and the biotechnology industry, *see* B. Verbeure, E. Van Zimmeren, G. Matthijs & G. Van Overwalle, *Patent Pools and Diagnostic Testing*, TRENDS IN BIOTECHNOLOGY, Vol. 24, No. 3, pp. 115-120 (2006) and for the World Intellectual Property Organization's open innovation "WIPO Re:Search" project for neglected diseases, *see* http://www.wipo.int/wipo_magazine/en/2011/06/article_0001.html. For a historical discussion of the "first privately formed patent pool," *see* Adam Mossoff, *The Rise and Fall of the First American Patent Thicket: The Sewing Machine War of the 1850s*, 53 ARIZ. L. REV. 165 (2011). For a survey of various patent pooling arrangements from the nineteenth century to the present, *see* David Serafino, *Survey of Patent Pools Demonstrates Variety of Purposes and Management Structures*, KNOWLEDGE ECOLOGY INT'L, June 4, 2007. And for more on MPEG LA, *see* http://www.mpegla.com/main/default.aspx. Patent pools are also becoming more prominent in the biotechnology space, both in the commercial context and in the context of facilitating access to essential medicines for developing countries. *See* Esther van Zimmeren et al., *Patent Pools and Clearinghouses in the Life Sciences*, in TRENDS IN BIOTECHNOLOGY, Vol. 29 569-576 (July 2011).

4. *The Misuse Doctrine Diluted.* Patent misuse is a common law, equitable doctrine that focuses on whether the patentee exploited his patent rights beyond its lawful statutory scope. *See Windsurfing Int'l Inc. v. AMF, Inc.*, 782 F.2d 995, 1001 (Fed. Cir. 1986) (stating a finding of misuse "requires that the alleged infringer show that the patentee has impermissibly broadened the 'physical or temporal scope' of the patent grant with anticompetitive effect"). What this means exactly is difficult to fully grasp, but misuse has typically applied (or is asserted) in the context of certain types of licensing arrangements, namely tying or post-expiration royalty provisions (i.e., royalty payments made after the patent expires).

Over the past several years, however, the misuse doctrine has been greatly weakened both statutorily and judicially. Beginning in 1952, Congress enacted section 271(d), which precludes a patent owner being found "guilty of misuse or illegal extension of the patent right" if he:

> (1) derived revenue from acts which if performed by another without his consent would constitute contributory infringement of the patent; (2) licensed or authorized another to perform acts which if performed without his consent would constitute contributory infringement of the patent; (3) sought to enforce his patent rights against infringement or contributory infringement.

In *Dawson Chemical Co. v. Rohm & Haas Co.*, 448 U.S. 176 (1980), the Supreme Court provided a lengthy historical analysis of events that led to the enactment of section 271(d). In *Dawson*, the Court held that the patentee's practice of conditioning the licensing of its process patent on the purchase of an unpatented product was not misuse because the product did not have a substantial noninfringing use—it had "no use except through practice of the patented method." *Id.* at 199.

Two additional provisions were added to section 271(d) in 1988:

> (4) refused to license or use any rights to the patent; or (5) conditioned the license of any rights to the patent or the sale of the patented product on the acquisition of a license to rights in another patent or purchase of a separate product, unless, in view of the circumstances, the patent owner has market power in the relevant market for the patent or patented product on which the license or sale is conditioned.

Subsection (4) reflects the longstanding principle in the United States that—in contrast to countries such as Brazil and India—the patent owner has no duty to work, sell, or license his patented invention. *See Continental Paper Bag Co. v. Eastern Paper Bag Co.*, 210 U.S. 405, 429 (1908) (stating "exclusion may be said to have been of the very essence of the right conferred by the patent, as it is the privilege of any owner of property to use or not use it, without question of motive"). In contrast, under Indian patent law, the patentee may be required to submit to the government information relating "to the extent to which the patented invention has been commercially worked in India." *See* Indian Patent Act §146(1)-(3) (1970). The U.S. principle—"no duty to work" the patented invention—will be reexamined in section B on antitrust in the context of a refusal to deal scenario. Subsection (5) of section 271(d) is explored in greater detail in Comment 4, immediately below.

There have also been judicial pronouncements that question the economic soundness of the misuse doctrine (and whether there is room for such a doctrine in the light of antitrust law). *See USM Corp. v. SPS Technologies, Inc.*, 694 F.2d 505 (7th Cir. 1982) (stating the traditional formulation of misuse is "too vague . . . to be useful" and "taken seriously it would put all patent rights at hazard"), or that place significant limits on the applicability of the doctrine. *See Mallinckrodt, Inc. v. Medipart, Inc.*, 976 F.2d 700 (Fed. Cir. 1992), which is the next principal case. *See also Illinois Tool Works, Inc. v. Independent Ink, Inc.*, 547 U.S. 28, 35 (2006) (stating "[o]ver the years, this Court's strong disapproval of tying arrangements has substantially diminished").

5. *The Differences Between Misuse and Antitrust.* There are a few important differences between misuse and antitrust. Misuse has its origins in equity and arose from the doctrine of unclean hands. *See C.R. Bard, Inc. v. M3 Systems, Inc.*, 157 F.3d 1340, 1372 (Fed. Cir. 1998). It is an affirmative defense that has the effect of rendering the patent unenforceable, not invalid. Unenforceability, however, lasts only until the misuse is purged, meaning that the impermissible activity stops and the effects of misuse have dissipated. *Id.* Antitrust is employed as a counterclaim that can result in an award of damages. Thus, antitrust is more of a sword, whereas misuse assumes the role of a shield. Antitrust also has narrower applicability in that misuse may attach to a given scenario even though there is no antitrust violation. *See B. Braun Medical, Inc. v. Abbott Laboratories, Inc.*, 124 F.3d 1419, 1427 (Fed. Cir. 1997) (stating "[p]atent misuse arose, as an equitable defense available to the accused infringer, from the desire 'to restrain practices that did not in themselves violate any law, but that drew anticompetitive strength from the patent right, and thus were deemed to be contrary to public policy.' When used successfully, this defense results in rendering the patent unenforceable until the misuse is purged. It does not, however, result in an award of damages to the accused infringer.").

b. Field-of-Use and Other Licensing Restrictions

MALLINCKRODT v. MEDIPART
976 F.2d 700 (Fed. Cir. 1992)

NEWMAN, Circuit Judge.

This action for patent infringement and inducement to infringe relates to the use of a patented medical device in violation of a "single use only" notice that accompanied the sale of the device. Mallinckrodt sold its patented device to hospitals, which after initial use of the devices sent them to Medipart for servicing that enabled the hospitals to use the device again. Mallinckrodt claimed that Medipart thus induced infringement by the hospitals and itself infringed the patent.

The district court held that violation of the "single use only" notice cannot be remedied by suit for patent infringement, and granted summary judgment of noninfringement.

* * *

[T]he district court held that no restriction whatsoever could be imposed under the patent law, whether or not the restriction was enforceable under some other law, and whether or not this was a first sale to a purchaser with notice. This ruling is incorrect, for if Mallinckrodt's restriction was a valid condition of the sale, then in accordance with *General Talking Pictures Corp. v. Western Electric Co.*, it was not excluded from enforcement under the patent law.

We conclude that the district court misapplied precedent in holding that there can be no restriction on use imposed as a matter of law, even on the first purchaser. The restriction here at issue does not per se violate the doctrine of patent misuse or the antitrust law. Use in violation of a valid restriction may be remedied under the patent law, provided that no other law prevents enforcement of the patent. The district court's misapplication of precedent also led to an incorrect application of the law of repair/reconstruction, for if reuse is established to have been validly restricted, then even repair may constitute patent infringement.

BACKGROUND

The patented device is an apparatus for delivery of radioactive or therapeutic material in aerosol mist form to the lungs of a patient, for diagnosis and treatment of pulmonary disease. Radioactive material is delivered primarily for image scanning in diagnosis of lung conditions. Therapeutic agents may be administered to patients suffering various lung diseases.

The device is manufactured by Mallinckrodt, who sells it to hospitals as a unitary kit that consists of a "nebulizer" which generates a mist of the radioactive material or the prescribed drug, a "manifold" that directs the flow of oxygen or air and the active material, a filter, tubing, a mouthpiece, and a nose clip. In use, the radioactive material or drug is placed in the nebulizer, is atomized, and the patient inhales and exhales through the closed system. The device traps and retains any radioactive or other toxic material in the exhalate. The device fits into a lead-shielded container that is provided by Mallinckrodt to minimize exposure to radiation and for safe disposal after use.

The device is marked with the appropriate patent numbers, and bears the trademarks "Mallinckrodt" and "UltraVent" and the inscription "Single Use Only." The package insert provided with each unit states "For Single Patient Use Only" and instructs that the entire contaminated apparatus be disposed of in accordance with procedures for the disposal of biohazardous waste. The hospital is instructed to seal the used apparatus in the radiation-shielded container prior to proper disposal. The hospitals whose activities led to this action do not dispose of the UltraVent apparatus, or limit it to a single use.

Instead, the hospitals ship the used manifold/nebulizer assemblies to Medipart, Inc. Medipart in turn packages the assemblies and sends them to Radiation Sterilizers Inc., who exposes the packages to at least 2.5 megarads of gamma radiation, and returns them to Medipart. Medipart personnel then check each assembly for damage and leaks, and place the assembly in a plastic bag together with a new filter, tubing, mouthpiece, and nose clip. The "reconditioned" units, as Medipart calls them, are shipped back to the hospitals from whence they came. Neither Radiation Sterilizers nor Medipart tests the reconditioned units for any residual biological activity or for radioactivity. The assemblies still bear the inscription "Single Use Only" and the trademarks "Mallinckrodt" and "UltraVent."

Mallinckrodt filed suit against Medipart, asserting patent infringement and inducement to infringe. . . .

The district court granted Medipart's motion on the patent infringement counts, holding that the "Single Use Only" restriction could not be enforced by suit for patent infringement. The court also held that Medipart's activities were permissible repair, not impermissible reconstruction, of the patented apparatus. . . .

The district court also enjoined Mallinckrodt *recomp lite* from distributing a new notice to its hospital customers. The proposed new notice emphasized the "Single Use Only" restriction and stated that the purpose of this restriction is to protect the hospital and its patients from potential adverse consequences of reconditioning, such as infectious disease transmission, material instability, and/or decreased diagnostic performance; that the UltraVent device is covered by certain patents; that the hospital is licensed under these patents to use the device only once; and that reuse of the device would be deemed infringement of the patents.

Mallinckrodt appeals the grant of summary judgment on the infringement issue, and the grant of the preliminary injunction.

I

The Restriction on Reuse

Mallinckrodt describes the restriction on reuse as a label license for a specified field of use, wherein the field is single (*i.e.*, disposable) use. On this motion for summary judgment, there was no issue of whether this form of license gave notice of the restriction. Notice was not disputed. Nor was it disputed that sale to the hospitals was the first sale of the patented device. The issue that the district court decided on summary judgment was the enforceability of the restriction by suit for patent infringement. The court's premise was that even if the notice was sufficient to constitute a valid condition of sale, violation of that condition cannot be remedied under the patent law.

Mallinckrodt states that the restriction to single patient use is valid and enforceable under the patent law because the use is within the scope of the patent grant, and the restriction does not enlarge the patent grant. Mallinckrodt states that a license to less than all uses of a patented article is well recognized and a valid practice under patent law, and that such license does not violate the antitrust laws and is not patent misuse. Mallinckrodt also states that the restriction here imposed is reasonable because it is based on health, safety, efficacy, and liability considerations and violates no public policy. Thus Mallinckrodt argues that the restriction is valid and enforceable under the patent law. Mallinckrodt concludes that use in violation of the restriction is patent infringement, and that the district court erred in holding otherwise.

Medipart states that the restriction is unenforceable, for the reason that "the *Bauer* trilogy and *Motion Picture Patents* clearly established that *no* restriction is enforceable under patent law upon a purchaser of a sold article." (Medipart's emphasis). The district court so held. The district court also held that since the hospitals purchased the device from the patentee, not from a manufacturing licensee, no restraint on the use of the device could lawfully be imposed under the patent law.

* * *

The enforceability of restrictions on the use of patented goods derives from the patent grant, which is in classical terms of property: the right to exclude.

> 35 U.S.C. § 154. Every patent shall contain . . . a grant . . . for the term of seventeen years . . . of the right to exclude others from making, using, or selling the invention throughout the United States. . . .

This right to exclude may be waived in whole or in part. The conditions of such waiver are subject to patent, contract, antitrust, and any other applicable law, as well as equitable considerations such as are reflected in the law of patent misuse. As in other areas of commerce, private parties may contract as they choose, provided that no law is violated thereby:

> [T]he rule is, with few exceptions, that any conditions which are not in their very nature illegal with regard to this kind of property, imposed by the patentee and agreed to by the licensee for the right to manufacture or use or sell the [patented] article, will be upheld by the courts.

E. Bement & Sons v. National Harrow Co., 186 U.S. 70, 91 (1902).

The district court's ruling that Mallinckrodt's restriction on reuse was unenforceable was an application of the doctrine of patent misuse, although the court declined to use that designation. The concept of patent misuse arose to restrain practices that did not in themselves violate any law, but that drew anticompetitive strength from the patent right, and thus were deemed to be contrary to public policy. The policy purpose was to prevent a patentee from using the patent to obtain market benefit beyond that which inheres in the statutory patent right.

The district court's holding that Mallinckrodt's restriction to single patient use was unenforceable was, as we have remarked, based on "policy" considerations. The district court relied on a group of cases wherein resale price-fixing of patented goods was held illegal, viz. *Bauer & Cie. v. O'Donnell*; *Straus v. Victor Talking Machine Co.*; *Boston Store of Chicago v. American Graphophone Co.* ("the *Bauer* trilogy"), and that barred patent-enforced tie-ins, viz. *Motion Picture Patents Co. v. Universal Film Mfg. Co.*

* * *

These cases established that price-fixing and tying restrictions accompanying the sale of patented goods were per se illegal. These cases did not hold, and it did not follow, that all restrictions accompanying the sale of patented goods were deemed illegal. In *General Talking Pictures* the Court, discussing restrictions on use, summarized the state of the law as follows:

> That a restrictive license is legal seems clear. *Mitchell v. Hawley* [83 U.S.], 16 Wall. 544 (1873). As was said in *United States v. General Electric Co.*, 272 U.S. 476, 489 (1926), the patentee may grant a license "upon any condition the performance of which is reasonably within the reward which the patentee by the grant of the patent is entitled to secure." . . .

The practice of granting licenses for restricted use is an old one, *see Rubber Company v. Goodyear.* So far as it appears, its legality has never been questioned. 305 U.S. at 127.

In *General Talking Pictures* the patentee had authorized the licensee to make and sell amplifiers embodying the patented invention for a specified use (home radios). The defendant had purchased the patented amplifier from the manufacturing licensee, with knowledge of the patentee's restriction on use. The Supreme Court stated the question as "whether the restriction in the license is to be given effect" against a purchaser who had notice of the restriction. The Court observed that a restrictive license to a particular use was permissible, and treated the purchaser's unauthorized use as infringement of the patent, deeming the goods to be unlicensed as purchased from the manufacturer.

The Court, in its opinion on rehearing, stated that it

> [did not] consider what the rights of the parties would have been if the amplifier had been manufactured under the patent and had passed into the hands of a purchaser in the ordinary channels of trade.

305 U.S. at 127. The district court interpreted this reservation as requiring that since the hospitals purchased the UltraVent device from the patentee Mallinckrodt, not from a manufacturing licensee, no restraint on the purchasers' use of the device could be imposed under the patent law. However, in *General Talking Pictures* the Court did not hold that there must be an intervening manufacturing licensee before the patent can be enforced against a purchaser with notice of the restriction. The Court did not decide the situation where the patentee was the manufacturer and the device reached a purchaser in ordinary channels of trade.

The UltraVent device was manufactured by the patentee; but the sale to the hospitals was the first sale and was with notice of the restriction. Medipart offers neither law, public policy, nor logic, for the proposition that the enforceability of a restriction to a particular use is determined by whether the purchaser acquired the device from a manufacturing licensee or from a manufacturing patentee. We decline to make a distinction for which there appears to be no foundation. Indeed, Mallinckrodt has pointed out how easily such a criterion could be circumvented. That the viability of a restriction should depend on how the transaction is structured was denigrated as "formalistic line drawing" in *Continental T.V., Inc. v. GTE Sylvania, Inc.,* 433 U.S. 36, 57-59 (1977), the Court explaining, in overruling *United States v. Arnold, Schwinn & Co.,* 388 U.S. 365 (1967), that the legality of attempts by a manufacturer to regulate resale does not turn on whether the reseller had purchased the merchandise or was merely acting as an agent of the manufacturer. The Court having disapproved reliance on formalistic distinctions of no economic consequence in antitrust analysis, we discern no reason to preserve formalistic distinctions of no economic consequence, simply because the goods are patented.

The district court, holding Mallinckrodt's restriction unenforceable, described the holding of *General Talking Pictures* as in "some tension" with the earlier price-fixing and tie-in cases. The district court observed that the Supreme Court did not cite the *Bauer, Boston Store,* or *Motion Picture Patents* cases when it upheld the use restriction in *General Talking Pictures.* That observation is correct, but it should not be remarkable. By the time of *General Talking Pictures,* price-fixing and tie-ins were generally prohibited under the antitrust law as well as the misuse law, while other conditions were generally recognized as within the patent grant. The prohibitions against price-fixing and tying did not make all other restrictions per se invalid and unenforceable. [footnote omitted] Further, the Court could not have been unaware of the *Bauer* trilogy in deciding *General Talking Pictures*, because Justice Black's dissent is built upon those cases.

Restrictions on use are judged in terms of their relation to the patentee's right to exclude from all or part of the patent grant, and where an anticompetitive effect is asserted, the rule of reason is the basis of determining the legality of the provision. In *Windsurfing International, Inc. v. AMF, Inc.*, this court stated:

> To sustain a misuse defense involving a licensing arrangement not held to have been per se anticompetitive by the Supreme Court, a factual determination must reveal that the overall effect of the license tends to restrain competition unlawfully in an appropriately defined relevant market.

782 F.2d at 1001-1002. The district court, stating that it "refuse[s] to limit *Bauer* and *Motion Picture Patents* to tying and price-fixing not only because their language suggests broader application, but because there is a strong public interest in not stretching the patent laws to authorize restrictions on the use of purchased goods," *Mallinckrodt*, 15 U.S.P.Q.2d at 1119, has contravened this precedent.

* * *

Viewing the entire group of these early cases, it appears that the Court simply applied, to a variety of factual situations, the rule of contract law that sale may be conditioned. *Adams v. Burke* and its kindred cases do not stand for the proposition that no restriction or condition may be placed upon the sale of a patented article. It was error for the district court to derive that proposition from the precedent. Unless the condition violates some other law or policy (in the patent field, notably the misuse or antitrust law, e.g., *United States v. Univis Lens Co.*, 316 U.S. 241 (1942)), private parties retain the freedom to contract concerning conditions of sale. As we have discussed, the district court cited the price-fixing and tying cases as reflecting what the court deemed to be the correct policy, viz., that no condition can be placed on the sale of patented goods, for any reason. However, this is not a price-fixing or tying case, and the per se antitrust and misuse violations found in the *Bauer* trilogy and *Motion Picture Patents* are not here present. The appropriate criterion is whether Mallinckrodt's restriction is reasonably within the patent grant, or whether the patentee has ventured beyond the patent grant and into behavior having an anticompetitive effect not justifiable under the rule of reason.

Should the restriction be found to be reasonably within the patent grant, i.e., that it relates to subject matter within the scope of the patent claims, that ends the inquiry. However, should such inquiry lead to the conclusion that there are anticompetitive effects extending beyond the patentee's statutory right to exclude, these effects do not automatically impeach the restriction. Anticompetitive effects that are not per se violations of law are reviewed in accordance with the rule of reason. Patent owners should not be in a worse position, by virtue of the patent right to exclude, than owners of other property used in trade.

We conclude that the district court erred in holding that the restriction on reuse was, as a matter of law, unenforceable under the patent law. If the sale of the UltraVent was validly conditioned under the applicable law such as the law governing sales and licenses, and if the restriction on reuse was within the scope of the patent grant or otherwise justified, then violation of the restriction may be remedied by action for patent infringement. The grant of summary judgment is reversed, and the cause is remanded.

QUANTA COMPUTER, INC. v. LG ELECTRONICS, INC.
553 U.S. 617 (2008)

Justice THOMAS delivered the opinion of the Court.

For over 150 years this Court has applied the doctrine of patent exhaustion to limit the patent rights that survive the initial authorized sale of a patented item. In this case, we decide whether patent exhaustion applies to the sale of components of a patented system that must be combined with additional components in order to practice the patented methods. The Court of Appeals for the Federal Circuit held that the doctrine does not apply to method patents at all and, in the alternative, that it does not apply here because the sales were not authorized by the license agreement. We disagree on both scores. Because the exhaustion doctrine applies to method patents, and because the license authorizes the sale of components that substantially embody the patents in suit, the sale exhausted the patents.

I

Respondent LG Electronics, Inc. (LGE), purchased a portfolio of computer technology patents in 1999, including the three patents at issue here: U.S. Patent Nos. 4,939,641 ('641); 5,379,379 ('379); and 5,077,733 ('733) (collectively LGE Patents). . . .

* * *

LGE licensed a patent portfolio, including the LGE Patents, to Intel Corporation (Intel). The cross-licensing agreement (License Agreement) permits Intel to manufacture and sell microprocessors and chipsets that use the LGE Patents (the Intel Products). The License Agreement authorizes Intel to "'make, use, sell (directly or indirectly), offer to sell, import or otherwise dispose of'" its own products practicing the LGE Patents. Notwithstanding this broad language, the License Agreement contains some limitations. Relevant here, it stipulates that no license

> is granted by either party hereto . . . to any third party for the combination by a third party of Licensed Products of either party with items, components, or the like acquired . . . from sources other than a party hereto, or for the use, import, offer for sale or sale of such combination.

The License Agreement purports not to alter the usual rules of patent exhaustion, however, providing that, "'[n]otwithstanding anything to the contrary contained in this Agreement, the parties agree that nothing herein shall in any way limit or alter the effect of patent exhaustion that would otherwise apply when a party hereto sells any of its Licensed Products.'" Brief for Petitioners 8.

In a separate agreement (Master Agreement), Intel agreed to give written notice to its own customers informing them that, while it had obtained a broad license "'ensur[ing] that any Intel product that you purchase is licensed by LGE and thus does not infringe any patent held by LGE,'" the license "'does not extend, expressly or by implication, to any product that you make by combining an Intel product with any non-Intel product.'" Brief for Respondent 9. The Master Agreement also provides that "'a breach of this Agreement shall have no effect on and shall not be grounds for termination of the Patent License.'" Brief for Petitioners 9.

Petitioners, including Quanta Computer (collectively Quanta), are a group of computer manufacturers. Quanta purchased microprocessors and chipsets from Intel and received the notice required by the Master Agreement. Nonetheless, Quanta manufactured computers using Intel parts in combination with non-Intel memory and buses in ways that practice the LGE Patents. Quanta does not modify the Intel components and follows Intel's specifications to incorporate the parts into its own systems.

LGE filed a complaint against Quanta, asserting that the combination of the Intel Products with non-Intel memory and buses infringed the LGE Patents. The District Court granted summary judgment to Quanta, holding that, for purposes of the patent exhaustion doctrine, the license LGE granted to Intel resulted in forfeiture of any potential infringement actions against legitimate purchasers of the Intel Products. The court found that, although the Intel Products do not fully practice any of the patents at issue, they have no reasonable noninfringing use and therefore their authorized sale exhausted patent rights in the completed computers under *United States v. Univis Lens Co.*, 316 U.S. 241 (1942). In a subsequent order limiting its summary judgment ruling, the court held that patent exhaustion applies only to apparatus or composition-of-matter claims that describe a physical object, and does not apply to process, or method, claims that describe operations to make or use a product. Because each of the LGE Patents includes method claims, exhaustion did not apply.

The Court of Appeals for the Federal Circuit affirmed in part and reversed in part. It agreed that the doctrine of patent exhaustion does not apply to method claims. In the alternative, it concluded that exhaustion did not apply because LGE did not license Intel to sell the Intel Products to Quanta for use in combination with non-Intel products.

We granted certiorari.

II

The longstanding doctrine of patent exhaustion provides that the initial authorized sale of a patented item terminates all patent rights to that item. This Court first applied the doctrine in 19th-century cases addressing patent extensions on the Woodworth planing machine. Purchasers of licenses to sell and use the machine for the duration of the original patent term sought to continue using the licenses through the extended term. The Court held that the extension of the patent term did not affect the rights already secured by purchasers who bought the item for use "in the ordinary pursuits of life." *Bloomer v. McQuewan*, 14 How. 539, 549 (1853). In *Adams v. Burke*, 17 Wall. 453 (1873), the Court affirmed the dismissal of a patent holder's suit alleging that a licensee had violated postsale restrictions on where patented coffin-lids could be used. "[W]here a person ha[s] purchased a patented machine of the patentee or his assignee," the Court held, "this purchase carrie[s] with it the right to the use of that machine so long as it [is] capable of use." *Id.*, at 455. . . .

This Court most recently discussed patent exhaustion in *Univis,* 316 U.S. 241, on which the District Court relied. Univis Lens Company, the holder of patents on eyeglass lenses, licensed a purchaser to manufacture lens blanks by fusing together different lens segments to create bi- and tri-focal lenses and to sell them to other Univis licensees at agreed-upon rates. Wholesalers were licensed to grind the blanks into the patented finished lenses, which they would then sell to Univis-licensed prescription retailers for resale at a fixed rate. Finishing retailers, after grinding the blanks into patented lenses, would sell the finished lenses to consumers at the same fixed rate. The United States sued Univis under the Sherman Act, 15 U.S.C. §§ 1, 3, 15, alleging unlawful restraints on trade. Univis asserted its patent monopoly rights as a defense to the antitrust suit. The Court granted certiorari to determine whether Univis' patent monopoly survived the sale of the lens blanks by the licensed manufacturer and therefore shielded Univis' pricing scheme from the Sherman Act.

The Court assumed that the Univis patents containing claims for finished lenses were practiced in part by the wholesalers and finishing retailers who ground the blanks into lenses, and held that the sale of the lens blanks exhausted the patents on the finished lenses. *Univis,* 316 U.S., at 248-249. The Court explained that the lens blanks "embodi[ed] essential features of the patented device and [were] without utility until . . . ground and polished as the finished lens of the patent." *Id.,* at 249. The Court noted that:

> where one has sold an uncompleted article which, because it embodies essential features of his patented invention, is within the protection of his patent, and has destined the article to be finished by the purchaser in conformity to the patent, he has sold his invention so far as it is or may be embodied in that particular article." *Id.,* at 250-251.

In sum, the Court concluded that the traditional bar on patent restrictions following the sale of an item applies when the item sufficiently embodies the patent—even if it does not completely practice the patent—such that its only and intended use is to be finished under the terms of the patent.

With this history of the patent exhaustion doctrine in mind, we turn to the parties' arguments.

III

A

LGE argues that the exhaustion doctrine is inapplicable here because it does not apply to method claims, which are contained in each of the LGE Patents. LGE reasons that, because method patents are linked not to a tangible article but to a process, they can never be exhausted through a sale. Rather, practicing the patent—which occurs upon each use of an article embodying a method patent—is permissible only to the extent rights are transferred in an assignment contract. Quanta, in turn, argues that there is no reason to preclude exhaustion of method claims, and points out that both this Court and the Federal Circuit have applied exhaustion to method claims. It argues that any other rule would allow patent holders to avoid exhaustion entirely by inserting method claims in their patent specifications.

Quanta has the better of this argument. Nothing in this Court's approach to patent exhaustion supports LGE's argument that method patents cannot be exhausted. It is true that a patented method may not be sold in the same way as an article or device, but methods nonetheless may be "embodied" in a product, the sale of which exhausts patent rights. Our precedents do not differentiate transactions involving embodiments of patented methods or processes from those involving patented apparatuses or materials. To the contrary, this Court has repeatedly held that method patents were exhausted by the sale of an item that embodied the method. . . .

Eliminating exhaustion for method patents would seriously undermine the exhaustion doctrine. Patentees seeking to avoid patent exhaustion could simply draft their patent claims to describe a method rather than an apparatus. Apparatus and method claims "may approach each other so nearly that it will be difficult to distinguish the process from the function of the apparatus." *United States ex rel. Steinmetz v. Allen*, 192 U.S. 543, 559 (1904). By characterizing their claims as method instead of apparatus claims, or including a method claim for the machine's patented method of performing its task, a patent drafter could shield practically any patented item from exhaustion.

This case illustrates the danger of allowing such an end-run around exhaustion. On LGE's theory, although Intel is authorized to sell a completed computer system that practices the LGE Patents, any downstream purchasers of the system could nonetheless be liable for patent infringement. Such a result would violate the longstanding principle that, when a patented item is "once lawfully made and sold, there is no restriction on [its] *use* to be implied for the benefit of the patentee." *Adams,* 17 Wall., at 457. We therefore reject LGE's argument that method claims, as a category, are never exhaustible.

B

We next consider the extent to which a product must embody a patent in order to trigger exhaustion. Quanta argues that, although sales of an incomplete article do not necessarily exhaust the patent in that article, the sale of the microprocessors and chipsets exhausted LGE's patents in the same way the sale of the lens blanks exhausted the patents in *Univis.* Just as the lens blanks in *Univis* did not fully practice the patents at issue because they had not been ground into finished lenses, Quanta observes, the Intel Products cannot practice the LGE Patents—or indeed, function at all—until they are combined with memory and buses in a computer system. If, as in *Univis,* patent rights are exhausted by the sale of the incomplete item, then LGE has no postsale right to require that the patents be practiced using only Intel parts. Quanta also argues that exhaustion doctrine will be a dead letter unless it is triggered by the sale of components that essentially, even if not completely, embody an invention. Otherwise, patent holders could authorize the sale of computers that are complete with the exception of one minor step—say, inserting the microprocessor into a socket—and extend their rights through each downstream purchaser all the way to the end user.

LGE, for its part, argues that *Univis* is inapplicable here for three reasons. First, it maintains that *Univis* should be limited to products that contain all the physical aspects needed to practice the patent. On that theory, the Intel Products cannot embody the patents because additional physical components are required before the patents can be practiced. Second, LGE asserts that in *Univis* there was no "patentable distinction" between the lens blanks and the patented finished lenses since they were both subject to the same patent. In contrast, it describes the Intel Products as "independent and distinct products" from the systems using the LGE Patents and subject to "independent patents." Finally, LGE argues that *Univis* does not apply because the Intel Products are analogous to individual elements of a combination patent, and allowing sale of those components to exhaust the patent would impermissibly "ascrib[e] to one element of the patented combination the status of the patented invention in itself." *Aro Mfg. Co. v. Convertible Top Replacement Co.*, 365 U.S. 336, 344-345 (1961).

We agree with Quanta that *Univis* governs this case. As the Court there explained, exhaustion was triggered by the sale of the lens blanks because their only reasonable and intended use was to practice the patent and because they "embodie[d] essential features of [the] patented invention." 316 U.S., at 249-251. Each of those attributes is shared by the microprocessors and chipsets Intel sold to Quanta under the License Agreement.

First, *Univis* held that "the authorized sale of an article which is capable of use only in practicing the patent is a relinquishment of the patent monopoly with respect to the article sold." *Id.*, at 249. The lens blanks in *Univis* met this standard because they were "without utility until [they were] ground and polished as the finished lens of the patent." *Ibid.* Accordingly, "the only object of the sale [was] to enable the [finishing retailer] to grind and polish it for use as a lens by the prospective wearer." *Ibid.* Here, LGE has suggested no reasonable use for the Intel Products other than incorporating them into computer systems that practice the LGE Patents. Nor can we can discern one: A microprocessor or chipset cannot function until it is connected to buses and memory. And here, as in *Univis*, the only apparent object of Intel's sales to Quanta was to permit Quanta to incorporate the Intel Products into computers that would practice the patents.

Second, the lens blanks in *Univis* "embodie[d] essential features of [the] patented invention." *Id.*, at 250-251. The essential, or inventive, feature of the Univis lens patents was the fusing together of different lens segments to create bi- and tri-focal lenses. The finishing process performed by the finishing and prescription retailers after the fusing was not unique. As the United States explained:

> The finishing licensees finish Univis lens blanks in precisely the same manner as they finish all other bifocal lens blanks. Indeed, appellees have never contended that their licensing system is supported by patents covering methods or processes relating to the finishing of lens blanks. Consequently, it appears that appellees perform all of the operations which contribute any claimed element of novelty to Univis lenses. Brief for United States in *United States v. Univis Lens Co.*, O.T. 1941, No. 855 et al., p. 10.

While the Court assumed that the finishing process was covered by the patents, and the District Court found that it was necessary to make a working lens, the grinding process was not central to the patents. That standard process was not included in detail in any of the patents and was not referred to at all in two of the patents. Those that did mention the finishing process treated it as incidental to the invention, noting, for example, that "[t]he blank is then ground in the usual manner," or simply that the blank is "then ground and polished." Tr. of Record in *United States v. Univis Lens Co.*, O.T. 1941, No. 855 et al., pp. 516, 498.

Like the Univis lens blanks, the Intel Products constitute a material part of the patented invention and all but completely practice the patent. Here, as in

Univis, the incomplete article substantially embodies the patent because the only step necessary to practice the patent is the application of common processes or the addition of standard parts. Everything inventive about each patent is embodied in the Intel Products. They control access to main and cache memory, practicing the '641 and '379 patents by checking cache memory against main memory and comparing read and write requests. They also control priority of bus access by various other computer components under the '733 patent. Naturally, the Intel Products cannot carry out these functions unless they are attached to memory and buses, but those additions are standard components in the system, providing the material that enables the microprocessors and chipsets to function. The Intel Products were specifically designed to function only when memory or buses are attached; Quanta was not required to make any creative or inventive decision when it added those parts. Indeed, Quanta had no alternative but to follow Intel's specifications in incorporating the Intel Products into its computers because it did not know their internal structure, which Intel guards as a trade secret. Intel all but practiced the patent itself by designing its products to practice the patents, lacking only the addition of standard parts.

We are unpersuaded by LGE's attempts to distinguish *Univis.* First, there is no reason to distinguish the two cases on the ground that the articles in *Univis* required the *removal* of material to practice the patent while the Intel Products require the *addition* of components to practice the patent. LGE characterizes the lens blanks and lenses as sharing a "basic nature" by virtue of their physical similarity, while the Intel Products embody only some of the "patentably distinct elements and steps" involved in the LGE Patents. But we think that the nature of the final step, rather than whether it consists of adding or deleting material, is the relevant characteristic. In each case, the final step to practice the patent is common and noninventive: grinding a lens to the customer's prescription, or connecting a microprocessor or chipset to buses or memory. The Intel Products embody the essential features of the LGE Patents because they carry out all the inventive processes when combined, according to their design, with standard components.

With regard to LGE's argument that exhaustion does not apply across patents, we agree on the general principle: The sale of a device that practices patent A does not, by virtue of practicing patent A, exhaust patent B. But if the device practices patent A *while substantially embodying* patent B, its relationship to patent A does not prevent exhaustion of patent B. For example, if the Univis lens blanks had been composed of shatter-resistant glass under patent A, the blanks would nonetheless have substantially embodied, and therefore exhausted, patent B for the finished lenses. This case is no different. While each Intel microprocessor and chipset practices thousands of individual patents, including some LGE patents not at issue in this case, the exhaustion analysis is not altered by the fact that more than one patent is practiced by the same product. The relevant consideration is whether the Intel Products that partially practice a patent—by, for example, embodying its essential features—exhaust *that* patent.

Finally, LGE's reliance on *Aro* is misplaced because that case dealt only with the question whether replacement of one part of a patented combination infringes the patent. First, the replacement question is not at issue here. Second, and more importantly, *Aro* is not squarely applicable to the exhaustion of patents like the LGE Patents that do not disclose a new combination of existing parts. *Aro* described combination patents as "cover[ing] only the totality of the elements in the claim [so] that no element, separately viewed, is within the grant." 365 U.S., at 344. Aro's warning that no element can be viewed as central to or equivalent to the invention is specific to the context in which the combination itself is the only inventive aspect of the patent. In this case, the inventive part of the patent is not the fact that memory and buses are combined with a microprocessor or chipset; rather, it is included in the design of the Intel Products themselves and the way these products access the memory or bus.

C

Having concluded that the Intel Products embodied the patents, we next consider whether their sale to Quanta exhausted LGE's patent rights. Exhaustion is triggered only by a sale authorized by the patent holder.

LGE argues that there was no authorized sale here because the License Agreement does not permit Intel to sell its products for use in combination with non-Intel products to practice the LGE Patents. It cites *General Talking Pictures Corp. v. Western Elec. Co.*, 304 U.S. 175 (1938), and *General Talking Pictures Corp. v. Western Elec. Co.*, 305 U.S. 124 (1938), in which the manufacturer sold patented amplifiers for commercial use, thereby breaching a license that limited the buyer to selling the amplifiers for private and home use. The Court held that exhaustion did not apply because the manufacturer had no authority to sell the amplifiers for commercial use, and the manufacturer "could not convey to petitioner what both knew it was not authorized to sell." *General Talking Pictures, supra,* at 181. LGE argues that the same principle applies here: Intel could not convey to Quanta what both knew it was not authorized to sell, *i.e.,* the right to practice the patents with non-Intel parts.

LGE overlooks important aspects of the structure of the Intel-LGE transaction. Nothing in the License Agreement restricts Intel's right to sell its microprocessors and chipsets to purchasers who intend to combine them with non-Intel parts. It broadly permits Intel to "'make, use, [or] sell'" products free of LGE's patent claims. To be sure, LGE did require Intel to give notice to its customers, including Quanta, that LGE had not licensed those customers to practice its patents. But neither party contends that Intel breached the agreement in that respect. In any event, the provision requiring notice to Quanta appeared only in the Master Agreement, and LGE does not suggest that a breach of that agreement would constitute a breach of the License Agreement. Hence, Intel's authority to sell its products embodying the LGE Patents was not conditioned on the notice or on Quanta's decision to abide by LGE's directions in that notice.

LGE points out that the License Agreement specifically disclaimed any license to third parties to practice the patents by combining licensed products with other components. But the question whether third parties received implied licenses is irrelevant because Quanta asserts its right to practice the patents based not on implied license but on exhaustion. And exhaustion turns only on Intel's own license to sell products practicing the LGE Patents.

Alternatively, LGE invokes the principle that patent exhaustion does not apply to postsale restrictions on "making" an article. But this is simply a rephrasing of its argument that combining the Intel Products with other components adds more than standard finishing to complete a patented article. As explained above, making a product that substantially embodies a patent is, for exhaustion purposes, no different from making the patented article itself. In other words, no further "making" results from the addition of standard parts—here, the buses and memory—to a product that already substantially embodies the patent.

The License Agreement authorized Intel to sell products that practiced the LGE Patents. No conditions limited Intel's authority to sell products substantially embodying the patents. Because Intel was authorized to sell its products to Quanta, the doctrine of patent exhaustion prevents LGE from further asserting its patent rights with respect to the patents substantially embodied by those products.[7]

IV

The authorized sale of an article that substantially embodies a patent exhausts the patent holder's rights and prevents the patent holder from invoking patent law to control postsale use of the article. Here, LGE licensed Intel to practice any of its patents and to sell products practicing those patents. Intel's microprocessors and chipsets substantially embodied the LGE Patents because they had no reasonable noninfringing use and included all the inventive aspects of the patented methods. Nothing in the License Agreement limited Intel's ability to sell its products practicing the LGE Patents. Intel's authorized sale to Quanta thus took its products outside the scope of the patent monopoly, and as a result, LGE can no longer assert its patent rights against Quanta. Accordingly, the judgment of the Court of Appeals is reversed.

Comments

1. ***Conditional Licensing and the Exhaustion Doctrine.*** In *Mallinckrodt*, the restriction was "single use only" for the patented device, which can be characterized as a "field-of-use" license. A field-of-use contract can impose geographic and use restrictions (as well as other types of restrictions), which allows the patentee to exercise greater control over his patented technology while also enhancing his financial return. This form of restrictive licensing, according to an early twentieth-century commentator, is "based on the assumption that the right to exclude from use given by the patent statute is not a single, indivisible right which must be retained in toto or parted with in toto." Thomas Reed Powell, *The Nature of a Patent Right*, 17 COLUM. L. REV. 663, 667 (1917). Rather, the patent owner has "many separate and distinct rights, a composite, rather than a simple, right." *Id.* Thus, if he saw fit, the patentee can exclude others from using his claimed invention "in Chicago, plus a right to exclude them from using in New York, plus separate and distinct rights to exclude from use in each of all the other territorial divisions of the country." Moreover, "[h]e has a right to exclude from use on Mondays, plus a right to

---

7. We note that the authorized nature of the sale to Quanta does not necessarily limit LGE's other contract rights. LGE's complaint does not include a breach-of-contract claim, and we express no opinion on whether contract damages might be available even though exhaustion operates to eliminate patent damages. See *Keeler v. Standard Folding Bed Co.*, 157 U.S. 659, 666 (1895) ("Whether a patentee may protect himself and his assignees by special contracts brought home to the purchasers is not a question before us, and upon which we express no opinion. It is, however, obvious that such a question would arise as a question of contract, and not as one under the inherent meaning and effect of the patent laws.").

exclude on Tuesdays, etc." *Id.* If viewed as "a bundle of an indefinite number of separate rights to exclude from separate specific uses," the patent owner "may part with one of these rights and still retain the others" as part of his right to exclude. *Id.* As two property theorists note, "[a] willing buyer and a willing seller can create an infinite variety of enforceable contracts for the exchange of recognized property rights, and can describe these property rights along a multitude of physical dimensions and prices." Thomas W. Merrill & Henry E. Smith, *Optimal Standardization in the Law of Property: The* Numerus Clausus *Principle*, 110 YALE L.J. 1, 5 (2000).

But these restrictive licenses are not without costs for the licensor, namely potentially high transactions costs such as identifying, negotiating, and overseeing what are oftentimes several licenses. These extra costs can be worth the effort, however, "when more than one company is needed to fully develop a technology's potential, when different licensees are needed to address different markets, or when field-of-use licensing has the potential to significantly increase the financial return from a technology." S.L. Shotwell, *Field-of-Use Licensing* in INTELLECTUAL PROPERTY MANAGEMENT IN HEALTH AND AGRICULTURAL INNOVATION: A HANDBOOK OF BEST PRACTICES 1113 (A. Krattiger et al. eds., 2007). And according to the Department of Justice study on the relationship between antitrust and licensing intellectual property, field-of-use contracts can be precompetitive by

> by allowing the licensor to exploit its property as efficiently and effectively as possible. These various forms of exclusivity can be used to give a licensee an incentive to invest in the commercialization and distribution of products embodying the licensed intellectual property and to develop additional applications for the licensed property. The restrictions may do so, for example, by protecting the licensee against free-riding on the licensee's investments by other licensees or by the licensor. They may also increase the licensor's incentive to license, for example, by protecting the licensor from competition in the licensor's own technology in a market niche that it prefers to keep to itself. These benefits of licensing restrictions apply to patent, copyright, and trade secret licenses, and to know-how agreements.

ANTITRUST GUIDELINES FOR THE LICENSING OF INTELLECTUAL PROPERTY (Dep't of Justice and Federal Trade Commission §2.3 (1995). *See also* Makan Delrahim, *The Long and Winding Road: Convergence in the Application of Antitrust to Intellectual Property*, 13 GEO. MASON L. REV. 259, 264 (2005) (discussing how field-of-use restrictions allow for pro-competitive behavior and social welfare benefits based on the patentee's ability to price discriminate). *But see* Mark R. Patterson, *Contractual Expansion of the Scope of Patent Infringement Through Field-of-Use Licensing*, 49 WM. & MARY L. REV 157, 192 (2007) (discussing potential anticompetitive effects of field-of-use licenses and how they impermissibly allow patentees to "to transform permissible conduct into infringement only by adoption of the use restrictions").

What is clear from *Mallinckrodt* (at least until *Quanta* was decided—see Comment 2) is that the principle of exhaustion can be contractually restricted as long as the contract does not have an anticompetitive effect and is "reasonably within the patent grant." The court has repeatedly viewed the patent grant as an in rem right and affirmed the patentee's ability to restrict the exhaustion principle. *See, e.g., Monsanto v. McFarling*, 302 F.3d

1291 (Fed. Cir. 2002) (rejecting McFarling's claim that contract restriction in "Technology Agreement" limiting McFarling's use of patented seed to "single season," and prohibiting him from supplying seed to third parties or saving "any crop produced" from seed "for replanting" violated misuse and exhaustion doctrines); *B. Braun Med., Inc. v. Abbott Labs.*, 124 F.3d 1419, 1426 (Fed. Cir. 1997) (stating "exhaustion doctrine does not apply to an expressly conditional sale or license" because "[i]n such a transaction, it is more reasonable to infer that the parties negotiated a price that reflects only the value of the 'use' rights conferred by the patentee. As a result, express conditions accompanying the sale or license of a patented product are generally upheld"); *USM Corp. v. SPS Technologies, Inc.*, 694 F.2d 505, 510-511 (7th Cir. 1982) (stating "[t]he patentee who insists on limiting the freedom of his purchaser or licensee—whether to price, to use complementary inputs of the purchaser's choice, or to make competing items—will have to compensate the purchaser for the restriction by charging a lower price for the use of the patent"). Moreover, recall the repair-reconstruction doctrine comes into play when there is an unconditional sale. As such, the doctrine is inapplicable in the face of a conditional license. *See Mallinckrodt*, 976 F.2d at 709 (stating in the light of the single-use restriction, there is "no need to choose between repair and reconstruction" because "even repair of an unlicensed device constitutes infringement").

The Federal Circuit's approach to the role of contract and the scope of patent rights is perhaps better appreciated in the light of the proposition that a patentee has no duty to sell, license, or use his patented product. As the Supreme Court stated in *Continental Paper Bag Co. v. Eastern Paper Bag Co.*, 210 U.S. 405, 429 (1908), "exclusion may be said to have been of the very essence of the right conferred by the patent, as it is the privilege of any owner of property to use or not use it, without question of motive." *See also Ethyl Gasoline Corp. v. United States*, 309 U.S. 436, 457 (1940) (patentee has right to refuse to license or sell its patented product). (This proposition will be reexamined in section B on antitrust in the context of the refusal to deal cases.) The rationale of *Mallinckrodt* was applied in *Arizona Cartridge Remanufacturers Ass'n, Inc. v. Lexmark Int'l, Inc.*, 421 F.3d 981 (9th Cir. 2005). Lexmark made and sold laser printers and toner (printer) cartridges, and also remanufactured its cartridges. As part of its "Prebate" program, Lexmark gave consumers an upfront discount on its patented printer cartridges. The Prebate cartridges cost consumers on average $30 (or 20 percent) less than a regular cartridge. In return, Lexmark required the consumer to return the depleted cartridge to Lexmark or its agent. The Prebate cartridge package set forth the following terms on the outside of the package:

RETURN EMPTY CARTRIDGE TO L'MARK FOR REMANUFACTURING AND RECYCLING

Please read before opening. Opening of this package or using the patented cartridge inside confirms your acceptance of the following license agreement. The patented cartridge is sold at a special price subject to a restriction that it may be used only once. Following this initial use, you agree to return the empty cartridge only to L'Mark for remanufacturing and recycling. If you don't accept these terms, return the unopened package to your point of purchase. A regular price cartridge without these terms is available.

Consumers can opt to buy L'Mark cartridges without the Prebate post-sale restriction, but at the higher price. According to Lexmark, its post-sale restriction on reusing the Prebate cartridges does not require consumers to return the cartridge at all; it only precludes giving the cartridge to another remanufacturer. ACRA, which represents wholesalers that remanufacture emptied Lexmark printer cartridges for reuse, alleged that Lexmark engaged in anticompetitive behavior. The Ninth Circuit disagreed and held that the terms on the package created a valid contract, and that under *Mallinckrodt* Lexmark could restrict the use of its patented product.

2. **Quanta's *Effect on* Mallinckrodt?** The Supreme Court arguably chiseled away at the Federal Circuit's in rem view of patent rights, and qualified *Mallinckrodt's* reach and raised concerns for licensors who participate in markets with a significant number of downstream players. In *Quanta*, the license agreement neither expressly precluded Intel from selling its products for combination with non-Intel products, nor expressly authorized customers of Intel to combine Intel's products with non-Intel products. Under the terms of a separate Master Agreement, Intel was required to provide notice to its customers that its license from LG covered articles containing only Intel products, and that combination of Intel products with non-Intel products was not permitted.

Quanta purchased products from Intel (chipsets and microprocessors) that were covered by the license, and combined these products with non-Intel products to make computers. As a result, LG sued Quanta. The Supreme Court held that LG's patent rights were exhausted, noting that the license agreement between LG and Intel was unconditional, and therefore, Intel's sell of chip sets and micro processors to Quanta was authorized. According to the Court:

> Nothing in the License Agreement restricts Intel's right to sell its microprocessors and chipsets to purchasers who intend to combine them with non-Intel parts. [T]he question whether third parties received implied licenses is irrelevant because Quanta asserts its right to practice the patents based not on implied license but on exhaustion.

Id. at 636 (emphasis added).

An important question is what is *Quanta's* effect on *Mallinckrodt?* While this question plays out in the courts, a plausible argument can be made for a narrow reading of *Quanta*, one based largely on poor contract drafting. Clause 3.8 of the license agreement between LG and Intel provided:

> Notwithstanding anything to the contrary in this agreement, the parties agree that nothing herein shall in any way limit or alter the effect of patent exhaustion that would otherwise apply when a party hereto sells any of its licensed products.

The license agreement between LG and Intel did not set conditions (in contrast to the limitation in *Mallinckrodt, Monsanto,* and *General Talking Pictures*), or expressly preclude Intel from selling products that can be combined with non-Intel products, thus invoking exhaustion as a default rule was straightforward. And the Court did not directly address contractual reach-through conditions that were at play in *Mallinckrodt*. Thus, a license that expressly provides for a conditional sale may be enforceable. Indeed, the Court seemed to implicitly allow for some conditions, expressly stating "No conditions limited

Intel's authority to sell products substantially embodying the patents." *Id.* at 2122. This reading would be consistent with Supreme Court precedent. *See Adams v. Burke*, 84 U.S. 453, 456 (1873) ("The right to manufacture, the right to sell, and the right to use are each substantive rights, and may be granted or conferred separately by the patentee."); *General Talking Pictures Corp. v. Western Elec. Co.*, 304 U.S. 175, 181 (1938) ("Unquestionably, the owner of a patent may grant licenses to manufacture, use, or sell upon conditions not inconsistent with the scope of the monopoly."). *See also* Michael Risch, *Patent Challenges and Royalty Inflation*, 85 IND. L.J. 1003, 1012 n.55 (2010) (asserting *Quanta* implied "that patent exhaustion might not apply if license agreement forbade downstream sales").

But there is also a case to be made for a broader reading of *Quanta*, one whereby contractual limitations on exhaustion (like those present in *Mallinckrodt*) are prohibited. The Court—relying heavily on *United States v. Univis Lens Co.*—sees the exhaustion doctrine as playing a more prominent role in transactions involving patents. If the broad reading is correct, questions and concerns about licensing arrangements and business dealings become more important. Will patentees seek to maximize revenue from first-tier licensees, knowing that extracting royalties from downstream purchasers is an uncertain proposition? Will there be fewer deals if willing parties cannot pick and choose among a bundle of rights in the context of contracting? What if a potential licensee can only afford a stick or two from the entire bundle or if licensing something less than the full bundle is more efficient? Will transaction costs rise because the need for side-bargains designed to achieve their principal goals? Is the term "substantially embodied" likely to result in higher transaction costs and greater uncertainty for licensing parties? How much of the patented invention has to be embodied in downstream products before exhaustion kicks in? What practical steps would you employ in drafting licensing agreements on behalf of patentees? Should patentees—if feasible—seek to license end users directly rather than suppliers? And what about limiting the licensee's rights to making, but not using and selling, thus allowing the patentee to retain more control? Several of these questions will have to be addressed by the Federal Circuit through its common law powers, as well as by the response of private actors who participate in industries that have robust licensing arrangements.

The Federal Circuit had an opportunity to apply *Quanta* in *TransCore LP v. Electronic Transaction Consultants Corp.*, 563 F.3d 1271 (Fed. Cir. 2009). The patentee, TransCore, owned patents related to automated toll-road collection systems such as the E-ZPass. TransCore entered into a settlement agreement with Mark IV Industries, whereby Mark IV paid TransCore $4.5 million and TransCore provided an unconditional covenant not to sue Mark IV for patent infringement. Mark IV thereafter sold a toll collection system to ETC, who won a bid to install a toll-collection system in Illinois. TranCore sued ETC for patent infringement. The court—relying on *Quanta*—held that the covenant not to sue between TransCore and Mark IV is indistinguishable from a license with respect to "authorization," and therefore, exhausts the TransCore's rights:

The language of the TransCore-Mark IV settlement agreement is unambiguous: "[TransCore] agrees and covenants not to bring any demand, claim, lawsuit, or action against Mark IV for future infringement. . . ." This term, without apparent restriction or limitation, thus authorizes all acts that would otherwise be infringements: making, using, offering for sale, selling, or importing. TransCore did not, as it could have, limit this authorization to, for example, "making" or "using." And indeed, at oral argument, TransCore conceded that the TransCore-Mark IV settlement agreement does not include a restriction on sales.

Id. at 1276. What is noteworthy about this quote is that it strongly suggests that explicit settlement language limiting the covenant not to sue to "making" or "using" would not have exhausted TransCore's patent rights with respect to Mark IV's *selling* the automated toll road system. Presumably, similar limiting language in a license agreement would also have the same effect. In fact, the Federal Circuit quoted the *Quanta* Court's characterization of the LG-Intel license agreement to support its position that TransCore could have contractually limited the exhaustion principle: "[n]othing in the License Agreement restricts [licensee's] right to sell its microprocessors and chipsets to purchasers who intend to combine them with non-Intel parts. It broadly permits Intel to 'make, use, [or] sell' products free of [licensor's] patent claims." *Quanta*, 128 S. Ct. at 2121. As counsel, what other language would you employ to limit the application of exhaustion?

3. ***What Is the Remedy for Breach of the Condition of Sale?*** Assuming contractual limitations are permissible, the question becomes one of remedy. Namely, is the remedy for breach of contract based on contract law or patent law? Will a breach of contract lead to, on the one hand, a simple state law contract claim and contractual damages; or, on the other hand, patent infringement and accompanying damages? Recall the district court in *Mallinckrodt* held that "no restriction whatsoever could be imposed under the patent law, whether or not the restriction was enforceable under some other law." The Federal Circuit reversed this holding, noting that under *General Talking Pictures*, Mallinckrodt's field-of-use restriction was a "valid condition of the sale" that "was not excluded from enforcement under the patent law." In other words, a breach of the condition would result in patent infringement.

Germane to this point, the Supreme Court in *Quanta* wrote in footnote 7, "We note that the authorized nature of the sale to Quanta does not necessarily limit LGE's other contract rights. LGE's complaint does not include a breach-of-contract claim, and we express no opinion on whether contract damages might be available even though exhaustion operates to eliminate patent damages." Thus, the Supreme Court may arguably view the patentee's remedy as one of breach of contract, not patent infringement. In particular, the Court quoted language from the *Keeler* case: "It is . . . obvious that such a question would arise as a question of contract, and not as one under the inherent meaning and effect of the patent laws." Some commentators agree with this approach. *See* Patterson, *Contractual Expansion, supra* Comment 1, at 192 (arguing that "[i]f the conduct at issue would not be infringement in the absence of the license, as would be the case for permissible repair, a breach of a contract should not constitute patent infringement"). *But see General Talking Pictures, supra,* Comment 2 (holding breach of licensing terms leads to patent infringement). How the Federal Circuit interprets *Quanta* (and this footnote in particular) is an open question.

One concern patentees may have with contract law as an enforcement mechanism is that the patent owner/licensor will have to show privity with downstream purchasers, a showing that can be quite challenging. In *Quanta*, for instance, it is uncertain that LG would be able to successfully sue Quanta for breach of contract because Intel complied with the license it had with LG. In other words, LG would have difficulty proving privity with Quanta. And while Mallinckrodt may be able to establish privity with the hospitals that purchased the "Ultravent," it is doubtful Mallinckrodt could show the same type of relationship with Medipart.

4. *"Essential Features."* LG argued that Quanta's combination of the microprocessors and chipsets with other components infringed LG system patents that were not directly part of LGE-Intel relationship. Yet the Court held these system patents were exhausted because the microprocessors and chipsets were an "essential feature" of the resulting combination. As the Court wrote:

> exhaustion was triggered [in *Univis*] by the sale of the lens blanks because their *only reasonable and intended use* was to practice the patent and because they "embodie[d] *essential features* of [the] patented invention." 316 U.S., at 249-251. Each of those attributes is shared by the microprocessors and chipsets Intel sold to Quanta under the License Agreement.

553 U.S. at 631 (Emphasis added). The Court continued that, "LGE has suggested no reasonable use for the Intel Products other than incorporating them into computer systems that practice the LGE Patents." Justice Breyer captured this line of reasoning when he offered the following hypothetical during oral argument:

> Imagine that I want to buy some [patented] bicycle pedals, so I go to the bicycle shop. These are fabulous pedals. The inventor has licensed somebody to make them, and he sold them to the shop. . . . I go buy the pedals. I put it in my bicycle. I start pedaling down the road. . . . Why can't I look at this as saying that patent is exhausted, the patent on the pedals and the patent for those bicycles insofar as that patent for the bicycles says I have a patent on inserting the pedal into a bicycle.

See John W. Osborne, *Justice Breyer's Bicycle and the Ignored Elephant of Patent Exhaustion: An Avoidable Collision in Quanta v. LGE*, 7 J. MARSHALL REV. INTELL. PROP. L. 245 (quoting from Transcript of *Quanta* Oral Argument at 29-30). The Intel Products—specifically the microprocessors and chipsets—are like Justice Breyer's pedals. In Justice Breyer's hypothetical (and under *Univis*), exhaustion would apply to the *patent on the use* of the pedals if the pedals were deemed an "essential feature" of the use patent. Similarly, LG having a separate patent on the system does not preclude application of exhaustion once it was determined that the microprocessor and chipsets were essential features of the asserted system patent. As the Court noted, "Quanta was not required to make any creative or inventive decision when it added" the Intel products. In fact, "Intel all but practiced the patent itself by designing its products to practice the patents, lacking only the addition of standard parts."

5. *The Power of the Contract-Patent Combination.* The *Mallinckrodt* case highlights the power of using contract and property rights in combination. Recall in *Mallinckrodt* the single-use notice applied to the entire patented device, and therefore (assuming the license is valid) the hospitals reuse of the inhaler

would be direct infringement, and Medipart would be liable for indirect infringement. Contrast this scenario with *Kendall Co. v. Progressive Medical Technology, Inc.*, 85 F.3d 1570 (Fed. Cir. 1996). In *Kendall*, the patent related to a medical device — known as the SCD System — for applying compressive pressure to a patient's limbs in order to increase blood flow. The patent claiming the SCD System comprised several limitations, one of which was "elongated pressure sleeves." The sleeves were not covered by a separate patent. Kendall sold its SCD System to medical care facilities, with the understanding that customers would replace the pressure sleeves to reduce the risk of contamination. Indeed, Kendall marked "FOR SINGLE PATIENT USE ONLY. DO NOT REUSE" on the packaging of the replacement sleeves that it sold to its customers. Some patients purchased replacement sleeves from Kendall, but others purchased sleeves from the defendant, Progressive, which supplied the medical care facilities with the replacement sleeves. Kendall sued Progressive for indirect infringement. Relying on *Mallinckrodt*, Kendall asserted it placed a valid single-use restriction on the use of the sleeves.

The Federal Circuit held *Mallinckrodt* was not helpful to Kendall's position. According to the court:

> In . . . *Mallinckrodt*, the patentee, sold patented inhalers to hospitals subject to a notice that they were for "single use only." The "single use only" notice referred to reuse of the entire patented device. The hospitals *disregarded* that notice and permitted the defendant, Medipart, to collect used inhalers from the hospitals, recondition them, and sell them back to the hospitals for reuse. . . . Here, unlike the facts in *Mallinckrodt*, Kendall's customers *followed* rather than disregarded the single-use notice. They replaced the pressure sleeves after each use. Also, Kendall's customers did not agree to purchase replacement sleeves *from Kendall*. Kendall argued in the district court that such an obligation existed in view of the statement in its product literature that, "To ensure product safety and efficiency, the Kendall SCD Compression System must only be used with SCD Sleeves and Tubing Assemblies." The district court correctly recognized that this language did not have contractual significance; by its terms, it was only the manufacturer's recommendation for purposes of "safety and efficiency," not a customer obligation.

Id. at 1575-1576 (emphasis in original). Thus, in retrospect, Kendall should have done a few things differently. First, if possible, it should have patented the "elongated pressure sleeves," thus rendering Progressive a direct infringer. Second, Kendall could have crafted its contractual language in a more binding manner, perhaps requiring its customers to purchase the entire patented product, or purchase replacement sleeves from Kendall.

BOWMAN v. MONSANTO COMPANY
133 S. Ct. 1761 (2013)

Justice KAGAN delivered the opinion of the Court.

Under the doctrine of patent exhaustion, the authorized sale of a patented article gives the purchaser, or any subsequent owner, a right to use or resell that article. Such a sale, however, does not allow the purchaser to make new copies of the patented invention. The question in this case is whether a farmer who buys patented seeds may reproduce them through planting and harvesting without the patent holder's permission. We hold that he may not.

I

Respondent Monsanto invented a genetic modification that enables soybean plants to survive exposure to glyphosate, the active ingredient in many herbicides (including Monsanto's own Roundup). Monsanto markets soybean seed containing this altered genetic material as Roundup Ready seed. Farmers planting that seed can use a glyphosate-based herbicide to kill weeds without damaging their crops. Two patents issued to Monsanto cover various aspects of its Roundup Ready technology, including a seed incorporating the genetic alteration.

Monsanto sells, and allows other companies to sell, Roundup Ready soybean seeds to growers who assent to a special licensing agreement. That agreement permits a grower to plant the purchased seeds in one (and only one) season. He can then consume the resulting crop or sell it as a commodity, usually to a grain elevator or agricultural processor. But under the agreement, the farmer may not save any of the harvested soybeans for replanting, nor may he supply them to anyone else for that purpose. These restrictions reflect the ease of producing new generations of Roundup Ready seed. Because glyphosate resistance comes from the seed's genetic material, that trait is passed on from the planted seed to the harvested soybeans: Indeed, a single Roundup Ready seed can grow a plant containing dozens of genetically identical beans, each of which, if replanted, can grow another such plant—and so on and so on. The agreement's terms prevent the farmer from co-opting that process to produce his own Roundup Ready seeds, forcing him instead to buy from Monsanto each season.

Petitioner Vernon Bowman is a farmer in Indiana who, it is fair to say, appreciates Roundup Ready soybean seed. He purchased Roundup Ready each year, from a company affiliated with Monsanto, for his first crop of the season. In accord with the agreement just described, he used all of that seed for planting, and sold his entire crop to a grain elevator (which typically would resell it to an agricultural processor for human or animal consumption).

Bowman, however, devised a less orthodox approach for his second crop of each season. Because he thought such late-season planting "risky," he did not want to pay the premium price that Monsanto charges for Roundup Ready seed. He therefore went to a grain elevator; purchased "commodity soybeans" intended for human or animal consumption; and planted them in his fields.[1] Those soybeans came from prior harvests of other local farmers. And because most of those farmers also used Roundup Ready seed, Bowman could anticipate that many of the purchased soybeans would contain Monsanto's patented technology. When he applied a glyphosate-based herbicide to his fields, he confirmed that this was so; a significant proportion of the new plants survived the treatment, and produced in their turn a new crop of soybeans with the Roundup Ready trait. Bowman saved seed from that crop to use in his late-season planting

---

1. Grain elevators, as indicated above, purchase grain from farmers and sell it for consumption; under federal and state law, they generally cannot package or market their grain for use as agricultural seed. See 7 U.S.C. §1571; Ind. Code §15-15-1-32 (2012). But because soybeans are themselves seeds, nothing (except, as we shall see, the law) prevented Bowman from planting, rather than consuming, the product he bought from the grain elevator.

the next year—and then the next, and the next, until he had harvested eight crops in that way. Each year, that is, he planted saved seed from the year before (sometimes adding more soybeans bought from the grain elevator), sprayed his fields with glyphosate to kill weeds (and any non-resistant plants), and produced a new crop of glyphosate-resistant—*i.e.*, Roundup Ready—soybeans.

After discovering this practice, Monsanto sued Bowman for infringing its patents on Roundup Ready seed. Bowman raised patent exhaustion as a defense, arguing that Monsanto could not control his use of the soybeans because they were the subject of a prior authorized sale (from local farmers to the grain elevator). The District Court rejected that argument, and awarded damages to Monsanto of $84,456. The Federal Circuit affirmed. It reasoned that patent exhaustion did not protect Bowman because he had "created a newly infringing article." 657 F.3d, at 1348. The "right to use" a patented article following an authorized sale, the court explained, "does not include the right to construct an essentially new article on the template of the original, for the right to make the article remains with the patentee." *Ibid.* (brackets and internal quotation marks omitted). Accordingly, Bowman could not " 'replicate' Monsanto's patented technology by planting it in the ground to create newly infringing genetic material, seeds, and plants." *Ibid.*

We granted certiorari to consider the important question of patent law raised in this case, and now affirm.

II

The doctrine of patent exhaustion limits a patentee's right to control what others can do with an article embodying or containing an invention. Under the doctrine, "the initial authorized sale of a patented item terminates all patent rights to that item." *Quanta Computer, Inc. v. LG Electronics, Inc.*, 553 U.S. 617, 625 (2008). And by "exhaust[ing] the [patentee's] monopoly" in that item, the sale confers on the purchaser, or any subsequent owner, "the right to use [or] sell" the thing as he sees fit. *United States v. Univis Lens Co.*, 316 U.S. 241, 249-250 (1942). We have explained the basis for the doctrine as follows: "[T]he purpose of the patent law is fulfilled with respect to any particular article when the patentee has received his reward . . . by the sale of the article"; once that "purpose is realized the patent law affords no basis for restraining the use and enjoyment of the thing sold." *Id.*, at 251.

Consistent with that rationale, the doctrine restricts a patentee's rights only as to the "particular article" sold, *ibid.*; it leaves untouched the patentee's ability to prevent a buyer from making new copies of the patented item. "[T]he purchaser of the [patented] machine . . . does not acquire any right to construct another machine either for his own use or to be vended to another." *Mitchell v. Hawley*, 16 Wall. 544, 548 (1873); see *Wilbur-Ellis Co. v. Kuther*, 377 U.S. 422, 424 (1964) (holding that a purchaser's "reconstruction" of a patented machine "would impinge on the patentee's right '*to exclude others from making*' . . . the article" (quoting 35 U.S.C. §154 (1964 ed.))). Rather, "a second creation" of the patented item "call[s] the monopoly, conferred by the patent grant, into play for a second time." *Aro Mfg. Co. v. Convertible Top Replacement Co.*, 365 U.S. 336, 346 (1961). That is because the patent holder has "received his reward" only for the actual article sold, and not for subsequent recreations of it. *Univis*, 316 U.S., at 251. If the purchaser of that article could make and sell endless copies, the patent would effectively protect the invention for just a single sale.

Bowman himself disputes none of this analysis as a general matter: He forthrightly acknowledges the "well settled" principle "that the exhaustion doctrine does not extend to the right to 'make' a new product." Brief for Petitioner 37 (citing *Aro*, 365 U.S., at 346).

Unfortunately for Bowman, that principle decides this case against him. Under the patent exhaustion doctrine, Bowman could resell the patented soybeans he purchased from the grain elevator; so too he could consume the beans himself or feed them to his animals. Monsanto, although the patent holder, would have no business interfering in those uses of Roundup Ready beans. But the exhaustion doctrine does not enable Bowman to make *additional* patented soybeans without Monsanto's permission (either express or implied). And that is precisely what Bowman did. He took the soybeans he purchased home; planted them in his fields at the time he thought best; applied glyphosate to kill weeds (as well as any soy plants lacking the Roundup Ready trait); and finally harvested more (many more) beans than he started with. That is how "to 'make' a new product," to use Bowman's words, when the original product is a seed. See Webster's Third New International Dictionary 1363 (1961) ("make" means "cause to exist, occur, or appear," or more specifically, "plant and raise (a crop)"). Because Bowman thus reproduced Monsanto's patented invention, the exhaustion doctrine does not protect him.[3]

Were the matter otherwise, Monsanto's patent would provide scant benefit. After inventing the Roundup Ready trait, Monsanto would, to be sure, "receiv[e] [its] reward" for the first seeds it sells. *Univis*, 316 U.S., at 251. But in short order, other seed companies could reproduce the product and market it to growers, thus depriving Monsanto of its monopoly. And farmers themselves need only buy the seed once, whether from Monsanto, a competitor, or (as here) a grain elevator. The grower could multiply his initial purchase, and then multiply that new creation, *ad infinitum*—each time profiting from the patented seed without compensating its inventor. Bowman's late-season plantings offer a prime illustration. After buying beans for a single harvest, Bowman saved enough seed each year to reduce or eliminate the need for additional purchases. Monsanto still held its patent, but received no gain from Bowman's annual production and sale of Roundup Ready soybeans. The exhaustion doctrine is limited to the "particular item" sold to avoid just such a mismatch between invention and reward.

Our holding today also follows from *J.E.M. Ag Supply, Inc. v. Pioneer Hi-Bred Int'l, Inc.*, 534 U.S. 124 (2001). We considered there whether an inventor could get a patent on a seed or plant, or only a certificate issued under the Plant Variety Protection Act (PVPA), 7 U.S.C. §2321 *et seq*. We decided a patent was available, rejecting the claim that the PVPA implicitly repealed the Patent Act's coverage of seeds and plants. On our view, the two statutes established different, but

---

3. This conclusion applies however Bowman acquired Roundup Ready seed: The doctrine of patent exhaustion no more protected Bowman's reproduction of the seed he purchased for his first crop (from a Monsanto-affiliated seed company) than the beans he bought for his second (from a grain elevator). The difference between the two purchases was that the first—but not the second—came with a license from Monsanto to plant the seed and then harvest and market one crop of beans. We do not here confront a case in which Monsanto (or an affiliated seed company) sold Roundup Ready to a farmer without an express license agreement. For reasons we explain below, we think that case unlikely to arise. And in the event it did, the farmer might reasonably claim that the sale came with an implied license to plant and harvest one soybean crop.

not conflicting schemes: The requirements for getting a patent "are more stringent than those for obtaining a PVP certificate, and the protections afforded" by a patent are correspondingly greater. *J.E.M.*, 534 U.S., at 142. Most notable here, we explained that only a patent holder (not a certificate holder) could prohibit "[a] farmer who legally purchases and plants" a protected seed from saving harvested seed "for replanting." *Id.*, at 140; see *id.*, at 143 (noting that the Patent Act, unlike the PVPA, contains "no exemptio[n]" for "saving seed"). That statement is inconsistent with applying exhaustion to protect conduct like Bowman's. If a sale cut off the right to control a patented seed's progeny, then (contrary to *J.E.M.*) the patentee could *not* prevent the buyer from saving harvested seed. Indeed, the patentee could not stop the buyer from *selling* such seed, which even a PVP certificate owner (who, recall, is supposed to have fewer rights) can usually accomplish. See 7 U.S.C. §§2541, 2543. Those limitations would turn upside-down the statutory scheme *J.E.M.* described.

Bowman principally argues that exhaustion should apply here because seeds are meant to be planted. The exhaustion doctrine, he reminds us, typically prevents a patentee from controlling the use of a patented product following an authorized sale. And in planting Roundup Ready seeds, Bowman continues, he is merely using them in the normal way farmers do. Bowman thus concludes that allowing Monsanto to interfere with that use would "creat[e] an impermissible exception to the exhaustion doctrine" for patented seeds and other "self-replicating technologies."

But it is really Bowman who is asking for an unprecedented exception — to what he concedes is the "well settled" rule that "the exhaustion doctrine does not extend to the right to 'make' a new product." Reproducing a patented article no doubt "uses" it after a fashion. But as already explained, we have always drawn the boundaries of the exhaustion doctrine to exclude that activity, so that the patentee retains an undiminished right to prohibit others from making the thing his patent protects. *See, e.g., Cotton-Tie Co. v. Simmons*, 106 U.S. 89, 93-94 (1882) (holding that a purchaser could not "use" the buckle from a patented cotton-bale tie to "make" a new tie). That is because, once again, if simple copying were a protected use, a patent would plummet in value after the first sale of the first item containing the invention. The undiluted patent monopoly, it might be said, would extend not for 20 years (as the Patent Act promises), but for only one transaction. And that would result in less incentive for innovation than Congress wanted. Hence our repeated insistence that exhaustion applies only to the particular item sold, and not to reproductions.

Nor do we think that rule will prevent farmers from making appropriate use of the Roundup Ready seed they buy. Bowman himself stands in a peculiarly poor position to assert such a claim. As noted earlier, the commodity soybeans he purchased were intended not for planting, but for consumption. Indeed, Bowman conceded in deposition testimony that he knew of no other farmer who employed beans bought from a grain elevator to grow a new crop. So a non-replicating use of the commodity beans at issue here was not just available, but standard fare. And in the more ordinary case, when a farmer purchases Roundup Ready seed *qua* seed — that is, seed intended to grow a crop — he will be able to plant it. Monsanto, to be sure, conditions the farmer's ability to reproduce Roundup Ready; but it does not — could not realistically — preclude all planting. No sane farmer, after all, would buy the product without some ability to grow soybeans from it. And so Monsanto, predictably enough, sells Roundup

Ready seed to farmers with a license to use it to make a crop. Applying our usual rule in this context therefore will allow farmers to benefit from Roundup Ready, even as it rewards Monsanto for its innovation.

Still, Bowman has another seeds-are-special argument: that soybeans naturally "self-replicate or 'sprout' unless stored in a controlled manner," and thus "it was the planted soybean, not Bowman" himself, that made replicas of Monsanto's patented invention. Brief for Petitioner 42; see Tr. of Oral Arg. 14 ("[F]armers, when they plant seeds, they don't exercise any control . . . over their crop" or "over the creative process"). But we think that blame-the-bean defense tough to credit. Bowman was not a passive observer of his soybeans' multiplication; or put another way, the seeds he purchased (miraculous though they might be in other respects) did not spontaneously create eight successive soybean crops. As we have explained, Bowman devised and executed a novel way to harvest crops from Roundup Ready seeds without paying the usual premium. He purchased beans from a grain elevator anticipating that many would be Roundup Ready; applied a glyphosate-based herbicide in a way that culled any plants without the patented trait; and saved beans from the rest for the next season. He then planted those Roundup Ready beans at a chosen time; tended and treated them, including by exploiting their patented glyphosate-resistance; and harvested many more seeds, which he either marketed or saved to begin the next cycle. In all this, the bean surely figured. But it was Bowman, and not the bean, who controlled the reproduction (unto the eighth generation) of Monsanto's patented invention.

Our holding today is limited—addressing the situation before us, rather than every one involving a self-replicating product. We recognize that such inventions are becoming ever more prevalent, complex, and diverse. In another case, the article's self-replication might occur outside the purchaser's control. Or it might be a necessary but incidental step in using the item for another purpose. Cf. 17 U.S.C. §117(a)(1) ("[I]t is not [a copyright] infringement for the owner of a copy of a computer program to make . . . another copy or adaptation of that computer program provide[d] that such a new copy or adaptation is created as an essential step in the utilization of the computer program"). We need not address here whether or how the doctrine of patent exhaustion would apply in such circumstances. In the case at hand, Bowman planted Monsanto's patented soybeans solely to make and market replicas of them, thus depriving the company of the reward patent law provides for the sale of each article. Patent exhaustion provides no haven for that conduct. We accordingly affirm the judgment of the Court of Appeals for the Federal Circuit.

It is so ordered.

Comments

1. ***Replication as Reconstruction.*** Monsanto's patented seed is a self-replicating technology. While Mr. Bowman or any farmer could successfully claim exhaustion applies to the use of a lawfully purchased patented seed, the Court held the exhaustion principle does not apply to subsequent generations of the patented seed. Bowman unsuccessfully argued that he did not make (or reconstruct) the next generation seed that was subject to an original

purchase; rather, it was the seed that replicated itself. As Bowman stated: "If patent rights in seeds sold in an authorized sale are exhausted, patent rights in seeds grown by lawful planting must be exhausted as well." The Court was unpersuaded by this "blame-the-bean defense" because "Bowman was not a passive observer of his soybeans' multiplication." In short, "it was Bowman, and not the bean, who controlled the reproduction (unto the eighth generation) of Monsanto's patented invention." If the holding were otherwise, stated the Court, "a patent would plummet in value after the first sale of the first item containing the invention" and "[t]he undiluted patent monopoly, it might be said, would extend not for 20 years (as the Patent Act promises), but for only one transaction."

The Federal Circuit also did not apply the exhaustion doctrine, because the "seeds grown from the original batch had never been sold," and therefore, the "price paid by the purchaser 'reflects only the value of the use rights conferred by the patentee.'" 657 F.3d at 1347 (citing *B. Braun Med.*). For the Federal Circuit, "[e]ven if Monsanto's patent rights in the commodity seeds are exhausted, such a conclusion would be of no consequence because once a grower, like Bowman, plants the commodity seeds containing Monsanto's Roundup Ready® technology and the next generation of seed develops, the grower has created a newly infringing article." *Id.* at 1348. The self-replicating capacity of the patented seeds does not grant Mr. Bowman the right to use replicated copies of the technology, and "'[a]pplying the first sale doctrine to subsequent generations of self-replicating technology would eviscerate the rights of the patent holder'" (citing *Scruggs*). *Id.* The court concluded, quoting from *Jazz Photo*, "[t]he right to use 'do[es] not include the right to construct an essentially new article on the template of the original, for the right to make the article remains with the patentee.'" *Id.*

The Federal Circuit also disagreed with Mr. Bowman's argument, which relied on *Quanta*, that the patented seeds "substantially embody" later generations. At least with respect to commodity seeds "nothing in the record indicates that the 'only reasonable and intended use of commodity seeds is for replanting them to create new seeds.'" As the court stated:

> Indeed, there are various uses for commodity seeds, including use as feed. While farmers, like Bowman, may have the right to use commodity seeds as feed, or for any other conceivable use, they cannot "replicate" Monsanto's patented technology by planting it in the ground to create newly infringing genetic material, seeds, and plants.

Id. at 1348. Interestingly, the Solicitor General advised against granting certiorari, but was nonetheless very critical of Federal Circuit's precedent on exhaustion, highlighting that it was inconsistent with Supreme Court precedent.

2. **Bowman, *the Use of Contract, and Conditional Sales.*** The *Bowman* case tells us very little about the appropriate use of contract to restrict the exhaustion principle. Monsanto's "Technology Agreement" did not come into play because Bowman impermissibly used subsequent generations of the patented seed, which, under the repair-reconstruction doctrine, leads to patent infringement regardless of the presence of a single use (or field-of-use) contract. *See* Comments following *Jazz Photo* in section A.1. As the *Bowman* Court stated in footnote 3, the exhaustion doctrine does not protect Bowman "however [he] acquired Roundup Ready seed."

The interesting question, one that neither *Quanta* nor *Bowman* directly addressed, is how would the Supreme Court view a patentee who — like in *Mallinckrokdt* — contractually limited the exhaustion doctrine against an alleged infringer who breaches the contract and re-uses the actual patented item sold (i.e., did not make or use a new item). In fact, during oral argument, Justice Sotomayor asked whether "we were explicit enough in *Quanta* and we don't have to address whatever lingering confusion the Federal Circuit may have with respect to conditional sales at all in this case?"

Currently, this breach of contract leads to patent infringement under *Mallinckrokdt*. In footnote 7 of *Quanta*, however, the Court recognized LGE's contract rights, but suggested that a breach of contract in this context would lead to contract damages, not damages associated with patent infringement.

c. Contractual Provisions Relating to Royalty Payments

BRULOTTE v. THYS CO.
379 U.S. 29 (1964)

Justice DOUGLAS delivered the opinion of the Court.

Respondent, owner of various patents for hop-picking, sold a machine to each of the petitioners for a flat sum and issued a license for its use. Under that license there is payable a minimum royalty of $500 for each hop picking season or $3.33 1/3 per 200 pounds of dried hops harvested by the machine, whichever is greater. The licenses by their terms may not be assigned nor may the machines be removed from Yakima County. The licenses issued to petitioners listed 12 patents relating to hop-picking machines; but only seven were incorporated into the machines sold to and licensed for use by petitioners. Of those seven all expired on or before 1957. But the licenses issued by respondent to them continued for terms beyond that date.

Petitioners refused to make royalty payments accruing both before and after the expiration of the patents. This suit followed. One defense was misuse of the patents through extension of the license agreements beyond the expiration date of the patents. The trial court rendered judgment for respondent and the Supreme Court of Washington affirmed. The case is here on a writ of certiorari.

We conclude that the judgment below must be reversed insofar as it allows royalties to be collected which accrued after the last of the patents incorporated into the machines had expired.

The Constitution by Art. I, §8 authorizes Congress to secure "for limited times" to inventors "the exclusive right" to their discoveries. Congress exercised that power by 35 U.S.C. §154 which provides in part as follows:

> Every patent shall contain a short title of the invention and a grant to the patentee, his heirs or assigns, for the term of seventeen years, of the right to exclude others from making, using, or selling the invention throughout the United States, referring to the specification for the particulars thereof. . . .

The right to make, the right to sell, and the right to use "may be granted or conferred separately by the patentee." *Adams v. Burke*, 17 Wall. 453, 456. But these rights become public property once the 17-year period expires. As stated by Chief Justice Stone, speaking for the Court in *Scott Paper Co. v. Marcalus Mfg. Co.*, 326 U.S. 249, 256:

> . . . any attempted reservation or continuation in the patentee or those claiming under him of the patent monopoly, after the patent expires, whatever the legal device employed, runs counter to the policy and purpose of the patent laws.

The Supreme Court of Washington held that in the present case the period during which royalties were required was only "a reasonable amount of time over which to spread the payments for the use of the patent." 382 P.2d, at 275. But there is intrinsic evidence that the agreements were not designed with that limited view. As we have seen, [footnote omitted] the purchase price in each case was a flat sum, the annual payments not being part of the purchase price but royalties for use of the machine during that year. The royalty payments due for the post-expiration period are by their terms for use during that period, and are not deferred payments for use during the pre-expiration period. Nor is the case like the hypothetical ones put to us where non patented articles are marketed at prices based on use. The machines in issue here were patented articles and the royalties exacted were the same for the post-expiration period as they were for the period of the patent. That is peculiarly significant in this case in view of other provisions of the license agreements. The license agreements prevent assignment of the machines or their removal from Yakima County after, as well as before, the expiration of the patents.

Those restrictions are apt and pertinent to protection of the patent monopoly; and their applicability to the post-expiration period is a telltale sign that the licensor was using the licenses to project its monopoly beyond the patent period. They forcefully negate the suggestion that we have here a bare arrangement for a sale or a lease at an undetermined price based on use. The sale or lease of unpatented machines on long-term payments based on a deferred purchase price or on use would present wholly different considerations. Those arrangements seldom rise to the level of a federal question. But patents arc in the federal domain; and "whatever the legal device employed" (*Scott Paper Co. v. Marcalus Mfg. Co.*, 326 U.S., at 256) a projection of the patent monopoly after the patent expires is not enforceable. The present licenses draw no line between the term of the patent and the post-expiration period. The same provisions as respects both use and royalties are applicable to each. The contracts are, therefore, on their face a bald attempt to exact the same terms and conditions for the period after the patents have expired as they do for the monopoly period. We are, therefore, unable to conjecture what the bargaining position of the parties might have been and what resultant arrangement might have emerged had the provision for post-expiration royalties been divorced from the patent and nowise subject to its leverage.

In light of those considerations, we conclude that a patentee's use of a royalty agreement that projects beyond the expiration date of the patent is unlawful per se. If that device were available to patentees, the free market visualized for the post-expiration period would be subject to monopoly influences that have no proper place there.

Automatic Radio Mfg. Co. v. Hazeltine Research, Inc., 339 U.S. 827, is not in point. While some of the patents under that license apparently had expired, the royalties claimed were not for a period when all of them had expired. That license covered several hundred patents and the royalty was based on the licensee's sales, even when no patents were used. The Court held that the computation of royalty payments by that formula was a convenient and reasonable device. We decline the invitation to extend it so as to project the patent monopoly beyond the 17-year period.

A patent empowers the owner to exact royalties as high as he can negotiate with the leverage of that monopoly. But to use that leverage to project those royalty payments beyond the life of the patent is analogous to an effort to enlarge the monopoly of the patent by tieing the sale or use of the patented article to the purchase or use of unpatented ones. *See Ethyl Gasoline Corp. v. United States*, 309 U.S. 436; *Mercoid Corp. v. Mid-Continent Inv. Co.*, 320 U.S. 661, 664-665, and cases cited. The exaction of royalties for use of a machine after the patent has expired is an assertion of monopoly power in the post-expiration period when, as we have seen, the patent has entered the public domain. We share the views of the Court of Appeals in *Ar-Tik Systems, Inc. v. Dairy Queen, Inc.*, 3 Cir., 302 F.2d 496, 510, that after expiration of the last of the patents incorporated in the machines "the grant of patent monopoly was spent" and that an attempt to project it into another term by continuation of the licensing agreement is unenforceable.

Justice HARLAN, dissenting.

The Court holds that the Thys Company unlawfully misused its patent monopoly by contracting with purchasers of its patented machines for royalty payments based on use beyond the patent term. I think that more discriminating analysis than the Court has seen fit to give this case produces a different result.

The patent laws prohibit post-expiration restrictions on the use of patented ideas; they have no bearing on use restrictions upon nonpatented, tangible machines. We have before us a mixed case involving the sale of a tangible machine which incorporates an intangible, patented idea. My effort in what follows is to separate out these two notions, to show that there is no substantial restriction on the use of the Thys idea, and to demonstrate that what slight restriction there may be is less objectionable than other post-expiration use restrictions which are clearly acceptable.

I.

It surely cannot be questioned that Thys could have lawfully set a fixed price for its machine and extended credit terms beyond the patent period. It is equally unquestionable, I take it, that if Thys had had no patent or if its patent had expired, it could have sold its machines at a flexible, undetermined price based on use; for example, a phonograph record manufacturer could sell a recording of a song in the public domain to a juke-box owner for an undetermined consideration based on the number of times the record was played.

Conversely it should be equally clear that if Thys licensed another manufacturer to produce hop-picking machines incorporating any of the Thys patents, royalties could not be exacted beyond the patent term. Such royalties would restrict the manufacturer's exploitation of the idea after it falls into the public domain, and no such restriction should be valid. To give another example unconnected with a tangible machine, a song writer could charge a royalty every time his song—his idea—was sung for profit during the period of copyright. But once the song falls into the public domain each and every member of the public should be free to sing it.

In fact Thys sells both a machine and the use of an idea. The company should be free to restrict the use of its machine, as in the first two examples given above. It may not restrict the use of its patented idea once it has fallen into the public domain. Whether it has done so must be the point of inquiry.

Consider the situation as of the day the patent monopoly ends. Any manufacturer is completely free to produce Thys-type hop-pickers. The farmer who has previously purchased a Thys machine is free to buy and use any other kind of machine whether or not it incorporates the Thys idea, or make one himself if he is able. Of course, he is not entitled as against Thys to the free use of any Thys machine. The Court's opinion must therefore ultimately rest on the proposition that the purchasing farmer is restricted in using his particular machine, embodying as it does an application of the patented idea, by the fact that royalties are tied directly to use.

To test this proposition I again put a hypothetical. Assume that a Thys contract called for neither an initial flat-sum payment nor any annual minimum royalties; Thys' sole recompense for giving up ownership of its machine was a royalty payment extending beyond the patent term based on use, without any requirement either to use the machine or not to use a competitor's. A moment's thought reveals that, despite the clear restriction on use both before and after the expiration of the patent term, the arrangement would involve no misuse of patent leverage. Unless the Court's opinion rests on technicalities of contract draftsmanship and not on the economic substance of the transaction, the distinction between the hypothetical and the actual case lies only in the cumulative investment consisting of the initial and minimum payments independent of use, which the purchaser obligated himself to make to Thys. I fail to see why this distinguishing feature should be critical. If anything the investment will encourage the purchaser to use his machine in order to amortize the machine's fixed cost over as large a production base as possible. Yet the gravamen of the majority opinion is restriction, not encouragement, of use.

II.

The essence of the majority opinion may lie in some notion that "patent leverage" being used by Thys to exact use payments extending beyond the patent term somehow allows Thys to extract more onerous payments from the farmers than would otherwise be obtainable. If this be the case, the Court must in some way distinguish long-term use payments from long-term installment payments of a flat-sum purchase price. For the danger which it seems to fear would appear to inhere equally in both, and as I read the Court's opinion, the latter type of arrangement is lawful despite the fact that failure to pay an installment under a conditional sales contract would permit the seller to recapture the machine, thus terminating—not merely restricting—the farmer's use of it. Furthermore, since the judgments against petitioners were based almost entirely on defaults in paying the $500 minimums and not on failures to pay for above minimum use, any such distinction of extended use payments and extended installments, even if accepted, would not justify eradicating all petitioners' obligations beyond the patent term, but only those based on use above the stated minimums; for the minimums by themselves, being payable whether or not a machine has been used, are precisely identical in substantive economic effect to flat installments.

In fact a distinction should not be accepted based on the assumption that Thys, which exploits its patents by selling its patented machines rather than licensing others to manufacture them, can use its patent leverage to exact more onerous payments from farmers by gearing price to use instead of charging a flat sum. Four possible situations must be considered. The purchasing farmer could overestimate, exactly estimate, underestimate, or have no firm estimate of his use requirements for a Thys machine. If he overestimates or exactly estimates, the farmer will be fully aware of what the machine will cost him in the long run, and it is unrealistic to suppose that in such circumstances he would be willing to pay more to have the machine on use than on straight terms. If the farmer underestimates, the thought may be that Thys will take advantage of him; but surely the farmer is in a better position than Thys or anyone else to estimate his own requirements and is hardly in need of the Court's protection in this respect. If the farmer has no fixed estimate of his use requirements he may have good business reasons entirely unconnected with "patent leverage" for wanting payments tied to use, and may indeed be willing to pay more in the long run to obtain such an arrangement. One final example should illustrate my point:

At the time when the Thys patent term still has a few years to run, a farmer who has been picking his hops by hand comes into the Thys retail outlet to inquire about the mechanical pickers. The salesman concludes his description of the advantages of the Thys machine with the price tag—$20,000. Value to the farmer depends completely on the use he will derive from the machine; he is willing to obligate himself on long credit terms to pay $10,000, but unless the machine can substantially outpick his old hand-picking methods, it is worth no more to him. He therefore offers to pay $2,000 down, $400 annually for 20 years, and an additional payment during the contract term for any production he can derive from the machine over and above the minimum amount he could pick by hand. Thys accepts, and by doing so, according to the majority, commits a per se misuse of its patent. I cannot believe that this is good law.

Furthermore, it should not be overlooked that we are dealing here with a patent, not an antitrust, case, there being no basis in the record for concluding that Thys' arrangements with its licensees were such as to run afoul of the antitrust laws.

III.

The possibility remains that the Court is basing its decision on the technical framing of the contract and would have treated the case differently if title had been declared to pass at the termination instead of the outset of the contract term, or if the use payments had been verbally disassociated from the patent licenses and described as a convenient means of spreading out payments for the machine. If indeed the impact of the opinion is that Thys must redraft its contracts to achieve the same economic results, the decision is not only wrong, but conspicuously ineffectual.

Comments

1. *Criticism of* **Brulotte.** The *Brulotte* decision has not been immune from criticism (as you will see after reading Judge Posner's *Scheiber* opinion, below). Building on Justice Harlan's dissent, William Landes and Richard Posner write:

After the patent expires, anyone can make the patented process or product without being guilty of patent infringement. As the patent can no longer be used to exclude anybody from such production, expiration has accomplished what is was supposed to accomplish. If the licensee agrees to continue paying royalties after the patent expires, the royalty rate will be lower during the period before expiration. The duration of the patent fixes the limit of the patentee's power to extract royalties; it is a detail whether he extracts them at a higher rate over a shorter period of time or at a lower rate over a longer period of time.

WILLIAM M. LANDES & RICHARD A. POSNER, THE ECONOMIC STRUCTURE OF INTELLECTUAL PROPERTY LAW 380 (2003). *See also* Rochelle Cooper Dreyfuss, *Dethroning* Lear: *Licensee Estoppel and the Incentive to Innovate*, 72 VA. L. REV. 677, 709 (1986) (noting that the *Brulotte* decision is "vulnerable on several grounds").

2. *Many Ways to Slice a License.* One of the primary criticisms of *Brulotte* is that it ignores the preferences of the contracting parties. A license—which is nothing more than a contract—can provide for a variety of payment methods. A licensee can agree to pay all royalties at the end or the beginning of the term; or prefer to make installment payments that go beyond the patent's statutory term simply because he was financially unable to make the necessary payments during the life of the patent.

SCHEIBER v. DOLBY LABORATORIES, INC.

293 F.3d 1014 (7th Cir. 2002)

POSNER, Circuit Judge.

The plaintiff in a suit to enforce a patent licensing agreement appeals to us from the grant of summary judgment to the defendants, Dolby for short. Scheiber, the plaintiff, a musician turned inventor who held U.S. and Canadian patents on the audio system known as "surround sound," sued Dolby in 1983 for infringement of his patents. The parties settled the suit by agreeing that Scheiber would license his patents to Dolby in exchange for royalties. The last U.S. patent covered by the agreement was scheduled to expire in May 1993, while the last Canadian patent was not scheduled to expire until September 1995. During the settlement negotiations Dolby suggested to Scheiber that in exchange for a lower royalty rate the license agreement provide that royalties on all the patents would continue until the Canadian patent expired, including, therefore, patents that had already expired. That way Dolby could, it hoped, pass on the entire royalty expense to its sublicensees without their balking at the rate. Scheiber acceded to the suggestion and the agreement was drafted accordingly, but Dolby later refused to pay royalties on any patent after it expired, precipitating this suit. Federal jurisdiction over the suit is based on diversity of citizenship, because a suit to enforce a patent licensing agreement does not arise under federal patent law.

Dolby argues that the duty to pay royalties on any patent covered by the agreement expired by the terms of the agreement itself as soon as the patent expired, because the royalties were to be based on Dolby's sales of equipment within the scope of the patents and once a patent expires, Dolby argues, there is no equipment within its scope. The argument would make meaningless the provision that Dolby itself proposed for continuing the payment of royalties until the last patent expired. Anyway the reference to equipment within the scope of the patent was clearly meant to *identify* the equipment on which royalties would be based (Dolby makes equipment that does not utilize Scheiber's patents as well as equipment that does) rather than to limit the duration of the obligation to pay royalties.

Dolby's principal argument is that the Supreme Court held in a decision that has never been overruled that a patent owner may not enforce a contract for the payment of patent royalties beyond the expiration date of the patent. The decision was *Brulotte v. Thys Co.*, 379 U.S. 29 (1964), dutifully followed by lower courts. *Brulotte* involved an agreement licensing patents that expired at different dates, just like this case; the two cases are indistinguishable. The decision has, it is true, been severely, and as it seems to us, with all due respect, justly, criticized, beginning with Justice Harlan's dissent, 379 U.S. at 34, and continuing with our opinion in *USM Corp. v. SPS Technologies, Inc.*, 694 F.2d 505, 510-11 (7th Cir. 1982). The Supreme Court's majority opinion reasoned that by extracting a promise to continue paying royalties after expiration of the patent, the patentee extends the patent beyond the term fixed in the patent statute and therefore in violation of the law. That is not true. After the patent expires, anyone can make the patented process or product without being guilty of patent infringement. The patent can no longer be used to exclude anybody from such production. Expiration thus accomplishes what it is supposed to accomplish. For a licensee in accordance with a provision in the license agreement to go on paying royalties after the patent expires does not extend the duration of the patent either technically or practically, because, as this case demonstrates, if the licensee agrees to continue paying royalties after the patent expires the royalty rate will be lower. The duration of the patent fixes the limit of the patentee's power to extract royalties; it is a detail whether he extracts them at a higher rate over a shorter period of time or a lower rate over a longer period of time.

This insight is not original with us. "The *Brulotte* rule incorrectly assumes that a patent license has significance after the patent terminates. When the patent term ends, the exclusive right to make, use or sell the licensed invention also ends. Because the invention is available to the world, the license in fact ceases to have value. Presumably, licensees know this when they enter into a licensing agreement. If the licensing agreement calls for royalty payments beyond the patent term, the parties base those payments on the licensees' assessment of the value of the license during the patent period. These payments, therefore, do not represent an extension in time of the patent monopoly. . . . Courts do not remove the obligation of the consignee to pay because payment after receipt is an extension of market power—it is simply a division of the payment-for-delivery transaction. Royalties beyond the patent term are no different. If royalties are calculated on post-patent term sales, the calculation is simply a risk-shifting credit arrangement between patentee and licensee. The arrangement can be no more than that, because the patentee at that time has nothing else to sell." Harold See & Frank M. Caprio, *The Trouble with* Brulotte: *The Patent Royalty Term and Patent Monopoly Extension*, 1990 UTAH L. REV. 813, 814, 851.

These criticisms might be wide of the mark if *Brulotte* had been based on an interpretation of the patent clause of the Constitution, or of the patent statute or any other statute; but it seems rather to have been a free-floating product of a misplaced fear of monopoly ("a patentee's use of a royalty agreement that projects beyond the expiration date of the patent is unlawful *per se*. If that device were available to patentees, the free market visualized for the post-expiration period would be subject to monopoly influences that have no proper place there," 379 U.S. at 32-33) that was not even tied to one of the antitrust statutes. The doctrinal basis of the decision was the doctrine of patent misuse, of which more later.

A patent confers a monopoly, and the longer the term of the patent the greater the monopoly. The limitation of the term of a patent, besides being commanded by the Constitution, and necessary to avoid impossible tracing problems (imagine if some caveman had gotten a perpetual patent on the wheel), serves to limit the monopoly power conferred on the patentee. But as we have pointed out, charging royalties beyond the term of the patent does not lengthen the patentee's monopoly; it merely alters the timing of royalty payments. This would be obvious if the license agreement between Scheiber and Dolby had become effective a month before the last patent expired. The parties could have agreed that Dolby would pay royalties for the next 100 years, but obviously the royalty rate would be minuscule because of the imminence of the patent's expiration.

However, we have no authority to overrule a Supreme Court decision no matter how dubious its reasoning strikes us, or even how out of touch with the Supreme Court's current thinking the decision seems. In *Agostini v. Felton*, 521 U.S. 203, 237 (1997), the Supreme Court "reaffirm[ed] that '[i]f a precedent of this Court has direct application in a case, yet appears to rest on reasons rejected in some other line of decisions, the Court of Appeals should follow the case which directly controls, leaving to this Court the prerogative of overruling its own decisions,'" quoting *Rodriguez de Quijas v. Shearson/American Express, Inc.*, 490 U.S. 477, 484 (1989). In *Khan*, the lower court (namely us), pointing out that the Supreme Court decision that we refused to declare defunct was clearly out of touch with the Court's current antitrust thinking, invited the Court to reverse, see *Khan v. State Oil Co.*, 93 F.3d 1358, 1363 (7th Cir. 1996), vacated and remanded, and it did, but pointedly noted that we had been right to leave the execution and interment of the Court's discredited precedent to the Court.

Now it is true that in *Aronson v. Quick Point Pencil Co.*, 440 U.S. 257 (1979), a case decided some years after *Brulotte*, the Supreme Court upheld an agreement superficially similar to the one invalidated in *Brulotte* and at issue in the present case: a patent applicant granted a license for the invention it hoped to patent to a firm that agreed, if a patent were not granted, to pay the inventor-applicant royalties for as long as the firm sold products embodying the invention. The Court was careful to distinguish *Brulotte*, and not a single Justice suggested that any cloud had been cast over the earlier decision. Since no patent was granted, the doctrine of patent misuse could not be brought into play, and there was no other federal ground for invalidating the license. The Court emphasized that *Brulotte* had been based on the "leverage" that the patent had granted the patentee to extract royalties beyond the date of expiration, 440 U.S. at 265, and that leverage was of course missing in *Aronson*.

If *Aronson* and *Brulotte* were inconsistent with each other and the Court had not reaffirmed *Brulotte* in *Aronson*, then we would have to follow *Aronson*, the later opinion, since to follow *Brulotte* in those circumstances would be to overrule *Aronson*. But the reaffirmation of *Brulotte* in *Aronson* tells us that the Court did not deem the cases inconsistent, and so, whether we agree or not, we have no warrant for declaring *Brulotte* overruled.

Scheiber argues further, however, that *Brulotte* has been superseded by a 1988 amendment to the patent statute which provides, so far as bears on this case, that "no patent owner otherwise entitled to relief for infringement . . . shall be . . . deemed guilty of misuse or illegal extension of the patent right by reason of his having . . . conditioned the license of any rights to the patent or the sale of the patented product on the acquisition of a license to rights in another patent or purchase of a separate product" unless the patentee has market power in the market for the conditioning product (which is not argued here). 35 U.S.C. §271(d)(5). The statute is doubly inapplicable to this case. It merely limits defenses to infringement suits, and Scheiber isn't suing for infringement; he's suing to enforce a license agreement. He can't sue for infringement; his patents have expired. Scheiber argues that since the agreement was in settlement of his infringement suit, the only effect of limiting the statute to such suits would be to dissuade patentees from settling them. Not so. Had Scheiber pressed his 1983 infringement suit against Dolby to judgment, he would not have obtained royalties beyond the expiration date of his patents, because Dolby had not as yet agreed to pay any royalties; there was no license agreement before the case was settled. The significance of the statute is that if some subsequent infringer should point to the license agreement with Dolby as a misuse of Scheiber's patent by reason of the tying together of different patents, Scheiber could plead the statute as a bar to the infringer's defense of patent misuse.

In any event, the new statutory defense is explicitly limited to tying, *Lasercomb America, Inc. v. Reynolds,* 911 F.2d 970, 976 and n.15 (4th Cir. 1990); normally of a nonpatented product to a patented product, as in a number of famous patent misuse cases, such as *Henry v. A.B. Dick Co.,* 224 U.S. 1 (1912), and antitrust tying cases, such as *International Business Machines Corp. v. United States,* 298 U.S. 131 (1936). The 1988 amendment limited the tying doctrine, in cases in which the tying product is a patent, to situations in which the patentee has real market power, not merely the technical monopoly (right to exclude) that every patent confers. *Virginia Panel Corp. v. MAC Panel Co.,* 133 F.3d at 869. There are multiple products here, and they are tied together in the sense of having been licensed as a package. The more exact term is bundling, because a single price is charged for the tied goods, rather than separate prices as in the canonical tying cases. *United States v. Microsoft Corp.,* 253 F.3d 34, 87, 96 (D.C. Cir. 2001) (*en banc*). We may assume that the statute encompasses bundling. We can't find a case on the point, but certainly the statutory language encompasses it and the objections to tying and bundling, such as they are, are the same. (The naive objection is that they extend monopoly; the sophisticated objection is that they facilitate price discrimination.) But it is not the bundling of the U.S. and Canadian patents on which Dolby pitches its refusal to pay royalties; it is the duration of the royalty obligation. The objection would be the same if there were a single patent and the agreement required the licensee to continue paying royalties after the patent expired.

. . . There just is no evidence that Congress in the 1988 amendment wanted to go or did go beyond tying. Had it wanted to, it would have chosen different words. We are not literalists, but there must be *some* semantic handle on which to hang a proposed statutory interpretation, and there is none here, though we have found a district court case that did hold that the 1988 amendment had overruled *Brulotte.*

Comment

A Scenario Waiting for the Supreme Court. With *Scheiber* in mind, *Brulotte* seems to be one of those cases waiting to be revisited by the Supreme Court. Of course, circuit courts have their hands tied when applying Supreme Court precedent even though they and a significant majority of commentators disagree with the precedent. This was the scenario in *Independent Ink, Inc. v. Illinois Tool Works, Inc.*, 396 F.3d 1342 (Fed. Cir. 2005), which addressed the issue of patents and market power. In arguing that a patent should not give rise to a presumption of market power, the defendants cited dissents and concurrences from Supreme Court cases and a great deal of academic commentary. But the Federal Circuit clearly understood its institutional limitations:

> The fundamental error in all of defendants' arguments is that they ignore the fact that it is the duty of a court of appeals to follow the precedents of the Supreme Court until the Court itself chooses to expressly overrule them. This message has been conveyed repeatedly by the Court. The Court's "decisions remain binding precedent until [it] see[s] fit to reconsider them, regardless of whether subsequent cases have raised doubts about their continuing vitality." *Hohn v. United States*, 524 U.S. 236, 252-53 (1998). "If a precedent of th[e] Court has direct application in a case, yet appears to rest on reasons rejected in some other line of decisions, the Court of Appeals should follow the case which directly controls, leaving to th[e] Court the prerogative of overruling its own decisions." *Rodriguez de Quijas v. Shearson/American Exp., Inc.*, 490 U.S. 477, 484 (1989). Even where a Supreme Court precedent contains many "infirmities" and rests upon "wobbly, moth-eaten foundations," it remains the "Court's prerogative alone to overrule one of its precedents." *State Oil Co. v. Khan*, 522 U.S. 3, 20 (1997). None of the authorities that defendants present . . . constituted an express overruling of [Supreme Court precedent]. . . . The time may have come to abandon the doctrine, but it is up to the Congress or the Supreme Court to make this judgment.

Id. at 1351. The Federal Circuit "teed" the issue up for the Supreme Court, knowing if the Court decided to hear the case, it would most likely reverse the Federal Circuit. The Supreme Court did grant certiorari in *Independent Ink*, and, as expected, reversed the Federal Circuit. *Independent Ink* is a principal case in section B, below.

3. Contractual and Jurisdictional Restrictions Relating to Challenging Patent Validity

The principal cases of *Lear* and *MedImmune* explore, respectively, whether licensees should be able to challenge the validity of the licensed patent, and, if so, under what conditions can a licensee invoke the declaratory judgment jurisdiction of a district court. The *SanDisk* case involves not a license, but an alleged infringer's ability to invoke declaratory judgment jurisdiction after receiving a communication from a patentee, a common scenario in patent litigation. The nature of the communication and the signals it sends are important considerations, particularly in the light of the *MedImmune* case.

a. Licensee's Ability to Challenge Patent Validity

LEAR, INC. v. ADKINS
395 U.S. 653 (1969)

Justice HARLAN delivered the opinion of the Court.

In January of 1952, John Adkins, an inventor and mechanical engineer, was hired by Lear, Incorporated, for the purpose of solving a vexing problem the company had encountered in its efforts to develop a gyroscope which would meet the increasingly demanding requirements of the aviation industry. The gyroscope is an essential component of the navigational system in all aircraft, enabling the pilot to learn the direction and altitude of his airplane. With the development of the faster airplanes of the 1950's, more accurate gyroscopes were needed, and the gyro industry consequently was casting about for new techniques which would satisfy this need in an economical fashion. Shortly after Adkins was hired, he developed a method of construction at the company's California facilities which improved gyroscope accuracy at a low cost. Lear almost immediately incorporated Adkins' improvements into its production process to its substantial advantage.

The question that remains unsettled in this case, after eight years of litigation in the California courts, is whether Adkins will receive compensation for Lear's use of those improvements which the inventor has subsequently patented. At every stage of this lawsuit, Lear has sought to prove that, despite the grant of a patent by the Patent Office, none of Adkins' improvements were sufficiently novel to warrant the award of a monopoly under the standards delineated in the governing federal statutes. Moreover, the company has sought to prove that Adkins obtained his patent by means of a fraud on the Patent Office. In response, the inventor has argued that since Lear had entered into a licensing agreement with Adkins, it was obliged to pay the agreed royalties regardless of the validity of the underlying patent.

The Supreme Court of California unanimously vindicated the inventor's position. While the court recognized that generally a manufacturer is free to challenge the validity of an inventor's patent, it held that "one of the oldest doctrines in the field of patent law establishes that so long as a licensee is operating under a license agreement he is estopped to deny the validity of his licensor's patent in a suit for royalties under the agreement. The theory underlying this doctrine is that a licensee should not be permitted to enjoy the benefit afforded by the agreement while simultaneously urging that the patent which forms the basis of the agreement is void."

Almost 20 years ago, in its last consideration of the doctrine, this Court also invoked an estoppel to deny a licensee the right to prove that his licensor was demanding royalties for the use of an idea which was in reality a part of the public domain. *Automatic Radio Manufacturing Co. v. Hazeltine Research, Inc.*, 339 U.S. 827, 836 (1950). We granted certiorari in the present case to reconsider the validity of the *Hazeltine* rule in the light of our recent decisions emphasizing the strong federal policy favoring free competition in ideas which do not merit patent protection. *Sears, Roebuck v. Stiffel Co.*, 376 U.S. 225 (1964); *Compco Corp. v. Day-Brite Lighting, Inc.*, 376 U.S. 234 (1964).

I.

At the very beginning of the parties' relationship, Lear and Adkins entered into a rudimentary one-page agreement which provided that although "[a]ll new ideas, discoveries, inventions, etc., related to . . . vertical gyros become the property of Mr. John S. Adkins," the inventor promised to grant Lear a license as to all ideas he might develop "on a mutually satisfactory royalty basis." As soon as Adkins' labors yielded tangible results, it quickly became apparent to the inventor that further steps should be taken to place his rights to his ideas on a firmer basis. On February 4, 1954, Adkins filed an application with the Patent Office in an effort to gain federal protection for his improvements. At about the same time, he entered into a lengthy period of negotiations with Lear in an effort to conclude a licensing agreement which would clearly establish the amount of royalties that would be paid.

These negotiations finally bore fruit on September 15, 1955, when the parties approved a complex 17-page contract which carefully delineated the conditions upon which Lear promised to pay royalties for Adkins' improvements. The parties agreed that if "the U.S. Patent Office refuses to issue a patent on the substantial claims (contained in Adkins' original patent application) or if such a patent so issued is subsequently held invalid, then in any of such events Lear at its option shall have the right forthwith to terminate the specific license so affected or to terminate this entire Agreement. . . ."

. . . The [Patent Office] regulations do not require the Office to make a final judgment on an invention's patentability on the basis of the inventor's original application. While it sometimes happens that a patent is granted at this early stage, it is far more common for the Office to find that although certain of the applicant's claims may be patentable, certain others have been fully anticipated by the earlier developments in the art. In such a situation, the Patent Office does not attempt to separate the wheat from the chaff on its own initiative. Instead, it rejects the application, giving the inventor the right to make an amendment which narrows his claim to cover only those aspects of the invention which are truly novel. . . .

The progress of Adkins' effort to obtain a patent followed the typical pattern. In his initial application, the inventor made the ambitious claim that his entire method of constructing gyroscopes was sufficiently novel to merit protection. The Patent Office, however, rejected this initial claim, as well as two subsequent amendments, which progressively narrowed the scope of the invention sought to be protected. Finally, Adkins narrowed his claim drastically to assert only that the design of the apparatus used to achieve gyroscope accuracy was novel. In response, the Office issued its 1960 patent, granting a 17-year monopoly on this more modest claim.

During the long period in which Adkins was attempting to convince the Patent Office of the novelty of his ideas, however, Lear had become convinced that Adkins would never receive a patent on his invention and that it should not continue to pay substantial royalties on ideas which had not contributed substantially to the development of the art of gyroscopy. In 1957, after Adkins' patent application had been rejected twice, Lear announced that it had searched the Patent Office's files and had found a patent which it believed had fully anticipated Adkins' discovery. As a result, the company stated that it would no longer pay royalties on the large number of gyroscopes it was producing at its plant in Grand Rapids, Michigan (the Michigan gyros). Payments were continued on the smaller number of gyros produced at the company's California plant (the California gyros) for two more years until they too were terminated on April 8, 1959.

[The California Supreme Court] rejected the District Court of Appeal's conclusion that the 1955 license gave Lear the right to terminate its royalty obligations in 1959. Since the 1955 agreement was still in effect, the court concluded, relying on the language we have already quoted, that the doctrine of estoppel barred Lear from questioning the propriety of the Patent Office's grant. The court's adherence to estoppel, however, was not without qualification. After noting Lear's claim that it had developed its Michigan gyros independently, the court tested this contention by considering "whether what is being built by Lear (in Michigan) springs entirely" . . . from the prior art. Applying this test, it found that Lear had in fact "utilized the apparatus patented by Adkins throughout the period in question," and reinstated the jury's $888,000 verdict on this branch of the case.

II.

* * *

A.

While the roots of the doctrine have often been celebrated in tradition, we have found only one 19th century case in this Court that invoked estoppel in a considered manner. And that case was decided before the Sherman Act made it clear that the grant of monopoly power to a patent owner constituted a limited exception to the general federal policy favoring free competition. . . .

In the very next year, this Court found the doctrine of patent estoppel so inequitable that it refused to grant an injunction to enforce a licensee's promise never to contest the validity of the underlying patent. "It is as important to the public that competition should not be repressed by worthless patents, as that the patentee of a really valuable invention should be protected in his monopoly. . . ." *Pope Manufacturing Co. v. Gormully*, 144 U.S. 224, 234 (1892).

Although this Court invoked an estoppel in 1905 without citing or considering Pope's powerful argument, the doctrine was not to be applied again in this Court until it was revived in *Automatic Radio Manufacturing Co. v. Hazeltine Research, Inc., supra*, which declared, without prolonged analysis, that licensee estoppel was "the general rule." 339 U.S., at 836. In so holding, the majority ignored the teachings of a series of decisions this Court had rendered during the 45 years since *Harvey* had been decided. During this period, each time a patentee sought to rely upon his estoppel privilege before this Court, the majority created a new exception to permit judicial scrutiny into the validity of the Patent Office's grant. Long before *Hazeltine* was decided, the estoppel doctrine had been so eroded that it could no longer be considered the "general rule," but was only to be invoked in an ever narrowing set of circumstances.

* * *

III.

The uncertain status of licensee estoppel in the case law is a product of judicial efforts to accommodate the competing demands of the common law of contracts and the federal law of patents. On the one hand, the law of contracts forbids a purchaser to repudiate his promises simply because he later becomes dissatisfied with the bargain he has made. On the other hand, federal law requires, that all ideas in general circulation be dedicated to the common good unless they are protected by a valid patent. *Sears, Roebuck v. Stiffel Co., supra*; *Compco Corp. v. Day-Brite Lighting, Inc., supra.* When faced with this basic conflict in policy, both this Court and courts throughout the land have naturally sought to develop an intermediate position which somehow would remain responsive to the radically different concerns of the two different worlds of contract and patent. The result has been a failure. Rather than creative compromise, there has been a chaos of conflicting case law, proceeding on inconsistent premises. Before renewing the search for an acceptable middle ground, we must reconsider on their own merits the arguments which may properly be advanced on both sides of the estoppel question.

A.

It will simplify matters greatly if we first consider the most typical situation in which patent licenses are negotiated. In contrast to the present case, most manufacturers obtain a license after a patent has issued. Since the Patent Office makes an inventor's ideas public when it issues its grant of a limited monopoly, a potential licensee has access to the inventor's ideas even if he does not enter into an agreement with the patent owner. Consequently, a manufacturer gains only two benefits if he chooses to enter a licensing agreement after the patent has issued. First, by accepting a license and paying royalties for a time, the licensee may have avoided the necessity of defending an expensive infringement action during the period when he may be least able to afford one. Second, the existence of an unchallenged patent may deter others from attempting to compete with the licensee.

Under ordinary contract principles the mere fact that some benefit is received is enough to require the enforcement of the contract, regardless of the validity of the underlying patent. Nevertheless, if one tests this result by the standard of good-faith commercial dealing, it seems far from satisfactory. For the simple contract approach entirely ignores the position of the licensor who is seeking to invoke the court's assistance on his behalf. Consider, for example, the equities of the licensor who has obtained his patent through a fraud on the Patent Office. It is difficult to perceive why good faith requires that courts should permit him to recover royalties despite his licensee's attempts to show that the patent is invalid.

Even in the more typical cases, not involving conscious wrongdoing, the licensor's equities are far from compelling. A patent, in the last analysis, simply represents a legal conclusion reached by the Patent Office. Moreover, the legal conclusion is predicated on factors as to which reasonable men can differ widely. Yet the Patent Office is often obliged to reach its decision in an ex parte proceeding, without the aid of the arguments which could be advanced by parties interested in proving patent invalidity. Consequently, it does not seem to us to be unfair to require a patentee to defend the Patent Office's judgment when his licensee places the question in issue, especially since the licensor's case is buttressed by the presumption of validity which attaches to his patent. Thus, although licensee estoppel may be consistent with the letter of contractual doctrine, we cannot say that it is compelled by the spirit of contract law, which seeks to balance the claims of promisor and estoppel in accord with the requirements of good faith.

Surely the equities of the licensor do not weigh very heavily when they are balanced against the important public interest in permitting full and free competition in the use of ideas which are in reality a part of the public domain. Licensees may often be the only individuals with enough economic incentive to challenge the patentability of an inventor's discovery. If they are muzzled, the public may continually be required to pay tribute to would-be monopolists without need or justification. We think it plain that the technical requirements of contract doctrine must give way before the demands of the public interest in the typical situation involving the negotiation of a license after a patent has issued.

We are satisfied that *Automatic Radio Manufacturing Co. v. Hazeltine Research, Inc.*, supra, itself the product of a clouded history, should no longer be regarded as sound law with respect to its "estoppel" holding, and that holding is now overruled.

B.

The case before us, however, presents a far more complicated estoppel problem than the one which arises in the most common licensing context. The problem arises out of the fact that Lear obtained its license in 1955, more than four years before Adkins received his 1960 patent. Indeed, from the very outset of the relationship, Lear obtained special access to Adkins' ideas in return for its promise to pay satisfactory compensation.

Thus, during the lengthy period in which Adkins was attempting to obtain a patent, Lear gained an important benefit not generally obtained by the typical licensee. For until a patent issues, a potential licensee may not learn his licensor's ideas simply by requesting the information from the Patent Office. During the time the inventor is seeking patent protection, the governing federal statute requires the Patent Office to hold an inventor's patent application in confidence. If a potential licensee hopes to use the ideas contained in a secret patent application, he must deal with the inventor himself, unless the inventor chooses to publicize his ideas to the world at large. By promising to pay Adkins royalties from the very outset of their relationship, Lear gained immediate access to ideas which it may well not have learned until the Patent Office published the details of Adkins' invention in 1960. At the core of this case, then, is the difficult question whether federal patent policy bars a State from enforcing a contract regulating access to an unpatented secret idea.

Adkins takes an extreme position on this question. The inventor does not merely argue that since Lear obtained privileged access to his ideas before 1960, the company should be required to pay royalties accruing before 1960 regardless of the validity of the patent which ultimately issued. He also argues that since Lear obtained special benefits before 1960, it should also pay royalties during the entire patent period (1960-1977), without regard to the validity of the Patent Office's grant. We cannot accept so broad an argument.

Adkins' position would permit inventors to negotiate all important licenses during the lengthy period while their applications were still pending at the Patent Office, thereby disabling entirely all those who have the strongest incentive to show that a patent is worthless. While the equities supporting Adkins' position are somewhat more appealing than those supporting the typical licensor, we cannot say that there is enough of a difference to justify such a substantial impairment of overriding federal policy.

Nor can we accept a second argument which may be advanced to support Adkins' claim to at least a portion of his post-patent royalties, regardless of the validity of the Patent Office grant. The terms of the 1955 agreement provide that royalties are to be paid until such time as the "patent . . . is held invalid," § 6, and the fact remains that the question of patent validity has not been finally determined in this case. Thus, it may be suggested that although Lear must be allowed to raise the question of patent validity in the present lawsuit, it must also be required to comply with its contract and continue to pay royalties until its claim is finally vindicated in the courts.

The parties' contract, however, is no more controlling on this issue than is the State's doctrine of estoppel, which is also rooted in contract principles. The decisive question is whether overriding federal policies would be significantly frustrated if licensees could be required to continue to pay royalties during the time they are challenging patent validity in the courts.

It seems to us that such a requirement would be inconsistent with the aims of federal patent policy. Enforcing this contractual provision would give the licensor an additional economic incentive to devise every conceivable dilatory tactic in an effort to postpone the day of final judicial reckoning. We can perceive no reason to encourage dilatory court tactics in this way. Moreover, the cost of prosecuting slow-moving trial proceedings and defending an inevitable appeal might well deter many licensees from attempting to prove patent invalidity in the courts. The deterrent effect would be particularly severe in the many scientific fields in which invention is proceeding at a rapid rate. In these areas, a patent may well become obsolete long before its 17-year term has expired. If a licensee has reason to believe that he will replace a patented idea with a new one in the near future, he will have little incentive to initiate lengthy court proceedings, unless he is freed from liability at least from the time he refuses to pay the contractual royalties. Lastly, enforcing this contractual provision would undermine the strong federal policy favoring the full and free use of ideas in the public domain. For all these reasons, we hold that Lear must be permitted to avoid the payment of all royalties accruing after Adkins' 1960 patent issued if Lear can prove patent invalidity.

C.

Adkins' claim to contractual royalties accruing before the 1960 patent issued is, however, a much more difficult one, since it squarely raises the question whether, and to what extent, the States may protect the owners of unpatented inventions who are willing to disclose their ideas to manufacturers only upon payment of royalties. The California Supreme Court did not address itself to this issue with precision, for it believed that the venerable doctrine of estoppel provided a sufficient answer to all of Lear's claims based upon federal patent law. Thus, we do not know whether the Supreme Court would have awarded Adkins recovery even on his pre-patent royalties if it had recognized that previously established estoppel doctrine could no longer be properly invoked with regard to royalties accruing during the 17-year patent period. Our decision today will, of course, require the state courts to reconsider the theoretical basis of their decisions enforcing the contractual rights of inventors and it is impossible to predict the extent to which this reevaluation may revolutionize the law of any particular State in this regard. Given the difficulty and importance of this task, it should be undertaken only after the state courts have, after fully focused inquiry, determined the extent to which they will respect the contractual rights of such inventors in the future. Indeed, on remand, the California courts may well reconcile the competing demands of patent and contract law in a way which would not warrant further review in this Court.

MEDIMMUNE, INC. v. GENENTECH, INC.

549 U.S. 118 (2007)

Justice SCALIA delivered the opinion of the Court.

We must decide whether Article III's limitation of federal courts' jurisdiction to "Cases" and "Controversies," reflected in the "actual controversy" requirement of the Declaratory Judgment Act, 28 U.S.C. § 2201(a), requires a patent licensee to terminate or be in breach of its license agreement before it can seek a declaratory judgment that the underlying patent is invalid, unenforceable, or not infringed.

I

Because the declaratory-judgment claims in this case were disposed of at the motion-to-dismiss stage, we take the following facts from the allegations in petitioner's amended complaint and the unopposed declarations that petitioner submitted in response to the motion to dismiss. MedImmune, Inc., manufactures Synagis, a drug used to prevent respiratory tract disease in infants and young children. In 1997, petitioner entered into a patent license agreement with respondent Genentech, Inc. (which acted on behalf of itself as patent assignee and on behalf of the coassignee, respondent City of Hope). The license covered an existing patent relating to the production of "chimeric antibodies" and a then-pending patent application relating to "the coexpression of immunoglobulin chains in recombinant host cells." Petitioner agreed to pay royalties on sales of "Licensed Products," and respondents granted petitioner the right to make, use, and sell them. The agreement defined "Licensed Products" as a specified antibody, "the manufacture, use or sale of which . . . would, if not licensed under th[e] Agreement, infringe one or more claims of either or both of [the covered patents,] which have neither expired nor been held invalid by a court or other body of competent jurisdiction from which no appeal has been or may be taken." App. 399. The license agreement gave petitioner the right to terminate upon six months' written notice.

In December 2001, the "coexpression" application covered by the 1997 license agreement matured into the "Cabilly II" patent. Soon thereafter, respondent Genentech delivered petitioner a letter expressing its belief that Synagis was covered by the Cabilly II patent and its expectation that petitioner would pay royalties beginning March 1, 2002. Petitioner did not think royalties were owing, believing that the Cabilly II patent was invalid and unenforceable, and that its claims were in any event not infringed by Synagis. Nevertheless, petitioner considered the letter to be a clear threat to enforce the Cabilly II patent, terminate the 1997 license agreement, and sue for patent infringement if petitioner did not make royalty payments as demanded. If respondents were to prevail in a patent infringement action, petitioner could be ordered to pay treble damages and attorney's fees, and could be enjoined from selling Synagis, a product that has accounted for more than 80 percent of its revenue from sales since 1999. Unwilling to risk such serious consequences, petitioner paid the demanded royalties "under protest and with reservation of all of [its] rights." *Id.*, at 426. This declaratory-judgment action followed.

Petitioner sought the declaratory relief discussed in detail in Part II below. Petitioner also requested damages and an injunction with respect to other federal and state claims not relevant here. The District Court granted respondents' motion to dismiss the declaratory-judgment claims for lack of subject-matter jurisdiction, relying on the decision of the United States Court of Appeals for the Federal Circuit in *Gen-Probe Inc. v. Vysis, Inc.,* 359 F.3d 1376 (2004). *Gen-Probe* had held that a patent licensee in good standing cannot establish an Article III case or controversy with regard to validity, enforceability, or scope of the patent because the license agreement "obliterate[s] any reasonable apprehension" that the licensee will be sued for infringement. *Id.*, at 1381. The Federal Circuit affirmed the District Court, also relying on *Gen-Probe.* 427 F.3d 958 (2005). We granted certiorari.

* * *

III

The Declaratory Judgment Act provides that, "[i]n a case of actual controversy within its jurisdiction . . . any court of the United States . . . may declare the rights and other legal relations of any interested party seeking such declaration, whether or not further relief is or could be sought." 28 U.S.C. § 2201(a). There was a time when this Court harbored doubts about the compatibility of declaratory-judgment actions with Article III's case-or-controversy requirement. We dispelled those doubts, however, in *Nashville, C. & St. L. R. Co. v. Wallace,* 288 U.S. 249 (1933), holding (in a case involving a declaratory judgment rendered in state court) that an appropriate action for declaratory relief *can* be a case or controversy under Article III. The federal Declaratory Judgment Act was signed into law the following year, and we upheld its constitutionality in *Aetna Life Ins. Co. v. Haworth,* 300 U.S. 227 (1937). Our opinion explained that the phrase "case of actual controversy" in the Act refers to the type of "Cases" and "Controversies" that are justiciable under Article III. *Id.*, at 240.

Aetna and the cases following it do not draw the brightest of lines between those declaratory-judgment actions that satisfy the case-or-controversy requirement and those that do not. Our decisions have required that the dispute be "definite and concrete, touching the legal relations of parties having adverse legal interests"; and that it be "real and substantial" and "admi[t] of specific relief through a decree of a conclusive character, as distinguished from an opinion advising what the law would be upon a hypothetical state of facts." *Id.*, at 240-241. In *Maryland Casualty Co. v. Pacific Coal & Oil Co.,* 312 U.S. 270, 273 (1941), we summarized as follows: "Basically, the question in each case is whether the facts alleged, under all the circumstances, show that there is a substantial controversy, between parties having adverse legal interests, of sufficient immediacy and reality to warrant the issuance of a declaratory judgment."

There is no dispute that these standards would have been satisfied if petitioner had taken the final step of refusing to make royalty payments under the 1997 license agreement. Respondents claim a right to royalties under the licensing agreement. Petitioner asserts that no royalties are owing because the Cabilly II patent is invalid and not infringed; and alleges (without contradiction) a threat by respondents to enjoin sales if royalties are not forthcoming. The factual and legal dimensions of the dispute are well defined and, but for petitioner's continuing to make royalty payments, nothing about the dispute would render it unfit for judicial resolution. Assuming (without deciding) that respondents here could not claim an anticipatory breach and repudiate the license, the continuation of royalty payments makes what would otherwise be an imminent threat at least remote, if not nonexistent. As long as those payments are made, there is no risk that respondents will seek to enjoin petitioner's sales. Petitioner's own acts, in other words, eliminate the imminent threat of harm. The question before us is whether this causes the dispute no longer to be a case or controversy within the meaning of Article III.

Our analysis must begin with the recognition that, where threatened action by *government* is concerned, we do not require a plaintiff to expose himself to liability before bringing suit to challenge the basis for the threat—for example, the constitutionality of a law threatened to be enforced. The plaintiff's own action (or inaction) in failing to violate the law eliminates the imminent threat of prosecution, but nonetheless does not eliminate Article III jurisdiction. For example, in *Terrace v. Thompson,* 263 U.S. 197 (1923), the State threatened the plaintiff with forfeiture of his farm, fines, and penalties if he entered into a lease with an alien in violation of the State's anti-alien land law. Given this genuine threat of enforcement, we did not require, as a prerequisite to testing the validity of the law in a suit for injunction, that the plaintiff bet the farm, so to speak, by taking the violative action. *Id.,* at 216. Likewise, in *Steffel v. Thompson,* 415 U.S. 452 (1974), we did not require the plaintiff to proceed to distribute handbills and risk actual prosecution before he could seek a declaratory judgment regarding the constitutionality of a state statute prohibiting such distribution. *Id.,* at 458-460. As then-Justice Rehnquist put it in his concurrence, "the declaratory judgment procedure is an alternative to pursuit of the arguably illegal activity." *Id.,* at 480. In each of these cases, the plaintiff had eliminated the imminent threat of harm by simply not doing what he claimed the right to do (enter into a lease, or distribute handbills at the shopping center). That did not preclude subject-matter jurisdiction because the threat-eliminating behavior was effectively coerced. See *Terrace, supra,* at 215-216; *Steffel, supra,* at 459. The dilemma posed by that coercion—putting the challenger to the choice between abandoning his rights or risking prosecution—is "a dilemma that it was the very purpose of the Declaratory Judgment Act to ameliorate." *Abbott Laboratories v. Gardner,* 387 U.S. 136, 152 (1967).

Supreme Court jurisprudence is more rare regarding application of the Declaratory Judgment Act to situations in which the plaintiff's self-avoidance of imminent injury is coerced by threatened enforcement action of *a private party* rather than the government. Lower federal courts, however (and state courts interpreting declaratory judgment Acts requiring "actual controversy"), have long accepted jurisdiction in such cases.

The only Supreme Court decision in point is, fortuitously, close on its facts to the case before us. *Altvater v. Freeman,* 319 U.S. 359 (1943), held that a licensee's failure to cease its payment of royalties did not render nonjusticiable a dispute over the validity of the patent. In that litigation, several patentees had sued their licensees to enforce territorial restrictions in the license. The licensees filed a counterclaim for declaratory judgment that the underlying patents were invalid, in the meantime paying "under protest" royalties required by an injunction the patentees had obtained in an earlier case. The patentees argued that "so long as [licensees] continue to pay royalties, there is only an academic, not a real controversy, between the parties." *Id.*, at 364. We rejected that argument and held that the declaratory-judgment claim presented a justiciable case or controversy: "The fact that royalties were being paid did not make this a 'difference or dispute of a hypothetical or abstract character.'" *Ibid.* (quoting *Aetna*, 300 U.S., at 240). The royalties "were being paid under protest and under the compulsion of an injunction decree," and "[u]nless the injunction decree were modified, the only other course [of action] was to defy it, and to risk not only actual but treble damages in infringement suits." 319 U.S., at 365. We concluded that "the requirements of [a] case or controversy are met where payment of a claim is demanded as of right and where payment is made, but where the involuntary or coercive nature of the exaction preserves the right to recover the sums paid or to challenge the legality of the claim." *Ibid.*

The Federal Circuit's *Gen-Probe* decision distinguished *Altvater* on the ground that it involved the compulsion of an injunction. But *Altvater* cannot be so readily dismissed. Never mind that the injunction had been privately obtained and was ultimately within the control of the patentees, who could permit its modification. More fundamentally, and contrary to the Federal Circuit's conclusion, *Altvater* did not say that the coercion dispositive of the case was governmental, but suggested just the opposite. The opinion acknowledged that the licensees had the option of stopping payments in defiance of the injunction, but explained that the *consequence* of doing so would be to risk "actual [and] treble damages in infringement suits" by the patentees. 319 U.S., at 365. It significantly did not mention the threat of prosecution for contempt, or any other sort of governmental sanction. Moreover, it cited approvingly a treatise which said that an "actual or threatened serious injury to business or employment" by a private party can be as coercive as other forms of coercion supporting restitution actions at common law; and that "[t]o imperil a man's livelihood, his business enterprises, or his solvency, [was] ordinarily quite as coercive" as, for example, "detaining his property." F. Woodward, The Law of Quasi Contracts §218 (1913), cited in *Altvater, supra*, at 365.[11]

Jurisdiction over the present case is not contradicted by *Willing v. Chicago Auditorium Association*, 277 U.S. 274. There a ground lessee wanted to demolish an antiquated auditorium and replace it with a modern commercial building. The lessee believed it had the right to do this without the lessors' consent, but was unwilling to drop the wrecking ball first and test its belief later. Because

---

11. Even if *Altvater* could be distinguished as an "injunction" case, it would still contradict the Federal Circuit's "reasonable apprehension of suit" test (or, in its evolved form, the "reasonable apprehension of *imminent* suit" test, *Teva Pharms. USA, Inc. v. Pfizer, Inc.*, 395 F.3d 1324, 1333 (2005)). A licensee who pays royalties under compulsion of an injunction has no more apprehension of imminent harm than a licensee who pays royalties for fear of treble damages and an injunction fatal to his business. The reasonable-apprehension-of-suit test also conflicts with our decisions in *Maryland Casualty Co. v. Pacific Coal & Oil Co.*, 312 U.S. 270, 273 (1941), where jurisdiction obtained even though the collision-victim defendant could not have sued the declaratory-judgment plaintiff-insurer without first obtaining a judgment against the insured; and *Aetna Life Ins. Co. v. Haworth*, 300 U.S. 227, 239 (1937), where jurisdiction obtained even though the very reason the insurer sought declaratory relief was that the insured had given no indication that he would file suit. It is also in tension with *Cardinal Chemical Co. v. Morton Int'l, Inc.*, 508 U.S. 83, 98 (1993), which held that appellate affirmance of a judgment of noninfringement, eliminating any apprehension of suit, does not moot a declaratory judgment counterclaim of patent invalidity.

there was no declaratory judgment act at the time under federal or applicable state law, the lessee filed an action to remove a "cloud" on its lease. This Court held that an Article III case or controversy had not arisen because "[n]o defendant ha[d] wronged the plaintiff or ha[d] threatened to do so." *Id.*, at 288, 290. It was true that one of the colessors had disagreed with the lessee's interpretation of the lease, but that happened in an "informal, friendly, private conversation," *id.*, at 286, a year before the lawsuit was filed; and the lessee never even bothered to approach the other co-lessors. The Court went on to remark that "[w]hat the plaintiff seeks is simply a declaratory judgment," and "[t]o grant that relief is beyond the power conferred upon the federal judiciary." *Id.*, at 289. Had *Willing* been decided after the enactment (and our upholding) of the Declaratory Judgment Act, and had the legal disagreement between the parties been as lively as this one, we are confident a different result would have obtained. The rule that a plaintiff must destroy a large building, bet the farm, or (as here) risk treble damages and the loss of 80 percent of its business, before seeking a declaration of its actively contested legal rights finds no support in Article III.

Respondents assert that the parties in effect settled this dispute when they entered into the 1997 license agreement. When a licensee enters such an agreement, they contend, it essentially purchases an insurance policy, immunizing it from suits for infringement so long as it continues to pay royalties and does not challenge the covered patents. Permitting it to challenge the validity of the patent without terminating or breaking the agreement alters the deal, allowing the licensee to continue enjoying its immunity while bringing a suit, the elimination of which was part of the patentee's *quid pro quo*. Of course even if it were valid, this argument would have no force with regard to petitioner's claim that the agreement does not call for royalties because their product does not infringe the patent. But even as to the patent invalidity claim, the point seems to us mistaken. To begin with, it is not clear where the prohibition against challenging the validity of the patents is to be found. It can hardly be implied from the mere promise to pay royalties on patents "which have neither expired nor been held invalid by a court or other body of competent jurisdiction from which no appeal has been or may be taken," App. 399. Promising to pay royalties on patents that have not been held invalid does not amount to a promise *not to seek* a holding of their invalidity.

Respondents appeal to the common-law rule that a party to a contract cannot at one and the same time challenge its validity and continue to reap its benefits, citing *Commodity Credit Corp. v. Rosenberg Bros. & Co.*, 243 F.2d 504, 512 (C.A.9 1957), and *Kingman & Co. v. Stoddard*, 85 F. 740, 745 (C.A.7 1898). *Lear*, they contend, did not suspend that rule for patent licensing agreements, since the plaintiff in that case had already repudiated the contract. Even if *Lear*'s repudiation of the doctrine of licensee estoppel was so limited (a point on which, as we have said earlier, we do not opine), it is hard to see how the common-law rule has any application here. Petitioner is not repudiating or impugning the contract while continuing to reap its benefits. Rather, it is asserting that the contract, properly interpreted, does not prevent it from challenging the patents, and does not require the payment of royalties because the patents do not cover its products and are invalid. Of course even if respondents were correct that the licensing agreement or the common-law rule precludes this suit, the consequence would be that respondents win this case *on the merits*— *not* that the very genuine contract dispute disappears, so that Article III jurisdiction is somehow defeated. In short, Article III jurisdiction has nothing to do with this "insurance-policy" contention.

* * *

We hold that petitioner was not required, insofar as Article III is concerned, to break or terminate its 1997 license agreement before seeking a declaratory judgment in federal court that the underlying patent is invalid, unenforceable, or not infringed. The Court of Appeals erred in affirming the dismissal of this action for lack of subject-matter jurisdiction.

Comments

1. *Licensee Estoppel.* The doctrine of licensee estoppel was rejected by the *Lear* Court, which held that a licensee may challenge the validity of a patent—he is not estopped. The Court cited that the public interest is served by having the licensee weed out bad patents. As the Court noted, "[l]icensees may often be the only individuals with enough economic incentive to challenge the patentability of the inventor's discovery." But as Joseph Miller points out, "[a] court judgment that a patent claim is invalid is a public good, [a]nd obtaining such a judgment requires the expensive, up-front cost of patent litigation." Therefore, because third-party competitors of the challenger do not have to bear these costs, "profit-maximizing firms will supply definitive patent challenges at a less-than-optimal rate." Joseph Scott Miller, *Building a Better Bounty: Litigation-Stage Rewards for Defeating Patents*, 19 BERKELEY TECH. L.J. 667, 688 (2004).

   But what about the interest of the patentee and the validity of the contract the licensee signed agreeing to pay royalties? What incentives are created by allowing licensees to challenge patent validity? Will there be fewer licenses? More express license terms prohibiting licensees from challenging validity? Indeed, *Lear* is not without criticism, particularly relating to its interference with private ordering and contractual allocation of risk. *See, e.g.,* Rochelle Cooper Dreyfuss, *Dethroning Lear: Licensee Estoppel and the Incentive to Innovate*, 72 VA. L. REV. 677, 680-681 (1986) (stating *Lear* failed to appreciate the "economic function" of licensee estoppel and eliminating estoppels has increased "inventors' exposure to litigation and prevent[ed] them from allocating to others the risk that their patents will be invalidated").

2. **MedImmune** *and Its Effect on Licensing Practice.* *MedImmune* was concerned with declaratory-judgment plaintiffs having to expose themselves to liability before bringing suit, and held that a licensee does not have to breach an agreement before seeking a declaratory judgment of invalidity or non-infringement. Is *MedImmune* consistent with the rationale of *Lear*—that is, the policy of weeding out "bad" patents trumps contractual obligations? In *Lear,* the licensee repudiated the contract. In contrast, MedImmune did not breach the license agreement; thus, was MedImmune simply asking the Court to determine what its liability (if any) would be if it decided to breach?

   The results of *MedImmune* may be that fewer licenses are negotiated and consummated because of patentee-licensor fears of looking over his shoulder during the entire term of the license. Fewer licenses—or license/settle-ments —may lead to more litigation and greater inefficiencies in the use and exploitation of patent rights. Nonetheless, licensing will remain a sig-nificant part of patent law. The question is: How will *MedImmune* alter licens-ing clauses from the licensor's perspective to deter licensee challenges? As you consider the following possibilities, ask yourself whether the suggested contractual clauses would violate *Lear*, or at least, be contrary to the spirit of *Lear* and *MedImmune* (Of course, whether licensees would agree to these contractual provisions is dependent on several factors, including bargaining power and lawyering skills.):

1. Require licensee to provide advanced notice before a validity challenge and identify prior art, thus allowing for more time to negotiate a settle-ment, or invoke reexamination proceeding (i.e., ask the USPTO to "reex-amine" the patent in the light of the licensee's prior art);
2. Require licensee to pay significant up-front payment, larger milestone payments (if applicable), or bigger minimum yearly royalties;
3. Require high early milestone payments;
4. Require that litigation must be brought in licensor's choice of forum (this provision was used prior to *MedImmune*);
5. Require licensee to pay licensor's legal fees and continue to pay royalties (as in *MedImmune*) while the patent is being challenged;
6. Require increased royalty payments if challenge fails, as the patent will be more valuable after surviving challenge. Alternatively and more aggres-sively, require increased royalty payments if challenge is invoked, and even higher royalty payments if challenge fails;
7. Terminate license upon challenge; or, less drastic, require conversion of license to non-exclusive upon challenge. Even less drastic would be to convert license to non-exclusive only if challenge fails.
8. Prevent refund of royalties paid if patent is challenged. (Under *Lear*, licensee is not liable for royalties once patent is invalidated.)

Another provision that is more controversial is a no-challenge clause, that is, a provision preventing the licensee from challenging the validity of the patent. Several circuit courts (prior to the creation of the Federal Circuit) —relying primarily on *Lear* and nineteenth-century Supreme Court case law—have held such clauses unenforceable. *See, e.g., Pope Mfg. Co. v. Gormully,* 144 U.S. 224 (1892) (holding non-challenge clause unenforceable); *Panther Pumps & Equip. Co. v. Hydrocraft, Inc.,* 468 F.2d 225, 230-232 (7th Cir. 1972); *Massillon-Cleveland-Akron Sign Co. v. Golden State Advertising Co.,* 444 F.2d 425, 427 (9th Cir. 1971). Yet *Lear* did not hold that non-challenge clauses are void; and dicta in *MedImmune* suggested that such clauses are enforceable. *See MedImmune,* 549 U.S. at 135 (referring to the license agree-ment at issue, the court stated "it is not clear where the prohibition against challenging the validity of patents is to be found. It can hardly be implied from the mere promise to pay royalties. . . . Promising to pay royalties on patents that have not been held invalid does not amount to a promise *not to seek* a holding of their invalidity") (emphasis in original). *See also* Rochelle Cooper Dreyfuss & Lawrence S. Pope, *Dethroning* Lear*? Incentives to Innovate After* MedImmune, 24 BERKELEY TECH. L.J. 971, 976 (2009) (stating "while *Lear* is understood as prohibiting the enforcement of any contract provision that reduces the licensee's incentive to challenge validity, *MedImmune* can be interpreted as permitting patent holders to bargain for such restrictions").

For more on *MedImmune*'s effect on licensing and post-*MedImmune* licensing strategies, *see* Michael Risch, *Patent Challenges and Royalty Inflation*, 85 IND. L.J. 1003 (2010); John W. Schicher, *Patent Licensing, What to Do After MedImmune v. Genentech*, 89 J. PAT. & TRADEMARK OFF. SOC'Y 364 (2007); Jennifer L. Collins & Michael A. Cicero, *The Impact of* MedImmune *upon Both Licensing and Litigation*, 89 J. PAT. & TRADEMARK OFF. SOC'Y 748 (2007).

3. *Assignor Estoppel.* The related doctrine of assignor estoppels precludes an assignor from challenging the validity of the patent. In *Diamond Scientific Co. v. Ambico, Inc.*, 848 F.2d 1220, 1224 (Fed. Cir. 1988), the court distinguished licensee estoppel and *Lear* in upholding the doctrine of assignor estoppel. The court focused on preventing the assignor from "benefitting from his own wrong" and to "prevent unfairness and injustice."

b. Declaratory Judgment Jurisdiction

The *MedImmune* ruling has implications beyond the licensor/licensee scenario. In footnote 11, the Court seemingly overruled the Federal Circuit's "reasonable apprehension" test and, as a result, expanded opportunities of alleged infringers to invoke declaratory judgment jurisdiction. In fact, in patent litigation, a declaratory judgment action—or "DJ"—is most commonly employed by alleged infringers or parties whom the patentee believes are infringing. The DJ allows the alleged infringer to take the initiative and assume greater control over the litigation, particularly with respect to choice of venue. But to invoke the DJ jurisdiction, the alleged infringer/DJ plaintiff must show there is an "actual controversy" under the Declaratory Judgment Act, which provides, in relevant part, that

> [i]n a case of actual controversy within its jurisdiction . . . any court of the United States, upon the filing of an appropriate pleading, may declare the rights and other legal relations of any interested party seeking such declaration, whether or not further relief is or could be sought.

28 U.S.C. § 2201(a). The *SanDisk* case explores the circumstances under which a party thought to be infringing can bring suit—alleging an "actual controversy"—after receiving a communication from a patentee. The nature of the communication (e.g., threatening litigation or asking for a license) is an important consideration.

SANDISK CORP. v. ST MICROELECTRONICS, INC.

480 F.3d 1372 (Fed. Cir. 2007)

LINN, Circuit Judge.

SanDisk Corporation ("SanDisk") appeals from a decision of the U.S. District Court for the Northern District of California granting ST Microelectronics' ("ST's") motion to dismiss SanDisk's second through twenty-ninth claims relating to declaratory judgment of noninfringement and invalidity for failure to present an actual controversy. Because the district court erred in dismissing the declaratory judgment claims for lack of subject matter jurisdiction, we vacate the judgment and remand the case to the district court.

BACKGROUND

SanDisk is in the flash memory storage market and owns several patents related to flash memory storage products. ST, traditionally in the market of semiconductor integrated circuits, more recently entered the flash memory market and has a sizeable portfolio of patents related to flash memory storage products. On April 16, 2004, ST's vice president of intellectual property and licensing, Lisa Jorgenson ("Jorgenson"), sent a letter to SanDisk's chief executive officer requesting a meeting to discuss a cross-license agreement. The letter listed eight patents owned by ST that Jorgenson believed "may be of interest" to SanDisk. On April 28, 2004, SanDisk responded that it would need time to review the listed patents and would be in touch in several weeks to discuss the possibility of meeting in June.

On July 12, 2004, having heard nothing further from SanDisk, Jorgenson sent a letter to SanDisk reiterating her request to meet in July to discuss a cross-license agreement and listing four additional ST patents that "may also be of interest" to SanDisk. On July 21, 2004, SanDisk's chief intellectual property counsel and senior director, E. Earle Thompson ("Thompson"), responded to ST's letter by informing Jorgenson of his "understanding that both sides wish to continue . . . friendly discussions" such as those between the business representatives in May and June. The discussions of May and June that Thompson referred to were discussions among managers and vice presidents of SanDisk and ST at business meetings held on May 18, 2004, and June 9, 2004, to explore the possibility of ST's selling flash memory products to SanDisk. The business meetings were unrelated to any patents. Thompson also requested that Jorgenson join the next business meeting on August 5, 2005. On July 27, 2004, Jorgenson replied, again urging a meeting with Thompson, noting that it was "best to separate the business discussions from the patent license discussions."

On August 5, 2004, when the business representatives next met, SanDisk presented an analysis of three of its patents and orally offered ST a license. ST declined to present an analysis of any of its patents, stating instead that any patent and licensing issues should be discussed in a separate meeting with Jorgenson. Later that same day, Thompson wrote a letter to Jorgenson objecting to separating business and intellectual property issues and stating that "[i]t has been SanDisk's hope and desire to enter into a mutually beneficial discussion without the rattling of sabers." On August 11, 2004, Jorgenson replied, stating that it was her understanding that the parties were going to have a licensing/intellectual property meeting later that month "to discuss the possibility for a patent cross-license." Letter from Jorgenson to Thompson (Aug. 11, 2004). She said that SanDisk should come to that meeting prepared to present an analysis of the three SanDisk patents it identified during the August 5th business meeting, as well as "any infringement analyses of an ST device or need for ST to have a license to these patents." *Id.* She also said that ST would be prepared at that meeting to discuss the twelve patents identified in her prior letters. In closing, Jorgenson said that ST was "look[ing] forward to open and frank discussions with SanDisk concerning fair and reasonable terms for a broad cross-license agreement." *Id.*

On August 27, 2004, the licensing meeting was held. Jorgenson, two ST licensing attorneys, and three technical experts retained by ST to perform the infringement analyses of SanDisk's products, attended on behalf of ST.

Thompson and an engineer attended on behalf of SanDisk. At the meeting, Jorgenson requested that the parties' discussions be treated as "settlement discussions" under Federal Rule of Evidence 408.[1] ST then presented a slide show which compared statistics regarding SanDisk's and ST's patent portfolios, revenue, and research and development expenses, and listed SanDisk's various "unlicensed activities." This slide show was followed by a four- to five-hour presentation by ST's technical experts, during which they identified and discussed the specific claims of each patent and alleged that they were infringed by SanDisk. According to Thompson, the presentation by ST's technical experts included "mapp[ing] the elements of each of the allegedly infringed claims to the aspects of the accused SanDisk products alleged to practice the elements." Thompson declares that "the experts liberally referred to SanDisk's (alleged) infringement of [ST's] products." SanDisk's engineer then made a presentation, describing several of SanDisk's patents and analyzing how a semiconductor chip product sold by ST infringes.

At the end of the meeting, Jorgenson handed Thompson a packet of materials containing, for each of ST's fourteen patents under discussion, a copy of the patent, reverse engineering reports for certain of SanDisk's products, and diagrams showing how elements of ST's patent claims cover SanDisk's products. According to SanDisk, Jorgenson indicated (in words to this effect):

> I know that this is material that would allow SanDisk to DJ [ST] on. We have had some internal discussions on whether I should be giving you a copy of these materials in light of that fact. But I have decided that I will go ahead and give you these materials.

Jorgenson further told Thompson that "ST has absolutely no plan whatsoever to sue SanDisk." Thompson responded to Jorgenson that "SanDisk is not going to sue you on Monday" and that another meeting might be appropriate.

On September 1, 2004, Jorgenson wrote to Thompson, enclosing copies of ST's general slide presentation from the August meeting and also enclosing a hard copy booklet containing each of the engineering reports "for each claim on all products where ST demonstrated coverage by the 14 ST patents to-date [sic]." Jorgenson requested that SanDisk provide ST with a copy of SanDisk's presentation and information about the three SanDisk patents presented. On September 8, 2004, Thompson replied by e-mail, confirming receipt of the package from ST, attaching a copy of SanDisk's presentation, indicating it was his "personal feeling . . . that we have got to trust one another during these negotiations," and seeking a non-disclosure agreement. Thompson also wrote "I still owe you the rates quoted."

On September 15, 2004, Thompson again corresponded with Jorgenson, this time by letter, enclosing a confidential version of SanDisk's cross licensing offer,

---

1. To avoid the risk of a declaratory judgment action, ST could have sought SanDisk's agreement to the terms of a suitable confidentiality agreement. The record before us reflects that the parties did not enter into such an agreement. Rather, ST sought to condition its open licensing discussions and the infringement study on adherence to Federal Rule of Evidence 408. That rule expressly relates to evidence of efforts toward compromising or attempting to compromise a claim in litigation and does not prevent SanDisk from relying on the licensing discussions and infringement study to support its claims. See Fed. R. Evid. 408. Furthermore, ST's presentation was made outside the context of litigation, and there is nothing on the record to indicate that it could be properly considered an "offer" to settle a claim which was then in dispute.

which noted that the offer would expire on September 27, 2004. Jorgenson destroyed this confidential offer and did not retain a copy, and, on September 16, 2004, sent Thompson an e-mail requesting that a non-confidential version be sent for ST's consideration. SanDisk refused to send a non-confidential version. Instead, on September 27, 2004, Thompson offered to send another confidential version, or to communicate the offer orally. Thompson also indicated that SanDisk did not need additional information regarding ST's patents because SanDisk was "quite comfortable with its position" and that it was "time to let our business people talk and see if a peaceful resolution is possible." On September 28, 2004, Jorgenson repeated her request for a written non-confidential version of SanDisk's licensing offer. The following day, Thompson e-mailed Jorgenson another confidential version of SanDisk's offer.

On October 15, 2004, after several further e-mails and phone calls between the business representatives trying to establish another meeting, SanDisk filed the instant lawsuit. SanDisk alleged infringement of one of its patents and sought a declaratory judgment of noninfringement and invalidity of the fourteen ST patents that had been discussed during the cross licensing negotiations. On December 3, 2004, ST filed a motion to dismiss SanDisk's declaratory judgment claims for lack of subject matter jurisdiction, maintaining that there was no actual controversy at the time SanDisk filed its complaint.

The district court granted ST's motion to dismiss, holding that no actual controversy existed for purposes of the Declaratory Judgment Act because SanDisk did not have an objectively reasonable apprehension of suit, even though it may have subjectively believed that ST would bring an infringement suit. The district court reasoned that "SanDisk has presented no evidence that ST threatened it with litigation at any time during the parties' negotiations, nor has SanDisk shown other conduct by ST rising to a level sufficient to indicate an intent on the part of ST to initiate an infringement action." The district court found that the studied and determined infringement analyses that ST presented to SanDisk did not constitute the requisite "express charges [of infringement] carrying with them the threat of enforcement." The district court also found that the totality of the circumstances did not evince an actual controversy because ST told SanDisk that it did not intend to sue SanDisk for infringement.

II. DISCUSSION

* * *

B. Analysis

SanDisk argues that the district court erred as a matter of law by requiring an express accusation of patent infringement coupled with an explicit threat of judicial enforcement to support declaratory judgment jurisdiction, and that, under the correct legal standard articulated by this court in *Arrowhead*, 846 F.2d at 736, the facts of this case illustrate that SanDisk's apprehension of an infringement suit was objectively reasonable. SanDisk asserts that the infringement analysis presented by ST and its experts at the August 27, 2004 licensing meeting constituted an allegation of infringement and that the totality of the circumstances shows that ST's conduct gave rise to an actual case or controversy. SanDisk further points out that negotiations regarding licensing had ceased by the time SanDisk filed its claims for declaratory judgment.

ST counters that the district court applied the correct legal standard and argues that SanDisk ignores the line of cases that have followed and interpreted *Arrowhead*. ST asserts that the cases following *Arrowhead* reveal that the bare mention of infringement, particularly during license negotiations, is not sufficient to meet the standard set forth in *Arrowhead*. ST asserts that its conduct at the August 27, 2004 licensing meeting was to strengthen its position during licensing negotiations and that, under the totality of the circumstances, SanDisk has not shown that ST's conduct gave rise to declaratory judgment jurisdiction. Moreover, ST argues that the district court did not abuse its discretion when it concluded, as an alternative basis for its ruling, that it would exercise discretion to decline to decide SanDisk's claims.

1. Case or Controversy

The first question we address is whether the facts alleged in this case show that there is a case or controversy within the meaning of the Declaratory Judgment Act, 28 U.S.C. §2201(a).

The Declaratory Judgment Act provides, in relevant part, that

> [i]n a case of actual controversy within its jurisdiction . . . any court of the United States, upon the filing of an appropriate pleading, may declare the rights and other legal relations of any interested party seeking such declaration, whether or not further relief is or could be sought.

28 U.S.C. §2201(a). The "actual controversy" requirement of the Declaratory Judgment Act is rooted in Article III of the Constitution, which provides for federal jurisdiction over only "cases and controversies." Thus, our jurisdiction extends only to matters that are Article III cases or controversies.

The Supreme Court, in the context of a patent license dispute, recently examined Article III's case or controversy requirement as it relates to the Declaratory Judgment Act. *See MedImmune, Inc. v. Genentech, Inc.,* 127 S. Ct. 764 (2007). In *MedImmune,* the Supreme Court considered "whether Article III's limitation of federal courts' jurisdiction to 'Cases' and 'Controversies,' reflected in the 'actual controversy' requirement of the Declaratory Judgment Act, 28 U.S.C. §2201(a), requires a patent licensee to terminate or be in breach of its license agreement before it can seek a declaratory judgment that the underlying patent is invalid, unenforceable, or not infringed." *Id.* at 767.

The Supreme Court began its analysis

> with the recognition that, where threatened action by government is concerned, [the Court] do[es] not require a plaintiff to expose himself to liability before bringing suit to challenge the basis for the threat—for example, the constitutionality of a law threatened to be enforced. The plaintiff's own action (or inaction) in failing to violate the law eliminates the imminent threat of prosecution, but nonetheless does not eliminate Article III jurisdiction.

Id. at 772. The Supreme Court quoted its earlier decision in *Maryland Casualty Co. v. Pacific Coal & Oil Co.,* 312 U.S. 270, 273 (1941), where the Court stated that "the question in each case is whether the facts alleged, under all the circumstances, show that there is a substantial controversy, between parties having adverse legal interests, of sufficient immediacy and reality to warrant the issuance of a declaratory judgment." *MedImmune,* 127 S. Ct. at 771. The Supreme Court emphasized that Article III requires that the dispute at issue be "'definite and concrete, touching the legal relations of parties having adverse legal interests'; and that it be 'real and substantial' and 'admi[t] of specific relief through a decree of a conclusive character, as distinguished from an opinion advising what the law would be upon a hypothetical state of facts.'" *Id.* (quoting *Aetna Life Ins. Co. v. Haworth,* 300 U.S. 227, 240-41 (1937)). The Supreme Court stated that, when faced with a genuine threat of enforcement that the government will penalize a certain private action, Article III "d[oes] not require, as a prerequisite to testing the validity of the law in a suit for injunction, that the plaintiff bet the farm, so to speak, by taking the violative action." *Id.* at 772. As the Supreme Court noted, "the declaratory judgment procedure is an alternative to pursuit of the arguably illegal activity." *Id.* The Supreme Court clarified that, although a declaratory judgment plaintiff may eliminate an "imminent threat of harm by simply not doing what he claimed the right to do[,] . . . [t]hat did not preclude subject-matter jurisdiction [where] the threat-eliminating behavior was effectively coerced." *Id.* "The dilemma posed by that coercion—putting the challenger to the choice between abandoning his rights or risking prosecution—is a dilemma that it was the very purpose of the Declaratory Judgment Act to ameliorate." *Id.* at 773.

The Supreme Court then applied these principles to the facts of the case and remarked that "the requirements of [a] case or controversy are met where payment of a claim is demanded as of right and where payment is made, but where the involuntary or coercive nature of the exaction preserves the right to recover the sums paid or to challenge the legality of the claim." *Id.* The Supreme Court held that "[t]he rule that a plaintiff must destroy a large building, bet the farm, or (as here) risk treble damages and the loss of 80 percent of its business, before seeking a declaration of its actively contested legal rights finds no support in Article III." *Id.* at 775.

With regard to patent disputes, prior to *MedImmune,* this court articulated a two-part test that first considers whether conduct by the patentee creates a reasonable apprehension on the part of the declaratory judgment plaintiff that it will face an infringement suit, and second examines whether conduct by the declaratory judgment plaintiff amounts to infringing activity or demonstrates concrete steps taken with the intent to conduct such activity. *See Arrowhead,* 846 F.2d at 736. The Supreme Court, in *MedImmune,* addressed the "reasonable apprehension of suit" aspect of this court's two-part test and concluded that it conflicts with *Aetna Life Insurance* and *Maryland Casualty,* and is in tension with *Cardinal Chemical Co. v. Morton International, Inc.,* 508 U.S. 83, 98 (1993).

In *Aetna Life Insurance,* an insurer sought a declaratory judgment that the insured was not relieved of his duty to continue to pay insurance premiums and that, since the insured had stopped making the payments, the insurance policy had lapsed. In that case, the Supreme Court first upheld the constitutionality of the federal Declaratory Judgment Act. 300 U.S. at 240-41. The Supreme Court then held that, although the insured party gave no indication that he would file suit, *id.* at 239, the case nevertheless presented a controversy under Article III because the parties had taken adverse positions with regard to their obligations, each side presenting a concrete claim of a specific right—the insured claiming that he had become disabled and therefore was relieved of making insurance premium payments and the insurer claiming that the insured was not disabled and that the failure to make payments caused the policy to lapse, *id.* at 244. Similarly, in *Maryland Casualty,* the declaratory judgment plaintiff, an insurance company which had agreed to indemnify and defend the insured against actions brought by third parties against the insured, sought a declaration that it had no duty to defend or to indemnify the insured. 312 U.S. at 272. In that case, the insured could not have sued the declaratory judgment plaintiff without first obtaining a judgment against the third party and the underlying action against the third party "[a]pparently . . . ha[d] not proceeded to judgment." *Id.* at 271. Nevertheless, the Supreme Court held that "[i]t is clear that there is an actual controversy between petitioner and the insured" since the insured was in the process of seeking a judgment and had a statutory right to proceed against the declaratory judgment plaintiff if such judgment were obtained and not satisfied. *Id.* at 274. Finally, in *Cardinal Chemical,* the Supreme Court held that this court's affirmance of a judgment of noninfringement does not necessarily moot a declaratory judgment counterclaim of patent invalidity. 508 U.S. at 98. The Supreme Court's rationale for holding that the declaratory judgment action can proceed consistent with Article III was that a contrary result would create the potential for relitigation or uncertainty with regard to the validity of patents and would be contrary to *Blonder-Tongue Laboratories, Inc. v. University of Illinois Foundation,* 402 U.S. 313 (1971).

The Supreme Court's opinion in *MedImmune* represents a rejection of our reasonable apprehension of suit test.[2] The Court first noted that "the continuation of royalty payments makes what would otherwise be an imminent threat at least remote, if not nonexistent. . . . Petitioner's own acts, in other words, eliminate the imminent threat of harm." *MedImmune,* 127 S. Ct. at 772. The Court nonetheless concluded that declaratory judgment jurisdiction existed relying in particular on its earlier decision in *Altvater v. Freeman,* 319 U.S. 359 (1943). There, the patentee brought suit to enjoin patent infringement, and the accused infringer filed declaratory judgment counterclaims of invalidity. The district court found that there was no infringement and that the patent was invalid. *Id.* at 362. The appellate court affirmed the finding of noninfringement but vacated the finding of invalidity as moot. *Id.* The Supreme Court held that the declaratory judgment counterclaims were not mooted by the finding of noninfringement. *Id.* at 365-66. In finding declaratory judgment jurisdiction in *MedImmune,* the Court specifically addressed and rejected our reasonable apprehension test:

> [e]ven if *Altvater* could be distinguished as an "injunction" case, it would still contradict the Federal Circuit's "reasonable apprehension of suit" test (or, in its evolved form, the "reasonable apprehension of imminent suit" test. A licensee who pays royalties under compulsion of an injunction has no more apprehension of imminent harm than a licensee who pays royalties for fear of treble damages and an injunction fatal to his business. The reasonable-apprehension-of-suit test also conflicts with our decisions in *Maryland Casualty Co. v. Pacific Coal & Oil Co.,* 312 U.S. 270, 273 (1941), where jurisdiction obtained even though the collision-victim defendant could not have sued the declaratory-judgment plaintiff-insurer without first obtaining a judgment against the insured; and *Aetna Life Ins. Co. v. Haworth,* 300 U.S. 227, 239 (1937), where jurisdiction obtained even though the very reason the insurer sought declaratory relief was that the insured had given no indication

---

2. In this case, we address only the first prong of this court's two-part test. There is no dispute that the second prong is met. We therefore leave to another day the effect of *MedImmune,* if any, on the second prong.

that he would file suit. It is also in tension with *Cardinal Chemical Co. v. Morton Int'l, Inc.*, 508 U.S. 83, 98 (1993), which held that appellate affirmance of a judgment of noninfringement, eliminating any apprehension of suit, does not moot a declaratory judgment counterclaim of patent invalidity.

MedImmune, 127 S. Ct. at 774 n.11.

The Supreme Court in *MedImmune* addressed declaratory judgment jurisdiction in the context of a signed license. In the context of conduct prior to the existence of a license, declaratory judgment jurisdiction generally will not arise merely on the basis that a party learns of the existence of a patent owned by another or even perceives such a patent to pose a risk of infringement, without some affirmative act by the patentee. But Article III jurisdiction may be met where the patentee takes a position that puts the declaratory judgment plaintiff in the position of either pursuing arguably illegal behavior or abandoning that which he claims a right to do. We need not define the outer boundaries of declaratory judgment jurisdiction, which will depend on the application of the principles of declaratory judgment jurisdiction to the facts and circumstances of each case. We hold only that where a patentee asserts rights under a patent based on certain identified ongoing or planned activity of another party, and where that party contends that it has the right to engage in the accused activity without license, an Article III case or controversy will arise and the party need not risk a suit for infringement by engaging in the identified activity before seeking a declaration of its legal rights. *See id. Contra Cygnus Therapeutics Sys. v. ALZA Corp.*, 92 F.3d 1153 (Fed. Cir. 1996) (holding that declaratory judgment jurisdiction was not supported where the "patentee does nothing more than exercise its lawful commercial prerogatives and, in so doing, puts a competitor in the position of having to choose between abandoning a particular business venture or bringing matters to a head by engaging in arguably infringing activity").

* * *

Under the facts alleged in this case, SanDisk has established an Article III case or controversy that gives rise to declaratory judgment jurisdiction. ST sought a right to a royalty under its patents based on specific, identified activity by SanDisk. For example, at the August 27, 2004 licensing meeting, ST presented, as part of the "license negotiations," a thorough infringement analysis presented by seasoned litigation experts, detailing that one or more claims of its patents read on one or more of SanDisk's identified products. At that meeting, ST presented SanDisk with a detailed presentation which identified, on an element-by-element basis, the manner in which ST believed each of SanDisk's products infringed the specific claims of each of ST's patents. During discussions, the experts liberally referred to SanDisk's present, ongoing infringement of ST's patents and the need for SanDisk to license those patents. ST also gave SanDisk a packet of materials, over 300 pages in length, containing, for each of ST's fourteen patents under discussion, a copy of the patent, reverse engineering reports for certain of SanDisk's products, and diagrams showing a detailed infringement analysis of SanDisk's products. ST communicated to SanDisk that it had made a studied and determined infringement determination and asserted the right to a royalty based on this determination. SanDisk, on the other hand, maintained that it could proceed in its conduct without the payment of royalties to ST. These facts evince that the conditions of creating "a substantial controversy, between parties having adverse legal interest, of suffi-cient immediacy and reality to warrant the issuance of a declaratory judgment" were fulfilled. SanDisk need not "bet the farm," so to speak, and risk a suit for infringement by cutting off licensing discussions[3] and continuing in the identi-fied activity before seeking a declaration of its legal rights. *See MedImmune*, 127 S. Ct. at 774 n.11. *Contra Phillips Plastics Corp. v. Kato Hatsujou Kabushiki Kaisha*, 57 F.3d 1051 (Fed. Cir. 1995) ("When there are proposed or ongoing license negotiations, a litigation controversy normally does not arise until the negotia-tions have broken down.").

2. *Promise Not to Sue*

We next address whether Jorgenson's direct and unequivocal statement that "ST has absolutely no plan whatsoever to sue SanDisk" eliminates any actual controversy and renders SanDisk's declaratory judgment claims moot.

We decline to hold that Jorgenson's statement that ST would not sue SanDisk eliminates the justiciable controversy created by ST's actions, because ST has engaged in a course of conduct that shows a preparedness and willingness to enforce its patent rights despite Jorgenson's statement. Having approached SanDisk, having made a studied and considered determination of infringement by SanDisk, having communicated that determination to SanDisk, and then saying that it does not intend to sue, ST is engaging in the kinds of "extra-judicial patent enforcement with scare-the-customer-and-run tactics" that the Declaratory Judgment Act was intended to obviate. *Arrowhead*, 846 F.2d at 735. ST's statement that it does not intend to sue does not moot the actual contro-versy created by its acts.

* * *

Bryson, Circuit Judge, concurring in the result.

Under our law, as things stood before the Supreme Court's decision in *MedImmune*, the district court's order in this case was correct. ST, the patentee, had offered a license to SanDisk, but had not threatened suit and had sought to continue licensing negotiations. Although ST had made a detailed showing as to why it believed SanDisk's products were within the scope of its patent rights, there is nothing exceptional in that. In the typical case, we would expect com-petent patent counsel who offers a license to another party to be prepared to demonstrate why such a license is required. By the time the suit was brought, ST had done nothing to give SanDisk cause to be in reasonable apprehension of suit, and in fact ST had expressly stated that it did not intend to sue SanDisk. In short, ST was simply availing itself of the safe haven our cases had created for patentees to offer licenses without opening themselves up to expensive litigation.

The decision in *MedImmune* dealt with a narrow issue: whether a declaratory judgment action can be brought by a patent licensee without terminating the licensing agreement. Footnote 11 of the *MedImmune* opinion, however, went further and criticized this court's "reasonable apprehension of suit" test for

---

3. Although the district court found that licensing negotiations had not been terminated, we note that SanDisk in fact declined to participate in further negotiations, effectively bringing them to an end. Regardless, however, a party to licensing negotiations is of course within its rights to terminate negotiations when it appears that they will be unproductive.

declaratory judgment jurisdiction. I agree with the court that the footnote calls our case law into question and would appear to make declaratory judgments more readily available to parties who are approached by patentees seeking to license their patents. In particular, the reasoning of the *MedImmune* footnote seems to require us to hold that the district court in this case had jurisdiction to entertain SanDisk's declaratory judgment action. For that reason I concur in the judgment of the court in this case reversing the jurisdictional dismissal of the complaint.

I think it is important, however, to point out the implications of the footnote in *MedImmune* as applied here, because the implications are broader than one might suppose from reading the court's opinion in this case. While noting that it is not necessary to define the outer boundaries of declaratory judgment jurisdiction, the court holds that "where a patentee asserts rights under a patent based on certain identified ongoing or planned activity of another party, and where that party contends that it has the right to engage in the accused activity without license," the party may bring a declaratory judgment action. Applying that principle, the court concludes that in this case, where "ST sought a right to a royalty under its patents based on specific, identified activity by SanDisk," an Article III case or controversy has arisen.

In practical application, the new test will not be confined to cases with facts similar to this one. If a patentee offers a license for a fee, the offer typically will be accompanied by a suggestion that the other party's conduct is within the scope of the patentee's patent rights, or it will be apparent that the patentee believes that to be the case. Offers to license a patent are not requests for gratuitous contributions to the patentee; the rationale underlying a license offer is the patentee's express or implied suggestion that the other party's current or planned conduct falls within the scope of the patent. Therefore, it would appear that under the court's standard virtually any invitation to take a paid license relating to the prospective licensee's activities would give rise to an Article III case or controversy if the prospective licensee elects to assert that its conduct does not fall within the scope of the patent. Indeed, as the court makes clear, even a representation by the patentee that it does not propose to file suit against the prospective licensee will not suffice to avoid the risk that the patentee will face a declaratory judgment action. And if there is any uncertainty on that score, all the prospective licensee has to do in order to dispel any doubt is to inquire of the patentee whether the patentee believes its activities are within the scope of the patent. If the patentee says "no," it will have made a damaging admission that will make it very hard ever to litigate the issue, and thus will effectively end its licensing efforts. If it says "yes" or equivocates, it will have satisfied the court's test and will have set itself up for a declaratory judgment lawsuit.

For these reasons, I see nothing about the particular facts surrounding this licensing negotiation in this case that triggers SanDisk's right to bring a declaratory judgment action under the new standard. The court emphasizes that ST made a "detailed presentation [to SanDisk] which identified, on an element-by-element basis, the manner in which ST believed each of SanDisk's products infringed the specific claims of each of ST's patents." The court summarizes ST's presentation by stating that "ST communicated to SanDisk that it had made a studied and determined infringement determination and asserted a right to a royalty based on this determination" and that SanDisk "maintained that it could proceed in its conduct without the payment of royalties to ST." Those facts, the court concludes, evinced a sufficient controversy to entitle SanDisk to institute its declaratory judgment suit.

But what is the significance of those facts? The court's legal test does not suggest that the case would come out differently if ST had been less forthcoming about why it believed SanDisk should take a license, or even if ST had simply contacted SanDisk, provided copies of its patents, and suggested that SanDisk consider taking a license. I doubt the court would hold that there was no controversy in that setting, as long as SanDisk was prepared to assert that it believed its products were not within the scope of ST's valid patent rights. If SanDisk's lawyers had any question about whether this court would permit them to seek a declaratory judgment under those circumstances, they could readily resolve that question by sending a "put up or shut up" response to ST's licensing offer—asking ST to state expressly whether it regarded SanDisk's products to be within the scope of ST's patents and to identify with particularity how SanDisk's products read on particular claims of those patents. Any response by ST would either end its licensing efforts or expose it to a declaratory judgment action.[1]

In sum, the rule adopted by the court in this case will effect a sweeping change in our law regarding declaratory judgment jurisdiction. Despite the references in the court's opinion to the particular facts of this case, I see no practical stopping point short of allowing declaratory judgment actions in virtually any case in which the recipient of an invitation to take a patent license elects to dispute the need for a license and then to sue the patentee. Although I have reservations about the wisdom of embarking on such a course, I agree with the court that a fair reading of footnote 11 of the Supreme Court's opinion in *MedImmune* compels that result, and I therefore concur in the judgment reversing the district court's dismissal order in this case.

Comments

1. ***Opening DJ's Doors.*** As the *SanDisk* case reveals, it is easier to obtain declaratory judgment jurisdiction post-*MedImmune*. *See Micron Tech., Inc. v. Mosaid Techs., Inc.*, 518 F.3d 897, 902 (Fed. Cir. 2008) ("[T]he now more lenient legal standard facilitates or enhances the availability of declaratory judgment jurisdiction in patent cases."). For Judge Bryson, the standard was too lenient as interpreted by the *SanDisk* court:

   > [I]t would appear that under the court's standard virtually any invitation to take a paid license relating to the prospective licensee's activities would give rise to an Article III case or controversy if the prospective licensee elects to assert that its conduct does not fall within the scope of the patent.

   480 F.3d at 1384.

---

1. The court suggests that ST could have avoided the risk of a declaratory judgment action by obtaining a suitable confidentiality agreement. The problem with that suggestion is that it would normally work only when it was not needed—only a party that was not interested in bringing a declaratory judgment action would enter into such an agreement. A party that contemplates bringing a declaratory judgment action or at least keeping that option open would have no incentive to enter into such an agreement.

2. **MedImmune and Its Effort on Licensing Practice.** The Federal Circuit has understandably interpreted *MedImmune*'s footnote 11 as a rejection of the court's "reasonable apprehension" test. *See Teva Pharmaceuticals USA, Inc. v. Novartis Pharmaceuticals Corp.*, 482 F.3d 1330, 1339 (Fed. Cir. 2007) (stating "because the Supreme Court in *MedImmune* cautioned that our declaratory judgment 'reasonable-apprehension-of-suit' test 'contradict[s]' and 'conflicts' with its precedent, these Federal Circuit tests have been 'overruled by . . . an intervening . . . Supreme Court decision'"). In its place, the question is "whether the facts alleged, under all the circumstances, show that there is a substantial controversy, between the parties having adverse legal interests, of sufficient immediacy and reality to warrant the issuance of a declaratory judgment." DJ jurisdiction will not arise by the mere existence of a patent or even if a DJ plaintiff—without some affirmative act by the patentee—perceives a risk of infringement. For there to be a case or controversy under Article III, the dispute must be "definite and concrete, touching the legal relations of parties having adverse legal interests," "real and substantial," and "admi[t] of specific relief through a decree of a conclusive character, as distinguished from an opinion advising what the law would be upon a hypothetical state of facts." *Prasco LLC v. Medicis Pharmaceutical Corp.*, 537 F.3d 1329, 1335 (Fed. Cir. 2008) (quoting *MedImmune*, 549 U.S. at 127). As the *SanDisk* court noted, "Article III jurisdiction may be met where the patentee takes a position that puts the declaratory judgment plaintiff in the position of either pursuing arguably illegal behavior or abandoning that which he claims a right to do." *SanDisk*, 480 F.3d at 1381. In other words, DJ jurisdiction exists "where a patentee asserts rights under a patent based on certain identified ongoing or planned activity of another party, and where that party contends that it has the right to engage in the accused activity without license." *Id.* While there is no bright line rule that triggers a "case or controversy," certain patterns can be gleaned from Federal Circuit cases.

For example, in *Matthews Int'l Corp. v. Biosafe Eng'g, LLC*, 695 F.3d 1322 (Fed. Cir. 2012), the court emphasized two facts that must be met before DJ jurisdiction can be established: immediacy and reality. The alleged infringer (Matthews) marketed a product called "Bio Cremation," which employed a more "environmentally friendly" process compared to "flame-based cremation." Matthews alleged that in a phone conversation he had with Biosafe's president, he was informed "that [Matthews's] sale of Bio Cremation equipment would infringe [Biosafe's] alleged intellectual property rights." In response to a request by Matthews for a letter detailing the infringement claim, Biosafe wrote "that Biosafe could pursue 'a variety of remedies for disputes involving intellectual property rights.'" Matthews subsequently filed a declaratory judgment action asserting invalidity. The district court dismissed Matthews's complaint because the Bio Cremation product was still "fluid and indeterminate" and that "Matthews' devices [were] not settled and those devices could 'be operated with parameters outside of the various ones specified' in the [Biosafe's] patents.'" The Federal Circuit affirmed. The court noted that a "justiciable controversy" exists only where a dispute is "definite and concrete." And while there is "no facile, all-purpose standard to police the line between declaratory judgment actions which satisfy the case or controversy requirement and those that do not," the court must determine whether the specific facts of a given case "show that there is a substantial controversy, between parties having adverse legal interests, of sufficient immediacy and reality to warrant the issuance of a declaratory judgment."

Immediacy was lacking here "because there is no evidence as to when, if ever, the Bio Cremation equipment will be used in a manner that could potentially infringe" Biosafe's patents. The reality requirement was also lacking because Matthews's product was too "fluid and indeterminate." As the court noted, "[t]he greater the variability of the subject of a declaratory-judgment suit, particularly as to its potentially infringing features, the greater the chance that the court's judgment will be purely advisory, detached from the eventual, actual content of that subject—in short, detached from eventual reality." Matthews did not provide sufficient evidence of specific parameters relating to infringement; in other words, Bio Creation was not "substantially fixed" as the "equipment can be operated using a variety of process parameters, some of which would not infringe the Biosafe's patents."

Another scenario where DJ jurisdiction was lacking related to a letter from the patentee that merely identifies a patent and the recipient's product. But correspondence setting forth detailed claim charts and infringement analysis are likely to give rise to declaratory jurisdiction. In *Sony Electronics, Inc. v. Guardian Media Tech. Ltd.*, 497 F.3d 1271 (Fed. Cir. 2007), the patentee sent the accused infringer correspondence having detailed infringement charts explaining how the accused products fell within the patentee's claims, and offered to license its patents. Correspondence between the parties continued for five years. Eventually, Sony filed for a declaratory judgment. The Federal Circuit held the DJ jurisdiction existed, rejecting Guardian's assertion "that there can be no jurisdiction in the courts because it was at all times willing to negotiate a "business resolution" to the dispute." *Id.* at 1286. The court continued: "[B]ecause Guardian asserts that it is owed royalties based on specific past and ongoing activities by Sony, and because Sony contends that it has a right to engage in those activities without a license, there is an actual controversy between the parties within the meaning of the Declaratory Judgment Act." *Id.*

In *Hewlett-Packard Co. v. Acceleron LLC*, 587 F.3d 1358 (Fed. Cir. 2009), the patentee, Acceleron, wrote Hewlett-Packard twice and each time imposed a two-week deadline for H-P to respond. Acceleron also noted that if H-P did not respond by the deadline, "it would understand that HP did not 'have anything to say about the merits of this patent, or its relevance to [HP's] Blade Server products.'" *Id.* at 1363. There was no threat of infringement or detailed claim charts in the correspondence. The Federal Circuit found DJ jurisdiction existed, stating "[t]he purpose of a declaratory judgment action cannot be defeated simply by the stratagem of a correspondence that avoids the magic words such as 'litigation' or 'infringement.' . . . But it is implausible (especially after *MedImmune* and several post *MedImmune* decisions from this court) to expect that a competent lawyer drafting such correspondence for a patent owner would identify specific claims, present claim charts, and explicitly allege infringement." *Id.* at 1363. Moreover, the court was influenced by the fact that Acceleron was a patent holding company and not a competitor of H-P. Accordingly, the court agreed with the district court's finding that "the receipt of . . . correspondence from a non-competitor patent holding company . . . may invoke a different reaction than would a meet-and-discuss inquiry by a competitor, presumably with intellectual property of its own to place on the bargaining table." *Id.*

In *3M v. Avery Dennison Corp.*, 673 F.3d 1372 (Fed. Cir. 2012), the chief IP counsel—Sardesai—of the patentee (Avery), spoke by telephone with his counterpart at 3M—Rhodes—informing him that a 3M product line "may infringe" Avery's Heenan patents and "licenses are available." A few days later, the attorneys spoke again (this time Rhodes telephoned), and 3M informed Avery that it is not interested in a license. Sardesai responded that it analyzed 3M's products and will "send claim charts." No charts were ever sent, but 3M nonetheless filed a DJ action. The district dismissed 3M's DJ, but the Federal Circuit vacated and remanded. The court initially noted, quoting *Hewlett-Packard*, that "[t]o establish the existence of a 'definite and concrete' dispute, more is required than 'a communication from a patent owner to another party, merely identifying its patent and the other party's product line.'" *Id.* at 1378-1379. But the content of the communications in the present case "would be sufficient to constitute a case or controversy between 3M and Avery." According to the court, "[t]hat Sardesai employed the term 'may infringe' instead of 'does infringe' is immaterial in light of his offer to license the Heenan patents, his representation that Avery had analyzed [3M accused products], and his statement that claim charts would be forthcoming." *Id. See Hewlett-Packard*, 587 F.3d at 1362 (explaining that the purpose of a declaratory judgment action cannot be defeated by avoiding "magic words" and noting that, post-*MedImmune*, it is implausible to expect that correspondence from a patentee would "identify specific claims, present claim charts, and explicitly allege infringement").

The Federal Circuit has denied DJ jurisdiction in other cases. For example, in *Prasco LLC, supra*, the DJ plaintiff—Prasco—based jurisdiction on the fact that Medicis (the patentee) marked its commercial products with patent numbers and filed a patent infringement suit against another competitor. Medicis did not know that Prasco planned on marketing a competing product until the DJ suit was filed. The court noted that a DJ "controversy must be based on a *real* and *immediate* injury or threat of future injury that is *caused by the defendants*—an objective standard that cannot be met by a purely subjective or speculative fear of future harm." *Id.* at 1338 (emphasis in original).

In *Panavise Products, Inc. v. National Products, Inc.*, 306 Fed. Appx. 570 (Fed. Cir. 2009), the court rejected DJ jurisdiction based on Panavise's (the DJ plaintiff) following claims: (1) Panavise "manufactured and produced," "publicly used and displayed," "distributed and continued to distribute samples of," and "[would] begin or had begun distribution and sales of" a "potentially infringing device known as the Model '811 Series"; (2) the patentee observed the Model 811 Series at a trade show in Las Vegas in January 2008; and (3) the patentee has filed various lawsuits against various entities, alleging infringement of NPI's patents, including the patent Panavise is challenging. *Id.* at 571.

And in *Innovative Therapies, Inc. v. Kinetic Concepts, Inc.*, 599 F.3d 1377 (Fed. Cir. 2010), the Federal Circuit agreed with the district court's holding denying DJ jurisdiction. KCI had not seen the ITI device, had not examined it for possible infringement of any KCI patent, and had not accused ITI of infringement. Nonetheless, Innovative Therapies (ITI) asserted an actual controversy existed based on (1) ITI's representations to the FDA, (2) ITI's phone calls to KCI executives, and (3) KCI's patent enforcement history. ITI received expedited pre-marketing approval of its device based on ITI representations to the FDA that its device has the "same technological characteristics" as KCI's previously approved wound therapy device and other FDA-approved devices that KCI has charged with infringement. The court stated "representations to a third person about "technological characteristics" do not establish a justiciable controversy with the patentee." The same would hold true even if KCI had knowledge of ITI's representations to the FDA. *Id.* at 1380. Regarding phone calls made by ITI to KCI to gauge KCI's response to ITI introducing its device, ITI argues that KCI executives suggested the KCI would act aggressively and enforce its patent rights. The district court held—and the Federal Circuit agreed—these phone calls represented a "sub rosa" attempt to establish DJ jurisdiction "by initiating telephone conversations to employees of the patentee who were not in decision-making positions and who were not informed of the real purpose behind the conversations." *Id.* at 1381. And, lastly, with respect to KCI's enforcement history, the Federal Circuit, citing *Prasco,* stated "the fact that KCI had filed infringement suits against other parties for other products does not, in the absence of any act directed toward ITI, meet the minimum standard discussed in *MedImmune.*" *Id.* at 1382.

3. ***Strategies to Avoid DJ Jurisdiction.*** What strategies would you employ to avoid DJ jurisdiction while also seeking to protect your client's patent rights? What do think of the following?
    1. Dispatch an *"innocuous" demand letter* that simply puts the alleged infringer on notice of your client's patent rights absent claim charts, infringement analysis, or demands for licensing negotiations. How effective are such letters likely to be?
    2. Enter into a *confidentiality agreement* with the alleged infringer prior to negotiations. Recall the *SanDisk* court's statement in footnote 1: "To avoid the risk of a declaratory judgment action, ST could have sought SanDisk's agreement to the terms of a suitable confidentiality agreement." Why is this type of agreement useful in avoiding DJ jurisdiction? Is it because confidential communications cannot be used to establish DJ jurisdiction? How likely is it that a sophisticated alleged infringer/potential licensee would sign such an agreement? The answer may depend on how sophisticated and financially secure the patentee is.
    3. Seek a six-month or one-year *standstill agreement* whereby the parties agree not to bring suit.
    4. File suit *before* sending a demand letter in a forum of choice that is most convenient for the parties, thus limiting the possibility of transfer based on the first-to-file rule (FTF rule). The FTF rule holds that the first court to have jurisdiction of the parties and issues has priority over a subsequent court when the issues largely overlap. *See Genentech, Inc. v. Eli Lilly and Co.,* 998 F.3d 931, 937 (Fed. Cir. 2003) ("We prefer to apply in patent cases the general rule whereby the forum of the first-filed case is favored, unless considerations of judicial and litigant economy, and the just and effective disposition of disputes, require otherwise."). *But see Micron Technology, Inc. v. Mosaid Technologies, Inc.,* 518 F.3d 897, 904 (Fed. Cir. 2008) (arguably weakening "first-to-file" rule in the context of declaratory judgment by providing "added significance" to exceptions to FTF rule such as "convenience factors").

5. A patentee may file suit without formally serving the alleged infringer for 120 days. Therefore, a demand letter sent after filing, but before service, may enhance the chances of successful negotiations and illustrate to the alleged infringer that the patentee is serious about enforcing its patent rights.

4. **DJ Jurisdiction and the Notice Requirement.** A patentee will not be able to recover damages until the alleged infringer has actual or constructive notice, and then damages will be available only for subsequent infringing activity. *See* 35 U.S.C. § 287(a). *See also Maxwell v. J. Baker, Inc.*, 86 F.3d 1098, 1111 (Fed. Cir. 1996). In the light of *SanDisk* and *MedImmune*, therefore, can a patentee satisfy the actual notice requirement without opening the door to a declaratory judgment claim of invalidity or noninfringement? This may be one of the broad implications that Judge Bryson was referring to regarding the majority's reading of *MedImmune*'s footnote 11.

B. ANTITRUST

This section explores the relationship between patent law and antitrust law. Antitrust law and patent law have a long and contentious history. Traditionally, it was thought that these two areas of law had inconsistent goals. On the one hand, patent law was seen as creating monopolies, whereas antitrust law was focused on dismantling them. But economic thinking on the subject—beginning in the late 1970s and 1980s—portrays a more complementary relationship with each body of law viewed as vehicles to promote innovation and competition, albeit by different means.[8] Despite this greater harmony, however, certain forms of patentee behavior can have antitrust implications.

The first issue addressed, in *Illinois Tool Works*, relates to patents and market power, a notion that is at the core of antitrust doctrine. Thereafter, various forms of patentee behavior are examined through the lens of antitrust law, including—in *Nobelpharma*—enforcement of a fraudulently obtained patent; a patentee's refusal to license his patent in *Independent Service Organizations Antitrust Litigation*; and, lastly, settlement agreements, particularly between a name-brand pharmaceutical company and a generic concern, in *Tamoxifen Citrate Antitrust Litigation*.

1. Patents and Market Power

Market power can be defined as the ability of a firm to price a product above its marginal cost without losing substantial sales, or as the "ability profitably

---

8. *See, e.g.,* ANTITRUST GUIDELINES FOR THE LICENSING OF INTELLECTUAL PROPERTY §1.0 (Department of Justice and Federal Trade Commission 1995) (stating "intellectual property laws and the antitrust laws share the common purpose of promoting innovation and enhancing consumer welfare"); *Intergraph Corp. v. Intel Corp.*, 195 F.3d 1346, 1362 (Fed. Cir. 1999) (stating "[t]he patent and antitrust laws are complementary, the patent system serving to encourage invention and the bringing of new products to market by adjusting investment-based risk, and the antitrust laws serving to foster industrial competition"). *See also* Thomas F. Cotter, *Reflections on the Antitrust Modernization Commission's Report and Recommendations Relating to the Antitrust/IP Interface*, 53 ANTITRUST BULL. 745 (2008).

to maintain prices above, or output below, competitive levels for a significant period of time."[9] In a perfectly competitive market, no firm has market power or what can be called an *economic* monopoly. Patent rights give rise to a *legal* monopoly because the patentee can exclude others from making, using, or selling goods that fall within its claim scope. Importantly, however, patent rights seldom give rise to an *economic* monopoly or market power because there are almost always viable substitutes. The *Illinois Tool* case explores the issue of patents and market power.

ILLINOIS TOOL WORKS INC. v. INDEPENDENT INK, INC.

547 U.S. 28 (2006)

Justice STEVENS delivered the opinion of the Court.

The question presented to us today is whether the presumption of market power in a patented product should survive as a matter of antitrust law despite its demise in patent law. We conclude that the mere fact that a tying product is patented does not support such a presumption.

I

Petitioners, Trident, Inc., and its parent, Illinois Tool Works Inc., manufacture and market printing systems that include three relevant components: (1) a patented piezoelectric impulse ink jet printhead; (2) a patented ink container, consisting of a bottle and valved cap, which attaches to the printhead; and (3) specially designed, but unpatented, ink. Petitioners sell their systems to original equipment manufacturers (OEMs) who are licensed to incorporate the printheads and containers into printers that are in turn sold to companies for use in printing barcodes on cartons and packaging materials. The OEMs agree that they will purchase their ink exclusively from petitioners, and that neither they nor their customers will refill the patented containers with ink of any kind.

Respondent, Independent Ink, Inc. has developed an ink with the same chemical composition as the ink sold by petitioners. After an infringement action brought by Trident against Independent was dismissed for lack of personal jurisdiction, Independent filed suit against Trident seeking a judgment of noninfringement and invalidity of Trident's patents. In an amended complaint, it alleged that petitioners are engaged in illegal tying and monopolization in violation of §§1 and 2 of the Sherman Act. 15 U.S.C. §§1, 2.

After a careful review of the "long history of Supreme Court consideration of the legality of tying arrangements," 396 F.3d 1342, 1346 (2005), the Court of Appeals for the Federal Circuit reversed the District Court's decision as to respondent's §1 claim, *id.*, at 1354. Placing special reliance on our decisions in *International Salt Co. v. United States,* and *Loew's,* as well as our *Jefferson Parish* dictum, and after taking note of the academic criticism of those cases, it concluded that the "fundamental error" in petitioners' submission was its disregard of "the duty of a court of appeals to follow the precedents of the Supreme Court until the Court itself chooses to expressly overrule them." 396 F.3d, at 1351. We

---

9. ANTITRUST GUIDELINES FOR THE LICENSING OF INTELLECTUAL PROPERTY §2.2 (Dep't of Justice and Federal Trade Commission 1995).

granted certiorari to undertake a fresh examination of the history of both the judicial and legislative appraisals of tying arrangements. Our review is informed by extensive scholarly comment and a change in position by the administrative agencies charged with enforcement of the antitrust laws.

II

Over the years this Court's strong disapproval of tying arrangements has substantially diminished. Rather than relying on assumptions, in its more recent opinions the Court has required a showing of market power in the tying product.

In rejecting the application of a *per se* rule that all tying arrangements constitute antitrust violations, we explained:

> [W]e have condemned tying arrangements when the seller has some special ability—usually called "market power"—to force a purchaser to do something that he would not do in a competitive market. . . .

Per se condemnation—condemnation without inquiry into actual market conditions—is only appropriate if the existence of forcing is probable. Thus, application of the *per se* rule focuses on the probability of anticompetitive consequences. . . .

> For example, if the Government has granted the seller a patent or similar monopoly over a product, it is fair to presume that the inability to buy the product elsewhere gives the seller market power. *United States v. Loew's Inc.,* 371 U.S., at 45-47. Any effort to enlarge the scope of the patent monopoly by using the market power it confers to restrain competition in the market for a second product will undermine competition on the merits in that second market. Thus, the sale or lease of a patented item on condition that the buyer make all his purchases of a separate tied product from the patentee is unlawful.

Jefferson, 466 U.S. at 13-16.

Notably, nothing in our opinion suggested a rebuttable presumption of market power applicable to tying arrangements involving a patent on the tying good. Instead, it described the rule that a contract to sell a patented product on condition that the purchaser buy unpatented goods exclusively from the patentee is a *per se* violation of §1 of the Sherman Act.

Justice O'Connor wrote separately in *Jefferson Parish,* concurring in the judgment on the ground that the case did not involve a true tying arrangement because, in her view, surgical services and anesthesia were not separate products. In her opinion, she questioned not only the propriety of treating any tying arrangement as a *per se* violation of the Sherman Act, but also the validity of the presumption that a patent always gives the patentee significant market power, observing that the presumption was actually a product of our patent misuse cases rather than our antitrust jurisprudence. It is that presumption, a vestige of the Court's historical distrust of tying arrangements, that we address squarely today.

III

Justice O'Connor was, of course, correct in her assertion that the presumption that a patent confers market power arose outside the antitrust context as part of the patent misuse doctrine. That doctrine had its origins in *Motion Picture*

Patents Co. v. Universal Film Mfg. Co., 243 U.S. 502 (1917), which found no support in the patent laws for the proposition that a patentee may "prescribe by notice attached to a patented machine the conditions of its use and the supplies which must be used in the operation of it, under pain of infringement of the patent," *id.,* at 509. Although *Motion Picture Patents Co.* simply narrowed the scope of possible patent infringement claims, it formed the basis for the Court's subsequent decisions creating a patent misuse defense to infringement claims when a patentee uses its patent "as the effective means of restraining competition with its sale of an unpatented article." *Morton Salt Co. v. G.S. Suppiger Co.,* 314 U.S. 488, 490 (1942).

Without any analysis of actual market conditions, these patent misuse decisions assumed that, by tying the purchase of unpatented goods to the sale of the patented good, the patentee was "restraining competition," *Morton Salt,* 314 U.S., at 490, or "secur[ing] a limited monopoly of an unpatented material," *Mercoid,* 320 U.S., at 664. In other words, these decisions presumed "[t]he requisite economic power" over the tying product such that the patentee could "extend [its] economic control to unpatented products." *Loew's,* 371 U.S., at 45-46.

The presumption that a patent confers market power migrated from patent law to antitrust law in *International Salt Co. v. United States,* 332 U.S. 392 (1947). In that case, we affirmed a District Court decision holding that leases of patented machines requiring the lessees to use the defendant's unpatented salt products violated § 1 of the Sherman Act and § 3 of the Clayton Act as a matter of law. *Id.,* at 396. Although the Court's opinion does not discuss market power or the patent misuse doctrine, it assumes that "[t]he volume of business affected by these contracts cannot be said to be insignificant or insubstantial and the tendency of the arrangement to accomplishment of monopoly seems obvious." *Ibid.*

IV

Although the patent misuse doctrine and our antitrust jurisprudence became intertwined in *International Salt,* subsequent events initiated their untwining. This process has ultimately led to today's reexamination of the presumption of *per se* illegality of a tying arrangement involving a patented product, the first case since 1947 in which we have granted review to consider the presumption's continuing validity.

Three years before we decided *International Salt,* this Court had expanded the scope of the patent misuse doctrine to include not only supplies or materials used by a patented device, but also tying arrangements involving a combination patent and "unpatented material or [a] device [that] is itself an integral part of the structure embodying the patent." *Mercoid,* 320 U.S., at 665. In reaching this conclusion, the Court explained that it could see "no difference in principle" between cases involving elements essential to the inventive character of the patent and elements peripheral to it; both, in the Court's view, were attempts to "expan[d] the patent beyond the legitimate scope of its monopoly." *Mercoid,* 320 U.S., at 665.

Shortly thereafter, Congress codified the patent laws for the first time. At least partly in response to our *Mercoid* decision, Congress included a provision in its codification that excluded some conduct, such as a tying arrangement involving the sale of a patented product tied to an "essential" or "nonstaple" product that has no use except as part of the patented product or method, from the scope of the patent misuse doctrine. §271(d). Thus, at the same time that our antitrust jurisprudence continued to rely on the assumption that "tying arrangements generally serve no legitimate business purpose," *Fortner I,* 394 U.S., at 503, Congress began chipping away at the assumption in the patent misuse context from whence it came.

It is Congress' most recent narrowing of the patent misuse defense, however, that is directly relevant to this case. Four years after our decision in *Jefferson Parish* repeated the patent-equals-market-power presumption, 466 U.S., at 16, Congress amended the Patent Code to eliminate that presumption in the patent misuse context. The relevant provision reads:

> (d) No patent owner otherwise entitled to relief for infringement or contributory infringement of a patent shall be denied relief or deemed guilty of misuse or illegal extension of the patent right by reason of his having done one or more of the following: . . . (5) conditioned the license of any rights to the patent or the sale of the patented product on the acquisition of a license to rights in another patent or purchase of a separate product, *unless, in view of the circumstances, the patent owner has market power in the relevant market for the patent or patented product on which the license or sale is conditioned.*

35 U.S.C. §271(d)(5) (emphasis added).

The italicized clause makes it clear that Congress did not intend the mere existence of a patent to constitute the requisite "market power." Indeed, fairly read, it provides that without proof that Trident had market power in the relevant market, its conduct at issue in this case was neither "misuse" nor an "illegal extension of the patent right."

While the 1988 amendment does not expressly refer to the antitrust laws, it certainly invites a reappraisal of the *per se* rule announced in *International Salt.* A rule denying a patentee the right to enjoin an infringer is significantly less severe than a rule that makes the conduct at issue a federal crime punishable by up to 10 years in prison. It would be absurd to assume that Congress intended to provide that the use of a patent that merited punishment as a felony would not constitute "misuse." Moreover, given the fact that the patent misuse doctrine provided the basis for the market power presumption, it would be anomalous to preserve the presumption in antitrust after Congress has eliminated its foundation.

After considering the congressional judgment reflected in the 1988 amendment, we conclude that tying arrangements involving patented products should be evaluated under the standards applied in cases like *Fortner II* and *Jefferson Parish* rather than under the *per se* rule applied in *Morton Salt* and *Loew's.* While some such arrangements are still unlawful, such as those that are the product of a true monopoly or a marketwide conspiracy, that conclusion must be supported by proof of power in the relevant market rather than by a mere presumption thereof.[4]

V

Rather than arguing that we should retain the rule of *per se* illegality, respondent contends that we should endorse a rebuttable presumption that patentees

---

4. Our imposition of this requirement accords with the vast majority of academic literature on the subject.

possess market power when they condition the purchase of the patented product on an agreement to buy unpatented goods exclusively from the patentee. Respondent recognizes that a large number of valid patents have little, if any, commercial significance, but submits that those that are used to impose tying arrangements on unwilling purchasers likely do exert significant market power. Hence, in respondent's view, the presumption would have no impact on patents of only slight value and would be justified, subject to being rebutted by evidence offered by the patentee, in cases in which the patent has sufficient value to enable the patentee to insist on acceptance of the tie.

Respondent also offers a narrower alternative, suggesting that we differentiate between tying arrangements involving the simultaneous purchase of two products that are arguably two components of a single product—such as the provision of surgical services and anesthesiology in the same operation, *Jefferson Parish*, 466 U.S., at 43, or the licensing of one copyrighted film on condition that the licensee take a package of several films in the same transaction, and a tying arrangement involving the purchase of unpatented goods over a period of time, a so-called "requirements tie." According to respondent, we should recognize a presumption of market power when faced with the latter type of arrangements because they provide a means for charging large volume purchasers a higher royalty for use of the patent than small purchasers must pay, a form of discrimination that "is strong evidence of market power."

The opinion that imported the "patent equals market power" presumption into our antitrust jurisprudence, however, provides no support for respondent's proposed alternative. In *International Salt*, it was the existence of the patent on the tying product, rather than the use of a requirements tie, that led the Court to presume market power. Moreover, the requirements tie in that case did not involve any price discrimination between large volume and small volume purchasers or evidence of noncompetitive pricing. Instead, the leases at issue provided that if any competitor offered salt, the tied product, at a lower price, "the lessee should be free to buy in the open market, unless appellant would furnish the salt at an equal price." *Id.*, at 396.

As we have already noted, the vast majority of academic literature recognizes that a patent does not necessarily confer market power. Similarly, while price discrimination may provide evidence of market power, particularly if buttressed by evidence that the patentee has charged an above-market price for the tied package, it is generally recognized that it also occurs in fully competitive markets. We are not persuaded that the combination of these two factors should give rise to a presumption of market power when neither is sufficient to do so standing alone. Rather, the lesson to be learned from *International Salt* and the academic commentary is the same: Many tying arrangements, even those involving patents and requirements ties, are fully consistent with a free, competitive market. For this reason, we reject both respondent's proposed rebuttable presumption and their narrower alternative.

It is no doubt the virtual consensus among economists that has persuaded the enforcement agencies to reject the position that the Government took when it supported the *per se* rule that the Court adopted in the 1940's. In antitrust guidelines issued jointly by the Department of Justice and the Federal Trade Commission in 1995, the enforcement agencies stated that in the exercise of their prosecutorial discretion they "will not presume that a patent, copyright, or trade secret necessarily confers market power upon its owner." U.S. Dept. of

Justice and FTC, Antitrust Guidelines for the Licensing of Intellectual Property §2.2 (Apr. 6, 1995). While that choice is not binding on the Court, it would be unusual for the Judiciary to replace the normal rule of lenity that is applied in criminal cases with a rule of severity for a special category of antitrust cases.

Congress, the antitrust enforcement agencies, and most economists have all reached the conclusion that a patent does not necessarily confer market power upon the patentee. Today, we reach the same conclusion, and therefore hold that, in all cases involving a tying arrangement, the plaintiff must prove that the defendant has market power in the tying product.

VI

In this case, respondent reasonably relied on our prior opinions in moving for summary judgment without offering evidence defining the relevant market or proving that petitioners possess power within it. When the case returns to the District Court, respondent should therefore be given a fair opportunity to develop and introduce evidence on that issue, as well as any other issues that are relevant to its remaining §1 claims. Accordingly, the judgment of the Court of Appeals is vacated, and the case is remanded for further proceedings consistent with this opinion.

Comments

1. *Market Power and Patents.* Market power is the ability of a firm to price a product above its marginal cost without losing substantial sales. *See* Benjamin Klein, *Market Power in Antitrust: Economic Analysis After* Kodak, 3 SUP. CT. ECON. REV. 43, 72 (1993) ("Most economists . . . would label the situation where a firm can increase the price of its product without losing significant sales, and thereby can engage in price discrimination, as one where the firm possesses some market power"); Marcel Kahan & Ehud Kamar, *Price Discrimination in the Market for Corporate Law*, 86 CORNELL L. REV. 1205, 1210-1211 (2001) (stating "market power . . . is defined as the ability to charge more for a product than its marginal cost. Since charging more for a product than its marginal cost is a condition for earning a profit, the ability to earn a profit over an extended period of time is evidence that a producer has market power").

   There is an important distinction between, on the one hand, having market power or an *economic* monopoly, and, on the other hand, having a *legal* monopoly. A patent and its right to exclude confer a legal monopoly. But this right rarely gives rise to an economic monopoly because the claimed invention is usually accompanied by the availability of viable substitutes. The *Illinois Tool Works* case recognized this distinction, as have several scholars. *See, e.g., Panel Discussion: The Value of Patents and Other Legally Protected Commercial Rights*, 53 ANTITRUST L.J. 535, 547 (1985) (F.M. Scherer speaking) ("A patented product may well be unique. It may, however, face a lot of substitutes, perhaps equally unique; and, as a result of this extensive availability of substitutes, confer very little, if any, monopoly power. Statistical studies suggest that the vast majority of all patents confer very little monopoly power—at least, they are not very profitable."); 1 HERBERT HOVENKAMP, MARK D. JANIS & MARK A. LEMLEY, IP AND ANTITRUST §4.2a (2005) (noting a patent grant "is not even a guarantee of market success," let alone giving rise to an economic monopoly); WILLIAM M. LANDES & RICHARD A. POSNER, THE ECONOMIC STRUCTURE OF INTELLECTUAL PROPERTY LAW 374-375 (2003) (stating "[t]he *average* patent . . . confers too little market power on the patentee in a meaningful economic sense to interest a rational antitrust enforcer, and sometimes it confers no monopoly power at all") (emphasis in original); Michael A. Carrier, *Unraveling the Patent-Antitrust Paradox*, 150 U. PA. L. REV. 761, 791 (2002) (stating "patents typically do not demonstrate market power, and the set of technological substitutes that cannot be practiced because of the patent grant often has little overlap with the set of products that consumers view as economic substitutes").

But the lack of market power does not necessarily mean an absence of economic rents. Indeed, although a patent does not assure commercial success, the ability of a patentee to price its patented good above marginal cost is a principal benefit of having a patent. *See* Kenneth Dam, *The Economic Underpinnings of Patent Law*, 23 J. LEGAL STUD. 247, 250 (1994) (asserting a "patent that reduces the cost of making a product will permit the patentee to enjoy economic rent. To be sure, this statement assumes that other producers are not able to use the innovation to reduce cost, but that is precisely the purpose of the power to exclude from 'manufacture, use, and sale' granted by a patent"). This point is particularly germane to the pricing of pharmaceuticals, as discussed in Comment 3, below.

2. ***Distinguishing Between Anticompetitive and Legitimate Conduct.*** While discerning whether a patent confers market power is obviously important, a finding of market power does not necessarily lead to antitrust liability. The patentee must also engage in anticompetitive conduct. *See Verizon Communs., Inc. v. Law Offices of Curtis V. Trinko, LLP*, 540 U.S. 398, 407 (2004) ("The mere possession of monopoly power, and the concomitant charging of monopoly prices, is not only not unlawful; it is an important element of the free-market system. . . . To safeguard the incentive to innovate, the possession of monopoly power will not be found unlawful unless it is accompanied by an element of anticompetitive *conduct.*") (emphasis in original). This type of conduct has been defined as that which "serves no legitimate purpose, or is itself unprofitable, and is undertaken in order to exclude or weaken competitors in anticipation of increased market power and resulting supracompetitive recoupment." A. Douglas Melamed & Ali M. Stoeppelwerth, *The* CSU *Case: Facts, Formalism and the Intersection of Antitrust and Intellectual Property Law*, 10 GEO. MASON L. REV. 407, 419 (2002). (Two types of anticompetitive conduct—*Walker Process* claims and sham litigation—are explored in section B.2.) But market power and supracompetitive profits that result from "'a superior product, business acumen, or historic accident' do not violate the antitrust laws." ANTITRUST GUIDELINES FOR THE LICENSING OF INTELLECTUAL PROPERTY § 2.2 (Dep't of Justice and Federal Trade Commission 1995). *See also United States v. Grinnell Corp.*, 384 U.S. 563, 570-571 (1966) (distinguishing between "willful acquisition or maintenance of that power as distinguished from growth or development as a consequence of a superior product, business acumen, or historic accident"); *U.S. v. Aluminum Co. of America*, 148 F.2d 416, 430 (2d Cir. 1945) (Hand, J.) (stating "[t]he successful competitor, having been urged to compete, must not be turned upon when he wins").

3. *Pharmaceuticals and Market Power.* To the extent there is an exception to the principle that patents rarely confer market power, it is likely to reside with patented drugs. *See* Thomas F. Cotter, *Refining the "Presumptive Illegality" Approach to Settlements of Patent Disputes Involving Reverse Payments: A Commentary on Hovenkamp, Janis and Lemley*, 87 MINN. L. REV. 1789, 1814 n.94 (2003) (stating "pharmaceutical patents . . . sometimes do confer market power"); Douglas Gary Lichtman, *Pricing Prozac: Why the Government Should Subsidize the Purchase of Patented Pharmaceuticals*, 11 HARV. J.L. & TECH. 123, 123 n.2 (1997) (stating "[a]lthough patents always confer some degree of market power, pharmaceutical patents are likely an extreme case. There are, after all, few substitutes for a patented drug like Prozac. Moreover, consumers in the pharmaceutical market (unlike consumers more generally) have no realistic option to defer consumption and thereby hold out for lower prices"). *Cf.* M. Howard Morse, *Product Market Definition in the Pharmaceutical Industry*, 71 ANTITRUST L.J. 633, 676 (2003) ("[Antitrust] [p]laintiffs in pharmaceutical cases cannot simply assume the existence of market power from the existence of patents, from pricing above short-run marginal cost, from generic entry at prices below the price of a branded drug, or from reduced output of the branded drug upon generic entry. A plaintiff's proposed narrow market definition that does not include therapeutic substitutes should be rejected unless the plaintiff presents a 'formal test' showing the various drugs' impact on the price and quantity of sales.").

The market power of drugs is likely to be stronger when pharmaceutical companies astutely employ—as they often do—patent and trademark protections. The signaling effect of a trademark can have a profound influence on consumers and physicians. *See In re Brand Name Prescription Drugs Antitrust Litigation*, 186 F.3d 781, 787 (7th Cir. 1999) ("Brand name prescription drugs ordinarily are patented, and, though the patent may have expired, the physicians who prescribe the drug may continue to prescribe the branded version rather than the generic substitute, whether out of inertia, or because they think the branded version may be produced under better quality control (the rationale for trademarks), or because the patient may feel greater confidence in a familiar brand. The same thing is true if the original brand, whether or not still protected by a patent, now has a therapeutically close substitute sold under a brand name that is less familiar to physicians or patients than the original brand. It would not be surprising, therefore, if *every* manufacturer of brand name prescription drugs had some market power.") (emphasis in original). *See also* Gideon Parchomovsky & Peter Seigleman, *Toward an Integrated Theory of Intellectual Property*, 88 VA. L. REV. 1455, 1460-1461 (2002) (discussing how "both patents and trademarks allow firms to appropriate the benefits of investment in Research and Development ('R&D') and product quality").

2. Walker Process *and "Sham" Litigation*

Antitrust liability may arise if a patentee fraudulently obtains a patent right and employs that right in an anticompetitive manner, namely enforcing or threatening to enforce the patent. This type of antitrust violation is known as a *Walker*

Process claim. In addition, an antitrust action can be sustained against a patentee who enforces his patent rights merely to interfere with a competitor's business relationships; in other words, the patentee enforces his patent even though he knows his patent is either invalid (although not fraudulently obtained) or not infringed. This type of antitrust violated is called a *Handgards* claim. Both *Walker Process* and *Handgards* claims are explored in *Nobelpharma*.

NOBELPHARMA AB v. IMPLANT INNOVATIONS, INC.

141 F.3d 1059 (Fed. Cir. 1998)

LOURIE, Circuit Judge.

Nobelpharma AB and Nobelpharma USA, Inc. (collectively, NP) appeal from the judgment of the United States District Court for the Northern District of Illinois holding that . . . (3) NP was not entitled to JMOL or, in the alternative, a new trial following the jury verdict in favor of 3I [Implant Innovations Inc.] on its antitrust counterclaim against NP, Dr. Per-Ingvar Branemark, and the Institute for Applied Biotechnology. We conclude that the district court did not err in . . . denying NP's motion for JMOL or a new trial on the antitrust counterclaim. Accordingly, the decision of the district court is affirmed.

BACKGROUND

Drs. Branemark and Bo-Thuresson af Ekenstam are the named inventors on the '891 patent, the application for which was filed in 1980 and claimed priority from a Swedish patent application that was filed in 1979. The patent claims "an element intended for implantation into bone tissue." This "element," when used as part of a dental implant, is placed directly into the jawbone where it acts as a tooth root substitute. The implants described and claimed in the patent are preferably made of titanium and have a network of particularly-sized and particularly-spaced "micropits." These micropits, which have diameters in the range of about 10 to 1000 nanometers or, preferably, 10 to 300 nanometers, allow a secure connection to form between the implant and growing bone tissue through a process called "osseointegration."

Branemark is also one of the authors of a book published in 1977, entitled "Osseointegrated Implants in the Treatment of the Edentulous Jaw Experienced from a 10-Year Period" (hereinafter "the 1977 Book"). As its title suggests, this book describes a decade-long clinical evaluation of patients who had received dental implants. The 1977 Book includes a single page containing four scanning electron micrographs (SEMs) of titanium implants that exhibit micropits. The caption describing these SEMs reads, in part: "Irregularities are produced during manufacturing in order to increase the retention of the implants within the mineralized tissue." 3I determined, based on measurements and calculations that it presented to the trial court, that the micropits shown in the 1977 Book have diameters within the range claimed in the '891 patent. However, the 1977 Book does not specifically refer to "micropits."

In preparing to file the Swedish patent application, af Ekenstam submitted a draft written description of the invention to the inventors' Swedish patent agent, Mr. Barnieske. This draft referred to the 1977 Book in the following translated passage:

> In ten years of material pertaining to titanium jaw implants in man, Branemark et al. [in the 1977 Book] have shown that a very high frequency of healing, as stated above, can be achieved by utilizing a carefully developed surgical technique and adequately produced implants.

However, Barnieske deleted all reference to the 1977 Book from the patent application that was ultimately filed in Sweden. Similarly, the 1977 Book is not mentioned in the U.S. patent application filed by Barnieske on behalf of Branemark and af Ekenstam.

In June 1980, while the U.S. patent application was pending, Branemark entered into an exclusive license agreement with NP covering the claimed technology. Barnieske kept NP informed of the prosecution of the U.S. patent application and received assistance from NP's U.S. patent agent. The '891 patent issued in 1982; NP has since asserted it in at least three patent infringement suits.

In July 1991, while Branemark was a member of NP's Board of Directors, NP brought this suit alleging that certain of 3I's dental implants infringed the '891 patent. 3I defended on the grounds of invalidity, unenforceability, and non-infringement. 3I also brought an antitrust counterclaim, based in part on the assertion that NP attempted to enforce a patent that it knew was invalid and unenforceable. Specifically, 3I alleged that when NP brought suit, NP was aware that the inventors' intentional failure to disclose the 1977 Book to the U.S. Patent and Trademark Office (PTO) would render the '891 patent unenforceable.

During its case-in-chief, NP introduced portions of a deposition of Branemark that apparently was conducted several years before this trial began in connection with a lawsuit involving neither NP nor 3I. NP also introduced into evidence portions of that deposition that were counter-designated for introduction by 3I. Branemark's deposition testimony included his admissions that one "could consider" the procedure used to manufacture the micropitted surface a trade secret, and "it might be" that there are details "important to making" the micropitted surface that are not disclosed in the patent. At the close of NP's case-in-chief, the district court granted 3I's motion for JMOL of invalidity and non infringement. The court held that the patent was invalid under §112, ¶1, for failure to disclose the best mode and that NP had failed to prove infringement. The court then denied NP's motion for JMOL on 3I's antitrust counterclaim, proceeded to inform the jury that the court had held the patent invalid, and allowed 3I to present the counterclaim to the jury.

After trial limited to the antitrust issue, the jury found in special verdicts, *inter alia*, that 3I had proven that (1) "the inventors or their agents or attorneys obtained the '891 patent through fraud," (2) NP "had knowledge that the '891 patent was obtained by fraud at the time this action was commenced against 3I," and (3) NP "brought this lawsuit against 3I knowing that the '891 patent was either invalid or unenforceable and with the intent of interfering directly with 3I's ability to compete in the relevant market." The jury awarded 3I approximately $3.3 million in compensatory damages, an amount the court trebled pursuant to section 4 of the Clayton Act, 15 U.S.C. §15 (1994). The court declined to rule on whether the patent was unenforceable for inequitable conduct, concluding that its judgment of invalidity rendered the issue of enforceability moot.

NP appealed to this court, challenging the district court's grant of 3I's motion for JMOL of invalidity and non-infringement and its denial of the post-verdict motion for JMOL or a new trial.

DISCUSSION

* * *

I. Antitrust Liability

I.

After the jury returned its verdict in favor of 3I on its counterclaim that NP violated the antitrust laws by bringing suit against 3I, the court denied NP's motion for JMOL or, in the alternative, for a new trial under Fed. R. Civ. P. 50(b). In denying NP's motion, the district court held that the verdict was supported, *inter alia*, by the jury's factual findings that the patent was obtained through "NP's knowing fraud upon, or intentional misrepresentations to, the [PTO]" and that "NP maintained and enforced the patent with knowledge of the patent's fraudulent derivation" and with the intent of interfering directly with 3I's ability to compete in the relevant market. The court further held, based on these findings, that the jury need not have considered whether NP's suit was "objectively baseless."

In support of its position that the court erred in denying its renewed motion for JMOL, NP argues that there was a lack of substantial evidence to support the jury's findings that the patent was obtained through "fraud" and that NP was aware of that conduct when it brought suit against 3I. NP also argues that these findings, even if supported by substantial evidence, do not provide a legal basis for the imposition of antitrust liability. Finally, NP argues that it is entitled to a new trial because the court failed to instruct the jury that bringing a lawsuit cannot be the basis for antitrust liability if that suit is not "objectively baseless."

3I responds that the jury's explicit findings that the patent was procured through fraudulent conduct and that NP knew of that conduct when it brought suit were supported by substantial evidence, and that these findings provide a sound basis for imposing antitrust liability on NP. Responding to NP's arguments for a new trial, 3I argues that an "objectively reasonable" or "objectively baseless" jury instruction was not necessary because the district court required that 3I prove that NP had actual knowledge of the fraud when it brought suit and that even if such an instruction had been necessary, NP waived this argument by failing to propose a jury instruction relating to an "objectively baseless" standard. We agree with 3I that the court did not err in denying NP's motion for JMOL because substantial evidence supports the jury's findings that the patent was fraudulently obtained and that NP sought to enforce the patent with knowledge of its fraudulent origin. Similarly, the court did not err in denying NP's motion for a new trial because NP was not prejudiced by any legally erroneous jury instruction.

II.

* * *

Whether conduct in the prosecution of a patent is sufficient to strip a patentee of its immunity from the antitrust laws is one of those issues that clearly involves our exclusive jurisdiction over patent cases. It follows that whether a patent infringement suit is based on a fraudulently procured patent impacts our exclusive jurisdiction.

Moreover, an antitrust claim premised on stripping a patentee of its immunity from the antitrust laws is typically raised as a counterclaim by a defendant in a patent infringement suit. *See Argus Chem. Corp. v. Fibre Glass-Evercoat Co.*, 812 F.2d 1381, 1383 (Fed. Cir. 1987) (*"Walker Process*, like the present case, was a patent infringement suit in which an accused infringer filed an antitrust counterclaim"). Because most cases involving these issues will therefore be appealed to this court, we conclude that we should decide these issues as a matter of Federal Circuit law, rather than rely on various regional precedents. We arrive at this conclusion because we are in the best position to create a uniform body of federal law on this subject and thereby avoid the "danger of confusion [that] might be enhanced if this court were to embark on an effort to interpret the laws" of the regional circuits. *Forman v. United States*, 767 F.2d 875, 880 n.6 (Fed. Cir. 1985). Accordingly, we hereby change our precedent and hold that whether conduct in procuring or enforcing a patent is sufficient to strip a patentee of its immunity from the antitrust laws is to be decided as a question of Federal Circuit law. This conclusion applies equally to all antitrust claims premised on the bringing of a patent infringement suit. Therefore, *Cygnus*, 92 F.3d at 1161, *Loctite*, 781 F.2d at 875, and *Atari*, 747 F.2d at 1438-40, are expressly overruled to the extent they hold otherwise. However, we will continue to apply the law of the appropriate regional circuit to issues involving other elements of antitrust law such as relevant market, market power, damages, etc., as those issues are not unique to patent law, which is subject to our exclusive jurisdiction.

III.

A patentee who brings an infringement suit may be subject to antitrust liability for the anti-competitive effects of that suit if the alleged infringer (the antitrust plaintiff) proves (1) that the asserted patent was obtained through knowing and willful fraud within the meaning of *Walker Process Equipment, Inc. v. Food Machinery & Chemical Corp.*, 382 U.S. 172, 177 (1965), or (2) that the infringement suit was "a mere sham to cover what is actually nothing more than an attempt to interfere directly with the business relationships of a competitor," *Eastern R.R. Presidents Conference v. Noerr Motor Freight, Inc.*, 365 U.S. 127, 144 (1961); *California Motor Transp. Co. v. Trucking Unlimited*, 404 U.S. 508, 510 (1972) (holding that *Noerr* "governs the approach of citizens or groups of them . . . to courts, the third branch of Government"). *See Professional Real Estate Investors, Inc. v. Columbia Pictures Indus., Inc.*, 508 U.S. 49, 62 n.6 (1993) (PRE) (declining to decide "whether and, if so, to what extent *Noerr* permits the imposition of antitrust liability for a litigant's fraud or other misrepresentations").

In *Walker Process*, the Supreme Court held that in order "to strip [a patentee] of its exemption from the antitrust laws" because of its attempting to enforce its patent monopoly, an antitrust plaintiff is first required to prove that the patentee "obtained the patent by knowingly and willfully misrepresenting facts to the [PTO]." 382 U.S. at 177. The plaintiff in the patent infringement suit must also have been aware of the fraud when bringing suit. *Id.* at 177 & n.6. The Court cited prior decisions that involved the knowing and willful misrepresentation of specific facts to the Patent Office: *Precision Instrument Manufacturing v. Automotive Maintenance Machinery Co.*, 324 U.S. 806 (1945) (misrepresenting that the inventor had conceived, disclosed, and reduced to practice the invention on certain dates); *Hazel-Atlas Glass Co. v. Hartford-Empire Co.*, 322 U.S. 238 (1944) (misrepresenting that a widely known expert had authored an article praising the invention); and *Keystone Driller Co. v. General Excavator Co.*, 290 U.S. 240 (1933) (involving an agreement to suppress evidence in the course of litigation). These cases indicate the context in which the Court established the knowing and willful misrepresentation test.

Justice Harlan, in a concurring opinion, emphasized that to "achiev[e] a suitable accommodation in this area between the differing policies of the patent and antitrust laws," a distinction must be maintained between patents procured by "deliberate fraud" and those rendered invalid or unenforceable for other reasons. *Walker Process*, 382 U.S. at 179-80. He then stated:

> [T]o hold, as we do not, that private antitrust suits might also reach monopolies practiced under patents that for one reason or another may turn out to be voidable under one or more of the numerous technicalities attending the issuance of a patent, might well chill the disclosure of inventions through the obtaining of a patent because of fear of the vexations or punitive consequences of treble-damage suits. Hence, this private antitrust remedy should not be deemed available to reach [Sherman Act] §2 monopolies carried on under a nonfraudulently procured patent.

Id. at 180.

Consistent with the Supreme Court's analysis in *Walker Process*, as well as Justice Harlan's concurring opinion, we have distinguished "inequitable conduct" from *Walker Process* fraud, noting that inequitable conduct is a broader, more inclusive concept than the common law fraud needed to support a *Walker Process* counterclaim. Inequitable conduct in fact is a lesser offense than common law fraud, and includes types of conduct less serious than "knowing and willful" fraud.

In *Norton v. Curtiss*, 433 F.2d 779, 792-94 & n.12 (1970), our predecessor court explicitly distinguished inequitable conduct from "fraud," as that term was used by the Supreme Court in *Walker Process*. The court noted that

> the concept of "fraud" has most often been used by the courts, in general, to refer to a type of conduct so reprehensible that it could alone form the basis of an actionable wrong (e.g., the common law action for deceit). . . . Because severe penalties are usually meted out to the party found guilty of such conduct, technical fraud[5] is generally held not to exist unless the following indispensable elements are found to be present: (1) a representation of a material fact, (2) the falsity of that representation, (3) the intent to deceive or, at least, a state of mind so reckless as to the consequences that it is held to be the equivalent of intent (scienter), (4) a justifiable reliance upon the misrepresentation by the party deceived which induces him to act thereon, and (5) injury to the party deceived as a result of his reliance on the misrepresentation.

Id. at 792-93. The court then contrasted such independently actionable common law fraud with lesser misconduct, including what we now refer to as inequitable conduct, which "fail[s], for one reason or another, to satisfy all the elements of the technical offense." *Norton*, 433 F.2d at 793. Regarding such misconduct, "the courts appear to look at the equities of the particular case and determine whether the conduct before them . . . was still so reprehensible as to justify the court's refusing to enforce the rights of the party guilty of such conduct." *Id.*

---

5. We understand from the enumeration of elements that the term "technical fraud" was used by the court to mean common law fraud.

Inequitable conduct is thus an equitable defense in a patent infringement action and serves as a shield, while a more serious finding of fraud potentially exposes a patentee to antitrust liability and thus serves as a sword. Antitrust liability can include treble damages. In contrast, the remedies for inequitable conduct, while serious enough, only include unenforceability of the affected patent or patents and possible attorney fees. *See* 35 U.S.C. §§282, 285 (1994). Simply put, *Walker Process* fraud is a more serious offense than inequitable conduct.

In this case, the jury was instructed that a finding of fraud could be premised on "a knowing, willful and intentional act, misrepresentation or omission before the [PTO]." This instruction was not inconsistent with various opinions of the courts stating that omissions, as well as misrepresentations, may in limited circumstances support a finding of *Walker Process* fraud. We agree that if the evidence shows that the asserted patent was acquired by means of either a fraudulent misrepresentation or a fraudulent omission and that the party asserting the patent was aware of the fraud when bringing suit, such conduct can expose a patentee to liability under the antitrust laws. We arrive at this conclusion because a fraudulent omission can be just as reprehensible as a fraudulent misrepresentation. In addition, of course, in order to find liability, the necessary additional elements of a violation of the antitrust laws must be established. *See Walker Process*, 382 U.S. at 178.

Such a misrepresentation or omission must evidence a clear intent to deceive the examiner and thereby cause the PTO to grant an invalid patent. *See id.* at 794 ("[T]he fact misrepresented must be 'the efficient, inducing, and proximate cause, or the determining ground' of the action taken in reliance thereon.") (quoting 37 C.J.S. Fraud §18 (1943)). In contrast, a conclusion of inequitable conduct may be based on evidence of a lesser misrepresentation or an omission, such as omission of a reference that would merely have been considered important to the patentability of a claim by a reasonable examiner. A finding of *Walker Process* fraud requires higher threshold showings of both intent and materiality than does a finding of inequitable conduct. Moreover, unlike a finding of inequitable conduct, a finding of *Walker Process* fraud may not be based upon an equitable balancing of lesser degrees of materiality and intent. Rather, it must be based on independent and clear evidence of deceptive intent together with a clear showing of reliance, i.e., that the patent would not have issued but for the misrepresentation or omission. Therefore, for an omission such as a failure to cite a piece of prior art to support a finding of *Walker Process* fraud, the withholding of the reference must show evidence of fraudulent intent. A mere failure to cite a reference to the PTO will not suffice.

IV.

The district court observed that the Supreme Court, in footnote six of its *PRE* opinion, "left unresolved the issue of how '*Noerr* applies to the ex parte application process,' and in particular, how it applies to the *Walker Process* claim." 930 F. Supp. at 1253. The court also accurately pointed out that we have twice declined to resolve this issue. Therefore, after reviewing three opinions from the Ninth and District of Columbia Circuit Courts of Appeals, the district court made its own determination that *PRE*'s two-part test for a sham is inapplicable to an antitrust claim based on the assertion of a patent obtained by knowing and willful fraud. We do not agree with that determination. *PRE* and *Walker Process* provide alternative legal grounds on which a patentee may be stripped of its immunity from the antitrust laws; both legal theories may be applied to the same conduct. Moreover, we need not find a way to merge these decisions. Each provides its own basis for depriving a patent owner of immunity from the antitrust laws; either or both may be applicable to a particular party's conduct in obtaining and enforcing a patent. The Supreme Court saw no need to merge these separate lines of cases and neither do we.

Consequently, if the above-described elements of *Walker Process* fraud, as well as the other criteria for antitrust liability, are met, such liability can be imposed without the additional sham inquiry required under *PRE*. That is because *Walker Process* antitrust liability is based on the knowing assertion of a patent procured by fraud on the PTO, very specific conduct that is clearly reprehensible. On the other hand, irrespective of the patent applicant's conduct before the PTO, an antitrust claim can also be based on a *PRE* allegation that a suit is baseless; in order to prove that a suit was within *Noerr*'s "sham" exception to immunity, an antitrust plaintiff must prove that the suit was both *objectively* baseless and *subjectively* motivated by a desire to impose collateral, anti-competitive injury rather than to obtain a justifiable legal remedy. *PRE*, 508 U.S. at 60-61. As the Supreme Court stated:

> First, the lawsuit must be objectively baseless in the sense that no reasonable litigant could realistically expect success on the merits. If an objective litigant could conclude that the suit is reasonably calculated to elicit a favorable outcome, the suit is immunized under *Noerr*, and an antitrust claim premised on the sham exception must fail. Only if challenged litigation is objectively meritless may a court examine the litigant's subjective motivation. Under this second part of our definition of sham, the court should focus on whether the baseless lawsuit conceals "an attempt to interfere *directly* with the business relationships of a competitor," through the "use [of] the governmental *process*—as opposed to the *outcome* of that process—as an anticompetitive weapon." . . . Of course, even a plaintiff who defeats the defendant's claim to *Noerr* immunity by demonstrating both the objective and the subjective components of a sham must still prove a substantive antitrust violation. Proof of a sham merely deprives the defendant of immunity; it does not relieve the plaintiff of the obligation to establish all other elements of his claim.

Id. Thus, under *PRE*, a sham suit must be both subjectively brought in bad faith and based on a theory of either infringement or validity that is objectively baseless. Accordingly, if a suit is not objectively baseless, an antitrust defendant's subjective motivation is immaterial. *Id.* In contrast with a *Walker Process* claim, a patentee's activities in procuring the patent are not necessarily at issue. It is the bringing of the lawsuit that is subjectively and objectively baseless that must be proved.

V.

As for the present case, we conclude that there exists substantial evidence upon which a reasonable fact finder could strip NP of its immunity from antitrust liability. In particular, there exists substantial evidence that the 1977 Book was fraudulently kept from the PTO during patent prosecution. The jury could reasonably have found that the 1977 Book was fraudulently withheld and that it disclosed the claimed invention. First, the jury could reasonably have concluded that Branemark, through his Swedish patent agent, Barnieske, withheld the 1977 Book with the requisite intent to defraud the PTO. The initial disclosure to Barnieske, provided by Branemark's co-inventor, af Ekenstam, indicated that the studies described in the 1977 Book verified the utility of the claimed invention. While Barnieske did testify that he did not recall his thoughts during the prosecution of the patent and that he would have submitted the 1977 Book to the PTO if he had considered it relevant, the jury was free to disbelieve him. Barnieske could not explain, even in retrospect, why he deleted all reference to the 1977 Book. Importantly, the 1977 Book was thought by at least one inventor to be relevant, as evidenced by the initial disclosure to the patent agent, but it was inexplicably not later disclosed to the PTO. Also, as the author of the 1977 Book and an inventor, Branemark presumably knew of the book's relevance to the invention and could have directed Barnieske not to disclose the book to the PTO. Thus, the jury could properly have inferred that Branemark had the requisite intent to defraud the PTO based on his failure to disclose the reference to the PTO. Such a scheme to defraud is the type of conduct contemplated by *Walker Process.*

Second, substantial evidence upon which a reasonable jury could have relied also indicates that the 1977 Book was sufficiently material to justify a finding of fraud. 3I's expert witness, Dr. Donald Brunette, testified that the SEMs of the 1977 Book depict dental implants having all the elements of the claims asserted by NP. Specifically, he explained how he had determined that the SEMs depict a "biologically flawless material" suitable for use as a dental implant. He also explained how he determined that the depicted micropits have diameters within the claimed range of approximately 10 to 1000 nanometers. Even Branemark, in this deposition testimony, conceded that it would not have been difficult to calculate the size of the micropits depicted in the 1977 Book, given the magnification factors provided in the captions to the SEMs. Accordingly, a reasonable jury could have found, based on the unambiguous claim language, that the 1977 Book anticipated the patent and that the examiner would not have granted the patent if he had been aware of the 1977 Book.

Third, the record indicates that a reasonable jury could have found that NP brought suit against 3I with knowledge of the applicants' fraud. A reasonable jury could have found that two of NP's then-officers, Dr. Ralph Green, Jr. and Mr. Mats Nilsson, were aware of the fraud based on Green's testimony that Nilsson told him: "[I]f the Patent Office did not receive a copy of [the 1977 Book], and if that were true, then we would have a larger problem and that was fraud." Green's testimony also indicates that NP was aware that the 1977 Book was highly material and, in fact, likely rendered the patent invalid. Green testified that he, Nilsson, and Mr. George Vande Sande obtained a legal opinion from NP's attorney, Mr. David Lindley, who indicated that if "we were to sue anyone on the patent we would lose in the first round. . . . [T]here was prior art, not the least of which was this textbook [the 1977 Book] that would invalidate the patent."

Regarding NP's motion for a new trial, we have concluded that the court's instructions to the jury regarding fraud, to which NP did not object, substantially comport with the law. Specifically, the court emphasized to the jury that to strip NP of its immunity from the antitrust laws, 3I "must prove that the '891 patent was fraudulently . . . obtained by clear and convincing 'evidence.'" The court also pointed out that only "knowing, willful and intentional acts, misrepresentations or omission" may support a finding of fraud and that the jury should approach such a finding with "great care." As to reliance, the court instructed the jury that "[m]ateriality is shown if but for the misrepresentation or omission the '891 patent would not have been issued." These instructions were not legally erroneous.

Because we conclude that the finding of *Walker Process* fraud was supported by substantial evidence and was based upon a jury instruction that was not legally erroneous or prejudicial, we affirm the denial of NP's motion for JMOL. NP was properly deprived of its immunity from the antitrust laws under *Walker Process*, and it could not have benefited from additional jury instructions regarding *PRE* or *Noerr*. The court's refusal to so instruct the jury therefore does not require a new trial.

We have also considered NP's alternative arguments in support of its motion for a new trial, including its assertions that the district court erred in permitting Green to testify, in prohibiting Dr. Hodosh and Messrs. Vande Sande and Martens from testifying, in allowing 3I to present a theory of joint venture liability to the jury, and in impugning the credibility of NP's arguments before the jury. We do not find these arguments persuasive. The district court did not abuse its discretion or misapply the law of attorney-client privilege in making its evidentiary rulings, nor did it prejudice NP's substantive rights by allowing the jury to consider a joint venture theory of liability or by commenting on NP's arguments during the trial. Accordingly, the court did not abuse its discretion in denying NP's motion for a new trial.

CONCLUSION

The district court did not err . . . in denying NP's motion for JMOL or a new trial on 3I's antitrust counterclaim. A reasonable jury, applying the correct law, could have found that the facts of this case were sufficient to constitute fraud within the meaning of *Walker Process*.

Comments

1. **Noerr-Pennington** *Immunity.* A basic principle of antitrust law is that the act of invoking the machinery of government (e.g., executive agencies or courts) is, by itself, not a violation of the antitrust laws. This immunity is referred to as the *Noerr-Pennington* doctrine. *See Eastern R.R. President's Conf. v. Noerr Motor Freight*, 365 U.S. 127, 135 (1961) ("We accept the same basic construction of the Sherman Act adopted by the courts below that no violation of the Act can be predicated upon mere attempts to influence the passage or enforcement of laws."), and *United Mine Workers v. Pennington*, 381 U.S. 657, 670 (1965) ("*Noerr* shields from the Sherman Act a concerted effort to influence public officials regardless of intent of purpose."). The doctrine is ground in First Amendment principles under the assumption that petitioning the government should not give rise to liability. *See Noerr*, 365 U.S. at 137 ("In a representative democracy . . . the whole concept of representation depends upon the ability of the people to make their wishes known to their representatives. To hold that the government retains the power to act in this representative capacity and yet hold, at the same time, that the people cannot freely inform the government of their wishes would impute to the Sherman Act a purpose to regulate, not business activity, but political activity, a purpose which would have no basis whatever in the legislative history of that Act."); Herbert

Hovenkamp, *Standards Ownership and Competition Policy*, 48 B.C. L. Rᴇᴠ. 87, 107 (2007) ("The Supreme Court applied the historical *Noerr* rule that private parties have a right, essentially protected by the First Amendment of the U.S. Constitution, to petition the government for even anticompetitive actions.").

Immunity extends to the petitioning of all branches of government, including the courts. *See California Motor Transport Co. v. Trucking Unlimited*, 404 U.S. 508, 612 (1972) ("Certainly the right to petition extends to all departments of the Government. The right of access to the courts is indeed but one aspect of the right of petition."). Thus, filing an infringement action in federal district court is—by itself—not a violation of antitrust law. An exception to *Noerr-Pennington* immunity is the so-called sham petition; that is, invoking the judiciary, not to legitimately influence a court, but to interfere with the business relationships of a competitor. See Comment 3 and the discussion of *Handgards* claims. Importantly, absence of immunity does not necessarily lead to an antitrust violation; the antitrust plaintiff must still meet his burden of proof, showing the existence of the requisite elements of an antitrust cause of action.

2. **Walker Process** *Claim.* A *Walker Process* antitrust claim can be traced to *Walker Process Equipment v. Food Machinery & Chemical*, 382 U.S. 172 (1965). In *Walker Process*, the Court "concluded that the enforcement of a patent procured by fraud on the Patent Office may be violative of §2 of the Sherman Act provided the other elements necessary to a §2 case are present." *Id.* at 174. The underlying contention of a *Walker Process* claim is that a patentee who engaged in fraud to obtain a patent and thereafter enforced it should not be able to seek refuge in *Noerr-Pennington* immunity. *See Dippin' Dots, Inc. v. Mosey*, 476 F.3d 1337, 1346 (Fed. Cir. 2007) (stating "[p]roof that a patentee has 'obtained the patent by knowingly and willfully misrepresenting facts to the Patent Office . . . [is] sufficient to strip [the patentee] of its exemption from the antitrust laws.'" (quoting *Walker Process*)).

Nobelpharma applied principles of common law fraud, which is narrower and more serious than what is required for inequitable conduct. The fraud for *Walker Process* "must evidence a clear intent to deceive the examiner and thereby cause the PTO to grant the patent." Common law fraud consists of:

> (1) a representation of a material fact, (2) the falsity of that representation, (3) the intent to deceive or, at least, a state of mind so reckless as to the consequences that it is held to be the equivalent of intent (scienter), (4) a justifiable reliance upon the misrepresentation by the party deceived which induces him to act thereon, and (5) injury to the party deceived as a result of his reliance on the misrepresentation.

In re Spalding Sports Worldwide, Inc., 203 F.3d 800, 807 (Fed. Cir. 2000). Thus, mere omission of a prior art reference is not enough to constitute *Walker Process* fraud. *See Dippin' Dots*, 476 F.3d at 1347 (stating "to find a prosecution omission fraudulent there must be evidence of intent separable from the simple fact of the omission. A false or clearly misleading prosecution statement may permit an inference that the statement was made with deceptive intent. For instance, evidence may establish that a patent applicant knew one fact and presented another, thus allowing the factfinder to conclude that the applicant intended by the misrepresentation to deceive the examiner. That is not the case with an omission, which could happen for any number of non-fraudulent reasons—the applicant could have had a good-faith belief that disclosure was not necessary, or simply have forgotten to make the required disclosure").

Once immunity is stripped, a *Walker Process* claimant must then prove "the other elements necessary to a §2 [Sherman Act] case." In *Unitherm Food Systems, Inc. v. Swift-Eckrich, Inc.*, 375 F.3d 1341, 1355 (Fed. Cir. 2004), the Federal Circuit stated:

> The elimination of [the patentee's] antitrust immunity would mark only the beginning of the antitrust inquiry, not its endpoint. To establish monopolization or attempt to monopolize a part of trade or commerce under §2 of the Sherman Act, it would then be necessary to appraise the exclusionary power of the illegal patent claim in terms of the relevant market for the product involved. Without a definition of that market there is no way to measure [the patentee's] ability to lessen or destroy competition. It may be that the patented process "does not comprise a relevant market. There may be effective substitutes . . . which do not infringe the patent."
>
> In order to prevail on its *Walker Process* claim, [the plaintiff] must therefore establish: that [the patentee] attempted to enforce the patent; that the patent issued because [the patentee] defrauded the PTO; that ConAgra's attempted enforcement threatened to lessen competition in a relevant antitrust market; that [the plaintiff] suffered antitrust damages; and that all other elements of attempted monopolization are met. These requirements frame our antitrust inquiry.

3. **Handgards *Claim*.** *Walker Process* dealt with the enforcement of a fraudulently obtained patent. A *Handgards* claim differs from *Walker Process* in that the former relates to the enforcement of a patent that was not obtained by fraud, but was asserted with knowledge that it was either invalid or not infringed. In other words, the focus is on the patentee's bad-faith enforcement or sham litigation, irrespective of his conduct before the PTO. *See Handgards, Inc. v. Ethicon, Inc.*, 601 F.2d 986 (9th Cir. 1979).

A patentee who engages in sham litigation does not enjoy *Noerr-Pennington* immunity. *See Noerr*, 365 U.S. at 144 (concluding that "application of the Sherman Act would be justified" where petitioning the government, "ostensibly directed toward influencing governmental action, is a mere sham to cover what is actually nothing more than an attempt to interfere directly with the business relationships of a competitor. . . ."); *City of Columbia v. Omni Outdoor Advertising, Inc.*, 499 U.S. 365, 380 (1991) ("The 'sham' exception to *Noerr* encompasses situations in which persons use the governmental *process*—as opposed to the *outcome* of that process—as an anticompetitive weapon. A classic example is the filing of frivolous objections to the license application of a competitor, with no expectation of achieving denial of the license but simply in order to impose expense and delay."); *California Motor Transp. Co. v. Trucking Unlimited*, 404 U.S. 508, 515 (1972) ("First Amendment rights may not be used as the means or the pretext for achieving 'substantive evils' . . . which the legislature has the power to control.").

In *Professional Real Estate Investors, Inc. v. Columbia Pictures Indus., Inc.*, 508 U.S. 49 (1993) (*PRE*), the Supreme Court provided a framework to prove a *Handgards* claim. The *PRE* Court set forth a two-part test, comprising an objective and subjective component. According to the Court, "the lawsuit must be objectively baseless in the sense that no reasonable litigant could realistically expect success on the merits." If an antitrust plaintiff is able to prove that the lawsuit was objectively meritless, "may a court examine the litigant's subjective motivation? Under this second part of our definition of sham, the court should focus on whether the baseless lawsuit conceals 'an attempt to interfere *directly* with the business relationships of a competitor, through the use [of] the governmental *process*—as opposed to the *outcome* of that process—as an anticompetitive weapon.'" 508 U.S. at 60-61.

3. Settlements

As a general policy, settlement is encouraged as an efficient alternative to litigation. Patent litigation is very expensive, and judicial resources are increasingly strained. Moreover, a consensual settlement between private parties is likely to accurately reflect the preferences of the parties, add prospective certainty to business dealings, and enhance social welfare. But patent settlements—which are usually horizontal (i.e., between competitors) — can also be anticompetitive. One particular form of settlement that has come under heavy antitrust scrutiny in the pharmaceutical industry involves so-called reverse settlements—payments made by the patentee to the alleged infringer to abandon the market. This type of settlement was at issue in *FTC v. Actavis, Inc.*

FEDERAL TRADE COMMISSION v. ACTAVIS, INC.
133 S. Ct. 2223 (2013)

Justice BREYER delivered the opinion of the Court.

Company A sues Company B for patent infringement. The two companies settle under terms that require (1) Company B, the claimed infringer, not to produce the patented product until the patent's term expires, and (2) Company A, the patentee, to pay B many millions of dollars. Because the settlement requires the patentee to pay the alleged infringer, rather than the other way around, this kind of settlement agreement is often called a "reverse payment" settlement agreement. And the basic question here is whether such an agreement can sometimes unreasonably diminish competition in violation of the antitrust laws. See, *e.g.,* 15 U.S.C. §1 (Sherman Act prohibition of "restraint[s] of trade or commerce").

In this case, the Eleventh Circuit dismissed a Federal Trade Commission (FTC) complaint claiming that a particular reverse payment settlement agreement violated the antitrust laws. In doing so, the Circuit stated that a reverse payment settlement agreement generally is "immune from antitrust attack so long as its anticompetitive effects fall within the scope of the exclusionary potential of the patent." *FTC v. Watson Pharmaceuticals, Inc.,* 677 F.3d 1298, 1312 (2012). And since the alleged infringer's promise not to enter the patentee's market expired before the patent's term ended, the Circuit found the agreement legal and dismissed the FTC complaint. *Id.,* at 1315. In our view, however, reverse payment settlements such as the agreement alleged in the complaint before us can sometimes violate the antitrust laws. We consequently hold that the Eleventh Circuit should have allowed the FTC's lawsuit to proceed.

I

A

Apparently most if not all reverse payment settlement agreements arise in the context of pharmaceutical drug regulation, and specifically in the context of suits brought under statutory provisions allowing a generic drug manufacturer (seeking speedy marketing approval) to challenge the validity of a patent owned by an already-approved brand-name drug owner. We consequently describe four key features of the relevant drug-regulatory framework established by the Drug Price Competition and Patent Term Restoration Act of 1984, 98 Stat. 1585, as amended. That Act is commonly known as the Hatch-Waxman Act.

First, a drug manufacturer, wishing to market a new prescription drug, must submit a New Drug Application to the federal Food and Drug Administration (FDA) and undergo a long, comprehensive, and costly testing process, after which, if successful, the manufacturer will receive marketing approval from the FDA. See 21 U.S.C. §355(b)(1) (requiring, among other things, "full reports of investigations" into safety and effectiveness; "a full list of the articles used as components"; and a "full description" of how the drug is manufactured, processed, and packed).

Second, once the FDA has approved a brand-name drug for marketing, a manufacturer of a generic drug can obtain similar marketing approval through use of abbreviated procedures. The Hatch-Waxman Act permits a generic manufacturer to file an Abbreviated New Drug Application specifying that the generic has the "same active ingredients as," and is "biologically equivalent" to, the already-approved brand-name drug. In this way the generic manufacturer can obtain approval while avoiding the "costly and time-consuming studies" needed to obtain approval "for a pioneer drug." See *Eli Lilly & Co.* v. *Medtronic, Inc.*, 496 U.S. 661, 676 (1990). The Hatch-Waxman process, by allowing the generic to piggy-back on the pioneer's approval efforts, "speed[s] the introduction of low-cost generic drugs to market," thereby furthering drug competition.

Third, the Hatch-Waxman Act sets forth special procedures for identifying, and resolving, related patent disputes. It requires the pioneer brand-name manufacturer to list in its New Drug Application the "number and the expiration date" of any relevant patent. See 21 U.S.C. §355(b)(1). And it requires the generic manufacturer in its Abbreviated New Drug Application to "assure the FDA" that the generic "will not infringe" the brand-name's patents.

The generic can provide this assurance in one of several ways. It can certify that the brand-name manufacturer has not listed any relevant patents. It can certify that any relevant patents have expired. It can request approval to market beginning when any still-in-force patents expire. Or, it can certify that any listed, relevant patent "is invalid or will not be infringed by the manufacture, use, or sale" of the drug described in the Abbreviated New Drug Application. Taking this last-mentioned route (called the "paragraph IV" route), automatically counts as patent infringement, and often "means provoking litigation." If the brand-name patentee brings an infringement suit within 45 days, the FDA then must withhold approving the generic, usually for a 30-month period, while the parties litigate patent validity (or infringement) in court. If the courts decide the matter within that period, the FDA follows that determination; if they do not, the FDA may go forward and give approval to market the generic product.

Fourth, Hatch-Waxman provides a special incentive for a generic to be the first to file an Abbreviated New Drug Application taking the paragraph IV route. That applicant will enjoy a period of 180 days of exclusivity (from the first commercial marketing of its drug). During that period of exclusivity no other generic can compete with the brand-name drug. If the first-to-file generic manufacturer can overcome any patent obstacle and bring the generic to market, this 180-day period of exclusivity can prove valuable, possibly "worth several hundred million dollars." Indeed, the Generic Pharmaceutical Association said in 2006 that the "'vast majority of potential profits for a generic drug manufacturer materialize during the 180-day exclusivity period.'" The 180-day exclusivity period, however, can belong only to the first generic to file. Should that first-to-file generic forfeit the exclusivity right in one of the ways specified by statute, no other generic can obtain it.

B

1

In 1999, Solvay Pharmaceuticals, a respondent here, filed a New Drug Application for a brand-name drug called AndroGel. The FDA approved the application in 2000. In 2003, Solvay obtained a relevant patent and disclosed that fact to the FDA, as Hatch-Waxman requires.

Later the same year another respondent, Actavis, Inc. (then known as Watson Pharmaceuticals), filed an Abbreviated New Drug Application for a generic drug modeled after AndroGel. Subsequently, Paddock Laboratories, also a respondent, separately filed an Abbreviated New Drug Application for its own generic product. Both Actavis and Paddock certified under paragraph IV that Solvay's listed patent was invalid and their drugs did not infringe it. A fourth manufacturer, Par Pharmaceutical, likewise a respondent, did not file an application of its own but joined forces with Paddock, agreeing to share the patent litigation costs in return for a share of profits if Paddock obtained approval for its generic drug.

Solvay initiated paragraph IV patent litigation against Actavis and Paddock. Thirty months later the FDA approved Actavis' first-to-file generic product, but, in 2006, the patent-litigation parties all settled. Under the terms of the settlement Actavis agreed that it would not bring its generic to market until August 31, 2015, 65 months before Solvay's patent expired (unless someone else marketed a generic sooner). Actavis also agreed to promote AndroGel to urologists. The other generic manufacturers made roughly similar promises. And Solvay agreed to pay millions of dollars to each generic—$12 million in total to Paddock; $60 million in total to Par; and an estimated $19-$30 million annually, for nine years, to Actavis. The companies described these payments as compensation for other services the generics promised to perform, but the FTC contends the other services had little value. According to the FTC the true point of the payments was to compensate the generics for agreeing not to compete against AndroGel until 2015.

On January 29, 2009, the FTC filed this lawsuit against all the settling parties, namely, Solvay, Actavis, Paddock, and Par. The FTC's complaint (as since amended) alleged that respondents violated §5 of the Federal Trade Commission

Act, 15 U.S.C. §45, by unlawfully agreeing "to share in Solvay's monopoly profits, abandon their patent challenges, and refrain from launching their low-cost generic products to compete with AndroGel for nine years." See generally *FTC v. Indiana Federation of Dentists*, 476 U.S. 447, 454 (1986) (Section 5 "encompass[es] . . . practices that violate the Sherman Act and the other antitrust laws"). The District Court held that these allegations did not set forth an antitrust law violation. It accordingly dismissed the FTC's complaint. The FTC appealed.

The Court of Appeals for the Eleventh Circuit affirmed the District Court. It wrote that "absent sham litigation or fraud in obtaining the patent, a reverse payment settlement is immune from antitrust attack so long as its anticompetitive effects fall within the scope of the exclusionary potential of the patent." 677 F.3d, at 1312. The court recognized that "antitrust laws typically prohibit agreements where one company pays a potential competitor not to enter the market." *Id.*, at 1307 (citing *Valley Drug Co. v. Geneva Pharmaceuticals, Inc.*, 344 F.3d 1294, 1304 (CA11 2003)). But, the court found that "reverse payment settlements of patent litigation presen[t] atypical cases because one of the parties owns a patent." 677 F.3d, at 1307. Patent holders have a "lawful right to exclude others from the market," *ibid*; thus a patent "conveys the right to cripple competition." *Id.*, at 1310. The court recognized that, if the parties to this sort of case do not settle, a court might declare the patent invalid. But, in light of the public policy favoring settlement of disputes (among other considerations) it held that the courts could not require the parties to continue to litigate in order to avoid antitrust liability.

The FTC sought certiorari. Because different courts have reached different conclusions about the application of the antitrust laws to Hatch-Waxman-related patent settlements, we granted the FTC's petition.

II

A

Solvay's patent, if valid and infringed, might have permitted it to charge drug prices sufficient to recoup the reverse settlement payments it agreed to make to its potential generic competitors. And we are willing to take this fact as evidence that the agreement's "anticompetitive effects fall within the scope of the exclusionary potential of the patent." 677 F.3d, at 1312. But we do not agree that that fact, or characterization, can immunize the agreement from antitrust attack.

For one thing, to refer, as the Circuit referred, simply to what the holder of a valid patent could do does not by itself answer the antitrust question. The patent here may or may not be valid, and may or may not be infringed. "[A] *valid* patent excludes all except its owner from the use of the protected process or product," *United States v. Line Material Co.*, 333 U.S. 287, 308 (1948) (emphasis added). And that exclusion may permit the patent owner to charge a higher-than-competitive price for the patented product. But an *invalidated* patent carries with it no such right. And even a valid patent confers no right to exclude products or processes that do not actually infringe. The paragraph IV litigation in this case put the patent's validity at issue, as well as its actual preclusive scope. The parties' settlement ended that litigation. The FTC alleges that in substance, the plaintiff agreed to pay the defendants many millions of dollars to stay out of its market, even though the defendants did not have any claim that the plaintiff was liable to them for damages. That form of settlement is unusual. And, for reasons discussed in Part II-B, *infra*, there is reason for concern that settlements taking this form tend to have significant adverse effects on competition.

Given these factors, it would be incongruous to determine antitrust legality by measuring the settlement's anticompetitive effects solely against patent law policy, rather than by measuring them against pro-competitive antitrust policies as well. And indeed, contrary to the Circuit's view that the only pertinent question is whether "the settlement agreement . . . fall[s] within" the legitimate "scope" of the patent's "exclusionary potential," 677 F.3d, at 1309, 1312, this Court has indicated that patent and antitrust policies are both relevant in determining the "scope of the patent monopoly"—and consequently antitrust law immunity—that is conferred by a patent.

. . . [R]ather than measure the length or amount of a restriction solely against the length of the patent's term or its earning potential, as the Court of Appeals apparently did here, this Court answered the antitrust question by considering traditional antitrust factors such as likely anticompetitive effects, redeeming virtues, market power, and potentially offsetting legal considerations present in the circumstances, such as here those related to patents. See Part II-B, *infra*. Whether a particular restraint lies "beyond the limits of the patent monopoly" is a *conclusion* that flows from that analysis and not, as The Chief Justice suggests, its starting point. (Dissenting opinion).

. . . [Our precedent] does not simply ask whether a hypothetically valid patent's holder would be able to charge, *e.g.*, the high prices that the challenged patent-related term allowed. Rather, they seek to accommodate patent and antitrust policies, finding challenged terms and conditions unlawful unless patent law policy offsets the antitrust law policy strongly favoring competition.

Thus, contrary to the dissent's suggestion, there is nothing novel about our approach. What *does* appear novel are the dissent's suggestions that a patent holder may simply "pa[y] a competitor to respect its patent" and quit its patent invalidity or noninfringement claim without any antitrust scrutiny whatever, and that "such settlements . . . are a well-known feature of intellectual property litigation." Closer examination casts doubt on these claims. The dissent does not identify any patent statute that it understands to grant such a right to a patentee, whether expressly or by fair implication. It would be difficult to reconcile the proposed right with the patent-related policy of eliminating unwarranted patent grants so the public will not "continually be required to pay tribute to would-be monopolists without need or justification." *Lear, Inc. v. Adkins*, 395 U.S. 653, 670 (1969). And the authorities cited for this proposition (none from this Court, and none an antitrust case) are not on point. Some of them say that when Company A sues Company B for patent infringement and demands, say, $100 million in damages, it is not uncommon for B (the defendant) to pay A (the plaintiff) some amount less than the full demand as part of the settlement—$40 million, for example. The cited authorities also indicate that if B has a counterclaim for damages against A, the original infringement plaintiff, A might end up paying B to settle B's counterclaim. Insofar as the dissent urges that settlements taking these commonplace forms have not been thought for that reason alone subject to antitrust liability, we agree, and do not intend to alter that understanding. But the dissent appears also to suggest that reverse payment settlements—*e.g.*, in which A, the plaintiff, pays money to defendant B purely so B will give up the patent fight—should be viewed for antitrust purposes in the same light as these familiar settlement forms. We cannot agree. In the traditional examples cited above, a party with a claim (or counterclaim) for damages receives a sum equal to or less than the value of its claim. In reverse payment settlements, in contrast, a party with no claim for damages (something that is usually true of a paragraph IV litigation defendant) walks away with money simply so it will stay away from the patentee's market. That, we think, is something quite different. . . .

B

The Eleventh Circuit's conclusion finds some degree of support in a general legal policy favoring the settlement of disputes. The Circuit's related underlying practical concern consists of its fear that antitrust scrutiny of a reverse payment agreement would require the parties to litigate the validity of the patent in order to demonstrate what would have happened to competition in the absence of the settlement. Any such litigation will prove time consuming, complex, and expensive. The antitrust game, the Circuit may believe, would not be worth that litigation candle.

We recognize the value of settlements and the patent litigation problem. But we nonetheless conclude that this patent-related factor should not determine the result here. Rather, five sets of considerations lead us to conclude that the FTC should have been given the opportunity to prove its antitrust claim.

First, the specific restraint at issue has the "potential for genuine adverse effects on competition." The payment in effect amounts to a purchase by the patentee of the exclusive right to sell its product, a right it already claims but would lose if the patent litigation were to continue and the patent were held invalid or not infringed by the generic product. Suppose, for example, that the exclusive right to sell produces $50 million in supracompetitive profits per year for the patentee. And suppose further that the patent has 10 more years to run. Continued litigation, if it results in patent invalidation or a finding of noninfringement, could cost the patentee $500 million in lost revenues, a sum that then would flow in large part to consumers in the form of lower prices.

We concede that settlement on terms permitting the patent challenger to enter the market before the patent expires would also bring about competition, again to the consumer's benefit. But settlement on the terms said by the FTC to be at issue here—payment in return for staying out of the market—simply keeps prices at patentee-set levels, potentially producing the full patent-related $500 million monopoly return while dividing that return between the challenged patentee and the patent challenger. The patentee and the challenger gain; the consumer loses. Indeed, there are indications that patentees sometimes pay a generic challenger a sum even larger than what the generic would gain in profits if it won the paragraph IV litigation and entered the market. The rationale behind a payment of this size cannot in every case be supported by traditional settlement considerations. The payment may instead provide strong evidence that the patentee seeks to induce the generic challenger to abandon its claim with a share of its monopoly profits that would otherwise be lost in the competitive market.

But, one might ask, as a practical matter would the parties be able to enter into such an anticompetitive agreement? Would not a high reverse payment signal to other potential challengers that the patentee lacks confidence in its patent, thereby provoking additional challenges, perhaps too many for the patentee to "buy off"? Two special features of Hatch-Waxman mean that the answer to this question is "not necessarily so." First, under Hatch-Waxman only the first challenger gains the special advantage of 180 days of an exclusive right to sell a generic version of the brand-name product. See Part I-A, *supra*. And as noted, that right has proved valuable—indeed, it can be worth several hundred million dollars. See Hemphill, *supra*, at 1579; Brief for Petitioner 6. Subsequent challengers cannot secure that exclusivity period, and thus stand to win significantly less than the first if they bring a successful paragraph IV challenge. That is, if subsequent litigation results in invalidation of the patent, or a ruling that the patent is not infringed, that litigation victory will free not just the challenger to compete, but all other potential competitors too (once they obtain FDA approval). The potential reward available to a subsequent challenger being significantly less, the patentee's payment to the initial challenger (in return for not pressing the patent challenge) will not necessarily provoke subsequent challenges. Second, a generic that files a paragraph IV after learning that the first filer has settled will (if sued by the brand-name) have to wait out a stay period of (roughly) 30 months before the FDA may approve its application, just as the first filer did. These features together mean that a reverse payment settlement with the first filer (or, as in this case, *all* of the initial filers) removes from consideration the most motivated challenger, and the one closest to introducing competition. The dissent may doubt these provisions matter, but scholars in the field tell us that "where only one party owns a patent, it is virtually unheard of outside of pharmaceuticals for that party to pay an accused infringer to settle the lawsuit." 1 H. Hovenkamp, M. Janis, M. Lemley, & C. Leslie, IP and Antitrust §15.3, p. 15-45, n.161 (2d ed. Supp. 2011). It may well be that Hatch-Waxman's unique regulatory framework, including the special advantage that the 180-day exclusivity period gives to first filers, does much to explain why in this context, but not others, the patentee's ordinary incentives to resist paying off challengers (*i.e.,* the fear of provoking myriad other challengers) appear to be more frequently overcome.

Second, these anticompetitive consequences will at least sometimes prove unjustified. As the FTC admits, offsetting or redeeming virtues are sometimes present. The reverse payment, for example, may amount to no more than a rough approximation of the litigation expenses saved through the settlement. That payment may reflect compensation for other services that the generic has promised to perform—such as distributing the patented item or helping to develop a market for that item. There may be other justifications. Where a reverse payment reflects traditional settlement considerations, such as avoided litigation costs or fair value for services, there is not the same concern that a patentee is using its monopoly profits to avoid the risk of patent invalidation or a finding of noninfringement. In such cases, the parties may have provided for a reverse payment without having sought or brought about the anticompetitive consequences we mentioned above. But that possibility does not justify dismissing the FTC's complaint. An antitrust defendant may show in the antitrust proceeding that legitimate justifications are present, thereby explaining the presence of the challenged term and showing the lawfulness of that term under the rule of reason.

Third, where a reverse payment threatens to work unjustified anticompetitive harm, the patentee likely possesses the power to bring that harm about in practice. At least, the "size of the payment from a branded drug manufacturer to a prospective generic is itself a strong indicator of power"—namely, the power to charge prices higher than the competitive level. An important patent itself helps to assure such power. Neither is a firm without that power likely to pay "large sums" to induce "others to stay out of its market." In any event, the Commission has referred to studies showing that reverse payment agreements are associated with the presence of higher-than-competitive profits—a strong indication of market power.

Fourth, an antitrust action is likely to prove more feasible administratively than the Eleventh Circuit believed. The Circuit's holding does avoid the need to litigate the patent's validity (and also, any question of infringement). But to do so, it throws the baby out with the bath water, and there is no need to take that drastic step. That is because it is normally not necessary to litigate patent validity to answer the antitrust question (unless, perhaps, to determine whether the patent litigation is a sham, see 677 F.3d, at 1312). An unexplained large reverse payment itself would normally suggest that the patentee has serious doubts about the patent's survival. And that fact, in turn, suggests that the payment's objective is to maintain supracompetitive prices to be shared among the patentee and the challenger rather than face what might have been a competitive market—the very anticompetitive consequence that underlies the claim of antitrust unlawfulness. The owner of a particularly valuable patent might contend, of course, that even a small risk of invalidity justifies a large payment. But, be that as it may, the payment (if otherwise unexplained) likely seeks to prevent the risk of competition. And, as we have said, that consequence constitutes the relevant anticompetitive harm. In a word, the size of the unexplained reverse payment can provide a workable surrogate for a patent's weakness, all without forcing a court to conduct a detailed exploration of the validity of the patent itself.

Fifth, the fact that a large, unjustified reverse payment risks antitrust liability does not prevent litigating parties from settling their lawsuit. They may, as in other industries, settle in other ways, for example, by allowing the generic manufacturer to enter the patentee's market prior to the patent's expiration, without the patentee paying the challenger to stay out prior to that point. Although the parties may have reasons to prefer settlements that include reverse payments, the relevant antitrust question is: What are those reasons? If the basic reason is a desire to maintain and to share patent-generated monopoly profits, then, in the absence of some other justification, the antitrust laws are likely to forbid the arrangement.

In sum, a reverse payment, where large and unjustified, can bring with it the risk of significant anticompetitive effects; one who makes such a payment may be unable to explain and to justify it; such a firm or individual may well possess market power derived from the patent; a court, by examining the size of the payment, may well be able to assess its likely anticompetitive effects along with its potential justifications without litigating the validity of the patent; and parties may well find ways to settle patent disputes without the use of reverse payments. In our view, these considerations, taken together, outweigh the single strong consideration—the desirability of settlements—that led the Eleventh Circuit to provide near-automatic antitrust immunity to reverse payment settlements.

III

The FTC urges us to hold that reverse payment settlement agreements are presumptively unlawful and that courts reviewing such agreements should proceed via a "quick look" approach, rather than applying a "rule of reason." See *California Dental,* 526 U.S., at 775, n.12 ("Quick-look analysis in effect" shifts to "a

defendant the burden to show empirical evidence of procompetitive effects").
We decline to do so. In *California Dental,* we held (unanimously) that abandonment of the "rule of reason" in favor of presumptive rules (or a "quick-look"
approach) is appropriate only where "an observer with even a rudimentary
understanding of economics could conclude that the arrangements in question
would have an anticompetitive effect on customers and markets." 526 U.S., at
770; *id.,* at 781. We do not believe that reverse payment settlements, in the context we here discuss, meet this criterion.

That is because the likelihood of a reverse payment bringing about anticompetitive effects depends upon its size, its scale in relation to the payor's anticipated future litigation costs, its independence from other services for which it
might represent payment, and the lack of any other convincing justification.
The existence and degree of any anticompetitive consequence may also vary as
among industries. These complexities lead us to conclude that the FTC must
prove its case as in other rule-of-reason cases.

To say this is not to require the courts to insist, contrary to what we have said,
that the Commission need litigate the patent's validity, empirically demonstrate
the virtues or vices of the patent system, present every possible supporting fact
or refute every possible pro-defense theory. As a leading antitrust scholar has
pointed out, "'[t]here is always something of a sliding scale in appraising reasonableness,'" and as such "'the quality of proof required should vary with the
circumstances.'" *California Dental, supra,* at 780 (quoting with approval 7 Areeda
¶1507, at 402 (1986)).

As in other areas of law, trial courts can structure antitrust litigation so as to
avoid, on the one hand, the use of antitrust theories too abbreviated to permit
proper analysis, and, on the other, consideration of every possible fact or theory
irrespective of the minimal light it may shed on the basic question — that of the
presence of significant unjustified anticompetitive consequences. We therefore
leave to the lower courts the structuring of the present rule-of-reason antitrust
litigation. We reverse the judgment of the Eleventh Circuit. And we remand the
case for further proceedings consistent with this opinion.

It is so ordered.

Chief Justice ROBERTS, with whom Justice SCALIA and Justice THOMAS join,
dissenting.

* * *

A patent carves out an exception to the applicability of antitrust laws. The
correct approach should therefore be to ask whether the settlement gives Solvay
monopoly power beyond what the patent already gave it. The Court, however,
departs from this approach, and would instead use antitrust law's amorphous
rule of reason to inquire into the anticompetitive effects of such settlements.
This novel approach is without support in any statute, and will discourage the
settlement of patent litigation. I respectfully dissent.

I

The point of antitrust law is to encourage competitive markets to promote
consumer welfare. The point of patent law is to grant limited monopolies as
a way of encouraging innovation. Thus, a patent grants "the right to exclude
others from profiting by the patented invention." *Dawson Chemical Co. v. Rohm*

& Haas Co., 448 U.S. 176, 215 (1980). In doing so it provides an exception to antitrust law, and the scope of the patent—*i.e.*, the rights conferred by the patent—forms the zone within which the patent holder may operate without facing antitrust liability.

This should go without saying, in part because we've said it so many times. Thus, although it is *per se* unlawful to fix prices under antitrust law, we have long recognized that a patent holder is entitled to license a competitor to sell its product on the condition that the competitor charge a certain, fixed price.

We have never held that it violates antitrust law for a competitor to refrain from challenging a patent. And by extension, we have long recognized that the settlement of patent litigation does not by itself violate the antitrust laws. Like most litigation, patent litigation is settled all the time, and such settlements—which can include agreements that clearly violate antitrust law, such as licenses that fix prices, or agreements among competitors to divide territory—do not ordinarily subject the litigants to antitrust liability.

The key, of course, is that the patent holder—when doing anything, including settling—must act within the scope of the patent. If its actions go beyond the monopoly powers conferred by the patent, we have held that such actions are subject to antitrust scrutiny. If its actions are within the scope of the patent, they are not subject to antitrust scrutiny, with two exceptions concededly not applicable here: (1) when the parties settle sham litigation, cf. *Professional Real Estate Investors, Inc. v. Columbia Pictures Industries, Inc.*; and (2) when the litigation involves a patent obtained through fraud on the Patent and Trademark Office. *Walker Process Equipment.*

Thus, under our precedent, this is a fairly straight-forward case. Solvay paid a competitor to respect its patent—conduct which did not exceed the scope of its patent. No one alleges that there was sham litigation, or that Solvay's patent was obtained through fraud on the PTO. As in any settlement, Solvay gave its competitors something of value (money) and, in exchange, its competitors gave it something of value (dropping their legal claims). In doing so, they put an end to litigation that had been dragging on for three years. Ordinarily, we would think this a good thing.

* * *

III

The majority's rule will discourage settlement of patent litigation. Simply put, there would be no incentive to settle if, immediately after settling, the parties would have to litigate the same issue—the question of patent validity—as part of a defense against an antitrust suit. In that suit, the alleged infringer would be in the especially awkward position of being for the patent after being against it. . . . This is unfortunate because patent litigation is particularly complex, and particularly costly. . . . The majority seems to think that *even if* the patent is valid, a patent holder violates the antitrust laws merely because the settlement took away some chance that his patent would be declared invalid by a court.

First, a patent is either valid or invalid. The parties of course don't know the answer with certainty at the outset of litigation; hence the litigation. But the same is true of any hard legal question that is yet to be adjudicated. Just because people don't know the answer doesn't mean there is no answer until a court declares one. Yet the majority would impose antitrust liability based on the parties' subjective uncertainty about that legal conclusion.

The Court does so on the assumption that offering a "large" sum is reliable evidence that the patent holder has serious doubts about the patent. Not true. A patent holder may be 95% sure about the validity of its patent, but particularly risk averse or litigation averse, and willing to pay a good deal of money to rid itself of the 5% chance of a finding of invalidity. What is actually motivating a patent holder is apparently a question district courts will have to resolve on a case-by-case basis. The task of trying to discern whether a patent holder is motivated by uncertainty about its patent, or other legitimate factors like risk aversion, will be made all the more difficult by the fact that much of the evidence about the party's motivation may be embedded in legal advice from its attorney, which would presumably be shielded from discovery.

Second, the majority's position leads to absurd results. Let's say in 2005, a patent holder sues a competitor for infringement and faces a counterclaim that its patent is invalid. The patent holder determines that the risk of losing on the question of validity is low, but after a year of litigating, grows increasingly risk averse, tired of litigation, and concerned about the company's image, so it pays the competitor a "large" payment, in exchange for having the competitor honor its patent. Then let's say in 2006, a different competitor, inspired by the first competitor's success, sues the patent holder and seeks a similar payment. The patent holder, recognizing that this dynamic is unsustainable, litigates this suit to conclusion, all the way to the Supreme Court, which unanimously decides the patent was valid. According to the majority, the first settlement would violate the antitrust laws even though the patent was ultimately declared valid, because that first settlement took away some chance that the patent would be invalidated in the first go around. Under this approach, a patent holder may be found liable under antitrust law for doing what its perfectly valid patent allowed it to do in the first place; its sin was to settle, rather than prove the correctness of its position by litigating until the bitter end.

Third, this logic — that taking away any *chance* that a patent will be invalidated is itself an antitrust problem — cannot possibly be limited to reverse-payment agreements, or those that are "large." The Government's brief acknowledges as much, suggesting that if antitrust scrutiny is invited for such cash payments, it may also be required for "other consideration" and "alternative arrangements." For example, when a patent holder licenses its product to a licensee at a fixed monopoly price, surely it takes away some chance that its patent will be challenged by that licensee. According to the majority's reasoning, that's an antitrust problem that must be analyzed under the rule of reason. Indeed, the Court's own solution — that patent holders should negotiate to allow generics into the market sooner, rather than paying them money — also takes away some chance that the generic would have litigated until the patent was invalidated.

Thus, although the question posed by this case is fundamentally a question of patent law — *i.e.*, whether Solvay's patent was valid and therefore permitted Solvay to pay competitors to honor the scope of its patent — the majority declares that such questions should henceforth be scrutinized by antitrust law's unruly rule of reason. Good luck to the district courts that must, when faced with a patent settlement, weigh the "likely anticompetitive effects, redeeming virtues, market power, and potentially offsetting legal considerations present in the circumstances."

* * *

The irony of all this is that the majority's decision may very well discourage generics from challenging pharmaceutical patents in the first place. Patent litigation is costly, time consuming, and uncertain. Generics "enter this risky terrain only after careful analysis of the potential gains if they prevail and the potential exposure if they lose." Taking the prospect of settlements off the table—or limiting settlements to an earlier entry date for the generic, which may still be many years in the future—puts a damper on the generic's expected value going into litigation, and decreases its incentive to sue in the first place. The majority assures us, with no support, that everything will be okay because the parties can settle by simply negotiating an earlier entry date for the generic drug manufacturer, rather than settling with money. But it's a matter of common sense, confirmed by experience, that parties are more likely to settle when they have a broader set of valuable things to trade.

V

The majority today departs from the settled approach separating patent and antitrust law, weakens the protections afforded to innovators by patents, frustrates the public policy in favor of settling, and likely undermines the very policy it seeks to promote by forcing generics who step into the litigation ring to do so without the prospect of cash settlements. I would keep things as they were and not subject basic questions of patent law to an unbounded inquiry under antitrust law, with its treble damages and famously burdensome discovery. I respectfully dissent.

Comments

1. *Settlement of Patent Litigation.* Empirical scholarship on patent litigation suggests that only about 1.5 percent of patents are litigated. *See* Mark A. Lemley, *Rational Ignorance at the Patent Office*, 95 Nw. L. Rev. 1495, 1501 (2001). Of this small percentage, about 11.5 percent were adjudicated (summary judgment or trial). *See* PatentStats.org. And a significant majority of the remaining cases are resolved through some form of settlement. *Id. See also* Jay P. Kesan & Gwendolyn G. Ball, *How Are Patent Cases Resolved? An Empirical Examination of the Adjudication and Settlement of Patent Disputes*, 84 Wash. U. L. Rev. 237 (2006). Thus, an overwhelming majority of patent litigation is settled, a result our legal system generally encourages. *See* Robert D. Willig & John P. Bigelow, *Antitrust Policy Towards Agreements That Settle Patent Litigation*, 49 Antitrust Bull. 655, 660-662 (2004).

2. *Exclusion Payments and the Courts.* Generally, patent litigation is very expensive, and a settlement dollar amount that is less than what it would cost to litigate is economically sound. But the combination of the pioneer's 30-month stay and the generic's 180-day exclusivity provide fertile ground for creative settlement agreements, which have generated a great deal of scrutiny. The pioneer wants to keep the generic drug off the market and retain the presumption of validity of its patent; and generics are drawn to cash in hand and want to keep other generic producers from entering the market. Importantly, prior to 2004, the 180-day exclusivity enjoyed by the first generic filer does

not begin until either the Secretary of Health and Human Services receives notice that the generic drug has been commercially marketed or a court holds the pioneer's patent invalid or not infringed. Thus, prior to 2004, if the settlement agreement delayed generic entry, the 180-day period was also delayed indefinitely. *See In re Cardizem CD Antitrust Litigation*, 332 F.3d 896 (6th Cir. 2003) (finding indefinite delay through periodic payments to generic firm a per se illegal restraint of trade). In 2004, Congress addressed this indefinite delay by providing the generic firm forfeits its 180-day exclusivity if it does not market the generic drug in a timely fashion. *See* Erika King Lietzan, *A Brief History of 180-Day Exclusivity Under the Hatch-Waxman Amendments to the Federal Food, Drug, and Cosmetic Act*, 59 FOOD & DRUG L.J. 287 (2004).

How these preferences play out in settlement agreements and the antitrust implications have been the subject of numerous court cases and FTC scrutiny, culminating in the principal case of *FTC v. Actavis*. Absent a patent right, exclusion payments would most likely be deemed per se illegal. One firm is paying another firm to stay off the market. Therefore, the existence of a patent right is significant. The FTC's adverse position notwithstanding and until the *Actavis* case, the federal appellate courts have tended to view exclusion payments as permissible under the antitrust laws. Courts had placed a high priority on encouraging settlement and emphasized the patent's presumption of validity and concomitant right to exclude, as the dissent did in *Actavis*. Unless antitrust plaintiffs can meet the "clear and convincing" standard to defeat the presumption of patent validity or show that the generic drug did not infringe the pioneer's patent (and the parties were aware of that fact at the time of settlement), courts generally have not assumed that a settlement including an exclusion payment exceeded the scope of the patent.

But the Supreme Court, armed with its five considerations, held the rule-of-reason applies and it is up to the district courts to fashion the rule-of-reason test when determining the lawfulness of these types of settlements. This will be a challenging endeavor. The districts courts are to apply the rule-of-reason analysis, which does not offer much guidance, in the context of the Hatch-Waxman framework and patent law policy. The dissent would have taken a much simpler approach, focusing merely on the scope of the right to exclude and the benefits of settlement.

Many commentators and policymakers who are skeptical of these types of settlements have argued that all settlements with exclusion payments should create a presumption that the patent holder exceeded the scope of its patent, because, unlike licensing agreements or negotiated entry dates for the generic drugs, exclusion payments allow the patent holder to maintain its legal monopoly that is disproportionate with the probability that the patent would withstand a trial verdict. Such a presumption, which the Supreme Court refused to adopt, would require the parties to the settlement to show that the settlement had pro-competitive effects by bringing more competition or efficiency to the market. The courts, however, have refused to treat exclusion payments as presumptively illegal.

In a 2010 study of pharmaceutical patent litigation, RBC Capital Markets examined 370 Paragraph IV challenges. The study states that "patent challenges have become the rule rather than the exception," with 65 challenges filed in 2009; 51 were filed in 2008, 24 in 2005, and 13 in 2003. *See* page 3 at http://amlawdaily.typepad.com/pharmareport.pdf. Interestingly, RBC found that generics won 48 percent of adjudicated cases, but the generic success rate increased dramatically—to 76 percent—when settlements were included. According to the report, "[s]ettlements provide clarity for the company and shareholders and we see them as a win-win for the generic and brand company." *Id.* at 4.

There has also been a great deal of commentary on this issue. *See, e.g.,* Michael A. Carrier, *Unsettling Drug Patent Settlements: A Framework for Presumptive Illegality,* 108 Mich. L. Rev. 37 (2009); Christopher M. Holman, *Do Reverse Payment Settlements Violate the Antitrust Laws?,* 23 Santa Clara Computer & High Tech. L.J. 489 (2007); Herbert Hovenkamp, Mark Janis & Mark A. Lemley, *Anticompetitive Settlement of Intellectual Property Disputes,* 87 Minn. L. Rev. 1719 (2003); Thomas F. Cotter, *Refining the "Presumptive Illegality" Approach to Settlements of Patent Disputes Involving Reverse Payments: A Commentary on Hovenkamp, Janis & Lemley,* 87 Minn. L. Rev. 1789 (2003); Jeremy Bulow, *The Gaming of Pharmaceutical Patents,* in 4 Innovation Policy and the Economy 145 (Adam B. Jaffe et al. eds., 2004); C. Scott Hemphill, *Paying for Delay: Pharmaceutical Patent Settlement as a Regulatory Design Problem,* 81 N.Y.U. L. Rev. 1553 (2006); Robert D. Willig & John P. Bigelow, *Antitrust Policy Toward Agreements That Settle Patent Litigation,* 49 Antitrust Bull. 655 (2004).

3. *The Architecture of Hatch-Waxman.* To fully appreciate the antitrust issues relating to exclusion payments (sometimes called "reverse payments"), it would be helpful to have a basic outline of the Hatch-Waxman legislation, formally known as the Drug Price Competition and Patent Term Restoration Act. In 1984, Congress passed the Hatch-Waxman Act, which focused on the relationship between the incentives of pioneer pharmaceutical companies and the desire for prompt market access to bio-equivalent generic alternatives. Under the provisions of the legislation, the pioneer, when filing its New Drug Application (NDA) as part of the FDA approval process, must list—in what is commonly referred to as the "Orange Book"[10]—any patents that would be infringed by a generic company. 21 U.S.C. §355(b)(1)(F). An Orange Book listing is a particularly powerful tool for the pioneer because it allows him to potentially secure a 30-month delay of FDA approval for the generic drug if the patentee sues for infringement.

A generic company, who seeks to introduce a generic drug into the market, can file an Abbreviated New Drug Application (ANDA) with the FDA. By filing an ANDA, the generic company does not have to undergo the rigorous and costly FDA clinical trials that the pioneer company endured.[11]

---

10. The "Orange Book"—which lists all approved drugs—is formally known as the "Approved Drug Products and Therapeutic Equivalents" that is published by the FDA. It is called the Orange Book because prior to it being available on the FDA website, the agency published a hardcopy that had an orange cover. *See* www.fda.gov/cder/ob.

11. The FDA new drug approval process is typically associated with three clinical phases. Phase I relates to the safety of the drug, but is restricted to a small number of human volunteers. Phase II pertains to determining preliminary efficacy and establishing proper dosage. And Phase III involves a large number of human patients that actually have the disease or ailment the drug is designed to treat. This phase seeks to determine both safety and efficacy.

But the generic company must prove bio-equivalency between the generic drug and the pioneer drug, meaning that the generic drug has the same active ingredient (although not necessarily the same inactive ingredients), dosage, and strength. If a pioneer's patent is listed in the Orange Book, however, the generic company is required to file a certification that discusses how the pioneer's listed patents will affect the generic company's plan to market a generic version of the pioneer drug. Most relevantly, the generic company has the option of filing a Paragraph IV certification, which asserts that the pioneer's patent is either invalid or not infringed. 21 U.S.C. §355(j)(2)(A)(vii)(IV). Importantly, the Hatch-Waxman Act provides the generic company who first files an ANDA and Paragraph IV certification with a 180-day period of exclusivity. This period of exclusivity bars other generic companies from marketing their generic version for 180 days after the first generic drug is commercialized or the pioneer patent is invalidated or held not to be infringed, whichever is earlier. The 180-day exclusivity is a powerful incentive for generics to challenge pioneer patents.

If the generic company opts for a Paragraph IV certification, it must also provide the pioneer with notice and details of its claim of invalidity or non-infringement within 20 days of the ANDA filing. 21 U.S.C. §355(j)(2)(B)(i)-(ii). At this point, the pioneer can take advantage of the aforementioned 30-month stay provision (a preliminary injunction for all practical purposes) for ANDA approval, but only if the pioneer files a patent infringement suit against the generic concern within 45 days from the generic's notice. (As of 2004, the pioneer is limited to one 30-month stay — *see* 21 U.S.C. §355(j)(2) and (5).) The ANDA will be approved "immediately" if the pioneer does not file suit. (Another option, infrequently used, is for the pioneer not to file suit, and to allow the ANDA to be approved and the generic drug introduced. This strategy, while risky, gives the pioneer the option to sue for damages.) Once suit is filed, a federal court will decide if the patent is proved invalid or not infringed, or vice versa. If the result is the former, then the FDA can approve the ANDA, and the generic will hit the market, even if the district court's determination occurs within the 30-month period. If the latter, the court will issue an injunction to keep the generic from entering the market until the pioneer's patent expires. 21 U.S.C. § 355(j)(5)(B)(iii). And the FDA will not be permitted to approve the ANDA until the patent expires. For a discussion of the Hatch-Waxman procedures, *see Mova Pharmaceutical Corp. v. Shalala*, 140 F.3d 1060, 1063-1065 (D.C. Cir. 1998).

4. Refusal to Deal

A basic tenet of patent law is the patentee enjoys the right to exclude others from making, using, and selling the claimed invention, which includes the right not to use, sell, or license its patent rights. But the right to exclude is not boundless and must be exercised in a manner consistent with antitrust principles. *Independent Service Organizations* explores the limits of the patentee's right to exclude in the context of a unilateral, unconditional refusal to sell its patented technology and the antitrust implications arising therefrom.

IN RE INDEPENDENT SERVICE ORGANIZATIONS
ANTITRUST LITIGATION

203 F.3d 1322 (Fed. Cir. 2000)

MAYER, Chief Judge.

CSU, L.L.C. appeals the judgment of the United States District Court for the District of Kansas, dismissing on summary judgment CSU's claims that Xerox's refusal to sell patented parts and copyrighted manuals and to license copyrighted software violate the antitrust laws. Because we agree with the district court that CSU has not raised a genuine issue as to any material fact and that Xerox is entitled to judgment as a matter of law, we affirm.

BACKGROUND

Xerox manufactures, sells, and services high-volume copiers. Beginning in 1984, it established a policy of not selling parts unique to its series 10 copiers to independent service organizations ("ISOs"), including CSU, unless they were also end-users of the copiers. In 1987, the policy was expanded to include all new products as well as existing series 9 copiers. Enforcement of this policy was tightened in 1989, and Xerox cut off CSU's direct purchase of restricted parts. Xerox also implemented an "on-site end-user verification" procedure to confirm that the parts ordered by certain ISOs or their customers were actually for their end-user use. Initially this procedure applied to only the six most successful ISOs, which included CSU.

To maintain its existing business of servicing Xerox equipment, CSU used parts cannibalized from used Xerox equipment, parts obtained from other ISOs, and parts purchased through a limited number of its customers. For approximately one year, CSU also obtained parts from Rank Xerox, a majority-owned European affiliate of Xerox, until Xerox forced Rank Xerox to stop selling parts to CSU and other ISOs. In 1994, Xerox settled an antitrust lawsuit with a class of ISOs by which it agreed to suspend its restrictive parts policy for six and one-half years and to license its diagnostic software for four and one-half years. CSU opted out of that settlement and filed this suit alleging that Xerox violated the Sherman Act by setting the prices on its patented parts much higher for ISOs than for end-users to force ISOs to raise their prices. This would eliminate ISOs in general and CSU in particular as competitors in the relevant service markets for high speed copiers and printers.

Xerox counterclaimed for patent and copyright infringement and contested CSU's antitrust claims as relying on injury solely caused by Xerox's lawful refusal to sell or license patented parts and copyrighted software. Xerox also claimed that CSU could not assert a patent or copyright misuse defense to Xerox's infringement counterclaims based on Xerox's refusal to deal.

The district court granted summary judgment to Xerox dismissing CSU's antitrust claims and holding that if a patent or copyright is lawfully acquired, the patent or copyright holder's unilateral refusal to sell or license its patented invention or copyrighted expression is not unlawful exclusionary conduct under the antitrust laws, even if the refusal to deal impacts competition in more than one market. The court also held, in both the patent and copyright contexts, that the right holder's intent in refusing to deal and any other alleged exclusionary acts committed by the right holder are irrelevant to antitrust law. This appeal followed.

DISCUSSION

The issue is whether the district court erred in granting Xerox's motion for summary judgment on CSU's antitrust claims. . . .

As a general proposition, when reviewing a district court's judgment involving federal antitrust law, we are guided by the law of the regional circuit in which that district court sits, in this case the Tenth Circuit. We apply our own law, not regional circuit law, to resolve issues that clearly involve our exclusive jurisdiction. "Whether conduct in procuring or enforcing a patent is sufficient to strip a patentee of its immunity from the antitrust laws is to be decided as a question of Federal Circuit law." *Nobelpharma,* 141 F.3d at 1068; *see Midwest Indus., Inc. v. Karavan Trailers, Inc.,* 175 F.3d 1356, 1360 (Fed. Cir. 1999) (*en banc* in relevant part) ("*Pro-Mold* and *Nobelpharma* make clear that our responsibility as the tribunal having sole appellate responsibility for the development of patent law requires that we do more than simply apply our law to questions of substantive patent law. In order to fulfill our obligation of promoting uniformity in the field of patent law, it is equally important to apply our construction of patent law to the questions whether and to what extent patent law preempts or conflicts with other causes of action."). The district court's grant of summary judgment as to CSU's antitrust claims arising from Xerox's refusal to sell its patented parts is therefore reviewed as a matter of Federal Circuit law, while consideration of the antitrust claim based on Xerox's refusal to sell or license its copyrighted manuals and software is under Tenth Circuit law.

A.

Intellectual property rights do not confer a privilege to violate the antitrust laws. *See Intergraph Corp. v. Intel Corp.,* 195 F.3d 1346, 1362 (Fed. Cir. 1999). "But it is also correct that the antitrust laws do not negate the patentee's right to exclude others from patent property." *Id.* "The commercial advantage gained by new technology and its statutory protection by patent do not convert the possessor thereof into a prohibited monopolist." *Abbott Lab. v. Brennan,* 952 F.2d 1346, 1354 (Fed. Cir. 1991). "The patent right must be 'coupled with violations of §2,' and the elements of violation of 15 U.S.C. §2 must be met."[1] *Id.* "Determination of whether the patentee meets the Sherman Act elements of monopolization or attempt to monopolize is governed by the rules of application of the antitrust laws to market participants, with due consideration to the exclusivity that inheres in the patent grant." *Id.* at 1354-55.

A patent alone does not demonstrate market power. The United States Department of Justice and Federal Trade Commission have issued guidance that, even where it exists, such "market power does not 'impose on the intellectual property owner an obligation to license the use of that property to others.'" *Intergraph,* 195 F.3d at 1362 (citing United States Department of Justice and Federal Trade Comm'n Antitrust Guidelines for the Licensing of Intellectual Property 4 (1995)). There is "no reported case in which a court ha[s] imposed antitrust liability for a unilateral refusal to sell or license a patent. . . ." *Id.* (citing

---

1. Section 2 of the Sherman Act, 15 U.S.C. §2, prohibits monopolization or attempts to monopolize: "Every person who shall monopolize, or attempt to monopolize, or combine or conspire with any other person or persons, to monopolize any part of the trade or commerce among the several States, or with foreign nations, shall be deemed guilty of a felony. . . ."

Image Technical Servs. v. Eastman Kodak Co., 125 F.3d 1195, 1216 (9th Cir. 1997)). The patentee's right to exclude is further supported by section 271(d) of the Patent Act which states, in pertinent part, that "[n]o patent owner otherwise entitled to relief . . . shall be denied relief or deemed guilty of misuse or *illegal extension of the patent right* by reason of his having . . . (4) refused to license or use any rights to the patent. . . ." 35 U.S.C. §271(d) (1999) (emphasis added).

The patentee's right to exclude, however, is not without limit. As we recently observed in *Glass Equipment Development Inc. v. Besten, Inc.*, a patent owner who brings suit to enforce the statutory right to exclude others from making, using, or selling the claimed invention is exempt from the antitrust laws, even though such a suit may have an anticompetitive effect, unless the infringement defendant proves one of two conditions. 174 F.3d 1337, 1343 (Fed. Cir. 1999). First, he may prove that the asserted patent was obtained through knowing and willful fraud within the meaning of *Walker Process Equipment, Inc. v. Food Machinery & Chemical Corp.*, 382 U.S. 172, 177 (1965). Or he may demonstrate that the infringement suit was a mere sham to cover what is actually no more than an attempt to interfere directly with the business relationships of a competitor. *See id.* (citing *Eastern R.R. Presidents Conference v. Noerr Motor Freight, Inc.*, 365 U.S. 127, 144 (1961)). Here, CSU makes no claim that Xerox obtained its patents through fraud in the Patent and Trademark Office; the *Walker Process* analysis is not implicated.

"[I]rrespective of the patent applicant's conduct before the [Patent and Trademark Office], an antitrust claim can also be based on [an] allegation that a suit is baseless; in order to prove that a suit was within *Noerr*'s 'sham' exception to immunity, [see *Noerr*, 365 U.S. at 144], an antitrust plaintiff must prove that the suit was both *objectively* baseless and *subjectively* motivated by a desire to impose collateral, anti-competitive injury rather than to obtain a justifiable legal remedy." *Nobelpharma*, 141 F.3d at 1071 (citing *Professional Real Estate Investors, Inc. v. Columbia Pictures Indus., Inc.*, 508 U.S. 49, 60-61 (1993)). "Accordingly, if a suit is not objectively baseless, an antitrust defendant's subjective motivation is immaterial." *Id.* at 1072. CSU has alleged that Xerox misused its patents but has not claimed that Xerox's patent infringement counterclaims were shams.

To support its argument that Xerox illegally sought to leverage its presumably legitimate dominance in the equipment and parts market into dominance in the service market, CSU relies on a footnote in *Eastman Kodak Co. v. Image Technical Services, Inc.*, 504 U.S. 451, 480 n.29 (1992), that "[t]he Court has held many times that power gained through some natural and legal advantage such as a patent, . . . can give rise to liability if 'a seller exploits his dominant position in one market to expand his empire into the next.'" Notably, *Kodak* was a tying case when it came before the Supreme Court, and no patents had been asserted in defense of the antitrust claims against Kodak. Conversely, there are no claims in this case of illegally tying the sale of Xerox's patented parts to unpatented products. Therefore, the issue was not resolved by the *Kodak* language cited by CSU. Properly viewed within the framework of a tying case, the footnote can be interpreted as restating the undisputed premise that the patent holder cannot use his statutory right to refuse to sell patented parts to gain a monopoly in a market *beyond the scope of the patent.*

The cited language from *Kodak* does nothing to limit the right of the patentee to refuse to sell or license in markets within the scope of the statutory patent grant. In fact, we have expressly held that, absent exceptional circumstances, a patent may confer the right to exclude competition altogether in more than one antitrust market.

CSU further relies on the Ninth Circuit's holding on remand in *Image Technical Services* that "while exclusionary conduct can include a monopolist's unilateral refusal to license a [patent] or to sell its patented . . . work, a monopolist's 'desire to exclude others from its [protected] work is a presumptively valid business justification for any immediate harm to consumers.'" 125 F.3d at 1218. By that case, the Ninth Circuit adopted a rebuttable presumption that the exercise of the statutory right to exclude provides a valid business justification for consumer harm, but then excused as harmless the district court's error in failing to give any instruction on the effect of intellectual property rights on the application of the antitrust laws. *See id.* at 1219-20. It concluded that the jury must have rejected the presumptively valid business justification as pretextual. *See id.* This logic requires an evaluation of the patentee's subjective motivation for refusing to sell or license its patented products for pretext. We decline to follow *Image Technical Services.*

We have held that "if a [patent infringement] suit is not objectively baseless, an antitrust defendant's subjective motivation is immaterial." *Nobelpharma,* 141 F.3d at 1072. We see no more reason to inquire into the subjective motivation of Xerox in refusing to sell or license its patented works than we found in evaluating the subjective motivation of a patentee in bringing suit to enforce that same right. In the absence of any indication of illegal tying, fraud in the Patent and Trademark Office, or sham litigation, the patent holder may enforce the statutory right to exclude others from making, using, or selling the claimed invention free from liability under the antitrust laws. We therefore will not inquire into his subjective motivation for exerting his statutory rights, even though his refusal to sell or license his patented invention may have an anticompetitive effect, so long as that anticompetitive effect is not illegally extended beyond the statutory patent grant. It is the infringement defendant and not the patentee that bears the burden to show that one of these exceptional situations exists and, in the absence of such proof, we will not inquire into the patentee's motivations for asserting his statutory right to exclude. Even in cases where the infringement defendant has met this burden, which CSU has not, he must then also prove the elements of the Sherman Act violation.

We answer the threshold question of whether Xerox's refusal to sell its patented parts exceeds the scope of the patent grant in the negative.[2] Therefore, our inquiry is at an end. Xerox was under no obligation to sell or license its patented parts and did not violate the antitrust laws by refusing to do so.

Comments

1. *Unilateral and Unconditional Refusals to Deal.* In the United States it has long been recognized that the patent owner has no duty to use, sell, or license his patented invention. *See Continental Paper Bag Co. v. Eastern Paper Bag Co.,* 210 U.S. 405, 429 (1908) (stating "exclusion may be said to have been of the very

---

2. Having concluded that Xerox's actions fell within the statutory patent grant, we need not separately consider CSU's allegations of patent misuse and they are rejected.

essence of the right conferred by the patent, as it is the privilege of any owner of property to use or not use it, without question of motive"); *Ethyl Gasoline Corp. v. United States,* 309 U.S. 436, 457 (1940) (patentee has right to refuse to license or sell its patented product); *United States v. Westinghouse Elec. Corp.,* 648 F.2d 642, 647 (9th Cir. 1981) (stating "Westinghouse has done no more than to license some of its patents and refuse to license others. '(T)he right to invoke the State's power to prevent others from utilizing his discovery without his consent' is the essence of the patentee's statutory monopoly. The right to license that patent, exclusively or otherwise, or to refuse to license at all, is 'the untrammeled right' of the patentee."). But the applicability of section 271(d)(4)—which expressly precludes a finding of misuse for a patentee's refusal to "license or use any rights to the patent"—to antitrust immunity is subject to debate. *See* ANTITRUST ENFORCEMENT AND INTELLECTUAL PROPERTY RIGHTS: PROMOTING INNOVATION AND COMPETITION 25-27 (Dep't of Justice and Federal Trade Commission, April 2007) (discussing whether section 271(d)(4) applies to unilateral refusals to deal).

With this tenet in mind, *ISO* can be viewed as holding a patentee who unilaterally and unconditionally refuses to deal with a third party is merely exercising his statutory rights under the patent code in a manner not inconsistent with antitrust laws. *See* Peter M. Boyle, Penelope M. Lister & J. Clayton Everett, Jr., *Antitrust Law at the Federal Circuit: Red Light or Green Light at the IP-Antitrust Intersection?*, 69 ANTITRUST L.J. 739, 747 (2002) ("We agree with others who have read *Xerox* [i.e., *ISO*] as standing for the limited proposition that an intellectual property owner may unilaterally and unconditionally refuse to license or sell products covered by lawfully acquired and valid patents or copyrights free from any antitrust liability. Although marred by murky reasoning and thin support on critical points, this holding finds support in orthodox antitrust principles."). In a speech given shortly after the *ISO* case, then chairman of the FTC, Robert Pitofsky, stated "I have no quarrel with the fundamental rule that a patent holder has no obligation to license or sell in the first instance. A patent holder is not under any general obligation to create competition against itself within the scope of its patent." Robert Pitofsky, *Challenges to the New Economy: Issues at the Intersection of Antitrust and Intellectual Property* (June 15, 2000—American Antitrust Institute Conference: An Agenda for Antitrust in the 21st Century, available at http://www.ftc.gov/speeches/pitofsky/000615speech).

The refusal to deal debate typically centers on two opposing theories. On the one hand, imposing a duty to use or sell arguably has short-term social welfare benefits because of increased competition and speedier improvement activity. But on the other hand, the long-term cost to ex ante incentives can be significant. *See* COMPETITION AND MONOPOLY: SINGLE-FIRM CONDUCT UNDER SECTION 2 OF THE SHERMAN ACT, Chapter 7 (Dep't of Justice 2009) (stating while forced sharing may lead to the appearance that consumers are better off, the innovator's "incentives to spend the necessary time and resources to innovate may be diminished," as will "the incentives of other firms to invest and innovate," thereby harming consumers in the long run). Moreover, courts have been skeptical of the ability of government authorities to regulate and supervise compulsory use. *See Verizon Commc'ns, Inc. v. Law Offices of Curtis V. Trinko, LLP*, 540 U.S. 398, 408, 415 (2004) (stating "[a]n antitrust court is unlikely to be an effective day-to-day enforcer of these detailed sharing obligations. . . . Enforced sharing . . . requires antitrust courts to act as central planners, identifying the proper price, quantity, and other terms of dealing—a role for which they are ill suited. Moreover, compelling negotiation between competitors may facilitate the supreme evil of antitrust: collusion"). Another concern with imposing antitrust liability is that it penalizes potentially beneficial price discrimination, which can serve markets that otherwise would not have access to the patented invention. *See* ANTITRUST ENFORCEMENT AND INTELLECTUAL PROPERTY RIGHTS, *supra*, at 24.

The *ISO* case can also be read as endorsing the proposition that when antitrust law and patent law are in conflict, patent law is favored. This notion finds support in *Simpson v. Union Oil Co. of Cal.*, 377 U.S. 13, 24 (1964) (stating "[t]he patent laws . . . are in pari materia with the antitrust laws and modify them pro tanto"). *See also Miller Insituform, Inc. v. Insituform of North America, Inc.*, 830 F.2d 606, 608 (6th Cir. 1987) (citing *Simpson*); *Data General Corp. v. Grumman Systems Support Corp.*, 36 F.3d 1146 (1st Cir. 1994) (stating "[t]he courts appear to have partly settled an analogous conflict between the patent laws and the antitrust laws, treating the former as creating an implied limited exception to the latter" (citing *Simpson*)); *SCM Corp. v. Xerox Corp.*, 645 F.2d 1195, 1204 (2d Cir. 1981) (stating a patentee's unilateral refusal to license "expressly permitted by the patent laws").

But the question remains why would a patentee refuse to license (or work) its patented invention? Michael Jacobs and Alan Devlin offer two reasons. First, the patentee may have imperfect information about pricing. For instance, "the IP has great value now in certain markets or applications, but may have even greater value in other markets or applications not yet identified." Michael Jacobs & Alan Devlin, *The Riddle Underlying Refusal-to-Deal Theory*, 105 NW. L. REV. 1, 3 (2010). Second, assuming the patentee does possess adequate pricing information, this "information might lead the firm to conclude that the costs outweigh the benefits, and that therefore agreeing to license would not be the profit-maximizing strategy." *Id.*

2. ***Conditional Refusals and "Beyond the Scope of the Patent."*** While the right to exclude under 35 U.S.C. § 154 is strong, it does not provide an absolute right of exclusion. The *ISO* court identified three situations where the patentee would violate section 2 of the Sherman Act: (1) *Walker Process* fraud, (2) sham litigation, and (3) illegal tying. But the court also recognized the "undisputed premise that the patent holder cannot use his statutory right to refuse to sell patented parts to gain a monopoly in a market *beyond the scope of the patent*" (emphasis in original). Thus, it may be too narrow a reading of *ISO* that violations of antitrust law are limited to the three instances expressly mentioned by the court. *See* ANTITRUST ENFORCEMENT AND INTELLECTUAL PROPERTY RIGHTS, *supra*, at 18-19 (criticizing *ISO* dicta limiting antitrust liability to illegal tying, fraud on the PTO, and sham litigation); Boyle et al., *Antitrust Law at the Federal Circuit, supra*, at 758 (stating "[t]here is no reason to believe that the three 'exceptions' to a patentee's 'antitrust immunity' enumerated in [*ISO*] exhaust the possibilities of anticompetitive acts involving the exercise of patent rights").

An example of a patentee using his patent rights in this manner (i.e., beyond the scope of his patent) is the *conditional* refusal to deal, as opposed to an unconditional and unilateral refusal. The *ISO* court did not address conditional refusals directly, but it is far from certain that the court would come out the same way as it did when presented with an unconditional refusal. In a conditional refusal context, the patentee is not simply saying "no, I refuse to deal, period," as in a unilateral refusal; rather, he says, "no, I refuse to deal, unless . . ." or "I will deal if. . . ." For example, "suppose a patent holder refuses to sell except on condition that the purchaser not buy from a potential competitor." Pitofsky, *Challenges to the New Economy.* Or a patentee "seeks to compel certain types of conduct or obligations from its licensees rather than merely to distinguish between groups of buyers" or tries to obtain "promises by licensees to act or refrain from acting in certain ways in the future." Herbert Hovenkamp, Mark D. Janis & Mark A. Lemley, *Unilateral Refusals to Deal in the U.S.,* 2 J. COMPETITION L. & ECON. 1, 38-39 (2006). *See also* David McGowan, *Innovation, Uncertainty, and Stability in Antitrust Law,* 16 BERKELEY TECH. L.J. 729, 781-782 (2001) (stating that "[a] unilateral refusal to license a work protected by a lawfully acquired intellectual property right is nothing more than the exercise of economic power that Congress has granted, and it should not be made the basis for a claim under the antitrust laws. Conditional refusals are different; they may extend a patentee's economic power beyond the scope of an intellectual property right. Conditional refusals therefore pose a risk of welfare-reducing strategic behavior that goes beyond the scope of power granted by Congress and which therefore may require antitrust analysis"); ANTITRUST ENFORCEMENT AND INTELLECTUAL PROPERTY RIGHTS, *supra,* at 6 (stating "[c]onditional refusals to license that cause competitive harm are subject to antitrust liability").

C. INEQUITABLE CONDUCT AND THE DUTY OF CANDOR

A patent applicant and other individuals associated with filing and prosecuting patent applications (e.g., the applicant's attorney) owe a duty of candor in dealing with the PTO. This means that for each pending claim information known to be "material" to patentability must be disclosed to the PTO. The duty of candor, grounded in 37 C.F.R. §1.56, is based on the notion that the "public interest is best served when, at the time an application is being examined, the Office is aware of and evaluates the teachings of all information material to patentability." Rule 1.56(a). An individual who violates this duty of candor is guilty of *inequitable conduct,* which is the subject of the *Therasense* case.

THERASENSE, INC. v. BECTON, DICKINSON AND CO.
649 F.3d 1276 (Fed. Cir. 2011) (en banc)

RADER, Chief Judge.

The United States District Court for the Northern District of California found U.S. Patent No. 5,820,551 ("the '551 patent") unenforceable due to inequitable conduct. (*"Trial Opinion"*). Therasense, Inc. (now Abbott Diabetes Care, Inc.) and Abbott Laboratories (collectively, "Abbott") appeal that judgment. This court vacates and remands for further proceedings consistent with this opinion.

I.

The '551 patent involves disposable blood glucose test strips for diabetes management. These strips employ electrochemical sensors to measure the level of glucose in a sample of blood. When blood contacts a test strip, glucose in the blood reacts with an enzyme on the strip, resulting in the transfer of electrons from the glucose to the enzyme. A mediator transfers these electrons to an electrode on the strip. Then, the electrons flow from the strip to a glucose meter, which calculates the glucose concentration based on the electrical current.

The '551 patent claims a test strip with an electrochemical sensor for testing whole blood without a membrane over the electrode:

1. A single use disposable electrode strip for attachment to the signal readout circuitry of a sensor to detect a current representative of the concentration of a compound in a drop of a whole blood sample comprising:

a) an elongated support having a substantially flat, planar surface, adapted for releasable attachment to said readout circuitry;

b) a first conductor extending along said surface and comprising a conductive element for connection to said readout circuitry;

c) an active electrode on said strip in electrical contact with said first conductor and positioned to contact said whole blood sample;

d) a second conductor extending along said surface comprising a conductive element for connection to said read out circuitry; and

e) a reference counterelectrode in electrical contact with said second conductor and positioned to contact said whole blood sample,

wherein said active electrode is configured to be exposed to said whole blood sample without an intervening membrane or other whole blood filtering member. . . .

'551 patent col. 13 l.29-col. 14 l.3 (emphasis added). "Whole blood," an important term in the claim, means blood that contains all of its components, including red blood cells.

In the prior art, some sensors employed diffusion-limiting membranes to control the flow of glucose to the electrode because the slower mediators of the time could not deal with a rapid influx of glucose. Other prior art sensors used protective membranes to prevent "fouling." Fouling occurs when red blood cells stick to the active electrode and interfere with electron transfer to the electrode. Protective membranes permit glucose molecules to pass, but not red blood cells.

Abbott filed the original application leading to the '551 patent in 1984. Over thirteen years, that original application saw multiple rejections for anticipation and obviousness, including repeated rejections over U.S. Patent No. 4,545,382 ("the '382 patent"), another patent owned by Abbott. The '382 patent specification discussed protective membranes in the following terms: "Optionally, but preferably when being used on live blood, a protective membrane surrounds both the enzyme and the mediator layers, permeable to water and glucose molecules." Col. 4 ll.63-66. "Live blood" refers to blood within a body.

In 1997, Lawrence Pope, Abbott's patent attorney, and Dr. Gordon Sanghera, Abbott's Director of Research and Development, studied the novel features of their application and decided to present a new reason for a patent. Pope presented new claims to the examiner based on a new sensor that did not require a protective membrane for whole blood. Pope asserted that this distinction would overcome the prior art '382 patent, whose electrodes allegedly required a protective membrane. The examiner requested an affidavit to show that the prior art required a membrane for whole blood at the time of the invention.

To meet this evidentiary request, Dr. Sanghera submitted a declaration to the U.S. Patent and Trademark Office ("PTO") stating:

> [O]ne skilled in the art would have felt that an active electrode comprising an enzyme and a mediator would require a protective membrane if it were to be used with a whole blood sample. . . . [O]ne skilled in the art would not read lines 63 to 65 of column 4 of [the '382 patent] to teach that the use of a protective membrane with a whole blood sample is optionally or merely preferred.

Pope, in submitting Sanghera's affidavit, represented:

> The art continued to believe [following the '382 patent] that a barrier layer for [a] whole blood sample was necessary. . . .

> One skilled in the art would *not* have read the disclosure of the ['382 patent] as teaching that the use of a protective membrane with whole blood samples was optional. He would not, especially in view of the working examples, have read the "optionally, but preferably" language at line 63 of column [4] as a technical teaching but rather mere patent phraseology.

> . . .

> There is no teaching or suggestion of unprotected active electrodes for use with whole blood specimens in [the '382 patent]. . . .

Several years earlier, while prosecuting the European counterpart to the '382 patent, European Patent EP 0 078 636 ("EP '636"), Abbott made representations to the European Patent Office ("EPO") regarding the same "optionally, but preferably" language in the European specification. On January 12, 1994, to distinguish a German reference labeled D1, which required a diffusion-limiting membrane, Abbott's European patent counsel argued that their invention did not require a diffusion-limiting membrane:

> *Contrary to the semipermeable membrane of D1, the protective membrane optionally utilized with the glucose sensor of the patent is [sic] suit is not controlling the permeability of the substrate.* . . . Rather, in accordance with column 5, lines 30 to 33 of the patent in suit:
>
>> Optionally, but preferably when being used on live blood, a protective membrane surrounds both the enzyme and the mediator layers, permeable to water and glucose molecules.
>
> See also claim 10 of the patent in suit as granted according to which the sensor electrode has an outermost protective membrane (11) permeable to water and glucose molecules. . . . Accordingly, *the purpose of the protective membrane of the patent in suit, preferably to be used with in vivo measurements, is a safety measurement to prevent any course [sic] particles coming off during use but not a permeability control for the substrate.*

(emphases added).

On May 23, 1995, Abbott's European patent counsel submitted another explanation about the D1 reference and EP '636.

> "Optionally, but preferably when being used on live blood, a protective membrane surrounds both the enzyme and the mediator layers, permeable to water and glucose molecules."

It is submitted that this disclosure is unequivocally clear. The protective membrane is optional, however, it is preferred when used on live blood in order to prevent the larger constituents of the blood, in particular erythrocytes from interfering with the electrode sensor. Furthermore it is said, that said protective membrane should not prevent the glucose molecules from penetration, the membrane is "permeable" to glucose molecules. This teaches the skilled artisan that, whereas the [D1 membrane] must . . . control the permeability of the glucose . . . the purpose of the protective membrane in the patent in suit is not to control the permeation of the glucose molecules. For this very reason *the sensor electrode as claimed does not have (and must not have) a semipermeable membrane in the sense of D1.*

(first and third emphases added).

II.

In March 2004, Becton, Dickinson and Co. ("Becton") sued Abbott in the District of Massachusetts seeking a declaratory judgment of noninfringement of U.S. Patent Nos. 6,143,164 ("the '164 patent") and 6,592,745 ("the '745 patent"). Becton's product was a blood glucose test strip, the BD Test Strip. Abbott countersued Becton in the Northern District of California alleging that Becton's strip infringed the '164, '745, and '551 patents.

. . . Of primary relevance here, the district court held the '551 patent unenforceable for inequitable conduct because Abbott did not disclose to the PTO its briefs to the EPO filed on January 12, 1994 and May 23, 1995. Abbott appealed. . . . On unenforceability, the panel also affirmed, but with a dissent. . . . Recognizing the problems created by the expansion and overuse of the inequitable conduct doctrine, this court granted Abbott's petition for rehearing en banc and vacated the judgment of the panel. This court now vacates the district court's inequitable conduct judgment and remands.

III.

Inequitable conduct is an equitable defense to patent infringement that, if proved, bars enforcement of a patent. This judge-made doctrine evolved from a trio of Supreme Court cases that applied the doctrine of unclean hands to dismiss patent cases involving egregious misconduct. . . .

IV.

The unclean hands cases of *Keystone, Hazel-Atlas,* and *Precision* formed the basis for a new doctrine of inequitable conduct that developed and evolved over time. Each of these unclean hands cases before the Supreme Court dealt with particularly egregious misconduct, including perjury, the manufacture of false evidence, and the suppression of evidence. Moreover, they all involved "deliberately planned and carefully executed scheme[s] to defraud" not only the PTO but also the courts. As the inequitable conduct doctrine evolved from these unclean hands cases, it came to embrace a broader scope of misconduct, including not only egregious affirmative acts of misconduct intended to deceive both the PTO and the courts but also the mere nondisclosure of information to the PTO. Inequitable conduct also diverged from the doctrine of unclean hands by adopting a different and more potent remedy—unenforceability of the entire patent rather than mere dismissal of the instant suit.

In line with this wider scope and stronger remedy, inequitable conduct came to require a finding of both intent to deceive and materiality. *Star Scientific Inc. v. R.J. Reynolds Tobacco Co.,* 537 F.3d 1357, 1365 (Fed. Cir. 2008). To prevail on the defense of inequitable conduct, the accused infringer must prove that the applicant misrepresented or omitted material information with the specific intent to deceive the PTO. *Id.* The accused infringer must prove both elements—intent and materiality—by clear and convincing evidence. *Id.* If the accused infringer meets its burden, then the district court must weigh the equities to determine whether the applicant's conduct before the PTO warrants rendering the entire patent unenforceable. *Id.*

As inequitable conduct emerged from unclean hands, the standards for intent to deceive and materiality have fluctuated over time. . . . This court embraced reduced standards for intent and materiality to foster full disclosure to the PTO. This new focus on encouraging disclosure has had numerous unforeseen and unintended consequences. Most prominently, inequitable conduct has become a significant litigation strategy. A charge of inequitable conduct conveniently expands discovery into corporate practices before patent filing and disqualifies the prosecuting attorney from the patentee's litigation team. *See* Stephen A. Merrill et al., Nat'l Research Council of the Nat'l Academies, *A Patent System for the 21st Century* 122 (2004).[12] Moreover, inequitable conduct charges cast a dark cloud over the patent's validity and paint the patentee as a bad actor. Because the doctrine focuses on the moral turpitude of the patentee with ruinous consequences for the reputation of his patent attorney, it discourages settlement and deflects attention from the merits of validity and infringement issues. Committee Position Paper, *The Doctrine of Inequitable Conduct and the Duty of Candor in Patent Prosecution: Its Current Adverse Impact on the Operation of the United States Patent System*, 16 AIPLA Q.J. 74, 75 (1988). Inequitable conduct disputes also "increas[e] the complexity, duration and cost of patent infringement litigation that is already notorious for its complexity and high cost." Brief and Appendix of the American Bar Ass'n as Amicus Curiae at 9.

Perhaps most importantly, the remedy for inequitable conduct is the "atomic bomb" of patent law. *Aventis Pharma S.A. v. Amphastar Pharm., Inc.*, 525 F.3d 1334, 1349 (Fed. Cir. 2008) (Rader, J., dissenting). Unlike validity defenses, which are claim specific, inequitable conduct regarding any single claim renders the entire patent unenforceable. *Kingsdown Med. Consultants, Ltd. v. Hollister Inc.*, 863 F.2d 867, 877 (Fed. Cir. 1988). Unlike other deficiencies, inequitable conduct cannot be cured by reissue, or reexamination. Moreover, the taint of a finding of inequitable conduct can spread from a single patent to render unenforceable other related patents and applications in the same technology family. Thus, a finding of inequitable conduct may endanger a substantial portion of a company's patent portfolio. A finding of inequitable conduct may also spawn antitrust and unfair competition claims. Further, prevailing on a claim of inequitable conduct often makes a case "exceptional," leading potentially to an award of attorneys' fees under 35 U.S.C. §285. A finding of inequitable conduct may also prove the crime or fraud exception to the attorney-client privilege.

While honesty at the PTO is essential, low standards for intent and materiality have inadvertently led to many unintended consequences, among them, increased adjudication cost and complexity, reduced likelihood of settlement, burdened courts, strained PTO resources, increased PTO backlog, and impaired

---

12. [The Merrill et al. study is available on the casebook website—http://law.case.edu/lawofpatents/—under "Documents and Literature."—ED.]

patent quality. This court now tightens the standards for finding both intent and materiality in order to redirect a doctrine that has been overused to the detriment of the public.

V.

To prevail on a claim of inequitable conduct, the accused infringer must prove that the patentee acted with the specific intent to deceive the PTO. A finding that the misrepresentation or omission amounts to gross negligence or negligence under a "should have known" standard does not satisfy this intent requirement. "In a case involving nondisclosure of information, clear and convincing evidence must show that the applicant *made a deliberate decision* to withhold a *known* material reference." *Molins,* 48 F.3d at 1181 (emphases added). In other words, the accused infringer must prove by clear and convincing evidence that the applicant knew of the reference, knew that it was material, and made a deliberate decision to withhold it. This requirement of knowledge and deliberate action has origins in the trio of Supreme Court cases that set in motion the development of the inequitable conduct doctrine. In each of those cases, the patentee acted knowingly and deliberately with the purpose of defrauding the PTO and the courts.

Intent and materiality are separate requirements. A district court should not use a "sliding scale," where a weak showing of intent may be found sufficient based on a strong showing of materiality, and vice versa. Moreover, a district court may not infer intent solely from materiality. Instead, a court must weigh the evidence of intent to deceive independent of its analysis of materiality. Proving that the applicant knew of a reference, should have known of its materiality, and decided not to submit it to the PTO does not prove specific intent to deceive.

Because direct evidence of deceptive intent is rare, a district court may infer intent from indirect and circumstantial evidence. However, to meet the clear and convincing evidence standard, the specific intent to deceive must be "the single most reasonable inference able to be drawn from the evidence." *Star,* 537 F.3d at 1366. Indeed, the evidence "must be sufficient to *require* a finding of deceitful intent in the light of all the circumstances." *Kingsdown,* 863 F.2d at 873 (emphasis added). Hence, when there are multiple reasonable inferences that may be drawn, intent to deceive cannot be found. This court reviews the district court's factual findings regarding what reasonable inferences may be drawn from the evidence for clear error.

Because the party alleging inequitable conduct bears the burden of proof, the "patentee need not offer any good faith explanation unless the accused infringer first . . . prove[s] a threshold level of intent to deceive by clear and convincing evidence." *Star,* 537 F.3d at 1368. The absence of a good faith explanation for withholding a material reference does not, by itself, prove intent to deceive.

VI.

This court holds that, as a general matter, the materiality required to establish inequitable conduct is but-for materiality. When an applicant fails to disclose prior art to the PTO, that prior art is but-for material if the PTO would not have allowed a claim had it been aware of the undisclosed prior art. Hence, in assessing the materiality of a withheld reference, the court must determine whether the PTO would have allowed the claim if it had been aware of the undisclosed reference. In making this patentability determination, the court should apply the preponderance of the evidence standard and give claims their broadest reasonable construction. Often the patentability of a claim will be congruent with the validity determination—if a claim is properly invalidated in district court based on the deliberately withheld reference, then that reference is necessarily material because a finding of invalidity in a district court requires clear and convincing evidence, a higher evidentiary burden than that used in prosecution at the PTO. However, even if a district court does not invalidate a claim based on a deliberately withheld reference, the reference may be material if it would have blocked patent issuance under the PTO's different evidentiary standards.

As an equitable doctrine, inequitable conduct hinges on basic fairness. "[T]he remedy imposed by a court of equity should be commensurate with the violation." *Columbus Bd. of Educ. v. Penick*, 443 U.S. 449, 465 (1979). Because inequitable conduct renders an entire patent (or even a patent family) unenforceable, as a general rule, this doctrine should only be applied in instances where the patentee's misconduct resulted in the unfair benefit of receiving an unwarranted claim. Moreover, enforcement of an otherwise valid patent does not injure the public merely because of misconduct, lurking somewhere in patent prosecution, that was immaterial to the patent's issuance.

Although but-for materiality generally must be proved to satisfy the materiality prong of inequitable conduct, this court recognizes an exception in cases of affirmative egregious misconduct. This exception to the general rule requiring but-for proof incorporates elements of the early unclean hands cases before the Supreme Court, which dealt with "deliberately planned and carefully executed scheme[s]" to defraud the PTO and the courts. When the patentee has engaged in affirmative acts of egregious misconduct, such as the filing of an unmistakably false affidavit, the misconduct is material. After all, a patentee is unlikely to go to great lengths to deceive the PTO with a falsehood unless it believes that the falsehood will affect issuance of the patent. Because neither mere nondisclosure of prior art references to the PTO nor failure to mention prior art references in an affidavit constitutes affirmative egregious misconduct, claims of inequitable conduct that are based on such omissions require proof of but-for materiality. By creating an exception to punish affirmative egregious acts without penalizing the failure to disclose information that would not have changed the issuance decision, this court strikes a necessary balance between encouraging honesty before the PTO and preventing unfounded accusations of inequitable conduct.

[T]he materiality standard set forth in this opinion includes an exception for affirmative acts of egregious misconduct, not just the filing of false affidavits. Accordingly, the general rule requiring but-for materiality provides clear guidance to patent practitioners and courts, while the egregious misconduct exception gives the test sufficient flexibility to capture extraordinary circumstances. Thus, not only is this court's approach sensitive to varied facts and equitable considerations, it is also consistent with the early unclean hands cases—all of which dealt with egregious misconduct.

This court does not adopt the definition of materiality in PTO Rule 56. As an initial matter, this court is not bound by the definition of materiality in PTO rules. While this court respects the PTO's knowledge in its area of expertise, the routine invocation of inequitable conduct in patent litigation has had adverse ramifications beyond its effect on the PTO. Tying the materiality standard for inequitable conduct to PTO rules, which understandably change from time to time, has led to uncertainty and inconsistency in the development of the inequitable conduct doctrine.

This court declines to adopt the current version of Rule 56 in defining inequitable conduct because reliance on this standard has resulted in the very problems this court sought to address by taking this case en banc. Rule 56 provides that information is material if it is not cumulative and:

> (1) It establishes, by itself or in combination with other information, a prima facie case of unpatentability of a claim; or
> (2) It refutes, or is inconsistent with, a position the applicant takes in:
> > (i) Opposing an argument of unpatentability relied on by the Office, or
> > (ii) Asserting an argument of patentability.

37 C.F.R. §1.56. Rule 56 further provides that a "prima facie case of unpatentability is established when the information compels a conclusion that a claim is unpatentable . . . *before any consideration is given to evidence which may be submitted in an attempt to establish a contrary conclusion of patentability.*" *Id.* (emphasis added). The first prong of Rule 56 is overly broad because information is considered material even if the information would be rendered irrelevant in light of subsequent argument or explanation by the patentee. Under this standard, inequitable conduct could be found based on an applicant's failure to disclose information that a patent examiner would readily agree was not relevant to the prosecution after considering the patentee's argument. Likewise, the second prong of Rule 56 broadly encompasses anything that could be considered marginally relevant to patentability. If an applicant were to assert that his invention would have been non-obvious, for example, anything bearing any relation to obviousness could be found material under the second prong of Rule 56. Because Rule 56 sets such a low bar for materiality, adopting this standard would inevitably result in patent prosecutors continuing the existing practice of disclosing too much prior art of marginal relevance and patent litigators continuing to charge inequitable conduct in nearly every case as a litigation strategy.

VII.

In this case, the district court held the '551 patent unenforceable for inequitable conduct because Abbott did not disclose briefs it submitted to the EPO regarding the European counterpart of the '382 patent. Because the district court found statements made in the EPO briefs material under the PTO's Rule 56 materiality standard, not under the but-for materiality standard set forth in this opinion, this court vacates the district court's findings of materiality. On remand, the district court should determine whether the PTO would not have granted the patent but for Abbott's failure to disclose the EPO briefs. In particular, the district court must determine whether the PTO would have found Sanghera's declaration and Pope's accompanying submission unpersuasive in overcoming the obviousness rejection over the '382 patent if Abbott had disclosed the EPO briefs.

The district court found intent to deceive based on the absence of a good faith explanation for failing to disclose the EPO briefs. However, a "patentee need not offer any good faith explanation unless the accused infringer first

. . . prove[s] a threshold level of intent to deceive by clear and convincing evidence." *Star*, 537 F.3d at 1368. The district court also relied upon the "should have known" negligence standard in reaching its finding of intent. *See Trial Opinion* at 1113 ("Attorney Pope knew or should have known that the withheld information would have been highly material to the examiner"). Because the district court did not find intent to deceive under the knowing and deliberate standard set forth in this opinion, this court vacates the district court's findings of intent. On remand, the district court should determine whether there is clear and convincing evidence demonstrating that Sanghera or Pope knew of the EPO briefs, knew of their materiality, and made the conscious decision not to disclose them in order to deceive the PTO.

For the foregoing reasons, this court vacates the district court's finding of inequitable conduct and remands for further proceedings consistent with this opinion.

Comments

1. ***The "Atomic Bomb of Patent Law."*** From as early as 1988, the Federal Circuit has expressed concerns with the inequitable conduct doctrine. For instance, in *Burlington Industries, Inc. v. Dayco Corp.*, 849 F.2d 1418, 1422 (Fed. Cir. 1988), the court noted, "the habit of charging inequitable conduct in almost every major patent case has become an absolute plague," as "[r]eputable lawyers seem to feel compelled to make the charge against other reputable lawyers on the slenderest grounds. . . ." These concerns continued over the years, culminating in *Therasense*, where the court referred to the devastating consequences resulting from a finding of inequitable conduct, namely unenforceability, as the "atomic bomb." These consequences—coupled with what the court viewed as the relatively low evidentiary requirements of intent and materiality and a laundry list of "unintended consequences"—influenced the court's opinion. Accordingly, with an eye toward greater certainty and addressing this "plague," the court "tighten[ed] the standards for finding both intent and materiality in order to redirect a doctrine that has been overused to the detriment of the public."

   But will this tightening also result in unintended consequences? Will fewer prior art disclosures lead to lower patent quality? In a noteworthy empirical study of patents that have been held unenforceable due to inequitable conduct, Lee Petherbridge, Jason Rantanen, and R. Polk Wagner found that these patents "have statistically significantly fewer citations to prior art than nearly all other types of patents," yet "they are also apparently among the most complex patents . . . in that they surpass all patents, including all other intensely litigated patents in length of pendency, and nearly all other patents in number of claims." Lee Petherbridge, Jason Rantanen & R. Polk Wagner, *Unenforceability Research Report* 2 (Nov. 16, 2012), available at unenforceability. fedcir.org. The authors conclude that their "results indicate that doctrine is likely to be operating better than the conventional wisdom would suggest."

2. ***Intent.*** The court adopted a "specific intent" standard. This standard is likely to be particularly germane to *undisclosed* material information. The omission of certain types of material information can be troubling from a patent

law perspective. For example, as the court noted in a prior case, "conceal-ment of sales information can be particularly egregious because, unlike the applicant's failure to disclose a material patent reference, the examiner has no way of securing the information on his own." *Paragon Podiatry Lab., Inc. v. KLM Labs. Inc.*, 984 F.2d 1182, 1193 (Fed. Cir. 1993). In *Therasense*, the court, while presumably aware of the perils of non-disclosure, nonetheless expressly reaffirmed the principle that "clear and convincing evidence must show that the applicant made a deliberate decision to withhold a known material reference." As such, the applicant must not only have known of the reference, but deliberately withheld it.

Moreover, the court eliminated the so-called sliding scale approach whereby a court could require less evidence of intent in the light of a highly material reference. In jettisoning this inverse relationship, the court stressed that intent and materiality are separate elements that should be weighed independent of each other.

Finally, proving intent in any setting is difficult. In the context of ineq-uitable conduct, rarely is there a "smoking gun." But this type of explicit evidence has not been necessary to satisfy the intent prong, as courts have inferred intent from the facts and circumstances relating to the applicant's conduct. Inferential findings of intent are still permitted under *Therasense*, but the court adopted the "single most reasonable inference" principle, which means that "the evidence must be sufficient to *require* a finding of deceitful intent in the light of all the circumstances." Thus, when multiple reasonable inferences are present, intent to deceive cannot be found.

3. ***Materiality.*** The *Therasense* court rejected the USPTO definition of material-ity set forth in 37 C.F.R. Rule 56, and adopted the more rigorous "but-for" approach; that is, a reference will be deemed material "if the PTO would not have allowed a claim had it been aware of the undisclosed" reference. The but-for test is thought to provide more certainty than prior definitions of materiality and discourage the disclosure of marginally relevant references. The dissent bemoaned the majority's new "hard and fast rules" that replaced the doctrine's longstanding flexibility, which, according to the dissent, could accommodate divergent scenarios. (The dissent's point reflects yet another instance of the rules-standards debate that we first encountered in Chapter 5—see pages 367-369, Comment 3.) The dissent would have adopted the USPTO's Rule 56 definition because the (1) "PTO is in the best position to know what information examiners need to conduct effective and efficient examinations, i.e., what information is material to the examination process"; and "the higher standard of materiality adopted by the majority will not pro-vide appropriate incentives for patent applicants to comply with the disclo-sure obligations the PTO places upon them."

In addition to the but-for test, the majority notably attached the prepon-derance of the evidence standard to this determination, rather than the more demanding clear and convincing evidence standard that applies to invalid-ity challenges. By definition, a reference that leads to a finding of invalidity (which is subject to a clear and convincing evidence standard) is material under the but-for test. Yet given the lower standard of proof under the but-for analysis, a reference may still be material even if it does not give rise to an invalidity finding. The preponderance of the evidence standard was affirmed in the post-*Therasense* case of *American Calcar, Inc. v. American Honda Motor*

Co., 651 F.3d 1318, 1335 (Fed. Cir. 2011) ("Even though the jury rejected Honda's invalidity arguments, both on anticipation and obviousness, as to the [patents-in-suit] based on the 96RL system, the withheld information may be material if it would have blocked patent issuance under the PTO's preponderance of the evidence standard, giving those patents' claims their broadest reasonable construction.").

The but-for test was also viewed by the court as consistent with social welfare. Enforcement of a valid patent does not harm the public, even though the applicant may have withheld a reference that a reasonable examiner would consider relevant to the claimed invention. Is there public harm if a patent would nonetheless have issued if the examiner was aware of the reference? Is there any harm to the public in this context? The dissent asserted that the majority—particularly its definition of materiality—"comes close to abolishing" the doctrine of inequitable conduct. Is this accurate? What about patent quality, a common concern over the past several years? Given the specific intent and materiality definitions, will applicants disclose fewer references, leading to lower quality patents?

4. *The Carve-Out: "Affirmative Acts of Egregious Misconduct."* The court seemed to think the public could be harmed by egregious behavior such as filing an "unmistakenly false affidavit" with the PTO. This type of behavior, according to the court, is material. Is this "misconduct" material only if a patent would not have issued but for the misconduct? The court writes of "encouraging honesty before the PTO," but are all dishonest acts "egregious"? Can an applicant tell a non-material lie to an examiner? Is there a difference between an "unmistakenly false affidavit" and a mere "false affidavit"?

This carve out was intended to provide "sufficient flexibility to capture extraordinary circumstances." Yet what these circumstances are remains to be determined. The majority noted that the three Supreme Court cases dealing with unclean hands concerned "perjury, the manufacture of false evidence, and the suppression of evidence" as well as "deliberately planned and carefully executed scheme[s] to defraud not only the PTO but also the courts." If the exception proves to be overly accommodating as applied by the district courts, the majority's tilt toward rule-based certainty could be diluted.

5. *On Remand.* The district court, on remand, found the European Patent Office briefs material under the but-for standard, and that Abbott's attorney and director of research had specific intent to deceive the USPTO by withholding the briefs. *See Therasense, Inc. v. Becton, Dickinson and Co.*, 864 F. Supp. 2d 856 (N.D. Cal. 2012).

6. *Supplemental Examination.* The AIA's new post-grant supplemental examination—which can be seen as a replacement for ex parte reexamination proceedings—serves as a sort of amnesty or second chance for patentees who may be concerned about plausible charges of inequitable conduct. (The patentee/requester does not have to admit—even if it were true—that the submitted references were improperly withheld from the USPTO during the initial examination.) The AIA amends section 257 and allows patentees to submit relevant information post-issuance. If the new information survives supplemental review without prompting a reexamination, or survives reexamination, the submitted information cannot be used later as a basis for an inequitable conduct claim. But, as the prior sentence implies, the new prior art may give rise to a "substantial new question of patentability" and

potentially lead to the invalidation of the claims in question. A request for supplemental examination becomes public as soon the request is given a filing date by the USPTO. Supplemental examination became effective on September 16, 2012.

D. EXPERIMENTAL USE

There are two forms of experimental use—statutory and common law. Regarding the former, under section 271(e) certain activities are exempted from infringement, namely activity that is "solely for uses reasonably related to the development and submission of information" under federal food and drug laws. This safe harbor is known as the Bolar Amendment or FDA exemption, and the breadth of its reach was at issue in *Merck v. Integra Lifesciences I*, the principal case below. The common law exemption, while it remains, is not robust and is explored in *Madey v. Duke*, the principal case in section D.2. Indeed, the Federal Circuit has never applied the doctrine in a manner that would absolve infringement liability.

1. Statutory Experimental Use Under Section 271(e)(1)

MERCK v. INTEGRA LIFESCIENCES I
545 U.S. 193 (2005)

Justice SCALIA delivered the opinion of the Court.

This case presents the question whether uses of patented inventions in preclinical research, the results of which are not ultimately included in a submission to the Food and Drug Administration (FDA), are exempted from infringement by 35 U.S.C. § 271(e)(1).

I

It is generally an act of patent infringement to "mak[e], us[e], offe[r] to sell, or sel[l] any patented invention . . . during the term of the patent therefor." § 271(a). In 1984, Congress enacted an exemption to this general rule, see Drug Price Competition and Patent Term Restoration Act of 1984 as amended, 35 U.S.C. § 271(e)(1), which provides:

> It shall not be an act of infringement to make, use, offer to sell, or sell within the United States or import into the United States a patented invention (other than a new animal drug or veterinary biological product (as those terms are used in the Federal Food, Drug, and Cosmetic Act and the Act of March 4, 1913) . . .) solely for uses reasonably related to the development and submission of information under a Federal law which regulates the manufacture, use, or sale of drugs. . . .

The Federal Food, Drug, and Cosmetic Act (FDCA), is "a Federal law which regulates the manufacture, use, or sale of drugs." See 21 U.S.C. § 355(a). Under the FDCA, a drugmaker must submit research data to the FDA at two general stages of new-drug development.[1] First, a drugmaker must gain authorization to conduct clinical trials (tests on humans) by submitting an investigational new drug application (IND). See 21 U.S.C. § 355(i). The IND must describe "preclinical tests (including tests on animals) of [the] drug adequate to justify the proposed clinical testing." 21 U.S.C. § 355(i)(1)(A); see 21 CFR §§ 312.23(a)(5) and (a)(8) (specifying necessary information from preclinical tests). Second, to obtain authorization to market a new drug, a drugmaker must submit a new drug application (NDA), containing "full reports of investigations which have been made to show whether or not [the] drug is safe for use and whether [the] drug is effective in use." 21 U.S.C. § 355(b)(1). Pursuant to FDA regulations, the NDA must include all clinical studies, as well as preclinical studies related to a drug's efficacy, toxicity, and pharmacological properties.

II

A

Respondents Integra Lifesciences I, Ltd., and the Burnham Institute, own five patents related to the tripeptide sequence Arg-Gly-Asp, known in single-letter notation as the "RGD peptide." U.S. Patent Nos. 4,988,621, 4,792,525, 5,695,997, 4,879,237, and 4,789,734. The RGD peptide promotes cell adhesion by attaching to αvβ3 integrins, receptors commonly located on the outer surface of certain endothelial cells.

Beginning in 1988, petitioner Merck KGaA provided funding for angiogenesis research conducted by Dr. David Cheresh at the Scripps Research Institute (Scripps). Angiogenesis is the process by which new blood vessels sprout from existing vessels; it plays a critical role in many diseases, including solid tumor cancers, diabetic retinopathy, and rheumatoid arthritis. In the course of his research, Dr. Cheresh discovered that it was possible to inhibit angiogenesis by blocking the αvβ3 integrins on proliferating endothelial cells. In 1994, Dr. Cheresh succeeded in reversing tumor growth in chicken embryos, first using a monoclonal antibody (LM609) he developed himself and later using a cyclic RGD peptide (EMD 66203) provided by petitioner. Dr. Cheresh's discoveries were announced in leading medical journals and received attention in the general media.

With petitioner's agreement to fund research at Scripps due to expire in July 1995, Dr. Cheresh submitted a detailed proposal for expanded collaboration between Scripps and petitioner on February 1, 1995. The proposal set forth a 3-year timetable in which to develop "integrin antagonists as angiogenesis inhibitors," beginning with *in vitro* and *in vivo* testing of RGD peptides at Scripps in year one and culminating with the submission of an IND to the FDA in year three. Petitioner agreed to the material terms of the proposal on February 20, 1995, and on April 13, 1995, pledged $6 million over three years to fund research at Scripps. Petitioner's April 13 letter specified that Scripps would

---

1. Drugmakers that desire to market a generic drug (a drug containing the same active ingredients as a drug already approved for the market) may file an abbreviated new drug application (ANDA) with the FDA. See 21 U.S.C. § 355(j). The sponsor of a generic drug does not have to make an independent showing that the drug is safe and effective, either in preclinical or clinical studies. See § 355(j)(2)(A). It need only show that the drug includes the same active ingredients as, and is bioequivalent to, the drug that it is mimicking. See §§ 355(j)(2)(A)(ii) and (iv); § 355(j)(8)(B).

be responsible for testing RGD peptides produced by petitioner as potential drug candidates but that, once a primary candidate for clinical testing was in "the pipeline," petitioner would perform the toxicology tests necessary for FDA approval to proceed to clinical trials.

Pursuant to the agreement, Dr. Cheresh directed *in vitro* and *in vivo* experiments on RGD peptides provided by petitioner from 1995 to 1998. These experiments focused on EMD 66203 and two closely related derivatives, EMD 85189 and EMD 121974, and were designed to evaluate the suitability of each of the peptides as potential drug candidates. Accordingly, the tests measured the efficacy, specificity, and toxicity of the particular peptides as angiogenesis inhibitors, and evaluated their mechanism of action and pharmacokinetics in animals. Based on the test results, Scripps decided in 1997 that EMD 121974 was the most promising candidate for testing in humans. Over the same period, Scripps performed similar tests on LM609, a monoclonal antibody developed by Dr. Cheresh. Scripps also conducted more basic research on organic mimetics designed to block $\alpha v\beta 3$ integrins in a manner similar to the RGD peptides; it appears that Scripps used the RGD peptides in these tests as "positive controls" against which to measure the efficacy of the mimetics.

In November 1996, petitioner initiated a formal project to guide one of its RGD peptides through the regulatory approval process in the United States and Europe. Petitioner originally directed its efforts at EMD 85189, but switched focus in April 1997 to EMD 121974. Petitioner subsequently discussed EMD 121974 with officials at the FDA. In October 1998, petitioner shared its research on RGD peptides with the National Cancer Institute (NCI), which agreed to sponsor clinical trials.

B

On July 18, 1996, respondents filed a patent-infringement suit against petitioner, Scripps, and Dr. Cheresh in the District Court for the Southern District of California. Respondents' complaint alleged that petitioner willfully infringed and induced others to infringe respondents' patents by supplying the RGD peptide to Scripps, and that Dr. Cheresh and Scripps infringed the same patents by using the RGD peptide in experiments related to angiogenesis. Respondents sought damages from petitioner and a declaratory judgment against Dr. Cheresh and Scripps. Petitioner answered that its actions involving the RGD peptides did not infringe respondents' patents, and that in any event they were protected by the common-law research exemption and 35 U.S.C. § 271(e)(1).

At the conclusion of trial, the District Court held that, with one exception, petitioner's pre-1995 actions related to the RGD peptides were protected by the common-law research exemption, but that a question of fact remained as to whether petitioner's use of the RGD peptides after 1995 fell within the § 271(e)(1) safe harbor. . . . The jury found that petitioner, Dr. Cheresh, and Scripps infringed respondents' patents and that petitioner had failed to show that its activities were protected by § 271(e)(1). It awarded damages of $15 million.

A divided panel of the Court of Appeals for the Federal Circuit affirmed in part, and reversed in part. The panel majority affirmed the denial of judgment as a matter of law to petitioner, on the ground that § 271(e)(1)'s safe harbor did not apply because "the Scripps work sponsored by [petitioner] was not clinical testing to supply information to the FDA, but only general biomedical research to identify new pharmaceutical compounds."

III

As described earlier, 35 U.S.C. §271(e)(1) provides that "[i]t shall not be an act of infringement to . . . use . . . or import into the United States a patented invention . . . solely for uses reasonably related to the development and submission of information under a Federal law which regulates the . . . use . . . of drugs." Though the contours of this provision are not exact in every respect, the statutory text makes clear that it provides a wide berth for the use of patented drugs in activities related to the federal regulatory process.

As an initial matter, we think it apparent from the statutory text that §271(e)(1)'s exemption from infringement extends to all uses of patented inventions that are reasonably related to the development and submission of *any* information under the FDCA. This necessarily includes preclinical studies of patented compounds that are appropriate for submission to the FDA in the regulatory process. There is simply no room in the statute for excluding certain information from the exemption on the basis of the phase of research in which it is developed or the particular submission in which it could be included.

Respondents concede the breadth of §271(e)(1) in this regard, but argue that the only preclinical data of interest to the FDA is that which pertains to the safety of the drug in humans. In respondents' view, preclinical studies related to a drug's efficacy, mechanism of action, pharmacokinetics, and pharmacology are not reasonably included in an IND or an NDA, and are therefore outside the scope of the exemption. We do not understand the FDA's interest in information gathered in preclinical studies to be so constrained. To be sure, its regulations provide that the agency's "primary objectives in reviewing an IND are . . . to assure the safety and rights of subjects," 21 CFR 312.22(a) (2005), but it does not follow that the FDA is not interested in reviewing information related to other characteristics of a drug. To the contrary, the FDA requires that applicants include in an IND summaries of the pharmacological, toxicological, pharmacokinetic, and biological qualities of the drug in animals. *See* §312.23(a)(5). The primary (and, in some cases, only) way in which a drugmaker may obtain such information is through preclinical *in vitro* and *in vivo* studies.

Moreover, the FDA does not evaluate the safety of proposed clinical experiments in a vacuum; rather, as the statute and regulations reflect, it asks whether the proposed clinical trial poses an "unreasonable risk." 21 U.S.C. §355(i)(3)(B)(i). This assessment involves a comparison of the risks and the benefits associated with the proposed clinical trials. As the Government's brief, filed on behalf of the FDA, explains, the "FDA might allow clinical testing of a drug that posed significant safety concerns if the drug had a sufficiently positive potential to address a serious disease, although the agency would not accept similar risks for a drug that was less likely to succeed or that would treat a less serious medical condition." Brief for United States as *Amicus Curiae* 10. Accordingly, the FDA directs that an IND must provide sufficient information for the investigator to "make his/her own unbiased risk-benefit assessment of the appropriateness of the proposed trial." Department of Health and Human Services, Guidance for Industry, Good Clinical Practice: Consolidated Guidance 43 (Apr. 1996). Such information necessarily includes preclinical studies of a drug's efficacy in achieving particular results.

Respondents contend that, even accepting that the FDA is interested in preclinical research concerning drug characteristics other than safety, the experiments in question here are necessarily disqualified because they were not conducted in conformity with the FDA's good laboratory practices regulations. This argument fails for at least two reasons. First, the FDA's requirement that preclinical studies be conducted under "good laboratory practices" applies only to experiments on drugs "to determine their safety," 21 CFR §58.3(d). See 21 CFR §58.1(a); §312.23(a)(8)(iii) (2005) (only "nonclinical laboratory study subject to the good laboratory practice regulations under part 58" must certify compliance with good laboratory practice regulations). The good laboratory practice regulations do not apply to preclinical studies of a drug's efficacy, mechanism of action, pharmacology, or pharmacokinetics. Second, FDA regulations do not provide that even safety-related experiments not conducted in compliance with good laboratory practices regulations are not suitable for submission in an IND. Rather, such studies must include "a brief statement of the reason for the noncompliance." *Ibid.*

The Court of Appeals' conclusion that §271(e)(1) did not protect petitioner's provision of the patented RGD peptides for research at Scripps appeared to rest on two somewhat related propositions. First, the court credited the fact that the "Scripps-Merck experiments did not supply information for submission to the [FDA], but instead identified the best drug candidate to subject to future clinical testing under the FDA processes." 331 F.3d, at 865. The court explained:

> The FDA has no interest in the hunt for drugs that may or may not later undergo clinical testing for FDA approval. For instance, the FDA does not require information about drugs other than the compound featured in an [IND] application. Thus, the Scripps work sponsored by [petitioner] was not "solely for uses reasonably related to" clinical testing for FDA.

Second, the court concluded that the exemption "does not globally embrace all experimental activity that at some point, however attenuated, may lead to an FDA approval process." *Id.*, at 867.[7]

We do not quibble with the latter statement. Basic scientific research on a particular compound, performed without the intent to develop a particular drug or a reasonable belief that the compound will cause the sort of physiological effect the researcher intends to induce, is surely not "reasonably related to the development and submission of information" to the FDA. It does not follow from this, however, that §271(e)(1)'s exemption from infringement categorically excludes either (1) experimentation on drugs that are not ultimately the subject of an FDA submission or (2) use of patented compounds in experiments that are not ultimately submitted to the FDA. Under certain conditions, we think the exemption is sufficiently broad to protect the use of patented compounds in both situations.

As to the first proposition, it disregards the reality that, even at late stages in the development of a new drug, scientific testing is a process of trial and

---

7. The Court of Appeals also suggested that a limited construction of §271(e)(1) is necessary to avoid depriving so-called "research tools" of the complete value of their patents. Respondents have never argued the RGD peptides were used at Scripps as research tools, and it is apparent from the record that they were not. See 331 F.3d, at 878 (Newman, J., dissenting) ("Use of an existing tool in one's research is quite different from study of the tool itself"). We therefore need not—and do not—express a view about whether, or to what extent, §271(e)(1) exempts from infringement the use of "research tools" in the development of information for the regulatory process.

error. In the vast majority of cases, neither the drugmaker nor its scientists have any way of knowing whether an initially promising candidate will prove successful over a battery of experiments. That is the reason they conduct the experiments. Thus, to construe §271(e)(1), as the Court of Appeals did, not to protect research conducted on patented compounds for which an IND is not ultimately filed is effectively to limit assurance of exemption to the activities necessary to seek approval of a generic drug: One can know at the outset that a particular compound will be the subject of an eventual application to the FDA only if the active ingredient in the drug being tested is identical to that in a drug that has already been approved.

The statutory text does not require such a result. Congress did not limit §271(e)(1)'s safe harbor to the development of information for inclusion in a submission to the FDA; nor did it create an exemption applicable only to the research relevant to filing an ANDA for approval of a generic drug. Rather, it exempted from infringement *all* uses of patented compounds "reasonably related" to the process of developing information for submission under *any* federal law regulating the manufacture, use, or distribution of drugs. We decline to read the "reasonable relation" requirement so narrowly as to render §271(e)(1)'s stated protection of activities leading to FDA approval for all drugs illusory. Properly construed, §271(e)(1) leaves adequate space for experimentation and failure on the road to regulatory approval: At least where a drugmaker has a reasonable basis for believing that a patented compound may work, through a particular biological process, to produce a particular physiological effect, and uses the compound in research that, if successful, would be appropriate to include in a submission to the FDA, that use is "reasonably related" to the "development and submission of information under . . . Federal law." §271(e)(1).

For similar reasons, the use of a patented compound in experiments that are not themselves included in a "submission of information" to the FDA does not, standing alone, render the use infringing. The relationship of the use of a patented compound in a particular experiment to the "development and submission of information" to the FDA does not become more attenuated (or less reasonable) simply because the data from that experiment are left out of the submission that is ultimately passed along to the FDA. Moreover, many of the uncertainties that exist with respect to the selection of a specific drug exist as well with respect to the decision of what research to include in an IND or NDA. As a District Court has observed, "[I]t will not always be clear to parties setting out to seek FDA approval for their new product exactly which kinds of information, and in what quantities, it will take to win that agency's approval." *Intermedics, Inc. v. Ventritex, Inc.*, 775 F. Supp. 1269, 1280 (N.D. Cal. 1991), *aff'd*, 991 F.2d 808 (C.A. Fed. 1993). This is especially true at the preclinical stage of drug approval. FDA regulations provide only that "[t]he amount of information on a particular drug that must be submitted in an IND . . . depends upon such factors as the novelty of the drug, the extent to which it has been studied previously, the known or suspected risks, and the developmental phase of the drug." 21 CFR §312.22(b). We thus agree with the Government that the use of patented compounds in preclinical studies is protected under §271(e)(1) as long as there is a reasonable basis for believing that the experiments will produce "the types of information that are relevant to an IND or NDA." Brief of United States as *Amicus Curiae* 23.

Before the Court of Appeals, petitioner challenged the sufficiency of the evidence supporting the jury's finding that it failed to show that "all of the accused activities are covered by [§271(e)(1)]." That court rejected the challenge on the basis of a construction of §271(e)(1) that was not consistent with the text of that provision or the relevant jury instruction.[8] Thus, the evidence presented at trial has yet to be reviewed under the standards set forth in the jury instruction, which we believe to be consistent with, if less detailed than, the construction of §271(e)(1) that we adopt today. We decline to undertake a review of the sufficiency of the evidence under a proper construction of §271(e)(1) for the first time here. Accordingly, we vacate the judgment of the Court of Appeals and remand the case for proceedings consistent with this opinion.

Comments

1. **On Remand.** The Federal Circuit reversed the district court's infringement finding, stating the challenged experiments, all of which were conducted after discovery of the anti-angiogenesis property of the experimental RGD peptide provided by Merck, meet the criteria of being reasonably related to research that, if successful, would be appropriate to include in a submission to the FDA. *Integra Lifesciences I, Ltd. v. Merck KGaA*, 496 F.3d 1334 (Fed. Cir. 2007).

2. **Drug Development and the FDA Regulatory Process.** Drug development is expensive, reaching into the hundreds of millions of dollars. *See* Joseph A. DiMasi et al., *The Price of Innovation: New Estimates of Drug Development Costs*, 22 J. HEALTH ECON. 151 (2003). *Cf.* Public Citizen, *Tufts Drug Study Sample Is Skewed; True Figure of R&D Costs Likely Is 75 Percent Lower* (Dec. 4, 2001). And a majority of prospective molecules/drugs get weeded out before clinical trials or ultimately do not get approved by the FDA. The development spectrum typically begins with basic research, then moves to preclinical studies, and finally clinical studies that invoke the FDA approval process. Basic research focuses on general understanding of particular diseases and large screening studies of various biological compounds. The preclinical phase centers on fewer compounds and information gathering that can lead to clinical studies, which focus of safety and efficacy through testing on human subjects.

3. **Preclinical Testing, Research Tools, and the Supreme Court's Expansive Reading.** The Bolar Amendment was narrowly interpreted by the Federal Circuit, which held that the exemption applies to experimentation that "would contribute (relatively directly) to information the FDA considers in approving a drug" (e.g., New Drug Application (NDA) to the FDA, which contain the results of clinical trials and must be approved by the FDA before a drug is marketed). *Integra Lifesciences I, Ltd. v. Merck KGaA*, 331 F.3d 860, 867 (Fed. Cir. 2004).

---

8. The relevant jury instruction provided only that there must be a "decent prospect that the accused activities would contribute, relatively directly, to the generation of the kinds of information that are likely to be relevant in the processes by which the FDA would decide whether to approve the product in question." App. 57a. It did not say that, to fall within §271(e)(1)'s exemption from infringement, the patented compound used in experimentation must be the subject of an eventual application to the FDA. And it expressly rejected the notion that the exemption only included experiments that produced information included in an IND or NDA. *Ibid.*

Thus, on the development spectrum ranging from basic upstream research to the downstream clinical/NDA stage, the Federal Circuit erred on the side of downstream application when interpreting the exemption. And the court, while not expressly holding that the exemption only applies to generic drug development, suggested as much in dicta. According to the Federal Circuit:

> The exemption viewed in this context does not endorse an interpretation of §271(e)(1) that would encompass drug development activities far beyond those necessary to acquire information for FDA approval of a patented pioneer drug already on the market. It does not, for instance, expand the phrase "reasonably related" to embrace all stages of the development of new drugs merely because those new products will also need FDA approval. Thus, §271(e)(1) simply does not globally embrace all experimental activity that at some point, however attenuated, may lead to an FDA approval process. The safe harbor does not reach any exploratory research that may rationally form only a predicate for future FDA clinical tests.

331 F.3d at 867. A broader reading of section 271(e), stated the court, "would swallow the whole benefit of the Patent Act for some categories of biotechnological inventions." *Id.* One category the court was referring to was upstream discoveries such as research tool patents. Research tools, such as peptides, enzymes, and non-diagnostic antibodies, are very important for screening drug candidates and for drug discovery. They are also important revenue generators for biotechnology companies.

The Supreme Court moved the exemption further upstream to include pre-clinical use of patented inventions, but footnote 7 expressly noted the Court need not decide whether the FDA exemption applies to research tools. But in *Proveris Scientific Corp. v. Innovasystems, Inc.*, 536 F.3d 1256 (Fed. Cir. 2008), the Federal Circuit rejected the alleged infringer's argument that the exemption applies to research tools. According to the court, because the alleged infringer "device . . . is not subject to a required FDCA approval process, it does not need the safe harbor protection afforded by" section 271(e)(1). *Id.* at 1266. Moreover, section 271(e)(1) "does not apply to information that may be routinely reported to the FDA, long after marketing approval has been obtained"; indeed, "[e]very decision examining the statute has appreciated that section 271(e)(1) is directed to premarketing approval of generic counterparts before patent expiration." *Classen Immunotherapies, Inc. v. Biogen IDEC*, 659 F.3d 1057, 1070-1071 (Fed. Cir. 2011). *Cf. Momenta Pharms. v. Amphastar Pharms.* 686 F.3d 1348 (Fed. Cir. 2012) (distinguishing *Classen* and finding certain post-approval activities are protected by the safe harbor of section 271(e)(1)).

2. Common Law Experimental Use

<u>MADEY v. DUKE</u>

307 F.3d 1351 (Fed. Cir. 2002)

GAJARSA, Circuit Judge.

Dr. John M.J. Madey ("Madey") appeals from a judgment of the United States District Court for the Middle District of North Carolina. Madey sued Duke University ("Duke"), bringing claims of patent infringement and various other federal and state law claims. For a first set of alleged infringing acts, the court held that the experimental use defense applied to Duke's use of Madey's patented laser technology. The district court erred in applying the experimental use defense.

BACKGROUND

In the mid-1980s Madey was a tenured research professor at Stanford University. At Stanford, he had an innovative laser research program, which was highly regarded in the scientific community. An opportunity arose for Madey to consider leaving Stanford and take a tenured position at Duke. Duke recruited Madey, and in 1988 he left Stanford for a position in Duke's physics department. In 1989 Madey moved his free electron laser ("FEL") research lab from Stanford to Duke. The FEL lab contained substantial equipment, requiring Duke to build an addition to its physics building to house the lab. In addition, during his time at Stanford, Madey had obtained sole ownership of two patents practiced by some of the equipment in the FEL lab.

At Duke, Madey served for almost a decade as director of the FEL lab. During that time the lab continued to achieve success in both research funding and scientific breakthroughs. However, a dispute arose between Madey and Duke. Duke contends that, despite his scientific prowess, Madey ineffectively managed the lab. Madey contends that Duke sought to use the lab's equipment for research areas outside the allocated scope of certain government funding, and that when he objected, Duke sought to remove him as lab director. Duke eventually did remove Madey as director of the lab in 1997. The removal is not at issue in this appeal, however, it is the genesis of this unique patent infringement case. As a result of the removal, Madey resigned from Duke in 1998. Duke, however, continued to operate some of the equipment in the lab. Madey then sued Duke for patent infringement of his two patents, and brought a variety of other claims.

A. The Patents and Infringing Equipment

One of Madey's patents, U.S. Patent No. 4,641,103 ("the '103 patent"), covers a "Microwave Electron Gun" used in connection with free electron lasers. The other patent, U.S. Patent No. 5,130,994 ("the '994 patent"), is titled "Free-Electron Laser Oscillator For Simultaneous Narrow Spectral Resolution And Fast Time Resolution Spectroscopy." The details of these two patents are not material to the issues on appeal. Their use in the lab, however, as embodied in certain equipment, is central to this appeal.

The three alleged infringing devices are the Mark III FEL, the Storage Ring FEL, and the Microwave Gun Test Stand. Although it is not clear from the record, perhaps because Duke defended by asserting experimental use and government license defenses, Duke seems to concede that the alleged infringing devices and methods read on the claims of the patents.

The Patent Motion and the Experimental Use Defense

The district court acknowledged a common law "exception" for patent infringement liability for uses that, in the district court's words, are "solely for research, academic or experimental purposes." The district court recognized the debate over the scope of the experimental use defense, but cited this court's opinion in *Embrex, Inc. v. Service Engineering Corp.*, 216 F.3d 1343, 1349 (Fed. Cir.

2000) to hold that the defense was viable for experimental, non-profit purposes, citing *Embrex*, 216 F.3d at 1349 (noting that courts should not "construe the experimental use rule so broadly as to allow a violation of the patent laws in the guise of 'scientific inquiry,' when that inquiry has definite, cognizable, and not insubstantial commercial purposes" (quoting *Roche Prods., Inc. v. Bolar Pharm. Co.*, 733 F.2d 858, 863 (Fed. Cir. 1984)).[3]

After having recognized the experimental use defense, the district court then fashioned the defense for application to Madey in the passage set forth below.

> Given this standard [for experimental use], for [Madey] to overcome his burden of establishing actionable infringement in this case, he must establish that [Duke] has not used the equipment at issue "solely for an experimental or other non-profit purpose." 5 Donald S. Chisum, *Chisum on Patents* § 16.03[1] (2000). More specifically, [Madey] must sufficiently establish that [Duke's] use of the patent had "definite, cognizable, and not insubstantial commercial purposes." *Roche Prods., Inc. v. Bolar Pharm. Co.*

On appeal, Madey attacks this passage as improperly shifting the burden to the plaintiff to allege and prove that the defendant's use was not experimental.

Before the district court, Madey argued that Duke's research in its FEL lab was commercial in character and intent. Madey relied on *Pitcairn v. United States*, 547 F.2d 1106 (1976), where the government used patented rotor structures and control systems for a helicopter to test the "lifting ability" and other attributes of the patented technology. The *Pitcairn* court held that the helicopters were not built solely for experimental purposes because they were also built to benefit the government in its legitimate business. Based on language in Duke's patent policy, Madey argues that Duke is in the business of "obtaining grants and developing possible commercial applications for the fruits of its 'academic research.'"

The district court rejected Madey's argument, relying on another statement in the preamble of the Duke patent policy which stated that Duke was "dedicated to teaching, research, and the expansion of knowledge . . . [and] does not undertake research or development work principally for the purpose of developing patents and commercial applications." The district court reasoned that these statements from the patent policy refute any contention that Duke is "in the business" of developing technology for commercial applications. According to the district court, Madey's "evidence" was mere speculation,[4] and thus Madey did not meet his burden of proof to create a genuine issue of material fact. The court went on to state that "[w]ithout more concrete evidence to rebut [Duke's] stated purpose with respect to its research in the FEL lab, Plaintiff has failed to meet its burden of establishing patent infringement by a preponderance of the evidence."

---

3. The accused infringer in *Roche* sought to assert the experimental use defense to allow early development of a generic drug. After the *Roche* decision, however, Congress changed the law, overruling *Roche* in part, but without impacting the experimental use doctrine. Congress provided limited ability for a company to practice a patent in furtherance of a drug approval application.

4. Madey also argued that Duke's acceptance of funding from the government and private foundations was evidence of developing patented devices with commercial intent. The district court also rejected this proposition. *Summary Judgment Opinion* at 13 (citing *Ruth v. Stearns-Roger Mfg. Co.*, 13 F. Supp. 697, 713 (D. Colo. 1935) (concluding that the experimental use defense applies when a university uses a patented device in furtherance of its educational purpose).

II. DISCUSSION

C. The District Court's Application of Experimental Use

On appeal, Madey asserts three primary errors related to experimental use. First, Madey claims that the district court improperly shifted the burden to Madey to prove that Duke's use was not experimental. Second, Madey argues that the district court applied an overly broad version of the very narrow experimental use defense inconsistent with our precedent. Third, Madey attacks the supporting evidence relied on by the district court as overly general and not indicative of the specific propositions and findings required by the experimental use defense, and further argues that there is no support in the record before us to allow any court to apply the very narrow experimental use defense to Duke's ongoing FEL lab operation. We substantially agree with Madey on all three points. In addition, Madey makes a threshold argument concerning the continued existence of the experimental use doctrine in any form, which we turn to first. Our precedent, to which we are bound, continues to recognize the judicially created experimental use defense, however, in a very limited form.

The Experimental Use Defense

Citing the concurring opinion in *Embrex,* Madey contends that the Supreme Court's opinion in *Warner-Jenkinson Co. v. Hilton Davis Chem. Co.,* 520 U.S. 17 (1997), eliminates the experimental use defense. The Supreme Court held in *Warner-Jenkinson* that intent plays no role in the application of the doctrine of equivalents. Madey implicitly argues that the experimental use defense necessarily incorporates an intent inquiry, and thus is inconsistent with *Warner-Jenkinson.* Like the majority in *Embrex,* we do not view such an inconsistency as inescapable, and conclude the experimental use defense persists albeit in the very narrow form articulated by this court in *Embrex,* 216 F.3d at 1349, and in *Roche,* 733 F.2d at 863.

The District Court Improperly Shifted the Burden to Madey

As a precursor to the burden-shifting issue, Madey argues that the experimental use defense is an affirmative defense that Duke must plead or lose. We disagree. Madey points to no source of authority for its assertion that experimental use is an affirmative defense. Indeed, we have referred to the defense in a variety of ways. *See Roche,* 733 F.2d at 862 (referring to experimental use as both an exception and a defense). Given this lack of precise treatment in the precedent, Madey has no basis to support its affirmative defense argument. The district court and the parties in the present case joined the issue during the summary judgment briefing. We see no mandate from our precedent, nor any compelling reason from other considerations, why the opportunity to raise the defense if not raised in the responsive pleading should not also be available at the later stages of a case, within the procedural discretion typically afforded the trial court judge.

The district court held that in order for Madey to overcome his burden to establish actionable infringement, he must establish that Duke did not use the patent-covered free electron laser equipment solely for experimental or other non-profit purposes. Madey argues that this improperly shifts the burden to the patentee and conflates the experimental use defense with the initial infringement inquiry.

We agree with Madey that the district court improperly shifted the burden to him. The district court folded the experimental use defense into the baseline assessment as to whether Duke infringed the patents. Duke characterizes the district court's holding as expressing the following sequence: first, the court recognized that Madey carried his burden of proof on infringement; second, the court held that Duke carried its burden of proof on the experimental use defense; and third, the court held that Madey was unable to marshal sufficient evidence to rebut Duke's shifting of the burden. We disagree with Duke's reading of the district court's opinion. The district court explicitly contradicts Duke's argument by stating that Madey failed to "meet its burden to establish patent infringement by a preponderance of the evidence." This statement is an assessment of whether Madey supported his initial infringement claim. It is not an assessment of which party carried or shifted the burden of evidence related to the experimental use defense. Thus, the district court did not conclude that Madey failed to rebut Duke's assertion of the experimental use defense. Instead, it erroneously required Madey to show as a part of his initial claim that Duke's use was not experimental. The defense, if available at all, must be established by Duke.

The District Court's Overly Broad Conception of Experimental Use

Madey argues, and we agree, that the district court had an overly broad conception of the very narrow and strictly limited experimental use defense. The district court stated that the experimental use defense inoculated uses that "were solely for research, academic, or experimental purposes," and that the defense covered use that "is made for experimental, non-profit purposes only." Both formulations are too broad and stand in sharp contrast to our admonitions in *Embrex* and *Roche* that the experimental use defense is very narrow and strictly limited. In *Embrex,* we followed the teachings of *Roche* and *Pitcairn* to hold that the defense was very narrow and limited to actions performed "for amusement, to satisfy idle curiosity, or for strictly philosophical inquiry." *Embrex,* 216 F.3d at 1349. Further, use does not qualify for the experimental use defense when it is undertaken in the "guise of scientific inquiry" but has "definite, cognizable, and not insubstantial commercial purposes." *Id.* (quoting *Roche,* 733 F.2d at 863). The concurring opinion in *Embrex* expresses a similar view: use is disqualified from the defense if it has the "slightest commercial implication." *Id.* at 1353. Moreover, use in keeping with the legitimate business of the alleged infringer does not qualify for the experimental use defense. The district court supported its conclusion with a citation to *Ruth v. Stearns-Roger Mfg. Co.,* 13 F. Supp. 697, 713 (D. Colo. 1935), a case that is not binding precedent for this court.

The *Ruth* case represents the conceptual dilemma that may have led the district court astray. Cases evaluating the experimental use defense are few, and those involving non-profit, educational alleged infringers are even fewer. In *Ruth,* the court concluded that a manufacturer of equipment covered by patents was not liable for contributory infringement because the end-user purchaser was the Colorado School of Mines, which used the equipment in furtherance of its educational purpose. *Id.* Thus, the combination of apparent lack of commerciality, with the non-profit status of an educational institution, prompted the court in *Ruth,* without any detailed analysis of the character, nature and effect of the use, to hold that the experimental use defense applied. *Id.* This is not consistent with the binding precedent of our case law postulated by *Embrex, Roche* and *Pitcairn.*

Our precedent clearly does not immunize use that is in any way commercial in nature. Similarly, our precedent does not immunize any conduct that is in keeping with the alleged infringer's legitimate business, regardless of commercial implications. For example, major research universities, such as Duke, often sanction and fund research projects with arguably no commercial application whatsoever. However, these projects unmistakably further the institution's legitimate business objectives, including educating and enlightening students and faculty participating in these projects. These projects also serve, for example, to increase the status of the institution and lure lucrative research grants, students and faculty.

In short, regardless of whether a particular institution or entity is engaged in an endeavor for commercial gain, so long as the act is in furtherance of the alleged infringer's legitimate business and is not solely for amusement, to satisfy idle curiosity, or for strictly philosophical inquiry, the act does not qualify for the very narrow and strictly limited experimental use defense. Moreover, the profit or non-profit status of the user is not determinative.

In the present case, the district court attached too great a weight to the non-profit, educational status of Duke, effectively suppressing the fact that Duke's acts appear to be in accordance with any reasonable interpretation of Duke's legitimate business objectives.[7] On remand, the district court will have to significantly narrow and limit its conception of the experimental use defense. The correct focus should not be on the non-profit status of Duke but on the legitimate business Duke is involved in and whether or not the use was solely for amusement, to satisfy idle curiosity, or for strictly philosophical inquiry.

Comments

1. ***Historical Development.*** The common law experimental use doctrine finds its origin in an opinion by Justice Story in *Whittemore v. Cutter*, 29 F. Cas. 1120 (C.C.D. Mass. 1813). Justice Story famously wrote that "it could never have been the intention of the legislature to punish a man, who constructed such a machine merely for philosophical experiments, or for the purpose of ascertaining the sufficiency of the machine to produce its described effects." *Id.* at 1121. In that same year, Justice Story wrote in *Sawin v. Guild*, 21 F. Cas. 554 (C.C.D. 1813), that "the making of a patented machine to be an offence within the purview of it, must be the making with an intent to use for profit, and not for the mere purpose of philosophical experiment, or to ascertain the verity and exactness of the specification [citing *Whittemore*]."

2. ***The Federal Circuit's Treatment of Experimental Use.*** The Federal Circuit has taken a very narrow view of the common law experimental use exemption. For instance, in *Embrex Inc. v. Service Engineering Corp.*, 216 F.3d 1343 (Fed. Cir.

---

7. Duke's patent and licensing policy may support its primary function as an educational institution. *See Duke University Policy on Inventions, Patents, and Technology Transfer* (1996), *available at http://www.ors.duke.edu/policies/patpol.htm* (last visited Oct. 3, 2002). Duke, however, like other major research institutions of higher learning, is not shy in pursuing an aggressive patent licensing program from which it derives a not insubstantial revenue stream. *See id.*

2000), the patent in suit concerned "methods for inoculating birds against disease by injecting vaccines into a specified region of the egg before hatching." *Id.* at 1346. The court held that an infringer's acts of having two scientists test a prototype machine cannot be deemed experimental use or de minimis. The tests were not for "scientific inquiry," but rather for commercial purpose, to wit, to demonstrate to potential customers the usefulness of the methods performed by the machines. That the infringer was unsuccessful in selling its machines conferred no immunity for the infringing acts of unauthorized testing. The court noted that it has "construed both the experimental use and de minimis exceptions very narrowly [citing *Roche*]." Notably, Judge Rader filed a concurrence wherein he stated that the "Patent Act leaves no room for any de minimis or experimental use excuses for infringement." *Id.* at 1352. For Judge Rader, experimental use cannot survive *Warner-Jenkinson* because that Court held intent is irrelevant to patent infringement. The *Madey* court rejected Judge Rader's reasoning, stating "we do not view such an inconsistency as inescapable, and conclude the experimental use defense persists albeit in the very narrow form articulated by this court in *Embrex*."

3. ***Criticism of Federal Circuit's Experimental Use Doctrine.*** A number of commentators have criticized the Federal Circuit's treatment of the experimental use exemption and called for a more vigorous experimental use exemption. *See, e.g.,* Janice M. Mueller, *The Evanescent Experimental Use Exemption from United States Patent Infringement Liability: Implications for University and Nonprofit Research and Development*, 56 BAYLOR L. REV. 917 (2004); Janice M. Mueller, *No "Dilettante Affair": Rethinking the Experimental Use Exception to Patent Infringement for Biomedical Research Tools*, 76 WASH. L. REV. 1 (2001); Rebecca S. Eisenberg, *Proprietary Rights and the Norms of Science in Biotechnology Research*, 97 YALE L.J. 177 (1987); Arti Kaur Rai, *Regulating Scientific Research: Intellectual Property Rights and the Norms of Science*, 94 NW. U. L. REV. 77 (1999).

E. INVENTORSHIP

United States patent law requires that the correct inventors be named in the patent application. This requirement stems from the patent and copyright clause of the Constitution, namely that Congress has the power "[t]o promote the progress of . . . useful arts, by securing for limited times to . . . *inventors* the exclusive right to their . . . discoveries" (emphasis added). The *Hess* and *Acromed* cases explore the issue of inventorship, and the type of contribution one has to make before he legally qualifies as an "inventor."

HESS v. ADVANCED CARDIOVASCULAR SYSTEMS, INC.
106 F.3d 976 (Fed. Cir. 1997)

FRIEDMAN, Senior Circuit Judge.

This appeal challenges the decision of the United States District Court for the Northern District of California that the materials and suggestions the appellant

Robert L. Hess provided to the listed inventors of a patent did not make him a co-inventor of the patented device. We affirm.

I.

A.

United States Patent No. 4,323,071 (the '071 patent), which listed Drs. John B. Simpson and Edward W. Robert as the inventors, covers a balloon angioplasty catheter that is inserted into a patient's artery which has a partial blockage, or stenosis. The balloon, fitted to the catheter, is inflated by forcing a radiographic fluid into it under pressure; the resulting expansion of the balloon eliminates or reduces the blockage of the artery.

While developing the catheter, Drs. Simpson and Robert were postdoctoral Cardiology Fellows at Stanford University Medical Center. A Swiss physician, Dr. Gruntzig, had pioneered the development of balloon angioplasty. After hearing Dr. Gruntzig speak at a cardiology conference at Stanford in March 1977 and later meeting him, Dr. Simpson spent time with Dr. Gruntzig in Europe, observing him perform balloon angioplasty procedures.

Upon returning to the United States Dr. Simpson discovered that Gruntzig catheters, made only in Switzerland, were in short supply. Drs. Simpson and Robert then decided to construct their own catheter. They had not examined the Gruntzig catheter in detail, but knew it had a balloon mounted on a shaft.

In attempting to find a material from which a balloon could be made, the doctors first experimented with a plastic called polyvinylchloride, which was ineffective, and next tried Teflon tubing, which produced unsatisfactory balloons. One of their Stanford colleagues (Bill Sanders) then referred them to the appellant Mr. Hess, an engineer at Raychem Corporation. At that time Mr. Hess was a technical liaison between Raychem's domestic and foreign operations; prior to that he had headed a business development group. Sanders made the suggestion because Raychem was one of the largest manufacturers of heat shrinkable materials and "might have some material" with which they could work.

The doctors told Mr. Hess, who had no previous experience with angioplasty, about the Gruntzig catheter. They stated they "wanted to . . . build a catheter . . . that incorporated a balloon on the end of a shaft." They explained what they were attempting to do, the problems they had encountered in finding a suitable material for the balloon, and that they were looking for a new material. They stated that the materials they had tried did not enable them properly to control balloon expansion.

Mr. Hess suggested that the doctors try Raychem's heat shrinkable irradiated modified polyolefin tubing and demonstrated how such a material could be used to form a balloon by heating the tubing above its crystalline melting point, applying pressure, and then cooling the material. Mr. Hess also suggested the use of an adhesive-free seal to attach the balloon to the catheter. He described how one end of the tubing could be shrunk fit onto the central shaft of the catheter without the use of any potentially-toxic adhesive chemicals. Mr. Hess stated that "the basic principles which I taught them"—involving heating the tubing "above its crystalline melting point, expanding it while it remains heated using internal pressure and then cooling it in its expanded state while your [sic] maintaining the pressure"—were "in various published textbooks and the like" and "was a generally known process to a number of companies."

Mr. Hess provided "multiple samples of . . . tubing," with which the doctors "experimented." At that meeting and in further discussions with the doctors, Mr. Hess also suggested "approaches to construction of the catheter" using the Raychem tubing.

Using that tubing, Drs. Simpson and Robert then developed and built their catheter. They had "difficulty . . . developing the . . . catheter" and spent "hours and days trying to configure this system to make it work," including "experimentation . . . with the tubing" Mr. Hess "gave" them. The two doctors worked on the catheter "virtually every day [for] four or five hours or more." The doctors finally developed the balloon using a technique called free-blowing, a technique which Mr. Hess admittedly did not suggest. Pursuant to Mr. Hess's suggestion, the doctors attempted to avoid the use of adhesives and shrink fit the balloon to the catheter shaft, but they encountered leakage problems. Without Mr. Hess's assistance and after further experimentation, the doctors ultimately developed an acceptable adhesive-free seal. Mr. Hess did not participate in the day-to-day experimentation.

The doctors applied for a patent on their catheter in April, 1978 and the '071 patent issued with twenty-one claims (the "original claims") in April, 1982. The two inventors organized the appellee company Advanced Cardiovascular Systems, Inc. (ACS), to which they assigned the '071 patent, and began manufacturing and selling the catheter. An ACS officer stated that the "catheter gained widespread success in the marketplace, and sales of the product grew rapidly," and that the Simpson-Robert catheter "was profitable" to ACS. Raychem supplied ACS with tubing for manufacturing the catheters.

B.

In 1987, ACS sued SciMed Life Systems, Inc. (SciMed) in the United States District Court for the District of Minnesota for infringement of the '071 patent. The district court granted SciMed's motion for summary judgment of noninfringement, based on its interpretation of the claims. This court, however, vacated and remanded, rejecting the district court's claim interpretation.

The question of Mr. Hess's alleged co-inventorship apparently first arose when in its answer SciMed asserted, as one ground for challenging the validity of the patent, that there was a "failure of the patentees to join Hess as a co-patentee." In a declaration Mr. Hess executed in 1988, which SciMed filed in the patent infringement case, he described the aid he had given to Drs. Simpson and Robert in connection with the development of their catheter. In a 1990 affidavit, he repeated those statements and asserted that he "made substantive contributions to the subject matter disclosed" in the '071 patent and "should be named as a co-inventor thereof."

In September, 1987, ACS requested reexamination of certain claims in the '071 patent. In May 1990, the Patent and Trademark Office issued a reexamination certificate, which upheld the original claims and added claims 22-52 (the "reexamination claims").

In the summer of 1990, Mr. Hess intervened in the ACS-SciMed suit to file a cross-complaint against ACS seeking a declaration that he was a joint inventor of the catheter the '071 patent covered and seeking correction of the patent to reflect his status. The district court dismissed Mr. Hess's cross-complaint for failing to state a claim on which relief could be granted because the complaint was barred by laches. This court vacated the dismissal and remanded, holding that there were disputed issues of material fact with respect to laches that precluded dismissal.

While that appeal was pending, Mr. Hess filed suit in United States District Court for the Northern District of California against ACS, alleging that he was a co-inventor of the catheter the reexamination claims covered.

On the eve of trial ACS and SciMed settled their infringement suit. The Minnesota District Court then transferred to the Northern District of California Court the remaining portion of the case, which was Mr. Hess's cross-complaint asserting his co-inventorship of the catheter the '071 patent covers. The California District Court consolidated the two cases.

The California District Court granted summary judgment that Mr. Hess's claim of co-inventorship of the catheter the original claims covered was barred by laches, and set for trial the co-ownership issue with respect to the reexamination claims.

After a bench trial, the district court held that the evidence did not establish Mr. Hess's claim of co-inventorship of the catheter the reexamination claims covered. Ruling from the bench, the court determined that Mr. Hess was required to prove co-inventorship by clear and convincing evidence. The court stated:

> [A]ll that Mr. Hess needs to establish is that he conceived some important element or some important claim that is claimed in the patent. . . . I don't think it's necessary for Mr. Hess to conceive of every feature of the catheter, but that he have some conceptual role in at least an important or a necessary element, or important and necessary claim.

The court noted:

> [I]nventors can obtain the services and ideas and product of others without losing their exclusive right to ownership. . . . So merely that Mr. Hess was consulted, Mr. Hess made some contribution, doesn't in and of itself rise to the level of conception particularly if he's doing nothing more than explaining to the inventors what the then state of the art was and supplying a product to them for use in their invention.

The court found that

> the information provided by Mr. Hess really didn't rise to the level of conception; that most, if not all, of his discussion with them were [sic] telling them what was available in the marketplace by way of product, and telling them how the product worked, and they, that is, Simpson and Robert, were the ones who used the product or used the—yes, used the product provided in their work. . . . [W]hen they were meeting with Mr. Hess, I think what Mr. Hess was doing was showing them available product, telling them its properties, telling them how it could be used, and how it might be used. . . . Raychem became a supplier of product to Simpson and Robert, really all of which really leaves [sic] me to the conclusion that Mr. Hess' role was really as a representative of Raychem who is making available to a customer or potential customer the product that Raychem has, and its property uses and adaptation to what the inventors here wanted to do. . . . [I]t's [sic] also clear from the record that Mr. Hess didn't know anything about angioplasty or medical catheters until discussion with Dr. Robert and Dr. Simpson.

Finally, the court stated:

> I do wish to state for the record that on a factual basis after having heard the evidence in the case, I'm also concluding that the evidence did not establish

coinventorship of the original claims in the '071 patent and not just the reissue claims for that patent.

II.

The patent laws provide that whoever "invents" patentable subject matter is entitled to a patent thereon, 35 U.S.C. § 101 (1994), and that when an "invention" is "made by two or more persons jointly, they shall apply for [a] patent jointly." 35 U.S.C. § 116 (1994). The statute also deals with the situation where an inventor is not named in the application or the issued patent. 35 U.S.C. §§ 116, 256 (1994). Section 256 provides that if "through [inadvertent] error an inventor is not named in an issued patent . . . the Commissioner [of Patents] may . . . issue a certificate correcting such error," and that "[t]he court . . . may order correction of the patent . . . and the Commissioner shall issue a certificate accordingly."

The district court held that Mr. Hess had to prove his claim of co-inventorship by clear and convincing evidence, and that Mr. Hess had not done so. Mr. Hess challenges both of these rulings.

A.

As the Court of Claims stated in *Garrett Corp. v. United States,* 422 F.2d 874, 880 (1970), "[t]he burden of showing misjoinder or nonjoinder of inventors is a heavy one and must be proved by clear and convincing evidence." Although the case involved section 116, which governs patent applications, and the present case involves section 256, which covers issued patents, the pertinent statutory language is virtually identical, and the burden of proof on this issue is the same under both sections.

The rule rests on important policy considerations. "The inventors as named in an issued patent are presumed to be correct." *Amax Fly Ash Corp. v. United States,* 206 Ct. Cl. 756, 514 F.2d 1041, 1047 (1975). As the court there stated, in holding that one claiming that the inventor listed in the patent derived the invention from the claimant's work must show derivation by clear and convincing evidence, "the temptation for even honest witnesses to reconstruct, in a manner favorable to their own position, what their state of mind may have been years earlier, is simply too great to permit a lower standard." *Id.* at 1047. This language is similarly applicable to claims of co-inventorship made after a patent has been issued—particularly where, as here, the patent has been outstanding for a considerable time and the patented device has been successful. In that situation, too, there is an equally strong temptation for persons who consulted with the inventor and provided him with materials and advice, to reconstruct, so as to further their own position, the extent of their contribution to the conception of the invention. In these circumstances, it would be inappropriate to permit a lower standard than clear and convincing evidence.

Mr. Hess apparently suggests that because of the particular circumstances of his participation in the activities of Drs. Simpson and Robert, the proper evidentiary standard for determining his co-inventorship claim should be preponderance rather than clear and convincing. Once the standard of proof has been determined, however—and we have held that it is clear and convincing evidence for determining co-inventorship—it applies without regard to the circumstances of a particular case. Permitting the exception Mr. Hess urges could significantly undermine the designated standard of proof, since litigants always can assert, and sometimes effectively, that their cases involve special circumstances.

B.

Mr. Hess concedes that the district court "articulat[ed] the appropriate test for inventorship." The district court's standard was whether Mr. Hess "conceived some important element or some important claim that is claimed in the patent," and whether he had "some conceptual role in at least an important or a necessary element, or important and necessary claim." Mr. Hess argues, however, that the court "completely misapplied" that standard "in finding that Hess's contributions were not inventive." This argument, however, is in reality only a reformulation of the contention that the district court's findings upon which the court based its conclusion that Mr. Hess had not established co-inventorship, are clearly erroneous.

We have carefully reviewed the evidence in the record. Although there is some conflict on the question of co-inventorship, the district court's findings that Mr. Hess was not a co-inventor of the catheter claimed in the '071 patent are not clearly erroneous.

When Drs. Simpson and Robert first met with Mr. Hess, he was totally unfamiliar with angioplasty catheterization and the problems it involved. They explained to him what they were trying to do, and what difficulties they encountered. He recommended a Raychem product that he believed would be suitable for making a balloon, showed them how a balloon could be formed by heating both ends of the tube (a procedure they did not use in making their patented catheter), and made other suggestions for making the catheter, using the Raychem tubing. Although the doctors followed and utilized some of Mr. Hess's suggestions in their extensive further research, testing and construction of their catheter, the district court justifiably concluded on this record that it was they, and not Mr. Hess, who actually conceived and made the patented invention and that Mr. Hess's contributions to the inventions did not constitute the conception necessary to establish co-inventorship.

More than 140 years ago the Supreme Court, in holding that Samuel Morse's discussions with scientists in connection with his invention of the telegraph did not alter his status of the sole inventor of that device, stated:

> No invention can possibly be made, consisting of a combination of different elements . . . without a thorough knowledge of the properties of each of them, and the mode in which they operate on each other. And it can make no difference, in this respect, whether [the inventor] derives his information from books, or from conversation with men skilled in the science. If it were otherwise, no patent, in which a combination of different elements is used, could ever be obtained.

O'Reilly v. Morse, 56 U.S. (15 How.) 62, 111 (1853).

Similarly, in *Shatterproof Glass*, this court stated that

> [a]n inventor "may use the services, ideas, and aid of others in the process of perfecting his invention without losing his right to a patent."

Shatterproof Glass Corp. v. Libbey-Owens Ford Co., 758 F.2d 613, 624 (Fed. Cir. 1985).

Mr. Hess relies on the following statement in the 1914 district court opinion in *DeLaski & Thropp Circular Woven Tire Co. v. William R. Thropp & Sons Co.*, 218 F. 458, 464 (D.N.J. 1914), *aff'd*, 226 F. 941 (3d Cir. 1915), which he describes as "the controlling legal standard."

> The conception of the entire device may be due to one, but if the other makes suggestions of practical value, which assisted in working out the main idea and making it operative, or contributes an independent part of the entire invention, which is united with the parts produced by the other and creates the whole, he is a joint inventor, even though his contribution be of comparatively minor importance and merely the application of an old idea.

That language, of course, is not binding precedent in this court, and its focus appears inconsistent with the approach the Supreme Court took in *Morse* and this court took in *Shatterproof Glass*. In any event, whether particular suggestions and contributions of third persons amount to co-inventorship turns on the facts of the particular case.

Here the district court found that in his consultations with Drs. Simpson and Robert, Mr. Hess was "doing nothing more than explaining to the inventors what the then state of the art was and supplying a product to them for use in their invention"; that "most, if not all, of his discussion with them were [sic] telling them what was available in the marketplace by way of product, and telling them how the product worked"; and that "what Mr. Hess was doing was showing them available product, telling them its properties, telling them how it could be used, and how it might be used." The principles Mr. Hess explained to them were well known and found in textbooks. Mr. Hess did no more than a skilled salesman would do in explaining how his employer's product could be used to meet a customer's requirements. The extensive research and development work that produced the catheter was done by Drs. Simpson and Robert. Our review of the record satisfies us that those findings are not clearly erroneous, and that they support the district court's conclusion that whatever contribution Mr. Hess made to Drs. Simpson and Robert did not constitute conception and therefore did not make Mr. Hess a co-inventor of the catheter claimed in the '071 patent.

Mr. Hess relies on snippets of the doctors' testimony in which, he asserts, the doctors conceded that Mr. Hess was responsible for significant portions of the invention the '071 patent disclosed. Those statements, however, cannot bear the weight Mr. Hess gives them. In the context of the entire record, they do not refute the factual sufficiency of the evidence supporting the district court's decision.

III.

Mr. Hess also argues that the district court erroneously dismissed on summary judgment, as barred by laches, that portion of his case that claimed co-inventorship of the invention disclosed in the original claims. That issue, however, is moot in view of the district court's ruling that "on a factual basis after having heard the evidence in the case, I'm also concluding that the evidence did not establish co-inventorship of the original claims in the '071 patent and not just the reissue claims for that patent." Accordingly, we do not consider it.

CONCLUSION

The judgment of the district court that Mr. Hess has not established his claim to co-inventorship of the catheter disclosed in the '071 patent is affirmed.

ACROMED CORP. v. SOFAMOR DANEK GROUP, INC.
253 F.3d 1371 (Fed. Cir. 2001)

RADER, Circuit Judge.

At the close of evidence, the United States District Court for the Northern District of Ohio granted judgment as a matter of law (JMOL) that AcroMed Corporation's (AcroMed's) U.S. Patent No. 4,696,290 ('290 patent) is not invalid for improper inventorship. The jury's verdict found that Sofamor Danek Group, Inc., and Danek Medical, Inc., (collectively Danek) literally infringed the claims of the '290 patent and AcroMed's U.S. Patent No. 4,854,311 ('311 patent). The jury further found the claims of the '311 patent not invalid. Because the district court correctly found insufficient evidence to invalidate the '290 patent and correctly upheld the jury verdict that the claims of the '311 patent were infringed and not invalid, this court affirms.

I

AcroMed is assignee of the '290 patent which names Dr. Arthur D. Steffee as its sole inventor. The '290 patent discloses a plate for surgical implantation onto a patient's spinal column. The spine plate straightens a spine misshapen by disc degeneration or fracture. This invention can thus alleviate pain and restore a patient's mobility.

In his first spine straightening operations, Dr. Steffee hooked and wired rods to patients' spines. This early method straightened spines somewhat, but the rods would later slip, thereby undercutting the effectiveness of the operation. To prevent slippage, Dr. Steffee began to use a plate-and-screw system similar to that described in the '290 patent.

Dr. Steffee's first plate-and-screw system used a long plate with fixed location screw holes. Dr. Steffee implanted this type of plate-and-screw system by drilling or tapping holes into a patient's vertebrae, aligning the vertebral holes with holes in the plate, and then attaching the plate with bone screws. Dr. Steffee typically installed two such plates, one on each side of the spine. These systems fixed the vertebrae more rigidly than wire and rod systems. The plates with holes in fixed locations, however, were difficult to install and adapt to different patients because the holes were rarely spaced identically to pedicle distances between a patient's vertebrae.

Dr. Steffee thus improved his plate-and-screw system in 1982 while working at a hospital in Cleveland. He conceived of headless screws that would permit him to first optimally locate such screws in each vertebral pedicle, and then attach the spine plate to the installed screws. Dr. Steffee took his regular bone screws to the Cleveland Research Institute (CRI) hospital machine shop, and asked Frank Janson, a machinist, to cut the heads off of the screws. Without screw heads, Dr. Steffee needed to find another means to attach the plate to the screws in the spine. He conceived of using a tapered, conical nut from a Hagie pin, a pin commonly used by orthopedists to fix broken hips in children.

Next, Dr. Steffee recognized that he would need to modify the fixed location screw holes in the plate to facilitate attachment at different pedical distances between vertebrae. Dr. Steffee looked to another well-known device—a small, slotted Egger's plate which orthopedic surgeons use to fix long bone fractures. Dr. Steffee asked Mr. Janson to make a bigger Egger's plate to accommodate a spine.

Dr. Steffee's final problem was that the slots in the plate could slide along the screws and defeat proper fixation of the plate to the spine. To solve this problem, Dr. Steffee told Mr. Janson that he needed a plate designed so that the Hagie pin nut "sinks in and stays right there." Mr. Janson responded to this instruction by putting nests in the slots. The '290 patent claims the resulting combination.

The disclosed spine plate (30) has a series of elongated slots (52) configured with a series of nests, or arcuate recesses (116). Claim 1 of the '290 patent recites:

> An apparatus for use with fasteners for maintaining vertebrae in a desired relationship, said apparatus comprising:
>
> an elongated plate for connecting at least two vertebrae . . .
>
> said elongated plate also having at least one elongated slot extending there through . . .
>
> said slot being capable of receiving a fastener therein . . . and
>
> said slot being defined by opposed slot surfaces extending longitudinally of said elongated plate and *arcuate recesses* in said opposed slot surfaces and spaced there along, the recesses in one of said opposed slot surfaces being aligned with the recesses in the other of said opposed slot surfaces to define said plurality of locations, *said recesses comprising means for blocking sliding movement* of [s]aid elongated plate relative to the fastener and of said elongated plate relative to the vertebrae when the fastener is located in a pair of aligned recesses

(emphasis added).

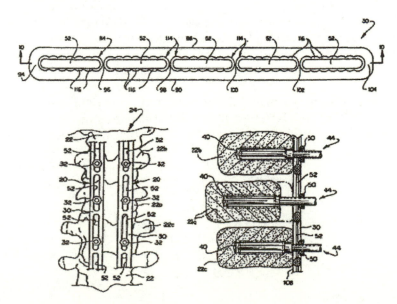

Dr. Steffee also improved the headless bone screw. The '311 patent discloses a bone screw with an elongated shank to, *e.g.*, fasten the plate of the '290 patent to a spine, connect broken bones, or connect prostheses to bones in any part of the body. The '311 patent describes the bone screw as having three identifiable segments: (1) a first externally threaded portion (142) for receiving a connecting member, such as a nut; (2) a cylindrical body portion for projecting into and engaging the bone opening surface (182); and (3) a second threaded portion for attaching the screw to the bone (144).

Bones have a hard outer shell (called cortical bone) and a spongy center (called cancellous bone). Cancellous bone contains blood vessels. Thus, once a hole is drilled or tapped into a bone, effluence (blood and other bodily fluids) may leak into the hole. This effluence can corrode and weaken the screw. According to the '311 patent, the claimed bone screw has a cylindrical body portion and a shoulder portion (184) that act as a sort of stopper, blocking effluence from leaking out of the bone. Claim 5 of the '311 patent recites:

> A bone screw for connecting a bone portion with a bone connecting member, said bone screw comprising:
>
> an elongated shank having a longitudinal central axis, a first externally threaded portion for receiving an internally threaded nut and a second externally threaded portion for threaded engagement with a surface defining an opening in the bone portion to attach the bone screw to the bone portion; and
>
> *means* integral with said shank and having a transverse cross-section at least equal to the transverse cross-section of the opening in the bone portion for projecting into the opening and *for engaging a portion of the surface defining the opening in the bone portion* to restrict movement of said bone screw relative to the bone portion in a direction transverse to the longitudinal central axis of said shank and *to block effluence from the opening in the bone portion,* said means being located intermediate said first externally threaded portion and said second externally threaded portion

(emphasis added).

Dr. Steffee and another colleague founded AcroMed in 1983. Dr. Steffee assigned all of his rights in the '290 and '311 patents to AcroMed. In 1988, CRI disbanded and Mr. Janson went to work at AcroMed. When Mr. Janson began working for AcroMed, he completed an Employment Agreement requiring him to disclose any pre-existing invention in which he had an interest. Mr. Janson checked the box marked "Employee has no such property," and signed that agreement.

Mr. Janson worked as a machinist at AcroMed until 1992, and then continued as a consultant for AcroMed until June 1994. In June 1994, Mr. Janson met with Danek's counsel on two occasions. Later that year AcroMed requested

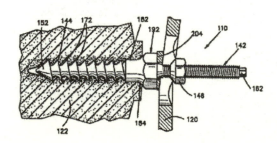

Mr. Janson to sign a declaration and power of attorney to add him as a co-inventor of the '290 patent. AcroMed also requested Mr. Janson to assign his rights in the '290 patent if he signed the declaration. Mr. Janson declined to sign either the declaration or the assignment. Instead, on January 25, 1995, Mr. Janson signed an agreement with Danek to assign his "patent rights" to Danek for $150,000.

AcroMed first sued Danek for infringement of the '290 patent by Danek's "Luque" system in 1988. The Luque was a semi-constrained plate-and-screw system without a way to hold the screws completely rigid to the plate. In March 1989, the parties entered a settlement agreement whereby AcroMed granted Danek a limited license under the '290 patent. In return, Danek paid AcroMed a license fee until 1996.

In 1992, Danek changed its technology into a constrained system. Danek developed several constrained systems, including the "DYNA-LOK" and "Z-PLATE" systems. In June 1993, AcroMed again filed suit claiming that Danek's DYNA-LOK, Z-PLATE, and various other spine plate systems infringe the '311 and 290 patents. Danek counterclaimed that AcroMed's '290 patent is invalid for failure to name Mr. Janson as an inventor. Danek further counterclaimed that AcroMed's '311 patent is invalid due to anticipation by United States Patent No. 3,554,193 to Ilias Konstantinou (Konstantinou patent).

As depicted below, the Konstantinou patent discloses a hip-pinning device for repair of hip fractures. The device uses a lag screw to attach a bone plate to the upper region of a femur. The lag screw has a rounded head portion (38) that permits the screw to be angularly displaced within a hole in a bone plate. A surgeon can, thus, vary the angle at which he attaches the screw to the bone while maintaining the plate in a desired location.

After a ten-day jury trial, the district court judge granted AcroMed's motion for JMOL that the '290 patent was not invalid for improper inventorship. The jury returned a verdict that Danek's DYNA-LOK and Z-PLATE spine plates infringed the asserted claims of the '290 patent. The jury further found that Danek's DYNA-LOK and Z-PLATE 5.5 mm bone bolts infringed claims 5, 10, 14, and 16 of the 311 patent and that Danek's DYNA-LOK and Z-PLATE larger diameter bone bolts infringed claims 5, 10, 12, 13, 14, and 16. The jury additionally found all asserted claims of both the '290 and '311 patent to be neither anticipated nor obvious over prior art. The jury awarded AcroMed $32,913,444 in damages and found that Danek had willfully infringed the '290 patent.

After the jury verdict, Danek renewed its motions for JMOL that the '290 patent is invalid for omitting an inventor, that its spine plates and screws do not infringe the '311 patent, and that the Konstantinou patent anticipates the '311 patent. The district court denied all of these motions. The district court then increased the damages to $47,806,701 to account for post-verdict damages and prejudgment interest. Danek appealed.

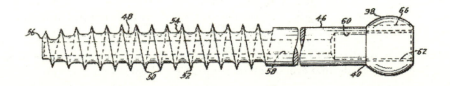

II.

Inventorship is a question of law that this court reviews without deference.

Inventorship

The Patent Act accords each patent a presumption of validity. 35 U.S.C. § 282. Under this doctrine, each patent also receives the presumption that its named inventors are the true and only inventors. *Hess v. Advanced Cardiovascular Sys., Inc.* In order to rebut this presumption, a party challenging patent validity for omission of an inventor must present clear and convincing evidence that the omitted individual actually invented the claimed invention.

When an invention is the work of several inventors, they must jointly apply for the patent. 35 U.S.C. § 116; 35 U.S.C. § 111. Omission of an inventor can invalidate a patent unless the omission was an error "without any deceptive intention." 35 U.S.C. § 256; 35 U.S.C. § 102(f). Danek argues that Mr. Janson was an inventor of the '290 patent. Because Mr. Janson was not named as an inventor of the '290 patent, Danek asserts that a reasonable jury would have found the '290 patent invalid.

"Inventorship is a question of who actually invented the subject matter claimed in a patent." *Sewall v. Walters*, 21 F.3d 411, 417 (Fed. Cir. 1994). "Conception is the touchstone of inventorship." *Burroughs Wellcome*, 40 F.3d at 1227. Accordingly, each person claiming to be a joint inventor must have contributed to the conception of the invention. *Fina Oil & Chem. Co. v. Ewen*, 123 F.3d 1466, 1473 (Fed. Cir. 1997). To prove that contribution, the purported inventor must "provide corroborating evidence of any asserted contributions to the conception." *Id.* at 1474. Beyond conception, a purported inventor must show that he made "a contribution to the claimed invention that is not insignificant in quality, when that contribution is measured against the dimension of the full invention, and [did] more than merely explain to the real inventors well-known concepts and/or the current state of the art." *Pannu v. Iolab Corp.,* 155 F.3d 1344, 1351 (Fed. Cir. 1998).

Danek asserts that Mr. Janson conceived the arcuate recesses recited in claim 1 of the '290 patent. Danek argues that Mr. Janson's testimony that he invented the arcuate recesses and the conical nut is sufficient evidence of conception and contribution. The record, however, contains no evidence to corroborate this assertion.

Mr. Janson testified that he conceived of a conical nut and arcuate recesses to prevent sliding movement of a spine plate before Dr. Steffee ever mentioned problems with plate sliding. Mr. Janson further testified that he was the first to conceive of a spine plate with slots and the first to conceive of transforming regular bone screws into machine-threaded screws to accept a slotted plate. In other words, according to Mr. Janson, he conceived of the entire plate-and-screw combination. Danek, however, was not able to put forth other witnesses, dated drawings, or any other evidence to verify Mr. Janson's assertions. In fact, Mr. Janson himself admitted that he did not communicate his conceptions to anyone.

On appeal, Danek argues that Dr. Steffee's own testimony corroborates Mr. Janson's claims of conceiving the arcuate recesses. In particular, Danek quotes the following deposition testimony made by Dr. Steffee:

I have always said Frank Jansen [sic] was the one who put the nests in the slots, that's the only thing that Frank Jansen [sic] did. And I was right there when he asked me if he could do it. . . . He and I were standing there together, he asked me if he could put the drill press down and put those nest in, and I said, fine, it sounds like a good idea, let's do it.

AcroMed concedes that Mr. Janson cut the arcuate recesses into the spine plate. Countersinking the slots in the spine plate, however, was not an inventive conception. The record in context supports the district court's conclusion that Dr. Steffee alone conceived the invention. Specifically, Dr. Steffee testified that when he brought the slotted plate and conical nut to Mr. Janson, he explained: "When I drive the nut down, I have to have it so it sinks in and stays right there." Dr. Steffee thus instructed Mr. Janson to design the plate according to his conception. Mr. Janson's work of putting arcuate recesses in the slots "was simply the exercise of the normal skill expected of an ordinary" machinist. *Sewall*, 21 F.3d at 416. Danek, having had the burden of proof at trial, did not present adequate evidence to suggest otherwise. As explained by the district court: "Danek could have countered this by producing testimony at trial concerning what would or would not be obvious to one ordinarily skilled in the art of making plates. Danek never did."

Danek argues that the prosecution history of the '290 patent provides clear and convincing evidence that the arcuate recesses were an inventive conception. During prosecution of the '290 patent at the United States Patent and Trademark Office, the patent examiner rejected claim 1 as obvious over prior art. In its response, AcroMed explained that the prior art did not "disclose or suggest an *elongated plate with an elongated slot therein having arcuate recesses in the slot.*" AcroMed further explained that the prior art plates actually permitted sliding movement instead of the "blocking" it as recited in claim 1. Contrary to Danek's contentions, AcroMed did not assert that the arcuate recesses alone rendered claim 1 patentable. Rather, AcroMed observed that the combination of an elongated plate with slots having arcuate recesses blocked sliding movements.

Danek further argues that the arcuate recesses are the sole feature that makes claim 1 patentable over prior art cited during trial to invalidate the '290 patent for obviousness. These prior art references, however, do not provide substantial evidence that Mr. Janson's countersinking of the elongated slots was more than the work of an ordinarily skilled machinist following instructions.

Claim 1 of the '290 patent is a combination claim. This court has long established that "[c]ombination claims can consist of new combinations of old elements . . . for it may be that the combination of the old elements is novel and patentable." *Clearstream Wastewater Sys. v. Hydro-Action, Inc.*, 206 F.3d 1440, 1444 (Fed. Cir. 2000). In fact, all of the elements in claim 1 appear in the prior art. For example, the 290 spine plate was modeled after the Egger's plate, a plate with elongated slots. A patent cited by Danek, Great Britain Patent No. 780,652, discloses plates for spinal fixation that are designed to prevent relative movement between fastening bolts and the plates. In fact, United States Patent No. 3,596,656 cited by the examiner during prosecution shows that arcuate recesses, or countersinking around a hole in a plate, appeared in prior art as early as the 1960s. Claim 1, however, combined these various old features to produce a new and nonobvious invention. The entire combination, not the arcuate recesses alone, renders claim 1 patentable.

Without corroborating evidence, Danek did not present clear and convincing evidence at trial that Mr. Janson's countersinking of the elongated slots was an inventive conception. Thus, the record contains sufficient evidence to support the judgment that the '290 patent withstood challenges to its validity based on excluding Mr. Janson as an inventor.

Comments

1. *Naming the True and Original Inventor.* In a recent biography of Robert Noyce, considered to be the founding father of the microchip (along with Jack Kilby), Leslie Berlin writes, "If nearly any invention is examined closely enough, it almost immediately becomes apparent that the innovation was not the product of a single mind, even if it is attributed to one." Rather, "[i]nvention is best understood as a team effort." LESLIE BERLIN, THE MAN BEHIND THE MICROCHIP: ROBERT NOYCE AND THE INVENTION OF SILICON VALLEY 141 (2005). Indeed, ascertaining the identity of joint inventors is particularly difficult. As the Court of Claims said in *Jamesbury Corp. v. United States*, 518 F.2d 1384, 1396 (Ct. Cl. 1975), determining the "exact parameters of what constitutes joint inventorship . . . is one of the muddiest concepts in the muddy metaphysics of the patent law." Nonetheless, as unrealistic or difficult as it may be, a patent application must identify the true and original inventor, that is, the person who is responsible for inventing what is set forth in the claims. (Inventorship is different from ownership.) Not correctly naming the true and original inventor can result in invalidation of the patent.

2. *Joint Inventors.* In a joint or multi-inventor context, one can be an inventor without making a contribution equal to the other inventors; nor does being an inventor require an inventive contribution to every claim. Section 116 of the patent code reflects this view:

   > When an invention is made by two or more persons jointly, they shall apply for patent jointly and each make the required oath. . . . Inventors may apply for a patent jointly even though (1) they did not physically work together or at the same time, (2) each did not make the same type or amount of contribution, or (3) each did not make a contribution to the subject matter of every claim of the patent.

   In *Tavory v. NTP, Inc.*, 297 Fed. Appx. 976, 979 (Fed. Cir. 2008), the Federal Circuit elaborated on section 116 and the need for the contribution to relate to inventive conception:

   > A co-inventor must prove he contributed to this conception of the claimed invention. The contribution must be more than simply the exercise of ordinary skill in the art. Simply reducing to practice that which has been conceived by others is insufficient for co-inventorship.

   > However, a co-inventor need not contribute to the conception of every claim of a patent; a single claim is sufficient. And he need not "make the same type or amount of contribution" as the other co-inventors. 35 U.S.C. §116. As a result, no individual co-inventor need have a "definite and permanent idea of the complete and operative invention" so long as all of the co-inventors collectively satisfy that requirement. *See* 35 U.S.C. §116.

In *University of Pittsburgh v. Hedrick*, the court wrote, in the context of an inventorship dispute, that conception does not require "scientific certainty." Rather,

> [c]onception requires a definite and permanent idea of the operative invention, and necessarily turns on the inventor's ability to describe his invention. Proof that the invention works to a scientific certainty is reduction to practice. . . . [The inventors] had disclosed a completed thought expressed in such clear terms as to enable those skilled in the art to make the invention.

573 F.3d 1290, 1299 (Fed. Cir. 2009).

For joint inventorship to hold, there must be some type of collaboration or joint behavior such as "one inventor seeing a relevant report and building upon it or hearing another's suggestions at a meeting." *Kimberly-Clark Corp. v. Procter & Gamble Distrib. Co.*, 973 F.2d 911, 917 (Fed. Cir. 1992). Moreover, "each contributor need not have their own contemporaneous picture of the final claimed invention" to qualify as a joint inventor; "[r]ather, the qualitative contribution of each collaborator is the key—each inventor must contribute to the joint arrival at a definite and permanent idea of the invention as it will be used in practice." *Vanderbilt Univ. v. ICOS Corp.*, 601 F.3d 1297, 1303 (Fed. Cir. 2010).

Federal law explicitly provides that patents have the attributes of personal property, and that both patents and applications for patents are assignable. And, importantly, there is a recording statute for patents; so the chain of title should be searched before any assignment is executed. *See* 35 U.S.C. §261.

3. *Correcting Inventorship and "Deceptive Intention."* Patent law provides for the correction of nondeceptive misjoinder and nonjoinder of inventors. There are two specific statutory sections: 116 and 256. The former pertains to pending applications and allows a patentee to correct inventorship that "arose without any deceptive intention." Section 256, which relates to issued patents, permits correction of inventorship that was done without "deceptive intention."

4. *Ownership vs. Inventorship.* Absent a contractual obligation, patent rights vest in the inventor, even if he conceived or reduced to practice in the course of his employment. *See Teets v. Chromalloy Gas Turbine Corp.*, 83 F.3d 403, 407 (Fed. Cir. 1996). Under section 262, joint inventors are also joint owners; that is, tenants-in-common, who—in the absence of any agreement to the contrary—can practice the claimed invention or license others without the consent of and without an accounting to the other cotenants. Thus, anyone interested in owning a patent must be very careful to get an assignment from each and every individual who contributed to the conception of any claim in that patent. It is the norm, however, for employees, as part of their employment contract, to assign ownership rights in inventions to the employer. And even if there is not a contract, an employer may obtain a "shop right" in the employee's invention. A "shop right," based on the fact that the employer assisted the employee's inventive efforts in some manner, is a common law doctrine that allows an employer to use an invention patented by one or more of its employees without liability for infringement. For a discussion of the "shop right," *see McElmurry v. Arkansas Power & Light Co.*, 995 F.2d 1576, 1580 (Fed. Cir. 1993).

F. PREEMPTION

Article VI of the Constitution—commonly known as the "Supremacy Clause"—states that the "Laws of the United States . . ." (i.e., federal law) "shall be the supreme Law of the land." This means that when there is a conflict between state law and federal law, the latter will preempt the former. Broadly conceived, patent law reflects a balance of competing considerations, and states cannot enact laws that conflict with this balance. The following principal cases unpack the preemption doctrine and explore under what circumstances federal law preempts state legislation.

1. The Framework of Preemption Analysis

PHARMACEUTICAL RESEARCH AND MANUFACTURERS OF AMERICA v. DISTRICT OF COLUMBIA

406 F. Supp. 2d 56 (D.D.C. 2005)*

LEON, District Judge.

On October 12, 2005, Plaintiff, Pharmaceutical Research and Manufacturers of America ("PhRMA"), filed a motion for a temporary restraining order and a preliminary injunction against the District of Columbia, Anthony A. Williams, in his official capacity as Mayor of the District of Columbia, the Office of the Attorney General of the District of Columbia, Robert J. Spagnoletti, in his official capacity as the Attorney General of the District of Columbia, the Office of Documents and Administrative Issuances of the District of Columbia, and Arnold R. Finlayson, in his official capacity as Administrator of the Office of Documents and Administrative Issuances (collectively the "District"), contending that D.C. Act 16-171, the Prescription Drug Excessive Pricing Act of 2005 (the "D.C. Act" or the "Act"), violates the Supremacy, Commerce, and Foreign Commerce Clauses of the United States Constitution. The motion for a temporary restraining order was denied the next day and a briefing schedule was set on October 21, 2005 for the motion for a preliminary injunction.

The same day, PhRMA filed a motion for an order consolidating the merits of the plaintiff's action for a declaratory judgment with its application for a preliminary injunction pursuant to Federal Rules of Civil Procedure 57 and 65(a)(2).

The next day Biotechnology Industry Organization ("BIO") filed its complaint seeking the same declaratory relief as PhRMA against the District. In the interests of judicial efficiency, the actions by PhRMA and BIO were consolidated on November 8, 2005, and the ruling on the merits and prayer for injunctive relief under Rule 65(a)(2) were eventually consolidated.

Based on the pleadings, oral arguments, and record, the Court finds the D.C. Act unconstitutional and GRANTS the plaintiffs' claims for declaratory and injunctive relief.

---

*This decision was affirmed by the Federal Circuit on August 1, 2007. *See* 496 F.3d 1362 (Fed. Cir. 2007).

BACKGROUND FACTS

I. Legislative History

The Prescription Drug Excessive Pricing Act of 2005 was initially introduced as legislation to the District of Columbia's City Council (the "Council") on February 1, 2005. The legislation was an effort by the Council "to restrain the excessive prices of prescription drugs," D.C. Act § 28-4551(3), which it found to be threatening the "health, safety, and welfare of [the District's] residents." *Id.* at § 28-4551(2).[3] Ultimately, the D.C. Act was passed by the Council on September 20, 2005, and signed on October 4, 2005 by Mayor Williams.

II. The D.C. Act

The D.C. Act specifically makes it "unlawful for any drug manufacturer or licensee thereof, *excluding a point of sale retail seller,* to sell or supply for sale or impose minimum resale requirements for a patented prescription drug *that results in* the prescription drug being sold in the District for an excessive price," D.C. Act § 28-4553 (emphasis added), and empowers any "affected party" to bring a suit in the Superior Court of the District of Columbia for damages and injunctive relief against the manufacturers or licensees. *Id.* at § 28-4555. By prohibiting excessive retail sales prices, while excluding retail sellers from enforcement, the Act necessarily directs "affected" parties to target the manufacturers' wholesale prices, and the casual relation, if any, between those wholesale prices and the allegedly "excessive" prices set by retailers that result therefrom.

Although it does not specifically define what makes a price "excessive," the Council did include in the statute a formulaic mechanism as an optional way for a plaintiff to establish a prima facie case of excessiveness. *See* D.C. Act § 28-4554(a). Specifically, a prima facie case of excessive pricing "shall be established where the wholesale price of a patented prescription drug" sold in the District of Columbia is "30% higher than the comparable price" in either the United Kingdom, Germany, Canada, or Australia, if the drug is protected in those countries "by patents or other exclusive marketing rights." *Id.* Upon doing so, the burden shifts from the affected party to the manufacturer of the patented prescription drug to prove, by a preponderance of the evidence, that the price of the drug, presumably at the retail level, is not excessive. *Id.* at § 28-4554(b). The D.C. Act does not state whether this formulaic approach is the only way to

---

3. The purpose and reasoning behind the D.C. Act is specifically set forth within three "Findings" pronounced in Section 4551 of the act:

   (1) The excessive prices of prescription drugs in the District of Columbia is threatening the health and welfare of the residents of the District as well as the District government's ability to ensure that all residents receive the health care they need, and these excessive prices directly and indirectly cause economic harm to the District and damage the health and safety of its residents;
   (2) The traditional police powers of the District of Columbia include protecting and promoting the health, safety, and welfare of its residents, regulating monopoly pricing of goods and services, and regulating to assure consumer protection and to prevent and sanction unfair trade practices; and
   (3) To promote the health, safety, and welfare of its residents, it is incumbent on the government of the District of Columbia to take action to restrain the excessive prices of prescription drugs through mechanisms that are consistent with District and federal law, including the Constitution.

52 D.C. Reg. at 9061; D.C. Act § 28-4551(1)-(3).

establish a prima facie case that a patented prescription drug is excessive. *Id.* It does specifically provide, however, that once a prima facie case is established the manufacturer of the drug can prove that the price of the drug is not excessive given the cost of inventing, developing, and producing the drug, the global sales and profits from the drug to date, the amount of "government funded research that supported the development of the drug, and the impact of price" of the drug to access to the drug by the District of Columbia government and its residents. D.C. Act § 28-4554(b).

If the manufacturer fails to meet its burden, and a Superior Court judge finds that "excessive pricing" was the "result" of the manufacturers' wholesale price, the judge can issue civil penalties and exercise any of the following additional options: "(1) Temporary, preliminary, or permanent injunctions to enjoin the sales of prescription drugs in the District at excessive prices; (2) Appropriate fines for each violation; (3) Damages, including treble damages; (4) Reasonable attorney's fees; (5) The cost of litigation; or (6) Any other relief the Court deems proper." D.C. Act § 28-4555(b)(1)-(6).

III. The Plaintiffs

PhRMA is a non-profit organization whose members consist of leading research based pharmaceutical and biotechnology companies who account for "close to 70% of the sales of prescription drugs in the United States. PhRMA serves as a "policy advocate" for its members and the pharmaceutical industry before federal and state government entities. BIO is a large biotechnology organization that consists of more than 1,100 members from around the world, BIO provides "advocacy, business development, and communications services" for its members and also represents other organizations which are related to the biotechnology field or provide services to the industry.

PhRMA's members manufacture and sell patented prescription drugs within the United States from facilities outside of the District of Columbia to wholesalers who are also located, for the most part, outside the District of Columbia. In most circumstances, patented prescription drugs that are manufactured by PhRMA's members are subsequently resold in the District of Columbia by retailers who are exempt from enforcement under the D.C. Act. BIO's members manufacture and sell patented prescription drugs and products which are mainly sold to entities outside of the District of Columbia. BIO represents companies that maintain patents and create patentable inventions.

While most of the wholesale sales by plaintiffs occur outside the District of Columbia, members of PhRMA and BIO both occasionally sell a small number of products, drugs, and therapies directly to doctors, hospitals, and pharmacies within the District of Columbia. *See* Powell Decl. ¶7 ("Although PhRMA members supply very limited quantities of patented prescription drugs directly to doctors and healthcare institutions in the District of Columbia, the vast majority of patented prescription drugs that are eventually provided to patients in the United States are initially sold by pharmaceutical manufacturers either to drug wholesalers . . . or to large retail pharmacy chains that warehouse their own drugs. . . ."); *see* Sachdev Aff. ¶8 ("The overwhelming majority of therapies produced by BIO members are supplied to customers outside the District of Columbia. Such therapies are rarely supplied directly from BIO members to doctors and healthcare institutions in the District.")

ANALYSIS

* * *

II. The Supremacy Clause Challenge

PhRMA and BIO each facially challenge the D.C. Act as violative of the Supremacy Clause of the United States Constitution. In essence, they contend that the law is preempted by the Supremacy Clause because it is a direct obstacle to the purposes and execution of the federal patent laws relative to manufactured drugs. The District disagrees, contending that the D.C. Act is not preempted by the Supremacy Clause since it neither excludes federal patent law, nor serves as an obstacle to the intended purpose of those laws as applied to the manufacturers of prescription drugs.

For the following reasons, the Court finds the D.C. Act, as drafted, is a clear obstacle to the accomplishment and execution of the purpose and objectives set by Congress in passing federal patent laws relating to prescription drugs and, therefore, finds it violates the Supremacy Clause of the United States Constitution.

A. Conflict Preemption

The Supremacy Clause of the United States Constitution states that "the Laws of the United States . . . shall be the supreme Law of the Land." U.S. Const. art. VI, § 1, cl. 2. Thus, where Congress legislates within the scope of its constitutionally granted powers, that legislation may displace state law. *Wardair Canada Inc. v. Fla. Dep't of Revenue*, 477 U.S. 1, 6 (1986) (holding that a state tax on aviation fuel did not violate the Commerce Clause of the Constitution and was not preempted by Congress); *Sears, Roebuck & Co. v. Stiffel Co.*, 376 U.S. 225, 229 (1964) (finding that a state's unfair competition law cannot prohibit the copying of a product that is not protected by a patent or copyright because the law "clashed" with the objectives of the federal patent laws).

Where federal legislation contains no specific preemption language, however, it is the duty of the federal courts to inquire whether an implied preemption exists in a given situation. *Gade v. Nat'l Solid Wastes Mgmt. Ass'n*, 505 U.S. 88, 98 (1992) (holding that a state's licensing laws were preempted to the extent that they conflicted with the Occupational Safety and Health Act of 1970). In that regard, two types of implied preemption have been recognized by the courts: field and conflict preemption. *Id.* Field preemption applies to those situations, unlike here, where the scheme of federal regulation is "so pervasive as to make reasonable the inference that Congress left no room for the States to supplement it." *Rice v. Santa Fe Elevator Corp.*, 331 U.S. 218, 230 (1947). *Hines* is a classic example of field preemption. 312 U.S. 52. In *Hines,* the Supreme Court found that the immigration system that Congress had enacted in regard to the registration of aliens was enacted in order to create "one uniform national registration system," and that the federal regulation was such that a state law could not be enforced when it interfered with the congressional regulation. 312 U.S. at 73-74.

Conflict preemption, on the other hand, applies to those situations where compliance with both state and federal regulations is either a "physical impossibility,"[8] or, as alleged here, "stands as an obstacle to the accomplishment and execution of the full purposes and objectives of Congress." *Id.* at 67. Plaintiffs contend that the D.C. Act is preempted by the Supremacy Clause because it poses such a conflict to the accomplishment and execution of the very purpose and objectives Congress had in mind when it passed the Patent Term Restoration Act and related non-patent market exclusivity statutes. How so?

Plaintiffs' argument is premised on its assertion that the federal patent laws and related pharmaceutical market exclusivity laws reflect Congress' considered judgment of the economic incentives and protections necessary to best promote the development of new medications. Indeed, plaintiffs contend that Congress gave pharmaceutical innovation even greater statutory protection than other types of innovation when it passed the Patent Term Restoration Act of 1984, which allowed pharmaceutical manufacturers to extend the terms of their patents and provided certain market exclusivity provisions that insulate manufacturers from generic competition *after* its original patent expires. *Id.* at 17; Patent Term Restoration Act of 1984, 35 U.S.C. § 156 (2005); 21 U.S.C. §§ 355 *et seq.* Unfortunately for the District, even a casual review of the congressional history attendant to these considerable legislative achievements bears out the truth of the plaintiffs' unmistakable assertion.

Congress' regulation of our nation's pharmaceutical industry is grounded in large part in a complex balance of economic forces and regulatory exclusivity designed to encourage and reward the innovation, research, and development of new drugs. Indeed, Congressman Henry Waxman, one of the principal sponsors of the Patent Term Restoration Act, articulated Congress' very purpose behind allowing pharmaceutical patent holders to set a price in their discretion:

> Because there is no one else in competition, and as a matter of public policy we, under the patent law, give that protection to the person who has put money into research and development for an innovative and new product. But at some point public policy calls for the free market system competition which will bring about the result of a lower price for the consumer. That is the purpose of the legislation.

130 Cong. Rec. 24,427 (1984) (statement of Rep. Waxman).[9] Not surprisingly, some of the federal courts have also acknowledged the same.

---

8. One such example of conflict preemption in which compliance with both federal law and state law was impossible occurred in *McDermott v. Wisconsin*, 228 U.S. 115 (1913). In *McDermott,* a state law made it criminal to offer for sale syrup that was not labeled in compliance with the state law, even though the syrup offered for sale did meet federal labeling requirements. *Id.* at 124-27. Here, the Supreme Court held that the state law was preempted by the federal regulation. *See id.* at 136-37.

9. Congressman Carlos Moorhead, when discussing the Patent Term Restoration Act, stated:

> We have struggled for a long time with this legislation, and most of the things that are in this bill . . . are the result of much effort and work over a long period of time and which resulted in compromises between various industries that are involved, the people that will be affected, the senior citizens of our country, the people who manufacture generics, and the people whose patents need to be protected to guarantee that they can get a recovery on the investment that they have made.

130 Cong. Rec. 24,428 (1984) (statement of Rep. Moorhead).

In *Pfizer Inc. v. Dr. Reddy's Laboratories, Ltd.*, the Federal Circuit specifically commented on the empirical balance within the Patent Term Restoration Act as follows:

> By restoring a portion of the patent term that is consumed during the approval phase, the incentive to develop and market products that require lengthy pre-marketing approval is intended to be preserved: The purpose of [the Patent Term Restoration Act] is to create a new incentive for increased expenditures for research and development of certain products which are subject to premarket government approval.

359 F.3d 1361, 1364 (Fed. Cir. 2004) (quoting H.R. Rep. No. 98-857, at 15 (1984)). And on a more general note, the Supreme Court itself has also recognized that the federal patent laws reflect a "carefully crafted bargain" among the various interests at stake. *Pfaff v. Wells Elecs., Inc.*, 525 U.S. 55, 63 (1998); *Bonito Boats, Inc. v. Thunder Craft Boats, Inc.*, 489 U.S. 141, 150-51 (1989) (stating that the patent system "embodies a carefully crafted bargain for encouraging the creation and disclosure of new, useful, and nonobvious advances in technology and design in return for the exclusive right to practice the invention for a period of years").

How then does the D.C. Act's thinly veiled effort to force manufacturers to limit the wholesale price of those drugs to less than 30% more than the wholesale price of the same patented drugs sold in four designated "high income" countries square with the congressional purpose and objectives inherent in the Patent Term Restoration Act? It doesn't!

B. The D.C. Act Is an Unmistakable Obstacle to Congress' Objectives

Although well motivated, the D.C. Act was unequivocally designed to force drug manufacturers who sell their products both in the District and in certain foreign countries to either limit the price of their product, or face the consequences of expensive litigation over an undefined standard of "excessiveness" which is likely to vary widely across the spectrum of judges on the Superior Court. Considering the relative ease of the *prima facie* case litigation option provided for in the statute, and the severity of the penalties at the judges' disposal, manufacturers will be hard pressed to chose to roll the dice on the expensive option of convincing a given Court that an application of the factors set forth in Section 4554(b) of the D.C. Act yields a non-excessive assessment or a lack of casual connection between the domestic wholesale price and the retailers' "excessive" price. Such choices give new meaning to that old expression: caught between a rock and a hard place. Most manufacturers who want to continue selling their products in the District will undoubtedly do exactly what the City Council wants: adjust their wholesale price to an amount no greater than 30% more than the wholesale price of the same product in the four designated foreign countries. And one need not speculate too long as to the likely collateral consequences throughout the pharmaceutical industry nationwide that such capitulations would cause. Punishing the holders of pharmaceutical patents in this manner flies directly in the face of a system of rewards calculated by Congress to insure the continued strength of an industry vital to our national interests. Ironically, the factors Congress weighed in calculating their system of rewards are the very same factors the Act requires manufacturers to litigate in Superior Court in response to a prima facie case. *See* D.C. Act §28-4554(b).

In short, using the litigation process to determine on a drug to drug basis the application of a given drug's pricing vis-à-vis that in a foreign country directly interferes with, and second guesses, the balance set by Congress in the current system of patents and market exclusivity for pharmaceutical products. Moreover, by allowing foreign drug prices to serve as the benchmark by which excessiveness may be determined in this country, the City Council is effectively substituting Congress' regulatory scheme for this industry with the regulatory system that has been formulated by these enumerated foreign countries. Because Congress' judgment in this area is supreme, the D.C. Act is preempted and therefore facially unconstitutional.

2. Preemption of State Law

KEWANEE OIL CO. v. BICRON
416 U.S. 470 (1974)

Chief Justice BURGER delivered the opinion of the Court.

We granted certiorari to resolve a question on which there is a conflict in the courts of appeals: whether state trade secret protection is pre-empted by operation of the federal patent law.

I

Harshaw Chemical Co., an unincorporated division of petitioner, is a leading manufacturer of a type of synthetic crystal which is useful in the detection of ionizing radiation. In 1949 Harshaw commenced research into the growth of this type crystal and was able to produce one less than two inches in diameter. By 1966, as the result of expenditures in excess of $1 million, Harshaw was able to grow a 17-inch crystal, something no one else had done previously. Harshaw had developed many processes, procedures, and manufacturing techniques in the purification of raw materials and the growth and encapsulation of the crystals which enabled it to accomplish this feat. Some of these processes Harshaw considers to be trade secrets.

The individual respondents are former employees of Harshaw who formed or later joined respondent Bicron. While at Harshaw the individual respondents executed, as a condition of employment, at least one agreement each, requiring them not to disclose confidential information or trade secrets obtained as employees of Harshaw. Bicron was formed in August 1969 to compete with Harshaw in the production of the crystals, and by April 1970, had grown a 17-inch crystal.

Petitioner brought this diversity action in United States District Court for the Northern District of Ohio seeking injunctive relief and damages for the misappropriation of trade secrets. The District Court, applying Ohio trade secret law, granted a permanent injunction against the disclosure or use by respondents of 20 of the 40 claimed trade secrets until such time as the trade secrets had been released to the public, had otherwise generally become available to the public, or had been obtained by respondents from sources having the legal right to convey the information.

The Court of Appeals for the Sixth Circuit held that the findings of fact by the District Court were not clearly erroneous, and that it was evident from the record that the individual Respondents appropriated to the benefit of Bicron secret information on processes obtained while they were employees at Harshaw. Further, the Court of Appeals held that the District Court properly applied Ohio law relating to trade secrets. Nevertheless, the Court of Appeals reversed the District Court, finding Ohio's trade secret law to be in conflict with the patent laws of the United States. The Court of Appeals reasoned that Ohio could not grant monopoly protection to processes and manufacturing techniques that were appropriate subjects for consideration under 35 U.S.C. §101 for a federal patent but which had been in commercial use for over one year and so were no longer eligible for patent protection under 35 U.S.C. §102(b).

We hold that Ohio's law of trade secrets is not preempted by the patent laws of the United States, and, accordingly, we reverse.

II

Ohio has adopted the widely relied-upon definition of a trade secret found at Restatement of Torts §757, comment b (1939). According to the Restatement,

(a) trade secret may consist of any formula, pattern, device or compilation of information which is used in one's business, and which gives him an opportunity to obtain an advantage over competitors who do not know or use it. It may be a formula for a chemical compound, a process of manufacturing, treating or preserving materials, a pattern for a machine or other device, or a list of customers.

The subject of a trade secret must be secret, and must not be of public knowledge or of a general knowledge in the trade or business. This necessary element of secrecy is not lost, however, if the holder of the trade secret reveals the trade secret to another "in confidence, and under an implied obligation not to use or disclose it." These others may include those of the holder's "employees to whom it is necessary to confide it, in order to apply it to the uses for which it is intended." Often the recipient of confidential knowledge of the subject of a trade secret is a licensee of its holder. *See Lear, Inc. v. Adkins*, 395 U.S. 653 (1969).

The protection accorded the trade secret holder is against the disclosure or unauthorized use of the trade secret by those to whom the secret has been confided under the express or implied restriction of nondisclosure or nonuse. The law also protects the holder of a trade secret against disclosure or use when the knowledge is gained, not by the owner's volition, but by some "improper means," Restatement of Torts §757(a), which may include theft, wiretapping, or even aerial reconnaissance. A trade secret law, however, does not offer protection against discovery by fair and honest means, such as by independent invention, accidental disclosure, or by so-called reverse engineering, that is by starting with the known product and working backward to divine the process which aided in its development or manufacture.

No person, having obtained possession of an article representing a trade secret or access thereto with the owner's consent, shall convert such article to his own use or that of another person, or thereafter without the owner's consent make or cause to be made a copy of such article, or exhibit such article to another.

Whoever violates section 1333.51 of the Revised Code shall be fined not more than five thousand dollars, imprisoned not less than one nor more than ten years, or both.

Novelty, in the patent law sense, is not required for a trade secret. "Quite clearly discovery is something less than invention." *A. O. Smith Corp. v. Petroleum Iron Works Co.*, 73 F.2d 531, 538 (C.A.6 1934). However, some novelty will be required if merely because that which does not possess novelty is usually known; secrecy, in the context of trade secrets, thus implies at least minimal novelty.

The subject matter of a patent is limited to a "process, machine, manufacture, or composition of matter, or . . . improvement thereof," 35 U.S.C. § 101, which fulfills the three conditions of novelty and utility as articulated and defined in 35 U.S.C. §§ 101 and 102, and nonobviousness, as set out in 35 U.S.C. § 103. If an invention meets the rigorous statutory tests for the issuance of a patent, the patent is granted, for a period of 17 years, giving what has been described as the "right of exclusion." This protection goes not only to copying the subject matter, which is forbidden under the Copyright Act, 17 U.S.C. §§ 1 et seq., but also to independent creation.

III

The first issue we deal with is whether the States are forbidden to act at all in the area of protection of the kinds of intellectual property which may make up the subject matter of trade secrets.

Article I, § 8, cl. 8, of the Constitution grants to the Congress the power

[t]o promote the Progress of Science and useful Arts, by securing for limited Times to Authors and Inventors the exclusive Right to their respective Writings and Discoveries. . . .

In the 1972 Term, in *Goldstein v. California*, 412 U.S. 546 (1973), we held that the cl. 8 grant of power to Congress was not exclusive and that, at least in the case of writings, the States were not prohibited from encouraging and protecting the efforts of those within their borders by appropriate legislation. The States could, therefore, protect against the unauthorized re-recording for sale of performances fixed on records or tapes, even though those performances qualified as "writings" in the constitutional sense and Congress was empowered to legislate regarding such performances and could preempt the area if it chose to do so. This determination was premised on the great diversity of interests in our Nation—the essentially non-uniform character of the appreciation of intellectual achievements in the various States. Evidence for this came from patents granted by the States in the 18th century. 412 U.S., at 557.

Just as the States may exercise regulatory power over writings so may the States regulate with respect to discoveries. States may hold diverse viewpoints in protecting intellectual property to invention as they do in protecting the intellectual property relating to the subject matter of copyright. The only limitation on the States is that in regulating the area of patents and copyrights they do not conflict with the operation of the laws in this area passed by Congress, and it is to that more difficult question we now turn.

IV

The question of whether the trade secret law of Ohio is void under the Supremacy Clause involves a consideration of whether that law "stands as an obstacle to the accomplishment and execution of the full purposes and objectives of Congress." We stated in *Sears, Roebuck & Co. v. Stiffel Co.*, 376 U.S. 225, 229 (1964), that when state law touches upon the area of federal statutes enacted pursuant to constitutional authority, "it is 'familiar doctrine' that the federal policy 'may not be set at naught, or its benefits denied' by the state law. This is true, of course, even if the state law is enacted in the exercise of otherwise undoubted state power."

The laws which the Court of Appeals in this case held to be in conflict with the Ohio law of trade secrets were the patent laws passed by the Congress in the unchallenged exercise of its clear power under Art. I, §8, cl. 8, of the Constitution. The patent law does not explicitly endorse or forbid the operation of trade secret law. However, as we have noted, if the scheme of protection developed by Ohio respecting trade secrets "clashes with the objectives of the federal patent laws," *Sears, Roebuck & Co. v. Stiffel Co.*, 376 U.S., at 231, then the state law must fall. To determine whether the Ohio law "clashes" with the federal law it is helpful to examine the objectives of both the patent and trade secret laws.

The stated objective of the Constitution in granting the power to Congress to legislate in the area of intellectual property is to "promote the Progress of Science and useful Arts." The patent laws promote this progress by offering a right of exclusion for a limited period as an incentive to inventors to risk the often enormous costs in terms of time, research, and development. The productive effort thereby fostered will have a positive effect on society through the introduction of new products and processes of manufacture into the economy, and the emanations by way of increased employment and better lives for our citizens. In return for the right of exclusion, this "reward for inventions," the patent laws impose upon the inventor a requirement of disclosure. To insure adequate and full disclosure so that upon the expiration of the 17-year period "the knowledge of the invention enures to the people, who are thus enabled without restriction to practice it and profit by its use," the patent laws require that the patent application shall include a full and clear description of the invention and "of the manner and process of making and using it" so that any person skilled in the art may make and use the invention. 35 U.S.C. §112. When a patent is granted and the information contained in it is circulated to the general public and those especially skilled in the trade, such additions to the general store of knowledge are of such importance to the public weal that the Federal Government is willing to pay the high price of 17 years of exclusive use for its disclosure, which disclosure, it is assumed, will stimulate ideas and the eventual development of further significant advances in the art. The Court has also articulated another policy of the patent law: that which is in the public domain cannot be removed therefrom by action of the States.

The maintenance of standards of commercial ethics and the encouragement of invention are the broadly stated policies behind trade secret law. "The necessity of good faith and honest, fair dealing, is the very life and spirit of the commercial world." *National Tube Co. v. Eastern Tube Co.*, 3 Ohio Cir. Cr. R., N.S. at 462. In *A. O. Smith Corp. v. Petroleum Iron Works Co.*, 73 F.2d, at 539, the Court emphasized that even though a discovery may not be patentable, that does not

> destroy the value of the discovery to one who makes it, or advantage the competitor who by unfair means, or as the beneficiary of a broken faith, obtains the desired knowledge without himself paying the price in labor, money, or machines expended by the discover.

Having now in mind the objectives of both the patent and trade secret law, we turn to an examination of the interaction of these systems of protection of intellectual property established by the Congress and the other by a State to determine whether and under what circumstances the latter might constitute "too great an encroachment on the federal patent system to be tolerated." *Sears, Roebuck & Co. v. Stiffel Co.*, 376 U.S., at 232.

As we noted earlier, trade secret law protects items which would not be proper subjects for consideration for patent protection under 35 U.S.C. §101. As in the case of the recordings in *Goldstein v. California*, Congress, with respect to nonpatentable subject matter, "has drawn no balance; rather, it has left the area unattended, and no reason exists why the State should not be free to act." *Goldstein v. California, supra*, 412 U.S., at 570.

Since no patent is available for a discovery, however useful, novel, and non-obvious, unless it falls within one of the express categories of patentable subject matter of 35 U.S.C. §101, the holder of such a discovery would have no reason to apply for a patent whether trade secret protection existed or not. Abolition of trade secret protection would, therefore, not result in increased disclosure to the public of discoveries in the area of nonpatentable subject matter. Also, it is hard to see how the public would be benefited by disclosure of customer lists or advertising campaigns; in fact, keeping such items secret encourages businesses to initiate new and individualized plans of operation, and constructive competition results. This, in turn, leads to a greater variety of business methods than would otherwise be the case if privately developed marketing and other data were passed illicitly among firms involved in the same enterprise.

Congress has spoken in the area of those discoveries which fall within one of the categories of patentable subject matter of 35 U.S.C. §101 and which are, therefore, of a nature that would be subject to consideration for a patent. Processes, machines, manufactures, compositions of matter and improvements thereof, which meet the tests of utility, novelty, and nonobviousness are entitled to be patented, but those which do not, are not. The question remains whether those items which are proper subjects for consideration for a patent may also have available the alternative protection accorded by trade secret law.

Certainly the patent policy of encouraging invention is not disturbed by the existence of another form of incentive to invention. In this respect the two systems are not and never would be in conflict. Similarly, the policy that matter once in the public domain must remain in the public domain is not incompatible with the existence of trade secret protection. By definition a trade secret has not been placed in the public domain.

The more difficult objective of the patent law to reconcile with trade secret law is that of disclosure, the quid pro quo of the right to exclude. We are helped in this stage of the analysis by Judge Henry Friendly's opinion in *Painton & Co. v. Bourns, Inc.*, 442 F.2d 216 (C.A.2 1971). There the Court of Appeals thought it useful, in determining whether inventors will refrain because of the existence of trade secret law from applying for patents, thereby depriving the public from learning of the invention, to distinguish between three categories of trade secrets:

> (1) the trade secret believed by its owner to constitute a validly patentable invention; (2) the trade secret known to its owner not to be so patentable; and (3) the trade secret whose valid patentability is considered dubious. *Id.*, at 224.

Trade secret protection in each of these categories would run against breaches of confidence—the employee and licensee situations—and theft and other forms of industrial espionage.

As to the trade secret known not to meet the standards of patentability, very little in the way of disclosure would be accomplished by abolishing trade secret protection. With trade secrets of nonpatentable subject matter, the patent alternative would not reasonably be available to the inventor. "There can be no public interest in stimulating developers of such (unpatentable) knowhow to flood an overburdened Patent Office with applications (for) what they do not consider patentable." *Ibid.* The mere filing of applications doomed to be turned down by the Patent Office will bring forth no new public knowledge or enlightenment, since under federal statute and regulation patent applications and abandoned patent applications are held by the Patent Office in confidence and are not open to public inspection.

Even as the extension of trade secret protection to patentable subject matter that the owner knows will not meet the standards of patentability will not conflict with the patent policy of disclosure, it will have a decidedly beneficial effect on society. Trade secret law will encourage invention in areas where patent law does not reach, and will prompt the independent innovator to proceed with the discovery and exploitation of his invention. Competition is fostered and the public is not deprived of the use of valuable, if not quite patentable, invention.

Even if trade secret protection against the faithless employee were abolished, inventive and exploitive effort in the area of patentable subject matter that did not meet the standards of patentability would continue, although at a reduced level. Alternatively with the effort that remained, however, would come an increase in the amount of self-help that innovative companies would employ. Knowledge would be widely dispersed among the employees of those still active in research. Security precautions necessarily would be increased, and salaries and fringe benefits of those few officers or employees who had to know the whole of the secret invention would be fixed in an amount thought sufficient to assure their loyalty. Smaller companies would be placed at a distinct economic disadvantage, since the costs of this kind of self-help could be great, and the cost to the public of the use of this invention would be increased. The innovative entrepreneur with limited resources would tend to confine his research efforts to himself and those few he felt he could trust without the ultimate assurance of legal protection against breaches of confidence. As a result, organized scientific and technological research could become fragmented, and society, as a whole, would suffer.

Another problem that would arise if state trade secret protection were precluded is in the area of licensing others to exploit secret processes. The holder of a trade secret would not likely share his secret with a manufacturer who cannot be placed under binding legal obligation to pay a license fee or to protect the secret. The result would be to hoard rather than disseminate knowledge. Instead, then, of licensing others to use his invention and making the most efficient use of existing manufacturing and marketing structures within the industry, the trade secret holder would tend either to limit his utilization of the invention, thereby depriving the public of the maximum benefit of its use, or engage in the time-consuming and economically wasteful enterprise of constructing duplicative manufacturing and marketing mechanisms for the exploitation of the invention. The detrimental misallocation of resources and economic waste that would thus take place if trade secret protection were abolished with respect to employees or licensees cannot be justified by reference to any policy that the federal patent law seeks to advance.

Nothing in the patent law requires that States refrain from action to prevent industrial espionage. In addition to the increased costs for protection from burglary, wire-tapping, bribery, and the other means used to misappropriate trade secrets, there is the inevitable cost to the basic decency of society when one firm steals from another. A most fundamental human right, that of privacy, is threatened when industrial espionage is condoned or is made profitable; the state interest in denying profit to such illegal ventures is unchallengeable.

The next category of patentable subject matter to deal with is the invention whose holder has a legitimate doubt as to its patentability. The risk of eventual patent invalidity by the courts and the costs associated with that risk may well impel some with a good-faith doubt as to patentability not to take the trouble to seek to obtain and defend patent protection for their discoveries, regardless of the existence of trade secret protection. Trade secret protection would assist those inventors in the more efficient exploitation of their discoveries and not conflict with the patent law. In most cases of genuine doubt as to patent validity the potential rewards of patent protection are so far superior to those accruing to holders of trade secrets, that the holders of such inventions will seek patent protection, ignoring the trade secret route. For those inventors "on the line" as to whether to seek patent protection, the abolition of trade secret protection might encourage some to apply for a patent who otherwise would not have done so. For some of those so encouraged, no patent will be granted and the result

> will have been an unnecessary postponement in the divulging of the trade secret to persons willing to pay for it. If (the patent does issue), it may well be invalid, yet many will prefer to pay a modest royalty than to contest it, even though Lear allows them to accept a license and pursue the contest without paying royalties while the fight goes on. The result in such a case would be unjustified royalty payments from many who would prefer not to pay them rather than agreed fees from one or a few who are entirely willing to do so. *Painton & Co. v. Bourns, Inc.*, 442 F.2d, at 225.

The point is that those who might be encouraged to file for patents by the absence of trade secret law will include inventors possessing the chaff as well as the wheat. Some of the chaff—the nonpatentable discoveries—will be thrown out by the Patent Office, but in the meantime society will have been deprived of use of those discoveries through trade secret-protected licensing. Some of the chaff may not be thrown out. This Court has noted the difference between the standards used by the Patent Office and the courts to determine patentability. *Graham v. John Deere Co.*, 383 U.S. 1, 18 (1966). In *Lear, Inc. v. Adkins*, 395 U.S. 653 (1969), the Court thought that an invalid patent was so serious a threat to the free use of ideas already in the public domain that the Court permitted licensees of the patent holder to challenge the validity of the patent. Better had the invalid patent never issued. More of those patents would likely issue if trade secret law were abolished. Eliminating trade secret law for the doubtfully patentable invention is thus likely to have deleterious effects on society and patent policy which we cannot say are balanced out by the speculative gain which might result from the encouragement of some inventors with doubtfully patentable inventions which deserve patent protection to come forward and apply for patents. There is no conflict, then, between trade secret law and the patent law policy of disclosure, at least insofar as the first two categories of patentable subject matter are concerned.

The final category of patentable subject matter to deal with is the clearly patentable invention, i.e., that invention which the owner believes to meet the standards of patentability. It is here that the federal interest in disclosure is at its peak; these inventions, novel, useful and nonobvious, are "the things which are worth to the public the embarrassment of an exclusive patent." *Graham v. John Deere Co.*, 383 U.S. at 9 (quoting Thomas Jefferson). The interest of the public is that the bargain of 17 years of exclusive use in return for disclosure be accepted. If a State, through a system of protection, were to cause a substantial risk that holders of patentable inventions would not seek patents, but rather would rely on the state protection, we would be compelled to hold that such a system could not constitutionally continue to exist. In the case of trade secret law no reasonable risk of deterrence from patent application by those who can reasonably expect to be granted patents exists.

Trade secret law provides far weaker protection in many respects than the patent law. While trade secret law does not forbid the discovery of the trade secret by fair and honest means, e.g., independent creation or reverse engineering, patent law operates "against the world," forbidding any use of the invention for whatever purpose for a significant length of time. The holder of a trade secret also takes a substantial risk that the secret will be passed on to his competitors, by theft or by breach of a confidential relationship, in a manner not easily susceptible of discovery or proof. Where patent law acts as a barrier, trade secret law functions relatively as a sieve. The possibility that an inventor who believes his invention meets the standards of patentability will sit back, rely on trade secret law, and after one year of use forfeit any right to patent protection, 35 U.S.C. § 102(b), is remote indeed.

Nor does society face much risk that scientific or technological progress will be impeded by the rare inventor with a patentable invention who chooses trade secret protection over patent protection. The ripeness-of-time concept of invention, developed from the study of the many independent multiple discoveries in history, predicts that if a particular individual had not made a particular discovery others would have, and in probably a relatively short period of time. If something is to be discovered at all very likely it will be discovered by more than one person. Even were an inventor to keep his discovery completely to himself, something that neither the patent nor trade secret laws forbid, there is a high probability that it will be soon independently developed. If the invention, though still a trade secret, is put into public use, the competition is alerted to the existence of the inventor's solution to the problem and may be encouraged to make an extra effort to independently find the solution thus known to be possible. The inventor faces pressures not only from private industry, but from the skilled scientists who work in our universities and our other great publicly supported centers of learning and research.

We conclude that the extension of trade secret protection to clearly patentable inventions does not conflict with the patent policy of disclosure. Perhaps because trade secret law does not produce any positive effects in the area of clearly patentable inventions, as opposed to the beneficial effects resulting from trade secret protection in the areas of the doubtfully patentable and the clearly unpatentable inventions, it has been suggested that partial pre-emption may be appropriate, and that courts should refuse to apply trade secret protection to inventions which the holder should have patented, and which would have been, thereby, disclosed. However, since there is no real possibility that trade secret law will conflict with the federal policy favoring disclosure of clearly patentable inventions partial pre-emption is inappropriate. Partial pre-emption, furthermore, could well create serious problems for state courts in the administration of trade secret law. As a preliminary matter in trade secret actions, state courts would be obliged to distinguish between what a reasonable inventor would and would not correctly consider to be clearly patentable, with the holder of the trade secret arguing that the invention was not patentable and the misappropriator of the trade secret arguing its undoubted novelty, utility, and non-obviousness. Federal courts have a difficult enough time trying to determine whether an invention, narrowed by the patent application procedure and fixed in the specifications which describe the invention for which the patent has been granted, is patentable. Although state courts in some circumstances must join federal courts in judging whether an issued patent is valid, *Lear, Inc. v. Adkins, supra*, it would be undesirable to impose the almost impossible burden on state courts to determine the patentability—in fact and in the mind of a reasonable inventor—of a discovery which has not been patented and remains entirely uncircumscribed by expert analysis in the administrative process. Neither complete nor partial pre-emption of state trade secret law is justified.

Trade secret law and patent law have co-existed in this country for over one hundred years. Each has its particular role to play, and the operation of one does not take away from the need for the other. Trade secret law encourages the development and exploitation of those items of lesser or different invention than might be accorded protection under the patent laws, but which items still have an important part to play in the technological and scientific advancement of the Nation. Trade secret law promotes the sharing of knowledge, and the efficient operation of industry; it permits the individual inventor to reap the rewards of his labor by contracting with a company large enough to develop and exploit it. Congress, by its silence over these many years, has seen the wisdom of allowing the States to enforce trade secret protection. Until Congress takes affirmative action to the contrary, States should be free to grant protection to trade secrets.

Justice DOUGLAS, with whom Justice BRENNAN concurs, dissenting.

Today's decision is at war with the philosophy of *Sears, Roebuck & Co. v. Stiffel Co., supra* and *Compco Corp. v. Day-Brite Lighting, Inc.* Those cases involved patents—one of a pole lamp and one of fluorescent lighting fixtures each of which was declared invalid. The lower courts held, however, that though the patents were invalid the sale of identical or confusingly similar products to the products of the patentees violated state unfair competition laws. We held that when an article is unprotected by a patent, state law may not forbid others to copy it, because every article not covered by a valid patent is in the public domain. Congress in the patent laws decided that where no patent existed, free competition should prevail; that where a patent is rightfully issued, the right to exclude others should obtain for no longer than 17 years, and that the States may not "under some other law, such as that forbidding unfair competition, give protection of a kind that clashes with the objectives of the federal patent laws," 376 U.S., at 231.

The product involved in this suit, sodium iodide synthetic crystals, was a product that could be patented but was not. Harshaw the inventor apparently contributed greatly to the technology in that field by developing processes, procedures, and techniques that produced much larger crystals than any competitor. These processes, procedures, and techniques were also patentable; but no patent was sought. Rather Harshaw sought to protect its trade secrets by contracts with its employees. And the District Court found that, as a result of those secrecy precautions, "not sufficient disclosure occurred so as to place the claimed trade secrets in the public domain"; and those findings were sustained by the Court of Appeals.

The District Court issued a permanent injunction against respondents, ex-employees, restraining them from using the processes used by Harshaw. By a patent which would require full disclosure Harshaw could have obtained a 17-year monopoly against the world. By the District Court's injunction, which the Court approves and reinstates, Harshaw gets a permanent injunction running into perpetuity against respondents. In *Sears*, as in the present case, an injunction against the unfair competitor issued. We said: "To allow a State by use of its law of unfair competition to prevent the copying of an article which represents too slight an advance to be patented would be to permit the State to block off from the public something which federal law has said belongs to the public. The result would be that while federal law grants only 14 or 17 years' protection to genuine inventions, see 35 U.S.C. §§ 154, 173, States could allow perpetual protection to articles too lacking in novelty to merit any patent at all under federal constitutional standards. This would be too great an encroachment on the federal patent system to be tolerated." 376 U.S., at 231-232.

The conflict with the patent laws is obvious. The decision of Congress to adopt a patent system was based on the idea that there will be much more innovation if discoveries are disclosed and patented than there will be when everyone works in secret. Society thus fosters a free exchange of technological information at the cost of a limited 17-year monopoly.

A trade secret, unlike a patent, has no property dimension. That was the view of the Court of Appeals, 478 F.2d 1074, 1081; and its decision is supported by what Mr. Justice Holmes said in *DuPont de Nemours Powder Co. v. Masland*, 244 U.S. 100, 102:

> The word property as applied to trade-marks and trade secrets is an unanalyzed expression of certain makes some rudimentary requirements of good faith. Whether the plaintiffs have any valuable secret or not the defendant knows the facts, whatever they are, through a special confidence that he accepted. The property may be denied but the confidence cannot be. Therefore the starting point for the present matter is not property or due process of law, but that the defendant stood in confidential relations with the plaintiffs, or one of them. These have given place to hostility, and the first thing to be made sure of is that the defendant shall not fraudulently abuse the trust reposed in him. It is the usual incident of confidential relations. If there is any disadvantage in the fact that he knew the plaintiffs' secrets he must take the burden with the good.

> The difference between the two things, letters-patent and copyright, may be illustrated by reference to the subjects just enumerated. Take the case of medicines. Certain mixtures are found to be of great value in the healing art. If the discoverer writes and publishes a book on the subject (as regular physicians generally do), he gains no exclusive right to the manufacture and sale of the medicine; he gives that

to the public. If he desires to acquire such exclusive right, he must obtain a patent for the mixture as a new art, manufacture, or composition of matter. He may copyright his book, if he pleases; but that only secures to him the exclusive right of printing and publishing his book. So of all other inventions or discoveries.

Baker v. Selden, 101 U.S. 99, 102-103.

A suit to redress theft of a trade secret is grounded in tort damages for breach of a contract a historic remedy, *Cataphote Corp. v. Hudson*, 5 Cir., 422 F.2d 1290. Damages for breach of a confidential relation are not pre-empted by this patent law, but an injunction against use is pre-empted because the patent law states the only monopoly over trade secrets that is enforceable by specific performance; and that monopoly exacts as a price full disclosure. A trade secret can be protected only by being kept secret. Damages for breach of a contract are one thing; an injunction barring disclosure does service for the protection accorded valid patents and is therefore pre-empted.

From the findings of fact of the lower courts, the process involved in this litigation was unique, such a great discovery as to make its patentability a virtual certainty. Yet the Court's opinion reflects a vigorous activist anti-patent philosophy. My objection is not because it is activist. This is a problem that involves no neutral principle. The Constitution in Art. I, § 8, cl. 8, expresses the activist policy which Congress has enforced by statutes. It is that constitutional policy which we should enforce, not our individual notions of the public good.

BONITO BOATS, INC. v. THUNDER CRAFT BOATS, INC.
489 U.S. 141 (1989)

Justice O'CONNOR delivered the opinion of the Court.

We must decide today what limits the operation of the federal patent system places on the States' ability to offer substantial protection to utilitarian and design ideas which the patent laws leave otherwise unprotected. In *Interpart Corp. v. Italia*, 777 F.2d 678 (1985), the Court of Appeals for the Federal Circuit concluded that a California law prohibiting the use of the "direct molding process" to duplicate unpatented articles posed no threat to the policies behind the federal patent laws. In this case, the Florida Supreme Court came to a contrary conclusion. It struck down a Florida statute which prohibits the use of the direct molding process to duplicate unpatented boat hulls, finding that the protection offered by the Florida law conflicted with the balance struck by Congress in the federal patent statute between the encouragement of invention and free competition in unpatented ideas. We granted certiorari to resolve the conflict, and we now affirm the judgment of the Florida Supreme Court.

I

In September 1976, petitioner Bonito Boats, Inc. (Bonito), a Florida corporation, developed a hull design for a fiberglass recreational boat which it marketed under the trade name Bonito Boat Model 5VBR. Designing the boat hull required substantial effort on the part of Bonito. A set of engineering drawings was prepared, from which a hardwood model was created. The hardwood model was then sprayed with fiberglass to create a mold, which then served to produce the finished fiberglass boats for sale. The 5VBR was placed on the market sometime in September 1976. There is no indication in the record that a patent application was ever filed for protection of the utilitarian or design aspects of the hull, or for the process by which the hull was manufactured. The 5VBR was favorably received by the boating public, and "a broad interstate market" developed for its sale.

In May 1983, after the Bonito 5VBR had been available to the public for over six years, the Florida Legislature enacted Fla. Stat. §559.94 (1987). The statute makes "[i]t . . . unlawful for any person to use the direct molding process to duplicate for the purpose of sale any manufactured vessel hull or component part of a vessel made by another without the written permission of that other person." §559.94(2). The statute also makes it unlawful for a person to "knowingly sell a vessel hull or component part of a vessel duplicated in violation of subsection (2)." §559.94(3). Damages, injunctive relief, and attorney's fees are made available to "[a]ny person who suffers injury or damage as the result of a violation" of the statute. §559.94(4). The statute was made applicable to vessel hulls or component parts duplicated through the use of direct molding after July 1, 1983. §559.94(5).

On December 21, 1984, Bonito filed this action in the Circuit Court of Orange County, Florida. The complaint alleged that respondent here, Thunder Craft Boats, Inc. (Thunder Craft), a Tennessee corporation, had violated the Florida statute by using the direct molding process to duplicate the Bonito 5VBR fiberglass hull, and had knowingly sold such duplicates in violation of the Florida statute. Bonito sought "a temporary and permanent injunction prohibiting [Thunder Craft] from continuing to unlawfully duplicate and sell Bonito Boat hulls or components," as well as an accounting of profits, treble damages, punitive damages, and attorney's fees. Respondent filed a motion to dismiss the complaint, arguing that under this Court's decisions in *Sears, Roebuck & Co. v. Stiffel Co.*, 376 U.S. 225 (1964), and *Compco Corp. v. Day-Brite Lighting, Inc.*, 376 U.S. 234 (1964), the Florida statute conflicted with federal patent law and was therefore invalid under the Supremacy Clause of the Federal Constitution.

On appeal, a sharply divided Florida Supreme Court agreed with the lower courts' conclusion that the Florida law impermissibly interfered with the scheme established by the federal patent laws. The majority read our decisions in *Sears* and *Compco* for the proposition that "when an article is introduced into the public domain, only a patent can eliminate the inherent risk of competition and then but for a limited time." 515 So. 2d, at 222. Relying on the Federal Circuit's decision in the *Interpart* case, the three dissenting judges argued that the Florida antidirect molding provision "does not prohibit the copying of an unpatented item. It prohibits one method of copying; the item remains in the public domain." 515 So. 2d, at 223.

II

Article I, §8, cl. 8, of the Constitution gives Congress the power "[t]o promote the Progress of Science and useful Arts, by securing for limited Times to Authors and Inventors the exclusive Right to their respective Writings and Discoveries." The Patent Clause itself reflects a balance between the need to encourage innovation and the avoidance of monopolies which stifle competition without any concomitant advance in the "Progress of Science and useful Arts." As we have noted in the past, the Clause contains both a grant of power and certain limitations upon the exercise of that power. Congress may not create patent monopolies of unlimited duration, nor may it "authorize the issuance of patents whose effects are to remove existent knowledge from the public domain, or to restrict free access to materials already available." *Graham v. John Deere Co. of Kansas City*, 383 U.S. 1, 6 (1966).

From their inception, the federal patent laws have embodied a careful balance between the need to promote innovation and the recognition that imitation and refinement through imitation are both necessary to invention itself and the very lifeblood of a competitive economy. . . . Protection is offered to "[w]hoever invents or discovers any new and useful process, machine, manufacture, or composition of matter, or any new and useful improvement thereof." 35 U.S.C. § 101. . . . The novelty requirement of patentability is presently expressed in 35 U.S.C. §§ 102(a) and (b). Sections 102(a) and (b) operate in tandem to exclude from consideration for patent protection knowledge that is already available to the public. They express a congressional determination that the creation of a monopoly in such information would not only serve no socially useful purpose, but would in fact injure the public by removing existing knowledge from public use. From the Patent Act of 1790 to the present day, the public sale of an unpatented article has acted as a complete bar to federal protection of the idea embodied in the article thus placed in public commerce. . . . In addition to the requirements of novelty and utility, the federal patent law has long required that an innovation not be anticipated by the prior art in the field. Even if a particular combination of elements is "novel" in the literal sense of the term, it will not qualify for federal patent protection if its contours are so traced by the existing technology in the field that the "improvement is the work of the skillful mechanic, not that of the inventor." *Hotchkiss v. Greenwood*, 11 How. 248, 267 (1851). In 1952, Congress codified this judicially developed requirement in 35 U.S.C. § 103. . . .

The attractiveness of such a bargain, and its effectiveness in inducing creative effort and disclosure of the results of that effort, depend almost entirely on a backdrop of free competition in the exploitation of unpatented designs and innovations. The novelty and nonobviousness requirements of patentability embody a congressional understanding, implicit in the Patent Clause itself, that free exploitation of ideas will be the rule, to which the protection of a federal patent is the exception. Moreover, the ultimate goal of the patent system is to bring new designs and technologies into the public domain through disclosure. State law protection for techniques and designs whose disclosure has already been induced by market rewards may conflict with the very purpose of the patent laws by decreasing the range of ideas available as the building blocks of further innovation. The offer of federal protection from competitive exploitation of intellectual property would be rendered meaningless in a world where substantially similar state law protections were readily available. To a limited extent, the federal patent laws must determine not only what is protected, but also what is free for all to use.

Thus our past decisions have made clear that state regulation of intellectual property must yield to the extent that it clashes with the balance struck by Congress in our patent laws. The tension between the desire to freely exploit the full potential of our inventive resources and the need to create an incentive to deploy those resources is constant. Where it is clear how the patent laws strike that balance in a particular circumstance, that is not a judgment the States may second-guess. We have long held that after the expiration of a federal patent, the subject matter of the patent passes to the free use of the public as a matter of federal law. Where the public has paid the congressionally mandated price for disclosure, the States may not render the exchange fruitless by offering patent-like protection to the subject matter of the expired patent. "It is self-evident that on the expiration of a patent the monopoly created by it ceases to exist, and the right to make the thing formerly covered by the patent becomes public property." *Singer,* 16 S. Ct., at 1008.

In our decisions in *Sears, Roebuck & Co. v. Stiffel Co.,* 376 U.S. 225 (1964), and *Compco Corp. v. Day-Brite Lighting, Inc.,* 376 U.S. 234 (1964), we found that publicly known design and utilitarian ideas which were unprotected by patent occupied much the same position as the subject matter of an expired patent. The *Sears* case involved a pole lamp originally designed by the plaintiff Stiffel, who had secured both design and mechanical patents on the lamp. Sears purchased unauthorized copies of the lamps, and was able to sell them at a retail price practically equivalent to the wholesale price of the original manufacturer. Stiffel brought an action against Sears in Federal District Court, alleging infringement of the two federal patents and unfair competition under Illinois law. The District Court found that Stiffel's patents were invalid due to anticipation in the prior art, but nonetheless enjoined Sears from further sales of the duplicate lamps based on a finding of consumer confusion under the Illinois law of unfair competition. The Court of Appeals affirmed, coming to the conclusion that the Illinois law of unfair competition prohibited product simulation even in the absence of evidence that the defendant took some further action to induce confusion as to source.

This Court reversed, finding that the unlimited protection against copying which the Illinois law accorded an unpatentable item whose design had been fully disclosed through public sales conflicted with the federal policy embodied in the patent laws. The Court stated:

> In the present case the "pole lamp" sold by Stiffel has been held not to be entitled to the protection of either a mechanical or a design patent. An unpatentable article, like an article on which the patent has expired, is in the public domain and may be made and sold by whoever chooses to do so. What Sears did was to copy Stiffel's design and sell lamps almost identical to those sold by Stiffel. This it had every right to do under the federal patent laws.

376 U.S., at 231.

A similar conclusion was reached in *Compco,* where the District Court had extended the protection of Illinois' unfair competition law to the functional aspects of an unpatented fluorescent lighting system. The injunction against copying of an unpatented article, freely available to the public, impermissibly "interfere[d] with the federal policy, found in Art. I, § 8, cl. 8, of the Constitution and in the implementing federal statutes, of allowing free access to copy whatever the federal patent and copyright laws leave in the public domain." *Compco,* 376 U.S., at 237.

The pre-emptive sweep of our decisions in *Sears* and *Compco* has been the subject of heated scholarly and judicial debate. Read at their highest level of generality, the two decisions could be taken to stand for the proposition that the States are completely disabled from offering any form of protection to articles or processes which fall within the broad scope of patentable subject matter. Since the potentially patentable includes "anything under the sun that is made by man," *Diamond v. Chakrabarty,* 447 U.S. 303, 309 (1980), the broadest reading of *Sears* would prohibit the States from regulating the deceptive simulation of trade dress or the tortious appropriation of private information.

That the extrapolation of such a broad pre-emptive principle from *Sears* is inappropriate is clear from the balance struck in *Sears* itself. The *Sears* Court made it plain that the States "may protect businesses in the use of their trademarks, labels, or distinctive dress in the packaging of goods so as to prevent others, by imitating such markings, from misleading purchasers as to the source of the goods." *Sears, supra,* 376 U.S., at 232. Trade dress is, of course, potentially the subject matter of design patents. Yet our decision in *Sears* clearly indicates that the States may place limited regulations on the circumstances in which such designs are used in order to prevent consumer confusion as to source. Thus, while *Sears* speaks in absolutist terms, its conclusion that the States may place some conditions on the use of trade dress indicates an implicit recognition that all state regulation of potentially patentable but unpatented subject matter is not *ipso facto* pre-empted by the federal patent laws.

What was implicit in our decision in *Sears,* we have made explicit in our subsequent decisions concerning the scope of federal pre-emption of state regulation of the subject matter of patent. Thus, in *Kewanee Oil Co. v. Bicron Corp.,* 416 U.S. 470 (1974), we held that state protection of trade secrets did not operate to frustrate the achievement of the congressional objectives served by the patent laws. Despite the fact that state law protection was available for ideas which clearly fell within the subject matter of patent, the Court concluded that the nature and degree of state protection did not conflict with the federal policies of encouragement of patentable invention and the prompt disclosure of such innovations. . . .

At the heart of *Sears* and *Compco* is the conclusion that the efficient operation of the federal patent system depends upon substantially free trade in publicly known, unpatented design and utilitarian conceptions. In *Sears,* the state law offered "the equivalent of a patent monopoly," 376 U.S., at 233, in the functional aspects of a product which had been placed in public commerce absent the protection of a valid patent. While, as noted above, our decisions since *Sears* have taken a decidedly less rigid view of the scope of federal pre-emption under the patent laws, *e.g., Kewanee, supra,* 416 U.S., at 479-480, we believe that the *Sears* Court correctly concluded that the States may not offer patent-like protection to intellectual creations which would otherwise remain unprotected as a matter of federal law. Both the novelty and the nonobviousness requirements of federal patent law are grounded in the notion that concepts within the public grasp, or those so obvious that they readily could be, are the tools of creation available to all. They provide the baseline of free competition upon which the patent system's incentive to creative effort depends. A state law that substantially interferes with the enjoyment of an unpatented utilitarian or design conception which has been freely disclosed by its author to the public at large impermissibly contravenes the ultimate goal of public disclosure and use which is the centerpiece of federal patent policy. Moreover, through the creation of patent-like rights, the States could essentially redirect inventive efforts away from the careful criteria of patentability developed by Congress over the last 200 years. We understand this to be the reasoning at the core of our decisions in *Sears* and *Compco,* and we reaffirm that reasoning today.

III

We believe that the Florida statute at issue in this case so substantially impedes the public use of the otherwise unprotected design and utilitarian ideas embodied in unpatented boat hulls as to run afoul of the teaching of our decisions in *Sears* and *Compco*. It is readily apparent that the Florida statute does not operate to prohibit "unfair competition" in the usual sense that the term is understood. The law of unfair competition has its roots in the common-law tort of deceit: its general concern is with protecting *consumers* from confusion as to source. While that concern may result in the creation of "quasi-property rights" in communicative symbols, the focus is on the protection of consumers, not the protection of producers as an incentive to product innovation. . . .

In contrast to the operation of unfair competition law, the Florida statute is aimed directly at preventing the exploitation of the design and utilitarian conceptions embodied in the product itself. The sparse legislative history surrounding its enactment indicates that it was intended to create an inducement for the improvement of boat hull designs. To accomplish this goal, the Florida statute endows the original boat hull manufacturer with rights against the world, similar in scope and operation to the rights accorded a federal patentee. Like the patentee, the beneficiary of the Florida statute may prevent a competitor from "making" the product in what is evidently the most efficient manner available and from "selling" the product when it is produced in that fashion. The Florida scheme offers this protection for an unlimited number of years to all boat hulls and their component parts, without regard to their ornamental or technological merit. Protection is available for subject matter for which patent protection has been denied or has expired, as well as for designs which have been freely revealed to the consuming public by their creators.

In this case, the Bonito 5VBR fiberglass hull has been freely exposed to the public for a period in excess of six years. For purposes of federal law, it stands in the same stead as an item for which a patent has expired or been denied: it is unpatented and unpatentable. See 35 U.S.C. § 102(b). Whether because of a determination of unpatentability or other commercial concerns, petitioner chose to expose its hull design to the public in the marketplace, eschewing the bargain held out by the federal patent system of disclosure in exchange for exclusive use. Yet, the Florida statute allows petitioner to reassert a substantial property right in the idea, thereby constricting the spectrum of useful public knowledge. Moreover, it does so without the careful protections of high standards of innovation and limited monopoly contained in the federal scheme. We think it clear that such protection conflicts with the federal policy "that all ideas in general circulation be dedicated to the common good unless they are protected by a valid patent." *Lear, Inc. v. Adkins*, 395 U.S., at 668.

That the Florida statute does not remove all means of reproduction and sale does not eliminate the conflict with the federal scheme. In essence, the Florida law prohibits the entire public from engaging in a form of reverse engineering of a product in the public domain. This is clearly one of the rights vested in the federal patent holder, but has never been a part of state protection under the law of unfair competition or trade secrets. See *Kewanee*, 416 U.S., at 476 ("A trade secret law, however, does not offer protection against discovery by . . . so-called reverse engineering, that is by starting with the known product and working backward to divine the process which aided in its development or manufacture"). The duplication of boat hulls and their component parts may be an essential part of innovation in the field of hydrodynamic design. Variations as to size and combination of various elements may lead to significant advances in the field. Reverse engineering of chemical and mechanical articles in the public domain often leads to significant advances in technology. If Florida may prohibit this particular method of study and recomposition of an unpatented article, we fail to see the principle that would prohibit a State from banning the use of chromatography in the reconstitution of unpatented chemical compounds, or the use of robotics in the duplication of machinery in the public domain.

Moreover, as we noted in *Kewanee*, the competitive reality of reverse engineering may act as a spur to the inventor, creating an incentive to develop inventions that meet the rigorous requirements of patentability. The Florida statute substantially reduces this competitive incentive, thus eroding the general rule of free competition upon which the attractiveness of the federal patent bargain depends. The protections of state trade secret law are most effective at the developmental stage, before a product has been marketed and the threat of reverse engineering becomes real. During this period, patentability will often be an uncertain prospect, and to a certain extent, the protection offered by trade secret law may "dovetail" with the incentives created by the federal patent monopoly. In contrast, under the Florida scheme, the would-be inventor is aware from the outset of his efforts that rights against the public are available regardless of his ability to satisfy the rigorous standards of patentability. Indeed, it appears that even the most mundane and obvious changes in the design of a boat hull will trigger the protections of the statute. See Fla. Stat. §559.94(2) (1987) (protecting "any manufactured vessel hull or component part"). Given the substantial protection offered by the Florida scheme, we cannot dismiss as hypothetical the possibility that it will become a significant competitor to the federal patent laws, offering investors similar protection without the *quid pro quo* of substantial creative effort required by the federal statute. The prospect of all 50 States establishing similar protections for preferred industries without the rigorous requirements of patentability prescribed by Congress could pose a substantial threat to the patent system's ability to accomplish its mission of promoting progress in the useful arts. . . .

Petitioner and its supporting *amici* place great weight on the contrary decision of the Court of Appeals for the Federal Circuit in *Interpart Corp. v. Italia*. In upholding the application of the California "antidirect molding" statute to the duplication of unpatented automobile mirrors, the Federal Circuit stated: "The statute prevents unscrupulous competitors from obtaining a product and using it as the 'plug' for making a mold. The statute does not prohibit copying the design of the product in any other way; the latter if in the public domain, is free for anyone to make, use or sell." 777 F.2d, at 685. The court went on to indicate that "the patent laws 'say nothing about the right to copy or the right to use, they speak only in terms of the right to exclude.'" *Ibid.*

We find this reasoning defective in several respects. The Federal Circuit apparently viewed the direct molding statute at issue in *Interpart* as a mere regulation of the use of chattels. Yet, the very purpose of antidirect molding statutes is to "reward" the "inventor" by offering substantial protection against public exploitation of his or her idea embodied in the product. Such statutes would be an exercise in futility if they did not have precisely the effect of substantially limiting the ability of the public to exploit an otherwise unprotected idea. As *amicus* points out, the direct molding process itself has been in use since the early 1950's. Indeed, U.S. Patent No. 3,419,646, issued to Robert L. Smith in 1968, explicitly discloses and claims a method for the direct molding of boat hulls. The specifications of the Smith Patent indicate that "[i]t is a major object of the present invention to provide a method for making large molded boat hull molds at very low cost, once a prototype hull has been provided." In fact, it appears that Bonito employed a similar process in the creation of its own production mold. It is difficult to conceive of a more effective method of creating substantial property rights in an intellectual creation than to eliminate the most efficient method for its exploitation. *Sears* and *Compco* protect more than the right of the public to contemplate the abstract beauty of an otherwise unprotected intellectual creation — they assure its efficient reduction to practice and sale in the marketplace. . . .

Our decisions since *Sears* and *Compco* have made it clear that the Patent and Copyright Clauses do not, by their own force or by negative implication, deprive the States of the power to adopt rules for the promotion of intellectual creation within their own jurisdictions. Thus, where "Congress determines that neither federal protection nor freedom from restraint is required by the national interest," *Goldstein, supra,* 412 U.S., at 559, the States remain free to promote originality and creativity in their own domains.

Nor does the fact that a particular item lies within the subject matter of the federal patent laws necessarily preclude the States from offering limited protection which does not impermissibly interfere with the federal patent scheme. As *Sears* itself makes clear, States may place limited regulations on the use of unpatented designs in order to prevent consumer confusion as to source. In *Kewanee,* we found that state protection of trade secrets, as applied to both patentable and unpatentable subject matter, did not conflict with the federal patent laws. In both situations, state protection was not aimed exclusively at the promotion of invention itself, and the state restrictions on the use of unpatented ideas were limited to those necessary to promote goals outside the contemplation of the federal patent scheme. Both the law of unfair competition and state trade secret law have coexisted harmoniously with federal patent protection for almost 200 years, and Congress has given no indication that their operation is inconsistent with the operation of the federal patent laws.

Indeed, there are affirmative indications from Congress that both the law of unfair competition and trade secret protection are consistent with the balance struck by the patent laws. Section 43(a) of the Lanham Act, 15 U.S.C. § 1125(a), creates a federal remedy for making "a false designation of origin, or any false description or representation, including words or other symbols tending falsely to describe or represent the same. . . ." Congress has thus given federal recognition to many of the concerns that underlie the state tort of unfair competition, and the application of *Sears* and *Compco* to nonfunctional aspects of a product which have been shown to identify source must take account of competing federal policies in this regard. Similarly, as Justice Marshall noted in his concurring opinion in *Kewanee:* "State trade secret laws and the federal patent laws have co-existed for many, many, years. During this time, Congress has repeatedly demonstrated its full awareness of the existence of the trade secret system, without any indication of disapproval. Indeed, Congress has in a number of instances given explicit federal protection to trade secret information provided to federal agencies." *Kewanee,* 416 U.S., at 494. The case for federal pre-emption is particularly weak where Congress has indicated its awareness of the operation of state law in a field of federal interest, and has nonetheless decided to "stand by both concepts and to tolerate whatever tension there [is] between them." *Silkwood v. Kerr-McGee Corp.,* 464 U.S. 238, 256 (1984). The same cannot be said of the Florida statute at issue here, which offers protection beyond that available under the law of unfair competition or trade secret, without any showing of consumer confusion, or breach of trust or secrecy.

The Florida statute is aimed directly at the promotion of intellectual creation by substantially restricting the public's ability to exploit ideas that the patent system mandates shall be free for all to use. Like the interpretation of Illinois unfair competition law in *Sears* and *Compco,* the Florida statute represents a break with the tradition of peaceful co-existence between state market regulation and federal patent policy. The Florida law substantially restricts the public's ability to exploit an unpatented design in general circulation, raising the specter of state-created monopolies in a host of useful shapes and processes for which patent protection has been denied or is otherwise unobtainable. It thus enters a field of regulation which the patent laws have reserved to Congress. The patent statute's careful balance between public right and private monopoly to promote certain creative activity is a "scheme of federal regulation . . . so pervasive as to make reasonable the inference that Congress left no room for the States to supplement it." *Rice v. Santa Fe Elevator Corp.,* 331 U.S. 218, 230 (1947).

. . . It is for Congress to determine if the present system of design and utility patents is ineffectual in promoting the useful arts in the context of industrial design. By offering patent-like protection for ideas deemed unprotected under the present federal scheme, the Florida statute conflicts with the "strong federal policy favoring free competition in ideas which do not merit patent protection." *Lear, Inc.,* 395 U.S., at 656. We therefore agree with the majority of the Florida Supreme Court that the Florida statute is preempted by the Supremacy Clause, and the judgment of that court is hereby affirmed.

Comments

1. *Three Grounds for Preemption.* The Supreme Court has established three grounds for preemption. First, explicit preemption based on Congress expressly providing for preemption of a state law; second, field preemption, where "the scheme of federal regulation is so pervasive as to make reasonable the inference that Congress left no room for the States to supplement it," *Gade v. National Solid Wastes Management Ass'n,* 505 U.S. 88, 98 (1992); and third, conflict preemption, "where compliance with both federal and state regulations is a physical impossibility, or where state law stands as an obstacle to the accomplishment and execution of the full purposes and objectives of Congress." *Id.* at 98.

2. *The Choice Between Patent and Trade Secret Protection.* The *Kewanee* Court stated that given a choice between patent and trade secret protection, the rational inventor would opt for patent protection because a trade secret provides weaker protection. In fact, the Court later wrote this "point was central to the Court's conclusion that trade secret protection did not conflict with either

the encouragement or disclosure policies of the federal patent law." *Bonito Boats*, 489 U.S. at 155. But survey evidence suggests trade secret protection is the appropriability mechanism of choice for in many industries, even though patent protection is available. *See, e.g.*, Wesley M. Cohen et al., *Protecting Their Intellectual Assets: Appropriability Conditions and Why U.S. Manufacturing Firms Patent (or Not)* 24 (Nat'l Bureau of Econ. Research, Working Paper No. 7552, 2000). There are often times good reasons to choose trade secrets. First, trade secret law does not require public disclosure of the invention. Thus, an innovator may choose trade secret protection because the value of the invention is derived from it not being disclosed, as would be required by patent law. Second, even if disclosure would not destroy the invention's value, opting for patent protection may induce design around activity or signal to competitors there is a market for follow-on research. And third, trade secret protection can last in perpetuity as long as the information remains secret and maintains its value whereas a patent expires 20 years from its filing date. As a result, an innovator with a patentable invention may opt for a trade secret if he believes that competitors will have difficulty reverse engineering or independently developing the invention.

The *Kewanee* Court also focused on economic efficiency concerns to support its conclusion there was no conflict between trade secret protection and patent law. Recall the Court's statement, "[t]he holder of a trade secret would not likely share his secret with a manufacturer who cannot be placed under binding legal obligation to pay a license fee or to protect the secret. The result would be to hoard rather than disseminate knowledge." As such, trade secret protection and patent protection have consistent goals, namely the efficient use and production of information that can enhance social welfare. In short, "[t]he detrimental misallocation of resources and economic waste that would thus take place if trade secret protection were abolished with respect to employees or licensees cannot be justified by reference to any policy that the federal patent law seeks to advance." *See* WILLIAM M. LANDES & RICHARD A. POSNER, THE ECONOMIC STRUCTURE OF INTELLECTUAL PROPERTY LAW 360 (2003) (stating the "patent route, because of its cost and required disclosures, often just is not attractive to an inventor of a patentable invention, so that to abolish or curtail trade secret would undermine incentives to innovate").

While *Sears/Compco* left room for the states to maneuver in the IP realm, the boat hull legislation of *Bonito* strayed too far into patent law's domain. Unlike the Ohio trade secret law (or trade secret law in general), the Florida statute in *Bonito Boats* was not seen by the Court as public-welfare enhancing. *See* Paul J. Heald, *Federal Intellectual Property Law and the Economics of Preemption*, 76 IOWA L. REV. 959, 987-988 (1991) (stating "the decision in *Bonito Boats* strongly suggests that, at a minimum, a state statute must attempt to offset monopoly costs by requiring an advance which benefits the public. . . . Rather than demanding the creation of value, the Florida law actually diminishes the availability of creations already in the public domain by making them the property of an individual").

Remedies

INTRODUCTION

This chapter explores the types of remedies available to a patentee. A patent owner is entitled to both money damages and equitable relief. Damages must be "adequate to compensate for the infringement," 35 U.S.C. §284, and are measured based on either lost profits or a reasonable royalty. And damages may be trebled if willful infringement is found. A court may also "grant injunctions . . . to prevent the violation of any" of the rights conferred by a patent. *See* 35 U.S.C. §283. The injunction is a remedy typically associated with a property right; and injunctive relief for patent infringement is conceptually similar to a real property owner enjoining a third party from trespassing on his land. A court has the power to issue preliminary and permanent injunctions. The patent code does not provide for criminal sanctions.

STATUTE: **Injunction**
35 U.S.C. §283

STATUTE: **Damages**
35 U.S.C. §284

STATUTE: **Attorney fees**
35 U.S.C. §285

STATUTE: **Time limitation on damages**
35 U.S.C. §286

STATUTE: **Limitation on damages and other remedies; marking and notice**
35 U.S.C. §287

A. MONEY DAMAGES

Money damages are usually measured by calculating the patent owner's *lost profits* or, if lost profits cannot be proved, by using a *reasonable royalty* method, which may be based on either an established or hypothetical royalty. The *Rite-Hite* and *Grain Processing* cases explore a lost profit analysis, and the *Trio Process* and *Lucent* cases discusses the framework for constructing a reasonable royalty.

1. Lost Profits

Lost profits are based on profits lost by the patentee, not the profits made by the infringer. The modern legal framework for determining lost profits can be found in *Panduit Corp. v. Stahlin Bros. Fibre Works.* In *Panduit*, the court stated:

> To obtain as damages the profits on sales he would have made absent the infringement, i.e., the sales made by the infringer, a patent owner must prove: (1) demand for the patented product, (2) the absence of acceptable noninfringing substitutes, (3) his manufacturing and marketing capability to exploit the demand, and (4) the amount of the profit he would have made.

575 F.2d 1152, 1156 (6th Cir. 1978). The parameters of *Panduit* are explored in *Rite-Hite* and *Grain Processing.*

RITE-HITE CORP. v. KELLEY CO., INC.

56 F.3d 1538 (Fed. Cir. 1995)

LOURIE, Circuit Judge.

Kelley Company appeals from a decision of the United States District Court for the Eastern District of Wisconsin, awarding damages for the infringement of U.S. Patent 4,373,847, owned by Rite-Hite Corporation. The district court determined that Rite-Hite was entitled to lost profits for lost sales of its devices that were in direct competition with the infringing devices, but which themselves were not covered by the patent in suit. The appeal has been taken *en banc* to determine whether such damages are legally compensable under 35 U.S.C. §284.

BACKGROUND

On March 22, 1983, Rite-Hite sued Kelley, alleging that Kelley's "Truk Stop" vehicle restraint infringed Rite-Hite's U.S. Patent 4,373,847 ("the '847 patent"). The '847 patent, issued February 15, 1983, is directed to a device for securing a vehicle to a loading dock to prevent the vehicle from separating from the dock during loading or unloading. Any such separation would create a gap between the vehicle and dock and create a danger for a forklift operator.

* * *

Rite-Hite sought damages calculated as lost profits for two types of vehicle restraints that it made and sold: the "Manual Dok-Lok" model 55 (MDL-55), which incorporated the invention covered by the '847 patent, and the "Automatic Dok-Lok" model 100 (ADL-100), which was not covered by the patent in suit. The ADL-100 was the first vehicle restraint Rite-Hite put on the market and it was covered by one or more patents other than the patent in suit. The Kelley Truk Stop restraint was designed to compete primarily with Rite-Hite's ADL-100. Both employed an electric motor and functioned automatically, and each sold for $1,000-$1,500 at the wholesale level, in contrast to the MDL-55, which sold for one-third to one-half the price of the motorized devices. Rite-Hite does not assert that Kelley's Truk Stop restraint infringed the patents covering the ADL-100.

Of the 3,825 infringing Truk Stop devices sold by Kelley, the district court found that, "but for" Kelley's infringement, Rite-Hite would have made 80 more sales of its MDL-55; 3,243 more sales of its ADL-100; and 1,692 more sales of dock levelers, a bridging platform sold with the restraints and used to bridge the edges of a vehicle and dock. The court awarded Rite-Hite as a manufacturer the wholesale profits that it lost on lost sales of the ADL-100 restraints, MDL-55 restraints, and restraint-leveler packages. . . .

On appeal, Kelley contends that the district court erred as a matter of law in its determination of damages. Kelley does not contest the award of damages for lost sales of the MDL-55 restraints; however, Kelley argues that the patent statute does not provide for damages based on Rite-Hite's lost profits on ADL-100 restraints because the ADL-100s are not covered by the patent in suit. . . .

We affirm the damage award with respect to Rite-Hite's lost profits as a manufacturer on its ADL-100 restraint sales. . . .

DISCUSSION

A. Kelley's Appeal

I. Lost Profits on the ADL-100 Restraints

The district court's decision to award lost profits damages pursuant to 35 U.S.C. §284 turned primarily upon the quality of Rite-Hite's proof of actual lost profits. The court found that, "but for" Kelley's infringing Truk Stop competition, Rite-Hite would have sold 3,243 additional ADL-100 restraints and 80 additional MDL-55 restraints. The court reasoned that awarding lost profits fulfilled the patent statute's goal of affording complete compensation for infringement and compensated Rite-Hite for the ADL-100 sales that Kelley "anticipated taking from Rite-Hite when it marketed the Truk Stop against the ADL-100." *Rite-Hite,* 774 F. Supp. at 1540, 21 USPQ2d at 1821. The court stated, "[t]he rule applied here therefore does not extend Rite-Hite's patent rights excessively, because Kelley could reasonably have foreseen that its infringement of the '847 patent would make it liable for lost ADL-100 sales in addition to lost MDL-55 sales." *Id.* . . .

Kelley maintains that Rite-Hite's lost sales of the ADL-100 restraints do not constitute an injury that is legally compensable by means of lost profits. It has uniformly been the law, Kelley argues, that to recover damages in the form of lost profits a patentee must prove that, "but for" the infringement, it would have sold a product covered by the patent in suit to the customers who bought from the infringer. Under the circumstances of this case, in Kelley's view, the patent statute provides only for damages calculated as a reasonable royalty. Rite-Hite, on the other hand, argues that the only restriction on an award of actual lost profits damages for patent infringement is proof of causation-in-fact. A patentee, in its view, is entitled to all the profits it would have made on any of its products "but for" the infringement. Each party argues that a judgment in favor of the other would frustrate the purposes of the patent statute. Whether the lost profits at issue are legally compensable is a question of law, which we review *de novo.*

Our analysis of this question necessarily begins with the patent statute. Implementing the constitutional power under Article I, section 8, to secure to inventors the exclusive right to their discoveries, Congress has provided in 35 U.S.C. §284. The statute mandates that a claimant receive damages "adequate" to compensate for infringement. Section 284 further instructs that a damage award shall be "in no event less than a reasonable royalty"; the purpose of this alternative is not to direct the form of compensation, but to set a floor below which damage awards may not fall. Thus, the language of the statute is expansive rather than limiting. It affirmatively states that damages must be adequate, while providing only a lower limit and no other limitation.

The Supreme Court spoke to the question of patent damages in *General Motors,* stating that, in enacting §284, Congress sought to "ensure that the patent owner would in fact receive full compensation for 'any damages' [the patentee] suffered as a result of the infringement." *General Motors,* 461 U.S. at 654; *see also* H.R. Rep. No. 1587, 79th Cong., 2d Sess., 1 (1946) (the Bill was intended to allow recovery of "any damages the complainant can prove"); S. Rep. No. 1503, 79th Cong., 2d Sess., 2 (1946), (same). Thus, while the statutory text states tersely that the patentee receive "adequate" damages, the Supreme Court has interpreted this to mean that "adequate" damages should approximate those damages that will *fully compensate* the patentee for infringement. Further, the Court has cautioned against imposing limitations on patent infringement damages, stating: "When Congress wished to limit an element of recovery in a patent infringement action, it said so explicitly." *General Motors,* 461 U.S. at 653 (refusing to impose limitation on court's authority to award interest).

In *Aro Mfg. Co. v. Convertible Top Replacement Co.,* 377 U.S. 476 (1964), the Court discussed the statutory standard for measuring patent infringement damages, explaining:

> The question to be asked in determining damages is "how much had the Patent Holder and Licensee suffered by the infringement. And that question [is] primarily: had the Infringer not infringed, what would the Patentee Holder-Licensee have made?"

377 U.S. at 507. This surely states a "but for" test. In accordance with the Court's guidance, we have held that the general rule for determining actual damages to a patentee that is itself producing the patented item is to determine the sales and profits lost to the patentee because of the infringement. To recover lost profits damages, the patentee must show a reasonable probability that, "but for" the infringement, it would have made the sales that were made by the infringer. *Id.; King Instrument Corp. v. Otari Corp.,* 767 F.2d 853, 863 (Fed. Cir. 1985).

Panduit Corp. v. Stahlin Bros. Fibre Works, Inc., 575 F.2d 1152 (6th Cir. 1978), articulated a four-factor test that has since been accepted as a useful, but nonexclusive, way for a patentee to prove entitlement to lost profits damages. The *Panduit* test requires that a patentee establish: (1) demand for the patented product; (2) absence of acceptable non-infringing substitutes; (3) manufacturing and marketing capability to exploit the demand; and (4) the amount of the profit it would have made. *Panduit,* 575 F.2d at 1156. A showing under *Panduit* permits a court to reasonably infer that the lost profits claimed were in fact caused by the infringing sales, thus establishing a patentee's *prima facie* case with respect to "but for" causation. A patentee need not negate every possibility that the purchaser might not have purchased a product other than its own, absent the infringement. The patentee need only show that there was a reasonable probability that the sales would have been made "but for" the infringement. When the patentee establishes the reasonableness of this inference, *e.g.,* by satisfying the *Panduit* test, it has sustained the burden of proving entitlement to lost profits due to the infringing sales. The burden then shifts to the infringer to show that the inference is unreasonable for some or all of the lost sales.

Applying *Panduit,* the district court found that Rite-Hite had established "but for" causation. In the court's view, this was sufficient to prove entitlement to lost profits damages on the ADL-100. Kelley does not challenge that Rite-Hite meets the *Panduit* test and therefore has proven "but for" causation; rather, Kelley argues that damages for the ADL-100, even if in fact caused by the infringement, are not legally compensable because the ADL-100 is not covered by the patent in suit.

Preliminarily, we wish to affirm that the "test" for compensability of damages under §284 is not solely a "but for" test in the sense that an infringer must compensate a patentee for any and all damages that proceed from the act of patent infringement. Notwithstanding the broad language of §284, judicial relief cannot redress every conceivable harm that can be traced to an alleged wrongdoing. For example, remote consequences, such as a heart attack of the inventor or loss in value of shares of common stock of a patentee corporation caused indirectly by infringement are not compensable. Thus, along with establishing that a particular injury suffered by a patentee is a "but for" consequence of infringement, there may also be a background question whether the asserted injury is of the type for which the patentee may be compensated.

Judicial limitations on damages, either for certain classes of plaintiffs or for certain types of injuries have been imposed in terms of "proximate cause" or "foreseeability." Such labels have been judicial tools used to limit legal responsibility for the consequences of one's conduct that are too remote to justify compensation. The general principles expressed in the common law tell us that the question of legal compensability is one "to be determined on the facts of each case upon mixed considerations of logic, common sense, justice, policy and precedent." *See* 1 Street, *Foundations of Legal Liability* 110 (1906) (quoted in W. Page Keeton et al., *Prosser & Keeton on the Law of Torts* §42, at 279 (5th ed. 1984)).

We believe that under §284 of the patent statute, the balance between full compensation, which is the meaning that the Supreme Court has attributed to the statute, and the reasonable limits of liability encompassed by general principles of law can best be viewed in terms of reasonable, objective foreseeability. If a particular injury was or should have been reasonably foreseeable by an infringing competitor in the relevant market, broadly defined, that injury is generally compensable absent a persuasive reason to the contrary. Here, the court determined that Rite-Hite's lost sales of the ADL-100, a product that directly competed with the infringing product, were reasonably foreseeable. We agree with that conclusion. Being responsible for lost sales of a competitive product is surely foreseeable; such losses constitute the full compensation set forth by Congress, as interpreted by the Supreme Court, while staying well within the traditional meaning of proximate cause. Such lost sales should therefore clearly be compensable.

Recovery for lost sales of a device not covered by the patent in suit is not of course expressly provided for by the patent statute. Express language is not required, however. Statutes speak in general terms rather than specifically expressing every detail. Under the patent statute, damages should be awarded "where necessary to afford the plaintiff full compensation for the infringement." *General Motors,* 461 U.S. at 654. Thus, to refuse to award reasonably foreseeable damages necessary to make Rite-Hite whole would be inconsistent with the meaning of §284.

Kelley asserts that to allow recovery for the ADL-100 would contravene the policy reason for which patents are granted: "[T]o promote the progress of . . . the useful arts." U.S. Const., art. I, §8, cl. 8. Because an inventor is only entitled to exclusivity to the extent he or she has invented and disclosed a novel, non-obvious, and useful device, Kelley argues, a patent may never be used to restrict competition in the sale of products not covered by the patent in suit. In support, Kelley cites antitrust case law condemning the use of a patent as a means to obtain a "monopoly" on unpatented material.

These cases are inapposite to the issue raised here. The present case does not involve expanding the limits of the patent grant in violation of the antitrust laws; it simply asks, once infringement of a valid patent is found, what compensable injuries result from that infringement, *i.e.,* how may the patentee be made whole. Rite-Hite is not attempting to exclude its competitors from making, using, or selling a product not within the scope of its patent. The Truk Stop restraint was found to infringe the '847 patent, and Rite-Hite is simply seeking adequate compensation for that infringement; this is not an antitrust issue. Allowing compensation for such damage will "promote the Progress of . . . the useful Arts" by providing a stimulus to the development of new products and industries.

Kelley further asserts that, as a policy matter, inventors should be encouraged by the law to practice their inventions. This is not a meaningful or persuasive argument, at least in this context. A patent is granted in exchange for a patentee's disclosure of an invention, not for the patentee's use of the invention. There is no requirement in this country that a patentee make, use, or sell its patented invention. If a patentee's failure to practice a patented invention frustrates an important public need for the invention, a court need not enjoin infringement of the patent. *See* 35 U.S.C. §283 (1988). Accordingly, courts have in rare instances exercised their discretion to deny injunctive relief in order to protect the public interest. Whether a patentee sells its patented invention is not crucial in determining lost profits damages. Normally, if the patentee is not selling a product, by definition there can be no lost profits. However, in this case, Rite-Hite did sell its own patented products, the MDL-55 and the ADL-100 restraints.

Kelley next argues that to award lost profits damages on Rite-Hite's ADL-100s would be contrary to precedent. Citing *Panduit,* Kelley argues that case law regarding lost profits uniformly requires that "the intrinsic value of the patent in suit is the only proper basis for a lost profits award." Kelley argues that each prong of the *Panduit* test focuses on the patented invention; thus, Kelley asserts, Rite-Hite cannot obtain damages consisting of lost profits on a product that is not the patented invention.

Generally, the *Panduit* test has been applied when a patentee is seeking lost profits for a device covered by the patent in suit. However, *Panduit* is not the *sine qua non* for proving "but for" causation. If there are other ways to show that the infringement in fact caused the patentee's lost profits, there is no reason why another test should not be acceptable. Moreover, other fact situations may require different means of evaluation, and failure to meet the *Panduit* test does not *ipso facto* disqualify a loss from being compensable.

In any event, the only *Panduit* factor that arguably was not met in the present fact situation is the second one, absence of acceptable non-infringing substitutes. Establishment of this factor tends to prove that the patentee would not have lost the sales to a non-infringing third party rather than to the infringer. That, however, goes only to the question of proof. Here, the only substitute for the patented device was the ADL-100, another of the patentee's devices. Such a substitute was not an "acceptable, non-infringing substitute" within the meaning of *Panduit* because, being patented by Rite-Hite, it was not available to customers except from Rite-Hite. Rite-Hite therefore would not have lost the sales to a third party. The second *Panduit* factor thus has been met. If, on the other hand, the ADL-100 had not been patented and was found to be an acceptable substitute, that would have been a different story, and Rite-Hite would have had to prove that its customers would not have obtained the ADL-100 from a third party in order to prove the second factor of *Panduit*. . . .

Kelley has thus not provided, nor do we find, any justification in the statute, precedent, policy, or logic to limit the compensability of lost sales of a patentee's device that directly competes with the infringing device if it is proven that those lost sales were caused in fact by the infringement. Such lost sales are reasonably foreseeable and the award of damages is necessary to provide adequate compensation for infringement under 35 U.S.C. § 284. Thus, Rite-Hite's ADL-100 lost sales are legally compensable and we affirm the award of lost profits on the 3,283 sales lost to Rite-Hite's wholesale business in ADL-100 restraints.

NIES, Circuit Judge, with whom ARCHER, Chief Judge, SMITH, Senior Circuit Judge, and MAYER, Circuit Judge join, dissenting-in-part.

The majority uses the provision in 35 U.S.C. § 284 for "damages" as a tool to expand the property rights granted by a patent. I dissent.

No one disputes that Rite-Hite is entitled to "full compensation for any damages suffered as a result of the infringement." *General Motors Corp. v. Devex Corp.*, 461 U.S. 648, 653-54 (1983). "Damages," however, is a word of art. "Damages in a legal sense means the compensation which the law will award for an injury done." *Recovery in Patent Infringement Suits: Hearings on H.R. 5231 [later H.R. 5311] Before the Committee on Patents*, 79th Cong., 2nd Sess. 9 (1946) (statement of Conder C. Henry, Asst. Comm'r of Patents) (hereinafter "House Hearings"). Thus, the question is, "What are the injuries for which full compensation must be paid?"

The majority divorces "actual damages" from injury to patent rights. The majority holds that a patentee is entitled to recover its lost profits caused by the infringer's competition with the patentee's business in ADL restraints, products not incorporating the invention of the patent in suit but assertedly protected by other unlitigated patents. Indeed, the majority states a broader rule for the award of lost profits on any goods of the patentee with which the infringing device competes, even products in the public domain.

I would hold that the diversion of ADL-100 sales is not an injury to patentee's property rights granted by the '847 patent. To constitute legal injury for which lost profits may be awarded, the infringer must interfere with the patentee's property right to an exclusive market in goods embodying the invention of the patent in suit. The patentee's property rights do not extend to its market in other goods unprotected by the litigated patent. Rite-Hite was compensated for the lost profits for 80 sales associated with the MDL-55, the only product it sells embodying the '847 invention. That is the totality of any possible entitlement to lost profits. Under 35 U.S.C. § 284, therefore, Rite-Hite is entitled to "damages" calculated as a reasonable royalty on the remainder of Kelley's infringing restraints. . . .

C. Property Rights Granted by Patent

An examination of pre-1946 Supreme Court precedent discloses that the legal scope of actual damages for patent infringement was limited to the extent of the defendant's interference with the patentee's market in goods embodying the invention of the patent in suit. This limitation reflects the underlying public policy of the patent statute to promote commerce in new products for the public's benefit. More importantly, it protects the only property rights of a patentee which are protectable, namely those granted by the patent. The patentee obtained as its property an exclusive market in the patented goods. "[I]nfringement was a tortious taking of a part of that property." *Dowagiac Mfg. Co. v. Minnesota Moline Plow Co.*, 235 U.S. 641, 648 (1915).

[I]n the United States, the grant of a patent did not convey to the inventor a right to make, use and vend his invention despite the statutory language originally to that effect. In interpreting a patentee's rights in *Crown Die & Tool Co. v. Nye Tool & Machine Works*, 261 U.S. 24, 26 (1923), the Supreme Court explained that an inventor has a natural right to make, use and sell his invention, and that a patent augments an inventor's position by making that natural right *exclusive* for a limited time. The statutory language was interpreted to give a right to *preclude others* from interfering with the patentee's exclusivity in providing the patented goods to the public. *Id.* at 34.

An inventor is entitled to a patent by meeting the statutory requirements respecting disclosure of the invention. Prior commercialization of the invention has never been a requirement in our law to *obtain* a patent. An inventor is merely required to teach others his invention in his patent application. Thus, when faced with the question of whether a patentee was entitled to enjoin an infringer despite the patentee's failure to use its invention, the Supreme Court held for the patentee. *Continental Paper Bag*, 210 U.S. at 424-430. Congress provided a right to exclusive use and to deny that privilege would destroy that right. *Id.* at 430. An injunction preserves the patentee's exclusive right to market embodiments of the patented invention.

These clearly established principles, however, do not lead to the conclusion that the patentee's failure to commercialize plays no role in determining damages. That the *quid pro quo* for *obtaining* a patent is disclosure of the invention does not dictate the answer to the question of the legal scope of damages. The patent system was not designed merely to build up a library of information by disclosure, valuable though that is, but to get new products into the marketplace during the period of exclusivity so that the public receives full benefits from the grant. The Congress of the fledgling country did not act so quickly in enacting the Patent Act of 1790 merely to further intellectual pursuits. . . .

Like the owner of a farm, a patentee may let his property lay fallow. In doing so, "he has but suppressed his own." *Bement*, 186 U.S. at 90. But it is anomalous to hold that Congress, by providing an incentive for the patentee to enter the market, intended the patentee to be rewarded the same for letting his property lay fallow during the term of the patent as for making the investment necessary to commercializing a new product or licensing others to do so, in order that the public benefits from the invention. The *status quo* may serve the patentee's interest, but that is not the only consideration. The patent grant "was never designed for [an inventor's] exclusive profit or advantage." *Kendall v. Winsor,* 62 U.S. (21 How.) 322, 328 (1858). . . .

G. "Foreseeability" Is Not the Test for Patent Damages

In the majority's view, the consideration of patent rights ends upon a finding of infringement. The separate question of damages under its test does not depend on patent rights but only on foreseeable competitive injury. This position cannot be squared with the premise that compensation is due only for injury to patent rights. Thus, the majority's foreseeability standard contains a false premise, namely, that the "relevant market" can be "broadly defined" to include all competitive truck restraints made by the patentee. The *relevant* market for determining damages is confined to the market for the invention in which the patentee holds exclusive property rights. . . . To paraphrase *Brunswick Corp,* 429 U.S. at 489, "[Plaintiffs] must prove more than injury causally linked to any illegal presence in the market [i.e., the infringing goods]. Plaintiffs must prove [patent infringement] injury, which is to say injury of the type the [patent] laws were intended to prevent." The injury, thus, must be to the protected market in goods made in accordance with the patent, not unprotected truck restraints. In sum, patent rights determine not only infringement but also damages.

The majority does not give a passing nod to long-standing precedent restricting a patentee's legal injury to diversion of sales it would have made of products containing the patented invention, much less does it explain why the precedent should be abandoned. It simply declares *ipse dixit:* "Whether a patentee sells its patented invention is not crucial in determining lost profits damages." While proximate cause limitations are acknowledged, the majority sees no problem here because the infringing devices were designed to compete with the ADL-100 devices and the "clear purpose of the patent law [is] to redress competitive damages resulting from infringement of the patent." This reasoning awards patent infringement damages as if for a kind of unfair competition with the patentee's business. However, infringement of a patent is not a species of common law unfair competition; it is a distinct and independent federal statutory claim. Moreover, the clear purpose of the patent system is to stimulate a patentee to put new products into the marketplace during the patent term, not to compensate the patentee "fully" while the public benefit from the invention is delayed until the invention falls into the public domain. Compensation in the form of lost profits for injury to the exclusive market in patented goods has provided the incentive to achieve that objective. . . .

Nothing in the statute supports the majority's "foreseeability" rule as the sole basis for patent damages. To the contrary, no-fault liability is imposed on "innocent" infringers, those who have no knowledge of the existence of a patent until suit is filed. Damages are recoverable for up to six years of unknowing infringement before suit. 35 U.S.C. § 286 (1988). "Foreseeability" is a wholly anomalous concept to interject as the basis for determining legal injury for patent infringement. While unknowing infringers cannot "foresee" any injury to the patentee, they are subject to liability for damages, including lost profits, for competition with the patentee's patented goods. Now they will be liable for diverting sales of the patentee's unprotected competitive products as well. . . .

The majority goes on to find the award of damages for lost sales of ADL-100s a *foreseeable* injury for infringement of the '847 patent. This is a remarkable finding. The facts are that Rite-Hite began marketing its ADL-100 motorized restraint in 1980. Kelley put out its Truk Stop restraint in June 1982. There is no dispute in this case that Kelley "designed around" the protection afforded by any patent related to the ADL-100 with which Kelley's Truk Stop restraint was intended to compete. Two years later, the '847 patent in suit issued on the later-developed alternative hook technology used in the MDL-55. Kelley would have to have had prescient vision to foresee that it would be held an infringer of the unknown claims of the subsequently issued '847 patent and that its *lawful competition* with the ADL-100 would be transformed into a compensable injury.

Kelley would also have had to foresee that, for the first time in over 200 years of patent infringement suits, a court would extend protection to a part of a patentee's business which is not dependent on the patentee's use of the patented technology. Moreover, the Supreme Court and all sister circuits which have spoken on the legal scope of damages have, without exception, rejected the majority's expansive view that the only limitations on patent infringement damages are (1) satisfaction of a "but-for" test applied to "foreseeable" injuries, and (2) the amount must not be too low. . . .

If damages are awardable based on lost sales of a patentee's business in established products not protected by the patent in suit, the patentee not only has an easier case as a matter of proof, but also would receive *greater* benefits in the form of lost profits on its established products than if the patentee had made the investment necessary to launch a new product. That lost profits on an established line are likely to be greater than on a new device cannot be gainsaid. This result is not in accordance with the purpose of the patent statute. Actual damages are meant to compensate a patentee for losing the reward of the marketplace which the patentee's use of the invention would otherwise reap. Without such loss, Congress has mandated compensation in the form of a reasonable royalty.

H. The ADL-100 Patents

Not only is the majority's basic idea of legal injury unsound based on "foreseeability" but also its specific test is equally flawed. For convenience, I have referred to the ADL-100 as "unprotected," meaning not covered by the patent in suit. However, a key factor in the majority's decision awarding damages for lost sales of the ADL-100 is that the "device" is "patented." The majority does not, nor did the parties, discuss what inventions the one or more patents on the ADL-100 cover. Nevertheless, the majority declares the ADL-100 provides the only alternative technology. While it is inappropriate for an appellate court to make findings, the finding by the majority is erroneous if one examines the record independently. There are other mechanisms for securing trucks to loading docks. Indeed, the Patent Office considered Kelley's Truk-Stop sufficiently different from the prior '847 patent to grant Kelley its own patent. Unfortunately for Kelley, this court earlier upheld the finding that its different structure was sufficient similar to the '847 patent to constitute infringement. But there were other alternatives which could be substituted. In any event, the one or more patents on technology used in the ADL-100 were never asserted against Kelley, and the validity of those patents is untested. If those patents are invalid, the majority's analysis collapses. As stated in *Lear, Inc. v. Adkins*, 395 U.S. 653, 668 (1969): "[F]ederal law requires that all ideas in general circulation be dedicated to the common good unless they are protected by a *valid* patent." (Emphasis added.)

GRAIN PROCESSING CORP. v. AMERICAN MAIZE-PRODUCTS CO.

185 F.3d 1341 (Fed. Cir. 1999)

RADER, Circuit Judge.

The United States District Court for the Northern District of Indiana denied Grain Processing Corporation lost profits for American Maize-Products' infringement of U.S. Patent No. 3,849,194 (the '194 patent). The district court instead awarded Grain Processing a 3% royalty on American Maize's infringing sales.

The district court found that American Maize proved that a noninfringing substitute was available, though not on the market or for sale, during the period of infringement. The court found further that this substitute was acceptable to all purchasers of the infringing product and concluded that American Maize rebutted the inference of "but for" causation for Grain Processing's alleged lost sales. Upholding the district court's findings and conclusions, this court affirms.

I.

This appeal culminates the lengthy and complex history of this case, spanning more than eighteen years and eight prior judicial opinions, three by this court. The patent featured in this infringement suit involves maltodextrins, a versatile family of food additives made from starch. Commercial food manufacturers purchase hundreds of millions of pounds of maltodextrins annually from producers such as Grain Processing and American Maize.

Maltodextrins serve well as food additives because they are bland in taste and clear in solution. They do not affect the natural taste or color of other ingredients in food products. Maltodextrins also improve the structure or behavior of food products. For instance, they inhibit crystal growth, add body, improve binding and viscosity, and preserve food properties in low temperatures. Consequently, food manufacturers use maltodextrins in a wide variety of products such as frostings, syrups, drinks, cereals, and frozen foods.

Maltodextrins belong to a category of chemical products known as "starch hydrolysates." Producers make starch hydrolysates by putting starch through hydrolysis, a chemical reaction with water. Hydrolysis breaks down the starch and converts some of it to dextrose. With adjustments, this process yields more dextrose. For instance, additional enzymes, time extensions, and increases in temperature or pH enhance the reaction. After hydrolysis, the producer typically refines, spray-dries, and packages the starch hydrolysate for sale in powder form.

Maltodextrins are starch hydrolysates that have a "dextrose equivalent" of less than 20. Dextrose equivalence (D.E.) is a percentage measurement of the "reducing sugars content" of the starch hydrolysate. D.E. reflects the degree to which the hydrolysis process broke down the starch and converted it into dextrose. Converting more starch into dextrose increases the D.E. of the resulting starch hydrolysate. Hence, pure starch has a D.E. of zero, pure dextrose a D.E. of 100. The D.E. value indicates functional properties of a maltodextrin. A 15 D.E. maltodextrin, for example, is slightly sweeter and more soluble than a 5 D.E. maltodextrin. On the other hand, the 5 D.E. maltodextrin has more prevalent binding, bodying, and crystal inhibiting properties.

Grain Processing is the assignee of the '194 patent, "Low D.E. Starch Conversion Products," which claims maltodextrins with particular attributes,

and processes for producing them. The claimed invention represents improvements in the "heavily explored" field of starch hydrolysates. Claim 12, the sole
claim on appeal, reads:

12. A *waxy* starch hydrolysate having

1. *a dextrose equivalent value between about 5 and about 25;*
2. *a descriptive ratio greater than about 2,* said descriptive ratio being the quotient
    obtained by dividing the sum of the percentage of saccharides, dry basis, hav-
    ing a degree of polymerization of 1 to 6, by the dextrose equivalent value;
3. a monosaccharide content in the range of from about 0.1 percent by weight,
    to about 2.4 percent by weight, dry basis;
4. a dissaccharide content in the range of from about 1.3 percent to about 9.7
    percent, by weight, dry basis; and
5. being further characterized as capable of producing an aqueous solution of
    exceptional clarity and substantially complete lack of opaqueness when said
    hydrolysate is added to water.

(Emphasis added.)

Grain Processing has manufactured and sold a line of maltodextrins under the
"Maltrin" brand name since 1969. The Maltrin line includes "Maltrin M100," a
10 D.E. maltodextrin. None of the Maltrin products, including M100, fall within
claim 12 because they are all made from a non-waxy starch.

American Maize began selling maltodextrins in 1974. It made and sold
several types of maltodextrins, including "Lo-Dex 10," a 10 D.E. waxy starch
maltodextrin. American Maize sold Lo-Dex 10 (called Fro-Dex 10 before 1982)
during the entire time Grain Processing owned the '194 patent rights, from
1979 until the patent expired in 1991. During this time, however, American
Maize used four different processes for producing Lo-Dex 10. The changes in
American Maize's production processes, and the slight chemical differences
in the Lo-Dex 10 from each process, are central to the lost profits issue in this
appeal.

American Maize used a first process (Process I) from June 1974 to July 1982.
In Process I, American Maize used a single enzyme (an alpha amylase) to facilitate starch hydrolysis. American Maize controlled the reaction to produce a
starch hydrolysate with the desired properties, including D.E. value.

Grain Processing sued American Maize for infringement on May 12, 1981,
based on American Maize's Lo-Dex 10 sales as well as sales of two other maltodextrins, Lo-Dex 5 and ARD 2370. Grain Processing asserted all fourteen claims
of the '194 patent, including product and process claims. The district court
bifurcated the infringement and damages issues for trial.

In August 1982, while the suit was pending, American Maize reduced the
amount of alpha amylase enzyme in its process to lower its production costs.
To achieve the same end result with less enzyme, American Maize continued
the reaction longer. American Maize used this process (Process II) exclusively
to produce Lo-Dex 10 from August 1982 to February 1988. Grain Processing
asserted in its lawsuit that Process II Lo-Dex 10 also infringed the '194 patent.

American Maize contended that Lo-Dex 10 (by both Processes I and II) did
not infringe claim 12 of the '194 patent because it did not have a "descriptive
ratio greater than about 2," as required by the claim. Descriptive ratio (D.R.) is
a function of the D.E. measurement. According to the formula in claim 12, D.R.
is inversely proportional to D.E. Because different scientific tests yield slightly

different D.E. measurements, the resulting D.R. values derived therefrom also vary slightly.

When Grain Processing accused American Maize of infringement, Grain Processing used the "Schoorl test" for measuring the D.E. of Lo-Dex 10. American Maize, on the other hand, used the "Lane-Eynon test," which it believed was the "industry standard," to measure D.E. The Schoorl test tends to yield a lower D.E. and therefore a higher D.R. than Lane-Eynon. Under the Lane-Eynon test, American Maize's measurements revealed that Lo-Dex 10 did not infringe claim 12, because all of its Lo-Dex 10 samples had a D.R. of less than 1.9. Grain Processing's Schoorl tests on the same samples, however, yielded a D.R. of greater than 2.

Following a bench trial, the district court held that Lo-Dex 10 did not infringe any of the claims because it did not meet the "exceptional clarity" limitation. This court reversed, holding that Lo-Dex 10 met the "exceptional clarity" limitation and therefore infringed claim 12 and its dependent claims 13-14. This court's decision, like the district court's, did not resolve the discrepancy between tests for measuring D.E. value. The district court subsequently entered an injunction on October 21, 1988, prohibiting American Maize from making or selling Lo-Dex 10 or any other waxy starch hydrolysate that infringed claims 12-14.

In response to the injunction, American Maize developed yet another process for producing Lo-Dex 10. In this new process (Process III), American Maize used more alpha amylase, adjusted the temperature and pH, and reduced the reaction time. American Maize used Process III exclusively to produce Lo-Dex 10 from March 1988 to April 1991.

American Maize believed Process III would yield a more uniform, noninfringing output of Lo-Dex 10. In fact, American Maize was "determined to avoid shipping a single bag of Lo-Dex 10 with a D.R. exceeding 1.9." Process III worked as American Maize intended. American Maize's measurements—using the Lane-Eynon test—showed that Process III Lo-Dex 10 samples all had descriptive ratios of less than 1.9 and therefore did not infringe. Moreover, American Maize's customers did not discern any difference between Process III Lo-Dex 10 and Lo-Dex 10 from Processes I or II.

In 1990, Grain Processing tested commercial samples of American Maize's Process III Lo-Dex 10. Grain Processing again used the Schoorl test to measure D.E. Grain Processing's measurements showed that American Maize's Process III output had a D.R. value of greater than 1.9 and therefore infringed. Grain Processing filed a contempt motion in the district court.

The district court initially held American Maize in contempt for continuing to sell an infringing product. However, the district court modified the order in 1991 to allow American Maize to use any scientifically acceptable method to show noninfringement. Because American Maize's Process III output consistently had a D.R. of less than 1.9 using Lane-Eynon, the district court ruled that it did not infringe. Grain Processing appealed. This court reversed in a nonprecedential opinion. Because the prosecution history of the '194 patent indicates that the inventor used the Schoorl test to measure D.E. of his invention, this court held that the Schoorl test, not Lane-Eynon, determines the relevant values in this case.

American Maize then adopted a fourth process (Process IV) for producing Lo-Dex 10. In Process IV, American Maize added a second enzyme, glucoamylase, to the reaction. Glucoamylase breaks down starch to a shorter average saccharide length. This shorter saccharide length yields a smaller D.R. without affecting D.E.

From the time American Maize began experimenting with the glucoamylase-alpha amylase combination, or the "dual enzyme method," it took only two weeks to perfect the reaction and begin mass producing Lo-Dex 10 using Process IV. According to the finding of the district court, this two-week development and production time is "practically instantaneous" for large-scale production. American Maize simply experimented with different combinations of glucoamylase and alpha amylase, along with pH, heat, and time of the reaction. American Maize did not change any equipment, source starches, or other ingredients from Process III. Glucoamylase has been commercially available and its effect in starch hydrolysis widely known since the early 1970's, before the '194 patent issued. American Maize had not used Process IV to produce Lo-Dex earlier because the high cost of glucoamylase makes Process IV more expensive than the other processes.

The parties agree that Process IV yielded only noninfringing Lo-Dex 10 and that consumers discerned no difference between Process IV Lo-Dex 10 and Lo-Dex 10 made by Processes I-III. American Maize used Process IV exclusively to produce Lo-Dex 10 from April 1991 until the '194 patent expired in November 1991, and then switched back to the cheaper Process III.

The district court commenced the damages portion of the trial on July 10, 1995. Grain Processing claimed lost profits in the form of lost sales of Maltrin M100, price erosion, and American Maize's accelerated market entry after the patent expired. Grain Processing further claimed that, for any of American Maize's infringing sales not covered by a lost profits award, Grain Processing should receive a 28% royalty. After a three day bench trial, the district court denied lost profits and determined that a 3% reasonable royalty was adequate to compensate Grain Processing. The royalty applies to all of American Maize's Lo-Dex 10 sales from May 12, 1981 (when Grain Processing filed suit) to April 1991 (when American Maize converted to Process IV, thereby producing a noninfringing product).

The trial court determined that Grain Processing could not establish causation for lost profits, because American Maize "could have produced" a noninfringing substitute 10 D.E. maltodextrin using Process IV. "With infringing Lo-Dex 10 banned, the customers' substitute is non-infringing Lo-Dex 10." *Id.* at 1392 (emphasis added). American Maize did not actually produce and sell this noninfringing substitute until April 1991, seven months before the '194 patent expired, but the district court nevertheless found that its availability "scotches [Grain Processing's] request for lost-profits damages."

The district court also found that American Maize's production cost difference between infringing and noninfringing Lo-Dex 10 effectively capped the reasonable royalty award. American Maize showed that it cost only 2.3% more to make noninfringing Process IV products than it did to make infringing Process I-III products. The district court also found that "buyers viewed as equivalent" the Process I-III and Process IV output: "Lo-Dex 10 made by Process IV had a lower D.R. [which is what makes it noninfringing] . . . but no one argues that any customer cared a whit about the product's descriptive ratio." The district court concluded that under these facts, American Maize, when faced with a hypothetical offer to license the '194 patent in 1974 (or to renegotiate the rate in 1979, when Grain Processing acquired the patent rights and its ability to collect damages began), would not have paid more than a 3% royalty rate. The court reasoned that this rate would reflect the cost difference between Processes I-III and Process IV, while also taking into account possible cost fluctuations (due to fluctuating enzyme prices) and the elimination of American Maize's risk of producing an infringing product, despite its best efforts. The court concluded that if Grain Processing had insisted on a rate greater than 3% in the hypothetical negotiations, American Maize instead would have chosen to invest in producing noninfringing Lo-Dex 10 with Process IV.

Grain Processing appealed the district court's denial of lost profits, alleging that American Maize cannot escape liability for lost profits on the basis of "a noninfringing substitute that did not exist during, and was not developed until after, the period of infringement." This court reversed and remanded. This court observed that "[t]he [district] court denied [Grain Processing's] request for lost profits because [American Maize] developed a new process of producing Lo-Dex 10 in 1991 [after years of infringement] that did not infringe the '194 patent." This court noted, however, that the mere fact of "switching to a noninfringing product years after the period of infringement [does] not establish the presence of a noninfringing substitute during the period of infringement." (citing *State Indus., Inc. v. Mor-Flo Industries, Inc.*; *Panduit Corp. v. Stahlin Brothers Fibre Works, Inc.*). This court noted that a product or process must be "available or on the market at the time of infringement" to qualify as an acceptable non-infringing substitute.

On remand, the district court again denied Grain Processing lost profits. The district court found that Process IV was "available" throughout the period of infringement. This factual finding, the district court explained, was not based merely on "the simple fact of switching [to Process IV]" but rather on several subsidiary factual findings regarding the technology of enzyme-assisted starch hydrolysis and the price and market structure for the patentee's and accused infringer's products. The trial court found that American Maize could obtain all of the materials needed for Process IV, including the glucoamylase enzyme, before 1979, and that the effects of the enzymes in starch hydrolysis were well known in the field by that time. American Maize also had all of the necessary equipment, know-how, and experience to implement Process IV whenever it chose to do so during the time of infringement. "The sole reason [American Maize did not use Process IV to produce Lo-Dex 10 prior to 1991] was economic: glucoamalyse is more expensive than the alpha amylase enzyme that [American Maize] had been using." *Id.* American Maize did not make the substitution sooner because its test results using the Lane-Eynon method convinced it that it was not infringing.

The district court concluded that "the profit lost from infringement is the cost and market price difference attributable to using glucoamylase." The court did not further address the amount of damages, having already found in that the infringement did not affect the market price of Lo-Dex 10, and having figured the 2.3% cost increase into the 3% royalty award.

The district court also went on to explain its denial of lost profits "from a different angle." The district court stated that *Panduit* and *Rite-Hite Corp. v. Kelley Co., Inc.,* 56 F.3d 1538 (Fed. Cir. 1995) (en banc) "identify demand for the patented product as an essential element of the patent holder's lost-profits claim." The district court recognized that there was "substantial demand for D.E. 10 maltodextrins." However, the district court stated the dispositive question as "whether there is economically significant demand for a product having all . . . attributes [of the claim in suit]," *i.e.*, whether consumers demand every claimed feature. The court found no such demand in this case because "[t]wo of the essential elements of the claim—that the starch be 'waxy' and that the 'descriptive ratio [be] greater than about 2'—are irrelevant to consumers." The court concluded that Grain Processing "does not have a patent on D.E. 10 maltodextrins, the economically significant product, and therefore cannot recover lost profits damages on account of [American Maize's] infringement."

Grain Processing appeals the district court's decision.

II.

Upon proof of infringement, Title 35, Section 284 provides that "the court shall award [the patent owner] damages adequate to compensate for the infringement but in no event less than a reasonable royalty for the use made of the invention by the infringer." 35 U.S.C. §284 (1998). The phrase "damages adequate to compensate" means "full compensation for 'any damages' [the patent owner] suffered as a result of the infringement." *General Motors Corp. v. Devex Corp.*, 461 U.S. 648, 654 (1983). Full compensation includes any foreseeable lost profits the patent owner can prove. *See Rite-Hite*, 56 F.3d at 1545-47.

To recover lost profits, the patent owner must show "causation in fact," establishing that "but for" the infringement, he would have made additional profits. *See King Instruments Corp. v. Perego*, 65 F.3d 941, 952 (Fed. Cir. 1995). When basing the alleged lost profits on lost sales, the patent owner has an initial burden to show a reasonable probability that he would have made the asserted sales "but for" the infringement. *See id.; Rite-Hite*, 56 F.3d at 1545. Once the patent owner establishes a reasonable probability of "but for" causation, "the burden then shifts to the accused infringer to show that [the patent owner's 'but for' causation claim] is unreasonable for some or all of the lost sales." *Id.* at 1544.

At trial, American Maize proved that Grain Processing's lost sales assertions were unreasonable. The district court adopted Grain Processing's initial premise that, because Grain Processing and American Maize competed head-to-head as the only significant suppliers of 10 D.E. maltodextrins, consumers logically would purchase Maltrin 100 if Lo-Dex 10 were not available. *See Lam, Inc. v. Johns-Manville Corp.*, 718 F.2d 1056, 1065 (Fed. Cir. 1983) (holding that the patent owner may satisfy his initial burden by inference in a two-supplier market). However, the district court found that American Maize proved that Process IV was available and that Process IV Lo-Dex 10 was an acceptable substitute for the claimed invention. In the face of this noninfringing substitute, Grain Processing could not prove lost profits.

American Maize concedes that it did not make or sell Lo-Dex 10 from Process IV until 1991, after the period of infringement. However, an alleged substitute not "on the market" or "for sale" during the infringement can figure prominently in determining whether a patentee would have made additional profits "but for" the infringement. As this court stated in *Grain Processing VII*, "to be an acceptable non-infringing substitute, the product or process must have been available *or* on the market at the time of infringement." (emphasis added). This statement is an apt summary of this court's precedent, which permits available alternatives—including but not limited to products on the market—to preclude lost profits damages.

In *Aro Manufacturing,* the Supreme Court stated that the statutory measure of "damages" is "the difference between [the patent owner's] pecuniary condition after the infringement, and what his condition would have been if the infringement had not occurred." *Aro Mfg. Co. v. Convertible Top Replacement Co.,* 377 U.S. 476, 507 (1964). The determinative question, the Supreme Court stated, is: "had the Infringer not infringed, what would the Patent Holder-Licensee have made?" *Aro,* 377 U.S. at 507. The "but for" inquiry therefore requires a reconstruction of the market, as it would have developed absent the infringing product, to determine what the patentee "would . . . have made."

Reconstructing the market, by definition a hypothetical enterprise, requires the patentee to project economic results that did not occur. To prevent the hypothetical from lapsing into pure speculation, this court requires sound economic proof of the nature of the market and likely outcomes with infringement factored out of the economic picture. Within this framework, trial courts, with this court's approval, consistently permit patentees to present market reconstruction theories showing all of the ways in which they would have been better off in the "but for world," and accordingly to recover lost profits in a wide variety of forms. *See, e.g., King Instruments,* 65 F.3d at 953 (upholding award for lost sales of patentee's unpatented goods that compete with the infringing goods); *Rite-Hite,* 56 F.3d at 1550 (holding that a patentee may recover lost profits on components that have a functional relationship with the patented invention); *Brooktree Corp.,* 977 F.2d at 1580 (upholding award for price erosion due to infringer's marketing activities). In sum, courts have given patentees significant latitude to prove and recover lost profits for a wide variety of foreseeable economic effects of the infringement.

By the same token, a fair and accurate reconstruction of the "but for" market also must take into account, where relevant, alternative actions the infringer foreseeably would have undertaken had he not infringed. Without the infringing product, a rational would-be infringer is likely to offer an acceptable noninfringing alternative, if available, to compete with the patent owner rather than leave the market altogether. The competitor in the "but for" marketplace is hardly likely to surrender its complete market share when faced with a patent, if it can compete in some other lawful manner. Moreover, only by comparing the patented invention to its next-best available alternative(s) — regardless of whether the alternative(s) were actually produced and sold during the infringement — can the court discern the market value of the patent owner's exclusive right, and therefore his expected profit or reward, had the infringer's activities not prevented him from taking full economic advantage of this right. Thus, an accurate reconstruction of the hypothetical "but for" market takes into account any alternatives available to the infringer.

Accordingly, this court in *Slimfold Manufacturing Co. v. Kinkead Industries, Inc.* held that an available technology not on the market during the infringement can constitute a noninfringing alternative. 932 F.2d 1453 (Fed. Cir. 1991). In *Slimfold,* the patent owner (Slimfold) claimed lost profits on its bi-fold doors with a patented pivot and guide rod assembly. This court noted, however, that Slimfold did not show "that the alleged infringer [Kinkead] would not have made a substantial portion or the same number of sales *had it continued with its old hardware* or with the hardware utilized by any of the other companies." *Id.* at 1458 (emphasis added). On the basis of this noninfringing substitute, which was not on the market at the time of infringement, this court affirmed the district court's denial of lost profits. This court determined that the record supported the district court's finding that this noninfringing "old hardware" was available to Kinkead at the time of the infringement. Specifically, Kinkead and others had used the substitute technology on other doors before the period of infringement. *See id.* Furthermore, consumers considered Kinkead's noninfringing alternative an acceptable substitute for the infringing doors. *See id.* Therefore, this court upheld the district court's award of a "small" royalty, rather than lost profits. *Id.* at 1458-59.

Several opinions of this court have noted that "market sales" provide significant evidence of availability as a substitute. These cases illustrate that market sales of an acceptable noninfringing substitute often suffice alone to defeat a case for lost profits. Focusing exclusively on this market sales principle, these opinions did not address availability without market sales. *See, e.g., Panduit,* 575 F.2d at 1162 ("[t]hat Stahlin's customers, no longer able to buy the patented product from Stahlin, were willing to buy something else from Stahlin, does not establish that there was *on the market* during the period of infringement a product which customers in general were . . . 'willing to buy in place of the infringing product.'") (emphasis added). Because these previous cases addressed only market sales, they did not consider that available substitutes, though not literally on sale, can affect market behavior as in the present case.

Nor does *Zygo* support Grain Processing's position equating availability with offers for sale. In *Zygo,* this court reviewed for clear error the district court's factual finding that the infringer's "SIRIs" interferometer was not an acceptable noninfringing substitute. *Zygo,* 79 F.3d at 1571. Like the accused infringer in the *Slimfold* case, the infringer in *Zygo* had "stopped marketing" the SIRIS when it began marketing the infringing interferometer. *See id.* In the words of this court, "[t]he central damages issue on appeal is whether . . . Wyko's SIRIS interferometer was . . . an *acceptable* noninfringing alternative. . . ." *Id.* (emphasis added). On that "central" point, this court noted "the insufficiency of the [district] court's findings" that the SIRIS interferometer was not acceptable, and observed that "the record evidence, while sparse, suggests a contrary conclusion." *Id.* Therefore, this court remanded for additional factual findings. *Id.* In addition to holding that the district court's decision lacked sufficient factual support, this court also opined: "[i]t is axiomatic . . . that if a device is not available for purchase, a defendant cannot argue that the device is an acceptable noninfringing alternative. . . ." *Id.* This statement beyond the premises necessary to resolve the legal issues in *Zygo* did not alter the standards for availability applied in the earlier *Slimfold* case and in subsequent cases. *See Gargoyles, Inc. v. United States,* 113 F.3d 1572 (Fed. Cir. 1997) (denying lost profits because a substitute that was not on sale was "available" to the relevant consumer, the Army); *Minco,* 95 F.3d at 1119 (considering allegedly available substitutes that were not on sale during the infringement); *Minnesota Mining & Mfg. Co.,* 976 F.2d at 1579 (determining that the infringer had an alternative available from a supplier in Europe, but that it was not acceptable). Rather, at most it reflects a finding on the record in *Zygo* that availability of the substitute in that case depended on direct market sales.

Grain Processing asserts that permitting the infringer to show substitute availability without market sales, thereby avoiding lost profits, under compensates for infringement. Section 284, however, sets the floor for "damages adequate to compensate for the infringement" as "a reasonable royalty." 35 U.S.C. § 284.

Thus, the statute specifically envisions a reasonable royalty as a form of adequate compensation. While "damages adequate to compensate" means "full compensation," *General Motors,* 461 U.S. at 654, "full compensation" does not entitle Grain Processing to lost profits in the absence of "but for" causation. *Rite-Hite,* 56 F.3d at 1545. Moreover, although Grain Processing stresses that American Maize should not reap the benefit of its "choice" to infringe rather than use the more expensive Process IV, Grain Processing does not allege willful infringement and the record shows none. To the extent that Grain Processing feels undercompensated, it must point out a reversible error in the district court's fact-finding, reasoning, or legal basis for denying lost profits or in its reasonable royalty determination.

III.

This court next turns to the district court's findings that Process IV was in fact "available" to American Maize for producing Lo-Dex 10 no later than October, 1979, and that consumers would consider Process IV Lo-Dex 10 an acceptable substitute.

The critical time period for determining availability of an alternative is the period of infringement for which the patent owner claims damages, *i.e.,* the "accounting period." Switching to a noninfringing substitute after the accounting period does not alone show availability of the noninfringing substitute during this critical time. When an alleged alternative is not on the market during the accounting period, a trial court may reasonably infer that it was not available as a noninfringing substitute at that time. The accused infringer then has the burden to overcome this inference by showing that the substitute was available during the accounting period. Mere speculation or conclusory assertions will not suffice to overcome the inference. After all, the infringer chose to produce the infringing, rather than noninfringing, product. Thus, the trial court must proceed with caution in assessing proof of the availability of substitutes not actually sold during the period of infringement. Acceptable substitutes that the infringer proves were available during the accounting period can preclude or limit lost profits; substitutes only theoretically possible will not.

In this case, the district court did not base its finding that Process IV was available no later than October 1979 on speculation or possibilities, but rather on several specific, concrete factual findings, none of which Grain Processing challenges on appeal. The district court found that American Maize could readily obtain all of the materials needed for Process IV, including the glucoamylase enzyme, before 1979. The court also found that the effects of the enzymes in starch hydrolysis were well known in the field at that time. Furthermore, the court found that American Maize had all of the necessary equipment, know-how, and experience to use Process IV to make Lo-Dex 10, whenever it chose to do so during the time it was instead using Processes I, II or III. American Maize "did not have to 'invent around' the patent," the district court observed; "all it had to do was use a glucoamaylase enzyme in its production process."

The trial court also explained that "the sole reason [American Maize did not use Process IV prior to 1991] was economic: glucoamylase is more expensive than the alpha amylase enzyme American Maize had been using," and American Maize reasonably believed it had a noninfringing product. While the high cost of a necessary material can conceivably render a substitute "unavailable," the facts of this case show that glucoamylase was not prohibitively expensive to American

Maize. The district court found that American Maize's "substantial profit margins" on Lo-Dex 10 were sufficient for it to absorb the 2.3% cost increase using glucoamylase.

Moreover, the district court's unchallenged finding that there is no "economically significant demand for a product having all of the [claimed] attributes" supports its conclusion of availability. Consumers demand "low-dextrose maltodextrins of which the patented product is just one *exemplar.*" Because consumers find the "waxy" and "descriptive ratio" elements of claim 12 "irrelevant," the prospect of an available, acceptable noninfringing substitute expands because a competitor may be able to drop or replace the "irrelevant" elements from its product. *Compare Rite-Hite,* 56 F.3d 1538 (upholding lost profits award for patentee's vehicle restraint—not covered by the patent in suit—because the patentee could exclude alleged substitute products with another patent) *with King Instrument,* 72 F.3d 855 (upholding only a *partial* award of lost profits for patentee's tape rewinder—not covered by any patent—due to the availability of alternatives acceptable to some consumers). Grain Processing cannot exclude Process IV Lo-Dex 10 because it does not have a patent on 10 D.E. maltodextrins, "the economically significant product" as the district court stated, but rather on a particular variety of 10 D.E. maltodextrins.

This court therefore does not detect, and the parties do not suggest, clear error in the district court's factual findings on the availability of Process IV. These factual findings support the district court's conclusion that Process IV was available to American Maize for making noninfringing Lo-Dex 10, no later than October 1991. American Maize had the necessary chemical materials, the equipment, the know-how and experience, and the economic incentive to produce Lo-Dex 10 by Process IV throughout the entire accounting period. Accordingly, this court holds that the district court did not clearly err in finding that Process IV Lo-Dex 10 was an available alternative throughout the accounting period.

Whether and to what extent American Maize's alleged alternative prevents Grain Processing from showing lost sales of Maltrin 100 depends not only on whether and when the alternative was available, but also on whether and to what extent it was acceptable as a substitute in the relevant market. Consumer demand defines the relevant market and relative substitutability among products therein. Important factors shaping demand may include consumers' intended use for the patentee's product, similarity of physical and functional attributes of the patentee's product to alleged competing products, and price. Where the alleged substitute differs from the patentee's product in one or more of these respects, the patentee often must adduce economic data supporting its theory of the relevant market in order to show "but for" causation. *See BIC,* 1 F.3d at 1218.

In this case, the parties vigorously dispute the precise scope of the relevant market. The district court's uncontroverted factual findings, however, render this dispute moot. In the eyes of consumers, according to the district court, Process IV Lo-Dex 10 was the same product, for the same price, from the same supplier as Lo-Dex 10 made by other processes. Process IV Lo-Dex 10 was a perfect substitute for previous versions, and therefore Grain Processing's efforts to show a distinct 10 D.E. maltodextrin market do not assist its lost profits case.

Market evidence in the record supports the district court's uncontroverted findings and conclusions on acceptability. First, for example, American Maize's high profit margin on Lo-Dex 10 and the consumers' sensitivity to price changes support the conclusion that American Maize would not have raised the price of Process IV Lo-Dex 10 to offset the cost of glucoamylase. Further, American Maize's sales records showed no significant changes when it introduced Process IV Lo-Dex 10 at the same price as previous versions, indicating that consumers considered its important properties to be effectively identical to previous versions. Witness testimony supported this market data. Thus, this court discerns no clear error in the district court's finding that Process IV Lo-Dex 10 was an acceptable substitute in the marketplace.

It follows from the district court's findings on availability and acceptability that Grain Processing's theory of "but for" causation fails. As the district court correctly noted, "[a]n [American Maize] using the dual-enzyme method between 1979 and 1991 . . . would have sold the same product, for the same price, as the actual [American Maize] did . . . " and consequently would have retained its Lo-Dex 10 sales. Grain Processing did not present any other evidence of lost profits, such as individual lost transactions as in *Rite-Hite Corp. v. Kelley Co.* Thus, the district court properly determined that, absent infringing Lo-Dex 10, Grain Processing would have sold no more and no less Maltrin 100 than it actually did.

IV.

In summary, this court requires reliable economic proof of the market that establishes an accurate context to project the likely results "but for" the infringement. The availability of substitutes invariably will influence the market forces defining this "but for" marketplace, as it did in this case. Moreover, a substitute need not be openly on sale to exert this influence. Thus, with proper economic proof of availability, as American Maize provided the district court in this case, an acceptable substitute not on the market during the infringement may nonetheless become part of the lost profits calculus and therefore limit or preclude those damages.

This court concludes that the district court did not err in considering an alternative not on the market during the period of infringement, nor did it clearly err in determining that the alternative was available, acceptable, and precluded any lost profits. Accordingly, the district court did not abuse its discretion in denying lost profits.

Comments

1. **The Panduit *Foundation and Manufacturing Capability.*** The *Panduit* test is commonly used for determining lost profits, although not an exclusive test. *Panduit* sets forth a standard "but-for" test; that is, the patentee must show a reasonable probability that he would have made the lost sales "but for" the infringing activity. Under *Panduit,*

> To obtain lost profits on sales he would have made absent the infringement, *i.e.*, the sales made by the infringer, a patent owner must prove: (1) demand for the patented product, (2) absence of acceptable noninfringing substitutes, (3) his manufacturing and marketing capability to exploit the demand, and (4) the amount of the profit he would have made.

575 F.2d at 1156. Thus, proving a causal relationship between the infringing conduct and lost profits is essential. *See BIC Leisure Products, Inc. v. Windsurfing Int'l Inc.*, 1 F.3d 1214, 1218 (Fed. Cir. 1993) (stating "[t]o recover lost profits as opposed to royalties, a patent owner must prove a causal relation between the infringement and its loss of profits. The patent owner must show that 'but for' the infringement, it would have made the infringer's sales. An award of lost profits may not be speculative. Rather the patent owner must show a reasonable probability that, absent the infringement, it would have made the infringer's sales").

2. *Noninfringing Substitutes.* Of *Panduit*'s four factors, the "absence of acceptable noninfringing substitutes" is perhaps the most important and controversial. Under *Panduit*, a patentee cannot recover lost profits if acceptable noninfringing substitutes are available because the consumer may have opted for the substitute—there is no but-for causality. Historically, the Federal Circuit required the substitute to actually be available on the market at the time of infringement. *See Zygo Corp. v. Wyko Corp.*, 79 F.3d 1563, 1571 (Fed. Cir. 1996) (stating "[i]t is axiomatic . . . that if a device is not available for purchase, a defendant cannot argue that the device is an acceptable noninfringing alternative for the purposes of avoiding a lost profits award. A lost profits award reflects the realities of sales actually lost, not the possibilities of a hypothetical market which the infringer might have created").

In recent years, the Federal Circuit has modified the second *Panduit* factor. For instance, in *BIC Leisure Prods., supra,* the court stated this factor, "properly applied, ensures that any proffered alternative competes in the same market for the same customers as the infringer's product." 1 F.3d at 1219. And in *Grain Processing*, the court—seemingly relaxing *Zygo*—held that a noninfringing substitute can be available—and therefore serve to deny lost profits—even though the substitute is not on the market. 185 F.3d at 1351 (stating "an available technology not on the market during the infringement can constitute a noninfringing alternative").

3. *The Market-Share Rule.* The *Panduit* test works well in a two-supplier market, where one can assume that consumers would have purchased the product from the patentee absent the infringing activity. *See State Indus., Inc. v. Mor-Flo, Inc.*, 883 F.2d 1573 (Fed. Cir. 1989) ("In the two-supplier market, it is reasonable to assume, provided the patent owner has the manufacturing and marketing capabilities, that it would have made the infringer's sales. In these instances, the *Panduit* test is usually straightforward and dispositive.").

The inference of the two-supplier assumption is weakened in a multi-supplier scenario because consumers have other options besides the patentee. The Federal Circuit addressed this problem in *State Indus., supra,* by adopting a "market share" approach. The market-share rule allows the patentee to recover lost profits based on market share, even though there are available noninfringing substitutes. The patentee is permitted to substitute market share for absence of noninfringing products because it nevertheless can prove, with reasonable probability, sales it would have made "but for" the infringement. *See BIC Leisure,* 1 F.3d at 1219 ("The market share approach allows a patentee to recover lost profits, despite the presence of acceptable, noninfringing substitutes, because it nevertheless can prove with reasonable probability sales it would have made 'but for' the infringement."). This approach assumes that the patentee, who, for example, has 30 percent of the market, would have made 30 percent of the sales absent infringing activity. Thus, *State Indus.* rendered neutral the "absence of acceptable noninfringing substitutes" factor. Importantly, as with the *Panduit* test, the market-share approach requires proof that the patentee and the infringer compete in the same market. This assumption was lacking in *BIC Leisure*, "because the record reveal[ed] that during the damages period the sailboard market was not a unitary market in which every competitor sold substantially the same product. Windsurfing and BIC sold different types of sailboards at different prices to different customers. [And] their sailboards differed significantly in terms of price, product characteristics, and marketing channels." *Id.*

4. **Manufacturing Capability.** The third *Panduit* factor requires the patentee have capability to meet market demand. This factor can be satisfied if the patentee can show that he has manufacturing capacity or although he does not currently have manufacturing capacity, he can increase his capacity or engage in licensing activity.

In *Wechsler v. Macke Int'l Trade, Inc.*, 486 F.3d 1286 (Fed. Cir. 2007), the Federal Circuit reversed the district court's award of lost profits because the patentee—Wechsler—failed to prove he had the capability to manufacture the patented product during the period of infringement. The alleged infringing activity began in late 1998 and ended in the spring of 2000, but it was "undisputed that Wechsler did not produce a product until April 2001, approximately one year after the period of infringement ended." Wechsler argued—based on later sales of the patented product—that he did indeed have the capability to manufacture the patented product during the period of infringement. The court was not convinced:

> The evidence of later manufacturing and marketing is not dispositive to the determination of whether the patentee had the ability to do so during the period of infringement. Only if it is indicative of the ability to manufacture and market the patented device during the period of infringement is it relevant.
>
> In the present case, the record demonstrates that, despite his later success manufacturing and marketing a product, Wechsler lacked the capability to manufacture his device during the period of infringement. In a letter dated April 24, 2000, Wechsler wrote to his factory stating that he "was disappointed to learn . . . that a rough production sample [of his device would] not be available until early June [2000]." Not until August 2000, four months after the Handi-Drink device was taken off the market, was Wechsler finally successful in producing his own device. As such, Wechsler clearly lacked the ability to manufacture his device during the period of infringement.

486 F.3d at 1293-1294.

5. **Foreseeability—Proximate Cause and Lost Profits.** In *Rite-Hite*, the court allowed for recovery of lost profits on products that were in competition with the infringing product, but were not covered by the patent-in-suit. (The patentee also commercialized the claimed invention, the MDL-55.) The key for the court was the foreseeability of the lost sales of the competitive product. As the court noted,

> [i]f a particular injury was or should have been reasonably foreseeable by an infringing competitor in the relevant market, broadly defined, that injury is generally compensable absent a persuasive reason to the contrary. . . . Being responsible for lost sales of a competitive product is surely foreseeable; such

losses constitute the full compensation set forth by Congress, as interpreted by the Supreme Court, while staying well within the traditional meaning of proximate cause. Such lost sales should therefore clearly be compensable.

Id. at 1546-1547. *Rite-Hite* is a departure from *Panduit*, which has traditionally been applied to products covered by the patent-in-suit. But as *Rite-Hite* noted, *Panduit* is not the *sine qua non* for proving "but for" causation. If there are other ways to show that the infringement in fact caused the patentee's lost profits, "there is no reason why another test should not be acceptable." *Id.* at 1548.

In dissent, Judge Nies did not see injury to the patentee's property right in an exclusive market for the patented goods. For her, allowing a patentee to recover lost profits of products not covered by the patent-in-suit is inconsistent with basic principles of patent law. For Judge Nies and other critics of *Rite-Hite*, patents are intended to cover the subject matter claimed by the patent, not necessarily markets.

A question prompted by *Rite-Hite* is whether a patentee can be compensated for lost profits on product sales it chose not to make; in other words, loss profits in a market it did not engage? The Federal Circuit answered in the affirmative in *King Instruments Corp. v. Perego*, 65 F.3d 941 (Fed. Cir. 1995). In *King*, the Federal Circuit extended the reasoning of *Rite-Hite*. In *King Instruments*, Tapematic was found to infringe claim 12 of King's '461 patent, but King did not sell or manufacture its patented invention, and the machine it did sell—the model 790—was not covered by the '461 patent. (King and Tapematic both sold competing machines that splice and wind magnetic tape.) The district court awarded King lost profits, noting that but for the infringement King would have sold more of its model 790 machine. The court rejected Tapematic's argument that lost profits are only available to patentees who sell or manufacture the claimed invention. The Federal Circuit affirmed:

> The 1952 Act, §154, clarified that a patent empowered its owner "to *exclude others* from making, using, or selling" the invention. 35 U.S.C. §154 (1952) (emphasis added). The 1952 amendment should have corrected any mistaken belief that patent rights somehow hinged upon the patentee's exploitation of the invention. Inventors possess the natural right to exploit their inventions (subject to the patent rights of others in a dominant patent) apart from any Government grant. Therefore, patent rights do not depend upon the exercise of rights already in the patentee's possession. Thus, the 1952 Act clarified that a patent confers the right to exclude others from exploiting an invention. It does not confer the right to exploit the invention already possessed by the inventor.

> This understanding of the right protected by section 284 informs the purpose and scope of the damages provision. Section 284 protects the right to exclude others from exploiting an invention. To invoke that protection, a patentee need not have exercised its natural right to itself make, use, or sell the invention.

> The damages section, section 284, protects the right to exclude, not the right to exploit. A patentee qualifies for damages adequate to compensate for infringement without exploiting its patent. . . . The patentee need not make, use, or sell the invention to sustain an injury to that right.

A patentee may suffer injury resulting from the violation of its right to exclude infringing, competing products. . . . The patentee's sale of a competing product not covered by the patent within that market does not change the policy justifications for restoring the parties to the positions they would have occupied absent the infringement.

The market may well dictate that the best use of a patent is to exclude infringing products, rather than market the invention. A patentee, perhaps burdened with costs of development, may not produce the patented invention as efficiently as an infringer. Indeed, the infringer's presence in the market may preclude a patentee from beginning or continuing manufacture of the patented product. Thus, as apparent in this case, the patentee may acquire better returns on its innovation investment by attempting to exclude infringers from competing with the patent holder's nonpatented substitute.

65 F.3d at 949.

2. Reasonable Royalty

Under section 284, "the court shall award the claimant damages adequate to compensate for the infringement, but in no event less than a reasonable royalty." Damages are determined using the "reasonable royalty" method when it is too difficult to prove lost profits or if lost profits are simply not claimed. Most damage awards are assessed within a reasonable royalty framework. As a recent study of patent litigation noted, "[r]easonable royalties are the kind of damages most frequently awarded in patent cases, constituting a greater share with each passing year."[1] In discerning a reasonable royalty, courts will usually look to established (extant) royalties or, if none exist, a hypothetical negotiation between what is referred to as a willing licensor and willing licensee. The time of the hypothetical negotiation is at the time the infringement began.

The common issues associated with the established royalty method are what constitutes an established royalty, how many licenses must exist before a royalty is "established," and how similar must the existing licensing agreements be to the relationship between the patentee and infringer.

TRIO PROCESS CORP. v. GOLDSTEIN'S SONS, INC.

612 F.2d 1353 (3d Cir. 1980)

ROSENN, Circuit Judge.

The infringement has been established and is no longer at issue. We are, however, revisited with the troublesome issue of damages. When this case was last before us on appeal from the original determination of damages, we vacated the judgment and remanded to the district court with instructions to recalculate the damages. We are now asked to decide whether the district court's action is consistent with our holding in that earlier appeal. We hold that it is not and, therefore, again vacate the district court's judgment.

---

1. 2013 PATENT LITIGATION STUDY 11 (PricewaterhouseCoopers).

I.

At the heart of this controversy is a patented process for removing insulation from copper wire in order to allow the copper to be salvaged. This process is covered by United States Patent No. 3,076,421, owned by Trio Process Corporation ("Trio"). In 1972 we upheld the validity of the patent and determined that it had been willfully infringed by L. Goldstein's Sons, Incorporated ("Goldstein"). The case was remanded to the district court for a determination of damages.

On remand the district court appointed a master to assist in the determination of damages. When we last reviewed the proceedings, we observed:

> The master approached the damage issue by comparing Goldstein's costs of operating the patented process with the costs of a similar, unpatented process. He found that use of the Trio process saved Goldstein $52,791 per furnace year in labor costs alone, and that other, smaller savings accrued to Goldstein from use of the patented method as well.

> In order to reach a "reasonable royalty" for use of the patent by the infringer, the master halved Goldstein's savings in labor costs, and concluded that $26,390 was a reasonable royalty for each furnace year. Multiplying this figure by the number of furnace years of infringement and making slight modifications, the master found damages of $1,564,804. The district court viewed the damage computation not with regard to the money saved by the defendant as a result of the infringement, as the master had, but in terms of what Trio had lost. It looked first to the initial sum of $2,600 per furnace year the amount actually charged by Trio for licenses in the 1960-1970 era. The district court then increased the $2,600 figure on the assumption that the open infringement had reduced the market price of the license, and proceeded to set damages at $7,800 per furnace year for the years prior to the decision by this Court on validity, a figure three times the rate charged by Trio during the 1960's. Damages were set at $15,000 per furnace year for the period following the 1972 adjudication. The employment of these two figures resulted in total primary damages of $653,839. The trial judge then proceeded to use a double multiplier in contrast to the master's trebling figure and denied attorneys' fees. With interest, the total damages computed by the district court were $1,726,525.

"Trio Process III."

On appeal we affirmed in part and reversed in part. *Trio Process III*, supra. We held that there was "no error in the first step of the district court's damage calculation, namely, focusing upon the losses suffered by the patent holder rather than upon the profits illegally made by the patent infringer." *Id.* at 129. We also affirmed the district court in its finding "that the license rate established by Trio in the 1960's may have been artificially depressed by Goldstein's ongoing infringement, and that the reasonable royalty should therefore be set at a level above the actual license rate."[1]

We held, however, that the district court had erred in two respects. First, it had calculated not one royalty rate but two: one for the period before our

---

1. Contrary to Trio's assertion, however, we did not hold that the reasonable royalty rate was, as a matter of law, higher than the actual license rate. We held only that it might be higher if the actual license rate had, in fact, been artificially depressed by Goldstein's infringement. Thus, we held in *Trio Process III* that the reasonable royalty should be set at a level above the actual license rate if it was demonstrated, on the basis of the submitted evidence, that Goldstein's infringing activities had artificially depressed the actual license rate established by Trio.

decision upholding the patent's validity and the second for the period after.[2] We held that a single reasonable royalty rate should be calculated for the entire period of infringement. The district court has done that and the point is no longer at issue. Second, and most importantly for purposes of deciding this appeal, there was a failure to articulate the reasons underlying the determination of the royalty rate. Thus, the cause was remanded to the trial court for reconsideration of the damages issue. We noted specifically that

> on remand, the district court should give proper regard to the rule that the extent of the deviation of existing license fees from a reasonable royalty must be determined solely on the basis of the submitted evidence and upon an evaluation of the factors that could affect the reasonable royalty rate, not upon mere conjecture.

Trio Process III, 533 F.2d at 130. This has not been done, however, and we therefore vacate the determination of damages.

II.

In calculating damages for patent infringement, a patent holder is entitled to receive compensation for the infringement but in no event less than a reasonable royalty. 35 U.S.C. §284. An exhaustive list of factors relevant to the determination of a reasonable royalty can be found in *Georgia-Pacific Corp. v. United States Plywood Corp.,* 318 F. Supp. 1116, 1120 (S.D.N.Y. 1970). The district court in this case found a number of those factors to be relevant in its own calculation of damages:

(1) (T)he existing value of the (patented) process to the licensor as a generator of sales of his non-patented items; and the extent of such derivative or convoyed sales.

(2) The duration of the patent and the term of the license.

(3) The established profitability of the product made under the patent; its commercial success; and its current popularity.

(4) The utility and advantages of the patent property over old modes or devices, if any, that had been used for working out similar results.

(5) The nature of the patent (process) . . . and the benefits to those who have used the (process).

(6) The extent to which the infringer has made use of the (patented process); and any evidence probative of the value of that use.

(7) The portion of the realizable profit that should be credited to the invention as distinguished from nonpatented elements, the manufacturing process, business risks, or significant features or improvements added by the infringer.

(8) The opinion testimony of qualified experts.

Applying the "willing buyer and willing seller" rule, the district court considered these factors in the context of hypothetical negotiations between the parties conducted in the absence of the infringing activity. The court found that the first two of the above factors would have had only a "minimal effect" in the determination of a reasonable royalty. As to the remaining factors, the court noted that "(they) all touch upon the benefits obtained by defendant through its infringing use of plaintiff's patented process." Thus, the court found

---

2. The district court had set damages based on a reasonable royalty of $7,800 per furnace year for the period prior to our adjudication of the patent's validity and $15,000 per furnace year for the period thereafter.

that "the license fee the parties would have agreed upon absent defendant's infringement would to a large extent have been determined by the economic benefits that were obtained through the use of plaintiff's patented process."

The court found that Goldstein had obtained four distinct benefits from its use of the Trio process: (1) a reduction in labor costs; (2) an increased recovery of copper from the scrap wire; (3) lower fuel consumption per ton of processed material; and (4) the ability to attract more electrical scrap for processing by advertising the advantages of the Trio process. The court, however, was unable to assign a dollar value to each of these benefits but indicated that "the only dollar figure available is the value of the direct and indirect labor savings achieved by defendant."

The court began its calculation of the labor savings with expert testimony, credited by the master, which indicated that Goldstein had realized labor savings of $52,791 per furnace year by virtue of its infringing use of the Trio process.[3] Because Goldstein operated a number of infringing furnaces over an eight and one-half year period, the court reduced this figure to $41,652 per furnace year, reflecting the wages prevailing in 1969, the mid-point in the infringing period. The court then found that "(i)n voluntary royalty negotiations untainted by defendant's infringing practices, defendant might well have been willing to split this saving with plaintiff and paid plaintiff a royalty of approximately $20,000 for each furnace year." For two reasons, however, the court further reduced this to $15,000 per furnace year. First, the court held that, as a seller of furnaces, "(Trio) would have been willing to accept somewhat less than the maximum royalty negotiable in order to promote its sales." Second, prior to the lawsuit, "plaintiff was unaware . . . of the exact extent of the labor savings that were obtainable through the use of its process." After multiplying $15,000 by the number of infringing furnaces, the court then doubled the primary damages and added interest of 6% per annum. The total damage award was $2,901,336 plus costs.

Georgia-Pacific lists first among the factors relevant to the determination of a reasonable royalty "(t)he royalties received by the patentee for the licensing of the patent in suit, proving or tending to prove an established royalty." *Georgia-Pacific*, 318 F. Supp. at 1120. In this case, the district court chose to disregard the license fees received by Trio because "they did not show that there was an established royalty and since the fees received were artificially depressed by defendant's ongoing infringement." The court noted its belief that "a royalty negotiated in the absence of defendant's infringement would have been several times higher than the license fees actually received by the plaintiff." We have not, however, been able to discover any evidence in this record to support this conclusion.

It is true that the actual license rate does not necessarily constitute a reasonable royalty. Thus, when the actual license rate is artificially low, a reasonable royalty may be set above that rate. *Trio Process III, supra*. Nevertheless, the actual license rate is an important factor in the determination of a reasonable royalty, at least when those royalties prove or tend to prove an established royalty. See *Georgia-Pacific*, 318 F. Supp. at 1120.

---

3. This figure was arrived at by comparing the cost of operating a similar, noninfringing furnace. Goldstein disputes the basis for this comparison but we need not address this issue in view of our disposition of the case.

We are mindful that the district court concluded that the royalties trio received under the license agreements did not constitute an established royalty. Nevertheless, the existing license rate does tend to show an established license rate. The evidence indicates little, if any, variation in the rate charged before or after the infringement. Further, the district court, in its first consideration of the damage issue, apparently found the actual license rate to be probative, although not conclusive, evidence of a reasonable royalty. Thus, the reasonable royalty rate determined by the district court in its first consideration of the damage issue was related to the actual license rate charged. That approach was correct. As we indicated in our earlier opinion, however, the district court erred in failing to demonstrate, on the basis of the evidence, the extent of the deviation of existing license fees from a reasonable royalty. That same void continues to exist in the district court's most recent damage calculation.

We are again unable to discover any support for the district court's conclusion that the existing license rate was depressed by Goldstein's infringement. Thus, its reliance on the rationale of *Tights, Inc. v. Kayser-Roth Corp.*, 442 F. Supp. 159 (M.D.N.C. 1977), is misplaced. In *Tights* the court disregarded the standard royalty rate, finding it had been artificially depressed "because it was established in an atmosphere of industry-wide infringement of and disrespect for the . . . patent." *Id.* at 165. The court thereupon calculated a reasonable royalty based on hypothetical negotiations between a "willing licensee" and a "willing licensor."[4] Unlike the instant case, the depressing effect in *Tights* was evident. There, the low license rate had been negotiated against a background of open industry-wide infringement. Further, there was evidence that the existing license rate had dramatically declined because of that infringement. Thus, there was a substantial factual basis which justified the court's decision to disregard the existing license rate. In the case before us, however, such factors are not present. The license rate agreed upon between Trio and Goldstein was arrived at in free and open negotiations conducted prior to any infringing activity by Goldstein.[5] Furthermore, there are no allegations in this case of industry-wide infringement. Unlike *Tights*, there is no indication that the license rates here declined after Goldstein's infringement. Indeed, even after Trio learned of the infringement, it offered Goldstein a license at the same rate as had been earlier agreed upon. Further, in the years following our decision upholding the validity of the patent, there were apparently no new licenses granted. Thus, the thrust of the evidence in this case indicates the absence of a depressing effect caused by Goldstein's infringement. Nor have we been referred to any permissible evidentiary basis to the contrary. Thus, we are compelled to vacate the court's assessment of damages.

* * *

4. In *Georgia-Pacific, supra*, the court also determined damages on the basis of the "willing buyer and willing seller" rule. This was used, however, only after the parties agreed there was no established royalty for the patented item. Indeed, the apparent policy of the patent holder was not to enter into licensing agreements but rather, to maintain its patent monopoly.

5. Goldstein and Trio entered into two license agreements in 1960. There is no indication in the record that Goldstein's infringing activities began any earlier than 1964 when it contracted with a metal fabricator for the construction of a copy of a furnace Goldstein had purchased from Trio.

IV.

We begin with the rule that we noted in our last opinion, that the extent of the deviation of the actual licensing rate from a reasonable royalty must be explained solely on the basis of the submitted evidence. In the absence of such an explanation, we must examine the record ourselves to determine whether it contains such evidence.

Trio itself did not utilize the patented process. Instead, its only use of the patent was to license it for use by others. The licenses sold were for five year periods. The first license was sold for $20,000. This amount covered the license and the furnace necessary to utilize the process; $7,000 represented the cost of the furnace and $13,000 the cost of the license, *i.e.*, $2,600 per furnace year. In 1960, Goldstein purchased two sets of licenses and furnaces, one for $20,000 and the other for $15,000. Between 1962 and 1969 four more buyers purchased licenses and furnaces at the $20,000 rate. In 1967, another company bought the package with a modified furnace for $25,000. Later that year the package was purchased by another buyer for $19,500. After a decision by Trio to raise the price, two more were sold in 1972 to purchasers other than Goldstein, for a price of $25,000. Thus, throughout this period, the license rate of $2,600 per furnace year appears to have remained relatively constant.

Goldstein's infringing activities began in 1965. However, Trio and Goldstein had in free and open negotiations previously agreed to a license rate of $2,600 per furnace year. The license rate Trio charged other licensees did not decline after Goldstein's infringement began. Consequently, if the infringing activity did have a depressing effect on the license rate it could only have been in deterring Trio from charging the rate it otherwise would have negotiated in the open market. The district court, however, disregarded the license fees received by Trio, because it believed they did not reveal an established royalty, and they were artificially depressed by the ongoing infringement. The court found that Trio was a seller of furnaces and thus in negotiating a royalty rate (prior to the infringement) "would have been willing to accept somewhat less than the maximum royalty negotiable in order to promote its sales." It further observed that prior to this lawsuit, Trio was unaware of the exact extent of the labor savings effected by the patented process. But the record indicates that even after learning of the infringement, Trio offered Goldstein a license for the infringing furnace "Under the same terms and conditions as the previous two incinerators."

It is true that "(a) patentee who has attempted to avoid costly and time-consuming litigation by settling for less than a reasonable royalty should not be penalized when an infringer forces full litigation." *Tights*, 442 F. Supp. at 165. Here, however, there is no reason to believe that the license rate negotiated by the parties was anything other than a balanced consideration by both Goldstein and Trio of those competing concerns that normally enter into the determination of price in an open marketplace economy. Trio consistently offered licenses at the rate of $2,600 per furnace year. Thus, the possibility that Trio, had it chosen to do so, might have obtained a higher license rate than that actually charged, is irrelevant. We believe the rate fixed by the parties prior to any infringement is pertinent and highly persuasive. Further, our examination of the record has not disclosed any reason to distrust the existing license rate as a measure of actual damages. Thus, we hold that the $2600 per furnace year rate negotiated between Trio and Goldstein prior to the infringement, constitutes a reasonable royalty.

LUCENT TECHNOLOGIES, INC. v. GATEWAY, INC.
580 F.3d 1301 (Fed. Cir. 2009)

MICHEL, Chief Judge.

Microsoft Corporation appeals the $357,693,056.18 jury award to Lucent Technologies, Inc. for Microsoft's infringement of the Day patent. Because the damages calculation lacked sufficient evidentiary support, we vacate and remand that portion of the case to the district court for further proceedings.[*]

BACKGROUND

In the 1970s, niche groups of hobbyists, including two teenagers in a Los Altos garage, built personal computers from scratch. In the early to mid-1980s, personal computing gained popularity although still in its infancy. In 1982, a fifteen-year-old high school student created the first public computer virus, spreading it among personal computers via floppy disks, most likely the 5 1/4-inch version, as the 3 1/2-inch disk wasn't introduced until a few years later. Commercially available operating systems at the time were mainly text-based with few, if any, graphical interfaces. In 1984, with its now famous "1984" commercial aired during Super Bowl XVIII on Black Sunday, Apple Computer announced the introduction of its Apple Macintosh, the first widely sold personal computer employing a graphical user interface. The following year, Microsoft introduced its own version of a graphical operating system, Windows 1.0.

In December 1986, three computer engineers at AT&T filed a patent application, which eventually issued as the Day patent. The patent is generally directed to a method of entering information into fields on a computer screen without using a keyboard. A user fills in the displayed fields by choosing concurrently displayed, predefined tools adapted to facilitate the inputting of the information in a particular field, wherein the predefined tools include an on-screen graphical keyboard, a menu, and a calculator. The system may display menus of information for filling in a particular field and may also be adapted to communicate with a host computer to obtain the information that is inserted into the fields. In addition, one of the displayed fields can be a bit-mapped graphics field, which the user fills in by writing on the touch screen using a stylus.

In 2002, Lucent [the assignee of Day patent] initiated the present action against Gateway, and Microsoft subsequently intervened.

At trial, Lucent charged infringement by Microsoft of claims 19 and 21, among others, of the Day patent. Lucent alleged indirect infringement of claim 19 based on the sales and use of Microsoft Money, Microsoft Outlook, and Windows Mobile. The jury found Microsoft liable on claim 19 as to all three products and on claim 21 as to Windows Mobile. The verdict awarded a single lump-sum against Microsoft for all products involved. The jury awarded $357,693,056.18 for Microsoft's infringement of the Day patent, excluding pre-judgment interest.

---

* [The Federal Circuit affirmed the district court's finding that the Day patent was infringed and not invalid. — ED.]

ANALYSIS

* * *

IV. Damages

Based on the evidence of record, Microsoft sold approximately 110 million units of the three software products capable of practicing the methods of the asserted claims. The total dollar value of the sales was approximately $8 billion. At trial, Lucent's theory of damages was based on 8% of sales revenue for the accused software products, and it asked the jury to award $561.9 million based on Microsoft's infringing sales. Microsoft countered that a lump-sum payment of $6.5 million would have been the correct amount for licensing the protected technology.

Microsoft challenges the jury's damages award on several bases. First, Microsoft argues that the jury should not have applied the entire market value rule to the value of its three software products. Microsoft's second argument for reversing the damages award is that, for method claims, *Dynacore Holdings Corp. v. U.S. Philips Corp.*, 363 F.3d 1263 (Fed. Cir. 2004), requires that damages be limited to the proven number of instances of actual infringing use. Microsoft states that, "[u]nder *Dynacore,* Lucent had to tie its damages claim to demonstrated instances of direct infringement." For the reasons stated below, we reject both arguments as presented by Microsoft. We agree, nevertheless, with Microsoft's argument that substantial evidence does not support the jury's verdict of a lump-sum royalty payment of $357,693,056.18. Further, to the extent the jury relied on an entire market value calculation to arrive at the lump-sum damages amount, that award is not supported by substantial evidence and is against the clear weight of the evidence.

A. *Reasonable Royalty*

"Upon finding for the claimant the court shall award the claimant damages adequate to compensate for the infringement, but in no event less than a reasonable royalty for the use made of the invention by the infringer, together with interest and costs as fixed by the court." 35 U.S.C. §284. As the Supreme Court has framed the general issue of determining damages, at least for competitors, a court must ask, "[H]ad the Infringer not infringed, what would [the] Patent Holder[ ] have made?" *Aro Mfg. Co. v. Convertible Top Replacement Co.*, 377 U.S. 476, 507 (1964); *see also Pall Corp. v. Micron Separations, Inc.*, 66 F.3d 1211, 1223 (Fed. Cir. 1995) ("[T]he purpose of compensatory damages is not to punish the infringer, but to make the patentee whole."). In the Supreme Court's words, awarding damages through litigation attempts to assess "the difference between [the patentee's] pecuniary condition after the infringement, and what his condition would have been if the infringement had not occurred." *Yale Lock Mfg. Co. v. Sargent,* 117 U.S. 536, 552, 6 S. Ct. 934, 29 L. Ed. 954 (1886).

The burden of proving damages falls on the patentee. Two alternative categories of infringement compensation are the patentee's lost profits and the reasonable royalty he would have received through arms-length bargaining. *See Panduit Corp. v. Stahlin Bros. Fibre Works.* Lost profits are not at issue in the present case. A reasonable royalty is, of course, "merely the floor below which damages shall not fall." *Bandag, Inc. v. Gerrard Tire Co.,* 704 F.2d 1578, 1583 (Fed. Cir. 1983).

Litigants routinely adopt several approaches for calculating a reasonable royalty. The first, the analytical method, focuses on the infringer's projections of profit for the infringing product. *See TWM Mfg. Co. v. Dura Corp.*, 789 F.2d 895, 899 (Fed. Cir. 1986) (describing the analytical method as "subtract[ing] the infringer's usual or acceptable net profit from its anticipated net profit realized from sales of infringing devices"). The second, more common approach, called the hypothetical negotiation or the "willing licensor-willing licensee" approach, attempts to ascertain the royalty upon which the parties would have agreed had they successfully negotiated an agreement just before infringement began. *See Georgia-Pacific Corp. v. U.S. Plywood Corp.*, 318 F. Supp. 1116, 1120 (S.D.N.Y. 1970). The hypothetical negotiation tries, as best as possible, to recreate the *ex ante* licensing negotiation scenario and to describe the resulting agreement. In other words, if infringement had not occurred, willing parties would have executed a license agreement specifying a certain royalty payment scheme. The hypothetical negotiation also assumes that the asserted patent claims are valid and infringed.

In the present appeal, the parties, in offering the damages evidence, each adopted the hypothetical negotiation approach, without objection. Both Microsoft and Lucent must therefore accept that any reasonable royalty analysis "necessarily involves an element of approximation and uncertainty." *Unisplay*, 69 F.3d at 517. We review the damages award within the *Georgia-Pacific* framework.

Before the district court, Lucent asked for a damages award based only on a running royalty. Microsoft, on the other hand, told the jury that the damages should be a lump-sum royalty payment of $6.5 million. Based on the verdict form, the jury decided on a lump-sum award, not a running royalty. The verdict form notes a lump-sum damages amount and no amount (i.e., zero or "N/A") on the lines for a running royalty. Faced with the jury's selection, our task is to determine whether substantial evidence supports a lump-sum, paid-in-full royalty of approximately $358 million for Microsoft's infringement of the Day patent. To do this, we must decide whether substantial evidence supports the jury's implicit finding that Microsoft would have agreed to, at the time of the hypothetical negotiation, a lump-sum, paid-in-full royalty of about $358 million. In performing this analysis, we focus mainly on the damages case as it applies to Microsoft Outlook, as infringement by the use of Outlook apparently constituted the vast majority of the award. We focus also on the relevant *Georgia-Pacific* factors, as presented to the jury through all the evidence and particularly the experts' testimony.

1. Factor 2

The second *Georgia-Pacific* factor is "[t]he rates paid by the licensee for the use of other patents comparable to the patent in suit." 318 F. Supp. at 1120. This factor examines whether the licenses relied on by the patentee in proving damages are sufficiently comparable to the hypothetical license at issue in suit. Subsumed within this factor is the question of whether the licensor and licensee would have agreed to a lump-sum payment or instead to a running royalty based on ongoing sales or usage.

Significant differences exist between a running royalty license and a lump-sum license. In a standard running royalty license, the amount of money payable by the licensee to the patentee is tied directly to how often the licensed invention is later used or incorporated into products by the licensee. A running royalty structure shifts many licensing risks to the licensor because he does not receive a guaranteed payment. Royalties are dependent on the level of sales or usage by the licensee, which the licensee can often control.

Compared to a running royalty analysis, a lump-sum analysis involves different considerations. A lump-sum license "benefits the patentholder in that it enables the company to raise a substantial amount of cash quickly and benefits the target [i.e., the licensee] by capping its liability and giving it the ability, usually for the remainder of the patent term, to actually use the patented technology in its own products without any further expenditure." Richard F. Cauley, *Winning the Patent Damages Case* 47 (2009). The lump-sum license removes or shifts certain risks inherent in most arms-length agreements. A lump-sum license removes any risk that the licensee using the patented invention will underreport, e.g., engage in false reporting, and therefore underpay, as can occur with a running royalty agreement. Additionally, for both contracting parties, the lump-sum license generally avoids ongoing administrative burdens of monitoring usage of the invention.

A further, important consideration is that an upfront, paid-in-full royalty removes, as an option for the licensee, the ability to reevaluate the usefulness, and thus the value, of the patented technology as it is used and/or sold by the licensee. As generally employed, once a lump-sum license is duly executed, the licensee is obligated to pay the entire, agreed-upon amount for the licensed technology, regardless of whether the technology is commercially successful or even used. A licensee to a lump-sum agreement, under usual licensing terms, cannot later ask for a refund from the licensor based on a subsequent decision not to use the patented technology. There is no provision for buyer's remorse.

The lump-sum structure also creates risks for both parties. The licensed technology may be wildly successful, and the licensee may have acquired the technology for far less than what later proved to be its economic value. The alternative risk, of course, is the licensee may have paid a lump-sum far in excess of what the patented invention is later shown to be worth in the marketplace.

As noted, Lucent's licensing expert, Roger Smith, argued for damages based solely on a running royalty rate. Smith emphasized his choice of a running royalty over a lump-sum payment.

> **Q:** Now, in each case, in the [other patents in suit] and then finally the Day 356 form entry patent, in each case you've selected a running royalty structure for your reasonable royalty; is that right?
> **A:** I certainly did, yes.

He also explained that "the running royalty in a hypothetical negotiation such as the one we're considering here would be appropriate, even though lump-sum does have the advantage that brings the money up front or at least some of it." *Id.*

On appeal, however, Lucent defends the damages award, contending that substantial evidence supports the lump-sum award of about $358 million. This is problematic for several reasons. First, no evidence of record establishes the parties' expectations about how often the patented method would be used by consumers. Second, the jury heard little factual testimony explaining how a license agreement structured as a running royalty agreement is probative of a lump-sum payment to which the parties would have agreed. Third, the license agreements for other groups of patents, invoked by Lucent, were created from events far different from a license negotiation to avoid infringement of the one patent here, the Day patent.

Parties agreeing to a lump-sum royalty agreement may, during the license negotiation, consider the expected or estimated usage (or, for devices, production) of a given invention, assuming proof is presented to support the expectation, because the more frequently most inventions are used, the more valuable they generally are and therefore the larger the lump-sum payment. Conversely, a minimally used feature, with all else being equal, will usually command a lower lump-sum payment. In this case, Lucent identifies no documentary evidence or testimony showing the parties' expectations as to usage of the claimed method. Lucent submitted no evidence upon which a jury could reasonably conclude that Microsoft and Lucent would have estimated, at the time of the negotiation, that the patented date-picker feature would have been so frequently used or valued as to command a lump-sum payment that amounts to approximately 8% of the sale price of Outlook.

Lucent's expert Mr. Smith did try to explain how one would calculate what an acceptable lump-sum would be.

> **Q:** Well, when one is considering what the magnitude of a lump-sum payment might be, does one ever look at what the expected royalty—total royalty would be produced by a running royalty based on the available information at that time?
> **A:** That generally is the way a lump sum would be determined, by looking at what the running royalty—what the value of each use of the patent might be and *then speculating as to the extent of the future use.*

(emphasis added). But an explanation urging jurors to rely on speculation, without more, is often insufficient.

Despite this shortcoming in its evidence, Lucent relies on eight varied license agreements which purportedly support the jury's lump-sum damages award. When we examine these license agreements, along with the relevant testimony, we are left with two strong conclusions. First, some of the license agreements are radically different from the hypothetical agreement under consideration for the Day patent. Second, with the other agreements, we are simply unable to ascertain from the evidence presented the subject matter of the agreements, and we therefore cannot understand how the jury could have adequately evaluated the probative value of those agreements.

Only four of the eight agreements purport to be lump-sum agreements. For the latter three, it is impossible for us, based on the record, to determine whether the agreements are at all comparable to the hypothetical agreement of the present suit. For the first agreement, what little explanation there is only underscores the differences between it and any hypothetical agreement for the Day patent.

Lucent candidly admits in its brief that "none of the real world licenses introduced at trial arose from circumstances identical to those presumed to prevail in the hypothetical royalty negotiation." Appellee's Br. 50. Moreover, the testimony excerpted above belies Lucent's claim of "present[ing] particularized expert testimony explaining how various differences between the real and hypothetical license negotiations . . . would factor into the appropriate royalty for Microsoft's infringement." *Id.* The testimony provides no analysis of those license agreements, other than, for example, noting the agreement was a cross-license of a large patent portfolio and the amount paid. Lucent had the burden to prove that the licenses were sufficiently comparable to support the lump-sum damages award. The law does not require an expert to convey all his knowledge to the jury about each license agreement in evidence, but a lump-sum damages award cannot stand solely on evidence which amounts to little more than a recitation of royalty numbers, one of which is arguably in the ballpark of the jury's award, particularly when it is doubtful that the technology of those license agreements is in any way similar to the technology being litigated here.

Lucent also cites four running-royalty license agreements which purportedly provide substantial evidence supporting a lump-sum damages award of approximately $358 million. A significant shortcoming of these agreements is their "running-royalty" nature, however. As we noted above, certain fundamental differences exist between lump-sum agreements and running-royalty agreements. This is not to say that a running-royalty license agreement cannot be relevant to a lump-sum damages award, and vice versa. For a jury to use a running-royalty agreement as a basis to award lump-sum damages, however, some basis for comparison must exist in the evidence presented to the jury. In the present case, the jury had almost no testimony with which to recalculate in a meaningful way the value of any of the running royalty agreements to arrive at the lump-sum damages award.

We now consider what Microsoft advocated, namely that the hypothetical negotiation would have yielded a lump-sum licensing agreement for $6.5 million. For whatever reason, Microsoft urged the jury to accept its theory based on a proffer of a single license Microsoft had executed for a graphical user interface technology. Thus, at a minimum, a reasonable jury could have awarded $6.5 million, or some larger amount as permitted by the evidence. *See Rite-Hite,* 56 F.3d at 1555 ("[W]hat an infringer would prefer to pay is not the test for damages.").

But we see little evidentiary basis under *Georgia-Pacific* Factor 2 for awarding roughly three to four times the average amount in the lump-sum agreements in evidence. Here the award was $358 million; there, the amounts were $80, 93, 100, and 290 million. That some licenses were cross-licenses or commuted-rate licenses—which may warrant a higher damages award—does not fill the evidentiary lacunae. Again, it was Lucent's burden to prove that the licenses relied on were sufficiently comparable to sustain a lump-sum damages award of $358 million. This is not an instance in which the jury chose a damages award somewhere between maximum and minimum lump-sum amounts advocated by the opposing parties. For the reasons stated, Factor 2 weighs strongly against the jury's award.

2. Factors 10 and 13

Factor 10 is "[t]he nature of the patented invention; the character of the commercial embodiment of it as owned and produced by the licensor; and the benefits to those who have used the invention." *Georgia-Pacific,* 318 F. Supp. at 1120. Factor 13 is "[t]he portion of the realizable profit that should be credited to the invention as distinguished from non-patented elements, the manufacturing process, business risks, or significant features or improvements added by the infringer." *Id.* These two factors, at least as applied to the facts of this case, both aim to elucidate how the parties would have valued the patented feature during the hypothetical negotiation.

The evidence can support only a finding that the infringing feature contained in Microsoft Outlook is but a tiny feature of one part of a much larger
software program. Microsoft's expert explained that Outlook's e-mail component is "the part of Outlook that's most commonly used by our customers."
Microsoft's witness also explained that, in addition to sending and receiving
e-mails, a user can create electronic tasks and notes. Additionally, Outlook can
be used as an electronic Rolodex, storing contact information, such as phone
numbers, addresses, and the like. It also has a fully functional calendar system,
in which a user can record appointments, meetings, and other items on one's
schedule. As Lucent's own expert testified, Outlook is a "personal organizer"
that is "an integrated suite of abilities to do e-mail, to set up contacts, to arrange
meetings, to maintain your personal calendar, et cetera." In short, Outlook is an
enormously complex software program comprising hundreds, if not thousands
or even more, features. We find it inconceivable to conclude, based on the present record, that the use of one small feature, the date-picker, constitutes a substantial portion of the value of Outlook.

The parties presented little evidence relating to Factor 13. Nonetheless,
the only reasonable conclusion is that most of the realizable profit must be
credited to non-patented elements, such as "the manufacturing process, business risks, or significant features or improvements added by [Microsoft]." As
explained by Microsoft's expert Mr. Kennedy, Outlook consists of millions of
lines of code, only a tiny fraction of which encodes the date-picker feature.
Although the weighing of Factor 13 cannot be reduced to a mere counting
of lines of code, the glaring imbalance between infringing and non-infringing
features must impact the analysis of how much profit can properly be attributed
to the use of the date-picker compared to non-patented elements and other features of Outlook. Here, numerous features other than the date-picker appear to
account for the overwhelming majority of the consumer demand and therefore
significant profit.

The only reasonable conclusion that can be drawn from this evidence is that
the infringing use of Outlook's date-picker feature is a minor aspect of a much
larger software program and that the portion of the profit that can be credited to the infringing use of the date-picker tool is exceedingly small. For these
reasons, Factors 10 and 13 of *Georgia-Pacific* provide little support for the jury's
lump-sum damages award of $357,693,056.18.

3. Factor 11

Factor 11 is "[t]he extent to which the infringer has made use of the invention; and any evidence probative of the value of that use." *Georgia-Pacific*, 318 F.
Supp. at 1120. As with Factors 10 and 13, the eleventh factor informs the court
and jury about how the parties would have valued the patented feature during
the hypothetical negotiation. In doing so, Factor 11 relies on evidence about
how much the patented invention has been used. Implicit in this factor is the
premise that an invention used frequently is generally more valuable than a
comparable invention used infrequently.

During oral argument, Microsoft characterized as irrelevant information
about how often the date-picker tool has in fact been used by consumers of
Microsoft products. That is so, according to Microsoft, because such facts post-
date the time of the hypothetical negotiation. *See Hanson v. Alpine Valley Ski Area,
Inc.*, 718 F.2d 1075, 1081 (Fed. Cir. 1983) ("The issue of the infringer's profit

is to be determined not on the basis of a hindsight evaluation of what actually happened, but on the basis of what the parties to the hypothetical license negotiations would have considered at the time of the negotiations."). But neither precedent nor economic logic requires us to ignore information about how often a patented invention has been used by infringers. Nor could they since frequency of expected use and predicted value are related.

In *Sinclair Refining Co. v. Jenkins Petroleum Process Co.*, 289 U.S. 689, 698 (1933), the Supreme Court recognized that factual developments occurring after the date of the hypothetical negotiation can inform the damages calculation:

> [A] different situation is presented if years have gone by before the evidence is offered. Experience is then available to correct uncertain prophecy. Here is a book of wisdom that courts may not neglect. We find no rule of law that sets a clasp upon its pages, and forbids us to look within.

Similarly, our case law affirms the availability of post-infringement evidence as probative in certain circumstances. In *Fromson v. Western Litho Plate & Supply Co.*, 853 F.2d 1568, 1575 (Fed. Cir. 1988), we observed that the hypothetical negotiation analysis "permits and often requires a court to look to events and facts that occurred thereafter and that could not have been known to or predicted by the hypothesized negotiators."

Consideration of evidence of usage after infringement started can, under appropriate circumstances, be helpful to the jury and the court in assessing whether a royalty is reasonable. Usage (or similar) data may provide information that the parties would frequently have estimated during the negotiation. Such data might, depending on the case, come from sales projections based on past sales, consumer surveys, focus group testing, and other sources. Even though parties to a license negotiation will usually not have precise data about future usage, they often have rough estimates as to the expected frequency of use. This quantitative information, assuming it meets admissibility requirements, ought to be given its proper weight, as determined by the circumstances of each case.

On the other hand, we have never laid down any rigid requirement that damages in all circumstances be limited to specific instances of infringement proven with direct evidence. Such a strict requirement could create a hypothetical negotiation far-removed from what parties regularly do during real-world licensing negotiations. As shown by the evidence in this case, companies in the high-tech computer industry often strike licensing deals in which the amount paid for a particular technology is not necessarily limited to the number of times a patented feature is used by a consumer. A company licensing a patented method often has strong reasons not to tie the royalty amount strictly to usage. The administrative cost of monitoring usage can be prohibitively expensive. Furthermore, with some inventions, say for example a method of detecting fires, value is added simply by having the patented invention available for use. Thus, potential licensors and licensees routinely agree to royalty payments regardless of whether the invention is used frequently or infrequently by the consumer.

With the foregoing in mind, we observe that the evidence of record is conspicuously devoid of any data about how often consumers use the patented date-picker invention. In one respect, Lucent believes the damages award is supported by the pervasive use of forms throughout the three software programs. What this position lacks is the requisite focus on the infringed claim. The damages award can't be supported by evidence that the infringers also used additional, non-infringing features. Only when the date-picker is used to fill out a form does infringement occur. All other means of filling out a form, such as typing in the entire date, do not infringe. The damages award ought to be correlated, in some respect, to the extent the infringing method is used by consumers. This is so because this is what the parties to the hypothetical negotiation would have considered. Lucent tries to stretch the claim scope so that claim 19 covers all pop-up tools. If this were the proper claim construction, we might have to reverse the validity ruling. But the claim construction—which neither party has appealed—is not so broad.

4. Other Factors

Other *Georgia-Pacific* factors applicable here include "[t]he nature and scope of the license, as exclusive or nonexclusive" (Factor 3); "[t]he licensor's established policy and marketing program to maintain his patent monopoly" (Factor 4); "[t]he commercial relationship between the licensor and the licensee" (Factor 5); "[t]he established profitability of the product made under the patent" (Factor 8); "[t]he utility and advantages of the patent property over the old modes or devices" (Factor 9); and "[t]he portion of the profit or of the selling price that may be customary . . . to allow for the use of the invention" (Factor 12). 318 F. Supp. at 1120. To the extent these factors are relevant, they appear somewhat to offset one another.

For instance, Factor 8, the profitability of the product made, supports a higher versus a lower reasonable royalty, given the unrebutted evidence that the products at issue are sold with an approximately 70-80% profit margin. Contrasting this evidence are Factors 3 and 9. Non-exclusive licenses generally command lower royalties. And, from the evidence presented, the infringing use of the date-picker seems to have, at best, only a slight advantage over what is arguably the closest prior art. We are mindful, however, that a jury could have reasonably concluded otherwise with several of the factors mentioned here. Even so, such reasonable conclusions, in this case, cannot overcome the substantial infirmities in the evidence for the other factors detailed above.

5. Conclusion on Lump-Sum Reasonable Royalty

Having examined the relevant *Georgia-Pacific* factors, we are left with the unmistakable conclusion that the jury's damages award is not supported by substantial evidence, but is based mainly on speculation or guesswork. When the evidence is viewed *in toto,* the jury's award of a lump-sum payment of about $358 million does not rest on substantial evidence and is likewise against the clear weight of the evidence. The evidence does not sustain a finding that, at the time of infringement, Microsoft and Lucent would have agreed to a lump-sum royalty payment subsequently amounting to approximately 8% of Microsoft's revenues for the sale of Outlook (and necessarily a larger percentage of Outlook's profits). We need not identify any particular *Georgia-Pacific* factor as being dispositive. Rather, the flexible analysis of all applicable *Georgia-Pacific* factors provides a useful and legally-required framework for assessing the damages award in this case.

Creating a licensing agreement for patented technology is, at best, an inexact science. In actual licensing negotiations, willing parties negotiating at arm's-length do not necessarily generate and analyze precise economic data concerning the perceived value of a patented invention. A complicated case this was, and the damages evidence of record was neither very powerful, nor presented very well by either party. Most jury damages awards reviewed on appeal have been held to be supported by substantial evidence. Nonetheless, on post-trial JMOL motions, district court judges must scrutinize the evidence carefully to ensure that the "substantial evidence" standard is satisfied, while keeping in mind that a reasonable royalty analysis "necessarily involves an element of approximation and uncertainty." *Unisplay,* 69 F.3d at 517.

B. Entire Market Value Analysis

Microsoft argues that the damages award must be reversed because the jury erroneously applied the entire market value rule. Despite the jury's indication on the verdict form that it was awarding a lump-sum reasonable royalty, Microsoft believes that the only way the jury could have calculated a figure of $357,693,056.18 was by applying a royalty percentage to a total sales figure of the infringing software products. Indeed, it is difficult to understand how the jury could have chosen its lump-sum figure down to the penny unless it used a running royalty calculation. Furthermore, as Microsoft explains in its brief, working the math backwards strongly suggests that the jury must have used some calculation of a rate applied to the entire market value of the software. Alternatively, the jury could have simply used a somewhat lower rate, such as about 5.5%, applied to the total sales figure. Assuming that the jury did apply the entire market value rule, such application would amount to legal error for two reasons.

In one sense, our law on the entire market value rule is quite clear. For the entire market value rule to apply, the patentee must prove that "the patent-related feature is the 'basis for customer demand.'" *Rite-Hite,* 56 F.3d at 1549; *TWM Mfg.,* 789 F.2d at 901 ("The entire market value rule allows for the recovery of damages based on the value of an entire apparatus containing several features, when the feature patented constitutes the basis for customer demand.").

In the distant past, before a contemporary appreciation of the economics of infringement damages, the Supreme Court seemingly set forth rigid rules concerning the entire market value rule. Shortly before the Civil War, in *Seymour v. McCormick,* 57 U.S. (16 How.) 480, 491 (1853), a case involving one of Cyrus McCormick's famous reaping machine inventions, the Court warned that it would be "a very grave error to instruct a jury 'that as to the measure of damages the same rule is to govern, whether the patent covers an entire machine or an improvement on a machine.'" About a century and a quarter ago, in *Garretson v. Clark,* the Court expressed further concern about basing damages on the value of the entire product:

> When a patent is for an improvement, and not for an entirely new machine or contrivance, the patentee must show in what particulars his improvement has added to the usefulness of the machine or contrivance. He must separate its results distinctly from those of the other parts, so that the benefits derived from it may be distinctly seen and appreciated. . . . The patentee . . . must in every case give evidence tending to separate or apportion the defendant's profits and the patentee's damages between the patented feature and the unpatented features, and such evidence must be reliable and tangible, and not conjectural or speculative; or he must show, by equally reliable and satisfactory evidence, that the profits and damages are to be calculated on the whole machine, for the reason that the

> entire value of the whole machine, as a marketable article, is properly and legally attributable to the patented feature.

111 U.S. 120, 121 (1884). And early last century, the Court elaborated on this theme:

> [An] invention may have been used in combination with valuable improvements made, or other patents appropriated by the infringer, and each may have jointly, but unequally, contributed to the profits. In such case, if plaintiff's patent only created a part of the profits, he is only entitled to recover that part of the net gains.

Westinghouse Elec. & Mfg. Co. v. Wagner Elec. & Mfg. Co., 225 U.S. 604, 614-15 (1912).

Translating the Court's early stylistic description into a precise, contemporary, economic paradigm presents a challenge. Notwithstanding this obstacle, the objective of the Court's concern has been two-fold: determining the correct (or at least approximately correct) value of the patented invention, when it is but one part or feature among many, and ascertaining what the parties would have agreed to in the context of a patent license negotiation. Litigants must realize that the two objectives do not always meet at the same precise number. Furthermore, licensors of patented technology often license an invention for more or less than its true "economic value." Such is the inherent risk in licensing intangible assets that may have no established market value.

The first flaw with any application of the entire market value rule in the present case is the lack of evidence demonstrating the patented method of the Day patent as the basis—or even a substantial basis—of the consumer demand for Outlook. As explained above, the only reasonable conclusion supported by the evidence is that the infringing use of the date-picker tool in Outlook is but a very small component of a much larger software program. The vast majority of the features, when used, do not infringe. The date-picker tool's minor role in the overall program is further confirmed when one considers the relative importance of certain other features, e.g., e-mail. Consistent with this description of Outlook, Lucent did not carry its evidentiary burden of proving that anyone purchased Outlook because of the patented method. Indeed, Lucent's damages expert conceded that there was no "evidence that anybody anywhere at any time ever bought Outlook, be it an equipment manufacturer or an individual consumer, . . . because it had a date picker." And when we consider the importance of the many features not covered by the Day patent compared to the one infringing feature in Outlook, we can only arrive at the unmistakable conclusion that the invention described in claim 19 of the Day patent is not the reason consumers purchase Outlook. Thus, Lucent did not satisfy its burden of proving the applicability of the entire market value rule.

As for Windows Mobile and Microsoft Money, a jury's conclusion might possibly be different. At this point in the litigation, we again need not decide these issues. Because the damages award based on the infringing date-picker feature of Outlook is not supported by substantial evidence and is contrary to the clear weight of the evidence, the damages award must be vacated. When the case is remanded to the trial court for further proceedings consistent with this opinion, it may be helpful to analyze the three infringing software products independently.

The second flaw with any application of the entire market value rule in this case lies in the approach adopted by Lucent's licensing expert. He had first tried to apply the entire market value rule to the sale of the "infringing" computers loaded with the software, opining that Microsoft and Lucent would have agreed to a 1% royalty based on the entire price of the computer containing Outlook. In response, Microsoft filed a motion *in limine* to exclude such testimony, which the district court granted. At trial, Lucent's expert changed his opinion, contending that the royalty base should be the price of the software (and not the entire computer) but also that the royalty rate should be increased to 8% (from 1%). This opinion contrasted starkly to the rates he proposed for the other patents in suit, which were in the 1% range. In choosing 8%, he reasoned that, "in a typical situation, if one applied a royalty to a smaller patented portion in a computer as opposed to the entire computer using typically infringed patents, 8-percent . . . of the fair market value of the patented portion would equate to 1-percent of the fair market value of the entire computer."

What Lucent's licensing expert proposed here does not comport with the purpose of damages law or the entire market value rule. Lucent's expert tried to reach the damages number he would have obtained had he used the price of the entire computer as a royalty base. Being precluded from using the computer as the royalty base, he used the price of the software, but inflated the royalty rate accordingly. This cannot be an acceptable way to conduct an analysis of what the parties would have agreed to in the hypothetical licensing context. The approach of Lucent's expert ignores what the district court's evidentiary ruling tried to accomplish. The district court implicitly recognized that any damages computation based on the value of the entire computer using common royalty rates (e.g., 1-5%) would be excessive.

Furthermore, Lucent's expert admitted that there was no evidence that Microsoft had ever agreed to pay an 8% royalty on an analogous patent. *See* J.A. 07824 ("Q: Did you find one license where Microsoft ever agreed to pay an eight percent royalty on Outlook for a tiny little feature? A: I didn't see any Microsoft licenses on Outlook, frankly.").

Although our law states certain mandatory conditions for applying the entire market value rule, courts must nevertheless be cognizant of a fundamental relationship between the entire market value rule and the calculation of a running royalty damages award. Simply put, the base used in a running royalty calculation can always be the value of the entire commercial embodiment, as long as the magnitude of the rate is within an acceptable range (as determined by the evidence). Indeed, all running royalties have at least two variables: the royalty base and the royalty rate. Microsoft surely would have little reason to complain about the supposed application of the entire market value rule had the jury applied a royalty rate of 0.1% (instead of 8%) to the market price of the infringing programs. Such a rate would have likely yielded a damages award of less than Microsoft's proposed $6.5 million. Thus, even when the patented invention is a small component of a much larger commercial product, awarding a reasonable royalty based on either sale price or number of units sold can be economically justified. *See, e.g., Kearns,* 32 F.3d at 1544 (awarding a reasonable royalty of 90 cents per vehicle that had the infringing intermittent windshield wipers, when the average car price was approximately $4000 to $6000).

Some commentators suggest that the entire market value rule should have little role in reasonable royalty law. *See, e.g.,* Mark A. Lemley, *Distinguishing Lost*

Profits from Reasonable Royalties, 51 WM. & MARY L. REV. 655, 656 (2009) (suggesting that "courts have distorted the reasonable royalty measure" by "importing inapposite concepts like the 'entire market value rule' in an effort to compensate patent owners whose real remedy probably should have been in the lost profits category"); Amy Landers, *Let the Games Begin: Incentives to Innovation in the New Economy of Intellectual Property Law,* 46 SANTA CLARA L. REV. 307, 362 (2006) ("The current iterations of the entire market value rule are inconsistent with the Patent Act's statutory language."). But such general propositions ignore the realities of patent licensing and the flexibility needed in transferring intellectual property rights. The evidence of record in the present dispute illustrates the importance the entire market value may have in reasonable royalty cases. The license agreements admitted into evidence (without objection from Microsoft, we note) highlight how sophisticated parties routinely enter into license agreements that base the value of the patented inventions as a percentage of the commercial products' sales price. There is nothing inherently wrong with using the market value of the entire product, especially when there is no established market value for the infringing component or feature, so long as the multiplier accounts for the proportion of the base represented by the infringing component or feature.

UNILOC USA, INC. v. MICROSOFT CORPORATION

632 F.3d 1292 (Fed. Cir. 2011)

LINN, Circuit Judge.

Uniloc USA, Inc. and Uniloc Singapore Private Limited (collectively, "Uniloc") appeals the district court's alternative grant of a new trial on damages. Microsoft cross-appeals the district court's denial of its motion for JMOL of invalidity of the '216 patent. . . . [The district court's award of JMOL that Microsoft was not liable for infringement is reversed, but] [b]ecause the jury's damages award was fundamentally tainted by the use of a legally inadequate methodology, this court affirms the grant of a new trial on damages.

I. BACKGROUND

Commercial software manufacturers like Microsoft lose significant sales as a result of the "casual copying" of software, where users install copies of a software program on multiple computers in violation of applicable software license conditions. Uniloc's '216 patent was an early attempt to combat such software piracy. There is no dispute as to the actual functioning of Uniloc's patented invention and Microsoft's accused products. The following background information is taken from the district court's opinion.

A. The '216 Patent

Uniloc's '216 patent is directed to a software registration system to deter copying of software. The system allows the software to run without restrictions (in "use mode") only if the system determines that the software installation is legitimate. A representative embodiment functions as follows. First, a user intending to use the software in "use mode" enters certain user information when prompted, which may include a software serial number and/or name and address information. An algorithm on the user's computer (a "local licensee unique ID generating means") combines the inputted information into "a registration number unique to an intending licensee" (a "local licensee unique ID"). '216 patent, Abstract. The user information is also sent to the vendor's system, which performs the identical algorithm (a "remote licensee unique ID generating means") to create a "remote licensee unique ID" for the user. When the application boots again, a "mode switching means" compares the local and remote licensee unique IDs. If they match, the program enters into "use mode." If they do not match, the program enters into "demo mode," wherein certain features are disabled. . . .

B. The Accused Product

The accused product is Microsoft's Product Activation feature that acts as a gatekeeper to Microsoft's Word XP, Word 2003, and Windows XP software programs. Upon receipt of Microsoft's retail software program, the user must enter a 25-character alphanumeric product key contained within the packaging of Microsoft's retail products. If the Key is valid, the user is asked to agree to the End User License Agreement ("EULA"), by which the licensor-licensee relationship is initiated.

At about this time, the software creates a Product ID ("PID") and a Hardware ID ("HWID") on the user's computer. The PID is formed from the combination of the Product Key, information from the software CD, and a random number from the user's computer. The HWID is generated from information about the user's computer. The user may use the software without initiating Product Activation, but such use is temporally limited (50 start-ups of Office and 30 days use of Windows until basic functions like saving and printing are deactivated) and functionally limited (no updates can be downloaded and installed). If the user elects to initiate Product Activation, the software sends a digital license request to Microsoft over the internet, which includes: the PID, the HWID, and additional activation information. At Microsoft's remote location, this information is entered into one of two software algorithms: the MD5 message digest algorithm ("MD5") for Office products and the SHA-1 secure hash algorithm ("SHA-1") for Windows products.

II. Discussion

***

C. New Trial on Damages

The jury here awarded Uniloc $388 million, based on the testimony of Uniloc's expert, Dr. Gemini. Dr. Gemini opined that damages should be $564,946,803. This was based on a hypothetical negotiation between Uniloc and Microsoft and the *Georgia-Pacific* factors. *See Georgia-Pacific Corp. v. U.S. Plywood Corp.*, 318 F. Supp. 1116 (S.D.N.Y. 1970). Gemini began with an internal pre-litigation Microsoft document that stated:

> Product Keys are valuable for two major reasons. First, since Product Keys can be used to install a product and create a valid Product ID, you can associate a monetary value to them. An appraisal process found that a Product Key is worth anywhere between $10 and $10,000 depending on usage. Secondly, Product Keys contain short digital signature technology that Microsoft Research created. For these reasons, it is crucial that Product Keys are handled with maximum security.

Gemini took the lowest value, $10, and testified that this is "the isolated value of Product Activation." Gemini then applied the so-called "25 percent rule of thumb," hypothesizing that 25% of the value of the product would go to the patent owner and the other 75% would remain with Microsoft, resulting in a baseline royalty rate of $2.50 per license issued. Gemini justified the use of the rule of thumb because it has "been accepted by Courts as an appropriate methodology in determining damages, in [his] experience, in other cases." He then considered several of the *Georgia-Pacific* factors, with the idea being "to adjust this 25% up or down depending on how [the *Georgia-Pacific* factors] favor[ ] either party." At bottom, he concluded that the factors in favor of Uniloc and Microsoft generally balanced out and did not change the royalty rate. He then multiplied the $2.50 royalty rate by the number of new licenses to Office and Windows products, 225,978,721, to get a final reasonable royalty of $564,946,803. Gemini then "did kind of a check to determine whether that number was reasonable. It's obviously, you know, a significant amount of money. I wanted to check to make sure it was a reasonable number." The "check" was performed by "estimating the gross revenues for the accused products" by multiplying the 225,978,721 licenses by the average sales price per license of $85. The resulting gross revenue value was $19.28 billion. Gemini then calculated that his damages calculation resulted in a royalty rate over the gross revenue of Office and Windows of approximately 2.9%. Gemini presented this information in a demonstrative pie chart to accompany his testimony. In response to Uniloc's attorney's question: "And have you prepared a chart or a graph or a pie chart to show us this comparison?" Uniloc's attorney, Mr. Cronin stated, "Your honor, there's no objection," and Microsoft attorney Mr. Scherkenbach stated, "Right, there is no objection." Gemini then opined that "in my experience, and data I've seen as far as industry royalty rates for software, which are generally above—on average, above 10% or 10, 11%, I felt that this royalty was reasonable and well within that range."

Microsoft had challenged the 25% rule *in limine* and attempted to exclude Mr. Gemini's testimony. The district court noted that "the concept of a 'rule of thumb' is perplexing in an area of the law where reliability and precision are deemed paramount," but rejected Microsoft's position because the rule has been widely accepted. The district court thus considered the use of the rule of thumb to be reasonable. *In Limine,* 632 F. Supp. 2d at 151. Microsoft contested Gemini's use of the entire market value rule "check" because Product Activation was not the basis of the consumer demand for Microsoft's Office and Windows products. The district court agreed with Microsoft, and granted a new trial on damages, because the "$19 billion cat was never put back into the bag" and the jury may have "used the $19 billion figure to 'check' its significant award of $388,000,000." *Uniloc II,* 640 F. Supp. 2d at 185.

On appeal, the parties present the court with three damages issues: 1) the propriety of using the 25 percent rule; 2) application of the entire market value rule as a "check"; and 3) excessiveness of damages. Because this court affirms the district court's conditional grant of a new trial on damages, this court need not reach the last issue.

1. 25 Percent Rule

Section 284 of Title 35 of the United States Code provides that on finding infringement of a valid patent, damages shall "in no event [be] less than a reasonable royalty for the use made of the invention by the infringer, together with interest and costs as fixed by the court." In litigation, a reasonable royalty is often determined on the basis of a hypothetical negotiation, occurring between the parties at the time that infringement began. *Wang Labs. Inc. v. Toshiba Corp.*, 993 F.2d 858, 869-70 (Fed. Cir. 1993). A reasonable royalty is the predominant measure of damages in patent infringement cases.

The 25 percent rule of thumb is a tool that has been used to approximate the reasonable royalty rate that the manufacturer of a patented product would be willing to offer to pay to the patentee during a hypothetical negotiation. Robert Goldscheider, John Jarosz and Carla Mulhern, *Use of the 25 Per Cent Rule in Valuing IP*, 37 *les Nouvelles* 123, 123 (Dec. 2002) ("*Valuing IP*"). "The Rule suggests that the licensee pay a royalty rate equivalent to 25 per cent of its expected profits for the product that incorporates the IP at issue." *Id.* As explained by its leading proponent, Robert Goldscheider, the rule takes the following form:

> An estimate is made of the licensee's expected profits for the product that embodies the IP at issue. Those profits are divided by the expected net sales over that same period to arrive at a profit rate. That resulting profit rate, say 16 per cent, is then multiplied by 25 per cent to arrive at a running royalty rate. In this example, the resulting royalty rate would be 4 per cent. Going forward (or calculating backwards, in the case of litigation), the 4 per cent royalty rate is applied to net sales to arrive at royalty payments due to the IP owner.

Id. at 124. The underlying "assumption is that the licensee should retain a majority (i.e. 75 percent) of the profits, because it has undertaken substantial development, operational and commercialization risks, contributed other technology/IP and/or brought to bear its own development, operational and commercialization contributions." *Id.*

The rule was originally based on Goldscheider's observations of commercial licenses entered into by a "Swiss subsidiary of a large American company, with 18 licensees around the world, each having an exclusive territory." *Id.* The rights transferred were a portfolio of patents and other intellectual property apparently related to the patented products. *Id.* The term of each of these licenses was for three years, with the expectation that the licenses would be renewed. *Id.* at 123. The licensees "faced strong competition," and "were either first or second in sales volume, and probably profitability, in their respective market." *Id.*

According to its proponents, the veracity of the 25 percent rule has been "confirmed by a careful examination of years of licensing and profit data, across companies and industries." John C. Jarosz, Carla S. Mulhern and Michael Wagner, *The 25% Rule Lives On*, IP Law360, Sept. 8, 2010. Goldscheider published a further empirical study in 2002, concluding that across all industries, the median royalty rate was 22.6 percent, and that the data supported the use of the 25 percent rule "as a tool of analysis." *Valuing IP*, 37 *les Nouvelles* at 132-33. Additionally, in a 1997 study of licensing organizations, 25 percent of the organizations indicated that they use the 25 percent rule as a starting point in negotiations. Stephen A. Degnan & Corwin Horton, *A Survey of Licensed Royalties*, 32 *les Nouvelles* 91, 95 (June 1997).

The 25 percent rule has, however, met its share of criticism that can be broadly separated into three categories. First, it fails to account for the unique relationship between the patent and the accused product. *See* Gregory K. Leonard and Lauren J. Stiroh, *Economic Approaches to Intellectual Property Policy, Litigation, and*

Management, 949 PLI/Pat 425, 454-55 (Sept.-Nov. 2008) ("[The 25 percent rule] takes no account of the importance of the patent to the profits of the product sold, the potential availability of close substitutes or equally noninfringing alternatives, or any of the other idiosyncrasies of the patent at issue that would have affected a real-world negotiation."); Richard S. Toikka, *Patent Licensing Under Competitive and Non-Competitive Conditions,* 82 J. Pat. & Trademark Off. Soc'y 279, 292-93 (Apr. 2000) (arguing that it fails to "distinguish between monopoly and normal profit. . . . Thus for narrow patents, the rule may be overly generous to the patentee, and for broad patents it may be overly stingy"). Second, it fails to account for the unique relationship between the parties. *See* Ted Hagelin, *Valuation of Patent Licenses,* Tex. Intell. Prop. L.J. 423, 425-26 (Spring 2004) (noting that the rule should not be used in isolation because it fails to "account[ ] for the different levels of risk assumed by a licensor and licensee"); *Hypothetical Negotiations* at 702 ("[T]he rule is unlikely to have any basis in the accused infringer's industry, in the technology involved in either the patent or the accused product or service, or in the claimed invention's contribution to the infringing product or service."). Finally, the rule is essentially arbitrary and does not fit within the model of the hypothetical negotiation within which it is based. *See* Roy J. Epstein and Alan J. Marcus, *Economic Analysis of the Reasonable Royalty: Simplification and Extension of the Georgia-Pacific Factors,* 85 J. Pat. & Trademark Off. Soc'y 55, 574 (July 2003) ("[The 25% and the 5%] rules of thumb are best understood as special cases [ ] that may be appropriate to a given situation only by chance."); Roy J. Epstein, *Modeling Patent Damages: Rigorous and Defensible Calculations* (2003) (paper presented at the AIPLA 2003 Annual Meeting) at 22 *available at* http://www.royepstein.com/epstein_aipla_2003_article_website.pdf (last accessed Nov. 19, 2010) (arguing that the 25% rule "shortcut" "is essentially arbitrary. Because it is based on ex post results, it does not necessarily relate to the results of a negotiation that took place prior to the infringement").

The admissibility of the bare 25 percent rule has never been squarely presented to this court. Nevertheless, this court has passively tolerated its use where its acceptability has not been the focus of the case, or where the parties disputed only the percentage to be applied (i.e. one-quarter to one-third), but agreed as to the rule's appropriateness. Lower courts have invariably admitted evidence based on the 25% rule, largely in reliance on its widespread acceptance or because its admissibility was uncontested. . . .

In *Daubert,* 509 U.S. at 589, and *Kumho Tire,* 526 U.S. 137, the Supreme Court assigned to the district courts the responsibility of ensuring that all expert testimony must pertain to "scientific, technical, or other specialized knowledge" under Federal Rule of Evidence ("FRE") 702, which in turn required the judge to determine that the testimony was based on a firm scientific or technical grounding. *Daubert,* 509 U.S. at 589-90; *Kumho Tire,* 526 U.S. at 148. "Expert testimony which does not relate to any issue in the case is not relevant and, ergo, non-helpful." *Daubert,* 509 U.S. at 591.

This court now holds as a matter of Federal Circuit law that the 25 percent rule of thumb is a fundamentally flawed tool for determining a baseline royalty rate in a hypothetical negotiation. Evidence relying on the 25 percent rule of thumb is thus inadmissible under *Daubert* and the Federal Rules of Evidence, because it fails to tie a reasonable royalty base to the facts of the case at issue.

The patentee bears the burden of proving damages. *Lucent Techs., Inc. v. Gateway, Inc.,* 580 F.3d 1301, 1324 (Fed. Cir. 2009). To properly carry this burden, the patentee must "sufficiently [tie the expert testimony on damages] to the facts of the case." *Daubert,* 509 U.S. at 591. If the patentee fails to tie the theory to the facts of the case, the testimony must be excluded. . . . The bottom line of *Kumho Tire* and *Joiner* is that one major determinant of whether an expert should be excluded under *Daubert* is whether he has justified the application of a general theory to the facts of the case. Consistent with this conclusion, this court has held that "[a]ny evidence unrelated to the claimed invention does not support compensation for infringement but punishes beyond the reach of the statute." *ResQNet.com, Inc. v. Lansa, Inc.,* 594 F.3d 860, 869 (Fed. Cir. 2010).

In *ResQNet, Lucent Technologies,* and *Wordtech Systems, Inc. v. Integrated Networks Solutions, Inc.,* 609 F.3d 1308 (Fed. Cir. 2010), this court determined that a patentee could not rely on license agreements that were "radically different from the hypothetical agreement under consideration" to determine a reasonable royalty. *Lucent Techs.,* 580 F.3d at 1327. *See also ResQNet,* 594 F.3d at 870-72 (holding that evidence of royalty rates from licenses without a relationship to the claimed invention could not form the basis of a reasonable royalty calculation). In *Lucent Technologies,* the patentee's expert relied in large part on "eight varied license agreements," four of which involved "PC-related patents," but either the specific subject matter of the patents was not explained to the jury or the license was "directed to a vastly different situation than the hypothetical licensing scenario of the present case," and four of which Lucent did not describe the relationship between the patented technology licensed therein and the licensee's products. *See* 580 F.3d at 1328-31. This court noted that the "licenses relied on by the patentee in proving damages [must be] sufficiently comparable to the hypothetical license at issue in suit," *id.* at 1325, and that the patentee's failure to do so "weighs strongly against the jury's award" relying on such non-comparable licenses, *id.* at 1332. Similarly, in *ResQNet,* the patentee's expert "used licenses with no relationship to the claimed invention to drive the royalty rate up to unjustified double-digit levels," looking at licenses that did not mention the patents and had no "other discernible link to the claimed technology." 594 F.3d at 870. This court rejected the expert's testimony, holding that the district court "must consider licenses that are commensurate with what the defendant has appropriated. If not, a prevailing plaintiff would be free to inflate the reasonable royalty analysis with conveniently selected licenses without an economic or other link to the technology in question." *Id.* at 872. This court held that on remand, "the trial court should not rely on unrelated licenses to increase the reasonable royalty rate above rates more clearly linked to the economic demand for the claimed technology." *Id.* at 872-73.

Similarly, in *Wordtech,* the patentee "introduced thirteen patent licenses that it previously granted to third parties for rights to some or all of the patents-in-suit" to argue to support the jury's damages determination. 609 F.3d at 1319. This court rejected eleven of the licenses because they were running royalty licenses (the patentee had only asked for a lump sum payment) and represented far lower rates than the jury returned. *Id.* at 1320-21. This court rejected the remaining two licenses (both for lump sum payments) because "[n]either license describe[d] how the parties calculated each lump sum, the licensees' intended products, or how many products each licensee expected to produce." *Id.* at 1320.

The meaning of these cases is clear: there must be a basis in fact to associate the royalty rates used in prior licenses to the particular hypothetical negotiation at issue in the case. The 25 percent rule of thumb as an abstract and largely theoretical construct fails to satisfy this fundamental requirement. The rule does not say anything about a particular hypothetical negotiation or reasonable royalty involving any particular technology, industry, or party. Relying on the 25 percent rule of thumb in a reasonable royalty calculation is far more unreliable and irrelevant than reliance on parties' unrelated licenses, which we rejected in *ResQNet* and *Lucent Technologies.* There, the prior licenses at least involved the same general industry and at least some of the same parties as the hypothetical negotiations at issue, and in *Wordtech* even involved licenses to the patents in suit entered into by the patentee-plaintiff. Lacking even these minimal connections, the 25 percent rule of thumb would predict that the same 25%/75% royalty split would begin royalty discussions between, for example, (a) TinyCo and IBM over a strong patent portfolio of twelve patents covering various aspects of a pioneering hard drive, and (b) Kodak and Fuji over a single patent to a tiny improvement in a specialty film emulsion.

It is of no moment that the 25 percent rule of thumb is offered merely as a starting point to which the *Georgia-Pacific* factors are then applied to bring the rate up or down. Beginning from a fundamentally flawed premise and adjusting it based on legitimate considerations specific to the facts of the case nevertheless results in a fundamentally flawed conclusion. This is reflected in *Lucent Technologies,* in which unrelated licenses were considered under *Georgia-Pacific* factor 1, but this court held that the entire royalty calculation was unsupported by substantial evidence.

To be admissible, expert testimony opining on a reasonable royalty rate must "carefully tie proof of damages to the claimed invention's footprint in the market place." *ResQNet,* 594 F.3d at 869. This court has sanctioned the use of the *Georgia-Pacific* factors to frame the reasonable royalty inquiry. Those factors properly tie the reasonable royalty calculation to the facts of the hypothetical negotiation at issue. This court's rejection of the 25 percent rule of thumb is not intended to limit the application of any of the *Georgia-Pacific* factors. In particular, factors 1 and 2—looking at royalties paid or received in licenses for the patent in suit or in comparable licenses—and factor 12—looking at the portion of profit that may be customarily allowed in the particular business for the use of the invention or similar inventions—remain valid and important factors in the determination of a reasonable royalty rate. However, evidence purporting to apply to these, and any other factors, must be tied to the relevant facts and circumstances of the particular case at issue and the hypothetical negotiations that would have taken place in light of those facts and circumstances at the relevant time.

In this case, it is clear that Gemini's testimony was based on the use of the 25% rule of thumb as an arbitrary, general rule, unrelated to the facts of this case. When asked the basis of his opinion that the rule of thumb would apply here, Gemini testified: "[i]t's generally accepted. I've used it. I've seen others use it. It's a widely accepted rule." Upon further questioning, Dr. Gemini revealed that he had been involved in only four or five non-litigation related negotiations, and had recommended the 25% rule only once in a case involving a power tool. He did not testify that the parties here had a practice of beginning negotiations with a 25%/75% split, or that the contribution of Product Activation to Office and Word justified such a split. He did not base his 25 percent baseline on other licenses involving the patent at issue or comparable licenses. In short, Gemini's starting point of a 25 percent royalty had no relation to the facts of the case, and as such, was arbitrary, unreliable, and irrelevant. The use of such a rule fails to pass muster under *Daubert* and taints the jury's damages calculation.

This court thus holds that Microsoft is entitled to a new trial on damages.

2. Entire Market Value Rule

As discussed above, Gemini performed "a check to determine whether" his $564,946,803 royalty figure was reasonable by comparing it to his calculation of Microsoft's approximate total revenue for Office and Windows of $19.28 billion. During trial, Gemini testified that his calculated royalty accounted for only 2.9% of Microsoft's revenue, and accented his point by reference to a prepared pie chart, showing Microsoft's $19.28 billion in revenue with a 2.9% sliver representing his calculated royalty rate. He concluded that 2.9% was a reasonable royalty based on his experience that royalty rates for software are "generally above—on average, above 10% or 10, 11%."

The entire market value rule allows a patentee to assess damages based on the entire market value of the accused product only where the patented feature creates the "basis for customer demand" or "substantially create[s] the value of the component parts." *Lucent Techs.*, 580 F.3d at 1336; *Rite-Hite Corp. v. Kelley Co.*, 56 F.3d 1538, 1549-50 (Fed. Cir. 1995). This rule is derived from Supreme Court precedent requiring that "the patentee . . . must in every case give evidence tending to separate or apportion the defendant's profits and the patentee's damages between the patented feature and the unpatented features, and such evidence must be reliable and tangible, and not conjectural or speculative," or show that "the entire value of the whole machine, as a marketable article, is properly and legally attributable to the patented feature." *Garretson v. Clark*, 111 U.S. 120, 121, 4 S. Ct. 291, 28 L. Ed. 371 (1884). *See also Lucent Techs.*, 580 F.3d at 1336-37 (tracing the origins of the entire market value to several Supreme Court cases including *Garretson*).

Microsoft argues that Uniloc employed the entire market value of Office and Windows by virtue of Gemini's pie chart, his comparison of his calculated royalty to the total revenue Microsoft earns through the accused products, and Uniloc's attorneys' belittlement of Microsoft's expert's royalty figure as representing only .0003% of total revenue. Microsoft argues that Uniloc's use of the entire market value rule was not proper because it is undisputed that Product Activation did not create the basis for customer demand or substantially create the value of the component parts. Microsoft continues that Gemini's testimony tainted the jury's damages deliberations, regardless of its categorization as a "check."

Uniloc responds that: (1) Microsoft did not object at trial and so waived any evidentiary argument to Gemini's testimony and demonstratives; (2) the entire market value of the product can be used if the royalty rate is low enough; and (3) the $19 billion figure was used only as a "check," and the jury was instructed not to base its damages determination on the entire market value, an instruction it should be presumed to have followed.

The district court agreed with Microsoft, and ordered a conditional new trial on damages. It noted that "Uniloc conceded customers do not buy Office or Windows because of [Product Activation] and said it would not base a royalty calculation on the entire market value of the products." *Uniloc II*, 640 F. Supp. 2d at 184-85. As such, the use of the entire market value of Office and Windows in the form of the $19 billion figure was "irrelevant" and "taint[ed]" the jury's damages award. *Id.* at 185. The district court also disagreed with Uniloc that Microsoft had waived its arguments to the entire market value, noting that "Microsoft objected specifically under the entire market value rule to use of a demonstrative pie chart," and that "[t]he Court preliminarily allowed it but after hearing the testimony instructed counsel to stay away from the $19 billion figure." *Id.*

This court agrees with Microsoft and the district court that Uniloc's use of the $19 billion "check" was improper under the entire market value rule. First, regarding Uniloc's assertion that Microsoft has waived the issue, this court will not second-guess the district court's explicit recognition of Microsoft's objections to Gemini's testimony. FRE 103(a) notes that "Error may not be predicated upon a ruling which admits or excludes evidence unless . . . (1) Objection.—In case the ruling is one admitting evidence, a timely objection or motion to strike appears of record. . . . Once the court makes a definitive ruling on the record admitting or excluding evidence, either at or before trial, a party need not renew an objection or offer of proof to preserve a claim of error for appeal." The district court here explicitly noted that Microsoft's objection fell into the exception at the last line of FRE 103(a): "Although Microsoft did not continue to repeat an objection, it made its position on this evidence sufficiently clear to preserve the instant challenge" to Gemini's use of the entire market value rule. This is supported by Microsoft's *in limine* filings and Uniloc's response, where Uniloc explicitly said that it would not be relying on the entire market value of the accused products. This court thus agrees with the district court that Microsoft has not waived its objection.

Uniloc argues that the entire market value of the products may appropriately be admitted if the royalty rate is low enough, relying on the following statement in *Lucent Technologies:*

> Simply put, the base used in a running royalty calculation can always be the value of the entire commercial embodiment, as long as the magnitude of the rate is within an acceptable range (as determined by the evidence). . . . Microsoft surely would have little reason to complain about the supposed application of the entire market value rule had the jury applied a royalty rate of .1% (instead of 8%) to the market price of the infringing programs.

580 F.3d at 1338-39. Just before this statement, however, this court held that one of the flaws in the use of the entire market value in that case was "the lack of evidence demonstrating the patented method of the Day patent as the basis—or even a substantial basis—of the consumer demand for Outlook. . . . The only reasonable conclusion supported by the evidence is that the infringing use of the date-picker tool in Outlook is but a very small component of a much larger software program." *Id.* at 1338. Thus, in context, the passage relied on by Uniloc does not support its position. The Supreme Court and this court's precedents do not allow consideration of the entire market value of accused products for minor patent improvements simply by asserting a low enough royalty rate. *Lucent Techs.*, 580 F.3d at 1336 ("In one sense, our law on the entire market value rule is quite clear. For the entire market value rule to apply, the patentee *must* prove that the patent-related feature is the basis for customer

demand" (emphasis added, internal citations omitted)); *Rite-Hite,* 56 F.3d at 1549 (same); *Bose Corp. v. JBL, Inc.,* 274 F.3d 1354, 1361 (Fed. Cir. 2001) (same); *TWM Mfg. Co. v. Dura Corp.,* 789 F.2d 895, 901 (Fed. Cir. 1986) ("The entire market value rule allows for the recovery of damages based on the value of an entire apparatus containing several features, when the feature patented constitutes the basis for customer demand.").

This case provides a good example of the danger of admitting consideration of the entire market value of the accused where the patented component does not create the basis for customer demand. As the district court aptly noted, "[t]he $19 billion cat was never put back into the bag even by Microsoft's cross-examination of Mr. Gemini and re-direct of Mr. Napper, and in spite of a final instruction that the jury may not award damages based on Microsoft's entire revenue from all the accused products in the case." *Uniloc II,* 640 F. Supp. 2d at 185. This is unsurprising. The disclosure that a company has made $19 billion dollars in revenue from an infringing product cannot help but skew the damages horizon for the jury, regardless of the contribution of the patented component to this revenue. Uniloc exacerbated the situation in colloquies like the following on cross-examination of Microsoft's damages expert, in which it implied a relationship between the entire market value of the accused products and the patent:

> Q [Uniloc]. You understand that there are approximately $20 billion in sales of infringing product, correct?
> A [Napper]. That's the calculation by Mr. Gemini, yes, the entire market value of those products.
> Q. And you understand your lump-sum max theory is $7 million?
> A. Yes.
> Q. And that would be an effective royalty of approximately .000035%?
> A. If one were inappropriately putting the entire market value of the products, that's what it would result in.
> Q. Uniloc invents it, correct?
> A. They have a patent, yes.
> Q. And under your theory, Microsoft goes out and infringes a valid patent, right?
> A. That's my assumption.
> Q. Under your theory, Microsoft brings in billions in revenue and sales from the sales of the infringing product, to wit, approximately 20, correct?
> A. The entire market value of those products, that's correct.
> Q. And at the end of the day, the infringer, Microsoft, who violated the patent law, they get to keep 99.9999% of the box and the inventor, whose patent they infringed, he gets the privilege of keeping .00003%?
> A. When expressed as the entire market value of the products, that's correct.
> Q. And that's reasonable to you?
> A. Yes.

This is in clear derogation of the entire market value rule, because the entire market value of the accused products has not been shown to be derived from the patented contribution.

Uniloc's final argument is that the use of the $19 billion figure was only as a check, and the jury must be presumed to have followed the jury instruction and not based its damages calculation on the entire market value rule. This argument attempts to gloss over the purpose of the check as lending legitimacy to the reasonableness of Gemini's $565 million damages calculation. Even if the jury's damages calculation was not based wholly on the entire market value check, the award was supported in part by the faulty foundation of the entire market value. Moreover, Uniloc's derision of Microsoft's damages expert by virtue of the .00003% of the entire market value that his damages calculation represented may have inappropriately contributed to the jury's rejection of his calculations. Thus, the fact that the entire market value was brought in as only a "check" is of no moment.

For the foregoing reasons, this court concludes that the district court did not abuse its discretion in granting a conditional new trial on damages for Uniloc's violation of the entire market value rule.

***

Comments

1. ***Statutory Basis for Reasonable Royalty.*** Section 284 of the patent code expressly provides a baseline amount of damages, stating that damages should be "in no event less than a reasonable royalty." It is up to the court, balancing several factors, to determine what is reasonable.

2. ***Reasonable Royalty Factors.*** The district court in *Georgia-Pacific Corp. v. United States Plywood Corp.*, 318 F. Supp. 1116, 1120 (S.D.N.Y. 1970), an oft-cited case, listed 15 factors relevant to the determination of the amount of a reasonable royalty. The *Trio Process* and *Lucent* courts relied on several of these factors. Perhaps the most important factors are those relating to established conditions within the market or industry. For instance, *Trio Process* placed a great deal of emphasis on the existence of an established royalty as a guide to what rate a willing licensee–willing licensor would have agreed. If the patentee had licensed the patent to five competitors at a 5 percent rate, there is a greater likelihood the patentee and defendant would have agreed on the same rate. Of course, an established royalty rate may not reflect the assumptions of an arm's-length negotiation between a willing licensee–willing licensor because the parties to the prior license may not be competitors, the market may not be fully developed at the time the license was negotiated, or the rate may be artificially low due to industry-wide infringement and lack of respect for the patent. For a detailed analysis relating to calculating a royalty base, *see Cornell Univ. v. Hewlett-Packard Co.*, 609 F. Supp. 2d 279 (N.D.N.Y. 2009) (Rader, J., sitting by designation). For more on calculating a reasonable royalty, *see* Daralyn J. Durie & Mark A. Lemley, *A Structured Approach to Calculating Reasonable Royalties*, 14 LEWIS & CLARK L. REV. 627 (2010).

3. ***Willing Licensor–Willing Licensee.*** As discussed in *Lucent*, courts oftentimes construct a hypothetical negotiation to arrive at a royalty rate. The timeframe for this negotiation is at the time defendant began infringing and is based on the assumption that the patent is not invalid. But this fictional construct is not without criticism. In *Georgia-Pacific*, for example, the court warned against placing the negotiation in a "vacuum of pure logic," outside a marketplace context that includes relative bargaining strength, commercial preferences of the parties, and commercial past performance of the claimed invention. 318 F. Supp. at 1121. And the *Lucent* case highlights, to use an established royalty, there must be a requisite connection between the

established licenses with the infringed patent. *See also ResQNet.com v. Lansa, Inc.*, 594 F.3d 860, 871 (Fed. Cir. 2010) (stating the "trial court, like the one in *Lucent* made no effort to link certain licenses to the infringed patent").

The 25 percent rule has historically been widely applied to approximate a reasonable royalty, particularly in the context of the *Georgia-Pacific* factors. The rule, as generally applied, estimates the licensee's expected profits to calculate an expected profit rate (say 10%, for example); divides the expected profits by the expected net sales over the period of infringing activity; multiplies the expected profit rate by 25 percent, thus reaching a royalty rate (10% x 25% = 2.5%). The *Uniloc* court referred to this rule as "fundamentally flawed" and "inadmissible under *Daubert*." For a vigorous defense of the 25 percent rule in the wake of *Uniloc, see* Robert Goldscheider, *The Classic 25% Rule and the Art of Intellectual Property Licensing*, 6 DUKE L. & TECH. REV. 1 (2011).

4. ***The Entire Market Value Rule.*** The entire market value (EVM) rule can be a powerful tool for patent owners. It is not uncommon for a product (particularly in the IT industry) to include several independently patented components (and some unpatented components). If it is deemed that an unauthorized use of such a product infringes only one of the product's patented features, the question becomes how to measure damages. How do you measure damages? Under the EMV rule, if the patentee proves the patent-related feature is the basis for customer demand for the product, the patentee can recover damages based on the value of an entire apparatus. In *Cornell University, supra*, at 286-287, Judge Rader, sitting by designation, identified three conditions that must be met before the EMV rule applies:

> The entire market value rule in the context of royalties requires adequate proof of three conditions: (1) the infringing components must be the basis for customer demand for the entire machine including the parts beyond the claimed invention; (2) the individual infringing and non-infringing components must be sold together so that they constitute a functional unit or are parts of a complete machine or single assembly of parts; and (3) the individual infringing and non-infringing components must be analogous to a single functioning unit. It is not enough that the infringing and non-infringing parts are sold together for mere business advantage.

This rule has come under increasing criticism, particularly among commentators and in Congress, which has sought (unsuccessfully) to enact patent damages reform that would dismantle the EMV rule. The judges in *Lucent* responded to this criticism by defending the EMV as reflecting the "realities of patent licensing and the flexibility needed in transferring intellectual property rights." While *Lucent* reiterated the longstanding principle of the EMV rule relating to consumer demand, the court also stated "the base used in a running royalty calculation can always be the value of the entire commercial embodiment, as long as the magnitude of the rate is within an acceptable range"; in other words, the royalty calculation can be based on the value of the commercial embodiment if the royalty rate is low enough—or the apportionment is already factored into the low royalty rate. As the *Lucent* court wrote, "Microsoft surely would have little reason to complain about the supposed application of the entire market value rule had the jury applied a royalty rate of 0.1 percent (instead of 8 percent) to the market price of the infringing programs." But the

Uniloc court appeared to clarify this language, emphasizing the importance of context in the application of the EMV rule and the need for establishing the basis for consumer demand of the patented component. In directly addressing *Lucent,* the court expressly noted that neither Supreme Court nor Federal Circuit precedents "allow consideration of the entire market value of accused products for minor patent improvements simply by asserting a low enough royalty rate." The court was concerned with "skew[ing] the damages horizon for the jury." As such, the facts in *Uniloc,* particularly evidence that "a company has made $19 billion dollars in revenue from an infringement product," provide "a good example of the danger of admitting consideration of the entire market value of the accused [products] where the patented component does not create the basis for consumer demand."

Moreover, the EMV rule is useful when "there is no established market value for the infringing component or feature." Thus, the problem with the EMV rule is one of application, which demands "the multiplier [to] account[] for the proportion of the base represented by the infringing component or feature." *See also Cornell, supra,* at 288 (greatly reducing the damage award due to the fact that "Cornell did not offer a single demand curve or any market evidence that Cornell's invention drove demand for" the HP's servers); *IP Innovation, LLC. v. Red Hat, Inc.,* 705 F. Supp. 2d 687, 691 (E.D.Texas 2010) (Rader, J., sitting by designation) (stating patentee's expert "improperly inflates both the royalty base and the royalty rate by relying on irrelevant or unreliable evidence and by failing to account for the economic realities of this claimed component as part of a larger system").

B. EQUITABLE RELIEF

Equitable relief can be broken down into two forms of injunctions: (1) preliminary; and (2) permanent. The latter is sought after a final ruling on the defendant's infringement liability, and is explored in *eBay.* The preliminary injunction—at issue in *Amazon.com*—is asked for by the patentee before a final ruling on the defendant's infringement liability. In this instance, the patentee is asserting that he will likely succeed on the merits regarding infringement and validity. Therefore, the court should enjoin the alleged infringing activity before a final ruling lest the patentee suffer irreparable harm.

1. Preliminary Injunctions

AMAZON.COM, INC. v. BARNESANDNOBLE.COM, INC.
239 F.3d 1343 (Fed. Cir. 2001)

CLEVENGER, Circuit Judge.

This is a patent infringement suit brought by Amazon.com, Inc. ("Amazon") against barnesandnoble.com, inc., and barnesandnoble.com llc (together, "BN"). Amazon moved for a preliminary injunction to prohibit BN's use of a feature of its web site called "Express Lane." BN resisted the preliminary injunction on several grounds, including that its Express Lane feature did not infringe the claims of Amazon's patent, and that substantial questions exist as to the validity of Amazon's patent. The United States District Court for the Western District of Washington rejected BN's contentions. Instead, the district court held that Amazon had presented a case showing a likelihood of infringement by BN, and that BN's challenges to the validity of the patent in suit lacked sufficient merit to avoid awarding extraordinary preliminary injunctive relief to Amazon. The district court granted Amazon's motion, and now BN brings its timely appeal from the order entering the preliminary injunction.

After careful review of the district court's opinion, the record, and the arguments advanced by the parties, we conclude that BN has mounted a substantial challenge to the validity of the patent in suit. Because Amazon is not entitled to preliminary injunctive relief under these circumstances, we vacate the order of the district court that set the preliminary injunction in place and remand the case for further proceedings.

I

This case involves United States Patent No. 5,960,411 ("the '411 patent"), which issued on September 28, 1999, and is assigned to Amazon. On October 21, 1999, Amazon brought suit against BN alleging infringement of the patent and seeking a preliminary injunction.

* * *

The '411 patent describes a method and system in which a consumer can complete a purchase order for an item via an electronic network using only a "single action," such as the click of a computer mouse button on the client computer system. Amazon developed the patent to cope with what it considered to be frustrations presented by what is known as the "shopping cart model" purchase system for electronic commerce purchasing events. In previous incarnations of the shopping cart model, a purchaser using a client computer system (such as a personal computer executing a web browser program) could select an item from an electronic catalog, typically by clicking on an "Add to Shopping Cart" icon, thereby placing the item in the "virtual" shopping cart. Other items from the catalog could be added to the shopping cart in the same manner. When the shopper completed the selecting process, the electronic commercial event would move to the check-out counter, so to speak. Then, information regarding the purchaser's identity, billing and shipping addresses, and credit payment method would be inserted into the transactional information base by the soon-to-be purchaser. Finally, the purchaser would "click" on a button displayed on the screen or somehow issue a command to execute the completed order, and the server computer system would verify and store the information concerning the transaction.

. . . The '411 patent sought to reduce the number of actions required from a consumer to effect a placed order. . . . How, one may ask, is the number of purchaser interactions reduced? The answer is that the number of purchaser interactions is reduced because the purchaser has previously visited the seller's web site and has previously entered into the database of the seller all of the required billing and shipping information that is needed to effect a sales transaction. Thereafter, when the purchaser visits the seller's web site and wishes to purchase a product from that site, the patent specifies that only a single action is necessary to place the order for the item. . . .

II

The '411 patent has 26 claims, 4 of which are independent. Independent claims 1 and 11 are method claims directed to placing an order for an item, while independent claim 6 is an apparatus claim directed to a client system for ordering an item, and independent claim 9 is an apparatus claim directed to a server system for generating an order. Amazon asserted claims 1-3, 5-12, 14- 17, and 21-24 against BN. Although there are significant differences among the various independent and dependent claims in issue, for purposes of this appeal we may initially direct our primary focus on the "single action" limitation that is included in each claim. This focus is appropriate because BN's appeal attacks the injunction on the grounds that either its accused method does not infringe the "single action" limitation present in all of the claims, that the "single action" feature of the patent is invalid, or both.

* * *

BN's Express Lane thus presents a product page that contains the description of the item to be purchased and a "description" of the single action to be taken to effect placement of the order. Because only a single action need be taken to complete the purchase order once the product page is displayed, the district court concluded that Amazon had made a showing of likelihood of success on its allegation of patent infringement.

In response to BN's contention that substantial questions exist as to the validity of the '411 patent, the district court reviewed the prior art references upon which BN's validity challenge rested. The district court concluded that none of the prior art references anticipated the claims of the '411 patent under 35 U.S.C. § 102 (1994) or rendered the claimed invention obvious under 35 U.S.C. § 103 (1994).

III

The grant or denial of a preliminary injunction under 35 U.S.C. § 283 (1994) is within the sound discretion of the district court. *Novo Nordisk of N. Am., Inc. v. Genentech, Inc.* "An abuse of discretion may be established by showing that the court made a clear error of judgment in weighing relevant factors or exercised its discretion based upon an error of law or clearly erroneous factual findings." 77 F.3d at 1367.

As the moving party, Amazon is entitled to a preliminary injunction if it can succeed in showing: (1) a reasonable likelihood of success on the merits; (2) irreparable harm if an injunction is not granted; (3) a balance of hardships tipping in its favor; and (4) the injunction's favorable impact on the public interest. "These factors, taken individually, are not dispositive; rather, the district court must weigh and measure each factor against the other factors and against the form and magnitude of the relief requested." *Hybritech, Inc. v. Abbott Labs.,* 849 F.2d 1446, 1451 (Fed. Cir. 1988).

Irreparable harm is presumed when a clear showing of patent validity and infringement has been made. *Bell & Howell Document Mgmt. Prods. Co. v. Altek Sys.* "This presumption derives in part from the finite term of the patent grant, for patent expiration is not suspended during litigation, and the passage of time can work irremediable harm." 132 F.3d at 708.

Our case law and logic both require that a movant cannot be granted a preliminary injunction unless it establishes *both* of the first two factors, *i.e.*, likelihood of success on the merits and irreparable harm.

In order to demonstrate a likelihood of success on the merits, Amazon must show that, in light of the presumptions and burdens that will inhere at trial on the merits, (1) Amazon will likely prove that BN infringes the '411 patent, and (2) Amazon's infringement claim will likely withstand BN's challenges to the validity and enforceability of the '411 patent. If BN raises a substantial question concerning either infringement or validity, *i.e.*, asserts an infringement or invalidity defense that the patentee cannot prove "lacks substantial merit," the preliminary injunction should not issue.

Of course, whether performed at the preliminary injunction stage or at some later stage in the course of a particular case, infringement and validity analyses must be performed on a claim-by-claim basis. Therefore, in cases involving multiple patent claims, to demonstrate a likelihood of success on the merits, the patentee must demonstrate that it will likely prove infringement of one or more claims of the patents-in-suit, and that at least one of those same allegedly infringed claims will also likely withstand the validity challenges presented by the accused infringer.

Both infringement and validity are at issue in this appeal. It is well settled that an infringement analysis involves two steps: the claim scope is first determined, and then the properly construed claim is compared with the accused device to determine whether all of the claim limitations are present either literally or by a substantial equivalent. Conceptually, the first step of an invalidity analysis based on anticipation and/or obviousness in view of prior art references is no different from that of an infringement analysis. "It is elementary in patent law that, in determining whether a patent is valid and, if valid, infringed, the first step is to determine the meaning and scope of each claim in suit." *Lemelson v. Gen. Mills, Inc.*, 968 F.2d 1202, 1206 (Fed. Cir. 1992). Because the claims of a patent measure the invention at issue, the claims must be interpreted and given the same meaning for purposes of both validity and infringement analyses.

IV

BN contends on appeal that the district court committed legal errors that undermine the legitimacy of the preliminary injunction. In particular, BN asserts that the district court construed key claim limitations one way for purposes of its infringement analysis, and another way when considering BN's validity challenges. BN asserts that under a consistent claim interpretation, its Express Lane feature either does not infringe the '411 patent, or that if the patent is interpreted so as to support the charge of infringement, then the claims of the patent are subject to a severe validity challenge. When the key claim limitations are properly interpreted, BN thus asserts, it will be clear that Amazon is not likely to succeed on the merits of its infringement claim, or that BN has succeeded in calling the validity of the '411 patent into serious question. In addition, BN asserts that the district court misunderstood the teaching of the prior art references, thereby committing clear error in the factual predicates it established for comprehension of the prior art references.

V

It is clear from the district court's opinion that the meaning it ascribed to the "single action" limitation includes a temporal consideration. The "single action" to be taken to complete the purchase order, according to the district court, only occurs after other events have transpired. These preliminary events required pursuant to the district court's claim interpretation are the presentation of a description of the item to be purchased and the presentation of the single action the user must take to complete the purchase order for the item.

* * *

[W]e ultimately agree with Amazon and construe all four independent claims (*i.e.,* claims 1, 6, 9, and 11) to call for the single action to be performed immediately after a display of information about an item and without any intervening action, but not necessarily immediately after the first display or every display.

* * *

VI

A

When the correct meaning of the single action limitation is read on the accused BN system, it becomes apparent that the limitations of claim 1 are likely met by the accused system. The evidence on the record concerning the operation of BN's "Express Lane" feature is not in dispute. At the time that the '411 patent was issued, BN offered customers two purchasing options. One was called "Shopping Cart," and the other was called "Express Lane." The Shopping Cart option involved the steps of adding items to a "virtual" shopping cart and then "checking out" to complete the purchase. In contrast, the Express Lane option allowed customers who had registered for the feature to purchase items simply by "clicking" on the "Express Lane" button provided on the "detail page" or "product page" describing and identifying the book or other item to be purchased. The text beneath the Express Lane button invited users to "Buy it now with just 1 click!"

* * *

We note that the district court concluded that "[b]arnesandnoble.com infringes claims 1, 2, 3, 5, 11, 12, 12, 14, 15, 16, 17, 21, 22, 23, [and] 24," and "also infringes claims 6-10 of the '411 patent." However, the relevant determination at the preliminary injunction stage is substantial likelihood of success by Amazon of its infringement claims, not a legal conclusion as to the ultimate issue of infringement. We therefore interpret the district court's conclusions as determining that Amazon had demonstrated a substantial likelihood of establishing literal infringement of the enumerated claims.

* * *

E

After full review of the record before us, we conclude that under a proper claim interpretation, Amazon has made the showing that it is likely to succeed at trial on its infringement case. Given that we conclude that Amazon has demonstrated likely literal infringement of at least the four independent claims in the

'411 patent, we need not consider infringement under the doctrine of equivalents. The question remaining, however, is whether the district court correctly determined that BN failed to mount a substantial challenge to the validity of the claims in the '411 patent.

VII

The district court considered, but ultimately rejected, the potentially invalidating impact of several prior art references cited by BN. Because the district court determined that BN likely infringed all of the asserted claims, it did not focus its analysis of the validity issue on any particular claim. Instead, in its validity analysis, the district court appears to have primarily directed its attention to determining whether the references cited by BN implemented the single action limitation.

* * *

In this case, we find that the district court committed clear error by misreading the factual content of the prior art references cited by BN and by failing to recognize that BN had raised a substantial question of invalidity of the asserted claims in view of these prior art references.

Validity challenges during preliminary injunction proceedings can be successful, that is, they may raise substantial questions of invalidity, on evidence that would not suffice to support a judgment of invalidity at trial. The test for invalidity at trial is by evidence that is clear and convincing. To succeed with a summary judgment motion of invalidity, for example, the movant must demonstrate a lack of genuine dispute about material facts and show that the facts not in dispute are clear and convincing in demonstrating invalidity. In resisting a preliminary injunction, however, one need not make out a case of actual invalidity. Vulnerability is the issue at the preliminary injunction stage, while validity is the issue at trial. The showing of a substantial question as to invalidity thus requires less proof than the clear and convincing showing necessary to establish invalidity itself. That this is so is plain from our cases.

When moving for the extraordinary relief of a preliminary injunction, a patentee need not establish the validity of a patent beyond question. The patentee must, however, present a clear case supporting the validity of the patent in suit. Such a case might be supported, for example, by showing that the patent in suit had successfully withstood previous validity challenges in other proceedings. Further support for such a clear case might come from a long period of industry acquiescence in the patent's validity. Neither of those considerations benefit Amazon in this case, however, because the '411 patent has yet to be tested by trial, and it was issued only a few weeks before the start of this litigation.

In *Helifix,* we recently confronted the situation in which a district court had granted a motion of summary judgment of invalidity based on allegedly anticipatory prior art references, and shortly thereafter denied a motion for a preliminary injunction based on a validity challenge using the same prior art references. 208 F.3d at 1344-45. On appeal, the patentee sought reversal of the summary judgment and claimed entitlement to a preliminary injunction. We held that the summary judgment could not stand, because disputed issues of material fact on invalidity remained for resolution at trial. *Id.* at 208 F.3d 1352. Nonetheless, we expressly held that the quantum of evidence put forth—while falling short of demonstrating invalidity itself—was sufficient to prevent issuance of the preliminary injunction. *Id.* Particularly instructive for purposes of this case is the treatment of the anticipation issue in *Helifix*. A particular reference which did not on its face disclose all the limitations of the claim in suit was argued to be anticipatory, even though there was a conflict in the testimony as to whether the reference would have taught one of ordinary skill in the art the claim limitations not expressly stated on the face of the reference. Although insufficient to demonstrate invalidity for the purposes of the summary judgment motion, the reference *was* enough to prevent issuance of the preliminary injunction. *Id.* at 208 F.3d 1351-52.

The situation before us is similar. Here, we have several references that were urged upon the court as invalidating the asserted claims. The district court dismissed those references, for purposes of its invalidity analysis, because it did not perceive them to recite each and every limitation of the claims in suit. As we explain below in our review of the asserted prior art in this case, each of the asserted references clearly teaches key limitations of the claims of the patent in suit. BN argued to the district court that one of ordinary skill in the art could fill in the gaps in the asserted references, given the opportunity to do so at trial.

When the heft of the asserted prior art is assessed in light of the correct legal standards, we conclude that BN has mounted a serious challenge to the validity of Amazon's patent. We hasten to add, however, that this conclusion only undermines the prerequisite for entry of a preliminary injunction. Our decision today on the validity issue in no way resolves the ultimate question of invalidity. That is a matter for resolution at trial. It remains to be learned whether there are other references that may be cited against the patent, and it surely remains to be learned whether any shortcomings in BN's initial preliminary validity challenge will be magnified or dissipated at trial. All we hold, in the meantime, is that BN cast enough doubt on the validity of the '411 patent to avoid a preliminary injunction, and that the validity issue should be resolved finally at trial.

* * *

CELSIS IN VITRO, INC. v. CELLZDIRECT, INC.

664 F.3d 922 (Fed. Cir. 2012)

RADER, Chief Judge.

The United States District Court for the Northern District of Illinois granted Celsis In Vitro, Inc.'s ("Celsis") motion for a preliminary injunction against CellzDirect, Inc. and Invitrogen Corporation, now Life Technologies Corporation ("LTC"). Based on the record, the district court did not abuse its discretion. This court affirms.

I.

Celsis is the assignee of U.S. Patent No. 7,604,929 (filed Apr. 21, 2005) ("the '929 patent"), which claims methods for preparing multi-cryopreserved hepatocytes (a type of liver cell). Claims 1 and 10 of the '929 patent are on appeal:

> 1. A method of producing a desired preparation of multi-cryopreserved hepatocytes, said hepatocytes, being capable of being frozen and thawed at least two times, and in which greater than 70% of the hepatocytes of said preparation are viable after the final thaw, said method comprising:

(A) subjecting hepatocytes that have been frozen and thawed to *density gradient fractionation* to separate viable hepatocytes from non-viable hepatocytes,

(B) recovering the separated viable hepatocytes, and

(C) cryopreserving the recovered viable hepatocytes to thereby form said desired preparation of hepatocytes *without requiring a density gradient step* after thawing the hepatocytes for the second time, wherein the hepatocytes are not plated between the first and second cryopreservations, and wherein greater than 70% of the hepatocytes of said preparation are viable after the final thaw.

10. A method of investigating in vitro drug metabolism comprising incubating hepatocytes of a multi-cryopreserved hepatocyte preparation in the presence of a xenobiotic, and determining the metabolic fate of the xenobiotic, or the affect of the xenobiotic on the hepatocytes or on an enzyme or metabolic activity thereof, wherein the hepatocytes have been frozen and thawed at least two times, and wherein greater than 70% of the hepatocytes of said preparation are viable *without requiring a density gradient step* after thawing the hepatocytes for the second time, wherein the hepatocytes are not plated between the first and second cryopreservations.

'929 patent col. 19 l. 56-col. 20 l. 19, ll. 49-59 (emphasis added to the disputed claim terms).

The specification of the '929 patent explains that human hepatocytes are a useful laboratory model for evaluating drug candidates. Two problems, however, have limited their use. First, hepatocytes have a short lifespan which causes an inconsistent and limited supply. Specifically, the only sources of fresh hepatocytes are liver resections or non-transplantable livers of multi-organ donors. Due to this reliance on liver donation, fresh hepatocytes become available at unpredictable times. Researchers must wait until a liver donation and must often resume or begin research with little advance warning. This unpredictability hinders laboratory studies, which usually require a consistent source of supplies. This supply problem also limits research geographically to the region near the liver donor.

To obtain a more consistent supply, scientists sought techniques for long-term storage of hepatocytes in the laboratory. The option of cryopreservation (freezing) did not work well because freezing extensively damages hepatocyte cells. Hepatocytes are extremely fragile and, once damaged, do not recover. Thus, even a single instance of cryopreservation can jeopardize the need for a sufficient level of viable hepatocytes. For this reason, experts in this field met initial attempts to freeze hepatocytes with skepticism.

The second problem is outlier data. If a researcher uses hepatocytes from only one or two donors, the results may not be representative of the larger population. To avoid this, the researcher needs a pool of hepatocytes from a larger group of different liver donors to minimize the effect of outliers. Once again, the unpredictability of liver donations jeopardizes the effort to accumulate a representative pool of hepatocytes. Of course, multiple liver donations are unlikely to occur at the same time. Therefore, the researcher must rely on preserving hepatocytes to accumulate a pool. Specifically, the researcher must combine frozen hepatocytes with fresh hepatocytes to create a pool. Because the pool must be used immediately, any unused cells are discarded; otherwise, refreezing would freeze the thawed cells a second time. Thus, preservation methods severely limit, or even preclude, pooled hepatocyte products.

The '929 patent intends to solve these problems while retaining substantial hepatocyte cell viability through a method of multi-cryopreserving hepatocyte cells. Celsis developed its LiverPool pooled multi-cryopreserved hepatocyte products, which it asserts are covered by the '929 patent. LTC also sells pooled multi-cryopreserved hepatocyte products, which Celsis alleges involve performing a process infringing the '929 patent ("the accused process"). For confidentiality reasons, this decision does not give the details of the accused process.

In June 2010, Celsis sued LTC for infringement of the '929 patent. Celsis moved for a preliminary injunction. After a month of discovery, the district court conducted a five-day evidentiary hearing. The district court, upon consideration of the testimony and written submissions, ruled from the bench and granted Celsis a preliminary injunction. LTC moved for a stay pending appeal, which the district court denied.

LTC appealed the district court's grant of a preliminary injunction. This court has jurisdiction under 28 U.S.C. §1292(c)(1).

II.

This court reviews a district court's decision to grant a motion for preliminary injunction for an abuse of discretion. *Abbott Labs. v. Sandoz, Inc.,* 544 F.3d 1341, 1345 (Fed. Cir. 2008). To constitute an abuse of discretion, a district court decision must either make a clear error of judgment in weighing relevant factors or exercise discretion based upon an error of law. *Id.*

The district court analyzes four factors when considering a preliminary injunction: (1) likelihood of success on the merits, (2) irreparable harm, (3) balance of hardships, and (4) public interest. *Id.* at 1344.

III.

The district court found that Celsis had shown a likelihood of success on the merits. The district court also considered LTC's defenses: non-infringement, obviousness, written description, and inequitable conduct. LTC has chosen to appeal only the first two.

As to infringement, the district court weighed the testimony of Celsis' expert Dr. Steven C. Strom against the testimony of LTC's marketing director Markus J. Hunkeler. The district court found Dr. Strom's testimony to be helpful in carefully explaining how LTC's accused process meets all the limitations of the asserted claims. In contrast, the district court found that Mr. Hunkeler "really didn't offer anything in the way of opinions to address the proper interpretation of the patent's claims." Preliminary Injunction Hr'g Tr. 4:10-12, Sept. 7, 2010.

Thus, the district court found that Celsis is likely to succeed in proving that LTC's accused process performs all the steps in the asserted claims. First, Dr. Strom gave testimony on the proper reading of the term "density gradient fractionation" in step (A) of claim 1. Then, he applied that term to the accused process. He testified that the accused process performs a density separation that satisfies the "density gradient fractionation" in step (A), because it separates viable from nonviable hepatocytes by density. Though Mr. Hunkeler testified that the accused process performs an "isodensity" separation that does not create a gradient, the district court found Celsis' expert Dr. Strom's testimony more persuasive.

Second, with that claim construction in place, LTC asserted an alternative non-infringement defense based on step (C). LTC presented documents showing that the accused process performs the same density separation after the first thaw (step A) and the second thaw (step C) only in a different medium. In contrast to step (A), step (C) includes the language "*without requiring* a density gradient step." '929 patent col. 20 l. 15, ll. 57-58 (emphasis added). LTC reads "without requiring" to mean "prohibiting," such that the accused process performs an action "prohibited" by step (C) and therefore does not infringe. LTC made the same argument about claim 10.

The district court found this argument to be "hokum" and an improper attempt to insert a limitation not in the claims. In finding for Celsis, the district court adopted Dr. Strom's expert testimony by reference to Celsis' post-hearing briefing. The district court concluded: "In sum, it is an understatement to say that Celsis has shown substantially more than a reasonable likelihood of success on the subject of infringement."

This record shows that the district court did not abuse its discretion in finding a likelihood of success on infringement. LTC errs in reading "without requiring" to mean "prohibiting." The claim language is not susceptible to this unnatural reading. Instead, "without requiring" means simply that the claim does not require the density gradient step. Thus, performance of that step does not preclude a finding of infringement. For that reason, this court need not reach LTC's subsequent argument concerning performance of the "density gradient step" in step (C).

As to non-obviousness, the district court reviewed the testimony and submissions of Celsis and LTC's fact and expert witnesses. It noted the "vast proliferation of authors and articles dealing with hepatocytes and use of cryopreservation." Hr'g Tr. 7:15-17. But, the district court found: "[N]ot a single one of that astonishingly large body of literature was devoted to the subject of *multi*-cryopreservation of hepatocytes." Hr'g Tr. 7:19-22 ("I have properly laid stress on 'multi.'").

The district court rejected LTC's attempt to fill that gap. LTC's expert Dr. Sanjeev Gupta opined that the only reference to multi-cryopreservation in the prior art is an article in 2002 that he co-authored ("the Malhi article"). *See* Harmeet Malhi et al., *Isolation of human progenitor liver epithelial cells with extensive replication capacity and differentiation into mature hepatocytes*, 115 (13) Journal of Cell Science 2679 (2002). The Malhi article discusses fetal hepatocytes as experiment models because they can replicate in laboratory conditions (unlike mature or adult hepatocytes). The essence of the article was not to introduce a new method or advance in cryopreservation but instead to focus on the advantages of using fetal hepatocytes due to their replication abilities. The Malhi article does report on the "poor viability of hepatocytes after cryopreservation."

The district court found Dr. Gupta's testimony unpersuasive and, as to the Malhi article, found that "nothing in that skeletal reference suggests or even hints at the advance conceived of by the inventor here." Hr'g Tr. 8:14-15. The district court instead credited Celsis' expert Dr. Strom who testified that due to the independent replication of the fetal hepatocytes, it could not be definitively determined whether the same cells were cryopreserved more than once. Dr. Gupta also conceded this same point. The district court found that LTC was attempting to make much of "a wisp of a term that is buried in the Malhi article." Hr'g Tr. 8:2-3. It deemed LTC's arguments to be nothing more than "second guessing and hindsight." Hr'g Tr. 8:17-18. The district court concluded that "again Celsis has demonstrated more than a substantial likelihood of success on the issue." Hr'g Tr. 10:8-9.

The issue on appeal is whether the district court erred in finding Celsis likely to succeed on non-obviousness in view of G. de Sousa et al., *Increase of cytochrome P-450 1A and glutathione transferase transcripts in cultured hepatocytes from dogs, monkeys, and humans after cryopreservation*, 12 Cell Biology and Toxicology 351 (1996) ("the de Sousa article"). On appeal, LTC does not assert its obviousness argument based on the Malhi article, despite LTC's own expert Dr. Gupta opining that Malhi was the only reference in the prior art that allegedly disclosed multi-cryopreservation. Instead of disclosing multi-cryopreservation, the de Sousa article analyzes whether single-cryopreserved hepatocytes can replace fresh hepatocytes as laboratory models, by comparing fresh versus (single) cryopreserved human, monkey, and dog hepatocytes. Specifically, while previous studies determined the effect of single cryopreservation on fresh hepatocytes by evaluating differences in cell viability, cell attachment, and protein synthesis, the aim of this article was to evaluate whether three different chemicals could induce (*i.e.* increase activity of) two different enzymes.

Under 35 U.S.C. §103, a patent claim is invalid "if the differences between the subject matter sought to be patented and the prior art are such that the subject matter as a whole would have been obvious at the time the invention was made to a person having ordinary skill in the art." The obviousness analysis is based on underlying factual inquiries including: (1) the scope and content of the prior art; (2) the level of ordinary skill in the art; (3) the differences between the claimed invention and the prior art; and (4) objective evidence of nonobviousness.

This preliminary record shows that the district court did not abuse its discretion in finding that Celsis has shown a likelihood of success on nonobviousness. LTC will have an opportunity at the merits stage to expand upon the arguments it made at the preliminary injunction stage. The record as it now stands, however, reveals no clear error by the district court. And this court does not opine on the final determination, which lays in the realm of the district court in the first instance.

As an initial matter, this court acknowledges that the present invention is in an art well-known for its unpredictability. As to the scope and content of the prior art, the district court correctly emphasized and found based on the preliminary record that the art was a crowded field for many years and yet there was not one reference to *multi*-cryopreservation. Moreover, the record shows that the prior art taught away from multiple freezings. A single round of freezing severely damages hepatocyte cells and results in lower cell viability. Celsis provided a sufficient showing at this preliminary injunction stage that, at the time of the invention, a person of ordinary skill would expect a second freezing on those damaged cells to kill even more cells than the first freezing. Celsis provides a helpful analogy. Imagine a runner who finishes one marathon and then immediately begins a second marathon. One would not expect the runner to perform the second in the same time as the first. More likely, the runner would not even finish the second marathon. Similarly, as Celsis' expert Dr. Strom testified, one would expect lower cell viability and a greater loss of cells after the second cryopreservation than after the first, thus teaching away from multi-cryopreservation.

With respect to the de Sousa article, this court sees no error in the district court's reliance on Dr. Strom's testimony that de Sousa does not describe or suggest more than one round of freezing, nor does it describe or suggest pooling.

Instead, de Sousa only discloses a single cryopreservation. Even LTC's expert Dr. Gupta did not testify that de Sousa discloses multi-cryopreservation. This court has not seen LTC identify any teaching, suggestion, or motivation in the de Sousa article that multiple rounds of freezing would somehow increase rather than decrease cell viability. Instead, to make this leap, LTC makes vague references to "market need" and testimony from its witnesses Dr. Gupta and Dr. Albert Li. Without more, this reference to "market need," properly linked to the claimed invention, is actually probative of long felt need under objective criteria analysis and supportive of non-obviousness.

Dr. Gupta opined on a "more resistance" theory, and Dr. Li opined on a "mathematical calculation" theory. Specifically, Dr. Gupta (opining specifically on the de Sousa article) claimed that cells that survived the first freeze would be "more resistant" and therefore more likely to survive a second freeze. Dr. Li (opining generally, not specifically on the de Sousa article) claimed that the same number of cells that survived the first freeze would survive the second freeze. The de Sousa article does not disclose either of these hindsight theories.

The district court did not find the testimony of LTC's experts Dr. Gupta and Dr. Li credible. The district court has wide discretion to weigh expert credibility. *Conoco, Inc. v. Energy & Envtl. Int'l, L.C.*, 460 F.3d 1349, 1362-63 (Fed. Cir. 2006) ("As for the relative weight given to the testimony of both sides' expert witnesses, we accord the trial court broad discretion in determining credibility because the court saw the witnesses and heard their testimony.") Thus, these determinations of credibility also buttress the record for nonobviousness.

Here, the district court found that the LTC expert's "revisionist history is unpersuasive." Hr'g Tr. 10:7-8; *see also* Hr'g Tr. 7:11-13 ("Instead of a more candid 'Why didn't I think of that,' we get [LTC arguing] 'Anybody reasonably skilled in the art would have thought of that.'"). Not one of LTC's experts testified to actually performing the claimed process or documenting their alleged understanding before the time of the invention, despite having the financial, scientific, and professional incentive to do so. The district court found that LTC's experts did not predict the results of the claimed methods at the time of the invention, nor could they find any reference in the prior art suggesting that any other scientist had. Hr'g Tr. 7:23-8:1 ("That was not the subject of numerous articles authored or assembled by Dr. Li or Dr. Gupta or by any of the other scientists who participated in the consortium about which Dr. Li testified, or for that matter by anybody else."). Accordingly, in this preliminary injunction context, this court determines that the district court did not clearly err in finding a person of ordinary skill in the art likely would not have found the invention obvious either.

In sum, the record supports the district court's conclusion that Celsis has shown a likelihood of success that a person of ordinary skill in the art would not have considered the claimed methods obvious at the time of the invention.

IV.

The district court found that Celsis would suffer irreparable harm absent a preliminary injunction. As the district court recognized, the simple fact that one could, if pressed, compute a money damages award does not always preclude a finding of irreparable harm. As its name implies, the irreparable harm inquiry seeks to measure harms that no damages payment, however great, could address. *See Altana Pharma AG v. Teva Pharm. USA, Inc.*, 566 F.3d 999, 1010 (Fed.

Cir. 2009); *see also Sampson v. Murray*, 415 U.S. 61, 90 (1974) ("The key word in this consideration is *irreparable*. Mere injuries, however substantial, in terms of money, time and energy necessarily expended in the absence of a stay, are not enough."). The district court found that the permanent, irreparable harm to Celsis would include price erosion, damage to ongoing customer relationships, loss of customer goodwill (*e.g.*, when an effort is later made to restore the original price), and loss of business opportunities. As the district court explained: "There is no effective way to measure the loss of sales or potential growth—to ascertain the people who do not knock on the door or to identify the specific persons who do not reorder because of the existence of the infringer." Hr'g Tr. 16:25-17:4.

Based on the record before the district court, this court sees no error in the district court's finding that Celsis would suffer irreparable harm absent a preliminary injunction. Price erosion, loss of goodwill, damage to reputation, and loss of business opportunities are all valid grounds for finding irreparable harm. Thus, contrary to LTC's assertions, the district court did not err as a matter of law in relying on such evidence. Further, the mere possibility of future monetary damages does not defeat a motion for preliminary injunction.

Celsis offered testimony from its expert Mark Peterson on irreparable harm. In contrast, LTC did not offer expert testimony in rebuttal. This court sees no error in the district court's reliance on Celsis' unrebutted expert testimony. To substantiate its claims, Celsis presented fact and expert testimony as well as specific financial records. Celsis presented evidence of LTC's significantly discounted prices as well as specific instances when customers purchased from LTC instead of Celsis. The record also shows that Celsis had a general no-discount policy to maintain its premium product pricing that it was forced to break in order to compete with LTC. The record included evidence that the LiverPool products are Celsis' flagship products and that the products are in their growth phase and will soon be entering the mature phase with the highest revenues and strongest market position. The record also included testimony that this market was particularly sensitive because customers buy in bulk and at irregular times, such that the loss of a single sale in this market may be more harmful than for products purchased daily.

Then, Celsis proffered expert testimony on the damage to Celsis' price, reputation, and business opportunities. Mr. Peterson testified to the irreversible price erosion. He also testified to the difficulty in quantifying the effect on reputation and business due to Celsis being precluded from marketing to potential and existing customers that it is the exclusive market leader. During the growth stage of a product, it is particularly crucial to be able to distinguish oneself from competitors. This includes building the brand, expanding the customer base, and establishing one's reputation and leadership in the market.

In light of the unrebutted expert testimony, this court finds no reason to reverse the district court's weighing of evidence and fact finding that Celsis would suffer irreparable harm absent a preliminary injunction.

V.

The district court concluded that "plainly the balancing of harms tilts heavily in Celsis's favor." Hr'g Tr. 17:11-12. This preliminary injunction factor is also affected by LTC's decision not to present expert testimony to rebut Celsis' expert testimony. The district court found that any asserted harm to LTC was "of lesser scope" than the harm to Celsis and also "protectable by a bond." Hr'g Tr. 17:9-11 (citing *PPG Indus., Inc. v. Guardian Indus. Corp.*, 75 F.3d 1558 (Fed. Cir. 1996)).

The district court did not clearly err in finding the balancing of harms favors Celsis. Absent a preliminary injunction, Celsis would lose the value of its patent as well as suffer the irreparable harms opined on by its expert. The losses alleged by LTC *upon* a preliminary injunction (loss of goodwill and reputation) would also be incurred by Celsis *absent* a preliminary injunction. Moreover, the record shows that the district court properly considered LTC's interest in fulfilling its current contract obligations. *See PPG Indus., Inc.*, 75 F.3d at 1567. In fact, the district court allowed LTC to complete some sales. This court sees no clear error in the district court rejecting the LTC witness Mr. Hunkeler's claims that it would have to shut down operations upon a preliminary injunction. Further, the preliminary record suggests that LTC's losses were the result of its own calculated risk in selling a product with knowledge of Celsis' patent. *See Sanofi-Synthelabo v. Apotex, Inc.*, 470 F.3d 1368, 1383 (Fed. Cir. 2006).

As to the bond, this court sees no abuse of discretion in the district court's bond amount. *See Sanofi-Synthelabo*, 470 F.3d at 1386 ("The amount of a bond is a determination that rests within the sound discretion of a trial court."). LTC argues that the bond is inadequate. But, the district court invited LTC to present additional evidence to substantiate a higher bond. LTC presented no such evidence.

VI.

The district court found that Celsis had carried its burden to prove that the public interest would favor a preliminary injunction. This court sees no error in the district court's conclusion. The public interest favors the enforcement of Celsis' patent rights here. *See Sanofi-Synthelabo v. Apotex, Inc.*, 470 F.3d 1368, 1383 (Fed. Cir. 2006) ("We have long acknowledged the importance of the patent system in encouraging innovation."). Such investment in drug research and development must be encouraged and protected by the exclusionary rights conveyed in valid patents. *See Abbott Labs. v. Sandoz, Inc.*, 544 F.3d 1341, 1362-63 (Fed. Cir. 2008). That incentive would be adversely affected by taking market benefits away from the patentee and giving them to the accused infringer in this case. *See id.* Though LTC argues that it sells products for drug research and development such that the public interest would disfavor enjoining LTC, both LTC and Celsis sell the same products and are in direct competition. In other words, the public can obtain the products from Celsis. The record shows that the district court has considered and properly addressed the public's interest in obtaining an adequate supply of pooled multi-cryopreserved hepatocyte products. *See PPG Indus., Inc.*, 75 F.3d at 1567.

VII.

The district court found that all four preliminary injunction factors favor Celsis. This court sees no reversible error in the district court's findings. Based on this record, the district court did not abuse its discretion in granting the motion for preliminary injunction. This court therefore affirms.

GAJARSA, Circuit Judge, dissenting.

I respectfully dissent from the majority's decision to uphold the "extraordinary and drastic remedy" of a preliminary injunction because, in my judgment,

CellzDirect, Inc. and Invitrogen Corporation (collectively, "LTC") raised a substantial question as to the validity of U.S. Patent No. 7,604,929 (the "'929 patent"). The grant or denial of a preliminary injunction is within the broad discretion of the district court. In this case, however, the district court committed legal error in granting the preliminary injunction. The district court's obviousness analysis was legally deficient, and it erroneously held LTC to a clear and convincing standard of proof regarding the '929 patent's invalidity. By affirming the injunction, the majority perpetuates these errors and reinvigorates the pre-*KSR* standard for obviousness, rigidly requiring an explicit teaching, suggestion, or motivation for multi-cryopreserving hepatocytes.

I.

The district court held that LTC had not proven that its obviousness defense had substantial merit because two limitations of the claimed invention were not present in the prior art: freezing and thawing hepatocytes a second time and making the density gradient fractionation optional after the second thaw.

Yet obviousness does not require that each element of the claimed invention must be present in the prior art. Indeed, the Patent Act precludes such a requirement by stating that obviousness depends on whether the "*differences between the subject matter sought to be patented and the prior art* are such that the subject matter as a whole would have been obvious at the time the invention was made to a person having ordinary skill in the art. . . ." 35 U.S.C. §103(a) (2006) (emphasis added). Furthermore, this court has recognized that proof of obviousness does not require that every element be present in the prior art.

Moreover, all of the claimed elements were present in the prior art. Properly interpreted, the claimed invention requires three steps: (1) thawing cryopreserved hepatocytes; (2) using density gradient fractionation to separate viable and non-viable cells; and (3) refreezing and rethawing the hepatocytes. Both cryopreservation and density gradient fractionation were well known in the art at the time of the invention. *See* '929 patent col. 2 ll. 41-54 (listing prior art references relating to cryopreservation); J.A. 2981 (Celsis Invitro, Inc.'s ("Celsis") expert Dr. Strom testified that use of density gradient fractionation to "enhance viability" of cells is "well-established to everyone in th[e] field."). The last "step" of the claimed invention requires nothing more than measuring the viability of cells thawed for a second time. If the cells have more than 70% viability, they meet this limitation; if they do not have 70% viability, they do not meet this limitation.

In other words, Celsis' invention uses two known techniques, repeats them, and happens to obtain 70 percent viability of hepatocytes. This "invention" is a "patent for a combination which only unites old elements with no change in their respective functions [and] obviously withdraws what already is known into the field of its monopoly," *Great Atl. & Pac. Tea Co. v. Supermarket Equip. Corp.*, 340 U.S. 147, 152-153 (1950), which is a "principal reason" for finding a patent obvious. *KSR Int'l Co. v. Teleflex Inc.*, 550 U.S. 398, 416 (2007). Repeating known steps to obtain a desired result is not inventive. *Perfect Web Techs., Inc. v. InfoUSA, Inc.*, 587 F.3d 1324, 1330-31 (Fed. Cir. 2009) (finding obvious a claimed invention that required performance of three steps known in the prior art, followed by repetition of those steps until a desired result was obtained).

The majority attempts to complicate the simplicity of the claimed invention by asserting that the art was unpredictable while simultaneously asserting that a person of ordinary skill in the art would have predicted low viability of hepato-cytes that had been frozen and thawed twice. *See Majority Op.* at 928. The major-ity cannot have it both ways. To the extent the art was unpredictable—an issue on which the district court was silent—this alone does not require a holding that the invention is not obvious. *See Pfizer, Inc. v. Apotex, Inc.,* 480 F.3d 1348, 1364 (Fed. Cir. 2007) ("[O]bviousness cannot be avoided simply by a showing of some degree of unpredictability in the art so long as there was a reasonable probability of success.").

The majority also faults LTC for failing to point out an explicit teaching, suggestion, or motivation to multi-cryopreserve hepatocytes. This is directly contrary to the Supreme Court's opinion in *KSR,* which the majority fails to rec-ognize. *KSR* explicitly rejected the rigid application of the teaching-suggestion-motivation test, explaining that "the analysis need not seek out precise teachings directed to the specific subject matter of the challenged claim, for a court can take account of the inferences and creative steps that a person of ordinary skill in the art would employ." 550 U.S. at 418. The majority fails to follow *KSR*'s man-date in deciding that LTC's obviousness defense lacked substantial merit.

Under the flexible approach of *KSR,* there is a substantial question of obvious-ness concerning the '929 patent. The patent spells out clearly—as does Celsis' brief—that there was a need in the art to multi-cryopreserve hepatocytes. The basic approach to determine whether hepatocytes could be frozen multiple times and remain viable was simply to pursue it. Celsis did and found that the hepatocytes were viable. This process is not entitled to be deemed an inven-tion. *See KSR,* 550 U.S. at 421, 127 S. Ct. 1727 ("When there is a design need or market pressure to solve a problem and there are a finite number of identified, predictable solutions, a person of ordinary skill in the art has good reason to pursue the known options within his or her technical grasp," the invention is likely obvious.); *see also Wyers v. Master Lock Co.,* 616 F.3d 1231, 1239 (Fed. Cir. 2010) ("*KSR* and our later cases establish that the legal determination of obvi-ousness may include recourse to logic, judgment, and common sense, in lieu of expert testimony." (citations omitted)). I would thus vacate the district court's grant of a preliminary injunction.

II.

The district court also erred in failing to appreciate that to avoid a prelimi-nary injunction, LTC needed only to offer proof that the '929 patent was vul-nerable, as opposed to clear and convincing evidence of its invalidity. As the patentee, Celsis bears the burden of proving that "in light of the presumptions and burdens that will inhere at trial on the merits," the '929 patent will with-stand LTC's challenges to its validity. *See Amazon.com, Inc. v. Barnesandnoble.com, Inc.,* 239 F.3d 1343, 1350 (Fed. Cir. 2001). Thus, if LTC raises a substantial ques-tion as to the '929 patent's validity, the preliminary injunction should not issue. *Id.* at 1350-51.

Importantly, it is unnecessary to prove a substantial question of invalidity by clear and convincing evidence. Rather, the party challenging the patent's valid-ity must show that the patent is vulnerable, which "requires less proof than the clear and convincing showing necessary to establish invalidity itself." *Amazon,* 239 F.3d at 1359. Here, the district court found that because LTC had not shown that every element of the claimed invention was present in the prior art, its obvi-ousness defense lacked substantial merit. But as explained *supra,* this is not the standard for obviousness. Moreover, requiring the defendant to prove obviousness improperly shifts the burden to the defendant. Instead, the district court must simply decide whether it is more likely than not that the patent will be proven invalid at trial.

The majority affirms the district court's erroneous analysis, stating that "LTC will have an opportunity at the merits stage to expand upon the arguments it made at the preliminary injunction stage." While the present record may not present a clear and convincing case for obviousness, it certainly raises a substantial question on that issue, which the majority implicitly recognizes. By relying on the patent and admissions from Celsis' expert, LTC demonstrated that all of the claim elements were present in the prior art. From there, based on the need for multi-cryopreserved hepatocytes, Celsis repeats the well-known steps to obtain its desired result.

CONCLUSION

In my judgment, the district court abused its discretion in finding that Celsis had demonstrated a likelihood of success on the merits because the claimed invention is nothing more than a repetition of steps already known in the art. Moreover, the majority perpetuates this error, and in so doing applies the wrong standard for obviousness and rationalizes the issuance of the preliminary injunction because it would prevent competition with a patented process which may be proven to be invalid. For these reasons, I dissent.

Comments

1. ***The Federal Circuit's Influence on Irreparable Harm.*** A preliminary injunction has historically been extremely difficult to obtain, particularly in the alleged infringing party was financially solvent. But in 1983, the Federal Circuit dramatically altered the irreparable harm analysis, in turn making it easier to acquire a preliminary injunction. Once a likelihood of success on the merits (validity and continuing infringement) is established, a presumption of irreparable harm would likely follow. This change came soon after the Federal Circuit was created and is consistent with the court's early work in strengthening patent rights. But this presumption is now dubious in the light of *eBay* (the next principal case). In *eBay,* the Supreme Court held that the general rule that a permanent injunction should issue following a finding of infringement is no longer valid. An important issue after *eBay*—in the context of preliminary injunctions—is the effect of *eBay* on the presumption of irreparable harm. In *Automated Merchandising Systems v. Crane Co.,* 357 Fed. Appx. 297 (Fed. Cir. 2009), a non-precedential opinion, the Federal Circuit held the presumption of harm is "no longer the law" after *eBay.*

2. ***Balance of Hardships.*** The balancing test focuses on the hardships of the patentee and the defendant. The Federal Circuit stated the hardship on a manufacturer, who is preliminarily enjoined, can be devastating because he must withdraw his produce from the market before trial. On the other hand, the hardship on a patentee denied an injunction after showing a strong likelihood of success on validity and infringement can also be quite harmful as his patent rights are of limited term.

3. *The Public Interest.* This factor can be the most controversial and difficult to apply. It has particular relevance in the pharmaceutical industry. In *Sanofi-Synthelabo, Inc. v. Apotex, Inc.*, 470 F.3d 1368 (Fed. Cir. 2006), for example, the court sided with the name-brand pharmaceutical company—Sanofi—in affirming the district court's grant of a preliminary injunction against a generic manufacturer. In particular, in the context of considering the public interest component, the generic manufacturer, Apotex, argued "that if the generic products were removed from the market, consumers would be inclined not to purchase their medication because of the accompanying price increase for the brand name drug, leading to possible deaths." In response, the Federal Circuit stated:

> While Apotex raises legitimate concerns, the district court did not abuse its discretion in concluding that those concerns were outweighed by the public interests identified by Sanofi. We have long acknowledged the importance of the patent system in encouraging innovation. Indeed, the "encouragement of investment-based risk is the fundamental purpose of the patent grant, and is based directly on the right to exclude." The district court relied on the testimony of Dr. Hausman in finding that the average cost of developing a blockbuster drug is $800 million. Importantly, the patent system provides incentive to the innovative drug companies to continue costly development efforts. We therefore find that the court did not clearly err in concluding that the significant "public interest in encouraging investment in drug development and protecting the exclusionary rights conveyed in valid pharmaceutical patents" tips the scales in favor of Sanofi.

Id. at 1383-1384.

2. Permanent Injunctions

EBAY INC. v. MERCEXCHANGE, L.L.C.
547 U.S. 388 (2006)

Justice THOMAS delivered the opinion of the Court.

Ordinarily, a federal court considering whether to award permanent injunctive relief to a prevailing plaintiff applies the four-factor test historically employed by courts of equity. Petitioners eBay Inc. and Half.com, Inc., argue that this traditional test applies to disputes arising under the Patent Act. We agree and, accordingly, vacate the judgment of the Court of Appeals.

I

Petitioner eBay operates a popular Internet Web site that allows private sellers to list goods they wish to sell, either through an auction or at a fixed price. Petitioner Half.com, now a wholly owned subsidiary of eBay, operates a similar Web site. Respondent MercExchange, L.L.C., holds a number of patents, including a business method patent for an electronic market designed to facilitate the sale of goods between private individuals by establishing a central authority to promote trust among participants. See U.S. Patent No. 5,845,265. MercExchange sought to license its patent to eBay and Half.com, as it had previously done with other companies, but the parties failed to reach an agreement.

MercExchange subsequently filed a patent infringement suit against eBay and Half.com in the United States District Court for the Eastern District of Virginia. A jury found that MercExchange's patent was valid, that eBay and Half.com had infringed that patent, and that an award of damages was appropriate.

Following the jury verdict, the District Court denied MercExchange's motion for permanent injunctive relief. 275 F. Supp. 2d 695 (2003). The Court of Appeals for the Federal Circuit reversed, applying its "general rule that courts will issue permanent injunctions against patent infringement absent exceptional circumstances." 401 F.3d 1323, 1339 (2005). We granted certiorari to determine the appropriateness of this general rule.

II

According to well-established principles of equity, a plaintiff seeking a permanent injunction must satisfy a four-factor test before a court may grant such relief. A plaintiff must demonstrate: (1) that it has suffered an irreparable injury; (2) that remedies available at law, such as monetary damages, are inadequate to compensate for that injury; (3) that, considering the balance of hardships between the plaintiff and defendant, a remedy in equity is warranted; and (4) that the public interest would not be disserved by a permanent injunction. See, *e.g.*, *Weinberger v. Romero-Barcelo*, 456 U.S. 305, 311-313, (1982); *Amoco Production Co. v. [Village of] Gambell*, 480 U.S. 531, 542 (1987). The decision to grant or deny permanent injunctive relief is an act of equitable discretion by the district court, reviewable on appeal for abuse of discretion.

These familiar principles apply with equal force to disputes arising under the Patent Act. As this Court has long recognized, "a major departure from the long tradition of equity practice should not be lightly implied." *Ibid.* Nothing in the Patent Act indicates that Congress intended such a departure. To the contrary, the Patent Act expressly provides that injunctions "may" issue "in accordance with the principles of equity." 35 U.S.C. §283.[2]

To be sure, the Patent Act also declares that "patents shall have the attributes of personal property," §261, including "the right to exclude others from making, using, offering for sale, or selling the invention," §154(a)(1). According to the Court of Appeals, this statutory right to exclude alone justifies its general rule in favor of permanent injunctive relief. But the creation of a right is distinct from the provision of remedies for violations of that right. Indeed, the Patent Act itself indicates that patents shall have the attributes of personal property "[s]ubject to the provisions of this title," 35 U.S.C. §261, including, presumably, the provision that injunctive relief "may" issue only "in accordance with the principles of equity," §283.

This approach is consistent with our treatment of injunctions under the Copyright Act. Like a patent owner, a copyright holder possesses "the right to exclude others from using his property." *Fox Film Corp. v. Doyal*, 286 U.S. 123, 127 (1932); see also *id.*, at 127-128 ("A copyright, like a patent, is at once the equivalent given by the public for benefits bestowed by the genius and meditations and skill of individuals, and the incentive to further efforts for the same

---

2. Section 283 provides that "[t]he several courts having jurisdiction of cases under this title may grant injunctions in accordance with the principles of equity to prevent the violation of any right secured by patent, on such terms as the court deems reasonable."

important objects"). Like the Patent Act, the Copyright Act provides that courts "may" grant injunctive relief "on such terms as it may deem reasonable to prevent or restrain infringement of a copyright." 17 U.S.C. §502(a). And as in our decision today, this Court has consistently rejected invitations to replace traditional equitable considerations with a rule that an injunction automatically follows a determination that a copyright has been infringed. See, *e.g., New York Times Co. v. Tasini*, 533 U.S. 483, 505 (2001) (citing *Campbell v. Acuff-Rose Music, Inc.*, 510 U.S. 569, 578 n.10 (1994)).

Neither the District Court nor the Court of Appeals below fairly applied these traditional equitable principles in deciding respondent's motion for a permanent injunction. Although the District Court recited the traditional four-factor test, it appeared to adopt certain expansive principles suggesting that injunctive relief could not issue in a broad swath of cases. Most notably, it concluded that a "plaintiff's willingness to license its patents" and "its lack of commercial activity in practicing the patents" would be sufficient to establish that the patent holder would not suffer irreparable harm if an injunction did not issue. But traditional equitable principles do not permit such broad classifications. For example, some patent holders, such as university researchers or self-made inventors, might reasonably prefer to license their patents, rather than undertake efforts to secure the financing necessary to bring their works to market themselves. Such patent holders may be able to satisfy the traditional four-factor test, and we see no basis for categorically denying them the opportunity to do so. To the extent that the District Court adopted such a categorical rule, then, its analysis cannot be squared with the principles of equity adopted by Congress. The court's categorical rule is also in tension with *Continental Paper Bag Co. v. Eastern Paper Bag Co.*, 210 U.S. 405, 422-430 (1908), which rejected the contention that a court of equity has no jurisdiction to grant injunctive relief to a patent holder who has unreasonably declined to use the patent.

In reversing the District Court, the Court of Appeals departed in the opposite direction from the four-factor test. The court articulated a "general rule," unique to patent disputes, "that a permanent injunction will issue once infringement and validity have been adjudged." The court further indicated that injunctions should be denied only in the "unusual" case, under "exceptional circumstances" and "'in rare instances . . . to protect the public interest.'" Just as the District Court erred in its categorical denial of injunctive relief, the Court of Appeals erred in its categorical grant of such relief. Cf. *Roche Products v. Bolar Pharmaceutical Co.*, 733 F.2d 858, 865 (C.A. Fed. 1984) (recognizing the "considerable discretion" district courts have "in determining whether the facts of a situation require it to issue an injunction").

Because we conclude that neither court below correctly applied the traditional four-factor framework that governs the award of injunctive relief, we vacate the judgment of the Court of Appeals, so that the District Court may apply that framework in the first instance. In doing so, we take no position on whether permanent injunctive relief should or should not issue in this particular case, or indeed in any number of other disputes arising under the Patent Act. We hold only that the decision whether to grant or deny injunctive relief rests within the equitable discretion of the district courts, and that such discretion must be exercised consistent with traditional principles of equity, in patent disputes no less than in other cases governed by such standards.

Accordingly, we vacate the judgment of the Court of Appeals, and remand for further proceedings consistent with this opinion.

Chief Justice ROBERTS, with whom Justice SCALIA and Justice GINSBURG join, concurring.

I agree with the Court's holding that "the decision whether to grant or deny injunctive relief rests within the equitable discretion of the district courts, and that such discretion must be exercised consistent with traditional principles of equity, in patent disputes no less than in other cases governed by such standards," and I join the opinion of the Court. That opinion rightly rests on the proposition that "a major departure from the long tradition of equity practice should not be lightly implied." *Weinberger v. Romero-Barcelo,* 456 U.S. 305, 320 (1982).

From at least the early 19th century, courts have granted injunctive relief upon a finding of infringement in the vast majority of patent cases. This "long tradition of equity practice" is not surprising, given the difficulty of protecting a right to *exclude* through monetary remedies that allow an infringer to *use* an invention against the patentee's wishes—a difficulty that often implicates the first two factors of the traditional four-factor test. This historical practice, as the Court holds, does not *entitle* a patentee to a permanent injunction or justify a *general rule* that such injunctions should issue. The Federal Circuit itself so recognized in *Roche Products, Inc. v. Bolar Pharmaceutical Co.,* 733 F.2d 858, 865-867 (1984). At the same time, there is a difference between exercising equitable discretion pursuant to the established four-factor test and writing on an entirely clean slate. "Discretion is not whim, and limiting discretion according to legal standards helps promote the basic principle of justice that like cases should be decided alike." *Martin v. Franklin Capital Corp.,* 126 S. Ct. 704, 710 (2005). When it comes to discerning and applying those standards, in this area as others, "a page of history is worth a volume of logic." *New York Trust Co. v. Eisner,* 256 U.S. 345, 349 (1921) (opinion for the Court by Holmes, J.).

Justice KENNEDY, with whom Justice STEVENS, Justice SOUTER, and Justice BREYER concurring.

The Court is correct, in my view, to hold that courts should apply the well-established, four-factor test—without resort to categorical rules—in deciding whether to grant injunctive relief in patent cases. The Chief Justice is also correct that history may be instructive in applying this test. The traditional practice of issuing injunctions against patent infringers, however, does not seem to rest on "the difficulty of protecting a right to *exclude* through monetary remedies that allow an infringer to *use* an invention against the patentee's wishes." (Roberts, C.J., concurring). Both the terms of the Patent Act and the traditional view of injunctive relief accept that the existence of a right to exclude does not dictate the remedy for a violation of that right. To the extent earlier cases establish a pattern of granting an injunction against patent infringers almost as a matter of course, this pattern simply illustrates the result of the four-factor test in the contexts then prevalent. The lesson of the historical practice, therefore, is most helpful and instructive when the circumstances of a case bear substantial parallels to litigation the courts have confronted before.

In cases now arising trial courts should bear in mind that in many instances the nature of the patent being enforced and the economic function of the patent holder present considerations quite unlike earlier cases. An industry has developed in which firms use patents not as a basis for producing and selling goods but, instead, primarily for obtaining licensing fees. See FTC, To PROMOTE INNOVATION: THE PROPER BALANCE OF COMPETITION AND PATENT LAW AND POLICY, ch. 3, pp. 38-39 (Oct. 2003), available at http://www.ftc.gov/os/2003/10/innovationrpt.pdf (as visited May 11, 2006, and available in Clerk of Court's case file). For these firms, an injunction, and the potentially serious sanctions arising from its violation, can be employed as a bargaining tool to charge exorbitant fees to companies that seek to buy licenses to practice the patent. See *ibid.* When the patented invention is but a small component of the product the companies seek to produce and the threat of an injunction is employed simply for undue leverage in negotiations, legal damages may well be sufficient to compensate for the infringement and an injunction may not serve the public interest. In addition injunctive relief may have different consequences for the burgeoning number of patents over business methods, which were not of much economic and legal significance in earlier times. The potential vagueness and suspect validity of some of these patents may affect the calculus under the four-factor test.

The equitable discretion over injunctions, granted by the Patent Act, is well suited to allow courts to adapt to the rapid technological and legal developments in the patent system. For these reasons it should be recognized that district courts must determine whether past practice fits the circumstances of the cases before them. With these observations, I join the opinion of the Court.

EDWARDS LIFESCIENCES v. COREVALVE, INC.
699 F.3d 1305 (Fed. Cir. 2012)

NEWMAN, Circuit Judge.

Edwards Lifesciences AG and Edwards Lifesciences LLC (collectively "Edwards") sued defendants CoreValve, Inc. and its successor in interest Medtronic CoreValve, LLC (collectively "CoreValve") for infringement of United States Patent No. 5,411,552 ("the '552 patent") issued May 2, 1995, entitled "Valve Prosthesis for Implantation in the Body and a Catheter for Implanting Such Valve Prosthesis." Two other patents, initially in suit, are not at issue. The inventors are Dr. Henning R. Andersen, an interventional cardiologist at Aarhus Medical School in Denmark, his surgical colleague Dr. John M. Hasenkam, and then medical student Lars L. Knudsen.

The invention is a prosthetic device called a "transcatheter heart valve." The valve is mounted on a stent and implanted in the heart by catheter, thereby avoiding open heart surgery and its associated risks. Suit for infringement was brought in the United States District Court for the District of Delaware, trial was to a jury, and the verdict was that the '552 patent is valid, that CoreValve's Generation 3 ReValving System infringed patent claim 1, and that the infringement was willful. The jury awarded damages of $72,645,555 in lost profits and $1,284,861 as a reasonable royalty.

The district court entered judgment on the verdict, but . . . declined to issue an injunction against future infringement, apparently on CoreValve's representation that, if enjoined, it would move its manufacturing operations to Mexico.

We affirm the district court's rulings, except that we remand for reconsideration of the court's denial of an injunction in view of the representation of
changed circumstances.

***

III

Remedies

B

Edwards requested entry of an injunction against future infringement, and
cited several equitable considerations, including the importance of establishing
customer relationships now that FDA approval has been obtained, and the fact
that Medtronic, as a large medical device manufacture, could overwhelm the
much smaller Edwards.

A patentee's right to exclude is a fundamental tenet of patent law. *Richardson
v. Suzuki Motor Co., Ltd.*, 868 F.2d 1226, 1247 (Fed. Cir. 1989) ("The right to
exclude recognized in a patent is but the essence of the concept of property.")
(quoting *Connell v. Sears, Roebuck & Co.*, 722 F.2d 1542, 1548 (Fed. Cir. 1983)).
The innovation incentive of the patent is grounded on the market exclusivity
whereby the inventor profits from his invention. Absent adverse equitable considerations, the winner of a judgment of validity and infringement may normally
expect to regain the exclusivity that was lost with the infringement. Edwards
argues that the Court's ruling in *eBay Inc. v. MercExchange, L.L.C.*, 547 U.S. 388
(2006), supports its position, for the willfulness of the infringement and other
equitable aspects weigh in favor of restoration of the exclusive patent right.

The Court in *eBay* did not hold that there is a presumption against exclusivity on successful infringement litigation. The Court did not cancel 35 U.S.C.
§154, which states that "Every patent shall contain . . . a grant . . . of the right to
exclude others from making, using, offering for sale, or selling the invention,"
nor did the Court overrule Article I section 8 of the Constitution, which grants
Congress the power to "secur[e] for limited Times to Authors and Inventors the
exclusive Right to their respective Writings and Discoveries." The Court held
that equitable aspects should always be considered, stating: "We hold only that
the decision whether to grant or deny injunctive relief rests within the equitable discretion of the district courts, and that such discretion must be exercised
consistent with traditional principles of equity, in patent disputes no less than
in other cases governed by such standards." *eBay*, 547 U.S. at 394. Statutory
and historical as well as commercial considerations impinge on every equitable
determination.

Precedent illustrates the variety of equitable considerations, and responsive
equitable remedy in patent cases; for example, the grant of a royalty-bearing
license instead of imposing an injunction in situations where the patentee
would experience no competitive injury, as in *ActiveVideo Networks, Inc. v. Verizon
Communications, Inc.*, U.S. App. LEXIS 18032, at *67-68 (Fed. Cir. Aug. 24, 2012);
or where there is an overriding public interest in continued provision of the
infringing product, as in *Bard Peripheral Vascular, Inc. v. W.L. Gore & Assocs., Inc.*,
No. 03-CV-0597 (D. Ariz. July 21, 2010), where the Gore vascular graft materials
were not available from the successful patentee Bard. Another form of equitable

response is illustrated in *Broadcom Corp. v. Qualcomm Inc.*, 543 F.3d 683, 704 (Fed. Cir. 2008), where the court postponed the effective date of an injunction for twenty months, to relieve hardship on the infringer.

In *Advanced Cardiovascular Sys. v. Medtronic Vascular, Inc.*, 579 F. Supp. 2d 554 (D. Del. 2008), the court observed that: "Courts awarding permanent injunctions typically do so under circumstances where plaintiff practices its invention and is a direct market competitor." *Id.* at 558. Edwards argues that these conditions here prevail. However, the district court declined to impose the requested injunction. First, the district court responded to Edwards' argument that without exclusivity it would lose first-mover advantage and market share and reputation, by stating that these had already been lost—although Edwards states that this is incorrect, for sales in the United States had not yet been authorized by the FDA, as to either the Edwards or the CoreValve/Medtronic product. The district court also stated that Edwards had given up exclusivity by licensing the '552 patent to another competitor. CoreValve does not dispute that the district court erred in its view of that transaction, and that no such license exists.

The district court's explanation of why it was withholding an injunction placed significant weight on CoreValve's statements that it was immediately moving this manufacturing operation to Mexico, and thus that infringement would terminate. *Edwards* at *29 ("The remaining two eBay factors do not alter the court's analysis, since the only practical effect of a permanent injunction would be that CoreValve would be forced to move its United States manufacturing operations for the accused product to Mexico."). The district court stated that if CoreValve should renew its infringing manufacture in the United States, then "[a]s it did in this case, Edwards can bring suit against CoreValve and seek damages if CoreValve continues its infringing manufacturing operations in spite of the judgment of infringement." *Id.* at *28. Edwards states on this appeal, and CoreValve does not deny, that CoreValve never stopped its infringing manufacture in California. Whether or not that representation was known to be false when made, the situation before us reflects, at least, changed circumstances.

In *TiVo Inc. v. EchoStar Corp.*, 646 F.3d 869, 890 n. 9 (Fed. Cir. 2011), this court *en banc* noted that "district courts are in the best position to fashion an injunction tailored to prevent or remedy infringement." Recognizing that the circumstances have not been fully explored in the record before us, we vacate the denial of the injunction, and remand to the district court for consideration in light of ensuing events and any other relevant factors.

Summary

The judgment of the district court is affirmed, with the exception that we remand for reconsideration by the district court, in view of changed circumstances, of the court's rulings on the permanent injunction.

ROBERT BOSCH LLC v. PYLON MANUFACTURING CORP.
659 F.3d 1142 (Fed. Cir. 2011)

O'MALLEY, Circuit Judge.

Robert Bosch LLC ("Bosch") appeals from the order of the United States District Court for the District of Delaware, denying Bosch's post-trial motion for entry of a permanent injunction. Because the district court abused its discretion when it denied a permanent injunction on this record, we reverse and remand with instructions to enter an appropriate injunction.

BACKGROUND

This is a patent infringement case involving windshield wiper technology, specifically beam-type wiper blades ("beam blades"). Beam blades are a relatively new technology that offers several advantages over conventional, or "bracketed," wiper blades, including more evenly distributed pressure across the length of the blade and better performance in inclement weather. Part of Bosch's business involves developing wiper blades, and Bosch owns patents covering various aspects of beam blade technology. In addition to its research and development efforts, Bosch sells blades to both original equipment manufacturers and aftermarket retailers. Pylon Manufacturing Corp., LLC ("Pylon") also sells beam blades and has competed with Bosch for business from retailers such as Wal-Mart.

In August 2008, Bosch sued Pylon in the District of Delaware, alleging infringement of U.S. Patent Nos. 6,292,974 ("the '974 Patent"), 6,675,434 ("the '434 Patent"), 6,944,905 ("the '905 Patent"), and 6,978,512 ("the '512 Patent"). On June 9, 2009, during a hearing regarding Bosch's alleged failure to produce certain financial data, the court informed the parties of its preference for bifurcating the issue of damages and suggested that this procedural mechanism may address the parties' discovery dispute. In response, Pylon moved to bifurcate the issues of damages and willfulness, a request that Bosch opposed. The district court granted Pylon's motion, noting its "determin[ation] that bifurcation is appropriate, if not necessary, in all but exceptional patent cases."

In light of the jury's determination that Pylon infringed valid claims of the '905 and '434 Patents, Bosch moved for entry of a permanent injunction. In a memorandum opinion dated November 3, 2010, the court denied the motion on grounds that Bosch failed to show that it would suffer irreparable harm. At the outset of its analysis, the district court noted an apparent difficulty faced by courts "struggling to balance the absence of a presumption of irreparable harm with a patentee's right to exclude," and observed that other courts had "frequently focused upon the nature of the competition between plaintiff and defendant in the relevant market in the context of evaluating irreparable harm and the adequacy of money damages." The court also discerned a tendency among district courts to award permanent injunctions: (1) "under circumstances in which the plaintiff practices its invention and is a direct market competitor"; and (2) where the plaintiff's "patented technology is at the core of its business. . . ."

With these factors in mind, the court proceeded to assess the nature of the competition between Bosch and Pylon. In doing so, the court identified deficiencies it perceived in Bosch's presentation of the competitive landscape, including a failure to "provide[ ] a clear, summary-level overview of the relevant market" and "a breakdown illuminating [the parties'] relative market percentages." The court also focused on the fact that "[t]his is not a clear case of a two-supplier market wherein a sale to Pylon necessarily represents the loss of a sale to Bosch" and "wiper blades alone are not at the core of [Bosch's] business." Based on: (1) its conclusion that Bosch "fail[ed] to define a relevant market"; (2) the "existence of additional competitors"; and (3) the "non-core nature of Bosch's wiper blade business in relation to its business as a whole," the court concluded that

Bosch failed to show it would suffer irreparable harm. *Id.* Finding the absence of irreparable harm fatal to Bosch's motion, the court denied the request for an injunction without addressing the remaining equitable factors of the permanent injunction inquiry.

Bosch timely appealed the district court's interlocutory order, asserting jurisdiction under 28 U.S.C. §§1291 and 1292. . . .

STANDARD OF REVIEW

This court reviews the denial of a permanent injunction for abuse of discretion. A district court abuses its discretion when it acts "based upon an error of law or clearly erroneous factual findings" or commits "a clear error of judgment." *Ecolab, Inc. v. FMC Corp.,* 569 F.3d 1335, 1352 (Fed. Cir. 2009). A clear error of judgment occurs when the "record contains no basis on which the district court rationally could have made its decision or if the judicial action is arbitrary, fanciful or clearly unreasonable." *Datascope Corp. v. SMEC, Inc.,* 879 F.2d 820, 828 (Fed. Cir. 1989). "To the extent the court's decision is based upon an issue of law, we review that issue de novo." *Ecolab,* 569 F.3d at 1352.

DISCUSSION

Consistent with traditional equitable principles, a patentee seeking a permanent injunction must make a four-part showing:

> (1) that it has suffered an irreparable injury; (2) that remedies available at law, such as monetary damages, are inadequate to compensate for that injury; (3) that, considering the balance of hardships between the plaintiff and the defendant, a remedy in equity is warranted; and (4) that the public interest would not be disserved by a permanent injunction.

eBay Inc. v. MercExchange, L.L.C., 547 U.S. 388, 391 (2006). Prior to the Supreme Court's decision in *eBay,* this court followed the general rule that a permanent injunction will issue once infringement and validity have been adjudged, absent a sound reason to deny such relief. In addition, at least in the context of preliminary injunctive relief, we applied an express presumption of irreparable harm upon finding that a plaintiff was likely to succeed on the merits of a patent infringement claim. *See Smith Int'l, Inc. v. Hughes Tool Co.,* 718 F.2d 1573, 1581 (Fed. Cir. 1983) ("We hold that where validity and continuing infringement have been clearly established, as in this case, immediate irreparable harm is presumed."). Based on our case law, district courts also have applied a presumption of irreparable harm following judgment of infringement and validity to support the issuance of permanent injunctions.[3]

In *eBay,* the Supreme Court made clear that "broad classifications" and "categorical rule[s]" have no place in this inquiry. 547 U.S. at 393. Instead, courts are to exercise their discretion in accordance with traditional principles of equity. The Supreme Court, however, did not expressly address the presumption of irreparable harm, and our subsequent cases have not definitively clarified whether that presumption remains intact. *See Broadcom Corp. v. Qualcomm*

---

3. Indeed, applying this presumption to permanent injunctions was entirely reasonable at the time, given that "[t]he standard for a preliminary injunction is essentially the same as for a permanent injunction with the exception that the plaintiff must show a likelihood of success on the merits rather than actual success." *Amoco Prod. Co. v. Village of Gambell,* 480 U.S. 531, 546 n.12 (1987).

Inc., 543 F.3d 683, 702 (Fed. Cir. 2008) ("It remains an open question whether there remains a rebuttable presumption of irreparable harm following *eBay*.").[4] Our statements on this topic have led one district court judge to conclude that "the presumption of irreparable harm is at best on life support." *Red Bend Ltd. v. Google, Inc.*, 2011 WL 1288503, at *18 (D. Mass. Mar. 31, 2011). We take this opportunity to put the question to rest and confirm that *eBay* jettisoned the presumption of irreparable harm as it applies to determining the appropriateness of injunctive relief. In so holding, we join at least two of our sister circuits that have reached the same conclusion as it relates to a similar presumption in copyright infringement matters.

Although *eBay* abolishes our general rule that an injunction normally will issue when a patent is found to have been valid and infringed, it does not swing the pendulum in the opposite direction. In other words, even though a successful patent infringement plaintiff can no longer rely on presumptions or other short-cuts to support a request for a permanent injunction, it does not follow that courts should entirely ignore the fundamental nature of patents as property rights granting the owner the right to exclude. Indeed, this right has its roots in the Constitution, as the Intellectual Property Clause of the Constitution itself refers to inventors' "*exclusive* Right to their respective . . . Discoveries." U.S. Const. art. I, §8, cl. 8 (emphasis added). Although the Supreme Court disapproved of this court's absolute reliance on the patentee's right to exclude as a basis for our prior rule favoring injunctions, that does not mean that the nature of patent rights has no place in the appropriate equitable analysis. *See eBay*, 547 U.S. at 392, 126 S. Ct. 1837 ("According to the Court of Appeals, this statutory right to exclude alone justifies its general rule in favor of permanent injunctive relief. But the creation of a right is distinct from the provision of remedies for violations of that right."). While the patentee's right to exclude alone cannot justify an injunction, it should not be ignored either. *See Acumed LLC v. Stryker Corp.*, 551 F.3d 1323, 1328 (Fed. Cir. 2008) (finding in a post-*eBay* decision that, "[i]n view of that right [to exclude], infringement may cause a patentee irreparable harm not remediable by a reasonable royalty").

The abolition of categorical rules and the district court's inherent discretion to fashion equitable relief, moreover, also do not mandate that district courts must act on a clean slate. "Discretion is not whim, and limiting discretion according to legal standards helps promote the basic principle of justice that like cases should be decided alike." *eBay*, 547 U.S. at 395, 126 S. Ct. 1837 (Roberts, J., concurring) (quoting *Martin v. Franklin Capital Corp.*, 546 U.S. 132, 139, 126 S. Ct. 704, 163 L. Ed. 2d 547 (2005)). In this area, as others, "a page of history is worth a volume of logic" when "it comes to discerning and applying those standards." *Id.* (quoting *New York Trust Co. v. Eisner*, 256 U.S. 345, 349 (1921) (Holmes, J.)). This wisdom is particularly apt in traditional cases, such as this, where the patentee and adjudged infringer both practice the patented technology. *See id.* at 396-97, 126 S. Ct. 1837 (Kennedy, J., concurring) (contrasting the relevant considerations in traditional patent infringement actions with certain cases arising now "in which firms use patents not as a basis for producing

---

4. In an unpublished decision, we stated without analysis, and without citation to our other cases describing the issue as an open question, that *eBay* discarded the presumption of irreparable harm. *Automated Merch. Sys., Inc. v. Crane Co.*, 357 Fed. Appx. 297, 301 (Fed. Cir. 2009).

and selling goods but, instead, primarily for obtaining licensing fees," "[w]hen the patented invention is but a small component of the product," and those involving "the burgeoning number of patents over business methods."

Over the past quarter-century, this court has encountered many cases involving a practicing patentee seeking to permanently enjoin a competitor upon an adjudication of infringement. In deciding these cases, we have developed certain legal standards that inform the four-factor inquiry and, in particular, the question of irreparable harm. While none of these standards alone may justify a general rule or an effectively irrebuttable presumption that an injunction should issue, a proper application of the standards to the facts of this case compels the conclusion that Bosch is entitled to the injunction it seeks. It is in ignoring these standards, and supplanting them with its own, that the district court abused its discretion.

We address each component of the four-factor test in turn.

I.

Bosch argues that the district court committed legal error by establishing categorical rules in its irreparable injury analysis. Specifically, Bosch contends that the district court adopted per se rules that "the existence of additional competitors" and "the non-core nature of Bosch's wiper blade business in relation to its business as a whole" each independently preclude a finding of irreparable harm. Bosch further argues that, on this record, no court acting within its discretion could find an absence of irreparable harm. In this regard, Bosch points to evidence of: (1) loss in market share and access to customers; (2) Pylon's inability to satisfy a judgment; and (3) direct competition between it and Pylon in "each and every distribution channel in [the relevant] market." According to Bosch, "decades of jurisprudence confirm that a patentee in [these] circumstances has suffered irreparable harm."

In response, Pylon argues that the district court never concluded that "there *had* to be a two-supplier market" or that "the wiper blade business *had* to be at the core of Bosch's business in order for an injunction to be warranted." Instead, Pylon contends, the district court applied the "proper legal standard to the evidence presented and concluded, as a factual matter, that the evidence presented was inadequate to establish irreparable harm."

While we agree that the district court did not establish categorical rules, we nevertheless conclude that the district court committed legal error by the weight given to the factors cited, and made a clear error in judgment in its analysis of the irreparable harm factor. Specifically, while facts relating to the nature of the competition between the parties undoubtedly are relevant to the irreparable harm inquiry, the court erred in relying exclusively on the presence of additional competitors and on the non-core nature of Bosch's wiper blade business. In addition, the court committed a clear error of judgment when it concluded that Bosch failed to demonstrate irreparable harm in the face of overwhelming evidence to the contrary. This is particularly true in light of Bosch's evidence of: (1) the parties' direct competition; (2) loss in market share and access to potential customers resulting from Pylon's introduction of infringing beam blades; and (3) Pylon's lack of financial wherewithal to satisfy a judgment. Given these facts, there is "no basis on which the district court rationally could have" concluded that Bosch failed to show irreparable harm. We first address the court's legal errors and then turn to the clear error of judgment.

A.

The court's first legal error lies in its conclusion that the presence of additional competitors, without more, cuts against a finding of irreparable harm. It is well-established that the "fact that other infringers may be in the marketplace does not negate irreparable harm." *Pfizer, Inc. v. Teva Pharms. USA, Inc.,* 429 F.3d 1364, 1381 (Fed. Cir. 2005). As we explained in *Pfizer,* a patentee need not sue all infringers at once. *Id.* "Picking off one infringer at a time is not inconsistent with being irreparably harmed." *Id.* Were we to conclude otherwise, we would effectively establish a presumption against irreparable harm whenever the market contains a plurality of players. Under such circumstances, the first infringer sued could always point to the existence of additional competitors. And, perversely, if that infringer were to succeed in defeating an injunction, subsequent adjudged infringers could point to the market presence of the first infringer when opposing a request for an injunction. Consequently, without additional facts showing that the presence of additional competitors renders the infringer's harm reparable, the absence of a two-supplier market does not weigh against a finding of irreparable harm.

This principle, moreover, is not incompatible with the cases cited by the district court, in which courts found irreparable harm based, in part, on the absence of additional competitors. While the existence of a two-player market may well serve as a substantial ground for *granting* an injunction—e.g., because it creates an inference that an infringing sale amounts to a lost sale for the patentee—the converse is not automatically true, especially where, as here, it is undisputed that the patentee has sought to enforce its rights against other infringers in the market. The record reveals that Bosch has diligently pursued infringers since the time it first learned of Pylon's infringing beam blades. Once it became aware of the infringement, Bosch immediately notified Pylon's supplier requesting that it cease production of infringing blades, to which it agreed. Later, in October 2007, Bosch sued Jamak Fabrication-Tex Ltd. in the District of Delaware, alleging infringement of its beam blade patents.

During the pendency of its suit against Jamak, Bosch learned that Pylon had started selling a new infringing product. Accordingly, in August 2008, three months after resolving its suit against Jamak, Bosch filed this action against Pylon. Bosch subsequently sued an additional competitor, Old World Industries, Inc., in March 2010 in the United States District Court for the Northern District of Illinois. For these reasons, the court erred in concluding that the absence of a two-player market effectively prohibits a finding of irreparable harm in this case.

B.

The court also erred in relying on the "non-core" nature of Bosch's wiper blade business in relation to its business as a whole. As other courts have concluded, the fact that an infringer's harm affects only a portion of a patentee's business says nothing about whether that harm can be rectified. Injuries that affect a "non-core" aspect of a patentee's business are equally capable of being irreparable as ones that affect more significant operations.

Under the district court's approach, for example, a large industrial corporation such as Bosch would find it easier to obtain an injunction if it subdivided its operations into child companies, with each focusing on a particular product line. Under such circumstances, Pylon's infringement would go to the core of the business of "Bosch Beam Blades LLC," which would increase the likelihood of irreparable harm. No one could seriously contend, however, that the irreparability of any particular injury should turn on incidental details such as a patentee's corporate structure. An injury is either of the irreparable sort, or it is not. Consequently, the district court erred in attributing weight to the non-core nature of Bosch's wiper blade business. *See Praxair, Inc. v. ATMI, Inc.,* 543 F.3d 1306, 1330 (Fed. Cir. 2008) (Lourie, J., concurring) ("[A] patent provides a right to exclude infringing competitors, regardless of the proportion that the infringing goods bear to a patentee's total business.").

It is true that some courts have referenced the fact that the patented product is at the core of a party's business when explaining their bases for *granting* an injunction. *TruePosition Inc. v. Andrew Corp.,* 568 F. Supp. 2d 500, 531 (D. Del. 2008) (granting a permanent injunction after finding that "[p]laintiffs are also frequently successful when their patented technology is at the core of its business. . . ."). The trial court's error in relying on these cases again arises from its conclusion that, if a fact supports the granting of an injunction, its absence likely compels denial of one. That is not the law, however.

C.

In addition to these legal errors, the district court committed a clear error in judgment when it concluded that Bosch failed to demonstrate irreparable harm. The record here contains undisputed evidence of direct competition in each of the market segments identified by the parties. Bosch also introduced unrebutted evidence of loss of market share and access to potential customers, as well as Pylon's inability to satisfy a judgment. The district court, however, did not address any of this evidence, but, instead, focused on: (1) the absence of a two-player market; (2) the non-core nature of Bosch's wiper blade business; and (3) Bosch's alleged failure to define a relevant market. In view of the entirety of the record, we are left with the firm conviction that there is no basis on which the district court rationally could have concluded that Bosch failed to demonstrate irreparable harm. We begin with an overview of the nature of competition between the parties before turning to the parties' arguments regarding harms arising from Pylon's competition with Bosch and Pylon's apparent inability to satisfy a judgment.

Although the parties dispute the finer details of the nature and extent of their competition, we agree with Bosch that the undisputed facts show that it competes with Pylon in all of the market segments identified by the parties. Neither Bosch nor Pylon sells directly to consumers. Instead, both offer their blades to intermediaries, who then sell the same to consumers. Before the district court, Bosch identified three channels of distribution in the relevant market: (1) mass merchandisers, such as Wal-Mart; (2) automotive specialty retailers; and (3) original equipment manufacturers ("OEMs"). Pylon did not dispute the existence of these distribution channels, nor did it identify the existence of additional channels within the relevant market. Rather, it disputed the extent of competition in each of these three markets. Specifically, Pylon argued, as it does now, that: (1) Bosch sells original wiping systems to OEMs for installation on new vehicles, while Pylon does not; (2) Bosch has a great concentration of customers in automotive specialty retailers, while Pylon lacks "a significant beam blade presence" in this market; and (3) "Bosch does not sell any beam blades to mass merchandisers." Thus, while the parties disputed the extent of competition within each distribution channel, there was no dispute regarding the contours of the relevant market. While Pylon now asserts that it does not agree "that these channels comprise the relevant market," it still fails to identify any additional distribution channels, and we reject its belated attempt to create a dispute as to this issue.

With respect to the mass-merchandiser channel, it is undisputed that both parties have competed for Wal-Mart's business, which alone represents a substantial portion of not only the mass-merchandiser channel, but also the aftermarket as a whole. Both Bosch and Pylon approached Wal-Mart in 2006 in an attempt to secure its beam blade business, and Wal-Mart initially agreed to distribute Bosch's ICON beam blades beginning in April 2007. Bosch, however, failed to make a timely initial delivery and, when it requested an extension, Wal-Mart refused, choosing to sell Pylon's infringing product instead. Since losing the account, Bosch has made numerous efforts to regain Wal-Mart's business and has even offered a new, cheaper blade in an attempt to compete with Pylon's lower prices. Thus, while it is true that Bosch has not succeeded in selling its beam blades in the mass-merchandiser channel, the evidence shows that it competes with Pylon for business with the largest participant in the aftermarket.

The record, likewise, shows direct competition in the aftermarket specialty store segment. Both parties have sold beam blades to AutoZone, and, although Pylon has had limited success in securing business from other specialty stores, it has competed against Bosch for business from at least five of AutoZone's competitors.

With respect to OEMs, Bosch sells its blades to most of the major car manufacturers, including BMW, Chrysler, Ford, General Motors, Hyundai, Mercedes Benz, Toyota, Volkswagen, and Volvo. Pylon admits that it has sold beam type wiper blades to at least one OEM, and has attempted sell beam blades to at least two additional manufacturers. The undisputed evidence, thus, demonstrates that the parties directly compete for customers in each of the relevant distribution channels.

Bosch argues that the harm caused by this competition is irreparable because it has suffered irreversible price erosion, loss of market share, loss of customers, and loss of access to potential customers. It also contends that Pylon's inability to satisfy a judgment renders its injury irreparable. As Bosch notes, the district court did not address any of these factors when concluding that an injunction should not issue.

In response, Pylon contends that, while "Bosch has preliminarily established that Pylon sells allegedly infringing beam blades, [it] has not established that Pylon's sales have had any definable impact on Bosch's sales of its own beam blades." According to Pylon, Bosch failed to prove that it was Pylon's competition, rather than that of other competitors, which caused it to suffer lost market share and price erosion. Pylon further argues that Bosch's evidence of Pylon's inability to pay is unsupported and speculative. We disagree.

While it is true that at least some of Bosch's loss of market share is attributable to other competitors, it is undisputed that it was Pylon that secured the Wal-Mart account, which alone accounts for a substantial portion of the entire market. Pylon argues that Bosch presumes "that Wal-Mart would turn to Bosch if Pylon were enjoined." Bosch, however, makes no such presumption. Rather, Bosch relies on the fact that it previously secured the Wal-Mart account as circumstantial evidence that it would reclaim Wal-Mart's business were Pylon enjoined. While the party seeking an injunction bears the burden of showing lost market share, this showing need not be made with direct evidence. Here, Bosch made a prima facie showing of lost market share, and Pylon proffered no evidence to rebut that showing.

Pylon, likewise, failed to rebut the testimony of Bosch's Director of Product Management, Martin Kashnowski, regarding its loss of access to potential customers. *See* Joint Appendix 954 ("[N]ot securing an account with Wal-Mart has made it much more difficult for Bosch to secure accounts with other mass-merchandisers, including Sears, Target and K-Mart. If Wal-Mart was carrying Bosch's beam blades, then its competitors would want to sell Bosch's beam blades as well to maintain a competitive position."). With respect to evidence of price erosion, although Bosch could have developed the effects of Pylon's conduct from that of other competitors more clearly, Mr. Kashnowski's testimony on this issue also stands unrebutted. Consequently, Pylon's arguments with respect to the sufficiency of Bosch's evidence of lost market share, the loss of access to potential customers, and irreversible price erosion are not well-taken.

As additional evidence of irreparable harm, Bosch introduced evidence showing that the financial condition of both Pylon and its corporate parent raised questions about Pylon's ability to satisfy a judgment. Specifically, Bosch submitted: (1) a Risk Management Report indicating that Pylon posed a "[m]oderate risk of severe financial stress, such a bankruptcy, over the next 12 months" and fell within the 49th percentile nationally in the category of "Financial Stress," JA 677; and (2) a public filing showing that Qualitor Inc., which holds 100% of Pylon's stock, obtained a five million dollar at a rate of 8.46%, JA827. In response, Pylon did not dispute the accuracy of these submissions, nor did it submit evidence demonstrating its ability to pay a damages award, either of past or future damages. Instead, Pylon responded with attorney speculation and argued that, if, "as Bosch alleges, Pylon sells so many beam blades, then there is little reason to suspect that Pylon will not have sufficient resources to pay a royalty to Bosch." JA 893.

While the burden of proving irreparable harm was of course Bosch's, Pylon's failure to submit rebuttal evidence regarding its ability to satisfy an award of money damages is troublesome given the procedural history of this case. Because the district court granted Pylon's motion to bifurcate damages, Bosch had no opportunity to obtain discovery relating to Pylon's financial condition, or that of its corporate parent before the court considered its request for injunctive relief. Consequently, facts relevant to Pylon's ability to satisfy a judgment were uniquely within its control. While Bosch's evidence of Pylon's inability to pay is not overwhelming—gleaned as it had to be from public records, in light of Pylon's failure to introduce any rebuttal evidence or to even argue below or to this court that Bosch's characterization of its financial status is inaccurate, and the unique procedural history of this case, we conclude that this factor favors a finding of irreparable harm.[6]

---

6. During a lengthy discussion at oral argument on this issue, Pylon's counsel, when asked directly, could not offer express assurances that Pylon could satisfy a damages judgment and a prospective royalty payment. Oral Argument (July 7, 2011) at 25:56-26:18, *available at* http:// www. cafc. uscourts. gov/oral-argument-recordings/all/pylon. html. In addition, when asked why Pylon did not produce evidence of its ability to satisfy a money damages judgment, Pylon's counsel said that, "our response is to argue, as we did to the district court, based on the evidence that was available, to make argument and then live with the decision that Judge Robinson ordered. . . ." *Id.* at 27:44-28:22. Pylon's counsel also contended, confusingly, that whether there was evidence "available" to show Pylon's ability to pay a judgment, and whether Pylon decided not to produce it, was a matter "we can and are debating." *Id.* at 29:28-36.

In view of the foregoing evidence, the record contains no basis on which the district court rationally could have concluded that Bosch failed to demonstrate irreparable harm or that a remedy other than injunction is sufficient to address its harm. Consequently, the court committed a clear error of judgment in analyzing this factor.

II.

Turning to the remaining equitable factors, we conclude that, on balance, they also favor entry of a permanent injunction.

With respect to the adequacy of money damages, Bosch argues that it will continue to suffer irreparable harm due to lost market share, lost business opportunities, and price erosion unless Pylon is permanently enjoined. According to Bosch, money damages alone cannot fully compensate Bosch for these harms. We agree. There is no reason to believe that Pylon will stop infringing, or that the irreparable harms resulting from its infringement will otherwise cease, absent an injunction. More importantly, the questionable financial condition of both Pylon and its parent company reinforces the inadequacy of a remedy at law. A district court should assess whether a damage remedy is a meaningful one in light of the financial condition of the infringer before the alternative of money damages can be deemed adequate. While competitive harms theoretically can be offset by monetary payments in certain circumstances, the likely availability of those monetary payments helps define the circumstances in which this is so.

Here, the only evidence of record is that Pylon likely will be faced with a substantial damages award for its past infringement and may be unable to pay even that. In the face of such evidence, the district court's failure to consider the extent to which a forward-looking monetary award is a viable or meaningful alternative to an injunction was error.

We also conclude that the third factor, the balance of hardships, favors Bosch. Pylon argues that "Bosch is an international conglomerate with a diverse product base," whereas "Pylon is a small, domestic corporation that focuses on the manufacture and sale of wiper blades," such that the parties' respective size and business models demonstrate that an injunction would burden Pylon more than the absence of an injunction would harm Bosch. We are not persuaded. A party cannot escape an injunction simply because it is smaller than the patentee or because its primary product is an infringing one. *See Windsurfing Int'l, Inc. v. AMF, Inc.*, 782 F.2d 995, 1003 n.12 (Fed. Cir. 1986) ("One who elects to build a business on a product found to infringe cannot be heard to complain if an injunction against continuing infringement destroys the business so elected."). On the other hand, requiring Bosch to compete against its own patented invention, with the resultant harms described above, places a substantial hardship on Bosch. This factor, therefore, favors entry of an injunction in this case.

As to the public interest, we find that this factor is neutral. Bosch argues that Pylon's inferior product "may potentially" compromise the public's safety, but there is no support in the record for that assertion. Although Bosch also cites its right to exclude and Pylon relies on its right to compete generally, neither party offers specific arguments as to why, in this case, the public interest would be served or disserved by an injunction. Although this final factor does not favor either party, the remaining considerations lead to only one reasonable conclusion: that Bosch has shown that it is entitled to a permanent injunction.

Because the undisputed evidence conclusively shows that permanent injunctive relief is warranted in this case, we do not believe that remand of this matter is appropriate. We agree with Bosch that, on the record as it stands, any alternative result on remand necessarily would be an abuse of discretion. Remand is particularly inappropriate here because it would only delay relief to which Bosch currently is entitled. Pylon has been competing against Bosch with a product that a jury has concluded infringes Bosch's valid patents, and it has done so for seventeen months since the jury's verdict and for nearly one year since the district court denied Bosch's motion for a permanent injunction. It also has done so despite a record which contains compelling evidence supporting injunctive relief in Bosch's favor. Further delay, which would amount to a stay of an injunction without a bond, would be inequitable.

We agree, as the dissent urges, that normally a district court should balance these equitable considerations in the first instance, but the facts of this case compel a different result. Unlike the cases on which the dissent relies, including *eBay* itself, where the district courts either could not have or did not apply the standard announced in *eBay,* the parties and the district court in this case were well aware of the *eBay* standard when developing and applying the record. Again, to the extent that bifurcation of the damages portion of the trial inhibited development of the record as it relates to injunctive relief, that was the result of Pylon's doing. Remanding the action for additional hearings prior to entry of injunctive relief would punish the patentee for the district court's decision, at Pylon's urging, to bifurcate the trial and for the district court's erroneous application of the law to the evidence before it. We cannot endorse that result.

CONCLUSION

For the foregoing reasons, and because we find that Pylon's remaining arguments are without merit, we reverse the district court's denial of Bosch's motion for entry of a permanent injunction and remand for entry of an appropriate injunction.

Comments

1. *A Fractured Supreme Court.* There were three separate opinions in *eBay.* In the majority, the Court retreated from what was considered "a given" by patent litigators, namely, an injunction would issue upon a finding of infringement (and, of course, that the patent was not invalid). This understanding was reflected in Federal Circuit precedent, and is consistent with treating a patent as a form of property. *See Richardson v. Suzuki Motor Co., Ltd.,* 868 F.2d 1226, 1246-1247 (Fed. Cir. 1989) ("Infringement having been established, it is contrary to the laws of property, of which the patent law partakes, to deny the patentee's right to exclude others from use of his property. . . . It is the general rule that an injunction will issue when infringement has been adjudged, absent a sound reason for denying it."). *See also* 35 U.S.C. §261 (stating patents "have the attributes of personal property").

   But in *eBay,* the "Supreme Court has since struck down that general rule . . . making clear that the traditional four-factor test for injunctions applies to patent cases." *Acumed LLC v. Stryker Corp.*, 483 F.3d 800, 811 (Fed. Cir. 2007). In *eBay*, the court noted that section 261 requires courts to look to other parts of Title 35. Indeed, section 261 states "*[s]ubject to the provisions of this title*, patents shall have the attributes of personal property." (Emphasis added.) The Court then turned to the permissive statutory language in section 283—an injunction "may" issue only "in accordance with the principles of equity."

The Court also rejected the district court's categorical approach that injunctions should be unavailable for patentees who do not commercialize their inventions. Justice Thomas cited university patentees and self-made inventors as entities that "might reasonably prefer to license their patents, rather than undertake efforts to secure the financing necessary to bring their works to market themselves." This language is important because the Court acknowledged there are entities that do not have the capacity to self-commercialize their inventions, and the patent system should not categorically treat them differently as a result. Thus, the Court implicitly distinguished between, on the one hand, "university patentees and self-made inventors" and, on the other hand, so-called patent trolls who, in the words of Justice Kennedy, "use patents not as a basis for producing and selling goods but, instead, . . . [as a] bargaining tool to charge exorbitant fees to companies that seek to buy licenses to practice the patent."

The two concurrences are interesting because Chief Justice Roberts looks to the past, and Justice Kennedy looks to the future. Chief Justice Roberts thinks district court judges should be informed by history. He looked to the nineteenth century and found that courts "granted injunctive relief upon a finding of infringement in the vast majority of patent cases." He found this practice unsurprising, given the "difficulty of protecting a right to *exclude* through monetary remedies that allow an infringer to *use* an invention against the patentee's wishes." (Emphasis in original.) Justice Kennedy, while recognizing the importance of history, noted that in contemporary patent cases, "the nature of the patent being enforced and the economic function of the patent holder present considerations quite unlike earlier cases." He also expressed his concern over so-called patent trolls (although he did not use this term), which are entities "that use patents not as a basis for producing and selling goods but, instead, primarily for obtaining licensing fees." (This dynamic received a great deal of press during the RIM/NTP litigation over the Blackberry® device.) In addition, Justice Kennedy noted that injunctions may have "different consequences" for business method patents, which are of "suspect validity."

2. ***The Effect on Innovation and Patent Litigation.*** Is giving the district court judge more discretion regarding equitable relief consistent with the right to exclude; will it lead to greater uncertainty, adversely affect innovation incentives, and diminish the likelihood of settlement? The pharmaceutical and biotechnology industries certainly think so. *See* Amicus Briefs of PhRMA and BIO in the *eBay* case.

But the software and electronics industries supported eBay. *See* Amicus Briefs of Intel, Microsoft, Oracle, and Micron. Justice Kennedy gave voice to the concerns of these industries in writing, "[w]hen the patented invention is but a small component of the product the companies seek to produce and the threat of an injunction is employed simply for undue leverage in negotiations, legal damages may well be sufficient to compensate for the infringement and an injunction may not serve the public interest." (Not surprisingly, RIM also filed an amicus brief supporting eBay.) The concern that an injunction would cause significant economic hardship and disruption can be traced to the mid-nineteenth century. In *Parker v. Brant*, 18 F. Cas. 1117 (1850), the court stated, "we feel a reluctance to stop two hundred mills . . . without giving the defendants a chance of making a settlement or compromise."

Professor Joseph Miller's blog, *The Fire of Genius*, has a "running list of the patent, copyright, and trademark cases in which courts have applied the *eBay* four-factor framework to grant or deny injunctive relief." *See* http://www.thefireofgenius.com/injunctions.

3. ***Direct Competition, "Small Component" Patentees, and the Injunction.*** As the principal cases suggested, district courts are much more likely to issue a permanent injunction if the patentee and infringer are competitors. *See TiVo, Inc. v. EchoStar Commc'ns Corp.*, 446 F. Supp. 2d 664, 669 (E.D. Tex. 2006); *Black & Decker Inc. v. Robert Bosch Tool Corp.*, Slip Copy, 2006 WL 3446144 (N.D. Ill.); *O2 Micro International, Ltd. v. Beyond Innovation Technology Co.*, Slip Copy, 2007 WL 869576, at *2 (E.D. Tex.) (stating "O2 Micro has demonstrated irreparable injury. O2 Micro competes directly with BiTEK, and this fact weighs heavily in the Court's analysis. This Court has recognized the high value of intellectual property when it is asserted against a direct competitor in the plaintiff's market"). Some courts, in the face of a "loss of market share" argument by a patentee, require the patentee to show "specific sales or market data to assist the court" and identify "precisely what market share, revenues, and customers" the patentee has lost to the infringer. *Praxair, Inc. v. ATMI, Inc.*, 479 F. Supp. 2d 440, 444 (D. Del. 2007).

The patent holding company (oftentimes referred to disparagingly as a "patent troll") whose patent forms a "small component" of the overall product at issue, has garnered less sympathy from district courts. (The holding company is structured to license its patent rights rather than manufacture or produce the patented product.) This should not be surprising given Justice Kennedy's concurrence in *eBay*:

> In cases now arising trial courts should bear in mind that in many instances the nature of the patent being enforced and the economic function of the patent holder present considerations quite unlike earlier cases. An industry has developed in which firms use patents not as a basis for producing and selling goods but, instead, primarily for obtaining licensing fees . . . and [f]or these firms, an injunction, and the potentially serious sanctions arising from its violation, can be employed as a bargaining tool to charge exorbitant fees to companies that seek to buy licenses to practice the patent. When the patented invention is but a small component of the product the companies seek to produce and the threat of an injunction is employed simply for undue leverage in negotiations, legal damages may well be sufficient to compensate for the infringement and an injunction may not serve the public interest.

126 S. Ct. at 1842. In *z4 Technologies, Inc. v. Microsoft Corp.*, 434 F. Supp. 2d 437 (E.D. Tex. 2006), the court denied injunctive relief even though Microsoft was found to willfully infringe. The court relied heavily on Justice Kennedy's

concurrence, stating the patentee's invention "is a very small component of the Microsoft Windows and Office software products that the jury found to infringe z4's patents. The infringing product activation component of the software is in no way related to the core functionality for which the software is purchased by consumers. Accordingly, Justice Kennedy's comments support the conclusion that monetary damages would be sufficient to compensate z4 for any future infringement by Microsoft." *Id.* at 441. *See also Paice LLC v. Toyota Motor Corp.*, 2006 WL 2385139 (E.D. Tex.).

4. ***The Demise of Irreparable Harm and the Rise of Property Rights.*** The *Bosch* court expressly confirmed that *eBay* "jettisoned the presumption of irreparable harm" in the context of permanent injunctions. But nonetheless the court wrote that while the historical "short-cuts" may be gone, let's not forget that patents are property rights grounded in the Constitution. The *Edwards Lifesciences* court also underscored that patents are property rights consistent with the Constitution; as the court noted, *eBay* "did not cancel 35 U.S.C. §154."

5. ***The Public Interest.*** District courts have—post-*eBay*—expressed the public interest consideration largely in favor of patentees and the patentee's interest in protecting his patent rights. For instance, the court in *O2 Micro International, Ltd. v. Beyond Innovation Technology Co.*, Slip Copy, 2007 WL 869576, at *3 (E.D. Tex.), the court stated "the public interest would be served by issuing an injunction to protect the patent rights at issue." The public interest factor was at issue in *Sanofi-Synthelabo, Inc. v. Apotex, Inc.*, 470 F.3d 1368 (Fed. Cir. 2006), discussed after the *Amazon.com* case above. Recall, the court sided with the name-brand pharmaceutical company—Sanofi—in affirming the district court's grant of a preliminary injunction against a generic manufacturer. The Federal Circuit stated:

> We have long acknowledged the importance of the patent system in encouraging innovation. Indeed, the "encouragement of investment-based risk is the fundamental purpose of the patent grant, and is based directly on the right to exclude." The district court relied on the testimony of Dr. Hausman in finding that the average cost of developing a blockbuster drug is $800 million. Importantly, the patent system provides incentive to the innovative drug companies to continue costly development efforts. We therefore find that the court did not clearly err in concluding that the significant "public interest in encouraging investment in drug development and protecting the exclusionary rights conveyed in valid pharmaceutical patents" tips the scales in favor of Sanofi.

Id. at 1383-1384. Does this imply that industries that do not have significant development cost will have greater difficulty obtaining injunctive relief? *See also i4i Ltd. P'ship v. Microsoft, Inc.*, 589 F.3d 1346, 1276 (Fed. Cir. 2009) (stating "[p]ast harm to a patentee's market share, revenues, and brand recognition is relevant for determining whether the patentee *has suffered* an irreparable injury") (emphasis in original).

In *Praxair, Inc. v. ATMI, Inc.*, 479 F. Supp. 2d 440 (D. Del. 2007), the patentee (Praxair) and the infringer (ATMI) were direct competitors, yet the court denied Praxair's motion for a permanent injunction because Praxair did not present sufficient evidence of irreparable harm and inadequacy of money damages:

Praxair's Uptime™ cylinder is in direct and head-to-head competition with ATMI's VAC® cylinder, as Uptime™ and VAC® are the only two mechanical-based systems for the controlled delivery of industrial gases on the market. VAC®, therefore, is taking sales from Uptime,™ an "important growth product" for Praxair, and (according to Praxair) continues to erode the exclusivity to which Praxair is entitled through the ownership of its patents. This "stolen" market share "work[s] a substantial and unjustifiable hardship on Praxair," which Praxair asserts cannot be remedied with money damages alone. . . . Praxair asserts that the public interest is generally served by the enforcement of patent rights. ATMI has presented evidence that an injunction would force its customers, semiconductor manufacturers running billion-dollar fabrication plants, to incur significant costs by shutting down operations to qualify an alternative gas source or to switch to alternate cylinders. Praxair has presented evidence that manufacturers could switch to other qualified non-infringing gas delivery sources during routine maintenance.

Under *eBay*, a plaintiff must prove that it is entitled to its statutory right to exclude by demonstrating, *inter alia,* irreparable injury and the inadequacy of legal remedies. Though the quantum of evidence required is relatively unclear, the court finds that Praxair has not met its burden under *eBay* to put forward sufficient proof vis-à-vis the broad scope of the relief requested. Praxair generally argues that VAC®'s presence in the market will cause Praxair to "likely lose additional market share, profits, and goodwill," without further detail. Praxair has not provided or described any specific sales or market data to assist the court, nor has it identified precisely what market share, revenues, and customers Praxair has lost to ATMI.

While money damages are generally considered inadequate to compensate for the violation of a patentee's right to exclude, Praxair nonetheless had a burden to iterate specific reasons why ATMI's infringement can not be compensated for with a money award. *TiVo, Inc. v. EchoStar Communications Corp.,* 446 F. Supp. 2d 664, 669-70 (E.D. Tex. 2006) (granting permanent injunction where plaintiff was "a relatively new company with only one primary product," and the parties agreed that customers tend to remain loyal to the company from which they obtained their first DVR recorder, "shaping the market to [p]laintiff's disadvantage and result[ing] in long-term customer loss"). Praxair has not explained why it may have "difficulties calculating damages going forward," nor how money damages could not adequately compensate for "lost market share" or any "lost research opportunities." Both parties cite to evidence demonstrating that the VAC®/UpTime™ sales are not critical to either party's overall corporate success. Praxair's desire to become a monopoly supplier in its product's market is hardly unique, and is not conclusive evidence of any factor.

Id. at 442-444.

6. ***The Comparison to Copyright Law.*** Justice Thomas looked to copyright law to support a more discretionary role for district court judges in deciding whether to issue an injunction. He cited *Tasini* and *Campbell,* which are cited regularly in academic circles for the proposition that injunctive relief in copyright cases need not be automatic. But in practice the presumption in favor of injunctions in copyright cases seems to be even stronger than it is in patent cases.

POLICY PERSPECTIVE
Property Rules, Liability Rules, and Patent Litigation

A patent is a personal property right that provides its owner with a right to exclude others. 35 U.S.C. §§ 154, 261. Thus, a patent right fits comfortably within a property-rights regime, for which the classic remedy is an injunction. But by giving judges more discretion, the Court opens the door for a liability rule approach whereby infringers infringe now and pay later. In their seminal article, Guido Calabresi and Douglas Melamed argued that when transaction costs are high and valuation is straightforward, a liability rule governs. In contrast, a property rule applies where transaction costs are low (e.g., prospect of a holdout is low) and valuation is difficult for the court. *See* Guido Calabresi & A. Douglas Melamed, *Property Rules, Liability Rules, and Inalienability: One View of the Cathedral*, 85 HARV. L. REV. 1089, 1106-1110 (1972). *See also* Keith N. Hylton, *Property Rules and Liability Rules, Once Again*, 2 REV. L. & ECON. 137 (2006) (reexamining the property/liability rule question in the light of bargaining theory literature). Was Justice Kennedy alluding to high transaction costs and, therefore, sympathetic to a liability rule approach when he wrote "[a]n industry has developed in which firms use patents not as a basis for producing and selling goods but, instead, primarily for obtaining licensing fees" and "[f]or these firms, an injunction, and the potentially serious sanctions arising from its violation, can be employed as a bargaining tool to charge exorbitant fees to companies that seek to buy licenses to practice the patent." Are these firms to be treated differently than university patentees and self-made inventors, who, as noted by the majority, frequently do not have the capability to commercialize their inventions on their own?

    There are shortcomings with a liability rule. Perhaps the most significant concern is that the market pricing mechanism is replaced by what the court thinks the proper price should be. Thus, the risk of under compensation is significant for no other reason than the state simply is not as familiar with the asset as its owner and the market. *See* Robert P. Merges, *Intellectual Property Rights and Bargaining Breakdown: The Case of Blocking Patents*, 62 TENN. L. REV. 75, 81 (1994) (stating "a property rule makes sense for patents because . . . a court setting the terms of the exchange would have a difficult time doing so quickly and cheaply, given the specialized nature of the assets and the varied and complex business environments in which the assets are deployed"). For a good discussion of the respective roles of property rules and liability rules in a technological context, see Mark A. Lemley & Philip J. Weiser, *Should Property or Liability Rules Govern Information?*, 85 TEX. L. REV. 783 (2007).

C. WILLFUL INFRINGEMENT AND ENHANCED DAMAGES

A finding of willful infringement allows for the assessment of treble damages and the awarding of attorneys' fees to the prevailing party. An alleged infringer may usually preclude a finding of willfulness if he obtained and properly relied on a competent opinion of counsel (the so-called noninfringement letter). But, as the *Knorr-Bremse* case holds, failure to obtain a letter will not necessarily lead to an adverse inference of willfulness. And, a few years after *Knorr*, the court, in *In re Seagate Technology*, raised the standard for a finding of willfulness and, importantly, eliminated the affirmative duty of care that typically accompanied actual notice of the alleged infringement. Both *Knorr* and *Seagate* are *en banc* opinions.

KNORR-BREMSE SYSTEME v. DANA CORP.

383 F.3d 1337 (Fed. Cir. 2004) (en banc)

NEWMAN, Circuit Judge.

Knorr-Bremse Systeme is the owner of United States Patent No. 5,927,445 (the '445 patent) entitled "Disk Brake For Vehicles Having Insertable Actuator," is sued on July 27, 1999. At trial to the United States District Court for the Eastern District of Virginia, the appellants Dana Corporation, Haldex Brake Products Corporation, and Haldex Brake Products AB were found liable for infringement and willful infringement. No damages were awarded, for there were no sales of the infringing brakes. Based on the finding of willful infringement the court awarded partial attorney fees under 35 U.S.C. §285.

The appellants seek reversal of the finding of willful infringement, arguing that an adverse inference should not have been drawn from the withholding by Haldex of an opinion of counsel concerning the patent issues, and from the failure of Dana to obtain its own opinion of counsel. Applying our precedent, the district court inferred that the opinion of counsel withheld by Haldex was unfavorable to the defendants. After argument of the appeal we took this case en banc in order to reconsider our precedent with respect to these aspects.

We now hold that no adverse inference that an opinion of counsel was or would have been unfavorable flows from an alleged infringer's failure to obtain or produce an exculpatory opinion of counsel. Precedent to the contrary is over-ruled. We therefore vacate the judgment of willful infringement and remand for re-determination, on consideration of the totality of the circumstances but without the evidentiary contribution or presumptive weight of an adverse inference that any opinion of counsel was or would have been unfavorable.

BACKGROUND

Knorr-Bremse, a German corporation, manufactures air disk brakes for use in heavy commercial vehicles, primarily Class 6-8 trucks known as eighteen wheelers, semis, or tractor-trailers. Knorr-Bremse states that air disk brake technology is superior to the previously dominant technology of hydraulically or pneumatically actuated drum brakes, and that air disk brakes have widely supplanted drum brakes for trucks in the European market.

Dana, an American corporation, and the Swedish company Haldex Brake Products AB and its United States affiliate, agreed to collaborate to sell in the United States an air disk brake manufactured by Haldex in Sweden. The appellants imported into the United States about 100 units of a Haldex brake designated the Mark II model. Between 1997 and 1999 the Mark II brake was installed in approximately eighteen trucks of Dana and various potential customers. The trucks were used in transport, and brake performance records were required to be kept and provided to Dana. Dana and Haldex advertised these brakes at trade shows and in industry media in the United States.

Knorr-Bremse in December 1998 orally notified Dana of patent disputes with Haldex in Europe involving the Mark II brake, and told the appellants that patent applications were pending in the United States. On August 31, 1999 Knorr-Bremse notified Dana in writing of infringement litigation against Haldex in Europe, and that Knorr-Bremse's United States '445 patent had issued on July 27, 1999. Knorr-Bremse filed this infringement suit on May 15, 2000. In September 2000 Haldex presented to the district court a modified brake design designated the Mark III, and moved for a summary declaration of non-infringement by the Mark III brake. Knorr-Bremse in turn moved for summary judgment of literal infringement by the Mark II brake, and infringement by the Mark III either literally or under the doctrine of equivalents. After a hearing in November 2000 the district court granted Knorr-Bremse's motion for summary judgment of literal infringement by the Mark II brake, and set for trial the issues with respect to the Mark III. Before and after the judgment of infringement by the Mark II, Dana and others continued to operate trucks in the United States containing the Mark II brake. Following a bench trial in January 2001, the district court found literal infringement by the Mark III brake.

On the issue of willful infringement, Haldex told the court that it had consulted European and United States counsel concerning Knorr-Bremse's patents, but declined to produce any legal opinion or to disclose the advice received, asserting the attorney-client privilege. Dana stated that it did not itself consult counsel, but relied on Haldex. Applying Federal Circuit precedent, the district court found: "It is reasonable to conclude that such opinions were unfavorable." The court discussed the evidence for and against willful infringement and concluded that "the totality of the circumstances compels the conclusion that defendants' use of the Mark II air disk brake, and indeed Dana's continued use of the Mark II air disk brake on various of its vehicles [after the judgment of infringement] amounts to willful infringement of the '445 patent." Based on the finding of willful infringement the court found that the case was "exceptional" under 35 U.S.C. § 285, and awarded Knorr-Bremse its attorney fees for the portion of the litigation that related to the Mark II brake, but not the Mark III.

The appellants appeal only the issue of willfulness of the infringement and the ensuing award of attorney fees.

I

Willful Infringement

In discussing "willful" behavior and its consequences, the Supreme Court has observed that "[t]he word 'willful' is widely used in the law, and, although it has not by any means been given a perfectly consistent interpretation, it is generally understood to refer to conduct that is not merely negligent," *McLaughlin v. Richland Shoe Co.*, 486 U.S. 128, 133 (1988), the Court citing conventional definitions such as "voluntary," "deliberate," and "intentional." *Id.* The concept of "willful infringement" is not simply a conduit for enhancement of damages; it is a statement that patent infringement, like other civil wrongs, is disfavored, and intentional disregard of legal rights warrants deterrence. Remedy for willful infringement is founded on 35 U.S.C. § 284 ("the court may increase the damages up to three times the amount found or assessed") and 35 U.S.C. §285 ("the court in exceptional cases may award reasonable attorney fees to the prevailing party").

Determination of willfulness is made on consideration of the totality of the circumstances, and may include contributions of several factors, as compiled, *e.g.,* in *Rolls-Royce Ltd. v. GTE Valeron Corp.,* 800 F.2d 1101, 1110 (Fed. Cir. 1986) and *Read Corp. v. Portec, Inc.,* 970 F.2d 816, 826-27 (Fed. Cir. 1992). These contributions are evaluated and weighed by the trier of fact, for, as this court remarked in *Rite-Hite Corp. v. Kelley Co.,* 819 F.2d 1120, 1125-26 (Fed. Cir. 1987), "'[w]illfulness' in infringement, as in life, is not an all-or-nothing trait, but one of degree. It recognizes that infringement may range from unknowing, or accidental, to deliberate, or reckless, disregard of a patentee's legal rights."

Fundamental to determination of willful infringement is the duty to act in accordance with law. Reinforcement of this duty was a foundation of the formation of the Federal Circuit court, at a time when widespread disregard of patent rights was undermining the national innovation incentive. Thus in *Underwater Devices, Inc. v. Morrison-Knudsen Co.,* 717 F.2d 1380 (Fed. Cir. 1983), the court stressed the legal obligation to respect valid patent rights. The court's opinion quoted the infringer's attorney who, without obtaining review by patent counsel of the patents at issue, advised the client to "continue to refuse to even discuss the payment of a royalty." *Id.* at 1385. The attorney advised that "[c]ourts, in recent years, have — in patent infringement cases — found the patents claimed to be infringed upon invalid in approximately 80% of the cases," and that for this reason the patentee would probably not risk filing suit. *Id.* On this record of flagrant disregard of presumptively valid patents without analysis, the Federal Circuit ruled that "where, as here, a potential infringer has actual notice of another's patent rights, he has an affirmative duty to exercise due care to determine whether or not he is infringing," including "the duty to seek and obtain competent legal advice from counsel before the initiation of any possible infringing activity." *Id.* at 1389-90.

Underwater Devices did not raise any issue of attorney-client privilege, while applying precedent that a finding of willfulness requires the factfinder to find by clear and convincing evidence "that the infringer acted in disregard of the patent," citing *Stickle v. Heublein, Inc.,* 716 F.2d 1550, 1565 (Fed. Cir. 1983). The aspect of privilege arose in *Kloster Speedsteel AB v. Crucible Inc.,* 793 F.2d 1565 (Fed. Cir. 1986), where the Federal Circuit observed that the infringer "has not even asserted that it sought advice of counsel when notified of the allowed claims and [the patentee's] warning, or at any time before it began this litigation," and held that the infringer's "silence on the subject, in alleged reliance on the attorney-client privilege, would warrant the conclusion that it either obtained no advice of counsel or did so and was advised that its importation and sale of the accused products would be an infringement of valid U.S. patents." *Id.* at 1580. Thus arose the adverse inference, reinforced in *Fromson v. Western Litho Plate & Supply Co.,* 853 F.2d 1568 (Fed. Cir. 1988), and establishing the general rule that "a court must be free to infer that either no opinion was obtained or, if an opinion were obtained, it was contrary to the infringer's desire to initiate or continue its use of the patentee's invention." *Id.* at 1572-73. Throughout this evolution the focus was not on attorney-client relationships, but on disrespect for law. However, implementation of this precedent has resulted in inappropriate burdens on the attorney-client relationship.

We took this case en banc to review this precedent. . . . The adverse inference that an opinion was or would have been unfavorable, flowing from the infringer's failure to obtain or produce an exculpatory opinion of counsel, is no longer warranted. Precedent authorizing such inference is overruled.

Question 1

When the attorney-client privilege and/or work-product privilege is invoked by a defendant in an infringement suit, is it appropriate for the trier of fact to draw an adverse inference with respect to willful infringement?

The answer is "no." Although the duty to respect the law is undiminished, no adverse inference shall arise from invocation of the attorney-client and/or work product privilege. The Supreme Court describes the attorney-client privilege as "the oldest of the privileges for confidential communications known to common law," and has stressed the public purpose

> to encourage full and frank communication between attorneys and their clients and thereby promote broader public interests in the observance of law and administration of justice. The privilege recognizes that sound legal advice or advocacy serves public ends and that such advice or advocacy depends upon the lawyer's being fully informed by the client.

Upjohn Co. v. United States, 449 U.S. 383, 389 (1981). Professor Wigmore has elaborated:

> The lawyer must have the whole of his client's case, or he cannot pretend to give any useful advice. . . . That the whole will not be told to counsel unless the privilege is confidential, is perfectly clear. A man who seeks advice, seeks it because he believes that he may do so safely; he will rarely make disclosure which may be used against him; rather than create an adverse witness in his lawyer, he will refuse all private arbitration, and take the chance of a trial.

8 J. Wigmore, *Evidence in Trials at Common Law* § 2291 at 548 (McNaughton rev. 1961).

Although this court has never suggested that opinions of counsel concerning patents are not privileged, the inference that withheld opinions are adverse to the client's actions can distort the attorney-client relationship, in derogation of the foundations of that relationship. We conclude that a special rule affecting attorney-client relationships in patent cases is not warranted. There should be no risk of liability in disclosures to and from counsel in patent matters; such risk can intrude upon full communication and ultimately the public interest in encouraging open and confident relationships between client and attorney. As Professor McCormick has explained, the attorney-client privilege protects "interests and relationships which . . . are regarded as of sufficient social importance to justify some sacrifice of availability of evidence relevant to the administration of justice." 1 *McCormick on Evidence* § 72, 299 (5th ed. 1999).

There is precedent for the drawing of adverse inferences in circumstances other than those involving attorney-client relationships; for example when a party's refusal to testify or produce evidence in civil suits creates a presumption of an intent to withhold damaging information that is material to the litigation. However, the courts have declined to impose adverse inferences on invocation of the attorney-client privilege. We now hold that this rule applies to the same extent in patent cases as in other areas of law. A defendant may of course choose to waive the privilege and produce the advice of counsel. However, the assertion of attorney-client and/or work-product privilege and the withholding of the advice of counsel shall no longer entail an adverse inference as to the nature of the advice.

Question 2

When the defendant had not obtained legal advice, is it appropriate to draw an adverse inference with respect to willful infringement?

The answer, again, is "no." The issue here is not of privilege, but whether there is a legal duty upon a potential infringer to consult with counsel, such that failure to do so will provide an inference or evidentiary presumption that such opinion would have been negative.

Dana Corporation did not seek independent legal advice, upon notice by Knorr-Bremse of the pendency of the '445 application in the United States and of the issuance of the '445 patent, followed by the charge of infringement. In tandem with our holding that it is inappropriate to draw an adverse inference that undisclosed legal advice for which attorney-client privilege is claimed was unfavorable, we also hold that it is inappropriate to draw a similar adverse inference from failure to consult counsel. The amici curiae describe the burdens and costs of the requirement, as pressed in litigation, for early and full study by counsel of every potentially adverse patent of which the defendant had knowledge, citing cases such as *Johns Hopkins Univ. v. Cellpro, Inc.,* 152 F.3d 1342, 1364 (Fed. Cir. 1998), wherein the court held that to avoid liability for willful infringement in that case, an exculpatory opinion of counsel must fully address all potential infringement and validity issues. Although other cases have imposed less rigorous criteria, the issue has occasioned extensive satellite litigation, distorting the "conceptual underpinnings" of *Underwater Devices* and *Kloster Speedsteel.* Although there continues to be "an affirmative duty of due care to avoid infringement of the known patent rights of others," *L.A. Gear Inc. v. Thom McAn Shoe Co.,* 988 F.2d 1117, 1127 (Fed. Cir. 1993), the failure to obtain an exculpatory opinion of counsel shall no longer provide an adverse inference or evidentiary presumption that such an opinion would have been unfavorable.

Question 3

If the court concludes that the law should be changed, and the adverse inference withdrawn as applied to this case, what are the consequences for this case?

A

The district court based its willfulness determination on several factors in addition to the adverse inference arising from the assertion of attorney-client privilege by Haldex and the failure of Dana to obtain legal advice. This court has explained that "there are no hard and fast per se rules" with respect to willfulness of infringement. Precedent illustrates various factors, some weighing on the side of culpability and some that are mitigating or ameliorating. *See Read v. Portec, supra.*

The district court found, on the evidence presented, that literal infringement by the Mark II brake was reasonably clear and did not present close legal or factual questions. As for the validity of the '445 patent, the court found that "given the quantity and quality of the evidence presented by defendants at trial on the issues of obviousness and indefiniteness, it cannot fairly be said that defendants, throughout the litigation, had a good faith belief that the '445 patent would ultimately be found invalid on these grounds." The court also found that the appellants failed to take prompt remedial action to terminate infringement after the judgment of literal infringement by the Mark II, stating that "Dana deliberately yielded to market pressures in deciding to continue using the infringing Mark II air disk brakes on test vehicles pending future receipt of replacement Mark III air disk brakes." *Id.* The court also found that "although Haldex indeed developed the Mark III air disk brake in a good faith effort to design around the '445 patent, Haldex nonetheless continued to use the Mark II air disk brake throughout the redesign effort, including displaying Mark II air disk brakes at various automotive conferences in the United States and distributing Mark II promotional literature to potential customers at these conferences," the court also noted that infringement was not then enjoined.

The district court also considered Haldex's invocation of the attorney-client privilege in order to withhold its opinions of counsel, and Dana's failure to obtain an independent legal opinion despite the warning and notice of infringement. The appellants argue that but for the adverse inference of unfavorable opinions drawn from these actions, the finding of willfulness of infringement is not supported. Knorr-Bremse responds that willful infringement is well supported by the remaining findings. Because elimination of the adverse inference as drawn by the district court is a material change in the totality of the circumstances, a fresh weighing of the evidence is required to determine whether the defendants committed willful infringement. This determination is the primary responsibility and authority of the district court. We therefore vacate the finding of willful infringement and remand for redetermination of the issue.

Several amici curiae raised the question of whether the trier of fact, particularly a jury, can or should be told whether or not counsel was consulted (albeit without any inference as to the nature of the advice received) as part of the totality of the circumstances relevant to the question of willful infringement. The amici pointed to various hypothetical circumstances in which such information could be relevant, even when there was no issue of attorney-client privilege. That aspect is not raised by this case, was not before the district court, and has not been briefed on this appeal. Today we resolve only the question of whether adverse inferences of unfavorable opinions can be drawn, and hold that they can not.

B

The appellants also argue that the award of attorney fees is a matter of punitive damages, and is therefore improper. Precedent and statute do not support this position. 35 U.S.C. §285 provides that "the court in exceptional cases may award reasonable attorney fees to the prevailing party"; and the court has confirmed that a finding of willful infringement may qualify a case as exceptional under §285. *See, e.g., Modine Mfg. Co. v. The Allen Group, Inc.*, 917 F.2d 538, 543 (Fed. Cir. 1990). That there were not actual damages does not render the award of attorney fees punitive. Attorney fees are compensatory, and may provide a fair remedy in appropriate cases. Upon a finding of willful infringement, the award of attorney fees is within the district court's sound discretion.

In view of our vacatur of the finding of willful infringement, the award of attorney fees is also vacated. On remand the award may be reconsidered, should the judgment of willful infringement be restored.

SUMMARY

An adverse inference that a legal opinion was or would have been unfavorable shall not be drawn from invocation of the attorney-client and/or work product privileges or from failure to consult with counsel. Contrary holdings and suggestions of precedent are overruled.

IN RE SEAGATE TECHNOLOGY, LLC
497 F.3d 1360 (Fed. Cir. 2007) (en banc)

MAYER, Circuit Judge.

Seagate Technology, LLC ("Seagate") petitions for a writ of mandamus directing the United States District Court for the Southern District of New York to vacate its orders compelling disclosure of materials and testimony that Seagate claims is covered by the attorney-client privilege and work product protection. We ordered en banc review, and now grant the petition. We overrule *Underwater Devices Inc. v. Morrison-Knudsen Co.,* 717 F.2d 1380 (1983), and we clarify the scope of the waiver of attorney-client privilege and work product protection that results when an accused patent infringer asserts an advice of counsel defense to a charge of willful infringement. . . .

The en banc order set out the following question[]:

> 3. Given the impact of the statutory duty of care standard announced in *Underwater Devices, Inc. v. Morrison-Knudsen Co.* on the issue of waiver of attorney-client privilege, should this court reconsider the decision in *Underwater Devices* and the duty of care standard itself?

DISCUSSION

Because patent infringement is a strict liability offense, the nature of the offense is only relevant in determining whether enhanced damages are warranted. Although a trial court's discretion in awarding enhanced damages has a long lineage in patent law,[3] the current statute, similar to its predecessors, is devoid of any standard for awarding them. Absent a statutory guide, we have held that an award of enhanced damages requires a showing of willful infringement. This well-established standard accords with Supreme Court precedent. *See Aro Mfg. Co. v. Convertible Top Replacement Co.,* 377 U.S. 479, 508 (1961) (enhanced damages were available for willful or bad faith infringement). But, a finding of willfulness does not require an award of enhanced damages; it merely permits it. *See* 35 U.S.C. § 284.

This court fashioned a standard for evaluating willful infringement in *Underwater Devices Inc. v. Morrison-Knudsen Co.,* 717 F.2d at 1389-90: "Where . . . a potential infringer has actual notice of another's patent rights, he has an affirmative duty to exercise due care to determine whether or not he is infringing. Such

---

3. Trial courts have had statutory discretion to enhance damages for patent infringement since 1836. 35 U.S.C. § 284 (2000); Act of Aug. 1, 1946, 60 Stat. 778; Patent Act of 1870, ch. 230, § 59, 16 Stat. 198, 207 (1870) (providing that "the court may enter judgment thereon for any sum above the amount found by the verdict as the actual damages sustained, according to the circumstances of the case, not exceeding three times the amount of such verdict, together with the costs"); Patent Act of 1836, ch. 357, 5 Stat. 117 (1836) (stating that "it shall be in the power of the court to render judgment for any sum above the amount found by such verdict . . . not exceeding three times the amount thereof, according to the circumstances of the case").

an affirmative duty includes, *inter alia,* the duty to seek and obtain competent legal advice from counsel *before* the initiation of any possible infringing activity." This standard was announced shortly after the creation of the court, and at a time "when widespread disregard of patent rights was undermining the national innovation incentive." *Knorr-Bremse Systeme Fuer Nutzfahrzeuge GmbH v. Dana Corp.,* 383 F.3d 1337, 1343 (Fed. Cir. 2004) (en banc). Indeed, in *Underwater Devices,* an attorney had advised the infringer that "[c]ourts, in recent years, have—in patent infringement cases—found [asserted patents] invalid in approximately 80% of the cases," and on that basis the attorney concluded that the patentee would not likely sue for infringement. 717 F.2d at 1385. Over time, our cases evolved to evaluate willfulness and its duty of due care under the totality of the circumstances, and we enumerated factors informing the inquiry.

In light of the duty of due care, accused willful infringers commonly assert an advice of counsel defense. Under this defense, an accused willful infringer aims to establish that due to reasonable reliance on advice from counsel, its continued accused activities were done in good faith. Typically, counsel's opinion concludes that the patent is invalid, unenforceable, and/or not infringed. Although an infringer's reliance on favorable advice of counsel, or conversely his failure to proffer any favorable advice, is not dispositive of the willfulness inquiry, it is crucial to the analysis. *E.g., Electro Med. Sys., S.A. v. Cooper Life Scis., Inc.,* 34 F.3d 1048, 1056 (Fed. Cir. 1994) ("Possession of a favorable opinion of counsel is not essential to avoid a willfulness determination; it is only one factor to be considered, albeit an important one.").

Since *Underwater Devices,* we have recognized the practical concerns stemming from our willfulness doctrine, particularly as related to the attorney-client privilege and work product doctrine. For instance, *Quantum Corp. v. Plus Development Corp.,* 940 F.2d 642, 643 (Fed. Cir. 1991), observed that "[p]roper resolution of the dilemma of an accused infringer who must choose between the lawful assertion of the attorney-client privilege and avoidance of a willfulness finding if infringement is found, is of great importance not only to the parties but to the fundamental values sought to be preserved by the attorney-client privilege." We cautioned there that an accused infringer "should not, without the trial court's careful consideration, be forced to choose between waiving the privilege in order to protect itself from a willfulness finding, in which case it may risk prejudicing itself on the question of liability, and maintaining the privilege, in which case it may risk being found to be a willful infringer if liability is found." *Id.* at 643-44. We advised that *in camera* review and bifurcating trials in appropriate cases would alleviate these concerns. *Id.* However, such procedures are often considered too onerous to be regularly employed.

Recently, in *Knorr-Bremse,* we addressed another outgrowth of our willfulness doctrine. Over the years, we had held that an accused infringer's failure to produce advice from counsel "would warrant the conclusion that it either obtained no advice of counsel or did so and was advised that its [activities] would be an infringement of valid U.S. Patents." *Knorr-Bremse,* 383 F.3d at 1343. Recognizing that this inference imposed "inappropriate burdens on the attorney-client relationship," *id.,* we held that invoking the attorney-client privilege or work product protection does not give rise to an adverse inference, *id.* at 1344-45. We further held that an accused infringer's failure to obtain legal advice does not give rise to an adverse inference with respect to willfulness. *Id.* at 1345-46.

More recently, in *EchoStar* we addressed the scope of waiver resulting from the advice of counsel defense. First, we concluded that relying on in-house counsel's advice to refute a charge of willfulness triggers waiver of the attorney-client privilege. *Echostar*, 448 F.3d at 1299. Second, we held that asserting the advice of counsel defense waives work product protection and the attorney-client privilege for all communications on the same subject matter, as well as any documents memorializing attorney-client communications. *Id.* at 1299, 1302-03. However, we held that waiver did not extend to work product that was not communicated to an accused infringer. *Id.* at 1303-04. *Echostar* did not consider waiver of the advice of counsel defense as it relates to trial counsel.

In this case, we confront the willfulness scheme and its functional relationship to the attorney-client privilege and work product protection. In light of Supreme Court opinions since *Underwater Devices* and the practical concerns facing litigants under the current regime, we take this opportunity to revisit our willfulness doctrine and to address whether waiver resulting from advice of counsel and work product defenses extend to trial counsel.

I. Willful Infringement

The term willful is not unique to patent law, and it has a well-established meaning in the civil context. For instance, our sister circuits have employed a recklessness standard for enhancing statutory damages for copyright infringement. Under the Copyright Act, a copyright owner can elect to receive statutory damages, and trial courts have discretion to enhance the damages, up to a statutory maximum, for willful infringement. 17 U.S.C. §504(c). Although the statute does not define willful, it has consistently been defined as including reckless behavior.

Just recently, the Supreme Court addressed the meaning of willfulness as a statutory condition of civil liability for punitive damages. *Safeco Ins. Co. of Am. v. Burr*, 127 S. Ct. 2201 (2007). Addressing the willfulness requirement, the Court concluded that the "standard civil usage" of "willful" includes reckless behavior. *Id.* Significantly, the Court said that this definition comports with the common law usage, "which treated actions in 'reckless disregard' of the law as 'willful' violations." *Id.*

In contrast, the duty of care announced in *Underwater Devices* sets a lower threshold for willful infringement that is more akin to negligence. This standard fails to comport with the general understanding of willfulness in the civil context, *Richland Shoe Co.*, 486 U.S. at 133 ("The word 'willful' . . . is generally understood to refer to conduct that is not merely negligent."), and it allows for punitive damages in a manner inconsistent with Supreme Court precedent, *see, e.g., Safeco*, 127 S. Ct. at 2209, 2214-15 n.20. Accordingly, we overrule the standard set out in *Underwater Devices* and hold that proof of willful infringement permitting enhanced damages requires at least a showing of objective recklessness. Because we abandon the affirmative duty of due care, we also reemphasize that there is no affirmative obligation to obtain opinion of counsel.

We fully recognize that "the term [reckless] is not self-defining." *Farmer v. Brennan*, 511 U.S. 825, 836 (1994). However, "[t]he civil law generally calls a person reckless who acts . . . in the face of an unjustifiably high risk of harm that is either known or so obvious that it should be known." *Id.* Accordingly, to establish willful infringement, a patentee must show by clear and convincing evidence that the infringer acted despite an objectively high likelihood that its actions constituted infringement of a valid patent. *See Safeco*, slip op. at 19 ("It is [a] high risk of harm, objectively assessed, that is the essence of recklessness at common law."). The state of mind of the accused infringer is not relevant to this objective inquiry. If this threshold objective standard is satisfied, the patentee must also demonstrate that this objectively-defined risk (determined by the record developed in the infringement proceeding) was either known or so obvious that it should have been known to the accused infringer. We leave it to future cases to further develop the application of this standard.[5]

Comments

1. *The Demise of the Adverse Inference Rule and Affirmative Duty of Care.* The *Knorr* court, citing *Underwater Devices*, stated that actual notice of another's patent right triggers an affirmative duty of due care. But in a unanimous en banc decision, the Federal Circuit eliminated the duty of care, as well as the duty to obtain opinion of counsel. *See In re Seagate Technology, LLC*, 497 F.3d at 1371 (Fed. Cir. 2007) (en banc) (stating "we abandon the affirmative duty of due care, [and] also reemphasize that there is no affirmative obligation to obtain opinion of counsel"). And in *Knorr*, the court held failure to obtain an exculpatory opinion of counsel or claiming attorney-client privilege for such a letter shall no longer provide an adverse inference or evidentiary presumption that such an opinion would have been unfavorable. (Although on remand, Judge Ellis of the E.D. of Virginia found willfulness, even in the light of the "now proscribed adverse inference." 372 F. Supp. 2d 833 (E.D. Va. 2005).)

And section 298 of the patent code (created by the America Invents Act) codified the rule against adverse inference:

> The failure of an infringer to obtain the advice of counsel with respect to any allegedly infringed patent, or the failure of the infringer to present such advice to the court or jury, may not be used to prove that the accused infringer willfully infringed the patent or that the infringer intended to induce infringement of the patent.

Moreover, in *Seagate*, the Federal Circuit stated "proof of willful infringement permitting enhanced damages requires at least a showing of objective recklessness." 497 F.3d at 1371. As such, "to establish willful infringement, a patentee must show by clear and convincing evidence that the infringer acted despite an objectively high likelihood that its actions constituted infringement of a valid patent." *Id.*

Seagate, *Knorr*, and section 298 make it more difficult for patentees to prove willfulness, and reduce the need for accused infringers to obtain an opinion of counsel relating to the alleged infringement. Thus, it is arguable that less time will be expended on establishing defenses to a willfulness charge, are more time spent on the nature of the alleged infringement.

But should competitors of a patentee nonetheless obtain competent opinion of counsel? What are the benefits? While an adverse inference is prohibited in the absence of an opinion, willful infringement can still be found to exist by a jury, thus increasing the changes of a judge enhancing the damages award. Therefore, obtaining a competent opinion can be an important

---

5. We would expect that the standards of commerce would be among the factors a court might consider.

insurance policy and provide strong evidence against a charge of willfulness. Moreover, opinions are also legal advice (not only litigation tools) that can offer "design around" suggestions, something that the Federal Circuit has encouraged. *See TiVo, Inc. v. EchoStar Corp.*, 646 F.3d 869, 883 (Fed. Cir. 2011) (en banc) (noting that "legitimate design-around efforts should always be encouraged as a path to spur further innovation").

2. ***District Court Discretion.*** Section 285 allows for treble damages, but says nothing about willfulness. As part of its common law, the Federal Circuit identified willful infringement as one instance where treble damages would be justified. Yet a finding of willful infringement does not require that damages be enhanced. Rather, this decision is left to the discretion of the district court judge. *See Modine Mfg. Co. v. Allen Group, Inc.*, 917 F.2d 538, 543 (Fed. Cir. 1990) (stating "a finding of willful infringement merely *authorizes,* but does not *mandate,* an award of increased damages") (emphasis in original).

3. ***Attorneys' Fees.*** Under section 285, a court may award attorneys' fees to the prevailing party in "exceptional cases." In *Waymark Corp. v. Porta Systems Corp.*, 334 F.3d 1358, 1362-1363 (Fed. Cir. 2003), the court stated:

> We have held that "[t]he determination of whether a case is exceptional and, thus, eligible for an award of attorney fees under §285 is a two-step process. First, the district court must determine whether a case is exceptional, a factual determination reviewed for clear error." The second step is that "the district court must determine whether attorney fees are appropriate, a determination that we review for an abuse of discretion."

Typically, an exceptional case is based on a finding of bad faith or utterly baseless claim. *See Interspiro USA, Inc. v. Figgie Int'l Inc.*, 18 F.3d 927, 934 (Fed. Cir. 1994) (stating "[t]he district court's finding of an exceptional case was premised on the court's determination that the question of infringement "was not close").

D. MARKING AND CONSTRUCTIVE NOTICE

To recover damages, a patentee must either mark its patented good or provide the infringer with notice of the infringement. According to section 287, "in the event of failure so to mark, no damages shall be recovered by the patentee in any action for infringement, except on proof that the infringer was notified of the infringement and continued to infringe thereafter, in which event damages may be recovered only for infringement occurring after such notice." The *Maxwell* case explores the marking requirement.

MAXWELL v. J. BAKER, INC.
86 F.3d 1098 (Fed. Cir. 1996)

LOURIE, Circuit Judge.

J. Baker, Inc. appeals from the final judgment of the United States District Court for the District of Minnesota in which the court denied J. Baker's motion for judgment as a matter of law after a jury verdict of infringement of claims 1, 2, and 3 of U.S. Patent 4,624,060, owned by the inventor, Susan M. Maxwell.

BACKGROUND

In retail shoe stores, pairs of shoes must be kept together to prevent them from becoming disorganized and mismatched. Typically, manufacturers connect pairs of shoes using plastic filaments threaded through each shoe's eyelets. However, some shoes do not have eyelets and cannot be connected in this manner. Thus, manufacturers have resorted to other methods of keeping the shoes together such as making a hole in the side of each shoe and threading a filament through these holes. This method creates problems for retailers and manufacturers because the shoes are damaged by the process.

Maxwell, an employee at a Target retail store, recognized this problem and invented a system for connecting shoes that do not have eyelets. She secured tabs along the inside of each shoe and connected the shoes with a filament threaded through a loop or hole in each tab. By securing the tabs inside the shoe, she preserved the integrity and appearance of the shoes.

Maxwell filed a patent application entitled "System for Attaching Mated Pairs of Shoes Together," which issued as the '060 patent on November 25, 1986.

* * *

J. Baker sells and distributes shoes through leased footwear departments in retail stores. Under a typical leasing arrangement, a retail store provides J. Baker with the exclusive right to operate a shoe department within the store. J. Baker selects the merchandise, stocks the shelves at the stores, and serves the customers. In exchange, the retail store receives a portion of the sales receipts.

J. Baker purchases the shoes it sells from independent manufacturers. Between the mid-1980's and 1990, J. Baker instructed its manufacturers to connect shoes together for sale using a fabric loop inserted under a shoe's sock lining (the "under the sock lining" version). In June 1990, Maxwell informed J. Baker's in-house counsel that she believed that J. Baker infringed the '060 patent. In response, J. Baker designed two alternate shoe connection systems. In the "counter pocket" version, a tab was stitched into the counter pocket of the shoe between the sole and the top of the shoe.

Maxwell sued J. Baker on December 12, 1990, alleging infringement of the '060 patent. After a month long trial, a jury returned a special verdict finding that the '060 patent was valid; J. Baker infringed claims 1, 2, and 3 of the patent; and J. Baker's infringement was willful after June 1990, when it received actual notice of the '060 patent. The jury also determined that Maxwell complied with the marking requirements of 35 U.S.C. § 287(a) as of November 1987. Thus, it awarded over $1.5 million in damages based on its determination that a reasonable royalty for use of Maxwell's patent was $.05 per pair of shoes and J. Baker sold 31 million infringing pairs of shoes.

J. Baker filed a motion for judgment as a matter of law and a motion for a new trial arguing, *inter alia,* that the marking date fixed by the jury was not supported by substantial evidence. The court denied J. Baker's motion.

DISCUSSION

* * *

C. Marking

J. Baker argues that the court erred by denying its JMOL motion on the issue of patent marking under 35 U.S.C. § 287(a). J. Baker asserts that, as a matter of law, no damages may be awarded for infringement occurring before it had actual notice of the alleged infringement in June 1990, and that substantial evidence does not support the jury's verdict that Maxwell complied with the marking statute as of November 1987. In support, J. Baker relies on evidence that at least 5% of the shoes sold by Maxwell's licensee, Target, were not properly marked because Target failed to instruct some of its manufacturers to mark the patented systems.

In response, Maxwell argues that substantial evidence supports the jury's verdict. In particular, Maxwell asserts that she was diligent in enforcing Target's duty to mark, and Target successfully marked 95% of the shoes sold with the attachment system. Thus, she maintains that the court did not err when it denied J. Baker's JMOL motion on the issue of marking. We agree.

Section 287(a) of the Patent Act provides:

> Patentees, and persons making or selling any patented article for or under them, may give notice to the public that the same is patented, either by fixing thereon the word "patent" or the abbreviation "pat.", together with the number of the patent. . . . In the event of failure so to mark, no damages shall be recovered by the patentee in any action for infringement, except on proof that the infringer was notified of the infringement and continued to infringe thereafter, in which event damages may be recovered only for infringement occurring after such notice.

35 U.S.C. § 287(a) (1994). Thus, the statute defines that "[a patentee] is entitled to damages from the time when it either began marking its product in compliance with section 287(a) [, constructive notice,] or when it actually notified [the accused infringer] of its infringement, whichever was earlier." *American Medical Sys., Inc. v. Medical Eng'g Corp.*, 6 F.3d 1523, 1537 (Fed. Cir. 1993). We have construed section 287(a) to require that "once marking has begun, it must be substantially consistent and continuous in order for the party to avail itself of the constructive notice provisions of the statute." *Id.* As the patentee, Maxwell had the burden of pleading and proving at trial that she complied with the statutory requirements. Compliance with section 287(a) is a question of fact, and we review the court's denial of JMOL on the jury's resolution of the issue for substantial evidence.

A patentee who makes, uses, or sells its own invention is obligated to comply with the marking provisions to obtain the benefit of constructive notice. *See American Medical*, 6 F.3d at 1538 ("Full compliance was not achieved until [the patentee] consistently marked substantially all of its patented products, and it was no longer distributing unmarked products."). The marking provisions also apply to "persons making or selling any patented article for or under [the patentees]." 35 U.S.C. § 287(a). Thus, licensees, such as Target, and other authorized parties, such as Target's manufacturers, must also comply. However, with third parties unrelated to the patentee, it is often more difficult for a patentee to ensure compliance with the marking provisions. A "rule of reason" approach is justified in such a case and substantial compliance may be found to satisfy the statute. Therefore, when third parties are involved, the number of shoes sold without proper marking is not conclusive of the issue whether the patentee's marking was "substantially consistent and continuous." When the failure to mark is caused by someone other than the patentee, the court may consider whether the patentee made reasonable efforts to ensure compliance with the marking requirements. The rule of reason is consistent with the purpose of the constructive notice provision—to encourage patentees to mark their products in order to provide notice to the public of the existence of the patent and to prevent innocent infringement.

Here, Maxwell, the patentee, made extensive and continuous efforts to ensure compliance by Target. There is evidence that Target, as licensee of Maxwell's patent, marked at least 95% of the shoes sold using the patented system. Because Target sold millions of pairs of shoes using the patented system, it is true that a numerically large number of shoes were sold without proper marking. Despite this, however, the evidence supports the jury's finding that Maxwell complied with the statute. Before the patent issued, Target agreed to mark "Patent Pending" on all pairs of shoes using Maxwell's shoe attachment system. After the patent issued on November 26, 1986, Maxwell notified Target to mark the patent number on all shoes using the patented system, as required by their license agreement. Initially, Target made no effort to change the marking from "Patent Pending" to recite the patent number. In response, Maxwell notified Target's manufacturers of the need to properly mark. Subsequently, Target agreed to properly mark shoes using the patented system by November 1987. Thereafter, on several occasions when Maxwell learned of Target's failure to properly mark shoes using the patented system after November 1987, she notified Target of the errors and requested that the shoes be properly marked in the future. Maxwell also presented evidence that, in response to her urging, Target used its best efforts to correct its failure to mark by instructing its manufacturers to properly mark in the future.

Thus, we find that substantial evidence supports the jury's determination that Maxwell complied with the marking statute as of November 1987. Most pairs of shoes using the patented attachment system were properly marked. Any deficiency in the marking was not due to Maxwell or any failure on her part to ensure compliance by her licensees; she diligently attempted to comply with the statutory marking requirements. Therefore, we affirm the district court's denial of J. Baker's JMOL motion on the issue of marking, [and] affirm the jury's conclusions that the '060 patent was not proved invalid and that Maxwell complied with the marking requirements of 35 U.S.C. § 287(a) as of November 1987.

Comments

1. *The Policy of Marking.* The marking requirement has its origins in the 1842 Patent Act. And the policies underlying this duty have not changed much since then. These policies include: (1) helping to avoid innocent infringement; (2) encouraging patentees to give notice to the public that the article is patented; and (3) aiding the public to identify whether an article is patented. *See Nike, Inc. v. Wal-Mart Stores, Inc.*, 138 F.3d 1437, 1443 (Fed. Cir.

1998). The role of notice was made clear in the Federal Circuit's decision in *American Medical Systems, Inc. v. Medical Engineering Corp.*, 6 F.3d 1523 (Fed. Cir. 1993):

> [C]ases under the 1952 Act have interpreted section 287(a) to allow damages from the time when marking begins in compliance with the statute or actual notice is given, whichever comes first. The plain language of section 287(a) does not provide any time limit by which marking must begin, nor does the legislative history indicate any such limitation. Congress structured the statute so as to tie failure to mark with disability to collect damages, not failure to mark *at the time of issuance* with disability to collect damages. Furthermore, allowing recovery of damages from the point of full compliance with the marking statute furthers the policy of encouraging marking to provide notice to the public, even if initial marking after issuance of the patent is delayed. The sooner one complies with the marking requirements, the more likely one is to maximize the period of time for recoverable damages. To prevent recovery of damages for failure to immediately mark, however, provides no incentive for a patentee who inadvertently or unavoidably fails to mark initially to mark in the future.

> * * *

> In light of the permissive wording of the present statute, and the policy of encouraging notice by marking, we construe section 287(a) to preclude recovery of damages only for infringement for any time prior to compliance with the marking or actual notice requirements of the statute. Therefore, a delay between issuance of the patent and compliance with the marking provisions of section 287(a) will not prevent recovery of damages after the date that marking has begun. We caution, however, that once marking has begun, it must be substantially consistent and continuous in order for the party to avail itself of the constructive notice provisions of the statute.

> * * *

> The date that AMS began marking its products is irrelevant for purposes of the statute, because marking alone without distribution provides no notice to the public where unmarked products are continuing to be shipped. The purpose of the constructive notice provision is "to give patentees the proper incentive to mark their products and thus place the world on notice of the existence of the patent." *Laitram Corp. v. Hewlett-Packard Co.*, 806 F. Supp. 1294, 1296 (E.D. La. 1992). The world cannot be "put on notice" if the patentee marks certain products, but continues to ship unmarked products. Therefore, AMS was not in full compliance with the marking statute while it continued to ship its unmarked products, which continued to mislead the public into thinking that the product was freely available. Full compliance was not achieved until AMS consistently marked substantially all of its patented products, and it was no longer distributing unmarked products.

Id. at 1537-1538. By the same token, a patentee may not engage in false marking "for purposes of deceiving the public. *See* 35 U.S.C. § 292. False marking includes both products that were never patented or on products that are no longer subject to patent protection. *See Pequignot v. Solo Cup Co.*, 608 F.3d 1356 (Fed. Cir. 2010).

2. *Constructive Notice.* A patentee can mark his goods at any point after issuance of the patent. Naturally, a patentee has an incentive to mark sooner than later so as to provide constructive notice and to begin the damages

clock. Constructive notice is provided when the patentee consistently marks substantially all of its patented products. Thus, infringers will be liable for damages even if they do not know of the existence of a patent. Such is the power of constructive notice. In addition, the notice must come from the patentee. *See American Medical,* 6 F.3d at 1537 n.18 (in response to patentee's argument that notice was satisfied because the infringer was notified that he was infringing by its own counsel, the court stated "[t]his is clearly not what was intended by the marking statute. Section 287(a) requires a party asserting infringement to either provide constructive notice (through marking) or actual notice in order to avail itself of damages. The notice of infringement must therefore come from the patentee, not the infringer").

3. *Marking and Method Claims.* Section 287 allows for the patentee to mark either the product or the packaging of the product. Package marking is permitted "when, from the character of the article" marking the product "can not be done." The key is that notice is provided. Not surprisingly, the marking requirement is not applicable to process or method inventions. How do you physically mark these types of inventions? *See American Medical, supra,* at 1538 ("The law is clear that the notice provisions of section 287 do not apply where the patent is directed to a process or method."); *State Contracting & Engineering Corp. v. Condotte America, Inc.,* 346 F.3d 1057, 1074 (Fed. Cir. 2003). And the marking requirement does not apply when only method claims are asserted on a patent that also includes product claims. *See Crown Packaging Technology, Inc. v. Rexam Beverage Can Co.,* 559 F.3d 1308, 1316-1317 (Fed. Cir. 2009), *cf. American Medical* (both method and apparatus claims were asserted). In *ActiveVideo Networks, Inc. v. Verizon Communications, Inc.,* 694 F.3d 1312 (Fed. Cir. 2012), the Federal Circuit rejected Verizon's argument that the rule not requiring marking of method patents should not apply when the patentee also asserts other patents that contain apparatus claims embodying the same invention, referring to such an approach as "a confusing mess for the district courts to try to apply." *Id.* at 1335.

4. *Patent Law's "Statute of Limitations."* Section 286 of the patent code provides a six-year "statute of limitations." But this provision is not a typical statute of limitations because it does not bar the patentee from bringing a patent infringement action. Rather, section 286 is a damages limitation rule, which states, "no recovery shall be had for any infringement committed more than six years prior to the filing of the complaint or counterclaim for infringement in the action." *Standard Oil Co. v. Nippon Shokubai Kagaku Kogyo Co.,* 754 F.2d 345, 348 (Fed. Cir. 1985) ("Since §286 cannot properly be called a 'statute of limitations' in the sense that it defeats the right to bring suit, it cannot be said that the statute 'begins to run' on some date or other. In the application of §286, one starts from the filing of a complaint or counterclaim and counts *backward* to determine the date before which infringing *acts* cannot give rise to a right to recover damages.") (emphasis in original); *A.C. Aukerman Co. v. R.L. Chaides Constr. Co.,* 960 F.2d 1020, 1030 (Fed. Cir. 1992) (explaining that section 286 is "not a statute of limitations in the sense of barring a suit for infringement" . . . but rather is a "limit to recovery to damages for infringing acts committed within six years of the date of the filing of the infringement action").

SECLECTED PATENT STATUTES

§101. Inventions patentable

Whoever invents or discovers any new and useful process, machine, manufacture, or composition of matter, or any new and useful improvement thereof, may obtain a patent therefor, subject to the conditions and requirements of this title.

§102. Conditions for patentability; novelty and loss of right to patent (Pre-AIA)

A person shall be entitled to a patent unless—

(a) the invention was known or used by others in this country, or patented or described in a printed publication in this or a foreign country, before the invention thereof by the applicant for patent, or

(b) the invention was patented or described in a printed publication in this or a foreign country or in public use or on sale in this country, more than one year prior to the date of the application for patent in the United States; . . .

(g) (1) during the course of an interference conducted under section 135 or section 291, another inventor involved therein establishes, to the extent permitted in section 104, that before such person's invention thereof the invention was made by such other inventor and not abandoned, suppressed, or concealed, or (2) before such person's invention thereof, the invention was made in this country by another inventor who had not abandoned, suppressed, or concealed it. In determining priority of invention under this subsection, there shall be considered not only the respective dates of conception and reduction to practice of the invention, but also the reasonable diligence of one who was first to conceive and last to reduce to practice, from a time prior to conception by the other.

§102. Conditions for Patentability; Novelty (Post-AIA)

(a) **NOVELTY; PRIOR ART**.—A person shall be entitled to a patent unless–

(1) the claimed invention was patented, described in a printed publication, or in public use, on sale, or otherwise available to the public before the effective filing date of the claimed invention; or

(2) the claimed invention was described in a patent issued under section 151, or in an application for patent published or deemed published under section 122(b), in which the patent or application, as the case may be, names another inventor and was effectively filed before the effective filing date of the claimed invention.

(b) **EXCEPTIONS**.—

(1) DISCLOSURES MADE 1 YEAR OR LESS BEFORE THE EFFECTIVE FILING DATE OF THE CLAIMED INVENTION.–A disclosure made 1 year

or less before the effective filing date of a claimed invention shall not be prior art to the claimed invention under subsection (a)(1) if–

  (A) the disclosure was made by the inventor or joint inventor or by another who obtained the subject matter disclosed directly or indirectly from the inventor or a joint inventor; or

  (B) the subject matter disclosed had, before such disclosure, been publicly disclosed by the inventor or a joint inventor or another who obtained the subject matter disclosed directly or indirectly from the inventor or a joint inventor.

 (2) **DISCLOSURES APPEARING IN APPLICATIONS AND PATENTS.**–A disclosure shall not be prior art to a claimed invention under subsection (a)(2) if–

  (A) the subject matter disclosed was obtained directly or indirectly from the inventor or a joint inventor;

  (B) the subject matter disclosed had, before such subject matter was effectively filed under subsection (a)(2), been publicly disclosed by the inventor or a joint inventor or another who obtained the subject matter disclosed directly or indirectly from the inventor or a joint inventor; or

  (C) the subject matter disclosed and the claimed invention, not later than the effective filing date of the claimed invention, were owned by the same person or subject to an obligation of assignment to the same person.

§103. Conditions for patentability; non-obvious subject matter (Pre-AIA)

(a) A patent may not be obtained though the invention is not identically disclosed or described as set forth in section 102 of this title, if the differences between the subject matter sought to be patented and the prior art are such that the subject matter as a whole would have been obvious at the time the invention was made to a person having ordinary skill in the art to which said subject matter pertains. Patentability shall not be negatived by the manner in which the invention was made.

§ 103. Conditions for patentability; non-obvious subject matter (Post-AIA)

A patent for a claimed invention may not be obtained, notwithstanding that the claimed invention is not identically disclosed as set forth in section 102, if the differences between the claimed invention and the prior art are such that the claimed invention as a whole would have been obvious before the effective filing date of the claimed invention to a person having ordinary skill in the art to which the claimed invention pertains. Patentability shall not be negated by the manner in which the invention was made.

§112. Specification

(a) In General.— The specification shall contain a written description of the invention, and of the manner and process of making and using it, in such full, clear, concise, and exact terms as to enable any person skilled in the art to which it pertains, or with which it is most nearly connected, to make and use the same, and shall set forth the best mode contemplated by the inventor of carrying out his invention.

(b) Conclusion.— The specification shall conclude with one or more claims particularly pointing out and distinctly claiming the subject matter which the applicant regards as his invention.

§154. Contents and term of patent; provisional rights

(a) In General.—

    (1) Contents.—Every patent shall contain a short title of the invention and a grant to the patentee, his heirs or assigns, of the right to exclude others from making, using, offering for sale, or selling the invention throughout the United States or importing the invention into the United States, and, if the invention is a process, of the right to exclude others from using, offering for sale or selling throughout the United States, or importing into the United States, products made by that process, referring to the specification for the particulars thereof.

    (2) Term.—Subject to the payment of fees under this title, such grant shall be for a term beginning on the date on which the patent issues and ending 20 years from the date on which the application for the patent was filed in the United States or, if the application contains a specific reference to an earlier filed application or applications under section 120, 121, or 365(c) of this title, from the date on which the earliest such application was filed.

§271. Infringement of patent

(a) Except as otherwise provided in this title, whoever without authority makes, uses, offers to sell, or sells any patented invention, within the United States or imports into the United States any patented invention during the term of the patent therefor, infringes the patent.

(b) Whoever actively induces infringement of a patent shall be liable as an infringer.

(c) Whoever offers to sell or sells within the United States or imports into the United States a component of a patented machine, manufacture, combination or composition, or a material or apparatus for use in practicing a patented process, constituting a material part of the invention, knowing the same to be especially made or especially adapted for use in an infringement of such patent, and not a staple article or commodity of commerce suitable for substantial noninfringing use, shall be liable as a contributory infringer.

§283. Injunction

The several courts having jurisdiction of cases under this title may grant injunctions in accordance with the principles of equity to prevent the violation of any right secured by patent, on such terms as the court deems reasonable.

§284. Damages

Upon finding for the claimant the court shall award the claimant damages adequate to compensate for the infringement, but in no event less than a reasonable royalty for the use made of the invention by the infringer, together with interest and costs as fixed by the court.

When the damages are not found by a jury, the court shall assess them. In either event the court may increase the damages up to three times the amount found or assessed. Increased damages under this paragraph shall not apply to provisional rights under section 154(d).

The court may receive expert testimony as an aid to the determination of damages or of what royalty would be reasonable under the circumstances.

TABLE OF CASES

Principal cases are denoted by italics.

INDEX